MW00356431

WILLIAM EMPSON

AGAINST THE CHRISTIANS

WILLIAM EMPSON

AGAINST THE
CHRISTIANS

JOHN HAFFENDEN

OXFORD
UNIVERSITY PRESS

OXFORD
UNIVERSITY PRESS

Great Clarendon Street, Oxford OX2 6DP
Oxford University Press is a department of the University of Oxford.
It furthers the University's objective of excellence in research, scholarship,
and education by publishing worldwide in

Oxford New York

Auckland Cape Town Dar es Salaam Hong Kong Karachi
Kuala Lumpur Madrid Melbourne Mexico City Nairobi
New Delhi Shanghai Taipei Toronto

With offices in

Argentina Austria Brazil Chile Czech Republic France Greece
Guatemala Hungary Italy Japan Poland Portugal Singapore
South Korea Switzerland Thailand Turkey Ukraine Vietnam

Oxford is a registered trade mark of Oxford University Press
in the UK and in certain other countries

Published in the United States
by Oxford University Press Inc., New York

British Library Cataloguing in Publication Data
Data available

Library of Congress Cataloging in Publication Data
Data available

Typeset by SPI Publisher Services, Pondicherry, India
Printed in Great Britain on acid-free paper by
Biddles, Ltd., King's Lynn

ISBN 0-19-927660-9 (Hbk.)   978-0-19-927660-8 (Hbk.)

ACKNOWLEDGEMENTS

I am indebted to the Empson family for their friendship and hospitality, and for entrusting me with this task—primarily (with regard to this volume) the late Hetta Empson, Mogador Empson, Jacob Empson, Simon Duval Smith—and to Sir William Empson for countenancing the very idea in the first place.

I am particularly grateful to Empson's literary executors for granting me permission to print in this volume, for the first time and exclusively, the verses entitled 'The Wife is Praised' (first drafted in 1948). The Estate of William Empson declined to include the poem in *Complete Poems* (2000) on a number of grounds: these included the judgement that it is an unfinished 'private' poem; that it is not of the same quality as the published poetry; and that Empson could have published it during his lifetime if he had so wished. My own view is that it is an ingenious and witty, as well as astonishingly frank, manifesto, albeit unpolished, and I had proposed to publish it in the collected volume of poetry (among various reasons) because I knew that Empson himself was averse to keeping any literary remains 'under wraps' (as he put it in a review). Empson further claimed in a related context: 'I stubbornly won't hide anything.' Notwithstanding, it has to be said that his Estate was faced with a genuine dilemma (since Empson did not apparently try to publish the poem, and did not leave testamentary directions about it) and acted in good faith. More recently, however, the executors have come to the view that the poem is yet an important autobiographical record in verse, and on that basis they believe it is now appropriate to publish the work in the context of this biography. I am grateful to them for their generosity and faith.

I am greatly indebted to the British Academy for a Research Readership in 1989–91, and for a later grant-in-aid; and no less to the Arts Council of Great Britain, the Society of Authors, the Leverhulme Trust, and the Research Fund of Sheffield University, which have helped to meet the costs of my research over the years. I could not have managed without them.

Many libraries and other organizations and institutions have been generous in affording me accommodation, or in providing research facilities of one sort or another, and in granting permission for the publication of the Empson letters under their control. I am eager first of all to thank the Houghton Library, Harvard University (custodian since 1986 of the Empson Papers), and in particular Leslie Morris (Curator of Manuscripts), Rodney G. Dennis (former Curator), and Elizabeth A. Falsey (who undertook the awesome job of preparing an inventory of the papers). I am deeply grateful too to the authorities of Beijing University, Peking, who kindly hosted my visit to China in 1984; the British Embassy, Peking (Alan Maley, First Secretary, Cultural Section, British Embassy, and Martin Davidson; David Marler, Cultural Counsellor, British Council Representative in China); the British Council, London (Angela Udall, Leigh Gibson, Specialist Tours Department; Martin Carney; Adrian Johnson, Cultural Counsellor and British Council Representative, Beijing); and the British Embassy Cultural Department, The British Council, Tokyo; BBC Play Library, Broadcasting House (Deborah A. Halfpenny); BBC Written Archives Centre, Caversham, Reading (Jacqueline Kavanagh, Written Archives Officer; Gwyniver Jones, Assistant-in-Charge, Enquiries; John Jordan, Enquiry Assistant); Beinecke Library, Yale University; Department of Manuscripts, The British Library (Sally Brown, Dr Chris Fletcher); Butler Library, Columbia University (Bernard R. Crystal, Curator of Manuscripts; Kenneth A. Lohf, former Curator); Chalmers Memorial Library, Kenyon College Archives (Thomas B. Greenslade, College Archivist); Chatto & Windus; Cornell University Library; Embassy of the People's Republic of China; Exeter University Library (Alistair Patterson); Harry Ransom Humanities Research Center, University of Texas at Austin (Ellen S. Dunlap, Research Librarian; Cathy Henderson, Research Associate; Elizabeth L. Garver, Intern); Modern Archives Centre, King's College, Cambridge (Dr R Moad, Dr P. K. McGuire); Manuscript Division, The Library of Congress, Washington, D. C. (Fred Bauman, Reference Librarian); Lilly Library, Indiana University; Magdalen College, Oxford; Magdalene College, Cambridge; John Rylands Library, University of Manchester; Mills Memorial Library, McMaster University (Carl Spadoni, Research Collections Librarian); the National Archives, Washington, D. C. (Kathie Nicastro); National Library of Scotland (Murray Simpson); Library/Information Service, National Sound Archive, British Library (Lee Taylor); Princeton University Library (Jean F. Preston, Curator of Manuscripts); Reading University Library (A. J. C Bainton, Michael Bott); Rockefeller Archive Centre, Tarrytown, New York;

St John's College, Oxford; School of Oriental and African Studies, London; Special Collections and Archives, The Library, University of Sheffield (Lawrence Aspden, former Curator); The Society of Authors; *Times* archive; The Library, University College London (Gill Furlong, archivist); The Library, University of Victoria, Victoria, B. C., Canada (Chris Petter, University Archivist and Head of Special Collections); and the Wren Library, Trinity College, Cambridge (Dr David McKitterick).

Individuals who have most kindly afforded me information, advice and assistance in various capacities include: Paul Allen, A. Alvarez, Professor Paul J. Alpers, the late Mulk Raj Anand, the late Professor Harry Armytage, Lawrence Aspden, Dr Charles Aylmer, Professor Shyamal Bagchee, Professor Bao Zhi-yi, Jonathan Barker, Sebastian Barker, A. Doak Barnett, Dr D. K. Barua, Professor Jonathan Bate, the late Professor Walter Jackson Bate, Trevor Baxter, Clark Beck (Librarian, Special Collections/ Archives, Rutgers University), Stephen Becker, Dr Teresa Bela, Jonathan Benthall, Eric Bentley, the late Sir Isaiah Berlin, Professor Francis Berry, Robert J. Bertholf (Curator, The Poetry/Rare Books Collection, State University of New York at Buffalo), Andrew Best, Dr Matthew Bevis, Professor Bian Zhi Lin, the late Professor Max Black, the late John Blofeld, Meifang Blofeld, the late Ralf Bonwit, Professor James Booth, the late Margaret Bottrall, Margot Bottrall, the late Ronald Bottrall, Zack Bowen, Gordon Bowker, the late Professor Muriel Bradbrook, Andrew Braybrook, Dr Elizabeth M. Brennan, Lord Briggs, Baroness Brigstocke, Professor David Bromwich, John Brown, the late Walter A. Brown, Derek Bryan, Stephen Burt, Barry Callaghan, James Campbell, the late Peter Carnell, the late Alan N. Cass, Chang Chiu-tse, Professor Chao Chao-hsiung, Professor Maurice Charney, Peter Chees'eman, Igor Chroustchoff, Ken Churchill (The British Council), the late Douglas Cleverdon, Mary Coleman, Professor Thomas E. Connolly, Peter Conradi, Dr John Constable, the late Alistair Cooke, Sir Hugh Cortazzi, Professor D. R. Cousin, Jenny Cowan, Professor C. B. Cox, Dr Matthew Creasy, Professor Sir Bernard Crick, Anthony Cronin, David Crook, Sir Colin Crowe, the late Margaret (Biddy) Crozier, Mrs C. Cruickshank (Archivist, Faber & Faber), D. W. Cruickshank, Peter Currie, Gordon Daniels, Natalie Davenport, Roger Davenport, the late Gwenda David, the late Hugh Sykes Davies, Professor Frank Day, Paul Dean, Professor J. S. Deas, Vicki Denby, J. B. Denson, Professor Martin Dodsworth, Professor John Doheny, the late Francis Doherty, Dr Penelope Doob, Duan Hui-sien, Professor Douglas Duncan, the late Elsie Duncan-Jones, Professor Katherine Duncan-Jones, Eamon Dyas (*Times* archivist), Vieta Dyer (Svetlana Rimsky-Korsakoff), Brian Dyson (Hull

University Library), H. J. Easterling, Professor Roger Ebbatson, the late Professor Richard Eberhart, Professor Philip Edwards, Professor Arthur Efron, Mrs Valerie Eliot, the late Charles Empson, the late Sir Charles and Lady Empson, Tsutung Emslie, the late D. J. Enright, the late Professor Martin Esslin, Garrett Evans, the late Professor Inga-Stina Ewbank Professor Dick Ewen, Maggie Fergusson (Royal Society of Literature), the late Professor Leslie Fiedler, Morris Fink, Father Peter A. Fiore, the late Professor C. P. Fitzgerald, Mirabel Fitzgerald, Barry Fox, Mrs Paddy Fraser, Michael Freeman, Professor Norman Fruman, Mrs Rintaro Fukuhara, Professor David Fuller, John Fuller, David Ganz, the late Professor Dame Helen Gardner, Helen Gardner (Society of Authors), Professor Averil Gardner, Harry M. Geduld, Professor Alex George, the late Roma Gill, Victoria Glendinning, Dr David Glover, the late Sir Ernst Gombrich, Reg Goodchild, Adrian Goodman, the late Mrs Celia Goodman, Prof. W. Terrence Gordon, W. G. Graham, Professor Gayle Greene, Dr Eric Griffiths, John Gross, Professor Jay L. Halio, Dr Michael Halls, the late Ian Hamilton, Saskia Hamilton, Dr Jason Harding, Dr Henry Hardy, Pamela Hardyment, Claire Harmon, Rachel Harris, Richard Harris, George Hartley, Professor Ihab Hassan, Selina Hastings, Coleen Hatrick, Professor Michael Hattaway, Professor David Hawkes, the late Desmond Hawkins, Mark Haymon, the late Sir William Hayter, the late Sir Robert Helpmann, Sandra Henry, Bernard Heringman, Tim Herrick, Annemarie Heywood, Christopher Heywood, the late Professor Christopher Hill, Geoff Hill, Andrew and Geraldine Hillier, Charles Hobday, the late Professor Philip Hobsbaum, Dr Anthony Hobson, Theodore Hofmann, Richard Holmes, Professor Michael Hollington, Dr Michael Holroyd, Dr Eric Homberger, Dr Janet Hopewell, the late Professor Graham Hough, Professor Nicholas Howe, Professor Huang Ming-yeh, Martyn Hughes, the late Judge W. H. Hughes, Professor G. K. Hunter, Professor Yukio Irie, Kevin Jackson, Professor John Israel, Professor A. N. Jeffares, Elizabeth Jenkins, Dr Nicholas Jenkins, Linda Jean Jenner (Hanson), Mary-Lou Jennings, Professor James Jensen, Professor Jin Di, Professor Jin Fa-xin, the late Professor Jin Yuelin, the late John Henry (David) Jones, Paul Kafno, Professor R. Kajiki, the late Professor Harry Kay, Brian Keeble, Paul Keegan, Anne Kelly, Professor Richard J. Kelly, Tim Kendall, Dr Gilbert Kennedy, Professor Sir Frank Kermode, the late David Kidd, Professor Kim Jong-gil (Kim Chi-gyu), Garry Kinnane, the late Professor L. C. Knights, Roger Kuin, Professor David Laird, the late James Laughlin, the late Professor Eric Laughton, Aviva Layton, the late Sir

Desmond Lee, Revd. J. Philip Lee-Woolf, Dr E. S. Leedham-Green, the late Professor Peter Levi, the late Professor Li Fu-ning, Professor Li Zhiwei, Professor Grevel Lindop, Joyce Linfoot, the late Earl Listowel, Liu Jo-tuan, Liu Ruoduan, Liu Yuan Zi, Professor James J. Y. Liu, Helen Lo, Yann Lovelock, Evan Luard, Dr Richard Luckett, the late Professor Hyam Maccoby, Jim McCue, Ian McEwan, the late Professor Maynard Mack, the late Dr Eric Mackerness, the late Professor Ian MacKillop, Alan and Robin McLean, Ben Maclean, Ken Mclean, the late Jenny McMorris, the late Professor Charles Madge, Hugh Major, Nick Malone, Professor Charles W. Mann, Joyce Marks, Dr D. H. Marrian, Janet Martin, Lauro Martines, Professor William H. Matchett, Professor Giorgio Melchiori, D. H. Mellor, M. C. Meredith (School Librarian, Eton College), Professor Karl Miller, Professor Earl Miner, the late Professor Edward Miller, Professor Neville Moray, Blake Morrison, Professor Derek Mosley, Professor Andrew Motion, the late Professor Kenneth Muir, Ross C. Murfin, Professor W. A. Murray, Professor Shigehisa Narita, Professor Leonard Nathan, the late Dr Joseph Needham, Sir Patrick Neill (All Souls College, Oxford), the late Jill Neville, Professor Christopher Norris, Professor A. D. Nuttall, Mrs Diana Oakeley, Dr Conor Cruise O'Brien, Professor Darcy O'Brien, Professor Kazuo Ogawa, Sumie Okada, Dr Duco van Oostrum, Timothy O'Sullivan, A. E. B. Owen (Keeper of Manuscripts, Cambridge University Library), Dr Barbara Ozieblo, Dr David Parker, Tjarda Parker, the late Ian Parsons, the late Marjorie Tulip (Trekkie) Parsons, Peng Jingfu, David Perry, John Oliver Perry, Dr Seamus Perry, Theophilus Peters, the late Professor Frank Pierce, Professor H. W. Piper, Dr David B. Pirie, the late N. W. (Bill) Pirie, Dr Adrian Poole, Mrs Dorothy Poynter (secretary to the late Professor Kathleen Coburn), Vic Pratt (Donor Access, The British Film Institute), John Press, Dr Kate Price, the late Professor F. T. Prince, Professor Qi Sheng-qiao, Qien Xuexi, the late Sir Peter Quennell, Jonathan Raban, Craig Raine, the late Dr Kathleen Raine, Professor Claude Rawson, the late Dr Theodore Redpath, Olive Renier, the late Mrs Dorothy Richards, Professor Christopher Ricks, the late Anne Ridler, Professor Andrew Roberts, Professor Mark Roberts, Professor Neil Roberts, Peter Robinson, the late George (Dadie) Rylands, Susan Rieger, John Robson, the late Professor W. W. Robson, Professor Thomas P. Roche Jr., Lisa A. Rodensky, Allan Rodway, Earl M. Rogers (Archivist, The University of Iowa), Derek Roper, Professor S. P. Rosenbaum, Andrew Roth, the late Dr A. L. Rowse, Professor Alan Rudrum, Professor John Paul Russo, the late Lorna Sage, Victor Sage, Professor Roger H. Sale, Leo Salingar, Deidre Sanders, the late Wilf Saunders,

Professor Michael Schmidt, Sumana Sen-Bagchee, Fritz Senn, Miranda Seymour, the late Martin Seymour-Smith, Sidney Shapiro, Dr Catherine Sharrock, Mr and Mrs Russell Sharrock, Dr Erica Sheen, Professor Dominic Shellard, C. D. W. Sheppard (Brotherton Library, University of Leeds), Professor T. T. Shui, Dr Murray Simpson, the late Marg Smale, the late Mrs Norah Smallwood, Bryan Smith, the late Janet Adam Smith, Professor Nigel Smith, Pat Smith, Dr Richard C. Smith, John Solomon, Professor George Soule, Professor Ray Southall, the late John Sparrow, the late Sir Stephen Spender, Lady Spender, the late Nikos Stangos, Susan Stephens (Assistant Registrar, University of Sheffield), Professor Herbert Stern, Professor and Mrs Harry Stoneback, the late Dr Alice Stewart, Sir Roy Strong, Sharon Sumpter (Archives Associate, The Archives of the University of Notre Dame, Indiana), Sun Yu-mei, Professor John Sutherland, Richard Sylvester, D. J. Taylor, Kevin Taylor, Mrs Eleen Thierry-Mieg, Sir Keith Thomas, Ed Thomason, Mark Thompson, John L. Thorn, Anthony Thwaite, the late Professor J. B. Trapp (Warburg Institute), Professor Jeremy Treglown, the late Julian Trevelyan, Christine Tucker (The Open University Library), the late Professor John Unterecker, the late Richard Usborne, Mrs Sybille van der Sprenkel, Robert Vas Dias, Professor William Vesterman, Professor Sue Vice, Professor Brian Vickes, the late Igor Vinogradoff, the late Professor John Wain, William Wain, the late Keith Walker, Stephen Wall, Jemma Walton, the late Professor Wang Zuo-liang, Ed Walkins Dr George Watson, John Webb, Professor Stanley Weintraub, Fay Weldon, Professor David West, the late W. J. West, John S. Whitley, Don Wiener, the late Ann Willett, the late John Willett, Professor J. H. Willis, Jr., David Wilson, Professor Mark Royden Winchell, the late Professor Robert Winter, Professor Lewis Wolpert, the late Gordon Woodcock, the late Professor Wu Fuheng, Professor Xu Guozhang, Professor Xu Yuan-zhong, Xu Zongying, Gladys Yang, the late Yang Xianyi, the late Professor Yang Zhouhan, Zhang Jin-yan, Professor Zhou Jue-liang, Professor Zhu Guang-tian, and the late Lord Zuckerman. The list is long, yet it is on my conscience that there are individuals whose names I have forgotten or mislaid over the years: I regret any such omissions.

As in the first volume, I am eager to acknowledge how much I owe to the example and the writings of my fellow critics and editors of Empson; in particular, I am indebted to John Constable, Frank Day, Terry Eagleton, Paul H. Fry, David Fuller, Philip and Averil Gardner, Philip Hobsbaum, James Jensen, John Henry Jones, Frank Kermode, Christopher Norris,

Christopher Ricks, Lisa A. Rodensky, Roger Sale, Mark Thompson, and John Wain.

Certain parts of the critical sections of this volume have previously appeared, in varying forms, in my introductions to the various posthumous volumes of Empson's writings that I have edited over the last twenty years.

At Oxford University Press, I greatly appreciate the friendliness and superb professional care of Andrew McNeillie, Tom Perridge, Val Shelley, Jacqueline Baker, Christine Rode, and other members of the team. Last but not least, I am grateful beyond words to Tom Chandler, who has worked brilliantly and tirelessly for many weeks to edit the text of this final volume of the biography—it is a long book, I am afraid, but before Tom's incisive intervention it had threatened to be an impossibly long book. He has saved me from umpteen errors and excesses; those that remain are all my fault.

CONTENTS

LIST OF ILLUSTRATIONS

ABBREVIATIONS

A	Empson, *Argufying: Essays on Literature and Culture* (London: Chatto & Windus, 1987)
BBC WAC	BBC Written Archives Centre
BL	British Library
Brotherton	Brotherton Library, Leeds University
CCBA	Chinese Central Broadcasting Administration
CCP	Chinese Communist Party
Constable	John Constable (ed.), *Critical Essays on William Empson* (Aldershot: Scolar Press, 1993)
CV	Empson, *Coleridge's Verse: A Selection* (London: Faber & Faber, 1972; with David Pirie)
Complete Poems	*Complete Poems of William Empson*, ed. J. Haffenden (London: Allen Lane, 2000)
EG	*Empson in Granta* (Tunbridge Wells: Foundling Press, 1993)
ESD	Eastern Service Director (of the BBC)
FO	Foreign Office
GS	Empson, *The Gathering Storm* (London: Faber & Faber, 1940)
Gill	R. Gill (ed.), *William Empson: The Man and His Work* (London: Routledge and Kegan Paul, 1974)
HE	Hetta Empson
Houghton	William Empson Papers, Houghton Library, Harvard University
IAR	I. A. Richards
JH	John Haffenden
KMT	Kuomintang (Chinese Nationalists)
Magdalene	I. A. Richards Papers, Old Library, Magdalene College, Cambridge
MG	Empson, *Milton's God* (rev. edn.; Cambridge: Cambridge University Press, 1981)
MOI	Ministry of Information
Peita	Peking National University

PLA	People's Liberation Army
Poems 1934	Empson, *Poems* (Tokyo, 1934)
PRC	People's Republic of China
PRO	Public Record Office
PWE	Political Warfare Executive
RB	Empson, *The Royal Beasts and Other Works* (London: Chatto & Windus, 1986)
Rodensky	Prefatory Note to *Some Versions of Pastoral* (Harmondsworth: Penguin, 1995)
SCW	Empson, *The Structure of Complex Words* (London: Chatto & Windus 1951; 3rd edn., 1977)
(Sheffield)	Sheffield University Library, Special Collections
SL	*Selected Letters of William Empson*, ed. J. Haffenden (Oxford: Oxford University Press, 2006)
SSS	Empson, *The Strengths of Shakespeare's Shrew* (Sheffield: Sheffield Academic Press, 1996)
STA	Empson, *Seven Types of Ambiguity* (London: Chatto & Windus, 1987)
SVP	Empson, *Some Versions of Pastoral* (London: Chatto & Windus, 1935)
TLS	*Times Literary Supplement*
TUC	Trades Union Congress
WE	William Empson

CHRONOLOGY

1906	27 September: born at Yokefleet Hall, Howden, near Goole, Yorkshire; youngest child of Arthur Reginald Empson (land-owner and squire) and his wife Laura Micklethwait; his siblings were John ('Jack', born 1891), Arthur (1892), Charles (1898), Maria ('Molly') Eleanor Katharine, (1902).
1914	16 May: death of eldest brother, a lieutenant in the Royal Flying Corps, in an aeroplane crash.
1914	Enrols at a preparatory school, Praetoria House School, near Folkestone, Kent, where mathematics becomes his forte.
1916	15 March: death of father, aged 63.
1920	Wins an entrance scholarship to Winchester College; specializes in mathematics and science; falls under 'the drug of Swinburne'. Writes first known poem, 'Mother, saying Anne good night', by 29 June, *aetat* 13.
1924	December: wins Milner Scholarship to Magdalene College, Cambridge.
1925	Wins English literature prize at Winchester; comes second (*proxime accessit*) to the future Labour MP Richard Crossman in competition for the Warden and Fellows' Prize for an English Essay (John Sparrow, future Warden of All Souls College, Oxford, is third).
	October: goes up to Cambridge, where his tutor for mathematics is A. S. Ramsey, father of the mathematical prodigy Frank Ramsey and the future Archbishop of Canterbury, Michael Ramsey. Joins humanist discussion society, The Heretics.
1926	February–March: T. S. Eliot delivers his Clark Lectures, 'The Metaphysical Poets of the Seventeenth Century', at Trinity College, Cambridge. Although Empson does not attend all the lectures, he benefits from informal conversations with Eliot. Participates in debates at the Union.
1926	12 June: publishes his first literary notice in *The Granta*.

1926   June: gains 1st class in Part I of the mathematical Tripos; awarded college prize.

1927   5 February: acts in a production at the Cambridge ADC of his one-act play, *Three Stories*, a melodrama.

1927   Begins reviewing film and theatre, as well as books, for *The Granta* and the *Cambridge Review*. For 1927–8, while still a student of mathematics, becomes 'Skipper' (literary editor) of *The Granta*.
         June: publishes first poem at Cambridge, 'Poem about a Ball in the Nineteenth Century'; he is influenced by seventeenth-century metaphysical poetry, especially John Donne.

1928   June: Senior Optime (Upper Second) in Part II of the mathematical Tripos: a disappointing result.
         October: registers for the English Tripos; tutored by I. A. Richards at Magdalene College; attends Richards's lectures on 'Practical Criticism'; begins work towards *Seven Types of Ambiguity*; becomes president of The Heretics.
         November: launches avant-garde magazine, *Experiment*, co-edited with Jacob Bronowski, Humphrey Jennings, and Hugh Sykes Davies (it runs for seven issues, the last in May 1931).

1929   20 January: gives a talk at Cambridge on ambiguity in literature.
         February: publishes 'Ambiguity in Shakespeare: Sonnet XVI' in *Experiment* (the essay will in due course form part of *Seven Types of Ambiguity*).
         March: takes title role in *The Tragedy of Tragedies: or the Life and Death of Tom Thumb the Great* by Henry Fielding, in a production by the Cambridge Mummers.
         June: gains first class with 'special distinction' in English Tripos; awarded a Magdalene college prize; elected to a Charles Kingsley Bye-Fellowship for 1929–30.
         July: discovered by college porters to be in possession of contraceptives; an extraordinary meeting of the Governing Body of Magdalene College resolves to deprive Empson of his Bye-Fellowship and remove his name from the college books. Empson removes himself to 65 Marchmont Street, London, where he lives as a freelance writer for the next two years; he is cultivated by literary figures including T. S. Eliot, Virginia Woolf, Harold Monro, and Sylvia Townsend Warner.
         October: *Letter IV* published by Heffer's of Cambridge. Six of the eighteen poems he has written to date feature in *Cambridge Poetry*

	1929, published by Leonard and Virginia Woolf at the Hogarth Press.
	November: publishes 'Some Notes on Mr Eliot' (a further preview of *Ambiguity*) in *Experiment*.
1930	November: *Seven Types of Ambiguity* published.
1931	29 August: begins three-year contract as a professor of English at Tokyo University of Literature and Science (Bunrika Daigaku); teaches also at Tokyo Imperial University.
1932	February: six poems are included in anthology, *New Signatures*, published by the Hogarth Press.
1934	*Poems*, in an edition of 100 copies, privately printed by The Fox & Daffodil Press, Kinuta-mura, near Tokyo
	8 July: returns to London, where he spends the next three years as a freelance writer.
1935	May: *Poems* published in London.
	October: *Some Versions of Pastoral* published.
	Publishes translations into Basic English of two works by J. B. S. Haldane, *The Outlook of Science* and *Science and Well-Being*.
	Gains MA, University of Cambridge.
1936	W. B. Yeats includes an Empson poem in the *Oxford Book of Modern Verse*; Michael Roberts picks six for *The Faber Book of Modern Verse*.
1937–8	August: takes up appointment at National Peking University, arriving just as the Japanese invade China; journeys through China with I. A. Richards and his wife; works with the exiled Peking universities—amalgamated as the Temporary University — from November 1937 to February 1938 on a mountain at Nan-Yueh, Hunan Province; journeys to Hong Kong.
1938–9	Continues university teaching with the National South-west Associated University in remote exile, first in the town of Mengtzu and then in Kunming, capital of Yunnan province, near the Indo-China (Vietnam) border. In the autumn of 1939, sets off to return home by way of the USA, where he spends a period in Cambridge, Mass. (broadcasting on Basic English).
1939	28 January: arrives back in England.
1940	26 June: joins the Monitoring Service of the BBC at Wood Norton Hall, near Evesham in Worcestershire, working as a sub-editor.
	September: *The Gathering Storm* published in London.
1941	Transfers to the BBC Overseas Service in London, where he becomes a Talks Assistant and then Chinese Editor, organising

talks to China and propaganda programmes for the Home Service; for two years, works alongside George Orwell.

1941   2 December: marries Hester Henrietta Crouse ('Hetta'), a South African artist, at St Stephen's Church, Hampstead, London.

1942   9 November: birth of first son, William Hendrik Mogador

1944   30 September: birth of second son, Jacob Arthur Calais.

1947–52 Teaches at National Peking University, his post being subsidized by the British Council; witnesses the civil war and the six-week siege of Peking late in 1948; the Communist takeover and the inauguration of the People's Republic of China, including the beginnings of reform and 'thought control'.

1948   24 March: *The Collected Poems of William Empson* published in New York.

        July–August: teaches at Kenyon College Summer School, Gambier, Ohio, USA, on leave from Peking.

1950   Further summer visit to the Kenyon College Summer School.

1951   July: *The Structure of Complex Words* published in London.

1952   Summer: returns with family from China to England.

        15 December: *The Poems of William Empson* broadcast by BBC.

1953   October: takes up Chair of English Literature at the University of Sheffield, where he works for the next 18 years, with occasional sabbaticals at American and Canadian universities.

1954   May: Gresham Professor in Rhetoric, Gresham College, London, lecturing on 'The last Plays of Shakespeare and their Relation to the Elizabethan Theatre'.

        June–July: Fellow of the School of Letters, Indiana University, Bloomington, Indiana.

        27 October: *The Birth of Steel: A Light Masque* performed for Queen Elizabeth II at the University of Sheffield.

1955   29 September: *Collected Poems* published in London.

1956   6 December: birth of Hetta Empson's third child, Simon Peter Duval Smith.

1961   February: *The Collected Poems of William Empson* (New York) issued in paperback.

1961   *Milton's God* published.

        William Empson Reading Selected Poems (*Listen* LPV3) issued.

1964   Autumn: Visiting Professor, English Department, University of Ghana, Legon, Accra, Ghana.

1968   Hon. D. Litt, University of East Anglia, Norwich.

        Ingram Merrill Foundation Award.

June–August: Visiting Professor, Department of English, State
University of New York at Buffalo.

1971   Hon. D. Litt, University of Bristol.
        Summer: retires from University of Sheffield.

1972   January–February: gives Waynflete Lectures on 'The editorial
        choice of the text of a poem', at Magdalen College, Oxford.
        Publishes *Coleridge's Verse: A Selection* (with David B. Pirie).

1973   Visiting Professor, York University, Toronto

1974   Lent Term: delivers Clark Lectures at Trinity College, Cam-
        bridge, on 'The Progress of Criticism'.
        Hon. D. Litt., University of Sheffield.
        Honorary member of the American Academy of Arts and
        Letters/The National Institute of Arts and Letters.

1974–5 Visiting Professor of English, Pennsylvania State University.

1976   Autumn: Visiting Professor, Department of English, University
        of Delaware, Newark, Delaware.
        Fellow of the British Academy.
        Honorary Fellow of the Modern Language Association of
        America.

1977   10 June: Hon. Litt. D., University of Cambridge.

1979   Knighted in New Year Honours for 'services to English litera-
        ture'.
        Elected Honorary Fellow, Magdalene College, Cambridge.

1982   January–April: Visiting Professor, University of Miami.

1984   15 April: dies in London.
        Collected Poems reissued; *Using Biography* published.

1986   *The Royal Beasts and Other Works* and *Essays on Shakespeare* pub-
        lished.

1987   *Argufying: Essays on Literature and Culture* and *Faustus and the Censor:
        The English Faust-Book and Marlowe's 'Doctor Faustus'* published.

1993   *Essays on Renaissance Literature*, vol. 1: *Donne and the New Astronomy*.

1994   *Essays on Renaissance Literature*, vol. 2: *The Drama*.

1996   *The Strengths of Shakespeare's Shrew: Essays, Memoirs and Reviews*.

2000   *Complete Poems of William Empson*.

2006   *Selected Letters of William Empson*.

1

The BBC War

People keep writing for propaganda, which I can't do, but I hope to cash in a little on pretending to know about China when I get home.

Letter to mother, 2 June 1939

I gave up writing for ten years because I really thought allied propaganda important...

Letter to Kenyon Review, Autumn 1949

I dropped all my literary interests...because I got absorbed in the war; I thought the defeat of Hitler so important that I could do nothing else (it was a time of great happiness, looking back, and anyway of considerable pleasure, but I have just a steady trickle of mental productiveness, and it was then all directed into propaganda). I still think the war was quite important enough for that, and a good deal of my previous poetry had been concerned to say so...

Letter to Christopher Ricks, 19 January 1975

'I had come back from China voluntarily for the war...I had returned feeling that the defeat of Hitler was of immense importance, to be sure, but also feeling reasonably confident that I would be allowed an interesting war by being let into the propaganda machine; and then again, I was protected by my obscurity, unlike the poet Auden who, I still think, was right in refusing to become the laureate of Churchill.'[1] Like Cyril Connolly, William Empson believed that the best artists of the age should be entitled and enabled to retain the purity of their work. He was modest about his own standing—he thought himself merely a 'minor' poet—but he would readily extend the compliment to Dylan Thomas: 'Dylan was deeply horrified by the raids, and by Hitler, but was also determined not to let his art become propaganda, not even against Hitler.'[2]

Empson had returned home in January 1940 in a run-down state. The months in China, devoid of any true relaxation, had taken a heavy toll, leaving him feeling bedraggled and withdrawn. Yet within a short while he had so far recovered his sense of well-being that he felt keen to pick up on society. T. S. Eliot related to John Hayward on 16 February: 'Bill Empson lunched with me on Saturday. Quiet voyage, but he says that if Winston's famous convoy was looking after his ship, it tactfully kept below the horizon, as he saw nothing of it. He is dirtier and more distrait than ever. It was most refreshing to see him.'[3] John Davenport, meeting up with him again at around the same time, reported to another old friend, Julian Trevelyan: 'I think Bill always does seem a little shy & reserved after these long oriental interludes. Not unnaturally I suppose.'[4] Eliot was to write again to Hayward, on 3 April: 'I dined a week ago with Ronald the Botulist [Bottrall], and Mrs. Bottles (both of whom I rather like)...And Bill the Lizard was there, his usual immaculate natty self, and mentioned that he had been stopping with the Davenports in the country. (I don't quite see what Bill ought to do with himself, except to get adopted into a tribe of gypseys, the Smiths or the Lees, and get a caravan. Otherwise, out of pure absence of mind and lack of self-protective instinct, he may either stop a bullet or die of sorosis of the liver).'[5] Empson did put down his name for military service, though he feared that his myopia might prevent him from being called up. In the meantime, he prepared his poems for publication by Faber & Faber, worked in the British Museum, went out drinking, and scouted about for some fit employment.

On 26 June 1940, four days after the fall of France and two weeks after Mussolini's declaration of war on the Allies, he joined the Monitoring Service of the BBC, which had recently taken over the delightful country estate of Wood Norton Hall, high above the River Avon and about two miles from the town of Evesham in Worcestershire. The purpose of the Monitoring Unit was to pluck information out of the airways of the world. To that end, most of its personnel were multi-linguists, their job being to translate into English the innumerable overseas broadcasts they tracked round the clock. Richard D'Arcy Marriott (later Assistant Director of Radio), who was appointed in June 1940 to build up the corps of monitors, gathered together an exceptionally talented troop, many of them anti-Nazi refugees, to bear the brunt of German broadcast propaganda. They included the future art historian Ernst (later Professor Sir Ernst)

Gombrich;[6] the future publisher George (Turli) Weidenfeld;[7] Anatol Goldberg (a Russian who was to rise to be Chief Commentator in the East European Service); Ilsa Barea (the charming, intelligent, forthright, Austrian-born and politically active wife of the Spanish Republican novelist Arturo Barea, who would himself later broadcast for the BBC Latin American service);[8] and Joe Pereszlenyi, a 22-year old from Budapest in Austro-Hungary who was to become better known as Martin Esslin, Head of BBC Radio Drama from 1963 to 1977.[9] Since several of the monitors were European émigrés whose standard of English fell short of scratch to varying degrees, their copy would be passed forward to a separate editorial team which was charged with writing up the material (or rendering it down, as the case might be) in a presentable English form, though without any loss of its original flavour, hint or implication.

Shortly before taking up his appointment, Empson wrote rather indiscreetly to a new American friend, the future spymaster and paranoid chief of the CIA's Office of Special Operations, James Jesus Angleton (whom he had met on a visit to Yale University in December 1939): 'the B.B.C. have given me a job sub-editing Lord Haw-Haw, doing during the night a precis of the day's foreign broadcasts.'[10] For the fair salary of £480 a year, Empson plied his fountain pen in the capacity of a sub-editor in Hut 23. He was helping to shape the hefty and ineptly-named 'Daily Digest of Foreign Broadcasts' and on occasion its concise offspring, the 'Monitoring Report' of some 3 or 4,000 words—which Lord Weidenfeld has described as 'absolutely indispensable background information and prime source for anybody dealing with propaganda to Europe or with information generally'.[11]

Unremitting and unquestionably valuable, the sub-editor's task called for a keen eye and self-restraint. Empson had to resist the temptation to gee-up a mulish piece of prose, since any misrepresentation of a bare fact or a bare-faced lie, let alone tricks of phrasing or tone, could prove disastrous. The job of cutting and selectively rephrasing the translations required a high level of analytical good sense and stylistic skill. But the work was not entirely a matter of dour concentration. Ewald Osers (later Vice-President of the International Federation of Translators) was heard to ask one day, 'Now, what is the English version of that fairy tale, you know, something like "The Booted Tomcat"?'[12]

Empson told Richards (in more guarded terms than he had used to Angleton): 'I am doing minor but satisfying work for the BBC and am safe and comfortable. It is on the side of incoming news . . .'[13] The Monitoring Unit was supposed to be secret: as Empson observed in a further letter to

Angleton, 'the country house has electrified wire round the estate, and we are challenged by four successive sentries in the dark before reaching the hut where we work till dawn; looking down from the hill at dawn you get the same level low-lying bank of fog that we did when isolated on the Sacred Mountain [at Nan-Yueh in China], a thing the Japanese paint very well.'[14] Naturally all personnel were rigorously vetted (Gwenda David, the first woman sub-editor on the team, recalled that her shelves were scrutinized by security investigators, who demanded to know why she possessed a copy of *Mein Kampf*), though none so thoroughly as the over-whelming majority of foreign nationals and refugees who came to join the roll at Wood Norton. It is symptomatic of the continuing wariness of officialdom that only the British nationals were permitted (and indeed obliged) to take fire-arms instruction: they had to learn how to handle a rifle. Similarly, the staff of Editorial, most of whom were British, 'felt themselves to be a group superior to, and somewhat withdrawn from, the mostly alien linguists.' According to another colleague, Richard Usborne (future editor of P. G. Wodehouse)—who considered Empson 'surely the best brain' of the whole editorial group—'some huts were for the heaven-born, others for the canaille'.[15]

The editorial élite worked on the Monitoring Report, distilling the day's inflow: David Hallett, Gustaaf Renier, Christopher (Kit) Saltmarshe (who had been a Cambridge contemporary of Empson), and Gilbert Harding (later famous for his irascible performances on the TV panel game 'What's My Line'). Empson would join that inner circle only when one of their permanent number was absent, as would another colleague, the self-igniting luminary of the literary world, Geoffrey Grigson. Empson and Grigson were known collectively as 'The Poets', even though, as Olive Renier remembers, 'they were very different' as individuals.[16] Acerbic, rude, and pushy, Grigson loathed his days in the Monitoring Service, which he later characterized as a 'concentration camp of incompatibles'.

Empson felt no such animus. Hardly ever given to gossiping or back-biting, he absorbed himself in a task which he believed to be profoundly useful to the war effort. Working the regulation 48-hour shift over a four-day period—twelve hours on (from 2 p.m. to 2 a.m.), twelve hours off—he nursed no sense of displeasure about either the kind of work he was doing or the humdrum conditions outside the BBC enclave, where he was billeted in the attic room of a redbrick terraced house at 69 Burford Road, Evesham: 'you don't see people much,' he observed flatly and without self-commiseration. He even felt good-humoured about doing his stint for the Home Guard, though it brought him some incidental difficulty. The duty 'involved sleeping with the clothes on in the earlier part of the night in the guards dormitory, after eating in the canteen . . . ,' he explained, 'and having eaten in the canteen I naturally had to be sick soon after lying down.'[17] At night, unearthly fiery skies to north and south-west indicated that Coventry, Birmingham and Bristol were burning after being bombed.

No one could complain that the material which passed across the sub-editors' desks lacked interest. Sometimes it was white hot propaganda or vital strategic information. The Monitoring Service soon became 'a lynch-pin of the whole BBC war-time organization,' as Asa Briggs has observed in his official history of BBC broadcasting. 'Both PWE [Political Warfare Executive] and the Ministry of Information attached the utmost import-ance to its growth and to the full co-ordination of the service with that of other related agencies inside or outside the BBC.'[18]

Occasionally, however, as the session in Hut 23 stretched into the small hours, with all personnel maintaining a dead silence in the face of urgent work, Empson would suddenly tell Gwenda David to listen while he recited a poem he had just written. (Although he gave her several of the poems announced in this fashion, she regrettably lost them some time ago.) Since the workload never slackened and the deadlines were always impending, the senior editor in the room would be very annoyed by such frivolous interruptions. Empson bicycled to and from work with a book propped against the handlebars of his Corporation Raleigh. Gwenda David witnessed this spectacle at least half a dozen times, and once watched in astonishment as he pedalled his way through a herd of cows without looking up from his reading. Richard Usborne recalled too that Empson would wear socks instead of gloves while cycling. He had no care for effect. Whether or not he was tipsy when he managed such feats is not to be known. But he did drink a good deal, often noticeably. All the same, drunk or sober, he could do the work as well as the next sub-editor. A few of his colleagues did once try to get him sacked on account of his drinking, but Gwenda David intervened on his behalf with the unanswerable argu-ment that no one could show any deficiency in his work. It seems quite likely that some spiteful colleagues, who had learned their trade in tough provincial journalism, resented his intellectualism and his poetry.

It was while working at Evesham that Empson met up once again with another poet with a mounting reputation as genius and drinker, Dylan Thomas (whom he had come to know in London in the mid-1930s). They were brought together on a visit in November 1940 to the home—Maltings

House at Marshfield, Gloucestershire—of Empson's friend John Davenport. (Davenport would presently join forces with Thomas in writing *The Death of the King's Canary*, their satirical fiction—in the modern tradition of Wyndham Lewis's *The Apes of God* and Roy Campbell's *The Georgiad*—about the writers and painters of Bohemia which incorporated a good parody by Thomas of an Empson poem.)[19] 'Bill Empson sends his love,' wrote Davenport to another old chum from Cambridge, Julian Trevelyan. 'He is smoking a cigarette, and sucking an orange & playing shove halfpenny & the whole room is in a ghastly condition.' Of Dylan Thomas, Empson would recall: 'I remember his telling me how frightening it was always to have nothing to do next day: sometimes, he said, "I buy a Mars Bar, and I think tomorrow I will eat that, so then I can go to sleep, because I have a plan." I did not much like this highly polished bit of tear-jerking, but there is little doubt that unemployment would have driven me to drink too.'[20] Another memory would crop up in a piece that Empson wrote over twenty years later: 'Dylan Thomas, with the dead earnestness which so often came as a surprise, told me it was curious he was such a martyr to attacks of neurotic guilt, as he led such an innocent life, but he found the only way to handle them was to hide in the country for a week or two, stopping drinking altogether, speaking to nobody, and so on. His meaning in using this term was clear; he felt struck down by guilt though by his own principles he had done no wrong; and it was easy to reflect that he had done wrong by the principles of the hostess of Fern Hill, his peasant aunt.'[21] Like virtually everyone who ever came into contact with Thomas, Empson found him 'immensely entertaining'—an 'entrancing talker'. But there was a price to pay. 'Drink was necessary to screw him up to the duty of entertainment, and because the whole party (however assembled) must be seduced into joining the feast of wit.'[22] Yet what is evident from the memoirs of those who witnessed the two poets in the hectic of conversation is that Empson did not just play the lay figure to the exuberant conversationalist Thomas. He could rival the Welsh bard for eloquence as well as for uttering poetry. Augustus John was to recall one evening in a pub when Empson looked like 'a late Michelangelo based on some recently unearthed and slightly damaged antiquity, while Dylan's face was round and his nose snub':

> Mr William Empson, although at this time enjoying none of the Welsh-man's notoriety, played no second fiddle but, as if under the spell of the *hwyl*, or divine afflatus, gave one at moments the illusion of riding like a bird above the ground! To achieve the Top of the World is worth taking a risk, no

doubt, but I wouldn't advise lesser men than Empson to try it. I was moved greatly by his performance, being something of an old mountaineer myself, and on a lower plane may call myself one of his fans.[23]

Like the very best part of boozy wit, however, most of the talk and the wit vanished in the next night's sleep.

But Empson was to become intensely loyal to Thomas—and not merely for the sentimental reasons of their happy acquaintance. He was devoted to the poetry, most especially the early poetry—of all contemporary poets, he would maintain, only Auden and Thomas had the 'true fire'—and became one of its most penetrating critics. Much of the poetry may seem obscure, even impenetrable, said Empson, but it should not be written off as meaningless, and certainly not as Symbolist. Despite the fact that Thomas would occasionally speak of his early poetry in terms of 'Symbolist patter', Empson knew that his friend did not actually credit the spurious tenets of Symbolism. 'I feel sure of this, not only from his subsequent work, but from a quaint moment in the pub . . . George Barker had just brought out a slim volume, and Dylan was spluttering over it: he said, "No man has the right to throw a bucket of sheer nonsense in the public's face," and I would have been tempted not to believe my ears, except that Davenport, who was much deeper in his counsels than I, clearly regarded this outburst as a healthy symptom. None of his good work, early or late, was written in obedience to that lethal theory . . .'[24] The key conviction in Thomas's work, Empson insisted (he was surely right), was 'a kind of pantheism'. He recognized this element in Thomas because he was inclined to credit a kind of quasi-pantheism—a belief in a world-soul, not a revealed personal godhead—for himself, but it would be false to say that he simply found what he was looking for. There is no doubt at all that he felt rapturous about Thomas's best poetry. 'We need not think of Dylan as a deluded or self-indulgent author,' he wrote. 'But, all the same, it is the first inspiration, the poems the young man hit the town with (overwhelmingly good, though one resisted them because one couldn't see why), which are the permanent challenge to a critic and in a way the decisive part of his work. I was disinclined to review the *Collected Poems* when it came out during his lifetime [in 1952], because I would have had to say I liked the early obscure ones best, and I was afraid this would distress him; so I now have one of those unavailing regrets about my timidity, because he knew all that kind of thing very well and could be distressed only by a refusal to say so.'[25]

Empson's own early poems, collected in *Poems* (1935), had gained for him too a reputation for obscurity (albeit different from Dylan Thomas's). If a fair number of his early poems address vexed moral and metaphysical issues with metaphors taken from scientific learning, for example, he also claimed that in his later poems—gathered up in *The Gathering Storm* (and issued by Faber & Faber in September 1940 in a slim black volume costing six shillings)—he was just as much of a political poet. The idea informing the verses, he said in a preface, 'is that there is a change in the style of the poems, whether good or bad, connected with the steady approach of war which we were conscious of during those years.'[26] (His political poetry can be seen to begin as early as the satirical 'Part of Mandevil's Travels' in 1928.) He is a political poet both in a general sense—the range of subjects encompasses the nature of aggression and warfare, dreams and despair, courage and fear, duty and desire, death and belief—and in the particular sense, since he writes also with deep commitment of Chinese endurance and survival ('China') and of his sense of solidarity with his university colleagues during their exile from Peking following the all-out Japanese military invasion in 1937 ('Autumn on Nan-Yueh').

> '[M]y second volume of verse The Gathering Storm [he was to write in a later year] meant by the title just what Winston Churchill did when he stole it, the gradual sinister confusing approach to the Second World War. Of course the title was chosen after writing the poems, during the early years of the war, but nearly all the poems really are considering this prospect, with which I had been fairly closely confronted, in China, Japan, Indochina and Korea.'[27]

T. S. Eliot, his editor at Faber & Faber, wrote for the book a blurb that was as cautious as it was precise in its claims: 'No poet of the younger generation has achieved reputation on a smaller output of verse than William Empson. His first volume made him known as the most brilliantly obscure of modern poets. This, his second volume, should not only increase the admiration of his admirers but bring him a larger public. For there is a remarkable development towards clarity and simplicity, and the expression, at times, of intense feeling.' Such a plaudit may seem half-hearted, and even ironic, but in fact there is little doubt that Eliot truly admired Empson's poetry. In October 1939 John Hayward, Eliot's friend (and Empson's), wrote to Frank Morley (a sometime editor at Faber's who was then working for the publishers Harcourt Brace & Company in New York) with a report of Eliot's eagerness to proselytize for Empson's verses:

> Ever since [Empson] sent me an extremely good poem by way of apology for being very drunk and uproarious and destructive in B. gardens [Hayward's flat in Bina Gardens, Kensington, London], I've pressed his claims on Tom [Eliot]. Now T. P. ['The Possum', Eliot's self-assumed nickname]

writes to say that 'Richards has shown me a couple of unpublished poems of Bill's which impressed me; damned if I don't think Bill has more brain power, as well as more resistance to the ills that flesh is heir to (Shakespeare, as quoted by Mr Sollory) than the rest of 'em poets'. He adds as a postscript: 'If Empson's poems have not been published in America, Harcourt B ought to get a lien on them, both published and unpublished. The new ones are almost as good as the one about the poison in the bloodstream ["Missing Dates"]'.[28]

'Missing Dates', a villanelle dating from July 1937, is a lament for lost opportunities in life and the poison released into the system, both personal and social, by a feeling of waste and unfulfilment; it closes sonorously and movingly:

> It is the poems you have lost, the ills
> From missing dates, at which the heart expires.
> Slowly the poison the whole blood stream fills.
> The waste remains, the waste remains and kills.

The Gathering Storm is made up of 21 poems (all of them composed between 1931 and 1937) including one lyric which commemorates the poet's sorry, abrupt affair with a Japanese woman in Tokyo ('Aubade'), and three translations from the Japanese of another young woman named Chiyoko Hatakeyama. It collects too Empson's indulgent satire, 'Just a Smack at Auden', on the left-wing doom-saying of Auden and his associates—the 'Auden Gang', as they became known—who foresaw not so much the world war that was to be unleashed in 1939 but that a decadent bourgeois society should die of its own demons: it would collapse from intolerable neuroses. In later years Empson would consistently maintain that he had admired Auden's admonitory stance in politics, despite the incantatory lampooning of his verses –

> Waiting for the end, boys, waiting for the end.
> What is there to be or do?
> What's become of me or you?
> Are we kind or are we true?
> Sitting two and two, boys, waiting for the end.

He wrote in 1983, for instance: 'I entirely agreed with Auden, though I could not express the opinion nearly so well, that War II was coming, and that backing the people's front was our only chance. I just thought his hammering at it had become counter-productive, and by the time he read my joke he thought the hammering had become a boring duty.'[29] Empson issues an urbane barracking to Auden and his pals.

One of Auden's most severe critics (and Empson's) was F. R. Leavis, who insisted upon the intent moral seriousness of the very best literature. It is not surprising, therefore, that another of Empson's poems pokes fun at the exacting puritanism of Leavis. 'Your Teeth are Ivory Towers' opens by referring to the researches of the Swiss psychologist Jean Piaget, who discovered (*The Language and Thought of the Child*, 1926) that young children exist in a state of egocentrism—'for the most part they are talking only to themselves,' he declared. Empson takes this insight as a metaphor for the poet's failure to communicate with his fit audience:

> There are some critics say our verse is bad
> Because Piaget's babies had the same affection,
> Proved by interview. These young were mad,
>
> They spoke not to Piaget but to themselves. Protection
> Indeed may safely grow less frank; a Ba
> Cordial in more than one direction
>
> Can speak well to itself and yet please Pa.
> So too Escape Verse has grown mortal sin.
> This gives just one advantage; a moral Ha
>
> Can now be retorted in kind. Panoplied in
> Virtuous indignation, gnawing his bone,
> A man like Leavis plans an Escape . . .

Escapism (the infamous ivory tower) or infantilism (including that of Auden and his fellow 'boys' who appeared sometimes to be fixated upon schoolday codes and values): such may be the wages of immaturity, or of failing to make contact with one's society and its burning issues. And yet, as Empson says in most of his poetry, life is fraught with contradictions that can't be resolved by analysis; those who think they hold the answers are commonly proposing simplistic solutions.

The paradoxical or ambiguous title of the fine poem, 'Courage means Running' (at once running in the race of life and running away), happily points to fear as the prerequisite of bravery. The most courageous individuals necessarily have the most immediate access to fear ('Usual for a man | Of Bunyan's courage to respect fear'); and strange but true as it may seem, both pleasure and pain 'presume fear'. These forces run so deep that they are not to be explained away; life itself is the condition of contradiction. So too, another poem, 'Ignorance of Death' takes the form of a witty and surprisingly comforting hymn to our saving ignorance of eschatalogy. It was Freud who pointed out that we are in love with death; and so Empson delights in the paradox that our love of death is 'civilizing'.

'Buddhists and Christians contrive to agree about death,| Making death their ideal basis for different ideals.| The Communists however disapprove of death | Except when practical.' Given our ignorance of the meaning of death, it is inevitably and wonderfully fruitful as an inspiration for human creativity—'It is the trigger of the literary man's biggest gun.' In a few of his poems from this period Empson takes pains to make use of the terza rima form, leapfrogging his rhymes and cascading his syntax in a way that propels the narrative enquiry in question. In 'Ignorance of Death' he makes use of a three-line form that looks at first glance like terza rima but is actually altogether more casual; in fact, it uses neither rhyme nor metre. The effect is to generate a jaunty mode for a daunting subject.

> Heaven me, when a man is ready to die about something
> Other than himself, and is in fact ready because of that,
> Not because of himself, that is something clear about him.
>
> Otherwise I feel very blank upon this topic,
> And think that though important, and proper for anyone to bring up,
> It is one that most people should be prepared to be blank upon.

Empson in these poems works his way through both wordly anguish and metaphysical consternation towards a point of philosophical resignation. The contradictions can perhaps never be reconciled, he comes to realize: and so it is that one's personal and philosophical worries must be surrendered to living a life in this world. Still, the sufferance can be sweet.

By the mid-1940s he had virtually given up writing poetry, and something of the reason for his apostasy can be comprehended when one lines up the unavailing 'talk' of 'Your Teeth are Ivory Towers' alongside the philosophical acceptance of 'blankness' in 'Ignorance of Death'. Not to give up the struggle to sort out ultimate purposes is the sure way to invite madness into one's mind. Thus one of his last lyrics is titled by way of a consoling directive, 'Let it go', for it takes the resigned measure of all the contradictions and the talk and the blankness:

> It is this deep blankness is the real thing strange.
>   The more things happen to you the more you can't
>   Tell or remember even what they were.
>
> The contradictions cover such a range.
>   The talk would talk and go so far aslant.
>   You don't want madhouse and the whole thing there.

Like Dr Johnson, Empson feared madness in proportion as he valued reason.

A related poem—an intent, gnomic paean called 'The Teasers'—puts in question the totalizing claims of religious or political doctrines; it opens balefully:

> Not but they die, the teasers and the dreams,
> Not but they die . . .

Creeds hold out the promise of absolving salvation, whether religious or secular; but they may be false, and they fail and die. Empson offered this gloss on the lines to an Australian poet named Hugh Major who had asked him about them: ' "Cock-teasers", when I was young, was a term for girls who excite sexual desire without intending to satisfy it; and [in 'The Teasers'] trust in Heaven or the Communist State is compared to them.'[30] So the poem closes with this humane and magnanimous advice:

> Make no escape
>   build up your love,
> Leave what you die for and be safe to die.

– which the poet likewise explained, in these terms: 'If you die feeling: "All right, call it a day; I have managed to do what I had to do", you feel safe about it. It does happen; I have known cases. The poem does not set out to mean more.' Such was the humanist morality to which Empson dedicated the best part of his life. If the groundbase of his poems from this period is fear, they also say much in favour of fulfilling duty and service.

Given the 'steady approach of war' which he believed to underpin much of this second collection, the poem called 'Reflection from Rochester' (notwithstanding its mild-mannered title) must be taken as a key work. Empson thought of this poem and 'Courage means Running' as essentially related, exploring the same theme from different angles. In 1953, in an untitled review of *Poems by John Wilmot, Earl of Rochester* (ed. by V. de S. Pinto), he had remarked of 'The Satire on Man': 'The most powerful section is an argument as with hammer-blows that all human actions proceed from fear.'[31] Accordingly, Empson's 'Reflection from Rochester' ruminates upon the traditional, even commonplace, contrast (deriving from Plutarch, Juvenal, Erasmus, and Hobbes) between ruthless human-kind and wild animals that forms the burden of Rochester's *A Satyr against Mankind* (1679). Taking his inspiration in a general way from Boileau's Satire VIII (which was itself based on Juvenal's Fifteenth Satire), Rochester contends that while wild animals kill only in order to eat—instinctively—human savagery is a function of treachery and caprice: our aggression is the product of vain self-interest or hypocritical self-protection. The lines that fire Empson's verses are the fulcrum of the poem, and he quotes them at the top and tail of his poem, like a sandwich:

> For hunger or for love they bite and tear,
> While wretched man is still in arms for fear.
> For fear he arms and is of arms afraid,
> From fear to fear successively betrayed . . . [32]

Empson's poem reflects upon the problem of war from a variety of perspectives: personal ambition, the arts of social coordination and political distraction, and sex and the paradoxes of sexual sublimation. Stanzas 5 to 7, for instance, read:

> Increasing power (it has increased a lot)
> Embarrasses 'attempted suicides',
> Narrows their margin. Politics that got
>
> 'Virility from war' get much besides;
> The mind, as well in mining as in gas
> War's parallel, now less easily decides
>
> On a good root-confusion to amass
> Much safety from irrelevant despair.
> Mere change in numbers made the process crass.

The quotation marks round 'Virility from war' have the effect of 'so-called': that is, they dissociate the speaker from the attitude or description implied without attributing it to anyone in particular, still less claiming an exact quotation. The idea that war is a manly activity and improves the virility of a race is traditional, but perhaps the 'Policies' to which the poem refers as being based on this idea are Fascist and Nazi ones, influenced by Nietzsche and his successors. The middle of the poem thus says that with increased numbers and more powerful technology we cannot afford this traditional idea of war. The close of the poem looks to the past for some workable precedent, but now it is our eyes that are 'blank': they are at once targets (an old sense of blank, as in *King Lear*), blind, uncomprehending:

> We now turn blank eyes for a pattern there
> Where first the race of armament was made;
> Where a less involute compulsion played.
> 'For hunger or for love they bit and tear.'

'Involute' means 'entangled, intricate', so those final lines look back to a less complicated world, a supposedly more innocent age, when biting had two clear (and yet not unrelated) primitive purposes: for tearing up food in the big game of survival and for affectionate play—as the sign of love. But there are no available patterns or precedents; the war machine devised by man has developed to such a monstrous scale that we cannot handle it.

Of all the poems collected in *The Gathering Storm*, those I have mentioned so far are perhaps the most successful: they represent what one critic justly called a 'triumph of poise' in the face of metaphysical, existential, moral, and political anxieties.[33] But one other poem is arguably even more teasing, beguiling and witty—and possibly more personally revealing—than all the others. 'Four Legs, Two Legs, Three Legs', first published in 1935 with the offhand title 'Travel Note', works in an apparently inconsequential way to conflate two sphinxes: the Greek one which set a poser for Oedipus and the battered Egyptian one which survives to this day. The poem appears to ask, casually—disingenuously?—about the meaning of the riddle and the effect of Oedipus's correct answer.

> Delphic and Theban and Corinthian,
> Three lines, by the odd chance, met at a point,
> The delta zero, the case trivial.
>
> A young man's cross-road but a shady one.
> Killing a mistaken black cat in the dark
> He had no other metaphysical trait.
>
> God walks in a mysterious way
> Neither delighteth he in any man's legs.
>
> The wrecked girl, still raddled with Napoleon's paint,
> Nose eaten by a less clear conqueror,
> Still orientated to the average dawn,
> Behind, Sahara, before, Nile and man
> A toy abandoned, sure, after so many,
> That the next sun will take her for a walk,
> Still lifts a touching dog's face eager for a sign.
>
> Not one for generalising his solutions
> Oedipus placed the riddle with a name.
> Another triumph for the commonplace.
> While too much to pretend she fell and burst
> It is a comfort that the Sphinx took such an answer.

The poem is more complicated than it might appear, with a remarkable range of allusiveness and 'stylization'. One cannot but wonder not only about what the poem seems to say—seeks to represent and express—about the contest between supernatural power and human being, but also about the mentality of Empson himself, since he depicts the monstrous feminine in terms first of a 'wrecked' girl, then as a 'toy' and a 'dog', and finally, by way of a subliminal allusion to the Acts of the Apostles, as the ultimate betrayer, Judas. The lack of strict coordination between wrecked girl, toy, dog, and Judas—they are such mixed metaphors—signifies to me that, one way or another, Empson was saying more than he knew. This very witty poem is thus available to many interpretations: ideological, psychological, aesthetic, moral, and maybe personal.

The Gathering Storm gathered only a few brief notices in the British press over the last dark months of 1940. Reviews were posted in the *Times Literary Supplement*, *Life & Letters*, *Scrutiny*, and *Poetry Review*. Stephen Spender, rounding up 'The Year's Poetry' in *Horizon* (February 1941), saw in the verses inklings of beauty and clarity, but his review erred towards the churlishly ignorant: 'When Empson's poetry overcomes obscurity it has moments of beautiful lucidity. If he can get rid of his mannerisms and decarbonize his system from an excess of undigested research into obscure topics, he may write the most lucid, instead of the most obscure, contemporary poetry.' It was left to G. S. Fraser, in a much later year, to pinpoint some of the excellences of the work:

> *The Gathering Storm* . . . is in the main a poetry of public events and the public tone of voice . . . The poems suggested a deep trust in the fundamental, sane anti-Fascism of the British people . . . and in a combination of prudence and courage in facing Axis aggression. There is nothing of the rather naïve belief of Auden . . . either that Western civilization is automatically running to an end or that we shall have Utopia tomorrow. The voice has a tart and humorous authority. The tone suggests political poets of the Restoration, like Dryden, Rochester, or Marvell in his satires much more than Donne: there is a kind of bulldog steadiness in it, and in a way it was appropriate that Churchill should choose the same title, *The Gathering Storm*, for his volume of memoirs about the 1930's. The tone of tense and intricate personal despair is replaced by one of humorous combative stoicism.[34]

Empson himself gave it little further thought: he became engrossed by his work at the BBC. His poetry was to be more fully appraised in the USA in the late 1940s, with the appearance of *Collected Poems of William Empson*, and in the UK only when his *Collected Poems* came out in 1955. When *The Gathering Storm* went out of print in January 1951, it was T. S. Eliot who prompted Empson's regular publishers, Chatto & Windus: 'I think it would be a great pity if Empson's poems ceased to be available.'[35] Eliot was to release the rights in the volume only in September that year.

Though seemingly impersonal in his usual demeanour, and giving away little of his private feelings, the one confidence Empson volunteered to Gwenda David while working at Wood Norton was his disappointment that he could not serve in the armed forces. He felt ashamed to be enjoying a sheltered wartime occupation. He did not undervalue the work of monitoring, but he desired a more constructive role. With his knowledge of Japan and China, he hoped to be of use in propaganda. As he would later say, he had no doubt that he was 'taking part in a crusade'.

Fate was on his side. According to Asa Briggs's *History of Broadcasting in the United Kingdom*, R. A. Butler wrote 'from the Foreign Office in February 1941 pressing for the appointment of BBC staff who would be capable of broadcasting to the Far East—staff whom Sir John Pratt, an expert on the Far East then working in the Ministry of Information, had also been demanding.'[36] Empson promptly volunteered himself for the job of preparing radio scripts for China; and at the same time, in a long letter to Sir Stephen Tallents, Controller of Overseas Services, he urged the BBC to broadcast propaganda to Japan as well.[37] The Japanese onslaught in China was the other half of the map of the world war, and some deft propaganda should help to forestall dreadful developments. He wrote on 12 February, with impressive prescience: 'A naval attack by Japan [against British territory] is possible and would be serious'; and he independently endorsed Butler's suggestion that 'nothing should be left undone to encourage resistance to Japan and to prevent her becoming actually involved in the war against us.'[38] Propaganda to China and Japan, 'even if done in a very small way, ought to be planned concurrently and with an effect of frankness,' Empson proposed. What the Japanese needed to be told was that they ought to be more suspicious of Germany and Russia than of Britain—'surely you Buddhists [the Japanese had to be reminded] can see through the jackdaw ignorance of [Hitler's] claim to racial superiority'.

As to Japan's policy towards China, the Japanese should acknowledge the unforeseen strength of Chinese nationalism, and that 'history surely proves that Japan need not be ashamed of making an agreed peace with her'. The aggressors could be reminded too: 'You do not want these conquests because you hate living anywhere but on the sacred soil of Japan.' On the other hand, Japanese imperialism had a forceful case 'which should be respected'.

With regard to the kind and size of audience that the BBC could expect to reach in Japan, the most likely owners of short-wave radios were those absolutely key figures, the industrialists, who 'are particularly disgruntled with the Japanese totalitarianism, which has always despised them . . .

Furthermore, at worst, the Japanese Government will certainly monitor foreign broadcasts and worry over them; and the truth is that we are getting there the kind of reader we most want. In China the position is of course different; the chief public aimed at is the local newspaper office, which generally has a receiving set; also many of the universities.'

Propaganda is the art of anticipating a response and thus of devising a form of persuasion which will secure acceptance and conviction; literary criticism is its close kin. In such terms, Empson's first 'screed' to the quiet, cultured and courteous Tallents (who had been secretary of the Empire Marketing Board before joining the BBC) was both imaginative and shrewdly judged. He showed an instinctively sure grasp of the business:

> For effective propaganda, the hearers should already have an inkling or suspicion that what the propagandist says is true; his function is largely to break the ice dividing what is frequently said in private talk from what it seems natural to write or find in print. These conditions are eminently fulfilled in Japan; the Japanese suspect the Germans as much as they do the British, and the Russians more than either.[39]

Sir John Pratt, to whom Empson posted a copy of his letter, responded from the Ministry of Information (MOI) to say he would warmly recommend the scheme to the BBC. Empson for his part told Ronald Bottrall, 'I am really not personally excited about getting the job, only about getting results . . . The business of pretending to have a propaganda service to Japan seems a bit irritating.'[40] It is tempting to believe that at least the MOI policy vis-à-vis broadcasting to Japan, which Pratt continued to urge upon the BBC, had been set in train by Empson, since Pratt's proposals went on reflecting Empson's very first suggestions. As Asa Briggs has noted: 'Pratt believed that broadcasts in Japanese might well influence Japanese policy—they would be listened to by monitors, if by no one else, and their contents would be summarized for the benefit of government officials . . .'[41] Words not unlike Empson's would accordingly echo down the corridors of power for months to come, though the seasoned Pratt would retire from the MOI during 1941. Once the Japanese Service was up and running, it would continue to operate without abatement until 1990.

Empson won considerable authority for himself in the Eastern Service simply because he took the initiative—not once but again, and again and again—in setting out a firm propaganda line on Japan which the BBC could reasonably pursue. In December 1941, when the Japanese finally declared war on the world, he leapt off his mark. 'The line required is simple, having only two parts, and I believe has the advantage of truth,' he argued in a seven-page policy paper submitted directly after the attack on Pearl Harbour and a week before the surrender of Hong Kong on Christmas Day. 'It is: "The Emperor has been misled by false admirers, especially German advisers" and "The Japanese people need not starve after an Axis defeat".'[42] He elaborated this with convincing confidence:

> The belief that Japan would starve after defeat is very widespread among Japanese, and must be combated. This is not 'appeasement' but an essential part of the war effort, the effort to make Japan accept defeat ... Our propaganda case about the Emperor is a very clear one ... it is urgent for us, during the war, to try to crack the Japanese shell of solidarity, and our only way in is the slogan: 'Remove the false advisers: restore the Emperor again to power'. An intelligent Japanese really feels the force of this slogan, because what the Emperor symbolises is at bottom only 'the head of the family', simple private Japanese nationalism ...

Empson's immediate superior was the scholar and diplomatist L. F. Rush-brook Williams, who was the first person to hold the post of Eastern Service Director: he had no more than ten weeks' experience of working for what Empson called 'this very queer organisation'.[43] Formerly a professor of modern history at the Universities of Allahabad and Delhi (he would pompously cling to the title of 'Professor' for the remainder of his career), and a valued servant of the Government of India, the intelligent and kindly Williams had no practical experience of the Far East, whether in China or Japan. It was common at this time for the British to speak of 'Asia' and mean just India, and Williams was wedded to Pakistan. All the same, though not the BBC's first choice for the Eastern Service office, he was an acute administrator and knew when to trust the expertise of a subordinate. Before taking over as BBC Eastern Service Director, he had been since 1939 head of the Middle East section of the Ministry of Information. The force of Empson's unsolicited essay on propaganda to the Japanese impressed him. 'I think Mr Empson's paper affords an excellent basis for discussion,' he wrote in an Internal Circulating Memo dated 15 December and marked 'Very Urgent', along with the proposal that it be sent forward to the Foreign Office. By implication, he was suggesting that Empson's submission could represent the official BBC position in talks with the Government. It was a singular compliment. R. A. (Tony) Rendall, Acting Controller of Overseas Services, whom Maurice Gorham described as 'a good example of the proverbial old head on young shoulders',[44] endorsed Williams's note with the comment that Empson's paper looked 'very interesting'. So far, so good. But the next step required them to subject Empson's promising plan to the gauntlet of bureaucracy. Rendall advised: 'I would suggest that the right course is to forward it to Far East Division M.O.I. for consideration for Far East Publicity Committee on which F.O. sits and we are represented by [A. F. N.] Thavenot [Assistant Director of Eastern Services]. If agreed Empson could also attend.'[45]

Perhaps not surprisingly, the proposals foundered in committee, even as Japanese forces lanced into the South Pacific. Singapore fell on 18 February 1942, Java ten days later. Asa Briggs has argued: 'In such times of flux and disaster Rushbrook Williams and many of his colleagues in the BBC thought of broadcasting in Japanese as at best a "stunt" . . . '[46] And yet Briggs's account of this matter gives a slightly false impression. Williams did indeed think it would probably be pointless to broadcast in Japanese on the 'occasional' basis proposed by the MOI; but in fact he was backing Empson, who had pressed as early as 10 October 1941 for a more regular service: 'Except in some very exceptional case it seems quite useless to broadcast from London anything less than a regular fifteen minutes a week.'[47] Thus both Williams and Empson, his internal adviser, believed it could be a waste of time to relay only an occasional feature. The MOI was 'keen' on the idea of setting up a 'stunt', Williams noted with regret (in the memo that was slightly miscontrued by Briggs); 'and I am afraid I have acted on the principle that the Corporation must meet any reasonable demands, however difficult, that may be made upon it!'[48] A regular propaganda slot would be quite different—maybe even an effective exercise. A month later, the BBC was told that until further notice the Far Eastern Division of the MOI would be directing its own propaganda to Japan and Japanese-occupied territories on behalf of the Political Warfare Executive, so that 'no Japanese broadcasts were required' from the BBC.[49] Nevertheless, the man from the Ministry 'agreed to discuss' with his superiors 'the possibility of Mr. Rushbrook Williams and Mr. Empson attending the committee now working on the basic plan of propaganda to Japan'. In sum, incredible as it may seem in retrospect, the Ministry of Information was evidently still working on a 'basic plan of propaganda to Japan' more than a year after Empson had made his first efforts to recommend a workable scheme to both the MOI and the BBC.

So long as there appeared to be any chance at all of inducing Japan to choke back her ambitions for world domination, Empson had urged, BBC broadcasts should seek to persuade the Japanese that they were being led astray by the Germans, not by the mandate of the Emperor. There might yet be time and a way to make them tread another path, to cultivate a better attitude. 'It is essential to give a feeling that world culture with its natural suggestion of friendship still exists,' he wrote in October. 'If done in this way the thing will not be mistaken for appeasement.'[50] When Japan unleashed her forces in the Pacific, leaving the western powers with no other recourse than to fight back, Empson's instinct as propagandist was to mock the enemy. To portray Japan as fiendish and powerful was to show too much respect for it. His tactic was to suggest that there was nothing fearful about the foe; on the contrary, it was pathetic and self-deluding, less bully than butt. At the end, however, Empson chose to depict the Japanese as so rootedly racist that they must be viewed with repugnance. They were unutterably alien beings, not merely puny pretenders.

But the argument that the Japanese are naturally contemptuous of other races would do little to downplay the danger they represented, as Empson presently realized; it would excite disgust in his listeners. He had enrolled in the Eastern Service hoping above all else to boost the morale of the Chinese, and to help in some small way to head off the threat of an escalation of the war in the Far East. Pouring scorn on the Japanese might gratify the Allies, but it would not sway minds at any deeper, more purposeful level. He would do better to dispel the notion that the Japanese were an iniquitous subspecies of humankind: they were less monstrous than misinformed and very muddled—though wickedly so.

Empson assumed this tack in a longer talk given towards the end of February 1942, the second of nine talks on 'The 20th Century Jap', which was first broadcast on the Overseas Service (to North America, Africa, and the Pacific) and then published in the *The Listener* under the title 'These Japanese'. It is probably the most effective broadcast he ever delivered during the war, since it is at once informative and disarmingly argued, with quite enough shocking surprises to fix the listener's attention. As Karl Miller has observed, Empson 'speaks here in his own voice, if more plainly and patiently than elsewhere, and every syllable is characteristic . . . sensible and humane'; above all, Empson's essay is 'refreshing'.[51] 'The Japanese are no more a separate race that the English,' Empson declares right off; 'they both live on the island beyond the continent, and the different waves of immigration can't get any further, so they all mix there. I think that is an important point, because the idea that the nations are fixed races does a lot of harm.' Both Germans and Japanese are telling lies when they propound the concept of 'inherent racial differences'. Just look at the Japanese: far from being the descendants of deities, they are nothing if not 'a very complete mixture of race'. Many of their fads and fancies are patently second-hand: even the kimono, which is a Chinese fashion of the T'ang dynasty. Take too the incidence of bandy legs and toothy smiles, and even weird responses such as their habit of hissing to show their politeness: there is no racial peculiarity about these characteristics ('My own brother does the hissing, I notice ... and I daresay he has never met a Japanese'), since they stem from training more than nature. 'Very little is known about teeth anyway, but they are much more affected by your state of mind than you think,' Empson ventured, 'and my own guess is that the rat teeth of the cartoon Japanese are produced by the condition of their nerves.' Perhaps everyone already knows that it is difficult for the Japanese to be friendly with foreigners, but it is worth knowing too that 'even between two Japanese, personal relations tend to be a bit blank'. Empson had personal evidence to enter here: 'I remember the great linguist Okakura saying an odd thing, apropos of nothing, as Japanese confidences do come; he said to me "It's one of our great difficulties that we have no colloquial Japanese; we can't talk to each other as equals, as the English do; there is always a formal relationship implied in the grammar." So again I don't think the curious stiffness which the world has noticed in the Japanese can be regarded as a racial or inherent character; it's a very direct result of their recent history and their political set-up.' Also, let no one labour under the delusion that the Japanese are smart-witted and decisive: they prefer everything to be considered in committee, and shrink from snap judgements. There follows 'a practical bit of advice': 'The Chinese guerrilla tactics are extremely powerful against the Japanese mind, because they continually give the Japanese subordinate a problem which his superiors had not foreseen. So what we must plan to give them is surprises.' As to the cult of suicide that everyone seems to have heard about, it only looks like bravery from the outside. 'They don't commit suicide traditionally as an operation of war, but out of despair.' Thus the Japanese are just ordinary beings who have hitched themselves to evil new doctrines. The final paragraph rises to the level of a ringing homily, though it includes a salutary piece of propaganda directed at the Japanese themselves—the message being that they can, and must, live with defeat:

> It would be a foolish thing to try to work up general hatred of the Japanese and all their works; they are not all going to kill themselves after this war, and what we have to aim at is a working relationship between the peoples of this planet. The Japanese have many graces and virtues, especially when they're back at home. Unfortunately they have taken it into their heads to be the rulers of a great Asiatic empire. Now that's the last thing they're any good at. They are extremely insular—they find it hard even to understand

outsiders; their contempt for the peoples they want to rule is as harsh even as the racial hatreds of the Germans; their perpetual anxiety for their dignity makes them liable to be brutal rulers; they have no political plans to offer except the theory that the Japanese are descended from the gods; and their idea of colonisation in Korea, where they could work it out in peace, has been simply to try to 'assimilate' the Koreans, that is, to prevent the teaching of Korean language and history, and to impose the very peculiar Japanese customs and written language. Now in any picture of a better world the south of Asia is one of the great obstacles, from its present state of politics, economics, education and everything else. That is getting better, and one of the few hopeful things about the present set-up is that the mere necessary resistance to Japan is likely to give it a real serious push forward. But if the Japanese get hold of all this area they will reverse the whole development; they will hold down these peoples and make them a running sore in the planet, an obstacle to all future plans for general betterment. The final and definite defeat of the Japanese, a defeat recognised as such by themselves, is an absolute prior necessity if the great hopes for a peaceful and progressing world, and a free and responsible Asia as an essential part of that world, are not to go down in misery and chaos.

Empson's talk hit the target hard. No less a person than the eloquent and histrionic propagandist Hans Fritzsche (sometime a lawyer) was stung into denouncing him by name. Broadcasting 'These Japanese', Empson would later say, 'was one of the events of my life I always look back on with satisfaction. It got under the Nazi skin somehow, and I was answered with some stock insults—called a "curly-headed Jew", I remember—but without any effective defence of the racial purity of the Japanese ally. This was done by Fritzsche himself, the top propagandist, in the peak hour.'[52] Lies and gross libels were Fritzsche's stock-in-trade.

In a later year Empson would argue that the poet John Milton was not 'corrupted' by working as a propagandist. He knew what he was talking about, claimed Empson, because his own employment in the same line had done him no lasting damage. In truth, making propaganda stretches the imagination. 'I wasn't in on any of the splendid tricks, such as Milton is accused of, but the cooked-up argufying I have experienced. To work at it forces you to imagine all the time what the enemy will reply; you are trying to get him into a corner. Such a training cannot narrow a man's understanding of other people's opinions, though it may well narrow his own opinions.' Milton 'can always imagine with all its force exactly what the reply of the opponent would be . . . [H]is style of attack is savagely wholehearted, but his depth of historical knowledge and imaginative sympathy keep having unexpected effects. He was not at all likely to feel that he had forfeited his independence of mind by such work.'[53]

Foremost among those whom Empson felt eager to heed at the BBC was an 'enemy alien', a German Jew named Ralf Bonwit, who joined the BBC soon after Pearl Harbour. Brought up in Frankfurt, where his father suffered a fatal heart attack brought about by a Nazi raid on the family home, Bonwit had fled first to Paris, where he studied Chinese at the Sorbonne, and then to London, where he was working for an MA in Japanese when he was interned on the Isle of Man at the outbreak of war. After being 'colleged'—that is, cleared for security ('The College' was a BBC committee supervised by the British Military Intelligence Security Service)—he followed the intensive BBC induction course, 'General Broadcasting Technique', run at Bedford College, University of London, where a lecture by R. J. T. Griffin, head of Intelligence in the European Services, persuaded him that he might be able to put his knowledge to best use as a Far East Intelligence Officer.[54]

In sharp contrast to the formality of the BBC training school (where one woman was severely reprimanded for wearing trousers), Bonwit was surprised when Empson chose to interview him in a pub. He told Empson he had learned to speak Chinese before he tackled English—to which Empson cracked, 'I can well believe it.'[55] Once enrolled in the Intelligence section, Bonwit proved to be an invaluable colleague; and indeed he was so tirelessly dedicated that he could often seem tiresome. 'His chief fault is that he is too keen on his work,' wrote Empson; 'he is liable to discuss things exhaustively when you have something else to do. But I have found that this can easily be dealt with by firm rudeness; you have only to say that you cannot now listen any more.'[56] But Empson did well to listen hard on the many occasions when 'specialist knowledge and pertinacious inquiry' were vital to the task in hand. Bonwit 'knows how the Chinese mind works,' Empson would come to believe.[57]

Empson's involvement in writing Feature programmes also brought him into close contact with Louis MacNeice, his fellow poet and exact contemporary, who looked sardonic and did not tolerate fools. But MacNeice proved to be 'a tower of strength' as a producer, Empson was to write (for a memorial):

> You could show him the rough material . . . and he knew at once what you could put over, what would do. Even with quite a complicated script, one run-through would be quite enough, after he had cut it, and the actors could

go out into the blackout and look for beer; he was always unruffled and very much the captain at the wheel of his ship. Of course this may have been because he thought it such tuppenny work that he wouldn't bother, but the results seemed to me very elegant. No wonder people like that wouldn't move over to television. He was very equable, one might think rather low-powered, but you had to look out when he began to look like a camel. That meant he had become decided.

For his part, MacNeice would in a later year characterize Empson as 'the oddest English poet who wrote between the two World Wars. And of his generation, he is probably unique in that he has not a trace of self-pity.'[58]

Empson's first collaboration with Bonwit (and with another colleague, Brigid Maas) was a two-hour Home Service Feature called *Japan Wants the Earth*—produced by Francis (or 'Jack', as he was called) Dillon—which was broadcast in half-hour episodes in alternate weeks beginning in the evening of 4 May 1942.[59] If the BBC could not broadcast propaganda directly to the Japanese, Empson believed, the least he could manage was to ensure that the home audience was left in no doubt of the gravity of the war in the Pacific. There was a danger that the immediate afflictions of the European front could so far overshadow the news from elsewhere that people might underestimate the scale of Japanese imperialism, which constituted a threat to the stability of the world every bit as severe as the horror of Nazism. Above all, the World War began in China in 1937, and arguably in 1931, and the Chinese had long been fighting their corner for the sake of the whole world. The Axis was a tripartite power, and the war could never be won until the total monster had been slain.

To that end, *Japan Wants the Earth* proposed to tell 'the story of the rise of Japan as a menace to our Civilisation'. Part 1, 'Plucky Little Japs', covered the period from the mid-nineteenth century to the Russo-Japanese War (during which the Japanese were 'adopted by the Western world as amusing pets'); Part 2, 'Made in Japan', reviewed the Japanese attempt to conquer the world by trade; Part 3, 'Asia for the Japanese', told over the history of Japanese aggression in China; and Part 4, 'Follow my Leader', showed how 'the Nazis force the pace'. Only half of the series now survives (Parts 1 and 3), but there is enough material to show that Empson and his colleagues were intent on putting across a simplified but serviceable account of Japanese megalomania and perfidy. Evidently written at speed, even as Japan's military carved into the flank of the Western Pacific, the surviving programmes include a number of slips of spelling and fact; but what they lack in polish, they make up in urgency.

Hindsight teaches us that in the last century the West was duped by the charming traditionalism and legendary self-discipline of the emergent Japan: so argues the episode called 'Plucky Little Japs'. Using the format of a semi-dramatized documentary, a compère introduces testimonies by the famous and the infamous, along with some historical sketches. Oscar Wilde, for instance, extolled Japanese art in 'Art and Decoration'; and in 1905 George Meredith sang the praises of the country's moral idealism in these words: 'Bushido, or the "way of the Samurai", has become almost an English word, so greatly has it impressed us with the principle of renunciation on behalf of the country's welfare. This splendid conception of duty has been displayed again and again, not only by the Samurai, but by a glorious commonalty imbued with the spirit of their chiefs.' Yet the truth is that the society of Old Japan had been shaped by centuries of coercion, as Lafcadio Hearn noted at about the same time: 'The kindliness and grace of manners were cultivated, for a thousand years, under the edge of the sword... Between the minds of these people and our own can exist no kinship of thought, no community of sentiment, no sympathy whatsoever.' As for the vaunted principles of the samurai warrior, in fact the warrior's duty of absolute loyalty to his overlord meant that no one else could trust him for anything. Expediently contradicting the very argument that Empson had placed at the centre of his earlier broadcast, 'These Japanese'—that the Japanese had no right to call themselves a separate people—the Chinese member of the cast (Dr Wu) is then given to say words which are inimitably Empson's: 'Now, speaking as a Chinese, I want to ask you to think of the Japanese as a separate people... The Japanese seem very queer to us Chinese as they do to you and the reason is that the political history of Japan is very queer, very unlike ours or yours.'

Going on from this blank assertion that the Japs are rum customers, the programme uses the technique of propaganda-by-parody to recount the modern history of the country.

JAPANESE 1: His Majesty decidedly has no function. He deigns to exist, and, by his existence, he carries through the ages the shining symbols of the divine mission of Japan, handed down to him by our ancestors, the Sun God.

JAPANESE 2: In other words, His Majesty is a God?

JAPANESE 3: Do you doubt?

JAPANESE 1: No, I daren't. I don't want to become the object of a physical correction by your Black Dragons, Mr. Toyama.

TOYAMA: Now, we've settled that the Emperor is divine and above politics. The more mighty we become, the more obviously divine becomes his Majesty.

A long-standing lord of the underworld, Toyama the revolutionary backed the Army Chief of Staff General Yamagata Aritomo in his determination to challenge Russia rather than the Western powers.

COMPÈRE: Japan on the March. In 1894 Japan fought and defeated China. This gave her a great deal of prestige; it let her get rid of extraterritoriality and make much more favourable treaty agreements.
CHINESE VOICE: Japan attacked China then without declaring war, by surprise. That was the first time. Maybe she would have won anyway. But we Chinese, do you see, cannot pretend to be very surprised about Pearl Harbour. Nor for that matter by the atrocities ordered from above at Hongkong. We Chinese have had plenty of time to get used to Japan.
COMPÈRE: After 1894, Germany took a hand in Far Eastern politics. Britain signed the Anglo-Japanese Treaty. Japan began her preparations for war against Russia.

The Chinese spokesman's remark about 'the atrocities ordered from above at Hongkong' prompts the listener to believe that those atrocities—which Anthony Eden had revealed to the House of Commons as recently as 10 March, less than two months before 'Plucky Little Japs'—had been sanctioned by imperial rescript. In fact, the commander of the regiments that laid siege to Hong Kong, Lieutenant General Sakai Takashi, did authorize the campaign of murderous brutality against the British colony, but there is no evidence that the responsibility ran higher than his own head.

That is a small example of what Empson called 'cooked-up argufying'; so is what the programme leaves out—including the fact that the 'compère' takes sufficient pains to mention the Anglo-Japanese Treaty of 1902, which the British had hastened to sign in order to prevent a Russo-Japanese alliance which was in the offing, but omits to explain its consequences. In February 1904, two years after Great Britain and Japan reached their accord, the Japanese Navy launched a surprise attack on Russia's Asiatic fleet, forcing it to take shelter in the harbour of Port Arthur. The British played a significant role in the subsequent destruction of the Russian Baltic fleet, which was entirely to the benefit of Japan.

Clearly it would have been bad propaganda for Empson to state on the Home Service that Britain had formerly helped Japan to trounce the Russian Navy and to gain territory in China as a first step towards its inroads of the 1930s. The point of the programme was to say that the British no longer had any excuse not to wake up to the skulduggery of Japan. Witness the bitter irony of history, remember that the Japanese have a record of declaring war only after they have launched a pre-emptive attack, and wince at the way the British cheered Japan in 1904/5. Indeed, the most successful aspect of 'Plucky Little Japs' is that the programme concludes by quoting what *The Times* and other newspapers had published that year; in May 1942, the sense of *déjà vu* must have felt sickening.

> TIMES: The Japanese Navy, thanks to the masculine decision of the Mikado and his advisers, has taken the initiative, and has opened the war by an act of daring. On the night of February 8 - 9 [1904], ten Japanese destoyers in three divisions surprised the Russian squadron in the outer roadstead at Port Arthur, and delivered their attack with such good effect that two of the best battleships of the Russian squadron and a cruiser were disabled . . .
> COMPÈRE: The Japanese tactic of surprise followed by a declaration of war. . . .
> TIMES: The objects for which Japan made war were the expulsion of the Russians from Manchuria, the freedom of Korea and China from Russian domination, and the conclusion of a lasting peace based on equal rights for all in the trade of the Far East, and adequate recognition of Japan's vital interests.

'What we've been trying to do, in collecting these quotations, is to show you what rubbish we all used to talk about Japan,' says the compère— though his apologia is more disingenuous than convincing:

> But the generous feelings behind all that are nothing to be ashamed of, and they weren't stupid either. The reason we were pleased about the Japanese victory, at bottom, was that we wanted to see Asia catching up with the modern world and standing on its own feet. We thought Japan was going to stand up for Asia. That was a mistake, because owing to their very peculiar political history the Japanese can't stand up for anybody but themselves. Anyway China is vastly larger, and the whole thing had [?has] yet to be done again more slowly and naturally by China. But we needn't blame ourselves because we welcomed and helped in every way the rise of an Asiatic power.

The other surviving instalment of the radio series, 'Asia for the Japanese', rehearses the history of Japanese aggression towards China during the 1930s. The free world had seen the emerging picture and done little to alter it; as a result, China had suffered both from Japan's military invasion and from international negligence. Indeed, the scale of China's sufferings staggers the imagination: the country had been pounded year after year by Japanese subversion, sabotage and aggression. Witness the fact (firmly established by 1942) that ever since the 1920s Japan had been peddling vast amounts of opium to the masses of Manchuria so as to undermine their resistance.

> COMPÈRE: Manchuria was flooded with cheap drugs—morphia and cocaine.
> JAP: The use of narcotics is unworthy of a superior race, like the Japanese. Only inferior races that are decadent, like the Chinese, the Europeans and the East Indians, are addicted to narcotics. That is why they are destined to become our servants and eventually disappear.
> COMPÈRE: In Japanese occupied territory, there was an enormous increase in the number of drug addicts.

As for the military assaults on China, the Japanese atrocities are written in blood in the annals of evil. Empson and his co-authors had no need to exaggerate what took place in Nanking, for example, where rapine and genocide began on 14 December 1937 and went on for no less than six weeks. The bare brutal facts said enough:

> VOICE: Chinese soldiers who gave up their arms were roped in batches of one hundred and shot—or bayonetted, as were all men of military age.
> VOICE: There were in total about twenty-four thousand murders of civilians—but this included women and children.
> VOICE: Of women from ten years to seventy, approximately ten thousand were raped . . .
> CHINESE: It is, we know, useless to give you details of the Japanese methods of atrocities. They are too horrible, and almost as horrid is the Japanese propaganda afterwards.
> JAPANESE: The Imperial Army entered the city, put their bayonets into their sheaths, and stretched forth merciful hands in order to examine and to heal, diffusing grace and favour to the excellent true citizens. Nanking is the best place for all countries to watch, for here one breathes the atmosphere of peaceful residence and happy work.
> COMPÈRE: The Japanese technique, hypocrisy, horror and efficiency.

According to the findings of the International Military Tribunal for the Far East, which sat in Tokyo from 1946 to 1948, no fewer that 20,000 women had been raped in Nanking and its environs; more than 200,000 men (at least a quarter of them civilians) were murdered.[60] In sum, the official post-war figures even doubled the estimates available in 1942.

Given such wickedness, how could Empson and his collaborators draw a positive lesson from this tale of criminality? The answer was to 'cook up' the pro-Chinese propaganda in their radio broadcast to a still greater degree, to depict the Chinese peoples not merely as victims but as staunch freedom-fighters. This passage shows the tactic at work:

CHINESE: In China we shall always remember with honour the battle of Shanghai 1932. The Japs brought in sixty thousand troops. Please remember we were not [at] war. They bombed Chapei, a suburb with a quarter of a million people. Our houses burn very fiercely and quickly, and so thousands of Chinese were burned to death. But our Fifth and Nineteenth Route Armies, who, before the Japs came, had been fighting each other, now combined and fought the Japanese. Japan was uniting China.

COMPÈRE: The Chinese stood up to Japan's assault, and threw it back. Only overwhelming weight of metal made the Chinese retire to positions twelve miles outside the city. By their heroic fighting resistance, the Chinese inflicted enormous loss on Japan—loss of face—which she has never regained in China. It showed the Western powers that, given weapons, China could resist Japan.

As the compère says, it is true that when hostilities broke out in Shanghai in January 1932 the Japanese marines detailed to 'protect' the Chinese borough of Chapei met a totally unexpected level of resistance from the Chinese 19th Route Army commanded by General Tsai Ting-kai, who declared that his force of 35,000 Cantonese would 'fight the Japanese to the last man if it has to dye the Whampo River red with its soldiers' blood'.[61] The Japanese naval landing force was driven back to the barricades of the Japanese settlement. Thereupon Admiral Shiozawa pounded the Chinese soldiers and *franc-tireurs* with bombs and shell-fire, but to no avail. 'For two weeks, despite Japanese numerical equality and fire-power superiority, the heroic young provincials of the Chinese 19th Route Army... refused to be driven from the native quarters of Shanghai.'[62] The Japanese had no choice but to commit more and more troops to the engagement, until—after many days of fruitless fighting—they were pitting a force of about 70,000 against a body of Chinese that had been cut down to some 20,000.

However, what Empson's compère skilfully leaves unclear is the outcome of the battle. The courageous Chinese Divisions were in fact beaten, though not until a month after the fighting broke out; and on the Japanese side army reinforcements had to relieve the beleaguered Imperial Navy. Japan gained nothing from her victory; after agreeing an armistice with Chiang Kai-shek, she withdrew her expeditionary force from Shanghai— thus hoping, albeit unsuccessfully, to impress the Lytton Commission with the level of her discipline. China, on the other hand, gained face over the inglorious Japanese; outmanned and outgunned, she had made a truly heroic stand before being totally defeated at the last. Yet the casual listener to this BBC broadcast could have been forgiven for thinking that the Chinese must have won the battle.

Yet more telling is the Chinese spokesman's boast that his country had established a united front against the invaders: 'our Fifth and Nineteenth Route Armies, who, before the Japs came, had been fighting each other, now combined and fought the Japanese. Japan was uniting China.' The facts tell another story. The officers of the 19th Route Army who elected to do battle at Shanghai belonged to the socialist Cantonese faction of the Kuomintang. They were Chiang Kai-shek's domestic opponents: idealistic agrarian reformers. When they entered the fray against the Japanese Imperial Marines, they trusted Chiang's pledge that he would send his personal 'guard divisions'—he had 40,000 men in the vicinity of Shanghai—to fight alongside them. But Chiang failed to honour his commitment; his divisions did not show up in time, and his navy withdrew up the Yangtse.

Knowingly or not, therefore, Empson and his co-authors were purveying Chinese propaganda when they declared that the Chinese had united their armies to defend their homeland. Since Chiang Kai-shek had committed himself to the annihilation of his Communist rivals, it now comes as no surprise to learn from David Bergamini: 'In later years the valiant 19th Route Army would go over to Chiang's open enemies, the Communists of Mao Tse-tung.'[63] Still, even in 1942 Empson and his colleagues must have known better than they said—that the battle of Shanghai had meant ignominy rather than unity—but they believed they had no other way to present the matter. It was a fundamental point of policy never to mention China's civil strife on the air; and throughout his time at the BBC Empson stuck to the principle that he should keep faith with the ideal of a China that was one and undivided. Thus the compère of 'Asia for the Japanese' praises China's single-mindedness: 'in spite of the clouds of Japanese propaganda, which appeared to confuse the world in 1937, we can now see the plan of Japanese aggression, as we can see the importance of the brilliant strategy of the Chinese leaders, and the heroic resistance of the Chinese peasants.' Still more, Chiang Kai-shek himself is given to deliver this high-minded speech as a climax to the programme: 'Since the beginning of this struggle, China has made it clear that she is fighting for her national existence and independence and for the cause of international peace and justice. The spirit of China is the spirit of humanity.' Hence, with respect to China, wishful thinking and the tricks of propaganda were all one. A lie was sometimes the very best hope.

The moral thrust of 'Asia for the Japanese' was characteristic of Empson's endeavours at the BBC. Although he believed he had some ideas to put forward in the way of belittling Japan, his top priority was to bolster China, which also meant building up British appreciation of China. He had felt a huge sense of relief on being transferred from Monitoring to the Overseas Service. Dealing with enemy broadcasts had come to feel like an increasingly passive and debilitating activity, and he ached for a constructive job. 'It seems fair to claim for myself,' he wrote in mid-1941, 'that after nearly a year of sub-editing Axis propaganda the whole thing seems accepted as filthier than I am or we are. But this is as false as can be; what I am asked to do is to educate the English to respect China, and I am not doing harm of any kind to anybody there.'

Black propaganda did not suit his character; he liked it best when he could pen hopeful sentiments, as in a short talk called 'China and the Future' which he delivered as a postscript to the Home News at 1 p.m. on 24 March 1942: 'it's very fortunately happening that China, the natural leader of the Far East, is rapidly working out as a great democracy with which we democratic Europeans can have a friendly, reliable relationship,' he wrote. And to conclude: 'Japanese propaganda is always saying that Japan is freeing Asia from domination. Of course, the only thing the Japanese do with the other Asiatics they can get hold of is to make slaves of them. But China really is freeing Asia, today only by the example of her determination and her military resistance, tomorrow perhaps also politically and intellectually by her leadership and her advice.'[64] Indeed, Empson became so enthusiastic about the bold rush of this pro-Chinese idea that he wrote too, in his first draft: 'But if we are to get any decent working world system after this war we have got to accept fully and seriously the equal importance of China with the other allies.'[65] At the time, China was still in the unhappy position of being an unequal ally—and Empson was not entitled to propose British Government policy in a News talk. The sentence had to be cut, as he realized even for himself. The Eastern Services Director approved the first draft, with the comment 'Excellent indeed', and all the editorial alterations—including the deletion of that overreaching sentence—are in Empson's hand.

It did not come easily, composing words with the right mix of fact, opinion and persuasion. Propaganda aims to be invisible, a seamless craft; and Empson would grind out many drafts before getting a piece more nearly right. In addition, he suffered from an urgent sense of responsibility about helping the Chinese. Occasionally the onus felt heavy enough to cause him real distress. It was his duty to promote China, and yet he felt

nervy and dithery; not incompetent but unconfident. Somehow his reputation seemed to be at stake, and just one bout of procrastination would set
him worrying. 'The maniac refusal to write a broadcast about China is
now reaching such a serious stage that it had better be dealt with by
starting a diary,' he wrote on 18 July 1941 (not long after joining the Eastern
Service).

> The mere fact that it is bound to be bad by the time they have finished
> mucking with it is not enough excuse. I am really fond of Chinese friends . . .
> and want to help and be praised . . . In Boston I got to the point of sitting in
> the lavatory in a pub near [radio station] WRUL and feeling maniac terror,
> I felt I couldn't possibly do the work there, not because it was intellectually
> hard or indeed had to be done cleverly but because the spoilt child's mind
> could not be held on such nonsense sufficiently to hold him from mere blank
> refusal, and mere blank refusal on a big scale means being taken to a lunatic
> asylum . . . The fear of not doing as terribly well as critics quite falsely said
> you did when you were younger may be a part of this neurotic refusal. But
> much more than that it is an inability of the imagination to start work on the
> thing put before it . . . I don't at my time of life dream about sex all the time.
> I dream about mathematics of a simpler type than I was educated to
> understand before I failed in mathematics. This seems an alarming feature.
> The drink it is surely stupid to be frightened about; God knows as soon
> as I can get interested in something else I stop drinking with pleasure.
> It would be worth giving up the drink to see if it helps, but my experience
> has been that getting a thing started requires drink and finishing it sobriety.
> If I can't start this broadcast drunk it looks as if I need psychoanalysis
> to start it sober.

The work was worth doing, he thought, but only if done very well indeed.

'China On the March' is the programme he struggled to write from the
first moment he joined the Eastern Service. Draft passages appear in
the notebook he kept at the Training School in the summer of 1941,
and the fullest draft was several times the length of the script as broadcast.
A half-hour Home Service programme, produced by the inventive 'Jack'
Dillon, it went out in the evening of 27 April 1942. Framed as a statement
of his faith in the Chinese, it mixes a good part of personal witness with a
lesser portion of pure hopefulness, all of which is purveyed through the
device of arranging a fictitious symposium. The speakers are a Scotsman
who was recently employed in China by a British firm, an English traveller, a missionary, and an American teacher from a Chinese university.
Rather than trot out passages of empty praise for poor little China,
however, Empson hoped to strike a balance between robust opinion and

a reasonable aspiration for that enormous, backward country. Ralf Bonwit would later advise his colleagues in the Eastern Department, 'The Chinese are both our Allies and equals: we are bestowing no favour when we treat them as such'—which was true enough. But Empson knew that no one could essay a portrait of China without admitting that she simply did not resemble a western democracy: it would be dangerously misleading to suggest otherwise. The vast majority of the people were illiterate peasants with no political representation. The domestic problems of the country might be of no concern to the western world, but they should be recognized for what they were—or else future relations would have rotten foundations. Empson counselled in a memo headed 'Propaganda about China for Home audiences': 'A bit more frankness would be more effective, especially in view of possible future complications. In this country at any rate propaganda has not grubbed out the roots of older settled opinions, and I think it would have been a bad thing if this had been achieved, but the effect is that a mere goodwill programme slides over the rooted opinions.'[66]

Thus 'China On the March' is introduced by a compère who has not been to China. This man is a romantic who rhapsodizes over the mysteries of the East, principally in order that he can be slapped down by the voice of realism. The English traveller manages a touch of meta-propaganda, breaking the illusion that we are about to hear an authentic discussion, when he objects to the compère's empty apostrophes: 'it is true, but it's the wrong line to take . . . I like the country. Nobody wants you to talk about it as if it was a circus, you know.' The effect is that when the compère still insists on making his point, that China is an admirable emergent nation, he continues to lard it on, though without really lying, and at the same time he expresses Empson's own best hopes: 'I fully agree it's no use thinking of China as a queer far-off story. The portent of the sturdy strength of China in the face of the blackest disaster and the mere fact of the sturdy sympathy of China for our side and our cause, don't underrate that. China is our friend. We'd have little enough hope of a real working settlement after the war if we hadn't got their friendship. China is now becoming one of the great democracies.'

Such is Empson's strategy: the differing viewpoints of the four speakers represent the range of his own hopes and doubts, while the programme as a whole successfully puts over one key idea—China has a glittering future, and you can rely on it. Her determination to shift her factories away from the coastal areas occupied by the Japanese and to rebuild an industrial base in the interior proves her heroism. So does the 'great popular movement' of her defensive mobilization against the Japanese invader. 'It was, and is, the peasants who support the guerrillas . . . Above all, you can't put through a scorched earth policy if the people won't let you.' Yet Empson was taking a leap in the dark when he gave the American teacher (whose view of China comes closest to his own) to posit 'a sturdy Central Government organisation' to which the whole country was rallying. The requirements of propaganda had to snuff out any flicker of dubiety on that score. Still it was safe to say that 'the ghost of Sun Yat Sen straddles or is recognised by both the Central Government and the Northern generals.' (Understandably, the script omits to mention that the Northern generals in question were Communists: enemies of Chiang Kai-shek.) 'That's why he is an important force for unity. He was never confused about what he wanted, ultimately: it was the modern, independent, democratic China.'

All the same, some other tough questions could not be ducked— whether political, concerning the tremendous gulf in her social structure; or plain prejudice as evinced by western attitudes toward 'footbinding' ('was it different from Victorian tightlacing?') and Asian cruelty ('historic-ally no more sadistic than any other nation'). All in all, Empson's half-hour programme satisfactorily covered many of the 'older settled opinions' that the West held against China, trumping them with the evidence that China was on course to become a modern democracy. He knew he was pontifi-cating (if only indirectly) on matters that were actually highly volatile. But it is not clear whether he appreciated the perils of discussing 'coolies', as he had been bold enough to do. It was only the next month, in May 1942, that Ralf Bonwit issued an Intelligence Memorandum headed ' "Don'ts" in relation to China', which included this strict warning: 'The word "coolie" is not really good Chinese and is certainly not good propaganda.' Simi-larly, while Empson made the views of a missionary prominent in his programme, Bonwit would counsel: 'Missionaries in China have undoubt-edly done great work, especially in helping the Chinese when the Japanese arrived. But there is still lingering a feeling of past misunderstandings. It is advisable, therefore, not to talk too much about missionaries, nor to give overmuch emphasis to the fact that a speaker is or was a missionary in China.'[67]

More gamely but unhappily, Empson in his propaganda had ventured to discuss, and even to appear to extenuate, the history of British policy in China, which was a sink of iniquity. Still more riskily, he gave his mission-ary to argue: 'we had a bad conscience about the Opium Wars. Mind you, Imperial China had to be opened to the world, and that was really what those wars were about. But it looked bad, and we took the stupid way out, as other nations have done since, because they felt in the wrong, so we spent a lot of time vilifying the Chinese. I think the present way of talking is much better than that one. But I do not like these violent changes, even in wartime, and I have my doubts about this startling gulf between the old China and the New.' Nor does anyone seek to discredit this missionary's position, which is allowed to stand. His last sentence is challenged by the Scottish trader, but more by way of moving forward the conversation than of demolishing a wrong-headed point of view.

A month earlier, when speaking in his own right in 'China and the Future', Empson had endorsed another apologia for the British record in China, in this case Sir John Pratt's disingenuous defence (in his book *Japan and the Modern World*) of a ghastly error: 'British diplomats, during the Manchurian affair, did not realise the immense importance which the Chinese attach to Manchuria as a part of China. Sir John Pratt, in defending British policy there, explains that we wanted chiefly to prevent Japan from attacking China proper, and that to prevent that great evil we thought a working arrangement might be made over Manchuria. There we made a mistake; I believe it's true to say that, even if the Japanese had been likely to agree to such a scheme, no Chinese Government *could* have agreed to it.'[68] Yet it scarcely seems likely that British diplomatists could have been quite so ignorant. Nor was it sensible for Empson to profess a defence of the British position which went so far to insult Chinese pride.

Ralf Bonwit's best piece of advice ran simply: 'British policy in the Far East is a subject best left alone.'[69] Empson took the advice, and never again introduced into his Feature programmes the subject of official policy. All in all, then, he did well to sustain the habit of professional collaboration with Bonwit, who kept him fully up to the mark. And in return for his good advice Empson taught Bonwit to write good English, though it was assuredly the case that the two men found they had little in common out of hours—and both seemed happy to keep things that way.

In August 1941 he reported to Bedford College, University of London, where the BBC's Staff Training Department, headed by a producer called E. A. F. (Archie) Harding, ran a two-week training course for new personnel. He was to become a Talks Assistant in the Far East section, at the good salary of £640 per annum. Although he would later dub this induction course the 'Liars' School', it was actually far less sinister than the sobriquet would suggest, since it was almost entirely concerned with describing programme techniques together with the engineering and administrative processes of the BBC. 'The Liars' School, I should perhaps explain,' he wrote later, 'had only dealt with lies in passing, and only under the form of warning us against the methods of the enemy. I chiefly remember two young disc jockeys who put on a very saucy turn with two gramophones and two copies of a record by Churchill; the familiar voice was made to leave out all the negatives, ending with "we will (hic) surrender".'[70]

The 'main business' of a Talks Assistant, the trainees were apprised, is 'to shorten without destroying the speaker's idiom' (as Empson recorded in his notebook). If a speaker fluffs a line more than once, they were instructed, they should deduce that 'it is a bolshie sentence with a psychological reason for stumbling. Anything you like to change? Make him (his own script) comfortable. Confidence in himself, then in the script, then in you, in order . . . (make him feel it's the best script ever written).'

As to the potentially fretful problem of censorship, the students learned, 'We are our own censors on behalf of Gov[ernment]. About 100 BBC censors acting for Govt. M[inistry] of I[nformation] can take the BBC over . . . Gov. can veto. BBC accepts in wartime the direction, general & particular, of M of I in matters the Minister regards as in the national interest . . . Passed by censor doesn't mean proper to broadcast. Censorship compulsory although we are selfcensoring, but not compulsory for the Press.' Whatever qualms these observations may have induced in Empson are not recorded: he had no experience as yet of trying to be both the lion and the cage. But he was obviously eager—or maybe merely amused—to copy down the following passage of official moral uplift: 'BBC executants of policy. But Gov. depts. agree that any idea wherever it comes from is to be welcomed by us. Hospitality of mind and creativeness are things to which we should all bend [sic] ourselves, and avoid like the plague the snottiness which won't accept suggestions from the cleaner or a Gov. dpt.' W. J. West observed, 'The BBC was subjected to a censorship more thorough than that imposed on any other media . . . Everything broadcast had to be submitted to the censor first; not a single word could be broadcast that had not been censored twice, once for security and once for policy.'[71] In general, however, issues of censorship were not altogether so alarming or sensational as West made out. Sensible precautions had obviously to be agreed;[72] and anyway it was BBC policy that 'We aren't tempted to add to the censorship', even though it might require a certain economy of means to keep up foreign confidence in the allied cause. 'Our declared objective,' declared the instructors of the Liars' School, 'is to convince Overseas that we are winning and that it will do good.' Perhaps it is only in retrospect that the formula, or slogan, has a chilling ring.

Certainly, the distinction to be made in wartime between public-service broadcasting and national propaganda was, to say the least, fine. As Michael Shelden has pointed out in his biography of George Orwell, 'The purpose of the Indian section of the Eastern Service was to make the voice of Britain heard in India . . . What it amounted to was a kind of cultural imperialism.'[73] While Empson would not positively wish to think of his work in quite such bald terms, much the same was also true of his work in the Far East section. In any event, a confidential BBC memo circulated in February 1942 by the Assistant Controller of Overseas Programmes was to stipulate in certain terms: 'The primary purpose of news commentaries is propaganda.'[74]

A tall, gaunt figure in frayed tweed jacket and corduroys, with a doleful lined countenance, a stripe of moustache and a crest of brown hair, turned out to be George Orwell, who would be working alongside Empson for the next two years. He resembled an intense, flat-voiced llama, though he would chuckle a lot too. (Henry Swanzy recalled with a degree of self-applause that he himself 'must have been the only person among the twenty odd people on the course who did not know that "E. A. Blair" was George Orwell. As a consequence, I treated him as a normal person, not with the somewhat hushed wariness, not to say obsequiousness, that some at least of our companions showed.'[75] He felt sure that Orwell resented 'the poets', including Empson, though other evidence suggests otherwise.)

Another student, a recent recruit to the African Service would share the rest of Empson's life. Hester Henrietta Crouse, who was always called Hetta, sat up and took notice of him during the screening of a propaganda film called 'Freedom Ferry', no. 15: 'Missions to Seamen', which took place at the Monseigneur Cinema at Marble Arch. As a merchant ship was seen to wallow through the sea, broadside to the camera, Empson cried out, 'What about the plimsoll line?!' In the midst of an unexciting programme, he had been remarkably attentive. What no one else had noticed was that the ship was manifestly overloaded and in danger of sinking, and he felt angry that a film which purported to celebrate the merchant marine was in fact recording a massive piece of naval incompetence which would nullify its propaganda value. 'That's my man!' thought Hetta Crouse, entranced by his alertness of mind and the fierceness of his declaration. She rushed out after him, gathering up the books and papers and hat that he had absent-mindedly left behind.

Hetta was born on 18 September 1915, in Kroonstad, a small town in the Orange Free State, where her father Johannes Jacobus Crouse was a

Lutheran cattle dealer: he would buy herds in south-west Africa and drive them 1500 miles up-country. 'My parents prayed for me, because they had three sons,' she would remark in a later year; 'and afterwards, from time to time, they said they wished they hadn't.' (A sister, Lilla, would follow her into the world.) Her family traced its ancestry back to a Huguenot refugee named David Sénécal (Senechal), born in Dieppe, who migrated to South Africa and became a farmer in the last decade of the seventeenth century, married a Parisienne in 1694, and sired eleven children. The name Crouse entered the fertile family tree when a daughter of the sixth generation married Hetta's grandfather. Her mother was called Magdalena (Maggie) Petronella Grobbelaar. The lineage was thus of pure Boer blood, though—at least according to Hetta—the family were very little concerned about the Boer War. 'My father probably fought on both sides, if he fought at all.'

Brought up with puritan strictness as a member of the Dutch Reformed Church ('I'm a lapsed Lutheran,' she would proclaim in later years), she went to church twice on Sundays as well as to a Sunday school. Indeed, there was nothing else she could do: she was not allowed to read or to play games on a Sunday. 'I grew up on the illimitable veldt,' she once said, perhaps ambiguously. Among her papers is this one draft page about her childhood on the veldt, and the dread influence of her father:

> A magical world it was, to get out of bed at four-thirty in the morning and catch the dawning on the veldt; all alone with the fairy tumble-weeds and the gigantic sun; red at first before it became golden. Everything was still, and immense, I felt it all belonged to me. I was six. Later there was a kaffir, a servant, who came with me and showed me how to mould the clay in the dongas into oxen. He could make a whole span of oxen very quickly. Wide horns, big shoulders, narrow flanks, he showed me how.
>
> Then one was not allowed. The tyrant, my father. No running around before daybreak. Off to school, and back at the break, home at once, and off to bed after the evening meal. Prayers before meals; all on your knees, and the servants in the doorways—even if they didn't understand a word of High-Dutch (a garbled version), the silly heathens, sons of Ham.
>
> Not a totally silly man, I suppose. He did what he did according to his beliefs. But I never did like him, though like the rest of us five children, I was in awe of him and helped him off with his boots, when every afternoon he used to yell for us, confusing the names, or maybe not; calling each name in turn, to unlace those high-laced, black, and rather deliciously-smelly boots. Often one fell back with a thud after pulling them off. He yelled with laughter then.

Mostly he was away from home, buying cattle in South-West Africa, and sending cryptic telegrams to my mother, like 'Everything in the garden lovely, home next week'.

It is likely that Hetta's highly developed sense of social justice was first bred of her early childhood association with the old farm labourer, who would tell her stories of African tribal life even as he encouraged her artistic temperament by showing her how to fashion oxen out of the red river clay. (She loved the river too, and in time she would also turn out to be a formidable sculler, rowing on the river in Kroonstad.)

Though the Crouses actually lived in town, Hetta spent a good deal of her childhood on farms owned by various relations. Everyone ate an enormous quantity of meat, both beef and venison, she was to recall in conversation (fish was not available on the inland plateau): from time to time her father and his friends would go off hunting and return with a lorry-load of buck. The family home was a typical homestead, shaded by a wide stoep. There was no internal plumbing. The story goes that Hetta was afflicted for a while by a case of 'penis envy', though not for the usual reasons. Her brothers, who were loth to go outside to relieve themselves in the cold Free State mornings, resourcefully rigged up a bull horn so that its tapering end fed through a hole in the wall to the outside. The boys were delighted they could urinate freely through this contraption without having to leave the comfort of their own room. By Hetta's account, she felt 'pissed off' by this astoundingly unfair situation; not to be outdone, however, she trained herself to urinate forwards while standing up. As a member of the family was to joke at her funeral, 'This may well be the origin of the oft-heard saying "The Crousers wear the Trousers".'[76]

She attended a bilingual local school (her mother had only a smattering of English), and went on to study Humanities at Bloemfontain University. But death stalked the family in rapid succession. Hetta's eldest brother died of food poisoning from eating an addled egg, and the third brother perished of typhoid. Then both father and mother died, leaving her orphaned at the age of 18, so that she left university after two years and returned to Kroonstad to live with the second brother, Hendrik. But Hendrik contracted typhoid during a trip to the Cape, just as she herself fell terribly ill while he was away from home. Since she began to be delirious with fever, she was hurriedly hospitalized; whereupon three doctors diagnosed typhoid in her case too. The circumstances of her recovery were weird: she had no idea that Hendrik had been struck down by illness until one night, at two o'clock in the morning, an aunt

came to her bedside and told her he was dead—'and I was no longer ill!'
But it took her a long time to recover from the shock of her dear brother's
death.

In due course she too departed for Cape Town, where she became an
apprentice to a well-regarded sculptor, Ivan Mitford-Barberton, in his
studio at no. 1 Bouquet Street. (Born in 1896, Mitford-Barberton had
been brought up in Kenya but studied at the Royal College of Art in
London and relocated to South Africa in 1930.) 'I was trained and spent a
number of years in the studio of I. Mitford-Barberton . . . ,' Hetta said in
a later job application, 'where I also obtained a great deal of experience in
carrying out decorative sculpture for architectural purposes. I am accustomed to work in all kinds of materials, such as clay for bronze casting,
stone, wood and cement.'[77] She became expert too in the designing and
hand-printing of textiles. Her works of the time included a bas-relief
cornucopia for the façade of the post office in Bloemfontein, and some
portrait busts. She lived with a community of artists below the Malay
quarter, on the slopes of Table Mountain. A seminal 'hippy', she was to be
long remembered for the fact that even in the 1930s she wore a kaftan and
walked barefoot. It was at this time that she met and befriended the artist
John Wright (who would later gain world renown as a master puppeteer).
Presently, with £300 in hand, she took off for Germany, to spend a year in
Munich where she enrolled in an art school. On returning to South Africa,
she earned her keep as publicity manager for a Communist-orientated
weekly newspaper, *The Guardian*, under the proprietorship of Betty Rad-
ford (Sacks). And she became a left-wing activist: during a six-month
period in Johannesburg she met a lot of 'old Communist Party people'
and got totally involved at last in the African situation. She organized the
laundry workers' union, was posted to a grim little town in the northern
Transvaal as a fund-raiser, and studied hard at all the Marxist classics.

But she was above all a passionate artist, and longed to spend time in the
galleries of Europe, despite the impending war. In Cape Town she fell in
love with a fellow artist, the German-born René Graetz (who had initially
trained as a printer and moved to South Africa in 1929, and who was
ultimately to win an international reputation for his work), and together
they undertook to do 'a dirty thing' (to use her own term) in order to raise
the sum of money they needed to buy a passage by sea.[78] With great
enterprise, they resolved to cash in on the centenary of the Great Trek of
1838—when the Afrikaners, or Boers, the descendants of seventeenth-
century Dutch settlers, sought to escape British domination by striking
out from Cape Colony and into the interior north of Orange River—by

designing an anniversary tie showing a woman in a bonnet alongside an ox-wagon. After buying just one tie for 1s. 6d. and selling it for 3s. 6d., they were in headlong business, printing ties day and night. She ran a workshop on the commercial exploitation of printed fabrics, and this was helpfully written up in the *Cape Argus*. As soon as she and Graetz had amassed £40 each, they took steerage on a Dutch steamer which conveyed them to Dunkirk. (While at sea, she made use of her experience as union organizer by working up a protest against the cramped, insanitary and ill-provisioned conditions that steerage passengers had to put up with.)

It was late in 1938. After visiting Paris they travelled to Switzerland; and then journeyed on to London, where Hetta changed her passport and became a British citizen. She adored her 'Darling Graetzl', as she called him, and anticipated marrying him, but his status as a German national would debar him from staying in England for very much longer. By 1940 he was taken into internment, first on the Isle of Man and subsequently at a camp in Canada, and for the first four months of their separation she received from him only a couple of postcards and one letter. She and Graetz had arrived in London with just three pounds between them, and matters did not improve when their Business Manager in South Africa failed to send on any of the profits from their sales: he was either incompetent or a fraud. She worked at menial jobs to pay the rent of 16 shillings a week on a studio room at 11 North Villas in Camden Town. 'I did some "char-ing", and then graduated to the status of model for emasculated English artists who measure you with a ruler to make sure they get the proportions right,' she related in a letter home in June 1939; '— with all their -isms they are more academic than the Royal Academy itself, hidebound, zealous, gutless little revolutionaries with no balls, to speak of— only now do they accept what the French artists discarded twenty years ago . . . '[79] Hetta was big and beautiful, with very blue eyes and very golden hair. One of the 'emasculated' artists for whom she posed in June 1939 was Vanessa Bell. 'I am treated justly and civilly enough,' she wrote directly after returning from Bell's studio, 'but am kept in my place—as a model should be, no doubt. Heigho! What does it matter?—Let them paint their laborious pictures, these English artists . . . '[80] Bell paid her 7s. 6d. for three hours of posing; at the Slade School of Art she earned 15s. for a 5-hour day. Among other adventures, Hetta attended a meeting of the Left Book Club at which Paul Robeson sang to an audience of some 20,000.

On the outbreak of war she undertook to drive an ambulance for the Auxiliary Ambulance Service (she had been able to drive since she was 14), based at a depot in St Pancras, and she continued to do so—on a 12-hour night shift and two 6-hour day shifts, and on occasion with 16-hour night shifts starting at 4 p.m. and ending at 8 a.m.—for the first six months of the Blitz that began on 7 September 1940 and battered on until 16 May 1941. On that first night, which was to become known as Black Saturday, 350 bombers escorted by fighter planes dropped their screaming payloads upon London, killing 430 people and injuring 1,600; after eight months, the unremitting airborne assault had accounted for 20,083 deaths. At first it was proposed that ambulances should not go out while the raids were in progress, but that proved to be unrealistic: she was soon taking her turn to go out at any time of day or night through the rubble and the raining bombs. 'It is not heroic,' she would insist to friends, 'it is humiliating.'[81]

> For a month now life has consisted of cowering at home at night in a basement, with gunfire and high explosive bombs overhead, rocking the very foundations [she wrote in October]; and at the [Ambulance] Station, sitting in a brick shelter in the garage, waiting for the telephone to ring for the next Ambulance out, and hoping that the worst of the bombing will have died down when one's turn comes to go out during the raid—and yet wishing that one could go out immediately, even envying those who go before.—anything to make this warfare seem less impersonal and detached, divorced from what once were the realities—anything to release one even temporarily from this humiliation which has been thrust upon one.
>
> Although when not out in it I do not feel any paralysing fear, rather an exhilarating excitement, and then comes the despair, perhaps days afterwards—with the continuous raids the feeling of futility grows . . . [But] I feel I cannot just leave, one's life becomes inextricably bound up with the events, almost incomprehensibly so. Travelling by underground at night, the platforms lined two deep with women, men, young and old, children too, lying or sitting with their bundles of blankets even food for the long night, and just staring mutely or helplessly sleeping close-packed, one knows one cannot escape merely because one happens to be able to leave the country. And then, in the early light of morning, long lines, dim forms, emerge tiredly from the undergrounds, wearily—and they go to work, whilst from early in the afternoon children, sent to keep the places in the long queue for the next night in the underground, stand or rest with the family's bundles on the sidewalks. What depths of humiliation—we are just creatures—sub-human, and without dignity. So one stays.[82]

The ambulance work paid her £1 18s. a week, which was enough to live on. Later, she managed to lift her income to £3 a week by changing her job. She took to driving a little van delivering addressing machines all over London (which she scarcely knew how to navigate: she was a stranger to the city, and in any case had a poor sense of direction). The size of the van disappointed the dauntlessly strong South African. 'I had thought, when taking this job that I should be given a whacking great truck to drive—my little van I could lift with one hand whilst changing the wheel . . . When there is heavy machinery I sometimes am given a ton van which is much more satisfying.'[83] She paid eleven shillings a week for a one-room flat above Eastman's furniture store near Camden Town Station—sharing it with 'a little nagging bitch of a Civil Servant' who fretted about conditions[84]—and applied herself to getting to know more and more of the artists of London. Quite soon she had managed to meet Rupert Shepherd (who was at a later stage in the war to paint a portrait of Empson that is now hidden away in storage at the National Portrait Gallery in London), Feliks Topolski, Herbert Read (who tried to help her by way of the good offices of the Committee of the Royal Academy in her efforts to get Graetz released from internment in Ottawa), Oskar Kokoschka ('a fine personality as well as a good painter—a jolly man with a warm heart and a sense of humour and *guts*'),[85] and Leslie Hurry, a tall, highly-strung, breathless man who later achieved deserved celebrity as a theatre designer. Hetta wrote of Hurry at the time, 'as soon as the raids start he leaves London because he finds he cannot work at all—I like his work very much'; and then again: 'he is a fine artist, the only one of english artists whose work I can admire and take seriously, except perhaps Henry Moore, who is of course also a serious artist but Leslie has more to say, more guts, and has not intellectualised his work as is the tendency in so many english artists.'[86] She also befriended the young Jomo Kenyatta.[87] In November, she moved into a shared house with some convivial people at 47 Downshire Hill, near Hampstead Heath; upstairs, for example, lived the great political photomontage artist John Heartfield (born Helmut Herzfeld). The house on Downshire Hill was home to the émigré artist and writer Manfred (Freddie) Uhlman, who had been interned for a year on the Isle of Man. When Uhlman was allowed back to London at the close of 1940 he was not entirely comfortable with all the quasi-bohemian folk ensconced in his house: they were not so much billeted as simply squatting. However, Uhlman and his wife Diana stayed for most of the rest of the war at Bambers Green in Essex, and set up in their London home an organization called the Artists' Refugee Committee which sought to find relief, including jobs and host families, for the families of German refugees (Hetta naturally became involved in its work), and later set up there the Free German League of Culture, bringing together thousands of German refugees to form an anti-Nazi organization. Although Hetta longed to return to her lovely studio in Camden Town, that proved to be literally impossible when the vibrations caused by the guns and the bombs falling nearby caused the entire glass roof to fall in.

But suddenly, on 22 June 1941, Hitler betrayed the Russo-German Pact by invading the Soviet Union, and the war became at once bigger and more purposeful for Hetta— who was a member of the Communist party. As Empson would later explain, 'Hetta, like many other high-minded people at the time, had been dubious about working directly for the Government until Hitler attacked Russia, though it had been all right to drive lorries or ambulances through the London blitz.'[88] (He remembered too that his friend George Orwell, the deep-dyed anti-Soviet, had 'jeered at those who expressed pleasure at having recently acquired the powerful ally'.)[89] Thus Hetta became a propagandist when she answered the BBC's advertisement for an Afrikaans-speaking member of staff; and she would become involved principally with two transmissions: (i) a women's magazine programme that included items on domestic economy, childcare and so forth, along with news of the Home Front; and (ii) a direct, pithy propaganda piece in a regular 3-minute slot that was designed to combat the gross amount of German propaganda broadcast to South Africa.

Whether drinking at The George, the BBC's local hostelry, or dining out at the Étoile in Soho, she and Empson hit it off from the start. With her slender good looks, her vivacity and force of character, it was very soon obvious that she could give him the 'backing and stiffening' he wanted from a wife. She was also, to his delight, an excellent cook. She was taken by his sure-fire intellect, his wit, and his steadiness of purpose. They became engaged within a few weeks, having reached such an instant understanding that Empson needed only to issue a sort of warning—or a promise: 'If you marry me, you'll have to go to China.' 'When?' she happily responded, and the thing was settled.

The Empsons got married on 3rd December in St Stephen's Church on Rosslyn Hill, one street away from the large red-brick Victorian house at the corner of Hampstead Hill Gardens where in five years' time they would establish their home. Empson's old friend Humphrey Jennings wrote to Cicely Jennings on 3 December, 'Bill Empson married—to a ravishing Africaans girl.'[90] The note of surprise in that missive was shared by many of Empson's friends, not only on account of his marrying a tall and tough and attractive Boer but simply because he was marrying at all: it was assumed that the bisexual Bill was one of Nature's lifelong bachelors. 'We were amazed,' said Gwenda David. 'Who was this woman who had won William, when we understood that he was not interested in women or marriage? She must be someone *very* special. She was. She was beautiful, had a very quick wit and a very sharp tongue; you couldn't play games with her; she was an arrogant woman who laughed easily and got angry easily.'[91] Hetta, aged 26, was married from a studio room above a garage at 99 Southend Road, near Keats Grove; Empson, 35, from some sordid bed-and-breakfast lodgings in Brunswick Square. It was a very low-key affair; and indeed they had a church wedding only in order to satisfy the Empson family. Empson's mother, who was unable to come to London for the wedding, had little time for sentimentality and wrote merely, 'My dearest William, I think your invitation wedding cards are very nice. I don't think any body will come, except Arthur, Molly, Monica [William's sister-in-law, wife to Charles] . . . With best love and all the good wishes in the world, Your very loving Mother.'[92] In the event, the witnesses were Empson's brother Arthur, who came up from Yorkshire, and Mabel Sharp, a good friend of Hetta's from the Ambulance Service who happened to be the ex-wife of the dean of St Stephen's (who officiated at the wedding). Empson's sister Molly did attend, and she presented them with some plates and saucers. Laurence Gilliam came from the BBC, and said it was the best Outside Broadcast he had ever heard—a remark which pleased Empson no end.

After a brief no-nonsense ceremony, the assembled company repaired to drink jugs of beer just down the road at 160A Haverstock Hill, a basement flat in a partly bombed building which the Empsons would inhabit for the remainder of the war. Their accommodation consisted of a living room, two bedrooms, kitchen, and bathroom, plus a small garden at the back where they kept two hens and grew sunflowers—'in the belief that they yield henfood'.[93] (The family would at least be able to cook an omelette with natural ingredients rather than a powdered egg substitute.) According to Hetta's own account, Dylan and Caitlin Thomas, who came along to the wedding party, ended up fighting furiously under the table. Even more remarkably, as the party wound to a close, Empson turned to Hetta and said, 'Well, I'll be going along, my dear'—and off he went to his erstwhile digs.[94] (He may have wanted to avoid the squalor of cleaning up after the party, but it is far more probable that he had drunk enough to forget he had got married and should be living with Hetta from then on.) Hetta had worn for her wedding a delicious new yellow felt hat, and she wore it every day for some weeks afterwards; and every night for some weeks Empson would patiently comb the lice out of her fine blonde hair. It took them a fair while to realize that the infestation came with the hat.

Just over eleven months later, on 9 November 1942, Hetta gave birth to their first son, in New End Hospital. They named the child William

Hendrik Mogador—'Mogador after a town in North Africa which was being occupied at the hour of birth,' as Empson needed to explain to anyone who dared to ask. 'I am told that the word is also the Yiddish for a muddle. That is, he was christened William Hendrik, but Mogador was added in the eyes of the law all right when he was registered.'[95] Both the parents and the child slept soundly as the bombs fell, or so Empson claimed. 'Nothing came this way, though the guns were very noisy,' he told his mother in response to an anxious telegram from her. 'In fact the child missed an early morning feed on the morning of the blitz because we all slept through it. However Hetta is determined to take William Hendrik into the Underground (or the new deep shelter which is being built even nearer to us) if things get seriously bad . . . Hetta is supposed to be starting work at the office again on the 1st of March, after doing work at home and broadcasting one day a week. But I hope we'll be able to wangle the work at home for a bit longer; she would have to wean the child before she went back to the office, and the longer it is nursed the better for it probably.'[96] Mogador grew into a buoyant, pudgy boy who seemed quite content to be left to crawl around in a creche while his parents went to work—'and the creche says he probably won't be able to walk till late because he is so fat,' Empson would report in June 1943; adding more dubiously: 'He is still very goodtempered, at home anyway, though I believe he objects to Voluntary Workers at the creche. I should think the longer he can be kept from walking the better.'[97]

George Orwell refused to come to the Empsons' wedding, though he was certainly invited. He seemed to be cross that Hetta had chosen to marry Empson, because he too had enjoyed her company in the Liars' School and afterwards. Instead, he sent the couple a carving knife and fork (which they rightly interpreted as an aggressive gift). Hetta became devoted to Orwell (and to his first wife Eileen), and loved arguing politics with him— though 'I was a Marxist, he was a Trot', and their quarrels could be terrible[98]—but she had no interest in developing their relationship beyond a deep friendship. She had told him not to talk silly when he offered to divorce his wife for her ('I didn't like him enough'), though she was certainly flattered by the gesture. But Orwell's foolish jealousy soon passed, and nothing ever marred their friendship. 'George was crazy about me for a bit, that's all.'[99] Empson and Orwell worked in harmonious close proximity for the next two years, and they remained on good terms even after Eileen's death in March 1945 and up to 1947 when the Empsons finally took ship for China.[100] For her part, more often than not, Hetta continued to find Orwell 'enchanting, very imaginative and very sweet; child-like in a way.' George Woodcock adroitly remarked that Orwell 'extracted a boyish enjoyment out of the hardships of the time';[101] and T. R. Fyvel noted his 'deliberately spartan way of life'.[102] Also, much as she found him endearing in so many ways, he was what she brilliantly called a 'wrong-footer', deliberately doing the contrary thing in order to antagonize other people. As another BBC colleague, John Morris—who never felt comfortable with Orwell, and whom Orwell would go out of his way to discomfort—would reflect, 'Nothing could have turned Orwell into a working-class man; yet I believe nothing gave him more pleasure than to be mistaken for one.'[103]

Empson remarked of Orwell, three decades later: 'It was lucky for me that George thought I was all right, as I admired him and wanted his friendship, and he might easily have decided I was not.'[104] He noted too that Orwell 'sounded a bit like what one had read of Lord Curzon, another isolated ailing and public-spirited Etonian who had cultivated a funny accent.'[105] After the first few weeks at Bush House, the two men worked through the winter months in the BBC offices at 55 Portland Place; later, from June 1942, they were to take up occupancy of adjacent offices on the high-ceilinged second floor of 200 Oxford Street (at Oxford Circus), the peacetime premises of the Peter Robinson's Men Shop, which housed— barricaded, wired, guarded—the Empire Service and other non-European Services of the BBC (in all, there were seventy-five editors and sub-editors). 'Some of the studios were so far below street level that the periodic sound of the Central Line trains of the London underground entering nearby Oxford Street tube station was clearly audible as a distant rumble and was picked up by the studio microphones, to be transmitted to all parts of the globe.'[106] It is almost universally agreed that the really rather good ground floor canteen, which could cater for a hundred at a time, with main meals for 1s. 6d. (though with no real milk or sugar), was the model for the canteen in *1984*. 'In the late hours there were few places in London where you could get a meal,' Maurice Gorham would recall, 'and many of our contacts got into the habit of dropping in to eat in our canteen, even if they were not broadcasting that night.'[107] The floor space of the department store had been subdivided into numerous austere little office compartments, each drab unit being screened from its neighbours by lath-and-plaster partitions rising to a height of about seven feet, so that the drones who worked there suffered from the continuously oppressive din of voices talking and dictating, footsteps, telephones, telex machines.

'My office is next door to George Orwell's and I find him excellent company,' Empson related to I. A. Richards; 'it is wonderful how he still

manages to do some writing.'[108] Among the writing that Orwell was keen
to share with his colleague was *Animal Farm*, though Empson, who read the
book with 'great excitement' and genuinely admired the beauty of its
limpid prose style, was to form the opinion—as he boldly and candidly
advised Orwell by letter in August 1945—that the allegory of the book was
in danger of being misunderstood by many readers.[109] Empson felt certain
too that it had been little short of a 'torture' for Orwell to write his fable:

> it was horrible to think of the evil men, stinking Tories, who would *gain* by
> his telling the truth, let alone jeer about it triumphantly.... With all the
> reviews ablaze he stayed cross at the reception of the book, so that we said:
> 'What more do you want, George? It's knocked them all right back. They all
> say it's terrific.' 'Grudging swine, they are,' he muttered at last, when
> coaxed and stroked into saying what was the matter; 'not one of them
> said it's a beautiful book.'[110]

George Ivan Smith, a journalist with the Australian Broadcasting Company who moved to London in 1941 to become head of Radio Pacific for
the BBC's Overseas Services, occupied the next cubbyhole along from
Empson and Orwell; he would recall in a later year:

> The fragrance of overheard conversations between the authors of Animal
> Farm and Seven Types of Ambiguity was strengthened by the fact that only
> a low partition lay between us. Empson came one day with swollen black
> eyes. 'I trod on a rake.' I enquired: 'In the garden?' He replied: 'No, in the
> hall. I was going to the bathroom to make a cup of tea.'
>   Near midnight at another time I was duty director and had to telephone
> his Hampstead home. 'William, where is your baby?' He consulted wife,
> Hetta. I reported that the police had telephoned me. The infant had not
> been collected from the creche.[111]

Another of Empson's colleagues noted of the arrangements at 200 Oxford
Street that 'the blending of claustrophobia with a denial of privacy' would
be 'well portrayed' in Orwell's book *1984*.[112] (It may be worth noting here
that Empson liked to refer to Broadcasting House, in Kafkaesque manner,
as 'The Machine'.) According to John Morris it was 'at times impossible to
carry on a telephone conversation'.[113] It is not really surprising that Orwell
came to regard the BBC set-up as being 'halfway between a girls' school
and a lunatic asylum'; and variously, in July 1943, as 'a mixture of whore-
shop and lunatic asylum'.[114]

   The quality of Orwell's contempt was brought home to Empson just a
few days after they first met, when he and H. G. Wells spent an evening
with the Orwells in what T. R. Fyvel called the 'reasonable discomfort' of

their small flat at 111 Langford Court, near Maida Vale.[115] The re-encounter between Orwell and Wells (they had enjoyed one previous meeting) could not have been more poorly timed, because Orwell had just published his excoriating essay 'Wells, Hitler and the World State' in the August issue of *Horizon*. Given this attack by Orwell, it was scarcely possible for the two men to avoid a quarrel when they met for dinner on 30 August; and as soon as the meal was over Wells and Orwell entered the fray. At one point Wells even accused his host of being defeatist—presumably because Orwell scorned his own faith in progressive rationalism. The novelist Inez Holden, who came in for coffee and so witnessed the contretemps, noted Empson's intervention:

> The poet Empson said that H. G. should take back the word defeatist considering Orwell had seen a considerable amount of fighting under the worst conditions. H. G. was clearly outraged and hurt by the wording of Orwell's article...Empson...said 'Great man Orwell I think we should appreciate his effort, there he is an Etonian and his honesty and fight against his upbringing compels him to say anything he wants in a rude manner. He is an Etonian. I am a Wykehamist, I can't write about anything that matters.[']...I remember H. G. saying it was not because Orwell was rude that he had been angry with him but because his values were wrong.
> Empson said 'No it was because Orwell was rude that H. G. had been angry.'[116]

Certainly, Empson sincerely admired the forthrightness with which Orwell would put opinions that were sure to offend other people. According to an unpublished memoir of Inez Holden by her friend Celia Goodman, the complete entry about the evening's spat in Holden's diary includes these additional remarks: 'While Orwell was in the kitchen making some more coffee William Empson volunteered a second remark on the subject of the conflict. Orwell, he thought, could be "rather flat-footed at times", and had been so in his criticism of Wells.'[117]

For his part, Empson was stubborn in his opinions and pugnacious in answering back; in fact, he could be quite as rude as Orwell to both friend and foe, for reasons set out at the very beginning of his career, in 1930:

> if you attack a view in any detail that proves you to have sympathy with it; there is already a conflict in you which mirrors the conflict in which you take part; that it why you understand it sufficiently to take part in it. Only because you can foresee and enter into the opposing arguments can you answer them; only because it is interesting to you do you engage in argument about it.

> For personally I am attracted by the notion of a hearty indifference to one's own and other people's feelings, when a fragment of the truth is in question...[118]

Orwell would wholeheartedly agree with that principle of empathy and impersonality; he had said as much in 'Wells, Hitler and the World State'.

Empson was conscious that he had grown up in a world of squirearchical privilege, but there is little evidence to suggest that he felt an uncommon degree of self-conflict when he came to profess political principles that might be thought to be at odds with his class, family and upbringing (any more than he found it a struggle to reject his family's religion). Like Orwell he became a libertarian socialist; but unlike Orwell he saw no point in posing as a proletarian. Empson was gravely mistaken when he wrote: ' "The working classes smell" was one of [Orwell's] famous debunking pronouncements... and this was a settled enough assumption in his mind to make him feel that only tramps and other down-and-outs were genuinely working class. It was a serious weakness in his political judgement, otherwise very good, and it clearly resulted from deep internal revulsions.' Empson even 'judged it to be connected with his firmly expressed distaste for homosexuality'.[119] In fact Orwell had written in *The Road to Wigan Pier* that he had been brought up by his family to believe that the working classes smell, obviously meaning that he had long since spurned such a crass prejudice. Empson went on to report the sorry fact that Orwell himself 'stank, and evidently knew it—well, his (first) wife talked to mine about it quite frankly'; it was impossible, he said, to pass an evening with him and not to notice the 'sweetish smell' of his rotting lungs. 'Bodily disgust, or rather a fear that a good man may at any moment be driven into some evil action by an unbearable amount of it, is deeply embedded in his best writing; and at the time I thought all this was easy to explain—he just hated his own smell.'[120] Probably Orwell did come to loathe the stench of his decaying bronchial tubes—like Robert Louis Stevenson before him, he was suffering from bronchiectasis—which may also help to explain why he indulged in such an acrid brand of shag, as a smokescreen. But it was a false equation for Empson to imply that Orwell chose to identify himself with the working classes at least partly on account of his own smell. It was a serious weakness in Empson's psychological insight, otherwise very good, and it may have resulted from his frankly admitted aversion to Orwell's body odour along with his puzzled effort to come to terms with Orwell's high-mindedness—'his immense power to convey a shaming rebuke, and how he sometimes turned this power on in a baffling manner', as well as his proletarian affectations. Possibly Empson was not fully in sympathy with Orwell or his ideological stance; or perhaps he ran foul once too often of what he regarded as Orwell's 'great power to make you feel ashamed of yourself'.[121]

Whatever slight reservations Empson had against Orwell's judgement, he and Orwell enjoyed entirely cordial working and social relations. In the later months of 1942 Empson welcomed the opportunity to participate in 'Voice', Orwell's six-part radio magazine about poetry which consisted of readings and rather low-key critical commentary—as W. J. West rightly suggested, the brief series 'pointed the way to the sort of poetry programmes that finally reached the wider British public after the war on the Third Programme'.[122] Other contributors to the broadcast programmes produced by Orwell included T. S. Eliot, Herbert Read, Edmund Blunden, J. M. Tambimuttu (the charming and gifted young Ceylonese editor of *Poetry London*), Dylan Thomas, Keidrich Rhys (editor of *Poetry Wales*) and his wife Lynette Roberts, and the Canadian libertarian anarchist George Woodcock (future author of *The Crystal Spirit*, a sympathetic critical study of Orwell).

Another regular contributor, more surprisingly, was Mulk Raj Anand, author of *Coolie* and *Untouchable* (and a veteran of the conflict in Spain, where he had been befriended by Orwell). Anand had become a conscientious objector at the outbreak of the Second World War, because most of the Indian leadership of the National Movement had been incarcerated by the British; and at first he declined Orwell's request for him to participate in BBC programmes. But he modified his position in 1942 when the Nazis started marching into Eurasia, forcing Indians to become aware that Hitler might repeat the ambitions of Alexander the Great in the third century BC. So it was that when his friend Orwell approached him again, he agreed to do casual broadcasts for the Indian Section of the BBC, and it was in that capacity that he renewed an old acquaintance with Empson. Anand had first come across Empson at Cambridge in the early 1930s, when the author of *Ambiguity*, with his reserved manners, sharp nose, searching eyes, black-rimmed spectacles and solemn poet's face, made a point of attending some meetings of the Indian Majlis. Empson was sympathetic to the cause of Indian freedom but made a point of asking Anand whether, in the event that the British were to quit India, the Indians were really capable of running a democracy for themselves? Anand told him about Karl Marx's three articles, published in the *New York Herald Tribune* in 1854, which pointed out that the British would inevitably have to leave India: once they introduced industrial development, the Indians were sure to ask for a share and eventually take over. Empson seemed to have a genuine feeling for Marxist thought, and on another occasion told Anand that he thought Christopher Caudwell's study *Illusion and Reality* was a more important work than his own *Ambiguity*. In 1936 Empson even joined the Conference of Intellectuals against Fascism which André Malraux, John Strachey, and Amabel Williams Ellis organized at Friends House in the Euston Road, London.[123]

One day, over lunch in the BBC's basement canteen, Anand told Empson that T. S. Eliot had once asked him if he had read the *Dhammapada: Sayings of the Buddha*? Anand had nodded firmly in reply, and said he had been in the Gandhi Movement and tried to be non-violent. 'The Buddha,' he told Eliot, 'is reincarnated in Gandhi!' Empson said to Anand: 'In the cocoon of our complacency before the Second World War, most of us saw the world only as the object of contemplation, not as something to be remade. Few intellectuals wanted to share common experience. Certainly, no one wanted to march with upraised fists with the communists. And Eliot had inclined towards reaction!'

Often the BBC broadcasters, including Orwell, Empson, and Anand, would go out drinking at a pub in Great Portland Street after a day's stint at the microphone.[124] On one such occasion Orwell told Empson about some of the horrible things he had been obliged to do as an officer in the Burma Police which he had not mentioned in *Burmese Days*. Empson went off and read the book again, and the next time they met he remarked that it had given him an insight into the real meaning of freedom.

'Perhaps poets only see the world from far away— except when they're in jail,' Empson volunteered with a flourish of self-deprecation.

Mulk Raj Anand took up the theme. 'The window of a jail cell is small, like the window of the soul. One looks out intently to see the things outside. Strange how Jawaharlal Nehru became conscious of the stars in heaven when he was sometimes allowed out of his prison cell. And he began to write letters to his young daughter about how the world began and what was the place of the earth in the galaxies.'

'After I left the Service,' Orwell recalled, in his flat-toned and monotonous voice, 'I felt I had emerged from a prison. I had new thoughts, new ideas, new feelings—'

'I suppose you went off to serve in French kitchens to see how the cook spits into the soup in chagrin,' Empson twitted him.

'Life in the kitchen as a dish washer certainly lifts the scales from one's eyes!'

'In India,' Anand ploughed on, 'we have never accepted Aristotle. Our poets responded to Shelley's *The Revolt of Islam*, Byron's *Isles of Greece*, Keats's talk of "the miseries of the world". Our old philosophy of illusionism—of reincarnation and salvation—is dead and gone. Gandhi says, "God comes to the poor in the form of bread." There's a transition from metaphysics to ethics.'

'Actually,' Empson corrected, 'Aristotle thought of tragedy as the conquest of grief.'

'It was to him an understanding of Fate,' argued Anand.

Orwell thrust in: 'Tragedy cannot be a substitute, in art, for chaos in life.'

'Now for absurdity of existence!' said Anand. 'Gandhi told me that writing is only expiation. One should confront reality directly. I told him Greek dramatists did that and cried out in horror against the pain of life.'

'Our purists think that the depiction of cruelty, of the horror of the tragic situation, is a failure of humanism,' Empson observed.

'They want symbolism,' said Orwell. 'I agree with Gandhi about the direct approach—though I have doubts about his political integrity.'

Both Empson and Anand looked at him askance.

'Why?' asked Anand.

'Gandhi slides back from position to position. Non-violence becomes violence against himself, when he undertakes a fast unto death.'

'This is an old Indian idea of the ascetic, taking on oneself the suffering of others,' Anand tried to explain.

'I should have thought it is genuine expiation,' ventured Empson.

'It is anti-life to take one's own life,' Orwell insisted. 'One must resist.'

'That may also bring death to the rebel,' Empson commented.

Orwell reacted sharply: 'The death of a rebel is heroic!'

'You sound like Byron.'

'Our times require revolt,' said Anand.

'Especially against the State—Hitler and Stalin,' Orwell hotly agreed.

'Also against Churchill,' Anand continued. 'I agree with Richard Hillary: "Our choice is to fight for the small lie against the big lie".'

Empson smiled his approval.

According to Anand, they ended up the conversation by agreeing that a sense of the misery with which armed force had filled the world was a necessary precondition for the struggle for justice.[125]

Empson and Orwell shared a sense of patriotic urgency about fighting the war against Fascism. 'I hold what half the men in this country would give their balls to have,' Orwell would remark to Empson, 'a yellow ticket.' This ticket meant that he could not be conscripted. 'But I don't want it.'

('In writing this,' reflected Empson in his memoir of Orwell, 'I paused and searched my memory, feeling that another bright phrase should come next; but no, he did not sustain his rhetoric, though he would use a phrase intending it to glitter. He was indignant at being told he was too ill to go abroad.')[126] Pacifism, Orwell strongly believed, was 'helpful towards totalitarianism'; and English pacifists tended towards active pro-Fascism.[127] Likewise Empson had long thought that pacifist idealism was phoney and self-deluding. In fact, his chat with Orwell and Anand touched on a subject he had weighed seriously for more than a decade, for it involved his interest in Buddhist teachings and the war between rationalism and transcendence. It was not by chance that in 'The Traps of Idealism', the first talk he ever drafted for the BBC (the twenty-minute piece, though scheduled for transmission on 3 September 1936, was ultimately pulled at the last minute),[128] he had written against the fallacies of unrealistic ideals such as pacifism. He maintained that people need to be protected against the traps of the ideals inherent in Christianity and Buddhism, where the desire to leave the struggles of the world was essentially a death-wish.

Later, on 4 September 1940 (about a year before he met Orwell), he attempted to intervene in a periodical controversy about the distinction between the terms *Pacifism* and *Pacificism*. The difference was not 'merely verbal', he suggested in a letter. 'A *pacifist* has commonly been a fanatic, and is now required to be such by the Conscription Boards; he has at least a definite opinion. The more refined *pacificist* sounds like a man in favour of being "pacific", wherever possible presumably, so he is *not* a man with a fixed doctrine.' Either way, he did not hesitate to insist upon his own bias on the issue. 'I think that Jesus and the Buddha could be outright pacifists without practical hypocrisy, not merely because they were celibates with no possessions, but also because they lived in warm fertile climates, and among peasants respectful to fanatics. Nobody in peacetime England or America who allows himself to be protected by the police is within reach of consistent pacifism. If he says he is he cheats.'[129]

When they joined the BBC, both Empson and Orwell felt that being a Talks Assistant was a second-best wartime occupation. But both fervently believed they should be agents of the truth, at once serving their country and supporting the interests of China and India respectively. But while Orwell came to feel that he was wasting his time and talent and left the BBC's employ on 24 November 1943, Empson knew he should stick it out. He had no doubt he was holding an important office, for the future of Anglo-Chinese relations might well depend on it—and 'it was a rather undeserved bonus to be approved by Orwell'.[130]

Faced with the menace of Nazism in Europe, Empson had no doubt where his duty lay. Only concerted action could ever win the day. As he wrote in a review of Jean-Paul Sartre's plays *No Exit* and *The Flies*, soon after the end of the war, Existentialism seemed to be a philosophy fit only for the defeated—the better value is to accept duty and to plan for action:

> [Existentialist philosophy is] a psychological method for keeping your self-respect when impotent and surrounded by evil. But so far as I can see it would not deserve respect under any other circumstances; because where there is any prospect of making things better by combined action existentialism would not encourage people to do it.[131]

One small riddle remains to be answered. Why did Orwell choose not to name William and Hetta Empson in the list of 'crypto-Communists & fellow-travellers' that he was to make available to the covert Information Research Department of the British Foreign Office in the spring of 1949?[132] The list does identify a few individuals who were known to Empson— Richard Crossman ('Political climber... Too dishonest to be outright FT'), John Davenport ('Well-disposed person, rather silly'), Kingsley Martin, editor of the *New Statesman* ('Probably no definite organisational connection... Decayed liberal'), Michael Redgrave ('People's Convention'), and Stephen Spender ('Sentimental sympathiser, & very unreliable. Easily influenced. Tendency towards homosexuality')—but of those few only Davenport was ever close enough to be called a friend. Orwell knew that Hetta was a Communist, and that Empson was sympathetic to the ideals of Communism. Also, he was not reluctant in May 1949 to make this fact known to the American editor Robert Giroux, who had brought out Empson's *Collected Poems* with the New York firm of Harcourt, Brace in 1948. 'Hetta, Empson's wife, is or used to be a Communist,' he declared in a letter to Giroux (who had sent him a copy of Empson's volume, very likely at Empson's request), '& he himself was not particularly hostile to Communism...'[133] This stark pronouncement to Giroux was made in the very month when Orwell was in correspondence with Celia Kirwan about identifying individuals who might give support to the activities of the Communist Party or show allegiance to the interests of the USSR.[134] It may just have been the case that he cared enough about Empson and his wife to wish to protect them from any possible future enquiry—and one may recall that he had sometime cared enough for Hetta to offer, however insincerely, to marry her. But it is doubtful whether he would have let personal loyalty get in the way of his convictions: the Communist enemy was bigger than the individual—and in any case he had been out of touch with the Empsons for some months, so loyalty was less of a live issue. It therefore seems far more likely that he simply did not see the Empsons as figuring in the category of potential fifth-columnists within the UK. For one obvious matter, they were safely out of the way in China, living under the new Chinese Communist regime, and they seemed set to stay there— the second sentence of his letter to Giroux reads, perhaps with a touch of relief, 'I note with interest from the Sewanee Review that Empson has decided to stay on in Pekin'—so that neither the Communist Hetta nor the possibly fellow-travelling Empson could be in any way operative in Britain. Hetta was a Communist, and Empson 'not particularly hostile to Communism,' he told Giroux—'but,' he went on, 'I doubt whether that would do them much good under a Chinese Communist régime.' The 'but' in that clause may serve to convey a vague amusement on Orwell's part that Hetta's Marxist brand of Communism was in any case misplaced in China. For Orwell, the real and present enemy was the USSR. Even when in London, Hetta was active only as artist and political scrapper: she had no direct, institutional political function or influence. Above all else, Orwell had worked alongside Empson for two years in the bureaucratic jungle of the BBC, and he knew that Empson was deeply patriotic, by no means a potential collaborator. When all is said and done, indeed, there is no doubt that he thought Empson a good fellow and no fellow-traveller. The double negative of his statement that Empson was 'not particularly hostile to Communism' need not imply anything like a positively pro-Soviet posture on Empson's part. In truth, a touch of warmth for his erstwhile colleague, his fellow worker on the treadmill of the BBC 'machine', is apparent in two sentences of his note to Giroux: 'I wonder if you are in touch with him? I should certainly be glad of any news of him.'

2

The War within the BBC

[A]ll propaganda has to admit that some opponents hold other views

Faustus and the Censor, p. 53

I ... thought it a duty to do propaganda against Hitler, and much of this was fun, but I had sometimes to eat dirt from people who replied to my advances that I must do my own dirty work.

Letter to Christopher Ricks, 6 May 1962

During the war I was a propagandist, and we were proud to explain that a stick of chalk was being put into every loaf of bread, which was enough to keep the kids from rickets though they didn't get eggs and so on. Then we reflected that for generations the baker who mixed chalk with his flour was considered the meanest kind of wicked man; and yet, every time holy religion converted a baker so that he renounced the current practice, he made a number of children cripples.

Letter to Mr Stuart Smith, 8 July 1966

RALF Bonwit's arrival at the BBC was all the more timely since it coincided with the advent of a new Counsellor at the Chinese Embassy who would serve as Director of the Chinese Ministry of Information. This illustrious personage was none other than Empson's old comrade-in-exile from Lianda days, George Yeh (Yeh Kung Chao), who landed in London at the end of May 1942. Empson had not seen him for nearly three years. Now in his late thirties (Empson was 35), Yeh had temporarily left China in September 1941, when he went to Singapore to take up duties both as Resident Representative of the Chinese Ministry of Information and as liaison officer between Chinese GHQ and the British Far Eastern Command and authorities in Malaya. On the outbreak of the Pacific War he had helped with mobilization for the defence of Straits Settlements' Chinese, and he escaped from Singapore to Java just a few days before the capitulation. In March 1942, after a tour of India, he reported back to Chungking, from where he was appointed to the London post; and *en route* for England he spent two weeks more in India, lecturing on China's struggle and meeting the Viceroy and General Wavell as well as Indian leaders of all parties. It seems somehow characteristic of the superabundant energy of the man that he even managed the air trip to London in record time.

Empson was delighted at the appointment, which would give him a fount of information and advice for his China lobby at the BBC. He felt equally pleased when the Pacific War caused another old friend, H. Vere (later Sir Vere) Redman, to be dispatched to London, where he was to serve as Director of the Far East Division of the Ministry of Information. In the 1930s, Vere Redman had been a university lecturer and journalist in Tokyo, where he lived throughout the decade and won a deservedly high reputation for his understanding of Japanese affairs; in 1939 he was made press attaché in the British Embassy, which he left for London at the end of 1942—though not before being arrested by the *Kempeitai* (the Japanese gestapo) and incarcerated in solitary confinement in Sugamo prison in Tokyo for eight cruel months.[1] Empson liked Redman's company—Redman was odd, short, portly, hospitable, witty, volatile, and sometimes rude and unconventional—and would tell I. A. Richards: 'It is very dreamlike to have Redman head of the Far East section in the MOI and George Yeh running the London Chinese MOI, or perhaps rather like a fancy dress ball. But they I think both feel they are in their proper places now.'[2] Concerning Yeh, he went on: 'He is still delightful company and I think is doing a lot of good for Anglo-Chinese relations, but you know how temperamental he is.' Son of the District Governor of Kiukiang, and descendant of a long line of high officials of the Chinese Empire, Yeh was not a man to tolerate any slight to China's dignity. Immensely cultivated, he was invariably polite and congenial; but as Ralf Bonwit well remembered, he could also be blunt.

For the rest of his career with the BBC Empson would have to keep a wary watch on four cardinal points of reference—his sometimes contumacious or recalcitrant superiors in the BBC, the Foreign Office, the British MOI, and the Chinese MOI—and much of his energy would be consumed by the need to please or appease George Yeh in particular. According to Bonwit, Empson saw the essential point of his work as being first and foremost to hold out a cultural lure for the Chinese. Yeh's varying humour became his litmus paper: any discoloration meant that Empson must have fallen short in his duty of enhancing Anglo-Chinese relations. It was really very stressful.

But Empson enjoyed to the full his social contacts with the Chinese. On one occasion, when a good-will mission of Chinese intellectuals arrived in town, he threw a party to which he gathered T. S. Eliot, Arthur Waley (who was now 'working his head off' in the MOI),[3] and other writers and artists including Tambi (Meary James Tambimuttu), the charismatic Tamil editor of *Poetry London* who had arrived in London in 1937 at the age of 22 and promptly made a name for himself as editor and talent-spotter.[4] When the flamboyant Tambi got drunk (as he often did), he launched into a quarrel with the Chinese about a Japanese writer whom he declared to be superior to many others. Empson, noting the annoyance of the Chinese, gestured at the coal-black Tambi and informed them disarmingly: 'You wanted to see British intellectual life in action; this *is* British intellectual life!'[5] (After enjoying another party at the Empsons' flat on Haverstock Hill in the winter of 1942, T. S. Eliot gossiped with evident glee to Mrs I. A. Richards: 'Tell Ivor that I dined with Bill Empson and his S. African wife last week: he is doing far east BBC work but is otherwise unchanged.')[6]

Possibly by coincidence, within a very few weeks of George Yeh's arrival in London the BBC Eastern Service stepped up the schedule of its broadcasts in Chinese. The Chinese News Service had in fact started on 5 May 1941 with weekly letters in Kuoyü (Mandarin or Standard Chinese). Quo Tai Chi, the Chinese Ambassador, and R. A. Butler gave the inaugural talks. In February 1942 the number of transmissions was increased to six a week. From 7 July, it was then decided, the broadcasts would go out on a daily basis at the prime time of 13.15 GMT, with a fifteen-minute period divided between a news bulletin and a news commentary (the normal ratio of news to commentary would be 2: 1, though a big commentary might oust some of the lesser items of news). Thus it was fortunate for all parties involved in this extended news service that Dr Yeh was available to give the inaugural talk, most especially because 7 July 1942 marked the fifth anniversary of the outbreak of the Sino-Japanese war.

Within a month of the launch of the extended Chinese News Service, the Far East experts of the BBC were recommending that the Corporation could serve its audience all the better if it put out not just hard news and news commentaries but also other kinds of feature, including talks on scientific and literary topics, which might be useful to Chinese universities. The response from R. A. Rendall, Acting Controller (Overseas Services), betrayed the depressingly common misapprehension that Asia was really all one: that what was true of India was probably also true of China. 'While I agree that we should not take too narrow a view of the type of commentary required from Chungking,' Rendall told Rushbrook Williams, 'I feel very dubious about the value of literary talks directed to students and intellectuals. After all, the similar appeal to an Indian audience in the Eastern Service, where there is much more time available, has not been a very marked success nor have we yet, unfortunately, any concrete indication of what Chungking wants.'[7]

Williams, whose experience might have inclined him to speak of Asia while thinking of India, took all the advice he could command and reported it with commendable firmness. 'On the question of the kind of commentaries which the Chinese want us to carry,' he insisted, 'the M of I Far East Dept, Dr Yeh, and Mr Empson are all in agreement. They strongly affirm that cultural commentaries are essential. This does not mean that "news" commentaries are excluded: it does mean that "news" must be given a very wide interpretation to cover cultural activities as well. I suggest that the Indian analogy does not help. The students and intellectuals are the backbone of Chinese armed resistance and their political importance far overshadows that of the corresponding class in India.'[8] That is precisely what Yeh and Empson would have told him.

The meaning of 'news commentary' was duly allowed to be flexible, with immediate effect; and Empson made it a regular (albeit 'haphazard') part of the schedule that the Tuesday commentary should cover a cultural topic, usually on a post-war problem, and the Saturday commentary a scientific topic. Some indication of the range of subjects tackled during the first months of the Chinese News Service is given by a surviving list of the 'postscripts' broadcast in the ten-day period 22 December 1942 to 2 January 1943. Dr Karl Mannheim spoke on 'Planned Society and Planned Education'; Professor F. Clarke on 'Education and World Order'; Professor W. H. Pearsall on 'Properties of Wet Soils' and 'Grasslands'; Stephen Spender on both 'What the Common Man thinks about War' (a talk that was subsequently felt to be 'controversial' vis-à-vis the issue of class in Britain) and 'The Common Man's hopes in the Post-war Period'.[9] Other commentators included Desmond Hawkins, fiction critic for the *Criterion*, whom Empson invited to talk to China about the novels of Ivy Compton-Burnett ('At the time it seemed a madly British gesture,' Hawkins would recall, 'almost sublime in its impracticality!');[10] the writer Hsiao Ch'ien, who was then based at the School of Oriental Studies in London;[11] and Dr Wellington Koo (Ku Wei-chün), the Chinese Ambassador to the UK. Empson in person seemed to Hawkins to be 'rather affectedly bohemian in a large overcoat with a great gash of a tear in it that hung and flapped'.

But Empson made the utmost use of George Yeh, who was ever-willing. All the same, it became a matter of urgent diplomatic necessity for Empson to ensure that his friend, the Chinese spokesman, was not confined to broadcasting only to his countrymen. Anglo-Chinese relations could be badly damaged if Yeh felt himself to be restricted and slighted. Accordingly, Empson worked very hard to induce the Home Service to put Dr Yeh on the air whenever possible. Among his first steps was to introduce Yeh to Mary Somerville, Director of School Broadcasting, who was delighted to accept Yeh's offer to present a series of programmes called 'If you were Chinese' which she had ready planned. In turn, Somerville—who considered Yeh 'an extremely well educated young man' as well as 'very pro-British' ('we had not thought,' she admitted, 'that a person of his eminence would wish to give the time to broadcasting to schools')—returned the favour by writing thus to A. P. (Pat) Ryan, Controller (News):

> I now understand from Mr. Empson that our action in inviting Dr. Yeh to broadcast in the Schools programme only is liable to be misunderstood among the Chinese and Mr. Empson is anxious that this situation should, if possible, be adjusted. He has asked me to suggest to you that Dr. Yeh might be given a Home Postscript on October 10th—the double '10th' being an important day in China, as it commemorates the revolution against the Manchu Emperors and the origin of the present Chinese Government. There is a 'Salute to China' programme on the following day (a Sunday) but Mr. Empson thinks it would be very helpful if there could be a short talk on the day itself.[12]

Ryan, whom Asa Briggs has described as a man of 'wide experience in the world of news and of intelligence', was inattentive and muddled on this occasion. 'Thanks,' he replied to Somerville. 'This was considered for a News Talk but dropped as there's a Feature programme on that day dealing with the Double Event.'[13] 'This' may refer either to Yeh or to Somerville's idea; but the reference to 'the Double Event' was simply ignorant, since it signifies that he failed to appreciate the significance of the anniversary; and the Feature programme was indeed scheduled, as Somerville said, for 11 October. In the event, Lady Cripps gave the Home News talk on 10 October, just as she had done on 7 July, the so-called Double Seventh—the anniversary of the outbreak of the Sino-Japanese war—which was suitably an appeal for the 'Aid to China' Fund; and Dr Yeh delivered a modest address on the Eastern Service. Little harm was done to the state of Anglo-Chinese relations by the fact that Yeh was not called upon by the Home Service that day. But Ryan's rooted indifference to the idea of putting Yeh in front of a Home microphone, which he saw not as an opportunity but as a luxury, is evident in the final line of his note to Mary Somerville: 'we'll, no doubt, be using him for [a news talk] on some day when we'd not be overloading the programmes.'

Empson must have done yet more nifty work behind the scenes, because Yeh made his first appearance on the Home Service just three days later, with a fifteen-minute talk on 'Education for All in Wartime China', detailing the resourceful ways in which the Chinese Government had coped with the exodus of students from the coastal cities to the interior provinces, and everyone's fortitude in the face of appallingly reduced circumstances. He gave such a solidly informed and inspiring talk, with no false sentiment, that it was repeated the next month on the Pacific Service. On 17 November he participated too in a discussion programme on China in the series 'World at War'. In sum, if the BBC's role in sustaining good Anglo-Chinese relations meant keeping George Yeh busy and happy, Empson had started off well.[14]

At this stage, in 1942, Empson was still (merely) a Talks Assistant in the Eastern Service, and as such very much a subordinate in an elaborate chain of command. In due course, as his authority became recognized and he was put in charge of the Chinese Service, he was afforded an assistant named Eleen Sam, a pretty, capable and forceful young woman of pure Chinese descent (albeit she did not speak Chinese): she had been born in British Guyana to Cantonese parents.[15] Thus, given Empson's experience of working in China, and the benefit of Bonwit's and Sam's advice, as well as his direct contacts with Chinese intelligence, especially through his relationship with George Yeh (who stood for the horse's mouth), he was often in a position to know better than his superiors what could or should be said to the Chinese listener. And so, inevitably, there were to be conflicts between his expertise and the administrative hierarchy that would seek to rein him in. As far as responsibility for the Chinese News Service bulletins was concerned, Bernard Moore managed to leave matters in a confused state with a memo of 6 July which emphatically stated both that the 'ultimate departmental responsibility for the bulletin as it goes on the air in Chinese' would rest with the Eastern Service Director (albeit the Empire News Editor should take responsibility for the script as first prepared in

English) and also that 'the final responsibility for the form and content of the script' would lie with the Chinese Editor. This arrangement would seem to provide three jockeys for the one horse, so it is not surprising that things could get out of hand.

One sharp clash of judgement occurred late in 1942, when Empson was given 'as a news item a statement of the new Japanese Foreign Minister, implying that there was no danger of an attack on Siberia.' He believed it 'an unsuitable item' to broadcast to China, as he later explained to Williams. And yet when he 'referred the problem upwards' to the Duty Officer, he was told that 'the item *must* be put on the air in Chinese whatever else was cut.' So he took it upon himself to cut the piece anyway. Bernard Moore, who was no longer Assistant but full Empire News Editor, consequently lambasted him in a memo to Williams:

> Mr Empson's note to you ... makes no mention at all of the fact that the passage concerned was deliberately omitted from the bulletin as broadcast in Chinese, despite the explicit instructions of the Duty Editor that it must be included. I must make the strongest protest against this grossly improper procedure and ask for an assurance that it will not be repeated. Several passages which were cut (including one for policy) were included ... If Mr Empson, Mr Hsieh [the newsreader] and the switch censor believed that the Duty's Editor's ruling was wrong, they should have referred either to you or to me and got the matter cleared. I agree with the Duty Editor that it is not only intolerable, but that it is contrary to all the Corporation's provisions for proper control of their output that they should arbitrarily remove any passage from the bulletin.[16]

Yet Empson's justification for his action seems not arbitrary but decidedly persuasive:

> My reasons for objecting to the item were (1) as a piece of news it must be so well known in Chungking that people there could only suppose we were repeating it for reasons of policy (2) even as a pointer to future events Mr. [Michael] Barkway [Chief Editor, Empire Services] will admit that it is not reliable; he himself said in a recent directive that a Japanese attack on Siberia is still possible though unlikely (3) Chungking, however unwisely, has been prophesying for the last few months that Japan would attack Siberia soon; if then we go out of our way to stress the failure of this prophecy we are annoying the Chungking advisers to no purpose; and, much more important (4) our repetition of Japanese propaganda will at once be interpreted by listeners all over China as evidence of pro-Japanese reflections in Britain.
>
> As you know, the Chinese Embassy was much disturbed by the use of Japanese propaganda on the BBC Home Service at the recent anniversary

of the Mukden Incident. Dr. Yeh explained at the time that there is still considerable suspicion in Chungking about British intentions towards China, and that any broadcasting of Japanese propaganda is liable to increase it. Surely the BBC broadcasts in Chinese ought to avoid this mistake.[17]

The whole fandango represented a confrontation of a classic order between the stickler for bureaucratic rules and the individualist following his nose on a point of political wisdom. There was right reason on both sides. But it is doubtful that Empson felt any remorse. As a champion of China, he knew he could not go far wrong if he monitored George Yeh's touchiness.

Empson and Ralf Bonwit went hand in glove on a more fundamental issue of policy. 28 August 1942 marked the centenary of the Treaty of Nanking, which China had been forced to sign after her humiliating defeat by the British in the 'Opium War'. That one-sided agreement became the model for all subsequent 'unequal treaties' and extraterritorial edicts, since Britain had been the first major power to clash with China in modern times. While the British naturally ignored an anniversary that could only seem morally disadvantageous in 1942, the Japanese propaganda organization (which included a celebratory speech by Wang Ching Wei, puppet ruler of Nanking, whom the BBC had a fixed policy never to mention on the air) capitalized on it by claiming that the war of liberation the Japanese were currently staging in Greater East Asia would wipe out 'a hundred years of shame for China'. Chiang Kai-shek, the Japanese alleged, was weakly trying to perpetuate the shame. Even the Chungking press took time to rehearse the lessons of the 'unequal treaty' system, and the ongoing obloquy. *Ta Kung Pao*, a popular newspaper, linked the significance of the Nanking Treaty to the notorious Protocol—'the consummation of all unequal treaties'—forced upon China after the Boxer troubles in 1901. 'So much did the foreigners then oppress China and so much did the overbearing attitude of the foreign missionaries disgust the Chinese, that a surge of anti-foreign feeling was natural ... Today Britain and America must have realised that the only achievement of the Protocol after 41 years has been the facilities it afforded Japan to attack China. Why do not Britain and America declare its abolition?'

In fact, as Empson despondently noted, the anniversary of the Treaty coincided with the clamour of 'increasing claims for Britain's strength on the third anniversary of the European war. The Chungking press had been demanding a "Pacific Charter", and this the Japanese are now promising.

Our propaganda has seldom before been so strikingly inferior to the enemy's.' He knew that broadcasts in Chinese normally ignored enemy propaganda, but he felt unusually exercised in this case. The Japanese were digging up all the dirt on the British record in China and rubbing Chinese noses in it. Not to answer such defiling propaganda would mean 'letting the case go by default', he told Rushbrook Williams:

> I ask therefore to be allowed to broadcast something like the following message: 'China is of course regarded as an equal nation among the Allied Nations, and one with equal rights. We do not commonly say this, because we take it for granted. As a party to the Lease-lend agreement with America, by which she both gives help and receives it, China is on the same footing as Britain. As to the details of China's relations with Britain, Britain is not acting hurriedly or dramatically. The United Nations state broad principles; they leave it to Japan and Germany to make detailed promises without knowing how to carry them out. But it follows from the principles already laid down that China will necessarily have an equal seat, this time, at the peace conference, as a full sovereign power. Just as she has admittedly shared in the sufferings of the other United Nations, so will she share in the construction of the better world for which we are fighting. The centenary of the Treaty of Nanking needed no Axis lies to make it a dramatic one. A hundred years ago Britain was fighting China, superficially in a very bad cause, more fundamentally to make the Manchu dynasty open China to world trade. Today Britain stands beside a renewed and united China in the fight for humanity. It is only in answer to the lies of the enemy that we find it necessary to state, what is obvious, that China is not merely equal to the other United Nations but among the greatest of them.'
>
> It would naturally be better if we could say something more definite and more reassuring.[18]

Of course the Eastern Service Director could not allow him to broadcast such a generous message in 1942. Neither he nor anyone else at the BBC was privileged to revise Government policy; and all this talk of unqualified equality—the notion that China should be seen 'as an equal nation among the Allied Nations, and one with equal rights'—overstepped the mark. The western powers had taken China as an ally out of wartime expediency, and were in no great hurry to lift the bondage, to rescind the unequal treaties, that they had long laid upon her.

For their part, the Chinese felt suspicious and critical not so much of western imperialism as of an 'alleged unwillingness to interfere with Japanese aggression', as Ralf Bonwit argued in an Intelligence Memo on

'Anglo-Chinese relations as affecting broadcasting' (31 October 1942). Within two weeks of Bonwit's memorandum, on 13 November 1942, Empson went about as far as he could on the Home Service in speaking for China as foremost equal ally and emergent democratic power. It was obviously no coincidence but a concerted application of right thinking on his part. 'War and the Peoples of China' was a 35-minute Feature produced by Francis Dillon (probably with help from Louis MacNeice), who rehearsed and broadcast the whole show in one eleven-hour day. Like the earlier 'Asia for the Japanese', from which it lifts certain passages, it is a semi-dramatized documentary on the modern history of Japanese aggression in China. It again quotes part of the 'Tanaka Memorial'; and again, like Bonwit in his memo, it stresses the two recent occasions on which the West let China down. The failure of the League of Nations to check Japan after the Manchurian Incident was 'the League's first failure,' says a Chinese voice. 'It encouraged Germany in her aggression, and in the end made the present war inevitable.' The compère picks up: 'In 1932 the Battle of Shanghai was fought. Japan brought in sixty thousand troops, but the Chinese, although under-equipped, with no tanks and hardly any aeroplanes, put up a heroic resistance which won the admiration of the world, and showed that, given arms, the Chinese could resist Japanese aggression.'

As that last passage exemplifies, 'War and the Peoples of China' differs from 'Asia for the Japanese' in seeking to cry up the Chinese and their military feats rather than to damn the Japanese. Empson determined to do away with the widespead insinuation that the Chinese could at best hold their ground against the invaders, but never strike back with effective might (in fact, he was so determined that he almost wrote off the Chinese air force: in the passage last cited, the typescript reads 'no tanks or aeroplanes', and the change is interpolated in another hand). Among the several voices who address the microphone, military and civilian, high and humble, one Chinese is quick to concede, though with something like sarcasm, that the problem of Anglo-Chinese misunderstanding is 'of course' a mutual one: '*we Chinese* often make mistakes about Britain and the British. We don't know each other very well, and I don't think you know much about the Japanese either.'

Probably the key thing to appreciate, the programme drives home, is that the Chinese are not lame-duck allies, they are awesome warriors. The compère explains that, although China is ill-supplied and has no facilities for making heavy weapons, the final victory at Changsha at the end of 1941 was the first major allied victory in the Pacific arena. Empson's urge to highlight his point with fluorescent colour is apparent; it gives an index of his exasperated ambition to make Great Britain sit up and salute the Chinese. The key words are sounded so thumpingly that the effect is almost as if the listener is being bullied into thinking of China as a victorious ally.

The other theme to be hammered home is that of democratic friendship; Empson ached to enkindle in his audience not just a sense of respect for the Chinese but a genuinely warm fellow-feeling, a note that is sustained in the paean of sentimentality by the compère which ends the programme:

> But it is the heroism of the whole Chinese people which has brought Japan's advance to a standstill; the peasants, the fishermen, small traders, labourers and craftsmen, all the humble folk who suffer first and most by resistance. Without their immediate, wholehearted, and loyal support, the actions of the trained and educated leaders are futile, and resistance ends. It is their faith which will bring victory, and it is their hatred which will destroy the Japanese invaders. The New China is theirs. A great democratic force—our friend—will secure peace in Asia.

Empson overdoes his enthusiasm to the point where the message feels factitious. The programme flops into the trap that Bonwit had warned against in his memo on Anglo-Chinese relations: 'It is important … to cultivate in our broadcasts the habit of mind that does really accept the Chinese as equals. No mere professions will convince them.'

Empson's methods might have been hectic and a little crude at times, but his purpose was admirable and far-sighted. It took a further six months for the British Government to catch up with the fine aspirations for Anglo-Chinese relations that he and Bonwit shared.

On 20 May 1943 the British and Chinese Governments did finally exchange instruments of ratification of a treaty by which Great Britain renounced extraterritorial rights and established equality in all dealings with China. The Sino-American Treaty was ratified in Washington at the same hour. Two months later, at a dinner given in London in honour of the Chinese Minister for Foreign Affairs (Dr Soong), Anthony Eden, the Foreign Secretary, pledged that British 'determination to defeat Japan is not one whit less than our determination to overthrow Hitler. In all these matters our cause and the cause of China is one, and we will be with them, as with our other allies, until we see this thing through.'[19]

In the meantime, in December 1942, the Overseas Planning Committee of the British Ministry of Information drew up a revised 'Plan of Propaganda to China'. This resolved among other things that British propaganda should aim 'to maintain China's determination to continue the struggle against Japan and to maintain China's confidence in Britain'; furthermore, it should 'seek to create a favourable basis for future Anglo-Chinese relations.' By the end of the year, the MOI decided in its revised secret plan to 'shift the emphasis of our propaganda to the Chinese, giving as much attention to the long-term development of satisfactory Anglo-Chinese relations as to the short-term policy of tiding over a critical situation.'[20] For many months, Empson had been putting just such a plan into practice at the BBC. He had anticipated every last provision of the MOI plan, including an item that related to his courtship of George Yeh: 'The technique of persuading the leading nationals of a target country to do our propaganda for us is particularly applicable to China.'

However, when the plan was passed over to the Political Intelligence Department of the Foreign Office, it came back with a number of proposed modifications in the form of a sniffy minute by A. L. Scott—which was notably endorsed by Robert Bruce Lockhart, head of the Political Warfare Executive (PWE): 'It is not the case that in the matter of the abolition of extraterritoriality we were dragged at the heels of the Americans . . . ' Scott's further amendments suggested more than a bad case of bureaucratic finicality: he meant both to give and to withhold what China, which was *de facto* Britain's major ally in the Far East, had every right to expect. China should not be encouraged to get above herself, let alone to pre-empt the prerogative of the imperialists.

But the habit of disdain dies hard; it is evident even in the original MOI document, which impertinently remarks in one place that the Chinese 'are assisting us in the fight against Japan (a point which must be brought home to the British public)'; and in another: 'there is no immediate prospect of the Chinese taking the offensive against the Japanese . . . ' Empson felt especially vexed by the last observation, because he knew full well that China was sending out regular communiqués about her battle fronts which the Home News contrived to ignore. It was all the more exasperating in view of the MOI's recommendation that the British public should be kept thoroughly informed about Chinese affairs.

In Bonwit's view, the directives put out by the MOI were 'idiotic'. He and Empson contrived to duck them whenever possible. At one MOI–BBC liaison meeting, Empson was asked who wrote the scripts for the Malayan Band? 'I can't find many signs of our advice,' said the chairman in a pique. Empson cracked back: 'Well, you know, these scripts are written by Mr Bonwit. You send me your advice under secret cover, and I put it in a case that's locked with a key. Mr Bonwit, as you probably know, is an enemy agent: he hasn't got the key.' Unhappily, the MOI took his satirical riposte at face value: from the next week, copies of the Ministry's directives were sent direct to Bonwit, who reckoned them to be 'rubbish'.

'I am really very happy and cosy,' wrote Empson to I. A. Richards in January 1943, 'but I write down this fact with some surprise, because I manage to find the propaganda business extremely worrying and liable to go wrong in quite unexpected ways and a great strain on the nerves and temper; maybe this is only the trick of inventing difficulties.'[21] Clearly, given the laggard handling of Chinese affairs by the MOI and the Foreign Office, and the BBC's tendency to distrust news supplied by China, he was not inventing difficulties or suspicions. In the very next month, George Yeh requested the BBC to supply Chungking with 'a full report of the BBC output concerned with China since Pearl Harbour'.[22] With one part of his mind Empson must have felt gratified that the BBC might be exposed to embarrassment from the Chinese quarter. However, it was never in his interest to aggravate the situation. He desired the BBC to take positive action to improve its service to China, and he accordingly urged his colleagues to make the best of their poor performance to date:

> As regards Talks, Feature Programmes and Plays, what is wanted is a list of the titles of the programmes, their dates, their authors' names, and whether they were for Home Service, Schools Department, European or Empire Service. I have sometimes been asked from the European side to help about programmes on China, and it would probably please Chungking to hear that programmes about China had been going out in that Service. Chungking may well be wanting to know whether the part of the BBC output which they can't monitor (Home and most of European) carries as much about China as the part which can (Empire etc.). My impression is that there has been a fair amount of Feature material about China on the Home Service but not as many Talks as on the Empire Service. It might be as well to point out that the reason is simply that Feature methods (sound effects and so on) are not well suited to short-wave radio.[23]

In fact, the tally of talks and feature programmes put out on the Home Service, Forces Programme, and Overseas Services looked better than Empson feared. Someone was talking about China, or adverting to China, on one or other wavelength virtually every week (and sometimes two or three times a week) in the period December 1941 to February 1943.

Yet Empson had reported too that Dr Yeh 'needed an indication of the proportion of BBC news time given to Chinese affairs', which—given the fact that on every day of the year there were 107 news bulletins in foreign languages, and 21 in English—was a very tall order indeed. J. B. Clark, in a letter to Yeh, regretted that he could not supply the Chinese Government with a schedule of the news items on China. But he went on to explain the BBC's policy on Chinese news in a way that can only be admired as a gem of equivocation: 'It is, however, the settled policy of the Corporation in news bulletins always to bring to the fore items of Chinese interest whenever the news from China, in relation to news from other quarters of the globe, makes this possible. Furthermore, variations of this policy are made according to the needs of the particular audience specially addressed in a news bulletin.'[24] The almost buried wiliness of the phrase 'in relation to news from other quarters of the globe' obviously gave the Controller the latitude to ignore the news from China if it did not seem relevant to news from elsewhere. Likewise, the second sentence, though it reads as a bonus, was actually nothing of the kind: it gave the Corporation the licence to omit the news of China's armed struggle if, at the BBC's discretion, an audience was somehow perceived not to need to know about it. Clark's account of the case was thus a tissue of conditions.

Dr Yeh was unimpressed by Clark's confection of bureacratic fudge. He could take stock for himself of how much the news from China was reported on the Home. As the sixth anniversary of the outbreak of Sino-Japanese hostilities (7 July, the Double Seventh) drew on, he felt depressed and refractory; on 15 May, five days before the signing of the treaty which abolished extraterritoriality in China, Empson had to inform Williams:

> George Yeh I find is extremely unwilling to broadcast on the Home and still less on any other air on the Double Seventh unless by that time some reasonable attempt is made to admit the war news from China onto the BBC Home News. I think I might get him to do it, but only on the agreement that he was not 'making himself ridiculous' by accepting the present decisions of the Home News. I do not suppose I am betraying his confidence, or indeed telling you anything you don't know, in telling you that Chungking is working up to a diplomatic row about the BBC Home News.[25]

To get over the difficulty, Empson propelled Yeh into the studio by way of a confidence trick. First he got permission from Pat Ryan to write and present a talk on 7 July; then, as if the wizard idea had just struck him, he suggested that Dr George Yeh—'an excellent broadcaster'—would be 'the diplomatically right man to speak at that time. My estimate is that he will be willing to say exactly what is wanted ... and from what he said a few days ago I understand that he is now willing to co-operate (chiefly because the Home News has been quoting the Chinese communiqué, I imagine, since that was the prestige point disturbing Chungking).'[26] Of course Empson's words were disingenuous, as Ryan must have suspected when he responded: 'Before you tackle Yeh can you & I have a talk—preferably after I've seen your draft? If not to talk over the draft.'[27] Pat Ryan, who had worked for the *Manchester Guardian* and the *Daily Telegraph*, and who became in later years an assistant editor on *The Times*, was a sharp newsman. However, having already agreed that a slot would be available on Home News for an address on the Double Seventh, Ryan was in no position to plead an overloaded schedule or any other evasive excuse.

Empson cautiously crowed home to his mother on 28 June: 'The BBC Home people have been ordered to put in more about China, partly because of Churchill's agreements in America and partly because Chungking protested at being left out, so our side gets asked in a bit more to help implement the policy. I was told to do a talk after the nine o'clock news on July the 7th, but after I'd written it I managed to induce Controller News to let George Yeh read it; or rather I first had to induce him to put it on the right day and then with only a fortnight to go spring the trap and say that George Yeh (whom he distrusts) would be willing to read what was put down for him. It is a great triumph getting George Yeh on the air for the Double Seventh; last year we failed to do it. In fact I suspect there may be a last minute snag even now. It's a pity they look so definitely askance at him.'[28] His ploy did in fact work: George Yeh duly gave the talk, 'Sixth Anniversary of Japanese attack on China', on 7 July.

Empson had no desire to indulge in machinations of that sort for their own sake, but he had little option other than to manipulate the 'machine'. He was faced with what amounted to a conspiracy to exclude China's news from the airwaves of Great Britain. This aversion on the part of Home News was all the more disturbing in so far as it ran counter to one of the putative objectives of the 'Plan for Propaganda to China' that the MOI had drawn up in December 1942: 'To convince the Chinese that Britain fully appreciates their long single-handed struggle against Japan and the contribution they have made and can make to victory.' Only indirect propaganda could achieve this 'important objective', the MOI emphasized, so it should 'mainly take the form of quoting back to China appreciative references made in Britain or elsewhere to Chinese achievements, and where possible on suitable occasions (e. g. anniversaries) of inspiring appreciative references which can be so quoted. In other words it is an objective which must mainly be tackled in this country.'[29]

'[T]here is little active fighting on the China front': so said the MOI in its 'Plan for Propaganda to China'. The events of May 1943 gave the lie to the MOI's condescending opinion of Chinese armed resistance, for China won a great victory against a tremendous Japanese assault upon the Upper Yangtze, in western Hupeh. The Chinese High Command termed it 'the Chinese battle of Stalingrad'; and General Chen Cheng, Commander-in-Chief of the Yangtze valley defences, considered it the most important engagement in the Sino-Japanese War since the start of hostilities in 1937.

In the dogged summer of 1943, Empson and Bonwit whooped at this news and promptly proposed to blazon China's victory in the form of a Home Service feature. In May and June, *The Times* gave prominent attention to the story—though always on page 3, in its 'Imperial and Foreign' columns, and hardly ever as the lead story—with headlines such as 'CHINESE VICTORY ON YANGTZE'.[30] But only a radio feature could make tactics and topography feel real to the listener. Moreover, as Empson and Bonwit foresaw with intense satisfaction, a feature could at once fulfil the MOI's directive to advertise China to the British audience and prove that the MOI itself had seriously underestimated China's capabilities. From every angle, the Chinese victory represented a godsent opportunity to create first-rate propaganda; and Empson and Bonwit exploited it to the full by arranging for 'The Battle of the Yangtze', a half-hour drama-documentary, to be broadcast on the key date of 10 October.[31]

Adroitly, the authors establish their credibility in the prologue to the piece by stating, twice, that the Chinese action against Japan constituted no more than a 'holding war'. At the same time, they stretched the truth on two counts: (i) by allowing the listener to infer that it was somehow part of the Allied strategy merely to hold off the Japanese, and not necessarily to drive them into the sea at the earliest possible moment; and (ii) by figuring that the time that had passed between July 1937 and October 1943 amounted to seven years, which is assuredly more heroic than the true sum.

More notably, the programme goes on to suggest that the USAAF and the Chinese Air Force had carried out a pre-emptive strike which destroyed all the warplanes that Japan proposed to deploy against the Yangtze gorges. 'Japanese Airport of Ichang out of action,' a Chinese Bomber Leader reports to base. 'Japanese Air Park destroyed'. An unidentified reporter comments: 'For the first time the Japanese had now to fight without air cover against local superiority in the air.' (Originally, the narrator was to have spoken those words, but in the event it was clearly more canny for the programme-makers to attribute them to a less authoritative and possibly even fallacious informant.) And yet on 29 June Colin McDonald, The *Times*' correspondent in Chungking, had sent home a report of an interview with the Chinese Commander-in-Chief. It is very much to be regretted, General Chen Cheng had said, 'that allied aircraft were few and the bases too far away, so that "during most of the time the air was controlled by the enemy." He pointed out that the Japanese air bases were a short distance from the Chinese lines and the Japanese aircraft were able to operate irrespective of the weather, machine-gunning and bombing for 16 hours a day, while the USAAF, starting from distant points, could attack only twice a day and for two hours at the longest.' Anyone who recalled, however vaguely, what *The Times* had published that day would have been staggered by the difference in the account put out by the BBC on 10 October. Maybe Empson and Bonwit had agreed to be lavish with the truth: after all, it was excellent propaganda to pretend that the Chinese Air Force and the USAAF had acted in decisive concert.

In fact, all such discrepancies in 'The Battle of the Yangtze' must probably be blamed not on the authors' readiness to flout facts but on their source of information. As Bonwit was to recall, time and again they asked the Chinese MOI to tell them exactly what took place on the Yangtze in the last two weeks of May 1943, but George Yeh and his officers could never settle for one straight story. First they said one thing, then another, or they havered. It might have been better not to have consulted them at all, but Empson and Bonwit had no other option. Likewise, if they had chosen to broadcast details that were at odds with what the Chinese told them, they would have caused a breach of confidence that could hardly be repaired. (Even when asked if the fortifications at Shipai stood to the east or west, or indeed to the north or south, of the Yangtze, said Bonwit, the Chinese MOI had difficulty supplying the right answer.) But no one could really blame the Chinese for claiming more than any independent witness could confirm—propaganda will always play second fiddle to national pride.

As Empson knew, his professional game was propaganda too; and it was not necessarily prejudice alone which made the Controller (News) decline so often to play his way. The BBC had established a reputation for telling the truth, and hated to be gulled into parroting propaganda in the guise of news. 'Keep the Chinese front in being for the Home listener,' Bonwit had urged in June 1943. 'If there are [*sic*] no news, say so ("There is no news from the Yangtse front").'[32] But the BBC preferred no news to being used;

and for want of corroboration of a piece of news, it chose to err on the side of mistrust. 'The problem about news,' Empson would acknowledge, 'especially from the BBC, is that half the time you are quoting a communiqué or some text which is the only authority for the story...' As a radio feature, 'The Battle of the Yangtze' was the stuff of lion-hearted fiction; as reliable news, nugatory.

All the same, there can be little doubt that the Chinese were substantially correct in feeling they had been relegated to the margin of media attention in Britain. If the BBC used abstracts of the Chinese communiqués for a while during the summer of 1943, matters had so far deteriorated by the autumn that George Yeh threatened to resign his post, though he had gained some popularity for his own skilled performances on the radio.

On 15 November Empson felt it necessary to submit to the Eastern Service Director a fervent personal memo on 'Anglo-Chinese Relations' in which he outlined George Yeh's (legitimate) complaints, the need to cultivate good East-West relations for the future, and the lack of coverage by the British media of the Chinese fighting.

Two days later he added, with honourable exasperation, 'the position has got worse ... George Yeh it appears is unwilling to appear either on the Brains Trust or in the film about Chinese activities. Irritating as he may be, his point is a reasonable one; it is that he cannot go on making appearances personally if he has failed to do what he was sent here to do, viz. to get a fair representation of the Chinese war effort in Britain... It is not important to put out Chinese war news on the Home News merely to please George Yeh. It is important because informed Chinese opinion would agree in feeling very suspicious of any further refusal.'[33] He said everything that needed to be said in his statement, and he said it well.

However, just over two months later again, the Director-General made it unarguably clear that the BBC would not favour an ally so far as to second their falsehoods on the air. Sir William Haley declared: 'We cannot commit ourselves to even a five-minute weekly dose of Chinese propaganda in the Home Service.'

'I haven't any cultural side to speak of, being now definitely an all-time propaganda hack,' Empson told I. A. Richards in January 1943; 'if I'm not fussing about broadcasting to the Far East I ought to be fussing about home BBC programmes on the Far East, the second is my artwork which I may do when I get home from the office. The BBC and MOI both sometimes nibble at the idea of using Basic, and I do then put in a word for it, but as you know what always frightens the BBC is that they can't advertise one product if its trade rivals are likely to complain, and it seems likely that persons describing themselves as trade rivals of Basic would complain.'[34] Very often he wrote many of the bulletins ('headline' news) and commentaries that were broadcast both on the Chinese News Service and on the Malaya (Overseas Chinese) band in what the *Times* would call the 'artificial idiom' of Basic English, in order to avoid complex verbiage and to clarify every item for a non-English audience.[35] This trick of verbal thinning-out was never noticed by Rushbrook Williams, and probably not by anyone else, such as the censor, who had occasion to read his stuff before it was translated into Kuoyü—though G. R. Tonkin, the Chinese News Editor (who was acknowledged as the principal news specialist on the Far East), liked the lucidity of his style without apparently recognizing its Basic medium.

What Empson had long taken for granted, Churchill chose to commend to the world in 1943. 'The kiss of death was the support of Sir Winston Churchill,' said Empson. In a speech at Harvard University on 6 September, Churchill praised Basic as 'a very carefully wrought plan for an international language'; and he went on to envision a chilling version of imperialism: 'The empires of the future are the empires of the mind.'[36]

Empson would later comment: 'I remember Miss Lockhart, the very able secretary or manager of the Basic organisation [Leonora W. Lockhart, Assistant Director of the Orthological Institute in London], attempting comfort after the speech and saying that all might yet be well, so it was recognised as harmful from the start. Churchill was well able to understand that other governments, not the British and American ones, would in the end decide the question; and if he had been serious about it he would have acted differently. It gave just what he wanted for his speech, breadth of post-war vision and cooperation between our two countries, and if it annoyed De Gaulle that was fun.'[37] (Within a month of Churchill's speech at Harvard, Empson participated in a debate on the merits of Basic English at the Churchill Club in London; his opponent was Rose Macaulay, and Lord Birkenhead made a patently sceptical chair.)[38] The BBC, which was forthwith consulted by a Committee of Ministers on Basic English, submitted a memorandum the same month.

These were merely the first moves in a debate about using Basic for broadcasting purposes that raged inside and outside the BBC for the next year or more. Because of his previous involvement Empson spoke on its behalf in print,[39] and also recommended himself as a Basic expert within the BBC. Unfortunately, neither Empson nor his superiors thought to involve the inventor of Basic in the trial programmes or in the start-up discussions. When Empson wrote to him in September 1944 for advice,[40] Ogden seemed not to be amused; the BBC had been considering the implementation of Basic for a year without consulting him or his team, and without any mention of payment. By October 1945, J. B. Clark, Controller of the Overseas Service, notified the BBC's representatives (and with evident relief) that no one should seek to resuscitate the dead letter of Basic English.

Empson had been willing to do his bit for Basic; but—just as with his argument that the BBC ought to broadcast the Chinese communiqués— no one was very willing to listen to him. He was trying to tread on snakes and scorpions. Yet not all his hopes and plans came to nothing. One practical initiative, taken at the end of 1942, promised to cheer up the whole future of Anglo-Chinese relations.

The BBC, with the help of the Central News Agency of China, determined to break the 'intellectual blockade' of Free China by regularly broadcasting to China abstracts of certain articles which the British branch of the Natural Science Society of China would select from the learned journals each month; and the MOI would send out the full texts by priority air mail, usually on microfilm. Since there were perhaps not more than a few dozen short-wave receivers even in the whole of the city of Chungking, local offices of the MOI and the British Council would use their mimeographic services to make copies of the digests and periodicals when they arrived.[41] Empson believed it was vital to shore up the bastions of the universities of China, in particular to aid the scientists who would otherwise fall out of touch with the wider academic community; and in February 1943 he confidently informed them that the BBC Chinese Service 'would speed the process up'. Asa Briggs has noted: 'in May 1943 the British Ambassador reported from Chungking to the Foreign Secretary that "intellectual broadcasts would be welcome". He had been given this advice by Dr Joseph Needham and Professor E. R. Dodds, who were on a visit to China dealing with Sino-British scientific and academic relations.'[42] Professor Dodds had seen for himself the parlous situation of the scientists in Chungking, Chengtu, and Kunming. Accordingly, he recommended as a matter of urgency 'that the Ministry of Information be asked to reserve a substantial proportion of whatever tonnage is assigned to it on the new R.A.F. service from Calcutta for the carriage of books and learned articles for distribution to Chinese universities and research institutes.'[43] But Empson needed no one to tell him such things: he had already contrived to make the BBC and the MOI set the business in train.

As well as initiating the science broadcasts, Empson went on to fight against all sorts of official obstruction and suppression to keep open the line of supply. Not long after the service was launched, for example, he asked the MOI to supply him with a list of the periodicals they were able to send to China; at first, the Ministry gave him a long list, but then—as he notified the Eastern Service Director in a state of 'vague general alarm'—a functionary told him that 'this whole MOI handout was sheer lies'.[44]

As far as Empson was concerned, the MOI's failure (or refusal) to give full cooperation meant that it had broken a concordat as much with China as with the BBC. His sometime friend from Tokyo, Vere Redman, whom he presumed to be an ally, was proving to be a disappointment, even a menace. He wrote to his mother on 28 June, 'My other old pal from the Far East, Redman who runs with Far East Section of the Ministry of Information, has been turning very nasty about the BBC because it won't let him have as much control as it wants; he has been trying to get all broadcasting to China from England stopped other than a short news service, so that he can start something else under his control in India, and suchlike. The clause that saves us I understand is that propaganda to an ally can't be classed as Political Warfare, which he could claim to run. But it now turns out that after promising me that he would send copies of the weekly "Nature" to China while we broadcast a weekly review of it he has stopped sending it so as to make us look untrustworthy. I call that a very mean little trick, but the appearances of friendship have to be kept up. Now that we've caught him out again I think it will be possible to force him to do it. You see how busy we all are.'[45]

It is astonishing that he could put on quite such a calm humour in that letter; and yet it was a point of principle that all his distresses should be minimized for mother's sake. Actually he felt ready to tear his hair out. Orwell, who was getting near to throwing up his job on account of its being 'an almost hopeless task', saluted Empson for his tenacious resolve:

> It is tremendously important from several points of view to try to promote decent cultural relations between Europe and Asia. Nine tenths of what one does in this direction is simply wasted labour, but now and again a pamphlet or a broadcast or something gets to the person it is intended for, and this does more good than fifty speeches by politicians. William Empson has worn himself out for two years trying to get them to broadcast intelligent stuff to China, and I think has succeeded to some small extent.[46]

(W. J. West was crucially mistaken when he proposed this libel: 'Empson remained a working colleague of Orwell's right through his time at the

BBC and stayed on considerably longer, not having the same moral imperatives that made him kick against the censorship and political cant current at the time.')[47]

Empson, who felt altogether more rattled and jittery than successful, would never claim more than Orwell's estimate for what he achieved. But the effort of the enterprise really did deserve the anonymous accolade that appeared in *London Calling* on 21 October 1943 (a month before Orwell quit his job with the Indian Service, calling it 'work that produces no result'). The article, headed 'BBC's Service to China Breaks the Intellectual Blockade', included these observations:

> The BBC broadcasts to China are probably the most 'intellectual' talks on the air, in the sense of the most technical; however, of course, there are limits to what anybody can take in from a radio talk, and these talks are tied as much as possible to advance description of material which is already being flown out to Chungking on microfilm.
>
> Among the writers who have contributed technical scripts or messages are the Archbishop of Canterbury, the Master of Balliol, Sir Stafford Cripps, Professor Andrade, Sir Lawrence Bragg, Professor Alan Ferguson, Sir John Russell, Lord Hankey, Sir Philip Hartog, Dr Karl Mannheim, and Sir Malcolm Watson.

In the bitter January of 1944, Empson became a senior member of the Chinese Section of the Far Eastern Service; soon thereafter he took over the editing of the Chinese News Service. 'I must say that the News Service has been conducted quite smoothly since you took over the Editorship,' reported a colleague called C. S. Wang, 'and it must have been quite a strain for you and Miss Buley to write two Bulletins each day.'[48]

On the face of it, Empson had now achieved a height of success and influence in the BBC, perhaps the highest he could attain. Yet he felt as frustrated and ineffectual as ever. In March there were grave doubts as to what extent, if any, the scientific and cultural materials sent out from Britain were actually being distributed to the Chinese universities. There was little point in advertising the goods if the customers never received them.[49] Then, at an MOI meeting in May, he heard from Redman (as he reported with barely controlled rage to Rushbrook Williams), 'we are no longer wanted to please the Chinese - as no doubt you know'.[50] At the foot of Empson's memo, his chief responded sanguinely from Room 214 at 200 Oxford Street: 'These things will happen ... They do not prevent us from using our own judgment.' And to Empson's agitated insistence that 'Britain needs friendship with a strong Asiatic power to win goodwill in the East as a whole, and ... an export trade (which China would help to absorb) more than America', the sage Williams, whom Orwell had considered 'very understanding and generous', affirmed too: 'I could not agree more: and will support you if you follow these lines.' All the same, however much Empson and his superior considered it a mandatory exercise to cast bread upon the waters, other officers of the BBC seemed to care all too little for the future of Anglo-Chinese relations.

By 22 May 1944 (two weeks before D-Day), Empson learned from Francis Dillon that their joint plan to broadcast the customary Home Feature on the Double Seventh anniversary had been squashed in the face of an MOI agreement, with respect to plans for propaganda *to* China, that 'certain major aims could only be achieved by reporting propaganda *about* China in this country.' He could not believe that the BBC would deliberately—whether from inertia or suppression, it was no matter— sabotage the Ministry's best intentions towards Britain's third major ally. 'This would be the first time,' he exclaimed to Williams, 'that the BBC Home Feature side had ignored the Double Seventh since China and Britain became allies. Various reasons for dropping it could occur to Chinese, American and British listeners, and they would all in my opinion be harmful ones.'[51] While Dillon entered an appeal at the next meeting of Home Features, Williams likewise lost no time in forwarding Empson's protest to the Acting Controller (Overseas Services); he endorsed it with characteristic coolness: 'It is written from the standpoint of a Chinese specialist without knowledge of Home Division's commitments or difficulties. But I believe [it] to be a serious argument: and from the standpoint of Eastern Services, I should be most grateful if you would represent the matter for reconsideration.'[52] Ralf Bonwit put in a firm oar as usual: in the opinion of Far East Intelligence, he averred, 'to pass the day in complete silence, ignore the Double Seventh with the possible exception of a Charity Appeal, will be such an anticlimax to what happened last year, that the Chinese will not easily forget it.' Also, pointedly echoing the MOI's words in its 'Plan for Propaganda to China', Bonwit reiterated the general rule: 'the Chinese will tend to interpret what the Home and Overseas sides do as the main expression of our attitude towards them.'[53] But neither Williams's suave diplomacy nor Bonwit's sharp digs had any effect.

It is a measure of the level of Empson's frustration, of his inability to make headway through any of the usual channels, that he next resorted to a direct personal appeal to one of the Governors of the BBC, Harold Nicolson—the only Governor he had met. The Double Seventh, he wrote, 'is an opportunity to remind people in this country that we are committed

to the Far Eastern war as well as to the defeat of Germany.'[54] The Eastern
Service Director, the MOI Far East Director, and the Foreign Office itself
('from what I am told') were all of one mind on the question of policy
towards China; 'it is a matter of getting the Home Side to do what is
wanted, and the Home side is very fully independent. But what they do is
what Chinese diplomatic opinion over here will take seriously, not any
performance on short waves'—that is, the Chinese Service broadcasts to
China proper.

The most that the Home Service audience could expect to hear on 7
July was the American point of view as given by the influential American
journalist and radio commentator Raymond Gram Swing, who was admired by Roosevelt, Churchill, and even Bernard Shaw.[55] 'This seems to
me an extraordinary attempt to pass the buck about the East (the East as a
whole) onto the Americans,' wrote Empson to Nicolson with just jealousy.
'It must be expected that Raymond Gram Swing if he takes on the job will
report a good deal of our new American low-down about China, which
you British don't seem to have caught up with yet.'

Harold Nicolson replied on 3 July, unperturbed by Empson's bid to go
over the heads of his superiors. 'Dear Empson... As you know in such
matters the Board are in the hands of P. W. E. and we are not supposed to
interfere. None the less I have many connections with P. W. E. and will try
to do my best in a private capacity. I am very glad that you should have
drawn my attention to this matter.'[56] But nothing further happened.

The Home Service seemed unimpressed by the Eastern Service Direct-
or's strategic pleas to hail an heroic China. At a period beginning in June
1944—when London was being pounded by the nerve-seering new flying-
bombs, the V1s, otherwise known as 'buzz bombs' or 'doodlebugs' (the
throbbing of the engine preceded a breath-stopping silence as the bomb
fell to earth), and soon afterwards, from 8 September, by the silent and
more lethal V2 (Vengeance Two) rocket-bombs which battered London
for a period of nearly seven months from 8 September 1944—the news and
rumours from home were hotter than tall stories filed from continents
away by unreliable Chinese. Some 2,500 V1s were launched at London
over a 10-month period. As for the V2s, there was initially a news blackout
lasting two months about the devastation they caused, but the facts could
not be held back for long in the face of conspicuous destruction. The V2
carried 1,650 pounds of explosive at an unstoppable speed of about 3,000
m.p.h.—no aircraft could catch it—and many thousands of Londoners
were to die in the assaults which went on until the 27 March 1945. Almost
half of the approximately 1,000 flying bombs launched against London hit

their target, and the full series of flying bombs killed 8,800 people in the country as a whole. Yet Empson claimed, probably so as to avoid frightening his mother, to see no reason to flap about the bombing: 'There is still nothing much from the flying bombs in this district. I gather that the defending forces generally manage to hit the petrol tank enough to make it leak a bit but not much, and the result is that places like Croydon have really been having a bad time, but they don't come north much. Distinguished persons who leave their offices early to go to their country homes in Surrey are rather sorry for themselves too, you generally find. However of course it may get worse yet.'[57] (On 26 December, a flying bomb killed sixty-eight people in Islington, about two miles from the Empson home. When the bombing ended in 1945, over 100,000 houses had been destroyed; about a third of the City of London had been razed.)

He and Hetta had to cope with the crawling infant Mogador, whom they sent off for a while to be cared for on a farm. Hetta was many months gone with another child, and Empson could report to his own mother only that 'the hospital doesn't seem to know when she's likely to have the baby; it may be earlier'—which was comically uninformative news. In due time Hetta gave birth to another son in Queen Charlotte Hospital on 30 September. What the happy parents had done unto their first, they did unto the second: they gave him three names —one South African, one English, and one commemorating a military activity on the day of birth—Jacobus Arthur Calais. Jacob Empson himself was later given to understand, 'I was almost called Dago Island because there was an engagement there which lasted all the day of my birth, but fortunately for me news came in at the last minute of the siege of Calais just before midnight.'[58] He was named Jacobus after an uncle on Hetta's side of the family, Arthur after his father's eldest brother. Fortunately there was an excellent Government Wartime Nursery just down the road from their home, so the parents' work was little affected by the new arrival.[59] Hetta could give Jacob his midday feed before bicycling off to the BBC, where she worked from 2 p.m. to 10 p.m.; William, who worked from 9 a.m. till 6 p.m., normally collected the children on his return home. He became such an enthusiast for the Government Daytime Nurseries that he pressed for the set-up to be kept going even after the defeat of Germany. Soon after Jacob's birth he stressed how much Mogador had benefited from the system, in a letter from which we may infer that Empson had assumed a fascinated if distinctly distanced posture towards the goings-on of the growing boy (his habit of referring to his son as 'it' is, I think, more accidental than telling):

> The child gets a medically planned diet and regular examination, with the immunizing injections at the right time; it is daily among other children, and this natural source of learning can't otherwise be got for children of small families; and in view of the housing shortage which is likely to continue in London it is important for a London child to have room to play in safely. Apparently there is a prejudice that the plan makes the child feel homeless or not enough helped by its parents, and this is held to outweigh the advantages. We think this idea evidently wrong, and our son though healthy is timid enough to be a fair test case. The routine gives it necessarily a day and a half every week at home with its mother; it is always taken to the nursery and fetched back by one or other parent, and you are told to give it specified meals at home before and after it sleeps at home. It certainly isn't homeless; it has both a home and an interesting routine ...

When the child contracted German measles, he had been taken 'by a male operator' to an Isolation Hospital and totally isolated from his parents for ten days. 'When my wife came to fetch it it screamed at her with horror. When I saw it at home it was beginning to get normal but would fall back at unexpected moments into screaming out No No No and twisting up its whole body as if to escape from a torture approaching from the right side.' Anything was preferable to such awful unkindness, which could not occur in the Daytime Nurseries where 'the mothers are too much on the spot'.

> Then by way of contrast the child was sent to a farm with two children of about the same age (this was merely because another nursery had been bombed and there was a double load; of course the child likes bombs as such and if it hears a buzzbomb explode says 'Bang'). The mutual jealousies of three small children with no others in reach were a great nuisance to the hostess and never got cleared up; the child learned to say 'shut up' and 'go away', but we were glad when it could return from family life to placid steady development in a Government Wartime Nursery.[60]

In the midst of life we are in death, Empson had cause to reflect at this time: his mother died on 20 August 1944, a month before Jacob's birth. When probate was granted on 3 February the following year, Empson learned she had left him the sum of £125, with the remainder of her estate going to the eldest son Arthur. It was later said that this legacy enabled Empson to buy in 1946 the leasehold in Studio House, formerly called 'Sunnycote'—a bright and very commodious house constructed of Luton purple bricks dressed with Suffolk reds, and incorporating a lofty artist's studio (it was built in 1875–6 for the minor painter John Ingle Lee)—on the corner of Rosslyn Hill and Hampstead Hill Gardens, which was to be their home for more than forty years. It is possible the legacy had served for a deposit, or else that Arthur kindly passed on to his youngest brother the bulk of the cash, running to more than £3,000, that had been willed to him by their mother, along with the family home and lands in Yorkshire.[61]

Also at this time there occurred another kind of loss which turned out to be far more disturbing than Empson anticipated. 'Our Director has walked out at a day's notice, nobody knows why,' he told his mother, 'and my old friend John Morris is doing it instead; which makes things rather cosier but not very different.'[62] (He had met Morris, who was to become Head of the Far Eastern service in 1943, while teaching in Japan in the early 1930s.) According to Ralf Bonwit, Williams had to leave because of some sort of intrigue with his secretary; and he was badly affected too by the buzz-bombs. From 1944 he was Asia specialist on *The Times* (writing leading articles on Asian affairs), and he apparently made it a condition of his resignation from the BBC that he could enjoy continued access to the counsel of Bonwit, whom he regarded as an expert on modern Chinese politics. Bonwit would turn up once a week for advisory tea at *The Times*. (However, Empson unwittingly spoiled their arrangement two years later, when he attended a reception for the new Chinese Ambassador on the Double Tenth of 1946. Being prone to impetuousness when drunk, and being quite drunk enough on this occasion, he brought Bonwit into a conversation with the reckless remark, 'You know Bonwit, don't you? He tells Rushbrook Williams what to write in the *Times*.' His indiscretion contained no malice aforethought; but within a week Williams informed Bonwit that he was too busy to receive him at *The Times* as heretofore. Williams was to remain with the newspaper until his retirement in 1955.)

Empson had enjoyed much support from Williams, and he believed he could expect nothing less from Morris, whom he thought 'liberal-minded'. (For one thing, Morris was brave enough to make no secret of his homosexuality.) As things turned out, he was wrong; and before long he would be complaining directly to the Director-General: 'so far as Mr Morris ... has ever made any proposals for the Chinese Service they have been bad ones.'

Notwithstanding Morris's credentials—he was to continue as Head of the Far Eastern service until 1952, when he became Controller of the Third Programme until his retirement in 1958 (one of his finest ultimate achievements was to persuade Samuel Beckett to contribute a number of plays to the BBC)—neither Empson nor Orwell spared much affection or even respect for the man. Empson's aversion was not based on any principle of inverted snobbery; he did not especially care that Morris was a pompous Tory, only that his professional behaviour was unsound.

'The obvious division' in the ranks of the BBC, Empson would write in a later year, 'was not between gents and proles but between the businessman types or civil-service types who decide policy and the artists who carry it out. The Corporation was and is an exclusive hierarchy, supposed to be secret but actually spurting out hot jets of leakage in every neighbouring bar. The administrators were evasively determined to avoid trouble . . . In fact, looking back, I can't remember Class raising its ugly head at all.'[63] In such terms, as far as Empson was concerned, Morris fell slap bang into the scorned category of 'civil-service types who decide policy' —just like J. B. Clark and R. A. Rendall—as against the 'artists' like himself and Francis Dillon who were trying to make exemplary and really useful programmes.

But Morris remembered another aspect of Empson's response which was altogether more significant. 'When I joined the BBC Empson was in charge of our Chinese programmes; and . . . he, quite unfairly I think, regarded me as some sort of enemy; because I made no secret of the fact that I had enjoyed my time in Japan and had acquired a number of lasting friendships (which still endure), I must therefore be against the Chinese . . . When I afterwards became head of the Eastern Service my personal relations with Empson were to become even more difficult, and the intimate friendship between him and Orwell undoubtedly affected the latter's attitude to me.' Empson thought he had grounds for believing that Morris favoured Japan before Britain's wartime ally China, and he reckoned that such a prejudice made Morris a professional liability.

'I was forced to believe, as time went on,' wrote Empson in January 1946, that Morris casually indulged 'his own tastes and preferences (to be sure, many of them were useful ones). He of course was mainly interested in Japan . . . '[64] In Bonwit's opinion, Morris was not a man of strong principle like Empson; his worst failing was that he was 'played up' as an authority on the Far East as a whole and yet made no attempt to quash this specious idea. Certainly he wanted to make decisions without reference to all available advice, which may have indicated not so much arrogance as insecurity. For the most part Morris avoided Bonwit, who thought him a 'phoney' albeit cultured. When he did ask Bonwit's advice about something and Bonwit duly gave it, Morris seemed utterly surprised: Bonwit had to remind him that it was part of his job to give advice on request. On the other hand, it may well have been the case that Morris simply felt badgered by Bonwit, who could be relentless in pressing his opinions, as Empson well knew. But it was not only Bonwit whom Morris tried to suppress: Empson was treated in a not dissimilar way. In spite of the strained relationship that developed while he and Morris were both

Talks Producers, Empson would recall, 'I did ... continue talking to Mr Morris after his appointment as E.S.D. until one day he shouted at me and said "This must Stop". I found in fact that he would not allow criticism and believed that it had been destroyed when it was silenced. This is not easily done to Mr Bonwit...'[65]

Matters bounded towards an abyss of recrimination soon after Morris took over as Eastern Service Director, when Empson started bombarding him with justifiably exasperated memoranda. 'It really seems to me urgent to stop the MOI sabotage of broadcast cultural and scientific material to China and get them let through in one way or another,' he wrote in October 1944.[66] A major part of the problem was that ever since the start of the Chinese Service in 1941 the BBC's arrangements inside China had been handled by the British MOI, whose representative in Chungking, Stanley Smith, was acknowledged by the BBC to be 'very anti-culture and anti-BBC'. Hollington Tong, the Chinese Minister of Information, even took the view (as Empson was given to understand) that 'the Chinese could not be expected to give relays [of the BBC broadcasts] against the advice of the British MOI man on the spot'.

Then, on 7 December, the Eastern Services Organizer, Clifford Lawson-Reece—a busybody whom Empson nicknamed 'Lies-and-Greese', and whom Bonwit dubbed 'the Broadcasting House spy, a stooge with nothing to do'—sent out a piece of curiously imprecise news in a 'Private and Confidential' memo addressed to Donald Stephenson, Director (from February 1944) of the BBC's New Delhi Office, who had been detailed to undertake a tour of inspection in China: 'We have more than once offered our news and programmes—particularly the cultural and scientific talks—for relay by CCBA [Chinese Central Broadcasting Authority] but they have never confirmed their intention of re-broadcasting any part of our Chinese output. None the less, they have retrospectively informed us that from time to time our cultural talks have been relayed by Chungking during the past two-and-half years and we have also had twenty or thirty reports from individuals that the Kuoyu News has been re-broadcast by Chungking.'[67] In other words, the state of play in China, where the reception of the BBC's long-range transmissions was so poor that it would be pointless to carry on broadcasting unless the CCBA relayed the programmes, was not necessarily dire. Lawson-Reece went on: 'It is clear that the Chinese will not commit themselves to a regular relay of BBC Chinese transmissions until they have a *quid pro quo* in the shape of a Home Service relay of material in English from Chungking.' In other words, the Chinese did not wish to see themselves only as a client nation; they had wares to trade in return for the BBC's bounty.

There can be no doubt that Lawson-Reece had recognized the character of the bait, for his next sentence reads very firmly: 'We see no possibility of accommodating regular relays of Chungking in the Home Service at the present time, but this question does not even arise until we know that Chungking is capable of giving a reliable signal.' He must have chuckled: his snottily bureaucratic language was delighting in the fact that the CCBA had become entrapped in a false position. He knew the Chinese broadcasters were aware that their equipment was inadequate to supply a good signal; he knew that in 1940 they had placed an order in the UK for a 100 KW shortwave transmitter, and that the transmitter had then been commandeered by the British Government; and he knew too that they had placed a further order for some high-power shortwave transmitters in the spring of 1943—and it had recently been reported that those transmitters too had been commandeered by HM Government. All in all, therefore, Lawson-Reece was in effect advising Stephenson that the BBC felt safe from the implied threats of the CCBA. It was hardly the BBC's fault if the CCBA did not have fit equipment; and that being the case, the BBC could not possibly meet the CCBA's request for a *quid pro quo*. 'All the Chinese that we have met either here or in China remain obdurately blind to the fact that the BBC is not a branch of Government,' Lawson-Reece lamented from on high.

It was only at the end of January 1945 that Stephenson confirmed in his report—a fear that Empson had been reluctant to admit to himself—that the CCBA was in fact doing no more than the minimum it had agreed with Dr Needham of the British Scientific Mission: 'XGOA relays, on the first Wednesday *only* of every month, the BBC Science Talk in Kuoyu.'

In the meantime, Needham himself returned to England for a short visit. Morris and Rendall pounced upon him. Under the guise of asking his advice about the prospects for broadcasting to China, they sought to ensure that he would confirm their prejudices. From Rendall's minute of their interview on 8 January, it is quite obvious that the representatives of the BBC, the Acting Controller (Overseas Services) and the Eastern Service Director, had already made up their minds and were intent on putting words into Needham's mouth. His authority could be used to back their own settled intentions, which were opposed to Empson's. 'In general Needham agreed to my conclusion that on the evidence which he had offered Chinese broadcasting from this country should be regarded entirely as a political warfare activity, i.e. it should be directed to Occupied China, since we had no audience worth the name in Free China.'[68]

This conclusion—or foregone resolution—threatened to devastate everything for which Empson had laboured since mid-1941. He cried out against it with a mixture of despair and anger. He told the Director-General in a measured letter a year later: 'My real shock came in January 1945, not long after [Morris] had been made Service Director, when he told me that he had decided to stop all cultural broadcasting in Chinese and allow only political warfare in that language; his decision was already made, he said, and it would be useless for me to express any opinion as Chinese editor. I did express opinions . . .'

To be sure, exactly a week after the date of Rendall's minute, Empson opened a memo to Morris with the words, 'I understand from you that it is proposed to turn the Chinese Service over entirely to what is called Political Warfare.'[69]

> What has to be kept in mind all the time is, that there are very strong anti-British feelings at present working in China, and dating back for a long time. The only reliable cross current in our favour is the belief that the British, though Imperialist, have got culture (more so than the Americans). If we send cultural and scientific material it is felt that we have something to say, and that we are showing a proper appreciation of China in saying it to her.[70]

His arguments apparently won the day, though not without leaving the Chinese Section with the feeling that it had been badly bloodied. It was not Morris but Rendall, Empson would inform the Director-General Sir William Haley the following year,

> who told me that the plan had been reconsidered, and the service would not after all be destroyed. Mr Morris then went on, very properly, to build up the cultural side of the Japanese service; and indeed I do not mean to say that permanent harm was done by these flurries, or that the Chinese service was prevented from doing any major thing it ought to have done. But it is necessary I think to recall these things to give the "atmosphere"; the Chinese service was living under threat, and all those who built it up before Mr Morris arrived were treated grudgingly. Miss [Eleen] Sam in particular, who was arranging the talks, always considered that great difficulties were put in her way, and that Mr Morris when not actually making difficulties threatened her work with rude indifference. I think it really was rather exhilarating for us to feel that we were fighting alone against the forces of evil, and it made us very keen on our work . . .[71]

His case had been proven, though only in part, by Stephenson's report to Rendall on 'Broadcasting in and to China', which emphasized that—as of January 1945—official Chinese policy was at once 'inherently anti-British' and 'blatantly' pro-American.[72] Empson must have felt faintly encouraged in his conviction that the policy he advocated for the BBC Chinese Service might help to assuage some of this anti-British sentiment; or, to put it contrariwise, that a switch to political warfare would have given the Chinese what he called 'a startling impression of ill-will'. Nevertheless, Stephenson's report suggested too that the most the BBC could hope to achieve would be an exercise in damage limitation, for his findings included this withering tip: 'The whole Chinese Central Administration is hopelessly corrupt and inefficient; from the latter stigma at least, the Central Broadcasting Administration is no exception.'

If it was depressing enough to be told that the CCBA was not run by reasonable and responsible professionals, it must have been crushing for Empson to hear also that radio receivers in China were as rare as a square meal. Stephenson worked out that there were 'not more than 250 to 500 sets in working order in the whole territory'—that is, in the whole territory of Free China, not just Chungking. The actual or potential audience for the BBC's Chinese Service therefore amounted to the tiniest fraction of a potential audience of many millions (the population of China in 1945 was ten times as large as that of the United Kingdom), though that fact alone would have justified Empson's policy of targeting a specific audience —the university scientists, a group whose professional needs could be ascertained and met to some small degree.

Perhaps the real value of the broadcasts was always reckoned to lie in the realm of public relations: it was quite as important that transmissions were known to be made as that they were listened to. Stephenson indeed reported that few people had ever heard a BBC transmission; and yet he notably reaffirmed too: 'There seems no doubt that the BBC is and will continue to be an important factor in the maintenance of British prestige in China.' In the face of that paradox it would have been folly to have altered course in 1945, to have made the Chinese Service not a medium of education but a weapon of war.

Evidently Morris preferred not to be convinced of the case for carrying on as before; he seemed to want to boycott those who advocated an altruistic policy in the Chinese Service. As Empson noted for example, 'many documents bearing on listener research were deliberately kept from Mr Bonwit.' The unfortunate Bonwit was eventually sacked from the Far Eastern Research department at Bush House in London. Fortunately, a little bird conveyed the news of Bonwit's plight to Christopher (Kit) Saltmarshe, who gave him a job in the Monitoring Service at Caversham Park near Reading—where he was to remain for the rest of his career.

For himself, Empson fared little better from his boss. So far from being supported in his programme-planning by the Far Eastern Service Director (as Morris was now styled), he encountered only more of the man's contrariness. As the eighth anniversary of the Double Seventh drew on, for example, he wrote to Morris with high hopes,

> I understand from this morning's meeting that it was considered possible that there might be
> (a) a statement from all three political parties asserting their determination to fight Japan;
> (b) the usual message from Churchill to Chiang Kai-shek, but released in time for announcement on the day (it would be an excellent thing if he would consent to record the message in his own voice);
> (c) a news release from Redman [of the MOI] about British preparations and activities in the war against Japan.[73]

Three days later, Morris returned Empson's memo with an unaccountable rebuttal at the bottom: 'No action as spoken'. A little later, on 12 June, James Langham, Assistant Director of Programme Planning, circulated an equally terse memo under the heading 'DOUBLE SEVENTH DAY: WEEK 27, SATURDAY, 7TH JULY': 'Will you please note that no action is to be taken this year in connection with this anniversary.'[74] That was all: no explanation.

Nor did Empson get any more satisfaction out of the Home Service during the last months of the war—not even after the sudden collapse of Japan, when he became especially keen that the United Kingdom should adopt a conspicuously cooperative stance towards China, her free though still disunited ally. When the Kuomintang and the Communists agreed to participate in an all-party conference in Chungking in October 1945, he correctly foresaw the Double Tenth anniversary that year, the first after V-J Day, as a day not of 'song and dance' but of 'solemn preparation'.[75]

But Empson lost this campaign. Though he was not without allies, no one seemed to know just who had issued the wrong-headed decree to scant the occasion. The mystery of the decision-making processes of the Home was never unravelled, but it seems not unlikely that John Morris had quashed the idea of giving serious attention to China's anniversary. In turn, Empson assumed an air of Confucian metaphor-making when he counselled Morris in a memo: 'The more anyone is frightened about the possibilities of China, the more he ought to try to be decently friendly to China. It is not a rational policy to poke an umbrella at the baby tiger while you have still got it behind the bars; the only thing you can do at that stage is to avoid spoiling its temper.'[76]

For the immediate future, Empson wanted—rather innocently as it turned out—to trust to the good faith of the political factions within China. Like the Roosevelt administration, he hoped that a joint national assembly could prove viable. 'I don't doubt that the Yenan [Communist] Government really has done wonders, and that many of the accusations made against Chungking are correct,' he wrote in a review of a book that jibbed at the Nationalists and praised Mao's Communists. 'But China is a large and complicated scene, and the only way to avoid civil war is by a deal between the major forces, both regional and general.'[77] Elsewhere, in the draft of an article called 'China and the World' written at this time, he conceded that the Communist sphere of influence emanating from Yenan 'made the greater appeal' to the Chinese masses. All the same, he believed, 'the picture of Chiang Kai Shek as a dictator, which has been spread, is a radically false one. He has always been a balancer, a reconciler of different groups and largely of regional groups . . .'[78] But in saying so much for the Chinese Nationalist leader he was projecting his personal wisdom on to a dictator; the concept of balancing and reconciling, which he had learned as an undergraduate from I. A. Richards, was a keynote of his own life, not of Chiang Kai-shek's. At this stage of his career Empson was still hoping that Chiang Kai-shek would prove himself worthy of the office of supreme leader. But Empson was out of touch with popular sentiment in China; it was already too late to speak well of the old order. Nonetheless he was right to forecast that partition—a Communist north (backed by Russia), a Nationalist south (backed by the USA)—was out of the question. Failing the negotiable option, that the Communists should be admitted to a share of power, civil war would be unavoidable. Everything depended on Chiang's next steps.

> I have been getting very wrapped up in the broadcasting [wrote Empson to I. A. Richards in July 1945], though of course I mean to leave it after the war; and have done no writing to speak of . . .
>
> Certainly the end of the war appears as the longed-for dawn all right; I mean I look forward to being back in a university where one could do some real work again, and yet feel I hardly know how I should start or what the light would reveal. A tired grey harried old man, I appear to myself . . .[79]

He was not exaggerating: he had told John Hayward in January that office life was 'so exhausting that it is making me quite ill'.[80] With the end of the war he did fall ill, with a painful stomach ulcer which kept him in bed for a month; he passed the time by reading novels in bed, eating baby food, and knitting squares. He was not quite 40 years old.

He stayed with the BBC for a further 16 months after the end of the war, never relaxing in his insistence that China deserved everyone's best attention. As to general policy on the subject of the war in China, he had always maintained, 'it is important to recognise the clearcut Chinese successes for the sake of general goodwill'; all the same, as he admitted even to John Morris, 'Chinese communiqués perhaps tend to exaggerate the weight of the fighting . . . '[81] Thus he had struggled to get China's news reported on the Home Service first and foremost because it was 'worthwhile to have China on the map of the news of war against Japan'. Just what he achieved during his five-and-a-half years with the Eastern Service is impossible to quantify, especially when he had to commit so much of his energy to overcoming the opposition— the indifference and the knavish tricks of his colleagues— within the institution of the BBC, as well as the continual suspicions that beset Sino-British broadcasting relations. Lord Briggs gave this sorry summary of the seeming failure of Empson's special branch of the BBC: 'China, the ally, one of the Big Four at most of the war-time international conferences, played almost as small a part in the pattern of war-time broadcasting as Japan, the enemy.'[82] Yet it came as no surprise to Empson to learn in January 1945 that the actual audience in China was miniscule; nor did it cause him much concern. Ralf Bonwit would happily recall forty years on, 'I always assumed that no one was listening.' It was the same for Empson. Both of them were strangely sanguine about that state of affairs because they reckoned that the value of the Chinese Service was more symbolic than practical—though Empson had hoped that his broadcasts on science would be of actual use to the universities with whose plight he identified. Accordingly, when he came to notify the British Council that he wished to return to China, he spoke of his achievements in a paradoxically negative fashion: 'I can promise you that no ill-will has been created to my knowledge by the BBC attempt to break the Japanese intellectual blockade.'[83] But perhaps Bonwit best summed up the role which his boss had honourably fulfilled during his years of broadcasting when he said: 'Empson was an outpost of China in the BBC.'[84]

Empson officially resigned from the BBC on 12 January 1947. Five days before his departure, John Morris commissioned from him a series of twenty 5-minute talks to be broadcast under the title of 'English by

Radio'. He delivered his scripts in just two weeks, on 24 January, and they were recorded by 11 February. It seems a sadly apt and ironic comment on Empson's relationship with the BBC that the scripts and the recordings are no longer held at the BBC Script Unit—they have been thrown away.[85]

Wartime London was not all professional enmities and petty irritability, telephones and anger. Austerity was relieved by a goodly amount of beer-drinking in pubs and at parties, and by flare-ups, flings, and casual affairs. Dorothea Richards was to take away her own rather prejudiced view of Empson, after meeting him again in the summer of 1946: 'black & bearded & manners not much improved "as thick skinned as a rhinoceros".'[86] But to the vast majority of his friends and acquaintances in London in the mid-1940s he seemed an altogether more charming, sharp-minded and generous figure, albeit with a fundamentally impersonal and intellectually abstracted mien. As a husband and the father of two new children, he was also far more alert and responsible than the peculiarly derelict figure that Mrs Richards persisted in imagining him to be. For instance: at one of the Empsons' easy-going parties (no one was introduced to anyone else, or obliged to talk to anybody else in particular, or even to circulate), the writer Joan Wyndham found herself being ogled by the thin, hawklike, twitchy figure of Lucian Freud. After he had chatted her up for a while he led her 'down some rickety stairs to a nursery where Empson's children were sleeping. He pushed me back against Mogador's cot and kissed me, but Empson came down in a great rage and shooed us up again.'[87] Empson was enraged purely by their carelessness of the sleeping child.

If he was a responsible father, however, he was also a complaisant husband. Hetta was not secretive about the lovers she invited home; and as their friends noticed, Empson seemed content in the capacity of cuckold. That part of him that was the child of a lord of the manor retained about him a large portion of the seigneur who disdained to be jealous of his wife; and at least, since he wanted to preserve for himself the prerogative of his bisexuality, he should allow his wife to fulfil her strong sexual needs. The refugee writer Elias Canetti, novelist, essayist, and dramatist, who had taken up residence in Hampstead in 1939, went to a number of Empson parties and noticed the acute differences between their two sorts of guest. On the one hand were the literary celebrities and artists—'intellectuals of any colour and provenance'—whether the courteous, proper T. S. Eliot or the romantic, decorous, softly-spoken, mystically-inclined Kathleen Raine, and with other party-goers including Tambimuttu, Mulk Raj Anand, and Louis MacNeice; and on the other hand, the more louche characters whom Hetta gathered up. The result was that the Empsons' parties were 'really quite lively and free of vanity and formality': democratic, alive, spontaneous, 'never boring'. To his immense regret, however, Canetti felt he was not among those who could hold his host's attention; he could never get close to the 'sharp, active, ramifying' mind of Empson. Born in Bulgaria in 1905 but brought up in Vienna (with an interval in Manchester, England), Canetti was an almost exact contemporary of Empson's; he was already hailed for the absurdist plays he had written in the 1930s and for a novel translated as *Auto-de-Fé* (1935), which was banned by the Nazis; and in 1938 he had fled Vienna for Paris and then London, where he would live not far from the Empsons. He had witnessed the burning of the Palace of Justice in Vienna in 1927 and would go on to write a remarkable analysis of the dynamics of crowd psychology and of Nazi abuses of power, *Masse und Macht* (1960), published in translation as *Crowds and Power* (1962), and ultimately to win the Nobel Prize for Literature in 1981. But still he could not induce Empson to distinguish his particular interests, to pay him the compliment of a sustained conversation about things they might have had in common—not even on the topic of Empson's experiences of crowd behaviour in Japan or China, though it would have fascinated Canetti to learn about them.

> So I was condemned to complete impotence with this man. It would never have occurred to him to talk to me about the Chinese masses. I would have been burningly interested if he had, but what would he have had to say to me? It would have appeared to him like small talk, which he despised.
>
> So I went gladly enough, but still somewhat shamefacedly, to the Empsons'. You were asked along, but for Empson it was as though you didn't exist.[88]

In truth, Empson was the complete democrat. He made no distinction of persons on the basis of celebrity; all he cared for was merit or mettle. Even if he did not choose to chat very much with Canetti, he had taken stock of the other man. '[W]hat little I know of Canetti is all in his favour,' he was to profess to Kathleen Raine in March 1948.[89] It was actually a diplomatic remark, since he would have known she was taken with Canetti. All the same, neither Empson nor his wife really took much of a liking to Canetti: he was not a terribly likeable person.

However, even though Canetti never became an intimate of the Empsons, he found one thing in particular quite remarkable: Hetta's bohemian openness about her sexual partners:

Her lovers, of whom there got to be quite a number over the years, she
sometimes even allowed into her quarters. Empson seemed not to have
anything against it at all ... You had the impression, coming to the house,
that each of them had their own life, without getting in the way of the other,
and respecting everything to do with it, even if it was diametrically opposed
to whatever he or she thought. Empson himself struck me as completely
asexual, it was a little perplexing that there were two boys from that union,
who grew up in the midst of their mother's tangled love life, without coming
to any apparent harm from it.[90]

It may have been the case, as Canetti implied, that Empson had a low sex
drive; that his sexuality was sublimated in, or compensated by, work of the
mind. But Empson had in fact persuaded himself that it was a vital point of
principle to be liberal and non-possessive about sex; it was progressive—'a
blow for freedom'—to seek to share one's wife with another man. And
perchance the wife would now and then share a lover with her husband? It
is the master narrative for which he found the model in Joyce's *Ulysses*.

Those who gained access to Empson's mind, or who engaged his
imagination and sympathy, were well rewarded with supportive kindness.
One such was the South African poet Roy Campbell, whose occasionally
buccaneering and bullying conduct left a lot of people feeling intimidated.
Campbell was a big, bombastic man, quickly confrontational when
crossed. Stephen Spender, to take a notable instance, was incensed by
Campbell's *Flowering Rifle* (1939) to the extent of writing a review, 'The
Talking Bronco' (*New Statesman*, 11 March 1939), which lambasted the
poem as 'an incoherent, biased, unobjective, highly coloured and distorted
account of one man's experience of the Spanish War, seen through the
eyes of a passionate partisan of Franco'. Campbell, who had indeed
supported the pro-Fascist side in the Civil War, would never forgive
Spender's indictment of his work; part of his revenge was to adopt the
headline of Spender's review as the title of a volume he published through
T. S. Eliot at Faber & Faber in May 1946. *Talking Bronco* is famous among
other things for Campbell's coinage of the term 'MacSpaunday' as a
contemptuous collective noun for the MacNeice–Spender–Auden–Day
Lewis confederacy of poets. Among the few reviewers who admired the
volume, Desmond MacCarthy in the *Sunday Times* (7 July 1946) praised
Campbell for expressing so beautifully 'a tragic sense of life', and singled
out 'The Skull in the Desert' as the 'finest poem of all' in *Talking Bronco*.
Anna Campbell, the poet's daughter, in an interview with the biographer
Joseph Pearce, concurs with MacCarthy's judgement: 'In that poem he
puts the importance of the Cross, of the bearing of the Cross, and almost

that you have got to love it because, if you don't, you can't get to Christ. What he is talking about is more or less what Christ must have felt in the desert, but also that moment on the Cross which, if we don't share, if we don't cling to, we can't save our soul.' But the virulence of Campbell's satirical verses aroused further ire from Spender, Day Lewis, and Mac-Neice (MacNeice even picked a fist-fight with Campbell in a pub near the BBC); and other reviewers were outraged by his attacks on the left-wing poets.[91]

Empson—who had first met Roy Campbell in company with Dylan Thomas in the early 1940s, and who was to meet him again when from July 1945 Campbell was given the position of Talks Producer in one of the 'funk-holes of the BBC' ('The vultures on the cook-house nest | Like poets on the BBC,' wrote Campbell in one of his poems)—genuinely liked the man and got on very well with him. He appreciated his passion. Campbell was possessed of the kind of forthright vigour that he loved in his South African wife. Not feeling at all concerned to keep on the good side of Spender or MacNeice, Empson wrote in Campbell's defence a brief letter to *Tribune* which carried immense quiet authority: 'Several Reviewers of Roy Campbell's *Talking Bronco*, while expressing their abhorrence of his political opinions, have claimed that his verse shows a marked falling-off. I think "The Skull in the Desert" in that volume is the finest poem he has written so far, which is saying a good deal.'[92]

Campbell recriprocated Empson's immense liking; and the following year, not long after the Empson family had departed for China, he penned an article, 'William Empson: Contemporary English Poet and Scholar', which was produced by the Central Office of Information and circulated through the offices of the British Council. After lauding his friend's poetry almost without reservation, Campbell wound up his piece with a personal sketch of Empson of unusually perceptive intimacy:

Mr Empson is one of the few English writers whose conversation is on a level with his writing. It is rare nowadays for anyone except an Irishman to speak English in complete sentences without hesitating; but when Empson gets well launched into one of his celebrated monologues he takes one back to the great days of English conversation in the eighteenth century. In listening to Empson's conversation one gets a key to the amazingly mathematical construction which underlies his poetry, for although his conversation sparkles with all the incidental brilliancies which are the delight of all convivial company, one is even more struck by the architectural design of his reasoning and the control which he exerts over the most abstruse and complicated matters.

He included passionate words for his fellow South African: 'Mrs Empson, like many other Boer women, combines beauty with domesticity and is at the same time a brilliant intellectual companion.' Hetta herself was as passionate in her loyalties as she was fierce with fools. (Campbell would be just as passionate in his loyalty to Edith Sitwell.) Empson admired full-blooded convictions, and with Campbell there were no half measures.[93]

Another wartime party hosted by the Empsons (on behalf of the British Council) took the form of a reception for the French poet Pierre Emmanuel. It was a movingly symbolic occasion, taking place as it did soon after VE-Day and the Liberation of France: Emmanuel stood as the representative of the newly freed ally. The poets and other writers of London turned out in force: T. S. Eliot, Michael Roberts, George Barker, Dylan Thomas, Rayner Heppenstall, Ruthven Todd, Paul Potts, Kathleen Raine, Anne Ridler, and John Heath-Stubbs. Edith Sitwell sent a message regretting that she could not attend; and the veteran poet Anna Wickham arrived late—she was welcomed with warmth and a good deal of fussing about chairs—and already slightly the worse for drink. The party was handled by the Empsons with pleasing informality. As John Heath-Stubbs was to recall in his autobiography, 'We were served beer in pint mugs— wine and spirits were hardly obtainable at this time—and most of us sat on the floor and ate lettuce sandwiches.'[94] Ruthven Todd pounced upon Eliot, rudely demanding to know what was being done to get Ezra Pound released from the mental hospital where he had been interned in Washington DC, following his arrest for treason. 'Eliot looked extremely embarrassed by this brash advance.'[95] But the most memorable and moving part of the occasion was the experience of hearing T. S. Eliot read—in his measured, reverberant tones—part of *The Dry Salvages* and then the 'Compound Ghost' section of *Little Gidding*.

The war years brought Empson several opportunities too to read his own poems, both in public and at private parties. His performances were extraordinary, and won new admirers who would oftentimes become his friends. At a British Council party for the Chilean poet Gabriela Mistral, G. S. Fraser watched Dylan Thomas and T. S. Eliot read their poems in their distinctive styles. But then Fraser was struck by a dimension of Empson's poems which was vividly brought out by the 'sprightliness' of his reading:

> with his head on one side, cocking it up a little with an alert and pleased look when he came, every three lines or so, to some pungent equivocation; and with his legs astride, and swaying to rest his weight, now on this foot,

now on that, to mark the broad movement of the rhythm. His gaiety, his physical enjoyment of his own poetry were infectious; the dryness of which some critics complain in his verses became a positive quality; one was no longer aware of his obscurities as hampering the communication of the total intention of the poem.[96]

Similarly, at a reading held in aid of Aid to China at the Wigmore Hall in September 1943—every poet of note was there again: T. S. Eliot, Kathleen Raine, Louis MacNeice, Osbert Sitwell, Edith Sitwell—Anne Ridler noted the way Empson read 'Bacchus'—'accompanied by his extraordinary dance of the limbs, which Louis MacNeice compared to a satyr.'[97] Eliot too thought it most remarkable: 'The hit of the afternoon was Bill Empson's reading of BACCHUS (the more obscure Bacchus of the two, with that stuff about the Arkitekt): the house reverberated with applause.'[98]

It was at the Wigmore Hall reading that Empson had approached Anne Ridler and asked her whether she knew the young poet G. S. Fraser, who had surprisingly (to her) published in Tambimuttu's magazine *Poetry London* a fine poem called 'Letter to Anne Ridler'. Empson admired the verses Fraser had put out during the war, and thereupon commanded Ridler to send a telegram to Fraser in Egypt—at once—which of course she didn't do.[99] Born in 1915 and brought up in Glasgow and Aberdeen, Fraser had gone on to St Andrews University and then to be a cub reporter; at the outbreak of war he volunteered for the army and joined the Black Watch, but he passed most of the war on journalistic duties in Egypt and Eritrea. It was only after being demobilized in December 1945, when he arrived in London, that he was able (through Tambimuttu) to meet up with Empson. ('I met George Fraser in a brothel,' Empson once said to the Cambridge don George Watson. 'George had a sporting attitude towards brothels.'[100] But the claim may have been a momentary tease: there is no other evidence of brothel-going in his career.) Empson presently assumed the role of mentor to the shy and ultra-sensitive young Scot, sharpening his intellect and teasing his personality. 'I had noticed in Empson's writing,' Fraser would write in his precocious autobiography, 'several pleasant little tricks, of the sort that keep a reader wakeful: a way of saying "of course", when drawing some conclusion that seemed likely to jar and startle; a habit of alluding to rather out-of-the-way quotations as "these famous lines". In conversation, Empson had similar ways of jogging one: a trick of saying "To be sure, to be sure", for instance, before taking hold of some vague and inept remark of one's own and handing it back twisted by irony or perception into some new and intriguing shape.'[101] (Elias Canetti was likewise to note that 'it wasn't in Empson to keep quiet, because he spoke incessantly, at an extremely high intellectual level, and never listened to anyone not speaking the same highly cultivated language . . . I often heard him speak, he had wit and verve, he was quick and confident, talked in streams of interpretative knowledge, very individual opinions and precise knowledge, perhaps the most fluent, inspired, clearest speaker I ever heard in England, among poets.')[102] Eagerly adopting the role of disciple, Fraser was nevertheless keen to argue every point with the Master. Yet Fraser was so 'snail-horn sensitive', as his wife was to say, that from time to time he would flare up in resentment at something Empson said; but their friendship would survive any such moments of goading and hurt.[103] Empson could be savage. 'You wrote your best poems when you were the scruffiest private in the British Army,' he once insisted to Fraser. 'Don't delude yourself that you can still do it.' Fraser's wife, who overheard that painful put-down, wondered if Empson was actually rebuking himself for his failure to write more poems.[104] For the very most part, however, Empson gave unconditional backing to Fraser. He became the ultimate dutch uncle to his unconfident protégé, and would willingly send off references to help him find employment at the BBC, or at this or that university (Fraser was to land up at Leicester in 1958.) He was happy too to attend the wedding of George and Paddy Fraser at St Andrew's Church, Chelsea, on 30 August 1946; so were the egregious Tambimuttu and the young poet Gavin Ewart.

In London, where Fraser had to earn his living for some years by way of literary journalism, he would encourage other writers at his home: but Empson came to think he was using up his energies on 'lame dogs'.[105] Fraser had genuine talent as a literary critic. The admiration was mutual. 'The boyish zest for life, that went with an extraordinary intellectual equipment,' enthused Fraser, 'was the most taking aspect of Empson's personality. He was a person it was impossible to be with and not like.'[106]

One biting evening, Fraser took along to visit the Empsons a young compatriot, the poet and critic Tom Scott. Their host began by performing his trick of concocting mulled beer by plunging a red-hot poker into a pint glass of mild ale. 'There was a sizzling pause, and a moment of suspense, while we all waited for the glass to crack, which it never did; a rich froth gathered on the beer and it acquired a delicious creamy flavour.'[107] By the end of the evening, Scott came away with such positive impressions that he wrote down this lucid paean to the worth of the man he had witnessed:

> I was surprised to find a short gypsy-dark man in bohemian clothes, with a
> Norse goddess of a wife. I suppose he is the most intensely intellectual

person I have met, with just a touch of that puckish, childish sentimentality about him. His degree of introversion was another surprise; I had imagined he would be rather arrogant and socially poised; instead, he has humility, is pedantic, keenly observant of people, intellectually precise, athletic-looking, and erudite. He is a born scholar, of complete integrity, and 'really what he is'. I was quite unable to take part in the conversation between him and G. S. F[raser]. I liked him best for his impersonal sincerity. He is not like the average denizen of these parts who delights in 'helping' others; he has too much respect for truth and candour to say things which are supposed to benefit the imagined psychology of a 'person' ... I liked him but felt out of place in his company. His wife has a wealth of physical rest in her.[108]

Paddy Fraser was rather more impressed with Hetta's sheer energy; 'rest' would seem to imply a power held in reserve, and Hetta was not one for restraining her emotions and reactions. She had an instinct of coiled steel. When the Empsons threw a party before their departure for China, Mrs Fraser carried away from the evening one vivid memory: it was the image of Empson's tall, handsome wife—'wild like a Maenad'—sweeping 'her guests out of the door late in the night, with a kitchen broom.'[109] Throughout their acquaintance, which endured until G. S. Fraser's death, Mrs Fraser remained astonished by the sheer force that was Hetta Empson:

> large-boned, half-way between a powerful Greek goddess and one of the large cats, tigerish, I suppose is the word, something fierce, even frightening at times, combined with a lithe strength. But this is too feline an image, too smooth: Hetta had a tremendous directness, a brutal frankness, a don't-give-a-damn attitude, which was surprising and refreshing: it was this, I believe, that attracted William from their earliest meeting... [S]he was so much herself, so totally unconventional. Once she raised me in her arms and threw me like a doll up to the ceiling; I was terrified.

Of Empson, Mrs Fraser would remember most vividly 'the speed and surprisingness' of his mind; his 'sprightliness'; his unpretentiousness; the austerity of his way of life, especially in later years at Sheffield; and the fact that he was 'gruff' only on the outside. 'He loved to play the eccentric, but not the teddy-bearish kind; he could be formidable but kind... at his most provocative, William was gleeful, outrageous, daring you to disagree.'[110]

In August 1946 there appeared in *Picture Post* an illustrated article headed 'A Nest of Singing Birds'—the title was presumably taken from Byron's lines in *Don Juan*, 'A nest of tuneful persons to my eye | Like four and twenty Blackbirds in a pie'—celebrating the surprising number of poets who were then working for the BBC: those featured included Louis

MacNeice and Roy Campbell as well as Empson.[111] It was a swan-song
moment for Empson, for it was not long before he would quit the BBC; not
long too before he would realize he had given up writing poems. For a
while, in the winter of 1945, he was tempted to apply for the King Edward
VII Chair of English Literature at Cambridge (vacated by the death of
'Q'—Sir Arthur Quiller-Couch). (Initially, he thought it was the Oxford
Chair in Poetry that was available, being unaware that the latter post,
which was in abeyance throughout the war, did not carry a proper salary.)
The only other candidates, he was told at one point, were J. B. Priestley
and George Barker. He even sought counsel about the position from T. S.
Eliot (who told him gnomically that one needed 'Influence at Downing
Street') and from John Hayward;[112] also from I. A. Richards, to whom he
added: 'please don't tell George Yeh I was asking about this, because he
might feel it was an attempt to break a promise [to return to the National
Peking University after the war]; but after all if I am setting out to educate
two children I had better try to earn some money.'

A little earlier, at a party thrown by Tom Harrisson not long before
D-Day, Empson had vainly helped to preserve the well-being of a celebrity
whose wartime broadcasts were credited with doing much to buoy up
British morale: it was none other than J. B. Priestley (who was supposedly
to be his rival for whatever Chair was going begging). Beer flowed, as did
the usual flirtations and antagonisms. One of the other guests was Woodrow Wyatt, the future politician and diarist, who was awaiting a posting
to his army unit in France; at the party, he became infuriated by the
boastfulness of Priestley, who was 'drunkenly explaining that some broadcasts he had made were the reason why we were winning the war; the
Government did not understand the nature of the British people; only he,
the blunt Yorkshireman, did.' When Wyatt shouted at him, 'Utter balls.
You're just a windbag', Priestley was roused to more furious and self-
applauding volubility. As luck fell out, at the end of the evening Wyatt was
obliged to install the great man in his jeep and drive him back to his
apartment in the Albany, and Empson lent a hand in easing the inebriated
Priestley into the open-topped military vehicle. But Wyatt was himself so
far gone in liquor that he could not quite remember the whereabouts of the
Albany, and ended up careering round and round the statue of Eros in
Piccadilly Circus. Priestley yelled to be allowed out of the crapulous merry-
go-round.

> The terrified Priestley [recalled Wyatt] had several times been prevented by
> William Empson from jumping out on to the road. Once in Jermyn Street,

almost at Albany, he managed it. He fell into the gutter. William Empson
and I got out and looked at his motionless but heavily breathing body.

'We'd better get him back into the jeep. You can't leave a distinguished
man like that lying in the gutter,' William said.

I prodded him with my foot. 'He's only a silly old dramatist.'[113]

Fecklessly, they abandoned the body of the distinguished person. Still, no
harm came to Priestley: he was to live and write, and to talk the talk, for
years to come—he survived for a further forty years and died only in 1984.

For himself, Empson acknowledged that neither Cambridge nor all the
boozing and battling of the latterday bohemia that he both enjoyed and
endured in London was to be his destiny. He had determined to go back—
this time with the complement of his young family—to another conflict in
another country.

3

━━◦•◦━━

Chinabound

I N 1930 Peter Quennell discovered during a visit to Peking—perhaps largely in comparison with the discomfortingly rigid year he had just spent in Tokyo—that 'mysteriously but unmistakably, "one can breathe", and China remains oddly sympathetic...'[1] Seventeen years later, the Empsons felt much the same easeful spirit still in place. Notwithstanding, after years of occupation and neglect, the fabric of Peiping, or 'Northern Peace' (as it had been called since 1938, when Nanking was designated the capital city—from October 1949 it would again be Peking, or 'Northern Capital'), looked worn and war-torn, a mixture of downtrodden imperial splendour and indigent modern bustle.

Something approaching three million people occupied the space of 707 square kilometres within the 25-mile oblong perimeter of its massive crenellated walls, which were 40 feet high and 'broader than Fifth Avenue' (as one American correspondent wrote home). Large, regular thorough-fares drove from one to another of the two-storeyed gate-towers, East and West, North and South, boxing the compass of the three constituent sectors of the city: the Imperial City, the Tartar City, and the Chinese City. The intersections of the major arteries were marked by glossy triumphal arches, called *p'ai-lou*, made of painted wood surmounted by high banks of coloured tiles. A medieval fortress of innumerable walls within walls, Peiping seemed almost wilfully to defy the symmetrical pattern outlined by its walls and highways. Off the major streets, which in the late 1940s added up to little more than 215 kilometres of sound road, lanes of trodden mud wove like an insoluble jigsaw puzzle between high and windowless grey walls that screened off courtyard homes, small businesses, and handicraft shops making everything from pots and pans to fans and carvings in ivory or jade. Countless street stalls would serve up seed cakes, hot *wun tun* soup, bean curd, meatballs, sweet potatoes, persimmons, pork dumplings, pastries. Flea markets and fairs, and hawkers with charcoal braziers, enlivened the throng of the streets. People got about either on foot or on two wheels: there were about 110,000 bicycles in the city. At the heart of the city, the divine centre of *Zhongguo*—the Middle Kingdom, the age-old Chinese world—stood the Forbidden City, the Imperial Palace of the Ming and Ching dynasties (since 1925, the Palace Museum), with its awesome walls of faded purplish pink topped by glazed imperial yellow tiles overbearing the world that bowed before its bastions.

The National Peking University (usually known by the abbreviation *Peita*),[2] which was first established in 1898 as the Imperial University, sat on the northeast shoulder of the Palace Museum, on the site of Ming buildings known as *Ma Shen Miao* (Temple of the God of Horses). During the period of less than 60 years since its foundation, the story of the university had become intimately linked to the development of China's politics, ideology, culture, and science. Among the foremost figures who had either taught or held office at the university were the educationalists and ideologists Yan Fu and Cai Yuanpei; Mao Tse-tung, Li Dazhou (the university librarian for whom Mao worked), and Chen Zuxui, who fired up the Chinese Communist Party; and the writer Lu Xun, the leader of the New Culture Movement. Peking University played a major role in the Chinese Democratic Revolution; and the students deserve their repute for making it what the official account calls 'the cradle of the anti-imperialist and anti-feudal May 4th Movement' of 1919, which rose up in revolt against the provisions of the Versailles Conference.

The focus of the modern university was a large red brick building called simply 'Red Building', built in 1910, which housed the College of Liberal Arts. Empson would be given an office on the second floor. Adjacent to it lay other colleges and student dormitories. The Empsons, who had left England in February 1947 (sailing from Southampton via Shanghai), were well housed in the north-west corner of a former Manchu palace alongside the main campus. Their university-owned accommodation at number 11 Tung Kao Fang consisted of several rooms linked by three courtyards (one of them including what Empson called 'an artful rockery topped with a seat to write poems on'), the whole area being entered from a typical dirt-paved lane or *hutung* by way of a *cha-lan men*, a roofed and copper-hinged 'barrier-gate' of crimson-lacquered wood, with brass fittings and with a high stone threshold. 'Every morning at eight o'clock William and I have a

Chinese lesson on the rockery,' wrote Hetta. 'Our teacher is a young man who is doing post-graduate work.'[3] Hetta got on well with the language, albeit she ended up speaking a Chinese that was peculiar to herself— 'incantatory, ululatory, full of despairing cadences,' as the scholar David Hawkes has described it. Hawkes came to the conclusion that Hetta was quite probably tone-deaf. So too was Empson, who never got on with Chinese: he found it an uncomfortable tongue, and gave it very little attention. Hawkes, who knew him from late 1948, only ever heard him say one word of Chinese—*Liangkaishui* ('cold boiled water').

With a circumvallation of high grey brick, their residential quarters were single-storeyed, with tiled roofs (by long-standing decree, no building in the city could overtop the Imperial Palace), all just as grey as the walls that fronted the lane but with latticed paper windows decorated in scarlet and green lacquer. In the summer, the lattice windows would be replaced by gauze screens which were designed to keep out insects; and matted canopies called *p'engs* could be fitted over the courtyards so as to extend the living space of the property. Their quarters had no bathroom as such, so they would bathe in a small room in a big round vessel known as a 'lotus jar', which had a hole in the bottom; one day, Hetta jumped out of her skin when she saw a snake slithering over the rim of the bathing jar. In the winter months, when fierce cold and overwhelming dust-dense winds roared out of the north, so-called 'coal balls' (coal dust compacted with clay) would be used to heat stoves.

The family retained both a young cook named Lao Yu (who would attempt to beat his brains out on the rockery when he was threatened with conscription to the army), and a stately old *amah*: this was an austere-looking Manchu lady in a long grey gown who took charge of the flaxen-haired children even though she had bound feet and could not pursue the prankish Mogador and Jacob—who eagerly took to befriending neighbours and pedicab drivers. After the silent and sly Lao Yu went berserk, he was replaced by an older cook named Guan-shifu, who was, like the *amah*, a Manchu and an ultra-conservative: he would always speak of the free-spirited Hetta with awed admiration—from of old, he had heard of Manchu ladies who carried on like Hetta. Neither the nurse nor the cooks could speak any English. Although the children were initially put to school in a French Catholic kindergarten, they picked up colloquial Chinese (including a full lexicon of swear words) far more quickly than English, and they would later need remedial instruction in their native tongue. (As Peter Quennell remarked, 'Profanity is eloquent in Peking.')[4] Their father, with small Chinese, found it hard to talk to the boys. At a later stage they were put to a Chinese school, the *Kong De Xiao Xue* (a pedicab driver was hired to take them to and from the school), and Empson would be delighted by the treatment they received there: 'My...children were going to a Chinese school, and they will never be so much petted again.'[5]

On weekends and holidays the family could walk or bicycle the short distance to Coal Hill (*Mei Shan*), otherwise known as *Jingshan* or Prospect Hill, an artifical square-cut eminence due north of the Forbidden City. Once the preserve of imperial officials, courtiers and ladies, Coal Hill is surmounted by five lacquered pavilions. The topmost pavilion, *Wan Ch'un T'ing* (pavilion of Ten Thousand Springs), provides a vantage point to survey the glories of the city, including the surprising discovery that Peking in 1947 was not just a maze of tall ashen grey walls. From Coal Hill, especially in the summer when the weather turns hot and humid, Peking resembled a forest or parkland, with trees and flowers—lindens, cypresses, acacia, magnolia, peonies, roses, asters, mimosas, chrysanthemums—surging up from thousands of courtyards. At a distance of some twenty miles to the north-west looms the misty arc of the Western Hills. In the immediate foreground, due south of Coal Hill, stands the oblong mile of the Forbidden City itself, incorporating some 9,000 rooms: the most grandiose and painfully privileged prison compound in the world. Imperial mustard yellow roofs, with eaves that curl and surge like stylised waves, lap away in punctilious perspective.

> I see few people, talk no Chinese, and take very little interest in the local arts [Empson wrote]. It is rather hard to say why I like being here so much, as I certainly do. One says one 'likes the Chinese', but I don't like the look of most of the people I am introduced to here, any more than anywhere else. What is meant I suppose is a much more general feeling of affection, chiefly for the people you see in the street. But I suppose most of them, though they have the great merit of not looking fussed or hurried, look pretty sordid from concentration on some half dishonest employment. The women do not raise my spirits at all. The weather and the beauty of the town do a bit, but not much. As far as I can see it comes down to a diffused homosexual feeling, that is, you will seldom go through a street without seeing at least one agreeable young man, and you feel affectionately towards him because he seems so content with himself, and there is no need for anything to be done. I do not think this is a peculiarity of mine; considering the high proportion of buggers among the foreigners who genuinely 'love China' it seems to be the chief thing the country has to offer. No doubt you could generalise it into saying you like to be in a place where there is no sense of

sin and no feeling that it is a duty to worry, combined with an adequate amount of hardheadness (of course I don't feel at all that the Chinese are delicious tender creatures, like the at present murderous but always kittenish inhabitants of south-east Asia; you don't feel outside the modern commercial world in China) but even so I should say you get this more general feeling through looking at working class young man—seldom from students, who do tend to be harried a bit, poor things.[6]

For years the students had been harried above all by the politics of poverty. Since late December 1945, President Truman had delegated the Marshall Mission to try to negotiate a coalition between the two sides in the Chinese Civil War, the Nationalist Government (KMT) of Chiang Kai-shek and Mao Tse-tung's Communist forces (which in July 1946 had been renamed the People's Liberation Army or PLA), even while continuing to supply the KMT with combat *matériel*—a supply which was temporarily embargoed, for a few months from September 1946, in an effort to give some credibility to General Marshall's services as a go-between. In January 1947, however, the American government recalled Marshall and formally declared that his mission had ended in failure. So far from arranging a marriage between Nationalist reactionaries and Communist revolutionaries, General Marshall could not even induce them to cohabit.

The Chinese student body had long sustained dire economic privations resulting from the fact that Chiang Kai-shek pillaged the public purse to feed his war machine. The government allocated a mere 4 per cent of the national budget to education. Both students and university faculty, who were exempt from military conscription, despaired of a peaceful political settlement to the conflict. In the first months of 1947, price indices rose by 50 to 100 per cent, and during just one 5-day period, 5 to 10 May, the index of commodity prices shot up by 15 per cent. When the Empsons arrived in Peking, the exchange rate for the pound sterling was 140,000 Chinese dollars; just three months later, in July, it had dropped to 40,000.[7] Like everyone else Empson became concerned about the giddily declining value of his income. His salary at the National Peking University was set at about CNC $8,800,000, the equivalent of £105 a year, which the British Council had undertaken to make up to about £950; in practice, the British Council paid him £60 a month, which left him £125 short of the guaranteed annual sum. Thus the official exchange rate gave a false picture of real purchasing power, as he justifiably argued in a 'disagreeable' letter to the Council: 'I submit that the open market rates are the only ones which bear any relation to actual living conditions.'

Hyperinflation took a heavier toll on his colleagues and students, and angry demonstrations against economic disruption and the Civil War broke out nationwide in May 1947, just a month after the Empsons' arrival. The national deficit rose to 70 per cent of expenditure during 1947, and then to 80 per cent in 1948; and the currency would collapse in August 1948: 'the wholesale price index in Shanghai reached a level 6,600,000 times that of 1937.'[8] It was hardly surprising, then, that such conditions led to wide-scale protests by both students and faculty, despite often vicious opposition by Chiang Kai-shek's forces.

On one such occasion, in the face of potentially ruthless opposition from police and military agencies, the 3,537 students of Peita advisedly withdrew their plans for a protest march on 2 June. All the same, as Hetta Empson wrote in an article published the next month in the South African paper *Die Suiderstem* (*Voice of the South*), under the headline 'Ontevredenheid Oor Burgeroorlog In China: Afrikaner Se Undrukke' ('Discontent over the Civil War in China: An Afrikaner's Impressions'), the level of official intimidation ran grimly high:

On the night of 1 June the Government imposed martial law and a curfew from 10 pm to 6 am. On that night all streets in the university quarter, where we live, were blocked with barbed wire barricades and ramparts of bricks in baskets. Soldiers mounted guard with bayonets drawn. The students announced a day before this that they did not intend to hold any public demonstrations. Their intention was merely to be absent from classes and to conduct a memorial service in the University building to commemorate their dead comrades. They took the massive barricades and the severance of the University from the city as an insult. The methods were used to isolate other universities at Yenching, Tsinghua and Fujen. My husband and I got out our bicycles . . .and we were persistently intercepted by surly militia. By good fortune a student showed us a way through a dried stream bed [the 'Big Ditch', as the students called it] between two guarded bridges. The word was that we should buy coal on that day in the face of escalating prices and our plan was to draw cash in another part of town. The rest of the city seemed entirely normal and we returned without further incident.

In the afternoon the Mayor of Peking visited the city with the news that the road blocks would be removed in the night. In the course of an interview with the students he was apparently severely taken to task over the isolation of the university area. The meeting was disrupted after his departure by thugs who set about laying into the students. The students took this intervention by non-uniformed elements to be a Government provocation. There was a rumour of a fascist coup designed to topple the Government.

Students resumed classes after two days but in Shanghai and certain other centres the strikes lasted longer. There was no further bloodshed. The general view is that the students acted with restraint in conducting no demonstrations.[9]

In April 1948 Empson reported: 'There is a strike on at present in the universities, owing to a series of attacks on students by the secret police; rather puzzling, I think, because it seems not at all to the advantage of the Government to make trouble, but no doubt the secret police are an independent power with its own abstruse game to play.'[10] Throughout his first year in Peiping, when he knew for certain relatively little of the full scale of the Communist floodtide, it was difficult to comprehend that the repressiveness of the Nationalist authorities was in truth a function of weakness and desperation.

As the cold end of the year closed in, the Empsons moved into the smaller rooms of their quarters, so as to benefit from their coal stoves: 'the seasons come late because there is such a long way to go from the heat to the cold or back again,' Empson wrote on 21 November, 'and the great swing from one to the other is rather like being at sea. The dollar is driving downwards with the same majestic determination but prices in pounds on the open market are pretty steady. The Americans here seem quite baffled to know what their government is going to do. The political situation seems likely to continue as a stalemate for some time.'[11] Everyone sighed for a settlement by the end of the year, but it would take yet another full year before the Civil War would reach its climacteric.

The year 1948—a year when General Fu Tso-yi, a man with a high reputation both for military ability and for honest leadership, was appointed Commander of a new North China Communist Suppression Headquarters centred in Peiping, and when a tight curfew was regularly enforced from midnight until early morning—became for the student body the year of 'Anti-Oppression Anti-Hunger'. Constantly repressed by authoritarian measures, as well as by penury and hunger that went unrelieved by the Nationalist government, the students organized themselves for far more concerted protests against an administration they now openly defied as 'anti-democratic'. Students of the National Peking University set up a Self-Governing Association under the overall control of the North China Student Union in order to contest the 'reactionary' treatment they suffered, the unjustifiable violence and random killings.

Perhaps the most impressive demonstration of the early part of the year took place within the university precincts on 7 January, soon after five students had been arrested by the Peiping Garrison Commander on charges of being Communist conspirators. A few days earlier, a number of students had been injured, and others arrested, during a demonstration at Tungchi University in Shanghai. The mass rally at Peita in January therefore aimed to show solidarity with the students of Tungchi University as well as to denounce the arrests in Peiping. Some 2,000 students assembled in the large central square of the university known as 'Democratic Ground', which had been plastered with handwritten newspapers, slogans and cartoons (including some that cried up the USA as an 'ally of reaction'), to hail student leaders and sympathetic professors who indicted the Kuomintang and the Central Government for betraying the people and the sacred word 'constitution'. After the speeches came several short plays and songs illustrating varieties of government oppression.[12]

Empson, who sat with the congregation of students, could follow the spirit if not the words of the sometimes shrilly emotional speakers, and he clearly associated himself with the just cause of the occasion, which he would never forget. What particularly moved him on the day was a performance of a modern work called the 'Yellow River Cantata', sung by about a hundred men and women, not only because it incorporated several indigenous folksongs and was scored for Western instruments— though it was 'not a bastard art,' he stressed[13]—but also because he appreciated that the subject of the cantata was Communist guerilla resistance to the Japanese: Chiang Kai-shek had proscribed any performance of the work. 'The peasant singing is...very unlike the strained voice of the Chinese ruling-class music, popular in the cities through opera,' Empson acutely noted. 'Basing the revolution on the peasants thus gave a fair case here for letting in European techniques...I thought it hauntingly beautiful, all the more in the late dusk in the great square with a tense audience waiting for the liberation of the city.'[14] The song seemed so much in tune with the hearts and hopes of the people, the common mass of both students and peasants, that Empson found himself weeping in sympathy with the clarion call it sounded.

According to one of his students, the literary scholar Jin Di, Empson himself manifested a courageous commitment to the anti-oppressive cause. In an article published soon after Empson's death, Professor Jin recalled:

One lively scene remains fresh in my memory....We two [Jin Di and WE] and his wife went out and found the streets blockaded by a large number of military police with muzzles aiming at the masses, and nobody was allowed to approach the paraders or enter the campus. Professor Empson was

burning with anger in spite of the white terror; he told us 'Let's go in' and
went forward against the rifles, just like entering an unpeopled land. When
the Kuomintang officers and soldiers saw such a tiny group of three daring
to break their blockade line, and especially when they saw a heavily-
bearded foreigner in the lead, they couldn't help making way for us.

Having entered the campus, Professor Empson didn't go further than to
discuss the situation with acquaintances among the crowds in 'Democracy
Square' behind 'Red Building'. However, he unequivocally showed his
concern and indignation and then went upstairs to observe those broken
windows. He hurried to share with the threatened masses a bitter hatred of
the enemy in such a severe atmosphere. No wonder his simple and un-
adorned image with his staring eyes should be deeply imprinted in our
minds.[15]

Even allowing for the straight-faced style of Jin Di's account, which takes
pains to square itself with the official history and idiolect of New China,
Empson did indeed feel 'concern and indignation' for the perils of the
university and his students. However, there is little other evidence to
suggest that in 1948 he felt in himself 'a bitter hatred of the enemy'—the
municipal and national authority of the Kuomintang—or that he yet
regarded Generalissimo Chiang Kai-shek as irredeemably unregenerate.
At least in 1947–8, most foreigners and many Chinese simply wanted an
end to the hostilities, even a coalition government if it were practicable.

Empson felt an emotional commitment to the welfare of his students
and colleagues which fell well short of the ideological identification with
Mao Tse-tung's campaign which increasing numbers of students avowed.
Hetta Empson, who was already a member of the Communist Party of
Great Britain, played a more active role in working for the progressive
cause in China. But even though Empson did not question her principled
position, he would not be quick to assume Communist doctrine for
himself. As in Japan in the early 1930s, and during the Chinese War of
Resistance later in the decade, when national politics impinged upon his
classroom, so in the late 1940s he sustained his long-standing policy of
pressing the students to quiz any creed and its specifics, whether political
or literary, rather than to swallow them whole.

At Peita, where the head of the English Department was a philologist
named Yuan Chia-hua—a sympathetic man whom Empson called 'our
chief friend here'[16]—he taught classes in Shakespeare; Seventeenth and
Eighteenth Century poetry; and modern British poetry (including Hardy,
Sidney Keyes, Hopkins, Housman, Yeats, Eliot, Pound, Lawrence, Auden,

Spender, Dylan Thomas, and even some of his own work: 'Legal Fiction' and 'Missing Dates'), as well as a fourth-year Composition class for students majoring in English. In addition, he gave a weekly lecture on Shakespeare at Tsinghua (Qinghua) University, about seven flat miles outside the walled city, where he would cycle in all weathers. In winter he would wear socks on his hands, cheerily picking himself up whenever he fell on the ice, though he would look exhausted when he got back home.[17] 'William still cycles every Monday, come hell come fine weather,' wrote Hetta to some friends at Christmas 1949. 'He fell off three times on the day of the big ice, but he says everyone else was falling off much more.'[18] Even an unpleasant dental appointment did not deter him from his duty: Hetta Empson had occasion to write to a friend one sultry April day in 1950 that their dentist had 'lanced poor William's gum where a piece of bone from his old tooth is trying to get out. Anyway he isn't having pains any more though the bone hasn't come out and off he went to Tsinghua on his bicycle this morning wearing his big fur hat though it was quite sunny and hot.'[19] Never arriving late for a class, he always wore the same clothes, and his only acknowledgement of the changing seasons—and his only preliminary action before launching into his lecture—would be to hurl his jacket into a corner of the room if the weather was warm.

For their part, the students had trouble following his rapid and usually unscripted delivery of information and ideas. He seemed to be so absorbed in intensely speaking thoughts that he could neither lift his voice out his beard nor moderate the speed of his delivery. Instead, with a piece of chalk in his right hand and an eraser in the left, he would write out the entirety of his lecture on a pair of blackboards, only occasionally changing a single word. When the second board was covered, he would rub out the first (using his sleeve if the rubber had gone missing), and so on until the class ended, with the result that he covered himself with a heavy layer of dust of which he seemed unaware. The handwriting was strong and beautiful, and some of the students tried to emulate it. Hardly ever looking at the class, he would roll his eyes upwards as he reflected and recited; all of which led James J. Y. Liu (later Professor of Chinese and Comparative Literature at Stanford University) to discern that his enthusiasm for writing on the blackboard stemmed from a wish to avoid 'eye contact'—'for he seemed to me a shy person'.[20] (This was not an unconscious mechanism on Empson's part: he was quite aware he had the 'trick' of preferring not to look anyone in the eye.) The students would thus be kept fully occupied—ears, eyes, hands—though many of them were so busy copying down the words on the blackboard that they failed to listen to him at the same time.

Now and again, the class would be startled out of its transcriptive absorption when Empson, lost in thought while stepping off to one side, gave the fallen rubber a mighty sudden kick.

He was by no means oblivious to the students' difficulties in following his speech and ideas. Indeed, he almost defiantly rationalized his classroom procedure. As he wrote in his first annual report for the British Council in November 1948, he had no time at all for the kind of lecturer who delayed everyone's progress until such time as the weakest member of the class developed the capacity to answer a random question in English:

> while anxious to be friendly I have always assumed that it is not my business to please the students. Beyond a certain point 'talking over their heads' would of course become a farce, but there is always a practical question whether you are helping perhaps only two or three people in the lecture-room or whether you are trying to raise the low level of the worst ten people. My own impression of going to lectures in Cambridge was that the only good ones were the rousing ones, and they were always admittedly difficult. I am employed to lecture to people in their last year or so at a university, and unless the standard is high there it is high nowhere, within the experience of the persons taught. I therefore always give lectures which I would be prepared to give anywhere else, and are probably beyond the capacity of most of the students. However this is not as harsh as it appears, because the real difficulty for the students does not lie in any general intellectual capacity (I have again and again been surprised by their capacities) but by the mere difficulty of listening to spoken English. I therefore write everything I have to say on the blackboard and read out everything I have written at least twice before I rub it out. I never ask the class to speak and indeed have such a fixed habit of not looking at the class that I often do not know when old friends are present. Long habit makes this writing process quite quick...Of course handwriting is also hard to read, as must be learned from the process of reading what is on the board, but this is a training in hearing spoken English. Most Chinese (or Japanese) students are good at reading but have no experience of the spoken English voice, and the combination is useful to them.[21]

Justifiably proud of his prowess as a teacher who 'carried his subject in his head', he lectured less about large themes and movements than about individual poets and poems. His method was that of close critical reading, all the time glossing bits of difficult diction and making extensive use of paraphrase to tease complexities into accessible sense. At least one of his students, Zhao Shaowei, copied down from the blackboard every single word he wrote in his course on Seventeenth and Eighteenth-Century Poetry, and she managed to preserve her two packed notebooks, running to more than 120 pages, even throughout the Cultural Revolution (which many Chinese now more aptly term the 'Severe Catastrophe'). Her transcriptions show that Empson covered a comprehensive range of the major poetry of the period, from Donne and Jonson to Cowper and Coleridge, and including Herrick, Herbert, Crashaw, Vaughan, Marvell, Milton (excluding *Paradise Lost*, because the course concentrated on lyric poetry), Lovelace, Denham, Dryden, Rochester, Pope, Gray, Collins, and Smart.

Most of his expositions are uncontentious, and always set out with the throwaway lucidity of his published writings and conversation. Yet the very limpidity of his often descriptive mode of analysis releases meaning in a way that is at once witty and illuminating, as well as being disarmingly encouraging to the anxious Chinese student, who all too often balked at the creative risks of critical worrying. Lovelace's 'The Grasshopper', Empson told his class, for example, 'uses the grasshopper (cicada) to show the shortness of life, and might be expected to tell you to take pleasure quickly, but it (more thoughtfully) tells you to imitate the summer grasshopper all through the winter; it is not quite clear how you can.'

Pope's 'Essay on Women' speaks exclusively of 'rich upperclass women':

> when he describes the faults all women have he means only this rather specialized kind of woman . . .
>
> Pope's attempts to flatter a woman now seem positively insulting; he betrays great contempt for all women while he is doing it. But at the time it seemed the height of delicacy and fashionable politeness . . .
>
> After a particularly savage attack Pope always moves round to end on a moral and affectionate tone.

Characteristically he goes on, with particular reference to Pope's 'Epistle to Dr Arbuthnot', to defend the sincerity of the poet's moral purposes on a basis of clear-sighted logic. 'Some critics recently have felt that the moralizing of Pope is hypocrisy and therefore disgusting, whereas the savage attacks are good jokes. This is a misreading, I think. Pope takes the moralizing seriously and thinks it is the basis for the attacks; also, if you had only the attacks not the warm-hearted paragraphs the poem would become nauseating.' (Donne's 'Love's Deity' provoked from him this personal observation: 'I can't believe men used to love women who scorned them.') On the same basis he is equally apt to dispel nonsense, as when writing about Dryden's 'To Mrs Killigrew': 'It is a handsome piece of flattery for which he was paid . . . Some critics say that his real enthusiasm for poetry in general is used to build up this piece of false praise. But after all it is rather a disgusting piece.'

Some of the lectures drew on the insights and arguments of *Seven Types of Ambiguity*; others rehearsed versions of *Some Versions of Pastoral*, showing once again how the literary device of 'putting the complex into the simple' can work to establish the virtue of 'a proper or beautiful relation between rich and poor'. He told his often radicalized Chinese students: 'The poet who says his art gives mysterious powers (the main romantic idea) usually also says he is including in himself his whole society; or simply (as in [Cowper's] "The Castaway") that he is parallel to the labouring man. This is the connection, rather obscure but recognised at the time, between the growth of romanticism and left-wing politics.' In an unscripted talk on 'The Castaway', broadcast by the BBC some seven years later, he expanded upon this idea of the paradoxically selfless (and ironically un-Christian) assumption of Romantic poetry, in a way that still chimes with his earlier theory of pastoral: 'It says that the artist has a duty to express his whole society, or the historical period which his society is just getting into, and that this process does good to the society; not to him, it's altruistic, and indeed it does good to later societies, and yet he can only do this—he can only discover what he has to express— by being ruthlessly sincere, which in effect means self-centred.'

Other lectures forge similar links between his writings on pastoral and his post-war campaign of anti-Christian revisionism. His first substantial piece on 'The Rime of the Ancient Mariner' (published in 1964), for example, is anticipated in these lecture-remarks at Peita: 'The poem has a "moral", two verses from the end, "He prayeth best that loveth best" . . . But taken simply this is an immoral moral; the Mariner did not deserve all this suffering for killing one bird, nor did the rest of the crew deserve to die for saying it brought good luck. The idea is crossed with a less religious and more primitive idea, that delight in the world when terrible gives you strength to control it.' Empson's consistency of thought on the subject becomes fully apparent when one compares those remarks with his comments on the 'Ancient Mariner' in an earlier essay, 'Marvell's Garden' (from *Some Versions of Pastoral*): 'by delight in Nature when terrible man gains strength to control it . . . The reason it was a magical crime for a sailor to kill an albatross is that it both occurs among terrible scenes of Nature and symbolises man's power to extract life from them, so ought doubly to be delighted in . . . This is what Coleridge meant by alternately saying that the poem has too much of the moral and too little; knowing what the conventional phrases of modern Christianity ought to mean he thought he could shift to a conventional moral that needs to be based upon the real one.'

Christian literary critics, he would later proclaim, insultingly reduce to pious paradox all too many productions of complex mental struggle: they offend authorial integrity by bleeding works of literature of their rational conflicts and moral resistances. Whereas Christianity applauds a wicked God whom the Gospels depict as being satisfied by the Crucifixion, a decently protestant morality can be sustained without deference to such a sadistic Revelation. Why posit a God in the image of humankind's basest characteristics? Continually distressed by the Christianizing orthodoxy of modern literary criticism, he had recently come across Aldous Huxley's digest, *The Perennial Philosophy* (1946), and he found in it the revelation of a humane dispensation, a godhead immanent in the world, which he would salute, if not formally espouse, for the rest of his life. In a later article entitled 'Resurrection' (1964), to take just one example from among many, he eagerly endorsed Huxley's 'answer' that 'one should stop believing in this all-executive Father [of Christianity], but accept an impersonal 'Divine Ground', as in Hinduism and in the mystics of all other religions; thus becoming morally free.' It was small wonder, then, that in Peking in 1948 he felt delighted to discover in Henry Vaughan's poem 'The Night' a compelling argument that satisfied his own quasi-Pantheistic liking (and which the consensus of later commentators has confirmed): 'He is a mystical writer who wants to be re-absorbed into the divine; he does not think of God as a clear-cut person, so the paradoxes on light and darkness are needed = the real brightness for him would be like darkness because like losing his own personality (Buddhist idea).'

So too, he rejoiced in the opportunity to rescue John Donne's independent and deeply questioning intelligence from the orthodox version which characterizes him as a playful lyricist who eventually made good as a devout divine: 'All Donne's conceits treating two lovers as a unique divine pattern for the rest of the world are a sort of parody of (or simply a comparison to) the idea of the Incarnation.' That succinct piece of pedagogy, as professed to an audience of Chinese youth in 1948, recapitulates the searching critique that informs Empson's abandoned novel, 'The Royal Beasts', dating from ten years earlier. More crucially, it prepared him for further combat the very next year, when he found that Rosemond Tuve (in her book *Elizabethan and Metaphysical Imagery*) had in a real sense depersonalized the fighting originality of the mind and conscience of John Donne by arguing for the central importance in his poetry of the rhetorical tradition. Empson snapped back at Tuve that Donne 'incessantly clashed the rhetorical claim that some individual or pair of individuals was the Logos against the new ideas of Copernicus, in the only form which made them a practical danger to theology—the idea that there is life on other planets, to which Christ presumably has not gone.' In 1957 he further prosecuted his claims for the fundamental scepticism of Donne in his long article 'Donne the Space Man', particularly in the key assertion that 'The young Donne, to judge from his poems, believed that every planet could have its Incarnation, and believed this with delight, because it automatically liberated an independent conscience from any earthly religious authority'; and he again expounded his views on Donne some years lates, in a fierce critique of Helen Gardner's edition of *The Elegies, and the Songs and Sonnets* (1966), which he believed worked to dismantle Donne's reputation as a thinker 'who cast an independent eye on Church and State'—and all because of the editor's obviously biased piousness.

Peita's students were plum products, intelligent, hard-working and determined; though in the year 1947–8 they seemed to Empson more keen to learn a given line than to think through texts and issues from a variety of angles. It is impossible to know how many of his students kept up with the uncompromisingly brisk pace he set through English poetry, his patiently basic commentaries and casual blazing insights: exemplary simplifications spiked with unorthodoxy. If they had even heard of *Seven Types of Ambiguity* before they encountered his peculiar method of teaching, they understood the book to be a 'marvellous flower' of Western literary criticism and were most unlikely to have read it. Politics felt more consumingly real, with greater relevance, than the academic matter of poetry. They well knew that in 1947 the Red Army had gone on the offensive against the Nationalists and was making significant territorial gains; and being so preoccupied by the progressive political situation, some few students started to leak away from Peiping to join the 'liberating' Communists. Those who remained, and gave their lessons serious attention, were overwhelmed by the perceptive genius with which Empson pinned their critical faculties to the text in hand. Many of them clearly grew to revere him, and to delight in his odd conduct. All the same, one of his best students of the year, as Empson himself reported at the time, 'remarked that he just could not keep awake in my lectures on *Hamlet*. He was busy falling into great confusion about politics, and in the end the awful day came (after thorough discussion all round) when he said that Communists wouldn't *have* him (quite understandably, I think) so he had much better have kept awake at the *Hamlet* lectures after all.'[22]

The students often felt particularly baffled by his weekly habit of asking them to spend a short period, perhaps no more than five minutes, writing a piece on a question of a general nature, as a test of knowledge as well as of their literacy in English; at other times, he would ask them to discuss the topic in class. His own account of the procedure makes rich reading: 'I want to pay a small tribute to what may be called the collective mind of the average Chinese class; which is relevant here because one so often finds students protesting that they are not trained psychologists or historians or whatever the topic may require. I have three times (lacking a text at the moment) asked a class to discuss why two and two make four. There are only about five answers to this question, and no one student ever gave all five; but each class always gave all five. This being all that the human mind can do, on a rather subtle question, I think that the spread of opinion provided by a small class of this type is likely to cover most questions that are brought up.'[23] Liu Jo-tuan, one of the students who were faced with this poser, remembers that she felt at a total loss.[24]

Samples of his comments on the essays of Chang Chin-yen (Zhang Jin-yan), who was to pursue a career in literary criticism as a direct consequence of Empson's teaching and influence (he was to become a Professor in the Institute of Philosophy at the Chinese Academy of Social Sciences in Beijing), illustrate the clarity and directness of his dealings with the students:

> This is a good piece of criticism. I wish you would go on and do detailed work like this on something else. I find, looking at the poem [Eliot's *Four Quartets*] again, that I admire it all except the last Quartet (and in that admire II). But it is a very airless kind of poetry.
>
> You pick out the really important idea in the essay and express it well, but you don't discuss whether metaphors can work by *un*likeness. I think Richards lets his generalization spread too widely there—you can't have a "disparity action", an effect from *un*likeness, unless you first have likeness.[25]

In general, he was to report, he found that the students in his class on Twentieth-century poetry handed in 'rather a flat line of final essay…because all these boys and girls are too "modern" for it; until you get to G. S. Fraser, whom they were usually prepared to praise. Eliot and Yeats for instance simply seemed Fascists and nothing you could say would get them away from that. But the same of course would be true if I were lecturing in Hampstead; the Chinese student audience, I am rather anxious to point out, is precisely like the Hampstead audience as soon as some rather minor obstacles such as language can be got over.'[26]

Despite the slowly dwindling attendance at class, and instances of lack of interest or serious displeasure evinced by the students, he simply refused to be thrown off professional balance. When one student decided at the end of the year to turn away from English literature as a worthwhile subject—a situation which any other teacher might lament with a measure of self-reproach—Empson construed the case as signalling a positively 'genuine reaction'. He related this merry story in his Inaugural lecture at Sheffield:

> I was rather pleased one year in China, when I had a course on modern poetry, *The Waste Land* and all that, and at the end a student wrote in a most friendly way to explain why he wasn't taking the exam. It wasn't that he couldn't understand *The Waste Land*, he said, in fact after my lectures the poem was perfectly clear; but it had turned out to be disgusting nonsense, and he had decided to join the engineering department. Now there a teacher is bound to feel solid satisfaction; he is getting definite results. What I do think is that the effect of having the extra language obstacle, and the practice of composing a written summary on the spot, to write on the blackboard, made what is really a universal difficulty rather simpler than usual.

He could be kindly and indulgent to the students. Huang Ming-yeh, who was later to teach at Peking University, remembers that the professor allowed him on one occasion to write for three hours during a two-hour exam.[27]

With a certain number of his students absconding to join the liberating army of the Communists, and the remainder grimly and understandably preoccupied with politics and poverty, it is a wonder that Empson managed to make any genuine progress with his teaching. Apart from the delight of discovering the uncommon talent of a student such as Jin Fa-shen, there is little doubt that he found the academic session ending in 1948 a real struggle. He conceded in his report to the British Council that on the whole his students tended to be uninterested in both metaphysical and modern poetry (and indeed he felt ready to cut out Donne and Eliot 'after the communists arrive', if only he could be kept on to profess another subject to which he felt convinced he had the key: the teaching of elementary English in Middle Schools, using a slightly modified version of Basic English), though he believed that 'the appallingly difficult language of the major Shakespeare plays' did not deter them a jot.[28] (At some time during 1948 the Empsons took part in a reading of *Othello* that was put on at the British Embassy: Hetta was the upright Desdemona to Empson's sonorously insidious Iago.)[29]

In 1948 the head of the British Council in China was Lynda Grier, an economist who had just been appointed to the Nanking office at the surprising age of 68, after serving for over a quarter of a century as the doughty and large-hearted principal of Lady Margaret Hall in Oxford.[30] Notwithstanding the fact that she had recently done a successful lecture-tour of China, she had no experience of running an organization of such far-flung and anfractuous complexity as the China branch of the British Council in a time of national emergency; and her response to Empson's report was so much the less substantive or helpfully constructive than glowingly insipid:

> I am delighted that you are prepared to stay on 'whatever'. For I am sure that work such as yours under any regime is likely to be appreciated & I have no doubt whatever that it will be worth while. So I strongly hope that circumstances will not arise which make it impossible for you to remain, & I cannot imagine such.
>
> Whether it was right to risk having the children there during the emergency time alone will show...Please take this not as a protest in a matter which is none of my business. But I always hoped that you would stay, for...I had heard so much of the work you were doing that I knew it would be a most serious loss to Peita, to Peiping, to the teaching of English in China, & to the work of the Council in China if you went...Perhaps it is merely jejune to ask why Shakespeare seems more genuine & sensible to the Chinese than any other writer. For I suppose it is just one more proof that not time or space or even somewhat archaic language can interfere with the appeal of genius. I sometimes feel it a little tame to be as constantly knocked out by Shakespeare as I am & it is nice to know that it happens to so many others in other lands...
>
> I sympathise with the Chinese students about modern poetry, but am rather surprised that they do not respond more to the mystics of the 17th century. But I do not think that there I have got at the Chinese mind, which is philosophical without being mystical...perhaps.[31]

Godmotherly fuss and flattery would not help to keep Empson's classes on course. Only through individual initiative could he achieve significant educational results, especially when more and more of his students seemed to be closing their minds to anything other than the nostrum of Communism. But that sort of self-blinkering was something he felt he could certainly alleviate: he would refuse to let them surrender their heads to the herd.

One of his first practical steps on arriving at Peita was to assemble and distribute an anthology of demanding English texts—including A. C. Bradley's 'Hegel's Theory of Tragedy' and I. A. Richards on metaphor (from *The Philosophy of Rhetoric*), as well as three humorous essays—for discussion in his Composition classes. In a preface to the collection he insisted that his choice of essays was designed to give the students 'practice at arguing in the language, using it to examine a theory...In an ideal case, the class has already expressed the various possible views on the subject, or divided fairly evenly for and against the author; so that the main thing the teacher has to do is to introduce the students to each others' minds. Without giving the names of the students whose sentences are written on the blackboard, and without needing to express any opinion of his own (though he had better not appear evasive), he can give the class a sort of map of the possible opinions and their interrelations; and meanwhile it becomes easy to show that "this" argument used a verbal fallacy, whereas "that" one may be quite sound but wasn't put in a way that would convince an opponent.' While the students, he went on, 'are expected to criticize the printed text,' the teacher 'should appeal all the time to the students' sense of fact, their sense of how far a text can be trusted.'

No one ever knew for sure how many of Peita's students were secret Communists, though informed estimates put the number of sympathizers as high as 50 per cent; certainly a majority were anti-Government, if not avowedly Leftist, and had lost faith in the prospect of a coalition government. But Empson insisted upon the supreme importance of independent judgement, and determined in his Composition class that the students should not be captivated by Communist dogma, or any other line of thought, without first examining it from every possible (and preferably sceptical) angle. If the students blandly praised a passage in the anthology, he would boldly write on the blackboard: 'So far this class has committed itself to agreeing with the following doctrines...If you believe everything you read you are much worse off than if you were unable to read at all. No Chinese peasant would believe this obvious nonsense that you pretend to agree with because you think teacher wants you to agree with it. Unless you learn to think for yourself your whole education is only a means of making you more purblind than if you had been left at home.'[32]

The students rose to his unremitting challenge after just a few weeks:

> Nobody had ever said this to them before in class and it really made their writing entirely different in the course of a short year. I know how elementary it will sound to you [he told Grier], but it does not seem so elementary in a civil war when half the class writes communist nonsense (and I have to teach them what Marx did say) and the other half talks anti-popular stuff (and I have to say Not even the British or the Americans believe that) and then I have to try to explain on the blackboard that any serious human problem is a permanent one, quite unaffected by the current civil war...
> Last year I thought the first replies from the Composition class were quite

unrecognisable as from the same authors as the last five or six replies. I recognise that this boast may appear offensive to my superiors in Peita, but the political facts of the situation are simple and well-known. It is not that I was clever (I am continually conscious of thoughtless mistakes) but that a Chinese teacher under civil war conditions cannot challenge his students to write quite freely, whereas a foreigner can. It is really a surprise to a semi-communist student, once he has been induced to feel that he can write freely, to find that he can be answered or rather included in a larger picture where his views turn out to be deduced from more general theories which need not necessarily support him. I do not claim ever to have converted a Communist student, still less that I know which communist students I had (even the students I know well are asked to write only their numbers on their essays) but I do consider I had a noticeably humanising effect on the communist students in the class, and if I can do that at all I want to go on doing it as long as I can.[33]

He had no stake in curbing the rise of Communist sympathy among his students, nor did his contract permit him to involve himself in politics; but he felt he should oblige the students to question easy alignments, whether party or literary, and the seductions of rhetoric. (Lynda Grier approved of his method: 'The composition class with its insistence on making the students criticise & think, & argue, seems to me invaluable from my small experience.')

Although no specific examples survive from his Composition classes, it is evident that many such discussions would have reflected the analytical concerns of the essays he was working on at the time, including 'A is B', which would find their way into *The Structure of Complex Words*. In that work he argued, the supposedly 'emotive' use of language in literature must be brought to public account, for words invariably assert propositions or arguments even as they conceal them by appealing to common understanding. Seemingly simple words such as 'wit', 'sense', 'honest', and 'all' include within themselves various senses, attitudes and (crucially) assertions. Empson regarded his 'attempt to codify some basic facts about language'—how individual words accumulate strata of senses and implications, and how literature exploits those layered suggestions—as an essentially linguistic pursuit. He set out to describe the 'logical structure' at work in the process. The process of 'unpacking' or atomising words is essentially a development of his earlier examination of ambiguity and pastoral: it insists that the commotion and conflict—'the complexity of meaning' in literature—must always be available to rational analysis. 'Roughly,' he wrote when summing up his first three books (and as he would have charged his Chinese students to heed), 'the moral is that a developing society decides practical questions more by the way it interprets words it thinks obvious and traditional than by its official statements of dogma.'

Thus, if questions about the relationship between Nationalism and Communism in China came up in his classroom, his response would have rehearsed thoughts such as these from *The Structure of Complex Words*:

> The practice of making deep philosophical assertions in the form 'A is B', obviously prominent among the Germans, seems to have come in with the first translations of the Hindu sacred texts. The 'That art Thou' of Hindu mysticism ('with the accent on the thou') may well have a historical connection with 'Might is Right'; though nationalism is about the last idea it was originally intended to convey. The idea that everything is One seems to have been particularly welcome, not merely where the intellectuals were moving away from Christianity, but where a lack of national unity made them feel insecure . . . The relations of Marxism to Hegel are a more baffling topic, but the One might be taken to imply either that the whole world should become communist or that no activity can be independent of the class struggle. I do not think that much weight can be put on this historical approach . . . But, if someone objects that my treatment of the 'A is B' slogan tends to drag in too much undigested philosophy, I can answer that slogans of this type have really been used to hint at these philosophical ideas.[34]

Nevertheless, history was rapidly outrunning theory. By the middle of 1948, when Empson was destined to go and lecture American students at the Kenyon summer school, the US government had ever more grievously provoked the Chinese students' sense of nationalism. Early in April, the China Aid Act authorised payment to the Chinese Nationalist Government of US $338 million in economic aid and $125 million in special grants for the next financial year. Thereafter, on 20 May, President Truman authorized the appropriation of $100 million in the same budget so as to rehabilitate the Japanese economy. Naturally, the Chinese intellectuals could not fail to recognize that the Americans would do everything in their power to support Chiang Kai-shek the anti-Communist; and they knew from the dread experience of recent history that a strong Japan could all too soon compound the civil war with a renewed external threat. Ambassador Leighton Stuart hollowly asserted on 4 June, 'I defy anyone to produce a single shred of evidence that any part of Japanese military power is being restored or that there is any intention on the part of the U.S. other than to assure that it will never rise again', and warned of the depressing consequences of a new upsurge of anti-American sentiment. 'In reply,' as

Suzanne Pepper has related, '437 professors from colleges and universities in Peiping addressed Dr. Stuart as their former colleague, offering evidence that the U.S. was indeed restoring Japan's military capabilities, and rebuilding Japan without any regard for the lessons of history, which taught that China would be the victim.'[35]

Students organized demonstrations throughout May and June to protest against the new American policy of rebuilding Japan—at Tsinghua, the week beginning 23 May became 'Oppose American Support of Japan Week'—and as always the Nationalist Government would be brutal in seeking to suppress them. On 9 June, for instance, the Peiping police fired on parading students, and attacked them with clubs and rocks. On 30 May the American Consul General in Shanghai, John M. Cabot, managed only to exacerbate the situation when he insultingly admonished the Chinese: 'Many [in the USA] will bitterly retort that students getting their education through the beneficence of Americans who have contributed their mites to knowledge and understanding—students whose very food depends upon the labor of the American farmer and the generosity of the American taxpayer—should not spread calumnies against the U.S.'

Like his Chinese colleagues and students, Empson had no doubt about the truth of the situation, and would have a severe political message to carry to the USA in June. In the meantime, in a letter of 18 May, he rightly anticipated the next crackdown in Peiping while sympathising with the students' inability to formulate a viable political programme of their own:

We were expecting a whirl of strikes and persecutions in May, but so far it is passing off quietly. Last month the government hired a mob of several thousand hooligans described as an anti-communist students' movement to attack the universities, and the foolish hooligans broke in to a compound for professors here and broke a lot of their windows before being whistled off. This had an excellent effect on the morale of the Peita professors, who came out on strike on their own account and signed a very firm document protesting against secret police illtreatment of students. The government has a baffling capacity for putting itself in the wrong (this is only one example)...Of course it is reasonable enough in the middle of a civil war for any government to try to put down propaganda for the enemy, and that is really a difficult job because the ideas of the students are so very woolly, though very right-minded I think, that you can hardly say which are communists even when they are being frank with you. Which, I mean, would become communists if they were to decide after being informed; the point is that they seem so very uninformed. But they are very patient and disciplined and indeed brave about their own movement, which is largely a matter of trying to protect fellow students. In general I think their political position is the unimpeachable but not very helpful one that the civil war had better stop and something sensible had better happen afterwards.[36]

He was left in no doubt that the Nationalist economy was on the brink of collapse when he went to buy his airline ticket to the USA. 'One could not give a cheque for the ticket, because that would take a day to pass through the bank, and then be worth much less. We carried to the air-line office a military duffle-bag full of the highest denomination of paper money, and four men counted it all day; towards the fall of eve, with patient triumph, they said: "You're two million short," but I was just in time to get this extra sop out of the bank, and the ticket was won.'[37]

The Communist army was certain to take Peiping; it was only a question of when they would make their move—'but with any luck we may be able to stay on. If they arrive when I am in America it may be embarrassing, as the family stays in China.'[38]

4

Sounding the South: Kenyon College, Summer 1948

'**O**HIO is nice after all those deserts,' Empson wrote from Gambier on 24 June (registration day at Kenyon), after travelling overland from the west coast:

it is damp with a lot of trees, and looks in a general way like England, though I don't know which county... As for me I am not corrupting anybody so far; no doubt they think me as dull as I do them... Kenyon College ... has rather pleasant early Victorian Gothic excessively hidden by creepers.[1]

According to John Crowe Ransom, the small town and the English visitor seemed in the beginning 'hopelessly alien' to each other. 'Empson ... kept his guard up for weeks, but at last it broke down. He was admired and venerated...'[2]

Empson seemed to be unaware that he cut a strange figure as he wandered round the green and beautifully arboreal campus with its grey buildings. His perceived peculiarities included the fact that he sported a resplendent bush of weird black beard and talked to himself as he chain-smoked through a long cigarette holder. One student would recall, 'He was the most detached, impartial person I have ever seen... He looked peculiar and he acted nervous. But there was something inside the man so much bigger than his peculiarities and his nervousness that his students loved his eccentricities.'[3] For his own part, Empson wrote: 'I so often find when I have been getting sick of the Americans that it is a salutary shock to come up against some of the British.'[4] In his room in the West Wing of the building called Old Kenyon, the men's dormitory, he got himself up in shorts and a silk shirt ('It is hot and sticky with frequent rain and thunder storms, very pleasant I think, but doesn't make one active').[5] Out of doors, he dressed day after day in the same off-white crumpled linen suit. Only at the end of his visit, in the last week of August, did he draw a witty but dubious lesson from the peculiar spectacle he presented to the world: 'after going to a few bars I realise for the first time how I am viewed here. A beard is not wildly eccentric, but wearing whites is; it means a claim that you can afford to pay enormous laundry bills. There is a faint suspicion that I may really be a millionaire, but it is obviously more probable that I am a boastful fool. I have not seen a single other person wearing them, even when it is really hot.'[6] Ed Watkins, another student, judged him 'very shy', though for a reason which perhaps indicates less shyness than a combination of short sight and mild silliness: 'when he wore a bath-towel folded on his head for protection from the rain he would look at no one.'[7] As Ransom aptly noted, Empson was 'not at all American in his habits and mores'.

The Kenyon School of English, funded by the Rockefeller Foundation (which undertook to support the School for three years), afforded a generous stipend of $1,250 for each Fellow for the 45-day session, which was to run from 24 June to 7 August. A total of seventy-five selected students were enrolled. 'The roster of instructors was enough to pop the eyes of any major in English,' wrote *Newsweek*;[8] and indeed Empson soon enough changed his first impression as to agree: 'these people are quite interesting really I think.' In addition to John Crowe Ransom, the avuncular and courtly leader of the pack, other Fellows included Cleanth Brooks, Richard Chase, F. O. Matthiessen, Austin Warren, and Allen Tate. Although Empson liked the Dean of the School, Charles Coffin, a scholar with interests in theology and literature (including the work of John Donne), he got on best of all with Matthiessen, whom he thought 'an honest chap'[9] and 'a levelheaded creature'.[10] As for the rest, he remarked at the beginning: 'Most of the other lecturers (Tate, Warren, Brooks) are Southerners, much more pro-Empson than Matthiessen, I mean pro-ambiguity-stuff, but have mixed it up with being pro-South, anti-Machine Age, and anti-Negro. I have not yet cared to plumb this rather disagreeable complex.'[11] That he did in due course try to fight his way through the Agrarian Complex, and without pulling his punches, is suggested by a memo that Ransom penned the following year. Empson is 'gentle by disposition,' Ransom noted. 'But he has a terrible wit that serves him as a weapon if he needs it. Sometimes one catches him seeming a little uncertain whether to turn on the wit or stick to gentleness.' Yet Ransom felt somehow moved to decide, after knowing Empson for no more than eight weeks: 'The gentleness is gaining on him as he grows older.'[12] Still Empson concluded, after struggling for a while to comprehend the sublime racism of the Southerners, that his colleagues were 'anti-negro in a very charitable style and concerned to keep up the "values" of the country gentleman, who is a humanist... [O]ld John Crowe Ransom certainly tried to be a gentleman all the time, but the only effect was to make him a kind of major-domo. I thought this was really funny but went on struggling not to be drawn into agreeing with him.'[13] (Ransom's reserved and courteous manner could be off-putting for anyone who would have preferred more spontaneity.)

He was nervously excitable about his teaching. Since he was just then putting the finishing touches to *The Structure of Complex Words*, he could draw like a dazzling conjuror on the 'little novelties' of the book—including chapters such as 'Fool in Lear', 'Honest in Othello', 'Wit in the Essay on Criticism', and 'Sense in the Prelude'—to bedeck the single course he offered: 'The Key Word in the Long Poem: Shakespeare, Pope, Wordsworth'. Of the seventy-five regular students and twenty-three full-time auditors at Kenyon (many of them enrolled under the provisions of the GI Bill), he attracted twenty dedicated students and ten auditors—the latter being 'listeners to lectures but too grand to be students,' as he wryly characterized them[14]—and the class met for the standard two-hour sessions, three mornings a week over the six weeks of the school. The students were 'nice', he decided; 'clearheaded and energetic and willing'.[15] They found him stunning and stimulating, a professor fit to venerate. 'His detractors accuse him of "reading too much into" a poem,' Charles Coffin later remarked, 'but I have heard him silence a hubbub of young critics with a firm but witty insistence that "Shakespeare must have meant precisely what he said".'[16] Eric Bentley recalled: 'I attended a lecture of his on key words in Shakespeare and found it brilliant, wild, ingenious, but further from literary criticism than his earlier work.'[17] Speaking for the students themselves, Ed Watkins extolled the sparkling wisdom of the English visitor: 'He lectured as breathlessly as he read his poems, with a long descending rush... His sense of humor was probably his finest grace. After expounding for a week a complex set of semantic "equations" for the analysis of "key words" in the long poem, he turned to the class, said, "Now, if you want to, you may consider all this nonsense," and proceeded to a brilliant exposition of the texts. His lectures were as logical as they were complex; his systems are probably over-ingenious, but his insight is almost unbelievable. The man seems to know, and to understand, everything.'[18]

John Crowe Ransom, in his seminal classificatory study *The New Criticism* (1940), he formulated the theory of what he called the 'structure-texture relations' within a poem, with the structure—loosely described as 'a logical discourse of almost any kind', though different from prose—being primary.[19] 'Such a formula,' he wrote, 'indicates that we can realize the *structure*, which is the logical thought, without sacrificing the *texture*, which is the free detail—or if anybody insists, which is the feelings that engage with the free detail.'[20] A poem might be defined, albeit vaguely, as a 'loose logical structure with an irrelevant local texture'.[21] Thus an examination of the 'ontologically distinct' nature of poetic discourse should distinguish the relationship between structure and texture. But no such 'ontological' critic had yet appeared on the scene. Empson's basic error, no matter his sensitivity and perception (Ransom argued), was to focus his critical expertise on the 'irrelevant particularities' of a poem, the behaviour of its 'local objects', with the consequence that his critical writings have all been 'valuable diversions, a little to the side of the great critical problems.'[22]

Empson felt baffled to be told that his critical works had been singularly concerned with extraneous 'textural particularities', and debated the issue at hot length with Ransom in person. Like Kenneth Burke, he judged that Ransom was too intent on separating structure and texture in poetry, and that really something more like a dialectical relationship was at work. For his part, Burke argued that Ransom's terminology was in fact inadequate to represent the distinctions he posited. 'Mr. Ransom could profitably round out his terminology by some such third term as the "structure of texture" '. Empson (in a tribute written for a *festschrift* on Ransom's 76th birthday in 1964) maintained that in any case nothing in a poem could be called 'irrelevant' or merely 'local', even if it seemed unaccountable to the critic; and that (speaking for himself) he was sure to be concerned with both texture and structure:

> I was especially keen just then [in 1948] on a programme for explaining all the sources of the beauty of a poem, finding a reason for everything. I was thus disconcerted by his distinction, which kept coming back into the debates, between the 'structure' of a poem and its 'texture', described as logically unrelated to the structure. In fact I suspected that he didn't fully realise what our literary sect was aiming at . . . but in coming to know him better I had sometimes occasion to observe under his own texture the iron of his structure.[23]

But it was very hard work for Empson, argufying with Ransom, regaling his class with ceaseless brilliance (or over-ingeniousness, according to taste), and prolonging the entertainment out of hours—as well as being unusually abstemious, so as to avoid inflaming his old ulcer. He wrote home to Peking after just four weeks, momentarily jaded:

> The absence of sex life and the perpetual duty of giving a kind answer (people will show me bad poems which have somehow to be praised) are making me feel fairly neurotic. However there is no doubt that I am somebody in the academic world here and not in England.[24]

All the same, the students manifestly repaid his tireless efforts in class, as he very decently acknowledged: 'the boys have made a variety of points which if I can remember them ought to be put in the book [*Complex Words*] before it is posted off. I am arranging to stay on here a week or two to finish it.'[25] Notably too, he had a direct hand (though he probably never knew it) in stimulating the work of another scholar. When he asked the students to produce a close reading of a poem of their own choice, Bernard Hering-man tackled Hart Crane's obscure 'Voyages III'. On principle, Empson felt challenged by Heringman's essay to produce his own detailed explica-tion of the poem, running to three packed pages, though modestly begin-ning 'Just a few minor points'. Subsequently, Heringman took both pieces back to Columbia University in New York (where he was working on an MA) and showed them to his class contemporary John Unterecker, who added further pages to the chance collaborative paper. All three parties came to think their exchange eminently publishable but, as things turned out, every periodical he tried turned down the unique collaborative offer-ing. As he reported to Empson, he found it 'shocking' that John Crowe Ransom refused the essay on behalf of *Kenyon Review* with the explanation: 'I hate to celebrate a homosexual poem.'[26] Nevertheless, their joint effort bore good long-term fruit, as Unterecker recalled for me in 1987: 'It has a particular interest for me since it represented my first reading, so far as I can remember, of anything by Hart Crane—certainly the first time I ever wrote anything on him, nearly 15 years before I was to start work on the biography... I think it's a very solid piece of work—a good example of three minds working on a difficult poem, each in turn learning from and transforming what the earlier commentator had to say.'[27]

Beyond all academic satisfactions, however, Empson felt perturbed every day by the unresolved fate of China. When Hetta sent him an account of events in Peiping, her letter left him with 'a great impression of suffering and poverty bravely endured,' he said.[28] He felt constantly outraged by the obscenely oppressive misrule of the Nationalist Govern-ment in China, which was supported by the American taxpayer.

Accordingly, when it came to be his turn to give a plenary address at the Kenyon School, he took as his title 'The Relevance of Verbal Analysis in Criticism' but audaciously opened his presentation by insisting upon the radical relevance of politics; as he reported back to Hetta:

> Last Wednesday I had a public lecture in my turn on Criticism and suchlike and started off by telling them how brave the students were against the secret police the Americans sponsor, and would not take food from the Americans because they are so wicked, and so far as there was any military danger from the Chinese communists for the Americans in case of war with Russia it was entirely the result of American policy. I do not know how far you would approve of my remarks, because I said that the Russians were extremely like the Americans, both tending to be extremist out of raw national vanity, and both having a bad tradition of mob violence and police cruelty owing to their rapid growth. This was anti-Russian enough to make it go down fairly comfortably. But anyway it was all rather a flop, I thought ...[29]

But he was mistaken in thinking that his political declaration had been 'all rather a flop'. Lois Chevalier, Director of Publicity for Kenyon College (and later Senior Editor of *The Ladies' Home Journal*), would remember for a long time afterwards the moment when he 'implied that perhaps no literary criticism was very important, in the same sense that the war in China or the suffering of individuals is important. And, for a moment, all the literary people forgot that they were literary.'[30]

Empson publicly pressed his pro-Chinese charge against America just once more, when he went to give another lecture on ambiguity in criticism at Iowa University—

> again opening my remarks with about a quarter of an hour about how brave the Chinese students were under the secret police supported by the Americans and how it was a lesson for us that literary criticism must not be too footling, a somewhat thin connection, which did not cover the remarks about how if there was any military danger to the Americans (in case of war with Russia) from China it was entirely due to their policy there in the last five years or so. No questions were asked about this, but the professors afterwards were willing for a little detached chat about the topic.[31]

But one particular professor, Paul Engle (director of the Iowa Writers Workshop at Iowa), whom Empson considered 'comically 100% American', waxed fiery both in defending American capitalism and foreign policy and in criticizing British socialism. Engle later backed his challenges by letter, to which Empson promptly replied with outspoken force.

Following a spat of more than three closely-typed pages, he wound up with little trace of appeasement:

> This seems an unfriendly letter, but I have felt for a long time that it is not really friendly to keep mum in dealing with Americans (or for that matter anyone else). The British policy for the last two generations or so has been that it is no use answering even the grossest libels by Americans; they will talk themselves out and maybe answer each other, and if they are not answered by us they are more likely to do something sensible in the end. I think the time has gone by for that, even if it was ever a reasonable plan; and I am sure you would rather be answered seriously.

He had earlier been offered a permanent post at Iowa; but after his tournament with Engle, he guessed (without too much regret): 'though everyone expressed good will I rather doubt whether they are still keen to give me a job.' Ohio State University also offered him an immediate senior appointment, as did other universities. He was genuinely surprised to find that he was viewed as such an eminence in America, and partly attributed his reputation to the kudos that the Kenyon summer school had acquired: 'we don't seem very glittering here,' he wondered sardonically. 'The students and the world at large do however seem to have a pathetic impression that we are almost devilishly glittering; I had no idea that I and the rather dull school of which I am a patriarch were having such a vogue.'[32]

Presently, Allen Tate relayed to him the further good news that Harcourt Brace in New York had finally agreed to publish his poetry (Empson had been grumbling to T. S. Eliot about Faber's failure to sell the American rights). When *The Collected Poems of William Empson* appeared in US print the next year, the critics were creditably perceptive in applauding the way Empson treated 'man in his "non-Euclidean predicament"', with the pathos of his lost communications,' as William Troy phrased it in *Poetry*.[33] The brilliant and suave young poet Richard Wilbur wrote in *Sewanee Review* that Empson was dealing with a very real modern world, 'unshaped by faith and nearing cultural bankruptcy', in poetry which communicated a 'well-worked-out despair ... a clear perception of the cultural and intellectual crisis.' He added, 'There is a more unqualified acceptance of waste and emptiness in Empson than one can find in *The Waste Land*', justly arguing too that whereas Eliot 'implies ... some amendment', Empson offers no such thing; instead, 'he pitches [his poems] on the level of wit and poignant jocularity...'[34] All in all, Empson's poetry earned a more distinguished and discerning press in the USA than it had received in the UK for several years.

Despite the acclaim that came his way in the literary periodicals, and the decisive enhancement of his reputation that flowed from his spirited work at Kenyon, Empson regarded the possibility of securing a job in the US more as an insurance policy than as a personal ambition; he had no plans to give up his work in China. For the moment, all he wanted was to bring to fulfilment the long-crafted *The Structure of Complex Words*, and then to hurry home to Hetta in Peiping. 'I have agreed,' he wrote to her on 8 August,

> to do three articles for literary magazines out of three chapters of this book, which ought to raise about $500 dollars so it would be silly not to do it, but it means I won't have the time here to polish off corrections of the book; however maybe I can do that on the boat and post the thing from the Pullipines [sic] or somewhere...
>
> I ought then to be seeing you again in about seven weeks time, which is hard to believe; I still feel rather trapped and with more hoops in front of me than I can jump through. However there is certainly nothing to complain of; I really couldn't have been more petted and fussed over. It [the Kenyon School Fellowship] has come at just the right time for me, because I was ready with something fresh to say... [35]

In the event, he was able to complete *Complex Words* in San Francisco, while waiting for a very slow boat to China to settle its date of departure. (The SS *Narrandera* was destined to call at Vancouver, Manila and Shanghai before reaching Tientsin.) 'I hope you like it,' he wrote to his publisher in a last-minute letter (23 August) accompanying the hefty typescript of his book. 'I feel it might be brisker if a lot of qualifications were left out, but it needs I think to give an impression of patient honesty rather than careless "brilliance"—some reviewers thought *Pastoral* was just dashed off, merely because I had taken so much pains to make it easy to read. So I thought a little show of effort this time would do no harm... About American publishers—I am keen to get this done in the States, where I think it would sell (I seem to be on the crest of a wave here, perhaps because they tend to be a bit behind the times, but never mind) and F. O. Matthiessen, who read some of this book, said he would put in a word...' [36]

The ship took such an age to cross the Pacific that the term at Peita was well under way by the time he made it home. But the trip was even more eventful than he cared to admit to everyone. He had anticipated some peril in a letter to Hetta: 'I am carrying a fair sum of money, originally cashed with the idea of bringing home $500, but it is now already just under that. However I have left between four and five hundred in the

Gambier bank. There are rumours in the papers of a new money issue in China, but I propose to buy a needle and thread somewhere on the way to sew the few remaining US dollars into my knickers. Or come to think of it these enormous shoulder pads on my white coats would be better able to stand a search by a really lowminded customs official.'[37] As things turned out, however, his wily precautions were unavailing, and in Manila he was robbed of more than $300.

It was a deeply regrettable loss, for the family would really need a stock of foreign currency in the coming months. Lack of cash could bring them closer to the level of hardship that their Chinese friends endured during the civil war. But as to fearing for their personal safety, the Empsons had survived the blitz in London and believed they should show solidarity with the Chinese—if and when Peiping came under military attack. It was fundamental to Empson's character that one should always look to the future with courage and hope. Ransom had taken the measure of Empson when he blazoned him on his way: 'He is a man of the spirit; he expects no evil.'[38]

5

Siege and Liberation

'WE have had a certain amount of distraction here,' Empson wrote on 19 November, just a few weeks after returning to the fray of Peiping.[1] Inflation had soared throughout the summer; food supplies plunged. As more and more government soldiers surged into Peiping, professors had to live 'cramped together in crowded compounds, almost penniless, too proud to speak of their destitution to the outer world,' as Derk Bodde (a Fulbright Fellow) noted in his journal.[2]

The purchasing power of money had become a nightmare. By August the exchange rate had depreciated to more than FP $7 million (Chinese National Dollars) to US $1, and at one point it pancaked to 12 million to one. On 19 August, in a desperately dishonest bid to stabilize the economy, the government introduced a new currency, the Gold Yuan (GY), calling in all old notes of denominations up to one million FP at an exchange rate of FP $3,000,000 for GY $1. Salaries and wages were frozen, strikes and protest meetings banned. As the *Cambridge History of China* sardonically comments, this obligatory swap of paper for paper did nothing to boost public confidence, for it amounted to nothing less than asset-grabbing, a massive financial swindle: 'When the programme was abandoned by the end of October, the only achievement anyone could think of was that it had allowed the government to confiscate US $170 million worth of gold, silver and foreign currencies from the public, in accordance with the regulation that all such holdings had to be exchanged for the new currency, the Gold Yuan.'[3] The Nationalist military machine continued to gorge 80–90 per cent of the national budget, and civilian China went hungry.

While the living standards of the university faculty and students were reduced to the level of peasants, refugee students from Communist-occupied territories, along with numbers of enforced evacuees, were herded into Peiping without provision for their welfare. Many squatted in the precincts of the Temple of Heaven on the south side of the city (more than fifty occupying the robing room of the Son of Heaven), with the result that the once sacred enclave became squalid and insanitary. Refugees ripped out the wooden furniture and fittings of empty houses, including window frames, to light their fires and cooking stoves.

At Peita, the male students of arts and social sciences occupying the ninety unglazed rooms of Third Court (once the Imperial School of Translation of the Ching Dynasty), with an average of five or six to a room, huddled round miserably inefficient stoves and slept on wooden-planked beds. According to one account, as many as one in ten of the students contracted tuberculosis in Peiping during this period.[4] The situation of the women's dormitory known as Gray Mansion was exceptional in that it enjoyed the uncommon luxury of central heating.

The radical alienation of the student body from the Nationalist government deepened into outrage, and the Communist resistance deployed an active and successful underground movement in the universities including Peita. Increasing numbers of students left university to join the People's Liberation Army as the Nationalist forces sustained more and more losses.

Yen Kuei-lai was at this period a student of Empson's who would later seek political asylum in Hong Kong; writing under the name of Maria Yen, she was to recall in her memoir *The Umbrella Garden*:

> Peita leaders [i. e. Communists] helped spread the rumor that students were going to be driven into the army to fight the Communists. On July 5th they incited 3,000 refugee students to march on the City Council to present a petition. But when the paraders arrived, everybody on the council had gone home. The students smashed everything breakable and smeared insulting slogans in black paint on the signboard over the gate. Then they marched on to the house of Hsu Hwei-tung, the head of the City Council. Because Mr. Hsu had already fled to a friend's place after asking the gendarmery to protect his property, soldiers from the 208th Division of the Youth Army blocked the students' advance with rifles, machine guns and a tank.
>
> For two hours the students argued with the officers commanding the troops. Tempers got short; minor scuffles started. Then shooting suddenly ripped out. The students wavered, broke ranks, and ran. Bursts from the machine guns chased them up the street; dozens of students dropped before somebody halted the firing. The official version claimed later that a student stole a pistol from an officer and opened fire first. Others said that a soldier enraged by the jeers thrown at him fired his rifle at his tormentors and that other soldiers had followed his lead. Whoever started it, from now on we students would call it Bloody July Fifth.

Bloodshed made the affair even better for the Communists. They helped us rally in a huge demonstration on July 9th to protest Bloody July Fifth and to honor our comrades martyred by the Youth Army.[5]

So too in Tientsin, the political situation rapidly deteriorated during the summer vacation. Otto van der Sprenkel reported: 'Mass arrests and beatings of students began in the middle of August, and some faculty members, including one from the Foreign Language Department, found it advisable to flee to the Liberated Area. By the time of the first semester of 1948-9 year opened we found, during registration week, that large numbers of our students had also fled. Among those that remained the mood was frightened, sullen and bitter.'[6] With an ingenuousness that perhaps says much about the ignorance or isolation of the diplomatic community in Nanking, the Indian Ambassador Panikkar said he found it surprising that so many of the faculty members he met at Peita, including foreign professors, became Communist sympathizers. Yet the vicious government clampdown on the universities left absolutely no other outlet for enlightened opinion. Even the Democratic League, which for a decade had enlisted those liberal intellectuals who rejected the autocracy of Chiang Kai-shek and aspired to reinvoke the democratic ideals of the original republic of 1913, had long been persecuted by the Kuomintang. After the failure of the Marshall Mission, the Nationalist government reasserted its undisguised authoritarianism and in October 1947 officially proscribed the League, assassinating some of its leading members and harrying many others into association with the professed egalitarianism of the Communists.

In the universities of Peiping, students and faculty, whether or not they openly aligned themselves with the 'progressives', were no less subject to assault and sometimes murderous treatment: it was enough to be fingered by random suspicion. Professor C. P. ('Pat') Fitzgerald, anthropologist, historian of China, and in the late 1940s British Council representative in Peiping (who had first met Empson at the remote southwestern town of Tali [Dali] in Yunnan province in 1938), wrote from personal knowledge in *The Birth of Communist China*: 'The universities were suffering the heavy hand of the "Te Wu", the special secret service of the regime. Sudden and secret arrests, mysterous disappearances, assassinations, a covert reign of terror prevailed in academic circles. Students were suspect, professors watched, freedom of thought, of publication and of speech suppressed. In so far as the choice between totalitarian and democratic government was concerned, it did not exist; the Chinese people groaned under a regime Fascist in every quality except efficiency. The Kuomintang had long lost the peasants; now they had cast away their only asset, the support of the scholars.'[7]

Empson knew a number of students who were seized for questioning by the Kuomintang, and admired their solidarity in the face of government repression. 'Students told us afterwards,' he wrote some ten years later, 'that in these arrests for questioning no actual Communist student was ever hit upon, and none of those arrested would point one out. A splendid claim, and it shows how many of the supporters considered they were only fellow-travellers.'[8]

One of the foremost foreign sympathizers with the progressive cause was an outgoing American professor at Tsinghua University. Since resigning his post as a professor of French at the University of Chicago, Robert Winter had been teaching in China continuously for 25 years; he was then in his sixties. He had embarked for China in a state of deep disillusionment with American society: 'The final straw [at Chicago] came in the spring of 1923 when I handed in my students' examination papers. The head of the department told me to "mark down" the Jews and Negroes in the class, "otherwise the university will be overrun by them." '[9] A tall, athletic, powerfully-built man of patrician appearance, with golden hair, blue eyes and a thin moustache, he was expert in both English and French literature as well as phonology and intonation; he was also a tremendous and tireless gossip, a music lover (with a large collection of gramophone records); and a passionate horticulturalist to boot. His students dubbed him a 'walking dictionary', and he taught them with exceptional vigour. During the war of resistance against Japan, while teaching at the refugee Southwest Associated University in Kunming (where he sported a pet monkey that once involved him in a fist-fight when it scratched someone in a queue outside a cinema), Winter courageously stood up for justice and against official ruthlessness.[10] Zhu Yongian later reported in a Chinese periodical: 'At the end of 1945, after [four] students had been butchered in the "December First Massacre", Winter took it on himself to go to the garrison HQ of Yunnan Province, where he confronted the chief instigator of the massacre, the garrison commander Guan Linzheng.'[11] (Independent sources confirm the story of that explosive encounter.) Furthermore, when a prominent member of the Democratic League, Li Kung-p'u, was assassinated by Kuomintang agents on 11 July 1946, Winter offered to stand guard outside the door of his friend, the poet Wen I-to [Wen Yiduo], who was an esteemed professor of Chinese literature, an artist (at night he would carve seals to supplement his income), and an equally outspoken reformist. The hired killers of the government would not dare to attack an

American citizen, Winter believed. Having prevailed upon him to abandon his post as body-guard, however, Wen was soon afterwards, on 15
July, shot to death while returning home from a Democratic League press
conference: the incident made Wen I-to's name a legend and a rallying-cry
in the cause for academic freedom in China.

Back in Peiping in the late 1940s, Winter involved himself on the side of
Communist idealism against the corruption of the Kuomintang, though he
never became a Communist (nor a citizen of China, where he would
remain until his death in 1986) and did not in general regard himself as
a 'political animal'.[12] He was the only foreigner among eighty signatories
to a letter of protest following the intemperate warning that John M. Cabot
had issued in May to the ungratefully anti-American students of China—
and that letter 'was reported in the Chinese press,' as Hetta Empson wrote
to her husband in the USA, 'so he got a severe letter from Rockefeller and
wrote back to say he'd sign one once a week if the opportunity arose.'[13]
Even more defiantly, according to a profile published in 1980 (when he was
still taking some classes in English at the age of 93, and had only recently
given up regular swimming at the Summer Palace),

> Professor Winter's early faith in the Communists led to his active partici-
> pation in their revolutionary activities. When some of his language students
> at Qinghua University became involved with the Communist movement,
> he carried parcels and letters for them to Tianjin and other cities. At a time
> when the Nationalist authorities were executing Communist sympathizers,
> Winter was brazen enough to make occasional deliveries of 'packages' that
> contained guns and ammunition.
>
> 'As a foreigner, I didn't arouse suspicion,' he said with a glint in his
> eye. 'It was a pretty exciting time to be in China. These people were
> actually trying to create a new type of society that would give dignity to
> the common man.'[14]

In August 1948, the government issued a blacklist of 250 students and
made many arrests in Peiping. In Tientsin too—as Hetta Empson wrote in
a daring bulletin which she addressed to 'progressive non-Government
elements in England'—'students have been arrested, the Universities
surrounded . . . and thorough searches carried out. In all cases, the students
were summoned to appear before the Special Criminal Court where
proceedings are held in secret and there is no opportunity for any kind
of legal defence. The orders for these measures came directly from Nanking . . . There is every indication that there will be even sterner suppression of liberal opinion in the near future, because it is estimated that, as a
result of the issuing of the new currency, prices may be stabilised for from

one to two months, after which time the old inflationary spiral will start again.'[15] Among the students blacklisted at Tsinghua University was a young woman named Fu Yi, whom Robert Winter secretly took to shelter in an inner room of his house. After a couple of days, when the KMT military police conducted a search of all university residences, Winter hid her in a large wardrobe which he locked. Inevitably—in a terrifying fashion made banal only by the clichés of postwar cinema—the police ordered him to open the wardrobe, but he protested that he had lost the key and had been unable to go to town to have a new one cut because of the curfew. Outfaced and consternated, the military policeman left the house, with the happy consequence that Fu Yi was still alive in 1984—when Winter himself was 98 years old.

Among several Chinese academics in mortal danger if they stayed in Peiping was Wu Han, a professor of Chinese history at Tsinghua University and a leading proponent of the Democratic League. Born in 1909, he had joined the League in 1943 while teaching at the Southwest Associated University, where he subsequently became editor of the *Democratic Weekly* and gained further renown as an orator and literary publicist; and he left Kunming just a month before the assassination of his close friend and associate Wen I-to. After returning to Peiping, where he first supported the Marshall Mission's abortive efforts to fashion a coalition of Nationalists and Communists, he allied himself more directly with the Communist Party and so became a marked man. Hetta Empson consulted with Professor Fei Hsiao-t'ung about means to help Wu Han, whom she considered 'one of those moderate elements who might be influential in the new regime'.[16] The 'excellent machine' of the British Council might rescue him with a visiting fellowship, or at least his travelling expenses, she calculated, if only the Foreign Office could be induced to grant the authority for him to visit the UK. With a courage that could well have imperilled her own safety, she wrote to England on 30 August to request help from Dorothy Woodman, stepmother of the *New Statesman* and 'wifely companion' (to use C. H. Rolph's antic phrase) of Kingsley Martin.

For unknown reasons, possibly because her plea never reached its destination, Hetta received no word back from Woodman. That very month, however, since Wu Han's situation was far too extreme to await any international recourse, he fled to Communist-held territory and had his first meeting with Mao Tse-tung; and after the liberation of Peiping he served for a long while, from November 1949, as deputy mayor of the capital, with special responsibility for culture, education, and health, officially joining the Communist Party in 1957—only to end up being persecuted during the Cultural Revolution (he has been posthumously rehabilitated).[17]

But Hetta Empson did succeed in helping other progressive professors and students escape the killing purges of the KMT, as Empson unclearly recalled in an article dating from 1959, 'Pei-Ta before the Siege'. Their quarters in Peiping, he related, 'also had a separate door, opening on a narrow passage with frequent right-angled turns, and this became a valuable escape route from the university when persecution became serious.'[18] What he was vaguely remembering ten years on, but must have twigged and turned a blind eye to in 1948, was that his wife managed to aid the students, who could not get out of the city, by smuggling them in the small hours through the courtyards of their dormitory and into a side street; thence they were spirited into neighbouring hospitals where they were put to bed and sheltered by sympathetic doctors.

Surprisingly, even while Peiping was beset by terrible inflation and the ruthless measures of the military, the foreign community both inside and outside the Legation Quarter kept up a full social life. As Sybille van der Sprenkel recalls, it seemed to be a 'semi-gilded' time, with gaiety running high before the gathering storm.[19] Hetta Empson took the children swimming at the International Club, and boating at the Summer Palace, and she both gave and received invitations to a series of parties. Renowned for her statuesque looks and flamboyant gregariousness, she became the cynosure of a large circle and brought a sense of dramatic moment to many tipsy get-togethers. Every party gained éclat from her presence, and from Empson's for his scholarly reputation—as well as a supply of tattle to feed the following days and nights. Often Empson would bedeck himself in a Chinese gown (a practical measure in the Peking winter); and he took to affecting a heavy dark beard, which he wore for many years, that fanned out from his jaw-line in a curious and almost sinister fashion—Hetta was constantly pointing out that it was dirty. The convivial disorder of their dormitory at 11 Tung Kao Fang—now with a complement of new servants (a 'very ladylike Manchurian' housekeeper and her nephew, the cook, who dearly loved concocting soup and 'booding')—became an almost obligatory staging-post for a succession of new friends including the research student David Hawkes (later Professor of Chinese at Oxford), whom Hetta found 'very agreeable and nice to have around', and two young American teachers at Tsinghua University, Walter Brown and David Kidd (b. 1927), who presently became Hetta's closest companions.[20] In time, Brown, who was short in stature but built like an athlete, would become Hetta's lover, and subsequently a devoted lifelong friend. David Kidd was to remember that it was Empson who propositioned Brown in these terms: 'Why don't you sleep with my wife? I think you like her, and I know she likes you.'[21] Brown also helped with tutoring the children.[22]

Also during the summer vacation in Peiping, C. P. Fitzgerald, with the assistance of Otto and Sybille van der Sprenkel, arranged an amazingly full programme of meetings, admission free, running daily from 17 August to 3 September, prior to the opening of a new British Council Centre and Library. Hetta crowned the whole show by helping to stage a production of *An Inspector Calls*, with a cast of students from Peita. It was sparsely attended but enthusiastically received, and the students had enormous fun in doing it. (Simple fun was otherwise in fairly short supply for the students: because of the civil war, many of them could not get home during the vacations, and life in their hostels was prison-like and drab.)

The Peiping office of the British Council acquired even more vim with the advent of a new 'Functional Officer', subsequently its Director, named Ronald A. Parker. He was an energetic and resourceful educationalist in his early thirties. Empson considered him a 'decent man who...knows how to do his stuff';[23] and Lynda Grier thought him 'the only genius I've ever met'.[24] Just as soon as he arrived, he set about the business of arranging still more concerts, readings, and theatrical productions. His ambitious programme for the New Year 1949 included a course of six lectures by Empson entitled 'Changes in Critical Taste', and a weekly series of public readings from English literature, including Empson's selection of 'The Poetry of Argument' and Hetta's 'A Bunch of Contrasts', along with his own anthology called 'Mild & Bitter'.

But the political and military convulsions of China would not stay for British cultural bounty. Throughout the enforced closure of the British Council Centre during the siege of Peiping, Parker 'worked industriously,' as Sybille van der Sprenkel was to recall, 'carving and dressing puppets for the quite impressive puppet theatre which he ran as a side-line (employing for the purpose a carpenter acquired in Sikkim and a Chinese seamstress). After the liberation he gave puppet performances of *The Merchant of Venice* with British residents speaking the text, and produced Emlyn Williams's *The Corn is Green*, with a cast of Chinese students (including the speeches in Welsh, drilled by a Welsh-speaking missionary).'

Empson was scheduled to teach seven hours a week, but the Communists' relentless onslaught in northern China put paid to Peita's planned programme. As the People's Liberation Army seized Nationalist strongholds in the provinces of Hopei, Shantung and Shansi, increasing numbers of students slipped away to join the winning side. One student witness, who stayed on in Peiping, estimated that more than a thousand students (over a quarter of the total number) deserted the Peita campus by the end of November alone. As a professor correctly remarked to his colleagues, 'What clearer sign do you want that the government is going to collapse!... The students have always been the weathercock of what is to come.'[25]

By the end of October the Communists took control of the entirety of the rich resources of Manchuria, including the plentiful stock of new arms that the Americans had supplied to the Kuomintang as well as leftover Japanese weapons. They knew that control of the north-east would enable them to thrust through the rest of China. Chiang Kai-shek shifted south again, and never came back. He left the capable General Fu Tso-yi, whom he distrusted and kept short of vital American armaments, to defend the North China plain. The brilliant Lin Piao, Communist victor in Manchuria, stood ready to propel his army down through the Shanhaikuan corridor and into Tientsin and Peiping. He had a combined force of 890,000 regular Communist troops to command against the 600,000 Nationalist soldiers left to Fu Tso-yi, lost leader of the 'North China Bandit Suppression Headquarters'.[26]

Within days of the liberation of Manchuria, 'non-essential' foreigners had been advised by their diplomatic representatives (with varying degrees of forcefulness) to leave Peiping and Tientsin. Alarmed by the increasingly strident warnings of the US embassy, by the end of the month over 60 per cent of a total number of 674 American nationals had abandoned Peiping.[27]

On 18 November, the Foreign Office announced that British consular officials and other foreign service staff would be 'expected to remain at their posts' as long as necessary, though the wives and children of consular personnel might be evacuated. While the American precipitancy annoyed the British Consul General in Shanghai because it could foolishly provoke anxiety and even panic throughout the foreign community, the Empsons had already made a firm decision to remain through the inevitable siege and likely fighting. Empson wrote to his publisher on 20 November:

> The trouble here is the difficulty of getting money from abroad [for trading on the black market], which may get easier or worse, but it is not as easy now as earlier. We propose to stay on and so does the British Council as far as anyone can prophesy its movements; the embarrassing thing for us would be if the university decided to make a pretence evacuation taking only professors and leaving everybody else in the lurch, but I do not think that probable (actually there is a professors meeting about it tomorrow). Of

course the Communists might take the town in the next few weeks but they are not expected to do it till the spring. The British have been behaving better than the Americans about refusing to evacuate. We have laid in a little food [some sacks of flour and rice, as well as a stock of coal] for the probably difficult period of turnover, but not too much because everybody knows everything and a real lot of food would invite looters. I confess we feel a bit unsettled, but so far everything is going according to longterm plan.[28]

The professors of Peita and Tsinghua did decide to maintain their university presence in Peiping (though Hu Shi, president of Peita, founding father of the Chinese literary renaissance and former Ambassador to the USA, had argued for evacuation). But the students still worried that the authorities might abandon them at the last moment. Empson felt encouraged to stay partly because he learned that the universities in Shantung province had been able to resume their work just a week after falling to the Communists, and even more positively because as a cultural ambassador he fervently hoped that the British might seize the initiative and build up their influence after the takeover—'an extremely rational sentiment I think,' he told John Crowe Ransom in one of his last letters before the start of the siege.

He also wrote, on 11 December, to his sister Molly (who had informed the British Council she would stand ready to 'ransom' her trapped relations if the need arose, which Empson found an amusing notion—'it sounds to me like putting ideas into their heads'), staunchly reassuring her that the foreign community seemed really 'very placid'. 'There are rumours that it is considering whether to back out of China, which I think would be a grotesque mistake; this is just the kind of occasion when the machine might turn out to be worth the public money spent on it.'[29] The siege of Peiping began just two days later.

'In all the records of modern warfare no other such improbable operation as the siege of Peking has occurred to enliven the task of the historian,' C. P. Fitzgerald has written. 'Yet for six weeks, from 13 December 1948, to 22 January 1949, this strange siege continued.'[30]

Some four weeks before the start of the siege, Hetta Empson had gained accreditation as a correspondent for the *Observer*—the press card allowing her certain privileges such as being allowed to break the curfew after 11 p.m.—which ran her first signed dispatch on 28 November, under the headline 'Life in Peking as City Awaits Communists' (p. 5). Although General Fu Tso-yi presently held secret talks with the People's Liberation Army with a view to surrendering the city he had been abandoned to garrison, few civilians knew anything whatever of his efforts to save them from a potentially calamitous bombardment. Thus Hetta could telegraph only the chilling common opinion that Fu was 'believed bitterender'—meaning that he would probably fight to the last. Rumour and suspicion dogged every doorway. Quite apart from the Communist forces speedily encircling the city, the other enemy already stalked the streets in the form of a Discipline Supervisory Corps—Kuomintang terror squads armed with submachine guns and swords, with the power of summary trial and execution—intent on suppressing all supposed Communist sympathizers. The students feared an ever more vicious and arbitrary crackdown by the government.

Worst of all fears was the dreadful prevalent apprehension that the Americans might help Chiang Kai-shek by destroying Peiping with a last-minute air raid. According to the Communist radio beamed into Peiping, if the USA gave any such direct military assistance to the Kuomintang, the People's Liberation Army would regard all American nationals in China as its declared enemies.

'British less panicky than Americans,' Hetta Empson closed her dispatch in a far-sighted passage which was omitted from the columns of the *Observer*— perhaps for reasons of space, perhaps diplomacy—'hope British attitude may influence American policy not precipitate crisis as believed this would thrust Chinese communists into arms Russians stop.' The Empsons could not know that on 27 November the Nationalist government had appealed to the American Congress for immediate aid—but really for rescue—'in America's self-interest'. Fortunately, Truman refused all requests to increase the supply of *matériel* and to appoint an American commander to direct the Kuomintang in crisis. The CIA advised him in a *Review of the World Situation* on 17 November: 'The situation in China has deteriorated to the point where its stabilization by the Nationalist Government is considered to be out of the question.'

Trusting to history, Hetta Empson hopefully affirmed that Peiping was the 'least dangerous uncomfortable place China with tradition peace luck stop'; and that the small but significant number of foreigners hanging on there had 'settled down await changeover thinking must get on with Communists some time'. The British diplomatic interest was left in the sole charge of a young Consul named Martin Buxton. Just 28 years old, and rather a shy intellectual by nature, he combined boyish good humour with upright imperturbability and promptly proved equal to the daunting job before him.[31] During the siege Buxton ministered to the British community as best he could; in particular, since the Shell Company had abandoned in the legation compound a large dump of oil, he sold off or simply handed out barrels of kerosene to each family unit so that they could obtain silver dollars or greenbacks to finance local expenses.[32] Empson, who found it nearly impossible to cash foreign cheques even before the siege bit hard upon the city, certainly considered him 'much better value than most consuls'.

While many wealthy Chinese families were hastily evacuating, a total number of about 150,000 ill-disciplined and ineffective Nationalist troops had been compressed into the city, either bivouacking in ancient public enclosures or being brusquely billeted, in what A. Doak Barnett fittingly called 'a sort of human osmosis', upon private houses. In the few days before the first cannonade on 13 December, innumerable military vehicles, bands of infantrymen in faded khaki uniforms with white sun cap-badges, and donkey-carts laden with ammunition and food, thrashed back and forth through the streets; yet still the foreigners and the remaining wealthy Chinese could gather in cafés to take coffee and cream cakes while discussing the perennially compelling topic of falling house prices. 'Chinese with big houses are offering to let foreigners live there practically rentfree,' wrote Empson, 'which is rather a temptation . . . But then we are rentfree here and in university property, which is rather like a consulate; if we went out we would lose this place, we couldn't really keep out looters and refugees as we would be supposed to do, we might at any moment be told to leave our new quarters or still worse to pay rent for them, which as foreign cheques are increasingly hard to cash might be actually impossible. I am therefore keen to stay where we are.'[33]

Inevitably, commodity prices soared; and for the first time in umpteen months of inflation American dollars yielded less on the black market exchange than the so-called Mexican (silver) dollars. Fighting was reported within a ten-mile range of Peiping, though the railway line to Tientsin somehow remained open until the last moment. A number of students, impatient for the turnover, trickled out to Communist areas; other folk, as if oblivious of the Red tide sweeping upon the city, diverted themselves by going skating on the thick ice of the former imperial lakes. Hetta Empson continued to telegraph dispatches to the *Observer*, though none of them reached print. 'Peiping all services functioning normally,' she wrote a day or two before the first artillery fire was heard to the west and north of the city, 'press censorship shanghai nanking not yet imposed peiping but letters censored . . . no reckless gaiety . . . busy trading life slow humour northerners unchanged . . . possibility travel get news stories if desired end.' With more than two million people waiting to be held hostage, the city seemed reluctant to suspend its natural animation.

'General Fu Tso-yi holds a beautifully delicate and priceless vase in his fingers,' said a Chinese observer. 'If anyone tries to take it, it will be destroyed.'[34] Indeed, the Communists had such a certain sense of the architectural and symbolic value of the city that, according to C. P. Fitzgerald, a curious incident took place in the early days of the siege:

> When it was found that Fu refused to surrender, Lin Piao had seriously envisaged carrying the city by assault, and as this would involve breaching the walls—immensely thick and sixty feet high—artillery would have been necessary.
>
> Before deciding on the point to be breached the Communist command asked Professor Liang Ssu-ch'eng, of Tsing Hua, the leading architect and archaeologist in China, whether the place the military favoured was objectionable on historical and aesthetic grounds. Professor Liang thought it was; he said that the spot chosen, a gate in the west wall of the south city, was one of the few pieces of unrestored Ming military architecture surviving and it would be a great loss to art and archaeology if it were destroyed. He suggested, in turn, another place, also opposite a vacant space within the walls, where bombardment would neither slay the citizens nor damage an historical monument. The Communist command accepted this change, but fortunately the surrender of the city obviated the need for any bombardment.[35]

In fact, the PLA fired very few rounds into the city throughout the forty days of the siege—as far as Yen Kuei-lai (Maria Yen) could remember, it was not until 15 December that 'the first shell from a Communist gun arched in over the old walls with a fluttering shriek and exploded on Nan Chi Tze'—while the jumpy defenders blasted away at everything in sight, whether in or out of range. 'Late at night . . . we could lie in bed and listen to the distant hammering of machine guns as the Nationalists fired blindly into the night.'[36] On 15 December the Communists seized the Shihching-shan electricity plant, shutting off the city's principal source of power and light, and five days later cut the Tientsin power lines. The curfew was called more and more early as the long days passed, eventually at 8 p.m., and a sudden black death would meet anyone who went out after dark.[37]

Empson drew deep on his inner resources and kept his head down to literary criticism. It is a tribute to his powers of concentration that during the oppressive distractions of the siege he planned and started writing for the *Kenyon Review* his combative essay 'Donne and the Rhetorical Tradition'. A gentleman does not complain lightly, not even about the strains of a military siege; though after three weeks, on 8 January, even he had to admit: 'we seem to be being rather badgered now in one way and another.'

By way of preparation for his essay, he managed in the course of the siege to read through Rosemund Tuve's *Elizabethan and Metaphysical Imagery*, along with *Shakespeare's Small Latin and Less Greek*, by T. W. Baldwin, and *Shakespeare's Use of the Arts of Language*, by Sister Miriam Joseph. They were 'comforting things to have in bed with one while the guns fired over Peking,' he granted in a letter to John Crowe Ransom—taking care to trick out self-pride in a casual public pronouncement.

On the far side of the mighty city wall, the Communist forces could bide their time while a process of attrition worked upon Peiping's nerves and stomach, and in the meantime they secured the state of siege by occupying the south airfield (Nan Yuan), five miles from the city. Imprisoned within Peiping, Fu Tso-yi commissioned an emergency landing strip to be built on the eastern stretch of the Tung-tan glacis, the rough open area covering three sides of the Legation Quarter (part of it laid out for a polo field), hard by the heart of the city. Immediately outside the perimeter wall, thousands of humble homes were needlessly razed by Kuomintang ukase, and with no more than nominal compensation if any, in order to make a defense cordon of dead ground; just inside the wall, other buildings had to give place to a military road. Foxholes and roadblocks were dug in numerous city streets, and yet more trees felled to make man-traps. For all such unpaid work in huge labour gangs, each *Chia* or unit of about sixty Chinese households in the city was commanded by martial law to make available a daily quota of between five and twenty able-bodied civilians, as well as requisitions of money, food, and other household goods: hay, lumber, rope, and gunny sacks.

By Christmas, a pack of ten Chinese cigarettes cost GY $10. The Empsons portioned out their limited stocks of food and coal. On 8 January, Empson wrote gamely to Ransom, 'Most people were estimating three months, and it is no use grumbling after one . . . I imagine most people in the town can only live on their stores. They can go on longer than this.'[38] In another letter of about the same date, written against a background of rumour, he expanded upon his stout faith in the short-term future:

> the food situation is not yet appalling - prices are very high compared to what people here are used to or can (most of them) afford . . . If the siege goes on the thing is no doubt bound to get very bad, and it is difficult to estimate . . .
>
> We are in good health and go along comfortably so far, though of course one must expect this dragging affair to lower one's spirits. I do not imagine we are in danger from the war, but there might well be a period of looting if the siege drags on, especially if there is an interregnum period.[39]

Outside the city, the district including Tsinghua and Yenching Universities
had been peacefully occupied by the PLA just three days after the start of
the offensive against Peiping. Three days later again, on 19 December,
Nationalist aircraft dropped five bombs on the Tsinghua campus; which,
as it was reliably reported, 'did much to destroy, among students and
faculty alike, what little pro-Kuomintang sentiment remained'.[40] Though
Kuomintang propaganda disseminated in the city horrifying rumours
that the PLA had slaughtered 2000 students and professors, in fact the
Communists kept their university wards alive for two months with supplies
of millet.

At the other extreme, Fujen, a private Catholic university within the city,
promptly closed down for the duration, leaving ten students who remained
in residence—the majority being tall Pekingese girls with straight short
hair or thick pigtails, and wearing long trousers under loose grey or blue
padded gowns—with the task of fending for themselves on an unvarying
diet of rice gruel and soya beans. One of the students was the 17-year-old
Svetlana Rimsky-Korsakoff (a grand-niece of the composer), whom
Empson considered 'a sturdy, sensible, willing, energetic, handsome and
unexcitable girl who will always be able to fit into life somehow'.[41] Feeling
very frightened during the siege, both for herself and for her parents
caught up in unimaginable circumstances behind the Communist lines,
as well as achingly strapped for money, she began to give secret lessons in
Russian so as to earn some of the coveted though illegal silver dollars.

Soon after Christmas, which she and the four other girls in her dormitory celebrated by getting 'howling drunk' on bad Chinese wine, and after
securing permission to leave the city in order to spend the New Year with
her parents, on 31 December she presented herself at the city gate and was
allowed out after a period of rude handling by the Kuomintang guards. In
the hope of avoiding any military on the road, she struck out directly across
the fields. But after a while she drew near a soldier stationed on a hill who
screamed at her vehemently and then fired a bullet in her direction;
unwilling to go back to the city, she persisted in walking up to the soldier
who thereupon explained that he had been desperately trying to deter her
from walking across a minefield. In due course she made it to the village
adjacent to Tsinghua, where a snowstorm had stopped any fighting, and
was astonished to be solicitously entertained to peanuts by the soldiers of
the Liberation Army before ascertaining that her parents were alive and
well. Three days later she returned to the city, only to find that the
Nationalist guards suspected her of being a Communist spy and were
aggressively reluctant to let her back inside.

On 25 December, the day after the Communists captured Kalgan, capital of Chahar province and one of the last remaining Nationalist strongholds in north China, Lin Piao and his political commissar broadcast a statement to the people of Peiping, ordering them among other things not to loot but to protect all private and public property, commercial and industrial concerns. The full 8-point programme promised that after takeover the Liberation Army and Democratic Government would protect schools, hospitals and public institutions; also that 'the lives and property of all foreigners will be protected'.[42]

Perhaps reassured by those promises, and by the strictly unofficial news that the PLA was not harming or interfering with the activities of civilians in its liberated areas, Empson decided to chance the trip to Tsinghua—by coincidence on the same day, 31 December, that Svetlana Rimsky-Korsakoff also intrepidly crossed the lines. A week later he explained in a letter:

> I spent the New Year at Tsing Hua University outside the town, which is in communist hands, having gone there to give my weekly lecture on *Macbeth*, but the boys did not want to be lectured to, so I have not gone this week. It was an interesting and pleasant trip across the lines, with a police pass you understand; I was invited to a students New Year party in the evening, with singing and dancing and so forth, and came back the next day. There seems to be no fighting around here at present. It is all more placid than you seem to expect, but of course the real question is how the food supply works out.[43]

'I thought it made an elegant New Year,' he told another correspondent.[44] (In *Milton's God*, which he would start to write some ten years later, he would characterize the adventure in these terms: 'Happening to cross the fighting lines by an unauthorized route during the siege of Peking, I was greatly struck by the beautiful evangelistic feelings of the [Communist] troops who captured me, all consciously and confidently redeeming and redeemed; and I admired the feelings of many other Chinese during the following two years.'[45]) Whether he really made the trip out of a pigheaded sense of duty or simply because he thought he might stretch his legs and so relieve his nerves of the claustrophobia of Peiping, he certainly reckoned it ever afterwards as one of the two occasions in his career when he had shown really professional grit: 'it is true that, besides sleeping on my blackboard when a refugee [in 1938],' he permitted himself to boast in his inaugural lecture at Sheffield University, 'I crossed the fighting lines during the siege of Peking to give my weekly lecture on *Macbeth* at a university outside the town; that does seem to make me a serious teacher.'[46]

Having cut off the city's electricity in the first days of the siege, with the New Year the PLA broadcast an offer to reconnect the supply on the grounds that they had no wish to inconvenience the people; when the Nationalist authorities reluctantly agreed to accept a partial return of power for essential needs, the people knew whom they had to thank. In the meantime, since the supply of running water depended largely on electric pumps, they had often been obliged to queue for drinking water at the nearest private well: happily, there were 7,000 wells in the city. The so-called 'night soil'—human excrement which in normal times would be carted out every night to fertilize the fields—accumulated in insanitary piles until the Communists graciously granted leave for the 'honey carts' ('fu-carts') to do their business. Although such PLA tactics had a decidedly lowering effect, punishing the morale of the military and civic authorities, Peiping as a whole remained calm.

On 12 January the PLA pressed for a speedier fall of the archaic fastness of the city by opening up a brief bombardment with light artillery, skilfully targeting the area in which the Kuomintang secret police had their headquarters. As C. P. Fitzgerald noted, 'The accuracy of this fire gave much satisfaction to the citizens.'[47] Two days later, having rejected Chiang Kai-shek's insincere offer of peace talks at the beginning of the month, Mao Tse-tung, Chairman of the Central Committee of the Chinese Communist Party, set out the implacable terms on which he would conduct peace negotiations:

(1) Severe punishment of war criminals. (2) Repeal of the bogus constitution. (3) Abolition of the bogus government structure. (4) Reorganization of all reactionary armies in accordance with democratic principles. (5) Confiscation of bureaucratic capital. (6) Implementation of agrarian reforms. (7) Abrogation of all treaties of national betrayal. (8) Convocation of a Political Consultative Conference, without participation of reactionary elements, in order to form a Democratic Coalition Government to take over the authority of the reactionary Kuomintang Government in Nanking and of its affiliated organizations in the provinces.[48]

While Chiang haughtily rejected such an offer, which amounted to a demand for unconditional surrender, Li Tsung-jen—the Vice-President, and head of a clique within the Kuomintang which regarded Chiang as the chief obstacle to a termination of hostilities—manoeuvred to sue for peace and so to supersede him. But even by the second week of January 1949 Li's belated day had still not arrived.

Tientsin, the largest industrial and commercial city in north China, had come under siege a few days earlier than Peiping, on 10 December; but unlike the historically precious Peiping it eventually fell to all-out military attack, on 15 January. Realizing in due time that the Garrison Commander at Tientsin would not give in without a hard fight (he had flooded an area on the outskirts in a vain attempt to impede the enemy advance), the PLA launched a ferocious artillery barrage, demolishing a large portion of the city and killing and wounding many civilians. The Communists took the city on the second day of their assault, capturing both the Garrison Commander and the so-called 'puppet mayor'.

General Fu Tso-yi was left with no alternative but to yield up the prize of Peiping as soon as he could negotiate clement terms for his surrender. In Nanking on 21 January, President Chiang Kai-shek chose not to resign but temporarily to retire from office, leaving Li Tsung-jen as acting president to pick up the lost cause of the Kuomintang. At six o'clock the following evening, Fu Tso-yi, who no longer needed to sustain his fealty to Chiang, formally announced the 'peace settlement' which gave Peiping over to the PLA. 'Peiping became the first major city in the Chinese civil war to come under Communist control by peaceful agreement between Communist and Nationalist leaders,' wrote A. Doak Barnett, 'rather than by capture or outright military surrender.'[49]

The fall of the finest fortress in China seemed almost an anti-climax. A Joint Administrative Office, staffed by a 'coalition' of four Communists and three members of the Kuomintang, was established to deal with 'all military and political problems' during a 'transitional period'. Over the following few days, it was decided, all Nationalist forces would be withdrawn from the city and eventually subsumed into the People's Liberation Army, while government bodies and public organisations should 'maintain the *status quo*' pending turnover. Recalcitrant Nationalist officials would be allowed to fly out of the city; those who remained might redeem their criminality as slaves of the Kuomintang by accepting integration into the Communist order. While General Fu Tso-yi in due time accommodated himself to the new regime, the president of Peita took the last opportunity to depart. Hu Shi had told John Leighton Stuart on 17 December that he considered Communism so 'implacable and intolerant, so diabolically thorough in its indoctrination, and so ruthless in enforcing its totalitarian control even in China, that Chiang Kai-shek should be supported';[50] and in the Spring of 1949 he reportedly expostulated to Empson's former colleague, George Yeh (who had become Vice-Minister of Foreign Affairs of the KMT): 'The only reason why liberal elements like us still prefer to string along with you people is that under your regime we at least enjoy the freedom of silence.'[51] Still later, in Nanking, Hu Shih called on Ambassador

Panikkar, lamenting the unarguable failure of Chinese liberalism: 'All this is the fault of us liberals. When we saw how things were shaping in 1936, how the Kuomintang was renouncing the democratic idea of the Revolution and was set on the path of dictatorship and reaction, we should have protested and organized ourselves into an effective opposition.'[52]

For their part, the ordinary civilian populace of Peiping could 'carry on life as usual', though the 8 o'clock curfew remained in force; and it would be difficult to sustain any kind of normal life while rampant inflation prevailed. In the course of one year the price of flour had risen 4,500 times, and at the very moment of Communist takeover the pound sterling could purchase only one silver dollar; a pound of sugar cost £1, ten cigarettes ten shillings.

At last, ten days after the official surrender, at 4 o'clock in the afternoon of Monday, 31 January, an advance guard of the PLA marched into the city, apparently without prior announcement, to occupy the billets that the KMT had only just quit. '*Ba Lu lai lo!*' ('The Eighth Route Army is here!'), people shouted down the streets.[53] The troops were headed by a sound truck blaring 'Welcome to the Liberation Army on its arrival in Peking!'

'Beside it and behind it, six abreast, marched some two or three hundred Communist soldiers in full battle equipment,' Derk Bodde observed. 'They moved briskly and seemed hot . . . All had a red-cheeked, healthy look and seemed in high spirits. As they marched up the street, the crowds lining the side-walks . . . burst into applause . . .

'Behind the soldiers marched students carrying two large portraits: one of Mao Tse-tung, the other presumably of Chu Teh, commander in chief of the People's Army. A military band came next, and finally a long line of trucks . . . In about ten minutes the parade was over.'[54]

Next, the PLA staged a truly impressive spectacle. On 3 February, when Peiping happened to be thrashed by an unremitting dust storm, masses of infantry and cavalry, together with literally hundreds of motorized units—jeeps, tanks, trucks (mostly captured American equipment) and artillery, machine guns and mortars (mostly Japanese)—paraded through the streets and down Ch'ang-an Chieh, the main East–West avenue running past the Forbidden City. The procession of weathered, expressionless soldiers, six abreast and with eyes fixed to the front, stretched for miles. 'For roughly six hours,' noted Barnett, 'the Red Army put on a show of force that made it quite clear that they had not captured Peiping by bluff.'[55] Whirling heavy clouds of dust and sand did nothing to mar the awesome discipline of the demonstration. 'Are you Lin Piao's troops?' two students asked some soldiers. 'No,' came the well-groomed answer. 'We are the people's troops.'[56] Thousands of students, workers and craftsmen joined in the display, singing and chanting, and flourishing banners—some decorated with Communist slogans, still others with portraits of Mao Tse-tung and other leaders—and coloured paper pennants. Many folk had got themselves up in traditional New Year costumes to strut the streets on stilts. Others danced to the insistent drum and cymbal music—'Chang, Chang! Chi-chang-chi!'—of the *Yang Ko*, the peasant 'planting dance' which presently became the craze of Peiping.

As for the Empsons, they certainly rushed along with the students to cheer the PLA. 'It seems natural in England by this time to give a pretty gloomy jeer at the term "liberation",' Empson commented later, 'but [the students] honestly did think they were liberated from serious danger when the Communist troops finally walked in; you might argue that on a long-term view they were deluded, but there is no doubt about what they were feeling at the time.'[57] Though he was by no means a convert to Communism, he acknowledged the political reality that Mao Tse-tung had won popular support and might serve the country well. Few people could doubt that Chiang Kai-shek had forfeited the legitimacy of his government by the abuse of power, with nepotism and inefficiency, and with corruption and terror. The Communists were conquering China by armed force, it is true, but equally they were cleverly taking great pains to carry the people with them.

Hetta Empson summed up the prevailing popular feeling in a contemporary cable: 'now great feeling general relief'.

'Of course my attitude has been all along that nothing but a communist government would be firm enough to get anything done in China,' Empson wrote on 19 June 1949, 'and there is no reason why it should hurt us if we keep our tempers—not always an easy assignment, I quite see.'[58]

The question that constantly nagged him and other sympathetic western observers, however, was whether the Chinese Communists would look to their country alone or presently leap into bed with the dictatorial body of Soviet Communism. He saw no reason why the Chinese should necessarily follow or be dominated by the Bolshevik model of totalitarianism.

As early as 1923, Bertrand and Dora Russell, in *The Prospects of Industrial Civilization*, had judged that the sick injustices of the capitalist system, including the presumed law of 'the sacredness of private property', should give place to the goal of international socialism.[59] An international world-state should therefore seek first to limit the sovereignty of separate nations, because a proliferation of national interests inevitably induces wars for supremacy. International warfare would be brought to an end when an alliance of socialist countries, even if dominated by one State, could serve to counterbalance the aggressive world power of Capitalist Imperialism.

Reading the Russells' treatise in 1946, Empson found it impossible to credit the claim that Soviet Communism was programmed to give issue to an ideal form of international socialism. There must be alternative brands of Communism, he believed, which would be serviceable to indigenous needs and not simply accountable to Cominformist doctrine. Although the ideal of international socialism would win his vote at all times, it would not help the distinct political, economic, and cultural requirements of China for its new leaders to bow to a heteronomy dictated from Moscow. On the contrary, he feared, Soviet hegemony seemed all the more likely to promote the world war that the Russells had foreshadowed. Far from seeking merely to make rapid progress with the urgent internal business of industrial development, the Soviet pattern of Communism as developed by Stalin had already acted upon expansionist ambitions as absolute as those of American imperialism: both polities acted as if aggrandisement had become a necessary and just function of nationalism.

Empson told Martin Buxton, the British Consul in Peiping, in 1949: 'whenever I hear anyone argue in theory either for pure capitalism or pure communism I feel the arguments against him to be very obvious.'[60] It seemed by no means certain that power was so well balanced as to deter global war, despite the Russells' 'very reasonable' proposition that the great blocs might create peace by becoming invulnerable to one another.

He had recently read *The Armed Vision: A Study in the Methods of Modern Literary Criticism*, in which Stanley Edgar Hyman had commented, in a chapter with the misapplied title 'William Empson and Categorical Criticism', that *Some Versions of Pastoral* was 'implicitly Marxist throughout'; and sometime in 1949 Empson felt entitled to respond to the charge: 'Your praise of me as a Marxist critic has (very falsely perhaps) given me a very strong leg in the Peking area. You might regret what you did here.'[61] Moreover, he took the opportunity in the same letter categorically and nobly to observe that he regarded both America and Russia as: 'patently lunatic (one of them says you mustn't get into a bath unless it is super-heated steam and the other says you mustn't unless it is a solid block of ice); and the only hope for the world is to find an independently strong country which will be able to refuse to listen to the nonsense talked by either side. Such was my opinion before my return to China in 1947, and the later events have not altered it.'

He composed his impatience with the polarization of the Superpowers in this untitled villanelle, a hymn to political temperance:

> The ages change, and they impose their rules.
> It would not do much good to miss the bus.
> We must endure, and stand between two fools.
>
> Two colonies of Europe now form schools
> Holding absolute power, both of them fatuous.
> The ages change, and they impose their rules.
>
> One claims the State is naked between ghouls
> The other makes it total Octopus.
> We must endure, and stand between two fools.
>
> A says No Both not Superheated Steams. B cools
> This off by Only Solid Ice. For us
> The ages change, and they impose their rules.
>
> Both base their pride upon ill-gotten tools
> And boast their history an Exodus.
> We must endure, and stand between two fools.
>
> There is world and time; the Fates have got large spools;
> There need not only Europe make a fuss.
> The ages change, and they impose their rules.
> We must endure, and stand between two fools.

If the Russians and the Americans continued to anathematize one other, and charged all other countries to fall into one or other orbit, there seemed to be no way forward. Moreover, if Stalinism purported to be the one true party of international socialism, could there be no alternative and still valid manifestation of Communism—except as a defiant deviation from doctrinal orthodoxy, the mandate of Moscow?

'I am not at all clear what is supposed to be the difference between Socialism and Communism in the controversies in England,' he wrote;

of course so far as the Russians say they are a socialist not communist state this can't be relevant to the Labour Party's fear of Communists. The Russell book foresees a great deal but not the extent to which free thought would collapse entirely under state socialism—the fact that national socialism is a reasonable description of Britain (1946) and both Russia and Germany (1939) is so confusing that there is hardly any language left to discuss politics in . . .

It seems clear that the best way out of the confusion of Communism with Russian nationalism would be to have some other communist state not in geographical contact with it. France would be a good one, being very nationalist and strong enough to have a casting vote in some circumstances. At present the Russians feel that they are absolutely better than everyone else and must therefore expect to be martyred. I suppose though that if a communist France differed with them on foreign policy they would at once say it wasn't truly communist; hence there would be no great gain.[62]

Two years later, Empson's hypothesis became a reality not in France but in Yugoslavia. On 28 June 1948, when premier Josip Broz Tito declined to meet the Kremlin's political and economic demands upon his country, he was denounced by Stalin, who forthwith expelled the Yugoslav Communist Party (KPJ) from the Comintern. Although the first Yugoslav constitution of 1946 had been modelled on the Soviet formula, Tito took this opportunity to decentralize his administration, to institute greater personal freedoms, and to stand aside from the military blocs of East and West. In so standing up to Stalin, while still sustaining a Socialist state, he set a provisional example of Communist national independence (albeit much against his real wishes, for he continued to favour the concept of 'socialist solidarity'); and the West, rejoicing in Tito's non-alignment, promptly courted his show of co-existence, resumed trade relations with Yugoslavia, and admitted it to the UN Security Council. 'Tito may be a scoundrel, but he's our scoundrel,' said Ernest Bevin, the British Foreign Minister.[63]

Like many China watchers, Empson applauded Tito's stand and tended to overlook the fact that the bold and charismatic premier regarded himself as misunderstood and had not actually taken the initiative in severing relations with Moscow. Surely, thought Empson, Communist China would prefer, and could be encouraged, to adopt a similar position vis-à-vis the overlord Stalin? Bertrand Russell had correctly judged in 1923 that a Communist government 'may acquire just as much nationalism as was shown by its capitalistic predecessor', though Marxist theorists denied the possibility that the Communist regime in China could be both nationalist and internationalist in proportionate measure.[64]

Empson set out his convictions even before the Communists took power in China, in a letter of 20 November 1948:

> I am strongly anti-Russian but think the urgent thing is not to drive the various Asiatic parties described as communist into fighting on the Russian side in a world war; if you can avoid that you may not have it, and if you do you certainly will. This sentence is a trifle ungrammatical but is not intended to be ambiguous. I am puzzled that so few Americans can be got to see the point. The difference between Rumania (say) and China, or Java (for that matter), is that one is under direct military control from Russia if the Russians chose and the other isn't. I am rather optimistic about the

longterm picture though a bit uneasy at the moment here. Of course I don't say the Chinese communists if successful would be sure to work out in this agreeable way, only that for people to try to make them seems the only reasonable bet.

In another, undated letter, addressed to John Crowe Ransom before the siege, he reiterated the urgent desirability of a separate Chinese communism: 'I have not yet seen anything to break my optimistic view that the Chinese communists aren't likely to jump into a world war to help Russia, and I wouldn't have thought it sensible to bring a family here without that as a prior calculation.'[65] Like Edgar Snow and Owen Lattimore, then, he became what David Caute has called 'a prophet of Third World non-alignment'.

All such calculations would be shaken, if not fully dashed, when Mao Tse-tung elected to mark the 28th Anniversary of the Chinese Communist Party on 1 July 1949 by publishing his unequivocal essay 'On the People's Democratic Dictatorship'. The creation of a Chinese nation-state led by the working class necessitated a policy of 'leaning to one side', Mao declared. 'This means allying ourselves with the Soviet Union, with every New Democratic country... This means forming an international united front... The Communist Party of the USSR is our very best teacher.'[66]

After visiting Peking for six weeks in July-September 1949, Michael Lindsay (who had spent four years with the Communists during the war, following a period of teaching at Yenching University in Peiping) reported to Chatham House in London on 1 November that there was 'an arguable case' for China's seemingly unpressured choice of a pro-Russian alignment.[67] His argument exactly rehearsed the situation that Bertrand Russell had viewed as a happy prospect in 1923: a military stand-off or offensive stalemate. 'Briefly, the argument is that the real danger of a third world war comes from the risk of American aggression and that the only way to stop it is by an anti-aggression front, so strong and so determined that it would deter the United States from starting a war. I think that is the reason for the anti-Tito policy: it is considered that Tito is breaking the anti-aggression front, thereby increasing the risk of war.' Indeed, the Chinese were given pretty good cause to suffer from what Lindsay termed 'a persecution mania about the west', and they internally incited it whenever it was not provoked from abroad (Mao is said to have believed that imperialism should be smashed by another world war, and proposed to secure a Socialist China within twenty years).[68]

Watching the anti-American enmity of the Chinese Communists, and the anti-Communist bellicosity of the Americans, Empson found little handy comfort in the concept of a balance of power. All the evidence available to him in Peiping over the ensuing months suggested that American foreign policy would soon force a war, and his attitude towards China represented a triumph of hope over experience.

Nevertheless, Empson continued to sow among his students and colleagues the germ of a 'separate' form of Chinese Communism. As he recalled in a letter dating from 1980, 'It was not original thinking at all, but what all our stripe of opinion thought. For that matter, Churchill had backed Tito in the war, and not some royalist Yugoslav, against much Tory opposition, because he was genuinely fighting Hitler. And, though it seems possible that what our stripe foresaw will eventually turn out to be right, as I hope it will, we were quite wrong at the time; we had not foreseen the Korean War.'[69] Just a year after the inauguration of the People's Republic of China, that is to say, the Chinese went to war on behalf of the united front of international socialism. For the time being, Empson did everything he could to keep his foot in the cultural door.

In Peiping the immediate changeover to Communist rule passed with no significant drama. Although Hetta Empson reported to the *Observer* on 4 February, 'apparently communists unexpected quick turnover signs of unpreparedness cope civic problems', the PLA was in fact expeditious in getting the city up and running. 'In human terms, it has been somewhat like a game of musical chairs,' Barnett reported. 'The top personnel of key organizations, together with certain titles and names, have been reshuffled and changed overnight, but the organizations continue to function much as they did before.' The Communists were nothing if not 'businesslike', he observed. Water and electricity came back on line; trams and buses resumed normal service, the city gates were opened, trains went back and forth to Tientsin, Mukden, and Tsinan; snow-covered streets were cleared of military debris. The 8 o'clock curfew remained in force, but no one seemed to bother if it was breached.

John King Fairbank has written that 'inflation was brought under control by the concerted use of several devices: control of all credit by taking over all the banking system, control of major commodities by setting up nation-wide trading associations in each line, and assurance to the public by paying all personnel in market-basket terms, that is, calculating salaries not in money but in basic commodities... This made individuals' salaries independent of the inflation and created a stable basis for commerce. The flow of goods and of money was thus brought into balance and the inflation reduced to about 15 percent a year. This was literally the salvation of the salaried class.'[70]

Although A. Doak Barnett reported in February 1949 that people grumbled about the so-called 'Communist millet economy' (at least when the KMT introduced payments in kind, it was argued, the professors and students had received their wages and subsidies in terms of wheat flour rather than coarse grains), the professional classes soon felt heartened to acquire this security of income, most especially since the payment of *hsiao-mi* (millet) helped to guard against the inflation they dreaded. The university salaries announced in May showed an increase of about one-third over their depressed and paperweight value in the latter part of 1949: a topmost professor (of several years' standing) might earn up to 1300 catties (equivalent at the time to US $30). By the end of the year, then, the Communists had taken satisfactory control of the economy. As Hetta Empson related in a letter: 'University teachers and professors are amongst the most highly paid classes now, all based rigidly on Hsiao Mi (price published day before salaries are issued). Of course prices have gone up in terms of the paper denominations, but then so has the hsiao mi, and it really is very just and equitable. William, for instance, is getting 1015 lbs of hsiao mi per month...'

Like the Nationalist forces of foul recent memory, many 'warriors of the liberation' were necessarily billeted on the citizens; but unlike the Nationalists, their conduct proved to be exemplary and beguiling: 'soldiers well-equipped wellfed wellbehaved impressing populace favourably excellent discipline,' wrote Hetta Empson. Some troops, caught short while waiting to enter their new headquarters in the former Japanese legation, politely asked the neighbours just over the way if they could use their toilet facilities: the British Embassy naturally said yes to such good manners. Alan Winnington seems not to have exaggerated the case when he recalled years later: 'PLA men, when offered space on the family brick bed, preferred to sleep under the broad eaves. They swept the courtyards, fetched water, carried night soil, made coal balls, asked for nothing, accepted nothing, sang, taught the children the Yangko dance, drank no alcohol, treated women with respect, held meetings and studied.'[71] They were acting under strict orders, working hard and wooing the natives. The brave new world had arrived, the students proclaimed: the City of Northern Peace had been liberated from 'Kuomintang reactionaries and American imperialists'.

Not surprisingly, the Communists swooped upon the private business interests of 'bourgeois capitalists'. But they moved just as swiftly to stem the flow of free news and movement. As early as 4 February, Hetta Empson cabled to the *Observer*, 'correspondents dejected no official press relations communists say too busy stop top officials incomunicado stop telegraphic communication rumoured ceasing shortly'; and in her last despatch, dated 11 February, she reported that the PLA was sustaining a policy of holding itself 'aloof' from all foreigners. On 1 February, the *North China Daily News* was transformed into the *People's Daily*; the Central News Agency became the New China News Agency (Hsinhua), with the prominent journalist Fan Ch'ang-chiang as editor. Thereafter, both government organs fed their audience on a diet of small news and copious propaganda derived mostly from *Pravda* and Tass, filleting factual information from home and abroad; and the government made no bones about exploiting the media principally to disseminate party policy. 'Every mention of the Soviet Union is laudatory...,' noted Barnett. 'Conversely, all United States action is portrayed as motivated by sinister imperialism.'[72]

According to the Communists, early in February two American journalists had mischievously reported that the majority of the people of Peiping (aside from the students and organized groups of workers) had given the PLA a far cooler welcome than they had afforded in 1937 to the invading Japanese. Whether or not the Communists deliberately distorted the story in what Barnett considered 'a bitter smear campaign', the newly-formed Communist union of journalists leapt at the chance to slate the meretricious Associated Press correspondents in question (neither of whom was in fact an American citizen). Moreover, as Hetta Empson observed, the 'popular complaints' against them were even 'stronger than [the] official' denunciations. Andrew Roth fairly summed up the incident: 'This brief flurry revealed the deep pool of anti-foreignism upon which the Communists can draw.'[73]

There was no suggestion yet that other individual foreigners would be victimized; but no one could doubt they were being isolated and treated at best with indifference. 'As for ordinary foreign nationals,' Mao Tse-tung announced, 'their legitimate interests will be protected and not encroached upon.' So it was that Empson wrote home in June: 'There is no noticeable anti-foreign feeling among ordinary people; the communist leaders simply don't meet foreigners.'[74]

Most threateningly, however, Mao refused to do business with foreign consulates, on the grounds that there could be no official contact without government recognition. He directed too that 'imperialist propaganda agencies' should be closed down. All foreigners were consequently left in the irregular position of having no diplomatic representation whatsoever;

even the consuls were effectively disjoined from their legal status, being regarded as nothing more than 'private citizens'. 'The Communists seem to regard all foreigners as spies and are extremely wary of them,' wrote Barnett. 'They have specifically warned the populace, through the newspapers, that all American newspapermen can be considered potential spies.'[75]

In such extraordinary circumstances, it had become an inevitable step for the Military Control Commission to give orders on 27 February that 'during the present military period, all foreign news agencies and news-papermen are forbidden to carry on any of their activities in this city.' For the English-speaking residents of Peiping, the radio remained the only way to keep in touch with outside news. Fully conscious of official censorship, Empson wrote in June to England (where his uncensored letter did arrive): 'We feel a good deal cut off, indeed, but not from any deliberate Iron Curtain business; the postal set-up is bound to be trying till the new government is set up and recognised, and our radio apparently can't be mended. The local papers are short of news.'[76] It was tactful coding.

Next, the Military Control Commission kept watch and ward on the citizenry of Peiping by requiring everyone to obtain residence certificates, and by restricting movement beyond the city limits. Travel permits were granted only for proven purposes, and for several months the Empsons could not venture farther than Tsinghua University and the Summer Palace some seven miles beyond the city walls.

Foreign nationals had also to attend for personal registration at the Bureau of Public Security, involving 'several visits', and 'the writing of quadruplicate answers in Chinese to a fairly detailed questionnaire', and submission of six photos. Nor was it unusual for Westerners to be paid intimidating 'house calls': at any time of the day or night, officials of the Public Security Bureau would burst into their homes and subject them to further close questioning about their personal lives and contacts.[77]

But the Empsons suffered no ordeal at all, as Hetta reported: 'Both William and I were very well received, separately. He, because of his refugee-ing with the University 1937-9 and because we seem to be quite well-known, and I took along my party cards and gave an account of my life since birth (the salient political facts, which is what they were interested in, took about thirty minutes) and they seemed to know enough about my personal life here not to want to ask any questions.'[78] It was at about this time too that Hetta, whose long-held faith in Communism seemed at last to be vindicated, wrote in a letter to a friend: 'I have written [to the British Communist Party in London] to say I want to be transferred to the

Chinese Party, now my Chinese is good enough to go to meetings (though I can't write yet) and friends here think that would be the best thing to do, while waiting for an answer from London, I have been invited to attend Branch meetings and discussions, but I'm rather shy of going until my credentials have been established.'[79] Although the Empsons had never been particularly discreet about their views and activities, it is likely too that a report on their personal lives and political conduct had been submitted to the authorities by their neighbour (and first teacher of Chinese), Ch'i Sheng-ch'iao—who, it emerged at this time, had long been an underground Communist at Peita. (Many years later, in 1972, Robert Winter wrote to Ivor and Dorothea Richards: 'It seems that he also learned from William habits of excessive drinking—usually the deadly "pei ka'rh" [*bai gar*, a white moonshine made from millet, with a taste like gasoline]. Ch'i is still devoted to the Empsons...')[80]

The Fourteenth All-China Student Representatives Conference, held in Peiping from 1 to 6 March, reinforced among the youth of China the conviction that there remained many opportunities to partake of the glory of the revolution, by participating in the task of nation-building. In the Peiping area alone, four centres were established to train new cadres, three of which—the North China University, the North China Military and Political University, the North China People's Revolutionary University— held competitive entrance examinations, normally for university and middle school graduates, and set out to teach their recruits for between four and six months. The PLA's Southward-bound Service Corps, which ran a six-week course specifically to prepare students to play supportive roles (chiefly as political workers) when Lin Piao's Fourth Field Army presently pushed on into southern China, adopted a policy of more open enrolment, and over 3,000 students had matriculated by the middle of March; a further 2,600 students were admitted in April.[81] Many university students in Peiping, newly exalted by the liberation, responded to the recruiting campaign: up to 678 students (out of a total body of 2,482) from Tsinghua alone, about 80 from Yenching, and a considerable proportion of Peita's roll.

On 19 June, Empson wrote home to England: 'We plan to stay on another university year, till next summer, anyway. I think it ought to be pleasant again when things settle down, the government is formed and so on (unless Hell breaks loose, of course, but in that case it doesn't much matter where you are). At present...our more intelligent student acquaintances have joined Southward-going Working Groups and after a brief display of their uniforms have actually gone south.'[82] Among them, one of his very best students, Jin Di, was prompt to join up. While Empson appreciated the patriotism that inspired his ardent pupils, and the redemptive cause for which they enlisted—just before Jin Di's departure with the Service Corps, the Empsons threw a party at which everyone sang the 'Internationale'—he made light of the fact that their absence coincided with a period when it had become disturbingly difficult to know just whose hand held the tiller of educational strategy.

For the first months of their rule, the Communists held back from heaving on the educational rudder; rather, they chose gradually to cultivate self-reform in the intellectual community, and only after a calming interim to set the schools, colleges, and universities on their predetermined course of revolutionary reorganization. Such an approach seemed to achieve its objective. In Michael Lindsay's judgement, by the second half of 1949 many of the Chinese professors in Peiping who had been educated overseas, in Britain and America, were giving 'fairly enthusiastic support' to the new regime. The 'prevailing opinion' could be illustrated by 'typical remarks' such as: 'Well, for the first time in China we have got a Government which really is honest, and which really means to get something done'. Lindsay hoped that the 'scientific Marxists', those who evolved their political principles and adjusted their practices according to popular democratic needs and criticism, would win the day over the doctrinaire Marxists, the adherents of a 'scholastic or superstitious Marxism'.[83]

Yet the paradoxical title of Mao's June essay 'On the People's Democratic Dictatorship' gave certain notice to liberal intellectuals that in due time their destiny would be dictated solely by the proletariat, and some still thought it a baleful prospect. Only by virtue of being classified as 'brain workers' were the intellectuals granted the hope that they might have a say in China's collective future: once re-educated, they would come to know their place under the leadership of the working class. For the moment, they could be won over, and perhaps the majority were being won over, principally because they were not immediately threatened with the scientific application of neo-totalitarian ideas to the old educational order. But even those who harboured no self-saving hopes of retaining the ideal of intellectual liberalism had lost every chance to fend off the future. Suzanne Pepper has pinpointed the failure of the former intellectual élite with this adroit formulation: 'Perhaps their greatest tragedy was, appropriately enough, more intellectual than political: they failed to comprehend the fact of their own irrelevance.'[84]

Well before the Communists arrived in Peiping, Empson had anticipated a very testing transitional period, whether under the Communists or under a coalition government, which he hoped to turn to the advantage of the British Council and the interests of English teaching in general. Though not a natural administrator (and too individualistic to enjoy manipulating committees or indulging in managerial games), he seems to have been the only foreign educationalist around who determined to put forward workable proposals: 'we can't go on as at present much longer,' he had written to I. A. Richards late in September 1948, 'and it is important to be ready with plans.'

His first thought was to challenge Richards himself to become the next great helmsman of the British Council in China; and he drafted this letter without undue deference:

> Are you clear in your mind that Miss Grier is appointed only for two years . . . and is too old and I gather too discouraged to want to go on. About the middle of next year a new appointment will therefore be made, and Fitzgerald (who is my boss here, but I am afraid the British Council seldom does what he wants, but still they appointed Miss Grier on his recommendation, and all she has done is to believe any cheat who comes up to her with stories against Fitzgerald—it is true sure enough that he is a bad business man . . .)—be that as it may, Fitzgerald is keen to have you take on the job next, and I quote this to show that a man who has listened to a lot of topgrade B. C. politics thinks it possible. . . . If you did take the job it would mean that the English teaching business could be put on a working footing just while a collapse of the process was otherwise inevitable.[85]

The bureaucratic trivialities of the British Council, he explained further, operated on 'a petty-sultan basis' and need not concern Richards, in particular because 'dear Miss Grier is spending her time with the nose down to the accounts, and her successor won't have the same worries, it will be a purified organism just waiting for somebody to put a little life into it.' So long as Richards could satisfy the British Council that he was not 'a local dictator' and did not support C. K. Ogden's unaccommodating jealousy vis-à-vis every article of the Basic English programme, the British Council would surely be happy to appoint a man of his distinction. In Empson's inimitably witty encapsulation, 'The British Council as such does not care how well English is taught in China, so long as there is no suggestion that English must be taught equally well to all the rest of the world.' As to the question of whether the Communists would anyway hold on to the British Council and English-language teaching, the only sure provision against their possible displeasure was for the British to have 'reasonable goods to offer'.

In any event, just like Robert Winter—who was 'roaring away in excellent health and temper' and 'rather banking on his very fine collection of gramophone records and his powers as a dramatic producer to make himself obviously useful even if the English language is totally abandoned'—Empson valiantly hoped to be able to remain and teach in China:

but I would be unable to offer anything but my language in its various reaches, and my only claim could be that I know how the language can be taught without the absurd effort which it at present costs. The last pronouncement by Hu Shih on the subject, earlier this year, was that he thought the middle schools had better give up all pretence of teaching English because they were obviously failing to do it altogether. My own impression was that we did the whole language teaching in the first two years at the university. However Hetta has just started taking a first-year Peita language class and their knowledge is very decent... We are unwilling at present to believe in progress, but actually the recovery in teaching levels since the war does seem to be real though modest. Total collapse is not after all on the cards... No doubt I am pattering round the subject rather tediously, but the point I am aiming at is that teaching of English language and historical background (if that is what literature may come to be called— it suits me all right) will go on being required. I should expect a Chinese communist government once in power to become pretty soon very nationalist, anxious to show it wasn't in the Russians' pocket but very nasty about Hongkong and Malaya and so on, meanwhile childishly eager to keep any customer it was being nasty to, and active in trying to revive the cultural life which is at present being starved. Of course my students who will rally at once to demonstrate against the present [KMT] government will say at once if asked 'suppose when the communists come they won't let you speak up'[,] 'of course if they try to suppress us we must resist them too'. The picture seen by the Peita student is very flat and moral and to be sure ignorant but not at all partisan. I like them very much, and think it obvious that no political change... would alter the basic educational requirements. And as regards my own conscience in taking British Government money, I think I earn it already, but I should feel I was likely to give better value for it behind communist lines than just in front of them. The more people or rather nations can be made not to take part in the prospective Russian-American war the more hope for the future, it seems to me, though I do not pretend to be heroic about my convictions and have always felt that avoiding any suspicion of becoming a traitor to my own nation would have to be the casting vote.

He typed out at least two versions of the letter to Richards; the final one, dispatched on 22 January 1949, was no less forcefully impressive:

The Chinese are a field you were forced to let drop, and I am sure you feel that at the right time that part of the career ought to be tidied up. Now is the time; no later period would give anything like the same opportunity. The decision may really come in the next year or two whether the Chinese go on learning English in bulk at all. It is time to put your oar in.

As to the politics, my point of view is simply that the Chinese communists had much better not be forced into the arms of Moscow, where they don't really want to be; this seems to be the attitude of most foreigners on the spot. So one could say that getting the Middle School English teaching here on a tolerable footing is really a matter of world importance in preventing the Third World War. How often do you receive calls of so high a character?[86]

To his great credit, Richards promptly rose to the bait of Empson's letter. 'Notable, isn't it, that they already think something can and should be done,' he appealed to the Rockefeller Foundation on 3 February. 'There is a kind of hopeful stir?'[87] And he agreed without hesitation that his name could be put forward. Unhappily, however, he did not get to lead the British Council in China, though he would return to Peking for a while in 1950.

But Empson remained undaunted in his aspiration to steer English-language-teaching into a belatedly sensible channel; and in view of the fact that language-teaching was neither his avowed profession nor part of his job at Peita, it has to be recognized that every time he spoke up for the Basic brief in China he was most loyally advocating the mission that his mentor had appeared to abandon over a decade before.

Soon after the arrival of the PLA, and before anyone else thought to make plans for perhaps unwelcome educational reconstruction, he seized the initiative by writing a formal letter to the university authorities—more than seven closely-typed pages—proselytizing for the advantages of using Basic as the set method for teaching English in secondary schools and universities.

'We must expect that when a political settlement is reached many questions about education will be reopened, and it looks as though this time may be not far off,' he began. 'Clearly it would be better for the universities so far as possible to be ready when the occasion arises with proposals of their own suited to the circumstances . . . We need . . . to recognise that a reduction of the hours given to learning English in Middle Schools may be required. The question as I see it is whether we can hope to obtain better results from less time, and I believe that is possible, though naturally it will require careful organisation and a "gearing-up" of the whole process.'[88] The 'guiding principles' had already been decided by the working party of the Ministry of Education in 1937, which he had attended with Richards. Chinese students needed above all else to be saved from drowning in the welter of English words, as well as all the 'minor subtleties' of the language (such as 'endless heaps of irregular verbs'), to which they had traditionally and woefully been subjected. Likewise, the bugaboo of trying to exact from the students any so-called 'correct' pronunciation was of no real consequence at all. Strict phoneticians had long laboured, for example, to make Chinese students say not CULTURAL but KULSHRL, he argued elsewhere, and with quite ridiculous results: 'A man who has been deliberately taught to say KULSHRL cannot speak up; he can only mumble with the air of a man going through a difficult gymnastic exercise.' A form of Basic English nimbly adapted to the requirements of the Chinese beginner represented the only viable scheme, he urged with extremely fine tact; I. A. Richards's *A First Book of English for Chinese Learners*, published in 1938, was the best textbook yet available—and Robert Winter already held a copy in Tsinghua University. (When Richards eventually made it known that he did not wish to reprint his primer, however, Empson acknowledged in a later letter, as he had thought to himself all along, that it was in fact far too 'intellectual': 'I remember first reading it with keen interest as a sort of disguised treatise on the English language, but you can't expect the average Middle School student to have the same line of interest.'[89] In due course Richards sent Empson copies of his new *Pocket Book* and its accompanying *Work Book*, along with some 'mechanical aids' including gramophone records.)

Even the secondary school student who does not go on to a university, Empson concluded his first open letter, 'ought to feel (especially if he has spent the present allowance of hours on English) "I know the language perfectly well, only of course I would have to learn any particular word that came up". At present he feels "I know thousands of words, but the language is a buzzing confusion and I dare not use any of it; the sensible thing is to forget it and say I know none". Surely this is the fundamental failure which we are all concerned to correct.'

When the Peiping universities were at last obliged in the rain-soaked summer of 1949 to face up to the Communist review of their courses, with the aim of making them more practical and efficient, Empson patiently and appealingly reiterated all the bonus points of Basic English, while admitting that he had 'practically no experience of language teaching as such and...no particular business to express views about it'. However much the Communists seek to overhaul the curricula of the Middle Schools, the universities must take responsibility for giving the schools a lead in language teaching, he insisted in a letter of 1 July 1949 to his former Lienda colleague, Chao Hsiung Chao, who had just been put in charge of the Western Languages Department at Tsinghua. (Chao, who had 'behaved so badly about Basic in Kunming',[90] now seemed 'energetic and ready to make changes,' he told Richards, 'and interested in getting collaboration with other universities, contact with Middle Schools etc. Of course he is rather unpopular and may not last.')[91] Even though Empson declared his own interest in an appropriately modified version of Basic English, he argued, matriculating students would be far better equipped than at present if they could only be taught while at school to read and write fluently with an 'agreed list of a thousand words'. '*Any* tolerably reasonable word-list would, it seems clear, be better than none.'

The amount of astute reflection he had given to the rigid word-list of the Basic scheme, and his practical experience and sheer good sense, are evident in this sampler from his detailed letter:

> No such list could avoid including the eighteen verbs used in Basic and the prepositions; the only practical question, I think, is whether it should have other verbs. Basic has been rather badly advertised by the claim that it is easy; the real point is that the prepositions and their uses with simple verbs (e.g. 'put up with' and other uses simpler than that) are really hard for Chinese students, but you have no idiomatic grasp of the language if you leave them out and learn verbs which the English speaker feels to be pedantic as a way of getting round them. The Basic scheme is I think clearly right in saying that the prepositions should be taught as beginning from a spatial meaning to which their other meanings can be attached; they are quite interesting if they are taught like this, whereas if the idioms are simply thrown at the student piecemeal he can only feel that the language is intolerably whimsical and gives him no chance to use his own judgement. The same kind of psychological argument applies to the limitation of irregular verbs ...
>
> Among the things that should clearly not be taught in Middle School *as for use when the students write in English* are 'should' (*ought to* is the safe alternative); the confusion in a sentence like 'It is a bad thing that women should have the vote', where the second clause seems a complete contradiction of the first, is a bad patch in the language and one that they had better simply keep out of. The straightforward alternative here is of course 'It is a bad thing *for* women *to* have the vote'. *Shall* and its elaborate complexities are not used by many reputable Englishspeaking groups and can only serve to horrify a Middle School student.[92]

He wound up: 'The only over-all view that I feel confident about is that even a considerable reduction of the hours given to teaching English in this country need not be incompatible with a greatly increased knowledge of the language; indeed I really feel that a reduction of hours might be a positive help if it forced people to consider the purpose in view and plan how to arrive at it.'

While it is impossible to know whether the short cut of Basic English was truly the best foundation for teaching Chinese learners, Empson's experience proved to his satisfaction that it worked. He had always found it beautifully effective for explaining even complex analytical points in his own lectures on literature. There can be little doubt that he was exceptionally wise before the event in anticipating that the Communists would soon curtail the teaching of the English language; but naturally he could not expect that the New China would eventually scotch English in favour of Russian. In the meantime, as he wrote in September, he found it emotionally exhausting to try to deal with the 'pokey situation' begotten by the bureaucracy of uncoordinated committees—'but I see nothing in my own judgement to make me doubt that the situation will turn out well if reasonably handled.'[93]

'It is not that conditions are bad once you get here,' he had written to Richards on 3 July; 'we are living very comfortably; but so far no British Council people (or teachers of any kind, that I know) have been allowed to come up here, even from Shanghai after liberation.'[94] He felt particularly dismayed when that 'sharp and well-intentioned old body', Lynda Grier—who 'became deservedly unpopular'—'starved Peking, where good relations with the incoming government might easily have been established, and formed a quaint enclave of her own pets in Nanking.'[95] Her favoured circle did not include C. P. Fitzgerald, whom she presently sacked from the Peiping office—'on the specific ground of knowing the Chinese language from what I gather,' Empson reported—while adding an observation that he knew could be taken to reflect a frankly unhappy irony on his own noble efforts at organization: 'No doubt he was rather unbusinesslike as well, but they really have been getting rid of sinologues or refusing to take them, [John] Blofeld and [Henry] Macaleavy for instance. It is very absurd; one could almost say that the Chinese don't take a foreigner seriously unless he knows the language.'[96] Even when the British Council office in Peiping eventually managed to run 'an innocent discussion series for Middle School teachers', in which Empson played a part, he formed the discouraging impression of 'the local figures', teachers and officiators, that 'the energetic ones are narrow and pretty benighted and [the] enlightenable ones very slack.'[97]

Sadly, the lack of cooperation between the universities resulted in the implementation of separate stratagems. While Yenching saw fit to leave its curriculum alone, Tsinghua (where Empson would continue to lecture once a week on Shakespeare) opted for the time being to increase to twelve hours a week the amount of language teaching it would offer to prospective English majors. Peita proposed to reduce its hours of English-language teaching, even for English majors, from five to three; but Empson judged that 'we are lucky in having Chu Kuan Tien as head of the W[estern]-L[anguages] department, politically a bit suspect in the past but a sturdy old organiser; rather pro-Basic than not, but of course a great fence-sitter. The man who used to be in charge of first and second year language teaching is very cross because it has been taken over by the Dean of Studies for centralising; I don't know that it makes the decisions come any quicker.' Nonetheless, with his usual optimism, Empson salvaged some constructive consolation from all this shuffling: 'There seems to be general agreement on a formula that language only is to be taught in the first two years and literature in the second two, but if the class is reading a text it may as well be worth reading, so the distinction isn't clear-cut.'[98]

As far as he could see in the middle months of 1949, therefore, the Communists were doing little more than gentle the universities towards revolutionary rectification, and he felt confident that he would be allowed to go on teaching what he called 'English language and historical back-ground'—meaning the great literature he hoped forever to profess.

Throughout the weeks when the Communists had been busy turning over the city, a great peeling portrait of Chiang Kai-shek had been left hanging on the Gate of Heavenly Peace, the main entrance to the Forbidden City. Come September, when the PLA had satisfactorily liberated the most part of China, Chiang's face gave place to an equally large picture of Chairman Mao, which was mounted not on the gate itself but on the wall of Tian'an-men. Likewise, on a huge flagpole in the centre of the plaza, which had been enlarged and festooned with banners and floodlights, flew the new national flag: a field of red with one large five-pointed star and an arc of four smaller stars, all in gold, in the canton.

On 1 October, a day of grey sky and drizzle, Mao Tse-tung and his Party leaders filled the nine bays of the lofty terrace beneath the double-eaved red-and-gold gate tower in order to inaugurate the People's Republic of China. China's new rulers 'looked oddly stiff and mechanical, like opera singers seen from the third balcony,' thought David Kidd.[99] Before the rostrum, there passed in review a huge military parade. Hetta Empson described the spectacle just a few days afterwards: 'It could only have been a small part of the Liberation Army that took part in the military display because the main forces must be fighting in the South, but it was extremely thrilling. They were well-equipped (with the best American equipment, captured from the KMT) and the cavalry was very surprising too, thousands of them on sturdy little Mongolian ponies riding past in formation, each unit formed of horses of the same colour.'[100] At dusk, when the two-hour military march-past had drawn to a close, units of hilarious students and other citizenry took their turns to process through the plaza, cheering, singing, dancing, waving red flags and banners, and carrying innumerable lanterns, 'so that it became as light as day, thousands upon thousands of columns.'[101] Each group saluted the rostrum with chants of '*Mao Tse-tung Chuhsi, wan sui!*' ('Long live Chairman Mao Tse-tung!'), and to every single acclamation Mao responded, in his surprisingly high voice: '*Chung Hwa Jen Min Kung Ho Kuo, wan sui!*' ('Long live the People's Republic of China!'). So unflaggingly did Mao cry out his answer to the marchers that after a time he could only respond with a hoarse '*Wan sui! ... Wan Sui!*' ('Long live!' - or literally translated, 'Ten Thousand years!'), and the crowd roared back: 'Wan sui, wan sui, WAN WAN SUI!'[102] Again and again too, the assembled masses sang 'The East Shines Red', a folk song reworded to anthem the Communist apocalypse:

> The East shines red,
> The sun arises,
> Mao Tse-tung appears in China,
> Toiling for the happiness of the people,
> The saviour of the people![103]

Teams of boys and girls clad in coloured silks, with their faces heavily powdered, eyebrows blackened and lips picked out in carmine, performed a highly stylized and synchronized version of the *yang-ko*, the Planting Dance, to the accompaniment of drums, cymbals and gongs. Other groups of marchers bore big lanterns in the shapes of Chinese characters which they ingeniously fitted together to make yet larger shapes: flags, pagodas, tanks, battleships, and even a glowing likeness of the Gate of Heavenly Peace. 'I have never seen anything more impressive than the spectacle ...,' wrote Hetta Empson soon afterwards. 'It was deeply inspiring.'[104] The city blazed with continuing festivities, dancing, and fantastic firework displays, for three days.

6

The New China

SHORTLY before the Inauguration, from 21 to 28 September, Mao Tse-tung had convened the first Plenary Session of the Chinese People's Political Consultative Conference, which was attended by 662 representatives from the CCP, the Democratic League, and other democratic groups, labour, peasants, business and industry.

'The Chinese people have stood up,' Mao declared in his opening address. 'China will never again be an insulted nation.' One of the most brilliant strokes of statesmanship of the modern era, fusing the otherwise distinct concepts of cultural nation and political nation, Mao's rhetoric seemed to deliver to the Chinese peoples the fulfilment of their dreams: a sovereign nation-state which would be ruled by no one but themselves. In respect of some regional and minority cultures, Mao was supplying them with a need they had never known they felt; but certainly his speech inscribed in the minds of the majority of the Han Chinese the ardent desire to make a reality of the nation-myth, to secure their country's integration, harmony and political self-determination. In short, he had mobilized the political will of the people. Nonetheless, in the absence of consensus, all policies would be decided for the people by the 'democratic centralism'—*min-chu chi-chung chih*—of the Party.

After designating Peiping as the official capital of China, and formally changing its name back to Peking (Beijing),[1] on 29 September the conference adopted the 'Common Programme', which would stand as the principal constitutional document of the People's Republic of China until 1954. Article 45 of the Programme prescribed: 'Literature and art shall be promoted to serve the people, to enlighten the political consciousness of the people, and to encourage the labour enthusiasm of the people.

Outstanding works of literature and the arts shall be encouraged and rewarded. The people's drama and cinema shall be developed.'[2] The people had been served or encouraged by a first dose of just such reconstruction as early as March, when the Cultural Control Committee banned fifty-seven plays and operas from the traditional repertoire, some because they were superstitious or licentious; others because they catered to 'slave morality' or glorified feudalism; and others again, perhaps with more artistic discrimination, because they were simply 'boring'—as well as seeking to suppress 'decadent' American films in favour of 'healthy' Russian specimens.

Impinging directly on Empson's professional prospects, Article 46 of the Common Programme provided: 'The method of education of the People's Government shall reform the old educational system, subject matter, and teaching methods systematically according to plan.' Such was the unspecific promise. In practice it meant that the Minister of Education, Ma Hsü-lun, immediately issued guidelines for a nation-wide programme of political study (*cheng-chih hsüeh-hsi*), which served to set under way a sustained process of ideological indoctrination.

Every university would presently be commanded to undergo the curricular shake-up that Philip West has described in an account of Yenching: 'New courses were introduced in which each week students and faculty met jointly for a two hour lecture, known as the *ta-k'o*, followed by discussion sessions in small groups formed in each of the various departments, with a student serving as chairman and a faculty member always present. All students were required to take Historical Materialism and Social Evolution the first semester and Principles of the New Democracy the second semester, each for three hours credit. In addition all students in the arts and social sciences were required to take six hours of Political Economy... This intensive program of political education was carried out largely by people within the university... The newly instilled revolutionary consciousness was intended to permeate all areas of life... The major enemies in the attack, labeled as feudalism, imperialism, and capitalism, were identified with forces outside the university.'[3]

The students were organized by their cadres into a complex and all-consuming network of 'mutual-aid circles', unions, sections, and squads, with student officers exercising control over both academic classes and political classes. The liberal bourgeois notion of privacy became defunct, for further Party or Youth League members took charge of 'floor groups' in the dormitories, watching the private lives and even the thoughts of their peers and submitting regular written reports on their attitudes and degrees of application. Likewise, casting off their long gowns or western-style suits—the remnants of feudalism and imperialism—the students became equally dedicated followers of the folk fashion. A grey uniform of short jacket, sweater, and trousers became the regular wear: everyone, the moneyed bourgeoisie as much as the students, wanted to look like—to identify with—the *lao pai hsing* (the common people, or literally 'old hundred names').

Although the flush of academic reconstruction induced by the Common Programme certainly unsettled his classes in the autumn, Empson refused to let it knock him off course. But the big wave of the new way sent a number of his Chinese colleagues reeling backwards. Early in the semester, an unprecedented conference of Peita's professors and students passed eight unanimous resolutions, including one that some teachers would at that time regard as unnerving: 'Teaching methods should be based upon a spirit of mutual assistance between teachers and students and mutual benefit between teaching and learning.'[4] Anodyne wording, perhaps, but the formula served to admit the rule that no course could proceed without the approval of the students. As Maria Yen recalled, the resolution caused many teachers 'to act very gingerly', for 'by this time our leaders selected by the Party and the Youth League had effective control over the rest of us, which meant that the Party was going to use us to impose the changes it wanted our teachers to make.'[5]

For a while, the most progressive students included Shakespeare 'in the blanket condemnation passed on all Western literature'; after all, they argued, most of Shakespeare's heroes were kings and noblemen concerned with personal honour or glory. However, as soon as it became known that Soviet literati did not regard Shakespeare as a reactionary, and in fact had a high respect for his works, the local progressives hurriedly reconstrued their doubts as 'deviations'. 'We all made a point of attending an exhibition of Shakespeare's works and a photographic display of his life and background at the British Council on the anniversary of the great man's birthday [in 1950],' wrote Yen. 'And to our immense satisfaction the most prominent figures at the show were the same progressives who had denounced England's greatest writer as a "reactionary" three months before.' Yet the study of Shakespeare, which students regarded as one of 'the more difficult required subjects' in the English department, was still made into an 'elective'.[6]

If such a change meant that Empson would have fewer students in his class, he claimed to find it neither a threat nor a bother; in truth, he made it rather a point of pedagogical principle that a lecturer 'ought to be willing and helpful to his students, but still I think it ought to be obvious that he is more interested in his subject than he is in them . . . as when Professor G. E. Moore is said to have gone through an entire course at Cambridge with unruffled dignity attended only by one student; who was I. A. Richards, and he of course was well worth doing it to.'[7]

Many students did drop Shakespeare, but mostly because they felt burdened by the difficulties of the texts; not because they could not follow, at one and the same time, Empson's patter about problems and his writing on the blackboard. It is true that he would not match up to a normative definition of a good teacher, because he was really more interested in questions that exercised his own mind than in what the students might find acceptable or accessible; but it is just as true that his best, most constant students were impressed by his prodigious memory and brilliant insights. Nonetheless, while defending his right to decide the content and line of his own courses, he wrote on 14 October: 'I have been rather uneasy till now whether the students were going to put up with me, as it takes the first three or four weeks of term to make them decide, but I feel I am doing well enough now. I still feel of course that this is the right place for me to be if I can stand the pace; or rather if the pace will go on listening to me while I say what I want to. There could hardly be any more interesting job of its humble placid kind.'[8]

Still the students, stirred up by the Student Union, pressed for far more radical reforms of the liberal curriculum, regularly drubbing their teachers with new suggestions and criticisms. Maria Yen, in *The Umbrella Garden* (1954), most notably described how she and her contemporaries tackled one particular, unnamed teacher who is unmistakably identifiable as Empson:

> One department boasted a foreign teacher who proved to be especially amenable to our ideas. Because I rather liked him, I won't mention his name. But I think some foreign readers would recognize it; he is a man of some standing in his field. In the classroom he was fuzzy and vague and sometimes delightful, as amiable as most foreigners are not. We kept offering him suggestions which he patiently accepted and tried to incorporate in his teaching. His prompt and unmurmuring compliance got to be something of a joke with us; he was rather naive about politics, and kept telling us that perhaps it was a good thing we had come into our own.
>
> The stresses we inflicted upon this scholar must have been greater than we realized, however. After a particularly complicated series of suggestions had been loaded upon him, his very progressive wife came to us and told us: 'Don't offer any more suggestions. What do you want to do—make him go

off somewhere and hang himself?' This shamed us into dropping what we
had looked upon as a perfectly harmless sport.[9]

Hetta was known to be *li-hai* (hot-tempered); a tiger in defence of Empson.

Whatever the truth of Yen's account—and no observer could deny the
fair comment that Empson could well seem 'fuzzy and vague', as well as
amiable—the pejorative implication that he was weakly accommodating
to the premature pressure of his students' views, whether provocative or
whimsical, is almost certainly false. Like any teacher, his usual practice was
to make use of his students' ideas and initiatives so long as they served the
purposes of the course and were not distractingly irrelevant. In his official
'Report on Work in Progress', dated 6 April 1950, he readily acknowledged
that he would normally try to comply with students' requests if they were
useful, but his words betray no sense that he felt in any way timorous
before their tyrannous conduct: 'In the Poetry class I have been trying to
put in more sociological background than usual, as the students have
requested, and I agree with them that this ought to be done.' Setting
aside the fact that a large number of students had chosen to withdraw from
the Shakespeare courses run by Empson—though it left him with just
three students in attendance at his course—there is no reason whatever to
doubt the honesty of this statement: 'My Shakespeare and Poetry classes
seem to me satisfactory and I have had no complaints about them.'

His course on Modern English Poetry ran from Hardy to Sidney Keyes,
and included among other poets Hopkins, Housman, Yeats, Eliot, Pound,
Lawrence, Auden, Spender, and Dylan Thomas. While he may have been
happy to incorporate in his teaching a larger amount of what he called
'sociological background'—to discuss, that is to say, the social and historical
context of the poetry—he was indifferent to any overt or implied suggestion
that he should defend the course by putting a suitably socialistic gloss on
each and every work. He went on purveying his singular brand of perception. He even discussed two of his own poems, 'Legal Fiction' and Missing
Dates', taking care to point out that his work had been stimulated by
seventeenth-century Metaphysical poetry and not by the political purposes
of some poets of the 1930s. In the 'Metaphysical' method, he explained,
'one of the standard dilemmas of life is described briefly and surprisingly so
as to throw light on it. My own verse was considered obscure, but once you
see the point there is no further trick: it is not like poetry which is meant to
work on you without understanding it, indeed it is much less rich.'

In the face of the developing political muscle of the student body,
therefore, none of Empson's recorded comments suggest that he felt shy

of continuing to insist on high academic standards, that he would modify his individual judgements and intellectual rigour for fear of being criticized either in or out of the classroom. Equally, he made no attempt to buttress his supposedly embattled authority by demanding of his students more work or discipline than before the Communist takeover; he continued simply to praise and encourage those who showed enthusiasm for the subject.

On many occasions he would invite a student home to talk about poetry, as Chang Chin-yen, who was subsequently a professor in the Chinese Academy of Social Sciences, recalls: 'My first visit to Empson proved very fruitful. He lent me Cleanth Brooks' *Understanding Poetry*, Stanley Hyman's *The Armed Vision*, and a novel by David Garnett [*The Grasshoppers Come*] . . . It was new to me that full appreciation can only be achieved by means of careful analysis. Until then it seemed to me that enjoying poetry was something incompatible with intellectual analysis . . . In retrospect, it is not an exaggeration to say that my lifelong interest in literary criticism depends on this visit.' Not in the least jealous of his personal possessions, Empson regarded his small library as an open feast for students to sample at will, without caring whether the books were returned in good time or condition.

To another student, Chow Chiang-tsu, he lent out no less than fifteen critical studies. In the summer of 1949 Chow, who had won a postgraduate place at Tsinghua University, was accused of being 'reactionary' and consequently lost his fellowship. That autumn, however, he passed the graduate school entrance examination to Peita, where Empson undertook to supervise his thesis on modern British poetry. But Chow found that he could not stomach the new China for himself. 'The intellectual climate was very oppressive; the prescribed approach was to be in line with Marxist-Leninist theories,' he recalls. 'After considerable soul-searching I decided to flee the country. Empson had a very long talk with me one night. He thought the regime was new and that I should give it a chance and be patient.' But Chow had made up his mind and chose not to heed that advice: he and his wife ran away to Hong Kong in the summer of 1951. Empson himself would recall in general: 'my business was to improve the minds of the sober majority, not to create a few disaffected persons . . . only after the liberation did I have a few anti-communists coming round, of a moderate character but not my business to encourage; I don't think I gave them bad advice.'

It is arguable that in the longer term Empson showed a degree of naivety or blindness in his view of the increasingly purgative policies of Communist China, especially during and after the most thoroughgoing 'thought reform' campaign late in 1951. In the short term, as a witness to the first heady months of reconstruction, he was by no means at fault in believing that the good of the cause, and the nature of the political programme, outweighed their bad incidental effects. As a socialist in the liberal democratic tradition, he felt he could work with the command that the 'scientific historical viewpoint' should be applied 'to the study and interpretation of history, economics, politics, culture, and international affairs', though principally by playing devil's advocate against absolutism. As an intellectual who valued the right and duty of independent judgement, he held it as an article of faith that a teacher should not suffer himself to become an instrument of indoctrination. In practice, then, he would make his own way between serving the needs of his students and subverting the totalizing claims of the state. Whereas the *apparatchiki* proposed to cut every thought to one cloth, he would labour to cultivate in his students an awareness that the wider world wore a coat of many colours.

Even so, at the beginning of the 1949–50 academic year, over half of the 1,190 students in Peita were found to hold 'erroneous views' about the Soviet Union; by the end of the session, following indoctrination, the official number of the misguided had declined to 100. To accomplish such a turnabout, as Maria Yen recalled, the Student Union at Peita had voted to intensify the 'study (*hsüeh-hsi*) movement' by ordering the students to devote between 54 and 62 hours a week to classroom work and supervised study:

> Our new daily schedule called for study or classroom attendance from eight in the morning until noon, from two to six, and from seven to ten. Our morning physical drill began at seven, and we had to go to bed at ten-thirty. More and more emphasis was also put upon 'collective study.' This was another part of the constant progress we were supposed to be making toward our final goal of 'collective living'. Few students could find any excuse not to participate, for fear of being accused of 'bourgeois individualism.'[10]

It is important to note that the effect of such an exorbitant consumption of the students' time and energies was indirectly, not purposely, detrimental to Empson's teaching. Far from feeling it their duty to relegate the study of Shakespeare, or to embarrass the professor, the three remaining students in his class were evidently sincere when they came to type out this letter in the summer of 1950:

> Dear Professor,
> In the first place we wish to beg your pardon for not having fulfilled our duty as students, and to express our regret for this fault of ours.

It is true we have neglected Shakespeare this term. Not that we meant to ignore it but that we failed to spare time for it. As a result of China's liberation, every university student is required to have a good knowledge of Marxism. The school authorities asked the senior students of 1950 to take up Dialectic Materialism and Political Economy at the same time (this costs an additional eighteen hours per week) so our classmates dropped Shakespeare along with other courses. Being interested in his work and delighted with your way of teaching, we can't bear to make the sacrifice. With great regret, therefore, we who have had the intention to study carefully this best English writer, find at the end of three months and a half that we have read little, not even done the assignment, Henry IV part 1. We now sincerely hope we may be permitted to make it up during the vacation. This is most improper, of course, but apparently the only remedy.

Dear professor, please forgive us for this kind of 'negociation' [*sic*] which, we can assure you, is by no means deliberate. We hereby promise to work with redoubled efforts next term and ever remain

Your respectful students
2635005 / 66 / 83

Empson accepted the excuse, seeing no reason to expect that the process of political straitening, engrossing such a large portion of academic life, would go on indefinitely. He had faith in the future, and was prepared to await it.

As yet, in the year of Communist takeover, no wholesale programme of reindoctrination had been forced upon the Chinese faculty, though none could long escape the order to offer themselves up to 'self-education and ideological remoulding'. Official statistics revealed that early in 1950 '470,000 intellectuals participated in political study either in political universities or short-term political classes'; and in June 1950, at the Chinese People's Political Consultative Conference, Kuo Mo-jo reported that the 'accomplishments' of the nation-wide political study campaign included the following items: 'Self-criticism is practised by many old-style intellectuals . . . The influence of the fallacious idea of a so-called "middle road" has, in the main, been eradicated . . . The concept that labour is the creator of civilization has been decisively established among the broad masses of the working people and the intellectuals . . . The idea of serving the people has become prevalent among intellectuals and government personnel. After political study, many intellectuals and young students have taken part in the work of revolution and reconstruction.'[11]

At the first 'literary evening' to be held in Peita after the Liberation, Maria Yen felt thunderstruck to discover just how speedily such 'fine progressive writers' as Ho Ch'i-fang and Pien Chih-lin (who had just undergone a special indoctrination course) had adapted their colours: 'Visiting students, who had walked in from other schools and waited two hours sitting on the floor to hear their two idols, sat dazed while they heard Ho and Pien denounce all of their own past work, the books which had been such inspiration to these young writers.'[12]

Some scholars may have danced ahead of the party tune, or been sharp-eared enough to hear it coming. But other prominent figures still felt free to question extremist responses and intemperate measures in the matter of educational reform.

The Empsons' friend Fei Hsiao-t'ung, for instance, publicly argued as late as mid-1950 that it was wrong to dismiss every aspect of the old education as a 'heap of garbage'. While acknowledging that education and ideology had to be developed to meet the needs of a modern indus-trialized state, he advised, an utter emphasis on practical service could result in 'degenerating educational and scientific work to narrow pragma-tism'. He rejoiced to find that the novel consultative procedures of the Communists seemed to be calculated to give everyone, high and low, a hearing. (The workers' representative on university committees would always be called *hsien sheng*—teacher—an honorific term previously re-served for educated members of the upper classes.) In the autumn of 1949 Fei had been elected to the first All-Circles Representative Conference, an assembly of 322 delegates charged with running the municipal government of Peking, its administrative policies and budget; by far the largest number of representatives were elected to serve on this 'People's Congress'.

Fei Hsiao-t'ung emphasized that autumn the sense of rejuvenation at large in the new China—in contrast to the terror of life under the KMT 'Gestapo'—and pronounced: 'The difference between now and then is like the difference between heaven and hell. Why could we listen peacefully and speak freely in the Peiping conference? It was because the reactionaries had been disarmed and suppressed. This is dictatorship to the reactionar-ies to be sure. But it is only through such a dictatorship that the rest of us can have democracy.'

Thus, however zealous or restive his colleagues and students became in the scrum of political realignment, Empson felt sympathetic to the initial progress of Communist China. Like Fei Hsiao-t'ung, a large number of progressives and liberals approved of the Communist campaign, which seemed willing to take constructive advice from all quarters, because the PLA had delivered them from years of living hell; even if they harboured misgivings about Marxist-Leninism, and the prospect of neototalitarianism, they would otherwise look around in vain for a better future. Some excesses seemed unavoidable, but no reasonable person could condemn all the positive steps that the Communists were taking to rectify the state of Nationalist misrule which Empson had seen in person.

Although he never attended—and was in fact kept out of—the round upon round of institutional meetings for criticism and self-criticism, even the business of rooting out corruption was by all accounts strict but not vindictive. He was fond of citing one particular story, told to him by Robert Winter, of what took place at Tsinghua University, whose business manager, a man named Pi, confessed to years of financial skulduggery.[13] Indeed, as late as 25 August 1950 Empson was repeating the story in a letter to John Hayward:

> There has been no victimization of teachers for political reasons, even if they belonged to Chiang's Youth Movement for instance, and there is no feeling of terror-stuff. There *was* of course under America's Chiang very serious torture and terror, affecting some of my own students, but now we have been liberated and there isn't any terror... However a good deal of what is most naturally described as Oxford Group behaviour goes on, confession of one's sins to one's committee...
>
> In my university (Peita) the confessions have been very placid (foreigners not performing anyhow you understand), nobody wanting to tease their colleagues particularly, but at Tsing Hua, the other one I lecture at, they seem to have been tweaking each other's tails with great vigour. The grandest incident was the confession of the business manager, for which so much ammunition had been prepared that it went on for nine hours until he has confessed embezzlements going back for twenty years and continuing after the liberation. You understand there were no officials present, and even after that he wasn't sacked though he ceased to be business manager. As a means of airing petty resentments and scandal it has a less impressive side, but it is obviously better than a lot of imprisonment shooting etc. even so. I really think the thing has been going well so far, and feel very pro-Chinese about it.[14]

Since he had not been present at any meetings, Empson's habit of winsomely jejune expression—his use of terms such as 'teasing' and 'tweaking tails'—may well give a false impression of the amount of cajolement that must have been applied, the humiliations endured, even during the first phase of university reconstruction. It is hard to imagine such close interrogations being conducted without a degree of bullying, let alone a 'free' confession of grave criminality. Nonetheless, if Empson's trick of understatement—and in this instance his schoolroom argot—seems misplaced in such a context, his main purpose (like that of Robert Winter and Fei Hsiao-t'ung) was to drive home the signal point of difference between the new kinds of openness—including confession and committee meetings which, to say the worst, seemed far less dread than dreary ('the professors grumble at having to go to so many long meetings but are otherwise better off')—and the nightmare, the oppression and the penury, that the Chinese people had suffered at the hands of the KMT. The Communists won a particularly high score in his estimation, judging from the evidence of life in Peking, because they renounced the use of physical coercion. 'The group confession process,' he emphasized, 'is obviously more workable as well as more humane than a purge with a lot of jailing and shooting'. Yet he was not so ingenuous as to withhold a note of caution: 'how it works out is of course still in the balance.'

Furthermore, the Empsons were impressed in the autumn of 1949 by the unfeigned eagerness with which students spoke about their revolutionary summer assignments—they had been sent into the countryside during the *fan shen* campaign, to help to 'turn over' the peasants—and in the next few months by the Communists' skill in recovering a more balanced economy (inflation was brought under control by March 1950), in improving labour conditions and communications. Hetta Empson wrote on 10 April 1950:

> The famine seems to be well in hand. In the last two weeks prices have dropped phenomenally—and I mean phenomenally, because it hasn't happened for years. Vast quantities of grain have come in and are being distributed from here. We have had some Spring rains already and if the weather holds, this year might well produce a bumper crop and with good communications and a good centralised system of distribution there ought to be enough progress to confuse all enemies. Last year it was simply stinking bad luck, first the drought and then unbelievable floods which ruined all the crops. All our students went out into the country to help with the land re-distribution and came back very enthusiastic even though they lived on sweet potatoes all through the holidays, because they lived in with the peasants. It was a completely new experience for most of them, because though they have been in the forefront of the movement they actually have had little real experience of life beyond the boundaries of the universities.

When Empson met up with the poet G. S. Fraser ('who seemed very reactionary as I told him') in Tokyo in the late summer of 1950, he spoke with equal warmth 'about young people living for the idea of the good, and making one self-questioning and almost ashamed of not being Communist'.

Everywhere the quality of life rose so markedly, only an inveterate cynic or enemy could fail to cheer all the shows of Communist success. One especially notable step was taken in November 1949, when the municipal government closed down the 237 brothels of Peking—Pa Ta Hutung, the red-light district outside the Chien Men Gate, was an age-old scandal— and conveyed the miserable prostitutes to a Women's Production and Education Institute, where they were taught to read and trained for jobs. 'The physical repair of these human beings was a long but comparatively simple task,' wrote Peter Townsend. 'Out of thirteen hundred registered prostitutes all but seventy-nine had venereal disease and all but two hundred and fifty were illiterate.'[15] Hetta Empson noted: 'Some horrible things about the goings-on in the brothels have come to light. Two very notorious procuresses are being held for trial . . . I suppose it's the first time in history that there has been such a dramatic exposure.'[16]

Not long afterwards, appropriately enough at a theatre near the Bridge of Heaven where they used to ply their trade, the former whores put on a play they had written themselves, *The Ice Breaks on the Frozen River*, depicting the horrors of their past. 'Excuse us if our acting's rough,' said a bespectacled middle-aged woman who introduced the presentation. 'We haven't had time for much preparation. But please, friends, don't cry. This is all over.' Yet the authenticity of the production, fleshed out with scenes of child slavery and the brutality of procurers and madams, reduced the players themselves to tears. The audiences wept too, day after day throughout the two-week run.

Jack Chen, a seasoned journalist whose father had served as China's foreign minister during the Wuhan Revolutionary Government in 1927 (and had died in Japanese captivity in the war), likewise found himself drowned in tears. 'This head-on assault on prostitution was accompanied by a press and radio propaganda campaign . . . ,' he recalled (in his book *Inside the Cultural Revolution*) twenty-five years later. 'The new Marriage Law had been passed [1 May 1950], and by dissolving unsuitable marriages, freeing concubines, and liberating women in general, more stable, happier family relationships were created.'[17]

Buoyed up by all the dynamism and confidence unleashed in Peking, Empson became more and more concerned that the People's Government should be given every credit for attempting to build a better society. Robert Winter spoke for a number of progressive westerners, including the Empsons, when he eagerly declared at the end of the first year of Communist rule in Peking: 'The fact that the government invites criticism and is quick to correct errors has released tremendous forces both inside the university and outside.'[17]

Yet in the weeks immediately following the inauguration of the People's Republic in October 1949, exultation was tempered with anxiety as foreign sympathizers waited to see if their governments would extend recognition to the new régime. As early as 30 April Mao Tse-tung had professed a readiness to negotiate for the establishment of diplomatic relations with foreign nations on the basis of equality, mutual benefit, and a mutual respect for territorial integrity—but on one absolute condition: every corresponding country would have to break off relations with 'the Chinese reactionaries', the Kuomintang. But although the ambassador, John Leighton Stuart, was willing to play the part of go-between, particularly in the hope of strengthening the 'more liberal anti-Soviet element in [the] CCP', President Harry S. Truman and Secretary of State Dean Acheson forbade him to make even a show of conciliation.

While the American government stalled over its China policy, however, Mao Tse-tung anticipated that his offer of rapprochement would be denied. On the same sorry day (1 July) that Acheson instructed Stuart not to deal with the Chinese Communists, he prematurely declared the CCP an ally of Moscow. Whatever his immediate motives for adopting a pro-Soviet line his annunciation of 'an international united front' tending to 'the realm of world Communism' undoubtedly gratified the long-entrenched anti-Communism of the USA, which had perennially aided and abetted Chiang Kai-shek while purporting to seek a just peace in China.

The American public, ignorant of the sham of Chinese Nationalism, had been persuaded since 1937 that Chiang Kai-shek stood against Japanese imperialism and insurgent Communism, and for a free and western-looking Asia. Mao was merely a peasant mugwump, a Soviet stooge intent on forswearing his heritage and annexing China to an alien power. From inside China, such an interpretation could only be perceived as a gross distortion of fact. Robert Winter, for instance, felt outraged by Acheson's 'illogical and callously imperialistic' *China White Paper*. 'I challenge any one [Winter wrote in his diary] to find any equivalent to our spending three and a half billion dollars to foment civil war in a friendly country which was recently an ally against Fascism . . .'[18]

Jen-min jih-pao (*People's Daily*), the official Communist newspaper, vehemently denounced the *White Paper*; and Theodore H. E. Chen reported that it was then assailed in every forum: 'At that time, the mass study programme had already been inaugurated in Peking, Tientsin, and other Communist cities, and for several weeks the "White Paper", or "opposing the White Paper", was the central theme of the "study" sessions . . . At Peking University, several hundred professors and staff members placed their signatures to a protest against American imperialism exposed in the "White Paper".'[19]

The Soviet Union recognized the People's Republic of China on 2 October, the day after its inauguration; satellite states followed suit over the next few weeks. Burma, India, and Pakistan extended formal relations within three months, as did the Communist regimes of North Korea and Vietnam. But the USA and Great Britain, reluctant to jilt the Nationalist Government, sat on their banns. Nevertheless, the Truman administration temporarily confined itself to supporting the Nationalists only with economic assistance, not with arms.

A week after saluting Stalin's seventieth birthday on 9 December (the same day the remnant KMT Government finally departed for Taiwan), Mao Tse-tung went abroad for the first time in his life—to strike a necessary bargain with Stalin, who 'suspected Mao of incipient Titoism'.[20] Contrary to the inimical judgement of many overseas commentators that Mohammed was duly going to the Mountain, that the Chinese delegation would bend the knee to the Soviets, in fact Mao's men went not to kneel but to negotiate a tough treaty.

Although it is true that China rapidly expanded her trade with Russia after signing the Treaty (from a level of 1.6 per cent in 1946, the account rose to 23.4 per cent even in 1950), it was primarily because western interests prevented it from doing otherwise. First, in the summer of 1949, the Nationalist government blockaded the mainland; then the Americans closed and locked the economic door.

Peter Townsend reasonably observed in 1955: 'A policy of "containment" must inevitably...drive its intended victim to counter-measures. China's answer was to shake off any illusions that she could turn to the Western nations for help and to strengthen her ties with Russia and Eastern Europe.'

Empson agreed. 'I think they [the Chinese] are going to have their hands quite full at home for a long time, and I am very uncertain how far they will go with the Russians, given a bit of time to look round. But of course the American policy has driven them into the arms of the Russians very strongly and dangerously.'

In the first weeks after 1st October 1949 the Empsons had set great store by the prospect that the United Kingdom would presently recognize the PRC; and the infectious enthusiasm of their many social contacts—gatherings with Chinese and foreign friends alike—sustained the hope. Max Bickerton, the New Zealand Communist whom Empson had last seen in Tokyo in 1933, turned up in Peking at this time and jumped at the offer of a teaching post at Peita. (The homosexual Bickerton grew very close to Hetta over the months in Peking, and, in a sort of way, he came to love her, though he was rather given to nagging her. Three years later, when the Communists threw him out of his job at the university and out of his room on the campus, only Hetta among the foreign community stepped in to house and feed him. Later, in England, he became her tenant in London and would remain in the house until his death.)

Also at the University, Hetta happily took on a regular class in English Conversation—'so I do four hours a week of gossiping with the students,' she reported. 'They are really quite good. I have twenty-six and the English Department got a better enrolment than people thought likely.'[20] Out of class, she and Walter Brown spent a good deal of time making the puppets for 'a real Punch and Judy show, because we discovered that Max Bickerton can do the manipulating and talking'. Typically, Bickerton could not resist adding a little more mischief to Punch and Judy: 'Max made the Doctor say to Punch, "I can't waste my time on lower middle class cases like yours." So Punch poked him in his lower middle until he was dead.' The upshot might have been predictable: when they presented their subversive show at the Peking Club, a number of tots had to be carried out screaming; and Mrs Clubb, wife of the U. S. Consul General, commented with splendid ambiguity: 'We should have asked more adults.'

When the ladies of the American Consulate mounted an art exhibition, Hetta submitted 'a rude torso in bone, about three inches high', and it was bravely displayed in a prominent position on a drape of black velvet. Her most successful work of those years was a bust of Sardar Panikkar, the Indian Ambassador, doyen of the diplomatic corps (India at that period was China's thousand-year-old friend). She also translated booklets of new Chinese woodcuts and captions.

The last weeks of the year passed in a continuous ferment of sociability: 'we've had a successful Christmas,' Hetta wrote, 'the usual Empson messy kind, with people in and out for days, Lao Chan [a servant] running a path to the wine shop for pounds of Pai Gar—we stick to that now because Vodka is rather high and also has deteriorated terribly. William drinks madly and happily in the mistaken belief that because he mixes large glasses of Pai Gar with boiling water it can't do his stomach ulcer (which I secretly don't believe in), any harm.' Not surprisingly, she had mixed thoughts on the season as a whole: 'Sometimes we feel gloomy because there are so few people we know but other times we seem to have the house full from morning to night and then William gets the jitters.'[21]

Still Hetta hoped to put the best part of her energies to the all-important task of building up the new China, both locally and internationally, and fearlessly undertook in this post-revolutionary period a few démarches of a political kind. She spoke of the seriousness of her commitment in a letter of 19 November: 'I have written [to the British Communist Party] to say I want to be transferred to the Chinese Party, now my Chinese is good enough to go to meetings (though I can't write yet)...I have been invited to attend Branch meetings and discussions, but I'm rather shy of going until my credentials have been established.' In company with Max Bickerton and David Hawkes, she collected 32 signatures from the British community and 'sent a cable, urging recognition on the grounds (amongst others) of "mutual advantage", to Mr. Bevin.'[22] 'We all think the British Government is very silly to hesitate about it,' she wrote in another letter of the same date, 'this is the one time they might get in before the Americans and show they're not slaves of Wall Street.'[23] By Christmas, though they received no direct reply from the Foreign Office, they could tap the thriving Peking grapevine with considerable satisfaction: 'Everyone thinks the British will recognise early in the year—we all hope so.'

To the annoyance of the USA, the United Kingdom extended recognition to the People's Republic of China on 6 January 1950.

Coincidentally, or provocatively, or perhaps even both (since the British had given official notice of their intentions over the radio), the Chinese applied a poultice to the inflamed issue of diplomatic relations on the very same day. The Peking Military Control Commission brusquely informed the British and American consulates general, as well as the French and Dutch embassy offices, that for reasons of 'military necessity' the premises of their 'former military barracks'—areas which had been exacted from the Empress Dowager under the terms of the 1901 Protocol following the Boxer Uprising—would be 'requisitioned' seven days from that date. The British territory in question was a pretty litter of shrubberies, ruins and a semi-derelict swimming pool. The American military compound, on the other hand, included the office of the Consulate General along with a 'terrific radio mast'. When the requisition order was unceremoniously enforced on 14 January, the US Government, claiming 'invasion of its property rights', closed down its diplomatic and consular establishments and withdrew all personnel from Communist China.

Yet the protest and the apparently direct retaliation by the USA stood on a weak footing. By agreement with the Kuomintang, all 'imperialist' countries, both American and European, had already relinquished their rights of 'extraterritoriality', including the legal immunities and franchises of the Legation Quarter, after the war.[24]

In Empson's opinion, the so-called 'Barracks Areas' were anyway 'no longer needed in Peking and were not demanded by Ambassadors in any other civilised capital'; and he was shocked by subsequent perversions of the matter. As late as August 1955, *Encounter* ran an article entitled 'The American Dilemma Over China' in which O. H. Brandon wrote: 'Events in China meanwhile further aroused the sense of danger among Americans. Mao Tse-tung concluded the Sino-Soviet Treaty and the Peking Government illegally confiscated American consular property and mistreated American consular officials. The fires of hatred were astir among Americans. It incensed them that the Government was powerless to do anything drastic in the face of these humiliations.'

Brandon's report was misleading on a number of counts. Indeed, the Sino-Soviet Treaty had not been concluded at the time. In addition, as Empson protested in a letter published in *Encounter* in November 1955, the phrase 'illegally confiscated' might have been 'true about incidents elsewhere in China but distracts attention from what happened in Peking. The American Government broke off diplomatic relations because of a demand to return the "military barrack" area of the American compound in the Legation Quarter... These relics of the past had always been insulting however necessary and now, on the return of the capital to Peking, stood out as absurd. The American State Department people on the spot, who were muzzled of course, thought this a very bad choice of talking-point for breaking off relations.'[25]

Predictably, the editors of *Encounter* declared themselves 'puzzled' by Empson's mis-statement that the American Government 'broke off diplomatic relations' because of the Peking incident: 'We have always been under the impression,' they sniffed, 'that diplomatic relations between the U.S. and Communist China never existed.' Not content with that easy score, they also scoffed at his other remarks: 'Mr. Empson's erudite discourse on American consular property in Peking serves only to bewilder us... So far as we can see, it is his remarks about Peking (which we regret we cannot accept as the last word on the subject) that serve as a distraction from what he calls "incidents elsewhere in China".'

Yet the editors of *Encounter*, sitting in better judgement behind their royal plural, were gravely in error. What happened in Peking, and its causes and consequences, had profound effects upon the international perception of Communist China, as well as dire repercussions for the individuals involved. In an unpublished letter of later date, Empson wrote: 'I liked and admired the American Consul-General, so far as I was privileged to meet him, and I am anxious now not to get him into further trouble; he certainly did not tell me his views, but other Americans did. He cabled home that it would be very bad propaganda to break off relations merely because the Chinese Government demanded back the Barracks for American troops, and could they not at least stall it off somehow. But the reply from Washington to the humiliation of losing their radio mast in Peking had to be immediate. He need not have worried, because the actual American reason for breaking off negotiations with Communist China has been completely forgotten.'

In September 1951, O. Edmund Clubb, the ousted American Consul-General, published an article entitled 'Chinese Communist Strategy in Foreign Relations', arguing with rigid loyalty that in January 1950 there had been 'no "military necessity" which would justify even temporary requisitioning of local private property, to say nothing of the public property of friendly states.' Passing on from the pretence that the USA had ever been a true 'friendly state' vis-à-vis China, Clubb declared that since 'non-Communist influence' had been 'thrust from China', the country had become 'a clear field for Soviet penetration'. Mao Tse-tung 'failed to observe that China, by effectively cutting itself off from relations with other countries not entirely to his liking, was thus making itself into a dependency of the U.S.S.R.'[26]

Clubb's show of jealous patriotism brought him small reward, as David Caute has related: 'Clubb returned from Peking when the US flag was hauled down in 1949, and was appointed Director of the Office of Chinese Affairs in the State Department. In December 1950 he was confronted with an interrogatory containing eight charges alleging fellow-travelling contacts with Chinese and American communists. Although the Loyalty Security Board ruled in December 1951 that there existed "no reasonable doubt" as to Clubb's loyalty, it nevertheless recommended separation from the Foreign Service on the ground that Clubb was a "security risk".'[27]

Casting his mind back over the witch-hunts of the early 1950s, Empson added to his unpublished letter these words of bitter regret for the way the American administration had lost the grand opportunity of establishing diplomatic ties with Communist China, and scorn for the way they later treated their man in the front line:

> For himself [Clubb], he had to worry, because he was sacked, like all other good men who had worked in China for the United States State Department. A scholar of Chinese, immensely well-informed about Chinese

affairs, so anti-Communistic as to be rather tiresome to talk to, I thought, he was none the less broken by the event, and so were all that impressive lot of Americans I peeped at while I was in China. The Diplomats of other nations, you can understand, I would sometimes become on easier terms with; and their point of view was that being an American diplomat was exactly like being a Russian diplomat; very unlike England or Denmark (or whoever I was talking to). Of course the Americans wouldn't shoot a man in the back of the neck while deciding to abandon his policy, but they would throw him out with a ruthlessness only like the Russians', and madly unlike the way the British and the rest of Western Europe still carry on diplomacy.

7

Changes in China; and Kenyon Again

However happy the Empsons felt that the United Kingdom had recognized the PRC, their pleasure was dampened when the Chinese chose not to reciprocate. The British Government hoped that diplomatic ties would serve to protect valuable trade exchanges, but the People's Republic declined to regularize full relations on the basis of such a patently self-interested gesture. As Peter Townsend later explained, 'China's hesitation to establish full diplomatic relations until, among other points, Britain voted in favour of seating China in the United Nations Assembly, was probably designed to force Britain to declare whether, in the final analysis, she was prepared to allow her commercial interests in China to suffer rather than run counter to America, and Britain's refusal to vote for China reinforced the belief that America was, and would remain, the arbiter of Western action.'[1]

As a result, the British envoys who presently transferred from Nanking to the capital Beijing had to establish themselves in an old local habitation but without the name of embassy. Thenceforth Ying Kuo Fu would be accredited only as a 'Negotiating Mission', with the former Minister-Counsellor in Shanghai, John Hutchison, now Chargé d'Affaires in Peking, acting as its one and only 'negotiating representative'.[2]

Protocol became a ticklish business, sometimes threatening to damage any prospect of better relations, at other times farcical, because the Wai Chiao Pu, the Ministry of Foreign Affairs, placed all foreign representatives in one of three categories or orders of merit (with peculiar subdivisions). No one could carelessly neglect to know their place. Those countries which had established full diplomatic ties with the People's Republic, notably the Eastern bloc, together with other nations including India, Burma, Pakistan, Switzerland, Sweden, and Denmark, basked in all the privileges of the first rank. Great Britain, the Netherlands, and Norway, who had recognized the PRC but were not formally accredited, made up the second-class category: though unofficially granted the customary privileges and immunities, the representatives of those three countries could never be sure if their presence at any particular function constituted a minor embarrassment or an intolerable solecism. France, Belgium, and Italy, which had not extended recognition to the PRC but retained temporary representation in Peking, had no standing and were consequently ostracized.

In April 1950—just when I. A. Richards, after an absence of 12 years, finally descended upon Peking for a four-month visit beginning on 6 April—Empson shared in the absurdist fun of one particular breach of etiquette which somehow passed off safely:

> the marriage of a young man [David Hawkes] sent from England to learn Chinese under the Scarborough plan, who has always been in and out of our house, and of course met all our friends, and when he at last got permission for his wife to come out he innocently invited everyone he knew. This is impossible in modern Peking and Hetta tried at the last moment to send out warnings, but it all happened and was like the sea giving up its dead. The British consul came, the secret British communists came, the Chinese police who spy on the foreigners came, the Christians came, the university came, and it was really a good party such as I have always thought one of the keenest pleasures in life.[3]

The pleasure of attending the wedding party of David and Jean Hawkes on 5 May 1950 (with the arrangements having been made by Hetta) was all the more keen because I. A. and Dorothea Richards also came, as Empson related, and Richards 'begged me to be let go early in this huge and tumultuous (indeed often indignant) party, but I pointed sternly at a communist prominent in the English Language Teaching Profession and said "That's your business; go and talk to him" and some hours afterwards as I picked my way through the pillared hall I saw him still talking away like a horse.'[4]

Over twenty years later, I. A. Richards would recall his return to Peking, which lasted from April to August, as an almost unequivocally intoxicating experience. 'It was a wonderful, wonderful moment. "Bliss was it, in those days, to be alive," as Wordsworth said about the French Revolution. It was really too beautiful for words, to see the Chinese returning to their natural pride and glory. But it wasn't easy.'[5] Apart from the last understated remark, his salutations were unqualified by the shadow of any better later knowledge.

Dividing his time between a lakeside house at Yenching University and a residence rented by the British Council in the heart of the city, Richards energetically undertook to give courses on Communication Theory, Techniques of Mass Instruction, Criticism, and Shakespeare; and wherever he went he tried to gain a just estimate of conditions of life under the new regime. Though noting with sensible canniness that 'naturally we hear most from those who are enthusiastic', and put off only by the fact that no Party officials would give him an audience, he was still very favourably impressed by the absence of fear or suspicion that he encountered, and by the freedom and tolerance with which staff and students would talk about indoctrination lectures, discussion groups, and 'the many spectacular conversions following self-criticism'. It was 'comforting' to find that people would even joke about the way other people had changed their views. (The only thing he and his wife found frustrating, being hyperactive and athletic individuals, was that all movement was restricted to within eight miles' radius of the city; so they sought much-needed exercise by walking in the grounds of the Empress's Summer Palace.)

'Spirits among students is [*sic*] high; among staff observant,' wrote the Richardses in the journal they shared.[6] All the same, they could not fail to see and report in all conscience that 'the pressure on the universities to conform in thought is alarming' and quite as 'prodigiously time-taking' as Empson would have told them.[7] 'Interference with regular studies is, of course, considerable,' they noted, along with the worry that 'the opinion-conformity pressure is unduly heavy, especially on students... There is anxiety for some that *in time* they may be expected to change their views more than they would find easy, but wide allowances seem to be being given in the matter of tempo.'[8] Like Empson, with his bias for looking on the bright side, Richards thus erred in favour of indulgence rather than scepticism. Perhaps as a way of making palatable a mode of indoctrination which he would otherwise (outside China) find distasteful, he compared the pressure placed upon individuals to 'that put on small minorities by a jury'.

From Richards's first days in Peking, indeed, the balance of his judgement had swung towards enthusiasm, as was reflected in two letters he wrote to the Rockefeller Foundation in April. While not denying that the methods of Communist re-education disturbed him, Richards was always at pains to put them in perspective. The political campaign might be deemed to be relentless, but at least it utterly repudiated the ruthlessness of the KMT. As far as he could judge, firm persuasion was the order of the day, not murderous suppression. Whereas he arrived in China expecting to witness the tyranny that American opponents hankered to hear about, he found to his obviously genuine astonishment that the work of reconstruction was 'all most moral & uplifting'.[9] Most importantly, popular sentiment, though always difficult to assess, struck him as running with the new regime. And yet, as he admitted in his diary, 'the old liberal in me sighs & wonders at times'.[10] Though hoping against the hopelessness being generated in the USA that China might have gained an altogether more decent administration than it had endured for many years, he had not looked for such extraordinary progress in so many fields. All told, he concurred with Empson's view that the Communist regime in China was infinitely preferable to the Nationalist government it had driven out. Yet the American Government and general public were primed to believe otherwise: 'In general the People's Gov. is a vast improvement on the KMT & I can't make out why we all should still be supporting Chiang— who is about the most discrediting associate possible.'[11] The main difficulty, as Richards knew only too well, would be to make the Americans admit that the Communists were doing any good at all by China.

In-between lectures and meetings, Richards worked at translating the *Iliad* into Basic English (Empson 'made helpful suggestions'),[12] and he gave a marathon solo performance of what he called his 'dramatic abstraction'—an adaptation of Homer—entitled The *Wrath of Achilles*. 'It was the greatest possible fun,' he would remember without a trace of modesty. 'One had to jump from being Achilles into being Agamemnon . . . I had to jump from point to point and put on a different air, and act it. My voice lasted for two and a half hours, which is something. I always felt that it was a good durable voice.'[13] What the perdurable audience thought of his show is not recorded. And on top of all his other activities in Peking, he would jump from point to point in order to expound the wherewithal for teaching Basic English.

Empson not only turned out for one of his mentor's public lectures but respectfully prinked himself up in suit and tie. 'Nor was [Richards] above calculating his effects,' he was to recall in a memorial essay published in 1980.

When he visited Peking after the Communist victory, he required among other props a folding card-table at the side of the stage, not an easy thing for the British Council to find, and he used it by leaning upon it, as he went out from his lecture, to say: 'In my end is my beginning.' He would not have done this in either of the Cambridges, but the Chinese students would find hearing English a serious effort, and would need a bit of action; it went over very well. He was expounding something about Plato, as I remember, but he literally did mean to return to Peking.[14]

Of recent years, while working in the Graduate School of Education at Harvard University, Richards had contracted a devout belief in the value of using visual aids for teaching the English language, and he proposed to deploy many such 'materials' in China. 'I'm inclined to think,' he wrote in 1949, 'that the film is the cure for the Chinese habit of textbook memorization.' But Empson was properly sceptical about the viability of hustling a backward and penurious country into adopting what amounted to relatively advanced technology. Richards's primary interest, Empson wrote in the draft of a letter home from the USA in July 1950,

> is to make them adopt his English-language-teaching methods, now very different from the Ogden formula, and when I left he was making an impression in the right quarters; the point is, not that they are keen on teaching the enemy language, but that they don't want to sack all the Middle School teachers who are accustomed to give most students six years of it (without the slightest result); they would like to make it three years and get some results (from the ones who haven't chosen Russian) instead; what they want then is a mass education method which can be learned by stupid teachers and imposed in some foolproof form.[15]

In any event, Empson was content to relinquish his thankless unofficial role as standard-bearer for Basic English. Richards would accomplish what he could, but Empson could now step back from that particular struggle. The signs of his tactful withdrawal are evident in this later letter to Richards: 'I hope you have left in Peking adequate material to be used about language teaching if people can be got to take interest. Sorry I haven't been more use about it, but I don't really see how to be; I am very willing if occasion offers.'

In November 1950 Richards went for debriefing at the Rockefeller Foundation, where his interviewer John Marshall learned that he 'has nothing but disdain for Communist doctrine' and so concluded: 'there seems to be every reason to take this report as the report of a detached, dispassionate, and, on the whole, well qualified observer.'[16] Perhaps not adequately realizing that Richards could be neither detached nor dispassionate, since he remained loyal to the potential of China and yearned to succeed in promoting English-language teaching there, Marshall reported in a memorandum: 'His advice was sought on the future improvement of the teaching of English, particularly for Chinese agents and diplomats abroad. He decided to accede to such requests in the general interest of a better international understanding. A knowledge of Russian or English is now required in all the universities. At first the students opportunistically took Russian, but the teaching and texts are so poor that they have increasingly turned to English.'

However, it is clear that Richards was not at all prepared to fool himself about the prospects for the advancement of English teaching. While in China he had conceded in his diary: 'the whole course of E. teaching here is quite doubtful. For the present the place of the West in official Ch. eyes is to be scaled down.' Such a self-admission would have been a severe blow to his plans for Basic English; the dismal word 'doubtful' was his acknowledgement of a temporary defeat which he would not willingly share with the Rockefeller Foundation. The spoils of his triumphant return to Peking were in that respect wasted, though he would never give up the cause. Empson wrote about Richards: 'It had always been central to his mind that an apparent intellectual conflict need not be a practical obstacle.' Yet the practical obstacles to disseminating the English language in China blocked productive conflict: ideology had already bested intellectual challenge.

Just as Richards was not prepared to betray any private apprehensions, neither would he expose his associates to criticism. The Rockefeller Foundation had asked before his departure for China, 'it would be interesting to know how Bob Winter and others are adjusting to the communist program for confining literary production to "socialist realism".'[17] According to a supplementary memorandum circulated in the Rockefeller Foundation, Richards 'had some difficulty in explaining Bob Winter's present position but seemed to feel that his attitudes, described as "left of the regime," were in part a defense mechanism of trying to prove that he was not an enemy alien.'[18] They clearly suspected Richards of being evasive.

With respect to Empson, Richards felt no need to mumble his opinion. He was shocked, much as a natural parent would be, to find that his protégé was drinking to excess and leading a messy life which he could only ascribe to occupational stress. One choice entry in the shared Richards diary encapsulates all their aversion to apparent delinquency: '10 April. On to Bill Empson—found him with a New Zealand communist Max Bickerton—Both sipping Pei Gar—Looks thin & v. worried: same queer, puzzled parrot. House a shambles, filthy beyond words—Two splendid but neglected children. Hetta out. Offered a room in a Court where the comrades dance & where the Hawkes live. Hastily caught bus back.'[19] (Curiously, Hetta Empson was to write in a letter dating from the very next day, though presumably with regard to an earlier visit when the Richardses did stay over for the night: 'The Richards came and went, that's why I'm up so early, they had to catch a nine o'clock bus. They are quite agreeable...')[20] Of another gathering, at the end of May, the Richardses recorded: 'Empsons arrived late very drunk. Everlasting dreary drunken party till 1.30 Empson spilling stuff on table, rowing with Hetta, each shouting each other down. David Hawkes got a book & read, leaving Jean Patterson in bed with tonsilitis—Hetta fed up now with Jean & urging him to leave her alone to pull herself together. David Kidd [their feline American friend] v. exquisite & contemptuous of Bill... Bill fell out of his chair several times & had to be held up by Hetta.'[21] (Hetta was to declare to a friend in May, after attending Richards's presentation of *The Wrath of Achilles*: 'We went to Richard's [sic] lecture on the Iliad which was very good and then to eat with them Saturday. Nothing happened except William fell over twice though he was far more lucid and entertaining than any of them and we all parted friends.')[22] Other friends and visitors who bore witness to the bohemia of the Empson establishment saw it less with dismay, as a place of squalid self-abandonment, than with delight, as the appropriate ambience for abstracted genius. The ebullient and scholarly Indian ambassador K. M. Panikkar wrote of Empson in his memoirs: 'The British community—forgetting that he was undoubtedly the most distinguished Englishman in Peking at the time—disapproved of his way of life and his refusal to conform to the suburban habits of its diplomats. Empson sported a strange type of beard, kept company with doubtful Chinese, and allowed his children to play in the backyards of Chinese houses where they grew up uninhibited. His house, in a not very clean part of Peking, was always... untidy... There Ezra Pound's *Pisan Cantos*, textbooks, detective novels and proofs of Empson's own *Structure of the Complex World* [sic] lay cheek by jowl with toys of children, Chinese new year paintings, and half finished sculptures by Hetta. Empson had been an intimate friend of Orwell and we had many interests in common.'[23] (Panikkar himself, as his compatriot Frank Moraes noted, could 'draw analogies and cite precedents with the ease of a conjuror extracting rabbits from a hat. ' "I make history," Panikkar once said in a mood of exaltation. "You mean you make it up," said his companion.')[24]

Whatever the putative unseemliness of the Empsons' ménage, they were not in fact a totally feckless couple, as Richards had begun to think. At worst they were simply eccentric, with a complex extended household and a thriving social life to support ('the house is always just like it always is,' wrote Hetta to Walter Brown, 'like a railway station waiting room, only no trains come').[25]

But, despite occasional protestations to the conrary, the principle of domestic order would be breached as often as honoured. For one matter, the servants fell to squabbling about the disproportions in their duties; and the upshot was that by the summer of 1950 Hetta had to sack two of them and cast about for other help. 'Kuan Shih Fu got very gloomy (chiefly because of all the dinners and that swine Lao Chan never stayed to help him) and said he wanted to leave, so this afternoon I have to sack Lao Chan and the old lady otherwise I think he really would, and I don't want to be without him, he is so reliable and does five times as much as they do together.'[26] Thereafter Mogador would nobly plod with his brother to early morning school. And as for pedicab drivers, Hetta argued, 'our sanlour [*san-luerh*, literally "three-wheelers"] at the corner are after all just as reliable as Lao Chan.'[27]

Another constant problem, which Empson approached with a high if ineffectual sense of responsibility, was the general discipline and awkward educational needs of the children, who hardly knew which way to turn for their first language. One fine winter day C. P. Fitzgerald was sitting with Empson in a courtyard—'Lovely dirty little house, isn't it?' Empson used to remark—when the boys started to suck pieces of ice from the gutter. Empson told Mogador to stop it, but Mogador simply ignored him and went on sucking the ice. Then Empson turned to Fitzgerald and said: 'No use talking to Jacob. He doesn't understand English and I can't speak Chinese.'[28] (Hetta wrote in the peach-blossoming spring of 1950, perhaps with double aptness: 'The children flourish like weeds.')[29]

Season by season, the Empsons would talk over the advisability of returning to England so that the boys could have a regular schooling, and, after returning from his summer visit to America, Empson would start to keep a watching brief on their progress. In good time, he resolved, they should be afforded a much more sound secondary education in England; and indeed, by the autumn of 1951, Mogador was officially put down for Winchester—though, as things turned out, he would not be enrolled there.[30]

Still the fact remains, as Richards lamented, that Empson was drinking far too heavily. While Empson would readily admit that the clash between prevalent university politics and his stubbornness on the question of 'academic freedom' did cause him 'a bit of a nervous strain', he disputed any suggestion that occupational stress drove him to drink. 'I always feel I can do the mediating process quite honestly.'[31] Rather, he believed, he drank more out of boredom than from neurosis: it was always a good time for a little something. Though not an alcoholic, he took it for granted that when writing the first drafts of an essay he should loosen his thoughts and allay the tension of the typewriter with good measures of whatever came to hand. Both he and Hetta insisted that they found life in Peking 'pleasant and stimulating', and they were not yet minded to start afresh in a world elsewhere. Moreover, Hetta had cause to admit: 'I'm pretty sure they wouldn't have me in America anyway [on account of her membershup of the British Communist Party], which is where William would have to go to make a living.'

Yet I. A. Richards would not be satisfied by explanations or excuses, and tried to frighten Empson off the bottle. Empson related in a draft of a letter addressed to John Hayward (which he appears not to have posted): 'He told me that Time magazine has a complete file of sexual and alcoholic scandal against me, which they have only not published on his personal intervention, and will prevent or conclude my employment in any American university as soon as they feel safe in publishing it. This is the kind of thing that makes a man feel important and gives him nerve (you understand I had already refused about eight offers from American universities; the post seems to let through nothing else). They [the editors of *Time*] would feel safe, I presume, though Richards would not agree to this distraction from his very affectionate moral diatribe, if they had also political grounds.'[32] (Henry Luce, proprietor of *Time*, was a zealot in the war against Communism and 'a fervent apologist for Taiwan'.)[33]

Richards's gambit may have been a bluff, since *Time*, for all its anti-Communist prejudice, had no reason to collect any materials on Empson beyond the few profiles it had garnered from Kenyon College a year earlier (and which it had already put to exiguous use in a review of his *Collected Poems* on 18 April 1949). Empson would never know for sure one way or the other, but he certainly needed to take a serious view of the possibility of persecution. At some time in 1949 he had been given to understand that 'the American consular people' in Peking were 'collecting dossiers of all foreigners here' (and indeed Peking was rife with 'rather full-blooded gossip'); and when he arrived in the USA in the summer of 1950, he was immediately told of a rumour that a *Time* reporter had been endeavouring to sniff him out. Ironically, as Empson's letter to Hayward suggests, the effect of Richards's solicitous but nonetheless disturbing intervention was not so much to make him scotch the boozing habit as to aggravate his feelings of irritation towards the USA.

Still, though bothered by I. A. Richards's accusation that he had taken to drinking too much out of neurotic anxiety, Empson believed he success-fully passed the test of public exposure at the Kenyon School of English that summer. In fact there is no doubt that he did both enjoy and distinguish himself at Kenyon, impressing everyone as 'a decent and regular gentleman'.[34] From the first moment of his arrival, Empson rel-ished the irony of being supported by a bizarre combination of employers. He had thought it quite amusing enough, when he stopped off in Tokyo, to learn from H. Vere Redman that 'the Japs are coming to feel they are a very attractive maiden with two rich suitors, and are making increasing demands on America as the price of their favours.'[35] But in America, he realized, he could hilariously go one better: 'My position here really seems to me very dramatic; there can be few other people in the world who are receiving pay simultaneously and without secrecy from the Chinese Com-munists, the British Socialists, and the capitalist Rockefeller machine. Practically a little friend of all the world.'[36] (As in 1948, he received a stipend of $1,500 out of the $40,000 subvention awarded to the School by the Rockefeller Foundation.)

'We all seem very friendly,' Empson wrote of the pride of literary lions who came to be corralled at Kenyon.[37] Other Fellows of the School, in addition to John Crowe Ransom and the admirably solicitous and schol-arly Charles M. Coffin, were Kenneth Burke, Robert Lowell, Arthur Mizener, Philip Blair Rice and Delmore Schwartz; together with just one other British visitor, L. C. Knights, who suffered horribly in the heat of Ohio. On 27 June Ransom would write to Allen Tate: 'The School is starting off in fine style ... A big session the other evening here with Rice, Coffin, Burke, Empson, and Knights gave me the sense that we'd have unusually intelligent and civil discussions this summer ... Cal [Lowell], Mizener, and Delmore are in good form.'[38] Empson found his compatriot Knights 'a very nice fellow but not very communicative'; they had never met before, even though they had been exact contemporaries at Cam-bridge.[39] According to Lauro Martines (a 22-year-old from Chicago, later a professional writer), the moody Knights complained during his time at Kenyon that there was no conversation in the US, and no breakfast except for that stuff that tastes like wet cardboard—cornflakes.[40] As fate fell out, just three years later Empson was to succeed what he cannily described as the 'impressive person' of Knights in the Chair of English Literature at

Sheffield University, where he was to joke in his inaugural lecture that in 1950 the Americans had regarded Knights's natural leanness as 'another proof that we are all starving to death in England'.

Although there were fewer students this time round, Empson found them just as game as ever. 'We came to the summer's enterprise with a zest that I suppose few of us had ever brought to our regular studies...,' recalled George Lanning, a visitor in 1948 and a student in 1950. 'Vigorously, we "explicated", in and out of class; we got so we could spot a Precious Object at a thousand yards; and where we couldn't find an ambiguity we made one. It was all tremendous fun, and if we were often foolish our elders let us take our heads.'[41]

In October 1949 Empson had advised Charles Coffin, 'I don't think you would find me so full of little novelties as last time, when I had just finished re-writing a ten-year-old book after a long fallow period', though he intimated that he had begun to think his way towards essays like 'Falstaff and Mr. Dover Wilson' (*Kenyon Review*, Spring 1953). 'A look at Falstaff and Henry V and the recent British fashion of presenting Shakespeare as a sturdy royalist is a topic I would like to fit into my course somewhere; he seems to me an intelligent politician, in a rather incidental way, who does not deserve to be praised as a sycophant of the Tudors.' But he was not yet ready to expatiate in public upon his argument that Shakespeare posed acute problems without supplying all the answers which critics had begun to stipulate. Instead, he chose again to rehearse at the summer school much of the material of *The Structure of Complex Words* (which appeared only in 1951, three years after he had submitted the finished manuscript) in a course he called 'The Word of Poetry: Studies in the English Tradition'.

Though the twenty-five students in his thrice-weekly class were at first perturbed by the rush of his delivery and his inveterate habit of talking *en face* to the blackboard, on which he would write a version of his lecture, they soon warmed to his energy and literary acumen, and the lack of arrogance or posturing in his manner (as Priscilla Sutcliffe, later the College Archivist, recalled).[42] Such was the eccentric professor's brilliant intensity in the classroom that he worried not a whit if the students found him all the more endearing on account of his peculiar Englishness: he merely looked nonplussed when everyone howled with laughter at the unwonted ambiguity of his remark apropos 'Ode on a Grecian Urn' that all the people in the poem were 'glued to the pot'.[43] When he attended lectures by other Fellows, he would sit in the front row and often fall asleep with his head tilted back.

Extracurricular activities were just as diverting, and Empson played a dedicated part in the almost nightly parties. The most diligent host was the elegant Arthur Mizener, who 'with his big convertible and striped polo shirts looked like an ad for the best Scotch whiskey'. (Mizener otherwise spent his time playing tennis with Delmore Schwartz.) Drinking mostly gin or vodka, Empson would argue vociferously with anyone who lurched into reach. Maurice Charney remembers him as 'a very open and lovable man': 'He made a strong impression on everyone because he was such a colorful figure who spoke his mind without any regard for your feelings or opinions. He seemed strikingly childlike and naive—even clownish in the best sense of the word, since he looked so strange in his neck beard.'[44] (Empson's 'Chinese beard' would 'spread nicely', Don Wiener recalls, 'as he floated on his back in the Kenyon pool.') He could also be a little childish when drinking: one evening, during a huddled discussion on a kitchen floor, Empson suddenly got up and disappeared, only to return and proclaim in a loud and slightly tipsy voice, 'I don't know where you go to pee—I go out in the garden.'[45]

The student song of the summer, devised by John Edwards, went:

> One two three four five six seven types of am-bi-gu-i-teee.
> One two three four five six seven types of am-bi-gu-i-teee.
> And that's not all:
> We've got some versions of the pas-torale . . .

'Empson was charmed by the composition,' George Lanning recalled, 'and when—as regularly at a certain point in the evening—it was sung, he would respond with imitations of English music hall singers.'[46] Lanning was especially pleased to discover that Empson shared his enthusiasm for reading murder mysteries—'but where my motive was the simple one of pleasure, his had a finer, a truly Empsonian quality about it: he read them, he told me, to see if he could guess the copyright date from internal evidence.'[47]

Wherever he went, Empson would read a book as he walked about the place; and when one of the students asked if he found it difficult to read while walking, his immediate response was: 'No. It is much more difficult while riding a bicycle.'[48] George Soule, who would sometimes walk with him from the dormitory to various parties (and then assist him to get home afterwards), did not know if he was being teased when Empson made a surprising revelation one day. While writing *Seven Types of Ambiguity*, he declared, he found he had so much to say that seven seemed to be as good a number as any for the book. When asked further about *Ambiguity*, and the time when he had been thrown out of Magdalene College in 1929, he again astonished everyone when he said he had no idea what point he had reached at that moment, because he had become so focused on what he was doing.[49] Another day, some of the students and faculty wrote a progressive sonnet; Soule remembers just one gnomic line (which reads as if ghosted by Stephen Dedalus)—'Anfractuous the modalities of the visible'—but not whether Empson wrote it.[50] (It seems not unlikely that the author of the verse was Delmore Schwartz, who was deeply preoccupied with Joyce that summer.)

On another occasion, Empson gave a reading from his poetry, and no one would easily forget his moving recital of the villanelle 'Missing Dates', with its haunting burden: 'The waste remains, the waste remains and kills'. Another Kenyon Fellow that summer, Robert Lowell, whose poetry Empson came to admire very highly, returned the compliment with considerable interest in a later year, 1958: 'It can't be denied that almost no praise would be too high for your poems. You have the stamina of Donne, yet a far more useful and empirical knowledge of modern science and English metrics. I think you are the most intelligent poet writing in our language and perhaps the best. I put you with Hardy and Graves and Auden and Philip Larkin.'[51]

Outside the classes and the parties, a favourite pursuit was the weekly softball game. Empson, who had natural athletic ability but sorrily poor vision, was put in command of one team, L. C. Knights of the other. Playing right field, Empson could not catch a thing—except once, when Don Wiener purposely hit a 'fly' in his direction and watched in dismay and disbelief as the famously short-sighted fielder clung to the ball that fell securely into his hands.[52] When it was Empson's turn to bat, he almost invariably missed the ball—except (again) once, during one of the last games of the session, when he managed a mighty big connection. George Soule remembers: 'Empson hit the ball very well—deep towards right field—but foul.' Soule, who had been forced to act as umpire after twisting an ankle, judged that Empson could not have seen where the ball went and that, since he interpreted baseball as a form of cricket, he had little idea of what a foul ball was. 'So I called it fair, and Empson ran determinedly all the way to second base. No one objected.'[53] (The momentous run is captured in a snapshot reproduced on the record-sleeve of Empson's *Selected Poems*.)

Among the faculty, Empson hit it off best not with the reticent and conscientious Knights but with the more expansive, warm, and accessible Kenneth Burke, whose staring eyes would appear almost to burst out of his head as he fixed his interlocutor with his gaze. Burke was invariably combative in a jolly, friendly way, and he was all the merrier if his opponent responded in kind. He was decidedly 'a live wire and much on my beat,' as Empson enthused of him.[54] Indeed, Empson and Burke, who shared Left-wing sympathies, were somewhat isolated from the rest of the faculty, which was dominated by the angry, noisy, right-wing crowd that included Mizener and Schwartz. Don Wiener has remarked of their encounters, 'Both were men with few pretensions and great intellectual integrity.'[55] Not unlike Ransom, who had criticized Empson's earlier writings, in particular *Seven Types of Ambiguity*, for paying too much attention to the 'texture' of poems and not enough to their 'structure', Burke embraced the larger analytical view. If Empson was the eclectic empiricist, Burke was a system-builder. His concern was to formulate a dominant theory of language. What he called his 'logogogical' engagement with literature, which amounted to an expanded mode of philology, aimed to extrapolate from the literary work a diagnosis of human motivation. Empson, though always chary of the overreaching claims of theory, was obliged to acknowledge a kinship with Burke: at the least, he had to admit, there might be just a manageable step between his own local analyses and disclosures and Burke's grand, albeit sometimes wanton, theoretical designs. All the same, the major difference is that Empson had come to reckon himself rather more responsible to historical and contextual usage, to the ways in which words work in literature, than headstrong with unparticularized ingenuity, especially in *The Structure of Complex Words* if not in *Seven Types of Ambiguity*. Of Burke's work he would say in a later year: 'I probably have been influenced by it but I wouldn't want to read much now, I don't think.'[56]

Marian Janssen, historian of the *Kenyon Review*, has recorded too: 'There is a story of Empson drunkenly yet brilliantly attacking Burke's views at four in the morning, at which a devoted student of Burke's got so upset that he woke Burke and pleaded with him to get dressed and let Empson have it; however, when Burke arrived, Empson had passed out, so Burke returned to his pajamas and bed. Nevertheless, the close associations, the social gatherings, games, and charades at the School prevented dogmatic isolation and bred tolerance and a broadening of views.'[57] Given that Empson and Burke promptly turned out to be 'great pals' at Kenyon, and that (because of timetable clashes) no student could attend both Empson's course on complex words and Burke's on poetry as symbolic action, the two men agreed to hold a joint lecture-seminar in order to spell out their differences.

During his hectic visit to Peking, I. A. Richards had read the proofs of *The Structure of Complex Words*, in which (among other matters) Empson quarrelled with his mentor's distinction between the emotive and cognitive uses of language, as well as quizzing his Theory of Value. Empson had looked forward to receiving from Richards either a cross confutation or an acknowledgement of the validity of his arguments. Where Empson hoped they might lock horns in a strong but respectful argument, however, not only did Richards reprove his personal conduct, he patronized his latest work with scant attention. The preoccupied Richards, Empson wrote rather pettishly, 'praised it but regarded it as solely about dictionary technique and advised me to get employed by the Oxford Dictionary, apparently because scandal would soon exclude me from all further contact with the growing mind. I believe in neither side of this unexpected drama (I was ready to stop the edition by cable if he had minded my attacks on him, but his mind is always on something else)...' In truth, Richards was more puzzled than outraged by the way in which (as he believed) Empson misrepresented his critical stance. He may well have shown real concern when he reprobated Empson's drinking; but, if Empson told the whole story, he was less than considerate when he depreciated his book. All the same, notwithstanding his dissatisfaction with Richards's negligent response to his work, and his disaffection, Empson was not given to nursing undying resentments.

Indeed, he graciously acknowledged that *The Structure of Complex Words* might turn out to be something less than epoch-making when Kenneth Burke offered him a similar opinion. In Empson's judgement, Burke was truly 'the king of the show' at Kenyon; and he was evidently prepared to allow that Burke may have got the better of their 'entertaining' public debate. He wrote to John Hayward at the time: 'talking to Kenneth Burke here does make me feel that my bombshell [the new book] like the atom bomb itself is more narrow in impact than the strategist would like to claim.'[58] Don Wiener confirms that Empson and Burke showed 'a great deal of respect for each other... The argument was handled with great good humor and affection on both sides.'[59] It was just the sort of constructive tussle that Empson sorely missed engaging in with his mentor Richards, to whom he wrote while on the journey back to Peking: 'reading Burke's new book [*A Rhetoric of Motives*] on the boat has made me think very highly of him indeed (he is a charming fellow to quarrel with in public in an arranged manner anyhow, but I never thought him first class till I settled down to the new book).'[60]

As for the good political row that Empson anticipated, the chance to set the record straight on China, precious few of his colleagues seemed eager to do battle with him: 'two years ago there was Matthiessen here, who was interested in the world picture and whose suicide was rather a disaster I think, but now we are as concentrated on our profession as a conference of dentists practically. Except for Kenneth Burke . . . '[61] Otherwise, only the 'shambling, sweaty, untidy' Delmore Schwartz picked any sort of fight, which his biographer James Atlas has attributed to his growing paranoia:

> When the Schwartzes gave a cocktail party that summer, he unleashed a furious attack on Allen Tate for his part in awarding the 1949 Bollingen Prize to Pound. (Among the judges were Eliot, Auden, Robert Penn Warren, and Robert Lowell.) It was a controversial issue, and Delmore would perhaps have been justified in objecting—as Irving Howe and others did in *Commentary* and *Partisan Review*—had he confined himself to the matter of Pound's politics or anti-Semitism. But he was certain that an intricate conspiracy implicating Eliot and other, more shadowy figures manipulated the committee into giving the award to a Fascist. Lowell was at the party and tried to placate Delmore, which only fueled his agitation. When William Empson, just back from China and sporting a Mao suit, volunteered that giving the Bollingen Prize to Pound was the best thing America had ever done, Delmore turned on him and accused him of being a traitor to England because he was a Communist.[62]

Empson later confined himself to one comment on the fracas: 'The dangerous figure there, I thought, was poor Delmore Schwartz, who when drunk expressed political suspicions of me; but I think he was won over before the end.'[63]

He finally found his own outlet towards the end of the session, when it came to be his turn to address the assembled school in a series of lectures on the state of the critical art. He anticipated the opportunity with splendidly aphoristic nerve in a letter of 2 July: 'I have to make a public speech as part of my employment here in two or three weeks time, at which I shall say whatever I think it important to say. The advantage or perhaps the limitation of being an obstinate man is that you don't have moral problems, only risks; what you ought to do is always clear . . . However it would be silly to dramatize the thing, and I do not expect any kind of publicity to follow my little talk.'[64] Adverse publicity was indeed a serious possibility, and the US State Department would not have overlooked it. A whiff of warning had been carried to him on his arrival in Ohio in June, when Ransom and Coffin went to meet him by car in Cleveland—'in part they said to guard against a *Time* reporter believed to be on the trail; but the arrival of John Foster Dulles in Japan on my airplane made it eighteen hours late starting back, so I missed them and had a night in Tokyo.'[65] Strangely enough, at a time when the unanticipated Korean conflict was making front-page news, almost everyone at Kenyon came to regard Empson as a strikingly apolitical person; so it is just possible that he warily kept his own counsel in private conversations.

In any event, when he gave his plenary lecture (as he recalled three years later), 'I gave my first quarter of an hour to a general political scolding of Americans about China, and indeed I had done [so] two years before; pretty absurdly really, because it was nothing to do with the School and also meant going against my contract with the British Council, in which you promise not to talk politics at all. But this legal clause is interpreted reasonably; it is obvious that there are many cases where a determined silence would only create suspicion, and I knew if I didn't tell this audience what I really thought about China they would be quite certain I thought something much worse. I would positively have smelt fishy if I hadn't scolded.'[66] What he told them, as he related soon after the event, was 'that the Chinese set-up isn't this-and-that at all, and that they think the Americans ridiculously wicked; but this went over as smoothly as a cup of tea, and it appeared that nobody disagreed so that one couldn't expect much "discussion".'[67]

Maybe Empson's audience took it on the chin because they were as little 'aware of politics'[68] as he had reckoned (or indeed as he seemed to them), or else they blinked politely at his killjoy impropriety. As Don Wiener recalls, they were otherwise having 'a hell of a great time'.[69] Yet another possibility is that he gave them his sharp political hiding at a time when many Americans had grown sick of the anti-Communist wolf-howls relayed in the press. On arrival in Ohio, he had perceptively judged the mood of the moment: 'The weeklies here other than *Time* seem to be swinging away from the Redbaiting; Senator McCarthy has been overdoing it absurdly, seems to be the feeling [in February, Joseph McCarthy had alleged that numerous Communists had penetrated the State Department as part of an international conspiracy]; however I daresay they will swing back.'[70] All the same, upon returning to Peking, he would write to Kathleen Raine of the wretched pusillanimity of the liberal American mind: 'The chief thing to report about my intellectual American friends . . . is that they are very gloomy about international affairs but don't feel they can do anything and don't want to stick their necks out . . . '

At the end of August he journeyed back behind the Iron Curtain— 'travelling third class in a large American liner carrying troops to Korea (it would then resume its normal life and go to Hongkong). It seemed clear that this conflict was merely intended to stoke up the Cold War, whoever had arranged it, on either side.' When the President Cleveland made a landing at Yokohama, Empson's younger friend and admirer, the poet and critic G. S. Fraser, accompanied by his wife and by Professor Rintaro Fukuhara (who had been Empson's boss in Tokyo), drove out to treat him for a day in Tokyo. Fraser was serving for two years, in succession to Edmund Blunden, as Cultural Adviser to the UK Liaison Mission in Tokyo. Fukuhara noted that Empson had thrown on his cabin bed a copy of *Middlemarch* and a book called *God is Love*. 'You can never tell what this chap is going to read next,' he thought. Sizing up Professor Fukuhara in the car, Empson felt 'shocked to see this naturally cheerful character looking so very sad, and . . . all the more struck because people in the streets of Tokyo, as I peeped out at them, looked to me as if they were feeling very successful.' For his part, after a lapse of sixteen years, Fukuhara expressed his pleasure at seeing that Empson had preserved all the 'confident buoyancy' he had brought to Japan in 1931. Puffing with animation on a pipe (he kept his tobacco in a spectacle case), Empson chatted 'eagerly and freely' with G. S. Fraser, who seemed 'dreadfully gloomy', he thought, and even 'very reactionary as I told him'.[71]

The British Ambassador, on being introduced to Empson in the Embassy Compound, seemed to be startled by his beard (beards were not common at the time, and Empson's was far more uncommon than most).

> 'Been in Peking, eh?' he asked warily.
> 'Yes,' responded Empson, impishly refusing further conversation.
> 'Must have been jolly interesting.'[72]

Empson 'was still the high-spirited young man we used to know,' wrote Fukuhara. 'When I remarked that the Americans were addicted to writing enormously long histories of American literature he said "Yes, it must be unpleasant work. You have to read such a lot of tripe".'[73] Empson's version of the exchange, written after Fukuhara's death over thirty years later, reads: 'the first thing to ask Fukuhara . . . was: "How did you get on under the American Occupation?" He may be described as putting on an act, though placidly; he became very Japanese. Spacing out the syllables, he said: "We are very sorry for them. They have to be loyal to their American classics." Then, in a different character, holding up his hand as an absurd pretence of hiding his mouth, he said: "The Scarlet Letter. Tee hee hee." No doubt he had been on a committee where American officials recommended books for the English Departments of Japanese Universities. Sorry for them one might really be.'[74] Empson's lack of admiration for the American classics was long-standing, but his distaste was surely compounded by a sense of vexation over the American response in Korea. As he would tellingly recall in the same piece too: 'I suppose I was travelling third class to avoid meeting the military officers.'

8

Quitting Communist China

The American obsession with Communism, which Empson had observed while at the Kenyon summer school, and which was exemplified by the bullying tactics of Senator Joe McCarthy at home, was every bit as virulent abroad in US foreign policy. But although the world waited—almost resignedly—for the Cold War to be transformed into violent conflagration, few anticipated that Korea would be the catalyst. General MacArthur had thrown down the gauntlet to the PRC in declaring for the nationalist cause over Taiwan: already incensed by this, the Chinese regarded American intervention in Korea as an act of blatant aggression.

After returning to Peking, Empson would not be swayed from his opinion that Communist China had earned its right to be treated as an equal member of the community of nations; nor shirk what he regarded as his responsibility to insist upon the claim. Early in October he wrote to Kathleen Raine, 'I gather the British are beginning to act a small amount more firmly over China Formosa etc. on the UN, which seems to be all that's required.'[1] As for the Korean conflict, he believed without cynicism, it had best be left to resolve itself as an internal issue rather than rip towards a war between the USA and China.

But the worst forecast seemed to be close to realization, filling him with a sense of defeat: 'I seem so fearfully blank; for so long now I seem to have been waiting to see whether something turns out all right, and there is always something, just now the Korean War of course, in which all right means avoiding world war because the Koreans are determined to get united and socialist anyway and will go through a lot of hell first anyway, so that the war news is merely depressing; but the feeling I am waiting for the end about is a bad habit, and probably a common one among literary chaps.'[2] He was alluding to his own poem, 'Just a Smack at Auden', written twelve years earlier, in which he had lampooned the poetry of what he called 'young Communist uplift' for sniping at a diseased social order and foretelling its doom. 'Waiting for the end, boys, waiting for the end. | What is there to be or do? | What's become of me or you?' In 1950, the irony was not lost on him.

The finest opportunity to stand up and be counted among those who applauded the achievement of Communist China occurred on 1 October 1950, at the huge parade in Peking to celebrate the first anniversary of the People's Republic. Shaking the buildings over a wide area, a salute of guns marked the moment when Chairman Mao Tse-t'ung, together with President Liu Shao-chi, Premier Chou En-lai and Marshal Chu Teh, took their places with the other bigwigs on the rostrum of Tiananmen in order to review a display of military and industrial power followed by a demonstration of mass enthusiasm.

From among the official British corps, only the 'Chargé d'Affaires to negotiate the establishment of diplomatic relations' enjoyed the honour of a seat on the tiers reserved for diplomats, fraternal delegations and foreign guests; other members of the British mission, quaffing beer and reflecting that there were after all some advantages to the Chinese policy of non-recognition, had to watch the swarming pomp and circumstance from a near distance—over the garden wall of the Embassy compound, at a diagonal to the rostrum.

Peking University would not have minded if William and Hetta Empson had chosen to absent themselves from the body it massed for the parade (as Peter Townsend noted, 'the Chinese are masters at the political art of staying away from obligatory performances'[3]). After all, for them to take part in a show of applause to the Communist state and its leaders meant giving a clear political signal. But they felt bound to show solidarity, and said to hell with compromising consequences. Empson wrote the next day:

> there was a marchpast of (they say) around half a million people, and Hetta and I with our university lot were waiting from about eight to one-thirty till our crowd was passed through, in a great solid mass all yelling slogans to Mao on the balcony with terrific red hangings and banners and all the rest of it. Dear Hetta suddenly clutched my arm at the crucial moment and said 'There's the British consul—don't catch his eye—I know he saw me—all those in the top hats are the British—Oh God I'm sure he noticed me— you're bound to get the sack'; the British have been recognised so far as to

get a seat on one of the grandstands. Of course I didn't see them myself, being very bad at seeing people, but I began explaining in the general uproar and hurry that the case was similar to any other meeting of acquaintances in questionable places—if you are wrong to be there so are they. But by this time we were passing the elaborately dressed Sinkiang notables and Tibetans and whatnot along the grandstand so there was no opportunity for much generalisation. Actually I don't think the local British are in the least likely to complain at my going along with my Trades Union on these occasions, but the world has become so tricky that one does tend to get these illusions of seeing two jumps ahead suddenly.[4]

It might be thought a 'Significant Detail', Empson would have one know, that he took with him on the march a copy of Evelyn Waugh's *Scott-King's Modern Europe*: a 'powerful little skit,' he said, 'a handy thing for the pocket'.

National Day was nonetheless a fateful day for China in the world. It marked the beginning of the end that Empson had long awaited so blankly. On that very day, General MacArthur called for the surrender of North Korean forces; South Korean troops penetrated north of the 38th parallel, followed a week later by US forces; and 'Mao circulated a secret directive that Chinese troops would enter the war, using the name of Chinese People's Volunteers (CPV) as a device to try to limit the war to the Korean peninsula.'

During the next few months the tension ratcheted up. At a news conference on 30 November, when Truman was asked if he had thought of deploying the atom bomb against Communist China, he responded, with a wretched lack of political caution: 'There has been active consideration of its use.'[5] This caused uproar in the British parliament, and Prime Minister Atlee rushed to confer with the President in Washington. In December Truman declared a national emergency.

On 1 February 1951, the United Nations, at the insistence of the US Congress, formally branded the People's Republic of China an aggressor. American forces regained Seoul on 15 March. Instead of enforcing their advantages over the exhausted Chinese, however, they remitted their efforts and began to talk of truce talks by July. Yet the misbegotten war slogged on for two more deadly years.

'Historical facts teach us,' Peking declared on 4 November 1950,

that a crisis in Korea has much to do with the security of China. With the lips gone, the teeth would be exposed to the cold; with the door open, the house itself would be in danger... To protect our own country, we must help the people of Korea.

Throughout the country the Chinese people are enthusiastically volunteering to resist American aggression, aid Korea, protect their homes and defend their country.[6]

Thousands of students and workers did volunteer, Peter Townsend recalled; so many, in fact, that only a rank sceptic could doubt the considerable spontaneity of the mobilization. 'Granted that the air of excitement was calculated to bring a patriotic lump into a young man's throat, and that soldiers and students, among the most active in politics, took the lead, the response was overwhelming.'[7]

On the home front, the Resist America, Aid Korea Association, prompted by the CCP, organized demonstrations of anti-American activity throughout the country. All the same, the Chinese Communists were 'at pains to distinguish governments and policies from people,' Townsend noted. 'The leading political figures of America, for example, were "American devils", "imperialists" and the like. The ordinary people were "decent" and "essentially friendly", if sometimes misled . . . '[8]

Empson likewise reported: 'Even outside the university work, we had no trouble with anti-foreign feeling, such as has in the past sometimes been very bad in China, and might be expected now. If we went to the grand new public swimming pool in Peking, for example, we would be sure to be chattered to, and asked questions, and probably asked first if we were Russians; there seemed to be rather a shortage of Russians to talk to, in fact; but the painful truth that we weren't Russians would not produce unfriendliness or stop the conversation.'

University branches of the 'Resist America, Aid Korea' Association were set to work in close co-operation with the 'study committees' of professors and students, whose urgent duty it became to bind education to the needs of national defence. On 4 November, 376 professors from Peking University signed an open letter to Mao Tse-tung denouncing the crimes of American imperialism; the next day, Professor Feng Yu-lan (a philosopher who had been a colleague of Empson's at the Southwest Associated University) published an article entitled 'To Aid Korea and to fight for peace'; and for two or more weeks, as Theodore Chen recorded, all regular classes were overborne by the instruction to scrutinise the American record in China (taking as their text a specially prepared handbook entitled 'Know America'). ' "Learning sessions" . . . dealt with the history, the nature, the menace, and the various manifestations of American "imperialism" not only in military aggression but also in political domination, economic exploitation, and cultural enslavement.'[9] In Peking alone, according to an editorial in *Jen-min jih-pao* (*People's Daily*), more than 30,000 college and high school students took themselves off to factories and farms to engage in propaganda.[10]

Some commentators have maintained that the hardliners of the Central Committee in Peking thus seized upon the Korean War as the excuse they had desired from the outset to tighten the screws of internal reform. That argument has substantial weight: the coincidence is too exact to be ignored.

For his part, Empson believed throughout the first months of the Korean War that the People's Republic of China was victim more than villain. As he understood the situation, China was beleaguered by American forces marching towards the Sino-Korean border, by their aggressive 'neutralization' of Taiwan, by bombing sorties over Manchuria, and by economic warfare. To add insult to injury, it was further belaboured by the blague of the UN's decision to condemn China as an aggressor. Empson and his wife acted upon their sympathy with China's affront so far as to make up a puppet-play (incorporating a caricature of MacArthur crafted by Hetta) depicting 'the unity of the world combating imperialism'; dubbed into Chinese by Jin Di, the piece was staged a number of times in Peking.[11] Apart from that one pro-Chinese demonstration, however, Empson kept to his contractual obligation not to involve himself in political activity; and Peking University willy-nilly helped to preserve his apolitical posture by excluding him from the remorseless meetings for ideological indoctrination, confession and self-criticism that it was obliged to initiate in the final months of 1951.[12]

In any event, the upshot of the Korean War laid waste his wish that Communist China and Great Britain (if not the USA) might come to terms, though he remained reluctant to give up all hope of a rapprochement. For the remainder of his employment in Peking, and for some time after returning to England in the summer of 1952, he kept faith with his happy and optimistic perception of the PRC as it was in the beginning, during the first year or so after liberation. Principally because he was to a considerable degree isolated from what was happening, he went on upholding—for too long—the picture of Peking as a place of popular exhilaration and high promise, as the vibrant centre of a Communist state that was generously accommodating in its policies. He felt bound to answer publications that libelled the regime, even when his apologia ran up against the mounting evidence which showed that the New China had progressed to more totalitarian aims and measures.

For the immediate future, with the world diving into the bloody maelstrom of the Korean War, he resolved to prove to his students that they should at all costs take the largest possible view of the tide of human affairs. Towards the end of 1950 Empson wrote for publication a statement that wonderfully encapsulates the fundamental conviction of his life and work:

> it is of great importance now that writers and other artists should try to keep a certain worldmindedness; that is one of the reasons why I as an Englishman like living in Peking and feel I may have a certain usefulness there. Without the literatures you cannot have a sense of history, and history is like the balancing-pole of the tightrope walker (it looks only a nuisance, but without it he would fall off); and nowadays we very much need the longer balancing-pole of not national but world history.

'The universities seem to have made up their minds to go on teaching English language and literature, after a year of some doubt,' Empson wrote in October 1950. 'Shakespeare is in effect "required" again this year at my place, whereas only a few, two or three, stalwarts did it last year. The internal affairs seem to be being handled very reasonably.' He was on the whole well disposed to cooperate with a sensible process of curriculum reform at Peita. Not only did the university deserve his support if it was to come into its own at a time of international aggression, he lamented the fact that the traditional curriculum made the students trudge through the gamut of English literature. Many of the classics left them gasping with incomprehension, so that they were forced to con available works of criticism and not to exercise their own judgements; likewise, the labyrinth of grammar and pronunciation had to be learned by rote, and not explored as the means to intelligent expression.

The First National Congress on Higher Education, held in July 1950, yet complained that most of the curricula in institutions of higher education were 'still not "new democratic"—not national, scientific, and popular, and not in conformity with the needs of new China's reconstruction work.' It therefore decreed that higher institutions 'must abolish politically reactionary curricula and offer "new democratic" revolutionary curricula, in order to eliminate feudalistic, comprador, and Fascist ideas and to develop the ideal of serving the people.'[13]

Empson's response to that ukase was ready and willing, albeit canny. While always insisting that the study of literature was primarily 'important in itself', he said, its 'important practical purpose' was to enable the student to understand 'the psychology or general background of the native speakers'. If revolutionary China needed graduates 'who are reliable translators or interpreters of English writing done recently, both American and English', he maintained, the students would most successfully learn to meet that practical task by first striving to comprehend the history of the English-speaking mind as mediated through the literature. 'A fair knowledge of Shakespeare can honestly be recommended from this practical point of view...,' he ventured, 'because he is much more often quoted than any other author.'[14]

However sound his argument for the relevance of historicity may have seemed to the university authorities, his students in the session 1950–1 nonetheless found grounds for complaint: not all his selected texts, after all, catered to the tendentious purpose of 'serving the cause of the revolution'.[15] Did the works of Yeats and Eliot help to cultivate the necessary scientific—specifically, Marxist—and popular attitude? Were they not, to some extent at least, politically reactionary? Unless they instilled in the reader the correct ideology, they should not be countenanced but thrown out of class. Though buffeted by such protests, Empson persisted with his classroom agenda in the certain knowledge that he knew better than their narrow-mindedness. Yet he had to admit to the British Council in July 1951, 'the students have been told to try teasing the teacher this year (and very rightly, because there really are a lot of bad teachers around, and the government policy here is that even in minor matters you would prefer to get the row started at the bottom). I have therefore been shot at a bit during the year, but have come out of it rather better thought of than before, I think; anyway the proposal that my wife should go back to England with the children this year was found to be too hard, there was too much desire that we should all stay, and we are staying.'[16] (Hetta Empson, who again gave conversation classes on a part-time basis—'My wife was thought very good at making her classes talk,' said Empson—was not so subject to doctrinaire chivvying. As she explained in a letter to Dinah Stock, 'there is a new stress on practical English—that is teaching the students to talk the language instead of just writing it, and the two things seem to be tending to separate—that is, pure literature and practical English'; so her courses would not readily run up against the accusation of being unacceptably polemical.) 'I hope it works out all right,' said Empson in the summer of 1951, not realizing that the next session would be programmed to break his professional resolve—if anything could do so.

On 29 September 1951, Chou En-lai delivered an exhaustive address to Peking University—it lasted for no less than five hours—to inaugurate the programme of radical reorientation. College teachers would have to purge themselves of reactionary ideology, he proclaimed; they should espouse the truth of a 'revolutionary standpoint, viewpoint and method'.[17] During the summer, Professor Ma Yin-ch'u, an economist who became President of

National Peking University on 1 June that year, had anticipated Premier Chou's call by organizing his faculty for 'reformative study' (*kai-tsao hsüeh-hsi*).[18] From now on, stressed an editorial published in the party paper *Jen-min jih-pao* (*People's Daily*) on 23 October, all staff, from the president down to junior instructors, must 'boldly criticize their erroneous and incorrect attitudes. On the one hand they must examine themselves and oppose the attitude of self-complacency and self-delusion, and, on the other hand, they must boldly criticize each other, discarding the hypocritical politeness which tries to offend nobody.'[19] In the same issue of the official organ, President Ma published the text of his own latest speech to Peita. Prompt to act upon Chou's coercive cue, he traduced the 'liberal and unorganised atmosphere' of the university and gave order that all employees should 'voluntarily undergo mind-reform' by way of 'a planned and systematic study movement'. Forsaking the 'influences of the Anglo-American reactionary capitalist class', along with all erroneous trends such as 'objectivism' and 'individualism', everyone should henceforth cleave to the pantology of Marxist-Leninism and the Thought of Mao Tse-tung. The responsibility of university education, the president decreed, was 'to train large numbers of revolutionary youths for the country... to train advanced technical personnel and principal cadres for national construction... to combine theory with practice.'[20] In short, every person and pursuit should be forced into the correct revolutionary shape.

'Professors in the universities obviously had to change what they thought and what they taught in order to accomplish this assignment,' commented Maria Yen. 'The reluctance of teachers to let go of the old and embrace the new during the first two years of the Liberation obviously agitated the Communist leaders. After the campaign to reform the intellectuals got under way, the Vice Minister of Education, Ch'ien Chun-ju, explained [in *Hsüeh Hsi* (*Study*, the chief theoretical journal of the party), 1 November 1951] just why it was necessary: "the slow rate and limited scope of change attained by the great majority of professors during the past two years".'[21] A week later, Professor Ch'ien Tuan-sheng, the Harvard-educated dean of the College of Law at the National Peking University, uttered a sentence of death upon the 'pedagogical philosophy of freedom of thought and freedom of learning': 'it not only becomes divorced from facts right from the beginning, but afterwards develops into each department or faculty governing itself, and leads to learning becoming opposed to politics... learning for learning's sake and other serious mistaken attitudes of mind which have not yet been eliminated.' From that moment on, Empson would profess to deaf ears that studying literature was 'important in itself'; English would survive as a fit subject for study only if it served to promote the ideology of revolutionary consciousness. Education is indoctrination, they said; 'the people's standpoint' must supplant any old 'personal standpoint'.[22]

Unwarily, Empson had written to I. A. Richards in March 1951: 'Of course a lot of foreigners have been going away, and to tell the truth a touch of boredom has been making itself felt; but I still think this one of the most interesting places to be, and it is certainly comfortable and friendly.'[23] Come September (albeit in a letter justifiably pressing the British Council for more financial support), he would refer to his job in Peking as 'this rather exacting and isolated post'.[24] He was excluded from the labour of mental rectification, including struggle meetings for criticism and self-criticism) though his wife voluntarily undertook self-criticism—to show her solidarity. Indeed, his colleagues took pains to protect him from that form of inquiry and assault. But he was obliged vigorously to defend the study of English literature, and to plan courses which would pass the severe test of directly contributing to 'new China's reconstruction work'. Willingly, without fear or favour, he set himself to review the parade of literature through the prism of politics.

In a long report written at the request of Professor Pien Chih-lin [Bian Zhilin], he again insisted with a stout heart that whatever employment the students were destined to take up, as graduates in English they ought to be able to penetrate the English-speaking mind and its history. A literary course 'ought to consider real history, rather cursorily, rather than literary history, and use the literary examples to show what the real history felt like.'[25]

Far from floundering in the gap between disinterested scholarship and the Communists' political purposes, he discovered (though he did not directly say so), the curriculum and pedagogical approach he had in mind coincided with his own recent work on the nature and action of complex (simple) words in English literature. The argument of *The Structure of Complex Words* is concerned with describing how the current suggestions of words behave as encapsulated thoughts or (sometimes dubiously) doctrines; with discovering the 'logical structure' at work in the process. Most notably, as he would later write in an essay entitled 'Professor Lewis on Linguistics', 'Readers need to be warned that a writer often means by a word something other than what their own background leads them to expect; a working understanding of the historical process of change of meaning, by giving this awareness, may be enough.'[26] Just so, he told Peita in 1951: 'The practical function of studying the literature of another country, I submit, is that it is a way to learn this background or psycho-logy... There is a case for studying modern poetry on this principle (as I would wish there to be) because it often puts important prevalent ideas in a conveniently striking and brief form.'

There would be no conflict of interest, he triumphantly determined, between his own critical forté and the educational edicts of the CCP; and there was no shyness or sophistry in the forceful case he sought to elaborate:

> The whole conception of 'psychological background' which I am writing from will perhaps seem either nationalistic or obscure; it may naturally be said: don't you only mean, at best, that the Chinese who are taught to handle English must learn to distinguish between different types of reac-tionary ideology? I certainly think they must, if they are not to make serious mistakes; the question is not so much the differences in ideology as how they are expressed in the language. And a historical attitude is always required for a political forecast, or rather the skill to pick out the part of the historical background which will be important in a particular country now; and you cannot start to make that difficult but sometimes important guess unless you know enough of the background.
>
> This suggests the question: how far ought the material to be political? The first reply I think is that it is like eating; what suits us is a mixed diet, and it is better to have a tiny surprise at every meal. Of course you may say it is all food, and all thought is at bottom political; but anybody gets bored unless there is the feeling that he or she is now going through an unex-pected experience which demands a new reaction or appraisal. If you want the students to learn, the way to help them is to give them variety. A steady diet of reactionary material is at first very stimulating (they denounce it) but soon they get a habit of denouncing it without bothering to read it except for a short look for 'talking points'. A steady diet of pro-government material of course has the same effect more quickly. The essential thing is to keep them feeling they have got to read the English text carefully because they don't yet know 'the answer'... If you want a technical skill, here or in engineering or in anything else, you must plan how to train people for it.[27]

As for specific examples of poetry to be studied, he went on, 'I think one might distinguish between verse to be read early as part of language-training (which needn't be at all inferior poetry) and verse to be read later as illustrating recent ideologies and changes of taste. It is not possible to show the point of the big poems by Yeats or Eliot or the earlier Auden without giving a fairly large background of this sort, and one could hardly show it in action more directly.'

Mindful of the current background of China's fierce antipathy towards American imperialism, he then offered this seemingly offhand but striking suggestion: 'There is no one English poem which any English-majoring student ought to have read; if you try to think of such a thing, perhaps the nearest is *The Ancient Mariner*, which could be taken fairly early, and by the way has an interesting political background in the sixteenth-century maritime empires and their guilt.' That political gesture was not merely a fetch for the Reds, however, since Empson had foreshadowed the argument in his pre-Liberation classes at Peita; and he would dwell on it for many years to come, until 1964, when he brought out his first magnificent essay on the subject. 'What then did one find,' he would write, 'reading in bulk the reports of the European maritime expansion, which made it suitable for the Mariner to be struck down by guilt? Surely the answer is plain once the question is asked; they reek of guilt. Indeed Columbus himself, returning to Europe in the first triumph of discovery...lamented that the Caribbeans were so innocent, unsuspicious, and doomed..."What use was their religion if it did not tell them that this was wrong?"—such was the way it would appear to Coleridge, who boasted to correspondents around this time that he did not examine religious doctrines as a mere arguer, but always in the light of their practical effects.' While the Chinese Communists might allow that 'The Ancient Mariner' could be construed as a political fable about the evils of imperialism, Empson judged that it served also to catechize Christianity, the wicked religion of the western world. Without feeling obliged to compromise either his critical integrity or his ethical principles to fit the Communist directive, he was pointing to at least one certain match of politics and poetry.

Likewise, he boldly advised the authorities, Marxist theory was neither the exclusive preserve of Communism nor even anathema in the West; he himself had been excited by it when writing *Some Versions of Pastoral*. 'No use supposing Marx left out by bourgeois states; long been fundamental to bourgeois criticism; his and Engels [*sic*] literary views long recognised and not as narrow as made by some disciples.' Naturally he was in no hurry to tell them that the lead essay in his book, 'Proletarian Literature' (first published in Japan in 1933), had arraigned the very concept of 'proletarian literature' as 'bogus'. 'One might define proletarian art as the propaganda of a factory-working class which feels its interests opposed to the factory owners'; this narrow sense is perhaps what is usually meant but not very interesting,' he had unerringly argued. 'You couldn't have proletarian literature in this sense in a successful socialist state.' While proposing that 'there must be some kind of resistance behind good writing', and even yet that 'this is no argument against communism as a political scheme', he had concluded with firm fine logic: 'It is only an argument against the communist aesthetic.' In the face of what Japan's rulers in the 1930s feared as the dangerous flood of international communism, Empson had judged that 'bourgeois' art would assuredly survive even in a proletarian state. While 'pure' proletarian literature might not be distinguishable from propaganda, the social conflicts of which the pastoral mode is evidence would continue to produce a genuine art of resistance: 'the most valuable works of art so often have a political implication which can be pounced on and called bourgeois . . . My own difficulty about proletarian literature is that when it comes off I find I am taking it as pastoral literature; I read into it, or find that the author has secretly put into it, these more subtle, far-reaching, and I think more permanent, ideas.' In sum, he believed, 'the prop of individualist theory' is at odds with 'a rigid proletarian aesthetic'.

'The Chinese communist short stories have great merit in limited numbers,' he allowed in July 1950, 'but it is a very narrow field (of course we know the chaps employed on translating them into English, and the whole subject of what should be sent abroad is one of frequent tedious discussion in my house).' Early the next year, one of his students, William Lee, showed him an unpolished translation of a pre-Liberation story by the celebrated Lao She, 'Outside the Temple of Great Mercy' (a fable about humiliation and guilt, the story later became available in an authorised translation entitled 'By the Temple of Great Compassion' in *Crescent Moon and Other Stories*, Beijing, 1985). Empson admired the subject matter and literary quality of the tale, and promptly sent it to John Hayward with the request that he try to place it with an English periodical. 'I seriously think the story so good that it ought to be known,' he declared in a draft of his letter.[28] Presumably his motive in asking Hayward to act as an agent was to persuade his students that the outside world would not scorn good Chinese literature on some xenophobic principle, and that Lao She's story would still, even in the midst of the Korean War, find an appreciative audience in the West; also that the students could trust him to support their own literary endeavours. 'I am kind of gambling my mystique on your being willing to play up . . . ,' he admitted to Hayward; 'if you can place this young man's translation it will make a great difference to his life.' Certainly he was not peddling Communist wares. At Empson's request, Lee submitted the piece to 'the official bureau, where we have friends of course . . . but the kind of thing he wants to translate isn't what they are interested in; however they are perfectly willing to have him place them abroad; so there is no smuggling or puzzle about this.'[29] Hayward ruled not only that the story held no more than a 'slight' interest for 'English readers unacquainted with Chinese mores' but also that the translation was too rough for publication. Never inclined to let friendship get in the way of a good quarrel, Empson riposted on 24 July 1951: 'do consider what the great translations from the nineteenth-century Russians into English are like—the clumsiness is a positive gain, because it forces the reader to imagine a quite different society, as he is ready to do, instead of confusing him by suggesting that these characters are all Englishmen behaving improbably... So please hand the text on like an honest man, and don't go on imagining that your reputation for appreciating the English prose of Lin Yu-tang might be robbed from you.'[30] When Hayward did nothing further, however, Empson let it go.

In fact, by 1951 the 'kind of thing' the official bureau was concerned to promote, following the 'proletarianization' of literature and art, turned violently against the kinds of merit that Empson discerned in Lao She's story. In July 1949 the party leaders had speedily assembled 750 delegates for the First All-China Conference of Writers and Artists, which duly set up the All-China Federation of Literary and Arts Circles and unanimously adopted Mao Tse-tung's dictates on revolutionary literature—Leninist theories adapted to Chinese circumstances—as the 'militant common programme for the literary and art movement in new China.'[31] (Ironically, Lao She was lecturing in the USA at the time, though he was assuredly present in spirit.) Mao had pronounced upon the party's literary line as early as May 1942, in two lectures published as *Talks at the Yenan Literary Meetings*: 'The revolutionary writers and artists of China... should permanently, unconditionally, and wholeheartedly go over to the worker–peasant–soldier masses.'[32] In May 1951, even as Empson was trying to purvey to the west a translation of Lao She's old-style story, Chou Yang (a senior communist literary critic and Vice-Minister of Cultural affairs) brusquely reaffirmed the doctrine in a speech at the Central Institute of Literature: 'It is only with a proletarian outlook that we can understand the workers, peasants, and other classes; it is only with a proletarian method of art (revolutionary realism) that we can mirror the lives of the workers, peasants, and other classes.'[33]

Born a Manchu in 1899, Lao She (his real name was Shu Ch'ing-ch'un) was brought up in Peking and went abroad for six years in 1924. He wrote his first three novels while teaching at the School of Oriental and African Studies in London. Thereafter he won considerable attention as a satirical novelist, finally achieving world-wide acclaim when an English translation of his masterpiece, *Lo-t'o Hsiang-tzu* (*Hsiang-tzu the Camel*, 1939), published under the title *Rickshaw Boy* (1945), became a Book-of-the-Month choice and a best-seller in the United States—though the author was shocked to discover that his tragic story of a kind-hearted rickshaw puller had acquired a sentimentally happy ending in the process of translation. For most of the war years he lived in Chungking, where he organized writers and artists to support the resistance; and in 1951 he was awarded the title of 'People's Artist' (later he became Vice-Chairman of both the All-China Federation of Literary and Arts Circles and the Chinese Writers' Association). Though he had won fame for the sophisticated satirical humour of his attacks on corruption and apathy in China, after Liberation he committed himself to the role of proletarian literary producer. In consequence, when the Standing Committee of the All-China Federation of Literary and Arts Circles launched its 'ideological reform' movement in November 1951, he promptly indicated the degree of his creative conformity in a single shamed or shameful remark: 'Unprincipled humour which encourages people to treat everything in a light-hearted manner is actually harmful to the people in that it promotes inaction and the attempt to get through by compromise.'[34] Furthermore, the following May, he published in the *People's Daily* an 'apology' which included these statements: 'I . . . became bewildered on learning Chairman Mao's principle of the subordination of literature and art to politics . . . As a result of incessant trials in writing and through listening to the opinions of others, I gradually realised the importance of giving top priority to political ideology and the mistake of being satisfied with a couple of smart phrases.'[35]

The Lao She who could write such things was not the artist whose earlier work Empson had been eager to advertise to the West as recently as the spring of 1951; and Empson would never again show a vital interest in post-Liberation Chinese literature. He would not have been in the least surprised to learn that an editorial in *People's Daily*, published on the same day as Lao She's statement, exhorted artists to 'Continue the Struggle for Mao Tse-tung's Literary and Art Line' because of the paucity of their output: 'Taken as a whole, our literary and art activities have up to now failed to meet the actual needs . . . In all phases of literary and art work, whether in creative writing, criticism, the teaching of literary and art theories, or in administrative leadership, there seems to be a total suspension of activities.' Finding themselves flummoxed by the effort to marry artistic value and prescriptive ideology, authors had settled for writing in terms of formula-and-concept; so the editorial went on: 'We lack compositions which are both *ideologically* and *artistically* satisfactory in the reflection of the mighty struggles of the Chinese people.'[36] Empson could have told them the sad but true source of the problem; he had pinpointed it in *Some Versions of Pastoral* over fifteen years earlier: 'To produce pure proletarian art the artist must be at one with the worker; this is impossible, not for political reasons, but because the artist never is at one with any public.' (Despite his loyalty to the state, Lao She died as a result of Red Guard harassment in 1966.)

In August 1951, Empson gaily and perhaps glibly observed about the political situation: 'As for the Chinese, it seems clear that they have plenty of traditional individualism, and may do well to have some practice in collective action.' He meant that the reconstruction of China obviously called for an unprecedented effort of cooperative organisation, which was all to the good; not that individual enterprise should be consigned to oblivion. He thought it proper that a government should be interventionist to some degree, for he 'warmly' favoured 'a Third Way between laissez-faire and totalitarianism' and consistently voted for 'the British brand of socialism'. Almost nothing he had seen for the last two years led him to expect that the CCP would force a totalitarian polity upon the country. In any case, he could not imagine his learned and worldly colleagues submitting themselves to a mental strait-jacket. He trusted to their individualistic intelligence to sustain a liberal education at the university; and he insisted that 'the feeling of "independence" is a very important one for general morale'.

In fact, when the command came down that the Chinese intelligentsia should overthrow their political backwardness, their bourgeois and petty-bourgeois tendencies, and avow the progressive ideology of the working class, they were told to see the transformation in themselves as a metabolic process. Nourished by the study of Marxism–Leninism–Maoism, everyone would grow to live and breathe the Revolution. Cells of the body politic, they would naturally think with the one proletarian mind. For his part, Empson interpreted the order to make education 'national, scientific and popular' in a more simple sense than that of ideological absolutism: he took it to mean that the curriculum should be angled towards practical utility. If 'New Democracy' required the students to have more vocational training and less 'pure' scholarship, he could meet the case without equivocation. By all means, he volunteered, let them 'read a fair amount of elementary science in English; the ideas ought to be taught sometime, and would be found interesting, and if properly written this kind of text does show the force of simple English and help to counteract any previous over-literary training'.[37] The author he recommended was his old Cambridge acquaintance J. B. S. Haldane (who was to sign up as a Communist), in particular his essay called 'On Being the Right Size' (from *Possible Worlds*). 'It was written before he became a communist, and ends with an expression of political doubt which though very harmless is I suppose more suited to the fourth year than earlier ones, but it could easily be cut anyway.'[38] So too with his course on Shakespeare: 'It would be a good thing to read the political ones more, e g. Julius Caesar and Coriolanus.' (In fact, on looking round the whole field of English drama from the point of view of the new Chinese requirements, he decided: 'Shakespeare and Bernard Shaw seem the only outstanding figures. Galsworthy is much more like actual modern speech, and this makes me find him rather dull, combined with the "obviousness" of his situations; but both qualities might make him good material to use; he is direct and not trivial.')

Always the well-wisher, though never a convertite—'I . . . do not pretend to have interest [in] as apart from sympathy with modern China; sympathy I think anybody ought to feel,' he stated earlier in the year[39]—he dismissed the idea that to give a political bias to his classes might do damage to his professional integrity. 'I thought a reasonable amount of Socialism was obviously needed in a country like China, as well as a firm government with enough popular support behind it,' he would recall two years later. 'So I could sincerely agree about a lot of these political questions; where I didn't agree I tended to keep quiet, sure enough, but I don't remember telling any lies, and I didn't have people trying to push me into the position of either disagreeing or telling lies. Of course it is different for a Chinese, because foreigners were not expected to go to the recent confession meetings.'

If he was happy to be accommodating on almost every count, however, he continued to stand his ground on one major issue. The students should be exposed to the widest possible range of English opinion and perception—the variousness of social and political views—as expressed in the best literature. The official communist version, promulgated with prejudice by a proletarian ideologue, would simply not fit them for their future jobs. Accordingly, he sent forward for official consideration, along with his other proposals, a synoptic survey of the modern fiction that he thought could be taught to advantage: 'there do not seem to be any big recent novelists,' he wrote by way of preface. 'There are a number of good novels to be picked out, and Chinese students had better read contemporary stuff.' His annotated reading-list reads rather like whimsical patter, almost like a parody of a bluffer's guide to recent fiction (though with a fair deal of idiosyncratic insight), as if he was teasing the austere new authorities of China, or even risking subversion. In truth, he meant it quite seriously to illustrate the splendidly mixed landscape of the literature. Empson's idiosyncratic choices for his proposed reading list ranged from the relative obscurity of *The Grasshoppers Come* by Richard Garnett, to E. M. Forster's classic, *A Passage to India*. The following comment on Christopher Isherwood's *Mr Norris Changes Trains* will serve to give a flavour of Empson's approach: 'A study of Berlin when the Nazis took power, not merely of the collapse of moral life but of the astonishment of one kind of collapsing man when faced with the assumptions of another kind of collapsing man. Profound as well as amusing, I always think.' The continual prodding of epithets he applied to his selections, such as 'true', 'real' and 'solid' suggests that he was most concerned to impress upon the Communists not so much the imaginative force as the factuality of the works he recommended. They could rely on these fictions, he was seeking to suggest, to give authentic information about the history, politics and psychology of the UK and (to a limited extent) the USA.

With regard to 'the whole European background of the English-speaking mind', the one work he thought 'a major piece of English literature' was the Revised Standard version of the Bible. He had thought of it on an earlier occasion, but had set it aside: 'it is very much less quoted now than it used to be, and I do not think that a Chinese who claimed to follow any recent newspaper editorial and so on in the English language would risk much by not knowing the English Bible.' But now, he thought in September 1951, there was a fair chance to test or tease the atheistic resolve of the authorities. If they said yes to the chief burden of his proposals—'it is important to give the students a sense of history'[40]—could they reasonably deny him the Bible? Thus he wrote to the university: 'I propose to begin with a fair amount of the Bible in English, chiefly for its historical importance, and give examples of prose styles from then onward up to the recent experiments of Joyce; the aim of course being not to attempt completeness but to show what the main different styles "feel like". A certain amount of background material is to be distributed with the typed material.'[41]

Two years later, in his inaugural lecture at Sheffield, he would recall the implicit response to his request, which he took to be affirmative, as one that reflected great credit upon the inalienable liberality of his colleagues:

> My own teaching didn't alter at all as a result of the political change. Except that there was one change in my last year there, when there was a general drive to make teaching more practical; for instance it was felt if they are

learning a language they must really learn to talk it, then my superiors with a touch of embarrassment said would I mind making my poetry course into a prose course this year. I said at once that I would like to very much, it would be most interesting, and I hoped there were plenty of Bibles about so that we didn't have to type it out, because I would need to begin with at least six weeks on the Bible. I thought this was trying them rather high, but they didn't even blink at it. Under the old system the government teachers were very separate from the missionary ones, and I had actually never lectured on the Bible before, in China or Japan. It seemed to me a rather comical result of the Communists trying to be practical, and I made little jokes about my Bible Class to my Chinese colleagues, but I could feel they were rather bored by this and didn't think it was funny. I think their attitude was: 'Of course Peita... will continue to give a liberal education; what did you expect?'[42]

'There was no official interference with my teaching at all,' Empson iterated. One might be tempted to feel sceptical about the claim, and to judge that he was very sadly deceiving himself when he deduced that the university positively desired him to carry on just as before. After all, it would seem more likely, throughout his final year at Peita, that his colleagues were so overwhelmed by the business of submitting themselves day after day to 'Thought Reform' that they could hardly attend to the outstanding anomaly of his 'liberal' classes. And yet the facts tell another story: plenty of copies of the Bible were produced, so there was no need for mimeographing, and he duly proceeded to lecture on it. 'I had rather a crowd for the first weeks.'

During all his years in China, however, the teaching he valued the most highly, more even that his courses on Shakespeare and on poetry, was his Composition Class, which was compulsory for all fourth-year students (though the numbers in attendance 'went down in the five years from just under thirty to just over ten, and that amount of reduction is perhaps reasonable'). Its purpose was to make the students read a text and argue in English about it, both on paper and in class. No other course afforded him such a legitimate opportunity to challenge the students to express their views: the classroom procedure ruled out their perennially passive habit of closing their minds while copying down the lesson of the day. It was the only class in which his skills as a critic came together with sometimes overtly political material—and naturally the students were quick to balk at what they saw as the controversial character of some of the documents he set before them. But he was prepared to defend its signal importance against all criticism.

He found it irritating when students complained either that they could not understand some of the pieces in the class anthology (let alone write and talk about them) or that certain texts were pretty obviously designed to undermine their faith in the final solution of Communism. He had felt enraged when the rumour reached him sometime in 1949 that the American Embassy was looking into his professional behaviour on the suspicion that he had been disseminating left-wing literature. On that occasion he had posted this combative justification to Martin Buxton at the British Consulate:

> No one could do this work decently without mentioning politics, because [the students] drag politics into every question. The best formula, I find, is to give them sensible but in an incidental way rather 'reactionary' material, which they will attack, and then point out the logical errors (as well as their errors of grammar) and explain that it is harder than they think to convince someone who disagrees with them. The technique has not changed since the siege except that I have introduced some rather more 'reactionary' material, not out of contrairiness but because the situation seemed more clear-cut; the students of course have not altered. In this teaching process, may I point out, I do not require them to express any political views, nor do I expound any views of my own (except what seems self-evident, that is, I don't make a fuss about having no opinions); I merely try to bring out the logical background of the opinions the students choose to express. They, unlike the American collectors of dossiers, consider me a self-confessed reactionary, but not more than they are willing to put up with. One could not do any useful work among present-day Chinese students without being considered a tolerably well-intentioned man, and if one is so considered one can I think make them a good deal more sensible in the course of a year.[43]

The next year, he returned to the offensive, prompt to nail the common complaint that 'the class wants to read and discuss material which bears on their own practice in their own lives, and not to waste their time puzzling over remote or academic problems. In short, they ought to be given essays about modern China of which they can thoroughly approve, and then they ought to write down that they thoroughly approve of them.' He answered:

> My point is that, however the major-English student from Peita may apply his training later on, whether for propaganda or political interpretation or diplomacy or business negotiation or anything else, he will always be wanted as the man who can really say what the English-speaking author of some document meant; how much is he to be suspected? Was he perhaps making a joke? Can it be assumed anyway that the obscure bit of the text doesn't matter? . . . The plan of my fourth-year English Composition Class

is to make them exercise their powers in this direction, and . . . the plan itself is one that a university cannot abandon . . .

The collection of essays which the Peita Press did for me seems to me now very unsatisfactory, and I would be glad to alter it. But I think the best ones are the ones which have raised most complaint from the class, that is, the merely funny ones where the question is 'what does the author really want you to believe?'—a very important problem about foreigners' jokes, and also the downright wicked ones (politically speaking): 'say why it is wrong'.[44]

'This rather coarse way of expressing it,' he later wrote, 'was I thought regarded by my superiors as merely the proper way to offer a defence in case a defence was needed; what they really thought was that they wished to continue giving a liberal education. I did not have any bother about it.'[45]

In 1951–2, when all institutions of higher education were strictly obliged to eliminate 'politically reactionary curricula' in favour of 'the ideal of serving the people', Empson's Composition Class was indeed an astonishing exception to the rule. Again it might be thought that he was allowed to go ahead under sufferance rather than on principle: his western-educated colleagues were in no position to dare to believe they could continue to provide a liberal education. Professor Ai Ssu-ch'i, chief exponent of Communist ideology, made it perfectly clear in his writings that the primary intention of the Thought Reform Programme was to purge from the minds of intellectuals, both professors and students, every kind of deviation, and most especially the 'ideology of the bourgeois class'. Yet the fact remains that Empson's Composition Class—a forum dedicated to discussing often highly unorthodox documentation—went ahead without any official intervention.

For their part, the students were in any case under enormous pressure throughout the months from October 1951 till June 1952. Not only were they required to spend a substantial amount of their time and energy absorbing revolutionary tracts and arguing in political discussion groups, they also had to participate in the enforcement of the current '3-Anti Movement'—a drive against corruption, waste, and bureaucratism in government and party organs and businesses—which soon merged with the '5-Anti Movement', aimed at eradicating bribery, tax evasion, fraud, and the theft of both state property and state economic secrets. Ralph and Nancy Lapwood (who were in general sympathetic to the New China) observed about the workings of the 3-Anti Movement at Yenching University that 'everyone was afraid of being wrongly charged without chance of explanation or rebuttal, and everyone who had held authority went about in a dark cloud of nervous apprehension.'[46] It is small wonder that the students felt unwilling to cope with the demands of the choice texts of Empson's Composition Class, which ranged from Boswell's *Journal of a Tour to the Hebrides with Samuel Johnson* to two essays by J. B. S. Haldane, 'Time Scales and H. G. Wells' and 'The Milky Way' (both taken from the volume *Science in Peace and War*).

Some of the Composition Class documents, as Empson admitted, were politically 'very hot'. They included a 6-page extract from *Road to Survival* (1948), by William A. Vogt, an American soil expert, which revealed the contentious fact that China's excessive exploitation of land—violating 'every canon of sound land use'—fatally compounded the 'demographic dilemma' of the country. Vogt's incisive analysis of the situation ends up with these words:

> Mighty plans have been dreamed to help China. Blueprints for TVAs, roads, railroads, and industrialization lie upon the desks and drawing boards of both Chinese and western engineers and economists. The possibility of such developments seems remote indeed, until China is able to establish internal peace; and this, in all probability, is a grimly satisfactory outlook both for China and for the rest of the world. For with internal peace and such 'improvements' as have been envisioned, China might well suffer such a population explosion as that of India, which increased 15 per cent in one decade. China quite *literally cannot feed more people.* Indeed, with unfavorable climatic conditions, such as a cycle of drought that might occur at any time, she cannot feed the people she has . . . There can be no way out. These men and women, boys and girls, must starve as tragic sacrifices on the twin altars of uncontrolled human reproduction and uncontrolled abuse of the land's resources.[47]

Given such an insult to national pride, 'even the anti-communist characters were regularly thrown into indignation by it,' said Empson. 'Before long this book was denounced by name by Mao Tse-tung in person,' he would recall,

> and this only made the discussion more vigorous, and the students more willing to borrow the full text. This is not in a way an interesting case, because they knew they had to denounce it and they had been getting a good deal of information which they felt was quite sufficient for the purpose; and of course I was always scrupulous about writing on the blackboard beforehand that it had been denounced. Here as elsewhere it is not the business of a teacher to try to get some of his students into trouble, but to make the ordinary loyal majority rather more intelligent about the subject in hand . . . We had much more puzzling cases to discuss, where the opinions of the class were various and divided; and I found it became a

reassuring point of technique to end the hour going over the discussion by saying 'This as far as I know is the official Communist point of view'; which made them feel they weren't being messed about, and I didn't have to say I agreed with it.[48]

(While the authorities would not countenance the idea of birth control—the official line being that there was no problem of overpopulation, only of underproduction—Empson's personal opinion was 'that China has a generation in hand after her prolonged disasters before population pressure will again be felt, and that if they can succeed meanwhile in raising the standard of living fast enough they will find that they have got over the hump and the problem has solved itself, as in Western Europe. This was always enough as a solution to make the lecture tolerable, though the IF is big and they would prefer not to have the subject raised—there is no accepted Soviet formula.' In June 1953 he would write further: 'The refusal even to recognize this subject in public has long seemed to me an obvious weakness in the Communist position.')[49]

What is most remarkable, however, at a time when Chinese professors were subjected to sometimes fierce harassment, is that for the most part the students went on showing a fair amount of decency and restraint when negotiating curriculum changes with Empson. Despite the fact that their position in the university had become 'remarkably strong' (as Empson knew), they conducted themselves as if they were still fundamentally concerned to answer to their professor as much as to call him officiously to order: 'only in the last year did the class make a positive refusal, in graceful letters expressed with much pleading, to read such documents as A. C. Bradley's opinion of Hegel's *Theory of Tragedy* in its full twenty pages or so,' Empson would recall. 'I considered this a step down in knowledge of English, because if a communist student can take the mere reading in his stride, as students in previous years had done, he has any amount to say about whether Marx did or did not agree with Hegel, a point I never became clear about.'

Though officially charged to discard 'the hypocritical politeness which tries to offend nobody', the students' continuing respect for Empson, and his steadfast determination to earn it, are fully evident from letters that were exchanged between them. But although they would make their requests for change deferentially, and indeed went to considerable lengths to explain their point of view, Empson would have none of it.

You must know your enemy, Empson admonished the students; or, as he would later—and most invigoratingly—phrase the same sentiment as a literary proposition in *Milton's God*: please understand that 'the central function of imaginative literature is to make you realize that other people act on moral convictions different from your own.'[50] We would prefer to toe the party line, the students replied with their winsomely insidious charm. No other teacher could have been so well qualified to supply them with just what they really needed, if China was ever to establish lines of communication with the world beyond the communist bloc: the benefit of his experience as both literary critic and wartime propagandist. Ironically, by assisting the Chinese in such a fashion, he would also be giving the best possible service that anyone in his position could offer to his own country. 'What you really want is the work of intelligence to go on,' he maintained, meaning that individuals must be free to express their opinions (as he believed that his Chinese colleagues at least would continue to do); even while admitting: 'It is true that the modern Chinese don't like to hear a foreigner disagree with their more especially fervent beliefs . . . but many other people feel like that.'

There are many examples in the correspondence of the pressure the students mounted to make Empson bend his teaching towards political relevance. His later remarks make it clear that the leverage had been kept up since September 1951. 'I did come to feel, I confess, during the last year, when things were getting rather warm, that I was undertaking to do a kind of lion-taming act every week, but that was a matter of keeping the good will of the students, or rather of getting them to hold their tempers, and not of the university authorities.'[51] But he would not be intimidated. On the contrary, he thought, the new habit of nagging did them much credit. In his opinion, it was the touchstone of civility that a country should renounce physical force for rational persuasion—and he somehow persuaded himself that the new China had done just that. 'The idea that good bargaining is partly a test of keeping your temper is of course rather deeply fixed in their minds. The attitude is not a brutal one; I found it very fixed in the minds of my students . . . that any form of cruelty was completely out of date, no longer worth discussing. The new world had no such problems, they felt.'

By remarkable coincidence, on 2 February 1952, the day after receiving a second letter from the students about his classes, Empson very reluctantly gave notice of his resignation to the National Peking University. As far as the British Council was concerned, it was not before time. William M. Emslie, who took up the post of Regional Director of the British Council, had written to the Foreign Office on 31 May 1951:

> There is now only Professor Empson at Peita working as a subsidized post. Holding such a post is not easy at the present time, and it is remarkable that

Mr. & Mrs. Empson have been able to continue without incident. I feel that after the withdrawal of Empson it will not be possible for a long time to gain a foothold inside any of the Universities even after the establishment of Diplomatic relations. The amount of work done in the University by Empson is not large (six hours of teaching a week) and I personally think that unless there is a major change in the University one more academic year is the most that can be hoped for. (Empson does not share this view but feels he is a fixture for as long as he wants to stay.) In the meantime the presence of an English family living on the University campus is probably the major contribution.[52]

Certainly the number of foreigners in Peking had declined very steeply: the British Embassy invited the entire British community to dinner on Christmas Day 1951, and just thirty-six people sat down to table (a year earlier, the Embassy staff alone added up to more than fifty).

Nonetheless, it was to the credit of the Foreign Office that it insisted to the British Council on 13 July: 'We do not think that Emslie should be withdrawn yet, nor that we have yet reached the stage where a cultural foothold in China is a liability rather than an asset. It is moreover just possible that there may be a Korean settlement and a consequent improvement of our relations with China. We therefore feel that Emslie and [Geoffrey] Hedley [Officiating Representative of the British Council in Shanghai] should hang on as long as possible unless conditions become quite intolerable, when we would of course consider their withdrawal.'[53] After conferring with the diplomatic corps in Peking, Emslie continued to press for the closure of British Council operations there. Lionel Lamb, for the British Negotiating Mission, addressed the Foreign Office on 8 October 1951: 'Both Emslie & I consider that in the circumstances Peking is not worth the money, which could be better spent elsewhere. Moreover, Emslie does not wish to renew contract, and there is no suitable successor available locally.'[54] Three months later, on 10 December, he repeated his defeatist plea: 'I do not (repeat not) believe that [the British Council-subsidised posts in Peking and Tientsin] any longer serve a useful purpose at either University and I therefore consider that they could be reasonably discontinued at the conclusion of the present academic year in June 1952 ... I have sounded Empson here. He gladly consents to leave China if he could find a suitable job in the United Kingdom, about which he has been making enquiries including Manchester University. Anyhow he is reconciled to the possibility of subsidies being withdrawn.'[55]

As a direct consequence, Empson wrote honourably and considerately to Professor Pien Chi-lin at Peita:

I pass on to you a letter in which the British Council says that they would agree if I and my family chose to leave now, before the end of the academic year (their 'agreeing', you understand, means simply that they would pay the passage money, which they would not do if they did not 'agree', and with luggage it is a considerable sum). It seems clear that I ought to show you the letter.

I do not know what problems you have to consider, and on my side I simply intend to carry out obligations unless released from them; doing my work to the end of the academic year is clearly an obligation. But I do not know what the feeling of the students will be when we reassemble for lectures, nor whether you are yourself doubtful whether to cut out the lectures I am giving. I have no reason to think I am unwelcome to individuals, but I realise that my whole plan of lecturing is not on the agreed line. I consider that my lectures obviously remained unaltered after liberation, because they were never reactionary, but still I am very willing to believe that different plans are now being made. In short I do not stand in your way; if you wish to abolish my lectures before term opens it would be a slight convenience to me, so far from annoying me; but if you prefer to keep them open, or some of them, I will continue to talk as seriously as I can.

May I say again that I am not asking you to release me, only showing to you that there would be no difficulty on my side if it seemed to you preferable.[56]

The fact that Peita did not immediately jump at the offer and release him from his contract gives a certain indication that they still valued his work, and that maybe, as Empson always believed, his colleagues hoped in some sort, however tenuously, to retain a liberal education at the university.

But the good fight was lost when the British Council wrote to Empson from London on 9 January 1952 that they would be unable to offer him any further renewal of contract after 31 August. 'As you know, the Council has suffered a progressive reduction in its grant-in-aid during the past two or three years which has meant a considerable decrease in the total number of posts, both at home and overseas, and I am sorry to say that the post you now occupy is amongst the number of those which will have to be cut next year.'[57] They would bear the cost of repatriating his family; and moreover he had accumulated an entitlement while in China to the maximum of five months' paid leave (one month for each year of his service). In the event, therefore, his appointment with the British Council was formally closed on 28 February 1953; he had been in service for just over five years, since 16 December 1946.[58]

Having made no move of his own to end his career in China, Empson wrote with sincere regret to Peita:

> the Council's letter forces us to decide one way or the other, and I had already been feeling that it was nearly time to go home; there was no room for hesitation about the answer.
>
> This is not at all because we dislike being here; indeed, so far as what we say has any importance, we are more use to China outside it than inside it. But I have been coming to feel less useful in general here. I am a specialist type of man, who needs to keep abreast of what is being done in his own field and so forth; this is rather hard to do in Peking, and the field is not one that is much use here. Then again, the children impose an early decision; this is about the last year in which the elder one could be moved over to the English system of education without too much strain. Our plan in coming here was to educate the children in China, but though we foresaw the Pa-Lu [Communist] victory we did not foresee the Korean war and its international effects.[59]

While hoping that his type of specialized course for small classes might be allowed to continue in the 'new Democracy', he had to admit all the same: 'it would be absurd of me to think that in the present case...What we would both like to feel, however, is that we may hope to be invited back to Peita eventually, when world conditions are more settled and fortunate.'[60]

The family 'advertised'—that is, took steps to obtain an exit permit by advertising in a newspaper, for three days in succession, their intention to emigrate (which served to notify any aggrieved Chinese that they should bring forward their objections)—in the first week of July.[61] Leavetakers had also to complete an inventory (twelve copies) of their personal possessions. All went smoothly until the family reached Tientsin, when Empson was at last touched by the darker workings of the Communist state: for unknown reasons, he was not immediately allowed to depart the country. Years later, in *Milton's God*, he would incidentally remark (without further explanation), 'When I was emerging from Communist China in 1952 there was a midnight eve-of-sailing removal of my passport, never explained, which gave me an interesting peep for two weeks at the nerve-racked foreign business community of Tientsin and its weeping but heroic bank managers.'[62] Naturally he repaired to the Tientsin Club, where foreign businessmen went to bemoan their lot. 'Many a European,' Svetlana Rimsky-Korsakoff would later recall, 'was denounced by neighbours, servants, or friends and instead of being on an ocean liner to Hong Kong, was put into prison for a year or two'; and, according to Hetta Empson, her husband was indeed 'roughed up' (her phrase) in some fashion during his unaccountable temporary detention in Tientsin—though the details were apparently never disclosed.[63] There is a further riddle here, however: ten years later, Empson would write to Martin Buxton to ask very warmly after the well-being of a Burmese diplomat who, he said, had 'smuggled out for me a small suitcase containing unfinished plays, an unfinished novel about Africa ['The Royal Beasts'], none of it to do with China; I have never looked at them since but revere Myat Tun [*sic*] for saving them with such firm instructions and energetic adroitness.'[64] Just why he should have needed to 'smuggle' out of China such innocuous papers must remain a mystery; all we can know is that it was a matter of importance and urgency for Empson—else why would he speak in terms of 'revering' Myint Thein for 'saving' his 'plays' (presumably a slip for 'poems') and his draft novel?

Hetta and the boys took ship to Hong Kong, and Empson turned up two weeks later, on 14 August—still none the wiser. (His arrival in Hong Kong was even reported in the *Times* of London on the following day. During the blissful respite in Hong Kong he was looked after by A. C. Scott, a cultural relations officer with the British Council who had come to know him during many months of service with the British Council on the mainland. One night, Scott and his wife Dorothea took Empson out to dinner at the Peninsula Hotel, where Empson absentmindedly set fire to his beard while smoking—it was something he often did, he remarked.[65]) According to Empson's report of the terribly harassing incident at Tientsin, however, he claimed to be disturbed much less by his temporary detention in China than by the prospect of life in the misguided West, which he illustrated with this contentious parable: 'The first newspaper I saw in Hongkong described the latest sex case in the homeland. A man had met a girl in Epping Forest and, after talking to her for half an hour, had offered to kiss her; four sweating policemen had bounded out of the bushes and arrested him, because she was a policewoman dressed up to seduce him. The magistrate dismissed the case, but as the culprit was a teacher like myself he would probably lose his job all the same. "Good God," I said, with an involuntary cry, "it takes a bit of nerve to go and live in that country." I was coming back under the power of Christianity, and the smell already hit me at the end of the world.'[66]

Nonetheless, he granted, the easing experience of finally sailing home from Hong Kong felt 'like diving out of intense heat into a deep cool pool'.

9

Final Reckoning: The Affair of Fei Hsiao-t'ung

E MPSON wrote in 1953, just a few months after returning to England: 'If you moved about in Peking you could not get an impression of widespread suspicion and anxiety... And the new China has something positive to offer; the idea that it must be dismal to return to England does seem to me at least intelligible.' Thus the outstanding question about his postwar career in China is: why did he choose, from 1952 until 1957, to become to a certain degree an apologist for the People's Republic of China, a Communist state that was indicted by much of the western world both for acts of naked international aggression and for the scale on which it abused human rights at home? Was he blind or misguided, or simply—even stupidly—economical with the truth?

His erstwhile colleague, George Yeh, who in 1949 became Foreign Minister of the Nationalist Government in Taiwan, declared at the UN General Assembly in November 1952 not only that the Chinese Communists acted as Stalin's stooges when they launched their 'massive manpower' upon Korea 'in an attempt to drive the United Nations into the sea' but also that the 'reign of terror on the mainland of China spares nothing... no less than 14,000,000 persons have been executed or otherwise put to death during the past five years'.

If it might otherwise be argued that the Foreign Minister of Taiwan—the enemy of the mainland People's Republic of China—would of course purvey a parcel of prejudice, the overwhelming majority of the evidence available to the West certainly supported his pronouncement. Although the exact number of executions will probably never be known, to this day historians have no doubt that the actual figure was still immense. In the absence of precise official statistics, says the *Cambridge History of China*, 'the primarily urban campaign against counter-revolutionaries may have resulted in as many as 500,000 to 800,000 deaths'. It was a 'righteous' duty to suppress counter-revolutionaries, said the party; and Mao Tse-tung: 'Our benevolence applies only to the people, and not to the reactionary acts of the reactionaries and reactionary classes outside the people.'[1] With regard to the 'official violence' of the Land Reform movement, John Gittings estimates the number of executions as 'several hundred thousand'.[2] If Empson knew of such purges, why did he not lend his voice to the outcry?

The answer is that he quite evidently knew very little of the sometimes appalling acts—the torture and the slaughter—carried out during those two campaigns. Since he was unable to understand the Chinese language, he had no direct access to media reports; and he had no reason to doubt the truth of what his enthusiastic students told him. More crucially, he never pretended to know the facts of what happened beyond his immediate ken in Peking. Indeed, as he said in this passage of his inaugural lecture at Sheffield: 'What was going on in the villages I naturally wouldn't know about, except that my students would often do what is called "being sent on Land Reform", that is, they would be sent by the Government to stay for five months or so in a village where land was being re-allocated, as part of their education. They would come back much in favour of it, even the ones who had been doubtful . . . '

Only after returning to England did he learn more about the excesses of the campaign against counter-revolutionaries; and then he made no attempt to dispute the fact that 'cruelty probably did beget cruelty during the military struggle, in various parts of the country'. If he knew about some of the executions while still in Peking, he had no way of ascertaining if they violated any civilized code of justice. Likewise, if he had known that any of the criminal proceedings involved torture, we may be sure (given his life-long horror of cruelty) that he would have been the first to voice his disgust at their obscenity. Nor was he anyway in favour of the programme of mandatory rural collectivization: 'Of course, a great deal of co-operative arrangement, small machine industry, and help from industrial chemists will be needed, but I suspect that they will have to stick to intensive land cultivation in the main areas, just to get the most off the land.'

However, the subject upon which Empson felt more qualified to press an opinion was what he correctly called 'one of the darker aspects of

Communism'—the campaign of *szu-hsiang kai-tso* or ideological remould-ing, also known as Thought Reform or 'Brainwashing':

> the dragooning of independent thought and the hysteria of the confession meetings...Naturally we heard a good deal of gossip about how it was going. It was not a Terror; that seems the first thing to say. I don't know of any of our Chinese colleagues who got sacked, let alone arrested, and some had been well-known political opponents of the regime; the test didn't come till two and a half years after the regime had taken over, and a man whose confession was refused, so that he was sent back to prepare another one, would go on teaching and being respected by the students who had heard his first confession. The attendance at meetings with your colleagues, where they each in turn discussed their past and their state of mind, had to be enormously long, and you might call it a deliberately calculated nagging process; but even so that is really different from a police terror.[3]

Yet the majority of foreign reports maintain that the experience was devastating for the university professors, leaving them abject and compli-ant. Even an impartial source, Merle Goldman ('The Party and the Intellectuals', *The Cambridge History of China*, vol. 14), records this observa-tion: 'Repeating Communist doctrine or the official line was insufficient; the individual had to give convincing evidence that his past ideas and behavior were totally wrong and his surrender to the Party's will totally complete.' If the Ideological Reform campaign was so designed to achieve the utter abasement of the intellectuals, the strict regimentation of their minds, how was it that Empson—who never saw the process in action but who assuredly knew many of the liberal scholars who had to participate in it—could still remain sanguine enough to describe it as something far short of a Terror?

Although the term 'brainwashing' can perhaps convey a less pernicious connotation when rendered as 'cleansing the mind',[4] few western com-mentators could ever allow that the object of the exercise was anything other than grotesque: the denunciation of the individual's past—including family and class background, education and ideas, the values of the 'old society', and the scholarly writings of a lifetime— coupled with a vow to be refashioned in the Communist image. To that end, Empson's colleagues were commanded to undergo a course of total ideological immersion and fervent self-reconstruction. The unremitting study of Marxist-Leninist doctrine and Mao Tse-tung's theory of the Chinese Revolution was ac-companied by a series of meetings for 'criticism and self-criticism' (*p'i p'ing tzu wo p'i p'ing*), which forbade them the freedom of silence; and the whole process might culminate in the *Tou-cheng Ta Hui*, a Mass Meeting for

Struggle, at which the apostate would recite his confession: a recantation and a firm purpose of amendment. Party cadres and students acted as tribunes of the people.

According to Robert Jay Lifton, such imposed experiences can give rise to 'the dangerous group excesses so characteristic of ideological totalism in any form'.[5] Certainly there are many well-documented accounts, by survivors and witnesses, of the cruelties sometimes perpetrated in the name of ideological remoulding, which fully deserve the obloquy of Empson's word 'hysteria'. There is no doubt that the 'criticism and self-criticism' meetings could be sometimes horrific, as attested by Ralph and Nancy Lapwood and Svetlana Rimsky-Korsakov,[6] but brutal excesses were the exception rather than the rule. The usual pattern of meetings for criticism and self-criticism, it seems clear, aimed to give issue not to a riot of denunciation but to a confession that was refulgent with convincing evidence of a happily earnest reformation. As Merle Goldman stresses, 'The Party did not want merely passive acquiescence, but positive conversion to its beliefs';[7] and Ralph and Nancy Lapwood observed at the time: 'People were taught not to be afraid of conflict and struggle, but to welcome it as the inevitable requisite of progress.'[8] Mutual criticism is equivalent to mutual help, said the Party. The procedure of thought reform, as Robert Jay Lifton pointed out, 'thus follows the classic Marxist sequence of harmony, struggle, harmony; in psychological terms—group identification, isolation and conflict, and reintegration.'[9]

Ironically, one of the first confessions to be published in Peking, in May 1949, stemmed from the pen of a distinguished historian, Ch'en Yüan, the elderly president of Fujen University: 'I realise for the first time that our whole study of history has been subjective, unscientific. Man's mind is determined by his society. We must study that society in order to understand the individual, and can reform the individual only through reforming the society. All culture follows politics and at the same time leads politics. The realization of this fact is the freedom that the government has brought to me.' 'Subjectivism' (*chu kuan chu i*), the Party ruled, set false store by a personal rather than a Marxist viewpoint.[10]

Since the Communists in a real sense deified Marxism-Leninism as 'the most correct, scientific, and revolutionary truth', they vilified other models of ultimate value such as that afforded by the Christian mission to China, which they regarded as an instrument of ideological colonialism. The Party also slated the 'subjective idealism and mysticism' of liberal thinkers such as John Dewey and his sometime student Hu Shih, who had propounded his mentor's philosophy in his role as leader of

China's 'New Thought Movement' and 'Literary Revolution' earlier in the century.

As the self-validating system of Marxist materialism not only opposed but disqualified philosophical idealism, Chinese philosophers of the old school had to revoke every article of their former theories. Their teaching had isolated theory from practice, more so than perhaps any other discipline, and they had no choice but to turn themselves inside out. As Professor Feng Yu-lan discovered, apparently to his satisfaction, 'A revolutionary philosophy for reforming the world is entirely different from the philosophy which maintains that it "interprets the world." It is precisely because of its inability to reform the world that it is also unable to interpret the world.'[11] Feng therefore denounced his numerous early writings, including his definitive work *History of Chinese Philosophy*, as erroneous. The premise of both *A New Treatise on Human Nature* and *A New Treatise on Moral Principles* had been individualistic, he acknowledged; henceforth he would devote his energies to dialectical materialism and the thought of Mao Tse-tung.

Another distinguished scholar who came to realize that intellect should be placed at the feet of activism was Professor Chin Yueh-lin, Empson's dear old comrade-in-exile: once upon a time, in the summer of 1938, they had traded Cambridge stories on an idyllic mountain in Hunan province. Regarded as China's authority on formal logic, Chin was at that time Chairman of the Department of Philosophy at Tsinghua University. The road to reformation was rocky, he found; and he was obliged to essay several confessions before coming up with a self-indictment that passed the test of popular approval. Born of a bureaucratic landlord family, he had spent his life in a condition of ideological depravity and professional dereliction, he began his public *mea culpa* in April 1952. He had lived abroad for eleven years, absorbing 'the way of life and the predilection for pleasure of the European and American bourgeoisie'; and for a full thirty years he had turned his back on 'realities' in order to play 'a game of concepts'. Always disseminating 'the trivialities of metaphysical idealism', he never cared to shoulder the responsibilities of privilege. Furthermore, he admitted, though he had always honestly loathed the Kuomintang, he had also opposed the Chinese Communists. Though now classifying himself as 'a criminal for having sinned against the people', he fully believed that Marxism-Leninism was 'concrete, militant, and should serve as the guide for our action.' From now on, therefore, he would dedicate himself to the forward march of reality: 'The old philosophy, being metaphysical, is fundamentally unscientific, while the new philosophy, being scientific, is the supreme truth. It was during the

curriculum-reform campaign of 1951 that I succeeded in realizing that the
mission of the Philosophy Department lies in the training of propaganda
personnel for the dissemination of Marxism-Leninism.'[12]

By almost any reckoning, Chin's ritualistic, reiterative and arguably
pitiful confession seems to have been a breathtaking somersault. In the
eyes of some few conservative students, such a bouleversement represented
not a genuine admission of decadence but a betrayal of principle and
integrity. Maria Yen repined: 'Our teachers, who in this manner "bowed
in front of the people," as the Communists call it, were the men who failed
to give us the leadership which might have helped save our generation
from capture by the Communist revolution.'[13] Yet Lionel Lamb, in a
commentary (written from the British Embassy in Peking in January
1952) on Professor Ch'ien Tuan-sheng's confession, discriminated the
fundamentally positive feature of thought reform: 'This new ideology is
the more plausible because it is identified with "service of the people" as
opposed to "personal inclination".'[14]

Empson reported early in 1953:

> The attendance at meetings with your colleagues, where they each in turn
> discussed their past and their state of mind, had to be enormously long, and
> you might call it a deliberately calculated nagging process; but even so that is
> really different from a police terror. What we would often ask, when we
> heard gossip from these meetings, was how far the confessions were sincere;
> but our Chinese friends would always feel quite sure they were
> sincere; nobody could go through all that and not be sincere at the end,
> because the audience could judge their sincerity... But some of these con-
> fessions by the internationally-minded Chinese seem very hard to estimate.

The methods of ideological remoulding 'though intense are extremely
non-violent,' he was given to understand; but he readily acknowledged:
'The technique of enforced discussion in small groups is a fearfully powerful one.' Yet, 'In all of this', wrote Robert Jay Lifton, 'it is most important
to realize that what we see as a set of coercive maneuvers, the Chinese
Communists view as a morally uplifting, harmonizing, and scientifically
therapeutic experience.'[15]

There were in fact many strong and honourable reasons why the
Chinese intellectual should be peculiarly susceptible to an offer to change
his ways: not least, the subliminal desire to reintegrate himself with his own
country and culture. Traditionally called a *Chün Tzu*, a scholar-gentleman,
he was (as Robert Jay Lifton properly recognized) the spiritual if not the
lineal descendant of the Confucian literati. Chinese intellectuals had

'always retained their aura of a learned élite and a sharp sense of separation from the rest of the mostly illiterate population'; as often as not, they had enjoyed the privilege of a foreign education, in England or the USA (if not both); and they knew in their hearts 'that sentimentalism and nepotism had long been barriers to Chinese progress.'[16] Their intellectual liberalism created too a problem of self-identity, 'since the individual Westernization which was likely to accompany any profound acceptance of liberal democratic ideas often led to a sense of being severed from Chinese roots.'[17] This 'undigested combination of filialism, Nationalism, and Western liberalism' engendered a state of 'emotional chaos'.[18] Consequently, Communism afforded the literati the means both to 'outgrow' the class characteristics of their bourgeois and petty bourgeois backgrounds (indeed, to emulate the example of Mao Tse-tung himself) and to overcome the personal and national traumas of modern history, their sense of self-estrangement and their country's long ignominy.[19]

Other well-informed commentators, including C. P. Fitzgerald, agreed that the intelligentsia were profoundly moved by a sense of shame.[20] Peter Townsend observed that self-criticism transcended the trick of formulism for one crucial reason: 'The conscious revolutionary desire to identify oneself with the working class and assume its qualities was supplemented by a less conscious social desire for affiliation.'[21] He added: 'It was not an emotional purgative, though it could act as such, but a preparation for better work.'[22]

According to Robert Jay Lifton, however, there was another aspect of Thought Reform which might give rise to doubts about some confessions: 'as totalist pressures turn confession into recurrent command performances, the element of histrionic public display takes precedence over genuine inner experience . . . The difficulty, of course, lies in the inevitable confusion between the actor's method and his separate personal reality, between the performer and the "real me".'[23]

In Empson's seemingly paradoxical opinion, his colleagues could in all honesty make a show of solidarity and retain their independence of mind. Though dunned by the process of criticism and self-criticism, they would not (clearly did not) emerge as dunderheads. While Party functionaries might denounce such a recourse as a cynical evasion, a betrayal of the wholesale commitment they called for, he thought it no slur on the sincerity of an individual's patriotism: 'I think the Chinese are natural actors anyway, very sensitive to social requirements, and in this case, of Chinese who have studied long overseas, there is often a deep feeling that they have neglected their own people and take a delight in returning to them if pressed in the right way.' From the point of view of some enemies of the regime, who believed that ideological remoulding created nothing less than Communist clones, Empson's statement would be a self-contradiction: no one could so pillage both their past and their principles and still pretend to keep a free head on their shoulders. Yet other antagonists, like Tsui Shu-chin, argued that the professors on the mainland were 'still spiritually alive': they would soon rise up and overthrow the 'autocratic rule' which had afflicted them with 'mental torture'.[24] Empson could credit neither of those equally contradictory eventualities, the mindless or the mutinous. His interpretation of the issue of thought reform coincided with C. P. Fitzgerald's: 'Men must not merely obey, they must obey intelligently, of their own free will, understanding the reasons for their actions, working towards an end which is comprehensible and desirable.'[25]

However horribly they were browbeaten into overstating their sins, Empson observed, his colleagues evidently believed that the new China continued to deserve their constructive support. In his Inaugural lecture at Sheffield, he ventured:

> The main fact, I think, is that the Communists when they conquered left the intellectuals alone for about three years, so that everyone was astonished at their not killing people, and then said 'It is time to go into the subject in group discussions'... The less ambitious life of the great universities has been badgered rather than terrorized, but I do not mean to deny that badgering is a large real thing. The danger of it is the danger of destroying the intellectual life of the country, especially the astonishing world-embracing hungry cleverness of the old Peita. But I do not think from what I have seen, and remember that we were there till the end of the big drive on cleaning up thoughts, always with the suggestion 'You mustn't sit quiet and think you've won the Korean War already, as you thought you had', that the Chinese universities are at all broken from independent thought by it, or are even intended to be.[26]

Empson's brand of fellow-travelling was in part the fruit of emotional and moral idealism. If his fault was to idealize or sentimentalize the mettle of his colleagues, he had seen for himself enough of the genuine terror of life under the Kuomintang to feel sure that the Communists were less brutal than the government they had ousted. The other source of his support for Communist China was his opposition to US foreign policy, which he was convinced had driven China out of the orbit of the free world. Ever since the Treaty of Nanking in 1842, when Hong Kong was ceded to the British, few observers could deny that China had been what the journalist Frank Moraes (editor of *The Times of India*) called 'the joint colony of international imperialism'.[27] Though a severe critic of Chinese Communism, the Oxford-educated Moraes had to admit that 'China, prey to conflicting imperialisms, was drained even while she was devoured.' It is little wonder that Empson reacted in favour of China when she suffered the canard of being identified as the aggressor in Korea, followed by a trade embargo enforced by military blockade. Moraes judged well when he wrote: 'Had America's policy of building a cordon sanitaire around Red China dislocated that country's internal economy and made closer approximation with Russia difficult, it would have served a purpose. But its only effect has been to heighten the tempo of China's internal efforts to achieve full socialism while strengthening Peking's communion with Moscow on the international plane.' Empson therefore made a perfectly tenable deduction: 'I thought that China might again become too rigid in mind, but was only likely to do so if squeezed too hard from outside.' (In a review of *Mandarin Red*, by the journalist James Cameron, who made an independent visit to China in the autumn of 1954, he declared: 'I am glad he happened to turn on The Voice of America in a hotel in Changsha, and realised that any Chinese who listens to it feels quite sure the Americans are aggressors, because of its tone.'[28])

Frank Moraes visited China as a member of an Indian Cultural Delegation from April to June of 1952, when Empson was still in residence in Peking. His trenchant account of the Communist regime, *Report on Mao's China*, was published in 1953; so was *Window on China*, by Raja Hutheesing, who had travelled with the same delegation. Empson, who reviewed both volumes for the *Listener* (8 October), observed: 'Mr. Moraes is much the more balanced and good-tempered, and ends with a reasoned defence of India's policy of neutrality... but both give a strong impression of dislike for the China they saw, and express some anxiety about its possible influence in Asia. On the other hand, if you pick out the admissions, they both say a great deal in favour of the Peking Government's reforms.'[29] It is in fact extremely difficult to pick out any such favourable admissions, apart from Moraes's criticisms of the drastically counter-productive effects of American foreign policy. One can only assume that Empson was being wilfully biased in his reading. Moraes's observations included this absolute statement: 'Of the many things that impressed and repelled me during our stay in China nothing burned itself so strongly in my mind as the mental furtiveness of her intellectuals... In China I discovered that a man's mind can be chained, tethered, and imprisoned.'[30] Since nothing in Empson's experience lent credence to such a remark, he drew the partisan conclusion that Moraes was in effect producing anti-Communist propaganda.

'Of course,' he admitted, 'both these authors travelled widely in China and saw a great deal more than I did; and much of what they say is of great interest; but it does seem reasonable to feel a certain suspicion about their ability to interpret what they saw.'[31] As he revealed by way of a personal anecdote in his review, he felt he had been given good grounds for suspecting Moraes of paranoia when the Indian visitor called at the Empsons' house in the university and asked among other matters 'if it was safe for my wife to go out alone; we gazed at him in astonishment'.[32] (Moraes made no mention in his book of having met the Empsons.) The question does indeed betray a certain prejudice and paranoia: Moraes must have assumed, or believed he had discovered, that China was a police state. Given that fact, Empson thought he could discountenance the burden of the book as a whole.

If Empson fleered at Moraes's objections to Communist China, he might be deemed by at least one critic to have damned himself when he put on record his endorsement of the views of another foreign tripper— who favoured the state of affairs he saw in 1952 and climaxed an account of his visit with the claim that he found in China 'a mood of triumph and achievement: a mood of angry indignation that the Chinese People's Government is still excluded from its rightful place in the United Nations'. David Caute has written in *The Fellow-Travellers: Intellectual Friends of Communism*:

> Basil Davidson, a socialist writer known for his championship of independent black Africa—and other notably 'progressive' one-party states— travelled to China during the last phase of the Korean War under the auspices of the Britain-China Friendship Association. Insistent that he had been invited 'unconditionally', and that he had seen a great deal of the country, Davidson readily digested the vocabulary offered by his hosts. The 'People's Democratic Dictatorship' was not (he granted) a parliamentary democracy, but this new Chinese dictatorship had 'nothing in common with Hitler's or Mussolini's'. (All dictatorships have certain qualities in common.) Davidson quoted Mao Tse-tung on the need to deprive reactionaries of political rights; quoted Mao on the sacred duty to give freedom of speech and association to the people; accepted the incorruptibility of the communist leadership; and embraced the 'intellectual remoulding' of the middle classes through self-criticism. . . .
>
> The right to strike? There was no need of that, Davidson thought, in a society possessed by a spirit of unity and harmony. Communism was about unselfishness . . . And what of intellectual freedom? Davidson was impressed: 'most of the intellectuals you meet . . . are manifestly at their ease,

full of projects for the future, and unobsessed by fear of sudden sanctions or some shadow-like terror in the background' [p. 136].

But who are the intellectuals 'you meet'? Davidson seemed oblivious to the operation known as the 'conducted tour' . . .

Empson reviewed Davidson's *Daybreak in China* in the *New Statesman and Nation* on 20 June 1953. Except for disagreeing with Davidson's acceptance of the need for collectivized farming in China, and with its failure to discuss the population problem, he readily backed his joyful tidings: 'It does seem rather a duty, though a placid one, to speak up and say that my experience agrees with Mr. Davidson's.'[33] In his Inaugural Lecture at Sheffield he had already said, with particular reference to Thought Reform, 'it wasn't a Terror, not like Hitler was doing for instance; nobody felt it as that, even when they were teased by it very hard.' His inveterate habit of employing unserious schoolroom cant such as 'teased' to describe such a grave subject is infelicitous. But David Caute would have taken far graver exception to the 'ideological duality characteristic of the fellow-traveller'—the 'outlook which dismisses much of what is admired in China as being irrelevant to the West, and vice versa'—that Empson evinced in his review.

According to a Marxist critic like David Caute, Empson would have been as guilty as Davidson: for reasons either of liberal naivety or equivocation, he was surely seeking to explain away the grotesqueries of the situation in China. Yet Nancy Lapwood, a Christian missionary who did not flinch from being critical when necessary, told a story that matched Empson's. When she left China for Australia in 1952 she related her news and observations to C. P. Fitzgerald, who passed them on to I. A. Richards: 'She takes the view that the regime is still supported by the overwhelming majority; that the Korean War is also now felt to be a national struggle, even if many people do not really believe the story about its origin, they feel that it is now a war in defence of the New China. Singularly inept of the West to have made this view so plausible. Her own evidence on the purges was that she knew of no family among the staff of any university, nor indeed among her other acquaintance who had any member accused, tried, or executed.'[34]

Subsequently, Fitzgerald—who considered himself 'by no means a socialist, rather a crusted Tory really'[35]—returned for a visit to China; and in *Flood Tide in China* (1958) he reported what he called 'the attitude of mind which he perceived to prevail among old friends, known for many years, who belong to the group who are suspected of having been subjected to this form of terrorization'—that is, brainwashing or even the threat of death: 'On the basis of this evidence it must be said that tokens of broken spirit, abject submission, fear and anxiety were not encountered.'[36]

Just like Empson again, Fitzgerald insisted: 'the Chinese people ... have no consciousness of having lived through a terror'; and also: 'China cannot afford a vast purge of the educated and the skilled; the explanation of the changed character of the scholar class, as of its present relatively favourable situation, is the fruit of the lesson learned from the Bolsheviks. There are better ways of transforming a society than by wholesale liquidation and massacre ... '[37] David Caute might well snap back that Fitzgerald, like Davidson, showed himself to be oblivious of the trick of the 'conducted tour' when he went on to claim that 'the Chinese are very willing to show the traveller anything he wishes to see', and that the visitor 'will be, no matter what reservations he feels on other questions, inevitably a witness speaking favourable things'.[38] But it would require an act of blindly prejudicial will to dismiss the entirety of Fitzgerald's testimony.

To anyone who believed that the Chinese People's Republic was the Death begotten by Stalin's Sin, or that all Communist states were equally evil because they subserved the Moscow monolith, Empson would realize, there was nothing to be said. Still he continued to defend the particular corner of Communism that was China, no matter that he was obliged to indulge in a touch of 'ideological duality'. But the case of the distinguished social anthropologist Fei Hsiao-t'ung (Fei Xiaotong) became a much-publicized test of Empson's contention that China's intelligentsia had not been clubbed into conformity by the Ideological Remoulding campaign of 1951–2.

Empson had known Fei Hsiao-t'ung (1910–2005) since before the Liberation, and believed him to be a conscientious individual as well as an outspoken critic of the political and social policies of the Nationalist Government (in 1946, after the assassination of Wen I-to, he had taken refuge in the American consulate in Kunming). Educated at Yenching (Yanjing) and Tsinghua (Qinghua) Universities, Fei had also studied under Bronislaw Malinowski at the London School of Economics, where he gained his Ph.D. His landmark study in anthropological field-work and theory, *Peasant Life in China* (1939), appeared with an enthusiastic preface by Malinowski. In 1943 he lectured and pursued research at Harvard and Chicago, and at the Institute of Pacific Relations in New York; and in 1946 he again visited England under the auspices of the British Council to work at the London School of Economics. After the Communist victory, his many posts included membership of the culture and education committee of the Government Administration Council. In June 1951 he was appointed vice-president of the Central Institute for National Minorities in Peking. Though a non-Communist who made known his misgivings about official moves to substitute pragmatism for systematic theoretical research, he was yet volubly 'progressive' and assented to the effort involved in developing the requisite proletarian consciousness.[39]

His troubles began not within China, where he seemed to thrive under the new regime, but in the form of an attack from overseas. His assailant was Karl August Wittfogel (1897–1988), an orientalist scholar and Director of the Chinese History Project at Columbia University. A former youth leader, and a refugee from Hitler, Wittfogel was trained in European Marxist thought but was to outrage orthodox Marxists by his determination to demonstrate an unbreakable link between economic centralization and political despotism. Helen Foster Snow (ex-wife of the legendary journalist Edgar Snow) would later write of Wittfogel with corrosive dislike: 'He was called a Trotskyist. If he had studied anthropology at all, he did not understand it... Wittfogel's mind and objectivity had been damaged by his victimization at the hands of the Nazis, who forced him to clean out latrines barefoot to the ankles to humiliate him and destroy his personality.'[40]

As a ferocious anti-Stalinist (and a participant in McCarthyism in the USA), Wittfogel castigated the polity of the Chinese People's Republic as nothing more than a derivative of Bolshevik bullying. He had presented his case in the September 1951 issue of *The Annals of the American Academy of Political and Social Science*, a volume which purported to 'lay before the American people a consistent and coherent body of facts and informed opinion about Communist China' but was evidently dedicated to damning the regime.[41] His next shot at the heresy of Stalinism-Maoism appeared in the *Review of Politics* in October 1954. The London Marx, the author of *Das Kapital*, he argued, would scorn the socio-historical role, the 'unilineal developmental scheme'—the procession from slavery to feudalism to capitalism—that both Stalinists and Chinese Communists claimed to sanction their establishment of a despotic apparatus state. Socialism means a planned economy with effective popular control, not a new enslavement of the workers. In sum, Wittfogel persuasively argued, the new China had set up a 'mixed' semi-managerial system, which 'probably involves tighter patterns of social and intellectual control than were practised in the U.S.S.R. prior to the collectivization'.[42] His summative work *Oriental Despotism* (1957) was to scandalize orthodox Marxists.[43]

Whatever the real merits of his theoretical arguments, Wittfogel played foul when his obsession with the subject impelled him to discredit the scholar Fei Hsiao-t'ung. Fei had betrayed his own scholarly integrity, Wittfogel sought to allege; and *Encounter* (a journal founded in 1953 and secretly founded by the CIA, edited by Stephen Spender and Irving Kristol) enabled him to mount his offensive. Before the Communist takeover of China, Wittfogel argued in the issue of January 1955, Fei had worked not only to analyse but also to improve the conditions of the Chinese peasants. He advocated a 'reasonable and effective land reform'; he genuinely believed he could work with the Communists; but he did not accept the Communist analysis of Chinese society. Even as recently as 1947–8, when he assembled the essays later published in the west as *China's Gentry* (1953), Fei had evidently opposed the official Soviet and Chinese Communist theory that China was plagued by the evils of private ownership in the shape of feudal landlords: he knew that China's problem was not the control of landed property but the sway of state power, the despotic order of a bureaucratic gentry. In his previous incarnation, that is to say, Fei had more or less agreed with Wittfogel. 'Despite these heretical views, Fei awaited the coming of the Communists with high hopes. And after they established their dominance, he wrote in praise of the "New Democracy." Soon he was singled out for unusual honouring: Mao Tse-tung talked with him face to face. Was it during this conversation that Mao ordered Fei to concentrate his researches on urban reconstruction, and to stop busying himself with the gentry, which the Communists understood better than he? Rumour has it so. In any case, Fei was given a place on various government boards and committees. But he was kept out of the villages, which in the past he had studied so intensely.' Judging from 'the scattered information to hand, and especially from the denunciations and exhortations in official directives', Wittfogel concluded, the redistribution of land in China would perpetuate an agrarian problem, leaving all the peasants in great hardship; and 'having known [Fei] personally, I consider it more than likely that in the depth of his heart he comprehends fully the tragedy which has overwhelmed him and his country.'[44] In so insinuating that Fei held opinions which were at odds with the Marxist-Leninist dogma of a state that Wittfogel himself believed to be the organizer of 'total terror', he was exposing a prominent official of that very state to possible victimization: it was, to say the least, a shockingly low blow.

Thus Cedric Dover, in the August 1955 issue of *Encounter*, justifiably protested: 'It is a very curious token of regard that Wittfogel should publish statements that, according to his own fantasy-pictures of China, could only lead Fei to prison or to the executioner.' But Wittfogel's report was untrue, Dover went on: Fei was in fact 'highly respected and personally integrated'. Dover had been close friends with him for twenty years, and during a recent conversation Fei had spoken of his pleasure at having 'become an "anthropologist in action,"' in an exhilarating atmosphere where "cooperative work with minorities" has already produced such outstanding results; and I agreed, from what I had seen of the new position of the minorities, that I envied him—as I sincerely do.'[45]

Empson too, recalling his own observations of the national minorities in the late 1930s (and the contempt that the Han Chinese had often expressed for them), argued in the same issue:

> The Chinese have a bad record as colonists in the past, not that they were at all racially prejudiced, but that a tribesman could not expect much unless he adopted Chinese culture. The present sturdy drive to encourage minority cultures . . . is a conscious attempt to correct the errors of the past. That is why I feel the casual assertion that Fei must be feeling ashamed of himself is a particularly bad guess, as well as being rather nasty.[46]

Wittfogel would not relent a word. In view of the known developments in Chinese villages, including 'forced collectivisation, famine, flight from the farms, and, in cases of overt defiance, brutal persecution, slave labour, and death', he wrote back, 'my assumption regarding Fei's state of mind now is reasonable and legitimate . . . Perhaps Fei's moral fibre is weaker than I, on the basis of a rather long friendship, believe. Perhaps today Fei is indeed an enthusiastic supporter of policies that were formerly alien to his way of thinking.' In any event, why is Fei 'no longer permitted to deal with the Chinese peasants' on which he is an expert, only with non-Chinese tribes? 'Any literate person knows—or ought to know,' Wittfogel hammered, 'that in Communist China free discussion of such matters is impossible.'[47]

Empson, while honestly admitting to himself that he could not explain why Fei had been seconded to work with the non-Chinese peoples, yet returned with an impeccably logical response published in *Encounter* in November 1955:

> I agree that it is a pity when an informed person [Fei] cannot contribute to a debate, also when a scholar after becoming an official is put to do work off his main line—even when it is important work, and nearly on his main line. But both things happen very often on this side of the Curtain. I doubt if Government officials anywhere are allowed to print articles criticising the policy of their superiors; and in this country it usually isn't considered decent to jeer at a Civil Servant for not answering when his position

requires him not to answer. Probably a large proportion of your readers have signed contracts like that in their time, as I have myself; and it did not make me feel tortured by remorse, as Mr Wittfogel presumes that Fei does... The Americans are not allowed to visit him, owing to the folly of their Government, and they make up bad-tempered stories instead. Why should you whistle up Americans to tell us about him, the one group of people who can't know?[48]

The editors of *Encounter* now declared their hand in the propaganda row, though edgeways, by levelling an attack upon Empson's logic. 'For a critic who is distinguished for his analysis of other men's ambiguities, Mr. Empson seems peculiarly insensitive to his own. After having asserted, in a previous letter, that Fei is happy as a Communist functionary, he now states that, because he is a functionary, Fei is in no position to say whether he is happy or not. We do not see how he can have it both ways.'[49]

They may well have felt goaded to intervene in the controversy, however feebly, by a seemingly gratuitous final paragraph of Empson's letter (written on 23 August) which they had cut from the published version:

> I see that dear Mr Fiedler is still carrying on in your magazine. Since it began, he has been positively praising whatever the reader is likely to think most disgusting in America at the moment; this time it isn't a monstrous legal killing, as in your first number, but only horror comics. Everybody likes a man to be gallant, but I don't think you are on to a really good line there. People might begin to think you were taking advantage of the young man's innocence, or something.[50]

He was referring to two articles by Leslie A. Fiedler, 'A Postscript to the Rosenberg Case' (in the very first issue of *Encounter* in October 1953), and 'The Middle Against Both Ends' (August 1955), which he signally misrepresented—though he hit upon a deep truth behind them.

When discussing the trial and execution of the spies Julius and Ethel Rosenberg, Fiedler had argued in the first piece, everyone must realize that there were in truth two cases: the actual 'open-and-shut' legal case, which established that, in Fiedler's words, the couple were 'flagrantly guilty' of spying; and the 'legendary' or symbolic case, the myth of martyrdom, which the Rosenbergs themselves did everything possible to promote—and indeed to win. 'In the Rosenberg case, a part of the world (that part, at least, still not hopelessly poisoned by Communism) turned to America for a symbolic demonstration that somewhere a government existed willing to risk the loss of political face for the sake of establishing an unequivocal moral position.'

Fiedler's contempt for the Rosenbergs, his atrabilious opinion of Communism, and his sense of frustration that America had missed a move to show that it held the high moral ground against all the Cold War odds: such major aspects of the essay are obvious. But in fact Fiedler did not, as Empson alleged, praise 'a monstrous legal killing'. All the same, it is difficult not to deduce that Fiedler was lamenting the loss of a propaganda coup—'a symbolic demonstration'—just as much as the failure of humanitarianism.[51]

Fiedler's other essay aimed to answer the critics of comic books, which he said were a kind of literature that 'comes first from us'. This 'apology' required him to attempt a two-pronged critical strategy: an estimate of the value of vulgar literature, and an attack on the politics and the pathology 'involved in the bourgeois hostility to popular literature'. Fiedler's case rested on the necessity to assent to a market-led cultural economy: 'to delegate taste to majority suffrage'. You must not force high art upon the masses, nor ban their vulgar diversions. Any attempt to do so means 'a drive for conformity on the level of the timid, sentimental, mindless-bodiless genteel'. It would also mean suppressing 'a peculiarly American phenomenon', of course, which is naturally impossible: 'To declare oneself against "the Americanisation of culture" is meaningless unless one is set resolutely against industrialisation and mass education.'[52] At the back of this 'apology' for the comic book, therefore, lay a patriotic salute: where America leads, the world will follow.

Stephen Spender considered Empson's crack at Fiedler extraneous to the 'main purport' of his letter, which was principally concerned with defending Fei Hsiao-t'ung and with justifying China's annexation of American consular property. But Empson had discerned a certain palpable link between *Encounter*'s attacks on Fei, its prejudicial account of the conduct of the Chinese People's Government in Peking, and its publication of transparently pro-American propaganda pieces by the likes of Leslie Fiedler. His summary of Fiedler's sophisticated argument apropos the Rosenberg case was bluntly and caustically reductive, especially since he chose to ignore its climactic point that the quality of American mercy should not have been strained. But he felt so righteous in exposing *Encounter* as a covert organ of Cold War propaganda that he had no hesitation in posting the censored paragraph to Fiedler himself, whom he had met while teaching the summer school at the School of Arts and Letters in Bloomington, Indiana, in 1954. 'It is widely understood over here that the magazine is taking foreign gold for an attempt to affect opinion in England,' he wrote scornfully in his covering letter to Fiedler (which he copied to Spender). 'Thus when you, for example, tell your views to the English public in it, you do so by foreign subsidy, presumably because they wouldn't sell on their own merits; and it is not only in my own case that the magazine has refused to print the retorts of the English reader. The Americans wouldn't like such an arrangement any more than the English do.'[53] Empson felt so incensed on behalf of Fei Hsiao-t'ung by the politically prejudiced stance of Stephen Spender and Irving Kristol (the latter being an American with a well-established reputation as an 'intellectual bruiser') that he set up a meeting at the offices of *Encounter* in Haymarket, London, in order to challenge the two editors over their pro-American propagandizing. However, he got no satisfaction for his trouble. Spender sought eagerly to reassure Fiedler that 'Irving Kristol and I are completely responsible for the policy of this magazine'—albeit that just a month after publishing Fiedler's article on the Rosenbergs, in a letter of 5 November 1953, he had conceded he thought Fiedler's piece betrayed 'rather obvious anti-communism'.[54] Paradoxically, too, Spender made it known to friends that he actually deplored Fiedler's piece; it was at least a serviceable way of 'letting British readers know just how awful a certain type of American intellectual could be.'[55] According to Spender's biographer, Kristol had in fact 'nurtured and painstakingly "edited"'— that is, rewritten—the article.[56] If Spender was not entirely sure which side his bread was buttered, it seems, he always claimed he had no idea at all where the butter came from.

Fiedler responded to Empson, with strained dignity: 'I not only did *not* support the execution of the Rosenbergs, but the main point of my essay was an explanation of why they should have been spared. As for my piece on Popular Culture, it quite specifically states that my attack on the opponents of the comics is not to be construed as a defence of the comics themselves . . . It seems to me that you are in a most unfortunate situation now which causes you to demean yourself and which may eventually obscure your justly won reputation. I can only sympathize with your plight, possessed as you are of so much political passion and so little political understanding.' He added by hand in a footnote: 'It occurs to me that you may not have read my articles at all—and were simply playing by ear!'[57]

A reader might take leave, as did Empson, to doubt whether Fiedler's summary does justice to all of the detail and the vehement implication of his own articles. In the judgement of Frances Stonor Saunders, author of a full analytical history of the CIA's covert cultural operations, Fiedler's text remains 'striking for its human meanness'.[58] Both E. M. Forster and

Czeslaw Milosz complained to the magazine about the article; and T. S. Eliot in a letter to Spender adjudged from Fiedler's piece that *Encounter* was 'obviously published under American auspices'.[59] Indeed, Fiedler could hardly be so ingenuous as not to be aware that both of his articles were infused with praise for the USA: its political and moral superiority over the Soviet bloc in the Rosenberg article, its literary leadership even in the matter of comic books. Spender (who carried on in apparent ignorance of the CIA subvention to his own magazine) was obliged to explain to his sponsors the force of Eliot's charge: 'The point is that Eliot here states the kind of reputation we have to try and live down of being a magazine disguising American propaganda under a veneer of British culture... [T]he implied criticism that I am putting in articles which serve American purposes is naturally very painful to me.'[60]

Empson retorted to Fiedler on 10 February, with his main political point following some sophistical but reasonable guesswork in the first paragraph:

> I was interested by the footnote in red pencil, saying that your two articles were attacks on their subjects, not defences of them as I thought, so probably I was 'playing by ear'. I certainly did read them at the time (it would be too much to go and look them up now), and what I said was not only the impression I got but what other people said when they mentioned the articles to me. Indeed, as I only claimed to be reporting the English reaction to them, in my letter to you, I might still be right though I *had* been playing only by ear. No such article can be purely pro or con, unless very narrow, and I daresay the proportion seemed quite different to you from what it did to the English reader. If so, it was just as well to tell you.
>
> There is one thing I feel I should try to make clear; so far as I know, I haven't changed my opinions about politics since I was a young man. At that time Spender was shouting away on the Left-Wing band-wagon, and I was commonly called reactionary. He is now shouting like you on the reactionary or pro-American band-wagon, whereas I am just where I was; and still think myself free to speak up whenever there is too much nonsense being talked on either side. I hope this partly relieves the fears you expressed for my future.
>
> As to 'foreign gold', of course I didn't mean to reproach you for taking it; I have often been employed abroad myself. I was asking you to realise the point of view of the English reader, and one would think the English editor. The magazine is generally understood to be supported by UNESCO, that is, largely by American money; and it is evidently very pro-American. This set-up is liable to be resented, so that it works out as anti-propaganda. It seems rather friendly of me, really, to warn you of that.[61]

Empson's genuinely angry belief that *Encounter* was 'taking foreign gold for an attempt to affect opinion in England' incited him over the following years to indulge in some waspish behaviour. Crucially, when he ran into Spender at a party thrown by Louis and Hedli MacNeice in the early summer of 1961 he followed him round the room chanting, 'Stephen's a cheat! Stephen's a cheat!' Spender became so irritated that he hurled his glass of wine in the face of the gadfly.[62] Subsequently, when Spender took the initiative in writing to make up the quarrel, Empson returned on 6 June:

> Dear Spender,
> ...I haven't ever felt cross in the slightest degree about the quarrel at Louis MacNeice's in front of the Austrian Ambassadress; I thought she was overwhelmingly charming, and that we had put on just the kind of show she would expect to see when she went out slumming to look at authors. I was told next day that you had thrown a glass of wine at me, but no decisive evidence could be found on my admittedly used garments, and my only impression was that I had made better cracks than you. I couldn't have been tempted to be cross about it.
>
> What we were arguing about, on the other hand, I would always feel had to be taken seriously. As I understood the position, and still do, you were and are taking American money, perfunctorily disguised as international money, to confront the British public with innocent-seeming American propaganda. You can't expect to do this without ever hearing a grumble; you wouldn't have got away with it in earlier times.
>
> It was later, I think, that I had to write to your magazine because of a gross libel which you printed against poor Fei Hsiao-tung...and nothing but a laborious effort of self-delusion, I think, can explain how you came to imagine that I was only cross because of some personal offence taken at one of Louis' parties.

On the following day, Empson wrote again in ostensibly more 'understanding' vein, though the purport of his letter was just as critical:

> On second thoughts, it is absurd to grumble about money as I did in writing to you last night. A man could be blamed for taking money to do what he knew to be wrong, while saying that he thought it right, but the real accusation would be against his sincerity. For all I can say, you may really believe your American propaganda, and regard the tricky devices for sustaining it as a necessary Cold-War duty.
>
> It is none the less true that I couldn't be on friendly terms with a man who held such beliefs.

I hope this makes the matter clear, and I wish to withdraw any irrelevant insults.

In a third letter (9 June) he elaborated his former criticisms, drawing on his own experience of propaganda during the war, and highlighting especially the CIA funding of the journal. Nevertheless, when Spender informed him that he had demanded of his colleagues whether the magazine was in any possible way funded by the CIA, and that he had been given a categorical assurance that it was not the case, Empson had no option but to accept Spender's word of honour that he was innocent.

> Oh, dear, I suppose I am being unreasonable [wrote Empson on 14 June]. What you have said almost completely exonerates you, and I don't think the magazine has carried anything similar after that case. No doubt Kristol took almost no interest in the case; I mean only that his attitude to propaganda seemed to me unscrupulous—no doubt he would think that a patriotic duty.[63]

Strangely—given the mild tone of this last letter from Empson—Spender wrote on 22 June 1961 from the offices of *Encounter* at 25 Haymarket, London (it is just possible that he had not yet received the more recent of WE's letters):

> Dear Empson,
> I agree that we (or I) should abandon the attempt to overcome the estrangement. The reasons for our not being able to overcome it are honourable to you, and the occasional brusqueness of your remarks should be ignored by me. Apart from this, I would like, on my side, to end by saying what I was all along trying to convey: that it pains me whenever I think (which I do often, as I read your poems often) that you might not realize what gratitude and admiration I feel not just for your poetry but for the person I feel present in it. What I also wanted to convey was that my saying this was not to ingratiate myself with you or to introduce any scruple into your thoughts about me. Probably this means nothing to you now. Still it might do some day.
> Yours sincerely
> Spender
>   (Houghton)

Alongside his signature Spender affixed a 2d. postage stamp, presumably in the hope that Empson might relent his antagonistic posture. He also took pains to write out a copy of the letter, complete with a handwritten sketch of the stamp, to pop into his own files. Yet for all Spender's intransigent ignorance of the facts, it was the case that the CIA itself had come to think *Encounter* 'our greatest asset'.[64]

Despite Spender's durable (and arguably wilful) state of unknowing, including his failure to investigate the matter beyond the reassurances he was accorded whenever he enquired of his immediate colleagues, Empson was not alone in sustaining dark suspicions of *Encounter*'s primary allegiance. Eight years later, in an article entitled 'Journal de Combat' (*New Statesman*, December 1963), Conor Cruise O'Brien sharply pointed out (independently of Empson) that—despite the claim of its very first editorial that '*Encounter* seeks to promote "no line" '—'Encounter's first loyalty is to America': 'It seeks rather to carry the impression that its anti-communist and pro-capitalist propaganda is not propaganda at all, but the spontaneous and almost uniform reaction of the culturally free, of truly civilized people . . . [A]lmost every issue has contained some cleverly written material favourable to the United States and hostile to the Soviet Union.' To cite one example, he went on, Leslie A. Fiedler's article on comic books 'was written at a time when hostile criticism of these works of art and literature was considered to be causing some damage to America's image in the world. Professor Fiedler's thesis, argued as cleverly as possible in the unpropitious circumstances, was to the effect that anti-comic-book talk was petty-bourgeois and middlebrow; the ordinary man likes these books and real intellectuals, like Professor Fiedler, at least tolerate them . . . The case for "comic books" was argued, in the pages of *Encounter*, within a specific political context. The United States (good) produces these books in enormous numbers; the Soviet Union (bad) neither produces nor imports them . . . ' Thus O'Brien judged, just like Empson before him, that *Encounter* assuredly pursued a cold-war strategy. 'Where the truth in question is uncomfortable for the Soviet Union it is promulgated; where it is uncomfortable for the United States it is mitigated . . . Great vigilance is shown about oppression in the communist world; apathy and inconsequence largely prevail where the oppression is non-communist or anti-communist.'[65]

Three years later, Stephen Spender was to resign from *Encounter* when it became public knowledge that the journal's sponsor, the Congress for Cultural Freedom, had been financed all along by the CIA. (Over the ten-year period 1953–63, it is estimated, the CCF, which was directly run by a CIA agent, had supported *Encounter* to the tune of a million dollars.) Spender discovered to his distress too that his own salary had for many years been funded by the British Government (his salary of £2,500 had been fixed for a decade); and that his co-editors, Irving Kristol and subsequently Melvyn Lasky, had known the real situation all along. It even became known that the magazine's long-serving office manager (later its managing director) was in fact an employee of the British Foreign Office. Spender objected to having been misled for fourteen years, 'and to having consequently in good faith defended *Encounter* upon information now shown to be untrue . . . On the information I had hitherto consistently been given, I had believed that, in having it printed in the pages of *Encounter* that it was sponsored by the CCF, its American interest was declared. But the interest of the CIA was not declared either to the general public or to the English literary co-editors.' On 24 April 1967, Spender was therefore to write honourably to WE (on headed notepaper from the English Department of Northwestern University at Evanston, Illinois): 'I have been meaning to write to you for some weeks about something in which I was wrong and you were right. It is quite true that from 1953 . . . *Encounter* was by way of the Congress for Cultural Freedom supported by the CIA.' Spender then offered an account of his loss of innocence (if such it was) and subsequent resignation, and ended up: 'The point of the letter—of stating all this—is that I owe you an apology.'

Notwithstanding that apology, Spender and Empson were never to be fully reconciled; they would always thereafter tread warily of one another. As late as 1985, just a year after Empson's death, Spender would say of his erstwhile antagonist: 'I never really got on with William Empson and I didn't know him very well. We were ideologically apart. There was a very communist side of Empson and he always regarded me as a bit of a renegade, I think. So I couldn't claim a friendship with him. But on the other hand, there was something we liked very much about each other.'[66] The insinuation that there was 'a very communist side of Empson' carried a false and self-excusing implication. Empson for his part distrusted Spender's posture of strained integrity, and was to lament in a note to a friend in 1983 (the last full year of his life): 'Isn't it awful that Spender has got a Knighthood. It takes all the point out of mine. Put not your trust in princes.'[67]

Little of that larger picture could help him in the affair of Fei Hsiao-t'ung, where it was a matter of his affirmation of loyalty standing against Wittfogel's charge that the Chinese scholar was a false apostate. It seemed that there could be no quittance to the matter unless Fei spoke up for himself. And fortunately, he did just that—in a letter written on 26 October 1955 and published in the February 1956 issue of *Encounter*. Wittfogel's so-called review of *China's Gentry*, Fei protested, was full of 'rumours and calumnies . . . describing me as a miserable figure without moral fibre under cruel persecution.' The truth stood to the contrary: 'if the American people had known the real situation in China . . . they would have rejoiced that China was starting a happy life, and they would never have sanctioned intrigues and attempts to restore the privileges of the few.' As to his own mind, he wrote, he had indeed changed it: 'The fact is that many of the opinions I expressed in pre-liberation days I have now discarded as untenable...Of course, I am not denying that in pre-liberation days I did hold the ideas and views expressed in the book, and as an historical document it perhaps has some justification.' The crux of his letter, however, was neither argument nor demonstration, only the old formula that he had recently learned: 'in pre-liberation days, I did hold the view that academic study was one thing and practical political activity another, and that they had nothing to do with each other. That view is out of touch with reality and therefore incorrect and untrue.'[68]

Wittfogel felt fully justified in pronouncing judgement against him: 'Dr. Fei is an official of a government which, possessing total power, exerts total control over the utterances of its subjects. Free discussion with him is therefore not feasible.'[69] But at least Fei had said his piece, so Empson could stand aside.

Fei even wrote a further article in English, published in *People's China* on 1 June 1956, reassuring his foreign friends of his unambiguous commitment: 'We love our present-day work, we love New China. All that I dreamed about in the past is now, or will soon be, reality.'[70] Likewise, Yue Daiyun, a young teacher at Peking University, recalled in after years: 'Everybody was excited in 1956; we thought the fight had finished and that we could concentrate finally on building our country'.[71] Chou En-lai rejoiced at the time: 'The overwhelming majority of the intellectuals have become government workers in the service of socialism and are already part of the working class.'[72]

Thus all the personal testimony coming out of China appeared to support Empson's affidavit of June 1955: 'The chief thing that emerges is that the Chinese, whether rightly or wrongly, are still feeling enthusiastic about it all; they feel they are at last getting ahead and recovering their natural position in the world.' Everyone seemed to agree that the mid-1950s should be trumpeted as 'golden years', as it was noted by Alan Winnington (who witnessed the revolution in Beijing): 'I was amazed at how swiftly the Communists had swept away corruption and made way for the honest, cheerful, friendly Chinese to flourish. Beijing was vivid, kaleidoscopic, optimistic.'

Yet the aftermath of the Hundred Flowers movement changed everything forever. 'Let a Hundred Flowers Bloom, a Hundred Schools of

Thought Contend,' proclaimed Mao Tse-tung in the spring of 1956—with a view to seeing a host of 'fragrant flowers' (*hsiang hua*) and not to extirpating 'poisonous weeds'—though a further year would pass before the slogan became action. So the central committee duly promulgated a new-style rectification movement on 30 April: for a period of six months, it decreed, everyone should feel completely free to speak out, to expose both 'contradictions among the people' and the failings of party functionaries. Open discussion, not coercion, became the order of the day. 'If you speak,' said the *People's Daily*—with Mao Tse-tung's total endorsement— 'it will not be held against you.'[73] After some understandable hesitation, the floodgates sprang open in the month of May: every aspect of party practice and policy came under attack. Even the famous writer Lao She ridiculed what he called 'so-called literary works that are filled with political slogans'.[74]

But not for long: the Party could not stand the tidal wave of criticism. As Robert Guillain reported in *Encounter* (December 1957), 'the discontented overshot the mark. The limits of permitted criticism were transgressed. The measure ran over. The party turned to the counter-offensive.'[75]

In the 'anti-rightist struggle' (*fan yu p'ai tou cheng*) launched on 8 June, with Chairman Mao to the fore of the assailants, an enormous number of intellectuals—as many as 400,000—were speedily denounced as 'rightist deviationists'; they had manifestly failed to unite with the workers and peasants, Mao thundered. Among them, Fei Hsiao-t'ung became a major target for nation-wide attack. Unable to extenuate his guilt, he had no option but to denounce himself as a reactionary. 'I hate my past,' he declared on 14 July 1957. 'I confess my sins, I shall continue to reflect, to struggle against the rightists, to study in the course of the struggle, in order to reform myself. I resolve to accept the education of the Party and to take the path of socialism under the leadership of the Party.'[76] (Following his self-criticism, he was cleared of the 'rightist' label in 1958; and in April 1959 he was elected to membership of the Third Chinese People's Political Consultative Conference.)

Empson was dragged into the mire when he was directly challenged in *Encounter*: 'One hopes that Professor Empson and Mr. Dover will now spring to Fei's defence, as they did before. His need, this time, would seem to be more urgent.'[77] Being quite unaware that Fei had incriminated himself, in Chinese opinion—and presently in his own, as his fiduciary confession made clear—by publishing 'reactionary' articles, Empson responded with entirely creditable (though radically uninformed) loyalty, in February 1958:

I think that all these public slanders against an expert by his colleagues are
very disgusting... We do not gather that [Fei] has lost his official position
because of the recent slanders against him, or is even likely to. Why you
think all this justifies Wittfogel I do not understand. You boys seem to think
it is quite all right to tell a lie as long as somebody else tells a different lie
later on... Perhaps I should make clear that the slanders come from
[Chinese] colleagues, not from any kind of independent MI5 system. Surely
it is clear that the same kind of nastiness against Fei was going on in both
these cases, though Wittfogel was writing from behind the American curtain; how readily we can all imagine Stephen Spender busying himself with
such work, if the British Government would only give him proper encouragement.[78]

Some months later, in August 1958, the *Spectator* likewise came down on his
head with an article, 'More Trouble in Tartary', by J. E. M. Arden: 'Has
not Professor Empson been let down by the purge of Chinese scholars
whose contented devotion to the regime he had just been asserting?'[79]
Again he valiantly responded in the next issue, first rehearsing the
facts—(i) Wittfogel had earlier insinuated that Fei 'must feel ashamed of
working for his Government'; (ii) in the Chinese purge campaign of 1957,
'Fei was very grossly blamed, and even on some occasion accused of being
an American spy'—and then countering:

> Knowing Fei, a very patriotic man, who is enthusiastic about his work, I felt
> sure they were both wrong; and I suspected that this kind of smear talk by
> American colleagues was one of the things that had set off the eager
> suspicions of Chinese colleagues. I therefore said that it was a very nasty
> article to have printed, and that it ought not to have been printed in
> England.
>   These attacks are done by learned colleagues, and encouraged by the
> [Chinese] Government, of course, but not directed; and I am afraid many
> intellectuals have enough jealousy and spite to make this an easy thing for
> Governments to do.[80]

The argument went on through two more exchanges, with Empson having
the last—though inconclusive—word on 3 October: 'It strikes me that
these Western propagandists have already got into an alarmingly totalitarian frame of mind.'[81] Empson scored one point, in answer to the
assertion by Arden that Empson had said 'Fei was an enthusiast for the
regime's treatment of its intellectuals'[82], to which he could reply in all
honesty: 'I did not say this, but that Fei would be genuinely keen on the
work he was doing; which Wittfogel in his lengthy insinuations had known
nothing about.'[83] But his long-standing claim that the Chinese scholar was

in no way a dissident could no longer be sustained when it became known that in July 1957 Fei had accused himself of a 'treasonable crime'—and had even thanked the Party for 'clubbing me in order to awaken me in good time.'[84]

If the events of the Hundred Flowers campaign proved the truth of Wittfogel's damaging accusations, equally they did nothing to disprove Empson's long-standing argument that the Chinese intellectuals had honestly tried to establish their 'solidarity and sincerity'. But one of the most distressing outcomes of the whole business—certainly it would have given him no cheer to realize it—was that the upshot of the campaign showed with dreadful irony just how right he had been on another fundamental question: as he argued in June 1953, the 'background opinions' of the intelligentsia had clearly been 'less permanently affected' by the Ideological Remoulding of 1951–2 than the spate of ghoulish western propaganda had reported at the time. The intellectuals had not become 'cowed and compliant', with their minds destroyed; they had remained 'very sturdy'. When the Party urged them again and again in May 1957 to voice their criticisms, they spoke out with courage—and only then were they truly punished.

Empson said nothing to extenuate the aftermath of the Hundred Flowers campaign. Indeed, all he had ever tried to maintain, since leaving China in 1952, was his trust that his old colleagues were not 'broken from independent thought . . . or . . . even intended to be.' So far from inaugurating a 'Terror State', he believed, the new regime had at first brought the country 'a vast return of national pride, which was eagerly desired by many classes. "It is like having the emperors back", as casual characters would say in the street, phrasing it as a joke but feeling it as praise; and they would call the dictator "lao tai tai", the old grandmother who controls the big house secretly from behind; not always a kind old woman, in the memories that are assumed, but not at all a person expected to leap into war; a very different object, I think, from all the previous dictators of the modern world.'

Frederick C. Teiwes, in his detailed study *Politics and Purges in China* (1979), covering the period 1950–65, has pointedly confirmed Empson's judgement: 'Besides the "ruthless struggles" of pre-Mao CCP leaders, the rectification approach was developed with another "negative example" in mind: the Stalinist Great Purge in the 1930s. As is well known, the Stalinist purge and CCP rectification differ significantly . . . But one of the most notable contrasts with the Stalinist period, the lack of "terror," has not been sufficiently emphasized.'[85] Defining the 'essence of terror' as 'its unpredictability and arbitrariness in striking someone regardless of whether he obeys the state's commands', Teiwes stresses that in the People's Republic of China 'the basic approach in dealing with individuals has been selective and surgical rather than arbitrary... [E]ven relatively coercive movements were marked by a substantial degree of predictability.'

Such was Empson's detestation for injurious propaganda, for imputing ugly motives, that as late as February 1958 he ventured to attribute to the Chinese dictator an entirely decent response towards the Hundred Flowers backlash: 'It is a melancholy thing that "the intelligentsia are weasel-minded," a remark made by Ezra Pound while pretending to translate Confucius; indeed, I expect Mao Tse-tung is feeling rather shocked by it, so far from having only intended his bit of encouragement for independent thinkers to work out as a trap for them.'[86] One can only conclude, therefore, his consistent expressions of optimism vis-à-vis the New China serve to highlight, not so much his political innocence—though something of that—as his really extraordinary faith in human nature. Whether or not Mao intended the Hundred Flowers to be a trap, the result was all one.[87] The New China had betrayed its intelligentsia—and Empson's faith. Once he finally learned about the vindictive upshot to the campaign, he never again published a word on behalf of Communist China.

If the events of 1957 made his estimate of Communist China obsolete, he had not been wrong to deny that his colleagues were terrorized during the first three years of the new regime. For the very most part, they had been subjected only to 'a deliberately calculated nagging process', as he averred on the basis of what he saw and heard reported; always adding, 'I do not mean to deny that badgering is a large real thing'. His mistake lay in being far too eager to generalize from local observation and report, so offering what he sometimes admitted might be 'too rosy a picture' of the country as a whole. By contrast with the certain terror of life under the Kuomintang, the Nationalist Government of Chiang Kai-shek, he firmly believed (and the majority of the Chinese assuredly agreed with him), the Communist administration initially afforded everyone the opportunity to rediscover dignity, to work for a better society.

For a description of a Terror, Empson maintained, one had only to read George Orwell's *1984* to know that China was utterly different. Ironically, a copy of the novel had reached him in Peking in 1949, just as the Communists came to power; it was posted from Buckinghamshire, with no indication of the sender, and came wrapped up in a Danish illustrated paper.[88] In his opinion, it was a harrowing novel, but it lacked imaginative authenticity; as he wrote to Kathleen Raine the following year: 'I thought the poor old chap was writing about his sense of exasperation and approaching personal death and had lost the ring of truth which all his previous writing had. It seemed a very remote heartcry when looked at behind the Bamboo Curtain.'[89] The effect of reading it was 'like a hot iron leaving a permanent scar on your imagination,' Empson felt. To test its 'truth', he related, he lent it to various Chinese colleagues; and they responded: 'It's tiresome; it's invented. My situation is bad enough, and very disagreeable; but it isn't like that.'[90] His small (and unscientific) market survey helped to convince him that Communist China could not be defined as totalitarian by the measure of *1984*.

Yet Robert Jay Lifton later commented on fundamental aspects of Chinese Communist ideology and language-usage in a way that remarkably coincides with the central concerns of Empson's contemporary writings on linguistics—specifically his attempt in *The Structure of Complex Words* (virtually completed in 1948) to codify the process by which 'our language is continually thrusting doctrines on us'—though he did not fully make the connection at the time. 'The totalist milieu,' Lifton argued, 'maintains an aura of sacredness around its basic dogma, holding it out as an ultimate moral vision for the ordering of human existence'; the 'claimed certitudes' are continually enforced by a jargon so constricted that it results in linguistic deprivation.[91] The primacy of doctrine, Lifton concluded, is evident from the way totalism always prefers the abstraction of experience before the experience itself. 'The human is thus subjugated to the ahuman.'[92]

Certainly Empson never erred on the side of defending a theory of words as 'plain representation'; nor did he suffer from the kind of 'logophobia' that has been ascribed to George Orwell. He understood that language is a complex cultural tool, freighted with history. But he knew too that the act of critical understanding often involved a process of undeceiving. 'Feelings in Words', the first chapter of *The Structure of Complex Words*, accordingly tries 'to separate various entities in the habitual uses of a single word, for example Senses, Implications, Emotions and Moods.' Then, in chapter 2—'Statements in Words'—he addresses the problem of how words carry 'compacted doctrines' or 'covert assertions.' 'A word may become a sort of solid entity, able to direct opinion, thought of as like a person . . . If our language is continually thrusting doctrines on us, perhaps very ill-considered ones, the sooner we understand the process the better.'[93] The most common tendency of the language, he explains, is to assert doctrines by way of what he calls 'equations', as in the 'A is B' formula. But that mode of predicative identification is always non-symmetrical—it can variously mean A entails B, A is part of B, A is like B, or A is typical of B— so that it can become 'a great source of delusion'.[94] A may be called B; but if you turn the sentence around, you invariably discover that it no longer holds good to say that 'B is A'. As the agreed subject of discussion, A suggests its context in terms of B, which therefore has a generalizing function, framing an adjectival arena of likely debate. Thus the process of apparent identification is by no means clear-cut. Yet the speaker asserts a 'doctrine' in terms of 'A is B' by 'claiming the connection is normal since the word is one thing. Also there is commonly an appeal to an outside body of opinion, which adds greatly to the power of this little trick; the idea is "everybody agrees with me; language itself agrees with me; but you the hearer seem not to know it well enough".'[95] What is conveyed is the assertion that the word itself proves the equation: the two senses of a word naturally belong together.

Admittedly, Empson is most concerned with the action of what he calls 'vague rich intimate' words, not the official language of a state; but it would take no effort to extend the theory to formulae such as 'Marxism is scientific', 'materialism is correct', or 'the proletarian standpoint is true' (with their negative counterparts such as 'the bourgeois viewpoint is incorrect' or 'idealism is backward'). In fact, he approached an exactly parallel application in chapter 19 of *Complex Words*, entitled 'A is B', where he discusses the extravagant implications, the multiple questions that are necessarily begged, by the formulae 'Right is Might' and 'Might is Right', which—like so many religious paradoxes—are altogether less denotative than assertive. As he remarked, in all such formulations—which include 'God is Love' and 'time is money', as well as the Hindu 'That art Thou'— 'the machinery of false identity is in play'.[96] With regard to the 'Might is Right' slogan, for instance, he suggested: 'Even the form "Efface discussion of right" could be taken to mean "We know that our might is of the ideal kind; do not admit any derogatory suggestion that it is not". The opponent, on the other hand, in holding the slogan up to detestation, takes it to mean that might is the "only real" kind of right in the sense that right will no longer be considered at all . . .'[97]

His conclusion to the subject might equally be applied to the Communist claims to have erected an 'ultimate science'—to hypostatize the state-established 'Word'—in the form of Marxist ideology. 'It is not so easy to fix on the point of agreement between "might is right" and "right is might", but it seems fair to say that both parties assume the State to be a demi-god.

Neither slogan is used about individuals, at any rate about individual men...A state which receives worship, or a people with a "destiny", are in the same position as God because they are expected partly to create the standard of rightness by which they are to be judged.'[98]

That assessment exactly matches Robert Jay Lifton's diagnosis of the totalist milieu:

> The assumption here is not so much that man can be God, but rather that man's *ideas* can be God: that an absolute science of ideas (and implicitly, an absolute science of man) exists, or is at least very close to being attained; that this science can be combined with an equally absolute body of moral principles; and that the resulting doctrine is true for all men at all times. Although no ideology goes quite this far in overt statement, such assumptions are implicit in totalist practice.[99]

Empson was fully aware too that any 'equation theory' needed to account for the 'pre-logical' habit—'the distinctive feature of the primitive mind' (long recognized by psychologists and anthropologists)—which continuously enables human beings to impute an identity between things that are known to be different; as when a profane matter is designated as mystical, or in cases of psychiatric transference—when a patient identifies the psychiatrist as the father. It should also be able to unravel bad logic and syllogisms: such as, in crude terms, the claim that (i) science is truth; (ii) Marxism is scientific; and that consequently (iii) Marxism is the truth.

He was prompt to insist at all times, as in *Milton's God* (1961):

> our minds have a wonderful readiness to satisfy themselves with admittedly false identities, but any orderly schooling needs to drive the process into the background of its area of practical work. I tried in my book *Complex Words* to show how very fundamental it is...but educated people rightly suspect it...The machine is best described in the terrible book *1984*, where it produces a number of horror-slogans such as 'War is Peace'.[100]

As he advised in *Complex Words*, the decision to regard an 'equation' as a general truth is 'a fairly serious step on the part of a zeitgeist or an individual.'[101] In such terms, the ideological remoulding ordained by the Chinese Communist state exploited this weakness of the 'pre-logical mind': it required the intelligentsia to accept what Lifton adroitly termed a 'blend of counterfeit science and back-door religion'.[102]

Empson thought it fundamental to any discussion of rational semantics, of politics or of ethics, that no one should wittingly surrender their minds to that 'pre-logical' tendency; nor that a state should usurp the prerogative of the independent intelligence. That principle alone explains why he claimed that his Chinese colleagues reserved their 'background opinions' during Thought Reform, though paradoxically not dissembling their support for the regime. Had they failed to do so, the Chinese state would have been a brutally totalitarian machine, not constructive and reformative but systematically punitive. The suggestion that after being subjected to thought reform an individual could be utterly sincere in avowing a statement he knew to be false, flouted Empson's root faith in human rationality. That a person (such as Fei Tsiao-t'ung) could change his mind was unarguable; that he could live and believe a lie, Empson found unconscionable.

The very idea of 'brainwashing' in a totalist sense struck him as so appalling that for a long time he evidently refused to believe it could be done. It would tear the heart out of his life's work: it would contradict his belief that language is always answerable to intelligence. Only a state that was evil or insane could enforce such a practice; and its subjects, its victims, would be bewitched or deranged.

All the same, his reading of Orwell's mind-boggling *1984*, in which Winston Smith is compelled to affirm the falsehood that '2 + 2 = 3', finally drove him to add this afterword of frustrated protest—written from Peking on 24 November 1950, before Ideological Reform or Ideological Remoulding (*ssu-hsiang kai-tsao*) was forced upon his Chinese colleagues— to his chapter on 'Statements in Words':

> The most striking recent work on the kind of linguistics I am trying to consider has been a very untechnical one; it is in the dreadful book *1984* which George Orwell wrote while dying. What he calls 'double-think', a process of intentional but genuine self-deception, easy to reach but hard to hold permanently, really does seem a positive capacity of the human mind, so curious and so important in its effects that any theory in this field needs to reckon with it. In the nightmare of his book the emotional ground of the process is a secret but fully justified fear, and the case is so hideously special that it seems rather hard to generalise (indeed the book itself, I think, tends to frighten the reader into believing the possibility of what he does not really think possible). But no doubt this kind of process does occur, and is based on emotional grounds; I am left uneasy whether my treatment here has a pureminded intellectualism which ignores the facts in view. I might protest that you can have a usable linguistic theory which doesn't apply to sheer madness . . . Actually I think . . . the kind of analysis I am attempting here could be applied even to the ghastly paradoxes of the Orwell world such as 'War is Peace'. Clearly this means that to be analysable doesn't make a bit of

language good, but it was never supposed to. While considering the possible equation forms I gave a paragraph about 'the paradoxes of the great religions'; and all I can find to add, after trying to mull over the question again, is that I think it would apply to the very worst religions too. But then again, to take this way out of the theoretical dilemma does seem only another way to make my position a null one. It is rather hard to see beforehand what a line of argument is letting you in for; but I suppose I really meant to argue all along that the human mind, that is, the public human mind as expressed in a language, is not irredeemably lunatic and cannot be made so. (p. 83)[103]

If China's vindictive treatment of its intelligentsia could not be defended after the Hundred Flowers campaign, it subsequently occurred to Empson that the anti-Communist propaganda suggested a new and sinister equation, which was also an allegory of the Cold War. Unknown to itself, western propaganda was steadily belabouring Communism for advancing a state of terror that was altogether equal to the historical record and ultimate ethical values of Christianity. To take one crucial instance, he would later argue, the Doctrine of the Trinity—the Athanasian doctrine, laid down by the Council of Nicaea, of the consubstantiality of the Son with the Father—'is a means of deceiving good men into accepting evil; it is the double-talk by which Christians hide from themselves the insane wickedness of their God.'[104] (Empson's 'double-talk' is clearly derived from Orwell's coinage 'double-think'.) The basis of his objection to such 'Orwellian' behaviour on the part of Christians is made clear in an article dating from 1963, in which he maintained: 'The doctrine of the Trinity is necessary, or the Father appears too evil in his "satisfaction" at the crucifixion of his Son. But to present Jesus as one with the Father only turns him into a hypocrite; when he prays for his enemies to be forgiven, he knows under his other title he will take revenge.'[105]

He first turned Orwell's fiction into an undifferentiated attack on Christianity in a private latter arguing about Gerard M. Hopkins's 'The Windhover'; this dates from December 1955: 'You say that the falcon swooping onto its prey is by that act a symbol of Christ humbling himself to our manhood, and that this is a Christian tradition familiar to those properly informed. I think this is a distortion of human sentiment so hideous that it recalls the slogans of George Orwell's *1984*, and by the way people do not realise that that book was meant to attack any system of power through inquisition, Christian quite as much as Communist.'[106] Some four years later, in a letter published about a year after it had become fully apparent to him that the People's Republic of China had truly started to terrorize his former colleagues, he would declare:

> Orwell considered that the ultimate betrayal of the Left, the worst thing about the way communism had developed, was that it had nearly got back to being as bad as Christianity. For a few centuries the enlightened sceptics had managed to prevent that loathsome system of torture-worship from burning people alive, but it would spring like a tiger again at any opportunity to revive its standard techniques; and in the increasingly crazy modern world, with whole continents regarding Christianity as the only alternative to communism, the opportunity was almost sure to come. Communism had no inherent need to be as torturing as Christianity, but had so far shown itself very ready to learn from its opponent. In the world of Orwell's book, it would be fatuous for the author to mention whether the capital in view was the post-communist or the post-Christian one, because they have become indistinguishable, and maintain a permanent half-hearted state of war merely to secure for both sets of rulers the pleasures of police terror. Surely Orwell made very clear that he considered it the ultimate shame for a man to hand over his conscience either to Stalin the Big Brother or to the incessantly gloating monster God the Father, so that he took pains in his writing to confuse them. Surely the conception of a Ministry of Love, whose towering office hag-rides the city because each citizen believes it has calculated for him the torture he would find most unbearable, corresponds to nothing in communism and a great deal in the history of Christianity.[107]

He offered not one word to explain away the terror-tactics lately perpetrated in China; on the contrary, he earnestly concurred with Orwell that it was 'the ultimate shame for a man to hand over his conscience' to the state.

Two years later he would incorporate that letter, in virtually the same words, into the body of *Milton's God*. And yet one particular change of phraseology is altogether telling: he altered the blank assertion that the concept of a Ministry of Love 'corresponds to nothing in communism' to the formulation that it is 'hard to relate to the ideals of communism'.[108] The shift from an absolute to a qualified statement is actually radical: it gives a sure indication that his days of fellow-travelling were over and done with. He too had come to believe that the People's Republic of China had betrayed its original ideal of establishing a 'popularly inspiriting Socialism',[109] which had formerly filled him with sympathy, and it no longer deserved his support. The Chinese Communists had finally committed what he considered the ultimate crime: they had set about to crush what he had always extolled as 'the astonishing world-embracing hungry cleverness of the old Peita.'

But at least his protracted campaign of answering bad propaganda had yielded him a new mission. From now on, he resolved, he would seek to vindicate the value of rational humanism over Christianity. The Christians, whether clerics or literary critics, must be hoist by their own propaganda. 'Of course,' he said, 'the reason is that I had begun teaching literature for the first time in a Christian country, and...found my colleagues telling pious lies...'

10

'A Mighty Raspberry': *The Structure of Complex Words*

I wanted to offer a coherent linguistic theory about ambiguity...

Letter to Roger Sale, 1973

By the way, the term Ambiguity, which I used in a book title, and as a kind of slogan, implying that the reader is left in doubt between two readings, is more or less superseded by the idea of a double meaning which is intended to be fitted into a definite structure.

SCW, p. 102

*T*HE *Structure of Complex Words*, though it was published on 31 July 1951, took nearly twenty years to drive forward from initial notion to final, albeit flawed, form. Empson can be found writing to his publisher Ian Parsons in October 1935: 'I want to do a real dull book on Language, using formulae, which is more than half written though still shapeless. I hope to be able to send that along next year, but you might well not want to handle it.'[1] Three years later, in February 1939, he seems to have forgotten quite what he had said to Parsons, for he wrote again, self-doubtingly: 'I am trying to pull together a language book, which is mostly finished really but seems to have no shape ... It really ought to be done by the autumn.'[2] He wrote in similar vein to Michael Roberts: 'I want to finish that confused book only it is all scattered in periodicals. It has an unpleasant way of seeming either trivial or crazy.'[3] Later the same month he disclosed to Roberts still more candidly that he was feeling frustrated by having to generate ideas in a critical vacuum: he needed libraries for stimulation and fresh material:

> this year is being a useful burial to get my beastly little linguistic book pulled into some order. There is a faint show of daylight in the jungle and I think it should be finished by July. I hanker after glitter, because the material seems so unreal unless pleasing, but getting rid of that there ought to be a short book making a few decent points. Well then, it is very nice being buried as long as I have that, but there isn't a great deal more I can spin out of my bowels, I don't believe, and it would be bad for me as well as nasty to live here another year with nothing to go home and write, after the lecture.[4]

The last three letters were written from south-west China, where he was putting up with life as a refugee university teacher in severe conditions. But the ambition of completing the work within five months proved to be excessively optimistic. Not least, his war work at the BBC was to absorb all his energies for the duration.

Upon returning to China in the spring of 1947 he resumed work on the book and wrote again to Parsons, as the autumn pressed towards grim winter: 'I am going on steadily with Intraverbal Structure but keep running into puzzles, in fact I am only inventing the theory after tidying up the literary evidence for it, so I don't know how long it shall still take. It is getting much better, I think.'[5] Parsons responded on 4 December 1947, expressing himself in a way that might seem to suggest the working title was already long fixed in the minds of both author and publisher: 'So glad to hear *Intraverbal Structure* is progressing steadily.'[6] It was in fact an exact provisional title, less misleading than the ambiguous title that was ultimately given to the work, but it was never to be referred to again after that exchange—perhaps because the Latinate term was judged to be too pompously rebarbative. By the spring of 1948 the volume was in large part finished, though Empson felt he still had to do a fair amount of tinkering with it. He made use of the flimsy but hefty typescript as his text for a course of lectures presented at the Kenyon Summer School in 1948, believing it did him good to have to expound it. As he wrote to Ian Parsons: 'I hope this process will result in making it less unreadable as I find out what the class can't swallow.'[7] By the end of the third week of August 1948 he paused in San Francisco, while en route back to China, to polish the work. To his wife he wrote, 'I have been through the text of the book again here and am now prepared to post it off tomorrow, and having reached that point am now drinking rather solemnly to see if that makes me think of broad points left out. Not drinking cuts one off very much . . .'[8]

Two days later he posted the text to London, including in his covering letter these less-than-sparkling extenuating reflections: 'I hope you like it. I feel it might be brisker if a lot of qualifications were left out, but it needs I think to give an impression of patient honesty rather than careless "brilliance"—some reviewers thought *Pastoral* was just dashed off, merely because I had taken so much pains to make it easy to read. So I thought a little show of effort this time would do no harm.'[9] (His anxiety that the style of this book should be as 'natural' as possible was to be reflected in another letter to Parsons written in late 1951, and not long after publication: 'I had been feeling that my prose style in the book was too tense and twitchy to be readable or even sound true, so I was comforted by an adverse review in *Tribune* which said the style was so slack, like a fireside chat.')[10] To Richard Eberhart, he wrote a few days later, from on board a freighter back to China, in more unbuttoned mode: 'This book...has been hanging round my neck for years...But I am now a tolerably free man again, and might even try to write some more verse after nearly ten years.'[11]

Over the following months he would dispatch to Chatto & Windus a number of afterthoughts and additional footnotes. Hetta Empson wrote to a friend at the close of 1949: 'William has just got the proofs of his book from England, and is correcting madly and rewriting bits he thinks are too gloomy.'[12] But even after returning the corrected (and partly rewritten) proofs, Empson would now and then submit extra bits and pieces: most notably, the long crucial note on Orwell's *1984* was sent off nearly a year later, on 24 November 1950.[13] More worryingly, Parsons realized as he was looking over the proofs that many of the quotations cited were inaccurate (there was nothing sinister about this, though it was certainly not creditable to the author: it was merely the case that he was careless of scholarly propriety and would anyway quote poetry largely from memory). Parsons had to set to and review all the passages quoted: he found that of the 900-odd quotations, 'about 90% needed corrections—some of a major order'.[14] Empson would in due course complain that Chatto & Windus had dilly-dallied for nearly three years before bringing out his book. He would not admit that a fair part of the delay was due to difficulties of his own making.

Sales were remarkably healthy for a critical work of its kind, and it would continue to sell in very reasonable numbers for several years. Chatto & Windus ordered an initial printing of 4,650 copies (of which 2,000 were to come out in the USA under the imprint of New Directions). By 11 September, just two months after publication, it was reported that

1,350 copies had been sold in the UK. In August 1952, 2,000 copies were required for the second impression; the third impression, in November 1963, called for a further 1,500. It was only in March 1969 that Parsons had to inform Empson that sales were down to 150-200 copies a year—still a fair figure for a literary-linguistic book then in its eighteenth year.

'Owing to a tug between two interests, the book has turned out like a sandwich,' wrote Empson. What he meant was that the beginning and the ending of the volume were predominantly taken up with linguistic theory; the larger layer of the book's filling comprised a series of exemplary critical interpretations of literary texts. Yet that is by no means all: the book actually embraces an extraordinary range of subject-matter, from ethics to the history of ideas and even symbolic logic. Cultural and philosophical development and change are equally to the fore. Nonetheless, balancing itself primarily 'on the borderland' between linguistic theory and literary criticism, *The Structure of Complex Words* is given additional purposeful energy by being what Empson termed (off the record) 'a mighty raspberry'.[15] It undertakes to mount a full-scale onslaught on the reductive theory propounded by his mentor, I. A. Richards, which holds that poetry is fundamentally an 'emotive' genre, and that the emotions in poetry are independent of their sense—and furthermore that any supposed ideas expressed in poetry are best understood as 'pseudo-statements' which cannot be expected to answer to cognitive analysis or even to what any actual person could be imagined to think in the real world. (For a logical positivist, a statement which can not be shown to be true or verifiable must be taken to be emotive.) Richards was ever eager to separate what he called the 'gesture' or 'emotive meaning' of a poem from its sense. Empson's counterblast held that sense and emotion interact with each other, since there cannot possibly be such a thing as a purely emotive use of language. Indeed, Richards's emotivist theory did unacceptable damage: it proposed to deny the words in poetry their right to function as deliberate, rational, explicable communication—and assuredly this amounted to a version of aestheticism. In the face of emotive theory, rational critical analysis would become redundant. Empson put his case thus (with a mildly provocative air) in a later essay: 'I think the "feelings" in the background, though not examined by the speaker, are commonly quite reasonable and can be treated so without further worry.'[16] More surprisingly, Empson maintained, the emotion in a word is supported by a judgement which the speaker would be prepared to back up if an explicit defence were to be called for. He thus believed that the performances of words in their historical contexts can be subjected to analysis in terms of definite logical and classifiable principles.

However, one of the potential problems of the book arises just here, because while Empson denies the idea that he is writing psychology, a number of his analyses do in practice treat unconscious mechanisms as though they are conscious. One of Empson's best contemporary critics, Richard Sleight, acutely remarked on this aspect of the theory: 'When discussing the mostly unconscious methods used by people to communicate verbally, the critic has to decide how much of the explanation is to be hung round what they are aware of, and how far he is going to neglect that and claim to know more about the "real" motives of their thought than they do themselves.'[17] Since most of Empson's examples are taken not from ordinary social discourse but from sophisticated literary texts, such a criticism is difficult to set aside; intention and meaning are not necessarily the same. Empson seeks to pre-empt the problem in his first chapter, when he remarks that 'something quite unconscious and unintentional, even if the hearer catches it like an infection, is not part of an act of communication'[18]—but that ruling might be taken less as a fully conclusive demonstration than as a gesture at foreclosure. All the same, the premise of the book, that language is a public object and therefore subject to forces including changing social circumstances and (especially) the speaker's attitude towards his words, is hard to fault. It had to be right for him to make the attempt, as he persuasively insists at all times, 'to write down the possible alternative structures and meanings in the words'.[19]

The title is at first glance misleading, since the book does not in fact discuss polysyllabic or self-evidently polyvalent words, nor words with complex etymologies, and nor even words which lend themselves to punning (such as 'tight' or 'enduring'), but what Empson described—in a book review dating from February 1936—as 'the individual forces that must be at work behind single words'.[20] (The American critic Cleanth Brooks, reflecting on the inaccuracy of the title *The Structure of Complex Words*, jokily and yet not unreasonably suggested that a better gambit might have been *Four Types of Identity Formation*, to match the earlier *Seven Types of Ambiguity*.)[21] Empson gave his attention to words which are culturally compounded and complex in their meaning in any given period: this is what he called the 'performance "in" the word'. The latter phrase is slightly misleading, as is Empson's frequent recourse to the concept of 'inherence'; it is perhaps easier to reckon that the complexity and the structure pertain less to words themselves than to their meaning or use. Accordingly, the introductory chapters, entitled 'Feelings in Words' and

'Statements in Words', set out the conceptual apparatus—the theory behind the sustained literary analyses which make up the body of the book. Empson came after a certain time to think his opening chapters 'malignant' in their difficulty, but actually they are fairly clear and well-focused, if a little too abstract. All poetry is cognitively accountable, they insist. Words incorporate senses and concomitant aspects which shift in usage from one socio-historical period to another, and from one context to another. As society changes, the senses and implications of simple words likewise shift in intimation and implication. The meanings of such semantic adaptations are central to Empson's enquiries. He aims to show how very often the simplest words, which we take for granted, may operate in the richest ways.

The interrelated entities of a word are Senses, Implications, Moods and Emotions. A *Sense* (Empson invariably and distractingly employs the capital letter to designate his own key terms) is more or less the same as a 'meaning'. A single word can convey two or more senses precisely because of the possibilities it embodies of coordinating and subordinating meanings. *Implications* are best understood as connotations. In all, *Complex Words* sets out five types of possible interrelations of major and secondary meanings and their sub-categories—it would serve no useful purpose to rehearse them all here. A Sense can also be subject to what Empson calls Pregnancy—Appreciative or Depreciative (positive or negative)—depending on whether it is expressed with greater warmth or coolness. It can also express *Moods* (by which the speaker says much 'about his own relations with the person addressed or the person described'). After all, words belong more to speakers than to the things denoted by them; and meaning lies in what the speaker feels about a thing and about his or her audience. Friendly Moods, for example, can convey patronage, while negative Moods tend towards irony.

Given the primacy of such meaningful characteristics in the performance of a word, *Emotions* are awkwardly relegated to the position of everything that is left after meaning has been accounted for—that is, whatever 'is left in the way of "feelings" when these other feelings have been cut out'. So the emotion in a word has to be understood as a public concern: as a function of analysable discourse. Empson is therefore primarily concerned with Senses and Implications. Moods and Emotions have a lesser capacity because they are consequent upon the Senses that correspond to them. 'The emotion in a word, as I am treating it, is an extremely public object, practically as much so as the Sense'; and so the emotions are reckoned to be 'comparatively permanent and simple, and they are used in building structures more elaborate and changeable than themselves. Normally they are dependent on a Sense which is believed to deserve them . . . ' And so this formula for determining 'intraverbal' functions does indeed add up to a radically outspoken assault on Richards's doctrine with regard to emotions and pseudo-statements. It proposes nothing less than to codify an 'inner grammar' (as Empson called it) of single words—corresponding to the 'overt grammar of sentences'—with the aim of weighing up the resourceful and wily conduct of simple but complex words as well as for derogating the sort of emotivist evaluation that Richards favoured. The language of a poem must be allowed to mean something—something relating to life—and not simply to convey factitious or numinal feelings. (The very notion of Richards' category 'pseudo-statement' radically undervalues the imagination; and indeed Richards tended to relegate, or not fully to comprehend, the fictive and dramatic character of literary experience. The point for Empson was not whether a poem speaks for assertions which are absolutely true or false; rather, one needs to imagine the state of mind of some other person for whom the statement could be authentic or true.) Empson noted: 'The trouble is I think that Professor Richards conceives the Sense of a word in a given use as something single, however "elaborate", and therefore thinks that anything beyond that Sense has got to be explained in terms of feelings, and feelings of course are Emotions, or Tones. But much of what appears to us as a "feeling" . . . will in fact be quite an elaborate structure of related meanings.'[22] A single word is thus more resonant with intended meaning and less 'emotive' than Richards would have it. Even a word that seems 'emotive' still carries ascertainable propositions.

What Empson calls 'Statements in Words' are examined in terms of 'Existence Assertions' and 'Equations'. In such terms, a word can incorporate a 'compacted doctrine' simply because of the deceptive manner in which its senses interact with one another. Certain words, on account of the way they function by common understanding within a given social context, are comprehended as conveying certain dubious 'assertions'. But these covert assertions are dangerous because the 'doctrines' they proclaim are so generalized as to become delusory. Crucially, a 'compacted doctrine' is to be differentiated from the use of ambiguity in a literary text, because in the latter case two meanings have been desired and devised: they are intended to be ambiguous. The author, as Empson maintained in *Ambiguity*, is usually aware of 'both the meanings' created 'by the immediate context, which has been twisted around to do it.' In other words the author has worked to stylize language into a double meaning—even 'as if by magic'. On the other hand, in the case of double meanings in the single words which generate covert assertions, the suggestion is: 'everyone agrees with this, so that language itself bears me out.' Such tricksy double meanings appear to be inherent in the nature of language itself. The term *native*, by way of example, may have started out as politically innocent and yet it very soon came to accrue unannounced layers of patronage and eventually rank prejudice. 'A word may become a sort of solid entity, able to direct opinion, thought of as like a person . . . ', Empson maintains. 'I am concerned here with the kind of suggestion in a word which seems to cling to it and can affect opinion . . . The decision . . . to regard the equation as a general truth, is a fairly serious step on the part of a zeitgeist or an individual.'

A moderately politicized little example is the Victorian trick with the word 'delicate'—as used by Oscar Wilde in *Lady Windermere's Fan*: 'Mr Hopper, I am very, very angry with you. You have taken Agatha out on the terrace, and she is so delicate'—which clearly intimates the snobbish notion that a refined young lady is inevitably delicate. Such is the dubious equation condensed into the period use of the word: its covert assertion. That is a simple case of 'A = B'. Yet the contrary disposition, 'B = A', makes one properly doubt the doctrine, since it is certainly not the case that all delicate young women are refined. It is as if two different truths or assertions are identified by way of the unexamined equation. Thus the arrangement in an equation is necessarily non-symmetrical: the predicative identification can really only run in the one direction. Different types of 'equations' arise according to whether 'A' or 'B' behaves as subject or predicate.

One of the reasons why Empson took so long to complete this book is almost certainly because he found he had to wrestle with the evidence before convincing himself that equations in words do not work easily when expressed in reverse order; and that in such perverse cases the assertions that can be generated, as in the case of Orwell's *1984*, may lead to delusion or deception. Even as late as November 1947, he wrote in his notes: 'I keep falling into muddles because I want the equation order to stay fixed, but it apparently has to swap over from "A is like B" or "A normal A is B" to "B is the type of A". In sense and sensibility we get the swap over without any change of order. But we don't in grammar, and we don't in a simple pregnancy like [Hamlet's] "he was a man". It may be because I want the order to stay the same whichever sense is demanded by the immediate context . . . ' A rationalist to the core, he ached to resist the manifest finding that a simple complex word can beget deceit and lies. While pondering a

crucial case in point, the persuasive trick of a false argument (in the chapter
'Mesopotamia')—namely, the age-old issue of whether grammar is to be
regarded as normative and regulatory or as a natural and evolving phenomenon in which 'rules' must needs subscribe to usage—he remarked to
himself: 'As to grammar, the alternatives for the Usage theory seemed to
be "correctness is merely usage" and "usage is the only real criterion for
grammar"—"how people actually talk is the typical part of what grammar
is about". Here there is a swap over, but the first equation may be merely a
delusion and "usage is correctness" could hold the field (the inverse for the
Authoritarian view only needs some Authority putting in it.) In short I still
don't at all understand the crucial point which has puzzled me all along.'[23]

He argues further, in his chapter on 'Metaphor', that 'a metaphor is the
opposite of an equation'.[24] An equation can be more potent than a
metaphor since it carries a covert assertion, whereas a metaphor feels
more 'like direct description.' 'A metaphor goes outside the ordinary
range of a word, and an equation "argues from" the ordinary range,
treating it as a source of traditional wisdom'. Strangely, a word can be
more wily in its behaviour than a metaphor.

Empson's stab at linguistics is meant to be applied; he believed there was
little purpose to a theory unless it contributed to the exegesis of literary
effects. He confesses in chapter two: 'Perhaps it is as well to explain that I
did most of the work on the large scale examples given in later chapters
before I had arrived at the classification of Types given in this one . . . Thus
I am more sure of the general literary account than I am of the classifying
fitted onto it.'[25] That disarmingly candid admission refers to the rewarding
literary-critical heart of the volume: specifically, the dozen chapters (3–14)
which explore what he styles 'key words' and the 'covert assertions' they
embody within a series of specific literary texts. To determine precisely
how 'pet words' can embody 'compacted doctrines' is the ultimate object
of the exercise. The key words discussed in detail are *wit, all, fool, dog, honest,
sense, sensibility*, and *candid*. (Empson also takes the incidental opportunity to
draw up a brilliant diagram of the range of meanings in *quite*.) On the face
of it, many of those words would seem to be unpromising, since they are
not the value-laden terminology of the official language (which might
include such terms as *nature, justice, truth, right, faith, God*); and yet Empson
chose to fasten upon such apparently unambitious or neutral words precisely because they stand apart from, and even dissent or detract from,
officialese. 'A man tends finally to make up his mind, in a practical
question of human relations, much more in terms of these vague rich
intimate words than in the clear words of his official language.'[26] He

explains why at many points, but this is an instance from 'The English Dog':

> It is surely a striking reflection that a great deal of the thought of a man like Dr Johnson, and probably the parts of his thought which are by this time most seriously and rightly admired, were not carried on his official verbal machinery but on colloquial phrases ...; phrases that he would have refused to analyse on grounds of dignity, even if he had been able to.... there is a claim to be made for the branch of study I am touching on here. You need to know, as well as the serious opinions of a man in the society, how much weight he would allow, when making a practical decision, to some odd little class of joke phrases, such as excite, he would feel, sentiments obvious to any agreeable person, and yet such as carry doctrines more really complex than the whole structure of his official view of the world.[27]

Accordingly, many of the words Empson investigates are deeply encoded with mischief and paradox. They also often criticize or defy the pronouncements of value ordained by Church or State. They are inherently a good deal more shifty, equivocal and critical than doctrinal or institutionally declarative words. Most of the examples are taken from Shakespeare (*King Lear*, *Timon of Athens*, *Othello*, *Measure for Measure*), though works by Milton, Pope, Wordsworth, and Jane Austen are also subjected to analysis, as well as numerous lesser instances ranging from Boswell's *Tour to the Western Islands* to Fielding's *Tom Jones*, and from *Pilgrim's Progress* to *The Beggar's Opera*. Not all of the essays are of an equally rewarding standard, but several do successfully illuminate the flexing intimations and implications of selected key words as they have been put to use.

Among the best chapters, 'Wit in the *Essay on Criticism*' explores the gambit of that 'smart flat little word' as Pope deploys it again and again, with divergent values, through the course of his poem. Chiefly, it is argued, Pope nimbly surmounts the severe limitations of the Augustan canons of criticism by exploiting the jokey play 'in' the word *wit* (a seemingly unassuming word with fun built into it) to hint at complex covert assertions within and beyond the immediate context. *Wit* as Pope makes use of it in his poetry wriggles itself between various meanings—primarily, wit as bright social talker, wit as critic, wit as poet—and the poetry develops both collusive and quasi-subversive 'equations' along that axis. Readers who appreciate the parodic effects Pope exploits derive the fullest enjoyment from the work. 'The equations are not supposed to show Pope's final opinions, only the basis of common assumption that he accepted and played upon.' Empson's sensitivity to social tone is in tune with Pope's sense of balance.[28]

Shakespeare inspires some of the most revelatory criticism in *The Structure of Complex Words*. Some critics of *Ambiguity* had found fault with the specific analyses Empson essayed, often because the passages scrutinized in it were extrapolated from their larger dramatic or fictional contexts. In the later volume Empson shows just how much he had heeded the criticism. While not forsaking the method of close analysis, he also (often but not always) raises his sights to offer critical estimates of plot, character, thematic development and overall meaning, and indeed the metaphysics of the literary works under consideration—readings generated by the reverberant or spinning behaviour of a single key term. In *King Lear*, for example, the word 'fool...is used (by the way) forty-seven times,' observes Empson in a curious phrase—as if the very high incidence of the term were almost an incidental matter. He goes on, therefore, in 'Fool in Lear', to take his cue from Erasmus's treatment, in *The Praise of Folly* (the subject of the preceding chapter), of the paradox by which types of simpleness and innocence—ranging from simpletons and children to madmen and saints—can be regarded as reflecting one another, and then applies it to a fresh view of the functions of the simple and the sophisticated in Shakespeare's theatre. Of the mirroring of clowns and madmen, he observes: 'it is true I think that the types both had a sort of magical aura; both were outside society and therefore in touch with wild forces, or anyway in a position to criticize society as aliens.'[29] As so often in Empson's work, the singular insight ramifies throughout the book to the point where it becomes a major motif; here the idea of clowns and madmen being interpreted as outsiders and critics harks back to one of the key themes of *Some Versions of Pastoral* which can also be seen to be threaded through several of the essays in *Complex Words*. 'The English Dog', for instance, ponders the code of values of the Restoration aristocrat, and then rapidly seizes upon— with a sense of surprise that obviously delights Empson—this dashing perception: 'Dog, it is absurd but half-true to say, became to the eighteenth-century sceptic what God had been to his ancestors, the last security behind human values...It is the pastoral idea, that there is a complete copy of the human world among dogs, as among swains or clowns.'[30] He pushes through to this seemingly topsy-turvy aperçu (one rather unimaginative critic was later to slight Empson's essay as a case of 'learned buffoonery')[31] by way of reflecting on what he terms the 'humanist application'—that is to say, 'something vaguely anti-Christian'—which throws up this profound further truth: 'The fundamental novelty was an idea that "Man is no longer an abortive deity, born in sin, necessarily incomplete in the world, but the most triumphant of the animals". To call him a dog playfully is thus to insist on his rights; he is better than a dog, but has the same reasons for being cheerful. It brings in a sort of pastoral feeling to do this; that there is a sweetness or richness in the simple thing, that to cut yourself off from it would be folly, that it holds *in posse* all later values.'[32] Likewise, the chapter called 'Honest Man' reflects upon the apparent redundancy or rudeness of being required, or choosing, to address or even praise someone else as 'honest'. And then—it is again expressed in a way that speaks for his genuine surprise at having followed through this formula—Empson breaks out into an invigorating riff, reeling off this string of logical paradoxes:

> But in the new [Restoration] sense the word at once developed irony. As something normally demanded, not something admired when pointed out, it could be used for patronage, especially by contrast with the hearty use among friends. A man you praised for mere honesty was in a position where it was hard to be honest, or could not be praised for anything else. The clash of this with the permanent claims of the word then gave convenient twists to express both pastoral sentiment and rogue sentiment; you could retain a touch of the patronage in warm praise for simple people, and also praise rogues with it as not being hypocrites, where one sense of the word is used directly though the effect is ironical. The hearty use among friends could then throw in both pretended patronage and a hint that the friend was a rogue; hence you could imply that you preferred your friend to be a fundamental rock-bottom man, and that this figure is independent of the laws of society. Also the truth-telling aspect then acquired the prominence which it still holds; this tended to imply that the rogue or friend was an amusing critic, ready to blow the gaff.[33]

Just such a minor 'pastoral idea' becomes central to *King Lear* because, as Empson discerns it, the dramatic paradoxes of the powerfully spinning word 'fool', which enable the likes of madmen and saints to mirror one another, are linked up with the major conception of pastoral as Empson reformulated it in *Some Versions of Pastoral*. His ultimately subversive demonstration in *Pastoral* was that any secular hero who functions as the scapegoat and sacrifice might stand as a secret rival to the Christ, the supreme redeemer and reconciler. So too, in assessing the meaning of *King Lear*, Empson questions the received wisdom, set down by A. C. Bradley in his *Shakespearian Tragedy* (1904), that the death of the king is the sign of religious reconciliation: a holy end to human suffering. He accepts the point that 'the root idea of tragedy [is] that the sacrifice of the hero re-unites his tribe with Nature or with supernatural forces', but he firmly jettisons the idea that Lear's death speaks for a pietistic closure: a blessed death in the hands of the Christian God. Empson's ultimate reading of the play may feel a bit bleak, but it is actually extremely subtle, capacious, and humane:

> It is thoroughly Christian to say that Nature is inadequate to the human spirit, and that the world will come to an end... On the other hand, of course, I do think that the suggestions of a fundamental horror in the play were meant to be prominent... [I]t was reasonable and not theologically suspicious to have this background of cosmic horror, because the play was about the huge evils which could follow from a false renunciation.
>
> Where there does seem room for a religious view is through a memory of the Erasmus fool, that is, by being such a complete fool Lear may become in some mystical way superlatively wise and holy. It seems hard to deny that this idea is knocking about, and yet I think it belongs to the play rather than the character.... And the scapegoat who has collected all this wisdom for us is viewed at the end with a sort of hushed envy, not I think really because he has become wise but because the general human desire for experience has been so glutted in him; he has been through everything.[34]

Such a mature interpretation correctly holds that the overall meaning or 'moral' of the play is larger than the suffering of Lear; and so indeed it properly puts the king back into the play. So too, it takes pains to reposition the play as a tragedy by challenging the sentimental view (enunciated by Bradley) that Lear dies of a passion of joy. Empson admired and often emulated in his own work Bradley's predominantly character-based criticism, but in this case he believed there was a deeper wisdom, albeit harsh, in George Orwell's argument that Lear is 'still cursing, still not understanding anything' at the end.[35] It is not surprising that even ten years after the publication of *Complex Words* he was disturbed to find himself named, and (as he felt) shamed, in an article by Barbara Everett, in a group of contemporary critics who echoed Bradley's sense of a fulfilling closure to *King Lear*.[36] He insisted in a published reply to Everett that he had been concerned in his book only to endorse the severe realism of Orwell's reading:

> I failed even to make anyone rebut this view; perhaps from not being clear enough, but anyhow it seems to be unmentionable. To accept it, one need not deny that Lear achieves his renunciation and regeneration, in the 'I will drink it' and 'birds in a cage' scenes. The point is that the story knocks him off his perch; when Cordelia is hanged, he again wants revenge and kills the slave who was doing it. What is more, we should think worse of him if he continued to be a non-attached yogi; the reason why the play has to kill

Cordelia, which has so often been found wanton, is that we need to know whether Lear's renunciation of the world will survive her death...

The Orwell view thus seems to me to make a better play, so far as the difference is noticeable. The reason why no one will mention it, I think, is that it doesn't feel religious enough...[37]

Such is the continuity of interests between *Pastoral* and *Complex Words* that it feels surprising that Empson did not make use of *King Lear* as a prime example of the pastoral mode in the earlier book. It is relevant at least to note that some of the essays in the two books were worked out virtually cheek-by-jowl, in parallel—and indeed, 'the choice of words was already made when I wrote my *Pastoral*'.[38]

It might readily be argued, and it was indeed to be argued by some reviewers of Empson's book, that other terms in *King Lear*—not least *Nature*, *animal*, and *division*—have as much linguistic and interpretative prominence and scope as the word *fool* upon which Empson had elected to centre his interpretation of the play. But no one can deny that the word *honest* is a master key to *Othello*. What Empson achieves in his chapter 'Honest in Othello' is at once to catch the word in its historical flight, at a time of rapid transition, and to offer a suggestive insight into Shakespeare's mentality. In the two preceding chapters, 'Honest Man' and 'Honest Numbers', Empson revelled in the flexibility of the word *honest* as it journeyed down to the Restoration. A word of multiple ironies, it gained status especially in terms of the cult of Independence, since it was useful for expressing both pastoral sentiment and rogue sentiment among men of higher class. When spoken in hearty fashion of, or to, a friend, *honest* might signify generous, loyal, amusing, courageous, unhampered by religion, not a Puritan. Empson expatiates further upon the word: 'There is an obscure paradox that the selfish man is the generous one, because he is not repressed, has "good nature", and so on. Also he tends to have "natural ease", which was then specially prominent as a test virtue of the gentleman.'[39] Still more, he contends, *honest* becomes hooked up to *rogue*, because the latter would readily be used with appreciably humorous irony—as between friends who chaff one another with slang words. In terms of pastoral: 'The swain may tell simple truths or illustrate profound ones but the rogue can only a get a foothold in the word honest by being "not a hypocrite".' All the same, *rogue* and *honest* would happily bed down together in their implicature when they moved up the social scale and were made use of for 'the affectionate pretence of insult' (a bantering trick which has carried on down even to the present day, albeit with a different lexis): 'you pretend that your friend is a rogue,' notes Empson, 'and this is not really insulting because you are supposed to pretend that you are one too. Rogue sentiment is then in play, with the idea "we can afford to talk like this, in our closed circle, among ourselves"'.[40]

The most extraordinary highlight in Empson's account of the word *honest* as Shakespeare deployed it, so conspicuously and so rangingly, in *Othello* is his remark that Shakespeare had somehow seen the future in the word and deplored its coming loucheness or decadence. For one thing, contemporary audience-response to the vicious rogue, Iago (to a degree, the audience was amused by him, and even indulgent towards him in a manner that ran close to connivance), made Shakespeare suspect the ironic trickery brewing up in that very wicked word. This explains why the prevalent ironic use of the word in Shakespeare leans invariably towards sarcasm and contempt, not to the fellow-feeling or rogue-sentiment that the Restoration would embrace with a will. 'Four columns of honest in the Shakespeare Concordance show that he never once allows the word a simple hearty use between equals,' Empson remarks. 'Some low characters get near it, but they are made to throw in contempt.'[41] Given the constraints that Shakespeare seems to have set upon *honest*, Empson argues that the playwright had anticipated the insidious suggestions growing up within the word. 'What Shakespeare hated in the word, I believe, was a peculiar use, at once hearty and individualist, which was then common among raffish low people but did not become upper-class till the Restoration...'[42] Whereas *honest* implies, at face value, qualities such as 'generous' and 'faithful to friends', the word was already—even by the turn of the seventeenth century—laced with still more unstable and equivocal insinuations. 'The suggestion of "stupid" in a patronizing use of *honest*... brings it near to *fool*; there is a chance for these two rich words to overlap. There is an aspect of Iago in which he is the Restoration "honest fellow", who is good company because he blows the gaff...'[43] In the elaborate make-up of Iago there is also a large proportion of the puritan, who 'despises his pleasures' even while gratifying himself with 'discovering enormous sins in the very act of being particularly righteous'. Yet at the same time Iago is thought by everyone else to be 'a worldly good fellow' (dependable, loyal, truth-telling—'a fundamental rock-bottom man'). Since he prides himself too on his sharp understanding of human nature and behaviour, it comes as an enormous dramatic and moral shock when Emilia eventually scorns him as 'such a fool'. 'The cynic had always hated to be treated as a harmless joker, and what finally roused him into stabbing her was perhaps that he thought she had called him a clown. The

Lion and the Fox are thus united in the word...'[44] There is not space enough here to do justice to Empson's full reading of the character and the play, but it is worth noting that his diagram of the word is actually set out with a winningly modest provisionality:

> there seems a suggestion of trickery or triviality about saying that the character is only made plausible by puns on one word...But it is clear I think that all the elements of the character are represented in the range of meanings of 'honest', and...that the confusion of moral theory in the audience, which would make them begin by approving of Iago (though perhaps only in the mixed form of the 'ironical cheer') was symbolised or echoed in a high degree by the confusion of the word.[45]

On the other hand, Empson is a good deal less comprehending with respect to Othello's conduct, principally—or so it would appear—because he felt, or had persuaded himself to feel, out of sympathy with sexual jealousy:

> I know that a critic ought at least to put up a claim to understand human nature, but I cannot show any expertise here; because it seems to me that Othello's principles about the matter were all wrong, let alone the way he applied them. The advent of contraceptives has taken a lot of strain off the topic, but I am not sure that the attitude of the Elizabethans was as simple as they pretended.[46]

The lore that jealous husbands boil over with a feeling of such grossly wounded pride that they are prompt to murder their wives is overplayed, he contends, since it belongs more to legend than to legal history. There is another tradition—that the happy cuckold, so far from feeling shamefully bothered by the jeering heaped upon him in the theatre and in popular verse, knew which side his bread was buttered on. After all, the complaisant husband may have more than one useful reason to be complacent. The arrangement could work out as affording a career opportunity, for example, and the cuckold is anyway saved a great deal of trouble and expense. Perhaps cuckolds arouse popular rancour simply because they have secured an advantage to themselves in some such way. Shakespeare had obviously experienced jealousy, Empson concedes, but he did not hold it up as a principle of behaviour. The argument might be felt to be dubious or cynical, but Empson was actually concerned to step up the propaganda for willing cuckolds. So far from being invariably contemptible or pathetic (as in popular songs), a cuckold might have calculated on an enlightened self-interest, or think of it as an act of friendship to share the wife with a man he fancies—or even longs for—for his own sake. This unusual line of argument that Empson expounded, and espoused, ran beyond theory: he felt it could be sustained by his own experience. All told, 'Honest in Othello' presents a very cogent account of Iago, but it is less convincing on Othello; less convincing in the suggestion that Othello's Honour speaks to Iago's honesty, or that both of them are 'versions of the Independent Man'—a very fine Empsonian slogan that is not fully worked out through the evidence. The *TLS* reviewer was to note that 'for the most part Empson ignores the various pointers directing us to concentrate attention on the nature of Othello himself—especially the heroic rhetoric...In general the reader may feel that one aspect of the play comes to obscure the whole.'[47] But what Empson is especially adroit at is in his outwitting of earlier critics such as E. E. Stoll who had quarrelled with the inconsistencies and improbabilities of the ways in which Othello and Iago are characterized. Why do we expect human nature to be ultimately so nice and tidy? 'Perhaps I am a bad judge of inconsistency,' Empson quips, 'because it seems to me that few writers have dared to make people as eccentric as they really are...' But the real trouble, with respect to his reading of this particular tragic hero, is that Empson does not quite credit Othello's wrathful jealousy.

If Empson's interpretation of *Othello*, and especially of the figure of Iago, is worked out with an impressive fullness by way of the varying manifestations and equations of *honest*, he does not manage quite so well with the word *sense* in *Measure for Measure*. Certainly it seems true that Shakespeare developed compound meanings from the word *sense*, most crucially in those passages in which Angelo is astonished to discover in himself an unprecedented degree of *sense* (in the sense of *sensuality*), whereas elsewhere in the play the term usually suggests knowledge or dark intelligence, and rarely sensibility. In the preceding essay, which borrows Jane Austen's title 'Sense and Sensibility', Empson keenly unfolds the interplay between those key terms as they had developed by the late eighteenth century. The logic with which he gathers up all the implications is exceptionally strong and pleasing, but for the sake of economy I must extrapolate only some of the steps. Sense and sensibility, he explains,

> both combine the ideas of reception-of-sensations and reaction-to-contexts [but] they make opposite covert assertions...[T]he ideas follow from the presumption that *sensibility* names a kind of special power of sensing, and that *sense* is radically opposed to it...For example *sense* does not imply that a good reaction is often painful and commonly outside your control, though this is true enough about reception of stimuli; the word considers sensations as means of knowledge not of suffering...[I]n the simple use of *sense* the

judgement and the sensation are admitted to be quite different, though they are compared; in the doctrinal use they are seriously included in one vast kingdom, and good judgement is made king of it . . . *[S]ense* is the simple and general word for all degrees of capacity, whereas *sensibility* brings in, through "ability" or what not, the idea of a high degree; it tends to imply some theoretical view of the matter, and perhaps by being a "long" word can suggest a high-falutin tone . . . In the more doctrinal uses, the individualist idea in *sense* will also tend to cut out emotion . . . [I]n *sensibility* people tend to feel that the judgement really is inherent in the sensations . . . It seems to me that to read equations into the words is the natural way to handle these broad but vague covert assertions, and if you take the whole development of *sense* you can hardly say that it has less inherence doctrine than sensibility.[48]

But the best part of Empson's analysis of *Measure for Measure* comes when he seeks to take the measure of every trait and action of the Duke that bothers the twentieth-century reader:

> *Measure for Measure* is I think one of the most striking cases where the feelings in his words jib at a wholehearted acceptance of the story . . . [T]he higher you pitch the ethics of the Duke, the more surprising you must find his character.
>
> It seems hard not to regard him as a comic character . . . [T]he combination of vanity and cowardice cannot be intended for praise . . .
>
> What is really offensive about the Duke is . . . that he should treat his subjects as puppets for the fun of making them twitch. But here, I suppose, the Character is saved by the Plot . . . [I]t amounts to pretending to write a romantic comedy and in fact keeping the audience's teeth slightly on edge.[49]

Measure for Measure may have started out as a morality play, but (as Empson deduces) Shakespeare 'found he did not like his saints when he had got them'. The argument was by no means new in 1951—W. W. Lawrence's *Shakespeare's Problem Comedies* (1931) had argued that the Duke is best construed as a function of the plot rather than as a fully realized character—but Empson certainly makes it feel new. That is one of the high moments, when the reader rejoices in Empson more for his clarifying insight than for all the teasing-out of equations and his heady reading into the word *sense* of 'broad but vague covert assertions'. He climaxes his analysis with the curious observation that 'the performance with . . . *sense* is made to echo the thought of the play very fully up to the end . . . [T]he word was made to echo controversial questions that were both subtle and pressing . . . but it was not made to come down on one side of the fence till considerably after his time.'[50] More usually, when Empson feels on rather stronger ground, he claims not that the words work as an echo to the sense but that they are equated with it.

For a long time, Romantic poetry had been regarded as a stumbling block for the methods of close critical analysis, so it was a bold but necessary step for Empson to test his theory of complex words against the poetry of Wordsworth. Surprisingly, 'Sense in *The Prelude*' is one of the sharpest chapters in the volume, demonstrating as it does just how Wordsworth brings together the extreme ends of a scale that runs all the dizzying way from Sensation to Imagination. In Wordsworth, the word *sense* (Empson maintains) 'means both the process of sensing and the supreme act of imagination, and unites them by a jump... [W]hat is jumped over is "good sense"; when Wordsworth has got his singing robes on he will not allow any mediating process to have occurred.'[51] Whereas some readers have seen muddle and bluster, or the usual visionary afflatus of the Romantics, Empson respectfully concludes of Wordsworth's poem: 'It does not seem unfair to say that he induced people to believe he had expounded a consistent philosophy through the firmness and assurance with which he used equations... equations whose claim was false, because they did not really erect a third concept as they pretended to...'[52] That is a very fair judgement. Empson felt no need to apologize for admiring the thrilling oratory orchestrated in *The Prelude* when he remarked that Wordsworth 'was much better at adumbrating his doctrine through rhetorical devices than in writing it out in full.'[53] As in all of the better essays in the volume, Empson manifests a keen historical awareness, an appreciation of the changing shape of words through evolving social contexts.

Given Empson's passion for semantics, it was natural that in the closing chapter of *The Structure of Complex Words* he should turn his critical attention not only to lexicography but also to metalexicography (the study of how words are treated in dictionaries). All available dictionaries, he discovered, fall short both in the way they represent shifts of meaning (often enough, they make no attempt to show how a word has developed) and in their modes of definition. To take an extreme but authentic example, he pointed out, a learner who looks up the phrase 'a rough claret' will be advised that *rough* can mean either or both *drastic* and *riotous*; so how on earth is the learner to tell which is the right one? The introduction to the *Compact Oxford English Dictionary* takes care to state that there is no especial significance to the order of synonyms supplied under any definition, with the consequence that the list of possible explanations for the word *rough* yields (among a spread of examples) *startling, hairy, entirely unwrought*. (Empson had written to I. A. Richards about this sort of egregious problem as early as 1939: 'Striking how Fowler can say the point about *broad* clearly and quickly in Modern English Usage but even in the later edition of the Concise Oxford seems to think he isn't allowed to—it can only be done by giving the difference from *wide*.')[54] Thus the learner has little choice other than to take pot luck, with the result that he may easily stumble into error or absurdity. The series of synonyms works most like a thesaurus; and yet when Empson took the trouble to ask the editors of the 'reckless' *NED* (later *OED*) whether they had proposed in practice to construct a thesaurus, this was denied. His conclusion seems impeccable: the *NED* is mistaken in its practice of numbering 'up to thirty meanings for a common word without showing the smallest interest in how anyone ever comes to pick out the right one, let alone how they overlap'; and 'once a dictionary has adopted the practice of circular definition, it is in a sense committed to compiling a thesaurus in a cumbrous manner'. A nice epitome of this genuine problem is provided in another chapter, on 'Sensible and Candid', where Empson cites headings 4 and 5 of the *NED*'s account of *candid*:

> 4 free from malice; 'not desirous to find fault', 'gentle, courteous'; favourably disposed, favourable, kindly (1633)
> 5 frank, open, ingenuous, straight-forward; sincere in what one says (1675).
>
> One must admire the great work in '4' for making the definitions grow slowly from the idea of the just judge to that of the judge prejudiced in your own favour. But '5' I think confuses ideas which are more seriously opposed; telling truth against yourself (the early one) and exposing other people to their faces (the late one). All the defining words cover both, and this hides a thing you want to know—the process that took the word from one to the other; I imagine it was a clear-cut jump due to irony.[55]

His recommendation, in the final chapter, 'Dictionaries', has a very fine logic to it: 'My general proposal is that the interactions of the senses of a word should be included... [W]hat would need a certain amount of space would be marking the turn to a new head sense at a given period, and the resulting change in equation structure.' The structures of complex words develop over time; so do their meanings, values and feelings; and yet dictionaries seem often to be content with denotation. Empson's point was that the challenge is not just lexicographical, it is philosophical. In short, dictionaries ought to practise the approach to usage and change, and the findings, set out in *Complex Words*. Yet he was realistic enough to know that such a constructive proposal would never be acted upon.

In October 1951 Empson wrote to his publisher with seeming surprise: 'The reviews seem very friendly...'[56] He had seen only some of the reviews of the UK edition. American reviews were not to reach him until more than six months after publication date. He still berated himself for the difficulties of his opening gambit, 'Feelings in Words'—'I feel now,' he went on in the same letter, 'that the first chapter is almost intolerable, as several people have delicately hinted, but maybe it gives a certain dignity if you bully the reader at the beginning and try to entertain him afterwards'—but in the main the British reviews found the book both demanding and rewarding. Even adverse reviewers recognized an access of maturity, as well as a conspicuous depth of thought and insight. It was not uncommon for critics to compliment portions of the work, usually the literary chapters, while feeling Empson was constructing an analytical mountain out of a theoretical molehill. One reviewer was to sum up this trend with this pronouncement: 'if Empson could bring himself to focus upon some larger critical issue and produce a book less narrowly concerned with pushing to extremes a minor obsession with semantics, he would do much to efface his reputation as an eccentric. Perhaps he likes that reputation, but in the best parts of *Complex Words* there is a rationality, a maturity of critical judgment, that ought to be given freer play.'[57] Other critics objected to the way he pursued off-hand judgements or recondite ideas: often amusingly but at times irrelevantly. Empson relished the business of having to justify himself by writing letters in response to foolish or aggressive reviews, so it was with evident disappointment that he reported to Parsons in January 1952: 'There has been no real theoretical attack that I have seen, though some expressions of distaste of course.'[58]

The one aspect of the book that was widely distasted by reviewers was Empson's endeavour to devise a system of symbols for each specific potential element—social, psychological, literary—implied in a single word's structure of meanings, so that their interplay could be observed and discussed. The complications of this quasi-mathematical approach— albeit Empson claimed that his symbols 'are no more mathematical than road-signs'—could ultimately produce such a terrifying formula as this equation: $3c + ? 2 = 1a - .1\$1$ (p. 89), which accounts for the trick of Pope's play with the word *wit* in *The Essay on Criticism*.[59] The introduction of what Empson dubbed his 'little bits of machinery' alienated a majority of reviewers. Austin Duncan-Jones called it an 'unbearable algebra prep', and observed further: 'Bits of machinery pop up here and there, but in the particularised discussions they become less and less conspicuous. They do not seem to hamper the workings of Mr Empson's penetrating intelligence, and indeed I suppose they must help it—perhaps as a private mnemonic.'[60] Cleanth Brooks too doubted whether the machinery really pays its way: 'is it worthwhile trying to pin down the semantic transaction on a chart so finely scaled?'[61] However, apart from that area of critical vexation, the book was treated with a good deal of respectful reflection.

Ian Watt, in the *Cambridge Review* (17 November 1951), felt some awe at the scope and depth of what Empson had achieved. '*The Structure of Complex Words* contains matter enough for several volumes of its size,' he declared, concluding: 'In the last analysis, what Mr Empson offers is not primarily semantic. He focuses on complex words because they are the most direct and valuable evidence for the understanding of our cultural tradition . . . The promise of the approach seems unbounded. The achievement is great, not only in originality, insight and entertainment, but in truth and substance. So great that Mr Empson's right to be called the most distinguished literary critic of his generation can hardly now be questioned.'

Richard Sleight drew towards the close of his intelligent critical evaluation of the book with an acknowledgement of the force of Empson's proposals vis-à-vis dictionaries. 'Oddly enough the logical analyses of sense in the *O.E.D.* work *against* their historical arrangement.' He concluded that in the book as a whole Empson 'successfully rebuts those critics who would describe his work as nonsense or unscientific, and a product of the haphazards of individual taste . . . Irritating, difficult and wrong-headed though it often is, *The Structure of Complex Words* is unquestionably the most important contribution to critical theory since [T. S. Eliot's] *The Sacred Wood*.'[62] On the other hand, the academic philosopher Austin Duncan-Jones ended up by finding fault with a number of aspects of the book, including both what he called its 'logical monstrosities' and the fact that the author gave 'some countenance to the biographical heresy—the opinion that to understand a work of the imagination is to reconstitute the experiences of its writer; from which it would follow that the ultimate tests of an interpretation were extraneous . . .'[63] Empson jumped at his opportunity to slug back at his opponent. 'I consider that I committed no "logical monstrosities" and indeed that I have no detailed criticism to answer under that head. The idea that "a logician" looks down on these matters from a height and somehow knows that you mustn't say a word is complex to mean that its operation is complex, seems to me absurd; if a training in logic makes a man stupider than he would be without it, that is only to its discredit.' And to follow that splendidly quasi-aphoristic rebuff he chose to fly in the face of contemporary critical doctrine: 'As to the "personalist [biographical] heresy", I think that a reader should try to decide what his author intended to say... Any theory designed to give a shorter answer, I think, loses touch with common sense.'[64] In answer to another review, he reiterated: 'I think a critic should have an insight into the mind of his author, and I don't approve of the attack on "The Fallacy of Intentionalism".'[65] Only a feebly doctrinaire Behaviourist would deny a critic of imaginative literature the natural right to imagine someone else's feelings. Unfortunately, Empson's riposte to Duncan-Jones was never published in *Mind*.

In the USA, the book received extensive and largely thoughtful coverage in periodicals ranging from *Arizona Quarterly* to *Kenyon Review*. Some critics, like Robert Gorham Davis in *Partisan Review*, found it a great achievement. In the 'primarily literary essays', wrote Davis, there is 'a wonderful wealth of original perceptions and recondite information, all fascinating in its own right.'[66] In *Hudson Review*, on the other hand, the flashy young Hugh Kenner was less hospitable. His objection to what he called an 'atomic theory of language' was that long poems 'can't really be reduced to the intricacies of their key-words'. *Ambiguity* had possessed an 'infectious zest... like that of a boy taking watches apart,' decreed Kenner; but in *Complex Words* Empson, 'whose charm has always depended on a sort of Alice-persona, has accommodated himself to his own image of the Victorian scientist'.[67]

Cleanth Brooks, in *Kenyon Review*, adjudged still more severely: 'This is the most mixed-up book that Empson has written to date. It makes excursions into linguistics, semantics, the history of ideas, social psychology, the history of the language, author psychology, anthropology, etc.'; Empson is ragged as 'the incorrigible amateur'. Brooks admired a number of local things in the book, and yet he still summed it up as 'provocative and seminal, but... also much more than the earlier books, a kind of ragbag'.[68] In addition, Brooks spoke for a majority of reviewers, both British and American, when he questioned—having felt irritated by Empson's analysis of the word *all* in *Paradise Lost*—'Why did Empson choose *all*? Because of its sheer statistical frequency? Or because Empson believes as he says, that Milton was an "all-or-none" man...? How does Empson know that Milton was an all-or-none man? And how does he know that "Milton's feelings were crying out against his appalling theology in favour of freedom, happiness and the pursuit of truth"?'[69]

Empson took the occasion to rebuff Brooks in a fashion that amounted to a snub to the whole 'school' of New Criticism (of which he was deemed by a number of readers, on the basis of *Ambiguity*, to be one of the founding fathers), for its narrow, quasi-behaviouristic doctrine that nothing must be countenanced in the act of criticism other than the written text (historical occasion and author's intention were declared to be extraneous to the poem and irrelevant to the critic):

> I feel I ought to answer the charge, in Mr Cleanth Brooks' friendly review of my book *Complex Words* that it is extremed mixed-up . . . He asks why I chose to talk about *all* in Milton, and how I know that Milton was an all-or-none man. Actually I chose because the Kenyon Summer School put me down for Milton by mistake, but it struck me this was good luck, because *all* is an interesting test case; it cannot be supposed to attract complex meanings, and yet it is clearly important for Milton's style, perhaps because he is clearly an all-or-none man. I would be a more 'responsible' literary critic, says Mr Cleanth Brooks, if I did not start hares like this. But I was being responsible about my linguistic theory, taking the case hardest for it to handle that I could think of; as to Milton, I am free to admit I know what every competent reader of him knows. What is really being felt by Mr Cleanth Brooks is that a literary critic must behave like a psychologist or what not; he must pretend he doesn't know what is ordinary knowledge till he has proved it by his direct analysis of the text before him. I think this claim to rigour often becomes a mere artificial elegance in the scientists, and then confuses them; it is obviously not needed for some kinds of literary criticism.[70]

Three years later, he stressed in a letter to Brooks (who went on trying to make him toe the New Critical line he was believed to have drawn in the first place):

> I do not know why you say that I have decisively abandoned some old positions that I may be said to have pioneered; I do not think I have abandoned any; but in any case I would always have been against any pig-headed cast-iron dogmatic position such as the Rejection of Intentionalism . . .
>
> As to 'impressionism', I seriously do think that a critic is no good unless he has impressions; and relies on them, apart from the processes of checking and making sure which nobody has argued against in principle. My book on Ambiguity, if I may go back to that, continually said that the analyses were only supposed to show what happened in the mind of the fit reader (and there were plenty of such readers). To say that the reader ought to abandon all attempt to use his imagination, especially in imagining what the author intended (but must instead follow rules laid down by some master critic) seems to me to abandon the whole instrument which is all we have for appreciating works of art.[71]

It is worth noting here that worthy attempts have been made from time to time to trace a line of critical-theoretical descent from Richards and Empson directly to the New Critics and thence to the more recent school of deconstructionists. Professor John Carey has commented: 'The vogue for "deconstruction" in the 1970s—regarded at the time as dazzlingly new and French—was basically a re-run of Empson's ideas' (the putative 'ideas' of *Seven Types of Ambiguity*, that is to say). However, if the pyrotechnics of *Ambiguity* gave Empson any cause for regret, it would surely have been because commentators took the improvident genius of that book as sufficient in itself to have him sire what he regarded as the pretentious rigour of those very schools of criticism. New Critics constantly made efforts to call him to order, especially when it seemed to them that he was behaving like the sow eating her own farrow, although he had distinguished his own practice from their doctrines at the earliest possible stage.

Were it necessary to make choice of forebear, a stronger case can be made for affiliating the more recent 'readers' to Richards rather than to Empson.[72] While Richards's principles can be found to coincide with the interpretative scepticism of the deconstructionists (although they themselves often argued against any likely link with him), Professor Christopher Norris, who studied under Empson at Sheffield, and who has done extremely well to divine points of likeness and unlikeness between Empson and deconstructionism, has intelligently concluded that it is 'impossible to claim Empson for either side in the current debate about literary theory'.[73]

On principle and in practice, Empson deplored 'the literary mystagoguery of France and the United States.'[74] However, Christopher Norris naturally thought it reasonable—having regard to the close interpretative practice that Jacques Derrida undertook in his early works—to encourage Empson to read them. (Jacques Derrida had emerged as a significant theoretical force within and out of France as early as 1967, with the publication of *Of Grammatology*, *Writing and Difference*, and *Speech and Phenomena*.) Empson responded with impatient distaste:

> I feel very bad not to have answered you for so long, and not to have read those horrible Frenchmen you posted to me. I did go through the first one, in translation, Jacques Nerrida, and nosed about in several others, but they seem to me so very disgusting, in a simple moral or social way, that I cannot stomach them. Nerrida does express the idea that, just as people were talking a grammar before grammarians arose, so there are other unnoticed regularities in human language and probably in other human systems. This is what I meant by the book-title *The Structure of Complex Words*, and it was not an out-of-the-way idea, indeed I may have got it from soneone else, but of

course it is no use unless you try to present an actual grammar, an actual grammar of the means by which a speaker makes his choice while using the language correctly. This I attempted to supply, and I do not notice that the French ever even try.

They use enormously fussy language, always pretending to be plumbing the very depths, and never putting your toe into the water. Please tell me I am wrong . . . [75]

Similarly, while he disassociated himself from the limiting formalistic criteria of organic form and intrinsic value, and had no truck with notions such as textual discontinuity, Empson also knew that his own criticism was concerned to establish meaning and never to rest content with 'indeterminacy' or 'undecidability'. Even when he first inscribed ambiguity as his analytical preference, he made no suggestion that 'unreadability' could ever be a happy outcome. Derrida's pronouncement that 'il n'y a pas de hors-texte' would have appalled him; and when Empson spoke at an early stage of 'this limiting critical impasse'—the impasse that regrettably stems from 'the idea that poetry is good in proportion as it is complicated'[76]—he resolved simply to analyse the poetry ever more deeply and to determine the meaning in it. His sense of ambiguity could never stand for the very different impasse of *aporia* in which deconstructionists rejoice.

All told, what he said in a radio broadcast entitled 'Literary Opinion' (on 20 October 1954) could well serve to represent his opinion both of the New Criticism and of the theoretical fashions that have emerged in more recent years:

There was a tremendous thing said by the poet A. E. Housman, in the preface to an edition of a Latin author; he said that the German professor A when he read the German professor B, must have felt like Sin when she brought forth Death. Now I am willing to confess I have sometimes felt like this when reading modern literary criticism, but not at all often. People aren't such fools as all that; the thing settles itself.

Challenged with exceptional rudeness about *Complex Words* in an article by Geoffrey Strickland,[77]—'In general it is difficult to believe that Mr Empson is not aware that his latest work is in many ways a solemn joke, a joke intended to disturb one by its display of erudition, its air of good common sense and its way of suggesting that in a world such as ours only the preposterous is sane and normal'—Empson gave himself the license to answer back with uncommonly extravagant defiance:

What I feel about the book, if there is any doubt, is easily told. I think it is wonderful; I think it goes up like a great aeroplane. A certain amount of noisy taxi-ing round the field at the start may be admitted, and the landing at the end is bumpy though I think without causing damage; but the power of the thing and the view during its flight I consider magnificent. When after long struggle it began to 'come out' I was astonished at its unity, at the way so many lines of effort which had felt somehow significant really did fit in (this must be what my critic takes to be its dreary paucity of ideas). When it was done I felt Nunc Dimittis; I was free, I was ready to die. I was to fly with the text from Peking to Ohio, where some final checking in libraries might well be done, and it was reasonable to leave at Peking a fully correct spare set in case of accident. There was little reason for alarm, but having to do this made me notice the firmness of my sentiments; I did not care about anything as long as the book got printed. This is disagreeably like writing an advertisement for myself, but consider how much more disagreeable it is for me to be told that I was cooking up a fatuously tiresome mass of spoof, licking my lips over the hope of jeering at anybody who was fool enough to take it seriously. The meanmindedness of anybody who can believe I did that feels to me quite sickening.

Thirty years later, Strickland had so far repented of his impertinence that he allowed H. A. Mason, in an article about contemporary literary criticism, to publicize the fact that he 'wishe[d] it to be known that he has changed his mind about *The Structure of Complex Words*, and, looking back, thinks that Empson had every right to be cross about the review'.[78] All the same, despite Empson's bravado at the time, not even he ever again made use of the theory of semantic grammar he had put forward in the volume. Contemporary readers were not yet ready for a cross-over between literary criticism and linguistics of the sort he was promulgating; and in any case his efforts would be overtaken within just a few years by the structuralism of Noam Chomsky. Ironically, one of Chomsky's key arguments in *Syntactic Structures* (1957) is that grammar is innate in the human mind—just as Empson had sought to show in *Complex Words* (1951). However, even if his linguistic theory has not enjoyed a continuing influence, there is no doubt that his specific critical analyses have an abiding importance.

'Empson has an annoying habit of bowing and scraping whenever he criticizes I. A. Richards,' said one review of *Complex Words*.[79] So it is: Empson does indeed fidget whenever he purposes to accost a point of principle held by Richards—'the source [as the dedication proclaims] of all ideas in this book, even the minor ones arrived at by disagreeing with him'—and so he offers politic obeisances every time he really means to drub his mentor. However, since so much of the book stems from the work of Richards, albeit by way of a counter-movement, it is worth ending this chapter with a closer look at Empson's critical disposition towards his mentor—beginning with a controversy in which he aimed to adjudicate between Richards and Cleanth Brooks, and culminating with the way in which, reluctantly but decisively, he endorses Richards's Theory of Value.

In accordance with Empson's focus upon equations in words of the type 'A = B' and variants thereof, it was natural that he took patient pains to intervene in the old quarrel relating to Keats's famous riddle in the 'Ode on a Grecian Urn': 'Beauty is truth, truth beauty'. While Cleanth Brooks, in *The Well-Wrought Urn* (1939), had argued that Keats's formulation added up to a coherent philosophical proposition, I. A. Richards mounted a putative defence which Empson judged to be scarcely a defence at all; rather, Richards was practically patronizing the poet. In the first chapter of *Complex Words* Empson uncompromisingly wipes the eye of his tutor, starting out by citing an unwarily damning passage from Richards's *Mencius on the Mind*. 'Urns induce states of mind in their beholders,' wrote Richards; 'they do not enunciate philosophical positions—not in this kind of poetry...' Empson pounced upon the potential condescension in that comment:

> I do not think poor Keats would have liked to be told he was writing 'this kind of poetry'. Professor Richards goes on to show that the ranges of meaning in Truth and Beauty overlap at three points, so that there are three ways of making 'Beauty is Truth' a mere tautology (not a sentence with any meaning). These possibilities, he says:
>
> 'account for its power in the poem (when, of course, it is not apprehended analytically) to convey that feeling of deep acceptance which is often a chief phase in the aesthetic experience.'
>
> Now it may well be that the lines are bad. But it seems to me that Professor Richards is not defending them; he is merely calling them bad in a complacent manner. And I should have thought, for that matter, that any word other than an exclamation or a swear-word has got to be apprehended as a meaning, giving room for a possible analysis of the meaning, if it is apprehended at all.[80]

There were no two ways about it: he was squaring up to Richards in a tone that was sniffy, not to say scornful. His manner of issuing this challenge amounts, as he gaily declared, to 'a mighty raspberry'—and there is no doubt whatever that the raspberry is being blown directly at Richards.[81] Surprisingly, with regard to the intraverbal equation enunciated by Keats's gnomic urn, 'Beauty is truth, truth beauty', Empson did not automatically align himself with Brooks's apologia for the sense of the adage, though he allowed that the idea was genuinely felt by the poet. 'Keats had wrestled with the idea in prose,' Empson correctly noted; and the poem is 'essentially about the unpleasantness of the life of the artist', and about the endeavour to transform suffering into artistic beauty. He therefore took up an intermediate position, granting a portion of justice to both Brooks and Richards. 'I do not think the lines need be regarded as purely Emotive or as a fully detached bit of philosophizing.'[82] All the same, *Complex Words* adds up to a derogation of the weaselly 'attitudes' and 'pseudo-statements' beloved of Richards; it functions as a manifesto for the centrality of meaning in poetic utterance.

In the beginning, in the early-to-mid-1930s, Richards had appeared to be totally in accord with Empson's efforts to elicit the structure of complex words. But, although his former pupil was rigorous in keeping him informed about the way his thoughts were developing, in the event, Richards was well and truly taken aback by the bite of *Complex Words*. Even as late as 1972 he read it again and jotted protests against a number of passages in his copy of the volume. For instance, against Empson's criticism of his remark (quoted above) that Keats was making use in 'Ode on a Grecian Urn' not of any kind of serious philosophy but of 'this kind of poetry', Richards seeks to justify his unhappy phrase: 'it was, for me, a form of *praise*'. Empson's comment that Richards's account of the possible meanings in Truth and Beauty added up to a way of 'merely calling [the lines] bad in a complacent manner', is met by the bluster of denial from Richards: 'Now, now, never, NO!' Likewise, when Empson declares that in any discussion of 'Ode on a Grecian Urn' 'a flat separation of Sense from Emotion would be merely a misreading', Richards merely questions: 'Who makes it?' Empson's carelessly unfair remark (on p. 14) that 'by the time Professor Richards came to write *The Philosophy of Rhetoric* and *Interpretation in Teaching*, he seems to have dropped the idea that a writer of poetry had better not worry about the Sense', is countered by the Professor's protest: 'He never had it, but he did point to an extreme possibility.' Against another slighting comment by Empson (also cited at n. 22 above), 'The trouble I think is that Professor Richards conceives the Sense of a word in a given use as something single, however "elaborate", and therefore thinks that anything beyond that Sense has got to be explained in terms of feelings, and feelings of course are Emotions, or Tones', Richards writes with deeply feeling impatience: 'No, no!' On the front flyleaf of his copy, Richards summed up thus his feelings about the challenges and criticisms that Empson had laid down in the volume:

Disagreements with IAR? ... These seem, in the theoretic Chapters (1 & 2) to be well-worth study. My feeling is that W.E. is almost always *right* in dissenting from what he takes I.A.R. to be saying, but nearly invariably wrong about that. In many instances, the two seem to me to be *trying* to say much the same thing in different ways. In others, some chance phrase of mine leads him to suppose in me a view I would violently disown: e.g. p. 6, my "this kind of poetry" meant to give higher rank to the lines than, say, to most of Davies, *Nosce Teipsum*. I am trying to say why I think them so good.[83]

In sum, Richards maintained, Empson was being wilful either in failing to understand him or in quite deliberately misrepresenting him. Yet Empson can scarcely be blamed for some of his misunderstandings.[84] Richards had been 'slightly wrong' in making a distinction between the affective and the referential modes of language, Empson later explained in an indulgently understated letter, and he himself had 'intended to restore the unity... What Richards and I both recognized was that analysis must be able [to] say when language is used dishonestly, as when a demagogue attempts to cheat his hearers by exploiting the emotive uses of words so as to prevent them from following up the referential uses.'[85] In any event, Richards's unstable early rhetoric had been a tremendous irritant to the younger Empson; as Christopher Norris has observed in a fine essay on Empson's criticism, *The Structure of Complex Words* was his 'full-scale rejoinder to Richards on the topic of language, poetry and truth.'[86]

More than two years before the publication of *Complex Words*, Empson had pondered in a letter to Ian Parsons (New Year 1949): 'Conceivably one would have a Reconsideration chapter towards the end of the book in which a lot of the wire-drawing of the theoretical position could be put'.[87] In fact, *Complex Words* does not wind up with a chapter in conclusion; there is no triumphant drawing-together of ideas. The final formal chapter is number 21, 'Dictionaries', exploring the inadequacies of existing English dictionaries, for reasons including the circularity of their definitions, their tendency to function as thesauruses, and their failure to take sufficient stock of shifts in usage. However, the literary filling of Empson's sandwich is ultimately buttressed by the bread of more theory in the form of three appendices on 'Theories of Value'—of which the first and most important picks up on emotivist theory and links it to a discussion of Richards's Theory of Value. Thus the appendix does in fact function very like a Reconsideration, since it allows the volume to begin and end with a critical discussion of Richards's two related theories. (It is astonishing to realize that Empson had adumbrated this appendix as early as 1932, twenty years before the appearance of the book, when he told Michael Roberts:

'I should like to write [for the young literary periodical *New Verse*] 3—5,000 words about Richards' pragmatism...; also about Richards' theory of value by addition, and how far it is valuable when you have left out the simpler fallacies in it which Richards now admits.'[88])

Richards's theory of value concerned itself centrally with what he called 'the effort to attain maximum satisfaction through coherent systematization'—'the systematization of impulses'.[89] Positive impulses he termed 'appetencies', and anything which worked to satisfy such impulses must be regarded as good or valuable. The full and ordered life necessarily maximized its varied satisfactions and minimized suppression and sacrifice. Given such a goal, the individual's accession to a life replete with self-realization and self-knowledge, poetry must take over the role of religion in the modern world. Poetry's intrinsic, vital and self-justifying function is to engender 'the best life . . . that in which as much as possible of our possible personality is engaged.'[90] In short, poetry fulfils itself in securing mental and moral health. In *The Foundations of Aesthetics* (1922; written with C. K. Ogden and James Wood), Richards stressed: 'A complete systematisation must take the form of such an adjustment as will preserve free play to every impulse, with entire avoidance of frustration . . . '[91]

Despite the evident frailties of his rhetoric in such writings, Richards more or less retained the theory of impulses in his later criticism. At the first, Empson seemed staunch in his loyalty, claiming without reservation or further enquiry in 1930 that Richards had 'produced a workable theory of aesthetic value.'[92] But in all honesty he registered misgivings from really quite an early stage, and by 1937 he reserved judgement in characterizing it as 'a police theory [which] helps you to stop the narrower theories from obstructing your practice.'[93] Then by 1950, in an essay on 'The Verbal Analysis'—scarcely a year in advance of *The Structure of Complex Words*—he seemed momentarily to surrender faith for scepticism:

> I do not deny that it may be a splendid thing to have a grand synthesis of human experience, a single coherent Theory of Value which could be applied to all works of art and presumably to all human situations; but it seems hardly reasonable to grumble, in the present state of affairs, that nobody has provided one; and if it did exist it would clearly be a philosophical synthesis rather than a literary one.[94]

According to the theory of value, poetry—which Richards later exalted as 'the supreme organ of the mind's self-ordering growth'[95]—can literally 'save' us. It will replace religion by relegating any Magical view of the world and enthroning a fundamental secularism. Richards arrived at this doctrine by way of a distinction already mentioned—between the language employed for enunciating true beliefs (essentially, scientific verities) and the language of poetry, which comprises 'pseudo-statements'. Pseudo-statements are 'not necessarily false,' he explained, but 'merely a form of words whose scientific truth or falsity is irrelevant to the purpose in hand.'[96] Thus his argument runs:

> Countless pseudo-statements—about God, about the universe, about human nature, the relations of mind to mind, about the soul, its rank and destiny—pseudo-statements which are pivotal points in the organization of the mind, vital to its well-being, have suddenly become, for sincere, honest and informed minds, impossible to believe as for centuries they have been believed....
>
> This is the contemporary situation. The remedy... is to cut our pseudo-statements free from that kind of belief which is appropriate to verified statements. So released they will be changed, of course, but they can still be the main instruments by which we order our attitudes to one another and to the world.[97]

Empson jumped upon the fallaciousness of Richards's logic. He deplored the way his mentor facilely linked an emotivist theory of literature (the idea that statements in literature cannot be regarded a either true or false, since they are actually pseudo-statements and so stand at a remove from real life) with his exaltation of a humanistic scale of values over any religious reckoning. He was quick to scotch Richards's error in terms that vindicate his very own book:

> [T]he idea that laying bare and outfacing the scandal about the universe was somehow the key to discovering and implementing the Emotive functions of language seems to me merely an unfortunate case of 'making it all fit in'. I think it has only delayed the treatment of emotions in words on their own terms.[98]

Yet that uncompromising dismissal of one part of Richards's thinking did not mean that he was equally dismissive of Richards' Theory of Value in general—though some critics of *Complex Words* most assuredly came away with the impression that he had indeed delivered a comprehensive knock-out blow to his mentor. Robert Gorham Davis noted in *Partisan Review*: 'Empson thinks that... the prudential most-impulses-satisfying value calculus of I. A. Richards [is] quite unworkable.'[99] Such a mistake on Gorham Davis's part was perfectly understandable, since the overall tone of Empson's appendix on 'Theories of Value', and especially its discussion of Richards's ideas, is querulous and sceptical, and even rather grudging in points of agreement. All the same, the clear burden of Empson's appendix, slightly shuffling and apologetic as it may be, is wholeheartedly to endorse Richards's positive thinking in respect of 'the maximum satisfaction of appetencies'. I extrapolate some of the key moments:

> It has the merit of making our judgements tolerably independent of theories about the universe ... The idea of measuring value has been objected to as such, but it is at least a traditional one, since the Christian God is to give us all marks on Judgement Day ... It is hard to write about the theory without facetiousness, because it seems to recommend a low view with so much pomp ... The theory is a consistent and serious attempt to touch rock-bottom in the matter, and so long as it is viewed as a painful truth I do not think it can be harmful. I do, on the other hand, think that believing more rosy things about the universe, on the specific ground that we will otherwise feel frustrated (and this is what the arguments that are preferred to us nowadays by nearly all religious leaders tend to make us do), is extremely harmful ... The belief to be defended at all cost, by fiction if nothing else will serve, is 'whatever is a good state of being is good in other people as well as me, so it is good to see that they get it'. It seems to me that anyone not insane will believe this by animal faith ... Surely this follows from the intellectuality of the creature: it does not depend on exciting emotions of fraternal love or what not ... It is part of the process of believing that there is a real world outside you ... No doubt the position I am recommending is what the philosophers like to call naïve realism, but I hope that need not be confused with religiosity.[100]

Ever afterwards, Empson was concerned to strengthen the foundations of the doctrine, to stop the holes in Richards's rhetoric of assertion, and he believed he could best do so by quizzing the theory, and even by pointing to its apparent shortcomings. For one matter, even though the Theory of Value was in no sense hedonistic, Richards put it forward in the language of Behaviourist psychology and hence made value an essentially unconscious gain. Empson proposed to prohibit a state of unknowing. As far as he was concerned, a theory of value must afford a sense of responsibility—it must strike a conscious balance between 'charity and a sense of social values'—for the final criterion is 'more nearly a political one'. So follows the crux of his argument, which informs all his writings on critical value as well as his later attack on Christianity: 'it is the intellectuality of the creature that turns a state of need into a state of pleasure.'

Empson thus became intent on refashioning what he regarded as Richards's theory of an essentially passive (because Behaviouristic) acquisition of value into a statement of conscious apprehension. 'It seems clear that consciousness is somehow involved in value, because if there was no consciousness we would at any rate feel there was no value,' he had declared in a letter to Richards of 2 April 1933.[101] Nonetheless, even though he worried away at Richards's Theory only in order to make it more purposeful, he would always stand up for Richards's secular morality —a morality derived from Jeremy Bentham's concept of the individual as a 'trustee for the community'. Richards's theory of the fullest satisfaction of positive impulses essentially constituted a reprise of Bentham's proposition that some kind of 'moral arithmetic' can determine the value of the pleasurable and the good, which is in itself socially serviceable. Richards expressed it in this form in *Principles of Literary Criticism*:

> the only reason which can be given for not satisfying a desire is that more important desires will thereby be thwarted. Thus morals become purely prudential, and ethical codes merely the expression of the most general scheme of expediency to which an individual or race has attained . . . Particularly is this so with regard to those satisfactions which require humane, sympathetic, and friendly relations between individuals. The charge of egoism, or selfishness, can be brought against a naturalistic or utilitarian morality such as this only by overloooking the importance of these satisfactions in any well-balanced life.[102]

Empson, who would continually seek to apply such an Helvetian principle in his own life and writings, was to reaffirm in 'The Hammer's Ring', a tribute to Richards published in 1973: 'The idea of making a calculation to secure the greatest happiness for the greatest number is inherently absurd, but it seems the only picture we can offer.' Among the best reasons for supporting this 'Calculable Value' theory, he believed, is the necessity both to avoid arrogantly self-confirming critical judgements (what Matthew Arnold called the fallacy of the 'personal estimate')—'the only alternatives to Bentham are arty and smarty moralising; giving unreasoned importance either to a whim of one's own or to the whim of a social clique'—and to appreciate different world-views without cultural prepossession. 'The main purpose of reading imaginative literature is to grasp a wide variety of experience, imagining people with codes and customs very unlike our own; and it cannot be done except in a Benthamite manner, that is, by thinking "how would such a code or custom work out?" '

In the postwar years he came more and more to believe that 'the whole of "Eng. Lit." as a University subject needs to return to the Benthamite position'.[103] In 'A Doctrine of Aesthetics' (1949), he observed, for instance: 'Perhaps the real test of an aesthetic theory, at any rate while so little is known about the matter, is how far it frees the individual to use his own taste and judgement; it must be judged in practice rather than abstract truth'[104]—so reaffirming the principle he had avouched at the outset of his career: 'the crucial judgement lies with taste,' he insisted in 1936; 'it is hard to feel that an adequate theory of literary criticism, if obtained, would be much more than a device for stopping inadequate theories from getting in your way.'[105] Twenty-five years later he reiterated that sentiment in 'Rhythm and Imagery in English Poetry': 'It is not even clear that you want a theory, because its findings must always be subject to the judgment of taste.'[106] Yet to the end of his life he carried on applauding Richards's Theory of Value, even while remaining doubtful that it had wholly and permanently defined the good effects of an aesthetic experience. Critics who ignore the theory, he felt, inevitably offend against the fundamental Benthamite spirit of capacious generosity. 'It was a fatal step, I always think,' he was to pronounce in 1959,

> when Leavis began attacking Richards' Theory of Value, which however hard to express properly is an essential plank in his platform; Leavis has never shown any philosophical grasp of mind, and took for granted that he could strut about on the rest of the platform without ever falling through the hole. The effect has been to turn his intensely moral line of criticism into a quaintly snobbish one, full of the airs and graces of an elite concerned to win social prestige, though this is much opposed to his real background and sympathies.[107]

Studying a literature, he insisted in that letter, 'is frivolous unless related to judgements of value, experience of life, some kind of trying out [of] the different kinds of attitude or world-view so as to decide which are good ones.'

If—as Empson was to bewail when he started working towards *Milton's God* in the mid-1950s—putatively Christian critics offend authorial integrity by bleeding works of literature of their moral conflicts and resistances, perhaps the worst charge that can be levelled against Empson is that he too indulged a *parti pris*—making his critical findings a function of his moral expectations and literary taste. Where the New Criticism hypostatized the concepts of semantic autonomy and intrinsic value, for instance, he insisted upon authorial rationality and critical common sense. If he could never be disinterested, however, he endeavoured always to resist reductivism, whether Christian or New Critical: the constrictions of doctrinaire morality or tidy theory. 'Mr. Empson, perhaps, will never elaborate a critical, political or metaphysical system,' Michael Roberts had shrewdly forecast in 1936.[108] Instinct told Empson that to enunciate any theory was to impose illogical and unnecessary limits on critical enquiry. Fiercely iconoclastic but never anarchistic, he stood out for the dignity of social order and the prerogative of individual human reason. If he also eschewed the call to proclaim a critical creed, however, reserving to his own practice all the rights of pragmatism, nevertheless it can be deduced from the bulk of his work that he avowed at least an implicit theory of the creative imagination itself. By definition, he maintained, the best literature is rationally protestant, often dissentient and rebellious, the expression not of neurosis but of real mental conflict, and it externalises the specific case in a publicly accountable form. Empson's theory (if it is one) thus works to emancipate the human mind from all dogma and to make literature continuous with all human experience.

Still, the single dogma he increasingly deplored was that of Christianity, and one of the insistent subtexts of *Complex Words*—indeed, it is so fervently reiterated that it is quite surprising that reviewers did not pick up on it—is the argument for what he termed the 'humanist application': that is, 'something vaguely anti-Christian'.[109] In 'The English Dog' he maintains: 'The web of European civilization seems to have been slung between the ideas of Christianity and those of a half-secret rival, centring perhaps (if you made it a system) round honour; one that stresses pride rather than humility, self-realization rather than self-denial, caste rather than either the communion of saints or the individual soul . . . '[110] He does not actually disclose in that instance that he himself upheld what he calls the 'half-secret rival' to Christianity; but as the book gathers pace, his salutations to the humanist 'system' become more and more blatant, even to the point of downright repetitiousness. Later in 'The English Dog' he declares, with manifest partiality, 'The fundamental novelty was an idea that "Man is no longer an abortive deity, born in sin, necessarily incomplete in the world [as in the Christian schema], but the most triumphant of the animals." '[111] In 'Timon's Dog' he says likewise: 'when you call a man a dog with obscure praise, or treat a dog as half-human, you do not much believe in the Fall of Man, you assume a rationalist view of man as the most triumphant of the animals.'[112] Speaking of 'the Restoration cult of independence', in the chapter 'Honest Man', he declares over again: 'There is now a covert assertion that a man who accepts his nature as it comes, who does not live by principle, will be fit for such warm uses of *honest* as imply "generous" and "faithful to friends", and to believe this is to disbelieve the Fall of Man.'[113] And he repeats the favoured formula yet once more in

'Honest in Othello', where he delights in the way in which 'a sort of jovial cult of independence' emerged in the word *honest*: 'the word came to have in it a covert assertion that the man who accepts the natural desires, who does not live by principle, will be fit for such warm uses of *honest* as imply "generous" and "faithful to friends", and to believe this is to disbelieve the Fall of Man.'[114]

Given such an enraptured repetition of the argument against Christianity, which is seeded throughout all such chapters, it was only a matter of time before Empson would feel obliged to tackle head-on the literary text that puts the Fall of Man at the centre of its dramatic complex. *Milton's God* was to appear in 1961. In later years, he would sometimes claim that he was forced to take up arms against what he contemptuously dubbed 'neo-Christian' readings of literary texts only when he realized that his students in England (when he began teaching at Sheffield from 1953) were unthinkingly regurgitating the supposed orthodoxies of the Christian faith. But in truth he was already working towards an anti-Christian campaign as early as the mid-1930s, when he started putting together the essays that became *Complex Words*. The point of no return, the declaration of combat, came when he pronounced, in 'All in *Paradise Lost*':

> I take it that Milton, while certainly not condoning either Fall, in Heaven or earth, knew that he was piling up the case in favour of Satan and our parents as strongly as he could ... That his feelings were crying out against his appalling theology in favour of freedom, happiness and the pursuit of truth was not I think obvious to him ... [115]

He was merely misremembering when he looked back in 1973: 'The topic did not seem to crop up in Complex Words.'[116] It had been on his mind, though not to the fore, since the 1930s; and it would finally burst into the open in *Milton's God*.

11

Homing to Yorkshire

I am sure you are a most valuable man to have as chairman, and you
must not let it weigh you down; when they complain, remind yourself
how lucky they are to have you there at all. That is the only way.

Letter to Kim Jong-Gil, 23 April 1965

THE family finally sailed from Hongkong on the P & O liner *Corfu* at
the end of August 1952, reaching London a month later. They were met
at London docks by Empson's sister Molly and brother Arthur, who drove
them back, past all the many vacant lots where bombed buildings were still
being cleared away, to Studio House in Hampstead. It was a dishevelled
and disheartening place to come home to. The house was still being used
as a camping ground by a variety of lodgers including A. G. (Dinah) Stock,
the author and anarchist, and John Wright (who had established in Studio
House, under the auspices of the Hampstead Artists' Council, a workshop
and studio for the puppet theatre that would become world-famous when
it was removed in 1961 to the Little Angel Theatre in Islington), as well as
others including Pat Miles, Barry Carmen, and Max Bickerton (who had
started a private English language school drawing pupils from among the
families of foreign embassies). The handsome red-brick house occupying
the corner of Hampstead Hill Gardens and Rosslyn Hill was filthy; the
blocked chimney a fire hazard—'no job for Pa,' as Hetta wrote to her far-
distant lover, 'but he doesn't care.' The fireplace smoked so intolerably
that Hetta came to think of it as 'like living in hell'. They were confined to
just three rooms of their big house—one for Hetta, one for the children,
and one for Empson himself (where he could get on with his writing)—with

kitchen and bathroom, all on the first floor. On one occasion, Hetta handmade some leather jackets for William and the boys; the only trouble was (as a close friend noted) 'they really *looked* home-made.'[1]

William 'sits at his desk in his room & types,' Hetta wrote in a despondent mood, 'just like always.'[2] Since Empson had no immediate prospect of a full-time income—the BBC initially invited him to do a 20-minute slot, broadcast on 4 December, in a series marking the 400th anniversary of the birth of Edmund Spenser, but such engagements brought in occasional fees only—it was just as well to import further lodgers, who were to include a number of Ugandans, Nigerians and South Africans in need of quarters. Indeed, their home would function as a paying apartment house for many years to come; and Max Bickerton would occasionally serve as the resident agent. Over the years, the list of lodgers included some names to conjure with. One such, in the late 1960s, was the young radio journalist Bob Harris—he came to occupy a room on the first floor, and was soon to find fame as a disc jockey on the legendary popular music programme 'The Old Grey Whistle Test'—who recalls in his memoirs: 'The place always seemed to be packed with people, mostly from the London School of Economics (famously militant at the time)... and the whole house had a vibrantly creative feeling. The atmosphere struck me as being totally amazing.'[3]

Bob Harris met William Empson on just one occasion during his residence at the house; but towards some of the lodgers Empson would adopt a kindly, paternalistic demeanour. For Lo Hui-min, a history student from Singapore who lodged at Studio House for several years, for instance, he took pains to help him to obtain extensions to his visa, to advance his education, and even to find him a speech therapist; though intelligent, Lo suffered in society from his curious mispronunciation of the English language. Empson was also 'particularly grateful' to Lo Hui-min (as he was to declare in 1956 in a draft petition written on Lo's behalf to the Home Secretary) 'for keeping up the interest and capacity of my two boys (now aged 12 and 14) in their knowledge of the Chinese language, which they would otherwise have lost'.[4]

Conditions of life were restricted in many ways: meat, bacon, eggs, cheese, and butter were still subject to rationing. The cost of living was high, and long queuing for rations became the order of the day; in addition, it was necessary to register for coal. A postwar grittiness was in the air; even the exhilarating moment of the landslide election of Clement Attlee's Labour Government, inaugurating the National Health Service and other major welfare reforms, had given way in 1951 to a return of a Conservative administration led by the ageing Winston Churchill.

Since the school year was imminent and there was no time to plan things, the children were put straight into a rather peculiar 'progressive' educational establishment (within walking distance of home) called Burgess Hill School. 'It was the only one which could take them,' as Hetta admitted. There were no formal lessons, and the children did not have to read and write unless they really felt like it; the only mandatory lesson was square dancing, solemnly conducted once a week. Empson made it clear to the headmaster that he wished his sons—Mogador was then nearly 10, Jacob just short of 8—to become proficient in the English language, and he was prepared to pay for extra cramming so that they should be able to enter the normal school system with a view to passing the Common Entrance exam: he looked forward to getting Mogador into Winchester within a year or two.[5] (He had told I. A. Richards even in 1950 that he wanted to raise his sons in England.) To assist with the boys' speedy acquisition of English he read to them, night after night, the entirety of *Huckleberry Finn* and *Tom Sawyer*.[6] He liked reading Kipling too: he thought 'The Flag of their Country' Kipling's best school story; and he once told his friend W. W. Robson, in a later year, 'that when he read "The Cat who Walked by Himself" to his children he wept so much that his children thought he had gone mad'.[7]

It did not take long for the experimentalism of Burgess Hill to be reckoned a failure, and by the next term the boys were more satisfactorily placed at Davies Preparatory School, a Hampstead crammer. A year later, they transferred to a regular preparatory school called The Hall (the writer and critic A. Alvarez was a former pupil), which did indeed prepare them, just as their father wished, to take in their stride the hurdle of the Common Entrance examination: they duly went on to Aldenham School at Elstree in Hertfordshire.

Hetta began by hating London, where she felt she lacked friends of first resort; she longed for the life she had lived in Beijing, and longed too for her lover, who was now teaching in Japan. Even though she learned too that the *News Chronicle* would welcome from her a series of personal articles about the situation in China, she felt she had no stomach for it. 'William keeps nagging I should write this book about China but I feel paralysed here, but paralysed.'[8] In fact, for many months after the return to London, Hetta felt herself descend into deep depression; she was to confess in May 1954: 'Jesus I was miserable to the point of suicide for an entire year'; but the needs of the children and the reconditioning of the house worked to repair her spirits.[9] In time too, as a friend of later vintage would remark, the green-fingered Hetta would create in the modest garden (which incorporated a small pond where frogs would breed a-plenty), an 'oasis of multi-coloured shrubbery: japonica, Japanese tree peony, clematis, forsythia, almond blossom, euphorbia, a rustic arch of rambling roses, all manner of bulbs, and a dwarf oak cut like a mushroom, a summer parasol for a marmalade cat'.[10]

Her husband, on the other hand, was promptly taken up again by what Hetta satirized as the 'literary parish'. He lost little time in getting together with old friends from the thirties and forties, including John Davenport and Louis MacNeice, who were cheered to see him back in town. He himself was delighted to catch sight of other famed survivors of the years; as he was to recall, for instance, in 1962: 'Stanley Spencer when observed at a party made everyone else look fretful, because he radiated so much expansive contentment—in fact, the scene would make a Stanley Spencer painting. All this stuff about how miserable he was seems absurd.'[11] The years of exile in Japan and China, both before and after the war, and the unremitting effort of his wartime work for the BBC, had left him feeling he had lived far longer than his years. He had lived hard in every sense, rarely letting up from the work and from the drinking that sustained it. Although his health was in general remarkably robust, he was prone to recurrent bouts of severe stomach ache at periods of emotional stress; he feared a recurrence of the ulcer that laid him low just as the strain of the war lifted—though he characteristically made light of the dread and the real pain that set him back from time to time. As to 'us office types,' he was to declare at Sheffield, 'our occupational hazard is Badgering, Causing Bellyache'.[12]

Yet parties and speaking engagements were to become routine in the following months, though the smogs of the postwar city made life unpleasant and indeed dangerous for anyone who ventured out. The Empsons had to grope for the number on the door of the MacNeices' house, where they had been invited to drink mulled wine ('all anyone can afford'), to make out if they had come to the right place.[13] This coincided with the Great London Smog, a five-day period (4–9 December 1952) during which London was suffocated by a fog laden with toxic pollutants such as sulphur dioxide, nitrogen dioxide, and soot: over 4,000 people were to die of it. Also, the Empsons began holding their own unbuttoned parties at which lodgers and literary figures mingled through the night; on occasion there were quarrels, intrigues, and flagrant sexual activity. Everyone from T. S. Eliot to Lucien Freud was pleased to attend such parties—which were 'happenings' before the term was coined.

One of the first of their fresh intake of lodgers was a young Chinese ex-diplomat and tennis champion named Kenneth Lo (born Lo Hsiao Chien in southern China in 1913). Lo had spent part of his youth in England, and he had studied under I. A. Richards at Cambridge in the 1930s. Soon after the Empsons re-established themselves in London, he brought his English wife Anne Brown to live at their place—at the time, he was running a flourishing business in Chinese greeting cards—and it was at Studio House that he began writing the cookery book that would launch his career as chef, restaurateur and writer. For the next forty years, he was to be the undisputed doyen of Chinese cuisine in England, writing more than 40 cookery books in all. (Empson would contribute the foreword to his *Peking Cookery* in 1971.)

'Studio House was an extraordinary place to live,' Lo was to recall:

William was one step removed from contemporary reality and seemed to stroll through life unhindered by its troublesome details . . . [L]iterary luminaries were a part of the furniture, all milling around, consuming vast amounts of alcohol and stubbing out their cigarettes on the Henry Moore sculptures, at the endless all-night parties.

But perhaps the main attraction at Studio House was Mrs Hetta Empson. She was a tall South African who was at least as handsome as Ingrid Bergman. Her main room, the Studio itself, was two storeys high and difficult to heat. Hetta built a huge brick bed, big enough for ten people to stretch out on. In North China such a construction was called the 'kang', a bed at night that doubled as a living platform to eat and sleep on during the day.

But Hetta was forbidden by the Hampstead bye-laws to heat her patent *kang* (measuring about twelve feet by six-and-a-half) by way of flues drawing hot air from an outside oven.

Having been thwarted by the Camden fire officer, Hetta, not to be daunted, erected a tent in the centre of the studio. By placing a smokeless fuel stove opposite the tent entrance, the radiating heat warmed the tent in no time, without having to heat up the cavernous room. Hetta was trying to recreate Inner Mongolia in NW3 . . .

Studio House was all a little avant-garde for Anne. People didn't appear to do any real work there! She was alarmed by the excess and noted, with sympathy, that while the adults slept off their hangovers, Mogador and Jacob could often be found on tiptoe in the kitchen, trying to reach up to the cooker to make themselves breakfast before setting off for school.[14]

The furniture the Empsons had packed up in Peking—over five tons of it—finally reached Hampstead (the costs of shipping had been met by the

British Embassy), so they were able to arrange the Studio into a striking room. Their fine drawing of the young Mao Tse-tung was given a prominent place. And for all the legendary wildness of the non-stop party life in Hampstead, their day-to-day activities were often as decorous as anyone else's. Ivor and Dorothea Richards, who called by at the end of June 1953, were impressed by the stylishness of the household and by their hosts' hospitable demeanour. 'Lively friendly talk . . . ,' Dorothea remarked in her journal afterwards. The youngsters were coming on well, she thought: 'Boys large & self possessed.' She noted too that Empson himself was 'pleased at increasing recognition.'[15]

He was suddenly much in demand, fêted like a prodigal son. He was invited to give talks on the BBC Third Programme and the Home Service, at the Institute of Contemporary Arts, and the International Institute of Oriental Affairs. Not only was he taken to be the lost literary leader, he was also cast as an authority on the New China, though he would perplex his audiences when he came to praise the Communist regime and uphold the Chinese line on the Korean War. Or else he would respond to hard questioning on his support for the new China with a gentle and very engaging, 'Well, I really don't know, you know', which was candid of him ('of course he *doesn't* know,' Hetta would remark with laughter) but could impress his hearers as either disingenuous or a lie. At Chatham House, where he was invited to give a talk about China, he perplexed everyone by saying of the Communists' treatment of the academics, 'They teased them a bit, you know', and grinding to a halt after twelve minutes.[16] Hetta had to admit that he probably did more good in speaking up for China than she would have done—'because I'd get cross'.[17]

He was more persuasive when he stuck to his professional line. On 15 December, he read his poems, with introduction and commentary, in a half-hour broadcast for the BBC Third Programme (for which he was paid 30 guineas). *The Poems of William Empson*, produced by Peter Duval Smith, was a splendid show, but one of the most noticeable aspects of the broadcast, which was in every sense polished, is that Empson seemed to put on two voices, one for the poetry and the other for the crisply executed prose. Few listeners would have thought to attribute this curious (and only marginally distracting) behaviour—or trick—to the effect of alcohol, but that is precisely how Empson tried to explain the matter in a draft letter to a listener who commented on the oral peculiarities of the production: 'I too hated the poetry-reading voice . . . The producer was keen to get the verse reading lush, and lushed me up for it on rum and Guinness mixed; not that

I blame him, I too thought that was probably the best method. It was certainly better than the trial version sober.'[18]

He had a patrician voice, with a slightly sardonic timbre, which there could be no disguising. The poet and critic G. S. Fraser, who got to know him well in the 1950s, wrote: 'everything that he writes, both in prose and in verse, has the run of his speaking voice, . . . an excellent instrument for expressing anger, scorn, and melancholy despair.'[19] Explanations or extenuations apart, the effect of Empson's poetry broadcast was riveting. Naomi Lewis gushed in the *New Statesman*: 'This was a most deliberate and exact performance; yet I have rarely been stirred to so lively an interest by a group of contemporary poems read by its author. Mr Empson keeps for his verse a special and indescribable voice.'[20]

That special voice was not reserved for his own poetry alone; a few weeks later, one of a series of talks on Shakespeare which he broadcast on the radio was similarly celebrated in the *Sunday Times*: 'It is fascinating to hear Mr Empson laying about him on "Some Problems in Shakespeare": he is as adventurous and forthright as he is learned. When he reads verse— his own or another's—his voice becomes that "sort of chaunt" which Hazlitt approved in Coleridge. There is everything to be said for it.'[21] According to Hetta, the poetry reading and the talks on Shakespeare— based on 'his new book of essays, which is nearly ready'—were making him 'big money'.[22] As with almost all of his undertakings, indeed, the nature of the lectures had been brewing for some years; in this case since 1949 when he notified C. M. Coffin, Dean of the Kenyon Summer School, about a course he had in prospect: 'A look at Falstaff and Henry V and the recent British fashion of presenting Shakespeare as a sturdy royalist is a topic I would like to fit into my course somewhere.'[23] All the same, since he was deeply nervous of the process of broadcasting, the production of the talks cost him a great deal in terms of apprehensiveness. For the first talk in the series, he resolved unnecessarily to put himself through the experiment of speaking for half an hour to the microphone not from a full script but merely from brief notes; he wrote to the producer in a manner so tense as to seem quite melodramatic: 'I write to you because I doubt whether my previous letter would make you realise the extreme violence of the conditions under which I propose to record *Hamlet I*. . . . If I can avoid it, I will not speak to anybody in the building before I record Hamlet I.[24]

In the event, the Shakespeare pieces were first published in one form or another in American periodicals, but then set aside—being overtaken by more urgent assaults against what he thought the sick new literary orthodoxy of neo-Christianity—until collected for the posthumous *Essays on*

Shakespeare (1986). 'Far too much has been written about Shakespeare,' he said once to his colleague and Professor of Philosophy at Sheffield, David Cousin.[25]

Just as he was deliberate and self-critical about his performances, so he was not actually as oblivious about his appearance and his effect upon others as some of his acquaintances later made out. At this time, and for many years, he affected to sport a bristly moustache and a beard that effloresced from the jawline and so made him look for all the world like a Chinese sage, though he preferred to call it a 'Newgate' beard—explaining when asked by anyone intrepid enough to touch on the subject that since the beard covered a fair portion of the throat, the rope would be less likely to burn the neck when one was hanged, or else indeed that such a beard enabled one to 'cheat the hangman'.[26] 'I am a proud man but not a vain man,' he once announced. 'Vanity is silly.' On his return to London his fame and physiognomy attracted such wide interest that a number of professional photographers, including Jane Bown of the *Observer*, sought to take his photograph. One of her most arresting portraits captures him in three-quarter face and in deeply contrasting light and shade, and with his mouth clenched round a darlingly long white cigarette-holder tipped by a half-finished fag that juts at right angles from the strong jaw and bisects the utter blackness of the left half of the frame; even though the subject himself is formally dressed in jacket, shirt and tie, and with his short hairstyle slicked into place, the beard looks like nothing so much as a weird muffler or a froth of ectoplasm. But even though he appeared to submit to being photographed with a good grace, albeit while invariably holding a tense closed expression, he was sufficiently self-conscious as to be wary of the image a photo might convey. Surprisingly, he wrote to one literary editor about his anxiety over the Bown photograph:

> My point of view is that I don't at all mind being a joke in a picture but I think people very soon get tired of a joke; and what is much worse they soon begin to suspect it is pretentious; as a photograph for regular use I think the one without a cigarette holder, though dull, has very much more wearing quality.[27]

Thus he had a keen eye for the way things might look—far more often than some people noticed in him. Being not quite the absent-minded don he was often taken for, he was concerned for his image—and he calculated on it.

He had been putting out feelers for a university post in England for quite a long time before the family ultimately left China, and friends looked around for him. In particular, the devotedly admiring Kathleen Raine made enquiries at universities including Birmingham (where Charles Madge, her ex-husband and Empson's friend, held a chair in the social sciences), at Hull (where Jacob Bronowski held a chair), and at Leeds (where Raine was close friends with Herbert Read). Edward Wilson at Cambridge was also notified of Empson's quest. Raine was jealous and avowedly critical of Hetta, but she preferred to have Empson back in England where she might at least see him from time to time. Despite her rather priggish attitude towards Hetta's character and political convictions, Raine worked hard on behalf of her old friend William and stirred others, including Bonamy Dobrée at Leeds,[28] into taking an interest.

Before he left China, Empson had been tipped off about a vacancy at the University of Sheffield. L. C. Knights was standing down after five years as Professor of English Literature to become Winterstoke Professor of English at Bristol; he actually departed from Sheffield in 1952, so his Chair was to stand empty for a year.[29] Even before an advertisement appeared in the press, Empson sent off to the registrar a sloppy and scantily informative letter of application. He even concluded with a discouraging piece of self-depreciation: 'It may be felt that my published work has been rather specialized, but I would try to provide what was wanted in the post and not merely indulge my specialities. I wish to add that I am myself a Yorkshireman, and my relations live there.'[30]

In October, back in England, he saw in *The Times* that the university wanted twenty copies of his application, with the names of three referees, and testimonials if available; so he hastily put his papers into the correct form.

Empson was invited for interview in the Council Room at the University of Sheffield on 29 January 1953. It is not known how many others were interviewed that day, but the long shortlist of candidates had included Kenneth Allott, Frank Kermode, and Harold Jenkins, each with a rising reputation as scholar and critic, and all of whom would very soon go on to gain chairs elsewhere. No candidate was especially invited to apply. References were taken up on 3 December, and for the most part both the nominated referees and the external assessors voiced their praise for Empson's achievements and talents, though a number also cast doubt on his suitability for a senior position which required good administrative skills. Did he have the taste or the ability to run the show? Basil Willey (King Edward VII Professor of English at the University of Cambridge), considered Empson to be 'of course in a class apart: he is a man of genius, & probably the most remarkable poet-critic we have. In a sense it would add great lustre to any University to have him ...'; and yet, one had to remember, there was the small problem of that universally acknowledged rumour about his incapacity for administration...Hugh Sykes Davies, one of Empson's referees, backed him with unequivocal praise; so did another contemporary and reliable friend, Ronald Bottrall, in a testimonial ('one of the most distinguished living critics and one of the most subtle and imaginative English poets...a man of unusual brilliance and distinction of mind').[31] L. C. Knights, who had got to know Empson in a small way at the Kenyon School of English in the summer of 1950, vouched that he found him 'hard-working, capable of tremendous application, and genuinely engaged in his work as a teacher... [I]f he were appointed he would, in my opinion, give himself to the work in hand, including the day-to-day routine.'

From across the Atlantic, John Crowe Ransom sang Empson's praises: 'I believe that before he is done Empson will rank as the leading literary critic of our time.' On a personal note, he added,

> Empson is a man of great probity, and of dignity, almost austerity. At first one thinks he is cold, but he is merely reserved; he is really very warmhearted, inclined to temper justice with generosity and humility. His public address is admirable; he speaks clearly, wittily, eloquently, and with a sincerity which obviously cannot put up with rhetorical tricks.

One of the most remarkable evaluations was sent in by E. M. W. Tillyard, if only because he chose to recollect Empson's achievements as a student, having examined him in the English Tripos at Cambridge in 1929:

> I shall never forget the brilliance of his papers. He has now an international reputation as critic and poet and in the eyes of the general literary world he would bring lustre on your English Chair in a way none of the other candidates could begin to do. He would command huge respect among the students. Unlike some modernists he has a catholic taste in Literature. He began as a scholar in mathematics and he has the logical penetration of the mathematician. In a certain kind of close literary analysis he has no equal. On the other hand his short flights are better than his long; and it was significant that his essay paper in the Tripos was ill-organised as a whole and much inferior to his other papers! And this brings me to my major doubt about him: whether he is suited to organising and running an important department. Could he, I ask myself, really be bothered? For enthralling talk in the small hours he could be relied on, but I just don't know whether he would submit to the duty of running a department. I fear it will be most difficult to get evidence on this, his teaching posts having been in China. So I am compelled to end on this large doubt.

I. A. Richards offered his full support to his finest pupil, though in an idiosyncratic style that must have given pause to some of the selection panel; Richards' unusual turns of phrase highlighted the eccentricity of Empson's genius, but left some doubts about the nature of his talent and temperament:

> As a critic and literary analyst, I think it might be fair to say that he has already done something of permanent kind to criticism. He is, as it were, the inventor and the first user of an ultra-microscope for the discernment of shades of meaning. The instrument is a tricky one and can introduce mirages, but about its powers in some uses there is no doubt. It is this, I think, which explains the fame and eminence accorded him by writers and critics of so many schools.
>
> This may suggest that his interests and activities are too recondite to find proper scope in the routine teaching of a Chair of English Literature. But he has been teaching classes for years in China and in Japan which needed to have the simplest essentials clarified and brought home to them. As to his scholarship, he has one of the most capacious and reflective minds I have ever encountered. Above all he has the gift of vivifying the interests of those around him, though he does present a daunting spectacle. I am not thinking of his beard, though that is terrifying, but of his intent concentration and regardlessness of all but the points in question.
>
> As a colleague and member of the Senate, he would be found most conscientious, cooperative and friendly (if sometimes absent-minded) and his extremely wide and active range of interests (he keeps up his mathematical pleasures and his reading is prodigious) make him a bracing influence on the intellectual tone of any community.

The overall impression conveyed by the references was that there was indeed one sure intellectual and critical star on the shortlist. What they left in doubt were his personality and capabilities; and what was in serious question was whether he could, or would be inclined to, undertake the ever-dreaded business of high administration. What is remarkable and even shocking is that, even though few if any of the referees and assessors had any personal knowledge of Empson's professional activities and conduct, they were yet so willing to express doubts about his capacity or inclination to run a university department—such is the force of rumour and hearsay in the academic world.

But the selection panel were men (all men) of distinction in their fields, and they prided themselves on their independence of judgement. In addition to the Vice-Chancellor and the Deputy Dean (L. C. Knights was Dean of the Faculty, but it was not proper for him to sit on the choice of his own successor in the Department), it ran to six professors including J. S. Deas (Music), D. R. Cousin (Philosophy), and H. W. Lawton (French), along with three members of the Faculty of Arts who were in in due course to be awarded personal chairs: F. F. Bruce (Biblical History and Litera-ture), Eric Laughton (Latin), and Richard M. Wilson (English Language).[32] All the same, as one of their number later admitted, in the days leading up to the interviews they all rushed around trying to get hold of a copy of *Seven Types of Ambiguity*; they also wondered quite what to expect when Empson appeared before them (the Vice-Chancellor had teased them in advance about his weirdly hirsute looks). Come the day, however, Empson was evidently too nervous to hold the floor, to put on a show of erudition and eloquence: his responses were singularly abrupt, though the questions asked of him were not such as to excite displays of captivating eloquence. The committee asked among other things about his work in the Far East; he would have told them about his teaching of Basic English, about giving classes from memory, and about how he had handled young Chinese communists in recalcitrant mood. To be sure, his experiences were un-orthodox but fascinating. Professor Lawton asked him which texts he felt it appropriate for first-year students to study when taking subsidiary Latin. 'Is it necessary for them to read anything in Latin?' Empson bravely queried by way of reply. Finally they asked, did he think he could manage the arduous and tiresome tasks expected of a Head of Department? 'I can do sums,' he responded. 'I shall be able to add up the marks.'[33] There is probably little doubt that he meant what he said to be taken as a serious answer, but after the laughter had died away this big issue was not pursued further. To be so adroit in making light of the matter, he must be one of them. The Vice-Chancellor, J. M. Whittaker, was a distinguished math-ematician in his own right (elected to the Chair of Mathematics at Liver-pool while still in his twenties); he knew of Empson's repute, and he relished such quick wit. Asked if he had any observations or comments to make, Empson emphasized again that he was a Yorkshireman and wanted to teach in Yorkshire. He also intimated that his domestic situation might prove a little awkward, and either he would have to commute from London or live beyond the usual boundaries—but the panel seemed fairly untroubled by practicalities.[34] ('I understood it to be agreed that a broad view would be taken,' he claimed afterwards.)[35] He was informed later the same day that his name would be recommended to the Senate, and his employment was to commence on 1 October. His starting salary was to be £1,850 per annum, with an additional family allowance of £50 for each child from birth until the end of the child's period of full-time education.

(For reasons that are not known, the contract was signed only on 12 November, some weeks after he took up his post at Sheffield: it is not impossible that it had been sent to him in London, and he lost the first issue.)

'I was considered a bold appointment,' Empson would say years later. 'They went in for bold appointments in those days.'[36] (Occasionally he would even refer to Sheffield as 'plucky little Sheff'.) What was particularly bold was that the university elected as its professor a strange and middle-aged man who had never before been employed in academic life in England; indeed, he had never even taught a native English-speaking student. To its credit, the committee was persuaded of his scholarly distinction; for the rest—the worry as to management skills—it was quite ready to take a gamble. Twenty years later, when Emeritus Professor William Empson was awarded an honorary degree by the university, he responded in his public oration: 'listening to that splendid praise given me by the Orator [Professor Brian Morris, his successor in the Department from 1971], it struck me that the University also deserved some praise for making the appointment. It was what is called bold; when I was made Professor here, I had actually never done any teaching in England at all.'[37]

As the years passed, he made a point too of taking up a posture along the lines of a *Guardian* interview in 1969: 'I regard Sheffield as the right place to be in as I come from Yorkshire.'[38] In truth, such a boast was window-dressing; he would have been just as willing to work in Manchester or Birmingham if the opportunity had arisen. One way or another, it was a mode (as he also readily allowed) of 'swagger'.[39] He would further play up to the idea of resuming his roots by announcing to a colleague at the beginning of term that he was off to Sheffield Market to buy (a) a Yorkshire hat or cap, and (b) a Yorkshire black pudding.

Whatever the selection panellists made of him, he professed to have felt very comfortable with them: they were his kind, they talked his language. But Hetta took one look at the ambience of postwar Sheffield and decided it was intolerable: a grim, grimey, smelly place. Industrial production in the steel furnaces on the east side of the city was again in full swing, but that meant only that a pall of smoke constantly pervaded the city—travellers from Derbyshire knew when they were nearing the city by the coal fug that lowered over it. The city centre had of course been bombed during the war, and utilitarian shopping precincts were being built to replace the clearances. Above all, with its predominantly cloth-cap, working-class culture, Sheffield struck the cosmopolitan Hetta as barren, a scrabble of mean redbrick streets; not a place to make one's permanent home. In any case, the children were already at school in London; and she was drawn to the arty-bohemian life of the capital. In 1965, when the Queen Mother visited Sheffield to open the new Arts Tower, and Hetta also put in one of her occasional appearances as Professor Empson's consort, it would amuse knowing bystanders to overhear Hetta's smart response to the question put to her in the royal receiving line. 'How long have you lived in Sheffield?' 'Thirteen years,' said Hetta brightly.

Empson would thereupon take a deliberate decision to live in Sheffield as simply and inexpensively as he could, so that the bulk of his salary could be reserved for keeping up the family's living arrangements in London, and of course for the school fees of the children. ('His salary just keeps us ticking over with an overdraft,' Hetta was to tell her friend and lover Walter Brown in May 1954.)[40] He would spend as little as possible on accommodation in the north, subsisting like a student in a ghastly bedsit. In any case, he had never looked for personal comfort, let alone luxury; and modest dwellings would serve in addition to absolve him from the obligation to keep up any sort of 'establishment' or entertain in fit professorial style 'at home'. His humble and unself-pitying disinclination to look to his own well-being is evident in this letter to Hetta which dates from the early weeks in Sheffield: 'You might bring a blanket or two if you have any spare, otherwise I shall buy some (I have borrowed from [John] Danby [his colleague] for tomorrow); also a pair of sheets will be wanted eventually; some butter would be a help.' But such a letter also shows the degree and kind of dependency she would have to supply in their relationship, for he was happy to refer to her for the stuff of practical life, and she became his fond brusque manager and forceful minder. 'When you come,' he similarly asked of her (early in his time at Sheffield), 'you might as well bring some butter, which is hard to get here without ration books'—adding a comment that anticipated by many years a famous advertising campaign: 'not that I can tell it from margarine anyhow.'[41] They would address one another only by their proper names, or as 'Pa' and 'Ma'; and they kept separate bedrooms from the time of their return to England; but that did not eclipse the bond of love between them. Even though they no longer slept together, they both embraced the terms of their relationship;[42] his letters to her would always open 'My dearest Hetta' or 'My darling Hetta'.

Yet there is no doubt that he did not relish all the months and years he would have to pass in his indigent-seeming solitude. If stoicism was bred in his bone, that did not mean he liked what he chose to put up with. Paddy

Fraser, wife of the poet and critic G. S Fraser, recalls this exchange from 1971:

> when he retired from Sheffield, he urged George to apply for the Professorship in English there, promising to back his application. He turned to me and said: 'The thing is, do *you* want to go to Sheffield?' 'Of course,' I said, 'if George wants to go, I'd be happy to go too. After all I do come from Yorkshire.' 'Good,' he said, 'that's *most* important, that you should want to go too.' That touched me greatly.[43]

As if to celebrate the Sheffield appointment, and to get out and see something more of the country (Hetta had only known England during the war, and even then not much more of it than the capital), Hetta bought an old, cheap, green-coloured delivery van to drive around in; and at Easter 1953 the family took off for ten days of camping, visiting Oxford, Blenheim, Stratford-on-Avon, Stonehenge, Salisbury, Tolpuddle, and finally Winchester (to 'show Mog what is going to happen to him if he's smart enough to be accepted when he's fourteen,' as Hetta sarcastically wrote).[44] Empson won fifty shillings by backing outsiders at a point-to-point meeting; and the sun shone every day. In the summer they drove *en famille* down through France and into northern Spain. (The village of Marcorignan became a place they would try to visit every summer for a while.) Empson made sure they visited the prehistoric cave paintings in the Dordogne which had always enthralled him. In typically contrary fashion, he resolved to be strict with himself while on holiday, though at a considerable emotional cost to everyone else. 'William, after heavy drinking for weeks on end in England (intolerable) got neurotic as soon as we began camping & doesn't drink or smoke and must have milk which is hard to get & turns sour, at once, anyway . . . ' They both habitually drank to excess—she for the hell of it, he to keep himself calm and steady.

It is not clear just how many digs he got through in his first months at Sheffield—he lodged briefly at 4 Elmore Road, and for a while in the winter of 1954 he took a room in the house of his colleague John Danby ('I am very depressed about moving lodgings again,' he wrote as late as January 1954)—but he ended up on the rear ground floor of a tenement dwelling at 17 Wharncliffe Road (which is about a quarter of a mile from the main university buildings). The postal address was not one he would choose to use for correspondence, because that would mean having to make his way to the front door of the large, three-storeyed, bald-fronted terraced edifice: he would take up his residence, that is to say, in the cellar, which was entered through a yard that led from a narrow alley or skillet linking the backs of this block of run-down houses. His accommodation consisted of a stark single room, about twelve feet square, along with a tiny kitchen area by the door; the floor was bare concrete, and an iron-framed single bed stood in the corner; there were two small open bookcases to left and right of the room, a naked lightbulb dangled from a flex in the ceiling, and a portable single-bar 14″ electric fire was the one permanent source of warmth—though he would also borrow 'for keeps' a pink paraffin stove as an occasional supplement, or for use during power strikes. The only decorations he ever put on the walls were his prized portrait of the young Mao Tse-tung and a wonderfully expressive photograph of a hippopotamus just surging from the water which he took pains to purchase from a national newspaper; he must have thought the latter an apt metaphor for his life and work in Sheffield. In the centre of the room stood a plain deal table. This drab place was where he would work: reading, making notes, turning down the pages of books and annotating them, 'smacking out' articles and chapters on his old Corona typewriter, and marking essays. Beyond an inner door, a stairway led to the floor above, where in theory he could make use of the toilet, but he soon came to feel he would prefer not to go that way. 'I won't tell you what I do,' he once remarked coyly to a colleague. (Invariably, he would urinate in the yard.) He occasionally had a bath in a colleague's house: at Francis and Nancy Berry's house, which was round the corner at 3 Victoria Road, or in a later year at Derek and Louise Roper's, which was further down the same road, at number 21, from 1958 until 1965. (The eccentric Berrys were unstinting in affording him food and warmth in their delightfully shaggy Victorian house, and they never trespassed on his life with criticism or helpful suggestions.) The upper floors were occupied by an assortment of tenants, including some Jamaican families. From time to time he would be disturbed by their loud music, and now and then the police would raid the premises on unexplained missions; and yet the shouting-matches of his fellow-tenants did not seem to bother him terribly much: some folk said he must have been used to rather bullish arguments with his wife.[45]

He would live in these conditions for the remainder of his time at Sheffield—no less than seventeen years—until 1971; and until the last year or so an old woman ('my old tortoise') would come in to 'do' for him; the West Indians used to 'jolly her up'. But she did not clean very thoroughly, and even Empson occasionally became concerned about the insanitary state of his dive. 'Would you walk into my burrow one day,' he wrote to Francis Berry in March 1959, for example, 'and remove any rotting food you find there; I don't believe brave kind old 80 can either see or smell it.'[46] Besides being dirty, his pied-à-terre was also damp at times in the winter; but its smallness made it relatively easy to heat. Empson would emphasize, rightly so far as most visitors could tell, that it really did not smell. Otherwise, the place did seem to agree with him: cheap and handy, it did not attract an excessive number of callers, and involved no time-consuming keeping-up of standards; and it left him perfectly independent. The door was never locked during term and not always during vacations: there was nothing to be stolen. He was the proverbial beggar who could sing before the thief.

Hetta felt bad, at least in the beginning, about leaving him to make do all by himself, so sadly and sordidly, in what was virtually a slum. 'I think I'll have to go look for a place in the country near Sheffield,' she wrote to her lover on 13 October. 'William can't go on being professor & head of the Department from a room for ever. But the children must finish this year (i.e. till next summer vac.) at their present school before they can move because they haven't caught up yet though they're supposed to be being crammed. Then they could be boarded & I'd be free. Meanwhile here I sit all alone in foggy London being a landlady... Isn't it pitiful.'[47] Yet for whatever reason she would never make any real move to set up a home in Sheffield—she committed herself instead to the work of refurbishing the Hampstead house, where Empson would invariably go home for the whole of the vacations—and Empson came to find that this arrangement suited him thoroughly well. He could get on with his work—he felt he could work best of all during the night—he could go out to the pub as and when he felt like it; and he was free to enjoy the occasional sexual encounter. More than ten years later, Hetta would therefore write to an old friend who had witnessed something of the Empsons' domestic life in Peking in the late 1940s and early 1950s: 'I think he is happy to be able to go off to his burrow [in Sheffield] and then come to the smoke refreshed from solitary life. He never was a family person was he.'[48]

In addition, the Derbyshire countryside was easily accessible for the walks that Empson loved; every autumn he would requisition colleagues for a hike to behold the 'autumnal tints'. His old and valued colleague Francis Berry was to write in a poem celebrating his retirement:

> ...let us praise the Yorkshire man
> Emerging from his 'burrow' to stalk the moors;
> In pork-pie hat, his county to scan—
> Strong in the line of East Riding squires.[49]

At some point (as Hetta indicated) Empson started referring to his tenement dwelling as 'The Burrow', and it swiftly became known as 'Empson's Burrow' throughout the university and beyond. For the most part he regarded his tenement as a fine and private place: simple, safe, undemanding and inexpensive. In the depths of his first winter he would write to his friend John Hayward: 'I feel very cosy having an absolutely solitary week end in my bedsitting room and looking at the falling snow (in the backyard from the basement). The silence is profound. As I won't arrange to have any post here I had better go out soon and try to buy The Times.'[50] Of course, 'bedsitting room' flattered the hovel.

But not all was always well in The Burrow, since Empson could—at least during the earlier part of his residence—too easily overlook for long stretches of time the necessity to keep himself fit and well. One very cold winter in the early 1960s, for example, he became so unwell that the doctor said it was imperative for him to be taken into care. His young colleague Christopher Heywood, with his wife Annemarie, gave him hospitality and nursing at their home at 86 Totley Brook Road. Annemarie Heywood recalls:

> [H]e asked me to phone [Hetta] and tell her what was going on. She was (understandably) very reserved; her affection showed in the great amount of detail she demanded to know and the tips she offered. However she did not come (as he may have hoped), and did not phone back. He did not have pneumonia, but apparently a total systemic collapse. What the physician told me was that the presenting symptoms were of gross malnutrition; that, left to himself, he could not survive much longer. His sturdy physique concealed how he had neglected and deprived himself over a length of time. What he needed was to be confined to bed, fed endless nourishing well-balanced meals, and kept from cigarettes and alcohol.

Annemarie Heywood did not like the idea of taking on the role of guard or keeper of Empson, whom she regarded as a sympathetic friend, but since he denied that he was 'ill' and refused to go into a hospital or nursing home, it was felt that she was his best hope.

> And he agreed. Meek as a lamb, he was delivered to our house. We had a drink and a cigarette in the living room, then I took him up to his cell and bed. It was awful; he was so obedient and meek. He kept himself busy by endlessly rehearsing knight's moves from chess in a little notebook, and turning over mathematical riddles in his mind. But he must have picked up tone; after a week or so (I think he stood it for a fortnight altogether, much less than the doctor had felt was required) I discovered a stealthy caterpillar of cigarette ash next to his bed. After the next meal I offered him a ciggie

myself, and we had a serious conversation about the verboten substances, and how we felt about him (or anyone else) 'killing themselves' by smoking, drinking or anything else. As for 'eating sensibly', he felt he had learnt his lesson and would stop forgetting to eat and wolfing the odd bun when he got seriously hungry. And so he did. He started taking long walks, and was soon declared fit again.[51]

But he was also perhaps irritated by, and maybe even jealous of, the attention they gave their daughter, and sped back to his basement as soon as possible.

Still, the Empson Burrow was to be the scene of a number of spontaneous and charismastic audiences. One such occurred during a visit by the artist Michael Ayrton, who was accommodated for a few days in a sad Student Residence while he acquitted himself as Visiting Artist and Lecturer under the auspices of the Sheffield University Fine Arts Society. Christopher Heywood took him in hand for various outings and delighted in doing so, since Ayrton had a fantastic repertoire of anecdotes from a literary ancestry going back to the Pre-Raphaelites. Ayrton was utterly unacquainted with the 'visionary dreariness' (Empson's favoured phrase from Wordsworth, to describe the Sheffield environment), so Heywood drove him out for a 'Tour of the Bay'—as Empson termed the trek into the Derbyshire countryside. Later that day, running out of ideas for entertaining the gloomy Ayrton, Heywood took him along to the Burrow. It was about 4.30 on a dreary November day.

> Instantly, out came the bottle of Teachers; out came two or three teacakes, butter, and honey; out of some twitchable fly-netted safe there emerged pickles of the type everyone relished in the postwar decade; toothmugs appeared; and water from the tap outside, plus a kettle with more water for tea. Up came the Empson phrases and gestures: completely incredibly, Michael's gloom melted, the memories of Roy Campbell, Augustus John and others fluttered around, the Teachers bottle was drained, and by 5.30 the adventure was over, as the prospect of Opening Time had by then approached the horizon. Later Michael said he had never encountered such magical powers, anywhere. It was a trifle 'to be sure', but yet, no one else known to me had that power of unlocking a glow in a wilderness, and I was delighted that it was acknowledged.[52]

Francis Berry's celebratory poem 'William Empson' (already cited) includes these pertinent lines:

> To finish this section—and with a grand slam:
> Let us now praise the Sheffield burrow!
> For eighteen sessions the Empson home.

> Often from here, when disaster did loom,
> Would he answer the Dean, or other such bother,
> With an eye-weeping frolic, dispersing the gloom.

By 1953, when Empson arrived on the scene at Sheffield, the university was small by today's standards: the total student body numbered about 2,000 (there has been more than a twelvefold increase in the half-century since that date). The Departments of English, French and Classics were located in nice red-brick houses almost adjacent to the principal university offices in Firth Court on Western Bank; the Scala Cinema was a few steps further down on the same side of the road. Cream-coloured double-decker trams shrieked and whined past the windows as they toiled uphill from the city centre to the choicer suburbs of Broomhill and Fulwood. Of about 260 students in the Department of English Literature, most were reading for Intermediate courses, with 80 taking Final General degrees, and about 30 Honours degrees. Numbers of staff were correspondingly small: in addition to the Professor, there were just two Senior Lecturers—John Danby and Douglas Hamer (who had been a candidate for Empson's post)—and four lecturers: Francis Berry, G. D. Klingopulos, W. A. Murray, and Patricia Thomson, and all of them were capable, energetic teachers, scholars, and critics.

If the staff felt apprehensive about their new Head, he readily admitted to feeling scared of them and of the daunting situation in which he now found himself; he wrote to Hetta after his first two weeks, on 23 October 1953: 'I still feel somehow depressed and uneasy here, not to say simply frightened, but there is no reason to and so far as I can see it will settle down all right. . . . But I am sure all that's required is to remain helpful and rather dull.' But there was no question of his ever seeming 'rather dull': no one could doubt on first encountering him that he was eccentric—from the start, for instance, when he invariably failed to remember the names of colleagues from other departments, he would unaffectedly address them by their subject—'Good morning, Professor Empson.' 'Good morning, History.'[53] Even the doughty Yorkshireman Richard Wilson (his counterpart in English Language), who made Empson feel a little timid, was hailed as 'Anglo-Saxon'.

Nor was the 'Catholic Poet' on his staff a figure whom anybody could reckon dull, though Empson had obviously feared he might be tiresomely pi. Born in Malaya in 1915, Francis Berry had gained his BA from the University of London in 1947 and straightaway obtained a lectureship at Sheffield; he was to become well known for his critical works, including

Poets' Grammar (1958), *Poetry and the Physical Voice* (1962), and *The Shakespeare Inset: Word and Picture* (1965). He once declared to a student interviewer, presumably teasingly: 'you'd be astonished to know how shy dons are. Any approach to any don at any time (within reason) and he would be delighted.'[54] The reverse tendency to shyness seemed uppermost in Berry's own persona: he was universally known and enjoyed for his bracingly forthright manner, his enthusiasm, and his passion for reciting poetry at tremendously high volume on every possible occasion. (He would put on in his Broomhall garden an annual performance of *Comus*, featuring suitably-attired colleagues and students; but perhaps the best part of the show was that his earthily philistine neighbours would hurl colourful abuse at the thespians so gathered and even cast doubt upon their manhoods.) His self-dramatizing lessons would reverberate through the Department of English Literature, so penetratingly that other tutors would have to pause in their teaching with an indulgent smile while Berry finished off a mighty period. 'Poetry is sound-waves—not printed signs *for* sound,' he declared once to a student interviewer. 'What are your reasons then for being eccentric?' his intrepid interviewer inconsequentially asked. 'Am I?—and whether I am or not, why the "then"? . . . Explanation: I behave as I am or (which might equally be the case, I don't know) I behave as I do to conceal, armour or protect what I am.'[55] One of Berry's favourite tricks in tutorial was to identify the (invariably female) student who would have, as he suspected, the lowest boredom threshold; striding to and fro while declaiming poetry he would scrutinize the suspected student for the tell-tale moment when she would try to glance at her watch, whereupon he would pounce upon her like a lunging fencer and ask with no abatement of volume: 'Pray, Madam, what doth the tick-tock say?'[56] Empson took instantly to Berry's eccentrically vigorous and outgoing personality. In 1957, when Berry first put in for a Chair elsewhere, Empson supported him with a full-hearted reference including these comments:

> He is generous to his students in time and energy, and has frequently helped them in readings and dramatic performances, sometimes in the garden of his own house. In lectures and tutorials he lays stress on 'delivery' and brings out the impact of the sound of the poem under consideration in an impressive manner. He is thus a stimulating teacher with a very definite point of view; but also a man of wide interests and intelligence, not inclined to impose his point of view. He is a reliable and friendly colleague, and would be found an asset in social activities. His wife (an Anglican, by the way) is an excellent hostess, cool and helpful.[57]

But Francis Berry was also on occasion scruffy and dirty, with food perhaps staining his clothes and his nails grime-rimmed, so his Professor may have found him all the more sympathetic in that respect—before the age of the zip, and for want of a seamstress, Empson himself would often adopt the makeshift remedy of fastening his flies with one or two safety pins.

'Let us praise the jovial man,' wrote Berry in his poem for Empson:

> His splitting jokes at various bars,
> Quick Chinese walk, the ruddy tan.
>
> And let us praise the lucky man,
> Chestnuts pulled for him from many fires,
> Endearing helplessness, as endear it can.

(Professor Kenneth Muir, on occasional visits to Sheffield, gathered the impression that it was Berry himself who sometimes pulled the chestnuts— for example in preventing Empson from quarrelling with the bureaucrats.)[58]

At the other extreme, the one member of his staff Empson could not abide, and would never get on terms with, was the next in line of seniority, Douglas Hamer (his rival for the Chair, Hamer would be promoted Reader within a year or two). Empson would disparagingly refer to Hamer, both in and out of the Department, as his 'sergeant'. He would even send written notes to 'Education' saying that 'My sergeant knows about these things' and so on.[59] Empson and Hamer had woefully little in common except for their anti-clericalism; scholastically even, they were poles apart; and Empson was distant too from Hamer's wife, Enid, who, according to the Hamers' daughter Janet Martin, probably had a better mind than her father—and who considered Empson a fraud.[60] Hamer had a taste for administration, without (according to colleagues of the time) being outstandingly good at all aspects of it: he was better than Empson about routine things like remembering dates and answering letters, and almost certainly saved Empson a good many scrapes, but then he also had his full share of obsessions and phobias, and he had little tact.[61] He therefore undertook all the administration he could, implying that Empson was a hopeless person to be in charge of a Department. In 1957 Empson was to write very honestly: 'I am lucky at Sheffield. Hamer retires in five years time, and he would be angry if I tried to take the work away from him (it isn't that I cheat him into doing my work).'[62] Hamer was an unrelaxed and unrelaxing man, and it was actually a sore trial to have him endlessly fussing about. While Empson was glad to have some chores taken off his hands, he might have made a better show of it if Hamer had not always been breathing down his neck. 'Father was not an easy man,' Janet Martin has recalled, 'but he was an admirable administrator and found it difficult and frustrating to have a head of department who was not.'

Empson's view of the matter figures in a letter to the personnel department of a later date: 'In 1953, when I arrived here, there was no Secretary; Mr Hamer was always scolding away at his juniors saying they hadn't done their work, or their share of the work, and they hated him for it. This quarterdeck approach to discipline has become rare (I think) in large departments during that short time. I have myself welcomed the change, but my staff find it so natural that it would have been difficult to resist. They resent being badgered by the Professor unless clearly and provably in the wrong, though of course he ought to know when this point is approaching.'[63]

At Department meetings they would sit uncomfortably side by side behind Empson's desk and endeavour to share the chair, Empson making an announcement or request which would usually be prompted by Hamer or contradicted by him. Once, they had a blazing row in front of the rest of the staff, with the choleric Hamer slamming the desk they shared. On the whole, however, Empson did not greatly oppose Hamer, and probably he did not dare to: after all, Hamer had been around for years, knew the Faculty regulations by heart, and had a decisive and irascible manner. Empson once—extraordinarily, perhaps revealingly—said of Hamer to another colleague: 'He's my wife!' Whenever he felt he could afford it, he would take his colleagues out to a meal in preference to holding a boring meeting: matters could be negotiated at sensitive length over food and drink. 'My party went off with the intended effect of holding at bay any alarm and despondency,' he wrote to Hetta at one period of crisis. 'Various little arrangements could be made, and it was obviously much better than "holding a department meeting", which when I took it over from L. C. Knights was only an insane scene of decorously suppressed fury.'[64]

In 1963 Empson was to announce to Francis Berry, full of glee: 'Hamer is retiring at the end of this session. I *am* glad I'm not retiring, I've got eight years to go.' And not long after Hamer's retirement, Derek Roper took the occasion to ask Empson how he felt about it. 'Like everybody else,' Empson replied, '—exactly like the grass when you take the roller off it.'[65] (Francis Berry was to take up much of the administrative burden formerly shouldered by Hamer.)

His colleague Eric Mackerness[66]—whom Empson turned into a Scotsman by stressing the second syllable of his name (though eventually he became simply 'Mac')—wrote in an obituary:

> During his years at Sheffield Empson acquired a reputation for being something of a 'character'. In personality he was endearingly eccentric and utterly uninterested in formal propriety. As departmental head his methods were distinctly unconventional and his apparent waywardness was often construed as negligence. The truth of the matter was, however, that in Empson's estimation the Department's duty to the student took precedence over administrative obfuscation.[67]

In that last sentence, of course, Mackerness was posing a false opposition, a specious contrast, but it is natural for academics to mock administrators. Yet it shows the strength of his commitment to Empson's priority, the teaching of students, over the pompous importunate paperchase of the bureaucrat's lot.

What sort of Head of Department and colleague did Empson become? Was he as feckless as some of his referees and assessors feared, or as Douglas Hamer endeavoured to make him out to be? The answer is that for the most part, surprising though it may seem, he acquitted himself with considerable professionalism, being in general extremely diligent in the performance of his duties. He was not sloppy in office. Students who needed references, for example, would be provided in no time at all with exact and detailed assessments of their characters, attainments, and potential (and long before anyone invented freedom of information, he would as often as not happily invite the student to peruse what he had written about him or her). He was dutiful too in tackling the background work that was required of him in his capacity as an examiner. Even during his first year, he had to undertake an oral examination of an MA thesis on the works of Jacob Tonson; although the subject was not in his direct line of interest, he nevertheless asked several searching questions about possible influences of the ballads published in Tonson's *Miscellanies*.[68] In his first year too, he took pains to start up a series of public readings by poets: the first to perform, at his invitation, was Edith Sitwell.[69] The gruffness or hauteur he sometimes assumed was recognized by most people who got to know him closely as a cover for nervousness; it made him remarkably sympathetic to the frailties of others, whom he usually treated with consideration and kindness. Loathing authoritarianism of any kind, and certainly of the bullying kind that Hamer would have favoured, and even fearful of anything that smacked of organized life, he cultivated naturally unforbidding relations with his staff and students. His single stated objective was to engage and stimulate young minds, not to bamboozle them.

If Empson himself attacked anyone, it was their foolish and misbegotten ideas (as he would see them) that he would attack, not the vulnerable human being. A quarrel was rarely personal—though admittedly it would be difficult on occasion for his opponent to appreciate the difference. 'I think So-and-so's going off his head,' he would invariably exclaim to Francis Berry with seemingly complete and sincere bewilderment about any colleague whose ideas struck him as unaccountably wrong-headed.

He was to claim, on receiving an honorary degree three years after his retirement:

> I did not arrive feeling any conscientious need to make radical changes. The danger of a bold appointment, of course, is that the man may want to destroy what has been built up before. The first thing to realise, I said to myself, is that you have here a working system, and it should not be tampered with except for strong reason. Actually there was a good deal of change in my time, and I seldom regretted it; but that basic attitude has become stronger in my mind now than it was at first. I think that Sheffield and the other universities of about the same age are in effect holding the fort; the very old universities and the very new ones have both given up, on this issue. We still, by and large, try to cover the field in the three years to the BA degree, without breaking it up into options.[70]

Despite the unorthodoxy of his views in so many other respects—notably including what he himself was to designate the 'heresy' of his blazing and principled antagonism to blindly Christian readings of literature—and the unconventionality of his temperament and conduct, he was to that degree a traditionalist. The students must needs be introduced to the fullest range of literature, to stretch their imaginations into other minds and other cultures.

The only other principle he brought to bear in his governance of his Department concerned the question of new appointments. In 1964 he was to declare in print: 'As an opinionated man myself, I have tried to appoint people with a variety of opinions which set one another off; this is particularly needed in English Literature, which admits greater variety of judgement than any other University Department.'[71] The sincerity of his paradoxical conviction in that respect is easily illustrated. Late in 1952 (not long after returning from China), he published in the *New Statesman* a predominantly derogatory review of Donald Davie's *Purity of Diction in*

English Verse (in which he detected what he called, in a memorable phrase, the 'strong smell of monks and commissars'[72]). A year later, when he was seeking permission from the Vice-Chancellor to fill a staff vacancy—the post held by the departing Danby—he was concerned initially to put forward the merits of his friend George Fraser as a candidate for the position (though Fraser indicated that he would probably not be able to live on the paltry salary on offer). If he failed to secure Fraser for the post, Empson went on (in a letter to Hetta): 'I might next try Donald Davie of Dublin who wrote that he wanted to come here, earlier.'[73] Thus, coming as it did only a few months on from his roasting of Davie's book, his suggestion that he might well invite Davie to put in for the job demonstrates that he meant exactly what he said about deliberately seeking a genuine diversity of approaches among his staff.

Empson's approach to interviewing could be idiosyncratic and disconcerting; his judgements uncalculable. In 1958 Elizabeth M. Brennan was shortlisted along with three men for an Assistant Lectureship; one of the candidates did not show up for the interview, so her chances jumped up by that margin. On the day of the interviews, it was not a secretary but the Head of Department himself who appeared at the door where the interviews were to be conducted. 'I am Empson,' he announced.[74] However, having been shown into the room, she was then subjected to what she recalls as 'the most aggressive interview I've ever experienced'.[75] Empson quizzed her for fifteen minutes on the subject of her dissertation, then turned to the other members of the panel and remarked: 'It's no good. She obviously knows her stuff.' The second candidate was a fine upstanding young Leavisite whose equally abrasive interview lasted for some twenty minutes. The third candidate was Derek Roper, and he was offered the job on the spot: his interview, or so it seemed, had lasted only about five minutes. Roper was to remain on strength at Sheffield for over thirty years.

It is not known on what grounds Brennan was turned down; on the face of it, she was well qualified. Probably, an unwise revelation that she was unread in modern literary criticism was held against her. But it is fairly unlikely that Empson had been prejudiced against her gender. Within a few years, in 1963, he was happy to give a job to the young, Yorkshire-born scholar, Roma Gill—whom Empson would refer to as 'Romagill', as if her names were one trisyllabic word. The Department secretary made it known to Romagill, after her interview, that Empson had been keen to appoint a woman—and this at a time before anyone had become terribly fussed about equal opportunities—even though, throughout the interview, he appeared to her to be hiding himself behind a newspaper. At the end, when she was bold enough to ask about her duties, he responded: 'Well, of course, my dear, you'll be teaching Elizabethan drama.' Gill had a very warm and natural manner, and a natural sense of the dramatic, and the students liked her. Empson respected her work on Marlowe, and would bandy quotations with her like a gentleman, though her churchiness must have given him pause. Derek Roper has remarked that Roma Gill's first years at Sheffield must have been happy: 'Academic life was more leisurely then, women lecturers were less numerous, and Roma, who could be amusing, was made much of: at lunchtime she was often found in the staff club bar surrounded by heads of departments She seemed in robust health, and with some of her friends she took up riding.' Within a few years the first symptoms of the multiple sclerosis that was to disrupt her career began to be apparent, but throughout the mid-1960s she and Empson developed a mutual and ever-dependable affection and regard: this was so solid that when in 1967 he had to undergo an eye operation at a local hospital and felt concerned about having to convalesce all on his own, he simply announced to her: 'I'll come and spend a few days with you.' He proved to be an undemanding but unorthodox after-care patient. He arrived with two half-bottles of brandy and gin, and would start to consume the brandy even before breakfast. She felt obliged to hide the gin bottle, because drinking gin seemed to make him quarrelsome. Still, he would get up and cook breakfast for both of them: onions and eggs, which he seemed to favour. And often he would disappear for a drink at the nearest pub, or head off for a walk by himself. On one occasion, he requested her to trim his unruly beard—'Every woman has scissors in her handbag,' he declared. She tackled the task well.[76] Still, it has to be said that she was the only woman Empson ever appointed to his staff.

Empson's slightly unnerving and wholly unpredictable demeanour at interviews was to continue even unto the end of his career at Sheffield, but he was delighted when interviewees or, for that matter, colleagues showed enough self-belief to argue for their ideas and convictions, and to defend their ideas if he ever challenged them—whether fairly or unfairly.

In his verses honouring Empson in 1974, Francis Berry aptly stressed:

> In the teaching of a variety of text,
> His policy was 'variety of opinion'.
> Remember the mixture that he mixed:
>
> Atheist, catholic, quaker, scrutineer;
> Oxford, marxist, la-dee-la and fiddle-de-dee;
> Post-christian roamer, the sweet-girl pagan.

The list was by no means random. If Empson was the atheist, and Berry the Catholic, the Quaker was Eric Mackerness, the scrutineer Mark Roberts, the 'Oxford' Derek Roper, and the Marxist Ray Southall. 'Post-christian roamer' is a punning reference to Roma Gill, who was a lifelong High Anglican. Empson's belief in a vitalizing opposition of views was realized at Sheffield.

For his own teaching, Empson would tutor both Honours and General (later Combined Subjects) students. At that time, groups numbered from four to eight, and he preferred a group to the one-to-one tutorial as formerly practised at Oxbridge—which he described emphatically as 'horrible'. He would take considerable pains to treat his groups with friendliness, tact and even-handedness. When his successor, Brian Morris, was to find in his desk a pair of dice and wondered how they found a place in his professional life, Empson happily explained his simple means of ensuring equity: 'Dice, or the spun coin, or the black spot, should always be used to decide which member of the tutorial group writes the essay to be read out next week. Students are rather prone to feel themselves imposed upon, but a sporting result disarms the suspicion, and I never found it resisted without good cause.'[77]

'I find it very stimulating being a university lecturer,' Empson was to say in a later year. 'You're forced to reconsider your opinions all the time.' He took a real interest in his students and their ideas, Derek Roper recalls, and would question them closely about the meaning of what they said or wrote, which often seemed to him strange enough; several of his later critical pieces take off from close encounters of this kind. He marked their essays very carefully, annotating freely in red ink and paying attention to punctuation and spelling as well as to content. 'If one, then the other,' he would write of parenthetical commas. He disliked the vague use of *however* as a linking word, and on one offending essay he annotated each appearance: 'needless however', 'baffling however', 'eerie however'. One student recorded an Empson comment on the handwriting of a fellow student: 'like a corpse crawling with worms'.[78] Eric Mackerness saw the pains that Empson took: 'I have never known any don so meticulous in the marking of students' essays.'[79] On the other hand, Empson respected the students enough to believe they could take tough criticism. 'He had a habit of writing exhaustive marginalia,' Mackerness noted, 'usually tendered in a vein which made it clear he was taking serious issue with the student, much as he might do with a correspondent in the *Times Literary Supplement*. For those unaccustomed to Empson's polemical mode, this could be disconcerting; but it gave the tyro a chance to see at first hand how a mind formed by frequent perusal of "the best that is known and thought in the world" sets about the business of creating "a current of true and fresh ideas".[80] And again, on his bearing in seminars: 'Empson is reluctant to make concessions to intransigence; yet he has always encouraged students who were bold enough to adopt an authentically personal approach.'

Not surprisingly, Empson became by and large extremely popular with the students for the direct way in which he engaged with them: he was felt to be not just an entertaining eccentric but a person of obvious genuineness and humanity. The eccentricity was apparent in his every action. At the beginning of one tutorial on Henry James, for example, he removed his shoes and socks; then he threw his socks on the fire; and finally he brought out a new pair of socks and put them on. 'James would have approved,' he remarked by way of inconsequential explanation. As Professor Harry Armytage—himself a brilliant educationalist, polymath and raconteur[81]—once insisted to me about this well-attested story, Empson was not a poseur: he unconsciously and naturally suited his actions to the subject.

(Socks feature as an incidental but fundamental leitmotiv in his life. Since he lived in very inadequate accommodation, and was not looking after himself at all well, he was forever bringing his wet socks into the library and draping them over a basement radiator, or the hot-water pipes, or on a plinth, or even on the shelves. 'I wonder if you've found my socks?' he would diffidently ask the staff. When it was not socks, it would be a famous filthy hat that he would leave around in the library: a thick tropical hat with a low crown. Later on, in the new library, he arrived at the book issue counter one day. 'Humph, humph—have you found a paper bag— large—Marks and Spencer—with a pair of pyjamas in it?' The staff always found him completely pleasant and polite—'a trouble-free library user,' as one of them described him.)[82]

To some students he became virtually a guru: they found his gnomic brilliance irresistible. Derek Roper was of the opinion too: 'One reason why our Department had an easier time than some others during the post-1968 student unrest may well be that its head was so clearly the reverse of a faceless bureaucrat.' For himself—especially after enduring such continual difficulties with his students in China—Empson described his British students, at least to begin with, as supremely 'dove-like'.[83] On his retirement he would ironically praise them: 'From my observations of Sheffield students I feel confident that they are equal in moral stature to those of China and Japan, though fortunately not so often called upon to be heroes.'

'As a lecturer,' Eric Mackerness remarked in his eulogy, 'he may well have seemed boring to the inattentive student, but for those sincerely interested in literature his modes of discourse opened up perspectives of a new and fascinating kind.' As with the tutoring, he did his full share of the lecturing, not granting himself any remission on account of his managerial duties. He liked to lecture best of all on Shakespeare, as well as other Renaissance poetries and drama. Quite often he brought no notes with him to the lecture podium, or at most a page of scribbles. His course of lectures on Shakespeare, for instance, consisted of a ramble through the works in roughly chronological order, dwelling on some and missing out others, and giving such facts and comments as occurred. On one occasion, he was desperate—or brave— enough to ask the class what he was supposed to be lecturing on. '*Antony and Cleopatra*,' they grudgingly replied. 'Who has read *Antony and Cleopatra*?' he asked. There was no response. 'Well, you'd better go away.'

As a rule, his lecturing style was conversational but remotely allusive— he had a horror of the obvious. He carried a one-volume Shakespeare from which pages or gatherings dropped as he hunted for a place. 'That's a nice old book and it's been with me all round the world, and it can fall to pieces when it likes.' The students enjoyed these performances, but it is not certain that they found them altogether helpful in the understanding of Shakespeare. Perhaps under the influence of his colleague Francis Berry, Empson seemed more interested in the sound and music of verse than he had been at the beginning of his career. He would tell his audience with emphasis how in *Richard III* 'suddenly the verse begins to sing!' Then he would read a few lines from Clarence's dream, culminating in 'That stabb'd me in the field by Tewksbury' (I. iv. 56), in the manner he called 'booing it out', which was something not unlike W. B. Yeats's 'chaunting'; but he did not explain what made the verse sing. In general, he was suspicious of much modern criticism, and his drift could seem oddly old-fashioned to a progressive listener.

He took great pains with his lecture on *Hamlet*, and put forward an original view: that much of the play, including the insufferable character of Hamlet himself, was to be explained as a parody of the *Ur-Hamlet*. The only reason Hamlet was a mystery is that he said he was a mystery, and he said this to tease the audience and exaggerate the absurdities of 'the old play'. This was an interesting view but, since the *Ur-Hamlet* is totally lost except for the two words 'Hamlet, revenge!', a hard one to challenge.

On the whole, Eric Mackerness's clever and slightly defensive eulogy does him fair justice: 'so far as the lax and indifferent student is concerned, his lecturing style conveys a good deal less than it is intended to; but for really keen and attentive listeners, the penetrating comments embedded in his discourse provide a stimulus which "personal magnetism" alone cannot account for. Empson's way of treating literary topics indicates that he habitually speaks out of a profundity of involvement and with a strikingly perceptive awareness of textual intricacies. Although not "academic" in the mundane sense of that word, he yet holds in reserve a vast amount of erudition—and the relevance of this is seldom lost on students who are prepared to meet the challenge of his provocative expressiveness.'[84] Some might have swallowed such kindly euphemisms only with a chaser of irony.

His Inaugural Lecture, given in the Mappin Hall towards the end of his first term (2 December), has become part of the stuff of the Empson legend. It is possible that he had never heard an inaugural lecture before and did not know of the convention that such a lecture should be a high-level, if not 'state-of-the-art', address in an area of academic specialization: a presentation of hard-earned wisdom made accessible for an audience of good but diverse intelligences. As if to emphasize his arrival at Sheffield as a watershed in his life, Empson chose to frame his lecture, 'Teaching English in the Far East and England', entirely in terms of autobiographical anecdote, telling about his career and adventures in the period 1931 to 1952: that is, his experiences in Japan and China, before and after the war, with just one linking paragraph on the BBC. His purpose may have been to attempt a bit of mild self-vindication, as if to answer those who would find fault with his want of experience of teaching English in England (whence the peculiar title of the lecture); he knew he had accumulated years of exotic and extreme experiences. But he was well aware too that the effect might seem rather egocentric and boastful. In November he wrote to Professor Bonamy Dobrée at Leeds:

> I write this in a mood of exhaustion after feeling my Inaugural is all right, at least it is over-length and can be cut freely, by my wife for example if she can be bothered. It is an extremely disgusting thing which has cost me a lot in whisky, because it is pure Show Off, and I *can* show off; the whole trouble about this silly thing, which has to be written for printing, is that is has to be a show-off in what *they* consider good taste. But never mind, I feel I have done it now, I don't have to shut myself up alone and drink beastly whisky to finish it, anyhow.[85]

On the big day, he looked presentable enough, in his freshly laundered brown suit and academical gown, but it soon became apparent to many in the audience that he may have primed himself too well. It seemed to

Professor Armytage that what Empson was clutching in his hands was a sheaf of toilet paper—this is how the legends begin—but in fact he had typed his talk onto tissue-thin paper: the sort used for letters sent 'by air' or for carbon copying. He was introduced by the Vice-Chancellor, Professor Whittaker, whose conspicuous nervousness would not have helped him to keep his own nerve.

> Well, ladies and gentlemen [Empson started off], I should explain in the first place, thinking of the title announced, that I have no business to lecture about teaching English literature in England, because I have only just begun to do it; my previous experience has all been in the Far East, three years in Japan and seven in China. But it seemed better to give this title, putting in England as well, because I *ought* to know something about doing it at home; that is, such experience as I have had ought to be some use to me in my work here. And I thought that, from your point of view, there might at least be, as they say, some curiosity-value in hearing an account of this experience; whether there is any other value in it I hardly know, and perhaps it is for others to decide rather than me. I am afraid it makes rather a trivial and gossipy Inaugural, but I also feel it is the main thing I have to offer on this occasion. I could talk, instead, about my theoretical books, which have been mainly about double meanings in literature, and the mechanics of how they have a literary effect; but I haven't found that that has much to do with teaching literature, in my experience so far; so it is perhaps not very relevant here. In fact, I have generally tried to put off my Far Eastern students from reading my books, which I thought would only worry and distract them. *They* have sometimes taught *me* something theoretical, or so I thought, when I had to consider why they found something difficult to learn; but that is another matter.[86]

That opening gambit, which was quite obviously calculated to be chatty and charmingly unpretentious, was misconstrued by a number of people in the audience who felt it sounded just too casual, too amateurish, too indifferent. So far from showing off, he seemed to them to be deprecating even his own professional project. Hearsay or gist reports of those introductory remarks have typically reduced them, with the passing of the years, to a crude vaunt: 'I suppose you want to know what you've bought . . .'[87] Thus his modesty, coupled with his speedy manner of speaking and throwaway delivery, struck some as a version of arrogance. When he reached the moment of describing his experience in China of bathing with water buffalo and climbing onto their slimy backs—'I strongly recommend them as toys for the bath; no rubber fish is anything like as good'—the charm of the anecdote was abrupted by an audible belch from the lecturer. Mrs Laughton, wife of the Professor of Latin, noticeably ducked her head. (Later it would be said that Professor Laughton had walked out.) Another anecdote went down equally badly. When the Communists came to power in China in 1949 and requested that he substitute a prose course for his poetry course, he related with a chuckle, 'I said...I would need to begin with at least six weeks on the Bible. I thought this was trying them rather high, but they didn't even blink at it. Under the old system the government teachers were very separate from the missionary ones, and I had actually never lectured on the Bible before, in China or Japan. It seemed to me a rather comical result of the Communists trying to be practical, and I made little jokes about my Bible Class to my Chinese colleagues, but I could feel they were rather bored by this and didn't think it was funny.' Yet nor was his seeming flippancy deemed to be funny by one or two members of his audience who made a serious profession of the Bible.

But the moment at which Empson really misjudged his tone, and was felt by some to have slipped up in taste, came early in the lecture, when he moved to fulfil the conventional duty of paying tribute to his predecessor:

> I ought also to say something about my predecessor in this Chair, Mr L. C. Knights, and I can praise him very sincerely. So far as I can make out, the way the English Literature Department now stands, which I suppose is largely due to him, is so right that my chief duty is to let it go on, the way it does, and try not to do anything to spoil it. Also he is an impressive person. The comment that does occur to me about him is that he is *too* conscientious; what Knights ought to do is to insist on making enough time to write his own excellent books, and he hasn't done that now for some while. I first met Knights...in 1950 in America, at the Kenyon Summer School, to which he had come from Sheffield largely by sea and I largely by air from Communist Peking. I remember the Korean War had just started at the time. Each of the lecturers at this Summer School has to do one speech to the assembled body, followed by a discussion; and I was in a way an old boy, as I had done it before in 1948; and Knights came to me, looking very worried as usual, and said 'I am very worried about my speech. I can't decide what I *ought* to say to them.' It seemed to me that our friends there didn't require any special tact, and I said 'Why, scold them, of course, tell them what's the matter with them. That's the only thing they wouldn't consider dull, it's the only thing they brought you here to do.' But his face got longer and longer and his eyes got rounder and rounder, and he said 'Do you think I really *have* to tell them what I think about them?' So I said 'Oh no, of course you don't have to, let it go, don't worry, I was only making a joke'; so I said, though I hadn't thought I was making a joke. They would

have put up with a lot of rudeness from him, because they thought him a kind of medieval saint, very reasonably; incidentally they thought his thinness was another proof that we are all starving to death in England. But he decided he didn't *have* to say what he thought about them, and the subject sank without a bubble into the depths of his mind. I don't know what it was, but I am sure he had better have said it. But you could tell it would have cost him too much; he would have blamed himself for it too much. It would be stupid not to admire this kind of character very warmly, but one would like more to come out.

This was felt to be going too far. Whereas it is the general rule simply to laud the public achievements of the predecessor, Empson in his candour over-personalized his portrait. Not only did he make a joke of Knights's famous skinniness, he depicted him as an austere, neurotic worrier; politic, cautious, and meticulous; such a ditherer that he did not get on with the activity he was best at: writing books.[88] Those in the audience who had worked with Knights assuredly recognized the portrait, but at best they could only smile wryly and nervously. It seemed that Empson was treading the razor's-edge of tact and might well have drunk enough to stumble over it at any moment.

Notwithstanding, the lecture as a whole amounted to a notable piece of personal testimony; it also enabled him to convey a timely political sub-text: to bear witness on behalf of China—albeit a China that had gone Communist.

Despite being chronically allergic to formal propriety, and his occasional over-indulgence in drink, Empson came to be valued by the large majority of his colleagues in other departments. 'Sheffield's Faculty of Arts was badly in need of a colourful character or two ...,' wrote Professor Stewart Deas (Head of the Department of Music from 1948 until 1968), 'and in my book Empson fitted the bill. He was often delightfully inconsequential, or seemingly so, but I suspect that his mind really just leapt over the insignificant intermediate details.'[89] In those early, much more formal days it was a shock to some in attendance to see Empson arrive an hour late for a meeting of the Senate and proceed to take off both his overcoat and his jacket: he was probably the first person at that forum to stand up and speak in his braces. At Senate and Faculty board meetings, which appeared to cause him agonies of boredom (they were the 'nannies'), he would do his best to distract himself with algebraic doodles—writing an equation and solving it, adding some new term and solving that, then adding another, and so on, so that the equations would propagate themselves across the page line after line.[90] He felt incited to speak only occasionally, though often to useful effect. It would be his purpose to dispel collective fug and above all to cut short the speechifying of others. Other individuals on the various committees would appreciate the odd succinct or witty comment from him. No doubt the effect of his interventions lay in their timing, the moment chosen.

The degree of affection he inspired in his colleagues can be deduced from an anecdote by Professor Edward Miller. Occasions when staffing was to be discussed were bound in general to provoke severe inter-departmental rivalries, but Miller found it remarkable to note how other Heads of Department made it their business to look after Empson's interests. 'I remember well one meeting of the Faculty of Arts committee for drawing up the Faculty's bids for new posts. Empson was present but seemed to have no demands to make; it was the other heads of department present who made a case for his department. I cannot imagine them doing so for anyone else.'[91]

However bored or dyspeptic Empson seemed, he missed little. Once, when the Department of Psychology brought forward a research proposal on the subject of 'the devising of a system for the measurement of fear', Empson sprang up, instantly alert. 'Is it proposed that there should be laboratory experiments on animals or human beings?' he interjected, being only too aware of the dangerous possibility that the Faculty might pass on the nod a license for cruelty. As if at his signal, other members spoke up against the proposal (though it is not known whether he and they prevailed that day).[92]

He was by no means innocent of the politicking that takes place in committees of whatever sort; indeed, he once reflected to himself, in some loose notes (no doubt with a backward glance at his work in 'propa-ganda' at the BBC): 'When as a member of a large committee I feel that we are being bamboozled or browbeaten I do not feel spontaneously indig-nant; I reflect that there may well be reasons we had better not be told, and that this is the proper way to swing the votes of a committee.' But in general he had no great respect for people who considered themselves good with committees. Towards the end of his career at Sheffield, at a time when student activists at last won the right for students to participate in the councils of the university, he was to write a valedictory piece welcoming that progressive step and including this wry, true observation: 'I am glad that the principle of Student Participation has been accepted by the English universities; for one thing, the ghostly student presence does seem to make us old men a bit less rude. But I hope the student representatives grasp that most work on committee is shockingly dull, except to people who are unlikely to get good results from it.'[93] Professor Laughton (Latin) told me that during his own period of duty as Dean (1961–4) he had welcomed Empson's 'illuminatingly simple points'; but it turned out that what he remembered best of all was a specific encounter with Empson, one day after a four-hour marathon in Faculty. To Laughton's weary-cheery remark that somehow they had managed to get through the entire agenda, Empson responded simply: 'Yes, we collapsed into agreement.'

There were few of his colleagues he disliked, though one was Professor R. J. Hopper (Ancient History), who was to insult him in some unknown way. In 1968, just three years before his retirement, he would write of Hopper: 'The Dean is no longer my enemy but is intriguing with me, not that I like that at all, but [at] least the silly pig doesn't bear me a grudge because he insulted me.'[94] Empson coined a superb simile for his harsh foe: 'Hopper has a voice like coke being poured out of a hod.'[95] Yet quite contrarily, it appears that Empson did bear Hopper a grudge: when on his retirement he discovered the name of Hopper on the list of subscribers to his leaving present, he insisted that the name be taken off and the contribution returned (this was done).[96] The only other member of the faculty he could never get on terms with was Maurice Bruce (Director of Extramural Studies at Sheffield from 1947 till his retirement in 1975), though the reason for the enmity has not been handed down. Perhaps to show his dislike, he did a vulgar thing at dinner with the Bruces one day: he asked for port, but they did not have any at home—so they were obliged to go out on a special trip to buy the liquor he required.[97]

With all other staff, especially if they simply accepted him as he was and did not seek to find fault, he was always on convivial and entertaining terms. At lunchtimes, he liked to patronize the Staff Club—originally located just off the entrance to Firth Hall, where there was also a refectory in the basement—and there he would be happy to chat with anyone about a wide variety of topics (though it was not always evident whether he could tell one person from another, from one day to another). Yet when he reached what he regarded as the end of the conversation he would simply get up and leave, without any formal courtesies or conventional 'signing-off' gestures.

Since Empson read every word of *The Times* and was keenly up with the world's agenda, as well as periodicals including the *New Statesman* and *New Scientist*, there was something fresh to talk about at all times. Often he was simply effervescent, and his explosions of mirth were delightful to see and to share. One day in the staff club, he literally loped over to Harry Kay to quiz him about a report in the *New Scientist* on the subject of Left-Handed Polar Bears: the piece purported in a sly way to explain why polar bears had the advantage over humans in a tight corner because a scientist had discovered that they are predominantly left-handed. This finding really tickled Empson's sense of humour, and he urged Kay as a psychologist to open up some research on the subject.[98] He accosted another colleague, Neville Moray (also a psychologist), with a similar barrage of questions. How could one tell the bears were left-handed? Perhaps when stalking their prey they had to cover the black tip of the nose so that they would not be seen by the prey, and used one paw rather than another for this purpose? 'He was a source of constant delight,' Moray recalls, 'and one of the people who gave the lie to the "two cultures" nonsense.'[99]

What colleagues took to be his 'other-worldiness', or detachment from the practicalities of life, is illustrated by an exchange overheard all too clearly by another colleague. Professor Armytage had to explain to Empson, very patiently, and almost in words of one syllable—as to a child—how he should handle some personal taxation problem. 'In the University we have a Department of Accountacy. There is a man named Whittington-Smith who is Head of it. You will find him at . . . and he will be able to tell you exactly what to do.' What particularly struck the bystander was that Armytage assumed—obviously correctly—that Empson would not have the faintest idea that the University had such a teaching department, and that he would not know Whittington-Smith—even though the University was so small at the time.[100]

His regular lunchtime drink was 'black and tan', an equal mixture of Guinness and draught bitter. He would sink a pint or two of this, and smoke some awful black tobacco—he was for many years a copious smoker—while chatting away. At other times he showed a penchant for a fairly rich mixture of gin and peppermint. He liked the drink better than the food—loathing sandwiches, he always took hot dishes—of which he often left a good deal. At other times he liked whisky, preferably Vat 69, with plenty of water. He disliked neat spirits, and would water a gin-and-French. He drank because he liked it, because it was a sociable activity—though he was essentially a loner, with a quality of remoteness about him that made a barrier to close relationships—and as a means of relaxing. Being a tense, 'highly-strung' person, he believed that a few drinks would take some of the tension out. Though never an alcoholic, he did not have an especially strong head, so there was always the danger that he would overdo the relaxing process—especially if he was upset, or nervous about some impending public or social event. When drunk, he spoke in a slurred, exaggerated drawl. He would close his eyes and sway his head, or his whole body, from side to side. From being genial he could quickly pass to being obtuse, then rude and aggressive, and finally incoherent. At such times his prejudices would emerge in their crudest forms. All this gave pain to his friends, pleasure to his enemies, and satisfaction to those who counted on him for entertainment. Sometimes, he may even have played up to such people. (He was very rarely sick when drunk, though on one occasion in the late 1960s he did manage to vomit over the counter of the Star and Garter pub, behind the University Arts Tower. Appalled on-lookers were nonetheless favourably impressed by the way he made up for his gross behaviour with elaborate and winning courtesy.)[101]

He was not often invited out for a meal, because there was always the distinct chance of his arriving very late and inebriated. Those who persisted were rewarded with wit and wisdom in return for the occasional flurry of embarrassment. When Professor Armytage came to collect him for dinner one day, Empson suddenly bethought himself: 'I must get something for your wife.' Dashing into an off-licence, he emerged with a box containing two dozen bottles of beer. At the end of the meal, when he absent-mindedly—and presumably drunkenly—moved to stub out his cigarettes in the remains of the mashed potatoes, his hosts rebuked him: 'There are people starving in China!' He replied merely, 'I know'—of course, he did know—and carried on stubbing out his cigarettes in the mash. He enjoyed a meal very often at the Berrys' house, but on one occasion, presumably out of sheer contrariness, he responded to an invitation: 'No, to tell you the truth, I don't like your wife's cooking.' But then he added, to soften the blow for his being so rude and curmudgeonly: 'Come to that, I don't like my wife's cooking either!'

All told, his first year at Sheffield amounted to a mixed experience. Inevitably there were times when he felt overborne by his unaccustomed duties, or fretful about the routine grind of business, or at times resentful. One day, for example, he would write to Hetta: 'It is going on all right here, though I can't get away from feeling cross with them often.' On another, he admitted, 'I feel more abreast of things now.'[102] The business of having to compile several batches of exam papers all at once in January each year invariably and comprehensibly shook his nerves.[103] Or again: 'It isn't only neurosis that makes me feel continually afraid that I [have] forgotten to do something...I have just been collecting myself...and doing a lot of the odd jobs which frighten me if I don't do them...'[104] By late April 1954, with the onset of his first summer term, he recovered some hopefulness: 'It is peaceful here at present, though I suppose some bother or other will soon rear its head. I got much more cheerful towards the end of the holiday, or rather shook off a state of neurotic gloom, and still feel much better; so much so that I have stopped drinking for a bit merely out of placidity.'[105] Hetta Empson was to claim in a miserable letter to a friend as late as May 1954: '[William] is entirely self-absorbed as usual, & hates Sheffield but is obstinately determined to go on with it.'[106] But that letter may have conveyed more of her own feelings than the full and just measure of Empson's sense of things. In truth, it is apparent that more and more, as the months went on, he was to find a great deal in his new role which gave him immense satisfaction. The balance was to shift decisively in favour of the life and the work at Sheffield.

Taken for all in all, he was delighted to have found his fit place in an English university. He really loved his teaching, he liked the society; for the very most part he enjoyed his colleagues; and the job gave him the time to do his writing. In addition, only the life of academia could accommodate his small eccentricities and relative waywardnesses. Moreover, he was delighted not to have to pursue a full-time career in literary journalism (the only really viable alternative for a person of his gifts, mentality, and manners), which he criticized for demanding rushed opinions and crudeness of writing. In 1959—in response to a questionnaire on this subject— he was to set out for Boris Ford his deeply-weighed profession of faith (a 'Personal Affirmation', as Ford called it) on the vital connection between literary criticism and the university.

> [Literary criticism] has become a much more powerful and interesting tool since about 1900, and many of the able literary young want to go in for it. They can I think certainly do it quite as well while employed as dons, though they should be warned against insisting they must be Professors, a capacity in which they are liable to get heavy extra chores. Bonamy Dobrée warned me like that when I was looking for a job after leaving Communist China ... I do not regret the way it fell. But at least a literary critic can become a university lecturer without feeling that he is wasting his talent, and indeed is likely to improve it that way.
>
> My students in Tutorials at Sheffield (of course the Professor just shares out with the other lecturers) don't seem to me as interesting as at Tokyo or Peking merely because they are less strange, but really they are just as much a problem; you need all the time to try to understand where the resistance comes from, and whether there is a good or in fact interesting reason behind it. I do not know how a literary critic could be in such close contact with the existing audience reaction anywhere else; he certainly won't do it by writing

journalism in obedience to the hunch of an editor. Even the process of lecturing, however much you consider it outdated by the invention of print, means for the lecturer that he acquires in the course of years a great familiarity with his subject. So long of course as he has not played the fatal trick of writing a lecture and reading it out more than once; this I have never done, and most lecturers don't. Indeed, the trouble is that distinguished old buffers like me rapidly reach the point where they can talk away about anything in their field but can't bear to write it down. A duty of high speed in writing should not be imagined, but they can do an article or one chapter of the book each holiday if they took that into their heads as the target, and they would come to it much fresher really than if they tried to write their book all the time. I think I would become gravely ill if I tried to write my book all the time.

But this alternative is not quite what is offered to us critics. You must remember that, if a young critic makes the great renunciation, saying "It is beneath me to read all these horrid essays", the next thing he will have to do is turn out a lot of shockingly coarse hackwork, which really is beneath him and will remain permanently in print to shame his later years. A university job does at least mean that you are free to print in a decently considered manner; and, so far from trying to stop you, most of the English universities make your promotion actually depend on eventually printing something good enough. It therefore seems to me very mistaken when young writers imagine that this is a shameful way to come to terms with the society they are living in; though I must say I never understand why they don't try [to] become postmen in country districts, surely much the best job for the type of writer who needs to feel uncontaminated.[107]

12

From Poetry to the Queen

EMPSON'S *Collected Poems* was published in the UK by Chatto & Windus on 29 September 1955, in an edition of 2,400 copies. It was a propitious moment for the reception of Empson's arguably rather specialized verses, for the volume won more comprehensive and searching evaluation than any of his poetry had been accorded for twenty years. The astringent, witty, problem-revolving aspects of the poems seemed to strike a chord with a reading public that felt eager to move on from the linguistic exuberances of a Dylan Thomas.

As might have been expected, however, for all the many reviews that celebrated the dense and challenging character of Empson's modest body of pragmatic, stoical, humane and wise verses, there were some few notices which judged his work to be the product primarily of superficial stylistic confection. The young poet (and Cambridge graduate) Thom Gunn, writing in *London Magazine*, allowed that 'when he cares, he can write passages of a positively Marlovian power', but most of his review was absorbed with discussing what he called 'five separate difficulties: muddled imagery, difficulty of reference, an excessive telescoping of statement, unclearness of tone, and some very odd ways with scansion'.[1] In the Oxford periodical *Essays in Criticism*, F. W. Bateson identified Empson as the Rochester to Auden's Dryden. Rochester and Empson, he suggested, 'flaunt an arrogant, ferocious *jusqu'-à-boutisme*, which gives their best passages a more distinctively personal flavour than those of the humaner, but also more colourless, Dryden and Auden'.[2]

Literary friends of the author were quick to anticipate, or to answer, the tired charge that the poetry was mostly a matter of style. G. S. Fraser stressed in the *Times Literary Supplement* that Empson's 'love of sanity springs not from phlegm but from passion.'[3] Kathleen Raine, an older friend of Empson's, declared: 'If imaginative depths are stirred (as they are both by Donne and by Empson) it is not by reason of their wit, but rather by the compulsive intensity of the passion by which both are driven to impose order on fields of knowledge and experience so contradictory as to threaten the mind that contains them with disintegration—the compulsion, as Empson writes [in 'This Last Pain'], to "learn a style from a despair".'[4] Charles Madge similarly laid emphasis upon the 'painful inner experience' of Empson's verses; if there is 'formal elegance' in the work, he added, it must be recognized that 'the elegance is used to "contain" a violent struggle, an all-out effort of emotion and intellect to confront the most desperate problems.'[5]

Yet it was by no means only Empson's friends who were discerning about the collected volume. Hilary Corke wrote in *The Listener* that the most accomplished poems were authentically 'concerned with human passions rather than metaphysical footnotes;'[6] and Naomi Lewis (*The Observer*), picking up on the customary comparison with John Donne, fairly discriminated: 'His range is more idiosyncratic; his wit is of a droller sort; his sadness is a quizzical melancholy, not the tremendous cry of the seventeenth-century divine ... Despair, that recurring word in Empson's poetry, carries with it undertones of an enquiring acceptance, a mocking resignation.'[7] Anne Ridler (*Manchester Guardian*) found in Empson 'a master of the subtleties of thought and language, and perhaps unique in our time in his power of using scientific knowledge for poetry'; he had too 'not only wit but an excellent sense of fun.'[8] From a slightly older generation, the distinguished poet Austin Clarke, reviewing the book for the *Irish Times*, praised Empson for not indulging 'in mystification for its own sake ... [H]e refuses sternly to compromise with the reader: his complex, concentrated lines are charged ...'[9] John Betjeman, who might have been expected to resist such clever poems—and who was not shy of admitting he felt mystified—positively owned up to finding the poems 'reluctantly fascinating. I turn to them again and again.'[10]

Pretty surprisingly, *Collected Poems* commanded remarkably good sales figures. Ian Parsons reported in January 1956, 'I'm glad to say the book is selling extremely well, nearly 1800 copies already, and orders coming in steadily. I hope you're pleased with the reviews.'[11] By 17 May 1956, a reprint of 1,250 copies was put in hand; and a further printing of 1,000 copies of *Collected Poems* was issued in 1962. (Royalties for all the books published by Chatto & Windus amounted in 1958 to the healthy sum of £224. 8s. 4d.) From the USA, Harcourt Brace relayed the extra welcome news that in 1959 they were going to issue a paperback edition of *Collected Poems* in their Harvest imprint: the normal printing would run to between 10,000 and 15,000 copies. Later, in 1972, Charles Monteith, poetry editor (and subsequently chairman) of Faber & Faber approached Chatto & Windus with a request that he would like to be allowed to produce a Faber paper covered edition of *Collected Poems*; he was turned down for the reason that Chatto & Windus (who had kept the hardback in print for seventeen years) proposed soon to put out a paperback of their own.[12] In the event, the first UK paperback edition of the poetry book was published under the Hogarth imprint only in the year of Empson's death.

Empson had been ambitious for *Collected Poems*; he told his publisher in about February 1954: 'I see the Poetry Book Club has now been started, and am hoping that proofs for my Collected Verse will be coming along soon.'[13] In the event, the poetry won him no prizes, but it did win several prominent fans and followers who were developing critical influence in their own right.

In 1955, after eight years of lecturing in English Literature at the University of Reading, the writer and literary critic John Wain, aged thirty, was to make the 'great renunciation' (as Empson called it)—he was to break loose from the academic life and endeavour to make his way as a freelance writer. In 1953 he had enjoyed a critical and popular success with his first book, the comic novel *Hurry on Down*, which was in essentials the forerunner of the so-called 'Angry Young Men' movement supposedly launched by John Osborne's *Look Back in Anger* in 1956; Kingsley Amis's *Lucky Jim* was also to follow it.[14] Wain's novel included a passage in which the anti-hero Charles Lumley (a wry version of the author) works himself into a state of such frantic stimulation that he is driven to invent variants on an epigrammatic line of verse by Empson—'And I a twister love what I abhor'—from the poem 'The Beautiful Train' (first published in 1940). Lumley thus rings the changes in his delirious mind: '*And I a lover twist what I abhor...And twister I, abhorring what I love...And I a whore, abtwisting what I love...Love eye and twist her and what I abhor.*'[15] The riddle was as entrancing to play with as the ravishing rhythm.

Wain was a passionate admirer of Empson's poetry, and freely and frankly imitated it in his own early verses; according to his friend and fellow critic A. Alvarez, he was 'besotted by Empson's sonorous villanelles'.[16] Absolutely enraptured by poetry, and taking a pride in his plainspokenness, Wain was a son of the Potteries and saw himself (to cite Alvarez's recollection) 'as a mixture of Dr Johnson, George Orwell and

J. B. Priestley'.[17] Most gratifyingly for Empson, one of Wain's very first published essays had been entitled 'Ambiguous Gifts: Notes on the Poetry of William Empson'; an intelligent celebration of the best of Empson, it came out in John Lehmann's *Penguin New Writing* (1950) and so attracted wide attention. It was much more than a generalized puff: it investigated the specific qualities of the poetry, demonstrating how Empson's conceits may be validly compared with Donne's, for example; and it presented good close readings of particular poems—'Arachne', for instance, is ably described as being 'not really about either soap-tension, or molecular structure, or the habits of water-spiders. These things are pivots on which a tragically sardonic love-poem is made to turn.'[18] Indeed, it is scarcely an exaggeration to say that Wain's piece set the terms for the post-war influence of Empson's poetry. By Empson's own account, when he was introduced to Wain, he hailed him: 'Hello, young man, I'm told you imitate me.' Wain replied, 'Imitate you? Why, I invented you!'—a reply which Empson said 'quite won my heart'. He must have been pleased to be treated to such a display of wit and nerve instead of sycophancy or embarrassment—though his response illustrates his generosity too. When Empson said rude things, Wain was quite prepared to hit back. Above all, Wain was to record in his precocious volume of autobiography *Sprightly Running* (published in 1962, when he was still three years shy of forty) that Empson showed real care when he tried to advise him.

> William Empson, when he heard of my decision [to leave academia and become a freelance writer], actually wrote me a letter offering to try to get me into a post abroad. 'I do advise against [resigning]; to make a success of it needs a lot of back-scratching, surely, which you can't think you are best at, and a lot of anxiety even if successful.' That letter helped me enormously. It did nothing to shake my decision to launch out, but it reassured me that I was parting friends with the academic world, since I had won the good-will of one of the most original and powerful minds in that world.[19]

John Wain was by no means alone among his near-contemporaries at Oxford in feeling excited by the enigmatic intensity of Empson's poetry. A. Alvarez declares: 'So far as I was concerned, Empson was the incarnation of brilliance ... and he was, briefly, a cult figure, the man who was going to lead British poetry out of the booming neo-romantic wildness of Dylan Thomas, George Barker and Edith Sitwell.'[20] As if to complement Wain's ardour for the villanelles, Alvarez 'imitated repeatedly Empson's spikier early poems,' he confessed, 'the ones that sounded like Donne in contemporary disguise: compressed and ironic and full of arcane learning,

just the style to appeal to a literary young man with intellectual pretensions.'[21] One of Alvarez's best pastiches was a poem called 'The Marks-
man' (published in *Oxford Poetry*), which takes its tone and diction straight
from Empson's 'The World's End' or 'High Dive':

> Our trim, cold shafts are keener now, not stronger,
> Thin as the air that lifts them, will fly longer;
>
> Plunge, then, through deeps of light and, thrusting, plunder
> Self-immolated Pantheon in the dark;
> Trace high the gap between the flash and thunder,
> Drop on the glinting bull's-eye all their arc.

In the summer of 1953 Empson made his first appearance in Oxford
(where he was to be invited back again and again by one group or
another). Wain, who heard him read his poems at a number of Oxford
venues, noted the difference between the public set pieces and the more
intimate occasions: 'When Empson reads to a large audience, he allows
himself a very wide range of sheer volume, shouting some passages like a
Neapolitan stevedore, laryngitically croaking others. When reading to
a handful of people in someone's sitting-room after dinner, he adopts a
much quieter style.'[22] Alan Brownjohn, another student contemporary,
came to the first of the Oxford readings and found himself in thrall; he
remembered, over thirty years later:

> when he eventually appeared at the Poetry Society [English Club] in the
> summer of 1953 his reading made a considerable impression. At that time
> his extraordinary reciting voice, which thinned to a hardly less remarkable
> whisper in his last years, was undiminished in volume: a loud sort of high-
> pitched drone, or boom, which would swoop down suddenly on the well-
> known lines and fling them away with a seeming disdain for his own
> highly-wrought ambiguities. It was a performance of unmistakable power.
> Empson *meant* his love poems, and charged their recital with surprising
> passion. For more than one undergraduate listener it was clear on that
> evening that there might be a modern metaphysical poetry in which wit and
> emotional intensity balanced and assisted each other. Empson might not
> provide student writers with an example which it was advisable to follow too
> slavishly, but he at least signposted one route out of the unthinking roman-
> ticism of the post-war years.[23]

Another time, Empson chose to take advantage of an invitation to the
English Club to proselytize for China (as he was always so concerned to
do in the months immediately following his return to England); even so,
the evening ended with the brilliantly lubricated Empson reciting his

translation of the Buddha's Fire Sermon—the piece that prefaced *Poems*—to a packed pub.[24]

It was one of Empson's earliest visits to Oxford that the young don George Watson (later author of *The Literary Critics*) would find memorable:

> His lecturing style might charitably be called grotesque. It was rather as if Buster Keaton had decided, after many years as a silent comic, to open his mouth and deliver a solemn parody of an academic lecture. His voice was rapid and soft, descending at times into a slurred mumble when the intensity of his convictions appeared to embarrass him. At such moments, on a platform, he would close his eyes in an intense, beatific expression that was not quite a smile and not quite a grimace. Behind the whimsy, you often felt, lay a certainty almost too deep to bear, and to hear him read aloud from his own poems was to realise that at heart he was less a Neo-Metaphysical poet in the style of Donne than a Neo-Romantic from the school of Swinburne. At other moments he would throw off an astonishing critical *aperçu* as if he were back in his local bar, and in an argot that took one back to the 1920s. Once, lecturing on *A Midsummer Night's Dream* and earnestly doubting whether Titania had ever had sexual designs on Bottom, he suddenly remarked: 'If she was wanting to have it off with a hairy worker, why did she have all these kids around?'[25]

Watson notes further that Empson seemed anti-Modernist in his critical remarks:

> This was the first time I ever heard a considered case made against T. S. Eliot and Paul Valéry by anyone who was not an old (or young) fogey, and the experience was memorable... The trouble with Eliot and Valéry, he told his Oxford audience, not to mention Ezra Pound, was that in the years in and around the first world war they had devised a poetic language in which it is all but impossible to say anything. 'I have just been to southwest France,' he explained, finding himself on the very coast that had once been the theme of Valéry's *Cimitière Marin*. 'In fact it's quite an interesting place—there is no fresh water there, and a shipwrecked sailor could die of thirst.' Then he looked contemptuous. 'That's why it's called the sea cemetery—but you could read and re-read Valéry's poem and never know it.' The point was characteristically radical, and an Oxford literary audience brought up to revere Eliot and Valéry shifted uneasily in their seats. Empson had let off his little bomb.[26]

F. W. Bateson, a learned, lively and lumbering-limbed don at Corpus Christi College who had edited the *Cambridge Bibliography of English Literature*, chose in 1951 to set up the literary quarterly, *Essays in Criticism*, in large part to follow the trail of serious literary criticism that Empson had blazed twenty years earlier. A. Alvarez, who was Bateson's pupil, was exhorted by him to overcome the after-effects of the vapidly 'appreciative' critical habits of the Oxford tradition by studying his Richards and his Empson. Alvarez came to feel so hugely inspired by Empson's work that he got together with three of his friends—David Thompson (later to be art critic of *The Times*), John Miles (a poet reading philosophy), and Graham Martin (who was to become Professor of English at the Open University)—to set up a student discussion group, the Critical Society, by way of tribute to Empson. Everything Empsonian, they resolved, was to be promulgated with relish.

Having steeped himself in Empson till his essays were brimming with ambiguity and his prose overflowing with the easier turns of Empson's style, Alvarez plucked up courage to invite the man himself to a party in Oxford. To the surprise of Alvarez and his peers, Empson agreed to come along. A reception was arranged in Lincoln College by a young don named W. W. Robson, a man of extensive learning who happened to suffer from writer's block and anxiety attacks; though deeply well read, he was also stuffed with neuroses and self-misgivings, and his abandoned appearance—greasy, long-haired, dandruff-laden—seemed a perfect match for his complex self-doubt.

When Alvarez and Robson met Empson off his train—the date is lost, but this must have been in 1953—they were taken aback by what Alvarez called his 'absurd neck beard'.[27] Worse still, he was grumpy: 'his eyes were like ice and he clearly didn't much like what he saw,' Alvarez has recalled.[28] After delivering a reportedly 'impenetrable' talk he appeared to become more cheerful at the party afterwards. However, according to Robson, 'there was one flare-up, when he rudely rebuffed the over-assiduous politeness of a young don' (Robson may have been referring to himself in the third person in that bleak recollection.)[29] As the long hours of the evening wore on, with Empson gulping down the plentiful supply of wine, everyone else felt increasingly bored and disappointed.

> It was a long wait [recalled Alvarez]. Around two in the morning, when we were all drunk and exhausted, Empson stretched back on Wallace's sofa and pronounced in his roller-coaster accents: 'When Eliot, in the *Four Quartets*, says: "Time past and time present are both perhaps present in time future", he's making a grammatical statement. What he's really saying is, the future perfect equals the ablative absolute.' There it was, the aphorism we had been waiting for, straight from the horse's mouth and not yet in print. It almost made our misery worthwhile.[30]

After Empson's departure the next day, Robson tried to comfort Alvarez
by explaining that Empson was a Wykehamist: he was a prime example of
how Winchester deforms its boys by trying to force them all into the same
mould.

Alvarez became convinced that Empson did not really like him and his
'lot'—'for the best possible reason—because he thought we were prigs
. . . [H]e smelt the Leavis contamination on everyone below a certain age
and he disliked me because I'd picked up some of the lingo and the disdain
that went with it.'[31] But it is possible that Empson had other reasons: he
may have taken greater exception than he would immediately or openly
admit to Alvarez's way of teasing him about the emotional foundations of
his poetry. As he wrote to Alvarez in 1956:

> You hinted in the pub after I had read my poems that I was playing to the
> gallery; which rather amused me, because I suspected you were disillu-
> sioned at not finding them esoteric enough. They weren't meant to be at all
> esoteric. They came from more isolation and suffering than is suited to
> public performance, but that is well known to be true of most performances,
> including clowns'.[32]

And yet he was generally able to take criticism of his work. On one
occasion, Alvarez and Robson queried a revision of a line in his poem
'Invitation to Juno'. He had altered 'Could not Professor Charles Darwin'
to 'Could not at one time even Darwin', which they told him was too weak.
He objected that he had made a simple error—Darwin had not been a
professor—but agreed the line was weak. For the fifth impression of
Collected Poems (1957), he amended the line again, to 'Did not once the
adroit Darwin', which suggests that he had acted on their initial friendly
criticism in the right positive spirit.

Wain, Alvarez and Robson met up with him a number of times over the
following years. 'The only problem,' as Robson recalled, 'was that he was
frequently drunk, and when in that condition he was unpredictable; he
could be charming, or horrible: there was no advance way of telling which
it would be.' Once, Robson accused Empson of being too patronizing
about F. R. Leavis; another time, to Robson's dismay, Empson behaved in
a 'childish' way and delivered a long harangue about his hatred of the
Christian god. On a further occasion Empson, again in the 1950s, lectured
at Lincoln College on *Hamlet*; evidently, he was still rehearsing the pieces
on Shakespeare that he believed would constitute his next book. Sadly,
Robson found the lecture unintelligible; and Alvarez, who had by that
time given up on Empson, whispered to Robson: 'Drunken nonsense'. But

the lecture was not nonsense: it was in essence identical with the piece printed in the posthumous *Essays on Shakespeare*. The problem lay with the manner of Empson's delivery of it.

Empson was only too well aware that a number of poets in the 1950s—especially Wain and Alvarez—took his work as a model, emulating what they considered to be the non-conformist, cool, scientific, and analytical cast of his poems, the distrust of rhetoric and sentiment, and the attempt to convey complicated states of thought and moral meaning.[33] They also admired his skills as a technician: his significant success in recuperating for contemporary English poetry forms including the villanelle and terza rima, as well as ottava rima and rime royal. All the same, since Empson recognized that the poetry of his admirers was primarily borrowing or mimicking the accidentals but not the driving emotion of his work—the 'isolation and suffering'—he was to observe in a BBC talk on 'Literary Opinion' in 1954:

> Recently the magazine *Encounter* had a joke poem, with very funny notes, meaning that Empson is a bad influence on young poets. Do you know, I rather often said this myself to young poets, both in England and America, who have kindly shown me their stuff. It seems to me that Empson's own poetry, though it comes from a rather limited and narrow talent anyhow, isn't nearly as narrow as what turns up when somebody imitates it; that does feel very narrow, and I wouldn't be sensible if I didn't agree.[34]

Though he liked Wain personally, he evidently felt that Wain and Alvarez were parroting the supposed devices of his poetry. He had been sincere in the writing of his own poetry; but their attempts ar emulation struck him as fundamentally factitious (as they were). Most importantly he was concerned in the BBC talk to insist that his work in literary criticism certainly did have real breadth, and it stood the test of time: 'Empson's type of literary criticism doesn't seem to me a bad influence or indeed, particularly narrow. And as for the present swing of fashion, which is in itself only a necessary self-correcting process, I think you can rely on it to swing back again far enough.'

Empson may have been lionized on his every appearance in Oxford, but he was by no means buoyed up by followers at all of his appearances elsewhere. His brief stint in the capacity of Gresham Professor in Rhetoric at Gresham College, Basinghall Street, in the City of London, went almost unremarked and unattended. Appointed in memory of Sir Thomas Gresham, the professor is required to give a series of four public lectures on a subject of his choice. The first Gresham lecturer was no less a person than Ben Jonson, and Empson derived much satisfaction from the distinguished line of succession.

He spoke about a wide range of Elizabethan and Jacobean plays from a great variety of angles, and the texts discussed or touched upon included *Macbeth*, *Richard II*, *The Arraignment of Paris*, *The Jew of Malta*, *Tamburlaine*, *The Duchess of Malfi*, *The White Devil*, *Women Beware Women*, *The Spanish Tragedy*, *Antonio's Revenge*, *Hamlet*, *Volpone*, *The Alchemist*, and *The Shoemaker's Holiday*. The theme of the code of honour being at odds with a Christian society is central to the lectures. In particular, revenge is opposed to the Christian ethic, Empson was keen to point out, 'and in a way the code of honour bears the same relationship to Christianity in the Renaissance that courtly love and its code did in the Middle Ages'. The Elizabethans liked to see conflicting forces play themselves out before an ultimate restoration of balance. In discussing this theme, Empson harked back to his analysis in the 1930s of the pastoral hero. In developing the theme of the individual overstepping the sanctions of his or her society, Empson went on, the intensity of revenge tragedy naturally served to beget the hero-revenger who is paradoxically sympathetic because he is so wretched—audiences like to feel associated with the feelings of despair expressed by a villain-hero such as Bosola in *The Duchess of Malfi*. 'The Jacobean audience had to be astonished, and the type of exasperated man represented by Bosola could astonish them.' As if echoing the final admonition of his own poem 'Let It Go'—'You don't want madhouse and the whole thing there'— Empson drew attention to the fact that no other great world theatre has given so much attention to madness as did the Elizabethans and Jacobeans: 'to understand the wretchedness and misery of the world one would become so overwhelmed that madness would result before one reached the bottom of misery. The human sensibility could not withstand the shock without going mad.'

In addition to extending the lessons of pastoral, Empson's lectures thus anticipated, in some cases by many years, several aspects of his essays of the later 1950s and the 1960s: notably in his pieces on *The Spanish Tragedy* and *The Duchess of Malfi*. What was remarkable about the lectures was that not only did he consider afresh such a large range of plays but that he worked to interpret them within various social and historical contexts at a time when this was not a very fashionable thing to do. What cannot be fully recovered, since these lectures do not survive in the form in which they were given in 1954, is his lively demonstrations of how the Elizabethan–Jacobean theatre of madness and the revenge tradition related to a previous literature and to a political society—in effect, his politicization of those themes—and of how particular plays work, the expressiveness of their plot structures and languages, and also their increasingly insistent enforcement of linguistic and social divisions.

However, maybe because of a last-minute rescheduling of the series, along with the rotten winter weather, it turned out that very few people came to the lectures. The audience consisted of a couple of local college students, a few folk off the street drawn by the warmth and shelter of the hall, and two American Fulbright scholars, David Laird and Robert O'Clair (the latter was later to edit the *Norton Anthology of Modern Poetry*, with Richard Ellmann)—with, always in attendance, Hetta Empson. According to David Laird, the lectures were 'exciting, original, provocative—clearly work to which he had devoted much time and energy, having recently re-read the major texts and responding with remarkable freshness and wit. The standard set in the first lecture . . . was pretty well sustained through the series.'[35] Feeling emboldened by the sparseness of the audience, Laird and O'Clair went up after the first lecture to introduce themselves, and then, since the chitchat seemed to promise well, to invite the Empsons for a drink at a local pub. Empson was carrying with him a copy of *Nature*, so they asked about his interest in science; he spoke with enthusiasm about the new biology and about competing models of scientific explanation. The lectures were scheduled at 5.30, so they were able to continue their get-togethers on the subsequent evenings of the week. Once, they went to a Greek restaurant and drank retsina, and once or twice back to the Empsons' place in Hampstead. They were impressed by Empson's ability to recite large amounts of literature by heart. The experience of teaching in China, he said, had accustomed him to quote from memory—sometimes, he admitted, to misquote. He read them his poem 'Just a Smack at Auden', with relish. It was all quite unfair to Auden, of course, but the rhythm was right: he liked it. 'He was an imposing figure,' remarked Laird, 'wiry, at times intense, at times composed, withdrawn . . . And there was always the protective, hovering presence of his wife upon whom it seemed he had come to rely in all sorts of transactions including the more mundane ones.' Hetta struck the two young Americans as extraordinarily generous, and yet spirited and independent. But the most remarkable thing of all, Laird reflected, was that Empson was so lacking in followers even in 1954, despite his singular contributions as poet and critic.

It must have been the sparsity of the audience that persuaded Empson, as he put it in a later year, the Gresham Chair was 'now so derelict that I gave it up after a year.'[36]

In utter contrast, Empson's visit to the USA in the summer of 1954—to teach the summer school as a Fellow of the School of Letters at Indiana University in Bloomington (the continuation since 1951 of the Kenyon School of English)—brought him more attention than even he might have wished. As soon as he spoke out in favour of the new regime in China (as he felt obliged to do in all conscience), his political views, his activities, and his background promptly became of interest to the secret police. The FBI and the CIA found good cause—or so they thought—to investigate his oration and his origins.

Early in 1953, at a time coinciding with his appointment at Sheffield, he was put forward as a Fellow for that summer, when he proposed a course on 'Some Poets of Our Own Age'. He said he might try 'to cover T. S. Eliot, W. B. Yeats, W. H. Auden, Dylan Thomas, and some more recent poets, and study in them the development of a technique which can express a wide-ranging thought with immediacy.' The problem with the vague rubric 'some more recent poets', as he told Richard B. Hudson (then Director of the School), was that there was 'practically no very good recent poetry...but that may be ignorance'. All the same, despite his lack of interest in contemporary poetry in general, he would have liked to say something favourable about the early poetry of Robert Lowell. He had enjoyed meeting Lowell at Kenyon College in 1950, and admired his dense and formal early work; nevertheless, he 'would rather leave him out than sound lukewarm about him.'[37] Also, for his public lecture in the 'Forum' series for 1953, he proposed a modest-seeming topic in which he hoped to issue a fatal counterblast to the anti-intentionalist dogma of the New Critics W. K. Wimsatt and Cleanth Brooks: 'The Critic and the Poet's Intention'.

He was very keen to take part in the school. Apart from his genuine interest in getting to know, or else keeping in touch with, some of the major American critics of the day, the stipend for the six-week term was $1,500 (which was equivalent to three months' salary in England); he was required to teach only a single graduate course of three classes a week; and all of his travelling expenses would be amply covered. But he was stupidly slow in applying for a visa (which just goes to illustrate something of his political innocence during the McCarthy era). By May 1953, when he finally got round to the business, he was given to understand that his period of residence in communist China would debar him from being issued with a visa on the instant: under the terms of the McCarran Act, the screening process could take up to three months, possibly as many as six—and not even the influence in Washington, DC, of his diplomat brother Charles could expedite matters.[38] 'I wish to make clear that there is no question of political suspicion,' Empson sought rather unconvincingly to reassure Richard Hudson; 'the American officials here are very definite in saying that it is only red tape, only a rule which they cannot break.'[39] Nonetheless, John W. Ashton, a Vice-President at Indiana (Dean of the College of Arts and Sciences), foresaw a good deal of bother, or else he smelled a rat; he suggested that the School should not extend an invitation to Empson for the following year—but John Crowe Ransom took no heed of his advice.

Dean Ashton had a fair point. The School of Letters was advised by the United States Department of Justice in November 1953: 'Under the provisions of the Immigration and Nationality Act (Public Law 414, which became effective on December 24, 1952), it is necessary that the prospective employer, in cases of this kind, file a petition with this Service for permission to import any alien whose services are sought for temporary employment.' As part of the protracted, paper-engrossing process of compiling a petition on Empson's behalf, it was necessary to furnish some character-references. Five eminent critics duly provided sworn affidavits. I. A. Richards bore his usual witness: 'In a fairly long experience I have never had a student of so much critical ability.' Philip Rahv, editor of *Partisan Review*, attested that Empson 'is in my view one of the leading literary critics and scholars in the English-speaking world'. Lionel Trilling, at Columbia University in New York City, declared him to be 'a critic and teacher of the very first importance. Indeed, his position in literary criticism may be said to be unique. Almost every notable critic in America is indebted to him for one point or another of critical doctrine.' John Crowe Ransom, creator of the summer school and a committed advocate of Empson, wrote also of his popularity and his effectiveness as a teacher: 'He is greatly sought by the students who come to us, and he conducts himself before them with extreme force, intelligence, and dignity.' The US Immigration and Naturalization Service duly granted 'nonimmigrant status' to Empson on 28 January 1954; a visa could be issued to him forthwith.

On 12 June he sailed for the USA. The summer school was to run for six weeks, from 19 June till 31 July. Bloomington, Indiana, he was interested to learn among other things, was the home town of 'the famous Sex Kinsey'.[40] The town was broiling ('the breeze this evening was almost painful, like fire from an oven'),[41] but the prospects looked bright. Arrangements had been made for him to sublet a nice but small university apartment; the students on his graduate course seemed 'quite lively and willing'; and it was good to pick up the latest gossip—'John Crowe

Ransom said he had made a list in some article of the ten best poets of this century, and Stephen Spender wrote to him and asked to be put on the list. I thought that was very funny.'[42] Having fought shy of modern poetry, he ran a course on 'Studies in Shakespeare', blending the line of argument of his Gresham lectures with the course on 'The last Plays of Shakespeare and their relation to the Elizabethan Theatre' that he had originally proposed for the Gresham series; he drew too on the essays on *Hamlet* and Falstaff recently published in the *Kenyon Review* and the *Sewanee Review*. 'I want to make some remarks on the Revenge Play in general, as background to *Hamlet*, and am keen by that time to have arrived at some opinion on the shaky topic of the last Shakespeare plays, their relation to Beaumont and Fletcher and so on . . . I shall talk mainly about the Hal-Falstaff trilogy, *Hamlet, Macbeth,* and the last plays, rather avoiding the plays treated by verbal analysis in my last book, though I stand by the treatment and wouldn't at all mind students bringing it up.'[43] It promised to be almost a research seminar. But after four weeks of classes, he wrote home: 'The students are quite lively and friendly but their minds are much wrapped up in philosophy—they struggle for a theory of literary criticism which philosophers would accept, which seems to me rather an odd ambition. Christianity is fairly prominent. I feel a bit tired of it, but I must say my stomach has been standing up to it wonderfully.'[44]

He was not expecting this time around to discover much liveliness among his colleagues on the teaching staff. In addition to himself and John Crowe Ransom, the faculty consisted of Harold Whitehall, Richard Blackmur, and the young Leslie A. Fiedler, who gave an early outing to some of the ideas that would eventually be polished into his wonderfully provocative study *Love and Death in the American Novel* (1960). Three months earlier, Empson had rather rudely written that he foresaw a certain solid dullness among the staff. 'I gather from the list of speakers,' he told Newton P. Stallknecht (the Director for 1954), 'that this is a case of the School settling into a respected middle age, where keen controversy is not really expected.'[45] In the event, if he feared the other staff would be staid and uninspiring, he certainly struck them as weird in his middle age, a bohemian with a crisp English accent. Leslie Fiedler was astonished, on entering Empson's apartment, to realize that the exalted and legendary critic lived like a sloppy student: dirty dishes seemed to be piled everywhere, stuck together, spilling over the floor. Empson must have noticed the shock in Fiedler's face. 'You Americans think we Brits are filthy,' he declared. 'Well, I *am* filthy.'[46]

1. BBC editorial staff producing the Daily Digest in the Monitoring Department at Evesham. Empson puffs a pipe. BBC.

2. Recording the poetry magazine *Voice*. Standing: George Orwell, Nancy Barratt, Empson. Sitting: Venu Chitale, J. M. Tambimuttu, T. S. Eliot, Una Marson, Mulk Raj Anand. BBC.

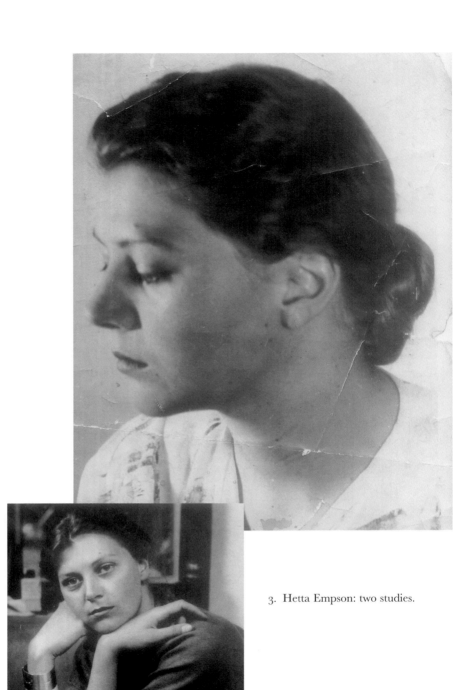

3. Hetta Empson: two studies.

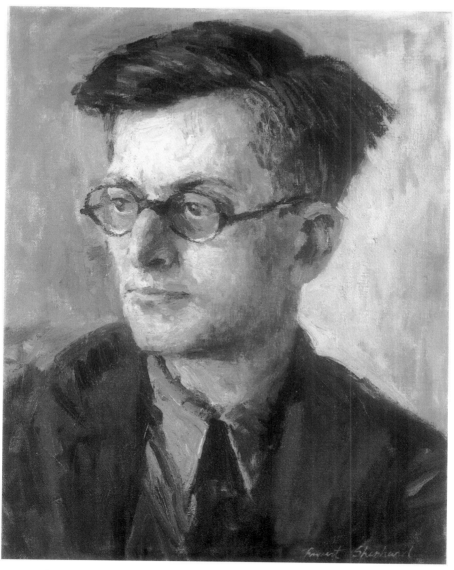

4. Portrait of Empson by Rupert Shephard, *c.*1944. National Portrait Gallery.

5. Severe, suited and bearded, in Peking.

6. Empson in his study at 11 Tung Kao Fang, near Peking National University, late 1940s.

7. Group portrait: taking tea in the Summer Palace at Peking. Seated from the left: David Kidd, Walter Brown, Hetta Empson, John Blofeld. Empson looks on, and smiles.

8. An alfresco meal in the courtyard of 11 Tung Kao Fang, Peking. The Empsons and their children, Mogador and Jacob.

9. The wedding of David Hawkes (later Professor of Chinese at Oxford University) and Jean Patterson, in Peking on 5 May 1950. Empson and I.A. Richards stand in snug formation to the left of the bride. Empson was to write of the wedding reception: 'The British consul came, the secret British communists came, the Chinese police who spy on the foreigners came, the Christians came, the university came, and it was really a good party such as I have always thought one of the keenest pleasures in like.'

10. A fancy dress party in Peking. Empson is the sinister Arab on the left. Hetta Empson, bedecked in black and white (and with a hand print on her dress) is being courted by the clown. Other figures in the picture include various personnel from the French and German embassies.

11. William and Hetta Empson enjoying the winter sun at home in Peking. To the right is their friend David Kidd.

12. Group portrait at Kenyon College, 1950. Standing, from left: Arthur Mizener, Robert Lowell, Kenneth Burke, Delmore Schwartz. Front row: Philip Blair Rice, Empson, John Crowe Ransom, L. C. Knights, Charles M. Coffin.

13. Playing softball at Kenyon College, 1950. George Soule remembers:
'Empson hit the ball very well—deep towards right field—but foul.' But
Empson did not quite understand the rules of the game; he thought it was
like cricket. 'So I called it fair, and Empson ran determinedly all the way to
second base. No one objected.'

14. Bright-eyed boys: Jacob and Mogador Empson in the 1950s.

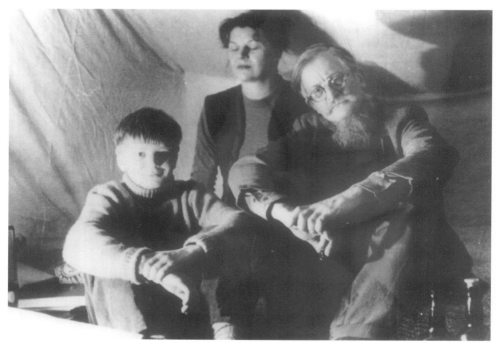

15. The Empsons and younger son, Jacob (aged 12), in a tent erected within the cold cavern of the studio at Studio House, 28 December 1956. Photograph by Irie Yukio.

16. Father and sons at Studio House in 1958.

17. Empson enjoying a pint with some students and friends.

18. Empson and Christopher Ricks at Studio House in the 1970s.

19. Portrait at Studio House, by Mark Gerson. The picture on the wall is a drawing of the young Mao Tse-tung given to Empson in the late 1930s. National Portrait Gallery.

20. Portrait of the old sage looking mischievous, by John Deakin.

21. British Museum: the portico. This atmospheric photograph by Eric de Maré happened to catch Empson shuffling in to work in the Reading Room; it was featured for many years on a British Museum postcard. Gordon Fraser Gallery.

22. Empson enjoying a drink and perusing an offprint at the Rosslyn Arms pub.

23. William and Hetta Empson sharing a joke. Photo by Judith Aronson.

24. The aged eagle, by Christopher Barker.

As for a 'keen controversy', Empson need not have feared: there was to be not a literary-critical controversy but a political one—and he was to be the cause of it. Ironically, the trouble came about in one respect at the specific invitation of the School of Letters. Professor Stallknecht had learned in March 1954 that for just one week, from 28 June till 4 July, the university would be hosting a congress on Oriental–Western literary and cultural relations; it was to run concurrently with the School of Letters. Knowing that Empson had taught for some while in the 'Orient', he therefore notified him in good faith—and in perfectly forgivable innocence: 'It has occurred to some of us that you might be willing to devote your lecture and forum discussion to some topic which would be of interest to people attending the congress.'[47] By a further irony, he also informed Empson in the same letter that Indiana State laws required the visiting lecturer to sign an oath agreeing that he would act in a positively pro-American manner while in the USA: indeed, his appointment at the School could not be legally finalized until such an oath had been filed with the university trustees.

'I am perfectly willing', Empson cannily forewarned Stallknecht, 'to talk about China and answer questions about it, and will do so to some extent whether I am billed as doing so or not, but [I] don't want to be billed as doing nothing else—in case I wanted to talk about literary criticism . . . Empson will speak both about China and about literary criticism, without pretending any connection between them. I . . . will certainly try to angle my speech to handle [the conference on Oriental-Western affairs]; but I won't promise beforehand not to make any remarks about literary criticism. Indeed I promise to talk about both.'[48] His reiterations must have seemed like a roundabout riddle or the mildest tease.

Not realizing that what Empson might want to say about China would be decidedly derogatory of US foreign policy, Stallknecht responded with equal good humour: 'It is not necessary for you to talk about China at all, although under the circumstances, I should feel a little bit more at ease if there were some open references, however brief or indirect, to the Orient.' He ended on a note of urbane geniality that can be seen with hindsight to compound the irony of his ill-advised initial request: 'Personally, it is my feeling that having our Oriental visitors present at your lecture will add, more or less, to the gayety of nations, and I very much appreciate your willingness to help us out.'[49]

Empson had understood the full scale of his dilemma when he turned up at the US Embassy in London in the Easter vacation of 1954 to sign an oath—witnessed on 23 March by the Vice-Consul—in accordance with

section 28–5114 of the Burns Indiana Annotated Statutes: 'I, William
Empson, solemnly swear that I will support the institutions and policies
of the United States during the period of my sojourn within the State of
Indiana.' But then, when sending off to Indiana his signed documentation
he enclosed a seemingly frank letter which flirted with disingenuousness
and equivocation:

> My opinions about China seem to me unalarming and indeed largely those
> of the British Government, but to express them does not seem like support-
> ing the policy of the U.S. Government, so after signing this I had definitely
> better not be billed as speaking about China in my public lecture. But in
> talking about literary criticism and the teaching of literature I imagine I am
> free to take a broad view and recall personal experiences.[50]

He knew full well that he had every intention of 'scolding' the Americans
about US policy vis-à-vis China. His only hope, as he saw it, was to delay
alerting the authorities; but it seems clear that he was not planning any sort
of show-down. On the other hand, there can be little doubt that on the day
itself he did decide to provoke maximum embarrassment to the Americans
in his audience (and perhaps to the 'Orientals' too) by donning for his
lecture the simple peasant suit that had become the statutory dress of the
victorious forces in China. In short, he had decided to parade before his
American hosts his allegiance to the new China: to embody in himself an
emblem of the Communist triumph.

Some twenty-three years later, I. A. Richards appeared in a radio
feature programme about Empson's life and work, and happened to
tell—evidently to illustrate with a vivid anecdote just what a wonderfully
colourful character Empson was—what he knew of the Bloomington
manifestation:

> When he came back from ten years' teaching in Peking he was invited to
> Bloomington, Indiana, to give a lecture or two; he carefully took with him
> his communist garments in which he had, as he put it, served Her Majesty
> for ten years in China. Well, the governor of the State was a particularly
> active anti-Communist, and the embarrassment of the University was really
> as colossal as you could make it.[51]

Although Richards's summary account of the incident is wrong about
certain factual details, the amused relish of his narration probably reflects
Empson's own tone in telling him about it as much as the quick gossip of
the academic grapevine. In Richards's version, it is particularly interesting
to note, there is no mention of the content and tone of Empson's speech in
itself. It is as if Empson's garb alone—which he 'carefully' took with him

(premeditating provocation?)—had set the red cat among the anti-Communist pigeons.

But what exactly did he say that interested some and inflamed others in his audience? While the notes he actually used during the lecture have not survived, another document still exists that probably conveys the substance and demeanour of his speech.[52] In July 1953, he was invited by the American periodical *The Nation* to write an article about his experiences in China—'suggesting,' as he put it, that he 'might want to say that the Chinese though of course very bad aren't quite so bad as somebody else.' To be sure, this typescript—'China', dated 23 July 1953—specifically addresses the American reader, and is intent on redressing false information:

> This is rather a tiresome job, because there is no point in it unless I try to pierce your intense complacency. I have to sound cross, though I have myself no reason to be cross. I have to address all Americans as 'you', which seems grossly unfair to Americans, also to Germans and Japanese, but you can't get away from that. You have been brought up, by hymns or something when young, to feel quite certain that all the rest of the world loves you and very nastily resentful as soon as you suspect they don't. But unless you realise they don't there is no point in discussing these questions with you.

After providing a little overview of his experience of teaching in China both before and after the war, he proceeded to explain why the Communist takeover had proved to be so popular with the ordinary Chinese peoples.[53]

> The Kuomintang Government [backed by the USA] was so badly thought of that many people welcomed its fall without being Communists, and more people came round to that when they found prices at last stable and other urgent things getting done. . . .
>
> People seemed to accept as evident truth, not as imposed by propaganda, that the American forces [in the Korean War] were driving towards Chinese territory, so that the Chinese entry into the war was merely a question of self-defence. . . . As to the Germ warfare business . . . to sit in Peking and listen to the Voice of America, announcing large outbreaks of plague in Manchuria, claiming leeringly that the atrocity story had only been invented to cover this, wheedling about it to the effect 'now you've got to give in. If you only give in you can have any number of the best doctors and nurses in the world. If you don't give in you will all die'—to hear that was to feel certain they had done it on purpose, and angry enough to resist desperately. . . .

The American State Department people in China [including O. Edmund Clubb], as I came across them, seemed to me to have a very good record; they really knew about the position and they were behaving reasonably. But then one heard that all these characters, even the most right-wing ones, were being tried as traitors and sacked without pension merely because they had done well what they were paid to do—they had advised their Government, surprisingly early, 'as a matter of fact, the Chinese Communists are going to win this civil war'. Now this is barbarism; it is like King David trying to kill the prophet because "he prophesied not good concerning me, but evil"; you cannot run a modern State like that. Nobody will work for you at that rate except fools or knaves.

It seems to me very disastrous to have international affairs drifting in their present direction, but I do not know what is likely to stop it. At any rate, it doesn't seem much use for you to wonder whether the Chinese are 'not quite so bad'; it would be more to the point if you could realise that they are still going to be there, whatever you think of them.[54]

Naturally it is not impossible, depending on just how much alcohol he had consumed before making his appearance, that his conference performance was more vituperative in his criticisms of the USA; but it is not entirely clear that the speech caused such instant wholesale consternation or outrage as the accretions of legend have come to suggest. Some members of his audience found the lecture amusing, though perhaps as much because of his drunken whimsicality as for anything he said.

But at least one of the other Fellows at the School did take earnest exception to Empson's remarks. Leslie Fiedler was not a man to pass up a controversy, or to stint an opinion of his own; according to his biographer, he spent one evening in a 'lively argument' with Empson 'over the charge that America had used germ warfare in Korea. Their dialogue began at 7:30 or eight in the evening and didn't conclude until four in the morning, when [Fiedler's wife] summoned the police, certain that there had been a terrible accident.'[55] Empson must have been referring to the same squabble when he wrote to Hetta, with surprising (or studied) casualness, on 10 July: 'Well, I have recovered my nerves, and feel the speech wasn't so bad. A certain amount of quarrelling about politics goes on late of an evening sometimes but not much. On the whole they take very little interest in it, anyway.'[56]

Two years later, when he sought to challenge Fiedler over the pro-American attitudes (as he saw it) of certain articles that the American had published in the British periodical *Encounter* (see pp. 252–5 above), Fiedler was to respond to him in a letter: 'There is...no point in your posing as an objective, fair-minded, somewhat patriotic English citizen appalled at American propaganda. From my memories of your extraordinary speech at Bloomington, I am convinced that your arguments must be understood as those of an apologist for a particular point of view. This does not, of course, prejudge them, but it puts them in a somewhat suspicious light. A man who believes in the cooked-up reports about germ warfare in Korea would be willing to believe anything.'[57] Although Fiedler concluded his letter on a note of conciliation—'I remember with some pleasure as well as exasperation our discussions at Bloomington when you too were being subsidized by "foreign gold" [Empson had levelled the phrase against *Encounter*], and I hope that it will always be possible for us to keep open channels of communication'—he copied his letter to Stephen Spender, co-editor of *Encounter*, with this dismissive comment on Empson: 'The poor bastard, I am convinced, is more than half mad at the present point and certainly his reactions are, I am sure, not reasonable ones.'[58]

Empson defended himself in a letter to Fiedler of February 1956: 'Going back to my "extraordinary" speech in Bloomington, you must remember that Churchill had just flown over to Washington to try to prevent the Americans from causing a world war over Indo-China; at least the English thought he did, and succeeded in it.'[59] A further observation in the same letter emphasizes that he was indeed aiming to make a clear political point about foreign policy differences between the UK and the USA: 'The point about my wearing my Communist uniform, as I hope I made clear, was not that I had one (a matter of no interest) but that Churchill had paid me to have one, all through the Korean War; I thought this would make everybody realise that the foreign policies of our two countries were actually different.'

In September 1954, less than three months after the lecture, the FBI noted down the evidence of an individual from the Office of the President at Indiana University who had been present at Empson's lecture; this person, it was written, 'recalled EMPSON stating something relative to a quilted coat which he had purchased in China and stating that he would wear it because he paid good money for it and there was still a lot of wear in it, regardless of where it came from.'[60] If that was indeed what Empson said in the lecture, we would have to deduce that he had suffered from a last-minute failure of nerve; those words would imply that he had dressed himself up in a Chinese uniform to deliver a keynote lecture at an international conference in the USA solely in the spirit of thrifty house-keeping—feeling unable to give up his suit until it was quite worn out. Such a disingenuous explanation would have been unworthy of him. His own letter to Fiedler, and Richards's amused anecdote, obviously represent the truth of his purpose in getting himself up in Communist guise. The Labour Government of Great Britain had subsidized (through the British Council) his appointment in China, and it had gone on employing him there even after the Communist victory; but it was a nonsense for him to suggest that the UK Government had paid him to dress literally in the style of the Chinese soldier. To cut the casuistry, Empson knew perfectly well that to sport his 'Communist uniform' in the heart of American capitalism was a sheerly provocative act; there can be no doubt, whatever his occasional equivocations to the contrary, that he intended it to give offence. To wear his quilted communist outfit in the sweltering heat of the Indiana summer would otherwise have been self-punitive to a masochistic degree.

 The FBI dossier on Empson's transgressive lecture runs to 13 pages. There are no biographical revelations in it, since most of the material included is nugatory in value or just flat-footed (at one point it was suggested to an FBI operative by the University of Indiana that the Bureau might find out more about Empson—or 'Epson' as he is spelled on one page—not by rooting among the files at Bloomington but by simply looking him up in the British *Who's Who*). He was reported to the FBI early in July not by a member of the School of Letters but by a participant at the conference on Western–Oriental Affairs—a self-declared opponent of free speech—who said 'he believed that a citizen of another country should not be allowed to enter this country and criticize it as EMPSON was reported to have done'. His specific complaint was that Empson 'did not stick to his subject matter, but instead spoke of the benefits and advantages of Communist China as compared to the United States'. The same stupid and unobservant informant also related that Empson 'was reported to be an Englishman'; he described him 'as having a goatee and wearing a Russian type quilted coat'.[61] In short, the FBI evidence-gathering began, and many agent-hours were to be wasted over the following weeks, on the basis of an initial misrepresentation. (Enquiries were conducted, among other sources of possible information, at the Bloomington Credit Bureau and at the Bloomington Police Department.)

 A few weeks later, after a search in the files of the Office of the President of Indiana University, an FBI agent reported that a university administrator

> explained . . . that on one occasion EMPSON was asked to sign a regulation loyalty oath which is normally signed by all instructors of Indiana Univer-

sity, a state university, and that this specific form was one which had been re-worded for those instructors who were not of American citizenship. [Proper name deleted] felt that EMPSON misunderstood the purpose of this form and, although he signed the form, he became very upset, and during one subsequent lecture he voiced very strong opinions concerning the way Americans and their Government handled the question of Communism and Socialism.[62]

The unidentified administrator in question was evidently shrewd and large-minded; he related that he himself had been present at the lecture, and—not perceiving Empson as a threat—offered the justly mitigating explanation 'that EMPSON was referring to freedom of education rather than espousing a Communist or Socialist line.' Nonetheless, Indiana University had been duly warned off Empson: they never again invited him to the summer school.

Later in the year, for a week beginning on 15 October, enquiries were also conducted in London; but the brief synopsis on file has been blanked out. By November 1954, the case was wound up, the dossier closed. We may infer that—despite the caution of the Information Resources Division of the US Department of Justice—no significant information had been ascertained.

'I think the affair has gone off all right,' Empson wrote home at the beginning of August.'[63] As to the 'affair' of the impertinent lecture and the affronting uniform, it is fair to say that the Department of Justice would not have been doing its job properly if it had not made some attempt to find out whether he was promoting sedition, though their actions are also a sad reflection on the Cold War. The best that can be said is that the FBI had the sense to drop the case when they realized he did not represent a continuing threat to political stability. For his part, Empson found the necessity to speak out about China a deeply stressful business. Yet he had a profound conviction that the USA was in effect besieging the new Communist administration in China which was being hailed with joy by the majority of its peoples; it was therefore a matter of conscience for him to speak out—though the effect of the speech was obviously mitigated by a degree of drunkenness in the speaker. There is no question but that it took courage for a loyal citizen of the UK to stand up and be counted a friend of the new China—which the propaganda of the free world was working to demonize. Leslie Fiedler was mistaken in implying that his speech had been unpatriotic.

He had more than three weeks to pass before sailing home from New York on the *Queen Mary* on 25 August 1954, and hoped to be able to call on W. H. Auden in New York or Robert Lowell in Boston, but neither replied to his letters (Lowell was in hospital suffering from a bout of manic depression, Auden was in Europe). In the event, he went on to stay for a few days with his diplomat brother Charles at 2339 'S' Street in Washington, DC, where he was delighted to discover that his niece Robin was 'a much nicer girl than I expected': 'I took her to "Cinerama" last night, and was glad she chose it because it is really an impressive machine.'[64] In New York, he met up with Antony West (embittered son of H. G. Wells and Rebecca West), whom he had known and liked at the BBC and who was currently working for *The New Yorker*; West hospitably took him off on his final weekend for some boating and swimming at his home in Connecticut.

The nice news awaiting his return home was that the Noonday Press (New York) wanted to publish a Meridian paperback edition of *Seven Types of Ambiguity*, with an advance of $10,000 (divided between Empson and New Directions in New York). 10,000 copies of the imprint were eventually issued, and it was reported that up to 8,000 had been sold by October 1959.

'Come to think of it, I had better write down . . . that I had only just time to take off my Communist uniform in Indiana and get home to train the actors to do the Masque for the Queen . . . What we were doing was telling the Queen she was God, a simple blasphemy which has never been done since the Stuarts . . . I was downright thrilled by the Queen, but I couldn't help also reflecting that it was good luck for me to have the Queen turn up just then in Sheffield; it puts my political face straight in a way . . . '[65]

On Wednesday, 27 October 1954, the Queen and the Duke of Edinburgh rather fleetingly descended upon the University of Sheffield in order to inaugurate its Jubilee Session. No other reigning Sovereign had visited the principal university buildings since King Edward VII opened them in 1905. Six months before the Queen's visit, the Vice-Chancellor, Professor J. M. Whittaker, put to his recently-appointed Professor of English Literature a 'general idea' with a much longer history—to celebrate the Queen's visit by reviving the masques with which Elizabeth I was greeted at Cambridge in 1564 and at Oxford in 1566 and 1592. Would Empson assist in the creation of a new masque by 'writing such parts of it as would be spoken or sung'? The vocal part should be in English and not Latin, Whittaker suggested; it should have 'literary value' and be in modern idiom rather than a pastiche of Elizabethan poetry. 'At any rate,' he gentled Empson, 'I hope you will turn the matter over in your mind and perhaps we could have a talk about it.'

As Roma Gill was to report many years later in the *Times Literary Supplement*, Empson advised the Vice-Chancellor that Elizabethan masquers would have told the Queen 'that she was God, and that she had invented steel.'[66] According to Empson himself, the Vice-Chancellor responded immediately and without temerity: ' "Tell her she's God again" ... And so I did. I thought this was magnificent Yorkshire behaviour.'[67] Empson forged ahead and sketched the outline of *The Birth of Steel* within a few days. It was 'entrancing' work, he wrote afterwards: 'it did not cross any of our minds that the "style" of the poet Empson was wanted; what the writing had to do was to put across the old savage fantastic thing very shortly and clearly.'[68] The plot tells how a medieval alchemist—inevitably named Smith—is baffled in his attempts to fashion a steel sword; mocked by his minions, he appeals to Minerva, Goddess of Wisdom, who thereupon enters in majesty and introduces the instruments of modern science. In other words, the key point for Empson was that the goddess on stage should take conspicuous pains to identify herself with the real Queen in the audience, who is therefore personally—and breathtakingly—credited with creating the steel industry.

The open-air production had more or less taken full shape during Empson's summer absence at Bloomington. The student producer, Peter Cheeseman (later Director of the New Victoria Theatre, North Staffordshire), together with the stage manager Alan Curtis, bulked up Empson's spare and insufficiently dramatic verse with 'alchemical mumbo-jumbo'; the composer Gilbert Kennedy ensured the grandness of the occasion with a score that incorporated blues and jazz rhythms, solemn chorales, and a triumphal tune to accompany Minerva's descent in a golden 'car'; and the architect Alec Daykin designed a covered stage and backcloth. The volunteer orchestra numbered sixty-six, with a large brass section provided by the Sheffield Transport Band; and a huge chorus included university undergraduates, students from the City of Sheffield Training College, and members of the Lydgate-Crosspool Choir. Such was the scale of the operation that the three groups—student orchestra, Transport Band, chorus—had to rehearse in separate venues, and they came together for the first time only a week before the performance. The assembled company filled half the quadrangle, with the conductor's rostrum being sited above a central fountain. To the other side, on the site of the former Chemistry Hut, a tiered grandstand was erected for spouses and special guests of the university staff. Pilkington Brothers manufactured a magnificent bullet-proof glass pavilion for the Queen, and so completed a setting—just as Empson had prefigured—fit for her audience with a goddess (Pamela Brown, a statuesque student contralto, playing Minerva). 'I have just come back from my first hearing of the Masque for the Queen rehearsed with full orchestra,' Empson wrote to Hetta on 19 October, 'and I must say it sounds staggeringly magnificent; I feel rather like The Sorcerer's Apprentice . . . I do feel it is rather a curiosity, which you might be sorry to have missed. I can't promise that we would both be presented to the Queen. Your loving husband William.'[69]

Before a coffee break at one rehearsal (which he found 'dismal'), he insisted upon addressing the entire cast and exhorting them that what they were preparing to stage was 'wildly strange; nobody had told royalty it was a divine creative spirit for three hundred years, and the whole lay-out of this ad-hoc theatre, with the Queen in a high glass cage before them . . . made it the strangest performance they were ever going to take part in. The mad king of Bavaria could not get what they were getting.' Afterwards, in the lavatory, he asked a severe-looking man whom he took to be an electrician what he had made of his 'harangue', as he thought it. 'His answer was surprisingly warm but from my point of view off the point. "It was plumb right," he said, "you got just the right timing. There's just a week to go, and they'll be all right once they feel in the straight (a metaphor from horse racing) but what they feel now is that they just can't bear any more rehearsing." The interest of this kind of thing, to me, if I may patiently explain, was that you could not get anybody to take the faintest interest in the historical revival of the Renaissance half-worship of the first Elizabeth; in one way they weren't bothered with any idea that you could treat the thing seriously, in another way they felt it was the only adequate reception for the present Queen.'[70]

It was at another meeting that he fought (as he indicated to Hetta) to retain the best joke in the show—which the producer and composer had agreed in their creative enthusiasm to throw out while he was in America:

it is just after Minerva has descended in her car, and her first words were to be:

> Majesty, I am yourself. As you would wish
> I now create SHEFFIELD. This poor fish

(presenting laboratory overalls to the Alchemist, who immediately dons them)

> I turn into a steel technician;
>
> And every worker to a real magician

      . . .

The difficulty was to get it into the head of the student actress, whose natural dignity was otherwise splendid for the part, that she really must look at the Queen and address her unofficially and as if otherwise un-heard—they are secretly plotting together. She said it was impossible (she had also to keep in time to background music) but I think she did it all right on the day. Anyhow, I won back that silly 'fish', and whether anybody in the audience realised it was a bad rhyme or not it did get the only laugh in the whole show. What I said in my harangue [to the cast] was 'You don't realise; this will become intolerable unless you force a laugh into it early enough', and when we had our delighted boasting-party after the show my opponents handsomely agreed I had been right.[71]

Soon after 4:30 on the day of the performance, a maroon Rolls-Royce bearing the Queen and the Duke of Edinburgh swept into the crescent at Western Bank: it was a few minutes behind schedule. To one side stood a cluster of photographers; to the other, under an awning, sat a rather bemused group of children from the Children's Hospital across the road, tucked into red blankets and waving little flags. The royal party was greeted by the tall figure of the Chancellor, Lord Halifax,[72] wearing his gold and blue robe, and carrying his gold-edged mortar board, and the Vice-Chancellor, in white and gold robe, along with the Lord Mayor and other civic dignitaries, and swept upstairs to Firth Hall for a formal exchange of speeches. The Queen's reply, enunciated in a clear and precise voice, was relayed outside by loudspeakers.

I thank you, the members of the University, for your loyal address and for your warm welcome to me and my husband. I am glad to have the opportunity of continuing the association of my family with the University and to see for myself something of the great progress made since my great-grandfather opened these buildings 50 years ago. Your achievement has been worth all the hope expressed on that occasion and gives strong assurance to the future... In this present age there is a growing necessity for men and women to take with them into life something of that store of human wisdom which may be acquired in the University... I am very glad to be able to attend these celebrations, which it gives me great pleasure to inaugurate.[73]

The Queen looked very tired, people remarked. Empson's heart sank: she looked 'as cross as a camel', he thought, and was obviously not going to enjoy the flattering little frippery he had written. But, as a member of the entourage later explained to Empson, delivering the speech was the most taxing part for the Queen; she was more at ease when chatting to dozens of strangers in line.

Following the 14-minute production of 'The Birth of Steel' in the quadrangle, the Queen was conducted down for tea in the Junior Common Room, which was decked out for the occasion with red velvet curtains and a feast of flowers. The Duke of Edinburgh promptly made himself at home, chatting and laughing. With a group of medical students he spoke about the film *Doctor in the House* and laughingly repeated the joke about the 'bleeding time'. He even poured out a cup of tea for himself, and licked his fingers after scoffing a sticky bun. At some point, the Duke also fell into absorbed discussion with Dr Gilbert Kennedy, the composer of the masque, on the subject of porphyrins.[74]

'I naturally had my piece to say to him about the masques done for the first Queen Elizabeth when on tour,' wrote Empson in a memoir of the event:

> and he caught me up sharp when I said they wouldn't have given her dancing because they couldn't do it. He says: Of course they could. Empson says: Yes, of course they had their own dancing, but they couldn't do *court* dancing, the *court* masque is an entirely different thing, with no audience at all really, because the Queen herself would often dance. But when on tour the first Elizabeth would always be received with a bit of music and a bit of poetry, just like we have here. This seemed enough to handle it, and then he said (of course he is very much an English military officer, a type of man who is very much pleasanter to deal with than the English legend pretends) that he thought it was a good plan to have this sort of show, because it gave a lot of them something to do, and they would always rather have something to do, really. Yes, I said, lying, and I crawled across and told this story exactly as if it was my own straight back to the Queen, because I had been briefed.[75]

All of a sudden he was told to keep the Queen in conversation until the composer, the director, and the cast could be gathered up to meet her. Dressed in his brown suit and an academic gown, and fully determined not to appear frightened, nor to be impudent or politically incorrect, he nevertheless began lecturing the Queen on his current pet subject—the differences between the court masque and the masques performed for Elizabeth I on her progresses. 'As always when lecturing, I shut my eyes,' he later reproached himself. 'This is a very stupid thing to do when talking to the Queen, because her face ought to be watched incessantly.' The Queen remarked that she liked the play because it was so light. He later thought to himself: 'The possibility of saying "Come, come, mam, what degree of blasphemous flattery *would* you call heavy?" not only could not but did not attract the mind of Empson.'

Suppressing his mischievous reflections, he ventured to the Queen: 'Well, it was meant to be funny, but the way it turned out, we only got one laugh in the whole show.'

'Yes, I was very interested in that too,' said the Queen; 'I was watching the audience with great interest. I *thought* that the reason why they didn't laugh at the jokes was that they had all heard them several times before.'

'Yes, mam, quite right,' said Empson—'lying again,' he admitted in his memoir.[76]

'When Minerva turned up in her full war-paint to meet the Queen at tea (please remember that the whole purpose of the play was to say that she is *identical* with the Queen) I cried out with a natural ironical rich friendly pleasure "Now, at last, they meet," and the Queen said "I envied you your ride in the car." She could not have answered better after a week of Sundays with ten committees. It was so gracious that it came pretty near accepting a legend.'[77]

Presently, the Queen was swept up again and driven off to the station; she had spent precisely 50 minutes on the university premises. But the awe was never to leave Empson. For the rest of his life he remained devoted to the Queen; and he would even collect pictures of her cut from newspapers.

A month later, when requesting that the masque should be included in his *Collected Poems*, he told his friend and publisher Ian Parsons: 'The Queen thought it funny and was sweet about it, to me and the composer (the music was terrific) and the two speaking parts. It isn't meant to be good poetry but it's somehow politically right (I mean, it combines queen-worship with pro-worker sentiment and fair claims for the university back-room boys) and it is really rather a curiosity... Now that it has gone off so very well (though unknown outside Sheffield) I don't see why it shouldn't be put in the book.'[78]

In truth, nothing quite like it had been achieved or attempted since Thomas Arne's masque *Alfred* (1740), produced for the Prince of Wales and chiefly memorable for including the first performance of 'Rule, Britannia'.[79] Within a few weeks—moved by the unique historical significance of the occasion and the awful implications of addressing the Queen as a goddess—he wrote the memoir that was published only posthumously as 'The Queen and I'.[80] And in a later year, when asked why he thought he had been knighted in 1979, he promptly quipped, perhaps with a touch of remembered awe: 'Well, you see, I once called her a goddess. What else could she do?'[81]

13

Ménage à Trois

Jealousy is drowned in a diffused bisexality

Brigid Brophy, *Fanny Hill*

THE day-to-day business of the university, with all its stimulations, irritations, backbitings, bickerings, and pockets of boredom—and full as it was of petty local intrigues as well as strategic decisions and longer-term developments—was probably the least dramatic element of Empson's life over the next few years. Sheffield meant regular professional diligence during a time when his domestic life turned rampantly melodramatic and inconstant. The threefold duties of the put-upon professor—teaching, administration, research—became all the more absorbing as his other life, his metropolitan marriage in the bohemian Studio House, threatened to go haywire and even break down. Being assiduous about his teaching in particular meant he could channel his mental and emotional energies and find a kind of steadiness. Many students were struck by the care and attentiveness he brought to his professional life.

'My overwhelming impression of him was of a combination of eccentric brilliance with extraordinary kindness and generosity (in accepting, and giving a lot of time to, a Swedish postgraduate student with unorthodox qualifications),' recalled Inga-Stina Ewbank (then Ekeblad).[1] Born in 1932, Ewbank had come to Sheffield in the autumn of 1954 to do a one-year MA by dissertation, working on the plays of Webster, Tourneur, and Middleton, with Empson as her supervisor. Usually they met in his office but occasionally in the 'Burrow', which was convenient for both of them: she had taken rooms with her father (who was recently widowed and retired, and shared the Sheffield year with her as a venture) at the top of a large house in Broomhall Place, over the road from Empson's tenement accommodation.

> In the context it somehow seemed quite normal that, in the 'Burrow', there was nothing but his unspeakably unmade and unlaundered bed to sit on, and that he should offer whiskey (in lieu of tea) in what was obviously a toothglass. I brought a piece of writing each week, and he would comment on it—chiefly on my punctuation. When it came to the content, he was very kind, anxious not to discourage and to praise rather than criticize. In effect, I suppose, he taught by example rather than precept: through monologues on whatever was the topic of the week—revenge tragedy or blank verse or iterative imagery—at the end of which, thrilled by the intellectual loops and twists I had witnessed, I would rush off to read more, because they stimulated more than they daunted. I particularly remember how he reacted to something I had written, *Scrutiny*-style, on the 'decadence' of the verse in *A Cure for a Cuckold* [by Webster and Rowley], by simply reading out loud the lines I had condemned, and how the reading itself became the most brilliant act of criticism, forever opening up the possibilities of late Jacobean blank verse to someone too blinkered to see and too deaf to hear.

The state of continuous intellectual excitement in which she found herself during that year convinced her she wanted to stay in English academic life—'and though Liverpool (where I went on a William Noble Fellowship) turned out to be in every sense a soberer place, I owe more to Empsonian Sheffield'.

Empson shared her commitment and expanded to her enthusiasm; 'please let me know if there is anything new about Tourneur,' he wrote to Bonamy Dobrée in Leeds soon after the beginning of the autumn term. 'My girl Swede is rather tough; she is trying to crack the Iron Curtain and get a learned article from a magazine in Bulgaria, and this makes me keen to give her any help I can.'[2]

In London, the equally energetic and yet extremely restless Hetta had started to 'hell around' (as she would put it) with a young lodger at Studio House. Empson knew his wife's lover very well and liked him. He was told of the affair and he smiled upon it. Since he and Hetta were no longer sleeping together, he felt it right and proper for her to seek sexual fulfilment outside the marriage.[3] 'I was brought up to believe that satisfying a woman was a courtesy, like being good at bridge,' Empson was to remark to Christopher Ricks. Why should he punish the wife for his own lack of performance? But it was not a discreet and closeted affair: Hetta and her young lover saw nothing to hide, and in any case they were so often intoxicated and over-excited with one another, and lavish and outrageous even in company, that everyone soon got to know of it.

The actor Trevor Baxter, who in 1954 became friends with Hetta's new lover, a raffish and liberated man named Peter Duval Smith, while drinking in the Dirty Duck at Stratford-upon-Avon, was thrilled to be invited to spend an evening at Studio House:

> However, by the time I arrived, Empson, his wife and Peter had all drunk so much that they were more or less beyond speech! I can see Empson so clearly. We sat at a lacquered table . . . Empson sat at the end of it looking at me all evening with a silent and owlish disdain . . . His wife spoke, telling me once or twice of how she wanted to have Peter's child. Peter was gurgling baby talk, only becoming slightly more coherent when he asked me if I would like to 'hold his little cocky' while he, too drunk to get up, peed into an earthenware bottle . . . When I left in the morning, looking for someone to say goodbye to and thank for my hospitality, I came across Peter, naked, draped around Mrs. Empson on a couch. I tiptoed away into the dawn.[4]

By the turn of the year 1955, Hetta was pregnant by her new lover; and she rejoiced in the pregnancy: she wholeheartedly desired this child by him. Openness and broadcast information were the order of the day. 'Ma has gone mad on pubs,' wrote the 11-year-old Jacob Empson to a friend, 'and she goes every day with a man called Peter Duval Smith, who is a radio producer. Ma is going to have a baby in about two weeks from 14 July, 7 o'clock in the evening.'[5] Kathleen Raine gossiped by letter to Dorothea Richards at this time: 'Hetta Empson is . . . expecting a baby any day now. Whether Bill is very happy about this I do not know . . . '[6]

Peter Duval Smith was twenty years younger than Empson, ten years younger than Hetta. He was in his mid-twenties when he met Empson at the BBC, and he presently came to occupy a room at Studio House. Born in Tanganyika in 1926, he had been brought up and educated in South Africa, a shared background that must have been one of the factors that attracted Hetta and Duval Smith to one another.[7] A man of slight stature, with small bones, fair curly hair, and a pale, chubby-cheeked, bespectacled face, Duval Smith compensated for his rather undistinguished looks with a soft, intimate voice which made him a natural for the wireless: once heard, his voice was not readily forgotten.[8] But he had more than an entrancing voice: he was highly intelligent and talented, he could be uproariously funny, and he was possessed of great energy and curiosity. He was hectic in his movements and in his enthusiasms—and he was also given to utter irresponsibility and excess. A dynamic figure, he would keep up his hunger for experience until his premature death at the age of 40. Richard West, who knew him in his last years, was to recall 'his exotic bitter romanticism . . . his zest for the outlandish and . . . his restless need for excitement'; 'he was one of those people who really enjoy danger'; 'he shouted in public places', and he 'enjoyed noise, especially in sexual intercourse'[9]—he was evidently highly sexed. But he indulged himself too (as Trevor Baxter remarked) in drunkenness and obscenity. Muriel Gardner was disgusted when at a party at her house he urinated into a sink, directly in her presence. Dorothea Richards recorded in her diary a visit to Studio House on 9 July 1954 (Empson was doing his stint at Bloomington), when she found Hetta Empson and Duval Smith on their worst behaviour: 'Peter Duval Smith came in kissed our hands, flopped onto the Kang [Chinese bed]—stared at us glassy eyed, made noises as if he were going to be sick repeated silly stories etc. Hetta got shoutey and irracible on political matters. Got away 11.45. Disgusted by finding Smith behaving like a dog.'

Another person who met him in the early period was the writer John Press, who was at the time a lecturer at the British Institute in Salonika, which Duval Smith visited in the spring of 1950. Duval Smith gave a lecture on T. S. Eliot's 'The Love Song of J. Alfred Prufrock', without a note: it was 'one of the best lectures I have ever heard,' recalls Press. 'He was delightful company, high-spirited, intelligent and funny.'[10] Then, in June 1950, Press spent a few days on duty in Athens, where he went to dinner twice with Louis and Hedli MacNeice. Duval Smith was a welcome guest on both occasions. MacNeice, who was at the time Director of the British Institute at Athens (on secondment from the BBC), shared Press's admiration for Duval Smith. But a number of colleagues at Athens gossiped to Press that Duval Smith's behaviour left a great deal to be desired. For one thing, he was infatuated with a novelist named Kay Wallis and more than once failed to turn up for a class on account of preferring to spend the time in her company. When teaching, he could be abusive: during one class he called a middle-aged woman a fool and threw a heavy dictionary at her. At a New Year's party hosted by Rachel Tatham, wife of the British Council Representative, Wilfred Tatham, he arrived sucking an orange which he threw away just before extending to her a sticky hand with pips still adhering to it. Such behaviour betrayed a very great deal of offensive arrogance in the young Duval Smith.

When Wilfred Tatham and Kenneth Johnstone (Deputy Director of the British Council) recommended to the British Council that he should forfeit one increment of his annual salary (for persistent unpunctuality among other things), Duval Smith promptly resigned from the Council.[11]

Louis MacNeice came to the rescue by finding him a job at the BBC. It
was a brilliant career move. Duval Smith's work for the BBC was to be
hugely successful, winning many plaudits. He is remembered above all for
his work on the TV programme *Bookstand* and the radio programme *The
World of Books*; among other assignments, he produced the fine broadcast of
Empson's poetry and several of his critical talks. But the standard of his
behaviour fell far short of his professional competence. Even MacNeice's
loyalty was subjected to huge strains, and matters finally reached a point
where MacNeice could no longer defend or endure him. Hedli MacNeice
told John Press about the climactic incident. One night, Duval Smith
dined at their home and would not leave, despite MacNeice's protestations
that he had to get up for a conference early the next morning. Duval Smith
refused to go home until he had finished a bottle of brandy he had started
to consume. When MacNeice persuaded him to take the bottle away, he
stood outside in their garden, draining the bottle and then hurling it
through their front window. That was the end of MacNeice's long affection
for Peter Duval Smith.[12]

Empson took a large amount of bohemian behaviour for granted in his
household. He had learned to live with turbulence and tempestuousness,
and when necessary he would join in slanging matches. After all, he had
chosen to marry a beautiful woman with a powerful personality: a woman
who (as one her close friends was to recall even at her funeral) 'had a very
quick wit and a very sharp tongue; you couldn't play games with her; she
was an arrogant woman who laughed easily and got angry easily'; and she
could be 'fierce' towards all kinds of stupidity.[13] Another friend was to say
of her, 'Hetta was a phenomenon, a white goddess, and at times, for better
or worse, a ball of fire.'[14] The charismatic, boisterous, albeit sometimes
self-indulgent, drunken, and loutish, Duval Smith would likewise have
appealed to Empson. His intellectual gifts were impressive, his excesses
often entertaining; and his tendency to mischief-making made him a man
after Empson's heart. Lewis Wolpert, who got to know him in a later year,
called him 'clever, funny, waspish, wild.'[15] Above all, Empson's experience
of Duval Smith as a radio producer impressed him a great deal. 'I have
formed a high opinion of him,' Empson was to write in a testimonial in
April 1956; 'he is professional, so to speak—he can realise what needs
doing in a new situation and is then keen to do it right. Of course he is not
an English academic figure, but he is undoubtedly "literary", a voracious
reader with severe canons of taste.'[16] By 'severe canons of taste' Empson
must have meant that Duval Smith could be downright opinionated, even

ruddy-mannered, in saying his piece; Empson greatly admired a decisive judgement, and a willingness to go to war for it.[17]

Nonetheless, if Empson was content to play the complaisant cuckold—*cornuto e contento*—to the talented and lively South African whom he had introduced into the household, it was another thing entirely for his wife to have a child by her lodger-lover. A cornutor could be lived with; but the advent of an illegitimate child would change the picture. Empson did not fuss when he learned of the pregnancy, but there is little doubt that he was perturbed by it. A close friend was to recall: 'William got as far as thinking it was a bit cool!'[18]

Very sadly, the baby girl, though brought to term, was stillborn. It is not clear where the father was at this moment, but it does seem clear that Hetta did not want her husband to be her support in the hospital; nor did he offer to stay at hand—all the better that he should look after the 'legitimate' children. A few months later, the Empsons' very loyal friend Max Bickerton (who occupied an attic flat at Studio House) filled out the picture for Walter Brown in Japan: 'Hetta is the same lovely creature . . . It was all very sad as she so much wanted a girl. I saw her in the hospital just a few minutes after they had taken the child away. It was pure bad luck—one chance in a million.'[19]

Empson's response to the grievous occurrence was mixed. Though positively content that Hetta should take a lover, he had in him enough of the Empson family code to deplore her begetting of a child outside the marriage. This letter, penned on 3 August (just a couple of days after she had delivered the dead baby), expresses calm good wishes but a refusal to mourn:

> My dearest Hetta,
> I am so sorry if you are unhappy about it. But I gather there is no reason to think you wouldn't succeed in another attempt if you choose to try. Of course, I haven't told anyone it wasn't mine, because we meant to do that later. I shall write and tell Arthur that he hasn't a new niece.
> We are all very contented here, and look forward to seeing you on the 11th. Give Peter my condolences and good wishes.
> Your loving husband
> William.

While both the salutation and the signing-off reconfirm his marital status and his deep affection for his wife, the first sentence betrays a tightness of feeling in the conditional 'if'; it refuses to grant any sorrow of his own. The second sentence is far more generous, extending to her the hope that her adulterous liaison might yet bring forth a child—if that is what she really wants of it. The third sentence is again rather insensitive—especially in referring to the child by the neuter pronoun 'it'—though it becomes inclusive for the first time with 'we'. The fourth sentence (which was of no concern whatever to Hetta) reminds her that he had dutifully observed the protocol of informing his eldest brother that he and his wife were at least expecting a child. Not to exhaust the complexity of the message conveyed by this terse and resolutely unmawkish letter, his formal extension of sympathy to the natural father of the child is surprisingly kindly: perhaps even more warm than merely formal.

An obvious question arises from this situation. Why did Empson appear to show virtually no jealousy of his wife? The route to an answer may begin with a remark made by Jacob Empson: 'It came as a surprise to my mother to realise my father was bisexual.' Empson was later to say of Coleridge, among other writers, that his sexuality had been 'mangled' in his youth, and quite possibly he felt the same about himself. Realizing in an early year that he was attracted towards both men and women, he had largely internalized the dual tendency in terms of self-division. Being queer at college was after all just a phase which one grew out of. At Cambridge he had first gone to bed with a confident older woman, but several of his poems of the time encode his desire for a male lover. In London he had bedded Alice Naish and then made no attempt to pursue her further after what turned out to be a one-night stand. Even during the war, when he suddenly got married to Hetta Crouse, some of his colleagues at the BBC, including Gwenda David, were taken aback only because they had assumed he was purely homosexual. It was probably only in China after the war that he had finally come to believe in the ideal happiness of the Consenting Triangle—if the other man in the case was willing to extend sexual favours to himself as well as to oblige the wife. It need not mean going in for sodomy; but even if anal penetration was a touch too far, as Empson argued elsewhere, it was a 'civilised arrangement' for a masturbating man to 'lend a hand' to another who was similarly inclined. All that was required of the young man was that he should 'make no bones about allowing him minor pleasures' (as he was to write in a late essay about the 'sexual constitution' of Andrew Marvell).[20] In other words, he came to feel not only complaisant but decidedly constructive.

Some sense of the nature of Empson's sexuality, and specifically of the way he saw homosexual desire as he grew older, may be gathered from his writings on Marvell. From the early 1970s at the latest, he became absorbed to the point of obsession with spelling out from Marvell's poetry and biography a construction of the poet's character and relations that was so particular and (so Empson insisted) commendable, that it seems fair to infer that to some degree he identified with a man he took to be peculiar and exemplary. As Empson interpreted the man and his works—in two detailed essays that were brought to completion only in the late 1970s but which took a long time to write—Marvell was bisexual; though seemingly attracted to women, it is agreed he felt very uneasy with them: 'he does not seem to like them much.'[21] Equally, he maintains, Marvell was evidently attracted to the figure of the mower in his verses: 'I think he fell in love with the Mower.' Damon the Mower (in the lyric of that title) 'keeps saying he is in despair for love of a woman, and this allows love to be talked about, but he would not have accepted the situation so passively. It is the poet who is in love with Damon; Freud calls the device "displacement", when interpreting dreams.'[22] Empson had thoroughly well understood the practice of displacement since the late 1920s, when he penned his series of 'Letter' poems to his Cambridge friend Desmond Lee, though he would always describe those poems as being about 'boy being afraid of girl'; the only difference is that he needed no Freud to tell him what his poetry was disguising, or concealing from overt analysis.

In his second closely-argued essay, 'The Marriage of Marvell', Empson sets out to prove that Marvell did in fact marry his landlady, albeit in secret (as the putative 'widow' Mrs Palmer had disclosed immediately upon the poet's death). But Empson was intent upon making Marvell into a married man not so as to discredit him, as a clandestine marriage to a social inferior might otherwise seem to do (and even those critics who have accepted the marriage as a likely fact have invariably argued that it serves only to damage Marvell's character), but perhaps rather surprisingly to praise him. 'I am keen to whitewash his character,' wrote Empson.[23] He thus proposes for Marvell an inner life which accounts for the way he wished to balance a desired marriage with his penchant for same-sex desire outside that marriage:

> When men get drunk together they often become affectionate, but do not want to make love, only to boast about their successes with women; and Marvell would long have felt that his embarrassment at this stage was itself a betrayal. He did not want to appear unresponsive, nor sexually timid, nor impotent, nor yet chaste . . . , and anyway he had few successes to boast of; but they were with young men, so that a true answer would amount to a demand for a perhaps unwelcome degree of confidence. This is presumably what A. E. Housman meant by the splendid line: 'Ask me no more, for fear I should reply' . . . Also (I expect) he had been much relieved to find that his

reactions when in bed with Mrs Palmer were entirely normal; his previous
experience had been very mangling. So he now felt equipped to get drunk
with men, and thus coax them into doing what he wanted.[24]

The logic of the psychology that Empson thus imagines for Marvell is
slightly difficult to follow, but it amounts to saying that the seventeenth-
century poet's discovery that he could enjoy normal sex with his 'wife' Mrs
Palmer released him to have affairs with men. (Some readers might deduce
that Empson is simply arguing for homosexuality.) Marvell would feel that
he had proved himself (to himself) as a 'normal' man, while at the same
time feeling he could pursue the sexual sideshow he also desired. In a
similar way, it is likely that Empson had found his own youthful sexual
encounters, whether with women or with men, somewhat 'mangling'—
almost certainly because he did not know how to resolve the question of
whether he was heterosexual or homosexual, when in truth he was
attracted both ways—and that he believed his experience of 'entirely
normal' sex with his wife Hetta had enabled him to clarify, or 'unmangle',
his sexuality. Moreover, there is no doubt that from the 1950s until his
retirement in 1971 he enjoyed a good relationship with Alice Stewart. 'I
never really expected at my age to be as sexually thrilled as I am,' he once
said of his long affair with Alice.[25] Indeed, Alice 'saved' him from any
bad, and possibly dangerous, encounters that might well have come his
way if he had been more active in seeking out casual same-sex encounters.
All the same, he would not deny his homosexual tendencies, and from time
to time he was moved to seek out what he called friendly and uncompli-
cated sex with nice young men. It was just such 'minor pleasures' that
Empson allowed himself in bed with Hetta and her lovers. It was merely an
act of kindness, he felt, and not exploitative (though such behaviour must
inevitably presume upon a degree of paternalistic licence).

A hitherto unpublished poem—printed for the first time in the Appendix
to this volume—entitled 'The Wife is Praised', drafted in 1948, takes the
form of an *hommage* or loving tribute to Hetta for her generosity in accommodating just such an arrangement in their loving life together. Many men
desire to share their wives with another man, he claims in the final lines:

> But it's true that few women can handle
>   What so many men want to do,
> Or (the phrase is) can 'hold up a candle'
>   To rival you.

This is presumably the polemical work he had in mind when he wrote to
the writer and editor Tambimuttu from Peking on 12 March 1948: he

proposed, he said, to finish *The Structure of Complex Words* by the end of the summer:

> Then I hope to look round a bit and see if I can still write verse. Don't you think it is time someone wrote a long didactic poem in terza rima telling people what to do in bed? Verse about the world situation was all right in the Thirties but does seem now to strike rather a chill. A new battle for freedom to print highminded advice about sex would strike something a bit warmer, wouldn't it?

—adding at the end of the letter this pointedly whimsical observation: ' "Of course his really important work can't be published yet; it will have to be posthumous"—That seems a very convenient thing to get people to say about one.'

In the event, the poem did not make use of terza rima; it borrows to joyously affirmative effect—it is not really didactic but generous—the form of Swinburne's 'Dolores'. The poem opens:

> Much astonished to find you were handy
> I proposed when we first got to bed;
> This was viewed as too pushing or randy
> And not what was usually said;
> I urged you have lovers beside me
> O lots, and I'd just as soon know.
> It took time and an angel to guide me
> To make the thing go.
>
> Did I love you as mine for possessing?
> Absurd as it seems, I forget;
> For the vision of love that was pressing
> And time has not falsified yet
> Was always a love with three corners
> I loved you in bed with young men,
> Your arousers and foils and adorners
> Who would yield to me then.

In short, what the poem is advocating (based on personal experience) is an arrangement so irregular that many folk would regard it as a perversion of normal marital relations. The notion amounts to pimping for the wife in the expectation not just of scopophiliac pleasure but even possibly of sharing the lover's favours.[26]

Throughout his adult career Empson maintained consistently anti-censorious views: every issue, he believed, should be available for literary treatment and criticism. It is surprising, in fact, to realize just how many of his early writings take on the topic of the relativity of ethical and moral standards. He was of course well aware that to dissent from the beliefs and *mores* of one's culture—religious, social, sexual—is to risk almost certain condemnation; let alone to propound alternative ways. Religious or cultural straitjackets deny one the birthright of a rational creature: the right to exercise freedom of thought and independence of conscience. Indeed, the concepts of *freedom* and *independence* underpin the essays in *Some Version of Pastoral*. In an article published a few years later, in 1963, he was to aver: 'the highest event in ethics [is] the moral discovery, which gets a man called a traitor by his own society.'[27] Modes of conduct which step beyond convention may well embody or convey truths which are neglected only because they appear, for a certain age, to infringe the dictates of religion or social custom. In other words, convention outlaws some kinds of activity simply because they can not be countenanced within the terms of its own provisionality.

On the other hand, for a man who is unable to accept the moral ideas of his society, he had argued in his early essay 'Alice in Wonderland', to base his dissent on intellectual dishonesty is 'to short-circuit it'. Thus Oscar Wilde and his associates, for example, must be seen as what Empson calls 'slavish':

> By their very hints that they deserved notice as sinners they pretended to accept all the moral ideas of society, because they wanted to succeed in it, and yet society only took them seriously because they were connected with an intellectual movement which refused to accept some of those ideas.[28]

Epater le bourgeois: that was not Empson's aim at all; rather, it was to reckon with the fact that the reach of the mind and personal conduct is larger than what any given society may regard as 'permissible'. We must realize that one of the supreme values of literary endeavour is 'precisely that of stepping outside preconceptions' (to cite a phrase he used in a 1930 review).

In another early essay (also drafted in the 1930s), on death and literary representations of death, he pointed out:

> There is a very nice postage-stamp collection of perversions in Romantic poetry by Mario Praz called *The Romantic Agony*, but it is prevented from being anything more important, I think, by its reproving tone. Also he is convinced that the appearance of perversions in literature is something peculiar to nineteenth century romanticism, an idea which is in any case untrue. The critic who takes a Freudian point of view is in the opposite difficulty: there is so much perversion at the back of the normal, and so much oddity about the position of the artist in particular, that there seems no way of deciding what version of a perversion is to be admired.

He did not draw the conclusion that whatever is, is natural and therefore good. He was himself deeply moral without being moralistic. Accordingly, the fact that unorthodoxy, in life as in art, can still be precisely moral and in certain circumstances acceptable is a fundamental paradox of his position.

'One rough principle can be invoked to avoid portentousness,' he argued in his essay on the literature of death:

> work known to be good by critics influenced by a fairly long series of changing fashions is not going to be spoilt by being explained. The combination of Freudian understanding and puritan sentiments is liable to be a paralysing one ... To say that the 'Ode to a Nightingale' involves death wishes and the 'Ode to Melancholy' masochism, or that Shakespeare uses the language of love about the pleasures of fighting, is to point out what was always on the surface; a psychoanalysis of the authors would not show why generations of various readers have found these versions of these perversions noble and sensible.

The tenor of 'The Wife is Praised' is enthusiastic: it is 'highminded advice', as he told Tambimuttu, and tested by experience. Indeed, it can be argued that it is cast as a work of moral idealism, not of perverse inclination, for it stands in the respectable tradition of utopianism. Plato's *Republic*, the origin of that tradition, ventured the morally progressive view that citizens of the state should go shares with each other in wives. Wives ought to be held in common (*koinēi*), Socrates is given to argue there, for the sake of the amity and unity of the association, and to remove temptations to selfishness and to rivalry between individuals. Aristotle, in his *Politics*, found Plato's idealism wanting in the face of his own partial scepticism, but he could scarcely impugn Plato's motive—only the putative naivety of his nobility of mind. Empson's endeavour is by no means so innocent of human nature, and he properly admits to a measure of special pleading in the case: 'I trace out a natural law,' the poem states; and equally:

> There is need for a quantum of terror
> In handling this secular theme;
> It is hubris and brash and an error
> To present it as strawberries and cream.

Nevertheless, what he wrote about La Rochefoucauld (in his essay on idealist ethical theories) is just as true of his own effort: 'the Maxims would not even be good writing if they did not carry a hint of paradox and self-contradiction.'

As with so many of Empson's verses, 'The Wife is Praised' is what he called an 'argufying' poem. It argues both for the happy triangle and to resolve his ambivalent response to Swinburne's 'Dolores'—ambivalent because he felt both intoxicated by it as poetry and deeply chary of the murky majesty of its meaning. 'Dolores' is unremittingly ceremonial, an invocation of dark and deathly lust in the form of the Queen of Passion. Empson overcomes its morbid message by adapting Swinburne's stanza-form to a great variety of attitudes and tones—including a kind of orator-ical eloquence, colloquial chattiness, and self-deprecation. Using the same rhyme-scheme but less rigid prosody, he makes the Swinburnian form amenable to a natural tone of voice and to informal reflection. In passages, admittedly, it plays with doggerel. The effect is analogous to the technique that Spenser discovered for *The Faerie Queene*—at least as Empson himself described it in his broadcast talk 'New Judgment on Edmund Spenser' (1952): 'what was needed was a regular idiom, so that you could go straight ahead and say *anything* in poetry, without getting flustered if some of it wasn't poetical.' Essentially, too, Empson casts out Swinburne's unwhole-someness with his own open speech, and with wit—as in this example of Gilbertian comic rhyming, boxing the compass between homosexuality and the extramarital allure of courtly love:

> Love is sodomy, love is adultery,
>   Say the sources; in pain you must roam.
> Nearly true, but I give to each cult a re-
>   Vision at home.

The two penultimate stanzas importantly shift away from Swinburne's pagan poem—ultimately rejecting the demoralizing 'Dolores' as betraying 'A puritan taint in the grain'—to the biography of James Joyce and to the meaning of *Ulysses*, in which (Empson argues) the character Bloom offers to negotiate a happy triangle with Stephen and Molly.

> I want it more homely and jolly—
>   This is coarse and like Leopold Bloom—
> But he craves to bed Stephen with Molly
>   On more grounds than the critics assume.
> With this Son in his bed he could sire one;
>   Ten years (since the death) he's felt barred;
> The theme is a bold and entire one;
>   Joyce hiding it hard.

> And the answer comes after the story:
>   Jeering Stephen became Mr Joyce

Knowing all of both Blooms to his glory,
    And how he got healed is your choice.
But I would not agree it's refining
    Not to care whether Bloom had a son.
Perhaps Joyce was ashamed he kept whining;
    The book's name says they won.

He first took it into his head that there might be a covert story, a secret subtext, to Joyce's *Ulysses* in September 1948, when he read the novel for a second time. He picked up a copy of the novel while at the Kenyon Summer School in Ohio, and read it during his passage back to China. It was a wonderfully funny novel, he found; it could reduce him to tears of laughter. And in a letter to Hetta written from on board his ship, the Narrandera, he outlined his theory in a lengthy paragraph from which I take key passages:

> I . . . think now that it has a 'point' which Joyce apparently was shy about and succeeded in hiding from his readers—I mean that Bloom has a quite specific neurosis about his wife which is going to be cured by his homosexual feelings about Stephen . . . Bloom wants another child but feels he can't copulate with her, and hasn't done for ten years since the first son died. If he can . . . get her to bed with Stephen, he feels, he will be able to try again . . . If Stephen is the author it is clear that he got out of this mental condition somehow, and a brief affair with Mrs B. before he leaves Ireland permanently for Zurich seems to fit the case very well . . . [I]t is a bold treatment of a subject which nobody else has dared to handle.[29]

The theory is difficult to get to grips with, but it seems to depend on the notion that a man who, for whatever neurotic reasons, has lost the desire to have sexual relations with his wife, might be enabled to sleep with her again by way of his homosexual desire for a younger friend whom he bids to sleep with the wife. The friend thus acts as a mediator, stimulating the husband once again to copulate with his wife and so to beget the child he has desired. 'Only a real son would count,' Empson insisted, 'and [Joyce] has laboured to present a special psychology for Bloom which makes a real son a possible result of this day.' To say the least, the psychology seems quite bewildering and even perverse; but Empson took the view that the means for dealing with this 'very specific neurosis' need not necessarily be regarded as 'scabrous'. 'Bloom is not impotent or homosexual or afraid of Molly,' he was to write in his first attempt at an article on the subject; 'he has simply this special trouble which has long upset his home life. He feels that if he could plant on her a lover he was fond of, who would even take his advice instead of jeering at him, he could even now have this son himself by his wife . . . ' Empson believed that if Stephen was to some extent a self-portrait of Joyce, the author himself must evidently have slept with just such an ur-Molly in his earlier life; the experience would have provided the 'actual homely example' that he would eventually deploy in his great layered and secretive book. 'I do not believe Joyce was capable of inventing such a good story, as it works out,' he claimed. Above all, as far as Empson was concerned, the idea gave a kind of moral credibility to the desired prospect of overcoming jealousy and sharing one's wife with one's friend. 'The situation that Joyce is envisaging,' Empson argued, 'especially in the note about Bertha [in Joyce's 'disgusting play' *Exiles*, which he believed to prefigure the radical theme of the novel] wanting their spiritual union, is clearly fundamental to *Ulysses*. Here is the healing process through which Bloom hopes even yet to produce a son. What Joyce has in view is a startling transformation of the Eternal Triangle; from being one of the inevitable grounds of greed and aggression it becomes, one would suppose, the highest or most evolved of all forms of human intimacy.'[30]

Hetta Empson was quite surprised to receive from her husband a letter outlining such a detailed account of his proposed exposition of Joyce's novel; she even showed it round to some friends (including the young scholar David Hawkes).[31] It may well be that she noted at once the likely applicability of Empson's explicatory ideas to some aspects of their own marital situation. Empson was to announce in private correspondence dating from the early 1950s that he no longer slept with his wife; and it is even possible that he had given up conjugal relations with her by the late 1940s, at the time when he noticed what he saw as a similar if not identical situation in Joyce's novel. It is also the case that he was himself a complaisant cuckold by the same date, when he took a benignant view of Hetta's affair with a young friend of theirs. Hetta must have wondered whether he was not trying in his letter to explain his own frame of mind vis-à-vis the affair, and to describe to her, or even to prescribe, the ideal happy triangle he would like to make up with her lover and herself. It is by no means necessary to suppose that he crudely projected on to Joyce's fiction a notion taken from his own life or even his fantasy life; merely that his personal experience gave him an intuition into certain aspects of the plot which moved him to work out the secret map of the whole novel.

Whether or not his insights about *Ulysses* to some degree matched his own experience in the 1940s, he was to remain possessed for the rest of his life by his contentious theory about the novel, and he would try to write it up on a number of occasions. Only a year after that letter to Hetta, for instance, he was to tell his publisher: 'I have written about 20,000 words about *Ulysses*.'[32]

His next attempt involved an extraordinary irony: on 'Bloomsday' 1954 he was to present his theory in the form of a talk, 'The Theme of *Ulysses*', broadcast on the BBC Third Programme, where his producer was none other than Peter Duval Smith—who seemed utterly enthused by Empson's thesis. Given that Empson was essaying a partly biographical reading of the novel, and that his interpretation was anyway obscure—was he actually alleging that Stephen-as-Joyce begot a child by one 'Mrs Bloom' before his marriage to Nora?—it is not altogether surprising to discover that the authorities at the BBC became nervous of his script on the basis of a partial misunderstanding. Duval Smith eagerly defended Empson's piece in an internal memorandum:

> Empson was willing to make a number of minor alterations in the script, with a view to sparing Mrs Joyce's feelings. I enclose an 'As-Recorded' script and a note from Empson giving his permission for the script to be shown to Mrs Joyce.
>
> All the same . . . there might be a policy objection because the script infers [*sic*] that Joyce had a son by a woman not his wife (the original of Mrs Bloom), and this might cause Mrs Joyce some embarrassment. In fact the script does not say this . . .
>
> I think you will agree that the script is not defamatory, unfair or unkind, after all. It seems to me most generous in tone, and as it is a remarkable contribution to the study of *Ulysses*, I hope it may be broadcast.[33]

However, even if Duval Smith was wholly persuaded by Empson's argument that *Ulysses* is underpinned by the covert plot of a happy triangle, that is not to say he embraced it as a viable way forward for his life with the Empsons.

Notwithstanding, Duval Smith did urge Empson also to print his essay, and Empson duly brought out 'The Theme of *Ulysses*' in the *Kenyon Review* in 1956. Then in 1969 Empson was to publish a summary statement of his argument apropos *Ulysses*, highlighting the demonstrable fact that 'the notes written by Joyce to advise himself how to write the play *Exiles* . . . show that he regarded the Consenting Triangle as an exalted and progressive ideal'.[34] Finally, his most extended discussion of Joyce's intentions in writing *Ulysses* ('The Ultimate Novel', in *Using Biography*) argues that the author assuredly 'thought the happy triangle a noble ideal, and tried to arrange one'. 'Why then does the book [*Ulysses*] make a secret of it?' Empson asks. 'Because the procedure which it regards as an innocent act of charity is heavily penalised by the law.'[35] The terms 'innocent' and 'charity' are loaded.

While Hugh Kenner, among other critics, regarded Empson's interpretation of Joyce's novel as an improper allegation (as Empson realized), Empson himself thought his exposition of the secret story in no way a slander on Joyce; rather that it was utterly to Joyce's credit: 'he would believe the practice to be quite usual, though treated with absurd secrecy.' He was concerned with rescuing, not damaging, Joyce's reputation; he believed it 'a high-minded thing' for Joyce to present 'a current problem'—'a blow for freedom'—' "Lots of advanced people are doing it nowadays, didn't you know?" '[36] Moreover, it may be relevant here to cite another early and disinterested attestation, from the 1930s: 'Really heroic love is superior to social convention,' he claimed in his essay 'The Beggar's Opera'.[37]

Such was Empson's ideal by the late 1940s—the contented triangle—and there is some reason, including the personal testimony of the poem, to believe that he and Hetta might have managed for a while to set up just such a relationship with a friend in Beijing—namely, with their American friend Walter Brown. One key to the arrangement was that Empson refused to take a romanticized view of sex: he came to think it a function of physical desire rather than of romantic love. Thus the bluff phrases about physical sex that he often used as an adult ('less hope of getting to bed together, of course, what else?' as he once told a correspondent who asked about the meaning of a line in one poem) may well have been part of a drive to exorcize the *princesse lointaine* complex which is so prominent in his early poems, notably in the 'Letter' series at Cambridge. To cite another example: in 1964, he read with interest a book on the poetry of Sir Thomas Wyatt by his young colleague Raymond Southall, *The Courtly Maker*. In one passage, Southall seems to be claiming credit for Wyatt because the poems show the pressure of real desire (and concomitant fear), not just Tudor convention. Empson wrote in his notes, with a ball-point pen, the blunt remark: 'He really *wanted* a poke. Why holy, though?'[38]

As Empson plotted it, the desiderated *ménage à trois* would sustain a paradox: it would both satisfy Hetta and enable them to keep their marriage together. All the same, since his own needs seem to have been focused so largely on the male lover in the ideal triangle he described, one might wonder whether he was not all along wholly homosexual in his orientation; whether he deluded himself into feeling he liked to sleep with a woman, and that the bisexuality he professed was not a fiction to save the probity of his marriage?

There are two points that are worth making in this context. On the one hand, in letters to friends, he is stubborn in defending homosexuality as normal: it is not a mental aberration or a disease in need of a cure. Nor did he hesitate to state his view in print: in *Milton's God* (1961), for example, he declared that he considered the current British law against homosexuality to be 'wicked'.[39] Still more strikingly, he gave it as his view on another page of *Milton's God*:

> As to the idea that Milton betrays homosexuality by letting angels love each other, which Robert Graves used as an accusation, and C. S. Lewis felt to need earnest rebuttal, I think that a sensitive man who took Milton's attitude to women, especially a classical scholar, would be bound to toy in fancy at least with the happiness of having an understanding partner who need not be continually snubbed. There is not much evidence that Milton felt so, but if he did it is to his credit.[40]

It is quite difficult to sort out the syntax and the clear meaning, if not the insinuation, of those remarks; but they seem to point to the recommendation that it would be right and proper for a man who suffers from an unsatisfactory wife to long for an 'understanding partner'—evidently a man.

On the other hand, and even in the same breath, Empson would deny the claim—or the allegation, as he might see it—which holds that any element of same-sex desire by a man only goes to prove that he is in fact exclusively homosexual. In 1957 he was to read with interest and enjoyment Professor G. Wilson Knight's latest book, *Lord Byron's Marriage*, and he would write a letter primarily to praise the author for his work but also to protest against the notion that Byron was essentially a closet homosexual whose 'effeminate' manners served only to betray his root feelings. It becomes clear from Empson's letter to Wilson Knight that—going against the consensus that there is no such being as a genuine, well-adjusted bisexual—he doubted whether there was anyone who was solely homosexual. Those who practised homosexuality alone were fooling themselves, for they were almost certainly bisexual. It is quite natural to swing both ways: 'you seem to assume,' he told Wilson Knight, 'that a "homosexual" is a distinct character, incapable of pleasure with women, whereas this is a very recent delusion.'[41]

Moreover, there is no doubt that he would become at times positively evangelistic about what he called 'the greater happiness' of a *ménage à trois* in which the various desires of all three parties would be generously satisfied. Of *Ulysses* he would write in 1970, with an exaltation that expresses a high degree of empathy, and a desire to pay personal tribute: 'the whole elaborate structure of the book, let alone the special psychology given to each of the three main characters, becomes pointless unless it [is] allowed to concentrate and interpret itself, as by a sudden revelation, upon making this great hope seem evidently possible even if hallucinatingly so, a "complete solution". Joyce was still near enough to the imagining of this great happiness to make a good book out of it, even though a sad one ... I can have no patience with the pretence that this kind of happiness does not often occur, is not genuine, must be some nasty madness.'[42] That markedly passionate passage comes from a letter to a young scholar named Darcy O'Brien, whose own article entitled 'Joyce and Sexuality' happened to come out in *20th Century Studies* (1969) alongside Empson's two-page epitome, or advertisement, on 'The Theme of *Ulysses*'. Following the joint appearance of their articles, O'Brien wrote privately to Empson, questioning his argument as to the so-called 'Bloom Offer'. Empson took great pains to formulate his reply to O'Brien, which survives in at least three different drafts dating from February and March 1970: it was clearly important to him to say it right, and to say it with fervent conviction. In the following passage in particular it seems justifiable to feel a degree of personal feeling, even self-identification, on Empson's part:

> To have your wife betray you with a leering cad, who jeers at you for it, would poison all relations with her; but suppose you made terms with jealousy, supposing you cannot live without her and do not at all know what she may require, by agreeing to a lover who is respectful to you and charming and will tell you all you want to know ... If you have agreed that the old pig of a husband must reduce his demands, well, what kind of terms can he make? If he is not to have any fun out of the lover, any more than out of the wife, he might just as well stop earning the money.[43]

The evidence from Empson's writings and letters, and from his demeanour in relation to Hetta and her lovers, adds up to show that he had made a great effort to overcome jealousy in himself—chiefly by asking his wife to be open about her affairs, so that he should not be left flailing in the monstrous dark—and he acknowledged to himself that he really could not live without her. The least painful path, and perhaps the most rewarding, was to find pleasure in Hetta's partners—at least to like them, if not to have 'fun out of' them. It is not known why he felt himself to be, or had proved to be, inadequate for her. Maybe he offered a partial hint when he once reminisced to a colleague about a man who had asked him, 'Have you ever been inside a woman and not been able to come?' Empson had replied, 'No, never; my trouble has always been just the opposite.' But of course the basis of the sexual failure would probably lie deeper, and be more complicated, than a case of premature ejaculation. The best and most rewarding way to keep his wife, he determined, was to show maximum generosity towards her, to look to her satisfaction wherever she chose to seek it out, and to compensate to himself, perhaps even to find a kind of happiness, by enjoying the charm, candour and largesse of her lovers.

Yet, whatever the ideal arrangement Empson may have projected when his wife first took up with her young lover, Peter Duval Smith was not to be the Stephen Dedalus to Empson's Bloom. This time round, the equation did not add up. Duval Smith was not unrelentingly heterosexual—indeed, he had definite bisexual tendencies, said his first wife Jill Neville (who discovered him kissing another man on at least one occasion)[44]—but he had fallen madly in love with Hetta. It seems almost certain that Hetta, for her part, continued to feel for Empson, then and for the rest of her life, 'a surprising amount of emotional dependence upon her reliable husband'.[45] But there is also little doubt that Duval Smith would have liked her to leave her husband. We do not know if Hetta's pregnancy was planned, but it is quite certain that she and Peter had come to feel passionately for one another and proposed to beget another child in the fullness of time; perhaps even more than one child.

For the time being, with the devastating loss of the child which Hetta had carried to full term, a potential crisis in the family could be set aside while their various lives went on. Jacob continued as a day boy at his prep school; a gentle child who had developed a great interest in animals, he was given a pet nanny goat which he would take for walks on Hampstead Heath. (A neighbour who was in advertising recognized the winning charm of Jacob and his goat, whereupon the pair—with Jacob sporting an uncannily white shirt and hefting the goat over his dazzling shoulder—presently appeared in a magazine advertisement for Oxydol, a washday whitener with an entirely new Oxygen formula generating a far greater whitening power than bleach itself!) Mogador was soon to become a boarder at Aldenham School. Empson returned to Sheffield for the next academic year. Hetta carried on with her affair with Duval Smith, and both of them went on living at the family home. Still, Hetta grieved for many months; in December she wrote: 'I seem to fall into despair all the time now—nothing's fun any more & no one.'[46] But the contradictions in their complex set of relations were not going to go away.

Notwithstanding, Hetta presently found an outlet for her tremendous energies in organizing an exhibition of painted scrolls by the Chinese artist Ch'i Pai-shih, under the auspices of the Britain-China Friendship Association: it toured from London to Oxford and Reading. Empson went to the opening at Oxford on 11th June 1955. By chance, among those who also came to the opening there was none other than Dr Alice Stewart, who had been carrying her candle for Empson since 1931. After yielding to what had seemed to be her fate—having slept with Empson for one night only, and having been rejected by him—she had married Ludovick Stewart in 1933 and had gone on to produce two children. After the war, Alice and Ludovick separated, and they were to finalize a divorce in the early 1950s. Although Alice was initially invited to Oxford as an assistant in clinical medicine, she eventually joined the new Department of Social Medicine.

To celebrate the opening of Hetta's exhibition in Oxford in the autumn of 1955, David Hawkes (the scholar of Chinese whose wedding in Beijing had been attended by both the Empsons and the Richardses) threw a party in his college rooms. Once during the war, but for one day only, Empson and Alice had somehow come across one another after a decade apart—'I remember getting this quick feeling again,' Alice Stewart was to recall, 'that we were pals'—but then nothing had come of it: yet again, they had gone their separate ways, in their different wartime occupations.[47] This time, at Oxford in the autumn of 1955, he not only invited her to dance, but they went on dancing all evening. They started an affair, and were to remain lovers until the last decade of Empson's life. Alice was pleased with him as a sexual partner; and Empson for his part had 'never expected to find such joy in sex' at his age, as he told her once.

Hetta was pleased for William, and relieved for herself, at this happy pass. At last they had achieved a balance: she was not the only one behaving 'badly'.[48] 'An old flame of William's turned up in our lives as a successful doctor,' she wrote, '& I blackmailed her into loaning me her Daimler while she went to Russia so we were very grand for three short weeks with bowing & scraping all round—even from the coppers.'[49] The Empsons cried off a prearranged Christmas visit to William's brother Arthur: the all-purpose goat needed to be milked and fed.[50] Instead, firm steps were taken to draft Alice into the family circle. Empson wrote to her in November: 'Hetta was asking whether you could come to London for Christmas, as we have decided not to go to Yorkshire this time. I hope to see you before then anyhow (and of course then too). Love, William.'[51]

Alice was surprised at the extremely warm welcome she received in Hampstead. 'I became as it were William's possession.'[52] She had no experience of an open marriage; but the symmetry of the Empson household—so inclusive as to be embracing a lover on both hands—made it a little easier for her to come to terms with the arrangement.

Still, it was to be a matter of continual disappointment to her that Empson would never make a serious attempt to leave Hetta for her. His purpose at all times was to preserve his marriage. Alice had bought a cottage in Fawler, a village outside Oxford, and more often than not Empson would choose to spend the occasional weekend away from Sheffield visiting Alice there rather than to take the train all the way to London, where he would have to cope with occasional rows as well as the friendly but none the less discomforting presence of Duval Smith. All the same, Empson took care to look to Hetta's interests before anyone else's.

In April, for reasons that are not clear, Peter Duval Smith left his job at the BBC (the gossip went round that he was sacked for gaining access to personal files and falsifying the details of the producer Laurence Gilliam).[53] Empson, despite feeling some misgiving about the professional dependability of his wife's lover, gave him a noble personal endorsement: he supported him in his bid for a post in the English Department at Hong Kong University, where Edmund Blunden held the Chair. 'I write to recommend my friend...', Empson began his letter of rather bodiless praise. Then, having praised Duval Smith's spirit of enterprise over the record of anyone else who might have taken a more routine academic path, he concluded his recommendation with this grand but unintentional grammatical ambiguity: 'You might, I should think, prefer to have a man with a rather open mind about what had best be done in the English Literature Department.'[54] It is possible that he was drinking even as he composed the reference, or else he may have felt in the back of his mind that something was false, for he signed himself: 'W. Empson. Professor of English Literature, Hongkong University.'

In September, Empson celebrated his fiftieth birthday with a splendid party at Studio House; the great and the good, the raffish and the respectable, all flocked along to cheer him. G. S. Fraser was so tickled by the occasion that he made up a dizzy poem 'For William Empson's Fiftieth Birthday' which was published to the world in the *New Statesman*; the opening lines run thus:

> The enormous room is crowded, the wine is red:
> The extraordinary luminous eyes in the backcast head

Of this institution, epithet, joke, sage
As famous as Pepsodent or Basic English
Confront their own world over our heads with a tinglish
Coiling shock. He is an electric eel
From whom our soft flat flounder thoughts rebound:
He stirs up in his own air his own sea
Of lithe prehensile ambiguity.[55]

Duval Smith got the job at Hong Kong, and he sailed away a few days after Empson's party. But Hetta was once again expecting a child by Duval Smith. Empson may have known of the pregnancy even as he wrote his woolly but warm reference for Peter the paramour: if he did actually know, it was the more magnanimous of him; if not, it must have struck him as both disturbing and ironic.

To Hetta, he did not bother to dissemble his dismay. She knew he did not want her to get pregnant by Duval Smith (though she seems to have hedged when asked about the possibility); but she had pursued only her own desire. For the first time—maybe the only time—in their married years, he addressed her in a letter not as 'My dearest Hetta' but crossly as 'Dear Hetta':

> Oh dear, it seems an awful prospect of bother about this baby again. Do you really want it? I could never make out.[56]

He rubbed in his displeasure by informing her in the next sentence that he would be sticking to his plan of spending the following weekend with Alice rather than altering his arrangements to meet with his wife at home. And yet he still signed his curt, hurt letter with: 'Your very loving husband William.'

A tense jealousy persisted between husband and wife for the remaining weeks of Hetta's pregnancy. On some days, they were distant; on others, fractious or furious. However, despite his annoyance with Hetta for getting pregnant without apparent regard for him or their children, he worked as hard as he possibly could to palliate her, to ease relations. Just a month before Hetta was due to deliver the baby, for example, he had agreed to give a talk in Cambridge on Thursday, 8 November. Kathleen Raine had stepped in with an offer to arrange a small dinner party for him, with selected guests, at Girton College on the Friday. 'Will you be able to come, or too near child-birth? he asked Hetta. 'Of course [Kathleen] would be very pleased if you would, but her note assumes that you couldn't. Do make it if you can.'[57] Hetta was far too shrewd not to be aware that Raine was in fact a jealous foe; she declined to accept an invitation from her so casually passed on by her husband, though it seems she did not make her reasons altogether clear to him. He was obliged to write up the dinner party with all the tact at his command: 'Your letter sounds very sad, and I am distressed you didn't come to Cambridge. I thought you were refusing because of the baby, not because Kathleen hadn't invited you properly; in fact I still think you were, really. She would certainly have been pleased if you had come. We just had a dinner party in Girton the day after my lecture, with C. S. Lewis and Basil Willey, neither of whom I had met before, and the old gentlemen chatted away civilly to each other. I don't know that you would have found it very exciting.'[58] In truth, however, despite this throwaway line, he would have been very pleased and proud for Hetta to have seen and heard in person the esteem in which he was held at Cambridge. C. S. Lewis, who had been appointed to the Chair of Medieval and Renaissance English there only two years earlier, told him (as he confirmed in a subsequent letter) how greatly he admired *The Structure of Complex Words*. Lewis told Empson too that he was working on a not dissimilar volume of his own—though it would 'not be controversial. I shall mention you . . . chiefly to explain that we're doing different things which overlap only at rare points. After that, a few agreements and disagreements as one would expect.'[59] (When *Studies in Words* appeared from Cambridge in 1960, Lewis was seen to have been as good as his word.) A few months later, when as an act of courtesy Empson sent Lewis a typescript of his essay 'Donne the Space Man', which included a couple of sly comments on Lewis's work, Lewis responded with enormous charm and friendliness:

> No one ever thought another man's account of what he said perfectly accurate, but there's nothing in either of your two references to me which I object to . . . I can't say I have so far seen any connection with journies [*sic*] to other planets in any of the passages you deal with. That may be the obtuseness of a sick man. Also, you and I clearly have opposite qualities. You seem to me liable to see in all poetry things that aren't there; and I no doubt seem to you constantly blind to what is. Both are probably right. Perhaps if we were rolled into one we'd make a quite decent critic . . . or wd. the result be deadlock and *aphasia*?'[60]

Empson was heartened by the warmth of Lewis's response. Much later in life, in 1969, he was to remark during an interview: 'I wish I had seen more of C. S. Lewis. You just can't believe people are going to die and then they do. But it would have been rather a tricky operation getting on to terms with him. I rather liked his being reckless and unscholarly, but *The Screwtape Letters* was a quite dreadful book.'[61]

In his letter to Hetta of November 1956 he moved further to sweeten her by inviting her to another event. 'Well then, if you feel able to move still, why not come this Friday to my staff dinner, from 7.0 for 7.30 at the Staff Club? You could get a taxi at the station; *send me a wire* if you are coming and I will meet you. It is just the staff again, but there is the new man a South African, and his wife who is from German South-West Africa and seems very nice ... She would certainly be delighted to meet you ... [D]o come now if you can.'[62] In short, he was doing everything he felt he possibly could to treat his wife with polite solicitude—everything short of showing a rapt interest in the final weeks of a pregnancy which was soon to thrust upon him the unwanted responsibility for a child by another man.

However, so resistant was he to thinking about the reality of the child at all that he filled up the final days of the Michaelmas Term with trivial speaking engagements: there was simply no time in his schedule for him to get home to Hampstead, he told Hetta with patent insincerity. 'Unfortunately I am to talk to the International Club here next Friday and talk in Cambridge again the Friday after, so I can't come home again till the week after that, near the end of term.[63] Down in London, the baby was due in the first week of December. Instead of breaking off relatively unimportant engagements to go down and support Hetta through the final anxious days, he posted her amusing stories:

> The International Club had no foreigners except a German metallurgist; a dumpy well-meaning small group. I had to say that Orwell was a Socialist and not a Christian, and was much distressed at deciding he ought to attack Stalin, and it seemed to come as a painful jolt to them. I felt desperately depressed next day, as I always do after having to tell an audience things they don't like. However I suppose there's no doubt it ought to be done. I got a civil letter of thanks from the lady who runs the thing, saying how they went on discussing it after I had gone—I gather they had just as soon get rid of me first. Well, looking at the bright side, I daresay they won't ask me again at all soon.[64]

In the same letter, written on Tuesday, 27 November, he bethought himself to pile up further obstacles to any more urgent mission to London: 'The end of term is about the 15th December. I ought to be able to come home next week, but come to think of it there is a Senate meeting that Friday, and I cried off the one last month. I am afraid it had better be the weekend after... With much love, and I wish I could come down, William.' Never was anyone so attached to a Senate meeting. The unhappy inference is unavoidable: he just did not want to be anywhere near Hetta when her by-child came into the world. He may have acquiesced in her affair, but for her to get pregnant by the other man went utterly against his wishes. Hetta had made it none of his business.

Hetta's child, named Simon Peter Duval Smith (and nicknamed 'Little Bear' by the delighted parents), was born ten days later, at 6.20 on the Friday evening, in the maternity wing of the Whittington Hospital on Highgate Hill. Empson was not around at the time. Hetta sent a telegram to her lover, and in a letter written just two hours after delivering the child she entertained him with her doting joy: 'I expect I was scared so the nurse was about to give me an injection to relax and he shoved just at that minute and came out with a kind of bubbling triumphant cry. They gave me him all puppy-dog wet... He just opened an eye then made kangaroo fists and went on yelling in a very absorbed kind of way... I just lay giggling and stroking... He's relaxed and... sucks like a diesel engine... He's got long legs, big feet and crumpled ears.'[65]

Duval Smith sent her a telegram ('Darling Maus'), and then a letter—addressing her not as Hetta Empson but by her maiden name, Hetta Crouse—full of excitement, and asking for details and a photograph; he had celebrated his fatherhood by getting drunk on champagne. It seems they had already talked about her going out to join him in Hong Kong after a few months. Now he urged her to come sooner rather than later: they could beget still more babies:

> if you are coming next autumn you may as well come now. Since we are going on together for good the sooner we start the better. If we are going to fit in another Small B, and perhaps a third, no time can be wasted. It is awfully nice here, but I don't enjoy it without my Maus.[66]

Pausing to consider the place of Hetta's husband, he added: 'About William, I don't know a bit, but I don't want him to feel too easily he has been cheated.' We may infer that he did indeed feel they were betraying Empson, who had played his complaisant part, confident that his wife was not going to be taken from him. But now Duval Smith was proposing exactly that: to cheat on their unspoken understanding—he wished after all to whisk Empson's wife away.

Hetta wrote also to her husband, and he responded by return of post:

My dearest Hetta,
Very glad to hear that all went well. I shall come home next Thursday 13th,
and will visit you on the Friday (if they allow that, as they presumably do; no
doubt Helena [Allen] will know). Helena wrote and told me how things
were going, also that she was improving Jacob's Latin.
Much love, and I am glad you are happy
William[67]

It was a kind, polite, restrained note; but if it were to be come across out of
context, no one could ever guess at the momentous occasion that
prompted it.

But Empson was never so much a proper son of the Empsons as when
he wrote to his eldest brother with constrained dignity on 11 December:

My dear Arthur,
    I have a piece of news which you clearly ought to be told, as head of the
family; I am not sure who else to tell it to at present. Hetta has just had a son
by Peter Duval Smith. He has promised to pay for its upbringing, adopt it in
his own name, and take out a life insurance policy in its favour. He is now a
lecturer at Hongkong University but means to come here next summer
vacation.
    It doesn't alter my feelings towards Hetta at all. What should make it
appear more sensible is that I don't see how I could have paid for another
child myself. Naturally I would like to have Peter's legal position on a tidy
footing, but once that is done none of us want to make a secret about it.
    At present it seems liable to look as if he has run away. But Hetta was in
favour of his putting in for this job, and I wrote recommendations for him
while expecting the child, so it really isn't like that. The child which died at
birth last year was his, and I expected at the time that that would finish it, so
I sent you a misleading letter, but she continued to carry out her intention.
It seems as well not to say much till the arrangements are more settled.
    The child is to be called Simon Peter and was born on December 6th.
Hetta in her letter from hospital sounds well and happy.
    Your affectionate brother
    William.[68]

Three aspects of that remarkable letter stand out in particular. The first is
that he makes an enormous effort, as the cuckold, to act as an apologist for
Hetta's lover, the father of her 'bastard' (he would use the blunt word at a
later date). The second is his claim that the situation made no difference to
his feelings for Hetta. To say the least, it was a most unusual response: most
men would regard a relationship as at an end if the wife persisted in both

loving another man and attempting to get herself pregnant by him. The third is the bizarre sentence 'What should make it appear more sensible is that I don't see how I could have paid for another child myself'. The exact meaning is obscure, but it seems to imply that since he felt too poor to afford a third child, it must be 'sensible' for Hetta to have the child by another man: that way, Hetta would get the additional child she wanted and the lover could pay for its upkeep—it seems almost as if he is congratulating himself upon winning both ways. A further implication would seem to be that, in addition to getting another child on the cheap, the household would continue much as before; and the natural father of the child, working abroad, would pay a visit the following summer.

Empson was home in London when Hetta returned from the hospital. Gwenda David, who sat with him as he waited for the taxi, recalls: 'We stood up; she ignored us and went straight upstairs carrying Si proudly.'[69] Hetta must have resolved that since her husband had been so stubborn in turning his back on her illegitimate child, she would in turn snub him with the child.

He went on turning his back. Unwilling or unable to talk through with Hetta the consequences for their marriage of the additional child, the effect on their future life together, or on their two existing sons, he took the classic male recourse: he sublimated all his energies in work. Over the Christmas vacation, even while everyone else in the house fussed over the new baby, he both finished off his long revisionist essay entitled 'Donne the Space Man' and started to plan his next volume of essays.

Two weeks later, back in Sheffield, he wrote to Hetta in a manner that was so preoccupied as to seem, in the circumstances, very strange; what is not said is as striking as what is said. He shows no interest in how Hetta fares; nor does he ask after Mogador and Jacob, let alone the new baby. Yet his concern for his own health may betray a psychosomatic strain arising from the repression of anger, or worry. Otherwise, he talked of the success of Alice Stewart's son in gaining admission to officer training— a son whom Hetta had probably never met, and could not care less about—and he sent news only of the 'donkey-work' in hand and of his 'interesting work' ahead.

Hetta, meanwhile, was making plans to go out to Hong Kong to be with Peter Duval Smith for an unspecified period. Since Empson had told his brother that Duval Smith would be visiting London during his next summer vacation from Hong Kong, it is clear he was not privy to the early stages of this plan. Meifang Blofeld, Chinese wife of the Sinologist and Buddhist John Blofeld,[70] had agreed to stay at Studio House during

Hetta's absence and take charge of young Jacob. Meifang is 'like my sister,' Hetta told her lover, 'and would ward off Alice and any bad kind of intrusion.'

Then Hetta asked Duval Smith: 'Shall I go to Sheffield and talk to William?'[71] She duly notified Empson of her proposed 'trip' to Hong Kong, and suggested she visit Sheffield to discuss things with him. 'I should love to have you come up...,' he responded on 23 January. 'The week-end is when I am free.' Alice was 'due to stop off here on Thursday night, tomorrow week that is [31 January], on her way to a committee meeting in Edinburgh'; so perhaps Hetta could come at the weekend, any day from the 25th? 'I daresay the Sunday trains are a bit worse than the others. I suggest Saturday.'[72] His way of wording himself seems to say, at first glance, that while Alice would be spending a night in Sheffield, maybe Hetta would come just for the day? Still it is clear that the reality of her suckling child had not come home to his mind; he does not even ask after the infant, let alone suggest how the baby might be accommodated for a day or a night—that is no business or concern of his. But then Empson went on in his letter to suggest that she might like to get together with one or other member of his Department staff: maybe for a meal with W. A. Murray? Anyone else would have seen the singular inappropriateness at such a time of going out to dinner with a member of the staff at Sheffield. Hetta's sole purpose in visiting him was to talk through the implications, familial and domestic, of her intention to spend time abroad with her lover. Empson would not put his heart to it, though he added as a postscript: 'Better wire if you would like me to fix up dinner with Murray on Saturday, but probably you don't.' As to the main matter, he aired his mind alongside other thoughts in the middle of his letter:

> Yes, I think you had much better have a trip to Hongkong if Peter will pay. I hope to God you don't mean he has chucked the University when you say he is 'due to finish with it next summer', as that would get me in the dog-house for recommending him; but I suppose you only mean he has a long summer holiday. The Kenyon Review has accepted my whole piece on Donne for publication at one go, so I am very pleased. The tum has got all right again, as it usually does after ten days.

The financial consideration is foremost—'if Peter will pay'—followed by a concern for his own professional reputation in the event that Duval Smith should turn out to be unreliable in his job at Hong Kong. (In his next letter he would say also: 'I trust he will stay two or three years, because otherwise they will feel they were cheated over the passage money.')[73] His professional pride seems to have mattered almost more than his feelings for his wife. Having said just so much, his attention promptly flits to concerns that seem more real or urgent to him: his article on Donne and the state of his 'tum'.

When she did not visit him on the very next weekend, he wrote again:

> My dear Hetta,
>   Still, I want to see you before you go, and I take it if you want to avoid the winter you are going to go fairly soon. . . . I asked the lawyer to send me a letter about Adoption procedure and such like, which he has done, but it doesn't make much sense to me; however, you might as well take it out for Peter to look at it [. . .] I will post it to you if you like, but I had much rather see you before you go anyhow. I could come to London really, but why shouldn't you peep at Sheffield?
>   Love
>   William.[74]

Curiously, he must have been in possession of the lawyer's letter explaining the Adoption Act 1950 for at least three weeks before he even got round to mentioning it to Hetta. Despite his assertion that he could not 'make much sense' of it, the burden of the lawyer's letter is in fact perfectly clear. 'As the child was born in wedlock there is a presumption of law that he is yours and until that presumption is upset you are and will remain liable for his upkeep, and he will be entitled for all purposes to regard you as his legal father. This presumption of legitimacy can be rebutted by evidence, but clearly such an enquiry would be distasteful and would be quite inappropriate in this case.' Duval Smith could apply to adopt the child, but he would have to be resident in England at the time, and 'the infant must have been continuously in [his] care and possession for at least three consecutive months'. A most important consideration that had to be weighed was that, if such an Adoption Order was approved, it would mean that both Empson and Hetta herself 'would cease to have any claim over the child or any right to his custody.' Above all, whether or not an adoption was to be agreed, it was essential that Duval Smith should be bound 'by deed . . . to provide for the maintenance of the child at a stated minimum rate until the child attains the age of 18 or finishes his full time education'.[75] There was no obscurity about the issue at all. The single problem that bore down on Empson was the question of how on earth Duval Smith might fulfil the conditions required before an Adoption Order could be put in hand; until such time, his headache was that the child was all his, to have and to support. There is no question, really, but that Empson understood what the solicitor had written; he just found it imponderably difficult to reconcile such recommendations with the untidy facts in this case.

Hetta visited Sheffield in the first week of February, and later she wondered why she had bothered to go at all. Her husband seemed to be incapable of comprehending the idea that she was going off to live with her lover, and he was still oblivious to the being of the baby. He could register Hetta's desire to go East only as a kind of tourist adventure. 'William was enthusiastic for me to go & look at things,' she told Peter, '—Nara, Angkor Wat & so on & I said maybe I couldn't go to all of them on account of SP [Simon Peter] & he said "You mean you're taking the baby with you! Oh no I shouldn't do that, you won't have any fun at all." As you say he's never really thought about you-and-me. Anyway he said I should wait till SP is a year old & I said I did not want to and we parted amiably as far as that goes & no bad feelings.'[76] The only way Empson could cope with the idea of her leaving him for a year or so was by way of offering advice on the best sights to see on her travels.

A couple of weeks later, after he had mulled over the matter, he wrote to her again; but his remarks seemed either irrelevant or to miss the point. His thoughts were so far removed from the reactions that might normally be expected of a man whose wife is leaving him and their legitimate children to go off with her lover and her by-blow, that he seemed to be detached from true emotions.

My dearest Hetta,
    Well, you obviously want to go very much, and I hope you have a nice time. I hoped you would decide not to, but I can't really see what reasonable objections there are. I very much hope you *will* come back in a year and a bit, and so of course will the boys. I'm rather afraid you may have an idea of softening the blow, whereas you *don't* really mean to come back. If it's like that I wish you would say so, because after all I only bought that house for you, and maybe I would do better to sell it if you positively don't want it. However I only say this in case. If you come back next year it isn't a very long time after all. And you may well find interesting things to do and see.
    I don't think I can go on paying you an allowance while you're with Peter; I go by imagining what other people would think too much perhaps, but surely that would be eccentric...And let me know when you are leaving; I must mind and come to London to see you before you go.[77]

Amidst all the reserve of feeling, the cool dignity, of that letter, the slight hint of petulance in the reference to his having bought the house 'only...

for you' reassures one that his feelings were not totally dissociated in the matter. But how is it possible he could find no 'reasonable objections' to her desertion of her marital family, most especially of her elder children Mogador and Jacob? Could he not be bothered to spell out all the excellent reasons? Or did he feel so guilty towards her—perhaps because of the sexual failure, and the feeling that she was justified in seeking out love with another man—that he felt he had forfeited his right to object to her going? Or was he simply too modest to make demands? In the event, all he would find to write to her was a phrase referring to Peter which in general usage strikes a note of remarkable finality, or else a quasi-paternal exhortation to a daughter eloping with a black sheep:

All my love, and make Peter turn out well,
Your loving husband,
William

It was as if he felt the game was up, the years of their life together over at last. Certainly his hopes for a happy Triangle had been dashed by this outcome. One stanza of 'The Wife is Praised' seems to have anticipated this eventuality:

> It is chiefly to know you are willing
>> And not what I get on the side
> That I find at once quieting and thrilling,
>> A peace, an insurance, a pride.
> And indeed when they care for you only
>> And think me a price they must pay
> That is proof I should really be lonely
>> With Hetta away.

Hetta's response was just as absolute, brooking no ambiguity or doubt:

My dearest Pa
[. . .] I can't imagine why you should think I am planning to bolt. I love you dearly and I have made elaborate arrangements to safeguard Mogador and Jacob against loss of feelings of security because I love them dearly. But I think I should go now even if it all ends in tears and I will come back in a year.[78]

Loving two men—though quite obviously she loved each in a different way—she was not ready to abnegate her need for the expression of love in sex. 'I love you & kiss your pp,' she informed Duval Smith in a letter of 20 February. Yet she was assuredly far from being without a bad conscience in deciding to go East. 'Everyone predicts dire things if I leave,' she fretted; 'I get uneasy.'[79]

She had recently taken to renting a cottage at Hare's Creek, on the River Orwell in Suffolk, for occasional weekends away with Duval Smith; and Empson placed enough trust in her undertaking that she would return in a year or so to agree to continue to meet the rent while she was away. The one thing that may very well have left him with a continuing qualm, a slight but lingering mistrust of Hetta's sincere intentions, was a letter he received from Peter Duval Smith ('I ought to have written to you before about this business of Hetta coming here'), who said he wanted to reassure Empson about what their 'movements' would be, not for the next year— the term that Hetta had put upon her trip—but 'for the next couple of years'. 'I guarantee at least,' wrote Duval Smith with a masterful mien, 'to send Hetta to England for the summer of 1958 (and I expect to come myself) so the boys will be able to have a proper family holiday then. The idea of all this flying around is of course that there will not be too much sad separation for the kids, and certainly no feelings of betrayal or anything disgusting like that.'[80] His rather arrogant and presumptuous asseverations would scarcely have been reassuring to Empson or to the kids. He hoped in addition, he suggested, that Empson might be willing to pay for Jacob to fly out in the summer to visit them in Japan (he was going to 'take' Hetta and their baby there for two months)—though 'I judged that Mogador could manage this summer holiday without his Ma, you will hardly want to pay two big fares even if you decide to do one. My present plan—to look at the next stage—is to stay here until the summer of 1959, and then return to England. I would feel I had played fair with the University and my sponsors by staying three years, on the other hand my contract is strictly only until September 1958, but of course almost certain to be renewed, and I may possibly leave then if I get too broke... Love from Peter.' His egotistical words served to place Empson in a totally passive posture: having to wait upon the wishes or the whims of Peter Duval Smith.

Hetta flew to Hong Kong via Bangkok on 23 March. Duval Smith met up with her in Bangkok, where they passed a few days—'ending each day in the Eastern style in the relaxed atmosphere of an opium den'.[81] Her ticket to fly had been bought by Empson on a 'hire-purchase scheme', and she was due to repay him by monthly instalments wired from Hong Kong. Nobly too, he wrote on the same day to smooth her path there. He hoped to reassure Edmund Blunden that there was no suggestion of antagonism or turpitude attaching to the irregular relations between Hetta and Peter Duval Smith; he himself was complaisant about Hetta bounding off to the arms of her lover.

My dear Blunden,

My wife Hetta is just setting out for Hongkong to stay with Peter Duval Smith, carrying his baby; she expects to come home to me and her elder children next year. She hopes to fit in some further travel with Hongkong as a base.

I thought I had better write and explain to you that there is no quarrel about this from my side, and that we all three expect the arrangement to work out sensibly.

Yours very sincerely
William Empson.[82]

What is interesting in a generous but otherwise flat and uncircumstantial letter (which he kindly showed to Hetta just before accompanying her to the airport) is his use of the phrase 'carrying his baby', which might normally be taken to refer to a condition of pregnancy rather than to a baby already born; and his trust that things would work out 'sensibly' is of course more of a velleity than a plan. Even Hetta had presently to admit, with unconscious wit (in a letter to an ex-lover written from Hong Kong in April): 'My position is rather ambiguous'.[83]

Empson's real plan was not to brood but to bury himself in work. The following day, he wrote to his publisher that he hoped to finish his new book, which was to include the essays on Joyce and Donne, by the autumn. 'I must try to clear the decks to do rapid typing in this holiday and the next, which has not been my habit. My wife has just flown off to Honkong meaning to return late next year.'[84] All the same, there is no question but that (as Annemarie Heywood feelingly noted) he endured a dark night of the soul throughout Hetta's absence, and coped in part by drinking far too much. 'There was no way in which he could tolerate being comforted, let alone "helped" when he was falling drunk,' she recalls. 'There was for him a constant low sky of melancholy or depression.'[85]

Just as he had feared, and almost as soon as Hetta reached Hong Kong, he received from Blunden a grumbling letter about Duval Smith. He relayed the gist to Hetta with some patronizing or paternalistic promptings of his own: 'So you mind and make him do it, my dear, and then things ought to be all right.'[86] She riposted to Empson's advice: 'Blunden appears to be nearly off his head with anxiety about everything. Peter is doing his work all right I'm sure.'[87] A month later she wrote again: 'We dined with Blunden last night—he was very affable in his twittering way.'[88] Hetta reported in addition: 'The baby grows & is good. Peter is very taken with him.'[89] But Empson never—in any of the many letters he was to send her—asked after Hetta's child by Peter; and in two letters only did he even spare greetings for Peter himself: 'My best wishes to Peter too' (24 November 1957); 'give my regards to Peter' (16 February 1958).

In June, Hetta and Duval Smith took ship for Japan, where they were entertained in Wakayama by Hetta's old flame Walter Brown, and by David Kidd. Empson took an interest in her letters only with regard to her travel news. She ought to do the things that he had done, and see the sights that he had seen, some twenty-five years earlier, when he had delighted in scenery and sites: she should re-enact his exotic journeys and the excitement of his discoveries.

Empson, having been obsessed with Buddha images in the 1930s, had naturally given her advance instructions about what to see; he was mindful too that she was herself a good sculptor, though she had produced no work since getting back to England. She was delighted to report a visit to Nara: 'at last I saw your gorgeous Maitreya & the large standing Kannon. The Kannon came as a great shock. It must be the most beautiful piece of sculpture in the world. The seated Maitreya is all that I expected only far warmer and more loving than the picture whereas the Kannon is sheer rigid beauty.'[90] He sent further firm directives: 'Look, I am glad you liked the statues but I don't gather that you have seen the Yumedono Kwannon, which is the one I was fussing about before. Do insist on that.'[91]

Returning to Hong Kong for the autumn term, Hetta and Duval Smith moved into a new and grander residence called Ascension House, at Tao Fong Shan in Shatin, with a fine view over the hills of the New Territories. When they could think of nothing better to do (as Duval Smith was later to tell his first wife, Jill Neville), he and Hetta would go and look at the local abattoir; or else they would make love in front of a picture window at their house, in flagrant view of the Chinese sitting on a hillside across the way.[92] Still Empson urged her on to tackle further journeys, especially to get over to Peking for Christmas or the New Year. 'In any case don't grizzle and invent problems on your mountain,' he admonished her like a brisk parent.[93] In the New Year of 1958 she did undertake a three-day journey by train to revisit Peking, though her account of the week-long visit both fascinated and troubled Empson.

But he was thrilled for her when she at last gained a commission to execute a bronze of a wealthy businessman in Hong Kong: standing ten feet tall, the statue was to be better than life-size. 'I am so very glad to hear your good news; I expect now that you have started doing sculpture again you will go on. Nothing exasperates a skilled person more than not using the skill, as I have often felt myself; and I always felt No Wonder you were cross living in the Studio and never doing any sculpture there. Also I expect it is a good market to be working for, because they won't nag at you and will be willing to realise they are lucky to have you for it.'[94] As if he were egging on a reluctant student, his words of patient encouragement may sound a trifle patronizing. But in truth he was honestly proud of her capability as an artist.

During Hetta's absence, his own skills as a literary critic were not so wholly dedicated to the speedily productive use he had proposed to Ian Parsons. Things went fairly smoothly for him all the while he was at Sheffield; but during the vacations, at Easter and in the summer, the grass widower had to give very much more of his time to his sons—despite the 'mothering' they received from the kind and willing Meifang Blofeld: 'the way I look at my life now,' he was to write, 'it is tiresomely full of entertaining incidents which I am yearning to thrust away so as to get back to the typewriter.' However, he also made a joke of it, as usual: 'As I know I fall into despair drink or actual sleep if left alone with the typewriter this seems the right arrangement for me; the old man could not be put under more suitable conditions, really.'[95]

His professional engagements included an appearance as an 'expert' at a seminar on 'A comparison between the British and Chinese approach to poetry'. Held under the joint auspices of PEN and the Arts and Sciences Committee of The Britain–China Friendship Association, the meeting was chaired by G. S. Fraser, who was just as much of an amateur of the subject as Empson himself. The one genuine expert of the evening was Arthur Waley, translator both of Chinese literature and of classical Japanese literature, who nevertheless disconcerted everyone by proceeding to read out 'three pages of joking refusal to talk only': he was not used to making speeches, he mumbled, and would say little.[96] Empson, who was left to make the best of his own anecdotal discourse, was further put out by the nature of the venue—two narrow interconnecting rooms—and the lack of a microphone, so that even his 'professional bellow' could scarcely be heard.

In another forum, he proposed to disrupt the placidity of the academic profession with his first 'rude' but sincere sally against the Christian God as portrayed in Milton's *Paradise Lost*. The gist of his argument, as he was to repeat it on many occasions—eventually in the devastatingly fierce and pellucid polemic of *Milton's God* (1961)—was that Milton's epic was para-doxically wonderful because it exposed the wickedness of the Christian godhead. His initial denunciation of that Deity took place at what he called a 'Professors Only Milton Only' weekend conference, as he was to tell John Crowe Ransom:

[Professor E. M. W.] Tillyard was to have been Raphael to my Satan; but he was taken very ill, and only pronounced out of danger during the conference. I felt shy about this, especially without Tillyard, and had to consider how to put my essay without hurting their feelings . . . It is always alarming to look back at the rough paper and consider what you left out, but I don't think now that there's more I positively ought to put in.[97]

That was early in May. Since he claimed that the business of having to 'mess about' being a professor prevented him from making rapid progress with his writing, it is surprising to realize just how much he did manage to get written during the vacations—considering that once Hetta had sailed away he had to fulfil his duties as a parent to an extent which he had never before been obliged to do. Indeed, the one, ironical bonus of Hetta's absence was that he got to know his sons, and to communicate with them, better than ever before. He was to take a close interest in their schooling; and he became intimately involved in organizing their lives and in planning their holidays.

Over Easter, he and Meifang Blofeld, after overcoming some initial difficulties of temperament and approach, worked out a modus vivendi that revolved around the needs of the children. The one bugbear was that his sister Molly, who had been on an extended trip through South America, arrived at Studio House for a visit lasting several days; as Empson feared, she could not stop herself behaving somewhat tactlessly, being highhanded with Meifang. But even after he had warned Molly that Meifang refused to be regarded as a servant and would take no wages for all her hard work, Empson's sister still behaved badly, even removing the family silver that Arthur had given William and Hetta as a wedding present, with the clear implication that Meifang might steal it. When Molly at last left the house Empson unconvincingly reassured Hetta, 'Meifang now feels the visit of Molly was funny and all right.'

Empson put his mind to the possibility that it might be good for Jacob to become a weekly boarder at his school, so that he should not be too solitary during term-time, but he decided against it—for kindly reasons as much as to save the expenses of the boarding. 'He doesn't strike me as moping at all, and he is doing much better at his lessons . . . He will have plenty of boarding from next year. For instance, he likes to go to the Natural History Museum and draw the Diplodocus, which it seems they provide paper and pencil for; I should think it is rather good, as well as nice, for him to be able to follow his own bent so much at that age. Max says he seems to have got over missing you, which no doubt he would do at first.'[98] Empson related also, with evident affection for his boy: 'He came for a walk with me and found a pair of buffalo horns in a wood which he carried home with great effort, and a flow of description of the safari-lie he can now tell.' He was equally observant and thoughtful with respect to Mogador: 'Mog asked me to take him round the British Museum again today (almost the only day with his father, and he may have thought it kind to the old man as I obviously hate any other form of entertainment); he is stubbornly inquiring and sensible though, and I always feel him worth talking to, as indeed I do Piggly, but Mog speaks up more.'[99]

In the summer, the boys spent ten days with the MacNeices holidaying on the Isle of Wight. Then the family including Empson spent a few days in Yorkshire, where Arthur took a kindly interest in his elder nephew Mogador and taught him how to shoot game: the teenager bagged a hare and a pigeon. Jacob was considered too young for a gun, but his father considerately noted that he 'doesn't seem to mind not being encouraged to shoot'. Mogador got on well with Arthur, and even began to think of taking up farming as a career. Arthur also came up trumps in terms of money: he made a deed of covenant in favour of Jacob, yielding £45 a year, and another arrangement for Mogador. It was nice too that Empson's kinsman, Air Marshal Sir Richard Atcherley, the survivor of the aviator twins, also decided at this time to take an interest in his young cousins; he flew the boys from London to Yorkshire. Another day, he even flew Jacob back to school—and the child 'had the keen pleasure of not being believed when he said so (he seemed to feel that was the best part).'[100]

Empson enjoyed himself so lavishly at one grand family lunch-party at Yokefleet that he fell over and broke his arm as he moved to rise from the table. 'I was so anxious to appear sober that I went on chatting politely.'[101] After his arm had been put in plaster, he would not let it hinder the next stage of their grand tour: they went on to spend a further ten days in Scotland with his colleague W. A. Murray, who had a share in a cooperative farm by Loch Fionn. The boys liked the country pursuits. 'The only thing [the broken arm] really kept me from doing in Scotland was rock-climbing,' boasted Empson to his brother.[102] By the time the children went back to school, he could claim with much, albeit muted, pride: 'They seem in good order and cheerful.' He had done wonderfully well as a parent over the holidays. He had also taken care to keep a concerned eye out for Meifang, the children's loyal young guardian (who was also catering very well for Empson himself): 'Meifang and Jacob have gone to see the new Chaplin film; she seems all right but is not really happy I think;

however she will go on with her schooling for a bit. She gave the I. A. Richards's . . . a very fine dinner . . .'[103]

For all the liberalism of his views on sexual morality, and the openness of his marriage, Empson was a surprisingly conventional parent when it came to worrying about his children. The perils of parenthood were not lost on him. If he worried about the expenses of their schooling, he worried still more about the possibility of waste if they failed to do well. He was never to feel so progressive as to imagine there could be any future for his offspring other than to get what he called 'the proper start in life': to make the necessary transit through university and into a profession, thereby putting themselves on a secure financial footing. He believed that for them to gain self-dependence in every sense was probably the major aim of their education, and anyway he did not want to have to shell out for ever to meet their needs.

'The children both have bad reports as usual,' he was obliged to tell Hetta ('Mrs Duval Smith' as he addressed her on the envelope) in January,

in the sense that they could do better if they tried, but Jacob's school is pretty sure he can pass Common Entrance, which he is to try this year, either earlier or later. The trouble about Mog, as his report pointed out, is that he has to take GCE, without passing which he can't go to a university, in a year and a half. He had been saying he really found his lessons too boring and had other interests (he has been reading about war in a stubborn way) but if he has so little time he really must start; I hadn't realised it was so quick. It does seem a bit absurd spending so much on his education if he can't be bothered to pass into college, and I would not know what to do with him next . . . Otherwise they are both doing nicely and continue to be social successes; Mog has begun giving parties.[104]

Indeed, thanks to the forebearance of Meifang (who must have found Empson, his sister's visit, and his parties far more trying than the two boys she was charged to look after), and the interest taken in the boys by family friends, the school year passed for the most part uneventfully, punctuated by pleasant breaks. But at Easter, while Jacob said he was willing to tag along with his father and Alice Stewart for a week or so of mountain-climbing in north Wales, Mogador, aged 14, expressed a desire not only to go off for the Easter vacation with a schoolfriend—it would be the first holiday he had taken away from one or other of his parents—but to tramp around France. Empson, who had more than enough on his plate at the time with staffing difficulties in the English Department, reacted like any anxious, over-responsible parent: he got into a terrible pompous fuss.

I am rather uneasy [he wrote to Alice Stewart] when I think of Mog confidently assuming he can 'hitch-hike' with his friend in France. Even if they get into this motor-car, what will they do when they eventually get off it? Surely, going to France with no idea in your head except waving at motor-cars does not give even a hope of reasonable life. Isn't there an elaborate scheme nowadays which he can't easily avoid joining?

Don't be alarmed, I have written the same kind of thing to him, and I expect he will answer sensibly. But the friend is a very silly boy, who will accept anything Mogador tells him, and I rather doubt whether it isn't cruel to let them expose themselves to the French like that.[105]

The tone and phraseology—'waving at motor-cars', 'expose themselves to the French'—have unmistakable comic echoes of the plays of Oscar Wilde or Noel Coward (perhaps his mother was coming out in him), but he did not see it that way: he was being indignantly protective towards his wilful elder son. Still, everything went well once Mogador joined the Youth Hostel Association (the 'elaborate scheme'); and by late April, when Mogador came home from France in happy good order, having taken full responsibility for himself, the father glowed with pride and relief to know that his elder son had passed a marker on the road to adulthood. 'What a comfort it is to have the child want to do something itself,' he told the wife, 'and come back successful and not resentful against anybody. They seem to be growing up all right so far.'[106]

He was proud too, when Jacob moved on to Aldenham in the autumn, to feel that Mogador was keeping a kindly eye out for his brother.[107] (Jacob was to arrive at the school in style, carrying the presents his mother had brought him upon her return from Hong Kong—400 mild cigarettes and an air gun.)

While Hetta was away, Alice Stewart began quite naturally to assume a more prominent place in Empson's life, and in the life of the Empson children. If the younger Meifang was the authorized childminder, Alice quite soon took up the role of 'stepparent'. (Biddy Crozier remembered with amusement that Meifang was ordered by Hetta to kill Alice if she gave excessively generous presents to the boys.)[108] It was to Alice that Empson turned in the first instance if he needed to let off steam, or to seek advice in general or in particular about the well-being of the children—after all, she was a divorcée, and a single parent, and her two children were some years older than the Empsons'. Not only did they go on holiday together, she would also spend increasing amounts of time at Studio House. He also took a genuinely supportive interest in her research in epidemiology; on one occasion he wrote for her (in 1971) a letter to *The Times* suggesting that research might be done on a possible connection between the spraying of tobacco with pesticides and an increase in the risk of chronic bronchitis and lung cancer. Is it not possible, she suggested through his words, that trace compounds of pesticide origin might add to the number of carcinogenic substances in tobacco smoke or else introduce a poisonous element into the situation by altering the way in which the tobacco burns?[109]

'I think there was a sigh of relief all round when Hetta went off,' Alice Stewart reflected in interview, 'because life had been getting too hectic.' Kathleen Raine hinted at a happier future by saying to her, 'Thank goodness for you. Hetta was very good for William when he was younger, but he really needs a quieter life now.'[110] Empson too felt she was enjoying being part of the family ('and I was, very much so'). So one day, while they were sitting at the kitchen table in Hampstead, he asked her: 'Would you like to marry me?' ('You can't imagine William making a great speech, can you?' she laughed with me, looking back. 'He didn't ever make a fuss, you know.') She felt that he wanted above all to please her by making the offer, not just to tidy things up for himself. The subject was put aside in a few moments. 'I didn't want to be a burden to him.'[111]

In any case, she reflected too: 'I remember, later on, he was really cut up because he didn't think that Mog had got the right share of the Yokefleet estate. I remember thinking: Yes, when it comes down to brass tacks, you do mind about the family.'

It was possibly at about the same time as he made his unpersuasive offer of marriage to Alice Stewart that he received a letter (now lost) from Hetta, who had come to feel that she should make him an offer of divorce: either so that he could retrieve his dignity by ceasing to be a complaisant cuckold, or else for the sake of her lover, who was reluctant to give her back to her husband. Whereas Alice really did love him, and would have married him like a shot if he had freed himself from Hetta, Empson saw Alice as a bosom friend, lover and confidante, but he resolved that his marriage to Hetta should be preserved as invincible if not sacrosanct. Whatever Alice might wish to the contrary, she would just have to swallow it:

> A nice letter from Hetta . . . but rather a bothering one as she offers to let me divorce her on grounds of desertion. This is no doubt a good time to do it if it is wanted, but I don't see who wants it, unless Peter does. On the other hand I had Molly and Arthur lunching at the [University Staff] Club here, and Arthur remarked in the lavatory that he had decided not to leave me any money but to divide my share equally among my three children. I have

written to him since reflecting on what he can have meant (what I have just said is merely what I *think* he meant) saying that neither Hetta nor Peter expect their child to get it, and I had insisted on informing him about the parentage exactly so that he wouldn't leave their child money. He hasn't answered, and I take it he means to punish me by leaving the money like that unless I divorce her. I think I had better refuse to tell her about it.[112]

It had become for him a point of jealous principle that Hetta's child by Peter Duval Smith should not benefit from Empson moneys. It was a matter of family honour, of which he had a plentiful supply, as well as a slight touch of vindictiveness. Above all, he had developed a distrust of Duval Smith's ability or willingness in the longer term to take full financial responsibility for his own child: for one thing, the young man, though undoubtedly talented in a high degree, showed little sign of being inclined to hold down a durable job.

Just so, his letter responding to Hetta's offer of divorce was characteristically framed in terms of the financial considerations involved. In it, since he chooses not to speak of his personal feelings, he does not tell Hetta he loves her; nor does he tell her that he loves Alice Stewart—though he does imply or take for granted an understanding that Alice has become a fast part of his life. Whether it is pride that makes him withhold any declaration of his feelings, or a genuine equivocation—knowing that he now loves two ways, and will hold to both ways if he can manage it—he sticks resolutely to practicalities.

The letter also refers to 'lying' and 'pretence' which he would find objectionable, alluding to the fact that he was a consenting cuckold: he had no desire to deny the case. He added a postscript: 'Of course, it would be important to start trying for a divorce before you come back to England, and not to come to Studio House when you arrive.[113] This was both tactical and true: if Hetta took steps to secure a divorce, she would need to appreciate that she would be homeless on her return to England. It would undo her petition to be found to be living with her husband. Curiously, but perhaps strategically, the one 'great advantage' for which he makes no allowance was the possibility that Hetta might love Duval Smith so deeply that she might actually wish to marry him; he allows only that Peter might be 'keen' on Hetta being divorced from him—so as to marry her. In the main, he prefers to stick to the recalcitrant facts, financial and legal.

Hetta's answer to his letter has been lost, but he sent to Alice (who was no doubt wounded by it) a very brief précis of her position: 'My dear

Alice . . . Hetta writes that she didn't want a divorce at all (only to clear the ground in a generous minded way as I hoped) and is expected back without Peter about July 1st. Love, William.'[114] Husband and wife had like minds in the matter. To Hetta herself he wrote back, six days before notifying Alice of her decision, that he was 'very relieved to get your letter, because I thought you hadn't answered because you were making up your mind to want a divorce.'[115]

Hetta was to leave Hong Kong at the end of May, making a leisurely journey by sea via Port Said and Marseilles. She hoped for a restful passage, but in the event it was rough and she was sick. Simon Peter, aged one-and-a-half, came with her; his father did not—Peter Duval Smith, for reasons that were not explained, wanted to go to Macao and write a book there over the summer, then to travel in Siam, Burma, and Nepal; and he would finally go back to England, at the end of his contract in Hong Kong, late in the year.[116]

Arriving in Marseilles at the end of June, Hetta received a brief typed letter from her husband in which, at long last, he devoted a single sentence to speaking of his feelings for her, and his keenness to see her: 'I love you and feel proud of you and am glad you are coming back.'[117] (At home, he had seemed eager to spread the news that he and Hetta would again make up a regular couple. 'I expect to be back at Studio House on the Friday, and Hetta should arrive back from Hongkong during the week-end,' he notified the Richardses. 'Looking forward to seeing you both.')[118] Furthermore, as he told Hetta, it would be especially 'convenient' to have her back because their landlords were (as always) raising difficulties about the kinds of improvements they had made to Studio House. To divide the building into separate flats would have been all right, the lessors maintained, but not the piecemeal improvements and the letting of rooms or flatlets that the Empsons had been undertaking—Empson was to pay out over the next few years for the installation of three bathrooms and three lavatories.

Hetta had kept her promise that she would return to her husband and her older children after a year (Empson had guessed it would be 'a year and a bit'). She had in fact been away for fifteen months. There is no suggestion that she and Peter had fallen out. Equally, she had not given Peter any undertaking that she would leave her husband. It is not even possible to infer any cooling-off in their relations. Duval Smith complained in a letter early in July that she had not written to him since her ship reached Djibouti, 'a fortnight ago', but there seems to be nothing suspicious about such a lapse: she must have been exceptionally busy during her first days back in London.

But what is certain is that Duval Smith still desired her exclusively for himself. He wanted her to give up on Empson and to live with him, perhaps at the cottage in Suffolk; and he had come to resent Empson for continually nagging him about taking out insurance and for pushing him to meet his financial obligations to the child. Peter's first letter on her return—addressed as usual to 'Hetta Crouse', since he could not bear her married name—says it all:

> What's it like in the menagerie? ... I hope the kids don't have any stored-up resentments, and that they like the Pieman (give him a bite for me), but I suppose they're too old now to be much help to him, I mean they would be bored. I'll fix a bank draft tomorrow for you to get £8 a month at the Midland Bank, sent from here by airmail on the 1st of each month, by cable this month. If William starts any of his nonsense tell him from me that I will eventually insure my life in the child's favour, but he is not to regard that as any of his business, and particularly that I won't enter into any kind of legal arrangement with him, even if you don't come to live with me, which is what I would like, severing yourself entirely from him. I don't like Happy Families: there'll be a big gate on that road at Hare's Creek if I live there. Bearbie, I love you, that's why I'm writing briskly. I can't bear to think of all that drunken yelling going on: I can quite see why people stopped coming to dinner. (Of course, it was all of us.) If William tries to ride you, just walk out and go to Hare's Creek and make a nest for the Bears, sweet Maus. I think we'll have to live together (at least I feel even worse without you), so we'll have to do something about our tempers and our manners. Enough.[119]

Apparently, little had changed during Hetta's absence, for all that she had spent months away. She made it clear to Empson that her relationship with Duval Smith would carry on when her lover came back to England. The signal difference is that she had got over her great excursion and would never again make a move to go off and live with Duval Smith. Empson's absences from Hampstead during the academic terms at Sheffield meant that they were already used to long weeks of separation; apart from those periods, husband and wife had resolved to continue living together. Still, Hetta would also keep up with her lover: she believed she could balance both of her men. Whether Duval Smith could stand being the lover rather than the husband remained to be seen; Empson, for his part, had made his choice to live with it (though of course he too was keeping a companion and lover of first resort).

Late in the autumn, Arthur Empson asked after his brother's affairs. The illegitimate child, and Hetta's long absence abroad with her lover, had bothered him on behalf of his youngest brother. It had bothered him even that his brother had glibly professed not to be very bothered by the situation. Arthur got his answer exactly five months after Hetta's return to the country, but whether he comprehended what his brother tried to convey to him must be seriously in doubt. To Arthur, a lifelong bachelor, Empson's angle on the moral world must have seemed muddled and incoherent, if not utterly zany.

> My dear Arthur, . . .
> the broad fact is that I was not withdrawing from telling you about my family affairs, only waiting till I had something to report about them. As to divorce, Hetta wrote from Hongkong and offered an undefended divorce, because it crossed her mind as a high-minded thing to do only, I am sure; but we high-minded characters are accustomed to feel that we are safer if we have made the alternative offer quite firmly. I wrote back earnestly offering to arrange a divorce if she expected to earn so much money as a sculptor that it would save money on our joint tax, and explaining that I could not possibly marry the woman I now love, divorced or not, because we both earn salaries which would be cut in half if we married. As lovers nobody objects to our appearing together, but if we married all informed persons would feel that the craving had become a bit sordid. Hetta really is, as I said to Molly some while ago, as strong as a horse and as brave as a lion, and I only hope she can manage to carry off her bet or fantastic choice and make something of Peter.
>   Oddly enough, I am almost as much against divorce as a Catholic, because I want to behave like an eighteenth century landlord. I wish I had had a third child, but as I am going I couldn't have afforded that. As long as Peter can afford it, I have nothing to grumble about; but that, as we will soon find out, may become a difficulty. I could not arrange to leave Hetta alone with a difficulty by telling lies to satisfy a disgusting law.[120]

What is omitted from the letter is some obvious kinds of argument that would have satisfied the brother: that Empson wanted to keep the marriage together for the sake of the children, or that he believed in the social imperatives of marriage even if, in his own case, he had abnegated sex with his wife. Or even that, however badly his wife behaved, he loved her and could not bear to lose her. Yet it is a feature of Empson as letter-writer that he would always seek to tell the truth as he saw it, even if his kind of truth might seem to the addressee as bizarre as could well be imagined. He was capable of equivocation, and of leaving out important facts or factors, but he would seek to avoid telling an outright lie. But perhaps the nearest he comes to being disingenuous here is when he writes 'I only hope she can manage to carry off her bet or fantastic choice and make something of

Peter', which seems to suggest that he is disassociating himself from Hetta's unconscionably weird determination to keep her lover going in tandem with her officially sanctioned marriage: probably he found himself phrasing the matter in such a way because he had tried too hard to put himself in Arthur's place. Modern women are beyond me, and a woman like Hetta is so headstrong that she just has to be allowed to follow her bent. A bold and daring gal, Arthur; we must see what she makes of this rum deal. In fact, of course, he had connived at Hetta's decision to go with her lover, and to go off with him, when he exhorted her in February 1957—in a phrase that is clearly echoed in this letter to Arthur—'make Peter turn out well'.

So too, the final paragraph precisely reiterates the sentiment he had expressed to Arthur exactly two years earlier (in the letter he composed a few days after the birth of Simon Peter). The one major difference from the earlier explanation is the positive declaration here: 'I wish I had had a third child.' The evident suggestion is once again that, but for his want of financial resources, the child might have been his legitimate offspring; as it was, Duval Smith could pick up the bill. For the sake of his brother, therefore, Empson was prepared to be disingenuous to that extent: it was easier to put the thing in terms of money, not of emotions or sexual difficulties. The final sentence, 'I could not arrange to leave Hetta alone with a difficulty by telling lies to satisfy a disgusting law' speaks to the code of honour that Arthur Empson would instantly understand and respect. Since the blackguard Duval Smith might fall down in his duty to support his love child, it was a noble thing for Empson to stand by his wife—in case he was required to supply the financial support she needed for the youngster: 'I will just have to pay for both.'

It seems most remarkable that he should address himself to precisely the same concerns—income and taxation—in the letter of March 1958 to his wife as in this of December to his brother. Indeed, what often goes unsaid in his letters is his positive desire to stay with Hetta, and his concomitant total willingness to acquiesce in her affairs so long as she will continue to be his wife. The money worries function almost as a displacement or disguise for this absolute wish: the bonds of fundamental affection that tied him to Hetta were ineradicable. Everything he says is predicated on his love for her, his desire to keep her his.

Everything changed within a year: turn and turn about. Hetta made it known to Duval Smith that she would not leave William, and Duval Smith, who took it hard, eventually opted to move out of Studio House into some gentlemen's chambers in St James's—but not before another young lodger had introduced another young woman into their lives. Lewis Wolpert, a South African, was to become a distinguished geneticist and one of the country's leading popularizers of science and a regular TV pundit; he was then in his late twenties and was living in a room at Studio House while researching for his Ph.D. at King's College, London. One day Wolpert brought back to Studio House a young, tall and very striking Australian named Jill Neville, whom he had once or twice taken out for a drink (they were not a couple at the time: he was to become Neville's third husband only in 1993). By the age of 20, she had saved enough to flee Australia and to risk her all on a passage to London, where she set up house, and quite soon afterwards a literary salon, on a houseboat in Chelsea. Hazel-eyed, with long auburn hair and a generous mobile mouth, Jill was friendly, funny, and avid for life; her zest and curiosity about everything, and her warm disposition, impressed everyone who met her.

But neither Hetta nor Duval Smith was in a fit condition to appreciate the woman whom Wolpert brought along to be introduced. (By coincidence, Jill was then living in a flat just across the road from Studio House.) Lying down in front of a fireplace, they were 'smashed out of their minds,' as Jill was to recall. Hetta, though drunk, was still beautiful; but Duval Smith, who was 'making baby movements with his hands', struck her as 'repulsive'.[121]

Nevertheless, a little while later she ran into Duval Smith at the York Minster pub (alias the French), and he started to besiege her with charm, wit and flattering attentiveness: he bombarded her with phone calls and flowers. A little while later again, she fell in love with him over lunch one day. Lewis Wolpert has written, reflecting on her capacity for falling in love with certain 'disastrous' individuals: 'She needed praise . . . Yet at the same time she loved her body, her own presence, and was a fool to flattering pursuit.'[122] Peter was an 'ardent lover', Jill discovered, and he was very prompt to propose marriage. He seemed, she remembered, quite desperately keen to marry her.

It is possible that the sheer ardour of his sudden determination to marry Jill Neville was fuelled, at least in part, by his fierce disappointment over Hetta. They were married without further delay at Hampstead Registry Office on 14 August 1959; and within two weeks she was pregnant. Five months later, in January 1960, he left her as fleetly as he had married her. He wanted to take up again with Hetta, and angled to move back in with her over the road at Studio House. The infatuation with Jill had been a mistake, he announced to her: she was a child by comparison with Hetta (she was in fact seventeen years Hetta's junior). He told Hetta how much he wanted her.

Hetta's initial reaction was to resist his ardent appeals to return to her bosom. She wrote to her husband in January 1960, a day or so before packing herself off for a much-needed holiday on the Continent: 'As to Peter, he is very repentant & full of golden promises but he has a great mess to deal with across the road and I want no part of it.'[123] But Jill Neville's autobiographical novel (*Fall-Girl*, 1966), and her recollections in a later interview, show that Duval Smith did indeed go back—perhaps not for long, but at least for a while—to live with Hetta at Studio House. 'I was out of their story,' reflects Neville's wounded protagonist in *Fall-Girl*. 'I was a minor character that had come in oddly for a few weeks and now I was out. I had just been a move in the destructive love-hate game they'd been having for years.'[124] That last sentence in particular has the very definite ring of truth. What is not clear is whether Duval Smith got back together with Hetta before the end of the year or else after February 1960, when Hetta returned home from her salutary trip abroad; either way, there can be very little doubt that Hetta was not in control of the situation; she was following her selfish fancy. She must have been gratified by the attention she received from Peter and by the access of power it gave her— he preferred her, he said, to the attractive young rival who had presumed to replace her.

Jill confessed to me that in fact she bombarbed Hetta with poison-pen letters; and one day—such was the fury in her hurt—she even tried to kill Hetta and Peter with a hammer. But that was by no means the end of the matter. The plot thickened, for Hetta had at this time—more or less simultaneously—taken up with a new younger lover (also seventeen years her junior) named Michael Avery, whom (for unknown reasons) she took to calling 'Josh'. He was an exotic-looking, sexy ex-sailor, with full lips, smooth olive complexion, broad nose, feline eyes, lustrous blue-black hair, and a short-statured, compact, muscular body. Normally considerate and courteous when sober, he was also painfully conscious of his lack of cultivation and tended to react with atrocious violence when he felt anyone was behaving in a condescending way towards him.[125]

After absconding from the navy, Avery had become part of the bohemian art set in Soho, whose base was the Colony Club. He was taken up by the likes of Dan Farson, Francis Bacon, and the photographer John Deakin who chose him as the model for Player's cigarette advertisements. It is not known how Hetta came to meet up with Michael (whom some of their friends took to be merely handsome, decent and dumb: a true toy boy *avant la lettre*)—whether in a pub or at a party—but by the end of 1959 he was more or less a fixture in Hampstead, and he remained so throughout the 1960s. Empson was to remark in 1966, on the subject of *Wuthering Heights*: 'the historical works of Robert Graves have made it clear that the instincts of a lady allow her to conduct a satisfactory sexual relation with the third footman without ever ceasing to treat him as the third footman.'[126] Such grand-seigneurial remarks are in line with the social code that Empson himself inherited and tacitly observed. If it is normal to take a lover from among the lower orders, it is fundamentally important that everyone still knows, and keeps to, their place in society. In this case, Hetta did not act in accordance with any such archaic code. Being more of a class warrior, she began from an early stage to treat Josh as her companion and her public escort. In many respects he was to become the surrogate husband: not merely a secret service but a social partner. It is not what her husband would have wanted, since it betrayed the cool convention that even his brother would have acknowledged and understood. But Empson was to try to take steps to ensure he remained master of the situation. Thus William and Hetta spent Christmas together at Studio House, and they were joined there by their respective lovers, Alice and 'Josh'. By 6 December Empson could be found writing to Alice in a manner which suggested that Hetta and Josh were rather routinely together. Hetta, he told his lover, 'invites you for Christmas at Studio House if you happen to be free, and indeed for this coming week-end; she and Michael will probably be in the country then . . .'[127] Empson liked Michael's looks and felt warmly towards him. He was amused to discover, for example, when he and Josh went for a country walk together, that for all his bravado and physical strength Josh was frightened of cows; it had never occurred to the country-bred Empson that one could be scared of a cow. So Christmas passed off convivially, though there were certain indications that the wild side of Michael could flare up when he was made to feel inadequate among intelligent conversationalists.

But not long after Empson returned to Sheffield for the winter term, Hetta was to write to him ('Dearest Pa') of a most alarming development:

> The boys went back to school in good order yesterday (Mogador rather counting terms to the end of his servitude). They had a very good party at Elizabeth Smart's (George Barker), where we all went. Unhappily Michael got cross again there and lashed out at me so unexpectedly that though Chisholm [the family doctor] does not think any ribs got broken, the bruise caused pheumonia, which has been exceedingly painful and I am still tied

across the middle with large strips of sticky tape & any quick movement is quite agonising. Anyway I don't feel so shaky any more, so please don't worry. I drove the boys to school and now all is peace & quiet and I can lie down & read a book. Michael has also gone away.[128]

Empson was quick to express his sympathy; but even though it was his wife who had been assaulted and genuinely battered, he preferred to offer a social and psychological explanation rather than to intervene in person. He offered no recourse, but his message was calm; and with regard to Michael he expressed kind understanding and a certain degree of constructive thinking:

> He is deeply upset by not being educated enough for his pretensions or for what he wants to do, and whenever he goes out and meets a large party he feels the other men don't take him seriously enough, as they couldn't do, so then he takes it out on Mum. This I am afraid is the basic thing, and the only way out for him is to buckle down and learn something he wants to know; it needn't be much more than a technical skill, but he must be proud of his skill at something before he can come away from a party with the people he likes to meet without feeling assertive and miserable.[129]

The following weekend (he added), he was booked to read poems at Durham University; still, he offered: 'I could come any weekend after that if wanted.'

Hetta underlined the high degree of her distress in an immediate reply:

> Dear Pa, I'm so sorry to be such a worry. I must go right away from London for a bit, say three or four weeks. It is too frightening to stay on here & I have only been waiting till I recovered a bit. The truth is that after unexpectedly & for no reason (or rather for reasons that you also give) banging me at the party & breaking a rib & of course black eye & the rest, Michael went home & later Jake & I drove home quite soberly & quietly to find Michael asleep, & as I thought, safely so. I went to sleep above Sye [Simon] & suddenly he [Michael] had jumped on me & was seriously trying to strangle me. He would certainly have succeeded, because it was so unexpected, except that dear Jake came in & hit him over the head with a hockey stick. As I said he left (he went to the Creek) & when he came for a moment & [was] very contrite, of course I explained that he must not return. Of course he managed to get into the house late one evening, & rather drunk naturally. Peter [Duval Smith] was here & his wife (behaving in hysterical fashion because he is leaving her). I quickly got Sye & drove away & spent the night with the Thompsons. I did mean to leave the next day but rather collapsed & have been recovering & trying to think what to do. Helena sleeps here [at Studio House] with me, but one can't go on being

scared to open the door. I think I'd better be quite alone for a bit so I'm going to see about going to Austria—it only costs £19 return to Vienna & I can manage that & it will be quite cheap for Sye & me... Please don't feel badgered about all this. It has been very disagreeable & upsetting but it's best for me to go away now for a bit.[130]

In the same letter she proclaimed that Peter would have to clear up the mess of his marriage by himself, for she wanted to have no further part in it.

A couple of weeks later, while Hetta was abroad, Jill Neville appealed to Empson for his help; she wanted him to get her husband away from Hetta.

'Dear Mrs Duval Smith,' he responded (the formality may have helped him to keep his distance, but it is quite possible that he had not even met her):

> I was glad to hear from you, as I naturally want to know about it; but I can't be much help. Please don't think that Hetta tried to break up your marriage, or even that Peter started to come back because he found there was a chivalrous duty to protect her. She was saying at the New Year that Peter was persecuting her by hanging about, and this was before Michael had hit her at all... Of course that doesn't sound helpful to you, but after all she had decided she wanted no more of Peter's mess a considerable time before. I hope that she doesn't have him back.[131]

While Hetta evidently dallied with the fancy of going back to Duval Smith, and spent one or two drunken days and nights with him, in a little while she successfully distanced herself from him and took up a more permanent arrangement with Michael Avery. Duval Smith and his misled and abused young wife went their separate ways; their marriage was to be dissolved in 1962. (For the first two years after separating from her husband, Jill Neville was to be the lover of the writer A. Alvarez.)[132] Though Josh lacked formal education or middle-class cultivation, Hetta recognized the worth of the man: his fundamental decency, his practical helpfulness, and his aspiration as artist and poet (albeit unavailing), and perhaps above all the esteem in which he generally held Empson. From time to time the bitterness Josh kept in check when sober erupted in fits of drunken violence against Hetta, but she was also physically strong and, being invariably as drunk as Josh on such occasions, gave back as good as she got. Lewis Wolpert recalls one day at Studio House when he heard Josh and Hetta fighting, and Hetta seriously shouting out for help. Wolpert intervened and knocked Josh to the ground—whereupon Hetta started beating up the apparently unconscious Josh.[133] However, the most appalling aspect of all such fights was that often enough the boys, Mogador and Jacob, were unavoidably witnesses to the drunken extravagance and the fisticuffs. Things became so bad that for most of his teenage years Mogador did not dare to bring a friend home to Studio House, for fear of finding his mother either self-abandoned or battling with her lover. On one occasion, the shocked and desparate boy shouted out, 'Why can't you just be normal?!' On another occasion, Mogador saw Josh punch his father in the stomach—Empson had recently undergone an operation on his stomach, so that Josh in his viciousness knew where to strike for maximum effect—and the boy saw red and leapt across the room to his father's defence, lashing out at Josh with a glass carafe. Josh was a boxer and knew how to duck, so that Mogador's weapon came crashing to the ground—if it had connected with Josh's head, the result could have been fatal. Both Mogador and Jacob were deeply disturbed by the harrowing scenes: some involved such terrible violence that blood flew from faces, and limbs would be broken. Whatever way one looks at it, the spectacle they had to witness must be reckoned to amount to a form of childhood abuse. Hetta chose rough, cruel lovers, and she would rough them up even as she was roughed up by them.

The pattern of occasional domestic violence waged between Josh and Hetta continued on and off through the 1960s, and the ferocity of it may not be underestimated. As much as he possibly could, Empson kept his distance from such domestic dramas. Friends now and then noticed that during his periods in Hampstead he would seem to be a detached lodger in his own house. Yet in truth the bond between Empson and Hetta was indivisible: there was never again to be any question of their separating. Both of them were happy that the other had an amenable lover, and Hetta was happy too in some fashion to share her lover with her husband.[134] 'The term "sexual perversion" is used rather trickily,' remarked Empson in *Milton's God* (which was being written even as the *ménage à trois* with Josh was being worked out); 'psychologists of all schools, I think, would agree that some emotional attachment upon others than the sexual mate is a basic requirement for a social animal, built into it by its evolution.'[135] Empson invariably found Josh to be amiable and highly respectful company. Josh was also on the whole quite biddable (as a friend noted).[136] 'I'm very fond of the dear boy,' Empson said of Josh one day. 'Good chap.'[137] Yet such bluff and seemingly condescending remarks said less than the complete truth: his tone was in all likelihood more protective of his privacy than patronizing towards Josh. Empson also felt responsible for him in every possible way, as though he had taken up a quasi-parental role—as

though, indeed, Josh had finally turned out to be the Dedalus to his own
Bloom, the fulfilment of his fantasy. And Josh found it natural even to
confide in his cuckold, as in this letter written after one of his separations
from Hetta:

> My Dear William,
>   I am writing to you because I feel so miserable from Hetta's absence, & as
> she is probably writing to you I would like to know how she is. I have
> accepted the fact that I am dead as far as she is concerned, but that doesn't
> make things any easier. I love her very deeply & my behaviour has robbed
> me of the finest thing that ever happened to me, & I, perhaps insincerely,
> wish her every happiness without me.

To say the least, Empson was at all times the paterfamilias in every sense.
Once, at a party, the writer Charles Osborne was to be knocked to the
floor by another guest (whom he left unidentified in his memoirs). Nigel
Richardson has been keen to name the assailant: 'I remember Josh
mentioning the episode to me; he'd thought Osborne was being lofty
and patronizing, asking whether Josh had really never heard of some
writer or painter or other or was he just affecting ignorance for *faux naif*
effect, to get inside someone's bluestocking knickers? Josh said this was the
kind of thing he had had to put up with all the time, in Hampstead
especially.' At the party, Empson rushed over to apologize to the shaken
Osborne. 'There's no need for you to apologise,' protested Osborne. 'Oh
but there is,' said Empson. 'He's my wife's lover.' His openness about his
open marriage preserved his dignity and self-respect. It is notable too that
there was a certain sense in which he derived a perverse pleasure from
Josh's antics; in June 1968, he happened to notice in *The Observer Review* that
Kenneth Tynan, in his column 'Shouts and Murmurs', mentioned just
such a kerfuffle—though without identifying 'Josh' by name:

> After an obstreperous party to celebrate a poetry reading in London last
> year, an American poet [John Berryman] fled back to his hotel and wet the
> bed in terror. Next day the management demanded that he should pay for a
> new mattress: he successfully charged it to the British Council.[138]

Empson thereupon sent the cutting to Hetta, seemingly with glee: 'Did you
see this joke by Kenneth Tynan? It must be the party wrecked by Josh.' We
can be sure of Empson's curious satisfaction in the allusion because he
added in his letter to Hetta: 'Please leave the cutting in my desk, for the
archives.'[139] The reference to any supposed 'archive' is unique in all of
Empson's writings.

Yet the *ménage* was by no means always histrionic or melodramatic; and certainly the open-marriage arrangement would turn out to suit Empson and his wife very well. In time, they became so free and easy in referring to it—as with Empson's unabashed remark to Osborne—that they could turn it into a fairly public joke, knowing it could disconcert others. Even as late as 1983, a few months before Empson's death, they went together to Cambridge for a party thrown by Christopher Ricks and his wife. Empson had made arrangements to sleep in Magdalene College, but it was not clear where Hetta would stay overnight until Graham Hough, an old friend, offered her a guest bedroom in his house in Grantchester—whereupon Hetta gaily called out to her husband,

'William, I'm sleeping with Graham Hough tonight.'
'Excellent, my dear. A very cosy plan.'
'Oh, he's just jealous he's not sleeping with Graham Hough!'[140]

For the most part, the Empson household worked well, and their friends were invariably enthralled to spend time with them. One friend of Hetta's was the writer Fay Weldon, who met her in 1960 and who would take happy inspiration from the invigorating robustness of her personality and views:

She was so powerful and extraordinary a personality . . . the resoluteness, the dangerous charm . . . She took me under her wing. I was terrified. I was an advertising copy writer: a much despised occupation in the circles I had just moved into, but which seemed like heaven to me: writers, sculptors, painters, layabouts, poets. I'd been living as a headmaster's wife in Acton [she had married Ronald Bateman in 1956]: my husband Master of a Masonic lodge: I was not used to wildness, or people acting, feeling, thinking with vigour and honesty. Hetta was witness at my wedding to Ron Weldon in 1963; after the wedding in St Pancras Town Hall we went to a Chinese restaurant in I believe Willesden. Hetta made me eat with chopsticks though I didn't know how—we ate English in Acton—and I asked for a spoon. But I learned. Her language could be savage. I was eight and a half months pregnant at the time: I think she liked that. But it wasn't exactly done, at the time—after the birth Ron and I went to The Creek; by the River Orwell . . . Hetta took us down to the river's edge to pick sea asparagus: I never forgot that: how astonishingly, delicately delicious. She could be so delicate: though her language could be so tough. She always knew things nobody else did; shared the wisdom, and the pleasure. And I always thought that bleak, flat, wind-swept landscape which she loved was a kind of English version of her native South Africa, plain, hot and dry though that was. She talked about that only once: her tall brothers, the fierce, powerful father: with the sjambok whip, running away at 17, out of there forever...

And William, awesome in a different way: *Seven Types of Ambiguity* reckoned just about the cleverest man in the world, there in the flesh, at Studio House. When you first met him he'd look at you hopefully, and engage you in conversation; and then his face would fall, he'd look disappointed, somehow or other one had failed intellectually: it happened to everyone, they said. After that it would be just down to the Roebuck for shove-halfpenny, and a talk about the merits of Heinz v. Campbell chicken soup. And Josh, of course. What parties, what madness, the walls of Studio House dented where heavy antique Chinese iron stirrups [which were used as ashtrays] had been hurled at someone's head, and missed: yet at the same time what kindness, what tenderness, what domesticity. There would be cucumber sandwiches, without crusts, cut in tiny triangles, for tea. I remember a dinner once, to which the Cuban cultural envoy and his beautiful, very elegant wife were invited: there we were dipping our strips of meat, with our chopsticks, in the boiling broth in the Tibetan wok—these meals were rituals, feasts—some incident occurred to do with the silkiness of the ambassadress's thigh, I think, crockery was on the verge of flying, everyone was on their feet: and the Cuban envoy said, 'My glimpse of English bohemian life. I have so longed to see this' and everyone sat down at once, determined not to gratify so suburban a spirit. They were wonderful days, hey-days: two archetypes, the brave and beautiful, outrageous Hetta; William, presenting himself as an absent-minded professor. I remember him coming to a party of ours wearing two ties—and John Rose—... brave, absurd John Rose, gay before men were allowed to be gay, a Scientologist when it was okay to be one, who believed cats ruled the earth—John Rose impertinently asked William what no-one else dared, 'William, why are you wearing two ties?' 'Because I couldn't find my belt,' William replied. A lateral thinker, before the term was invented. It seemed fair enough. And at a very early New Year party at Studio House, when 1960 turned to 1961, a kind of numerical palindrome, I heard him say, 'Ah, 1961, a year like a pencil sharpened at both ends.' I can never forget that, I still puzzle over it. And the cold, cold winter when the only solution to warming the vast studio was to erect a plastic tent inside it, and warm that—the Empsons were not just people in the arts; they were inventors, pioneers, explorers. Hetta as explorer—a good image, going where others dared not, to everyone's advantage.[141]

William and Hetta Empson finally broke up with their lovers at more or less the same time, in the very early 1970s. William, since he hated to have to discuss anything personal, was woundingly summary. Thus Mogador

Empson recalls a starkly memorable exchange at Studio House, not long after his father retired, when William told Alice Stewart that he would have to stop seeing her because 'he could no longer get it up!' In Mogador's mind, his father had decided to sever contact with Alice because he realized that from then on he would have to live a London life and keep things simple so that he could get his work done. 'His given reason was more information than I needed,' remarks Mogador, 'but then he was occasionally bloke-ish.' Josh was ultimately given his marching orders by Hetta when he became dangerously belligerent after drunkenly breaking a leg in the snow: he began to wield his crutches like clubs. He later took up with another woman who (it was claimed) was in many ways like Hetta.

14

The Anti-Christian: *Milton's God*

The advantage or perhaps the limitation of being an obstinate man is
that you don't have moral problems, only risks; what you ought to do
is always clear.

Letter to John Hayward, 2 July 1950

Paradise Lost... is evil unless you read it as Blake did...

Letter to Rosemond Tuve, 25 February 1953

THREE days before the grand performance of *The Birth of Steel* in
October 1954, Empson had lamented: 'I am getting guilt feelings
because I never get on with my book and other stuff I have promised to
write; nothing ever seems to get settled down; but I daresay it will. It upsets
me to feel on show all the time, but no doubt I shall come to be ignored
soon enough.'[1] Two years later, in 1956, he had come to feel that he had
two books on the go, though the volume of his essays on Shakespeare was
gradually yielding pride of place to the more urgent collection of his recent
essays.[2] Two years later again, in 1958, he told Ian Parsons at Chatto &
Windus that his next book would include 'essays on Donne Milton Fielding Joyce and a few extras, aiming at the general point that the neo-
Christian movement has greatly upset the natural and traditional way of
reading such authors; so that there has to be a certain air of challenge
about the book.'[3] The problem was, 'I have always worked slowly and
would still do so if I didn't have to mess about being a Professor, but I hope
you don't regard me as already dead.' The term 'neo-Christian' was his
own coinage; he meant it, as he said in another place, to designate what
amounted to a 'sect'. In the years following his appointment at Sheffield in

1953 he applied his energies, with increasingly hectic determination, to a campaign to combat the malignant morality of Christianity and the concomitant criticism of the 'neo-Christians'—the modern critics for whom the writings of Donne, George Herbert, and Milton were reduced willy-nilly to Christian writ. Critics such as W. K. Wimsatt and Hugh Kenner were 'neo-Christian', by which he meant that they were politically and socially reactionary, using Christianity to justify a pseudo-historical approach to literature and bullying students into suppressing their un-tutored (and Empson thought more healthy) reactions to famous works. However, even as he assailed the neo-Christians, he was forced from 1953 to answer critics who scorned the method and the validity of his own earlier writings, notably on Herbert and Hopkins. Soon, he was to turn defensive local scraps into large offensive sallies.

The two most serious—and, as time would tell, most ideologically disturbing—cases had been his climactic analyses in *Seven Types of Ambiguity* (1930) of George Herbert's 'The Sacrifice' and Gerard Manley Hopkins's 'The Windhover', in which he argued that the authors had felt obliged to confront rather than to accommodate themselves to the comforting but (as he thought) pernicious paradoxes of Christian doctrine. In other words, *Seven Types of Ambiguity* was already gathering the storm that was ultimately unleashed in *Milton's God* (1961). Stylistically and in many of its terms of reference, Empson's first critical book at once succeeded in changing the means of criticism and suffered because of its youthful extravagances. In substance, it not only purveyed a new mode of submitting imaginative literature to the test of the discursive reason, it had also culminated—artfully and gleefully—with two analyses that served to outrage Christian doctrine and history. While critics would eventually catch up with Empson's heterodoxy, the immediate reviewers had generally found themselves too stunned by his whole analytical approach to seize on his transgressiveness. But this is not to find fault with those readers who first winced or wondered at the resources of this new criticism. At the time of writing, not even Empson himself fully appreciated the import of his inflammatory insights, especially when (as he later came to think) they had been distract-ingly infected by the equally new and ravishing model of Freudian analysis.[4]

In 'The Sacrifice', he argued in *Ambiguity*, 'the various sets of conflicts in the Christian doctrine of the Sacrifice are stated with an assured and easy simplicity, a reliable and unassuming grandeur, extraordinary in any ma-terial, but unique as achieved by successive fireworks of contradiction, and a mind jumping like a flea.' His analysis reached its climax in discussing this stanza, which he sought to construe as paradoxically almost heretical:

> O all ye who pass by, behold and see;
> *Man stole the fruit, but I must climb the tree;*
> *The tree of life to all, but only me:*
> *Was ever grief like mine?*

'[Christ] climbs the tree to repay what was stolen, as if he was putting the apple back; but the phrase in itself implies rather that he was doing the stealing, that so far from sinless he is Prometheus and the criminal,' Empson observed. In other words, Christ is a figure of pastoral (as Empson himself was to redefine the form for *Pastoral*).

Twenty years on, the scholar Rosemond Tuve, in 'On Herbert's "Sacrifice"' (*Kenyon Review*, 12 (Winter 1950), 51–75), complained that 'a reader familiar with the traditions out of which this poem sprang will find Empson's reading inadequate.' In truth, she maintained, the conventions of the poem derive from the liturgical offices of Holy Week, and especially the Improperia or Reproaches of Good Friday. Accordingly, where Empson had perceived in the poem—with a beck towards I. A. Richards— 'contradictory impulses...held in equilibrium by the doctrine of the atonement', Tuve protested against the very notion of its imaginative uniqueness: 'the use of sharp antitheses ironically paralleling the tree of death with the tree of life is no novelty of a latter-day Metaphysical poet, and...a considerable naiveté is required of us as readers if we are to think that Herbert's particular phrasing of the convention makes us see Jesus as a son of the house, climbing in the orchard.'

Empson initially responded to Tuve's critical scholarship with a letter published in *Kenyon Review* in Autumn 1950 (*A*, 250–5). However, when Tuve, in *A Reading of George Herbert* (1952), continued to disparage his construction of the poem, he proceeded to draft a further, more aggressive and even patronizing rebuttal (which in the event was not published in his lifetime). 'I had not felt myself to be pulling any punches,' he wrote of Tuve,

> but it looks as though a rather more discourteous approach may be the only way to make contact with a mind so embedded in complacency. Her fuller version still says 'the phrase about climbing the tree (ascending the Cross) is the veriest commonplace' (p. 31), and 'Herbert uses the time-honoured "climb", for the ascent of the Cross' (p. 91), and still she offers among all her wealth of illustration not a single example of this...What has happened, I suspect, is something familiar among examination students: her head has got into a buzz with over-reading, so that it mixes things up. This then is also why she thinks that the style of Herbert is exactly like the style of the medieval liturgies (except for some mysterious personal quality which

she can't further describe); she has read so much on these themes that any one bit merely sets her head buzzing with all the others. She feels, as she is so fond of saying, 'it's a convention'.... Perhaps I should add that I am not myself a Christian, because the belief in a Supreme God who takes pleasure in giving torture seems to me ineradicable from the religion, and I find difficulty in imagining the minds of good men who accept it. But I do not think that this distracts my judgement when I feel that Herbert was far more conscious of the monstrosity than a composer of a medieval liturgy... I hope it is now clear that I claim to have a great deal of knowledge about Herbert, and do not claim as Rosemond Tuve asserts, that I can taste a poem better with no knowledge. I claim to know not only the traditional background of Herbert's poem (roughly but well enough) but also what was going on in Herbert's mind while he wrote it, without his knowledge and against his intention; and if she says that I cannot know such things, I answer that that is what critics do...

Having thus cavalierly spelled out his vexation, he yet retained enough gallantry to believe Tuve ought to be forewarned that he was proposing to publish a further snub to her scholarly authority; so in a letter of 7 January 1953 he offered her the right to reply. Tuve responded in February with a long and chatty letter. Cheerily conciliatory, she stood by the scholarship of her book, and saw no need to offer a further detailed rebuttal of Empson's readings. It was just such a pity that he invented 'arguments From Character of Author... You write excessive angry, but I don't think you are.'[5]

But there can be no doubt that he was sincerely angered by what he saw as the reactionary implications of her work on Herbert, her assuaging explanations of the poetry and its root theological conflicts. What Herbert confronted in his poetry, Empson insisted from first to last, was the fundamental opposition between the demands of the Christian God and the birthright of humanity, the responsibility to exercise individual judgement. Those imperatives are traditionally incompatible, and the conflict in poets who felt compelled to tackle the subject stems from the effort not to dissolve but to encompass its intolerable stresses. 'It was in the air of Herbert's time that the paradoxes of Christianity were a moral embarrassment,' he noted. 'The basic need of Metaphysical Wit, though seldom its conscious purpose, was to keep these new qualms at bay.'[6]

At the beginning of his second year at Sheffield he was also taken to task, in similar fashion, though more publicly—in the pages of the *TLS*—for his revelatory early reading of Hopkins's 'The Windhover'. In *Ambiguity* he had cited the 'proud but helpless suffering' of the poem as an example of his seventh type—in which 'the total effect is to show a fundamental division in the writer's mind'—for it conveys 'an indecision, and its reverberation in the mind'. His full analysis included these further observations:

> Confronted suddenly with the active physical beauty of the bird, [Hopkins] conceives it as the opposite of his patient spiritual renunciation; the statements of the poem appear to insist that his own life is superior, but he cannot decisively judge between them, and holds both with agony in his mind. 'My heart in hiding' would seem to imply that the 'more dangerous' life is that of the Windhover, but the last three lines insist it is 'no wonder' that the life of renunciation should be the more 'lovely'. 'Buckle' admits of two tenses and two meanings: 'they do buckle here', or 'come, and buckle yourself here'; 'buckle' like a military belt, for the discipline of heroic action, and buckle like a bicycle wheel, 'make useless, distorted, and incapable of its natural motion.' . . .
>
> Thus in the first three lines of the sestet we seem to have a clear case of the Freudian use of opposites, where two things thought of as incompatible, but desired intensely by different systems of judgements, are spoken of simultaneously by words applying to both; both desires are thus given a transient and exhausting satisfaction, and the two systems of judgement are forced into open conflict before the reader.[7]

Whereupon, years later—in 1954—it happened that an anonymous article, 'Pied Beauty in Spanish', reviewed the difficulties of putting into Spanish the sheer complexities of Hopkins's poetry, as Jose Manuel Gutiérrez Mora had managed to do in a monograph entitled *Hopkinsiana*. Among the many obstacles for a translator, the article cited the instance of Empson's treatment (following up an essay on Hopkins by I. A. Richards) of the ambiguities of the word 'buckle'. 'This is the perfect test-case for the deeper understanding of translator and interpreter . . . ,' the *TLS* writer noted. 'The word "buckle" is ambiguous in meaning and mood; it might be an imperative, a challenge to "brute beauty", or a statement; and it might mean either "buckle" in the sense of breaking down under strain, or "buckle" in the sense of preparing for military action, the two meanings Mr Empson quotes without deciding between them, because it is their simultaneous existence in the poet's consciousness and in the impact on the reader which gives "a transient and exhausting satisfaction".'[8]

F. N. Lees, in a letter to the *TLS* (3 September 1954), was irked by the reviewer's wholesale endorsement of Empson's attempt to balance contraries; Empson's negative paraphrase—his 'effectively contradictory development'—of the word 'buckle' in Hopkins could not be supported. In the weeks that followed, Empson had little trouble in seeing off a series of protests by Lees and others. But the following year, in a letter to the *TLS* (6 May 1955, p. 237), J. G. Ritz, writing from the Faculté des Lettres in Lyon, goaded Empson into an ideological rage with the religiosity of an inter-pretation of Hopkins which, as Ritz swaggered, 'answers all the difficulties of the sonnet, while rejecting far-fetched explanations'—specifically including Empson's. 'The whole poem,' Ritz declared, 'is at once one of Hopkins's splendid meditations on Christ's glory and sacrifice as God and Man-God, and one of his deep ponderings' over the necessity of imitating Christ. The windhover is symbolical of Christ who 'swooped down like a bird of prey': 'Christ's incarnation, his lowly life in Galilee, are "lovelier" and "more dangerous" since they imply the redemption of men and their salvation. To be Christ's prey is no small matter for Hopkins...' Any Christian can so imitate the Windhover: 'By gathering together and humbling his own gifts, his spiritual life will become far lovelier and more dangerous than the mere enjoyment of his mortal gifts.'

Empson answered two weeks later (20 May) with a letter which Derwent May, chronicler of the *TLS*, has called 'a classic example of his subtle yet commonsensical reading of poems':[9]

> I think the poem is about training and about the doubt in Hopkins's mind, expressed with painful force in later sonnets, as to whether the severe Jesuit training had only crippled him...
>
> Mr Ritz, on the other hand, takes the poem as about gloating over torture. Hopkins must have been 'stirred' by the hawk because he saw it, or imagined it, swoop and catch its prey, just as Christ has swooped and mangled Hopkins...
>
> Hopkins must have known, I agree, that the 'valour and act' of the bird, the source of its beauty of movement, was killing other creatures; and the idea of the fierceness of God was not strange to him; but if this is the point of the poem why is he so far from saying it?...
>
> The question, I think, has a larger bearing. Christian apologists now-adays, I seem to notice, have become rather defiantly keen on recalling the stark roots of primitive human sacrifice and their place in Christianity, even boasting in print (one is to suppose with a laugh) that the religion provides a more efficient sadistic drug than the forbidden Horror Comics.[10]

Ritz's sanctimonious and uninflected rendering of Hopkins's complex poem so galled Empson that later on in the year he returned to scold his opponent (even though the editor of the *TLS* had put a stop to the lengthy published correspondence).

In terms of Empson's critical career as a whole, therefore, his early pages on 'The Sacrifice' and on 'The Windhover' were to prove cardinal texts; dating from 1930, they seeded the catechizing writings of the post-war years, culminating in *Milton's God*. Nonetheless, at the time when he wrote about 'The Sacrifice' and 'The Windhover' his analyses seemed less perfidious than accepted good sense. By his reckoning, the damage was done to 'traditional' critical readings such as his own by the reactionary forces of the Christian religion, with T. S. Eliot as its literary high priest. In 1932 Eliot had put out a revisionist essay including the unsupported assertion, 'Donne was, I insist, no sceptic';[11] and in quick order other critics glibly bowed to the new wisdom.

Perhaps the one outstanding piece of contemporary literature to which Empson felt it all too appropriate to apply a Christian interpretation was *Waiting for Godot*. He enjoyed the play in its first English production by Peter Hall at the Arts Theatre in 1955, but the essential point of the thing, he felt, served to show just what a grotesque doctrine the Christian religion imposed upon its benighted adherents. In October 1955 he took part in a panel discussion at the Arts Theatre to consider whether the play was good, simply as entertainment. The ambiguous topic of the debate was: 'Do we or don't we wait for Godot?' As the *Bookseller* reported (8 October), other speakers included Harold Hobson, Peter Forster, and Peter Coates, and a vote taken at the end of the meeting gave those who were prepared to 'wait for Godot' a favourable majority of about 10 to 1. Empson wrote later: 'I was kindly invited to speak on the stage, as one of the two Devil's Advocates in the initial debate, when a packed house of enthusiasts for *Waiting for Godot* discussed in the theatre what they thought the play meant. No two of them agreed, and I came away strengthened in my own belief that this kind of religious education is a very unfair trick to play on a child.'[12] In the *TLS* there occurred a long-running debate on the meaning of Beckett's play; and when one contributor sought to maintain that *Waiting for Godot* was of course radically ambiguous, Empson jumped at his cue to submit a brief but sincerely scornful letter in March 1956:

> Mr [Philip H.] Bagby was quite right, I think, to point out the radical ambiguity of *Waiting for Godot*, but not all ambiguity is good. Here it expresses the sentiment: 'We cannot believe in Christianity and yet without that everything we do is hopelessly bad.' Such an attitude seems to be more frequent in Irish than either English or French writers, perhaps because in Ireland the religious training of children is particularly fierce. A child is brought up to believe that he would be wicked and miserable without God; then he stops believing in God; then he behaves like a dog with its back broken by a

car, screaming and thrashing on the public road, so that a passer-by can only wish for it to be put out of its misery. Surely we need not admire this result; the obvious reflection is that it was a very unfairly risky treatment to give to a child.

To be sure, we all ought to feel the mystery of the world, and there is bound to be a kind of literary merit in any play which makes us feel it so strongly; but we need not ourselves feel only exacerbated impotence about the world, and if we did we would be certain to behave badly. 'Oh, how I wish I could go to Hell! Why can't I go to Hell? It does seem a shame I can't go to Hell.' In itself this peculiar attitude deserves only a rather disgusted curiosity. But I would hate to suggest a moral censorship against the play; it is so well done that it is an enlarging experience, very different for different members of the audience. It would only be dangerous if it was liable to suck a member into the entire background to be presumed for the author, and that it cannot do.[13]

If the cumulative effect of his essays and ripostes on Herbert, Hopkins, and Donne did not reach a wide audience because they appeared only in little magazines in England and the USA, nevertheless his views on the wickedness of the Christian God became enormously well publicized with the appearance in 1961 of *Milton's God*, with its thesis following in the footsteps of Voltaire, Samuel Butler, Edward Gibbon (in his sorry account of Christianity in chapters 15 and 16 of *The History of the Decline and Fall of the Roman Empire*), H. T. Buckle, and J. M. Robertson. All the same, it is surprising to realize that he had actually made up his mind about the monstrous meaning of Milton's epic as early as 1953, just a year after his return from the Far East to England. After reading A. J. A. Waldock's study *'Paradise Lost' and Its Critics* (1947), he published an article that was as provisional and exhilarating as it was certain of a paradoxical truth:

I think that everything said by Waldock about the startling irreducible confusions in the story of *Paradise Lost* . . . is clearly true, could be added to considerably, and ought to be admitted by an opponent. But I think that these arguments, so far from proving that the poem is bad, explain *why* it is so good . . . I think it is horrible and wonderful; I regard it as I do the novels of Kafka, or for that matter Aztec or Benin sculpture; in short, I read it as Blake and Shelley did; and I am rather suspicious of any modern critic who claims not to feel anything so obvious . . . I am intrigued by a possibility that some part of Milton's unconscious mind (since Milton must have known enough theology to realise that his epic was making God entirely *un*-transcendental) intentionally left open through most of the poem a plausible case for the argument of Satan, which is that God is only a usurping angel and tells lies whenever he claims to be metaphysically unique . . . To worship the God of Milton, not only nagging and teasing even the good angels, from what we can gather, not only jeering with the meanness of a delinquent child whenever he gets the chance, but boasting of laying traps to make his helpless creatures incur further torments and then gloating when he has got them there, really is very close to what seemed so comical when Blake first said it, very close to worshipping the Devil. I have noticed critics saying austerely (after quoting Shelley perhaps) that this point of view must be rejected at once because it is quite unhistorical; it is always sad to have to spoil the innocence of an historian, but the fact is there had been a lot of arguing about theology long before Shelley...

The root of the startling power of Milton is that he could accept and express this downright horrible conception of God and yet keep somehow alive, underneath it, all the breadth and generosity, the welcome to all noble pleasure, which had been permanent just before it in the development of European history. No wonder his epic began to look a bit less dull when the critics began to ask what it meant.[14]

'Well, well, maybe it isn't true about Herbert anyhow; I think it is, but I don't care,' he had wearily conceded to Tuve about his reading of 'The Sacrifice', also in 1953. 'It really is true about *Paradise Lost*; that poem is evil unless you read it as Blake did, and I must say so till I die, and it raises exactly the same problems of interpretation.'[15] He minded very deeply about *Paradise Lost*, but it was not until early 1959 that he informed his publisher of his consummate plan. 'I have decided to do a short book on Milton, for around the celebrations people seem to be fixed on,' he wrote to Parsons.[16] Only two months after that announcement, he was so certain of the argument of the book he was projecting (most of which was to be written during 1959) that he could immediately submit on request from Parsons a full 'advance announcement' which, with an alteration of just one word, would in due course become the blurb on the book as published (moreover, the burden of the blurb was identical to that of the article on Milton he had published in 1953). At about this time too, he gave an unscripted talk on *Paradise Lost* at Lincoln College, Oxford; a good talk, though condensed, it showed that he had the argument of his entire book in his head. A simple but remarkable paradox was to be the crux of his argument (which no critic had ever quite said before): 'Milton's God... makes the poem so good just because he is so sickeningly bad.'[17] One need not doubt Milton's sincerity in his remarkable claim to be justifying the ways of God to man, to be setting out a theodicy, but the biblical facts relating to the awfulness of his God clearly defeated his honest object. By December 1959 the book was complete except for the final chapter which 'frightened' him, he reported.[18] The chapter was an outright indictment of Christianity which he believed to be 'shocking'; he hankered for it to prove so: 'this is the first time I have poked my nose in a book outside purely academic subjects,' he remarked.[19] Indeed, he was to carry on revising that chapter for a further year, though the book would be accepted for publication on 8 February 1960 (with a contract drawn up on 4 April giving the author an advance on royalties of £200). 'I haven't cut anything I thought honour required keeping in,' he told Parsons in January 1961, 'and I must say I find the chapter pretty oppressive to read. Still, it needn't be done again one would think; the next book ought to be able to illustrate the position quite light-heartedly.'[20] In truth, as F. W. Bateson was shrewdly to note, *Milton's God* is ultimately more about God than about Milton: Milton's epic is a stalking-horse to undo the infamy of the Christian God.[21] The book is nothing if not polemical; it is full of sardonic wit and sarcastic sharip focus. It is also the most readable of all Empson's books, the most relentless in its sharp focus, and the most courageous in its moral indignation, as well as the most invigorating and the most wilful.

Empson seriously expected the heavens to open when the book came out. 'I can believe one might get a prosecution for blasphemy now, though one wouldn't before the war,' he responded when his publisher pencilled on the manuscript a comment to the effect that he expected they would both be prosecuted for blasphemy (though Empson was quite sanguine about the prospect); 'I am not ready to suppress what I think the truth because of that, but am very ready to take care about the tone so as to have a strong case if necessary. When was the last prosecution of a book for blasphemy, I wonder?'[22] Not long after, he was gleefully announcing to W. W. Robson that he did expect to be prosecuted under the Blasphemy Act—'the first prosecution since Bradlaugh [in the 1880s].'[23]

He had a quick and chastening experience of a possible prosecution for printing inflammatory or libellous thoughts even as he polished off his chapter 'Christianity'. In January 1961 he reviewed for the *New Statesman* Arthur Koestler's latest tome entitled *The Lotus and the Robot*: Empson thought it silly stuff, and treated it in cavalier and sarcastic fashion:

> The chief moral of the book is that Koestler is now proud to be a Western European, as he is disillusioned with Zen and Yoga...
>
> The thesis of the book requires 'Europe' to be a single though growing entity; Christianity and science have always been one, and the only astronomers mentioned are Jesuits. A mention of "Judaeo-Christianity" is as much credit as the Semites can expect...It all brings comfort because it proves that the whites are genuinely superior. I think that this belief, even if true (it

is grotesquely untrue about Christianity), is not likely to do us good . . . Soon after the war, Koestler felt he hadn't enough petrol, and wrote to the *Partisan Review* [in November 1947], 'The Labour Party is betraying its trust. I have to cycle a mile and a half for my groceries. We old-established country squires are being wronged' (or words politically leaving that impression).[24]

Koestler felt he was being smeared as a quasi-fascist sympathizer, and claimed Empson had compounded his libellous insinuations by fabricating a quotation which inverted the authentic socialist sympathies of the genuine article. Empson was obliged, in consultation with the *New Statesman* and its solicitors, and with Koestler's solicitors, to put his signature to an apology that was published alongside Koestler's own letter of outraged protest: 'The sentences in quotation marks were meant to be a parody of the article in *Partisan Review*, which I had not seen since it was new. I thought I had made this clear and I am sorry if they were taken as a quotation, and for suggesting that Koestler used words "politically leaving that impression". I agree that unchecked reminiscing is a bad thing, since one's memory is likely to play one false, as it has admittedly done in this case.'[25] Walter Allen, editor of the *New Statesman*, had likewise to apologise in print for publishing an 'ironical paraphrase' by Empson. Empson could not say he had not been forewarned; the blasphemy law might be more swingeing than the law of libel from which he got away lightly in the Koestler episode. All the same, he felt he owed it to himself to print a libel upon the Christian God, and he was fully prepared to stand up in court to explain just why. 'Did you see Koestler kicking me in the New Statesman?' he asked his publisher, dashingly but perhaps not altogether convincingly. 'It had a useful effect perhaps in causing a sober approach to revising the last chapter. I did slip up there, but from too much sobriety oddly enough; I have had to stop drinking and smoking to avoid stomach-ache, and it has a very uneasy effect on the literary output.'[26]

Nevertheless, he had to confess himself a little bit worried about the effect the book might have on his professional standing at the University of Sheffield; he wrote in a note to the publicity department at New Directions (which was to publish in the USA in 1962 about a third— 1,040—of the copies printed by Chatto & Windus): 'The truth is, I rather want to avoid scandal than attract attention when the book first comes out; it will go on selling afterwards in a quiet steady way, I think you'll find. I am not so vain as to think I can alter the history of the religions, but to improve the moral tone of the literary critics a tiny bit should be within my range.'

But it was not just the American market which made him feel apprehensive about the possibility of a backlash from his employer. When Chatto & Windus identified him, on the title-page of a proof copy, as 'Professor of English Literature at Sheffield University', he quite pointlessly (and with uncharacteristic faintheartedness) asked them to delete it. 'They hate scandal in any form, and are sure to think this a rude book; I think they would want to be disassociated from it as much as possible. Of course they might be offended the other way, but that is less probable.'[27] All the same, he undertook some excellent advance publicity for the book: this included arranging three 20-minute talks to be broadcast by the BBC (directed in May by George MacBeth), which were then printed as a conspicuous series in *The Listener* during July 1960—the first of them even managed to misrepresent C. S. Lewis as saying that Milton's Satan 'must be meant to be funny'.[28]

Milton's God was published in the UK in an edition of 2,500 copies on 7 September 1961; reprints were called for in 1962 (500 copies) and 1963 (550). On 15 March 1965 a second edition appeared, with notes and a long appendix on the foisting into King Charles's I *Eikon Basilike* of the so-called Pamela's Prayer. Drawing on his own experience of being a 'propagandist' for the wartime BBC, Empson was virtually alone in standing out against the consensus of scholarly opinion: he sincerely believed that it would have been a wonderful achievement for Milton to have perpetrated a damaging fraud upon the supporters of the 'divinised' King Charles.[29] 'I think the additions change the tone of the book very much; it no longer ends in a blaze of indignation, but with placid interest in the results of the controversy,' he believed.[30]

The crux of his argument in *Milton's God* Empson left in no doubt at all, though subsequent critical misapprehensions—especially from critics who insisted on condemning him as an 'anti-Miltonist' (when in fact he felt nothing but admiration for Milton's courageous honesty, and for the power of his poetry, and when he was concerned to mount a 'defence' of *Paradise Lost*)—forced him to repeat it again and again, as in this letter from 1967: 'Shelley found it plain that, the more he reverenced the Son who endured, the more he must execrate the Father who was satisfied by his pain.'[31] Yet the very large majority of the reviewers found the book bracing for its critical intelligence and propagandist gusto while invariably regretting that it was nonetheless fundamentally wrong in its approach: wrong among other things in approaching an epic poem as if it were a detective novel, with God the Father being exposed as the supremely evil villain.[32] But the biggest snag in his liberal humanist approach, which certainly gave so many reviewers the opportunity to crab the book, lay in the very fact that he confronted the Christian God through a work of literary imagination, on the assumption that Milton's version of God could be identified with the 'truth' of the Gospel. While C. S. Lewis, in *A Preface to Paradise Lost* (1942), had convincingly demonstrated the broad orthodoxy of Milton's theology, other critics found poem and doctrine incommensurable and reasonably jibbed at Empson's evident equation. The book thus contrived to run up against an unforeseeable and perhaps insurmountable irony: that, as one notice deftly put it, 'Empson's every insult to God should prove a compliment to Milton'.[33] By arguing that Christianity was incoherent and morally ugly, he praised Milton's integrity in outstaring the embarrassments of the myth in poetry that was all the more brilliant because unblinking. John Bayley discriminated the central irony of Empson's approach when he noted, 'Unlike most critics, Lewis and Empson make a steadfast claim for Milton's complete moral coherence'.[34] The 'obstacles to grasping' the power of the poem, Empson wrote later, 'come from the basic fallacies of the Christian religion, or indeed the whole previous cult of human sacrifice. But Milton's treatment of the subject has to be approached through his language.'[35] And again: 'I am such an old academic that I agree with Blake and Shelley . . . I think the main points which have been found bad about *Paradise Lost* are precisely what made it so good, because they amount to a profound analysis of what is fundamentally wrong with the Christian God.'[36]

A defender of the faith, F. N. Lees (who had already taxed Empson in the pages of the *TLS* over his interpretation of 'The Windhover'), argued that 'many readers . . . would recognise a failure in the story-telling enterprise'; which is to say that the myth is simply unavailable for treatment as epic drama—and so Lees left himself short of argument, protesting only that 'Professor Empson is wrong about Christianity'.[37] The anonymous reviewer for the *TLS* likewise laughed the matter off as an impossible paradox: 'Once the critic strays from his text in order to exploit the many theoretical absurdities of an epic which has an omniscient character in it, there can be no end to the anti-Christian fun and games.'[38] But fun and games were not the point for Empson: it was a matter of true life and death, as he told the *TLS* the next week: 'I deny that a poem is a private self-subsisting world.'[39] (He was disheartened with the review coverage of his book; and he complained, three years later: 'it is not much use my trying to look moderate and goodhumoured; the book has not been reviewed in the trade papers (PMLA, RES and suchlike) and has made no dent in the armour of the Christian phalanx.')[40]

From inside the Christian camp, Helen Gardner issued a (perhaps surprisingly) urbane and generous piece of special pleading that is worth quoting at length:

> [Empson's] book has a radical flaw in its refusal to recognize that theology, like philosophy, has a history, and that Milton's highly individual emphasis on certain doctrines makes it impossible to equate his God with the Christian God ... [Milton] accepted by and large the form of the doctrine of the Atonement current in his day and presented it in a crude form. But I do not believe this doctrine meant much to him imaginatively or religiously. The interest of *Paradise Lost* does not lie here but in the doctrines that Milton lived by and to which he gave memorable expression: the doctrine of Creation, the doctrine of Providence, and the belief that the root of all goodness is freedom. Milton's passionate belief in God as Creator and Ruler, and in the freedom of the will, allied to his noble confidence in reason as the master faculty of the human mind, produces a God seen almost wholly in terms of Power and Will, who argues his case at the bar of human reason. This Being seems to have little relation to the 'Father' of Christ's discourses, and to have been created without reference to the fundamental Christian belief that the supreme revelation of the nature of the Deity is to be found in the life and death of Christ.[41]

Yet whatever discriminations apologists such as Gardner might make between religious absolutes and the evolution of Christian doctrine, it can hardly be disputed that Empson was in fact intently concerned with 'the life and death of Christ' in relation to 'the nature of the Deity'. Graham Hough seized the nub of Empson's matter: 'The Son who suffers on the cross is not the victim of a Father who can only be satisfied by blood; he is identical with the Father ... Whatever he came to believe later Milton seems to have been an orthodox Trinitarian at the time he wrote *Paradise Lost*. But Empson ... brushes off the consubstantiality of the Son with the Father as a mere form of words.[42] *Mere form of words*: few critics would dare argue that Empson was innocent of verbal complexities; and as for the doctrine of the Trinity, Empson saw it as an article of evasion, so to speak, a sophistical formulation obviously devised to overcome a morally execrable alternative.[43] Empson argued that Arius (AD 250–336) must have been in the right in believing Jesus Christ to be subordinate to God in Heaven, though in 325 Arianism was made a heresy at the Council of Nicaea, which proclaimed the consubstantiality of the Father and the Son. Gibbon too had believed that Athanasius (AD 296–373) had done damage to Christianity in the fourth century by imposing the wretchedly irrational doctrine of the Trinity. In conversation with W. W. Robson, Empson expressed bewilderment at the fact that so great and good a man (as he thought him) as C. S. Lewis had managed to make some kind of decent sense of the doctrine of the Atonement.

S. G. F. Brandon, in *The Judgment of the Dead* (1967), a volume which Empson reviewed some six years after publishing *Milton's God*, provided an objective assessment of the meaning and implications of Christ's ministry in terms that in no way shirk the issues that goaded Empson. Starting out from the eschatalogical tradition of Jewish apocalyptic belief that the Messiah would reward his faithful servants with everlasting bliss and damn his enemies to eternal torment, Brandon observes, Catholic Christianity presently emerged as 'a salvation-religion centred on a saviour-god.' Notwithstanding the increasing stress that the historical Church laid on a wholesome soteriology, however, 'Christ appears [in the liturgy] in two different, and logically contradictory roles, namely, as the Saviour and the Judge of mankind.' Brandon adds a footnote that presses home the terrible irony that this religion of merciful redemption somehow requires the sanction of everlasting punishment: 'Ideally, of course, the Christian moral code should be practised for love of God, and not for the hope of gaining Heaven or escaping Hell. Nevertheless, the validity of that code depends logically upon an ultimate distinction, made by God, between the just and the unjust.'[44]

By referring such observations back to the central argument of *Milton's God*, it is possible to see that Empson had reached an unerringly logical and devastating conclusion, as he was to frame it again in 'Herbert's Quaintness' (1963):

> The doctrine of the Trinity is necessary, or the Father appears too evil in his 'satisfaction' at the crucifixion of his Son. But to present Jesus as one with the Father only turns him into a hypocrite; when he prays for his enemies to be forgiven, he knows under his other title he will take revenge. (*A*, 257)

Kenneth Burke commented on Empson, 'by his stress upon "torture" rather than the sacrificial principle in general, he picturesquely deflects attention from the central relationship between religion and the social order.'[45] The adverb 'picturesquely' is of course a sarcastic euphemism: Burke also called him 'rabid', as did other critics who considered him 'vitriolic' in his fixation on the horrid meaning of what Burke terms 'the sacrificial principle in general'—a sentimental locution if ever there was one. Empson would later lament of Burke, in conversation: 'he really does like sacrifice, you see—he believes that the literature about sacrifice is splendid, as indeed it often is. But the idea that this would actually happen and that he is recommending a barbaric and very disagreeable thing simply cannot enter his mind. It's very remote from anything he would really like to happen—that's what I feel.'[46] Graham Hough remarked in a broadcast review that when Empson 'presents the early Christians as gloating over human sacrifice in a world otherwise civilised enough to have grown out of it, he ought to take a rest from the Rationalist Press classics and re-read Suetonius';[47] and yet, as Professor E. M. W. Tillyard agreed in private correspondence with Empson, any appeal to Suetonius must pale beside the evidence of Tertullian.[48]

Among the many Miltonists whom Empson took to task, in fact, Tillyard (former Master of Jesus College, Cambridge, author of a monograph on Milton, and examiner of the young Empson in the Cambridge English Tripos in 1929) considered himself well reproved by *Milton's God*: the book had interested him 'vastly', he told Empson (in an extraordinary and unexpected fan letter), largely because its thesis embodied a forceful *a priori* case: it fulfilled the principle enunciated by A. C. Bradley that the best way to comprehend Wordsworth's strangenesses was not by circumvention but by the approach direct. He applauded too Empson's coinage 'Neo-Christian', and said he feared writers such as Dorothy Sayers and Helen Gardner who manifested the neo-Christian tendency (though somehow not T. S. Eliot). As to the detail of the book, he went on, 'I have not been able to test your theses; but I do know that whether they will convert me or not they are vastly important in having put the poem in a new light. . . . You may have to wait several years before you get a fit return for your efforts. But you will get it . . . [Y]our book has thrilled me.' Empson felt so thrilled to receive such a letter from Tillyard, whom he had taken to be one of his arch-enemies, that he rushed around flourishing the two-page missive in front of anyone he could waylay in the university. In the months to come he would boast of Tillyard's 'nice' letter to Robert Lowell (who also praised him by post), and to his brother. Tillyard 'agrees with my book . . . all along the line, though I rather thought I was attacking him,' he related. 'I suppose he still considers himself an Anglican; he says that all the churches of Christendom ought to renounce the horrors of the Old Testament, as a precaution. Oh, well.'[49]

Empson may be faulted for inappropriately levelling his rational humanism at a transcendent and, in his terms, tyrannical deity—a God who not only held all the cards (gods will be theocratic) but also maliciously stacked them against mankind; perhaps more so for trying to deconstruct the Christian God by way of Milton's imagination. But his critical approach followed from principle: 'A man who believes in Hell can't help relating the prospect of it to his feelings about life in general,' he maintained in a letter to Frank Kermode.[50] That conviction explains precisely why he became so intent upon rescuing literature from Christian readings. In *Ambiguity* he had addressed 'the class of readers' who agreed with him about 'certain effects' in poetry; not perceiving himself as a polemicist, he had simply practised the close reading of literature in terms of what he considered 'depth psychology'. In his later years he resolved to reconstruct any and every kind of literary student—the mass of misreaders—for 'the intentions of the authors [they read],' he insisted in another letter, 'were very unlikely to be so nasty as those of your many-legged neo-Christian torture-worshippers'.[51]

In November 1962, a year after the publication of *Milton's God*, Empson went even further on the offensive by speaking at the Cambridge Union Debating Society in favour of the motion 'God is evil' (incidentally, it was the first occasion at which women were granted permission to speak at the Union Society); his celebrity opponent was Lord Longford, who pointed out that it was false to suggest, with Empson, that Christians 'gloated over suffering'. Longford argued that Christians had done much and were still doing a great deal to relieve suffering throughout the world. Empson, playing his devil's part, claimed 'Christianity is a frightfully slippery and unreliable engine. The idea that God does want suffering is the bad thing about Christianity.'[52] Yet his resolutely inflammatory rhetoric still failed to ignite more than two-thirds of the damp student body: the motion was defeated by 340 votes to 155.

Just so, the customary critical verdict on the post-war Empson is that he became exclusively obsessed with exploding the myths of Christianity, in toppling God: he had become bitterly negative, even virulent in his views, determined only to lam both the intrinsic wickedness and the wicked effects of worshipping the Christian God. And so, sadly, ends the story. But any such delimiting interpretation of his later career makes a grave mistake. On the strongest natural and moral grounds he felt sickened by the practice of cruelty or sadism; appalled at the notion of the Father in Heaven being 'well pleased' with witnessing the mortal sufferings of Christ (see 'The Satisfaction of the Father'). He had also studied the ethics of what he called 'the other half of Christian theology, let alone the other half of the old world—India and China and their satellites'. All of his reading convinced him that none of mankind's religious or social customs should be taken as absolute, only as relative. He hoped to deconstruct the Christian God, it is true, but he attacked only one version of godhead and thought it a sickening symptom of the very habit of mind he opposed that all too many critics interpreted his anti-Christianity as a blind attack on the One God. 'To say I hate God seems to me an example of pretending that Christianity is the only religion,' he protested in a letter; 'I hate Moloch, the god who was satisfied by crucifying his son.'[53] (Moloch, the god of the Ammonites, demanded human sacrifice as part of his worship (1 Kings 11: 7); the God of Israel did not, for the Mosaic law and the Hebrew prophets proscribe human sacrifice (Leviticus, 18: 21, 20: 1–5, Jeremiah, 7: 31, 19: 5, Ezekiel, 23: 39). Nevertheless, despite its Judaic foundations, Christianity as it developed arrogated to itself certain pagan elements such as the efficacy of human sacrifice.) A number of readers therefore see only the one facet of Empson, the supposed bigot who assailed Christianity. The side they neglect, which is in fact the concomitant and equally important aspect of his revisionary campaign, is the Empson who laboured to recover a positively hopeful and humane view of ethics and literary interpretation. Milton's God, he had argued, 'cannot be the metaphysical God of Aquinas...he has such a bad character'; and his postulate for a better version of godhead is assuredly set out in *Milton's God*, just as it is intimated in this later letter:

> The rebel angels...grant that a personal creator is conceivable, but such a being must satisfy the conditions of Aquinas, which include absolute omnipotence. (He must be built into the structure of the universe, as no creator can be.)...The poem sets out to explain why the world is bursting with sin and misery, and the only reason it can find is that God is tirelessly spiteful. He therefore cannot be the metaphysical God of Aquinas, and the heroic rebels were right on the essential point.[54]

The conception of an impersonal divinity somehow 'built into the structure of the universe' figures throughout his later writings, as his constructive alternative to the Christian God. It is a secularized version of godhead, following the Pantheistic paradigm; and he was pleased to find it in evidence in many authors, including Yeats[55] and Dylan Thomas; as an aspect of the early poetry of Kathleen Raine; and even in Tennyson's 'Tithonus'.[56] 'Dylan Thomas's religion is pantheistic and absorbs the Godhead into the world,' he declared in 1947. He had good reason for believing so, for in an early letter Thomas had delightedly cited a passage in Donne's *Devotions* 'where he describes man as earth of the earth'. T. S. Eliot's unacknowledged literary curates would of course pooh-pooh the ignorant fancy that Donne (if not Thomas) could have been signalling something pantheist, Empson acknowledged in 1965:

That would be 'provincial' no doubt, as Eliot called the beliefs of Yeats, so that they too become invisible. I do not mean to say that Dylan Thomas's philosophising, apart from its expression, is very recondite; he could have found most of it in Shelley, and probably did; but the indoctrinated modern reader is unwilling to find it anywhere.

If Empson trod on rocky ground in suspecting Milton's Trinitarianism, he almost certainly stumbled over his argument that even Milton might have been pointing to the same happy prospect—a fortunate future when God would 'dissolve into the landscape'. At least in this instance, his eagerness to repudiate the Christian God led him to too partial a reading of the textual evidence. In respect of Christianity he overlooked the principle that in general he practised so 'religiously', and for which he praised Arthur Waley in these terms: 'A large capacity to accept the assumptions of any world-view, without assuming any merit for our own, is the basic virtue of Waley's mind.' But as far as he was concerned Christianity was beyond tolerance. Looking for a redeeming feature in the way *Paradise Lost* depicts its God, he persuaded himself that Milton foresaw that God should abdicate his station. The passage in question is the Father's speech to the Son, ending

> Then thou thy regal sceptre shalt lay by,
> For regal sceptre then no more shall need,
> God shall be all in all   (III. 339–41)

—which it is in fact difficult to construe as anything other than a versification of St Paul's First Epistle to the Corinthians (15: 28): 'When all things shall be subdued unto him, then shall the Son also himself be subject unto him that put all things under him, that God may be all in all.' Empson once wrote, 'The standard literary training treats history pretty rough, but I don't'; yet here it seems likely that he had felt too avid to read into Milton's language a prospective dispensation on the order of Shelley's 'one Spirit'—at the expense of the more obvious theological gloss. Edward L. Hirsh accorded Empson the sideways compliment that his 'incredibly simplified view of Christian history and thought and his frank reliance on a totally secular humanism whose ethical prophet is Bentham together give *Milton's God* a certain clarity and honesty'; but, his review went on, severely though with some justice:

Unhindered by a knowledge of 17th-century or other Christian theology and biblical exegesis, he is able to conclude that Milton worked recalcitrantly, although necessarily, with the God of Moses, but left Him much better than he found Him and anticipated the day when He would abdicate His throne to become Spinoza's God of total immanence.[57]

It does indeed seem far-fetched for Empson to have conceived the idea that the Christian God might consign his status to that of an invisible, albeit material, soul; or even that, as Dr W. R. Matthews (Dean of St Paul's) put it, 'Milton could consciously abandon the dogma of the immutability of God'.[58] Only by divesting Milton's lines of their allusion could he have drawn such a happy lesson.[59]

Be that interpretative mishap as it may, Empson's belief that Christianity should die of its own destructive element went hand in hand with his genuine desire for a more generous scheme of life and death, not with scoffing at any or all possible religious or spiritual values. It entailed too his conviction that Christianity had exercised a withering effect upon literary interpretation, insultingly reducing to pious paradox all too many productions of complex mental struggle—whether Metaphysical poetry, Coleridge's 'The Ancient Mariner', or Yeats's Byzantium poems—and so robbing them of the largest part of their human and poetic value. 'The neo-Christian method of literary criticism leads to large and unpleasant misinterpretations,' he alleged. In place of the self-serving personal theocracy of Christianity, therefore, he advanced his interest in a religious scheme with a longer and more beneficent history: a scheme in which man humbly perceives himself as being at the service of the cosmos. Interestingly enough, this benign and unbigoted conception figures in Empson's thinking as early as 1935, in 'The Use of Poetry': 'all thoughtful egotists come to disbelieve in the individual. The event, not the person, is alone and unique and includes the universe in itself.' As against the widespread critical view that Empson's examination of religion was a post-war departure from his early work on semantics and society, his central concern with ethical values is likewise adumbrated in *Some Versions of Pastoral*, as the *TLS* review had perceived in 1935: '[Pastoral] is, in fact, though he does not say this explicitly, a form of the religious idea—a means of pitting the ideal creatively against the real.'[60] It was actually in Japan at the very beginning of the 1930s that he first felt drawn to a quasi-Buddhist faith in a Spirit of Nature, even then opposing it to the Christian God who purported to resolve the contradiction of being both loving redeemer and triumphalist torturer.

The problem for the critical reception of Empson has been that he invariably intimated his positive proposals so much less prominently (in occasional reviews and letters) in comparison with his overt vilification of the Christian God that readers could be forgiven for seeing him as exclusively negativistic. But in fact the plus side in his essays and reviews manifestly counterbalances the minus. 'I did not say [the Father] was bad because he created the world,' he insisted, 'and I think that idea a disgusting one . . . The world is equally good whether made by a personal God or not.' Likewise, in response to S. G. F. Brandon's account of the tortuous teachings of Church history (already cited), he observed in 'Heaven and Hell': 'The difference between right and wrong does not depend upon an arbitrary decision by a divine tyrant', while posing as a corollary this fundamental question: 'Why is it always taken for granted that the belief in life after death (always a very strained thing) actually produced better behaviour?'[61]—for his study of Buddhism had alerted him to the redeeming fact that 'the Chinese mind habitually winced away from the belief that there had to be a personal lawgiver before the laws of Nature, at all their levels, could exist, with at their summit the Natural Law of man'.

The western world frequently takes the conception of a 'Divine Ground' as eccentric or absurdly unconventional, as Empson well knew; it seems little more than a fad imported from beyond its narrow cultural ken. But he found authoritative grounds for believing that such a faith threaded prehistory, the Renaissance and the Romantic movement. A review-essay entitled 'The Active Universe', dating from 1963, provides historical evidence for that belief, along with his personal testimony and a philosophical and ecological aspiration that is as relevant today as it was in the beginning:

> The doctrine that Nature is a spirit peopled by spirits was a return to the science of the Renaissance, which made real discoveries by using it . . .
>
> The assertions about Nature were thus partly an allegory about human affairs, but they become trivial if viewed as that only. We are nowadays inclined to resist them as being too rosy, not realising that the rosy side of them was intended as a defiance to the torture-worship inherent in Christianity . . . It looks as though the race of man needs a feeling of being accepted by the universe, such as is immensely conveyed by Shelley, if it is to live with mental health or perhaps survive at all in the world presented by modern science.

From the early 1950s, Empson consistently pursued this point: that mankind should seek not for transcendence but for conciliation with a secular universe. The proposition is continuous with the underlying message of *Some Versions of Pastoral*, that (as Guy Hunter discerned in a contemporary review) 'the simple man in touch with Nature somehow knows everything.' Hunter went on pertinently: 'This book, to use the terminology of

Dr. Richards' *Science and Poetry* (which is very relevant here) is the Scientific View criticizing the Magical View.'[62] Some twenty years later, Empson recovered ancient wisdom as the best available answer to the modern crisis. '[The Chinese] insisted on an organic approach to Nature, and this (whether or not "scientific humanism" is a suitable term) will be found the only philosophy tolerable to man in the world he is discovering' ('The Wisdom of the East').

Just over twenty years later again, in 1976, he would observe about *The Epic of Gilgamesh*: 'The desire to find some kind of relation between civilized man and wild Nature...lies at the heart of the whole story.' And there again, he discovered, western readers need to be ticked off for glossing an alien—and as far as he was concerned superior—ethos by the nasty measure of Christian ethics. 'An obstinate determination may be observed among commentators on the epic to make the gods act on moral grounds, so that the sufferings of men are punishments for their sins... This mean-minded line of moralising runs through the schools of English Literature like a plague.' In place of the Christian quest for a personal immortality vouchsafed by an 'all-executive Father', Empson thus advocated what he considered a longer-standing and selfless tradition in which the individual is accommodated to an infinite impersonality: the 'world-spirit'. It was as near as he got to being a Buddhist.

'I am afraid that nothing can purge Christianity of the Father who was satisfied by the Crucifixion,' he was to state in a preface written in 1966 for a book by a Sheffield graduate, John R. Harrison, *The Reactionaries*; 'an impersonal Divine Ground, as in Aldous Huxley's *Perennial Philosophy*, is the only Supreme Being who can be worshipped without moral shame.' And in the same piece he makes this countercharge against anyone who might accuse him of taking improper licence in his revaluations: 'The books which ought to be banned for obscenity are those which pander to sadism, but what can you expect from a state religion whose symbol is a torture?'[63]

Some while later, he would write to Ian Parsons with composure: 'a slight suggestion of lunacy and bad temper necessarily attached to Milton's God, and is now cooling off I think.'[64]

15

'They think good literature is a tremendous scolding': From Sheffield to Legon

In the summer of 1960, Empson was very pleasantly surprised to be urged by W. H. Auden to agree to be nominated as the next Professor of Poetry at Oxford after Auden himself. (Three years before, some Oxford friends had asked him to accept nomination for the Chair of Poetry, but at that time he had said he would not presume to compete against Auden.) W. W. Robson hosted a lunch party at Lincoln College which was a signal success. The poets got on famously and cracked jokes about P. G. Wodehouse (the man and his foibles rather than his work); and Empson was persuaded to stand for the appointment so long as the statute limiting candidates to Oxford MAs could be overturned in due course. 'Auden told me to apply, and is busying himself,' he informed his publisher Ian Parsons, who also offered to take steps to drum up support for him.[1] Elsewhere he professed with some modesty that he had been exhorted to put himself forward partly for political reasons, to open up the contest to poets from outside Oxford and to keep out certain homegrown individuals: 'I am...told by my side (including Auden) that I must stand because otherwise a bad candidate would get in, almost certainly Helen Gardner, a very generous-minded woman in her way but a fanatical Christian. I offered to hold my candidature in reserve to swing in someone good; but I was told that further alterations to the statute, so as to make the conditions able to appoint good men, could only be made if I carried straight on from Auden with the same recommendations.'[2] (The reference to 'good men' can be seen to have betrayed an element of misogyny among those who were so keen to prefer Empson's candidature. In a few years' time, Empson would be at war with Helen Gardner over her edition of Donne's *Songs and Sonnets*, but in 1960 he had as yet no such feud in hand.)

His one qualm related to the possibility that his flagrantly anti-Christian polemic *Milton's God* might cost him votes at Oxford, though he remained resolute that nothing should hold up the publication of the book in the autumn of 1961 (which was to be the most likely time for an election by Convocation). In the event, it was decided to hold the election in February.

Within weeks, however, he had relinquished the great game of canvassing. Robert Graves had also consented to stand, and Empson had always said that just as he would not stand against Auden, so he would not go up against Graves. He was as good as his word. 'So call off your team,' he told Parsons. 'I shall always remember the proposal and wish I had seen it in action.'[3] He was particularly grateful for the good offices of Robson and went out of his way the next year to get him an excellent wedding present—a special kind of saucepan. Summing up their several encounters, Robson formed an overall estimate of Empson as 'a man of strong and deep feeling, kind and warm-hearted. But everything was constricted and under pressure.'

Destiny would have it that it was his turn to become Deputy Dean of the Faculty of Arts at Sheffield for a three-year period starting in September 1961, to be followed by a three-year stint as Dean, 1964–7. Empson so dreaded the burden of work of those offices (and almost certainly the expectation that he would have to spend longer periods in Sheffield than the bare term-times to which he had become accustomed) that he tried to use the Oxford position as a bargaining tool to secure himself a postponement of his turn of office at Sheffield. He wrote to David Cousin, the incumbent Dean, that the state of his health, notably the crippling stomach troubles to which he fell victim at times of stress, would not permit him at one and the same period to function as Deputy Dean and to deliver the lectures required of the visiting professor at Oxford. To put pressure on Sheffield, Empson told Cousin that he had made his candidature at Oxford conditional upon his being permitted to postpone his Faculty duties—and surely it would be appreciated that the prestigious Oxford post would redound to Sheffield's credit? Also, though he had just delivered the typescript of his next book, *Milton's God*, he had two further books in hand which needed to be made ready for publication in the near future.

To further his cause, within a week Empson had gone to the doctors for tests: 'it is not alarming, as I understand,' he reported without elaboration; 'they can't find a duodenal ulcer, and after one bout of tests they said it was general irritation to the upper intestine. It can get quite painful but is not expected to explode.'[4] (With the benefit of hindsight, it seems likely that his perennial complaint of severe pains at night was caused by the acidic burning of recurrent gastro-oesophageal reflux, a consequence of excessive smoking and drinking, and possibly oesophagitis, the chronic inflammation of the lining of the gullet; his continual recourse to antacid remedies would have given some local relief.)

David Cousin responded to Empson's plea with a sympathetic and sensible letter. While neither the Oxford Chair nor the non-specific stomach trouble were conclusive reasons for postponing the Faculty duties, he said, Professor Frank Pierce (Spanish) had kindly offered to be a very proactive Deputy, especially during the vacations, to assist Empson with his duties; and yet of course everyone has what they consider to be utterly urgent research to get done—could Empson possibly see his way to postponing his publication plans?[5]

The immediate medical advice he was given was to cut out alcohol and cigarettes. A month later, as he told his brother, the stomach-ache had not gone away; but—by a terrible paradox—to present such a complaint might work to his advantage: 'if it keeps me off drink and tobacco it probably makes me live longer, and if it gets me out of being Dean it will be really useful.'[6] Three months on, it seems both that his stomach pains had got better and that he had indeed been granted a stay of his term of Faculty office. 'I am going on not drinking or smoking,' he reported in January, 'and really don't feel like either, though I am quite out of pain since I stopped. Maybe I am afraid that if they caught me drinking they might make me Dean after all.'[7] The deliberations of the Faculty officers have not been recorded, but probably they had after all decided to be simply charitable to Empson, having acknowledged that he was in any case altogether too eccentric, too disorganized, and too *distrait* to acquit himself well in the office of the Dean. In any event, for the next decade until his retirement, he did escape the office.

Five years later, when Christopher Ricks offered to put him up again to become Oxford Professor of Poetry, Empson had to admit that he could not in all honesty reconcile himself to the hypocrisy of constantly claiming ill health at Sheffield while simultaneously desiring to undertake a demanding stint of lecturing work at Oxford. 'It is very kind of you indeed to propose me again as the Poetry Professor. But it would still be an unpopular move here (if I am too ill to take my share of being Dean why am I well enough to romp about at Oxford?) and I am not sure I *am* well enough—it would be quite a strain.'[8] Instead, he himself tried hard to get Robert Lowell into the ballot (and at Empson's request, Elizabeth Smart also tried to muster support for Lowell).[9]

Yet he was by no means disengaged from university business—bureaucracy, policy, planning. He was neither disinterested nor uninterested. In 1962, for instance, he involved himself in urging the Faculty of Arts to drop the so-called 'Four-Subject Intermediate', a scheme officially devised to give students a broad base to their studies but which was actually intended 'to drive students into the smaller departments'. He believed that the requirement to study four different subjects on arrival at the university would make many students shun Sheffield, but in the event the fight was soon won, and the four-subject intermediate requirement was rescinded.

To take another example: in the early 1960s he became involved very energetically with the Theatre planning committee; and he was furious when, after many meetings and the consideration of detailed plans, the whole project was dropped in a moment of craven submission to the University Grants Committee. 'Sheffield U. is building away and trying to expand,' he wrote to a friend, 'but afraid of getting bad students and cross at being done out of its theatre.'[10] One related anecdote may show how sensitive he was to colleagues. For the installation of R. A. Butler as University Chancellor, Professor Stewart Deas (Music) composed a fanfare which was duly performed by trumpeters from the army barracks at Catterick. At the ceremony Empson sat next to Deas in the organ gallery, and as soon as the resounding notes of the fanfare died away he took care to lean over to him and whisper: 'Splendid—most arresting!' As Deas would recall, no one else paid much heed to the music—and the official recording failed to pick it up.

One venture that Empson undertook at this time that he certainly felt put him under a lot of further constraint and pressure, but which might have made a small difference to the chance of his being elected Oxford Professor of Poetry, was to record his poems for a long-playing disc—*William Empson Reading Selected Poems*—that was to be issued by George Hartley on the *Listen* label (LPV3) produced by the Marvell Press in Hull.[11] 'My kind of verse is meant to be read rather than heard, and anything which further discouraged printing of suchlike stuff would seem to me bad,' he liked to insist.[12] He was referring to what he considered the truly wretched task of recording his poems. The prospect of having his poems evaluated in terms of his personal performance was an unnerving thing to him, being an essentially shy man who was all too aware that no reader could ever hope to convey, and no listener catch (especially not without simultaneously looking over the words on the page), the compounded meanings of his poetry. Hartley's enterprise was so bravely 'amateurish' that only 100 copies of the first pressing were released in March 1961 (Empson was to receive a royalty cheque for £15 in December that year), with the consequence that the record instantly became a collector's item. Copies are indeed rare.[13]

The critic John Wain, Empson's friend, who had heard many differing kinds of readings by Empson in a variety of venues, was in a strong position to evaluate the nature of this performance; he reviewed it for *The Observer*:

> It is more restrained than his performances in a public hall. When Empson reads to a large audience, he allows himself a very wide range of sheer volume, shouting some passages like a Neapolitan stevedore, laryngitically croaking others. When reading to a handful of people in someone's sitting-room after dinner, he adopts a much quieter style, and it is this quiet style that is to be heard here. Not that there are no variations; they are particularly noticeable where there is an abrupt change of subject-matter from poem to poem. For instance, the beautifully tender and gentle 'To an Old Lady' is followed immediately by the more boisterous 'Camping Out': the first describes a stately human ruin, the second the antics of fiercely alive young lovers; the poet's voice takes on an altogether different tone, though the curious angularity of rhythm, so attractive to some and so off-putting to others, is equally present in both.
>
> Buy this record. It is like a gulp of rough, red wine after an evening of sweet, bottled cider-substitute.[14]

Empson himself was not so pleased. 'It seems my poetry disc is out,' he told Parsons, 'and the reviews have said I sound frightfully snooty. I knew I did, because I was so cross at having to carry on my back the disc-editor from the suburbs of Hull. But you can never tell; they might even prefer it snooty.'[15] But that moment in March 1960 proved to be a false dawn; it was to be 1961 before the disc was actually issued. Empson commented: 'Not bad as a prestige object, somehow, is my impression, but very little good otherwise.'[16]

On 31 May 1961 Empson and his wife would enjoy featuring among the great and the good at a banquet hosted by the Lord Mayor of London in honour of the arts, the sciences and learning.[17] Other guests included T. S.

Eliot, Evelyn Waugh, John Betjeman, C. P. Snow, Dame Margot Fonteyn, and Yehudi Menuhin. Empson and his wife, inveterate outsiders, must have felt they had somehow arrived at the epicentre of the British establishment for the arts.

More immediately satisfying and successful, albeit ephemeral, was his performance in July 1961 during a week-long poetry festival at the Mermaid Theatre in London organized by John Wain. The event included readings by everyone who was anyone from Laurie Lee to Ted Hughes and George Seferis. Even a pop group, the Shadows, was called in to back a performance by a twenty-year-old poet named Royston Ellis. (The Shadows were to become even more famous when they joined up with Cliff Richard.) Empson featured in the line-up on the Saturday night, alongside others including John Heath-Stubbs and Nevill Coghill (who was to read passages from his versions of Chaucer). Sir Ralph Richardson and Dame Flora Robson were also billed to read. So popular was the gala night—on the Saturday—that the Mermaid Theatre, which had seating for 499, could not cope with the crowd. Empson brought along Hetta and Josh, but the tickets had sold out, so Hetta and Josh had to be seated in the green room. There Hetta promptly broke a rule of the theatre by asking people around her if they felt nervous.[18]

Empson was one of the few poets of the day, as a critic for the *New Statesman* noted, who managed to look like a poet;[19] and indeed he put on a classic show. The works he read out included 'Success', which he described as a poem 'about recovering from a love affair and saying it did you good.' He remarked further, arrestingly, 'I'm afraid I take . . . this clinical view of love: it's saving you from madness'; and wittily: 'I'm not so enthusiastic as other poets have been.' 'Chinese Ballad' he introduced as a peasant poem written by a Communist during the Civil War; the man is going off to battle, but the lovers 'can't be separated if they share these two mud dolls they have made together'. Someone who was doing a critique of the ballad had given him a transliteration and asked him to put it into good English. Empson said he burst into tears when it fell exactly into the international ballad metre. The poem moved Empson deeply: it seemed to him to be magically metaphysical.

'My villanelles are frightfully stiff,' he declared when introducing his poem 'Villanelle'. It could not stand comparison with a masterwork such as the villanelle that Auden writes in *The Sea and the Mirror*. Auden 'wiped the eye of everybody who tries to revive the villanelle,' he insisted, for he has the panting Miranda utter 'a perfect villanelle . . . he's a wonderful technician.' By comparison with such genius, Empson modestly concluded his commentary: 'My villanelle is very stiff. But it's like a tombstone—it's meant to be stiff!'[20]

Not long after that event, W. H. Auden came to Sheffield to receive an honorary degree and to give a poetry reading at the university. Although he was to be put up for the night by Eric Laughton, Professor of Latin, and his wife (who found him to be a discomfiting guest), Auden made it his business as soon as possible to seek out Empson, whom he had known since the 1930s and to whom he had spontaneously given generous financial assistance in New York late in 1939. The two poets sat opposite one another at lunch in the University Staff Club, talking about Stravinsky and gossiping about other poets. Laughton noted that while Empson ate nothing at all of the meal put in front of him, Auden asked the waitress for a bottle of port and consumed the entire contents.[21] Empson knew no bounds to his admiration for Auden as a poet; and when introducing his reading that night he found a memorable formula to express his appreciation. 'Among the poets of our time (of whom I am an unimportant and inconspicuous example) two alone stand out from the rest—Dylan Thomas and W. H. Auden. They alone have the divine fire.' (He said likewise in a monitory letter to David Holbrook, who was to write a censorious book about Thomas: 'Thomas ... and Auden are the only two real poets of my age and younger. The efforts of Leavisites to get them thought bad are nasty and ridiculous, but fortunately can have no lasting effect.')[22]

He was assiduous in inviting to the university a series of guest speakers, both critics and poets; he felt it good for the students—'the children'—to hear the views of a variety of international critics. Thus, every year, he sought out an American poet or academic to encourage the 'children' with insights into a particular American classic: one year, Professor Carl Bode spoke on *Walden*; the next, Leo Marx on *Huckleberry Finn*. In 1959 he took pains to secure Allen Tate as a visiting lecturer.

Empson felt grateful to Tate for his having taken generous constructive steps in the summer of 1948 (when they met at the Kenyon summer school) to recommend his poems for publication in the USA, and he never denied his sense of indebtedness; on the other hand, he deeply disliked Tate's right-wing and condescending politics: his nostalgia for a golden age of the South—the cultivation of a dubious aristocratic civility in a world of repressive privilege.

His rage against all modes of reactionary authoritarianism went deep into his soul. The display of his resentment may have been heightened, it is true, by the personal pain he had endured when he was thrown out of

Cambridge in the name of pure bigotry; but his feelings in favour of humane generosity and moral liberalism had gradually developed into a campaign erected on fierce moral principle. Notwithstanding his personal aversion to Tate's cultural and political ideas, however, Empson was just as deeply aware that his own faith in progressive liberalism meant that he had to resist any form of censorship. No matter that he believed Tate to be wrong in the convictions he purveyed, he believed the critic had a right to express them (and then had to stand up to being judged by them). Students needed to be open to every possible point of view: good sense and judgement would make them fit arbiters of decent thinking. Thus it was with no sense of hypocrisy that he invited Tate to address the students.

During 1959 too, he tried to get Robert Lowell—whom he had befriended at Kenyon College in 1948 and whose highly wrought early poetry he admired (Lowell had not yet published *Life Studies*, though he had been working on the volume for ten years)—to come to Sheffield as a Fulbright Visiting Professor for 1960–1.[23] But Lowell, who had initially embraced the idea, pulled out late in the year; he had recently spent two months in hospital through a bout of manic depression: 'the explosion jars for a long while.'[24] Lowell was not just offering lame excuses; he fully reciprocated Empson's friendly feelings, and he enormously admired Empson as both poet and critic. He had complimented him in 1958: 'it can't be denied that almost no praise would be too high for your poems. You have the stamina of Donne, yet a far more useful and empirical knowledge of modern science and English metrics. I think you are the most intelligent poet writing in our language and perhaps the best. I put you with Hardy and Graves and Auden and Philip Larkin.'[25] Elsewhere, he hailed Empson as 'the king of the critics', and spoke with enthusiasm of the 'intellect' in his poetry; though he was also to give this opinion, at a later time: 'Empson's best poems, half a dozen or more, though intellectual are forthright'—perhaps implying by the conditional that forthrightness is really the better part of poetry.[26] However, even if Lowell came in the long run to think of Empson-the-poet as more icon than inspiration, there is little doubt that much of Lowell's own early poetry, in the 1940s, took fire from Empson's.[27] Moreover, in 1960 Lowell delighted in the articles on Milton that Empson published in advance of *Milton's God*.[28]

Three years later, in the summer of 1963, Lowell made a visit to London and was at last able to spend some time in company with the Empsons' curiously extended family at home in Hampstead. In a letter to Elizabeth Bishop he offered this irresistibly vivid account of the bohemian ménage:

They live in a hideous 18 room house on the edge of Hampstead Heath. Each room is as dirty and messy as Auden's New York apartment. Strange household: Hetta Empson, six feet tall still quite beautiful, five or six young men, all sorts of failures at least financially, Hetta's lover [Josh], a horrible young man, dark, cloddish, thirty-ish, soon drunk, incoherent and offensive, William [. . .] red-faced, drinking gallons, but somehow quite uncorrupted, always soaring off from the conversation with a chortle. And what else? A very sweet son of 18 [Jacob], another, Hetta's [Simon], not William's, Harriet's age. Chinese dinners, Mongol dinners. The household had a weird, sordid nobility that made other Englishmen seem like a veneer.[29]

It may have been during this visit that Empson told Lowell, perhaps in too frank a fashion, that he should give up the confessional, free-verse mode he had been using since *Life Studies* in 1959 (he admired the early, formal, grandiloquent poetry); Mark Thompson, to whom Empson later related this contretemps, gathered that Lowell had been offended by Empson's candour: 'the gist was certainly that [Empson] had deplored Lowell's new mode to his face, and that some sort of break, temporary or not I do not know, ensued.'[30]

But Empson was to sustain his personal loyalty to Lowell throughout the years until Lowell's death in 1977; and he took care to show his feeling for his young friend in practical ways. In the summer of 1970, for example, when he learned that Lowell was in hospital in London for a bout of manic depression, he invited the American scholar Peter A. Fiore, who was a Catholic priest and a member of the Franciscan Order—and with whom Empson sometimes talked during the summer about the text of his essay 'Rescuing Donne'—to go with him on a visit to Lowell at the Wellington Hospital in St John's Wood. The visit was very brief, as Father Fiore was to recall, because it seemed that Lowell was highly medicated. But Fiore registered to the full Empson's tact and care. 'William was exceptionally good with him, very compassionate.'[31]

Lowell reciprocated Empson's esteem and affection; he was to write to him in 1966, with no betrayal of falseness: 'Let me say again ever since I first met you in 1939 I have loved and reverenced you as my friend and teacher, as the most important teacher in England, the greatest Englishman.'[32]

On 12 May 1959 the big catch of the century was hauled to Sheffield. T. S. Eliot's new young wife Valerie hailed from Yorkshire (her family still lived in Leeds), so Eliot was in any case well disposed to accept an invitation to open the new University Library at Sheffield.[33] In addition, Eliot looked forward to meeting up once again with Empson, whose work he greatly respected (he had been eager to publish *The Gathering Storm* in 1940, and he had felt it his moral duty to secure Empson a publisher in the USA. in the late 1940s—curiously, he told the young Robert Lowell in 1947 that Empson's poetry 'was good the way Marianne Moore was'),[34] and whose personal adventures had been good for harmless gossip over the years. It was a busy day for the ageing Eliot: first, he formally opened the library, then he was conferred with the honorary degree of Litt.D. (the ceremony being conducted within the main reading room of the library), and finally, in the evening, he gave a reading of his own poems. Empson had been drinking a little before the evening's entertainment, but he was reasonably in control when he got up to introduce the grand master. (There is a story that Empson introduced Eliot as 'my friend Auden', but that is not corroborated and so may be apocryphal.) He must have been divided in his feelings between respect for Eliot as poet and courtesy to him as guest, on the one hand, and on the other a compulsion to bear witness against him as a leading neo-Christian. But, not unlike Eliot himself, he liked to be surprising: he took the liberty on this occasion to identify him—he knew him quite well enough from various lunch engagements and occasional parties over a period of nearly thirty years to realize he could do so—as one of the major mischief-makers of Modernism. As he was to say a few years later, there was in Eliot 'a certain impishness, not far from a taste for practical jokes' (he knew from Eliot's erstwhile companion John Hayward that Eliot did indeed like practical jokes), so Eliot had evidently been keen in his early years to 'pull the legs' of his critics by introducing into a poem an allusion that would fox them—or so he clearly liked to think. Thus Empson's introductory remarks, in which he mostly praised Eliot's early poetry, centred on a point of annotation which he thought a fine joke on the scholars, as he would recount fifteen years later:

> Towards the end of his life he gave a poetry reading at Sheffield, which I was set to introduce, and I mentioned that, soon after he had published 'Marina' [in 1930], a Swedish Professor had written to me (I had just published my *Ambiguity*) asking where the Latin quotation [the epigraph to the poem: *Quis hic locus, quae | regio, quae mundi plaga?*] came from. I did not know, but I asked a brother poet Ronald Bottrall, who had done well at classics, and he paused, rolling the eight words over his tongue to taste the rhythms. He said, 'If it's poetry it's very unclassical poetry. It might be Seneca, for instance. In fact, it actually is from *Hercules Furens*', and he raised his eyes from the paper, 'My God what a thing.' He had grasped at once that the words nail the reader to a dramatic moment, eternally refusing to tell whether the traveller will reach his daughter on the island paradise or be

broken on the coastal rocks—the name 'Marina', recalling the happy ending in Shakespeare, is balanced or contradicted by the first words of Hercules emerging from the madness in which he had killed his children. So I wrote happily back to Sweden, saying that the quotation was from the *Hercules* and that was why the poem was so good. One could not grumble at the technique after seeing it achieve a success, though I think a modern edition should print '*Hercules Furens*' at the end of the Latin. This was the only bit of my lead-in that won a comment from Eliot after the show (of course nearly all of it was praise, on which he would not comment). He said: 'I didn't know Bottrall was a scholar. Seneca isn't in the school syllabus, so all the classical men were caught out.' The poem is splendid . . . but it is odd to reflect that this little tease was part of its basic planning.[35]

In his private thoughts—he did not even hint at them while introducing Eliot's reading at Sheffield—Empson liked to imagine there was much more significance to be derived from Eliot's citation of *Hercules Furens* than the poet himself could possibly have been aware of. Respect restrained him from saying it in his presence. Only after Eliot's death did he reflect on this nexus, in an article entitled 'The Style of the Master', with this startled observation: 'Of course he may have been wronging himself.' A notable analytical essay on 'Marina' that Empson drafted in the early 1930s, but which for unknown reasons he never completed, shows in just what way he suspected Eliot to be 'wronging himself': he felt that Eliot, by starting off his beautiful, redemptive poem 'Marina' with a specific reference to a moment of horror in Seneca, was betraying a fundamental sense of self-misgiving vis-à-vis his own conversion to Christianity. The 'motto', as Empson called it in this trial analysis, refers to:

> Hercules' first words in Seneca when he is recovering from the madness in which he has killed his children: a madness sent from heaven, through no fault of his own, after a successful descent into hell and a successful killing of his enemies . . .
>
> So heaven, which is desirable but dangerous to arrive at, is a place where you have been tricked into disaster—Eliot becoming a Christian, which doesn't work? Or it might mean you are now waking up and finding yourself a Christian.[36]

The realization that he was encroaching upon a point of possibly libelling the great living poet must have been what stopped Empson in his tracks. In his youthful critical analysis, that is to say, he had found himself aligning Eliot with poets such as Herbert and Hopkins as exponents of the seventh type of ambiguity—because the 'total effect' of their work expresses or betrays 'a fundamental division in the writer's mind.' For obvious reasons, it was not a revelation he felt he could risk in a published piece about the foremost living poet of the period. Thus he had abruptly abandoned his apprentice critical essay on 'Marina', straight after the passage just quoted, with a shrugging and almost embarrassed phrase: 'Rather ambiguity by vagueness, anyway.'

The memory of his youthful critical trespass must have been playing with some ironic and impish pleasure in the back of Empson's mind when he introduced Eliot to Sheffield University by way of such an otherwise obscure peroration apropos the epigraph to the poem 'Marina'. What he said aloud in Eliot's presence was simply that he found it 'thrilling' to be told the source of Eliot's epigraph, and to realize its implications; after all, *Hercules Furens* was not 'required reading,' he said—so it was a pretty good joke by Eliot to have succeeded in stumping his contemporary critics so smartly. (Eliot must have appreciated Empson's remarks to this degree: not long before, he himself had expressed disdain for the 'bogus scholarship' of his notes to *The Waste Land*.)

Many readers had complained of Eliot's early obscurity, Empson went on in his introductory lecture; but after reading the later poems and the plays he only hoped that Eliot would become obscure again as quickly as possible.

Eliot seemed unruffled by Empson's teasing introduction. In his reply he commented on the large audiences that came to poetry readings—'to find something else to criticise,' as he phrased it with choice ambiguity. After a few minutes, between two of the poems he turned to Empson and mentioned some learned matter—perhaps it was the remark about Ronald Bottrall—as though Empson, as a scholar and a gentleman, would appreciate the allusion. But by then Empson's eyes had glazed over and he gave only an owlish nod.

In his own lecturing and tutoring during the 1950s and 1960s, his peculiar appearance and mannerisms and comments struck alarm into a few of the students and disconcerted others. His personal get-up was unprepossessing and fusty: he seemed invariably to wear the same old brown suit, of which he professed to be proud. 'I've worn it since before the war,' he would claim; 'it wears very well.'[37] In truth, the ancient suit was moth-eaten, dowdy and discreditable; and his belly would swag in the waist-band. All the same, able students tended to become really rather fond of him, with his characteristic self-neglect and all. The catchment area of the university at the time was principally the North of England, and quite a number of students had never in their lives encountered such a flagrantly strange being as Empson, whose 'oriental' beard was the weirdest thing they had ever seen anyone got up in, and who gave the impression, particularly when walking, of ruminating upon far-off things. The Department was fairly small in those days, so it was almost inevitable that every student would be tutored by him at some stage of their career, and have the opportunity, if they were dedicated or simply diligent, to attend his somewhat uncoordinated lectures.

For all his personal oddity, however, he worked extremely hard in all sorts of ways to draw out the students, and to prod and develop their critical intelligences. While he definitely puzzled a good few of the undergraduates, he also introduced them to perspectives they could never have envisaged for themselves. Michael Freeman, a very gifted student who took his degree in the period 1956–9—and who has described himself as a 'first-generation grammar-school student from Tees-side, straight from school and insecure socially, intellectually'—has reflected, for instance: 'In retrospect, I took from him particularly: a *workable* critical stance for my own teaching.' In addition, when Freeman became president of the student literary society, he found Empson equally generous with encouragement and practical help.[38]

On the other hand, Empson could also be convincingly severe, when he felt occasion warranted it. (As another student has put it, 'He could be unexpectedly brisk on the pastoral side.')[39] Deidre Heaton—future 'agony aunt' under her married name of Sanders of *The Sun* newspaper ('Dear Deidre')—who was then editing the student newspaper *Darts*, recalls being summoned before Empson and Francis Berry to be given 'what I can only describe as a serious bollocking'. She was about to sit her Finals, but they felt she was spending far too much of her time on journalism, at the expense of her studies. There was no question but that Empson and Berry made a most alarming pair to answer to; all she could do was protest that she wanted to be a journalist when she graduated:

> 'A journalist,' said Empson, his lip curling above the mandarin beard as if I'd said I wanted to make a career of selling small children into slavery. 'So you want to spend your life grubbing around for the little Puddlington Gazette.' He clearly thought it the most seedy of occupations. Still, they frightened me enough to make me resign my editorship and I got a II. I.[40]

It seemed to many students that Empson found lecturing to be more of a chore than a pleasure. The lectures tended to be surprisingly plain in their approach, aiming to cover the life and works of an author in a fairly orthodox expository-analytical fashion. The trouble was that sometimes they seemed also to be ill-prepared, or difficult to follow, or else vagarious in substance and structure. What was surprising about Empson's approach was that his lectures did not take the form of propaganda for his own decided views upon particular works of literature, and he never even mentioned his own books. He invariably had the lectures in his head, which may of course go far to explain his ill-assorted, to-and-fro, or somewhat shapeless performances. Usually he would bring a text with him, but it was very impressively noticeable that he seemed always to recite passages more or less from memory. David Fuller remembers one day in his final year, when Empson was lecturing on Hart Crane the next day and could not find a text. All the same, Empson arrived at the lecture with a stencilled text of Crane's 'Voyages III' which he had reconstructed from memory, though by that time he had discovered a text and told the lecture class about his mistakes so they could correct them on the handout: it turned out that in a nineteen-line poem of notorious semantic and syntactic density he had introduced errors in just three phrases: writing in, for example, 'durst arrest' instead of 'must arrest'. There were only two students present at that lecture to witness such a feat of memory—on which Empson made no comment.[41] (Also, he had shown an unusual degree of preparation in printing out for the students Crane's letter to Harriet Monroe telling her just what senses to make of 'At Melville's Tomb'—a poem which he also typed out from the text he happened to have found.)

Sometimes the lectures could be passionate, and include passionate readings from the poems: most memorably in his readings from Milton. (In his room at the university he sat under a large print of Michelangelo's *Creation*; it was quite a spectacle for a student to walk in upon—God, Adam, and Empson all in the one frame—especially if Empson was to be found sipping from a cup of Alka-seltzer. The other conspicuous picture on his wall was Picasso's awesome *Guernica*.) Usually the lectures were also highly amusing: sometimes because of his throwaway remarks, but on occasion for his antics—as on the day when he decided to give the class an idea of how Elizabethan lyrics were set by playing some for them. 'Empson operating his record-player,' recalls David Fuller, 'trying to find the desired track, and so on, produced some splendid humour.'[42] The frequent and spontaneous but invariably spot-on moments of insight and humour were always worth noting down (as Fuller did). 'Poe looks back to Europe whereas Whitman thinks of all Europeans as slaves who need to be liberated.' On foreign words in Whitman: 'He's just welcoming the

Europeans who have come to live in America, but meaning "these are quaint old languages, but you had better give them up really".' Or—surprisingly for Empson, given his conviction that the critic's task is to elucidate meaning—on Hart Crane's 'Recitative': 'It's very fine, but I don't think you should try to make sense of it.'

For probably the majority of students, he proved to be much more stimulating as a tutor than as a lecturer. In his spoken comments he could be shrewd and incisive, as John S. Whitley remembers, despite his disconcerting habit of appearing to be utterly preoccupied with scribbling vast and intricate algebraic doodles on large pieces of blotting paper. In one tutorial, as Kim Jong-gil remembers, Empson had occasion to go over Philip Larkin's poem 'Church Going', and he expressed disappointment on remarking at the first reading that the rhythm breaks down in the final line.[43] Still, a number of students found themselves flailing to follow the ingenious, obscure, or private paths of his mind. David Fuller remembers too: 'Tutorials kept me on the edge of my seat because you never knew how he was going to react to things...I said to him once (this was later, after I'd left) how much I thought *Milton's God* had influenced me. "I suppose it drove you straight into the arms of the church," he said.' Few students could quite relax in his company, but equally few were not left with the impression of being in the presence of a great man with a great mind.

He was meticulous in his marking of tutorial essays. John Whitley has remarked, 'He could be waspish about failures of grammar, punctuation and handwriting (he once referred to me as a "malignant dotter") whereas he *could* be very generous in acceptance and discussion of approaches to literature which he found relatively unpalatable (like my studies of imagery). He was fond of saying that some badly-written and derivative piece on Milton or Dickens had "told me things I didn't know".'[44] Typically, Empson would like to take away routine course-essays, even before they had been read out and discussed in a tutorial, and return them to the student laden with corrections and a detailed, respectfully engaged commentary (though now and then he could certainly be rather facetious); and—what was most remarkable—he would complete the job of correction in no time at all. The same would be true for a postgraduate research essay or an MA thesis: a draft chapter of some 15,000 words would be returned to the student, often by return of post, copiously and fruitfully annotated. On one occasion, when a student gave him back a marked essay on *Robinson Crusoe* with comments on the tutor's comments, Empson was not averse to carrying on the dialogue and so adding more comments on the student's comments; his further considerations included a generous concession: 'My remarks were insolent and obscure. I shall always feel what I was saying, though, that you don't start by realising the subject, which is a great historical event happening to get recorded.'

Despite his elevated position, however, Empson was often willing to pay students the compliment of treating them in an easy and friendly way, without condescension. John S. Whitley graduated with a First Class in 1961 and proceeded to do a one-year MA on the subject of Dickens and America. For some reason, Empson read a chapter of the thesis as it was being written—though Whitley was left with the feeling that Empson did not appear to be 'very interested in the subject of his research, even though he examined the thesis with Douglas Hamer and John Jump. His comments on the one chapter were amiable and encouraging, but vague.' However, even though Empson scarcely knew Whitley, he was aware of him and acknowledged him as a whole human being. 'Once,' Whitley recalls, 'when I was undertaking research for my MA in the Sheffield University library, I found myself sitting opposite him and he suddenly leaned over and said quite loudly: "I think we've just got time for one before they close." He then rose and left his desk quite quickly, leaving me struggling to catch up with him. He was, during this rather brief drinks interval, unusually forthcoming and gave me some very sound advice about methods of research.' (Whitley went on to teach at Sussex University.)[45] Of course, Whitley's recollection probably serves also to illustrate something of Empson's radical loneliness. 'He struck me as in some ways a disappointed man,' reflects another student, Roger Ebbatson.[46]

Michael Freeman speaks for the experience of the smarter students from the 1950s and 1960s who came to delight in their inimitably odd, gifted tutor: 'He must have been bemused, baffled, tired by the general level of the undergraduates (Sheffield didn't attract very good students then, whatever happens these days)...but I'd want to stress the seriousness, the sheer moral concern underpinning the conscientious work he put into his teaching (though without being "high-minded" about it, the lightly graceful and joky manner even when worrying-out the moral point)... [W]hen I was doing my postgraduate Education course and later in my first years of school teaching he'd nudge me every so often to keep in touch (a meal, a chat, a letter &c).'[47]

One mature graduate student who quickly developed a candid and robust, and even rough-and-tumble, relationship with Empson from the late 1950s was Philip Hobsbaum, who had arrived at Sheffield after gaining extensive experience of encouraging creative writing by way of a group he had set up in London. Hobsbaum was therefore interested to hear Empson say on more than one occasion that he was still writing poetry 'but that the poems were no good because he wasn't old enough. Writing poetry was like taking baths, he said: necessary only for the young and the old. Middle-aged gents exempt.'[48]

Born in 1932, Hobsbaum had been brought up in Yorkshire and won an Open Exhibition from Belle Vue Grammar School to Downing College, Cambridge, where he became a keen pupil of F. R. Leavis. Of Leavis he has said, unusually: 'I found him very open-minded. It was like being taught by Coleridge or Dr Johnson.'[49] After school, he had spent two years working as a temporary clerk at a National Insurance office (poor eyesight kept him out of National Service), where—or so he claimed—he wrote 2,000 poems before going up to Cambridge. Thereafter, for seven years, he wrote no poems at all; it was only when he came to Sheffield that he started once again to write a lot of poetry. Empson, as he related in an interview, would read his poems in magazines—'and I gave him the Group anthology when it came out. He used to call us generically the Christie school of poetry, after John Christie the murderer, and he said our poems were full of torture and disgust. But he was never inimical, he was very humorous about it all.'[50] (Empson did not in fact claim credit for coining the phrase 'the Christie School'; he volunteered to George Fraser, who had complained that in a recent review Empson had been far too rude about the younger generation of poets: 'I do seem to have been ruder than I meant—Lowell and Larkin are very good poets I think, but they seem to me almost my own age. In grousing about the young I meant people like Peter Porter, the group in fact which Alvarez called the Christie poets very splendidly in a recent review. (They seem to be tidying the mouldy bits of chopped-up corpses they have collected). Such was what I had in mind, but I didn't want to name them.')[51] At Cambridge, Hobsbaum had edited the literary magazine *Delta*, where he published work by poets including Ted Hughes and Peter Redgrove. After graduation, he worked briefly in television, and as a supply teacher in no fewer than twelve tough secondary modern schools in London, before becoming in 1956 a full-time teacher in a pioneer comprehensive school, Tulse Hill, in south London—where the eleven-year-old Ken Livingstone, future Labour MP and Mayor of London, who had failed the eleven-plus examination, was one of his first pupils (had Hobsbaum not left Tulse Hill in 1958, Livingstone would later say in tribute, 'I would probably have stayed on for higher education').[52] From 1955 he ran a London creative writing group whose participants included

Peter Porter, Alan Brownjohn, Peter Redgrove, George MacBeth and Edward Lucie-Smith.

Miserable in his professional occupation in London, Hobsbaum was urged by his then wife Hannah to go in for a Ph.D. He duly applied to Empson, who 'said come up and see me and we got on quite well. I told Empson I'd like to do research into divergences among the critics, and he said, Righto, start off.'[53] However, although he began writing poetry again at Sheffield, beginning with a parody of Yeats, one of Empson, and one of Eliot—being released from the burden of schoolteaching released such energy in him that he wrote four collections of poetry during the nine years it took him to complete the Ph.D.—he was soon at loggerheads with his supervisor over a variety of issues of theory and practice in literature. 'Since he associated me with Leavis, whom he detested,' Hobsbaum has said, 'there was little chance of our agreeing on any particular issue.'[54] Arriving in Sheffield at the age of 28, and with some hard-won experience of standing up for himself in rough schools, Hobsbaum had the courage of his convictions to argue back at Empson's buffetings. Empson devised a working title for his thesis that might have been a parody of his own second book, *Some Versions of Pastoral*—'Some Reasons for the Great Variety of Response to Literature among Modern Literary Critics'—and it seems characteristic that he showed little patience with Hobsbaum's views when his responses differed markedly from his own. In a published memoir, 'Empson as Teacher: The Sheffield Years', Hobsbaum outlines a fascinating series of quarrels with his supervisor, some of them being fairly disinterested, but some unerringly personal, during the three years of his full-time research career, and then for a number of years (after Hobsbaum was appointed as a lecturer at Queen's University, Belfast) by rambunctious correspondence. His research project was to examine a large range of literature, from the Renaissance to contemporary poetry by the likes of W. S. Graham, so that each section of the work-in-progress challenged Empson to reconsider his own settled views on both specific works of art and theoretical approaches—and he would in turn endeavour to shake up Hobsbaum's opinions. In particular, as becomes clear from his letters, he found it disastrous for anyone to be a categorical Leavisite, as he suspected Hobsbaum of being. 'You take for granted that no qualified person could possibly disagree with the Leavisite party line,' he rebuked him in one undated letter, 'whereas most of the time I don't even know what it is.'

He was very keen, therefore, to defend Milton's way of describing Paradise, for instance, against Hobsbaum's supposedly Leavisite charge that *Paradise Lost* suffered from too many broad areas of generalization which were rescued by passages of local coherence. 'The description only prepares for the story,' countered Empson; 'it has therefore to fit all aspects of the story. [Milton] is recalling an Italian landscape painting, Venetian I should say. [The words] are merely in keeping; that is, so far as they make any suggestions, they make these ones. The style of *Comus* would be out of place.'[55] Thinking of his own current work towards *Milton's God* he tried to explain to Hobsbaum why many critics had found fault with *Paradise Lost*: 'What I would say is that each of them interprets the poem in accordance with his theology or world-view, but pretends to be making a purely Aesthetic judgement.'[56]

Similarly, Empson waxed eloquent in arguing for a warmly indulgent view of F. Scott Fitzgerald's representation of the glamorous and arguably meretricious values of the Great Gatsby. Of Fitzgerald's novels, he wrote: 'I think they are about "what Americans feel about millionaires".' Empson felt it fair and decent for the narrator Carraway to appreciate the finer qualities in Gatsby, of which Hobsbaum and the moralizing school of criticism were darkly suspicious. Essentially, Hobsbaum argued, admirers of Fitzgerald were too often, and wrongheadedly, advancing moral arguments, or so they thought, when they were in fact making aesthetic ones. Beauty and goodness were as different as celebrity and moral worth.

> I was much brought up on old Punches [responded Empson acutely], where newly rich people like Mr Buggs and Sir Gorgius Midas are treated as pathetically funny; so the American habit of treating them with religious awe seems to me entertainingly strange, not an evil which needs attack. This kind of difference is probably what lies behind the choice whether to attack the book with supposed proofs using these extremely slippery technical terms.[57]

The 'technical terms' he reviled included 'value' used as a form of judgement, when the term had not even been defined by the critic who wields it like the scales of justice. 'It is a disgusting piece of jargon, I think, and quite recent; probably due to Leavis,' he said, before going on to exemplify his own lucid judgement of proper kinds of value: 'One should always say *what* is believed to be valuable; the only reason for talking about Values in the void is to cheat. The duty not to tell oneself pleasant lies, whether out of self-indulgence or to gain position and influence, seems to me an important Value; so does being man enough to protect one's child [he was thinking of the case of King Lear's final act of reflex justice: 'I killed the slave who was ahanging thee']. Neither of these would ever occur to a person writing in this greasy literary style.'

With regard to Hobsbaum's evaluation of critical responses to Shelley's 'Ode to the West Wind', a poem which had been much snubbed by the likes of F. R. Leavis, Yvor Winters, and Allen Tate, Empson showed that he set a great deal of store by Shelley's conception of an organic cosmos. To begin with, Shelley's skyscape, which has been derided by many critics, earned Empson's endorsement: 'The clouds make *rain*, and this dissolves them but fertilizes the earth; hence they are *exactly* like the seed-bearing. Here all the critics you quote are just missing the point . . . The rainclouds building themselves up from the Pacific Ocean were a marvellous sight from 20,000 feet; they looked like a field of beans, and of course were a major source of world fertility.' He credited Shelley's sense of a secular godhead that was not transcendent but immanent, a pantheistic world-spirit. 'Why not remember all those Chinese landscape painters, up to a thousand years before,' he tried to impress upon Hobsbaum, 'convinced they were expressing a mystical view of Nature?'

Hobsbaum acknowledged the generosity articulated by his supervisor in his defence of Shelley, but he believed too that Empson was indulging himself with the fallacious tendency to deflect critical attention away from the text and toward biography. 'However self-denying Shelley's life,' Hobsbaum later remarked, very pertly, 'self-denial in itself would not make the "Ode to the West Wind" any the better—or any the worse—a poem.'[58] But Empson remained solid in defending Shelley as poet and man of principle, against the fashion of the twentieth century. 'The moral superiority spread by Eliot among readers of Shelley seems to me rather horrid farce,' he roundly declared to Hobsbaum.[59]

On occasion, Empson's comments on Hobsbaum's drafts, or 'enquiries' as he liked to call them, seemed not so much to address the material gathered on the page as to jump from it to reflections on the literary work in question. Hobsbaum had argued, for instance, that critics, however sophisticated, had invariably tended to oversimplify Marvell's 'The Garden'. Frank Kermode had interpreted the garden as a place of innocence; by contrast, Empson in *Some Versions of Pastoral* had gone for concupiscence. Empson reconsidered:

> I am inclined now to think we were all, including myself, too solemn about the poem to recognize the social realities of the case. As a Puritan Marvell would presumably feel he ought to be fighting against Charles, but he had found a splendidly cushy job which would obviously end in improving his worldly prospects. As a papa myself I would be cross with a young man who said he didn't need to learn any skill, because all the experience in the world just soaked into him as he sat in the garden. It is impudent, just as the boast

that he no longer requires women is impudent; in short, it really is witty. However it is *like* being in a mystical state, and an intense desire to keep out of the sordidness of the world must I think be felt in that verse of *Appleton House* 'Bind me ye woodbines...'; he really did feel at any rate that he was living in an enchanted peace.

However, this suits your interpretation very well, I think.

There is a Norwegian lady who has found that Fairfax was copying out a treatise on Hermetic philosophy, I forget what, so that Marvell might have been inserting definite mystical ideas to please his patron. But I think they would still only amount to a graceful compliment.

I don't quite agree with you that mystical states can't be expressed, but Marvell wasn't doing it—he implies that that would be an excessive claim for himself, and this modesty is what makes the impudent wit graceful.[60]

In Hobsbaum's opinion, Empson in such musings was moving away from the detailed analytical criticism of his early work to a worrying habit of trying to characterize the world of the poem and the person of the author. He seemed to become more and more intent on inventing a psychology, a context, a style of mind, behind a poem; and less on what is demonstrable from its language.

Furthermore, Hobsbaum came up ambitiously with the concept of the 'Misreadable Poem', meaning a poem so deeply obscure, so inadequate as communication, that no meaning could be shown to be valid; nor could one say if any reading is wrong. In 1961 he cited the case of a poem by W. S. Graham, 'The Nightfishing', claiming that it was too obscure to be fathomed. Empson made interesting stabs at glossing the poem for Hobsbaum; and in response to Hobsbaum's complaint that Graham had sacrificed structure to local poetic effect, he devised a generous aphorism—'good texture can be seen first and makes one decide that a meaning is worth looking for'—before falling back on stating his opinion of Graham (whom he had met at the BBC).

He agreed to do a piece for the BBC about his home village, mostly in prose, and returned to the village for the purpose; but annoyed the BBC by failing to produce it after the hour had been advertised. Really I think he has been fighting like a cat to get out of the home village and become a fisherman, but he recognizes, in a way, that this is the only interesting material he has, to make himself into an author with. I suspect that that conflict is what makes him incoherent, not anything about philosophy. A nice chap and a genuine talent, however distorted.

I think he could write good poetry, because this feels so like good poetry. But I have to agree with you I don't think it comes through.[61]

But Empson and his pupil fell out most fiercely over one specific text and one critical principle. The one was *King Lear*, the other, the issue of intentionalism. In 1961 Empson felt challenged by an article in *Critical Quarterly* to defend the realistic reading of *King Lear* that he proposed in *The Structure of Complex Words*: for too long, he had argued, religiose or merely sentimental interpreters had maintained that at the close of the drama, Lear and Cordelia reach a moment of sublime coming-together, so the final word is love and transcendent forgiveness. Exegetes long to take from the play such a message of redemption, but they deceive themselves, he insisted: 'The Orwell view [that the old man is 'still cursing, still not understanding anything' at the end] thus seems to me to make a better play, so far as the difference is noticeable. The reason why no one will mention it, I think, is that it doesn't feel religious enough . . . '[62]

Philip Hobsbaum, though himself an agnostic, felt aghast at the want of consolatory uplift in Empson's stern reading; he wrote later: 'My own view is that the character of Lear develops through the play and that in the last scene he is invested with a compassion and humanity he did not have before. In particular, the predicament of Cordelia leads him to think of another human being rather than himself. The tone [of Lear's final speech, including the baleful line 'Never never never never never'] seems to me curiously ecstatic . . . If, as some commentators and as Empson in his *Complex Words* contended, Lear ended up unregenerate, the play would be meaningless . . . '[63]

Empson would quarrel with Hobsbaum at terrific length, for much of the 1960s, about their utterly opposed views of the meaning of *Lear*. Even as late as 1969, after the thesis had been presented and passed, Empson was still concerned enough about the issue to seek to lambaste his student yet again.[64] Beyond the level of gratuitous personal abuse—having once hit upon an upbraiding vein of thought, Empson went at it with vehement rudeness—in a letter that extended to some eight pages he offered a goodly parcel of perceptive and persuasive comment on *King Lear*, for example:

> . . . You keep saying that the 'value' of the play lies in the 'reconciliation' of Lear and Cordelia (p. 289, say), and this is just as good if it happens unconsciously after they are dead (p. 272). This false sentiment is miles away from the play. They could not be more reconciled than they are when crying and kneeling to each other, but while they do this the text keeps insisting we should hear the drums of the approaching army which will kill Cordelia, because her father has not looked after her properly, the audience is to reflect. She makes clear that she is just being patient with him, realising he is deluded, so you have not much ground for trying to brighten the scene

by expecting her to commit incest with him. You express contempt for some
critic who said the play outrages our instincts; well, the accidental death of
Cordelia was intended at least to outrage normal expectation in the theatre,
and did, till the critical inventions of this century. When you start prating
that Lear as a result 'wins through to an order' you make me ashamed of my
profession. *What* order, for God's sake, can you extract from his few
desperate words? Does Leavis take this peculiarly nauseous line too? I
wouldn't know... [65]

If Hobsbaum registered the vociferousness of Empson's missive, he seems
not to have taken adequate stock of the many telling points given in it.
How many supervisors engage their research students at such stimulating
length? Empson's notes on the work-in-progress were just as full of insight
and provocation. Like all the best teachers, he was constantly pricking his
pupil to think again, to stretch his mind beyond prepossession and
closure. In 1993 Hobsbaum would allege that Empson had prematurely
closed his own mind to the supposedly ultimate (transcendent) suggestions
of *King Lear* because of his intransigent anti-Christian prejudice. But
Hobsbaum's mind may have been the more closed of the two: he could
not bring himself to accept any interpretation of the concluding moments
of the play that did not find in it a redeeming moral and spiritual significance. 'Cordelia's role seemed to me that of an intercessor, showing by
example the good life,' adjudged Hobsbaum. 'Lear, in this interpretation,
stood for the human soul as subject of the intercession. It... seems to me
the only interpretation which makes sense of Cordelia's death. The union
to which Lear and Cordelia aspire is not of this world. Empson, as a
militant atheist, necessarily attacked that standpoint. But, in so doing, he
forgot that it is possible to respect a work of literature with whose
philosophy one does not agree.'[66] Hobsbaum appears not to have realised
that such a summary of their exchanges on the subject is condescending
and unjust; his own notion of Lear's last speech as being 'curiously
ecstatic' (a phrase used also in the thesis itself)[67] is every bit as deeply
questionable: it is a predilection rather than an argument from the
evidence. To be sure, very many, if not most, critics have seen a radical
ambiguity in Lear's last utterances; and it is a readily sustainable argument that when Lear urges his company to 'Look there' upon the dead
Cordelia, he is deceived, or still deceiving himself: it makes the moment of
his death all the more harrowing. Hobsbaum's assertion that the speech
can be construed as 'ecstatic' begs for analytical evidence which he does
not supply. To say the least, when he wrote his memoir about the
challenges of being taught by Empson, he overlooked the fact that

Empson, in many of his earlier notes on Hobsbaum's 'enquiries', had shown the capacity again and again to reconsider his own views. The following notes sent off during the writing of the thesis (*c.* 1963) show full well that Empson was far from simply barking up his own tree, or that he 'forgot', in Hobsbaum's words, 'that it is possible to respect a work of literature with whose philosophy one does not agree':

> I don't deny, on second thoughts, that Shakespeare may have expected the audience to reflect that Cordelia would go to Heaven; some of them would do that anyway, no doubt. What is notable is that he gives them so little encouragement. They can't expect Lear to envisage Heaven for himself and Cordelia, because he is pre-Christian, as the play takes care to remind us. Gloucester has died of joy (or rather died of the shock) of finding Edgar still alive, and Lear and Gloucester have been treated in parallel all along. We need not suppose that Gloucester fell into ecstasy because he believed that, really, he was being cheated again and Edgar was in Heaven. Why must we apply such false sentiment to the parallel case?
>
> Two or three of my BA class, when the question was used in an exam, said that the Christian religion would have been proved false had not Lear died of joy. But this year they were all certain he hadn't—the brief remarks of Barbara E. ['The New King Lear' by Barbara Everett, in *Critical Quarterly*, 2: 4 (Winter 1960), 325–39] are presumably what had this decisive good effect.[68]
>
> Looking forward to seeing you.

In April 1967 Hobsbaum published in the *British Journal of Aesthetics* a chapter of his thesis containing an explicit statement of his basic theoretical position (which he did not include in the book of the thesis published in 1970 as *A Theory of Communication*). He decreed: 'The artist's intention is only evident if it is inescapably realized in the work; and in such a case it makes more sense to talk in terms of artistic achievement.'[69] His argument was in essence a rigid restatement of a key essay by W. K. Wimsatt, 'The Intentional Fallacy', which Empson deplored: it was the logical dead-end of the doctrine of the New Criticism, he believed. Moreover, in a review (published in *The Listener* in September 1965) of the second edition of *Milton's God*, Hobsbaum had recently impugned his supervisor: 'Too much of Professor Empson's book is bedevilled with intentionalism.'[70] Irked by such an impertinence, Empson wrote in a letter to the editor: 'of course you should try to decide what an author meant; to call it Committing the Fallacy of Intentionalism is the most absurd device for self-castration yet to emerge from America. Anti-intentionalist men are usually anti-Milton men, and they accuse him pretty freely of bad or paltry intentions. The doctrine is only invoked if you refute their accusations.'[71] Thus, not long before Hobsbaum published his piece in *The British Journal of Aesthetics*, Empson urged him not to be so absolute in excluding from consideration the importance of intention as an aid towards interpretation; in January 1966 he wrote him this charming and cajoling letter:

> I feel strongly about Intentionalism, but in a psychological not a theoretical way. Maybe, as an intention is only known as it is shown, all reference to intentions can in theory be avoided. The same is true of forces, in dynamics, which never come into the equations—one might say, they live in the equals sign, where the cause meets the effect. But all the same nobody could learn dynamics without learning the rules about forces, and using them all the time. This, by the way, is not 'like' empathy but the same fact of our natures. Still, I couldn't really agree that other people's intentions are meant to be by-passed in this way; it seems to me that the chief function of imaginative literature is to make you realise that other people are very various, many of them quite different from you, with different 'systems of value' as well; but the effect of almost any Orthodoxy is to hide this, and pretend that everybody *ought* to be like Homer or Dr Leavis.
>
> Just after reading your section on Intentionalism I picked up Kitto's *Form and Meaning in Drama* and found him starting off with a sheer paragraph of questions about what the intention of Aeschylus was in the *Agamemnon*, when he wrote things which seem to us confused or absurd. 'If he was a competent artist,' the argument runs, these details ought all to be useful pointers to us, showing what his theology was or what not. Here, I grant, he is presuming the author is good, but he says later that the plays have merely to be good enough to explain why they were admired and preserved; having got inside them by this assumption, he is quite prepared to decide that a detail was merely conventional or a bit of theology really confused. Without going to the intention, which I suppose amounts here to testing the coherence of a theory about the first productions of the plays, one could not overcome the historical difficulties in such a case. Euphemisms may be devised, so that one pretends not to be talking about the author's intention, but that is what the mind will be doing really, if what it does is any good.
>
> Also, I think there is a bad reason why you and your pals are so vociferous against Intentionalism; you will not let an opponent impute good intentions to an author, but you consider yourselves free to smear him with bad ones as fast as you can invent them.[72]

Such a lesson seems to have made some impression on Hobsbaum— though at heart, as time would show, he was in fact obdurate on the subject. (However, Hobsbaum would concede, in his 1993 memoir: 'He was still alert to the process of his own writing, which remained very spirited, and to faults in mine, which on occasion he drubbed vigorously. To this day I cannot use, nor can I let my pupils use, words like "subjectivity". My employment of New Critical terminology, which he called "pedants' jabber", has become exceedingly sparse.')[73]

By 1969, when he came to re-read the thesis at a time when Hobsbaum himself was concerned to turn it into a book for publication the following year, Empson lost patience with his pupil. In the last letter he would ever address to the intransigent, immodest Hobsbaum, he castigated him further:

> What is wrong with your whole position, I still believe, stems from the self-blinding theory that a critic is never allowed to gauge the author's Intention. I must not make extravagant claims for a process which all persons not insane are using in all their social experience; I have only to say that the effects of renouncing it (in the unique case of the most delicate and intimate formulations of intention) produces dirty nonsense all the time, with a sort of tireless unconscious inventiveness for new kinds of nonsense.
>
> Above all, it means that you can never get out of the circle of rival colleagues and consider the matter freshly, as it would have appeared to the author (authors of earlier times being necessarily free from our technical jargon). What you are offering is a recipe, for the unfortunate man who has fallen into the trade but knows he has no judgement, so that he can back the safest horse . . .
>
> I notice that when you pronounce on this matter of Intention you habitually say 'Never in all my experience have we found . . . ' (that considering the author's Intention does any good); well, of course you couldn't find anything, because whenever the right solution depended on doing that you remained boastfully and farcically ignorant. Habitually imputing bad or petty intentions, with a shameless disregard of your official theory, is the next step, and in my experience nearly all the addicts take it . . .
>
> Such being my general background impression, I feel a deep interest in your report on *King Lear*; it does seem a case which needs your police-dossier approach. I do not of course feel sympathy for a scholarly technique designed to tell an aspirant which is the safest herd to join, and your claim that the play is not worth Hob's attention unless it is holy enough for Hob strikes me as eerie. But in this case the movements of critical opinion are plainly worth separate study.
>
> You say as I understand that my view of the play makes it "a piece of nasty and irresponsible trifling, brutality for its own sake" (p. 292). I was relieved to hear you making this objection with such moral rigour, because such is the way I have long thought of your own poems, and those of your whole critical school. While I was emerging from a series of eye operations

[for cataracts] I was kindly allowed an extra machine to turn on the Third Programme in hospital, and was confronted by a whole programme by George MacBeth of readings from his Christie school, including yourself. This was good luck, as I do not normally hear the machine. The programme seemed to me pettily and wilfully disgusting, and you can hardly have felt more nausea and contempt than I did then when you read my chapter on *King Lear*. The first Shakespeare audiences, you see, assumed that they were being given a warning; 'we will be able to avoid this now,' they felt, 'we have been fairly warned'. But the Christie school gives a random impression, not one of broad avoidable causes. This does not make it any more 'spiritual' . . .

There was an odd detail where you remark that what I say about [Fielding's] *Tom Jones* and what a Chicago Aristotelian says do not seem to be about the same book, and the reader is clearly meant to deduce that Empson is wrong. The Germans began to interpret English Literature around 1780, and they have sometimes been right about it, but the English have always considered them farcically wrong. The American university tradition is crushingly German. I should feel considerable fear that I must be wrong if I found myself agreeing with this author. In short, the authorities you have now decided to trust as safe ones appear to me sinking or sunk already, and your own spiritual condition, upon which you appear to plume yourself in the book, impressed me as a record low even for you. Well, this is too hopeful. But such a bad and narrow fashion can't last for ever. I hope you will not boast of being my pupil any longer without admitting that I think all your present opinions harmfully and disgustingly wrong.

Yours very sincerely
William Empson

[P. S.] You know, it seems to me you are unusually bad at estimating other people's intentions, below normal there in fact, so that nursing a sheer theory you needn't even try at it is shockingly bad for you.[74]

Hobsbaum would later protest in his own defence, 'At no point, of course, had I denied the existence of intention; but it seems to me that Empson underestimated the difficulty of knowing what it is.'[75] But in truth there is no evidence to suggest that Empson actually underestimated any such difficulties; on the contrary, he maintained only that it is arrogant and presumptuous not at least to try to do so: the anti-intentionalist critic tends to lack humility, and so presumes to speak over and for an author rather than to come to terms with a different historical culture and a different style of mind.

Empson was angry that Hobsbaum in his thesis had so smugly and rudely set aside his own detailed interpretation of *King Lear*; it was for him a watershed in his dealings with his headstrong pupil. Some time later, during an interview (20 December 1970) with Christopher Norris and David B. Wilson, it was remarked to Empson that his reading of *King Lear* was 'very constructive' by comparison with that of a critic such as Maynard Mack. He responded eagerly, albeit with a parodic edge: 'I'm delighted to hear you say that. Now, it was one of the points at which we really exploded after my long attempt to improve the mind of Hobsbaum. He said that it wouldn't be worth his while reading *Lear* if he took an entirely nihilistic view of it like Empson. And he believed it meant we're all going to heaven & I thought it great impudence of Hobsbaum who didn't believe in anything of the kind. Why should *King Lear* not be good enough for Hobsbaum to read unless it told him he was going to heaven? I refused to teach Hobsbaum any more after that.'[76]

He had been given cause to feel grave misgivings about Hobsbaum's loyalty even as early as Hobsbaum's second year as a research student. In the *Times Literary Supplement* on 14 April 1961 there appeared an article by an unnamed 'Special Correspondent' entitled 'Hull, Leeds, and Sheffield'; it was the first of a series of special reports on the topic of 'University Writing'. The article opined that academic staff in the Department of English Literature at Sheffield seemed 'on the whole friendly but distant'. The staff have 'oddly divergent' views on the students, it went on: whereas some lamented that the students were far too dependent on the wisdom passed down to them, asking for 'nothing better than to be handed lots of ready-made ideas from their teachers' mind to regurgitate' in exams, 'Professor Empson finds that at least they are independently, up here in the rebellious north, seeming generally to feel that the main use of a university teacher is as someone to argue with.' The remainder of the report on Sheffield gave enormous weight to the views of the postgraduate student Philip Hobsbaum—identified as 'founder and spiritual director of the duplicated magazine *Poetry from Sheffield*'—because he was inclined to utter his opinions at length, without tact or restraint. Hobsbaum was, it was written, '[a] man inclined to strong opinions strongly expressed'. Hobsbaum was then credited with the opinion that the academic staff at Sheffield were to be blamed 'for their failure to encourage cultural activities or indeed have anything much to do with students at all':

> There seems to be a clearcut division between the Union and the staff; and a post-graduate, distrusted by both sides, has to choose. As for the staff themselves, those who try to fraternise with the students are liable to be ridiculed by their fellows, and may even find their social standing among the

staff or their chances of promotion impaired if they persist, on the principle
that a man who hob-nobs too much with students isn't really the sort you
could give a responsible job to.[77]

Empson was furious that Hobsbaum thought to slander the staff at
Sheffield, and the social and academic culture upheld by Empson himself,
quite so impudently. But in a published response Empson took the more
wise and adroit recourse of simply mocking the hubristic Hobsbaum
(whom he chose, at once graciously and dismissively, not even to name
in this letter):

> Sir,—Your article 'University Writing—I' reports a graduate student as
> saying that, at Sheffield University, 'As for the staff themselves, those who
> try to fraternise with the students are liable to be ridiculed by their fellows,
> and may even find their social standing among the staff or their chances of
> promotion impaired if they persist . . . ' In recommendations to Arts Faculty
> committees I have often heard as an extra reason for promotion that a man
> has done extra work with students. The idea of penalizing him for it would
> be received with astonishment. I have never heard any echo of ridicule for it
> either.
>   It is romantic, in a way, to have a graduate student who believes himself
> to be living at the court of Louis XIV; he arrived here already graduated
> and with firm convictions acquired elsewhere.
>   William Empson[78]

Notwithstanding, while Empson was given plenty of cause to dislike Hobsbaum—and he definitely did dislike his critical views—he harboured no
personal grudge. Within a matter of months, he was backing Hobsbaum in
his quest for an academic post, and taking care to advise him in May 1962:

> Dear Hobsbaum,
> There would be no harm in going to America, but you must mind and come
> back; it might be easier to get jobs here after the thesis is published, anyway.
> I will certainly recommend you to America, and I don't believe my name is
> a deterrent (they think me politically bad [he suspected that the gossip about
> his pro-Chinese and consequently 'un-American' views would have been
> widely disseminated], but that doesn't come off on you). However, my
> recommendations don't seem much good in the homeland either, though
> I promise you I have been writing warmly in your favour.
>   I hope you get Liverpool (or Keele), but it might be a good thing for you
> to have the visit to America early, anyhow.
>   Yours very sincerely
>   William Empson

Moreover, later in the same session, when the time came to appoint a replacement for Douglas Hamer (who had reached retirement age), Empson wrote of the situation without a hint of animus against his pupil Hobsbaum (whose thesis was not to be completed for a further six years). He was far more concerned to seek a balance of critical standpoints among his staff. He explained to Hetta his way of thinking on the matter: 'I have written asking for letters backing ten or twelve people, which I and [Richard M.] Wilson and [Francis] Berry will mull over and then invite six or seven for interview. Fiftythree applied. Berry doesn't seem mad to have a Catholic, but he is determined not to let me appoint the Leavisite Hobsbaum, which is what the third man on the staff [Mark] Roberts had begged me to do. Better not to let either of them have a co-mate. It means choosing somebody nobody's keen on who is "quiet", a bomb in a plain van very likely.'[79] The Assistant Lectureship went to Ray Southall, who was to remain at Sheffield for over ten years (eventually leaving for a Chair at the University of Wollongong). Empson later told Southall he felt the 'menagerie' was in need of another Marxist.[80] (He was labouring under the impression that Dr Eric Mackerness, a Quaker and supporter of the Co-op, was also a Marxist.) Philip Hobsbaum was appointed to Belfast the same year, and to Glasgow in 1966.[81]

Even though Empson could send Hobsbaum in 1969 that painfully drubbing denunciation of his theories and character, he did not shun or quarrel with him in person—as Hobsbaum was to recall, 'indeed, a year later we both got plastered in the Sheffield Staff Club arguing about "The Ancient Mariner".'[82] Empson behaved as if nobody should take personal criticisms too personally.

He was immensely gratified by the respect given to his work from elsewhere during the 1960s. In Oxford in particular he commanded attention as a living sage and not just as a legendary figure left over from the 1930s. Christopher Ricks (then a young Fellow of Worcester College) would remember that Empson's star shone bright at Oxford in large part because of 'the endearingly mischievous and animating F. W. Bateson', who gave Empson a regular forum for his reflections and ripostes in the pages of *Essays in Criticism*. Ricks remembered too: 'Empson used to come to read his poems to the students' Poetry Society, and thrilling those occasions were, the poems so alive with feeling and with thinking and with thinking about feeling, all delivered with flat-tongued wit. He used to come to talk with abrupt vividness to the Critical Society, a group corrugated of brow and mildly unhappy about Leavisite nasalities [and] very unhappy about our local Lord David Cecil's belletrist impressionism . . .'[83]

It was in 1960 that Ricks sent Empson out of the blue an offprint of an article he had just published on Middleton's *The Changeling*, with its argument indebted both to Empson on the sub-plot and to Empson on Complex Words; and he was deeply gratified to receive back a two-page critique of the piece. So began a friendship of profound liking and almost unimpaired respect that would thrive for over two decades, even till Empson's death. Often, a word, a hint, a critical remark in passing, would serve to stimulate the master. It was in 1963, for instance, that Empson began to think about writing at some length about Coleridge, and in particular about *The Ancient Mariner*; and one particular exchange of ideas with the young Ricks earned this warm acknowledgement: 'I was brought into the line of reason by your remarks about the Ancient Mariner, I somehow felt, or at least they added an important element to the brew of my attempt to decide. The first thing to admit or be bowled over by is that it is a highly magical work, however flawed—like the Epstein *Jacob and the Angel*.'[84] When Empson was introduced on a later occasion to Ricks's mother, he would offer the spontaneous tribute: 'Your son saved me.'[85] He meant he had found his ideal reader: someone who took his ideas seriously and would respond to them with respect. In 1970 he was to refer to Ricks, in a letter to his publisher, as 'my warmest supporter.'[86] There was enormous mutual affection. Equally, he was ready to dispute matters with Ricks, and to give him a tease on the occasions— albeit they would be rare—when he felt it was in order; in 1962, for instance, he would compliment Ricks with spirited ambiguity on an essay on *Great Expectations* which he had contributed to a volume of essays: 'I thought your essay on Dickens was much the best. A laborious rediscovery of the obvious, like reluctant sprouting in an overcast spring, seems often to go on among the young critics now; it should be welcomed contentedly but one can't feel much more. Your one had great sureness of feeling and almost made me want to read that painful book again.'[87]

Ricks, as soon as he too became one of the editors of *Essays in Criticism*, was adept at getting his idol to read and perchance to review books that he reckoned would most stimulate or provoke Empson. To cite a burning example: early in 1962, knowing of Empson's enormous admiration for the poetry of Dylan Thomas, Ricks made sure to supply him with a copy of David Holbrook's *Llareggub Revisited: Dylan Thomas and the State of Modern Poetry*, a critical volume dedicated to exposing Thomas as infantile, obscure and egotistical.

Empson's fighting defence of Dylan Thomas came out in *Essays in Criticism* 13: 2 (April 1963):

Mr Holbrook says that Thomas was incapable of generous love but craved for escape to the breast, for mothering; this allows denunciation of his later poems such as 'Fern Hill', which many people had thought a great turn for the better. For myself, I am thankful to have got out of being young; but it is absurd to denounce poets who find a mystical beauty in the child's delight and wonder at the new-made world. The child Dylan is always presented adventuring away from Mum, sitting on carthorses and suchlike... Dylan at seventeen or so was the Young Dog, determined to find sexual pleasure; like many other young men, he did not revere his childhood till he was safely past it. He did fear, we gather, that the precocious sensuality of his powerful imagination would warp his growth ('And I am dumb to tell the crooked rose | My youth is bent with the same wintry fever'); but even this serves to deepen his intuitive sympathy with all life... Mr Holbrook is always telling poets to brisk up and show public spirit, but when he is given it in the grand Dostoevsky manner he cannot imagine it...

The thought that events inside the skin of Dylan are like geographical or cosmic events outside it is inherently far from common social life, but cannot prove he had bad intentions about that; and he tends to present himself as the representative of mankind, but merely because any man would do as a specimen. Donne does the same thing. Mr Holbrook works up his denunciations about this to the point (p. 102) of accusing the jealous Thomas of telling Jesus to get back into the womb because he wants to be the Messiah himself. The idea that any man can become Christ, who is a universal, was a major sixteenth-century heresy and has been kept up among the poets... A prominent Malvolio has a duty of consistency in suppressing cakes and ale; if a poem laughs at Malvolios, he must say it 'reinforces untenderness. It is a cruel work, inviting our cruel laughter.' This is *Under Milk Wood*, which I find beautifully tender but at times a bit sentimental (the audiences at the play are obviously not being spurred to cruel laughter)... [Holbrook] aims to destroy in principle the poetry of Dylan Thomas, and one gathers that he would include any poetry of the Auden and Thomas generations which had the real fire. He wrote to the *Times Literary Supplement* explaining in defence of this attack on Thomas that he had to write it 'before I could take myself seriously as a poet at all'. As he is a poet whom no one else need take seriously this is rather a majestic enterprise, likeable in a way if not viewed too gravely.[88]

It was Oxford too that paid Empson the honour of devoting to his life and work a special issue of the literary periodical *the Review* (numbers 6 and 7), published in June 1963 by the 25-year-old poet and critic Ian Hamilton.[89] (The only other special issue to that date had been number 4, dedicated to T. S. Eliot.) The contributions included a well-researched essay by Martin Dodsworth on Empson's student work in the 1920s; a piece by John Fuller entitled 'Empson's Tone' which argues that the prose is almost certainly more influential (even upon other poets) than the verse; a fine exposition of the poem 'Legal Fiction' by Saul Touster; an overview of the poetry by the editor himself, who finds the early poems hampered by their intellectual jesting and pointless dexterity: 'In a sense it is the thirties and their terrible public events that expose the narrowness of Empson's early manner and demand from him the handful of poems, stanzas and single lines that argue his considerable potential.' ('Ignorance of Death' is among the very few poems to manifest the 'pressure of feeling' that Hamilton favours.) Empson's own student Philip Hobsbaum (who was at this time just three years into his long research), presumptuously offering his judgement on his research supervisor's merits as a 'critical practitioner', makes it abundantly clear in his essay that he finds Leavis the greater and more enduring critic of his two major teachers. 'How can one evaluate a Leavis as against an Empson?' he asks. 'The obvious distinction is one of moral concern: a critic like Leavis will feel that some poems are better for the universe than others ... This has produced an incomparable body of critical work, embracing many periods and literary forms. It is the way of the ideal reader ... ' He goes on:

> In comparison with Leavis, Empson seems to write only from special interests. He has not tackled any field systematically ... What [Empson's work] lacks in system and inclusiveness it makes up for in sharpness of perception. Empson is hard to read in bulk, bitty in argument, and liable to seem wrong-headed—especially on poems one doesn't onself like. But this is true of practitioner-critics such as Coleridge and Keats, who resemble Empson more than he does any of his contemporaries ...
>
> Leavis will always remain the critic for the educated man, in the best sense of the word: the man who wants to see literature whole. But Empson is likely to stay, thumbed and rumpled, at the bedside of the erratic and irreverent creative artist. (pp. 19–20)

Really, it should have come as no surprise to Hobsbaum that every so often Empson would feel outraged at his impertinence, and be aggressive back.

The most illuminating piece in the issue was also a unique item. 'William Empson in conversation with Christopher Ricks'—recorded in Oxford on 9 February and edited by early March—was the first published interview with Empson, who was then a few months into his fifty-sixth year. It is a charming, witty, self-deprecating performance, including some helpful comments on specific poems such as 'This Last Pain', 'The Teasers', 'Aubade', 'Courage means Running', and 'Let it Go', though it is also bulked up with enough crisp opinions and personal revelations to be true to his conversation.

> The first book [*Poems*, 1935], you see [he discloses among other things], is about the young man feeling frightened, frightened of women, frightened of jobs, frightened of everything, not knowing what he could possibly do. The second book is all about politics, saying we're going to have this second world war and we mustn't get too frightened about it. Well, dear me, if you call the first brave and the second cowardly, it seems to me that you haven't the faintest idea of what the poems are about. And so I do get irritated when I see these disciples of Dr Leavis still repeating that the second volume showed a failure of nerve. You may say it's a failure of nerve to stop writing altogether, but I don't know that I think that. It wasn't a failure of nerve to write *The Gathering Storm*: I still say that.

Asked about his influence upon poets of the 1950s, and by implication about his opinion of contemporary poetry, he claimed to have little interest in recent poetry: a stance splendidly justified by way of a parable out of Samuel Butler.

> Well, honestly, I don't like much of it. But it's largely because I'm an old buffer: the point has been reached where it is unusual for new poetry to seem very good to me. I haven't liked it very much; but I haven't liked any poetry, whether it's supposed to be imitating me or not. This seems a fairly irrelevant angle, but the fact is that I don't react very readily to any modern poetry. I was hearing a young poet give a reading of his work, and he was explaining afterwards how much he hated all the other ones his age. He was talking about one of these and I said 'He has a singing line, hasn't he?' Meaning, as I thought, that he had the root of the matter in him. This chap pounced and said 'That's it, you've got it! Just a writer of lyrics!' He thought that if it sounds pretty that means you're bad. Well, I thought he hadn't got the root of the matter in him. Milton could say 'God damn you to hell' and make it a singing line, but these people think it's got to sound ugly or they aren't sincere. I think it's Samuel Butler who describes a wallpaper of the Victorian period, with flowers on it, and he says that some bees came in and they went to every one of the flowers all the way down and then they went to every one of the flowers all the way up and they tested every one of these right across the area, and they never realised that *none* of the flowers had any honey.

When asked about the influence on himself of John Donne, on the other hand, he spoke with a sense of fervent personal association which would

come as a revelation to those readers who believed his poetry was all about
intellectual trickery; the true notes are conflict, courage, and the vanquish-
ing of madness:

> I still think he's wonderful. I think he meant something: I think he was
> attacking Christianity in his love poems. This has gone completely out, it's
> completely out of fashion to believe that . . . But this movement of fashion is
> all nonsense: it needs to be removed. Once you realise the love poems are
> defiant, you think they're good and courageous again. As long as you think
> they are only fribbles by a man who fully accepted the Church and State he
> was quarrelling with, you think it's in very bad taste. Of course it seems in
> very bad taste if you think it's all nonsense. So I think this misunderstanding
> of Donne is the result of the entirely mistaken criticism which was led by
> T. S. Eliot, in a book called *A Garland for John Donne*, which was, in fact, the
> kiss of death, the crown of thorns. When I was starting writing there was a
> lot being written—by Robert Graves as much as anybody—about how
> poetry ought to be about a conflict . . . [The] poem ought to be about a
> conflict which is raging in the mind of the writer but hasn't been solved. He
> should write about the things that really worry him, in fact worry him to the
> point of madness. The poem is a kind of clinical object, done to prevent him
> from going mad. It is therefore not addressed to any public, but it is useless
> to him unless it is in fact clear and readable, because he has to—as it were—
> address it to the audience within himself. It isn't expressed unless it's a thing
> which somebody else can read, so if it's obscure it actually fails in this
> therapeutic function, it isn't saving his sanity.

'I thought Hamilton had done some good editing on our recording, and I only
made small face-saving changes,' he told Ricks, along with a glum judgement on
his own performance: 'I think I sound very cross, not jovial at all.'[90]

In the early 1960s too, he enjoyed a brief moment as a pundit, or
'personality', on the television. In the summer of 1961, for instance, he
was engaged for a day to enlarge upon his opinions for a newly independent (commercial) TV channel on the subject of the European Common
Market. ('We'd be mad to join the Common Market,' he had declared one
day to a colleague at Sheffield. 'Underneath us the ground is constipated
with coal.' He was a Little Englander in his thinking on economics.) He
told his brother at the time: 'I understand they were canvassing English
opinion on the Common Market, housewife, bus-conductor, student and
so on, and thought Professor would go all right on the list.'[91]

More satisfactory, and more satisfying to himself, was his contribution to
a BBC *Bookstand* programme on W. H. Auden, in which he paid his usual

wholehearted tribute to that 'great' poet. He wished that he himself had been at Oxford, for he lacked what he called that 'curl of the tongue' which enabled Auden and his fellows to write so compellingly about the politics of the 1930s, including the need for a popular front against Hitler, for more socialism, and for the Welfare State. Some of the 'Pylon' poets had reneged on their early political convictions, he went on, but he never doubted they had been correct in their views: 'I think they were quite right, I just didn't know how to do this kind of poetry. And it does rather depend on the curl of the tongue.' If Auden was not writing so well in the 'gloomy' postwar world, Empson still spoke up for the greater poet: 'It may well be that he'll find interesting things to write about again; and, besides, a middle-aged poet often isn't very good: he often gets good again when he's old. I even hope it may happen to me.'[92]

He was back in Sheffield (where the bare Burrow had no television) when the programme was eventually broadcast in the autumn, but Hetta regaled him: 'Poor old Auden looked very broken on the box whereas Pa was splendidly whole and youthful. Al [Alvarez] talked at Auden in a reverential but kind of uncertain way, so that the whole thing came out rather oddly—Pa was vigorous and clear. We were all very admiring and love you.'[93]

Still more exciting was the prospect of being the subject of a BBC television profile in the 'Monitor' series, produced by Christopher Burstall. The production was to involve various segments of location film shooting, since the programme would cover the life from early years in Yorkshire to later fame. In March 1964 he made a reconnaissance trip to the family home and farmlands by the River Ouse, since Burstall was much taken by the poem 'Flighting for Duck' and wanted to film the photogenic poet, with his beard flying horizontally in the wind, against the backdrop of Yokefleet, the river, and the alluvial farmlands. The opening lines of the poem convey a rapt, exact description of a natural scene; they were proving irresistible to Burstall, though in the event they were not to be featured in the broadcast programme.

> Egyptian banks, an avenue of clay,
> Define the drain between constructed marshes
> (Two silted lakes, silver and brown, with grass,
> Without background, far from hills, at evening).
>   ...   ...
> The darker silhouette is where a barn
> Straddling two banks over a lesser channel
> Stands pillared upon treetrunks like a guildhall

> Empty, mudheaped, through which the alluvial scheme
> Flows temporary as the modern world.
> The mud's tough glue is drying our still feet.
> A mild but powerful flow moves through the flats
> Laden with soil to feed the further warping.

Empson explained the meaning of the lines in an anthology put out in 1951:

> This poem is about shooting on my brother's land, where I was brought up, in Yorkshire. We call it *flighting* when you wait round the marshes in the evening for the ducks to come and settle there to feed; they come at dusk and you go on as long as you can see. This country lies on the river Ouse, which joins the Humber estuary a mile further down, and the marshes are human products made for the purpose of *warping*, that is, enriching the soil with the river mud; you let the tides in on the selected fields for one or two years and then drain them again. All the land is under the hightide-level like coastal Holland, and indeed was drained by Dutch engineers in the seventeenth century, who are among my ancestors. The *Egyptian* diggings are of course the great drains, which may be up to forty feet deep and a mile or two long, ending with a lock gate at the river bank which shuts automatically as the tide comes in unless you are warping. I believe there has been no warping done there since the one I was writing about, but it will have to be done again some time if the value of the land is to be kept up; the effects only last for about a generation.[94]

'It seems quite fun so far,' Empson wrote to his brother after staying over for a night at Yokefleet Hall (where Burstall had insisted on scouting for locations), 'though I daresay it will get painful before the end.'[95] The programme, finally broadcast on Monday 26 January 1965, and introduced and edited by Jonathan Miller, was in fact to be a pure pleasure. Empson appears to be relaxed and genial in every shot—filming took place on the sea coast of Yorkshire, in and out of Yokefleet Hall, in the plain dull enclosure of the Burrow at Sheffield, and in a gallery of the British Museum where stood the wooden South Sea island statue creeping 'with all the creeds of the world' that had inspired the poem 'Homage to the British Museum'—and he showed a striking ease when speaking direct to camera. The opening shot shows Empson walking on a foreshore, with the sun-comprehending sea beyond, while a voice-over characterizes him as being 'full of fight and perky humour', as a man of 'clear sight, honesty, no self-pity'. The narration goes on to report that he had spent much of his teaching career in Japan and China, both before and after the war, where he took an interest in Far Eastern arts, notably images of the Buddha which Empson described as 'not all as we tend to imagine: not all snobbish, gluttonous or complacent.' Nowadays he works in Sheffield, a city full of factories and ringed by hills, 'looking,' as the voiceover teasingly suggests, 'in some lights anyway, like a latterday El Dorado.' We are then introduced to the pokey alley—'in a district which has known better times'—where Empson lives in his sorry burrow, across a rubbly 'area'. But he was born to another kind of outlook, we are told: the world of upper-class self-assurance that was represented by Yokefleet Hall near Goole.

The first of five poems to be featured in the programme was 'Homage to the British Museum', being recited by the actor Alan Dobie as the camera pulls back down a museum gallery to reveal Empson's 'supreme god'; details of the icon are lingered on. The poem, Empson explains, was 'a little joke against museums...or against the expectation that a broad culture will make us wiser.' After a cut to Yokefleet Hall, Empson reveals that the poem 'To an Old Lady' was about his mother. While the poem is recited, the camera dwells evocatively on deeply shaded facets of Yokefleet: 'What these pictures are meant to bring out,' Empson notes after the poem, 'is the romantic charm of the small estate where I was brought up. I was terribly shy about this as a young man...I felt it would be horrible bad taste to tell anyone else about Yokefleet, though I was secretly proud of it and thought it was very fine.'

Working in Japan in the early 1930s, when Japan was beginning its assault on Manchuria, the League of Nations collapsing into shame-facedness, and a world war appearing to be imminent, Empson next remarks, he wrote the poem 'Aubade' which links together 'a sordid love story and a grumble about world politics.' Of his fourth poem, 'Just a Smack at Auden', Empson amusingly reflected: 'My attempt at being worldly was a sad boss shot. Yet it does I think convey the exasperatingly farcical or hysterical effect of what Winston Churchill called the gathering storm: the slow devious approach of the second world war.'

To close the show, Alan Dobie recited the poem 'Missing Dates'—

> Slowly the poison the whole blood stream fills.
> The waste remains, the waste remains and kills.

—as the camera lingered on the poet's face as the light faded to a final darkness.

The Empson who came over on the TV was a civilized, clear-sighted, amiable, wry, and quizzical figure. Slightly paunchy, with keen dark pouchy eyes and fleecy beard, he looked perfectly respectable if strange; in every shot he wears what appears to be the same dark suit and tie, and a pale sleeveless pullover. The programme was indeed well received, by friends and strangers alike. The writer Anthony Burgess, for instance, who had just spent a week researching Joyce in Dublin, lamented in a column for the *Listener* the general absence from the TV screen of articulate artists who command the language.

> William Empson, for instance—cleanser of language, the revolutionary who saw how ambiguity, so shamelessly exploited by the politician, could be a legitimate tool of the poet. Well, he had his own piece in *Monitor*, and very moving it was, as well as enlightening. I'd been out of touch with his verse for some years (no excuse for that: there's not much of it), though I can recite some of his lines in pubs and did so in Dublin. I was sent back to his collected volume after Alan Dobie's fine readings and the poet's own good-humoured and lucid commentaries. The visual accompaniments to the poems were no mere marginal decorations. The corpses that illustrated the famous smack at Auden showed the depths under the gay ingenuity, and 'Aubade' ('It seemed the best thing to be up and go . . . The heart of standing is you cannot fly') was turned into a new experience by those Japanese earthquake scenes, which added the context of an *occasion*. The range of meanings was similarly extended for 'Legal Fiction'—which I can recite by rote but realize now that I never really understood. This programme brought out the seven, and more, enigmatic convolutions beneath the poet's genial, mandarin-bearded personality. At the end it merged his image into fire and sea and turned him into a myth.[96]

The only person to feel at all chary about the prospect of the broadcast was Empson's older brother Arthur, who contacted him just a week before it went out to ask whether he should not have been given the option to review the script to be broadcast, to pick up on anything that might strike a false note or trespass upon the family dignity or the family property. 'I am so sorry about this,' Empson blustered back by letter (seemingly calm but probably quite agitated by his brother's last-minute intervention); 'it never occurred to me that you should be shown the text of the part about Yokefleet, though of course they are liable to be in bad taste, and I was anxious not to let them be. I don't believe there is anything you would dislike, but I will write off at once and tell Burstall to let you see a copy of the script quickly. The thing is due to be peformed today week.'[97] Soon after the day of the broadcast, Arthur sent a telegram to his kid brother; things seemed in the main to have passed off all right, but it would be useful if William would comment on what he had said about his mother in the context of the poem 'To an Old Lady': it would not do to have exposed the old (and long-deceased) lady to any disrespect on the TV.

Thank you for your telegram [Empson responded by letter]. I think the TV worked out all right—it was frankly putting on a show, and the camera had always got something to work on.

What I meant by the line 'But in darkness is she visible' was that you only found out what a strong support she was when you were in real trouble; and this I felt very strongly when I was chucked out of Cambridge; but I must have written the poem before that, and do not remember now what example I was thinking of. Naturally I did not mean to blame Mother for trying to scold me into passing exams; I am feeling rather guilty just now for not driving on poor Jacob enough, and not at all tempted to blame parents. But I don't think other viewers thought I was meaning to blame her at all.

Oh well, it has passed off all right I hope.

Your affectionate brother

William.[98]

The sometime scapegrace still felt, at the age of 58, that he must keep in the good graces of his older sibling, the one-man watch committee of the family.

Still, his sister Molly liked it; she enthused by letter: 'It was excellent, quite gripping, I thought.'[99]

Yet it was always more important to Empson not merely to publicise himself but to speak out on issues of real public concern, whether literary or social. His published interventions were motivated by urgent moral concern; so it seemed to him not merely a literary or aesthetic matter to seek to correct the contemporary understanding of authors who were dear to him, especially when their works were being appropriated by smugly Christian interpreters. In matters of political and social conscience too, he did not hesitate to speak his mind. Specifically, for example, by 1957 he had come to believe, without hesitating on account of professional discretion, that he would have to speak out categorically against the further development of the nuclear bomb. In November 1957 J. B. Priestley was to publish in the *New Statesman* an article 'Britain and the Nuclear Bombs', which galvanized a campaign against the arms race, against the necessity for Britain to develop the hydrogen bomb.[100] Empson had written to the press on the selfsame issue on 30 September 1957:

Atomic Warfare

One is tempted to feel merely hopeless about the matter. If politicians have the power to destroy the human race they will almost certainly do it some time, and probably quite soon.

To be sure, a national leader who had only to press a button to make one last bang would be very likely to be cheated by his technicians; for example, Hitler before he killed himself would probably have pressed this button, and probably have found it was mysteriously out of order. But if the method is one of gradually poisoning the planet by 'trials, 'localised wars' and so forth, never knowing for certain which is the point of no return, with the fatal result merely that most of the childbirths produce lunatic cripples, then the world leaders all do seem desperately liable to blunder into it. The problem, of course, is not one the human race has been faced with before; till now, after any amount of destruction, however lunatic, there were always some people left alive somewhere else.

The only hope seems to lie in rousing very strong public opinion against this procedure, in all the countries with the technical skill to do it; and not merely on a basis of blaming other countries.

W. Empson
Sheffield University

When the Campaign for Nuclear Disarmament (CND) was launched on 17 February 1958, at a mass meeting at Central Hall in Westminster, Empson was among the first to pin his colours to the mast. He was prepared to turn out for a rally or a protest march—such shows of personal conviction and public feeling would remind him of his proud participation in the big parade marking the inauguration of the People's Republic of China in 1949, and at the anniversary parade in 1950—but he would feel himself to be of most use in writing letters to the press which would cry down false witness.

In an article with the deceptively disinterested title, 'The Question of the Bomb' (*The Spectator*, 18 April 1958), Irving Kristol—who was co-editor, with Stephen Spender, of *Encounter*—set out an impatient argument against advocates of nuclear disarmament. 'One listens in vain to their chorus for a clear response to the question of whether it is *ever* possible that no world should be preferable to some worlds. Are there in truth *no* circumstances to which they would feel that the destruction of human life presents itself as a reasonable alternative? ... The choice for Europe is not between servitude and survival on the one hand and catastrophe on the other. *That* choice is out of its hands. The real European choice is between a military readiness to defend itself with conventional arms, which means having to do without as many television sets, cigarettes and washing machines as it would like; and an unqualified reliance on the deterrent value of the Bomb, with all that implies.'[101] Of course, he implied in an ultimate cynical twist, no one is ever really prepared to make even such small sacrifices; *ergo*, the Bomb be it.

Deeply resentful of Kristol's possible complicity in the putative funding of *Encounter* by some arm of the CIA, Empson hurled off this letter:

> Sir,—To understand the mind of Mr Irving Kristol, I think, one must realise (and it is a very different thing from imputing low motives to him) that he is a dedicated American patriot, who thinks it his duty to help make her satellites do what she wants by absolutely any line of talk which might serve the purpose...
>
> What is intriguing about his proposal, that we should settle down to devoting our substance to providing America with cannon-fodder and 'conventional armaments', instead of trying to look important, is that it is so very close to the proposal for which he expresses such contempt, the proposal to renounce the atom bomb. It is tempting to suppose that he could realise what he was doing there; did he perhaps mean to kill the proposal by his eerie support for it?
>
> However, it does look from his high-minded first paragraphs about suicide as if he honestly cannot understand the objection to destroying all life on this planet, even the fishes at the bottom of the sea. Millions of years of evolution are expected for this planet, if only we do not prevent them; surely it is obvious that, at some point in that enormous tract of time, it would cease to seem very important whether the Americans or the Russians had won...[102]

A few days after the publication of his letter, Empson wrote to Alice Stewart: 'I was so frightened about that letter to the *Spectator* that I bought the paper in the morning and didn't dare look at it till I had had some drinks in the evening; because I am certain that he would be delighted to have an English libel action, with any amount of American money for propaganda to throw behind it. I am still rather frightened about what he will say tomorrow, but as soon as I could get myself to read it over I felt sure he couldn't actually fight a libel action on it.'[103] It was not just Cold War paranoia that led him to think in such a way: it was not very many years since he had come close to libelling Arthur Koestler. But there was to be no outraged and litigious letter from Irving Kristol: indeed, no further letter at all from him to the *Spectator*.

From 1960 to 1963 there was at Sheffield University a keen CND group which Empson's junior colleague Derek Roper helped to run. Empson was an early member, Roper recalls, and he would invariably come to the meetings (which would often be addressed by external speakers such as

Dr Antoinette Pirie). On one occasion Empson became very passionate, and mordantly ironical, about the idea that the Bomb might destroy all life on earth—not just human life but even, he emphasized (in an echo of his letter denouncing Kristol), 'the fishes at the bottom of the sea'. The thought was particularly abhorrent to him, and he was to repeat the phrase more than once.

During the Aldermaston marches of those years, the Empsons would invite the Sheffield contingent to sleep on the floor at Studio House (usually on the night before the march reached central London); and then Empson—who was anyway a fleet-footed walker—would usually join in the last leg of the march. He would face the march not grimly but in a spirit of carnival, for there could be some diverting incidents (as he told Robert Lowell in 1962):

> I generally do the first day of the Aldermaston March, as it is through nice country with a few spectators, and the Anglican parson of a parish along the route has been tending to crack up under it. He began by handing marchers his parish magazine, which explained that destruction of the world by the atom bomb was fully sanctioned by prophecy, and could be expected from the texts to be quite rapid and decisive, and after all it was high time, so why complain? 'I don't know how you feel, but this is how I see it' he was saying gruffly and very like an officer and gentleman as he first handed the copies out, some years ago now. But they came in greater and greater numbers, like locusts; I am told he began hitting out at them at random, and he is no longer seen along the route now, this year or last I think.[104]

Many years later, when reminiscing about the marches, Empson was to recall a nervous question put to them by a waiter in a hotel en route. Could anyone go on the march? 'Yes,' said Empson, 'you don't have to pass an exam!'[105]

The presence of his famous face among the motley marchers was even commemorated at the time in a poem by Alan Brownjohn, 'William Empson at Aldermaston'. While only the title refers directly to Empson, he is clearly identified—and indeed the title of the poem implicitly reckons him to be a moral leader—for his principled involvement in the demonstration against the 'trim, discreet pavilions of the State' at Aldermaston. For all the 'gaieties' of the day out, Brownjohn notes in his poem, there were uncanny differences between the marchers and the onlookers, whether policemen or civilians:

> This side there seemed
>
> Some thousands. while of death's there wasn't one.
> Just the white-braided police returned the stare

Of the boys with haversacks, or the fierce
Empirical gaze

Of the man with the Chinese beard . . .

All the 'tight and puzzled faces' looking out at the march from their houses were baffling to see, Brownjohn remarks. There were bands and there was singing, and guitars were being played; yet so many children stayed indoors.

No coloured hat, not one
In all the range of shirts and slogans worn,
Seemed odder than these faces. That deep blankness
Was the real thing strange.[106]

That final line pays ironic, allusive tribute to Empson's own puzzled poem, 'Let it go', which starts off: 'It is this deep blankness is the real thing strange.'

Empson's growing repute as a public figure who was unafraid to stand on principle was further acknowledged when another legendary campaigner, Bertrand Russell, invited him to join the British 'Who Killed Kennedy?' Committee set up in the wake of the Warren Report into the assassination of President John F. Kennedy. There were too many question-marks over the findings of the Warren Commission, it was widely acknowledged, especially in the light of the truly startling and impressive evidence subsequently gathered by Mark Lane, an American lawyer who had appeared before the Commission.[107] Lane had originally been retained by the mother of Lee Harvey Oswald to conduct a posthumous defence of her son, and his findings served to fuel the theories of a conspiracy reaching right to the heart of the American Government (which will probably never be resolved or explained).

'Dear Lord Russell,' Empson engagingly replied on 1 June 1964,

Thank you for the circular and enclosure, and I accept your offer; I agree to be on the British 'Who Killed Kennedy?' Committee. As you say, it seems harmful to let the matter remain in its present state of evident confusion.

The case for a gradual development of self-government among colonial peoples has always seemed to me strong, and whatever one may think about Kenya or the Congo valley it does seem clear that the liberation of Texas was premature.

Yours with much respect
William Empson.

Russell was almost certainly correct to suspect, as he did, more than a hint of irony in the second paragraph: a flourish of Empson's anti-American sarcasm. 'Thank you for your delightful letter of June 1st,' he replied conspiratorially. The formation of the committee, with other members including Michael Foot, Kingsley Martin, Sir Compton Mackenzie, J. B. Priestley, Sir Herbert Read, and Kenneth Tynan, was announced in the *Times* on 10 June.

However, Empson was not a man merely to put down his name and then sit on his hands. As the debate about the unconvincing findings of the Warren Commission raged on throughout the summer of 1964, he took pains to position himself among the disbelievers, in a letter to the *New Statesman* in October 1964:

> Sir,—May one suppose that the people who call it 'cynical' to doubt the Warren Report have not yet read the 'Comment on the Report' by Mark Lane? If they have, why do they not attempt any reply to his arguments? So decisively strong do these arguments appear to me that I have to make an effort not to suspect of cynicism the people who accept the report.[108]

Russell wrote in November to thank Empson for the impact of his contribution. 'It was most welcome and has considerably helped the work of our Committee which is unable to get many of its own letters published.'[109]

With the coming of the horrors of the Vietnam War, and the furious protests that took place in the mid-1960s, Empson was again prompt to declare himself against wretched foreign policy. At the Cochrane Theatre in London in mid-July 1966, a large gathering of British and Commonwealth artists, academics and journalists sought to demonstrate their dissent from the British Government's policies vis-à-vis Vietnam: specifically, that is, against Prime Minister Harold Wilson's expressed support for President L. B. Johnson. The speakers on the occasion included Phillipe Devillers, a Professor of Political Science and author of *The History of Vietnam, 1940–1952*, and Dorothy Woodman, author and specialist on south-east Asia; the actors Robert Lloyd, Ian Holm, and Patrick Stewart recited a roughly-cut version of Allen Ginsberg's compassionate poem 'Wichita Vortex Sutra'; and Diana Rigg read out Adrian Mitchell's 'To Whom It May Concern'. Among the several VIPs who filed forth to be seated on the stage for this brave, self-conscious, and rather pretentious event—they included John Arden, Brigid Brophy, John Mortimer, Kenneth Tynan, Arnold Wesker—was Empson.[110]

> I think my few good [poems] are all on the basis of expressing an unresolved conflict. It does seem to me a very good formula which applies to a lot of

kinds of poetry. I think it's completely out of fashion, isn't it? Nobody says that now. In a way, you see, as you approach middle age, though in fact you're a seething pit of scorpions, you don't recognise them in that form. You're getting things tidy: 'Can I get the boy to college?' and things like that are what you are thinking about.[111]

Empson was not indecisive or totally impractical, but he had a habit of thinking that his strong-willed wife would see to the day-to-day management of affairs. In the early 1960s, however, a series of unheralded problems arose with the children which would require some deft interventions by Empson himself to ensure the completion of their educational studies and the chance to find satisfactory careers for themselves. Living his semi-detached life between Sheffield and London, with most of his energies being absorbed by professional duties and the writing of criticism, it is perhaps not surprising that he came to presume his children's education was progressing in fine form at Aldenham, unless someone rang loud alarm bells. For himself, he would take stock of the boys during the holidays, and he felt proud to find them growing up into energetic and game teenagers who showed lots of initiative. In a way, he felt most comfortable simply to look in on their lives. Yet even during the holidays the boys had the closest interaction with their mother—though they would normally make the effort to go on holiday *en famille*: in 1962, for example, they enjoyed touring and camping in France. Empson may have fancied himself an eighteenth-century paterfamilias, but as a parent he was more of a nineteenth-century figure: fond and encouraging, though remote. In the summer of 1960 Mogador and Jacob had insisted on getting holiday jobs to earn some extra money, and their father, who had never thought to get holiday employment during his own schooldays from Winchester, looked with indulgence upon their enterprise as a rather pointless use of their time.

> The boys took it into their heads that they wanted to earn money this holidays [he told his brother Arthur], a quaint fashion it seems to me, as what they earn is such chicken-food compared to what I have to spend, but it is a healthy one in a way and certainly solves the problem of entertaining them. Mog worked in the London show-rooms and store-rooms of the Hudson Bay Fur Company, carrying specimens of mink and what not to the bulk buyers as they inspected it before the auctions. He seems to have met agreeable boys from universities who were doing the same holiday work, but I don't gather that any of them learnt much about furs. Jacob simply did a lot of house-painting. Maybe they are trying to get enough to buy motor-cycles, horribly dangerous. Mog has demanded extra tuition to

try to get into a university, and very sensible of Mog too; I thought the beastly school would do that as part of the fees.[112]

At the beginning of the school session 1961–2 Empson realized he had failed over the summer to give Mogador an effective pep talk, to instil in him a sense of purpose about striving to do well in his upcoming A-level exams. Indeed, he had probably felt shy of fluffing up his son in person, fearing that the very grown-up Mogador, who had become highly interested in the idea of making a good deal of money and gadding about with swish friends, might spurn him. He therefore took his preferred option of writing to his son a full, encouraging letter.

> However, I am not at all keen on your going to Cambridge, only on your going to a reasonable university, and the chief reason in my mind is that everyone agrees the friends you make at university last for the rest of your life in some way which the friends you make at school don't. To take English at Magdalene I am told is not bad now, because they have a good man, but English at Cambridge as a whole [at least as his friend Graham Hough advised him whenever he visited Cambridge] is frightfully bad, in fact hamstrung by quarrels among the dons. Plenty of the Redbricks would give you better teaching really, but what you really want is to be with other good students, and the children of course choose to go to Oxford Cambridge or London if their tickets are so good that they are allowed to choose, without knowing at all about where the teaching is good. Maybe it would be a bad thing to spend an extra year at home struggling to cram for Cambridge, granting that you have got to aim at English or History Honours, if you can get into a decent Redbrick right away. You would find you made friends all right; the cream has been skimmed off the milk to go to Oxford Cambridge or London, but what the examiners consider the cream doesn't by any means include all the agreeable and competent people who are going to do well later on . . .

He said a good Redbrick university would do just as well (though he did not favour the two universities suggested by Aldenham, namely Trinity College Dublin and Durham, because they were nominated by the public schools for snobbish reasons: as foundations that were as ancient as Oxford and Cambridge). Why not try for Bristol, for instance? Empson urged his son, but best of all be a farmer:

> When I say I want you to be a farmer, I really do think it would suit your temperament, but also I think it is the coming thing to be . . .
>
> You see, as soon as father says he will pay for a year on London crammers living at home before university, that gives you more freedom to choose

what you really want to do. I wish you would use the time to get out of the Arts side and learn enough Physics and Chemistry to be accepted by Reading as a genuine Farming student ...

I would not go on throwing money into your education, my dear Mogador, unless I thought you an able and sensible man capable to decide for himself what to do after having an adequate look round; and I have no doubt at the back of my mind there because both my brothers would agree Mogador ought to be given a proper start in life. In a way, it throws the weight back on you; you have more time to decide what life would suit you.

His devout hope that a career in farming might appeal to Mogador was not unrelated to his strategic aspiration that his son might become a big beneficiary of his brother's will, and so take up farming on the family estates at Yokefleet in Yorkshire. It was to no avail: the farmer's life was never to be for Mogador. But Mogador did agree to put his mind to sitting the entrance examination for the Magdalene group of colleges in 1962. 'After failing the Cambridge exam [Empson mapped out the grand plan for his brother's sake] he would have time to take other ones for Red Brick Universities. But he wants nice friends with shiny motor-cars.'[113] In the event, Mogador did not do as well as he might have done at his A-levels, so he left Aldenham in the summer of 1962 and for the following academic year took lessons in Chinese and French at Holborn College in London (where Hetta was doing some English language teaching).

Fortune smiled on the young Mogador in 1963. Even while studying in London he met and fell for Linden Zilliacus, the only daughter by a second marriage of the ageing but energetically controversial Member of Parliament, Konni Zilliacus. Hetta Empson thought of 'old Zill' as 'quite a tough reliable old thing'.[114] Although Empson had nothing against his son's involvement with Zilliacus's daughter, he felt it premature for the couple to choose to get married. Nevertheless, they were soon to do so, and a son, Saul, was to be born to Mr and Mrs Mogador Empson on 23 December 1963.

Mogador had enjoyed a further stroke of luck early in 1963 when he was accepted without great difficulty to read for a combined degree in Chinese and Economics in the Department of Chinese recently established at Leeds University by the famous American Sinologist Owen Lattimore, who had been hounded out of the USA after a prolonged assault during the McCarthy era. Empson, it turned out, had even met Lattimore some thirty years earlier:

the American who is opening a department of Chinese at Leeds University is an explorer who was in effect driven from Harvard by Macarthy's suspicions of his politics, and he wants modern Chinese, so he didn't demand from Mog the British A level in Chinese which means the ancient language. However, Mog's mother has succeeded in making him take it all the same, showing her strength, and it will probably be useful. [He did attain his A-level in Chinese in the summer of 1963.] All this is rather smart, and quite wipes out the shame of having failed to get to Magdalene to read English last year—I had much rather he equipped himself for the China trade. He looked in at Sheffield after winning Unconditional acceptance from Leeds and said handsomely that father's advice had for once been right. I had said he lost his only asset if he wouldn't speak Chinese, so for about three weeks before the interview he practised with Mei Fang the extravagantly affected noises required by the accent of Peking, which she pronounces with insolence. Unlike Oxford Cambridge and London, Leeds addressed him in Mandarin, and the whole interview was conducted with Mog growling and pinging as he had never pinged or growled before. No wonder he was accepted unconditionally. I can't find that Owen Lattimore has ever expressed any political opinions at all, though no doubt that gets him considered deep. About 1933 I was somehow taken to a reception at his house in Peking, where he was wearing a monocle, a reckless thing for an American to do.[115]

Empson was highly impressed to hear Owen Lattimore lecture the next year. 'I am told he will have four years in Leeds and will then retire for good.'[116]

Most fortunately and generously, Empson's dear friend Alice Stewart found at just this time that she had some capital to spare and decided to help Mogador and his new wife and their child by investing the money in a house in Windsor Terrace, off Woodhouse Lane, in Leeds, and installing the young family in a downstairs flat at the nominal rent of £2. 10s a week (the upper flat was occupied by a doctor at a higher rate). Mogador was pleased to make it known that he had discovered the house, and that its investment value was excellent. Mogador and Linden moved into the flat in September, before the start of his first year at the University. 'As the couple are already expecting a baby,' wrote Empson, 'they would find it extremely hard to hire lodgings in Leeds except by this special arrangement and Alice is charging them only half what the people upstairs pay. Mog wanted me to buy the house, which he is right in thinking he was clever to discover, and unrepentantly says he is sorry I refused the opportunity of making a lot of money, as Alice is now going to do. But I know I am no good at that sort of thing; it would only give me further distraction from earning money the only way I am good at.'[117]

Hetta Empson, who had not yet reached fifty years of age, informed a friend: 'Mogador as you know got married, rather defiantly—but it has turned out alright. Linden is keeping him to his books in Leeds and they now have a son called Saul, so I am a grandmother and wish I felt more like one, when does one reach an age of discretion and resignation and quietude?'[118]

Things did not look so promising for Jacob, who was quietly and yet unconfidently drifting along at Aldenham School. When the school casually but shockingly made it known in the summer of 1961 that his chances of getting to university on the Science side were really poor, and that he looked weak even for the Arts, Empson intervened with impressive decisiveness. Without giving due notice (it cost him a term's fees), he took his younger son away from the public school and placed him at Westminster City School, a state school about half a mile from Westminster Abbey in London (not to be confused with the private Westminster School), where he could specialise in the sciences: Botany, Physics and Chemistry. To some small degree, Empson suspected that Jacob had felt too comfortable and relaxed in the environment at Aldenham. More positively, however, Jacob made it known that he had felt inspired by the example of his father's charismatic old friend Norman Pirie (who was pursuing research at the Rothamsted Experimental Station in Hertfordshire) to take into his head the notion of becoming an agricultural botanist. His expressed ambition was sufficient for his father, who explained to the headmaster of Aldenham his reasons for such exigent decision-making: 'I think the boy may be shaken into trying hard enough at his real bent if put among grimmer surroundings and more anxious fellow-students.[119]

Jacob was to spend three years at Westminster City School (1961–4), leaving late—just short of twenty—because for one reason or another he had to struggle to gain the A-level grades he needed for university entrance. Empson spoke too soon when he announced to his brother in March 1963, 'I have just heard that Jacob was been unconditionally accepted by Nottingham University to do Botany next autumn; or rather, on condition of A level passes, and they will hold it open while he tries to get to Aberdeen, said to be better for Botany. So we can be fairly sure that both boys will get to a university next autumn. It has been getting so difficult that I was rather anxious.'[120] Botany was Jacob's strength, but he was to fail at physics and chemistry in the summer. Empson was shocked, but the truth was that Jacob had been putting on an act. Deeply unsure of himself, he did not want to let on to his parents that he was in danger of failing; and it seems that he even hid from them a school report which predicted a poor result. It is clear that during his long absences during term-times at Sheffield, Empson had not been available to pay attention to Jacob's progress; he merely trusted that all was going along fairly well—but the absent father could set no example of diligence; nor could he supervise his son. In practice, all too often Jacob had spent his evenings with his mother and Josh in the pub. Hetta could be a powerful figure, and extremely pushy, when she felt occasion warranted it, but she had no desire to pressurize her own children. Yet she was a slack parent in failing to insist that Jacob do his homework; she fell down in her duty of care.[121]

Empson lamented to a friend in February 1964,

> Poor Jacob . . . fell like a stone in the A level exams this summer, and just before his second shot this January told his mother he was no good at it and wanted to stop. For the last week I sent him to a crammer, who said he would need a lot more cramming to pass. So now we are waiting for the results, and a miracle may have happened, but otherwise I don't see how he can go to college at all. I feel very guilty, and suspect I ought to have realised that he was hiding the school reports, but he kept up such a firm front till the end that we assumed he was doing nicely.[122]

For the academic year 1964–5 Jacob travelled up to stay with Mogador and Linden at the house in Windsor Terrace, Leeds. Their parents were in any case committed to spending the months from October until Christmas 1964 at the University of Ghana, and it was agreed that Jacob should not even attempt to live at Studio House by himself. Taking up occupancy of a room above a garage behind the Leeds house, he went to classes at Leeds Technical College and ultimately did well in his A-levels. Empson said he was proud of his son for having been 'very unshaken, resisting all attempts to make him join the Air Force of a University in Australia'.[123] Jacob ended up with offers to read Psychology at both Durham and Sheffield, and he decided to take the course at Sheffield—where he would live not far from his father's Burrow. Once free of the Hampstead influence, he came into his own and prospered. 'Jacob is registered at Sheffield—', whooped Empson in October 1965; 'I am still afraid they may throw him out for not having taken Use of English, but we are pretty safe now as they consider it barbarous to retract a mistake.'[124] Jacob took naturally to psychology, gaining 83 per cent in his first university exam.

Much more surprisingly, the parents simply presumed too that during their absence in Ghana, Mogador, the young husband and father, should also look after the boy, Simon (who was still in primary school), at the house in Leeds. So it duly happened: Mogador received a double dose of fatherhood.

> I had a term at Legon University, in Ghana, just before the deposition of Nkrumah. He was becoming generally suspicious, and rather a problem for our Vice-Chancellor, Conor Cruise O'Brien, but I thought one of his complaints had a considerable ring of truth. The expensively imported teachers of 'Eng. Lit.,' he said, were inciting the students to revive human sacrifice and other savage customs, and in every way were resisting scientific progress in Ghana. With what astonishment my colleagues would have denied this (I do not think it was reported to them); and yet how could a vigorous-minded student in Ghana interpret their standard phraseology?[125]

Empson's reflection, written ten years after the occasion of his visit to Ghana for the autumn term of 1964, was not entirely reliable; like many anecdotes, this one was given a heightened colouring. It is possible that Empson may have learned that the president was grumbling about western teaching, and threatening retribution against supposedly reactionary lecturers—those who were regarded as imperialist and neo-colonialist subversives or counter-revolutionaries—and he probably jumped to the easy conclusion that President Kwame Nkrumah's professed socialist policies could be compared with the purging of western influence during Communist China's advance towards a secular-scientific new order. By 1973 Empson seemed willing to applaud almost anyone who saw through the evil influence of Christianity. In truth, however, there may well have been student 'spies' in his classroom in Ghana, but there was no direct interference with the teaching of English.

In 1957 Dr Nkrumah had enjoyed the distinction of leading the first African state to become independent of colonial rule; if there was a natural proponent of the emerging pan-African movement, it was he. Intelligent, charming, vain, self-dramatising, he had been educated in England and in the USA. He was elected president of Ghana—the former British colony that early European traders had named with rapacious aptness the Gold Coast, over five centuries ago—when it became a republic in 1960. The quondam University College of the Gold Coast, established in 1948 (and affiliated to the University of London), was reconstituted in 1961 as the University of Ghana, with President Nkrumah as its first chancellor. At the personal invitation of the president, the Irish diplomat and writer Conor Cruise O'Brien—who had recently served as the UN's representative to secessionist Katanga (a mission which ended in a debacle, though for reasons that were largely beyond his control)—consented to become Vice-Chancellor of Ghana's nationally-funded showpiece university for three years from 1962. O'Brien had won esteem for his anti-apartheid activism, for his utter integrity, and as a defender of freedom. In his dealings with Nkrumah, however, he soon found he had to face up to an increasingly autocratic policy and browbeatingly interventionist tactics—indeed, it is remarkable that he managed to serve out his term of office. Initially, his new Vice-Chancellor impressed and indeed influenced Nkrumah quite well enough for the president to recite at a graduation dinner in February 1963, without any significant modification, a speech drafted by O'Brien that professed an unwavering faith in academic autonomy. The Empsons, when they learned that Nkrumah was promoting socialist policies, were pleased; they were not to know that the president's administration was in fact corrupt and destined to ruin the country and its good governance in no time at all.

By 1964, Nkrumah had started to compel the University of Ghana to become an instrument for government propaganda; certain members of staff who were deemed to be dissident were arrested, and a handful of Europeans were deported. (There were to be more than 1,600 students by the session 1964–5—predominantly indigenous males—but expatriate lecturers were still in the majority: in 1962, only about a quarter of the teaching staff were African; three years later, some two-fifths were African.) In January 1964, one of the President's police guards attempted to assassinate him; he survived the gunfire but took to hiding in his palace and behaving in a paranoid and unpredictable fashion. Conor Cruise O'Brien, though harassed by Nkrumah (who declined to meet with him throughout his final year of office, and who clearly intended to humiliate him into resigning) defended academic liberty.

O'Brien had first encountered Empson in 1952, at a party held at Pratt's Club in London, to launch *Maria Cross*, O'Brien's study of modern Catholic writers. I. A. Richards had brought Empson along to meet the author (it was a motley gathering: C. K. Ogden was there; so was Alfred Munnings, famous for painting horses); and it may well have been Richards who put into O'Brien's mind the idea of inviting Empson to Africa in 1964.[126] Richards was to travel to Ghana just a few months before Empson's arrival, to see whether Basic English would be useful there. He gave classes for pupil teachers which were admired; but, as O'Brien later said, Richards was 'badly out of luck . . . As it was, his arrival coincided with the second attempt on the President's life and nothing really went right from that moment.'[127]

O'Brien had been working on a critical essay of his own about W. B. Yeats's intermittently pro-fascist writings—a shortened version was to appear as 'Yeats and Fascism' in the *New Statesman* (26 February 1965), and the full indictment as a chapter in *In Excited Reverie* (1965)—and he determined, being a longtime admirer of Empson's critical writings, to send Empson a draft of the piece for any comments he might like to offer.

> Empson's comments on this reached me one morning at breakfast-time [Cruise O'Brien would relate in his autobiography] while Ivor was staying with me. Empson described my essay as 'sordid' and this of course infuriated me.
>
> I brought the letter down to the breakfast-table, where I found Ivor eating a pineapple, a favourite Ghanaian delicacy. Furious, I showed Ivor Empson's letter hoping for some moral support. Ivor read the letter and his prominent and expressive eyes widened as he did so, fastening on the key word. Then he said, thoughtfully:
>
> 'Sordid... *Sordid*... do you suppose Bill Empson means that as a term of *praise*?'
>
> At that blessed word, all my irritation vanished and was replaced by exultation. I was able to write to Empson a letter of reasonable and amicable remonstrance, and we became friends.[128]

Empson seems in his letter (now lost) to have suggested that Yeats was 'anti-clerical for the same reason as James Joyce'—that is, because of the dogmatic dominance of the Catholic Church in Ireland—and to have protested that one could find 'many indications' of anti-Hitler feeling in Yeats's writings (though he gave no specific pointers); delighting in Yeats the poet, he fiercely reprobated O'Brien's attempt to hoist Yeats on the petard of pro-fascism.[129]

In Ghana, Empson and O'Brien were to enjoy their occasional encounters—though O'Brien was so grimly preoccupied with the political situation that social contacts were fewer than he would have wished. O'Brien had publicly criticized Nkrumah's dismissal of his Chief Justice and his relations with Government House plummeted, giving him a desperately difficult and unhappy year, so he was not at all his usual sociable self. Empson admired O'Brien for his sharpness, wit and vigour; and O'Brien for his part found it diverting to stimulate Empson to make mischief. Empson wrote home: 'I think I shall have to break to the students that Eliot didn't mean the same as they do by being a Christian (O'Brien

eggs me on to).'[130] He had taken the trouble to do some homework on
O'Brien before leaving for Ghana; but since he felt annoyed by the critical
severity of O'Brien's work on Yeats, he perused with some initial scepticism his recent apologia *To Katanga and Back* (about his work for the UN in
the Congo). However, within a month of getting to know O'Brien more
closely in Ghana, he was wholly persuaded of the good qualities of the
man. When he found out that the left-wing periodical *The New Statesman*
was looking for a new editor, Empson was prompt to recommend O'Brien
for the chair: 'He is a man of firm principles but much good humour and
good sense, and a really impressive power of not getting rattled.' It was to
no avail, however, for the selection committee decided against O'Brien.

Conor Cruise O'Brien's biographer has remarked: 'Several of the expatriate staff members were in Ghana out of a sense of moral or political
commitment to an emerging African nation.'[131] Certainly, William and
Hetta Empson, though they were visitors rather than permanent staff,
must have decided to risk spending some time in Ghana, even at this
period of growing crisis and possible danger, in very much of an idealistic
spirit: with partisan curiosity. Hetta was implacably opposed to the apartheid regime in South Africa, and eager to support a black African nation
that had established its independence from colonialism and was set upon
the road to socialism. She would hail the country for its triumph in casting
off its ruling white élite.

'My wife's a Boer, you know,' declared Empson at an early get-together
with the O'Briens. He would have made the statement out of mischief, in
hopes of disconcerting the party. But Maire O'Brien responded with what
appeared to be tight lips: 'It won't be held against her, if she's seen the
error of her ways.' Such a riposte must have been meant as a tease, but one
witness to the exchange noted that Hetta bristled; to her, Maire's sardonic
wit apparently felt like a snub.[132]

In general, judging by the demeanour of the folk he came across at the
University of Ghana, Empson gathered the favourable impression that the
Republic was pulling together and making proper social progress. 'It is
very good humoured and pleasant here . . . ,' he wrote. 'The country seems
to me to be going ahead very well, but rather too contented to force the
pace.'[133] It was his nature to try to see every affair in an optimistic light—
very much as he had found it inspiriting to be in China at the dawn of the
People's Republic—and yet even he was to find it increasingly difficult to
reconcile his hopes for socialism with the effects of Nkrumahism. O'Brien,
who started out by admiring the president's anti-colonialist record but who
was from the beginning sceptical of "Ghanaian socialism", was later to

lament most deeply of all that 'Nkrumah's state was one huge rip-off,' as he put it; the president created such a vast waste in the country—'the reckless running down of the currency reserves . . . [and] the destruction of the most valuable part of Ghana's inheritance from the colonial days: its honest and competent civil service.'[134] Empson related in his gossip home a choice piece of information (picked up on a trip to Kumasi) which offered a definite political insight—though he still chose to give the benefit of the doubt to President Nkrumah:

> The city treasurer of KUMASI, further north in Ghana, an accountant who had not previously left Lancashire, confided to Hetta his despair of even appearing to balance the books; but this is more or less what the dictator boasts of doing—straining the economy while the basic engineering is done in a rush. The Socialism still seems to me all right, but the business of worshipping Nkrumah, a high-minded and intelligent product of the London School of Economics, does seem hard on the Ghanaians, who don't take to it naturally as one might think.[135]

One feature of the strain put upon everyone in Ghana included censorship of the mail, so he was careful not to write anything questioning the dictator's regime while in the country. Although he hoped against hope that Ghana might grow into an enlightened socialist state, his honest feeling was that it was becoming a place of oppression—once out of Ghana, he was quick to admit that the neighbouring Nigeria 'certainly [felt] much more cheerful and outspoken.'[136] Sadly, Nkrumahism meant totalitarianism in the making.

The University of Ghana bestrode Legon Hill, where the expensively coordinated buildings struck the visitors as an amazing sight. The gleaming campus was like nothing else in Ghana, and the Empsons found the layout pleasantly reminiscent of the Summer Palace outside Peking; William wrote home that he thought the university 'a magnificent set of buildings . . . in simplified Chinese style'.[137] To begin with, they were put up in a visitors' house with a beautiful garden high up on Legon Hill, where they were looked after by a servant; but they did not like the isolation that such a swish residence imposed upon them, so they were moved down to a pokey flat in an ordinary apartment building. The house was nice enough in itself, but did not allow them to socialize in the impromptu fashion they liked—and the servant made them feel on show.

The Department of English ran to a staff of eight, five specializing in literature and three in language, and with just one African (a second was on leave, and a third was to be appointed the following year). Their number included a senior lecturer named Robin Mayhead, a Leavisite who had published several articles in *Scrutiny*—'a typical Leavisite (how astoundingly typical they are),' remarked Empson[138]—and Joan Bellamy, a lecturer in literature whose husband was Professor of Economics. Members of staff on short-term contracts included a couple from the University of British Columbia—Fred and Katharine (Kay) Stockholder—who got on well with the Empsons (Fred was an amateur anthropologist who endeavoured to make literature 'relevant' by quizzing his students on tribal customs). The Head of Department was (in his own words) a young and diffident lecturer named Douglas Duncan who was on a two-year secondment from the University of Southampton; he felt awed to learn that Empson was to be visiting professor during his own first term at Legon, but charmed by the modesty of Empson's first letter: 'Dear Professor Duncan . . . what would you like me to teach?'[139]

Duncan's predecessor at Ghana, T. A. Dunn (later of Lagos, and first professor at Stirling University), had devoted most of his energies to a massive revision of the curriculum, so Duncan was relieved of that problem. While there was certainly a little local pressure put upon them to teach more remedial English language and African literature, Duncan was conscious that international standards required them to cover major authors and periods from Chaucer on. Lecturers had to teach as many as 25–30 hours a week. Empson, being the visiting professor, was not expected to do quite so much teaching as the regular staff, but he was still assigned rather a heavy load. Duncan found his behaviour in the Department impeccable: he attended every weekly meeting and was quietly supportive, and he met all of his rather numerous classes—though he may not have been wholly understood. 'His public lectures were pretty disastrous,' remembers Duncan: 'one was a chapter from *Milton's God* recited from the page-proofs.'[140]

The University of Ghana was known as a mecca for left-wing radicals from around the globe, but the Empsons made no effort to seek out any such supposedly like-minded people. Instead, they approached Ghana in more of a holiday humour, being happy to enjoy the sun and the undemanding gossip both with Duncan—who liked the Empsons immensely and appreciated their generous warmth, but who felt he had little worthwhile conversation to offer them—and with the Stockholders. Certainly, as Duncan has recalled, he spent more time with them than he could actually spare, and found it highly enjoyable. At a time of maximum austerity in Ghana, it became one of Duncan's main tasks to locate the last surviving bottles of whisky on campus for the Empsons to consume. Among other activities, they made a trip into the bush, and Duncan was struck by the picture of Empson being solemnly received by a village chief who was obviously hugely impressed by his beard.

Empson, who liked the peoples he met, enjoyed all their outings. His most newsy letter shows just how entertaining everything seemed to him; he was essentially the English tourist: sympathetic, enquiring, forever diverted. Also, as always in his letters, he is considerately aware of his audience—in this case, his farmer brother—and picks out what will interest the addressee:

> It should be getting hot now at the end of the rainy season, but there has been very little rain and now heavy rain clouds are blowing over eastward, parallel to the coast, without ever coming down, so it is cool and pleasant. We went to the agricultural research station yesterday and the various kinds of cow looked fine but no plants were growing properly. We are determined to see rain forest but it is some way off. This is all grass and scrub and looks as if no food is grown, but much of what they eat grows on bushes (yams for instance) and we are told the grass carries all the cows it could without anyone bothering to make hay to feed them in the dry season. The cows are not used for milk and only occasionally eaten, at a feast; they are a mark of prestige used for buying high-class wives. There is plenty of food, and the people in their lazy way are very good-humoured. They believe that British troops only entered the capital of the King of Ashantee as Napoleon entered Moscow, so like the Sudanese and the Scotch they have no chip on the shoulder, no shame to avenge. We went to a fetish dance at a shrine and the drummers were reliably off their heads but the dancers would pretend to be but then stop when they got bored. Still, it was all dressed up very splendidly, and the shrine is considered efficient at dealing with barrenness in wives. There seems to be hardly any sculpture, we need to go to Nigeria for that.[141]

In Nigeria, Hetta greatly admired the objets d'art she discovered in markets and at shrines, and she purchased a number of curios. Yet her strict canons of taste in sculpture served to deprive her husband of an encounter with another form of curiosity that he had clearly anticipated with delight; still, he wrote it up as an incidental non-happening for Arthur's amusement:

> There was a prospect yesterday of being introduced to a German lady who has become a Yoruba priestess at a big shrine near Ife, visited by thousands on sacred days I understand with many sacrifices of goats, but Hetta decided her sculpture was bad (one could see it at the shrine) so we were let off. I thought it would be hard to know what to say to the lady, except 'Seen any good spooks lately?'[142]

On returning to the University of Ghana from their mid-term visit to Nigeria, they tended to make it known that they had of course loathed the fleshpots of Lagos and Ibadan—but perhaps primarily by way of consoling those who had to resign themselves to putting up with Ghanaian austerity.

They also made some trips with Douglas Duncan and the Stockholders to the extensive unspoilt beaches on the coast of Ghana, where the surf of the Atlantic ran rough and high along the Bight of Benin. 'William was wonderfully vigorous,' remembers Duncan, 'and would plunge into the surf and let it roll him up the beach like Odysseus. And he took long walks daily in the afternoon heat, wearing shorts and nothing on his head, [and] once wading through a swamp at evident risk of bilharzia.'[143] In a later year, Empson would muse aloud to John Willett about the visit to Ghana: 'Poor old Hetta, sweating like a pig.'[144]

In more private moments, Duncan was struck by the conspicuous strangenesses and paradoxes of the Empsons' personal relations. 'Hetta, I remember, was tigerish in her devotion to William's "greatness" (she used the word) and was extraordinarily quick to see signs of his being undervalued. On the other hand she would talk openly and longingly in his presence of the lover she had left behind in London. The mixture of professional boasting and sexual humiliation struck the Stockholders and myself as odd, though might not have done so if we had been more accustomed to the Hampstead scene.' It also became fairly clear to everyone who spent time with them in Ghana that Empson's complaisance or at least his broadmindedness was habitual. 'One couldn't help wondering how deeply this hurt him,' reflects Duncan. 'In many respects he and Hetta were very close (she was *there*, after all, and stayed the course for three months) and he was always genial with her in public, but I did have the impression that they didn't enjoy being alone together.'

The Empsons' choice of 'farewell party' seemed entirely characteristic. Nothing official was to be laid on, and the big Accra hotels did not appeal to them. Instead, the group went out together for a Lebanese meal, and then they settled into a very 'African' bar in an area where darkness and silence descended very early. One waiter struggled to stay awake through the night keeping the party supplied with beer while Empson declaimed and sang—eventually, as Duncan vividly remembers, 'greeting the dawn with a beautiful rendering of "Early one morning..."' Somehow, Duncan got them to the airport by 10 o'clock and lectured to his first-year class just an hour later.

Empson had entered with good spirit into the experience of teaching in a developing African country at a time of troubles, but he took no grand lessons away from it: no sense of special insight, let alone any authoritative opinions on the post-colonial situation. Rather, he quickly got back into the day-to-day business and busyness of Sheffield. But one bad taste lingered: because of exchange control difficulties in Ghana, he was not able to take out of the county the balance of his salary of £750. He complained to Conor Cruise O'Brien about this, and intimated too that his visit had turned out to be a waste of time; he felt he had been taken advantage of.[145] O'Brien responded in the only way he could: 'You must not feel that you wasted your time here . . . I know from talks with Duncan and some of the senior English students how much the stimulus of your presence and teaching meant to the English Department. Your company and Hetta's also meant a lot to Maire and myself in an otherwise rather oppressive period.'[146] In the mounting turmoil of Ghana, Conor Cruise O'Brien was almost certainly speaking for what should have been the case rather than what was. Yet the politics of the situation had been too all-consuming for any individual to leave much of a mark.

16

The Road to Retirement

B EFORE departing for Ghana, the Empsons upped and bought themselves a house in rural Wales. Empson was nearly 58 and really starting to feel his years, so retirement in the country felt like a desirable prospect. However, almost as soon as they got back from Ghana, they set about buying another house which circumstances had thrown in their way; and immediately the tranquil retirement in Wales looked somehow, and decisively, less attractive.

Back in October 1945 Empson had purchased a short leasehold interest of less than thirty years in Studio House; the original lease had a term of 99 years, but by 1965 there were only eight years to go. Assuming he would be retiring in 1971, at the usual age of 65, he and the family could be thrown out by the owner of Studio House just two years after that date. It therefore seemed sensible to make timely provision, and so at the end of August 1964, about six weeks before they were due to fly to Ghana, they set off to find a suitable farm in the general direction of Pembrokeshire. 'Nothing will do for Hetta really, I fear,' confided Empson to a colleague.[1] He had gathered together over recent years a small nest egg, comprised of royalties, overseas earnings, and dividends from the Empson family trust, and felt it was time to cash it all in for solid real estate. The house they speedily bought was called Stradmore Mansion, at Newcastle Emlyn, Carmarthenshire; although it was nicely sited on top of a hill, it was in need of some improvement (the electrics had been renewed but the kitchen wallpaper seemed to be breathing in and out). In fact, the only genuine peculiarity about the house was that it was faced not with stone or pebbledash but with corrugated iron: the story went that the mansion had once been owned by a judge, and one of the villains sent down by the judge returned in a later year and set fire to the house, so the corrugated cladding was meant to hold up the part of the house that had been damaged by the blaze. Empson found the neighbouring Pembrokeshire countryside beautiful, and Hetta fancied the idea of breeding ponies there.[2] He formed the fond idea that every so often he could simply walk down the hill to the A487 highway and catch a bus to Aberystwyth in order to do a day's work at the university library there.

Many months later, he would boast of the great property gamble: 'My son Mogador, who is studying Economics as well as Chinese, was astounded at my wisdom in selling out all nesteggs and scouring England for a house to buy, shortly before the Labour Government got in. How did you know? he delighted me by saying; he usually considers me as over-grown with moss.'[3]

But just then, only a month after their return from Ghana, by pure coincidence they were invited by 'the sharklike lady owner' of Studio House to purchase the freehold of their London home for the very reasonable sum of £11,500 (Empson had feared that it would not go for less than £40,000). Given the run-down state of the house even after twenty years of improvements by Hetta and by her lodgers, lovers, and decorators—dry rot was still flowering through the wall of one bath-room—they tried to persuade the owner to accept a lower price. 'I think it lucky that some of the dry rot happens to be visible when the surveyors come round,' Empson advised his wife. 'If you see them, remark (dressed rather sleasily) that the house is a bottomless pit into which your husband has sunk thousands of pounds merely out of insane fondness for it.'[4] In fact, the little white lie he proposed was not far from the truth. For a while, they hoped that they could buy both the Hampstead house and the house in Wales, but Empson's resources were by no means ample enough. In the event, he took out a small mortgage and sold Stradmore Mansion in order to meet the final agreed price of £11,000 for the London property: it was the shrewdest investment he ever made in his life.

'Of course I am mad to cling to [Studio House] ...,' admitted Hetta. 'I don't know... but I don't see myself stuck in Wales for keeps—not just yet anyway.'[5] Empson confessed likewise: 'we were all secretly afraid of having to go and live in the grim isolation of the house in Wales, beautiful though it is, or the lay-out of its trees at any rate.'[6] Coincidentally, Hetta came at this time into an amusingly small inheritance from South Africa—£8. 6. 8d. It ought to be spent on something that would last, she ironically determined, so she went out and bought 'a perfectly enormous vice' for use in her studio.[7]

In the summer of 1965 the whole family decamped to live for a while in
Wales, both to give Stradmore Mansion the semblance of being a settled
home—'to make a good appearance in the House while trying to sell it,' as
Empson put it[8] (though they had to sleep on camp beds while they did
so)—and to muck about with the decorative disorder of the great house.
George Melly, the jazz musician, writer, broadcaster, and aficionado of
fishing, was a close neighbour and so came to know the Empsons during
their brief tenure of the house (they gave him permission to fish their
stretch of the Teifi gratis):

> William, the famous poet and essayist, his dashing South African wife,
> stylishly dressed in the sado-masochistic mode, and hippyish young people
> ad lib, some of whom were their children, or perhaps stepchildren.
>
> It was a truly Bohemian set-up in the Augustus John tradition. There was
> for a start very little furniture; the ageing poet, his fine head partially framed
> by a long white beard growing from *under* his chin, sat in an otherwise empty
> room in a deck-chair reading, with calm concentration, a copy of *The Times*.
> The kitchen, however, presided over by his glamorous and lively chatelaine,
> was as restless and noisy as a troop of the bandalog. When it was time to eat,
> Empson carefully folding up his *Times*, we sat at a huge table on long
> benches (although our host and hostess had proper chairs at each end). As
> it was getting dark, one of the youngsters was dispatched to bring back a
> light bulb—they were apparently at a premium in the house—and, once it
> was plugged in, Madam served us huge helpings of pig from a great
> cauldron suspended over a burning tree. She told Diana [Melly] they'd
> bought a whole dismembered pig from a farmer, head and all (probably
> slaughtered illegally) and bunged the lot into the cauldron with a daily boost
> of vegetables. It was, while one couldn't help but wonder what part of the
> pig's anatomy had landed up on one's plate, delicious. Afterwards there was
> the rolling up and smoking of what *Private Eye* then called 'exotic cheroots',
> although I can't remember W.E. indulging. Indeed he was almost silent
> throughout the evening, but just now and again he would make an enig-
> matic if seerlike announcement, e.g. 'In Mandarin Chinese the word for
> "Alas" is the same as the word for "Hurrah".'
>
> It was a memorable evening but not to be repeated, as, very soon,
> although they hadn't been there long, they sold the house by auction.
> This was perhaps a wise move, as it was clear that Mrs E was a stranger
> to brooms, brushes, cloths, mops, soap and especially a flush brush.[9]

Melly could not resist dropping in at the auction, which was held in a
room above a pub, in the early autumn of 1965, and was amazed to hear
the Welsh auctioneer proclaim: 'People may wonder why the *distinguished*
poet who but recently added distinction to our little community by living

amongst us should, so comparatively soon after its purchase, have decided to sell his substantial house ... The reason is that Mr Empson has been summoned by the Government to occupy an important advisory post involving being called to Number 10, Downing Street at a moment's notice. Therefore ...'

'I looked at Empson during this absurd rigmarole,' Melly has recorded. 'He remained totally impassive. Indeed, I've often wondered if he hadn't fed the auctioneer the whole story.'[10] Melly's surmise was obviously correct. Altogether remarkably, by 31 October the Empsons had completed the sale of Stradmore for the sum of £6,700—which represented a 50 per cent profit on the sum they had paid for it just one year earlier.

After all their upheavals and transitions, Alice Stewart invited them to spend Christmas at her cottage near Oxford. Empson forewarned her that the irregular family Empson was now a very odd caboodle: 'Hetta, Josh, William, Jacob, Mog wife and baby, little Simon; eight mouths, four and a half beds.'[11] Jacob Empson recalls the bizarre events that ensued during the festive days:

> On arrival there was only one drink each, and then it transpired that Josh, Ma, Simon and I were to be billeted in a farmhouse down the lane. Alice had some Hungarian refugees in the house, so there wasn't room.
>
> Tempers got worse and worse, as the farmhouse was cold and without any drink. Ma sent Josh out to find firewood, and he pulled up a fence and built a nice big fire in the bedroom. He was then sent back to the house to get in and find the bottle of Marsala that was his Xmas present for Pa. Having drunk the Marsala, and perhaps more that he had found in the house, Ma got crosser and crosser, and started to kick the furniture to pieces, to provide more firewood.
>
> What with all the upset, Simon wet his bed (and so did Ma and Josh). Pa came over in the morning to tidy things up a bit (I remember him turning the mattresses) and smooth ruffled feathers. That was Christmas day, I think. It was not a very jolly Christmas lunch. (I remember a mad dash to the pub to get there before closing time.)
>
> The following morning Alice had been told about the farmer's fence, and had been over to inspect the other damages. We all had to leave. There was no public transport back to London, so David Hawkes was telephoned, and he came and got us all to take us into Oxford to stay at his house in Woodstock Road. The day after Boxing Day the buses were running, and we got one back to London, and a very chilly Studio House with not much food.
>
> Alice threw a real wobbler, as I remember, and I think it was the last I saw of her until Pa's funeral.[12]

Clearly Hetta's tantrums were set off in part by her having been relegated to a cold annexe—feeling herself to have been put in the position of 'second-best wife'. For the rest, it was a case of petulant self-indulgence—although Alice, knowing of Hetta's habit of hell-raising, had chosen to take the unwise course of behaving like a strict mistress in every sense.

Much of Empson's teaching during the period of his absence in Ghana was taken by a Fulbright Fellow from the University of Michigan, James Gindin, whose duties at Sheffield were divided between the Departments of English Literature and Education (from where he took the opportunity to visit some of the new comprehensive schools). Gindin was bidden by Empson to look after his first-year tutorial groups and his third-year lectures. The lectures, as Empson briefed Gindin in a letter, were to cover American poetry; a fairly standard list of poets was appended. Some students were beginning to show an interest in the poetry of Wallace Stevens, Empson noted, but he himself did not find it interesting; all the same, if Gindin wanted to give a lecture on Stevens, he should feel free to do so. When Gindin arrived in London in mid-September, Empson took him out to an alcohol-fuelled lunch; and only when the meal was almost over did Empson announce that they must have another drink because they had not yet discussed Gindin's teaching. 'Of course,' Empson then declared, 'some of the students want to talk about Stevens. But I can't read him. Let's leave him off the course.' Gindin was taken aback by this sudden reversal, particularly because he had spent part of his summer break reading Stevens in preparation for the Sheffield teaching—though in the event he went ahead and gave a lecture on Stevens. Empson ended up by amiably welcoming the visitor: he would be very glad to have him at Sheffield. Yet he tactlessly confided too: 'Of course, you understand, Robert Lowell would be the American I'd really want. But the Sheffield climate in winter would probably drive him into the asylum. Can't risk it.'

When Empson returned from Ghana to Sheffield in the new year 1965, Gindin was surprised to discover that he greatly enjoyed the experience of teaching in tandem with his host (just as he enjoyed talking with Empson about literature or politics on any occasion, since Empson could be relied upon to be quick and brilliant in his comments). They gave the Modern Poetry lectures together. Empson was a splendid teacher: lively, sharp, quick, engaged, with an instinct for what would interest the students without ever talking down to them. Sometimes Empson would talk for half an hour, then Gindin would do the same. On other occasions,

Empson would read out some poetry and ask Gindin to comment on it, followed by the students, and then he would comment on their observations. At other times again, they would agree to stage a dialogue for the students (it was all usually planned in about ten minutes before the class). Invariably, the classes worked well. But one particular class, which had more to do with criticism than with poetry, did not go so well, and Gindin and Empson began to discuss why it had not worked as they made their way over to the staff club for a lunchtime drink. Gindin, being honestly self-critical, suggested he may have lost the students by asking foggy questions of Empson. 'No, no,' said Empson, 'don't blame yourself. It's the mums.' Just then, they ran into someone who had to be introduced and Gindin was left wondering what flowers—chrysanthemums—had to do with a bad class. Only when they were deep into their first pints did he ask Empson what he had meant by 'mums'? Gindin recalls what followed: 'Out came a whole theory that mothers ambitious for status were pushing students to university who didn't really belong there and couldn't follow what was going on in either poetry or criticism. This, at the time, surprised me because his teaching itself was so gracious, so involved, so generally without condescension.'

Some of the staff, notably including Eric Mackerness (who had once held a visiting fellowship at Princeton), wanted to introduce more American literature into the Honours curriculum, and Gindin was asked to go over a suggested reading list and recommend the proposal at a Department meeting. At the meeting, however, Empson went through the motions of reviewing the list as if for the first time (though he had almost certainly seen it at an earlier moment): 'Yes, yes, mmm, yes, and *Huckleberry Finn*. Certainly, they should have read that. But, tell me, haven't their nannies read them that by the time they're nine years old?' The progressives seemed so put out by this snub that the subject was not brought up again, at least for the duration of that session.

Gindin was further taken aback by Empson's seemingly capricious stubbornness during the Finals examination meeting. Gindin and Vivien de Sola Pinto (the External Examiner that year)—Empson always called the latter simply 'Pinto'—agreed that one particular essay, on the fiction of William Faulkner, was brilliant; and the rest of the student's papers were by far the best: they therefore advocated a First for her. 'No, no,' said Empson (with support from Francis Berry), as he and Berry exchanged memories of something stupid the young woman had said during her first year. There was to be no first class that year, as indeed there had been no firsts for three or four years—not since John Whitley had graduated.

There do seem to have been touches of reflex misogyny in Empson's make-up, but there may have been better reasons for denying a First in this instance than the spin of the discombobulating anecdote that stuck in Gindin's mind.[13]

All the same, Empson's eccentric whimsicalities could on occasion betray a distinct wilfulness. One not untypical story seems to show him pushing obliviousness to the point of deliberately disconcerting rudeness. During their time in Sheffield, the Gindins had a son, their firstborn, late in May 1965. While Mrs Gindin and the child were still in hospital, Derek and Louise Roper invited James Gindin for a celebratory dinner, with fish as the main course. Louise Roper even went to the trouble of driving over to Hull that day, to acquire some special fresh fish in season. The guests gathered, Gindin arrived, drinks were served, and Louise went to the kitchen for spot-on timing. Just as she signalled that the fish was ready—it was 9.30 or 10—the doorbell rang, to reveal Empson dressed in a heavy coat on a warm spring evening. 'Derek, I can't seem to find those exam papers you were to give me this afternoon.' Roper went through the various capacious pockets of Empson's coat, all stuffed to bursting, and turned up the relevant set of exams. Empson looked up from the frisking of his pockets just as Louise was frantically signalling that the fish would be spoiled if there was any further delay, and airily remarked, 'Oh, don't bother about me. I can always go along to the Berrys and get a meal . . . But if you don't mind I'd really rather like to have a bath—it's so warm this evening.' Roper was obliged to escort him upstairs while the invited guests of the evening sat down to the meal. Later, they withdrew to the sitting room only to discover Empson apparelled in Roper's dressing gown and sitting in the deepest, most comfortable armchair, with a large tumbler of whisky and a siphon of soda water at his elbow. Gindin suspected, as with so many of Empson's apparent eccentricities, that he had planned every mischievous moment of the evening.

Not long before the Gindins were due to leave Sheffield, they drove out with their baby for lunch with Christopher and Annemarie Heywood at their house in Totley, on the outskirts of Sheffield. They agreed to give a lift to Empson, but they had bought their car in 1964 (before they learned of Mrs Gindin's pregnancy): it was a two-seater sports car, so Empson had to hunker into a space at the back that was more of a parcel shelf than a seat. When they stopped to buy some flowers for Annemarie Heywood, the uncomfortable and impatient Empson muttered, 'Why bring flowers to people who have gardens?' But the lunch was very pleasant, with much talk about psychology. 'I recall some surprise at Empson's acuity on what were then contemporary revisions of Freudianism. In short, I realized again the enormous range and speed of his mind—he was always coming out with the brilliant and unexpected remark—even though it's the eccentricity or the quick dismissal that remains quotable in memory rather than the brilliant remark.' Empson and Gindin parted on cordial terms (they had not grown close in a way that one would keep up)—'although he still wished that I'd been Robert Lowell.'

In general, Empson was keen to entertain visitors, and particularly enjoyed playing the grand seigneur by whisking them off for an afternoon or a day in Derbyshire, filling them up with beer during a pub lunch and then literally rushing them up hill and down dale at his naturally breakneck pace. It was childish fun to run young men ragged. Such outings anyway gave him the excuse to commandeer a colleague with a car and a few spare hours to be of service. It has to be said too that on occasion Empson liked to sport with his visitors. When the American Roger Sale, who had written on Empson in his study *Modern Heroism*, brought his wife and children to call on him on their way back from a holiday in the Dales, Empson naturally took them out for a Derbyshire walk, as was his wont. In what he called a 'German' forest they came upon a structure, a dam for a reservoir: Victorian Gothic. 'Can you date that?' he quizzed. 'Tower Bridge, 1890,' said Sale, pleased to feel that he could not be far wrong. 'No, no, my boy,' said Empson. 'Peter Pan, 1904.'[14] Though not quite a prepared put-down, it was a way of having the last word.

Another young man who got to know Empson as Head of the Department of English Literature in the mid-1960s was David Parker (who was ultimately to become Curator of the Dickens House Museum in London). Parker, having taken his first degree at Nottingham, transferred to Sheffield in the autumn of 1963 to work on a Ph.D. supervised by Empson (not unlike the thesis by Hobsbaum, his *Concepts of Modern Literary Criticism* gave some attention to the work of his supervisor). In 1965 he began doing some part-time tutoring for the Department, and from 1966 to 1968 he was a full-time temporary assistant lecturer. 'Towards students,' Empson was to write of Parker, 'he is appreciative, large-minded and firm.'[15] Parker found Empson 'at once forbidding and accommodating. He was very informal and friendly, even though he might forget who you were from time to time, but, though he would suffer fools gladly enough, he was courteously merciless about folly.' In response to one chapter of Parker's work—Parker himself later came to think it a desperately over-ingenious effort—Empson cheerily observed that it was 'quite all right, though rather what Virginia Woolf called the creak and screech of the brains in their weekly mangle'.[16] Of Parker's work he would write: 'My own critical writing was among the subjects to be discussed in his Thesis, which might have become embarrassing; but he gave this its minor place with entire firmness and directness. Probably this was what first made me notice the good sense which is his outstanding quality, but every other angle has reinforced it. Perhaps his essays on the Wife of Bath and the Sonnets of Shakespeare are the best examples of it. He is not an astonishing or revolutionary critic, but good sense on this scale presumes good taste and good judgment as well.'[17]

Although Empson would invariably be an amusing and stimulating companion at a graduate seminar, and especially in the pub after the seminar, few people, students or colleagues, ever felt they really got to know him well. There was often something distant, abstracted, or impersonal about him; he would usually avoid eye contact, and seemed not to invite close acquaintance. Also, his mind would leap at exceptional speed, not from A to B but from A to G, so that people thought him mad until they worked out the steps for themselves. His response to a request from a young colleague, Barry Argyle, seems to have been characteristically oblique. Argyle had come to Sheffield in the 1960s from a fairly formal department at the University of Geneva, and after a few months began to feel uncomfortable about having to address his senior as 'Professor Empson'. So he tackled him. 'Professor Empson,' he said, 'I feel over-formal always calling you that. What would you like me to call you?' 'A lot of people call me just "Empson",' he replied, 'but especially close friends tend to call me "Bill".' The story of the transaction is of course more illuminating than Empson's words alone: far from saying 'Do call me Bill', he did not offer Argyle any safely unembarrassed way out of his awkwardness.

On the other hand, Empson was fascinated by personalities very different from his own. One such was an American named Garrett F. Evans, a vigorous postgraduate who divided his energies between Romantic poetry and field sports, and who delighted in enunciating a *gung ho* Republican mentality. He would proudly and mischievously tell trendy young British liberals of the 1960s how his officer father, a distinguished colonel in the US Army Signal Corps, would deal with homosexuals detected in the US army. 'Sergeant,' Evans would boom, imitating his father, 'push that man downstairs and break his skull.' Empson remarked to David Parker: 'I can't understand how a man of his views can feel any sympathy for Shelley [whom Evans was working on].' But he said it with relish, and it was evident he enjoyed working on the paradox: reconciling opposites. When he completed his MA and moved on from Sheffield, Evans gave Empson an unusual and fine thank-you gift in the form of a Bowie knife (which inevitably ended up being chucked by Josh at the doors and floors of Studio House until it was ultimately lost).

Another characteristic of Empson's I encountered,' writes David Parker, 'was his habit of firmly making up his mind about you and your plans and ambitions. My lecturing contract at Sheffield was a temporary one. I had long been interested in the Far East and under his influence, felt that a spell there would be rather a good thing... So when the job I took in Kuala Lumpur was advertised, I was very interested and quickly applied. However, I wasn't resolved at all costs to go there, and I had applied to UK universities as well. I think it was Derek Roper who overheard Empson taking a call from Leicester about my application for a post there, and declaring firmly that it was no good treating such an application seriously: I was going to the Far East, and that was that. I was a bit surprised at this, but within a day or two I got a firm offer from the University of Malaya, and accepted that Empson and fate were on the same side.'[18] In later years Empson betrayed a bad conscience for having rushed Parker off to Malaya, and throughout the 1970s he would be writing testimonials for the 'very good-humoured and steady character' who had 'remained a friend' but who had presently decided that Kuala Lumpur was not to be his destiny after all. In one reference dating from 1972 Empson stated matter-of-factly that Parker 'would probably have been appointed to the staff [at Sheffield] if he had applied for a vacancy which came up, but he wanted to see the world, and went to Malaya'.[19] Five years earlier, however, he had admitted in self-defensive terms: 'it is rather on my conscience that I encouraged him.'[20] Parker was to resign his professorship in Malaya in 1975, and Empson was delighted when he finally took up his post at the Dickens House Museum.

Parker last saw his teacher on 21 September 1983, when Empson (with Hetta) attended the opening, by the Lord Mayor of London, of Dickens's 1839 drawing room, which Parker had reconstructed. Guests crammed the modest house, and the merriment was of a Dickensian order; it was all to Empson's taste. Parker remembers further: 'He had been quite rude about Dickens in print, complaining of Oliver Twist's innate middle-classness, and suggesting that the moral action recommended by the novel was going to the workhouse, picking out all the natural little gentlemen, and forgetting about the others. But his mind was too agile to get stuck in any kind of lasting hostility to a writer not positively wicked, and sufficiently complex to challenge the imagination. And I think he enjoyed meeting the great and good of the heritage establishment, not to mention old associates like Kathleen Tillotson and Philip Collins. He expressed himself pleased that, after some difficulty finding a suitable job when I came back to this country, I'd found my post at the Dickens House, and was doing unusual and interesting things.'[21]

To the undergraduate generations of the late 1960s and into the turn of the 1970s Empson would appear to be remote and preoccupied, quite old for his years, and not well coordinated; even a touch pathetic in his appearance and bearing. As Andrew Braybrook (one of his very last students at Sheffield) recalls, his tutorials would be set for 2.45 (a civilized hour to return from his 'liquid lunch' at the Star and Garter pub). The students would assemble in his room, under the watchful gaze of the formidable secretary Mrs Baehl, and Empson would arrive a few minutes later, mumble a greeting, hang his once-cream raincoat on the coat stand, and extract from his pocket the crumpled essay handed in that morning by the student who was slated to deliver it at the tutorial. But even as the student read out the essay of the day, the master would go through a distracting routine. He would take out a huge white tin of 'Neutradonna', his antacid of choice, spoon a generous measure into a glass, and top it up with water from a decanter and stir vigorously with whatever tool came to hand—usually a yellow 'Bic' biro. Even while the active liquid started fizzing in unseemly fashion, the valiant student would try to continue with his or her essay, and Empson would appear to stare vacantly out of the window and indulge in algebraic puzzles on his blotter. However, when the moment came for Empson to respond to the essay, and even as the students wondered whether he had paid any attention at all, Braybrook well remembers too: 'there was never the slightest hint on these occasions that he was anything but sober. There would follow a detailed and constructive evaluation of the essay which, for all the great man's complex writings, was a good deal more accessible and helpful than one might have imagined.'

Thus the delightful surprise about the rickety old man was that he was actually a kindly paternal figure, always concerned for students' well-being. For instance, he appreciated that students had very little money, so he would insist that reading lists contained the cheapest editions of the prescribed texts. During lectures he would endear himself to his audience with remarks such as: 'I shan't be saying anything about the third and fourth Cantos of Spenser's *Fairie Queene* because I've lost them.' And he went on to recommend that in order to read *The Faerie Queene* to best effect it was necessary to contract a heavy cold and retire to bed. Numerous similar aspects of the aged eagle inspired appreciation and affection. A lecture in which he argued that the English and Scottish ballads were amongst the finest things in all literature proved unforgettable. 'He gave us his own rendering of the most notable ones and I shall never forget the silent tears of emotion that ran down his cheeks as he did so. Indeed Empson was an accomplished singer of folk songs and would, if relevant, give his students an impromptu performance in tutorial.'[22]

The very idea of putting on creative writing courses at the University Empson disparaged as 'no doubt a good idea in places like America'.[23] Yet he was remarkably generous in giving praise and help to individual students who took up writing in one way or another. One such student was John Brown, who returned to Sheffield in 1968 (having taken his first degree in English in 1967, and having then spent a year in the USA) to write an MA thesis under Empson on an impressively progressive topic: *English Poetry of the last ten years—with particular reference to the work of Bob Dylan and Chuck Berry.*

In his final undergraduate year, Brown had pulled off the great coup, with the assistance of Richard Sylvester, of doing an interview with Empson that was published in the student magazine *Arrows* (no. 92, 1967), of which Brown was then the editor. Empson agreed to give the interview—it was one of only a handful he ever gave—at a time when he was extremely unwell (as is evident from the photographs which accompanied it), and it was all the more notable for eliciting responses to a medley of questions which he fielded with patience. To the encompassing question 'What common ground, if any, do you see as existing between European and Oriental cultures', he answered with good-humoured reasonableness: 'There is a great difference between North and South. There really is a difference whether you have a hard winter or not. As between the Northern Chinese and the English or Germans, I should think there is extremely little difference. In fact, I think the East is a delusion. It meant the way the boats went. Consider Morocco. It's due south of Sheffield and everybody would call that the East, in a film, say.' He was then bowled a wholly unrelated question 'On a more general level, is it true you were at one time a champion knife thrower and ski runner?'—which must have been prompted in part by gossip about the knife that Garrett Evans had given to Empson. 'No, I never threw knives at all. I wouldn't know how to. No is the answer,' he calmly explained. 'When I was a schoolboy I was taken out by my mother to a party, as one did then, skiing. It happened to be very bad snow and there was an International Ski Running race which was largely through mud and was only really for the lightly-built. It was a gift for a schoolboy, if you could sort of plough through the mud on skis. Taking twenty minutes for a race timed at seven, I was awarded, compassionately, the status of an International Ski Runner. This was of great use to me in later life. When people were timidly picking a party, deciding who were to stay in the hut in the pass and do the long run in the morning, I would say modestly "well, I am an International Ski Runner". They'd say "Good God, of course you can come." An important factor in my life. I do consider myself quite competent at rough skiing across country though no good at the elegant performances on the . . . you know, the things they test you for.' Asked about the 'primary function of art', he answered directly: 'The primary function of art is to be art and neither to teach or to please but to be good because it's good. I belong to that old Bloomsbury school, in fact.' Just a little later again, the student interviewers lobbed another large one: 'Do you agree with Yeats' belief that a successful man should be a man both of action and of thought?' Pausing only for a moment or two, Empson said: 'Successful? That's rather a baffling question, isn't it? The seventeenth century poets were all prepared to be Civil Servants. They needed three or four languages because English was little known abroad. You pick up a lot of information while learning three or four languages. I should say that a poet ought to be widely informed, but how much he need have done is another thing.' To the question 'Do you think the Arts Council (or anyone) should subsidise artists?' he offered the wise answer: 'I think they ought to subsidise literary magazines. It's silly to give a man a prize for writing a poem, because it doesn't make him write a poem . . . If you wanted to do anything to subsidise literature, it would have to be not tossing a bone to a pet but improving the whole level of payment for it.' On contemporary poetry, he responded just as sensibly: 'Oh, it doesn't matter. I'm an old buffer, do you see?' On audience participation at the theatre: 'I'm so deaf and blind I never go to the theatre at all. I suppose the more they shout away the better.' After asking his views on Henry Miller and William S. Burroughs, who were exhilarating prophets to the English-speaking youth of the 1960s, his young interviewers must have been slightly surprised to learn that he had indeed formed an opinion: 'Well, Miller is undoubtedly a good writer . . . As far as I can make out, Burroughs is appallingly boring. A very earnest artist, no doubt.' Nor was the 'buffer' ready to cast aspersions in response to this final question: 'Do you think the general public is culturally dead?' He responded: 'Of course it isn't. It's too easily taken in. There are more people wanting to be generous and understanding and like a piece of art which the next man can't like than there ever were before, I should have thought. I wish they had something better to look at.'

Equally, Empson kept up with the poetry that John Brown and his friends were managing to get published in the national periodicals, and he always commented on it constructively and, on occasions, favourably. Brown remembers further: 'He and Francis Berry used to award an annual poetry prize. Berry and I didn't get on and in the year when I was the likely front-runner he demanded that the prize go to a student of his who specialised in modern versions of Norse myths. Empson resisted this fairly strenuously and in the end they issued two prizes, one to me and one to Berry's choice.'

As a graduate student, Brown found himself living at 15 Brunswick Street, just a block down the road from Empson's Burrow. Since he was often away from Sheffield doing poetry shows, it proved almost impossible for him to arrange supervisions at the Department, so he and Empson tended to drop in on one another at home. At the Burrow, they would drink whiskey out of white porcelain pudding basins. Regardless of whether it was nine o'clock in the morning or eleven at night, the whiskey would be forthcoming. Empson's lodging was very dishevelled, but he could always lay his hand on any book he wanted in no time at all. He loved thrillers, Brown was interested to learn, with Allingham being a favourite; and on one occasion when they were discussing Chandler, Empson urged Brown seriously to take up Hammett because he was 'a much less sentimental writer than Chandler'.[24] John Brown noted that Empson was always much less disconcerted than his colleagues by 'the mid-sixties student world of psychedelic drugs and revolution'.

By the summer of 1971, when Empson retired, both he and Brown were resident in London, so Brown would drop in at Studio House from time to time over the next couple of years. Unlike in Sheffield, however, Brown felt that Empson was not relaxed in the Hampstead milieu: this was partly because of 'the number that was playing out between his wife and a late period Mailer clone called Josh', and partly because Hetta seemed to assume that Empson's male visitors were all gay and so 'having a scene with Empson' (though this was not the case with Brown): thus she appeared to treat his male visitors with some hostility.[25] So they would wander off to a pub where Empson liked to play shove-ha'penny. Sadly, the thesis that Brown had been working on was never to be completed.

Another student poet whom Empson was to encourage was Geoff Hill, who took a degree in Sociology in the summer of 1968. He came to Empson's attention with the poems he was publishing in student magazines, especially the glossy production called *Arrows*; he was also represented by no fewer than three poems in a noted Corgi paperback entitled *Love, love, love: the new love poetry*, which happened to be edited by yet another Sheffield graduate, Pete Roche. Empson thought Hill's poetry 'vigorous' and was prompt to recommend him for the Poetry Prize for 1968.

Among the poems which earned Hill the annual prize was 'The Sad Skyscraper', which took the form of a poster poem that borrowed from William Blake and Allen Ginsberg in arraigning the bleak erection that was the University Arts Tower, a high-rise building of glass and grey plastic panelling that had been opened for business only in 1966. English Literature was one of the departments that were shoe-horned into this sheer, unfeatured edifice over the summer of that year—though it was fortunate to be given offices that were no higher than the second floor. For an amusing while, Empson's door boasted the legend 'Professor Epsom'. Unusually among those who had to work in the Arts Tower, Empson rather liked the building, especially for its novel paternoster lift, a dumb waiter on a continuous loop which could carry two passengers in each open-sided box. Though it was not for the faint-hearted, Empson would urge visitors to travel to the top of the tower by this slow-motioning means. (In fact, the open-sided lift was such an alarming novelty that for a while, as Richard Sylvester remembers, caretakers had to be employed to push reluctant students into it.)[26] He wrote to his brother in May 1966, 'I have left out the Court news. The Queen Mother opens the Arts Tower next month, and Hetta is coming to the grand lunch with her, for the third time sticking to the rule that she comes only for royalty';[27] so too, with palpable excitement, to Christopher Ricks: 'The Queen Mother is opening it this month, and Hetta will come up for royalty as usual, the third time. You see how glutted with them we are. Hetta says it is the only time when Sheffield people are at all agreeable; she likes to hear them boasting about it.'[28]

Yet the new building was not an unmixed delight even for Empson: one morning, John Brown found him collapsed in front of the Arts Tower, and even as Brown was helping him to his feet and asking if he felt all right, Empson replied simply: 'These tall buildings do tend to overpower one so.'[29]

Geoff Hill's 'The Sad Skyscraper', which howls at the soulless Arts Tower, was to provoke a protest from the Architecture Department. It begins:

AVE Arts Tower, Supreme Steel, streamlined, steamironed

SAD earthbound wouldbe Superstellar Spaceship

ALL the sad scholars are waiting at your feet, waiting to feel your mighty
    rockets rumble & roar into life, waiting to feel the mighty thrust of your

Gigantic Pre-stressed Prick, waiting to be sucked into your Irresistible
Slipstream as you pull away to worlds of Infinite Possibility...

It ends up:

WHO DID IT? I MEAN WHO BUILT THIS UNFUCKING PLACE?

SOME bloke with pressed kneecaps & creases down his shins, with Regular
    Tubes & Cleanshaven Pubes who lechers after sculptures of Himself &
    wanks himself sterile in some Cool Clean Closet up there not forgetting
    to return his Cubic Pubic to its Allotted Place in the Departmental
    Refrigerator before he goes home at night...

AND hes not going to stop till the whole world looks like nothing on
    Earth...

WEVE gotta get out of this place if its the last thing we ever do

GIRL theres a better lie

        for me &

           yoooooooooooo ...

Though at odds with Empson's feeling for the building, it was one of the
poems that persuaded Empson to award the Poetry Prize to Hill; he must
have liked its mischievous energy. He told Hill he liked his 'virile' poetry.[30]

A handsome, long-haired man, Hill was cultivated by the 62-year-old
Empson (who was beginning to look all of his years). They would go out to
the pub together, and back to Empson's Burrow (where Hill noticed 'cheese
rinds and empty wine bottles'); and when Hill moved to London, he would
now and again go up to Studio House (where just like John Brown, he felt
that the living-in Josh was 'a Norman Mailer type'—'a wild boy' who gave
the impression of being drunk much of the time).[31] They would go out to a
local pub, or for a sprinting walk on Hampstead Heath. Once, at the fair on
the Heath, Empson pointed to the 'Haunted House' and said: 'Must be a
good few poems in there.' Empson would occasionally take the trouble to
call on Hill at his place in Notting Hill. Geoff Hill enjoyed Empson's casual
company: Empson was kind and caring, and both his formal conversation
and his chitchat were guaranteed to be instructive or amusing, or utterly
provocative, or at least startlingly novel. Empson once proposed to him, for
example, that 'it might be easier for two people to make love if they didn't
look into each other's eyes "since that can be too much—windows of the
soul, etc." ' Hill reflects on Empson's suggestion: 'Whether he regarded this
as a good general rule or just an occasional necessity I've no way of
knowing.'[32] Another time, he confided the opinion—*sotto voce* here—that
women were only finally allowed into the universities so that their future

husbands might be better able to talk to them 'afterwards'. On another occasion, when Hill probed him about a specifically literary subject—Structuralism—Empson was to show himself to be just as unreconstructed: 'That's a new name for an old thing.'[33]

There is no question but that Empson genuinely liked Hill and enjoyed his company, but it is also true to say that his interest in the young man was not entirely disinterested. 'I often thought his mind was on something else,' Hill has reflected. Every so often, indeed, Empson would make a pass at him of a rather old-fashioned kind that was neither convincing nor successful. Once, he even chased Hill round the kitchen table at his place in Notting Hill. On another occasion, fixing his mark with a fierce stare, he challenged him, 'Oh, you're not really into this long-haired business?' And another time: 'It'll make a good subject for your next novel.'[34] Perhaps to save embarrassment on both sides, Empson would make such suggestions in a take-it-or-leave-it fashion; he showed no resentment at rejection, and Hill rejected his advances.

Whichever way one interprets the deeper meaning of his behaviour, in truth Empson never exploited Hill. On the contrary, quite apart from feeling his odd surges of unrewarded sexual interest in his young friend, Empson was dedicated sbove all to Hill's talent as a writer. He took every opportunity to promote Hill's work in an entirely disinterested and uncompromised way. What especially impressed Empson was a full-length play entitled *The Heroes of Samsara*, which Hill himself directed for the Sheffield University Students Union Theatre Group in the summer of 1968. Empson found the work 'witty, imaginative and searching'.[35] He greatly enjoyed the play as performed at the Students Union. Being increasingly hard of hearing, he had come to dislike live theatre, so his praise for Hill's play represents an exceptional compliment.[36] Still more unusually, he found *The Heroes of Samsara* to be even more promising once he came to read the text. Indeed, he read it not once but a number of times over the next three years, each time commenting in detail on the language as well as the structure of the play, and urging both subtle and substantive revisions. By March 1969 he was recommending the play to a talent scout from the literary agency Curtis Brown. That same month, he pressed it upon the writer Karl Miller (editor of *The Listener*), in the sincere hope that Miller would recommend it to a commercial director or producer. Three years later again, when Bernard Miles, director of the Mermaid Theatre in London, approached Empson with a view to producing a staged entertainment in celebration of the tercentenary of John Donne, Empson did not forget his commitment to Hill's play. With undiminished enthusiasm he told Miles (as he would also tell his old friend Francis Dillon at the BBC), that the play 'was a terrific success here in the Students' Union, only four nights but that is as much as they do, crowded every night and [he said] altered every time'. At the end of a letter to Dillon which generously conveys the excitement he felt over Hill's fine work, he closes: 'I wish I knew who I could send it to next, instead of just sending it back to him. Peter Cheeseman isn't this line of country. Can't you suggest somebody who does produce plays for a younger audience? Surely there is that lady in the East End [Joan Littlewood]?'[37]

Unfortunately, nothing ever came of all his very warm advocacy; *The Heroes of Samsara* was never to find a producer who would stage it. All the same, Empson's tireless promotion of the play showed a degree of admiration for Hill's accomplishment that far outran his interest in the author's person.[38]

Empson was enthusiastic too about a work by another student—a poem— both because he felt it attained a high level of lyrical beauty (a lyricism which he believed was largely lacking in contemporary verse) and perhaps above all because he felt its subject-matter chimed with his own feelings for a quasi-pantheistic schema that was opposed to the personal godhead of the Christian myth: that is, it accorded with the notion of an impersonal 'Divine Ground', such as he had been delighted to find set out in Aldous Huxley's *The Perennial Philosophy* (1948), one of his favourite texts of the postwar era. From the late 1940s until the end, Empson consistently pursued this point—that humankind should seek not for transcendence but for conciliation with the universe. The proposition is continuous with the underlying message of *Some Versions of Pastoral*, that (as Guy Hunter discerned in a contemporary review) 'the simple man in touch with Nature somehow knows everything.' And in *Milton's God* he would explain:

> The idea of the re-absorption of the soul into the Absolute does get hinted at a good deal in the literature, if only in the form of complete self-abandonment to God; whereas the idea that God himself is wholly immanent in his creation belonged mainly to the high specialized output of the Cambridge Platonists. Marlowe's Faustus, in his final speech, desires to return his soul like a rain-drop to the sea rather than remain eternally as an individual in Hell, and this is a crucial image for grasping the Far-Eastern position ... [39]

Thus he was delighted in the final year of his career at Sheffield to discover a poem by a student that proved to express the specific organicist philosophy he desired to extol above a vengeful Christianity. Nick Malone, who was to graduate in Sociology in 1968, was chairman of the Arts Society, and so got to know Empson (the president of the society), albeit slightly, when they took guest speakers out for a meal before the meetings. Malone's poem, *The Burial of Crispin Pike*, a 505-line meditation in quasi-mystical vein on the processes, chemical and biological, whereby the deceased Pike is reabsorbed into the natural world, came to Empson's attention at a time coinciding with his retirement. (As Francis Berry was to note in a review of the published version, it is 'an extended meditation in the line of Lucretius, Donne's *Second Anniversarie* and *Gerontion*.')[40] Empson did not offer the author immediate, unqualified praise for the early draft he read, but he did recognize in it qualities he always enormously admired, most notably the 'singing line' and a sensuous ruminativeness that bowed not to a personal god but to an entrancement with Nature's processes. (It must have seemed to him that Malone's great effort was in some sort seeking to pick up the torch that had been dropped with the premature death of Dylan Thomas.) He wrote to Malone in August 1971, taking issue with him first on a technical matter—his aversion to the overuse of short (dimeter or trimeter) lines—and moving on to suggest that he overcome his 'modernist' rejection of narrative:

> Your poem is very good, I think, especially when one allows for the struggle you have to make against the appalling current fashion. I always hated those short lines even in Auden—I believe he adopted them from Laura Riding, who has no feeling for English at all; but in your case I think it is a way of hiding your natural power over the ten-syllable line, forbidden by Ezra Pound because he was bad at it ...
>
> There ought to be more story, I think; of course there is a kind of ghost of a story, but you feel you ought to apologise for it and hush it up. It is high time The Waste Land was turned into a car park.[41]

That he spoke so sharply and wittily to the young Malone shows that he took him very seriously as a poet: there was no point in fudging the fundamentals. If Malone was serious about his art, he ought to be able to take constructive criticism of the sort Empson proffered him. And presently, once Malone had polished up a full final version of the poem, Empson so heartily approved of it that he took it upon himself to 'act as barker' for it: he sent extracts from it to the editors Alan Ross (*London Magazine*) and Ian Hamilton (*the Review*), as well as to his own publisher, Chatto & Windus.

No periodical editor or trade imprint cared to take up the challenge to publish even short extracts from the poem, but by 1974 Malone had happily arranged for the Workshop Press in London to bring out the entire mini-epic. Best of all, Empson volunteered to write a critical preface for the publication. Malone's mentor was yet hesitant to commit his reputation to a claim which his hunch told him must be true, but of which he was not absolutely certain; he accordingly put to Malone in December 1973 a question he thought crucial:

> am I wrong in supposing that nobody writes poems about nature-spirits now? You seem to me very original there, but I read very little recent poetry. However, unless there is a great deal of it your originality can safely be praised.[42]

With his letter he included a draft of a spirited piece in praise of the poem which would in due course be printed, without alteration, as the Introduction to the volume as published in 1974. His reflections included these remarks generously locating Malone's work in a poetic tradition reaching back to the great Romantics, for whom negotiations with a divine Nature were all in all:

> Wordsworth and Shelley would both say that 'the cause of mind is probably unlike mind', and yet believed that *The Prelude* and *Prometheus Unbound* told some obscure truth about man's relation to Nature. If the poet is not allowed to enter that larger world he is in effect condemned to write about his personal worries, giving a stifling self-centred and pokey effect ... [43]

In January 1974 he would reconfirm for Malone his continuing faith in his work: 'Thank you for the poem, which is very sensitive and well-observed, I think.'[44] And in November that year, he would thus modestly acknowledge a finished copy of *The Burial of Crispin Pike*: 'Thank you for sending me the edition. I think it looks nice, except that Empson is rather too prominent.[45]

There is no question but that where Empson placed his faith, he would back it up with open praise and an abiding sense of personal commitment. For all that he would occasionally fancy the young men to whom he extended his patronage, first and foremost it was their literary talents that he cared for. Outings to the pub and tours of Hampstead Heath and its environs were a necessary aspect of the duty of mentoring; what mattered above all else was the literary promise of the students to whom he acted as patron. Never mind his lustful lunges, he was more fervent in his efforts to promote their work—and he would go on trying to stimulate the work, with a conscientiousness and a constancy that were remarkable, over a period of not months but years.

He did not see much of Malone through the 1970s, but in the autumn of 1979, when they had occasion to dine together, Malone ventured to say that he had been at work on another long poem, *Jason Smith's Nocturnal*

Opera; and then he asked Empson to look at a draft of this new work. As always, Empson lost no time in reading the typescript, and he was just as prompt to post off constructive encouragement:

> My dear Malone,
> Thank you for letting me see this... It is your poetry all right. I doubt whether the story of this one is so well suited to it as the last one, but I realise that it is not finished. You began outlining the plot at dinner, and I ought to have paid more attention, but felt I had better read the poem first. There will need to be prose introductions to each canto, or perhaps marginal glosses, like the Ancient Mariner ...
>
> In general, the reader needs to feel that the boldness of the writing is justified by an adequate theme, but I have no doubt you will fix it up. I am glad you still have your singing line.[46]

He was by no means alone in recognizing the qualities of Malone's poetry. A section from *Jason Smith's Noctural Opera*—'The Song of the expelled insects'—was to become a prizewinner in the National Poetry Competition 1979, judged by Brian Patten, Anne Stevenson, and Craig Raine.

Hard upon the New Year 1967, Ian Parsons urged Empson to think about his next book. Six years had passed since *Milton's God*, and there was a danger he could lose his public if further books were not forthcoming. Why not gather up the articles he had been putting out lately? Yes, Empson answered, he was eager to 'nail together' another volume; he was all too well aware that in four years' time he would have to retire, and he would need extra income to make up his pension (he did not stand to benefit from a full pension, since he had worked abroad in his younger years and had joined the universities' pension scheme only in 1953). Nonetheless, he was determined to work on his next book just as soon as he could find some free time. For the immediate future—during the summer vacation when he could normally get down to some writing—he had agreed to teach an American summer school at the State University of New York at Buffalo. He was doing the summer school principally for the immediate money, he said; he needed the cash for Capital Gains. (He was to say to Hetta, a little later: 'a richer future is always glimmering on the horizon.')[47] He concluded his letter to Parsons on a jaunty but slightly defensive note; the next book would be done in due time:

> I don't think I have [been] losing my public by only writing short articles, usually funny or rude. I suspect they are positively grateful to the old man

for not boring them with a book. Anyway, a slight suggestion of lunacy and badtemper necessarily attached to Milton's God, and is now cooling off I think. Many wicked teachers hate me, of course, but it does me good when they say so in their horrible magazines. I am rather surprised in fact at not being more of a back number; maybe it is just because the young are so dull.

High time to produce something, though, of course.[48]

He had indeed been looking to the near future in every respect. He had secured his home in Hampstead, with a small mortgage he could pay off with a lump-sum pension entitlement; and at the university he was pleased (after some difficulties and special pleading) to secure a personal chair for Francis Berry in 1967. This meant that the succession was also safe: Berry should be able to take over as Head of Department upon Empson's retirement. (All the same, he was to confide to Hetta, just a year and a bit later: 'Berry is already being piteous about being made to do administration.'[49]) While Empson actually held the sole established Chair of English Literature, he would seek to put a characteristically charitable construction on a suggestion by Berry that his personal professorship should somehow be limited to a specific area of the subject, such as poetry and poetics. Empson was not concerned for the standing of his own Chair, he insisted; as far as he was concerned, he and Berry were on an equal footing:

> The way I had always understood our Professorships is that they are equal and identical—there are simply two Profs of Eng. Lit.; and you of course continue when I go. But suppose you make yourself Professor of English Poetry and Poetics—the replacement Professor [for Empson himself] will be free to say that you have admittedly no say in whether half the novels studied shall be American ones since 1900 (for instance). I think it is very important for you to be an *all-round* Prof. of Eng. Lit., because in the coming years a defence of the whole stronghold will almost certainly have to be undertaken—though against whom I don't know.
>
> I assume that you speak out of modesty when you want to limit your field, and haven't any positive advantage in view.[50]

(He was also incidentally keen to wave away the illusory status conferred by the higher degree of MA—which, after all, he had not earned but merely purchased for a nominal fee: 'I should like to drop MA after both names [as on the Department notepaper]; it is an absurd thing to boast of, though essential to the promotion; and we both got it late and by arrangement.')

Robert Lowell was due to arrive in London at the beginning of March, to oversee a production at the Mermaid Theatre of his play *Benita Cereno*; he wrote to say he would like to pay a visit to Empson in Sheffield. Lowell had pictured Sheffield, as he correctly guessed, with a strangely eager relish, 'as a sort of British Pittsburg, blackness, iron and cutlery.'[51] Another very pleasing event was in prospect too: Empson and his wife were booked to go to Dublin for a few days, from 24 to 29 April, as Sheffield University representatives to the Dean Swift Tercentenary Celebration.

The only upset to the optimism of the New Year was the shocking news that Peter Duval Smith, Hetta's sometime lover and the father of her third child, Simon, had died suddenly while on assignment in Vietnam. The cause of death was never to be known, but it was thought he had suffered a heart attack in his hotel. He left a wife and a one-week-old daughter. Soon afterwards, Duval Smith's mother died in the Netherlands. Neither of them had made any testamentary provision for Simon. 'Very sorry to hear your news; it does seem special bad luck,' wrote Empson to Hetta. 'I suppose the trouble is that Simon's Granny might have left him some money but his aunts have no obligation to. I don't think you can blame yourself for this. Peter was extremely unwilling to be tied down, and nothing would have induced him to plan for the outside chance of the two deaths coming together in that order.'[52] Empson did not hesitate to take on the child: although there was to be no formal adoption, henceforth he was to treat Simon as one of his three.

But at the end of February all plans and promises had to be put on hold when Empson reported to his Sheffield doctor with a painful swelling in his throat. Local legend (possibly a Sheffield urban myth) has it that he was in the university staff club when he first complained about the lump, and a brilliant young medical colleague who happened to be there at the right moment was none other than Alan Usher, Head of the Department of Forensic Pathology (who was to become world-famous for performing many highly-publicized coroners' postmortems, and for taking part in almost 800 murder investigations): it is related that Usher took one look at Empson's swelling and ordered him to go directly to the medical centre.[53] Empson was diagnosed with cancer of the throat and rapidly referred for treatment to Guy's Hospital, London, where he had an immediate operation to remove a small growth on the uvula. Directly thereafter, he was put on a course of radiotherapy which went on for about four weeks, though he was allowed to go home after a week in hospital. Never patient with illness, he muttered to Alice Stewart: 'A quite unnecessary week in bed at Guy's Hospital, with the nervous stimulus of waiting for the answer, has been good for me I expect.'[54] Once discharged from the hospital, he had to report back for treatment every day throughout April. He was very relieved to think that the cancer had been caught in time, and that he might come through it quite quickly with the right treatment.

However, the radiotherapy caused severe irritation of the throat, and by early April he was scarcely able to talk; for days he could consume only some milk with a cold egg in it, or a little soup. By mid-April his throat felt so dreadfully raw—even the normally stoical Empson later admitted he had found it 'very trying'[55]—that he hoped to persuade the radio-therapist to reduce the daily dosage. To Professor C. B. Cox at Manchester University he remarked in a letter, 'I am in a very poor way from radio-therapy..., dumb and only able to swallow iced milk, but they say the prospects are good.'[56] But the therapist would not relent, and so the suffering Empson joked of him: 'He is a pawky reliable man who would obviously carry on with his treatment however much harm it was doing... The method of cure is a scorched-earth policy, liable to produce the disease if you go on long enough I believe. However I am lucky there is any method of cure of course.'[57]

Although the treatment left him feeling drained, he kept up his spirits and went on working through the afternoons directly after the morning visits to the hospital. Disconcertingly, he was not allowed to wash his face or to shave: a square of purple-black ink had been marked on each cheek to pinpoint the location for the radiotherapy. The effect was to make him look rather sinister, especially as hairs started to sprout where he had been used to shaving down to the jaw-line.[58] Yet he was surprised to find that his beard did not begin to fall out (as the radio-therapist had forewarned him it might); on the contrary, it was still 'growing sturdily'.[59] Mr Salmon, the surgeon at Guy's Hospital, proposed, not long after this initial severe and painful treatment, to cut out a swollen lymph node in the side of the neck to determine if it was cancerous. Empson wrote to his brother a letter that was a mixture of courage and querulous scepticism, closing with the revealing question: 'I don't think any of the ancestors died of cancer, did they?'[60]

He was a conscientious man, so the prospect of being unable to meet his professional obligations troubled him almost as deeply as the illness itself. At Sheffield—where he was due to give lectures on some American poets including Poe, Whitman, Dickinson, Hart Crane, and Frost (he had already 'covered' Ezra Pound when lecturing on Eliot) and on the prose writings of Bacon, Milton, Browne, and Walton—his colleagues Francis

Berry and Eric Mackerness agreed at short notice to fill in for him. 'Whoever does it,' he noted by way of slim encouragement, 'would have the first weekend of term in hand to look up quotes.'[61] He was determined to pick up his tutorials by the second week of term, in mid-May, and indeed he did just that. Moreover, he saw no good reason to go back on his undertaking to teach at a summer school in the USA in the summer. He was ferociously stubborn on the issue; it was not right to let people down, he protested: 'one had to think about the organisers of these affairs—they can't get somebody else at the last moment'.[62] Eventually, his surgeon at Guy's Hospital told him in short, sharp terms that it would be crazy for him even to attempt such a trip so soon after the cancer treatment.

The second operation, to excise the lump in the throat, took place on 2 June. The following day he was back to letter-writing, feeling at once hopeful and restless; he hated hospital fuss and was determined to get out like a shot:

> I feel much encouraged about it all, though a good deal badgered by life in hospital ...
> There is a drainage tube which is expected to stay in for two or three days—till then I am chained to the neighbourhood of the bed, but from then on I may hope to become an out-patient, surely.[63]

Although he was supposed to stay in for two weeks, he fretted after one week that he wanted to go for a walk on Hampstead Heath. The surgeon said OK: if he could manage such a walk, it was probably the best thing for him. At his own insistence too, he was allowed to go home after less than the two weeks.

By mid-June he was admitting to his publisher that the proposed book would not be forthcoming as quickly as he had anticipated back in January:

> Well, your warning that I had better write books while I can has been justified with eerie speed. I have just come out of hospital after an operation for cancer of the throat. It was caught early, and they say the prospects are good, but of course whether the disease has established itself elsewhere is always a gamble. So I am anxious now to get a draft of the next two books ready as soon as possible, hoping to be ready if the blow falls. A Long Vacation spent in what the Americans call Re-Search, rightly in my case because it is largely a matter of looking for things (historical evidence) which I used to know—that at least I may look forward to. But I won't confess I have been wasting my time; all this controversy in periodicals has been needed to know where I am, or what has been happening to my readers.

In a postscript he noted as a matter of psychological curiosity: 'How very self-centred the disease does make one; an absorbing experience, as they say.'[64]

A month later, despite the poorly condition of his throat, he valiantly stuck to a long-standing undertaking to recite his poetry at the first Poetry International festival at the Queen Elizabeth Hall and the Purcell Room on the South Bank in London, directed by Ted Hughes and Patrick Garland. There had been earlier poetry festivals at the Mermaid Theatre and the Royal Court Theatre, but nothing quite so ambitious as this one. A truly international pageant of poetry, the five-day event included appearances by Yehuda Amichai, W. H. Auden, John Berryman, Allen Ginsberg, Patrick Kavanagh, Hugh MacDiarmid, Pablo Neruda, Charles Olson, and Anne Sexton. Empson appeared at the Queen Elizabeth Hall on Wednesday, 12 July, when the line-up of poets—along with Empson there were Auden, Berryman, Spender, Neruda, Olson, and Hans Magnus Enzensburger[65]—was introduced by Malcolm Muggeridge; the following day, he appeared at the Purcell Room, introduced by his long-standing admirer A. Alvarez, together with Auden, Spender, Yves Bonnefoy, Neruda, and Enzensburger. (Translations, where required, were read by Ted Hughes and the actor Patrick Wymark.) Charles Osborne, who was then Assistant Secretary of the Poetry Book Society, retails in his memoirs some disobliging anecdotes from the occasion; according to Osborne, for example: 'On one evening, William Empson delivered a very long introduction to the poem he intended to read ['Bacchus'], and then sat down having forgotten to read it.'[66]

The summer brought along two occasions for celebration. The cancer appeared not to have taken permanent hold upon him, though he was to be monitored for a good while afterwards. In due course, it was officially admitted that the cancerous lump in his throat had almost certainly been benign: he need not, that is to say, have undergone the terrible radiation and the operations. Unfortunately, the treatment left one of his cheek muscles paralysed, with the effect that his speech became slightly slurred for the rest of his life—though he would never complain about it. The following year, he would write to Robert Lowell, without acrimony or even reproachfulness: 'I had five operations in six months, plus a bout of radio-therapy which was worse than any of them. And at last the great surgeon confessed that maybe I hadn't had cancer at all. However, it is agreed that I haven't got it now.'[67] A few years later, in July 1974, he was advised after a check-up at Guy's Hospital that there was no recurrence of neoplasia in the neck.

A more certain cause for rejoicing was the marriage in July of his son Jacob, aged 23, to a fellow student at Sheffield named Janet Beard (aged 21), the daughter of a tax inspector. A modest family wedding at Rickmansworth Parish Church—about fifty people attended, principally the family relations from both sides of the family (even Empson's brothers, Arthur and Charles, turned out for it)—was followed by a knees-up at Studio House.

Later in the month, to aid the process of Empson's convalescence, Hetta took him on a gentle motoring holiday on the Continent: she drove him down through southern France to Aix, and then over the border to Barcelona.

It was a necessary respite, because by mid-August he was back in Guy's for his third operation of the year. He had known for some years that he was suffering from cataracts (the milky opacity of the eyes is perceptible in his TV appearance for *Monitor*, filmed in 1964), but at his most recent check-up in 1965 he had been reassured that an operation might not be needed for 'many years'; at worst, it seemed, an increasing astigmatism could easily be corrected with new spectacles.[68] But the eye condition was thought to have been aggravated by the harsh treatment he had endured for the throat cancer. So then he had to have an operation to cut the cataract from his right eye. It was an operation that caused him to feel more anxious than the cancer: he was less afraid even of dying than of being left blind and unable to read and write to his heart's content. Indeed, the prospect of this operation put him in a 'very frightened' state, he said— though it would be over quickly. 'Hoping to *see* you,' he hailed Christopher Ricks with gallows wit.[69] 'Terrifying, I think,' he remarked just as candidly in another letter.[70] One comfort was that his fear had a specific actual cause, as he would joke too: 'Oh well, the troubles are good for the psychology up to a point, by removing neurotic guilt.' In the event, the operation was quickly and successfully carried out on 25 August.

Feeling that Ian Parsons' exhortation that he should produce a new book had put a hex on him, he wrote just as soon as the operation was over:

> The cure for cancer is thought to have gone off all right, though one never knows, of course; but one of the side effects of the radio-therapy has been to hurry on the cataract, and I have been having an eye operation. This cure has got over the anxious period (I hadn't realised so much anxiety was

usual) but I won't be reading easily for another six weeks or so. So the hoodoo on following your instructions is still pursuing, but I will write my book if I escape blindness and death.[71]

In consequence of this series of health problems and operations, Hetta and her eldest son became conscious as never before of the increasing frailty of Empson (now in his sixties); until this year, he had always seemed strong and sturdy, and even his stomach complaints had gone on for so many years that they seemed almost reliably unserious, and surely not life-threatening. Both of them wrote at this time to Francis Berry in Sheffield. Hetta urged that Empson needed to take things more easily: even though the latest operation had been a success it would be several weeks before he could read properly again; and she wanted him also to leave 'that beastly burrow of his. I think it is positively dangerous for him to go stumbling down those mouldering steps in the dark.'[72] So too, Mogador wanted him to move 'to a more sanitary flat'.[73] But although Mogador, who had recently finished his degree at Leeds and was in search of a job, was quite willing to go to Sheffield to help his father move from his dive into more suitable accommodation, Empson was not to be prevailed upon: he would stick to his Burrow for the remainder of his career at Sheffield.

By mid-September, Empson felt he was emerging from the shadow of death; his recovered jauntiness is manifest in this letter to Douglas Duncan (his young Head of Department at Ghana), in which he chooses to amuse himself by casting a sexist slur at Helen Gardner's pretensions to scholarship:

> I have been getting a lot of pleasure out of peering waspishly at the apparatus of Helen Gardner's edition of Donne. They will call me even more of a cad than they were doing already when I print my further reflections on her work; but after all why should she be allowed to destroy the text of Donne merely because a lady does not understand what he means? A lady used to know better than to seek out such a comical position.[74]

But his troubles were not yet over. By the beginning of October he was back in London for an operation for retinal detachment in the right eye. 'There is always the left eye, not yet operated on, if the right one goes,' he wrote to his sister; 'but still it means a lot more bother. Oh dear.'[75] For some reason, Alice Stewart came to Hampstead the next day to take matters in hand: she fixed an appointment in Sheffield for the Monday, and drove him up the motorway that morning. The operation to repair the damaged retina was performed without delay. But there may have been post-operative complications, because it was only on 2 December that he was at last discharged from hospital and went to be looked after for a while by his young colleague Roma Gill. Christopher Heywood, who drove him to Cambridge for a literary society meeting not long after the bandages had been taken from his eyes, recalls that throughout the journey down the A1 Empson observed that the landscape had the touch of heaven about it—he gasped about its Chinese qualities.[76]

Harry Kay, then Professor of Psychology at Sheffield, remembered the calm, impersonal way in which Empson seemed to weigh up his affliction:

> Late in his career at Sheffield he had a delicate eye operation, and since he could not be expected to return to his lonely cellar, and for reasons I can only guess, he could equally not go to London and be nursed by his wife, Dr Roma Gill looked after him. We went to dinner with them whilst Bill was still partly bandaged. I think the reason for asking me was ... [because] he was interested in the psychology of his half-blind-totally-blind state. I recall him turning his chair around in the middle of dinner so that he faced the wall, and staring at it earnestly for many minutes from a distance of a few inches. I could not imagine that he could 'see' anything from that position but I think he was considering it as an experimental condition in which he was recording primary data, perhaps impoverished stimulation[,] and examining what he made of it.[77]

It had been a year of dread symptoms and draining treatments.

The year 1968 opened in much more auspicious vein. Out of the blue he was awarded the Ingram Merrill Foundation Award in Literature for 1967—'for your distinguished contribution to many fields of literary criticism and for your excellence as a poet,' as the official citation had it.[78] In past years, the Foundation (based in New York) had 'played godmother' (as Empson put it) to writers including W. H. Auden, F. R. Leavis, Randall Jarrell, and Jorge Luis Borges. The nicest thing of all about this unsolicited accolade—'there are no dinners, speeches or anything else expected of you but that you shall accept,' he was reassured[79]—was a cheque for $5,000 (just over £2,000).

In 1968 too he agreed to teach for six weeks on the Fifth Summer Program in Modern Literature at the State University of New York at Buffalo. Though best known as a meat-packing town, Buffalo fielded a first-rate faculty, he was informed, including Leslie Fiedler, Charles Olson, Dorothy Van Ghent, and John Barth; a library with an outstanding collection of modern poetry; a symphony orchestra; and a museum devoted to abstract art. The directors of the programme had been patiently urging him to participate in the school since 1965, and at last he was to do so; but for the cancer diagnosis and hospital treatment, he would definitely have gone in 1967. 'I should say it might be quite a good thing, though a sweat,' he said.[80] Yet he would not undertake the trip if Hetta could not accompany him, he insisted; she had never before been to the USA. (In 1966 Hetta's lover Josh had said he would be quite miserable if Hetta went away with her husband for a period of several months in the USA; Empson had responded to the plaint: 'Tell Josh I am very sorry if it makes him unhappy, but it is only a short trip and ought to freshen her up.'[81] The use of the third-person pronoun 'her' puts Hetta at an obvious distance.) The only anxiety pertained to the question of whether Hetta could even manage to secure a visa to the USA; once upon a time, after all, she had been a member of the Communist Party of Great Britain. 'Do start getting your visa *at once* . . . ,' he had urged her in 1966. 'When you first break to them you were in Communist China say your husband was employed by the British Council. . . You have to vow you are not a Communist of course.'[82] He need not have worried: in the event, the US immigration authorities did not enquire too closely, and she was given a five-year visa starting in 1967. He wrote ahead to various friends including I. A. Richards and Robert Lowell to ensure that Hetta would have enough to do to fend off restlessness. 'Hetta really ought to be shown both the Buddhas and the shell-fish, for example the six different kinds of oyster, in Boston,' he prompted Richards.[83]

But nothing was entirely easy. For one matter, though he was invited to teach Modern Literature (as one might expect from the title of the school), he had been prompt even two years earlier to advise Buffalo, with spirited illogicality: 'I must not get into the position of pretending to know about recent literature in either England or America; there isn't much I have read, because there is very little I like. I suppose this is usual with old fogeys. Perhaps I could do a course on Shakespeare, or the Metaphysical Poets.'[84] (Although he was just 60 at the time of writing, 'old fogey' had become a settled posture.) Such was Buffalo's eagerness to secure his services, they immediately accepted his proposal: he would teach two classes three times a week; and they offered him a stipend of $3,600, which was $600 above their maximum, plus a further $100 if he would do a public reading of his poetry, and $50 if he participated in a symposium. He was even to be accorded the special status of distinguished professor, rather than professor *tout court*. Rather surprisingly, he nominated Helen Gardner's Penguin anthology *The Metaphysical Poets* as a set text for his course—albeit, he said, he expected to use her volume primarily 'to point out cases where I think her wrong.'[85] When he asked too for an air-conditioned classroom—'In my experience [in Ohio and Indiana], the sweating teacher can keep awake all right without it, but not the class'—one was allocated to him (though the summer in Buffalo is not very humid). Furthermore, when Daniel Seltzer, Director of the Loeb Drama Center at Harvard University, arranged (at I. A. Richards's express suggestion) to invite him to give a lecture there late in July, Empson asked Buffalo to allow him the necessary time out: and permission was promptly granted for such an excursion. 'What a lot of patience it must require to meet so many people's demands,' he graciously allowed at his own expense.'[86]

He even had to start a week late at Buffalo (where the summer school commenced on 24 June), on account of a prior appointment: on Friday 28 June he was present at a congregation held in St Andrews Hall of the University of East Anglia to receive the first honorary degree of his career. He was to be conferred by the Chancellor, Lord Franks, with the degree of D. Litt.[87] His fellow honorands included the 44-year-old sculptor Anthony Caro (who had been an assistant to Henry Moore from 1951 to 1953) and the great historian Christopher Hill (Master of Balliol College, Oxford), whose work he admired. When Empson took the opportunity (as he would later tell his publisher with enormous pleasure) to ask Hill what he thought of his thesis in *Milton's God*, Hill responded that initially he had thought it absurd for Empson to suggest that Milton expected God to abdicate—'but on deeper study he had found that plenty of people at the time considered it the only workable solution.'[88]

While at Buffalo, the Empsons lived in a rented apartment not far from the campus. But between classes they flitted about just as swiftly as they could manage: for the weekend of 13 July, for instance, they visited Stratford, Ontario; a week later, they flew to Boston so that Empson could lecture at the Fogg Museum of Art at Harvard. At the end of July they stayed in the grand two-floored apartment at 15 West 67th Street in New York that was home to Robert Lowell and his wife Elizabeth Hardwick (who were away at their country place in Castine, Maine); it was close to Central Park and the Lincoln Center. The Empsons found it such a delightful place (even though it lacked air conditioning) that they were tempted to sit tight: as Hetta enthused soon afterwards, 'it was the place one did not want to go out on the street from—at least that's how I felt.'[89] Also, Empson felt very flattered, as he would tell Lowell in his thank-you note, 'to see my own photo among the curios.'[90]

When Empson had been sent the list of visiting fellows at Buffalo that year, he remarked on just one of them—in a way that could not have seemed ominous at the time—'I shall be much interested to meet Hugh

Kenner.'[91] But Empson nurtured a radical antipathy for Kenner: he considered him a malignant anti-humanist who was set upon reading James Joyce in accordance with Roman Catholic illiberalism. Twelve years before, in 1956, Empson had reviewed Kenner's study *Dublin's Joyce* in a way that left no doubt about the fierceness with which he opposed Kenner's doctrinaire stance. Mr Kenner, he thundered,

> denies that Stephen represents the young Joyce at all, even in the *Portrait of an Artist as a Young Man*. Stephen represents a type incapable of development (p. 112), the heir of Hume, Shelley, H. G. Wells, and all *that* lot, for whom Joyce, we are to gather, felt the same unqualified contempt as Mr Kenner does . . .
>
> We didn't in England have such thorough controversy over 'humanism', twenty or thirty years ago, as the Americans did; though Dr Leavis has rather the same resonance. We do not therefore easily realise that the reason why Bloom, Stephen, Hume, Shelley and so forth are all treated as sub-human by Mr Kenner is that they are 'humanists'. It strikes me that the anti-humanists, now that they are a secure orthodoxy, are overplaying their hand.[92]

Thomas E. Connolly, director of the summer school, was thus acting in all good faith when he invited Empson to participate in a panel discussion, together with Hugh Kenner and Fritz Senn (an amateur authority on Joyce and editor of *The James Joyce Quarterly*), on the topic of 'The Novel since James Joyce'; he did not know that Empson might seek to scrap with his foe. 'The first sign that I had that something might go wrong came about a week before the date of the discussion,' he has recalled. 'Hugh Kenner came to me and said, "Tom, will you please explain to Empson the role of the moderator. He seems to think that he is like a referee in a boxing match." '[93] Evidently, Empson had been making verbal sallies at Kenner every time they passed one another on campus, and intimating that he could hardly wait for the big fight. Connolly remembers too: 'I later told Mr Empson that I would merely step in now and then to keep the discussion going.' He arranged that the speakers should present their opening statements in alphabetical order (thereby also ensuring, without being too obvious about it, that age would be honoured). Empson, primed to take advantage of this arrangement, leapt from his corner:

> Mr Empson stunned me and the audience with his opening statement: 'Ever since Mr Kenner spoiled the reading of *A Portrait of the Artist* for undergraduates some twenty years ago . . .' (I can't recall how he finished that sentence). When Kenner's turn came, I introduced him and held my breath. He graciously ignored the attack and made his statement. When

Fritz Senn's turn came he was so shocked that he could hardly speak (he's quite shy and sensitive). The rest of that hour is a blur in my memory. All I know is that no one spoke about the novel *after* Joyce.

Fritz Senn, who was a non-professional scholar, had no experience of teaching at a university; he had felt both flattered and awed to be invited to Buffalo as a visiting professor, but found himself scared of appearing on the panel, wondering and worrying about what to say. All the same, though he was preoccupied with his own nervous reflections, his memory of the occasion corroborates Connolly's account in all essentials: 'I remember that Empson started off by attacking Kenner outright, and even personally. The words "You have destroyed *A Portrait* for generations of readers" still ring in my memory (though I could not vouch for their accuracy). It seems that Kenner's ironic view of Stephen Dedalus in Joyce's *Portrait* had hurt Empson more than just as an attack on literature.' Senn remembers too that Kenner was obviously shocked by Empson's onslaught but handled it very well. 'The debate went on for a while, but I was probably more preoccupied by what I would have to say and I preserved what I hoped would be seen as Swiss diplomacy until the topic actually turned to The Novel after Joyce.'[94] Empson was avid to denounce the neo-Christian critic in the person of Kenner. However, even though onlookers found his assault rather embarrassing or improper, it must be reckoned too that his onslaught demonstrates the sincerity of his convictions and his deep moral courage.

Kenner may have seemed gracious on the night, but the memory of the effectiveness of Empson's attack on him clearly festered with the passing years. Many years later—in the year after Empson's death—he was to take his revenge by crudely scorning Empson's argument that George Orwell's target in *1984* was almost certainly not just the totalitarianism of Nazism or Communism but indeed all totaliatarianisms, centrally including Christianity:

> Orwell's wartime BBC acquaintance William Empson warned him in 1945 that 'Animal Farm' was liable to misinterpretation, and years later Empson himself provided an object lesson when he denied that 'Nineteen Eighty-Four' was 'about' some future Communism. It was 'about,' Empson insisted, as though the fact should have been obvious, that pit of infamy, the Roman Catholic Church. One thing that would have driven Empson to such a length was his need to leave the left unbesmirched by Orwell and Orwell untainted by any imputation that he'd besmirched the left. Empson summoned Orwell's shade to abet the hysteria he was indulging at the moment. He was writing about 'Paradise Lost,' contemplation of which appears to have unsettled his mind.[95]

Three years later again, in 1988, he would take further vulgar revenge when he commented in his book *A Sinking Island: The Modern English Writers*: 'Empson, in his late years "nutty as a fruitcake"—I'll not name my source for that judgment—came to hate whatever had been touched by Christianity'. In a footnote, equally negligent of the necessity to argue his case, he jeered at *Milton's God* that it was 'surely the maddest critical book of the century'.[96]

Once back in England, Empson would now and then refer to 'Buff and Sheff', as if the two cities were characters in a children's cartoon, or ancient gentlemen's outfitters, or as if there were really nothing much to choose between them.[97] He may have carried away some extra warmth for Buffalo on account of having—at least as he saw it—trumped and triumphed there.

Jacob Empson graduated from the Department of Psychology at Sheffield with an Upper Second degree in the summer of 1968 and was delighted when he was awarded a Medical Research Council scholarship for Ph.D. training in the MRC Unit for Metabolic Studies in Psychiatry, being based in Sheffield at the Middlewood Hospital and at the Psychiatry Department in Whiteley Woods Clinic, under the joint supervision of Professor Alec Jenner and Peter Clarke (a clinical psychologist). Empson would be very stimulated by this step in his younger son's career development; he thought it plucky of Jacob to go to work in a psychiatric hospital. 'Jacob is very gay but suspects he has got into a ramp [swindle],' he gaily reported to Hetta. 'His loony-bin has only one MANIC not a collection of them for study.'[98] Likewise, a few months later: 'Jacob is being allowed to examine the manics at the Whiteley Wood bin, but still not at the Middlewood bin.'[99] In addition to showing an enthralled interest in what Jacob was doing and discovering, he helped out by offering a gift of £30 to Jacob and Janet so that they could buy not only a secondhand scooter 'but two white shiny crash helmets and two black shiny macks [*sic*] ... I hope it won't fall apart ...'[100] That was a decidedly useful thing to do, since Jacob needed his own transport to scuttle back and forth between hospital and clinic.

Jacob was eventually to become an expert on the subject of sleep and brain-waves. His Ph.D. concerned the effects on memory of depriving people of rapid eye movement (REM) sleep, and since that work he has published two notable studies, *Human Brainwaves: The Psychological Significance of the Electroencephalogram* (1986) and *Sleep and Dreaming* (1989), which has gone through several editions. Since Empson was perennially interested in scientific ideas and the progress of research, he would become fascinated by his son's professional pursuits; in the summer of 1969, for example, he wrote eagerly from Hampstead: 'I don't believe your laborious German has asked the right question, viz: do the brain-waves begin at the same time as the belly-waves, or half an hour later, or in any such relation?'[101] And when Jacob came to publish his first research article in the periodical *Nature* in the summer of 1970, his father was very proud to notice it was mentioned in *The Times*.

In 1971 Jacob was appointed to a temporary post at Surrey University, and spent a year commuting from Sheffield on a weekly basis, often stopping off for a night or two at Studio House, though he also shared a house with two colleagues in Guildford. Despite the tiring demands of travelling back and forth between Sheffield and Surrey, he made excellent progress with his thesis and was able to deliver it by December 1971 (being examined early in 1972). Then in the summer of 1972 he was finally appointed as a Lecturer in Psychology at the University of Hull, where he would remain in post (and develop his work in a sleep laboratory) until taking early retirement in 1999.

His elder brother Mogador had graduated from Leeds in 1967, but to his shock and frustration he gained only a Pass in his joint degree in Chinese and Economics. Jacob, who had to convey the news to Empson in Sheffield, remembers that his father could scarcely believe that his firstborn, whose fluency in Chinese never failed to impress him, had only got a Pass degree—not that Mogador had passed at all. Still, refusing to be cast down, Mogador set about finding a job in which he could make use of his skill as a Chinese speaker, and in due course he gained employment with the firm of Bass Charrington: his job was to market French wines to Chinese restaurants. He brought Linden and baby Saul to live for some months at Studio House, and Linden produced a second son, Ben, on 4 July 1968.[102] In addition, very smartly, he secured a part-time job as a restaurant critic for *Egon Ronay*; Hetta happily posted the news to Sheffield: 'Mog has got himself rather a clever though daunting job on the side—eating two Chinese meals a day for a Guide (rather like the Michelin one). He has to get through sixty a month, for which they pay him £2 a go.'[103] All the same, his father hoped that sooner or later he would fulfil his talents by finding employment in his proper professional métier (as Empson saw it): the China trade. On occasion Empson would ask friends with useful contacts to tip him off about likely jobs for Mogador; and he was ready to play the 'Old School' card when he could, as when he contacted Lord Trevelyan (with whom he had been at Winchester) in hopes of finding the key to the China door. At one moment, it looked as though Mogador might turn journalist and take up his natural position as China correspondent of *The Daily Telegraph*, a prospect which his father fancied; but that chance came to nothing.[104] But eventually, a few years later, Empson was delighted to see his idea of his son's proper station in life realised when Mogador quit the wine trade and developed a career as a comprador, becoming employed by AEI as part of their drive to export heavy engineering plant (including power stations) to China: he was to be skilful and successful in that role.[105]

In 1968, with a loan from Uncle Arthur, his father's eldest brother, Mogador was able to purchase a house in Highgate, north London.[106] A year later, Hetta Empson conceived the notion of becoming the proprietor of a shop; it might have been a fine entrepreneurial venture, except for the fact that she seemed to have no idea what she might retail in her shop. 'Hetta wants to buy a pokey little shop next to Mog's house, for a vast sum, and doesn't even know what to sell in it,' Empson lamented to Jacob. 'She had much better have a pig-farm in Spain.'[107] Still, being ever unwilling to deny his wife her desires, Empson reluctantly, though with a good grace, agreed to put up £3,000 for the purchase of the shop; but he was relieved when Hetta gave up the idea after all. (One of his own wheezes to maximize a high-yield income was to take the $8,000 he had stockpiled in a bank in Buffalo—it was made up of his wages for the summer-school teaching and some fees accruing from articles published in the US—and to invest it in a Swiss bank account; he was temporarily thwarted by the information that he would need a minimum of $10,000 to open an account in Switzerland, and in due course he would relinquish that particular bid to get rich quick.) Yet as retirement approached, he worried more and more about his drop in income. Since his pension would yield only £500 a year (after eighteen years of pensionable service at the University), they decided to make a larger proportion of Studio House available for letting, and so Hetta set about a final reshaping of their accommodation. On Empson's retirement to the family home in 1971, they would occupy the renovated basement area which comprised a kitchen-dining-sitting area looking onto the much-loved back garden of the property (which they retained for themselves); off that communal area, on the same basement level, was to be a little corridor leading to some small bedrooms (including a bedroom-cum-study for Empson himself), while upstairs Hetta kept the big studio space for working, entertaining, and sleeping on her grand *k'ang*. Henceforth the large flat they had formerly occupied on the first floor generated additional rent. Empson wrote wryly: 'We are preparing the basement for the after-life, at great expense.'[108] This final conversion of the house bit £6,000 out of Empson's pension lump sum of £14,000; but the most staggering setback would come along when he was subjected to capital gains tax of £40,000 as a consequence of developing the luxury flat upstairs.

The constant financial worry that Empson suffered following his loss of a full salary would so possess him that he believed he had no option but to keep on accepting visiting appointments in the US and elsewhere, to boost his pension; for the next several years he would be torn between the desire to get on with his writing and the necessity, as he saw it, to lap up remunerations. As early as 1970, the year before he retired, he was offered a position at York University in Toronto, Canada, to begin just as soon as he had kicked free of Sheffield. Such a post would yield in the region of £10,000, he reckoned, which amounted to something approaching twice as much as his final salary at Sheffield; for the final year of his employment at Sheffield, in fact, his salary rose from £5,270 to £5,796. All the same, he put off York for a while, in the happy expectation that for the session 1971–72 he would be able to enjoy a 'year's holiday of plain living and high thinking in Hampstead.'[109] Nevertheless, the process of taking up temporary posts would get under way just as soon as he accepted a part-time teaching appointment at King's College, London—he was to do just over three hours of teaching a week ('We shall not expect you to do any departmental chores or examining,' he was also assured) for the Michaelmas and Trinity Terms, with an emolument of £1000 per term—even in the very first autumn of his retirement.[110]

Finally, young Simon, Hetta's son by Peter Duval Smith, who reached the age of twelve in 1968, was by this time going to a senior school in London; every day he would take the tube, toting an enormous black leather briefcase.

Within a month of returning home from the summer school at Buffalo in 1968, Empson found himself back in hospital for yet another operation: this was to cut the cataract from his left eye. He told Alice Stewart he hoped she might come and stay in Sheffield for a while so as to be able to visit him in hospital. By late September he was discharged, but with strict orders to take things slowly; 'the Sister made me promise to live under proper female supervision,' he dutifully related to Hetta.[111] Being as good as his word, every night at 10 o'clock he walked up the street to sleep at Jacob and Janet's house—though 'I didn't promise to eat her cooking too,' he joked to Alice.[112] Hetta was pleased to write to a friend a couple of weeks later—during which time she had come up and stayed for a few days with Jacob and Janet ('Jaket', as they had winsomely taken to referring to themselves)—that unlike the last time when he took no proper care of himself, William 'didn't bounce around after, so the retina stayed put and he ought to be seeing better than before.'[113]

The sole bonus of his spells in hospital during the 1960s was that it enabled him to get in touch with the revolution in pop music of the period:

> I had a long period in hospital, the later part with eye trouble [he was to tell interviewers in December 1970], so I was happy to listen to the mercifully piped radio, you know, and I found that I liked pop music very much. I'm a great admirer of the Beatles ever since—'Hello, Goodbye' is the only modern poem I admire since Philip Larkin, I think. I think there's a great deal more to be said for them than for the chaps without the guitar, you know, who just recite against a background.[114]

Smaller but cumulative health worries tended to nag him for his last two years of employment. In May 1969 he would write to Hetta, 'I am feeling much better now; I thought it was old age already, but of course I was a good deal pulled down by all that hospital-life.'[115] But his brave reassurances turned out to be slightly premature: by June he had developed such severe pains in his right leg that he was given an injection and made to wear a surgical bandage for three weeks; he suspected the root problem was rheumatism. The pains got less the more he walked around: which was OK, since he relished brisk walking. And yet the pains kept up for many months.

In spite of feeling quite run down after the series of minor operations he had endured, Empson was always ready and willing to respond positively to invitations to give talks or poetry readings at campuses and other venues around the country. As far as he was concerned, it was not so much a question of *noblesse oblige* as a fervent desire to rescue literary works by the likes of Donne, Marvell and Coleridge from the pernicious misinterpretations of the Christian critics. It was a welcome bonus if he was offered a fee, to salve his feeling of being perennially out of pocket. Thus, every month or so, he would catch the train to fulfil a variety of engagements. All this was exhausting work for a man in his early sixties who had been set back by lengthy illness. Yet he tried to give full measure both to his formal audiences and in the pubs or at the parties that were an inevitable follow-up to the performances.

Professor Kenneth Muir remembers a conference (not long after Empson's retirement) at which Empson was asked to read his poetry. But Empson arrived half an hour late and prefaced his reading with a startling question, 'Do you mind if I take out my teeth? I speak better without them.' He promptly removed the teeth and began reading—mumbling inaudibly. So after a few minutes a woman at the back of the hall shouted out 'CAN'T HEAR YOU!' The audience on this occasion was outraged at the interruption, and only later was Muir told that Hetta Empson had been entrusted by her husband with the task of bellowing at him when he could not be heard.[116]

Two years before his retirement, Empson wondered aloud in an interview, presumably disingenuously: 'It's funny, I get asked to lecture in Oxford, York, Liverpool, but not nearly so often in Cambridge. Once I spoke at the Cambridge Union with the mayor. He was a rationalist and he was wearing his chain of office at the time. Well, we both denounced the English churches [i.e., Christianity], and there was a considerable gap before I was asked again. It looks as though I am nursing a grudge. That won't do at all. Old men must always give the appearance of looking tidy.'[117] The run of his remarks as reported does not quite make sense, since Cambridge's failure to extend invitations to him on a more regular basis could scarcely be attributed by them to a grudge on his part; one suspects they were strung together from different parts of the recorded conversation. All the same, it is likely that he did harbour a grudge against Cambridge for the cruel way it had sent him packing exactly forty years before, in the summer of 1929; it felt natural and necessary to him to stick out his tongue whenever he came to deliver talks there. On the other hand, it is equally likely that he did feel a grudge because part of him always hoped he would eventually be taken back to the bosom of his alma mater. Indeed, if Cambridge had ever invited him back to take up a Chair, he would probably have felt he had to be big enough to accept it.

He went on: 'I think I'm in the straight now'—meaning that he was relishing the prospect of breasting the finishing-line of his career at Sheffield. Increasingly, and perhaps inevitably (he was now in his sixties), he found himself at odds with academia, its developments, its rancours, its rivalries. The sort of strain he always feared is illustrated by a story from his final year:

> For years a wicked Professor has been trying to make mischief in my Department by promoting them out of order, but this year [Ray Southall], who got wind somehow that they were trying to promote him out of order, wrote to me and said he would refuse to be made a Senior Lecturer unless [Derek] Roper got it too. This is the last time I shall have to be bully-ragged at this beastly committee, and it was a satisfaction to end with a firm show of good feeling from the staff and a decisive check-mate for my enemies. The other professors were afraid of what might come out at the inquiry which would follow the refusal, so they voted to put Roper ahead on the list...

A triumph in a way, but a nasty situation to be in, anyhow; I shall be glad to be out of it.[118]

Though he would never lose his enthusiasm for teaching, circumstances added up to make him feel tired of the daily struggle of academe. He believed his day as an academic had passed, that he was too old to cope with the necessity to update the system, let alone to comprehend or initiate any change. When his student John Brown returned in 1969 to do his MA, he found that students in Empson's Department were protesting in support of demands that the Departments of Language and Literature should award separate degrees, and that the degree results should be based, at least in part, on continuous assessment. In truth, the University had already decided to introduce both of those changes, but this fact had not been publicized. 'Empson spoke out, despite a very hostile reception, against the continuous assessment option on the basis that the students were ignoring the one real strength of externally assessed finals, namely that they acted as a check and balance on the power of the academics in the department to play teacher's pets.'[119] He was howled down, and the changes went forward.

Empson had failed to think through the issue in a sophisticated way: he had been unable to figure out that continuous assessment need not mean the demise of external examining, or to foresee that anonymous marking might be the solution; his point of principle was not in fact incompatible with the students' wishes, though he could not imagine it so. He wrote home, merely glumly: 'The students are demanding Continuous Assessment instead of exams. High time I left.'[120] At several British universities in the late 1960s, there were various and increasing manifestations of student unrest against the 'authorities', often of an anarchistic tendency, including a number of 'sit-ins'; greater openness was demanded, a greater say in the running of the show: maximum student participation. There was a little 'student unrest' at Sheffield, but nothing to rival that at Warwick, or Paris, or even in the USA; when John Webb, Empson's erstwhile research assistant, wrote to tell him of the goings-on at Buffalo, Empson could respond with relieved good humour at the end of the summer term of 1969:

What fun your letter is; I wish I could compete, but the placidity at present of the Sheffield students (won at the cost of incessant care and skill, you must remember, and liable to be destroyed at any moment, but still, aimed at by both parties to the dispute) is summed up by the announcement of the engagement of the President of the Students' Union to the Vice-Chancellor's daughter. He would not have dared confess to this intrigue till the end of his period of office. Your account of life abroad strikes a British note long familiar in the postbag of the islanders; it reminds me of one of my elder brothers [Charles the diplomat] saying proudly 'We always have plague in Baghdad'.[121]

Still, it was symptomatic of the onrush of his desire to retire that for the first time in his career he came to resent the quantity of examining he had to do. He would say with a sigh: 'Only twice more, two more years.'[122] He dreaded too the prospect of ever-increasing student numbers; in an article written for a student magazine in the year of his retirement, he reflected sympathetically for a moment on the question of 'qualified applicants for whom no room has been found.' But then he went on: 'But I do not mean to say they should be let in regardless of numbers; having viewed the startling results of that at Nanterre in Paris, I very much hope Sheffield may be spared them.'[123] The future he feared has come to pass, but he would not live so long.

Despite the process of slow yet inexorable disengagement from affairs at Sheffield, the one undertaking to which he remained committed to the end of his career was the establishment of a University Drama Studio. He would serve the Drama Committee with eagerness, and take pains to try to drum up money to fund the modest but imaginative plans that were put on the table by 1969. The efforts of Empson and his colleagues paid off with tremendous success: the Drama Studio, housed in the former Glossop Road Baptist Church (built in 1871), was to be opened on 30 June 1970. Twenty-five years later, it would be recorded that over 4,000 performances had taken place in the theatre, and there had been some 800 productions of plays, musicals, operettas, operas and dance shows, as well as some 400 concerts.[124] In October 1971 Empson would donate £150 to set up an annual prize for student drama at Sheffield (the first William Empson Prize was to be awarded to Martin Priestman), and he was pleased when Roma Gill agreed to assign to the fund any profits from the sale of the Festschrift, *William Empson: The Man and His Work* (1974).

Just weeks before he retired, Empson was honoured with a degree by Bristol University, where he and Hetta duly went to receive it on 20 May. It was the second of only four he was to be awarded.

Also before his retirement, he was momentarily taken aback when the administration at Sheffield asked him if he was prepared to nominate any critics and scholars who he thought should be invited to succeed him in the Chair of English Literature; he told Francis Berry: 'This is a surprise. If you have specific proposals and I agree (I have nothing in mind of my own choice), I had better support yours.'[125] But then, after taking a moment to remember a solid old loyalty, he asked G. S. Fraser if he would care to follow in his footsteps: 'Are you putting in for my Chair? I have had the routine request to say what I recommend and had better answer soon.'[126]

At a reception to mark his retirement in July 1971, Empson was presented with the best memento he could ever wish for: a set of the multi-volumed *Oxford English Dictionary*, the work which had informed so many years of his critical thinking but which he did not possess in person. Another colleague, Eric Mackerness, eulogized him in the University *Gazette*:

> No university teacher ever did more than he to uphold by his particular posture that reverence for the life of the imagination which alone justifies the advanced study of literature. In a sense, his career at Sheffield has been an open defiance of what Shelley called the 'selfish and calculating principle'. To have been allowed to work with him, as his colleagues here and elsewhere will testify, must be counted among the privileges of a lifetime.[127]

His friend and colleague Francis Berry, who had known and loved him for all of his eighteen years at Sheffield, would sing his praises in well-meant verses:

> Witty and lucky and plucky this man.
> He came as a legend, he left as a myth
> At the bars, by our fires, with his verse, with his prose,
> His extraordinary dares, his amazingly wise
> Or—his occasionally wild, quite lunatick—flairs
> He left with even more lustre than he began.[128]

A final interview was done by Ian Sainsbury, a journalist on the local newspaper, the *Morning Telegraph*, who would later put on record that he found Empson 'courtly, helpful, hospitable and effervescent, though he told someone he thought it rude of me to take notes over lunch.'[129] The headline of Sainsbury's piece, presuming upon a kind of teasing familiarity, picked up on Empson's customary self-characterisation—'An "old fogey" retires'—and Sainsbury himself was totally won over by the charm of the valedictorian Empson: 'one of the most remarkable men, not only in Sheffield, but in the world of contemporary English letters ... I have heard more than one Sheffield English graduate speak of his former professor with a fervent admiration that stops just this side idolatry ... Words bubble from him, he chuckles a good deal; though the amusement often seems to have a sardonic tinge.' Empson further revealed that he had spent a fair deal of time reflecting on the prospect of old age—he hoped he could be active for a further fifteen years—and of death: 'The man who once said "after the age of 80 you should be prepared to poison yourself" evidently has small faith in the concept of an ever-riper old age. He sees voluntary euthanasia, however, not as a categorical imperative but as "a decision that should be within personal choice".[130] (Sainsbury was citing an interview published just four years earlier, in 1967, when, in response to the question 'Would you like to grow very old?', Empson had announced with disconcerting decisiveness: 'The doctors are very dangerous today. They can keep you alive when useless. After the age of 80 you should be prepared to poison yourself.'[131])

A year later, the title of Professor Emeritus was conferred upon him by the University.

Three years later, in 1974, he was elected an honorary member of the American Academy of Arts and Letters and of its parent body, the National Institute of Arts and Letters, in recognition of his 'lifetime accomplishment'. Also in 1974 came the belated publication of the Festschrift, *William Empson: The Man and His Work*, edited by Roma Gill and with contributions by a good cross-section of his admirers including W. H. Auden, M. C. Bradbrook, Kathleen Raine, Karl Miller, Ronald Bottrall, George Fraser, Graham Hough, I. A. Richards, L. C. Knights, John Wain, Christopher Ricks, and Francis Berry. On 29 June, at a party at Studio House to celebrate the book, Empson was overheard defending the merits of a black roll-and-roll band which Professor Graham Hough had found fault with; and Jonathan Raban almost came to blows with someone (or so it was said).[132] It was a typical Empson triumph.

Kathleen Raine wrote to Dorothea Richards on the occasion of the volume:

> I hope William will be pleased by his festschrift. I was sorry to hear that several pieces were dropped on the grounds that they were not serious articles, for they are probably the ones Bill would have liked. Bill Pirie, for example, the biochemist [whom Empson had known since his years at Cambridge]. The photograph on the cover is splendid, is it not? What an impressive face!
>
> One day recently Brad [Muriel Bradbrook] and William came to me [at Girton College, Cambridge], (without Hetta, thank God) and it was poignant to see my old friend again so. He stayed after the others had gone; and I felt how thankless I had been to William for that *absolute* loyalty he has towards his friends, even a deserter such as I am. For I *am* a deserter from many of the things he stands for as a critic. Though never, at heart, from

our dear old friend whom we love. And what brash young critic can ever know the quality of William himself.[133]

In addition, Empson was awarded the degree of Litt. D. at the Annual Degree Congregation at Sheffield on 20 July 1974. The honour at once crowned and concluded his career at the university. The public orator for the occasion, held in Sheffield City Hall, was Empson's successor as Professor of English Literature, Brian Morris, who had been appointed to Sheffield from York University (where he had got to know Empson's arch-opponent, F. R. Leavis), and who did not mind hinting at his personal bias when he took considerable pains to celebrate Empson's 'impeccable civility of thought':

> 'Plus nominis horror quam tuus ensis aget. Minuit praesentia famam', said Claudian, the last great poet of the heathen world—the presence of a great man diminished his fame; and it may be that from 1953 to 1971, when William Empson was Professor of English, that the University of Sheffield was less than perpetually conscious that it had in its midst one of the most remarkable intellects of the age ... Empson is a product of Cambridge in the 1920s, the Cambridge of Russell, G. E. Moore, Wittgenstein, and I. A. Richards—there were giants in the earth in those days. Yet in literary criticism two names from those days still stand out: F. R. Leavis and William Empson, two mighty opposites perhaps best likened to Cavalier and Puritan in the Civil War. As Cromwell was to Prince Rupert, as John Pym was to King Charles, so was Leavis to Empson. The imperfect analogy serves to distinguish the rigour and the uncompromising dogmatism of Leavis on the one hand, and the graceful, seemingly careless, aristocratic intellectualism of Empson on the other.[134]

Empson's reply is a little masterpiece of wit and wisdom; a heartening statement of personal faith and pedagogical policy, it merits quotation in full:

> I am to give thanks, on behalf of my colleagues and myself, for the honour done to us by the University, and to express our consciousness of it.
>
> But I am too ignorant to say more about them, so I have to talk about me. That is bad, but I was a Professor of this University till I retired, for nearly twenty years, and perhaps I can say something about that. Indeed, listening to that splendid praise given me by the Orator, it struck me that the University also deserved some praise for making the appointment. It was what is called bold; when I was made Professor here, I had actually never done any teaching in England at all. When I was leaving Sheffield, about three years ago, I was given a farewell party, very friendly and generous, and when it was over I went to the bar, where I found one of my colleagues.

I said 'I'm glad they feel it has worked out all right, because at the time I was considered a bold appointment'. 'I know you were,' he said. 'I was a bold appointment too. They were making them then, but they don't now. That's what's the matter with the place.' I do not know whether this is true, but I thought it ought to be reported to you. I expect it is true; one can think of many reasons why it might seem inevitable.

I did not arrive feeling any conscientious need to make radical changes. The danger of a bold appointment, of course, is that the man may want to destroy what has been built up before. The first thing to realise, I said to myself, is that you have here a working system, and it should not be tampered with except for strong reason. Actually there was a good deal of change in my time, and I seldom regretted it; but that basic attitude has become stronger in my mind now than it was at first. I think that Sheffield and the other universities of about the same age are in effect holding the fort; the very old universities and the very new ones have both given up, on this issue. We still, by and large, try to cover the field in the three years to the BA degree, without breaking it up into options.

This would seem important when the basic planning was being done for new universities during the nineties of the last century. The students themselves wanted three years rather than four, and wanted a skilfully planned bit of packing to give them enough during those three years; in the fourth year, if all went well, they would be earning a salary, and they would get married on it. Almost every detail of this picture has become remote from the modern scene; no wonder that the pressure of the package deal has been so much moderated. And yet you really do want a student to have at least an impression of the whole field after three years. I can only speak for the subject of English Literature, but much the same problem crops up in other departments. You may meet a graduate (from some universities) who has deservedly been given a high class in his degree, and you say 'What do you think of Alexander Pope?', and his jaw drops, and he says 'Never heard of him'. So you try saying 'How about W. H. Auden', and his jaw drops; it becomes quite a familiar sight if you persevere; and he says 'Never heard of him'. At some point he will explain himself, defiantly or proudly, by saying 'I majored in Beowulf and Jane Austen'. Now, this is plainly not what you want, probably not even what the people who made his regulations wanted. Here, I think, is where Sheffield and the other universities of the same vintage have a claim; stodgy we may be, but we do still try to cover the field.

I was asked also to say something for those now taking their first degree, so as to encourage them in the life of learning. Something that applies very widely is needed here. I became interested in *Ecclesiastes* when we had it on the syllabus; the book has of course been enormously discussed, and it seemed clear that King James's translators understood it much better than later scholars. The preacher is a moody disgruntled old man, living in Alexandria (they say) when it was new and a centre for advanced thought, and very much a don; white-collar in class though not rich or notably successful; but he keeps coming back to the merits of 'labour', and you might think he is praising the worker, the labouring man. And yet all the time he is pretending to be Solomon, the ancient glorious king who had a thousand concubines; so that he is holding in mind all three conditions of life. The effect is certainly not cynical. I think he is saying: 'A man needs to be proud of his skill, and he is fortunate if it is one which he can still exercise when he is fairly old. Of course being a learned writer is rather a bore; not like a dictator or a jobbing plumber, who leads such a masterful life, and has so many people pleading with him; but it does give a man enough to go on with. You should keep that in mind' (such is the point of the tremendous last chapter) 'while you are still young'. He tries about five times to say what is good for a man, and I think his best shot at it is the first attempt in Chapter Two:

There is nothing better for a man, than that he should eat and drink, and make his soul enjoy good in his labour.

A strange phrase, and I should think very true about the human condition in general.[135]

17

Rescuing Donne and Coleridge

'[T]he highest event in ethics [is] the moral discovery, which gets a man called a traitor by his own society' WE, 'The Ancient Mariner' (1964)

E MPSON wrote to a friend, a former student, in April 1965: 'I am getting very wrapped up in trying to rebut the Christian revival among literary critics, which to most people with political interests seems very small beer.'[1] A few years later, high on the threshold of retirement, he relished the prospect of throwing off the inhibitions of his academic employment. Though never one to hide his views under a mantle of tact, he genuinely felt that after 1971 he need no longer watch his words so as not to displease or discredit his employer. 'I am still very keen on my subject but look forward to retirement so that I may speak my mind about it more freely.'[2]

His first opportunity to speak out followed hard at heel: he accepted an invitation to be Waynflete Lecturer at Oxford, for the Hilary Term of 1971–2, when (for a fee of £300) he elected to go to war over the texts of Donne and Coleridge. The title he proposed for his course of six lectures (beginning on 20 January 1972) left little to either succinctness or elegancy: 'How to Choose the text of a Poem—the literary side of the problems which face an editor: examples from Donne and Coleridge'. At the tactful suggestion of John Fuller, who hosted his visits to Magdalen College, it was trimmed down to 'The editorial choice of the text of a poem'. Empson gave his lectures in the Examination Schools—and one of them was to acquire additional magic and memorability because he chose to carry on talking in the face of a power black-out. As the poet and critic Peter Levi recalled: 'He gave almost the only Oxford lecture I ever heard that got a standing ovation; it was a discussion of Donne's manuscripts, delivered during an electricity cut, almost entirely in the dark. Later, he took everyone to a pub where he ordered gin, hot water, and peppermint cordial, which he believed was the ordinary drink of the working classes.'[3] Empson had by heart everything he burned to say about the texts of John Donne.

Two years after the Waynflete Lectures, the war was to be waged more thoroughly, on a more extended front, by way of the Clark Lectures, given at Trinity College Cambridge in the Lent Term of 1974. The title Empson chose for this course of six public lectures appeared to be critically innocuous or even historicist, 'The Progress of Criticism'—and by an amusing coincidence the next Clark Lecturer was to be I. A. Richards, who was set to talk about 'Some Futures for Criticism'. But Empson's lectures were to be quite specific, rehearsing all of his vehement concerns of recent years.

He was pleased to be back in Cambridge as a figure of celebrity. After all, it was forty-four years since he had been effectively expelled from Magdalene, and getting on for half a century since T. S. Eliot had delivered his celebrated Clark Lectures at Trinity in 1926, and now Empson had come back to pick a bone with Eliot's illiberal fiats. Though nervous of the august role he was about to fill, he felt otherwise buoyant, well disposed, mischievous. After his first lecture, on Tuesday 22 January, Leo Salingar of Trinity College hosted a drinks party and then took Empson in to dinner in Hall with two other guests who were well known to Empson: Muriel Bradbrook and Graham Hough. He also invited Edward Miller, Master of Fitzwilliam College, who had become acquainted with Empson when he had been Professor of History at Sheffield. Bradbrook signalled to Salingar that he should offer Empson a gown to wear at dinner, shrewdly guessing that Empson would like to sport an outward sign of formality on returning to a social occasion in his own university.

Salingar was impressed by an instance of Empson's thoughtfulness during the course of the Clark Lectures, at a time when Salingar suffered a slipped disc and had to spend some days in bed. He sent Empson a note of apology, explaining that he could no longer turn out to his lectures; and almost by return of post he received four well-worn paperback copies of Rex Stout (Nero Wolf) detective stories, with a covering note saying they were 'very good for convalescence'—as Empson had proven to himself during a number of recent periods in bed. 'I shall always remember this gesture by Empson as an example of literary—and personal—tact; and of kindness.'[4] As to the lectures themselves, Salingar remembers, 'to be quite candid, I felt embarrassed. The Mill Lane lecture room was packed. I remember introducing him and praising his stimulating influence as a critic as warmly as I could. Then, when he spoke, it became evident that he hadn't prepared his lecture or hadn't prepared adequately, so that he rambled on interminably.' George Watson noted too that while Empson was endeavouring to refer to critics of Marvell he pounced upon a piece of paper, held it aloft and twirled it as it unfurled before him; and then he smacked it back onto the lectern. 'Oh, I'm sure you know who they are.'[5]

As Salingar acknowledged, he himself was not able (because of the injury to his back) to attend the full course of lectures, so it is possible he heard only the first two. Nevertheless, it is a pity that he took so little from the lectures, which actually covered a range of texts and argued hard for reconstructive readings of them. A few draft passages survive which give a flavour of Empson's mode of address—though on the day itself (in February 1974) his opening gambit might have been presented differently from these engagingly chatty extracts:

When I was a student here I heard E. M. Forster giving *Aspects of the Novel* as a series of Clark Lectures [in 1927], and I thought they were a model; never noisy or rude, but continually amusing and even exciting, and one's attention was kept at stretch to hear the asides, which were mainly remarks about other writers, but they always seemed strictly part of the discussion.[6] And then, I couldn't get to Robert Graves's ones, but reading them I was struck by a remark that lectures for students ought to be addressed to the passions. Well, *which* passions is naturally a question; but it seems fair to say that a guest speaker ought to be tolerably entertaining. And yet, these lectures have to be printed, though the publisher is most pathetic about that, and says that no one will buy lectures now, any more than sermons; besides, on my own side, I am usually saying things that other people disagree with, and I need to present a much stronger case in print than I do in a lecture. It has been getting pretty near the point of just calling each other liars, so I ought to go out well wrapped up. There is an obvious solution to this problem, perhaps not a good one. The book can be longer than the lectures, so it can add in the more technical parts of the evidence; and the lectures need only give some of the more interesting conclusions, with enough evidence to bring out the point of them. I am afraid that the result will be rather a scrappy series of lectures, but, as you understand, so often in these things a change in the viewpoint automatically makes changes in the whole field, some of them more striking than others: and just picking out bits of them, with his long pointer perhaps, and then tapping for the next slide on the magic lantern, is about all a lecturer can do.

As to the title, I really do believe that progress goes on, it would be foolish not to think that, but often of course in a slow roundabout way; and it strikes me we are now coming to an important change, though the scene looks rather like dead water. A great burden is being gradually unloaded; the English tradition of T. S. Eliot; and the means of unloading is, one might say, a kind of silting up, the accumulation of historical knowledge.

On separate pages of the surviving typescript draft, he explained further:

the expense of altering a fallacy in the textbooks has become prodigious. But I think one major and much needed reform is now in progress, a decisive break away, if it can be pressed hard enough, from the iron rule of the T. S. Eliot men. It is the recognition that people held a great variety of religious or philosophical opinions in the sixteenth and seventeenth centuries, though they were cautious about printing it; instead of all having to agree with T. S. Eliot, because they knew no other... I therefore cannot express any respect for the higher morality upon which my opponents are so ready to preen themselves; instead, it is my duty to warn my listeners that these morals are simply bad morals. What the schools of English Literature have been going through, both here and in North America, is oddly enough a return to the naughty nineties, devil-worship and all. However, the reasons for it are complicated and I need not try to clear them up; I aim in this course of lectures merely at giving an answer, each time, to one or two critical problems, taking a series of cases...

All of these pieces have been published in posthumous collections, but it is relevant here to look more closely at the writings on Coleridge and Donne.

It was quite common in the 1960s for critics of Romantic literature to worry away at the relative merits of the various manifestations of *The Ancient Mariner* as Coleridge had felt moved, or indeed driven, to refashion the poem throughout the final thirty-odd years of his life. Beginning its published existence in 1798 as an anonymous, archaic ballad under the arch title, 'The Rime of the Ancyent Marinere, in Seven Parts', by the time of the final edition of the poet's lifetime (1834) it was made into a conspicuously re-orchestrated and more sophisticated production including a Latin epigraph and fifty-seven explanatory and interpretative glosses. The 'meaning' of the work depends in large part on the reader's view of the relation between the supposedly sixteenth-century ballad itself (though it was pretty quickly to be divested of its original orthography—'the comic Old English', as Empson styled it) and a commentary purportedly penned by a seventeenth-century pedant of moralizing bent.

William Wordsworth, who commissioned the work for *Lyrical Ballads*, found fault with it virtually from the start: 'the Poem of my Friend has indeed great defects,' he declared in print in January 1801; and one of the defects he understandably, if tactlessly, identified was that 'the events having no necessary connection do not produce each other'.[7] For the second edition of *Lyrical Ballads* (1801), in which the ballad continued to be anonymous, Coleridge was prompt not only to expunge from his work all Gothicisms but also to alter lines and stanzas. The poem ended up being 37 lines shorter than in the original version. More importantly, the introductory 'Argument' was changed. No longer did it gesture towards 'the strange things that befell' the ship and its crew; it pointed more directly to a statement of moral consequences: 'how the Ancient Mariner cruelly and in contempt of the laws of hospitality killed a Seabird and how he was followed by many and strange judgements'. By 1817, when it was finally published afresh, and over Coleridge's name, in *Sibylline Leaves*, the argument laid down a still more purposeful directive as to moral cause-and-effect: 'The Ancient Mariner inhospitably killeth the pious bird of good omen'. Empson choicely observes about this crux (in his first full essay on the poem, published in 1964): 'To call it a "pious bird" must be intended as a mild parsonical joke.' (Later he added: 'some tolerable implication might be found, but I can only see the Old Coleridge leering at the grown-ups; to insinuate: "holy lies before the kiddies, eh?" '[8]) He was by no means alone in disliking the way in which Coleridge imposed upon the deeply mysterious and moral-begging story of his initial invention an accountably moral meaning—concerning sin and redemption—that seems scarcely to match the main passage of the plot. Nevertheless, many readers over the years have been content with, and even grateful for, the adjustments Coleridge made, since they enabled the labyrinthine and gnomic Gothic Revival original to be reconciled with a crypto-Christian allegorical reading of later invention. Most critics and readers too have confined themselves to the 'grand text' (Empson's term)—the revised standard version edited in 1912 by the poet's grandson.

The ballad and its glosses are of course susceptible to various lines of sophisticated exegesis. Not the least persuasive critical argument is that the tiresomely moral pedant of the commentary is in any case not the poet Coleridge himself but a persona, so the poem calls for a dialectical reading rather than a straightforward reconciling of the poem and what Empson called its 'leering' allegorical glosses. But Empson preferred in effect to read the evolution of the poem backwards: it became a matter, as he later said, of 'unwinding the cocoon in reverse order' (*CV*, 54). He was at once gratified and appalled to learn that Coleridge, in *Aids to Reflection* (1825)—Aphorism XCVI. 2—undertook strenuously to remove doubts about 'Doctrines of Arbitrary Election and Reprobation, the Sentence to everlasting Torment by an eternal and necessitating Decree, vicarious Atonement, and the necessity of the Abasement, Agony and ignominious Death of a most holy and meritorious Person, to appease the wrath of God.' That passage from the writings of the older and avowedly Anglican apologist was by no means ironical: Coleridge was by that late date attacking all those who doubted such doctrines, particularly those who objected to the truth of eternal damnation, as destroyers of the foundations of morality. By contrast, as Seamus Perry has demonstrated, 'the young Coleridge who wrote the poem regarded orthodox Christianity with the same shuddering horror that Empson did. Coleridge was a Unitarian and almost became a Unitarian minister in the winter he was writing "The Ancient Mariner": being a Unitarian meant that, among other things, he disbelieved in the divinity of Jesus, in Original Sin, the miraculous conception, free will, the Holy Trinity, the Atonement . . . "[9] In one of his political lectures, delivered at Bristol in 1795, Coleridge had averred, 'the Doctrine of the Atonement . . . as it is now held, is perhaps the most irrational and gloomy Superstition that ever degraded the human mind.'[10] Thus it was not unreasonable for Empson to deplore the later, more orthodox and moralistic Christian Coleridge who set aside the authentic inclinations of his poem, and who introduced an allegorical interpretation into the received standard edition of his verses, because he had clearly fallen fundamentally out of sympathy with the Romantic visionary who wrote the original ballad. For one notable matter, the young poet had sincerely credited animism, the belief in a version of an immanent godhead that was considerably at odds with the transcendent, revealed God of the 'moloch priests' (as Coleridge called them even in 1796); the older and more reactionary Coleridge thus 'ratted' on the poem.

'Many critics,' wrote Empson, 'have felt sure that *The Ancient Mariner* is an allegory of the Atonement, or at least that it was turned into one when the author became a Christian and realized its meaning. But this doctrine was his chief point of resistance to Christianity, a resistance he never fully abandoned, so that he was very unlikely to have celebrated the doctrine in the *Mariner.*' (*CV,* 97) By the late 1960s he was in touch with a young scholar-critic of Romanticism named David Pirie, a lecturer in English at the University of Manchester, who shared his conviction that the text of certain of the poems, especially of 'The Ancient Mariner', needed to be rescued from the perverse adjustments of the 'Old Coleridge'. Empson and Pirie thereupon resolved to work together to edit a selection (to be published by Faber & Faber in 1972) which would restore the poetry to its peak performance, in accordance with the poet's authentic early designs. '[W]e have a primary duty,' Pirie concurred with Empson, 'to present the true Ancient Mariner at its most impressive.'[11] Naturally this turned out to be something much closer to, though not precisely identical with, the text as it was first put out in *Lyrical Ballads*. The premise of the edition they agreed upon is expressed by Empson in the opening pages of his Introduction (p. 14), which was itself a greatly developed version of his 1964 essay, and which was to be the basis of his Waynflete Lectures at Oxford and his Clark Lectures at Cambridge:

> an editor ... owes a loyalty to the author, or rather, to the person the author was when he wrote the poem. If the author made changes afterwards under duress ... the original text should plainly be restored; but sometimes, with the passage of years, the author has fallen out of sympathy with this work, or has rejected the beliefs which it expresses, so that by his changes he is in effect trying to write a different poem. It could be laid down, to avoid using the term 'intention', that the editor should print the poem as it was at the fullest and most characteristic stage of its development; but he is unlikely to pick this out if he does not think about the author. (*CV*, 14–15)

Yet obviously that rationale begged some big questions, not least because it curiously allowed that while an editor should *not* be permitted simply 'to print what he considers the best version', still the editor must be allowed to exercise his artistic judgement in determining exactly which state of the text does represent the poem at its 'fullest and most characteristic stage'.

Since Empson could sometimes be overbearing in matters of critical opinion, David Pirie turned out to be his ideal collaborator. Despite his relative youth (born in 1943, he was just entering his late twenties), he was very well able to stand up to the older man on behalf of his own editorial principles and judgement. Remarkably, they did see eye to eye on almost all the issues raised by the text, but one crux threatened to sink the whole project. After having reached a turning point in the text at lines 199–202–

> The Sun's rim dips; the stars rush out:
> At one stride comes the dark;
> With far-heard whisper, o'er the sea,
> Off shot the spectre-bark.

—Empson became fascinated by a footnote in E. H. Coleridge's 1912 edition (p. 195) which seemed to provide evidence that Coleridge in a notebook dating from October 1806 had tried out this variant wording of the lines:

> With never a whisper on the main
> Off shot the spectre ship;
> And stifled words and groans of pain
> Mix'd on each murmuring/trembling lip.

For reasons having to do with both story and sound, Empson determined therefore that the latter stanzas (which for Coleridge had almost certainly been an alternative formulation rather than an addition) should figure in the text after the stanza at lines 199–202 quoted. More controversially still, he resolved that the extra lines should take what amounted to a synthetic form which none of the known manuscript variants precisely authorized:

> With far-heard whisper on the main
> Off shot the spectre-ship;
> And stifled words and groans of pain
> Mix'd on each murmuring lip.

He was convinced that not only did it assist the progression of the story to introduce a baleful near-repetition of the lines at 220–1, it would also be psychologically apt and true to allow the seamen to express an emotional response (however it might be interpreted) as the spectre-ship speeds off. But, as Pirie politely but courageously continued to point out when subjected to a browbeating assault by post which would have broken a man of lesser principle:

In a number of places the 1817 passage can surely only be the work of a man polishing the 1806 lines. Take the lines . . . :
> The sky was dull & dark the night
> The Helmsman's Face by his lamp gleam'd bright,
is improved to:
> The stars were dim, and thick the night,
> The steersman's face by his lamp gleamed white;
No published text before 1817 has any equivalent for these lines. Surely therefore the 1806 passage must have been in front of Coleridge when he wrote the 1817 lines. Surely too the alterations he makes to the 1806 passage are desirable & can only have been dictated by literary considerations . . . I think he intended to leave the murmuring lip lines out & I don't think he was motivated by the kind of extraneous considerations which justify us in reversing his decision.[12]

Although Empson was presented with an immensely persuasive case by his
co-editor, the terrier in him would refuse to let it go until the exaggerated
contretemps very nearly brought a rancorous close to the collaboration.
Charles Monteith, who was then poetry editor at Faber & Faber (and later
chairman of the firm), had to intervene with a diplomatic plea for a
compromise before the two editors would agree to exhibit their differences
to the reader by way of publishing their preferred versions face-to-face on
pages 128–9 of their edition.[13] Even so, Empson was not in the least bit
gracious in dropping his bone of contention. He went on nagging at the
contested crux for two pages of his Introduction, and managed to throw
out his customary 'Eng. Lit.' slur in a manner that lassooed his co-editor:
'The idea that it is somehow artistic not to let the sailors groan when they
hear their fate strikes me as Eng. Lit. at its worst; I don't deny that
something like that may have influenced Coleridge when he cut the lines
in 1815, but if so we have an added reason for restoring what he planned
when in a healthier state of mind.'[14] The differences amounted to such a
battle between the principles of the disinterested editor and those of the
militant and tendentious critic, it seems truly a wonder that Empson and
Pirie agreed about so much else. Whereas Pirie, despite putting his head on
the block alongside Empson, still worried about the imperatives of textual
and editorial scholarship, Empson was almost exclusively intent on establishing what he called 'a consistent story'—always allowing of course that it
could not be Christian. Still, Empson greatly admired Pirie for his knowledge, and his editorial and critical acumen, and perhaps above all for his
capacity to 'stand up to the old man'; in a curious later reference, he would
say he had found his young collaborator 'sympathetic and rather fatherly
. . . a stimulating and inspiriting teacher'.

   In any event, the Empson–Pirie version of 'The Ancient Mariner' might
be thought to be severely compromised from the very start, precisely
because it seeks to establish an eclectic text—which in practice amounted
at times to rewriting the poem.[15] 'The chief difficulty in arriving at the right
text for *The Ancient Mariner*, a splendid poem which was much mangled by
its author for reasons of conscience,' declared Empson, 'is that though he
made harmful changes where he had fallen out of sympathy with its basic
ideas he kept on improving it in detail, even to the first posthumous edition
(1834). One needs therefore to form an eclectic text, always considering the
motives of the author in his successive changes, and only rejecting those
which conflict with the basic impulse and conception of the poem' (*CV*, 27).
Editorial decisions rest upon a priori interpretative decisions, and the
resulting text does not correspond to any single one of the received

printings. Empson and Pirie mix and match according to a preconceived idea of what they regard as the basic 'impulse and conception' of the work. As Jack Stillinger has pointed out in his study of the ballad, the first published version of the poem runs to 658 lines and 'varies substantively from the final [1834] text in about 90 lines'; but each of the eighteen known versions of the text (as Stillinger numbers them) is normally taken to be discrete.[16] It is not usual editorial practice for an editor to cross-pollinate as between the separate versions.

Stillinger notes too, in *Coleridge and Textual Instability: The Multiple Versions of the Major Poems* (1994), that Empson and Pirie 'concocted' their 1972 text according to a 'belief that nowadays is being challenged, and gradually replaced, by a pluralistic concept' of the text.[17] In the thirty and more years since the Empson–Pirie edition of *Coleridge's Verse: A Selection* (1972), there has indeed emerged a theoretical consensus which maintains that 'The Ancient Mariner' is paradoxically constituted by all of the 'authoritative versions one after another'. Stillinger remarks: 'If *The Ancient Mariner* is one poem, then in theory at least it has to be all its versions taken together.'[18] J. C. C. Mays calls his own variorum edition, in the *Collected Works of Samuel Taylor Coleridge* (2001), 'a storehouse of versions'; and he rejoices in the notion that '[d]iscrete texts float weightlessly, as it were without prejudice'.[19] (Yet Mays notes complacently, and therefore self-absolvingly, that Coleridge's intentions 'are always interesting, but I would be hard put to say always what they are; frequently they are contradictory and frequently they changed'—which is in effect another way of making Empson's point.)[20]

Among the crop of surprisingly sympathetic reviews of the eccentric Empson-Pirie edition (with its scarcely blunted edge of irritation swishing between the 'Introduction' by Empson and the 'Textual Commentary' by Pirie), the American pianist and writer on music and literature, Charles Rosen, wrote a keen but not uncritical piece for the *New York Review of Books* including an effective answer to the postmodern-pluralist position:

> Empson and Pirie's treatment of the text may be high-handed, but any edition with variant readings invites every reader to form just such a text for himself . . . However, it is not, strictly speaking, the "ideal" text that Empson and Pirie seek, but the one truest to the original idea of the poem.
>
> Their search implies an idealistic (and Romantic) view of literature in which none of the various stages of the text is the poem itself, but only approaches to it. That is indeed the only coherent view that permits genuinely interpretative criticism . . .

Empson treats Coleridge's betrayal of his poetry with generosity and sympathy, and he is wonderfully free of the pious moral airs expressed by recent critics faced with Coleridge's weaknesses... For Empson, indeed, the theme of the *Ancient Mariner* is the very reason that Coleridge betrayed the poem and tried to convince his readers and himself that it was about something else. The theme is a sense of guilt and revulsion from life greater than any possible motivation. The disparity between the shooting of the albatross and the subsequent horrors visited upon the Mariner and the crew is the most terrifying aspect of the poem... Almost as much as anything else, the *Ancient Mariner* warns us of the awesome consequences of religious guilt, and it is in this sense a deeply antireligious poem.[21]

Martin Amis, in an anonymous piece for the *Times Literary Supplement*, likewise applauded the bid to rescue the original pantheist poem from the later, and marred, Christian version, as well as the 'moving sympathy' that Empson evinced in writing of the troubled Coleridge: 'Professor Empson rightly takes the *Rime* as the work of a man who sees the universe as devoid of moral order, and his analysis of the poem as being fundamentally about "Neurotic Guilt" is more or less unanswerable.'[22]

Empson was by no means the first to pinpoint 'neurotic guilt' as a key feature of the ballad, but he was almost certainly the first critic of Coleridge to perceive a connection between that guilt and the 'maritime expansion of the Western Europeans'—including the long unadmitted horrors of the slave trade. Reports of the maritime expansion (on which Coleridge had drawn) 'reek of guilt,' said Empson in 1964. (Coleridge is known to have been an abolitionist from about 1795 to 1798.) Yet to say that the albatross is meant to symbolize 'ill-treated natives' would be glib; it would fail to reflect the complicated, unspecific nature of the guilt—'but the terrible cry "I didn't know it was wrong when I did it" belongs somehow naturally to the whole set-up of the exploring ship.'[23] Empson was to rephrase that observation in his Introduction to *Coleridge's Verse*: 'Horror of the Slave Trade does I think echo into the *Mariner* at one point, early on [when the 'Nightmare LIFE-IN-DEATH' advances in her 'spectre-bark']...; however, it cannot be part of the story—the explorers cannot foresee the remote consequences of their struggle... If Coleridge wanted the poem to symbolize the maritime expansion, and it seems plain that the idea entered his mind fairly early in the process of composition, to give it a mystery about guilt would be an inherent part of the programme.'[24] Since the ballad is 'magnificently externalized or unselfconscious', the point of it cannot be to invite the reader to solve a clue. Empson's lead in this regard has been tellingly followed up, and well filled out, by critics including J. R. Ebbatson, Peter J. Kitson, and Patrick J. Keane.[25] Debbie Lee, who highlights in her monograph *Coleridge and the Romantic Imagination* (2002) 'the intersection of slavery and disease', correctly notes that while 'the abatross is just one emblem of guilt ... the poem does not pinpoint any one source for the mariner's guilt'—though she does not appear to know of Empson's writings on the poem apart from the posthumous ' "The Ancient Mariner": An Answer to Warren'.[26]

But perhaps Empson's most important contribution to criticism of the 'Mariner'—and the most persuasive point of his argument in favour of the pre-Christian Coleridge—is his insistence upon the neoplatonic daemonography informing the work. What was new in the philosophy of the radical early Wordsworth and Coleridge was not so much pantheism (which was known even to Pope) but the more arcane animism: 'the belief in various kinds of Spirits which had been formative for Renaissance science.'[27] In *Coleridge's Verse* Empson explains further (pp. 42–3) that the dynamics of the poem are dependent on 'spirits of Nature' to such a fundamental degree that when the marginal glosses of 1817 try to pretend that the spirits animating the corpses are 'angels', the poet's holy larceny 'makes nonsense of nearly all the details about them, so nothing can be done to clarify the poem until the parasitic growth has been removed.' In truth, they are 'Spirits of the Air'—the 'middle spirits of Paracelsus'—what Coleridge was to call 'the invisible inhabitants of this planet, neither departed souls nor angels; concerning which the learned Jew, Josephus, and the Platonic Constantinopolitan, Michael Psellus, may be consulted.'[28] The earliest version of the ballad is thus appealing to an alternative belief; indeed it was by definition, and in its key terms, 'resistant to Christianity'.

Empson was ever eager to acknowledge that he derived his ideas about the age-old belief in the *animus mundi* from H. W. Piper's book *The Active Universe* (1962)—he had reviewed it on publication—which stressed the importance to the work of the young Romantics of 'the belief that this life could be found in each natural object and that, through the imagination, a real communication was possible between man and the forms of nature' (as cited in 'The Ancient Mariner' (1964)).[29] 'The fundamental doctrine of Unitarianism, and of the new quasi-pantheism generally, was that God's energy was the reality in the natural world,' noted Piper. Joseph Priestley, originator of Unitarianism, felt that neoplatonic doctrines of the soul, and in particular Ralph Cudworth's doctrine of the world-soul—as enunciated in *The True Intellectual System of the Universe* (1732), which Coleridge read in 1795—accorded with his own teaching.[30]

However, when H. W. Piper moved on to determine how such doctrines applied to 'The Ancient Mariner' he drew conclusions of such extraordinarily reconciling mildness that they were wholly at odds with Empson's view of the matter. 'The spirits who descend to work the ship,' wrote Piper, 'are ... natural forces, though they are described, not inconsistently, as angelic spirits in the gloss of 1815.'[31] So too, Piper professes in his book: 'Thus while it is true that nature in *The Ancient Mariner* is, in Coleridge's later phrase, supernatural or at least romantic, it is recognizably modelled on the supernatural or romantic aspect of that nature which Coleridge described in full belief in *Joan of Arc* and *Religious Musings*.'[32] In such terms (as Piper would have it), Coleridge could have it both ways at once. Piper's project to assimilate the neoplatonic Coleridge to the Christian Coleridge went on until as late as 1977, when he published an article which again professed to see no problem with atoning neoplatonic daemonography and Christian doctrine: 'the poem contains not only the symbolism of the natural world and of religion of Nature ... but also the language of biblical symbolism and prophecy... In the poem the two modes of symbolism are interfused... This makes the whole poem a figuration of the Apocalyptic story and gives it another spiritual significance ... recognizing implicitly and symbolically the sin, guilt, damnation and redemption which Coleridge's conscious Unitarianism rejected... "The Ancient Mariner" manages to combine a belief in the goodness of Nature with Coleridge's deepest apprehensions of guilt and damnation.'[33] Thus Piper argued that the Christian Coleridge was in the bud of the poem; the orthodox already somehow seeded in the heterodox.

Piper had read nothing of Empson's writings on Coleridge when he wrote his article in the mid-1970s, but he presently came across *Coleridge's Verse* and thought to send Empson an offprint of his piece. Empson was thunderstruck. He could scarcely comprehend how the author of *The Active Universe*, which he respected, had failed to take the obvious lesson of his own findings; but he responded with uncharacteristically calm restraint:

> I had assumed that, after proving that Coleridge when he wrote the poem believed in his spirits, you would use that to interpret the poem. Now that you have come across my book, I hope you will write telling me where you find it wrong; it has received no attention.
>
> The Coleridge of the Sibylline Books would be glad to have you say that he gradually discovered what had always been lurking [in] his mind about the poem; the objection to this view is that, when he wrote the poem, he would have considered it a malignant slander. And it is not enough to call him a silly child; all the Romantics thought the Atonement implied a wicked

God... Coleridge remarks in an early letter that one of his friends is particularly likeable, because 'he really *hates* God—with all his heart, with all his mind, with all his soul, with all his strength'. Coleridge himself does not have to join in, because he is searching for a philosophical God who has escaped from being a torture-monster, but any good man must feel earnest hatred for the God of the churches, and rather starve than accept bribes about it. He could not be a Unitarian pastor if it meant administering the sacrament: and surely this has to be recognised in an interpretation of the poem.

Such is my general position, but I am specially interested to know what you make of the spirits. Surely you agree that the author was lying when he called them angels, in 1815?[34]

Piper wrote back on 14 March 1978 that he did not think 'for a moment that the spirits were angels in 1797—they were Nature spirits... What I am trying to suggest in the article is that the guilt and fear of damnation from which he was trying so hard to escape through Unitarianism crept subterreaneously, so to speak, into the poem... I admired your book [*Coleridge's Verse*]... but the big point for me was that Unitarianism was an escape from a wicked God. I had thought the motive political, but I think you're right.'[35] Professor Piper confirmed for me, in a later year, that Empson was 'very distressed that I seemed to have given the poem an orthodox Christian interpretation (I thought I had seen his later orthodoxy looming) and that he hoped I would reconsider. I did and found I was wrong. I also saw that his Unitarianism, which I had thought mainly just radicalism was in fact a moral commitment that lasted down to 1805.'[36]

Another contemporary critic who took no stock of Empson on 'The Ancient Mariner' was James Twitchell, whose article 'The World above the Ancient Mariner' (1975) seeks to expound what he calls Coleridge's interest in 'spirits ... as the organic matrix between psyche and cosmos.'[37] In his piece Twitchell offers an insight that had already been fully analysed by Empson in 1972: 'in the 1798 version it is by no means clear who is propelling the ship. ... By 1817 it is not surprising to see Coleridge redesigning his hierarchy to make the angelic powers superior to the tutelary Spirit of the Pole. For by then a more orthodox Coleridge had begun to press the Christian hierarchies over his pagan systems.'[38] It is a pity that such critics ignored Empson's writings.[39] Andrew Bennett, in a review of Zachary Leader's *Revision and Romantic Authorship* (1996), wonders why Leader takes as his 'main target ... the now superseded 1972 edition of Coleridge's verse by William Empson and David Pirie, a focus of attack which ... seems somewhat beside the point.'[40] But the truth is that Leader was perfectly right in facing up to Empson's arguments.

Empson wrote to his wife in mid-July 1971: 'It [has] been rather a grim business trying to finish the Coleridge book in the heat with no bath and maggots cropping up in the food, but I have broken the back of it now and haven't much more to do.[41] It was the last piece of work he would finish off in the Burrow at Sheffield, at the height of the summer before his retirement; for the remainder of his years, he would work at home in London.

'No man really likes being promoted to the class of Licensed Buffoons,' he had written in 1966, at a time when he was given cause to reflect on his own critical reputation, 'but it has been an important post in England since the time of Jaques, I suppose, let alone Bernard Shaw.'[42] His status as a Licensed Buffoon was rehearsed, or rather ironically celebrated, by John Carey, Merton Professor of English Literature at the University of Oxford, in a review of Frank Kermode's *An Appetite for Poetry*. Empson, Carey writes, 'was pugnacious, irascible and dogmatic—a rottweiler to Kermode's pekinese. Far from sharing Kermode's courteous hospitality to divergent viewpoints, he thought he was right, and that anyone who disagreed with him was detestable and base. In fact, he was persistently wrong, indeed crack-brained, on some issues, as Kermode shows. He believed all his life that John Donne was interested in space travel, and in the theological problems of extra-terrestrial life-forms, and he once assured Kermode that Donne's "The Good Morrow" took place on the planet Venus. But even in these loopy seizures Empson compelled attention because he passionately believed in himself.'[43]

Given such a stalemate—Carey's humorous allegation that Empson was wrong when he thought he was right—it is worthwhile also to review and evaluate Empson's writings on Donne, which appeared over a period of no less than half a century, from 1930 to 1981, and to seek to understand why they have been patronized as divertissements, more or less irrelevant to the proper business of Donne scholarship.

Certainly the first point to be stressed is that, as Carey admits, Empson's arguments from Donne's poetry—specifically the love-poetry—were consistent from first to last. 'Practically all [Donne's] good poems,' Empson maintained, are concerned with enunciating a secret freedom from Church and State; far from being the fruits of waggishness, or 'typically capricious and inconstant' (to use Carey's phrase about Donne),[44] they are seriously sceptical, rebellious, and indeed revolutionary. Looking back in 1974, Empson remarked: 'It was not a new idea in 1935 that the love-poetry of Donne claims a defiant independence for the pair of lovers, especially by setting them to colonize some planet made habitable by Copernicus. A campaign to exterminate the idea was then in progress, using very little reasoned argument, and its success has naturally made the poems seem pretty trivial to a later generation.'[45] He was referring to his earliest sustained presentation of the theory, 'Double Plots' (1935), in which he argued that the Renaissance cultivated a 'desire to make the individual more independent than Christianity allowed', and that 'one did not want to submit to the inquisition of a central divine authority even at best...' The Copernican hypothesis, soon to be proved by scientific discovery, allowed an escape-route for the dissident. 'The idea that you can get right away to America, that human affairs are not organised round one certainly right authority (e.g. the Pope) is directly compared to the new idea that there are other worlds like this one, so that the inhabitants of each can live in their own way. These notions carry a considerable weight of implication, because they lead at once to a doubt either of the justice or the uniqueness of Christ.'[46]

If the Logos is at once 'the underlying Reason of the universe and ... the Christ who had saved man', to describe any other human being as fulfilling that dual role is to deny the singular Revelation of Christ as Creator and Redeemer. In 'The First Anniversarie' Donne gives 'an enormous picture of the complete decay of the universe, and this is caused by the death of a girl of no importance whom Donne had never seen. Ben Jonson said "if it had been written to the Virgin, it would have been something" but only Christ would be enough; only his removal from the world would explain the destruction foretold by astronomers. The only way to make the poem sensible is to accept Elizabeth Drury as the Logos.'[47] What all this adds up to, by Empson's reckoning, is a version of pastoral, whereby the poet—standing at a remove, 'because an artist never is at one with any public' (p. 14)—salutes the worth of individual conscience over institutionalised rule. Jonson was astute to think the *Anniversaries* 'profane and full of Blasphemies';[48] but as far as Empson was concerned, that heresy was creditable and indeed heroic: 'Blasphemy was a serious accusation, and we need not suppose that [Donne] expressed his deepest feeling in defending himself against it.'

Empson worked outside the current of Anglo-American criticism for most of the 1930s and 1940s, teaching in Japan and in China; so that the message he carried to his Far Eastern students, as in these unpublished notes linking the strategy of Donne's poetry to the political appropriation of Petrarchism by the Elizabethan court, reiterated what he took to be the orthodox view of the 'deeply sceptical and inquisitive' character of Donne's mind—albeit Donne may have 'felt the drama of scepticism rather than any rational necessity for it':

> The assertion that somebody *is* the whole world, or that their death will destroy the whole world, is always coming up in Donne's work... It is an ancient belief that the king or emperor has a magical effect on the country he rules; if there are floods and disasters, that proves he is insincere. In a sense he *is* everything, because he is magically connected to everything. In Donne's time this line of thought, partly because recovered from the classics, had been revived in a remarkable degree about Queen Elizabeth... But the metaphysical idea, that the person is everything just as whiteness is all white things, makes a different connection. Christ is the Logos in theology, that is, he is the underlying reason which keeps the universe obeying its laws, and he was also an individual man. And by his death he altered the conditions of the whole world. So what Donne says about his heroines was seriously believed about Christ. He is stealing fire from the two most sacred sources, royalty and religion, and the effect is to say with insolent force that he cares about nothing but the love-affair that he describes.[49]

Empson had to fight for his ground after the war, in 'Donne and the Rhetorical Tradition' (1949), where he argued that 'the final point' of the arcane research of Rosemond Tuve's *Elizabethan and Metaphysical Imagery*, as applied to Donne, 'turns out to be that he did not at all mean the kind of thing a modern critic admires him for, because Donne thought he was only applying the rules of rhetoric in a particularly rigorous and stringent manner.'[50] As he understood Tuve, he explained,

> she treats the Donne line of talk that the idealized woman is a world, or that the two happy lovers are a world, as a straightforward use of the trope *amplificatio*... I do not think you get anywhere with Donne unless you realize that he felt something different about his repeated metaphor of the separate world; it only stood for a subtle kind of truth, a metaphysical one if you like, and in a way it pretended to be a trope; but it stood for something so real that he could brood over it again and again... But [Miss Tuve] says that the astronomical images in Donne are 'dialectical counters in a war of wits,' and she has a firm footnote denying that 'what we like to think of as the peculiar character of metaphysical imagery' has among its causes 'the disturbed *Weltanschauung* which accompanied the acceptance of the Copernican world-picture.' ... I think it is obvious that his separate planet ... was connected with Copernicus; and I notice that Miss Tuve gives no reason for thinking otherwise. She merely finds it natural, as she is classify-

ing tropes, to assume that they are all fairly similar standard objects, rather like spare parts of machinery...

I deny, then, that Donne is simply 'using' a well-known trope, the standard howling hyperbole of the Counter-Reformation, when he identifies any person or pair of persons he chooses to praise with the Logos; because he regularly throws in the idea forbidden to Catholics of a separate planet, out of reach of the Pope, and this inherently lifts the old trope into a new intellectual air.

Thus Empson highlights in Donne's poetry this recurrent nexus: the syncretism of 'the metaphor of the separate planet', derived from the contemporary debate about astronomy or cosmology, with 'the trope based on the Logos', meaning that one might escape the sanctions of Christian dogma. Yet the generality of criticism in post-war years has tended to share Tuve's view that the astronomical metaphors in Donne are 'dialectical counters in a war of wits'; that he is at best brilliantly outrageous but hardly dissentient in any seriously sustained way. Professor Frank Kermode, for example, proposed that Donne's 'commonest device' was to depend 'heavily upon dialectical sleight-of-hand, arriving at the point of wit by subtle syllogistic misdirections ... making a new and striking point by a syllogism concealing a logical error'. The poet 'exercised his wit on the theme of sexual love, and ... was inclined to do this in a 'naturalist' way'.[51] To state only so much is to rest content with the bluff masculinity of Donne; let us delight in his audacious wit and look no further. Empson believed that Donne's celebrations of love amounted to a defiant doctrine, challenging canon law and received morality, and he wrote to Kermode: 'you take for granted that Donne does not mean what he says ...'

'I entirely agree that Donne must have been felt as a shock,' Kermode replied, 'and all the part of Miss Tuve's book which says he wasn't is not only wrong but easily shown to be so. Some of this shock is a matter of being a little risqué in theological matters, certainly....' However, Kermode went on, Donne 'always uses' the new-philosophy argument 'exactly as he uses alchemy, angelology and all the rest of it, as providing useful illustrations'.[52] For his part, Empson sought to credit Donne with being purposefully provocative, slicing through convention, with his imagery being not incidental but integrative.

The early Elegy XIX, 'To his Mistris Going to Bed', which Kermode was absolutely right to call 'magnificently erotic',[53] became for Empson a crucial measure of Donne's outrageousness. Spoken by a naked man, already abed, to a woman who is classily dressed in 'wyrie coronet', gown, and 'spangled brest-plate', the poem hurries her to bed— hustles her, if you will—with a blend of exaltation and rapt encouragement. 'Off with that girdle, like heavens zone glistering | But a farre fairer world encompassing.' As she doffs successive garments and accessories, the poet hymns her:

> Off with those shoes: and then safely tread
> In this loves hallow'd temple, this soft bed.
> In such white robes heavens Angels us'd to bee
> Receiv'd by men; Thou Angel bring'st with thee
> A heaven like Mahomets Paradise; and though
> Ill spirit walk in white, we easily know
> By this these Angels from an evill sprite:

> They set our haires, but these the flesh upright.
> Licence my roving hands, and let them goe
> Behind, before, above, between, below.
> Oh my America, my new found lande,
> My kingdome, safeliest when with one man man'd,
> My myne of precious stones, my Empiree,
> How blest am I in this discovering thee.
> To enter in these bonds is to be free...

And finally, to extol the virtue of shared nakedness, he claims that women:

> are mystique books, which only wee
> Whom their imputed grace will dignify
> Must see reveal'd. Then since I may knowe,
> As liberally as to a midwife show
> Thy selfe; cast all, yea this white linnen hence.
> There is no pennance due to innocence.
> To teach thee, I am naked first: Why than
> What need'st thou have more covering than a man.

Sex, says the poem, is not what the Churchmen say, it is not sinful but pure; there is no need to mortify ourselves. At least, that proposition is what the text of 1669 (the first to print the poem), as enshrined by Sir Herbert Grierson, says; it is the *textus receptus* which C. M. Coffin could celebrate in 1937 as needing 'no apology for treating love, unattenuated and unrefined by spiritual encumbrances, in a robust and downright manner.'[54] Empson thought it needed no apology for the vigour with which it confuted conventionality: its resolute heterodoxy. But the lovely line 46, 'There is no pennance due to innocence', is a textual crux; other manuscripts, arguably more authoritative, read variously 'There is no pennance, much less innocence' and 'Here is no pennance, much less innocence'— both of which reverse the meaning of the line, as Empson maintained, by scoffingly acknowledging the speaker's impenitent guilt. The wooer's expressions of urgent wonder turn into the rake's profession of bad faith. Grierson printed 'There is no pennance due to innocence', from the edition of 1669, on the grounds that it represented 'a softening of the original to make it compatible with the suggestion that the poem could be read as an epithalamium.'[55] Empson favoured that reading, but certainly not for its softening properties: 'we need not give much weight to [the] charitable idea that Donne wrote the poem for his own marriage,' he suggested.[56] The reason why the woman addressed and undressed is innocent, he argued, 'is that she is the Noble Savage, like Adam and Eve before the Fall (they are indeed the type case of lovers on a separate planet); she is America, where they are free as Nature made them, and not corrupted, as we are, by "late law". Sweet the line may well be called, but it was meant to take effect as a culminating bit of defiant heresy.' When determining a copy-text in this case, Empson thought, a key question is obvious: 'what was the origin of *due to*? It cannot be an unmeaning slip; it reverses the whole point of the line, wittily.'

Frank Kermode admires the poem for what Saintsbury termed its 'frank naturalism'; for cocking a snook at morality, but not for transgressing it in a deliberative way. 'I take this poem,' he told Empson, 'as being of the sort that does habitually say, "let's have no more of all that cant about 'honour', 'innocence' etc." "You certainly aren't penitent; thank god you're not 'innocent'; so off with that white linen." '[57] In short, for Kermode, the speaker vaunts his guiltiness, and expressly bows to conventionality through the very act of reckoning with it in such a manner. Empson constantly pressed the point that the poem must be honourably heretical, or else it is obscene and, if you follow the logic of its argument, insults the woman who is otherwise exhorted to share a free act of love; 'why is it essential,' he challenged Kermode, 'to suppose that the young Donne was not heretical, however much he appears to be? In other cases, the Christian critics are quite happy to say that an author had very wrong ideas till he was converted, but in the case of Donne they have somehow decided to twist both the text and the biography so as to pretend he never was ... '[58]

In a series of essays, published in 1957, 1966, 1972, and 1981, he returned to Elegy XIX as a touchstone of critical taste and judgement; perhaps most convincingly in an essay-review of Helen Gardner's edition of *The Elegies and The Songs and Sonnets*:

All through the poem, the lady is encouraged to undress by being told it is the right thing to do, for very exalted reasons ... [and] most of the comparisons are celestial: she is a better world, and her girdle is the Milky Way; she is one of Mahomet's angels, or a sacred or magical text, only to be read by men dignified through her 'imputed grace' (the Calvinist doctrine here implies an awestruck sense of unworthiness). There is a steady rise in these exhilarated claims, and he calls her 'innocent' when he gets to the top. Donne is fond of arguing his way through an apparently indefensible case, and his logic is habitually sustained; he would think it shame to collapse and confess himself guilty ... at the climax of a speech for the defence...

Indeed, a more general question imposes itself: 'Why is this not simply a dirty poem, please?' I think it becomes very dirty if you make the poem jab his contempt into the lady at the crisis of the scene of love, thus proving that all his earlier flattery of her must be interpreted as jeering.

In conclusion, he averred, the poem 'is defiant, and that is why it is not dirty; it is a challenge... It is only our modern orthodox young Donne who has to be made to express a specific sense of sin even while writing a love-poem.'

Nonetheless, it has been maintained, Donne's elegies are in any case only ingenious variations on subjects out of Ovid's *Amores*: displays of sheer cynical wit, or what J. B. Leishman termed 'discourses upon a broom-stick'[59]—outrageous in the degree to which they are impudent. Leishman classified Elegy XIX as a 'dramatic' elegy, smoothly witty and frankly suggestive *à la* Ovid, as opposed to certain others which might be considered in some way (speciously) logical or argumentative (p. 76). Yet few critics deny that Donne's elegies are much more than pastiches of Ovid's mode of sexual provocation; and Elegy XIX makes little sense at all unless it prosecutes a logical argument. One might also claim that the line 'Here is no pennance, much less innocence' is merely a superb example of *apodosis*, a rhetorical clincher that turns the argument on its head. Even so, the line still seems more like a sneering inversion, the crowing of a cad, than the thrillingly subversive 'There is no pennance due to innocence', which proposes a radically progressive principle.

All the same, J. B. Leishman enters a further caveat, which is to say that we must 'resist the temptation to regard such poems as autobiographical, or to infer from them anything about Donne's own conduct, morals and opinions' (p. 58). To that warning one must again reply: Donne was not just mimicking Ovid, he was reworking his model, reinventing the material, and we serve him ill to evade his individual meaning.[60] Indeed, it is a staggering irony that Empson's long campaign to prove the courageously heretical character of Donne's poetry, and to defend the poet from pietistic detractors, gains all the more point when you contrast his high-minded version with the portrait of the poet that John Carey presents in *John Donne: Life, Mind and Art* (1981). A number of Empson's readers (including Kermode) have judged that his account of Donne's style of mind and poetry is obsessively wayward; that he is at best describing himself in the image of Donne. John Carey's Donne, let it be said, is obnoxious. Donne's poetry is impelled by egotism, which is its 'consuming force', says Carey;[61] Donne is best understood as a shame-faced Recusant, driven by a lust for power; his art is the art of ambition, seething with self-regard and relentlessly on the make. Most likely taking his cue from Helen Gardner, who says that in the early poems 'one is aware of the dominance of the masculine partner who, if his mistress denies him what he wants, bullies or abuses her',[62] Carey describes Elegy XIX as a sadistic poem, exemplifying the 'almost pathological imperiousness' of Donne's 'urge to impose power'; it expresses 'a wish to insult, humiliate and punish'.[63] (Carey is not alone in offering such an extreme reading; Thomas Docherty has absurdly called the poem a study in 'auto-eroticism, masturbation', with the woman having 'no value in the poem'.[64]) Not surprisingly, Empson believed that his own account of the poet and the poetry rescued the work from such 'sordid and mean-minded' imputations. Whereas Empson compliments the poet's libertarianism, 'panting, bug-eyed' Carey commits a libel.[65] On the one hand, the poem is defiant and candidly sexy; on the other, indecent and punitive. So much depends, therefore—as Empson urged for 30 years—on the viciousness of the variant line 'Here is no pennance, much less innocence'. But for that line, readings like Carey's would be confounded, he argued:

> Donne is tenacious of an argument in a poem, and would not rat on it . . . Still, if the girl is a prostitute, as Dame Helen [Gardner] appears to tell us in an allusive footnote, there is nothing to rat on; both the characters are only pretending, and it is a comfort to them not to have to bother with holy scruples.
>
> Thus, on Dame Helen's view, the poem is deflated but still good humoured. On Carey's view, the man seduces an innocent girl by arguments purporting to prove that yielding will not be sinful, and then triumphs over her, at the very moment of penetration, by telling her she will go to hell for it. This is sadistic pornography, a very evil thing which Carey is right to be indignant about, but it has emerged from his own mind.[66]

Curiously, Empson and Carey come close to agreement on one central point of argument, when they seek to explain the covert meaning of what Carey calls the poet's 'transmutation' of 'private love into something of global significance' (p. 124). But whereas Carey sees this recurrent feature of the love poems as stemming from a process of compulsive substitution— Donne displacing the reality of his religious agitations on to 'the relatively innocuous department of sexual ethics' (p. 38)—Empson hails a campaign of exalted defiance, with the poet 'erecting personal love into a rival to Christianity'. This is the issue on which Carey highhandedly rated Empson for indulging in persistently 'crack-brained' notions, which he characterized as the belief that Donne 'was interested in space travel, and in the theological problems of extra-terrestrial life-forms'. To clear up that last matter first: Empson never said that Donne was interested in 'extra-terrestrial life-forms' *per se*, only as the metaphorical and metaphysical opportunity that he took to vindicate his claims for love. The idea of love as 'a mystery or cult' (as another editor, Theodore Redpath, calls it)[67] comes up very directly, for instance, in a number of poems including 'A Valediction: forbidding mourning' (which Donne may well have written just before a trip to France in 1611):

> So let us melt, and make no noise,
> No tear-floods, nor sigh-tempests move;
> 'Twere profanation of our joys
> To tell the laity our love.

Even Helen Gardner granted thus much: 'The superb *égoisme à deux* of these poems ... their stress on secrecy and insistence on the esoteric nature of love—a religion of which Donne and his mistress are the only saints ... —make these poems a quintessence of the romantic conception of passionate love as the *summum bonum*.'[68]

Yet it is a measure of Gardner's fundamental resistance to any heretical hidden agenda that she refused to countenance a staring impiety in another poem, 'The Relic', where the poet says that, in a future age of 'mis-devotion', 'Thou shalt be a Mary Magdalene, and I | A something else thereby.' Lots of readers feel sure that Donne must mean 'a Jesus Christ'; but Gardner would never suffer the notion: 'It has been suggested that Donne intended that his bone would be thought to be a bone of Christ and this has been supported by the revival of the hoary *canard* that Luther said that Christ and Mary Madgalen were lovers. But however sunk in 'mis-devotion' an age was it would surely be aware that the grave of Christ contained no relics other than his grave-clothes.'[69] Theodore Redpath exercises a long footnote on the line, deciding in favour of the 'very bold sense ... that people in that age of "mis-devotion" will take Donne's bone for one of Christ's'.[70] But even he, though sympathetic to Empson's arguments, failed to comprehend the more subtle and radically different point that Empson posed in 'Donne the Space Man': 'It has been objected that Jesus left no bone behind him on earth, and indeed this clearly made Donne safer; no doubt he himself would be ready with this objection if challenged. But '*a* Jesus Christ' would be logically a very different entity from the one Jesus, and the point I am trying to make all along is that this kind of poetry continually uses the idea that the attributes of the Christ can be applied to others.' Gardner expostulated to a draft of Empson's essay: 'Need you give currency to this notion of Mr. Redpath's[?] Surely even in the most wildly superstitious countries "a bone" dug up could not be taken as a relic of Christ, who left only grave-clothes in the tomb. The only physical relics ever referred to are the holy foreskin!'[71] Empson patiently explained: 'the central idea I am imputing to Donne is that there can be many incarnations, so the belief that Jesus left no bones on earth would not affect Donne's possible status as founder of a new religion ...'[72] She replied, with mounting indignation, 'I cannot see how you can believe that a bone with a love token round it could possibly be taken in the most deeply superstitious region ... for a bone of Christ.'[73] And he returned yet again, still placidly: 'I am puzzled you do not see that "*a* Jesus Christ" would be inherently different from "Jesus Christ".'[74]

In truth, the exchange is profoundly puzzling, for it reveals the imaginative limitations of Helen Gardner's literal-mindedness. From the outset, in her first letter (19 October 1956), she had misapprehended the radical burden of Empson's article: 'your main attitude towards Donne & his poetry I sympathize with very strongly,' she wrote, immediately after informing him that she had given a talk—'to an Anglican & Orthodox group'—which included quotations showing 'Donne conceiving, as you suggest, possibilities of salvation in Jesus Christ beyond a Church & beyond where the Gospel is preached'.[75] One would think that Empson had made himself perfectly explicit in 'Donne the Space Man', as in this observation: 'Theologically, the most reckless of Donne's poems are those in which he presents himself as ... the founder of a religion, the Christ of all future reckless lovers...'

Donne put the idea of space travel, as a corollary of the post-Copernican discovery of a possible plurality of inhabited worlds, to the service of 'denying the uniqueness of Jesus,' Empson maintained. 'In our time no less than in Donne's,' he wrote, 'to believe that there are rational creatures on other planets is very hard to reconcile with the belief that Salvation is only through Christ ...' Probably the only space-writer to have handled this 'real problem', he reckoned, was 'the Anglican C. S. Lewis; rather

brilliantly in *Out of the Silent Planet* (1938), where we find that our Earth
alone required the Incarnation because it had fallen in a unique degree
into the power of the Devil; but in the sequel *Voyage to Venus* (1943) we
gather that all future rational creatures will have to evolve in the image of
Man, throughout all galaxies, as a technical result of the Incarnation; and
this feels too parochial even to be a pleasant fantasy.' Respectfully, he
submitted a copy of 'Donne the Space Man' to C. S. Lewis, who reassured
him, 'there's nothing in either of your two references to me which I object
to,' and went on with an attractive grace: 'I can't say I have so far seen any
connection with journies to other planets in any of the passages you deal
with. That may be the obtuseness of a sick man. Also, you and I clearly
have opposite qualities. You seem to me liable to see in all poetry things
that aren't there; and I no doubt seem to you constantly blind to what is.
Both are probably right. Perhaps if we were rolled into one we'd make a
quite decent critic ... or wd. the result be deadlock and *aphasia*?' But at
least, unlike Helen Gardner, Lewis had taken the large point of the piece,
and acknowledged its significance. 'If you are right,' he conceded, 'it will
be most important.'[76] Clearly he had no doubt of the implications of
Empson's argument that 'The young Donne, to judge from his poems,
believed that every planet could have its Incarnation, and believed this
with delight, because it automatically liberated an independent conscience
from any earthly religious authority.'

To see into the heart of the matter of Donne's love-poetry, Empson thus felt
certain, a critic must arbitrate between two judgements. For the first, C. M.
Coffin is representative: 'It would be idle to say that Donne's love poems
are within the range of doctrinally conceived orthodoxy.'[77] The other
position is taken by M. F. Moloney, who argues that Donne's interest in
the new science, 'particularly in the new astronomy, was rather a popular
and poetic interest whereby he caught up new ideas, toyed with them,
wove them into the fabric of his poetry, but at no time saw in them a
challenge to the stability of traditional Christianity.'[78] Empson saw that no
one could balance those books. Donne's unorthodoxy can be appreciated
only if you allow for the full seriousness of his interest in the new science.
Frank Kermode told Empson, with reference to the explosive charge of
'The Relic', 'I entirely agree about "a something else thereby," finding it
strange that there has been so much hesitation over it. Donne's
mind worked theologically, he was all out to be épatant'; and yet he went
on: 'However, the "something else thereby" is in my view only an example
of the sort of thing liable to happen, not an example of a substantial and

persistent doctrine of Donne's.'[79] If there were still any doubt about where he stood, Kermode stated in a further letter: 'Donne makes precise use of doctrines for the truth of which, outside the poem, he does not vouch.'[80] In other words, for Kermode, Donne is the impresario of insincerity.

According to Empson, the truth stood to the contrary. Donne held genuine advanced views, he spoke up for 'liberation and enlightenment'. 'I think he was an earnest young man all the time he was working on his love poems,' he remarked to Kermode in conversation, 'instead of being a flibberty-gibbet as T. S. Eliot said... [T]he more you regard him as serious ... I mean as having a basis of conviction behind what he says ... even if talking in a riddle-like manner, I think that makes the poetry better.'[81] He waded in where others teetered: he was eager for the liberating extremism of Donne's new world. The motif of the separate planet 'leaps at you', he believed, in 'The Good-morrow', a poem on which he rested his case. I need quote only the last two stanzas (of three), including a small variant that Empson favoured:

> And now good-morrow to our waking souls,
> Which watch not one another out of fear;
> For love, all love of other sights controls,
> And makes one little room, an everywhere.
> Let sea-discoverers to new worlds have gone,
> Let maps to others, worlds on worlds have shown,
> Let us possess one world; each hath one, and is one.
>
> My face in thine eye, thine in mine appears,
> And true plain hearts do in the faces rest;
> Where can we find two better hemispheres,
> Without sharp North, without declining West?
> Whatever dies, was not mix'd equally;
> If our two loves be one, or, thou and I
> Love so alike, that none do slacken, none can die.

Empson's argument runs as follows: 'The world of the lovers, with its two "hemispheres", is one of the planets recently implied by Copernicus to be habitable; and the two lovers, jointly, have become the Intelligence or angel which pushes it round. There is a point in all this (which the editor [Helen Gardner] ignores), as in calling the lady of "Elegy XIX" his America; he is beyond the claims of Church and State. The slow line tolling out "one" has the awe of a space-landing.'[82] But where is the evidence for the stunning suggestion that Donne posits an independent dispensation for the lovers on a separate planet? It is manifest in these lines:

> Let sea-discoverers to new worlds have gone,
> Let maps to others, worlds on worlds have shown,
> Let us possess our world...

'The point of 'worlds *on* worlds',' Empson explained, 'is that you can get one planet lying behind another, further away';[83] in other words, the imaginative *mise-en-scène* is extra-terrestrial, in the realm of other habitable worlds. But do other critics go along with Empson? Clay Hunt, after worrying the evidence in *Donne's Poetry* (1954), concluded that Donne had in view only the New World of America; to which Empson responded, most acutely: 'Why are they both in the plural then? What does the line about maps add to the line about discoverers...?' Theodore Redpath offers the cautious gloss that ' "worlds" might be either "continents", or "worlds" in a sense which would include celestial bodies'; though he had earlier expressed the view that Empson's interpretation of the 'worlds' here was probably correct.[84] Most significantly, Helen Gardner does not comment at all on the phrase 'worlds on worlds'; she allows only that the 'maps' are 'probably "maps" of the heavens showing new spheres' (p. 198). Gardner is most reluctant to accept that Donne, even as late as 1610, might actually be referring to Galileo's discoveries, which 'powerfully supported the Copernican hypothesis' (as she has to acknowledge);[85] and thus— coming full circle—we understand that she dismisses the very idea of Empson's interpretation with respect to 'The Good-Morrow', which might have been written some years earlier still.

Gardner has to track a long way away from the line that Donne indubitably wrote in 'The Good-Morrow'—'Let maps to others, worlds on worlds have shown'—in order to explain it away by reference to a sonnet that the poet would write when he turned parson. In that sonnet, which begins 'I am a little world made cunningly', Donne bewails the fact that he has betrayed his body and soul into 'black sinne' and proceeds to an invocation which Carey rightly terms 'a vast gesture of despair'.[86] This is the end of the octet and the beginning of the sestet:

> You which beyond that heaven which was most high
> Have found new sphears, and of new lands can write,
> Powre new seas in mine eyes, that so I might
> Drowne my world with my weeping earnestly,
> Or wash it, if it must be drown'd no more:
> But oh it must be burnt...

Helen Gardner, who shies away from the likelihood that Donne, in calling upon 'new sphears' and 'new lands', is referring 'to the newly revealed immensity, and possibly to the infinity, of the universe', summons Alphonsus and Clavius to justify her tame suggestion 'that he is calling on discoverers generally: astronomers who find new spheres and explorers who find new lands'.[87] Her account makes Donne tidily conservative, not a man who is given to grasping the breathtaking implications of an infinite universe. 'I take it,' wrote Empson in 1957, 'that the converted Donne first reflected on his old idea of the separate planet, as an escape from the Christian Hell, and then wrote the poem specifically to renounce this heresy'; and earlier still, in 1949, when he put a gloss on the poem so penetrating and illuminating that no critic can better it: 'I think the remorseful hope of atonement with God is crossed with a shrinking hunger for annihilation and escape from God. Both of them are dominated by the image of the separate planet...' Later on, in a commentary he supplied to Frank Kermode, he added the sorry sardonic observation, 'it's a wonderfully thrifty use of his old material, to make the metaphor itself testify against his earlier uses of it.'[88] None of those acute comments were written merely to rally Gardner, for they develop his earliest discussion of the poem, in *Some Versions of Pastoral* (1935), where he had also relevantly perceived: '*Drowning* the world *no more* brings us back to Noah and an entirely pre-Copernican heaven...'[89] *Pace* Helen Gardner's evasion of the likelihood that Donne would be thinking of an infinite universe, and implicitly of plural worlds, when he featured 'new spheres' and 'new lands' in the sonnet 'I am a little world made cunningly', Empson noted that in *Ignatius his Conclave* (most probably written the very same year, 1610) Donne had specified 'the moone ... the planets, and other starrs, which are also thought to be worlds', and so stressed this judicious deduction: 'the opposition makes plain that *world* means '*inhabited* star'.' As to Carey's contemptuous misrepresentation of Empson's argument vis-à-vis 'the theological problems of extra-terrestrial life-forms', Empson actually left no room for doubt that what is being described is 'a continual metaphor.'[90] He told Kermode: 'I think that living on another planet is an extremely powerful Symbol for the claim of the lovers to have independent rights';[91] and elsewhere that in 'The Good-Morrow' Donne 'doesn't want to *discuss* space-travel; he is only comparing it to the situation of the lovers'.[92]

As well as introducing 'worlds on worlds' on top of the 'new worlds' lately discovered by seafarers, Donne goes on to ask in 'The Good-Morrow',

> Where can we find two better hemispheres,
> Without sharp North, without declining West?
> Whatever dies, was not mix'd equally;

> If our two loves be one, or, thou and I
> Love so alike, that none do slacken, none can die.

'It was a regular thing . . . ,' Empson explained, 'to have a pair of globes, for the earth and the stars; the young ladies in Oscar Wilde's plays are still being taught "the use of the globes," very properly. . . What Donne praises, in contrast to both these globes, is one made by combining the hemispheres of an eyeball from himself and an eyeball from his mistress, and he remarks with truth that this hasn't the usual properties of either of the public globes.'[93] It is practically ungainsayable that Donne makes a truly astonishing claim which sins against the fixed cosmology of current Christian dogma. The world constituted by the two hemispheres of the lovers— 'our world'—is 'better' than both the 'new worlds' of the Americas and the 'worlds on worlds' of the Christianized Ptolemaic scheme. It is undeclining and incorruptible, or—in Leishman's good phrase—'indestructible because irreducible';[94] in Empson's terms, the lovers have in effect (so much more explicitly than implicitly) colonized a planet beyond the sovereignty of Church or State. Theodore Redpath, seeming almost to hold his breath as he finds himself abetting this heresy, which he terms 'the bolder hypothesis', reaches exactly the same conclusion: 'if "none" in "none do slacken" refers to the lovers,' he writes, 'then "none" in "none can die" must surely most probably [*sic*] also refer to the lovers? Now, in that case, what the final lines of the poem will be saying is that if the lovers' love be actually a complete unity, *or* they love so similarly that neither of them slackens off in relation to the other's love, then the *lovers* will never die, i.e. they will achieve immortality. That would certainly give a strong meaning to the final lines.'[95] *Verbum sat.* Not unexpectedly, Helen Gardner's commentary provides an inverse index to the real presence of the poet's happy heresy: here she cannot wriggle out of agreeing with Empson's and Redpath's interpretation, but clings to Donne's 'If', as if to hold the poet's head above deep water: 'Conditional clauses must always suggest an element of doubt.'[96] 'The Good-Morrow' figures among the group of poems that she classifies, rather shiftily (that is, for want of a better word), as 'philosophic'; but she goes on to propose, flagrantly insulting the poet, that we need not imagine he means what he says: 'I do not intend by this to suggest that they were written to expound a philosophy of love.'[97]

If Donne does make use of the defiant implications of the new astronomy, as Empson insists, there are two consequential questions to be addressed. The first is a question of dating: was it only after about 1604, and so after his ruinous marriage to Ann More, that he learned enough of the scientific facts (as most critics seem to think) to exploit their implications in the challenging form of these poems? Second, if that is the case, and if the poems (or at least Empson's interpretation of them) collapse into inconsequentiality unless they are founded upon empirical science rather than speculation, is Donne speaking of his wife in the love-poems or merely imagining an all-consuming love?[98]

The two questions go together; and the received answers commonly lead to some extraordinary slurs on the poet. John Carey works to demonstrate the good case that 'we can discard the notion that the sexually promiscuous Donne who prowls through the elegies and the more wayward of the love lyrics was a figment of his imagination' (p. 73)—even though Carey seems to forget that on an earlier page of his book he has described the love poems in general as comprising a 'fantasy world' (p. 38). He claims for Donne's marriage, honourably and impressively, 'Donne's fidelity to Ann was absolute: when he had her, he wanted no other woman' (p. 73). But then, in the pages immediately following, he crushes any suggestion of sentimentality vis-à-vis the couple's life together: 'The world-obliterating ardour of the love poems ("She is all States, and all Princes, I, | Nothing else is") does not correspond to the realities of Donne's married life. Or rather, it corresponds to them if at all, in no simple way. To proclaim the all-sufficiency of the woman for whom he had sacrificed his career may have been the defiant response with which Donne's imagination faced worldly disaster. And it may have been made more defiant by the realization that she did not, after all, mean everything to him' (p. 75). In short, the love poems are fantastic concoctions; and again, either Donne does not mean what he says, or, even if he is imagining a sincere and unexampled state of love, his wife is about the last person he would have in mind. Empson agreed with just part of Carey's conjecture, that the love poems may in some sense have been 'the defiant response with which Donne's imagination faced worldly disaster' (p. 75), when he wrote in 1957 that Donne 'was keenly, if sardonically, interested in the theology of the separate planet—from fairly early, though he did not come to feel he was actually planted on one till he realized the full effects of his runaway marriage.' For the rest, he was disgusted, because Carey's argument requires the critic not merely to disparage Ann Donne (on the basis of negligible evidence) as unequal to her husband's gifts—she could inspire his love, it seems, but not the poetry—but also to depict Donne as self-aggrandizing, frustrated and insincere, a worldling who boasts of a fabulous love but entirely without conviction.

In 1608, seven years into his recklessly passionate marriage, Donne would pen this letter: 'I write from the fireside in my parler, and in the noise of three gamesome children, and by the side of her whom, because I have translated into such a wretched fortune, I must labour to disguise that from her by all honest devices, as giving her my company and discourse; therefore I steal from her all the time which I give this letter, and it is therefore that I take so short a list... But if I melt into a melancholy whilst I write, I shall be taken in the manner; and I sit by one too tender towards these impressions... '[99] Trawling for proof that Donne's 'dissatisfaction is discernible', Carey quotes only the first part of the letter and comments with stupefying bluntness (p. 74): 'Actually staying in the same room as his wife was, we gather from this, scarcely more than a benign duty.' (J. B. Leishman felt nothing of Carey's vulgar assurance when he commented on the same passage, 'Tenderness, yes, but tenderness, one might be tempted to think, more dutiful than spontaneous, though just how right or how wrong one would be I cannot really decide... '[100]) Empson's gloss is altogether more humane: 'we know that [Donne] felt compunction at having reduced Ann to such misery... [and] what crops up in the surviving letters, repeatedly, is this honourable sense of compunction.' In a later letter, dating from 1614, Donne would write of his wife, 'So much company, therefore, as I am, she shall not want; and we had not one another at so cheap a rate as that we should ever be weary of one another'[101]—on which Empson's comment seems plumb perfect: 'No convention made him talk like this.' Empson believed it an urgent duty to stand up for Donne against his denigrators.

Judging by what she falsely calls 'objective criteria'—(i) 'the kind of relation between a man and a woman that they assume'; and (ii) 'metrical form'—Helen Gardner groups all the poems I have discussed in the years of the poet's married life.[102] They must have been written, she believes, at a time when Donne really got cracking on 'recondite reading', that is between 1602 and 1614 (to which Empson responded acutely, 'what does she think the earlier Donne was busy at?'). Her tendentious and crypto-biographical classification thus licenses Carey's biographical aspersions. (Although Carey apparently jibs at her speculative specifics when he says of the *Songs and Sonnets* that 'there is not a single poem to which a precise date, about which all scholars agree, can be given', his inferences otherwise follow her scheme.[103]) If those poems were indeed written after Donne's marriage, and yet none of them to his wife, and if no adultery took place, they must be 'the product of an intense life of fantasy,' as Empson put it. Being convinced that to force such a shape on Donne's career simply invited critics to attribute base attitudes to Donne the man—they make him 'sulk and insult his wife'—Empson riposted: 'Professor Gardner does not realise what a strain it would be to elaborate and write up a series of hallucinatory erotic day-dreams, unsupported by any theory or framework, and entirely without self-approval...' For that generous reason at least, if for no other, he believed, 'about a dozen of the poems in her "Songs and Sonnets II" ought to be put back into "I", the group written before marriage, to avoid maligning the poet and allow an intelligible development of his character.'

However, saving Donne from a disobliging appearance as a husband can not be accomplished if the chronological parameters tell against it; and this brings back into blurry focus the question of the theology of plural worlds. If Donne was innocent of any extra-marital love-affair and yet did not write in homage to his wife, is it possible some of the poems that apotheosize love—specifically those that exploit the defiantly 'pastoral' device of linking 'the trope based on the Logos' with 'the metaphor of the separate planet'—were written before his marriage in January 1601, perhaps even in the 1590s? Predictably, John Carey, citing selective evidence, scoffs at the notion that Copernican astronomy may have spoken to the poet in any special way. Donne was indifferent to the truth or otherwise of the new theories: 'He wanted to feel free to entertain or dismiss them, and to play them off against his existing patterns of thought, as mood or occasion prompted... Ideas to him were plastic... Given humankind's imperfect faculties, all science was, on his reckoning, science fiction anyway, and he used it as a bargain basement' (pp. 249–50). Likewise Frank Kermode: 'It would be very unlike [Donne] to be much affected by the new philosophy.'[104] But what was the state of play of scientific discovery during Donne's early life? How deep did his knowledge run? And might he have speculated while the astronomers still searched?

Donne's eager interest in astronomy is evident in *Biathanatos* (possibly written by 1612, though not published till 1648), where he engrosses *De Stella Nova* so as to sneeze at 'Aristotles followers'—those 'Schollers [who] stubbornly maintain his Proposition still, though by many experiences of new Stars, the reason which moved Aristotle seems now to be utterly defeated.' Other references to cosmological transformation occur frequently in his works of this time—*c.* 1610–14—most notably including the stellar journey of Elizabeth Drury who 'baits not at the Moone, nor cares to trie | Whether in that new world, men live or die' ('The Second Anniversarie'); as well as in the satirical *Ignatius his Conclave*, where it is proposed that Loyola should be sent to found a *Lunatique Church* in the moon (Kepler seriously believed that the moon might be inhabitable): Donne's tract is replete with the very latest astronomical learning. In sum, no one need doubt that Donne was up with the stars and star-gazers.

Nevertheless, in the years between 1604 and 1614, the received wisdom maintains, Donne flittered or floundered. Unable to settle for Aristotelian metaphysics *or* neoplatonic mysticism *or* the disturbing implications of a reconstituted cosmos, his work seems torn by self-contradiction. Carey takes the view that this situation was fortunate, for it provoked the poet's creativity: 'Renaissance scepticism was a poetic advantage to Donne ... because it made all fact infinitely flexible, and so emancipated the imagin-ation ... When he writes about love his scepticism has a liberating and deepening effect.'[105] Yet both *Ignatius his Conclave* and 'The First Anniver-sarie' were written to meet specific occasions, to suit different peculiar audiences. 'We can select neither as Donne's 'real' response' to the new science.'[106] While still hoping for worldly advancement and so cultivating rich patrons, Donne had already set to work for what Carey rightly calls 'the Anglican propaganda machine'; and in due course he was virtually obliged, by King James I himself, to take Holy Orders in January 1615. It would be a wonder if he had not felt riven between Ptolemaic cosmology and the new world order. Moreover, as Empson observed, it would be difficult to 'deny that he was very capable of casuistry'. Thus Empson hazards: 'Probably he had come to accept the half-way theory of Tycho Brahe, which could be said to hold the field on the existing evidence; but there was nothing definite in that to disprove life on other planets, once you had got the idea into your head.'[107] However, by the same token that we cannot know Donne's deep beliefs about the revolutionary astronomy in the period after 1604, let alone after 1610—when he was on the brink of middle age and presently had to pummel himself into the mould of Anglican respectability—it is impossible to disprove Empson's argument that he could have taken the idea of plural worlds into his head at a much earlier stage, even during the 1590s. Those critics who have investigated Donne's concern with the 'new Philosophy, that denies a settlednesse ... but makes the Earth to move in that place, where we thought the Sunne had moved' (as he would put it in a sermon of 1626),[108] presume that he became excited and dispirited, turn and turn about, only after he got to know the evidence published by Kepler and Galileo. But that is the fallacy of literalism. It remains eminently possible that in an earlier year this notoriously sceptical poet was less shaken than stirred by the new science, and needed little more than speculation to seek to defy received religious and secular authority in a poem like 'The Good-Morrow'. Once he had made 'the obvious deduction from Copernicus', he could have 'toyed with it recklessly in his early poems'. Most likely, Empson further suggested, 'he took it seriously as a poet; and this doesn't at all mean taking it as a fancy, but concentrating on what the human consequences would be if it were true—treating it like a theologian, you might well say, though not like a scientist.' The reason why Donne's advanced ideas would need to be disguised in the poetry is well known: in the 1590s, progressive thinkers were still subject to persecution as heretics. As John Carey reminds his readers, 'Donne was born into a terror, and formed by it.'[109] Churchmen were assuredly angered and consternated by the new philosophy up to the time of Galileo. Clavius, the Aristotelian-Jesuit astronomer whom Helen Gardner adduces to disinfect Donne, attacked Copernicus as late as 1607. Earlier still, in *Initia Doctrinæ Physicæ* (1567), Philipp Melanchthon, *Preceptor Germaniæ*, indicted the infinity–plurality doctrine. Grant McColley paraphrases what he calls Melanchthon's 'most vital argument':

> there is but one Son of God, our Lord Jesus Christ, who was sent into the world, was dead, and was resurrected. He did not appear in other worlds, nor was He dead and resurrected there. Nor is it to be thought that if there are many worlds, something not to be imagined, that Christ was often dead and resurrected. Nor should it be considered that in any other world, without the sacrifice of the Son of God, men could be brought to eternal life. As Melanchthon reasons, to accept a plurality of worlds is to deny or to make a travesty of the Atonement.[110]

In sum, given Donne's up-to-the-minute fascination with the emerging new astronomy, and his known predisposition to affront authority, it is far from impossible to believe that he took advantage in his poetry of the potent philosophical implications of the Copernican revolution—not only to snub Church and State but to aver the autogeny and supreme value of human love—as when proclaiming in 'The Good-Morrow' that the lovers are 'two better hemispheres' and imperishable. That poem says that 'worlds on worlds *have shown*', which might suggest that it could not have been written before Galileo's *Sidereus Nuncius* had actually disclosed a welter of new stars; but the measure of its implied heresy may be reckoned retrospectively from a sermon Donne gave on 26 April 1625: 'The fulnesse, the compasse, the two *Hemispheres* of Heaven, are often designed to us, in these two names, *Joy* and *Glory*: if the *Crosse* of Christ, the *Death* of Christ, present us both these, how neare doth it bring, how fully doth it deliver Heaven it self to us in this life?' Critics often cite Donne the divine to prove that he always scoffed at

the problems of the new philosophy, just as Helen Gardner did when she
quoted to Empson this extract from *Fifty Sermons* (1649): 'There are an
infinite number of stars more than we can distinguish, and so, by God's
Grace, there may be an infinite number of souls saved, more than those of
whose salvation we discern the ways and means.'[111] And yet that late
passage is still allowing the conception of plural worlds, and admitting
that God alone knows how He will save those to whom the Gospel has
never been preached. At some time after 1611, it can be argued (it is an old
argument but no less sound for all that), Donne disciplined his mind
towards Anglican orthodoxy; forsaking the radically defiant Jack Donne,
he pressed himself into the ranks of Reaction. As Empson commented in an
unpublished draft letter, 'I would never impugn the desperate sincerity of
Donne when becoming a parson; he had gradually induced himself, and
the poems hint at it, to renounce the larger view of the world which had
been his heresy.'[112] Both Marjorie Nicolson and Grant McColley cite a
portion of the following passage from *Devotions upon Emergent Occasions*
(written 1623): 'Men that inhere upon *Nature* only, are so far from thinking,
that there is scarce anything *singular* in this world, as that they will scarce
thinke, that this world it selfe is *singular*, but that every *Planet*, and every
Starre, is another *world* like this: They finde reason to conceive, not onely a
pluralitie in every *Species* in the world, but a *pluralitie* of *worlds*; so that the
abhorrers of *Solitude*, are not solitary; for *God*, and *Nature*, and *Reason*
concurre against it.'[113] Nicolson thinks that the passage shows Donne
playing with the idea of plural worlds, without side; McColley that he is
making an adverse pronouncement. Both are plainly wrong, for the whole
thrust of Donne's argument is directed against singularity and solitude and
in favour of plurality—'all *plurall things*'—even by analogy with '*God* himself'
who accommodates 'a plurality of persons'. It is surely significant too that in
none of the sermons in which Donne adverts to the idea of plural worlds
does he disavow the discoveries of astronomical science.

Empson took it as a truth universally acknowledged that the young Donne
was an advanced thinker who 'held broad and enlightened views on
church and state, that he was influenced by the great recent scientific
discoveries, and that he used the theme of freedom in love partly as a
vehicle for these ideas to show what the ideological and sociological effects
of Paracelsus and Copernicus would turn out to be'. Indeed, he was
amazed that he had to battle for his position in later years. But Donne
was not at all interested in colonizing the planet Venus, a place liberated
from law and dogma, Empson had to explain—any such notions would be

'pretty flimsy'. Far more central to the love-poems, Empson argued in the 1960s and 1970s, is the idea that 'Donne and his woman are teachers in a school, or founders of a religion; they are founding the real religion of love, whereas Christianity, which had usurped that name, was busying itself with burning Christians alive [as in the case of Giordano Bruno]. I cannot believe that this line of talk was considered trivial or flippant.'

Hints of blasphemy are patently prevalent in Donne's poetry, if readers are prepared to see them. 'That love is a private religion, no less august than the public sects, was a thing he regularly argued in verse,' Empson maintained. 'It was a matter of believing too much, not of being a "sceptic"...' In particular, he argued, 'The Dream' bodies forth a blasphemy which is altogether more piercing than the 'splendid' jest that Gardner would have it. After reading Empson's account of this perfectly structured poem, John Sparrow (who had been a contemporary at Winchester College and who had edited *Devotions upon Emergent Occasions* while still a schoolboy) wrote to him in 1972: 'Your bull's eye—and Leishman is also a victim here—is *The Dream* ... where I am sure you are right.'[114]

> Dear love, for nothing less than thee
> Would I have broke this happy dream;
>   It was a theme
> For reason, much too strong for phantasy,
> Therefore thou wak'dst me wisely; yet
> My dream thou brok'st not, but continuedst it,
> Thou art so true, that thoughts of thee suffice
> To make dreams truths, and fables histories;
> Enter these arms, for since thou thought'st it best
> Not to dream all my dream, let's do the rest.
>
> As lightning, or a taper's light,
> Thine eye, and not thy noise, wak'd me;
>   Yet I thought thee
> (Thou lov'st truth) but an Angel, at first sight,
> But when I saw thou sawest my heart,
> And knew'st my thoughts, beyond an Angel's art,
> When thou knew'st what I dreamt, when thou knew'st when
> Excess of joy would wake me, and cam'st then,
> I do confess, I could not choose but be
> Profane, to think thee anything but thee.
>
> Coming and staying show'd thee, thee,
> But rising makes me doubt, that now
>   Thou art not thou.

That love is weak, where fear's as strong as he;
'Tis not all spirit, pure, and brave,
If mixture it of fear, shame, honour, have.
Perchance, as torches which must ready be
Men light and put out, so thou deal'st with me,
Thou cam'st to kindle, goest to come; thus I
Will dream that hope again, but else would die.

Curiously enough, although J. B. Leishman compliments the poem as
'dramatically convincing ... an absolutely consecutive and continuous
piece of argument from the first line to the last', he yet decides that
the situation is probably 'all dream ... purely dramatic and imaginary'
(p. 187). John Carey, stabbing a line out of context ('My dream thou
brok'st not, but continuedst it') declares that 'waking and sleeping life are
not distinguished but superimposed: girl blends into dream, dream into
girl' (p. 269)—which might be well said about Keats's 'The Eve of St
Agnes' but is inapplicable here. The poet tells the woman directly that he
broke off his dream when she woke him; nonetheless, since the dream
was 'too strong for phantasy', it is much to the good: she will fulfil his
dream, make it real, in person. After all, a love-dream that is 'too strong
for phantasy' is on the brink of becoming a wet dream ('Excess of joy
would wake me'), which would be a pity. What is happening between the
frank aplomb at the end of the first stanza—'Enter these arms ... let's do
the rest'—and line 1 of the third stanza, 'Coming and staying show'd
thee, thee', where the syntax must mean that she has proved to be a
phenomenon and not a figment of his imagination? The poet knows he
has not been dreaming of an apparition, for he has had palpable proof of
her presence. Thereafter, but only on getting up in the morning ('rising')—it has clearly been a night of stolen love, and she has left him
early—he starts to doubt the evidence of his senses; but he is reassured to
think she will come back at nightfall. Her absence will serve to stimulate
his passion anew, which is the purpose he imputes to her; and meanwhile
he will 'dream that hope again' (the 'happy dream' of line 2, that he is
making love with her). If she does not return, however, he 'would die'—
because his redoubled hopes will be laid waste. But the poem culminates
in self-reproach: he begins to fear that after a night of such glorious love,
such a blessing, she may not come back again; but it is an unworthy
thought, a false apprehension, reflecting badly on the poet himself (he
properly chides himself as 'weak', l. 24) for evincing a momentary loss of
faith in her supernal qualities.

Gardner places the poem in a group of four which she calls 'persuasions to a mistress to yield or arguments against honour'.[115] Since 'The Dream' is clearly not an argument against honour, this must mean that she thinks of it as a persuasion to a mistress to yield—an interpretation which flies so wide of the mark as to seem absolutely bizarre. Elsewhere she construes it as an example of the way in which Donne transforms the 'old Petrarchan theme of the love-dream ... by the brilliant stroke of bringing the lady herself into the room just as the dream reaches its climax of joy; and for the sadness of waking there is substituted disappointment in actuality and a return to the pleasures of dreaming.'[116] But her reading runs quite contrary to the words on the page: at no point does the poet suggest either that he is disappointed with the 'actuality' of the event or that he prefers dreaming. He has misgivings only when the woman leaves him. Irked by Gardner's 'grossly false' account, Empson took time to spell out the obvious: '*Comming* to his bed at just the right time showed her to be omniscient, like God, and *staying* was another action worthy of her divine nature; *rising* explains that while staying she got into bed. There is no hint of disappointment so far; it only appears when she goes away again... Rather than accept a life of mere fantasy, he would kill himself.' Theodore Redpath takes equal pains to note that one of the key features of Donne's originality here—as against the old habit of oneiric self-abuse in medieval Latin poetry and the Petrarchan tradition—is that he makes 'the girl appear in reality just when his sexual excitement had reached a high pitch in his dream'.[117] Gardner calls the 'climax' of that stanza a 'fine hyperbole', and we note the restrained, reluctant epithet. Donne's overstatement is so excessive, in other words, that she cannot believe him to be serious in dubbing the woman divine: the poem must be a fantasy. Whatever the case, it is worth remembering that Donne may not have titled the poem at all.

There are three textual cruces in the poem which reward an excursion—even though the plethora of manuscript evidence is infernally complicated, with a wealth of memorial corruption, scribal error, and 'contamination'. Furthermore, as Gardner points out, no manuscript collection contains 'solely the *Elegies* or solely the *Songs and Sonnets*'.[118] Thus Gardner's work involved a formidable business of collating *variae lectiones* from twenty-eight manuscripts, which she classified into five groups (IV is just one manuscript, the Westmoreland, written in the hand of Donne's friend Rowland Woodward, and includes only one of the *Songs and Sonnets*). For the purposes of constructing a text of the *Songs and Sonnets*, and so correcting where necessary the first (posthumous) edition of 1633, she determined, only Groups I, II, and III—with a little support from

their friends—had real value; with the proviso that 'the Group III manuscripts are further from Donne's papers than the manuscripts of Groups I
and II.' The relations of Groups I and II in particular allow for the
construction of *stemmata*. She observed in conclusion: 'Since the first
edition was based on the manuscripts of Groups I and II, [and] since in
many cases it is impossible on grounds of intrinsic merit to make any
choice between the readings when Group III reads against Groups I and
II ... I have retained the reading of the edition when it has the support of
Groups I and II and been content to record the reading of Group III as a
variant.'[119]

This amount of information may lead us readily to the first crux of 'The
Dream', which figures in the couplet (ll. 7–8)

> Thou art so truth, that thoughts of thee suffice
> To make dreams truths, and fables histories

Whereas Grierson printed 'Thou art so truth', as in the first edition,
Gardner opts for 'so true', which is endorsed only by Group III and a
medley of manuscripts from Group V which she otherwise (elsewhere)
finds grossly contaminated or 'sophisticated'. Yet 'so truth' has the support
of Groups I and II, so that one would expect the editor's own rule to apply.
Her self-exculpation runs as follows: 'In spite of Grierson's defence of "so
truth" as the more difficult reading and his quotation from Aquinas to
support the interpretation that Donne is equating the lady with God who is
truth itself, I find "so truth" a very forced expression and the repetition of
"truth ... truth" unpleasing to the ear. Also, to impute divinity to the lady
at this point is to spoil the fine audacious climax by anticipation.'[120]
Theodore Redpath, in his second edition of *The Songs and Sonets*, agrees
to print 'so true', adding the comment that he has 'searched in vain for a
parallel use of "so" to qualify a noun.'[121] Empson's commentary does away
with all mumbling objections: "truth—truth" is [would be] ugly, but the
slight vowel change with the plural makes *truths* all right ... *So truth* has
strong support from Groups I and II, and the objection that the expression
is 'forced' seems merely a resistance to the thought which it expresses.'

Helen Gardner jibs again at the next crux, in line 14, where again
Groups I and II agree in reading

> Yet I thought thee
> (Thou lov'st truth) but an Angel, at first sight

and she prints—this time agreeing with Grierson in retaining the reading
of *1633*—'(For thou lov'st truth) an Angell'. She concedes that, by itself, the

reading of Groups I and II makes 'a wittier line, the poet apologizing for having thought her merely an angel. But, taken with the following line which begins with 'But', 'but an Angel' is awkward; and taken with the whole stanza it makes the point too soon and spoils the fine hyperbole of the close.'[122] Redpath thinks Gardner's argument from the 'buts' a weak one; 'but an Angel', he feels, is not only more witty but intriguing.[123] The point here, as nobody can deny, is that the poet believes that the lady is only an angel until he realizes that she can read his thoughts (l. 16), which is a gift reserved only to God (*apud* Aquinas, angels are not mind-readers). Empson finds the *1633*–Grierson–Gardner line 'a pointless variant', for the sure-footed reason that Donne is driving an argument through the poem: an argument which Gardner either mistakes or misrepresents.

But the third crux is surely decisive, since it locks the logic tight. In lines 19–20 Gardner prints

> I doe confesse, it could not chuse but bee
> Prophane, to thinke thee anything but thee.

Her version thus matches neither *1633*, which provides 'I must confess', nor the manuscripts of I, II, and III—most of which read 'Profanenes'. She explains that she is prepared to be inconsistent (as a textual editor) in rejecting 'prophaneness'—'in spite of its high manuscript authority'—because she cannot believe that Donne wrote such 'a hopelessly unmetrical line'.[124] (Both J. C. Maxwell and F. W. Bateson saw no reason to deny the line on grounds of prosody; nor did Redpath.)[125] At all events, the reading of *1633* is agreed to be eclectic by most specialist critics; and some sort of bowdlerization of Donne's original looks to be evident. As Redpath gratifyingly explains, two distinct readings therefore seem to have been current before *1633*.[126] One is supported by Groups I and II and some other manuscripts:

> I doe confesse, it could not chuse but be
> Prophanesse, to think thee any thing but thee.

The other has a mixed bag of supporters, mostly from the ranks of Group V:

> I doe confesse, I could not chuse but be
> Prophane, to think thee any thing but thee.

Gardner glosses her mutated version of the lines in this fashion: 'Like the Deity she [the lady] cannot be defined or described: she is only she.' '*Like* the Deity', not '*As* the Deity': the clear inference to be drawn is that

Gardner prefers to soften the brunt of the blasphemy. Donne is allowed to liken the lady to God only in terms of her being incomparable and ineffable. To think that she is really God, or even better than God, would be profane: Donne is thus given to confess that it would profane God to believe the lady to be anything other than herself.

Yet, as Empson was the first to see, the poet has already identified the lady as God, since she shows the ability to read his mind; and therefore he must mean something more superbly nefarious at the end of the stanza, and not to signal a loss of nerve or shamefacedness. 'Donne says it would be profane to call the lady anything but herself,' wrote Empson in 'Donne in the New Edition', 'and as she is plainly not the Christian God he means she is something better—the cooing repetition of *thee* makes clear that *she* would be profaned, not God ... the poem though literally blasphemous does not insinuate any active and influential heresy'; and again in 'Rescuing Donne': 'the poet apologizes to the lady for mistaking her for God (as Petrarchan poets do) because he realizes now that, since she is better than God, she was insulted by the comparison.' As John Sparrow said, a 'bull's-eye'.

Empson felt that, 'though it is all right to be eclectic, one should not jump from one version to another, as the Gardner text does for *profane*, within one sentence.' Empson's colleague Mark Roberts went a good deal further, arguing in a powerful review of the Gardner text: 'What is unacceptable is the attempt to have it both ways, the erection of all this "scientific" apparatus as a cover for unregulated eclecticism, the pretence of principle when the only consistent principle is personal taste. It may be that the best way to edit Donne is to rely on one's literary judgment and select the readings that please one most. I doubt it, but this is at least a possible attitude.'[127] Empson, more indulgent on that score, limited himself to recording his distrust of Gardner's aesthetic and ideological taste: 'I think that she has arrived at a wrong belief about the poet on non-literary grounds, and that this vitiates a number of her conclusions; but, of course, she did right to form an opinion.' Moreover, he judged, 'An editor, I think, should not print a text censored by the author when under duress, or after having changed his beliefs so much as to be out of sympathy with it. The poem should appear as when geared up to its highest expressiveness and force.' Accordingly he constructed this account of what may have happened in the case of 'The Dream': 'All Group V report him saying "I do confess, I could not choose but be | Profane, to think thee anything but thee"; and when, in all manuscripts except the Group V ones, he is made to say "*it* could not choose ... | *Profaneness* ... ", it is plain that the poet himself got cold feet, and inserted a useless precaution. No one else would have thought that this tiny indirection would be enough to make him safe; and therefore the Group V manuscripts must be reporting his first version.' In general, he preferred the readings of Group V; and throughout his essays 'Donne in the New Edition' and 'Rescuing Donne' argued hectically, on occasion fancifully, that they preserved the poet's thrillingly iniquitous first locutions.

Professor Roberts, in his review of Gardner, propounds a strong case for believing that whereas Groups I and II—the manuscripts Gardner invariably favours—both represent revised texts (dating from about 1614 and 1625 respectively), and so have less authority: 'Group III MSS. are likely to give a somewhat tarnished, but possibly accurate, image of Donne's original version of a poem.'[128] He points out too the irony of Gardner's inconsistency: when editing the *Divine Poems* she proposed (pp. lxxvii–lxxviii) that Group III manuscripts often preserved the readings of Donne's original versions, but then she refused to let them hold the same reliable primary status in respect of the *Songs and Sonnets*. She argued in her latter edition, 'I see no evidence for any revision in the majority of the *Songs and Sonnets*. There is no particular reason why Donne should have wished to revise them. The *Satires* and the *Divine Poems* are a different matter... A man on the verge of ordination [i.e. in 1614] might well wish to make alterations in poems written some years before when he was a layman. There is no evidence that Donne regarded the *Elegies* and *Songs and Sonets* as poems likely to advance his career.' Yet there are obvious exceptions to that sweeping and slender judgement, as she has to allow when she constructs a mish-mash of 'The Dream'. Redpath seems little impressed by Gardner's grand assertions, for—like Roberts—he was to argue in 1983 that it is 'quite possible' that the Group III manuscripts of the *Songs and Sonnets* represent the earliest versions; in addition, 'it would seem likely that all other extant manuscript collections ... derive from manuscript material outside the tradition of both Groups [I and II], and *in circulation before 1614*.'[129] His statement therefore includes the Group V manuscripts that Empson laboured to extol for their heretical boldness. Indeed, Redpath's commentary on 'The Dream' goes far to vindicate Empson's acuity: 'I would guess that Professor Empson was quite possibly right in suggesting that Donne altered the lines when revising the poem, so as not to confess that he might be profane. If Professor Gardner is right in thinking that Group I MSS descend from a revised text of 1614, just before Donne's ordination, Professor Empson's suggestion would seem to have a fair degree of probability.'[130]

Furthermore, what neither Empson nor (presumably) Roberts realized when reviewing Gardner's edition of the *Songs and Sonnets*—she omitted to mention it in her apparatus—is that the Group V manuscripts of 'The Dream' are not alone in reading 'Prophane'. Gardner observes that the *consensus* of Groups I, II, and III (which she would usually find irresistible) reads 'Prophaneness', unlike *1633* which reads 'Prophane'. Most perplexingly, however, even while rejecting 'Prophaneness' on the grounds that Donne could not have spoiled the 'splendid' rhythmic run of his own stanza, she adds: 'I do not doubt that "Prophane" is a correction made in the copy for *1633* and do not regard its appearance in manuscripts outside the main groups as argument for its authenticity.'[131] In other words, even here she insists upon dismissing the evidence of Group V manuscripts, which offer 'Prophane', because they are inauthentic; rather than heed their degeneracy, she will trust her own ear for metrical beauty—which also just happens to yield up 'Prophane'. Theodore Redpath was the first scholar to reveal that two Group III manuscripts, Luttrell and O'Flaherty (*sigla: Lut* and *O'F*)—two out of the four manuscripts in that Group—also support Group V in reading 'Prophane'. *O'F*, which Gardner calls an 'edited' copy of *Lut*, was '*possibly corrected twice, from* Profane *to* Profanesse *and back again,*' he helpfully notes;[132] which might even allow for the possibility that its reading was first brought into line with Groups I and II, but that a shrewd scribe recognized the contamination and reinstated the author's original. Moreover, if Theodore Redpath is right in his conjecture—following Wesley Milgate's analysis of the *Satires*—that Group III manuscripts and the majority of the manuscripts in Gardner's category V (*A25, JC, D17, Cy, O, P, S,* and *K*) do represent the earliest versions of the *Songs and Sonnets*, it would seem at least possible that the same argument might apply to the *Elegies*. In addition to *Lut* and *O'F* from Group III, the following manuscripts from Group V support the reading 'Prophane' in 'The Dream': *HK2, A25, Cy, P, B* and *S*. Turning back to Elegy XIX, 'To His Mistress Going to Bed', we discover a teasing concurrence: the line that Empson battled to vindicate, 'There is no pennance due to innocence', is supported both by *JC, Cy, O, P, B,* and *S* from Group V and by the same separatist duo from Group III, *Lut* and its offspring *O'F*. This striking coincidence may or may not give aid to Empson's mighty argument—vis-à-vis 'To His Mistress Going to Bed'—against the massed ranks of Frank Kermode, John Carey and other critics, but it might give one pause before bowing to Dame Helen's determinative decree: 'I cannot regard the variant as anything but scribal in origin.'[133]

'Why will nobody believe a word I say about Donne?' Empson asked in 1973. 'The argument about the Songs and Sonnets looks to me so clear, and it does not get refuted, only treated with silent passive depression; maybe all right as a joke against Helen Gardner is the most they will say.'[134] Christopher Ricks, who sent him several words of praise for 'Rescuing Donne' in 1972, received a mild reproof in reply: 'Even you will not say it is right, or even sensible, but you allow me to be serious. The only other recipient who has answered at all is [Graham] Hough, who says it is a complete waste of time to tease the old woman, though everyone knows she is often silly.'[135] In an earlier year, before Empson had even begun to assail Gardner's textual scholarship, John Crowe Ransom accepted 'Donne the Space Man' for the *Kenyon Review* (1957) with this comment: 'I don't think [Donne] could be magnificent without the burden of thought which you attribute to him.'[136] Just four months before Ransom's letter, it is interesting to know, Gardner had written to Empson: 'I am now editing the Love Poems: Elegies and Songs and Sonnets and would that I *had* any evidence for dating them';[137] between that date (15 September 1956) and the publication of her edition in 1965, she had managed to construct what one critic has fairly called 'an absolute pyramid of speculation' about the dating and grouping of those poems, much of it based on the 'biographical inferences' she otherwise professed to find 'unsound': 'it is opinion,' wrote A. L. French, 'and should be clearly recognised as opinion.'[138]

For his part, Empson had no training at all as a bibliographer, so that his critiques are normally based on deep-seated aesthetic and ideological convictions, not to say prepossessions; but at least he did not fall into the error of applying print assumptions to a poet who, unlike Ben Jonson, was fiercely jealous of his manuscripts. Like Herbert Grierson, and indeed directly because of Grierson, Empson was deeply attached to the text of *1633*, as if an authorial imprimatur lay at the back of that first edition. But whereas Grierson allowed his aesthetic judgements to get the better of bibliographical objectives, Empson did instinctively focus his attention on a manuscript mentality and try to meet the case with a likely story of manuscript transmission. However, while Empson aimed to free the poet from the dual straightjacket of stemmata and sanctimoniousness, scoffing at Gardner's editorial methods and critical findings, another scholar has oppugned the idea that sensible readers must otherwise bow to Gardner's unassailable authority. In 1984, the year of Empson's death, Ted-Larry Pebworth argued that although Gardner and Milgate, in their respective editions, had been 'somewhat more accurate than Grierson', they still 'shared and even built upon their predecessor's anachronistic assumption of an authorially stabilized text'. Without even adequately showing that the old text needed to be revised in the first place, Gardner followed Grierson 'in ordering the manuscripts hierarchically according to their general agreements with the printed texts'; and yet she studied and reported far fewer manuscripts than were known to exist (in the case of *The Elegies and Songs and Sonnets*, just 43 out of more than 100 extant 'manuscript artifacts'), and her principal device was to substitute 'the Groups I and II manuscripts for the 1633 edition as preserving between them authorially set texts'. The fallacy of her practice of 'treating manuscripts of composite origins as if they had single origins' can be demonstrated from the case of British Library MS Lansdowne 740 (*L74*), which Gardner and Milgate feature as a member of Group II. In truth, 'the volume contains paper having eleven different watermarks and ... its contents were entered by at least twelve people over a period of more than a century. Specifically, its fifty Donne poems were copied in at least two hands on paper with four different watermarks.' Thus Gardner's 'monolithic view' of the manuscript groups is extravagantly specious; she built penthouses onto castles in air, as Pebworth puts it:

> Gardner's elaborate stemmata, supposing the existence of numerous unverified compilations, are constructed in order to account for the fact that the existing evidence does not support her conclusions. Rather than allowing the documentary evidence to dictate her theories of transmission, Gardner allows her preconceived theory of transmission to dictate the supposition of nonexistent manuscripts.
>
> To give Gardner her due, all of her theories of textual transmission are posited merely as suppositions. But she and Milgate nevertheless work from the assumption that her theories are facts... Moreover, Gardner and Milgate, like Grierson, print only selected variants from those relatively few manuscripts consulted; and those that they do report are presented in such a cryptic, often misleading fashion that it is virtually impossible to reconstruct from them the readings of any given manuscript.

Thus Pebworth's argument endorses Empson's damning complaint. 'In treating the groups as monoliths, and in most cases not even reporting individual readings that deviate from the majority, Gardner and Milgate obscure what may well be telling steps in the textual histories of individual poems.'[139] It is high time to look again at Empson's critique.

Certainly, by the 1960s, Empson won a reputation for revisionism, most notably in *Milton's God* (1961), but he was far from wishing simply to debunk Gardner when he fought to rescue Donne: he was in earnest in loathing the latterday picture of the poet and his poetry. On one point only did they agree, when Empson maintained, 'the estimate of probability turns on one's view of the interests, and the character, of the poet himself'; and Gardner: 'You may pay your money and take your choice. Neither Grierson, nor Professor Empson, nor I can claim to "prove" scientifically anything at all.'[140] Empson stated his case in 1967, when he wrote that his interpretation of John Donne had 'never been refuted, only swept out of fashion. Broadly, I think he meant what he said, and had experienced what he described. Surely, the onus of proof lies with the denier—who says that Donne never experienced mutual love, but cooked up fantasies about it, from his reading of pious and theoretical authors, while neglecting his wife.'[141] It seems rather likely that the onus of proof is still in the same court, with the advocates of a miserably domesticated Donne.

Empson remarked to Hugh Sykes Davies: 'Helen Gardner is a dangerous serpent, but not as dangerous as she thinks she is.'[142] To follow the first Waynflete Lecture at Oxford on 20 January 1972, Magdalen College invited the great and the good to attend a sherry party. Among those who were willing to cheer Empson on the occasion of his opening lecture on the text of Donne were John Sparrow (Warden of All Souls), Professor Richard Ellmann, Professor and Mrs David Hawkes (who had known him since the 1940s in China), and Peter Levi, a Fellow of St Catherine's College.

Among those who did not attend the reception was Helen Gardner, who replied to the invitation that she was unwilling to favour Empson: 'Dame Helen Gardner thanks the Vice President & the Tutors in English for their kind invitation to sherry on Thursday Jan 20th, but as she has no intention of attending Professor Empson's lectures begs to be excused for declining.[143] Empson later told Father Peter Fiore, editor of *Just So Much Honor*, he gathered that Gardner had cried because of the harsh attitude towards her that he expressed in print; he had never consciously intended to offend her, he said.[144] On the other hand, he could be gleeful in saying about any piece of evidence that he felt to be irrefutable: 'This will torpedo Helen Gardner!' For her part, Gardner was equally wont to disparage his critical scholarship thus: 'He knows as much about textual criticism as a babe unborn.'[145]

18

Roamings in Retirement: From Toronto to Miami

E MPSON told Christopher Ricks in 1965: 'In six years' time I have to retire (becoming 65 in 1971) and after so much fun abroad I only get £500 a year pension. I shall thus badly want congenial paid employment, and the money won't largely go in tax, as it would at present. I don't feel I shall be gaga in six years' time—I am relying on the retirement to finish various lines of research.' [1] (However, the royalties he earned on the books he published with Chatto's made up a not inconsiderable supplement: in 1971 he earned from his publisher £824.06, and for the financial year ending in April 1978 he was to receive £2,421.87. In 1981 Cambridge University Press issued a revised paperback edition, with Empson's 'Final Reflections', of *Milton's God*; it sold 893 copies in the first year, 357 in the UK.)

After his retirement in 1971, his first such visiting appointment—with a salary for the year of $30,000 (which was welcomed precisely for the chance it offered to make up for the seeming paucity of his pension)— was at a virtually new university in Canada. Founded only in 1959, York University had enrolled its first students in 1960; and the Faculty of Arts and Science opened in 1963. In 1965 the university established its principal campus, where Empson was to be based, at Keele Street and Steeles Avenue, a few miles to the northwest of downtown Toronto and the terrific sweep of Lake Ontario. Empson was offered a one-year appointment running from July 1972 to the end of June 1973. Such a lavish remuneration would in due course stir a certain amount of low-key grumbling among those of his colleagues who felt the visit had not been a success: the money might have been better spent, they felt, on hiring a couple of energetic junior faculty.[2] Professor Dick Ewen, who delighted in Empson's company, writes of the visit: 'Everyone, including me, wanted either to appropriate him or to pretend that they neither knew nor cared that he was there.'[3]

'Rather dull here, but friendly and sensible,' Empson noted in the autumn.[4] The university buildings were scarcely inspiring: the Keele campus consisted of a range of raw redbrick buildings constructed on open farmland on the outskirts of the city. Through the long winter months it would turn out to be a bleak, snow-whirling, alienating environment, and all too far from the city centre: an academic gulag. In its favour, on the other hand, was the reputation that it was more 'hip' than the fusty, much older, and more 'classy' University of Toronto; certainly, in the early 1970s, it seemed quite an offbeat and even avant-garde institution, and a number of Canada's leading writers and poets featured on the faculty. Hetta and Simon accompanied Empson for the year, and they rented an apartment (grimly designated Unit 12) at 21 Potsdam Road, in the district of Downsview not far from the campus. Simon was enrolled in a local school and would greatly enjoy his year abroad. The Empsons were keen to explore the ruggedly gorgeous countryside of Ontario, upstate of the modern city; and whenever Empson managed to free himself from the routines of teaching and writing, they would rent a car to sally forth for a day or so. 'The country is nice if you can get out,' Empson would report in postcard style to Frank Kermode in London; '—Hetta is hiring a car, and found the footprints of a bear in Algonquin Park, but it seemed pretty empty otherwise. Impressive, of course.'[5] At one point Empson's Sheffield colleague Roma Gill, whose health was declining as a consequence of multiple sclerosis, turned up for a visit, and Empson gamely pushed her wheelchair on outings.

On one occasion, Empson mildly (not complainingly) remarked that it had never been made clear to him exactly what he was expected to do at York University; surely it was not merely to fill in for whoever happened to be on sabbatical leave? In practice, he ran two classes: English 319, a large lecture course on Shakespeare (supported by a series of seminar classes run by other faculty and tutors), and English 626: 'Poetry 1580–1650'. English 319 was an undergraduate course for third and fourth year students, while English 626 was a graduate course covering the poetry of Sidney, Spenser, Donne, Carew, Herbert, Crashaw, Vaughan, and the non-dramatic poetry of Shakespeare and Jonson. Curiously but perhaps not surprisingly, he chose a rather outdated edition, Norman Ault's *Elizabethan Poems*, as one of the textbooks for English 626; the university bookstore had difficulty in

locating enough copies of it. Not many of the students (they included some
graduates from the University of Toronto who were keen to take advantage of the luminary's presence in the city) were prepared for their challenging and oblique encounters with the ageing, frail-looking, though in
fact surprisingly robust, Englishman whose utterances could assume a
muttering and even sardonic form, whose oddly military mien catered to
an eccentric effect, and whose full white moustache would often muffle the
rapid, darting outrush of his disconcerting remarks. Nicholas Howe recalls
of the Shakespeare course, which he found fascinating once he became
used to the style: 'Empson lectured by reading aloud from the text and
then commenting on words and passages, as well as discussing the larger
dramatic and thematic concerns of the play. For students accustomed to a
more formal style of lecturing, that is to say, a style that made taking notes
of the necessary points easy, Empson's method was alien and not very
successful. The large lecture dwindled quite quickly to a small group.'[6]
Much of the course, as another student remembers, seemed to be devoted
to an arcane debunking of the stage directions offered by John Dover
Wilson in his editions of the plays.

Empson's students included a few future professors of English such as
Shyamal Bagchee, later of the University of Alberta (and editor of the
Yeats-Eliot Review), who enrolled in his seventeenth-century course 'with
much enthusiasm and even joy'.[7] Bagchee was by no means alone in his
enthusiasm: another bright student reported to Professor Ewen, 'I live for
every Tuesday from 11 a.m. to 1 p.m. Professor Empson brings my mind to
life and makes the world better. Ah, Tuesday.' Indeed, Ewen's abiding
impression of Empson's visit is that 'he was anxious to earn his keep and
make a difference (as he did, but only to a large number of unconnected
individuals—he had an extraordinary power of seemingly detached and
absent-minded profound intimacy).

Aviva Layton, a teaching assistant who was married at the time to the
Canadian poet Irving Layton (himself a professor at York University),
remembers that the seminar group for English 626 sat around a table
with Empson at the head. Often, she remembers, Empson would look
bored or bewildered; or he would appear to be somewhere else altogether,
in the far-off country of his mind. At moments, indeed, he looked so
abstracted and inward that she was obliged to wonder whether he had
not in fact fallen asleep. Yet she would feel delighted by his sudden
interjections: what she regarded as his deliciously witty, dry, cryptic and
ironic comments.[8] John Morgenstern, on the other hand, remembers that
'the Empson we got was not quite the Empson who wrote [*Seven Types of*

Ambiguity]. He was certainly alert and in complete charge of his considerable faculties but he seemed somewhat more whimsical about reading
poetry than we were used to from our other professors. The thing that
I remember most vividly is his reading aloud long passages from *The Faerie
Queene* in a most beautiful and vibrant voice that seemed out of keeping
with the frail body from which it issued.'[9]

Bagchee remembers too Empson's shut eyes and soft speech. 'In one of
the early meetings the student who was to make his presentation sat
opposite the instructor, at the other end of the table. It is likely he was
not certain that WE was quite awake, or whether he would be able to hear
him clearly. At any rate, the student began reading his report a bit too
loudly for that small room, and WE interrupted pointing out that he was
not deaf, that he could hear quite alright, and that the student need not
"shout".'[10]

Despite his personal oddities, there were enormous gains to be made
from taking note of his stray but illuminating remarks or his acutely
attentive comments on student essays. Ben Jonson's 'A Journey' was a
'dirty poem', Empson announced one day. On another day, he pointed out
that the figure of Astrophel, in Sir Philip Sidney's *Astrophel and Stella*, is 'the
first fully developed personality in English literature'. Of Shakespeare's
sonnets, he remarked with solid good sense: 'Shakespeare did not intend
publication, so we should not object that the story is unfinished.'[11] John
Morgenstern recalls one other observation in particular: it was so important to Shakespeare's career as a playwright, said Empson, 'that he had
been admitted to the table of the Earl of Southampton, where he could
observe aristocratic behaviour.'[12]

Nicholas Howe, son of the critic Irving Howe (who is now a professor in
the Department of English, and Director of the Center for Medieval and
Renaissance Studies, at Ohio State University), remembers above all:

> he was enormously gentle with us, and kind in his criticism. Each week one
> of us would write a short paper (perhaps 3 or 4 pages) on the novel or poems
> assigned for that day, and then would read it aloud at the start of the two-
> hour class...The first paper of the course was by another student who
> wrote an allegorical interpretation of *Robinson Crusoe*. After the student
> finished, Empson paused for a moment and then said 'You mustn't make
> the same mistake as Tom Eliot, of reading everything as Christian.' It took
> all of us a few seconds to translate 'Tom Eliot' into T. S. Eliot and a few
> more to recognize that this was not name-dropping on his part. At that
> moment, something quite wonderful happened in the class: we realized that
> we were being taught by someone who knew poets like Eliot, and who also

had the human courtesy to respond in this way. Our mistakes, as readers, were not student mistakes in some embarrassing way; they were to him errors of interpretation that we shared with someone like Eliot. We all felt like we were being treated very seriously—probably far more so than we deserved. . . .

One moment of another sort stands out. I was reading a paper on one of Dryden's poems and he stopped me after I read a passage aloud to say that I had gotten the line wrong. He didn't know what it should be, he said, but he knew it wasn't right because it didn't scan properly. And of course we looked in our texts and found that he was right. That taught me something about what it meant to have an ear—not just to know the metrical types in some textbook fashion, as we had been taught them, but to listen so attentively to a twenty-year-old student reading aloud that you could catch that kind of slip.[13]

When Kenneth McLean asked Empson why he left the poetry of Thomas Traherne out of the course, Empson responded that it was all a matter of 'taste': he just did not get on with Traherne. 'Taste' indeed had become a by-word of his critical credo. Traherne did not measure up to his acid test for true poetry: the expression of an unappeased conflict—as in the moral wrestling of Donne's poetry. On the other hand, Empson felt unconstrained by the strict limits of the course. For reasons almost certainly having to do with protecting the curriculum monopoly of another professor, the Department had bizarrely specified that the syllabus for Empson's seminar on seventeenth-century poetry should not include coverage of Milton or Marvell, but in the event he did put on a good seminar on Marvell—except that the students could not quite figure out why he was primarily interested in the question of whether or not Marvell had married his landlady;[14] they were not to know that this issue, which amounted to a quest to vindicate Marvell's bisexuality, was to become a critical and moral hobbyhorse of Empson's throughout the 1970s.

For the final examination, he set questions of an unusually open kind; they were difficult in scope and yet curiously unforbidding, and highly inviting on the matter of taste. 'Describe the poetry of Wyatt. Do you find it too narrow in range?' or 'Discuss the influence of George Herbert upon Vaughan, Crashaw, and perhaps Herrick. Can he really have had much influence upon different authors?' or 'The moral allegory as written by Spenser was expected both to produce good poetry and to make the fit reader better. Do you consider it a viable form?—that is, *could* it do both these things at once? Also consider whether Spenser succeeds in making it work, on some occasions perhaps.'[15]

On the last day of the course, the six surviving students in English 626 gave him a bottle of good Scotch as a way of saying thanks, and he smiled with pleasure. Although he had not been particularly sociable with his students during the semester, he promptly invited all of them back for drinks at the apartment on Potsdam Road. Since he had recently written a review of the facsimile edition of *The Waste Land*, edited by the poet's relict, Valerie Eliot, one of his major conversational gambits during the party was to point out to the students the importance of Pound's revisions to Eliot's drafts.[16] At another moment, as Sumana Sen-Bagchee remembers, the topic of American writers cropped up in the conversation, and in particular the name of William Faulkner. Since Sumana was herself taking a graduate course on Faulkner, she pricked up her ears to hear what Empson might have to say about him; so did others. But then Hetta's voice was heard to be asking, 'Who's Fogner? Where's Fogner?' Empson was quick but soft and firm in his response: 'No one we need to worry about. No one.' Thus he smartly set aside a promising topic of conversation, though no one believed any malice had been intended and none was taken. 'I remember having a good laugh over the incident on our way home, late at night,' Mrs Bagchee recalls. 'We wondered, however, if Empson had ever read Faulkner, a question that remained unanswered.'[17]

And then, at a certain moment during the evening, Empson exclaimed, 'It's getting rather soggy down here'—he was obviously referring to his crotch—and forthwith disappeared for the rest of the evening. He was almost certainly far less comfortable with the students than was Hetta, who drank too much and supposedly propositioned some of the young men. Being a free, outspoken person, Hetta was equally quick to yell at a student who ventured to offer some observation about apartheid in South Africa: she left the poor staggered fellow with the thunderous impression that since he had no first-hand experience of the apartheid regime, he had no right whatever to offer any opinion about it.[18]

At faculty parties she would behave just as flamboyantly, drunkenly, sometimes rudely. Empson's colleagues were bright, witty, good-humoured individuals, and for the most part marvellous teachers. They enjoyed getting together for dinner parties and other occasions. But Hetta's exuberance and intoxication, and her open invitations to intimacy, taxed their goodwill. At one stuffy dinner party, she even danced on the table and whirled her skirt over her head.[19] In truth, her merry and predatory conduct made her just as memorable a figure at York as her quieter, more gentlemanly, and seemingly much more ancient or antic husband; rumours about her resonated for ages.

At a Burns Night party thrown by Dick Ewen in January 1973, both of the Empsons got—like the servants in *She Stoops to Conquer*—'as drunk as they could possibly be'. Hetta was dressed up in a toga-like garment worn off the shoulder, and she slunk about the place like a senior lioness on the prowl. As Ewen recalls, only four students happened to have been invited, two female and two male, and both of the guests of honour took an instant shine to one of them in particular, the handsome Nicholas Green—'and neither Empson attempted to conceal their appreciation of this fact'. This was the only occasion, as far as Dick Ewen can remember, when a prim onlooker might have found something to deplore in the Empsons' behaviour, and yet nobody did deplore them there. 'Both were so utterly without guile or meanness or self-importance.'[20] It was Nick Green who later in the evening discovered Empson on the brink of peeing into Ewen's bathtub (the door was left open); taking him gently by the shoulders Green reorientated the esteemed guest in the direction of the toilet bowl and left him to the rest.

Naturally, Empson relished the several parties of the academic session above all if he found the company stimulating, witty and inventive. He came across Kingsley Grahame, who was the other male student at Ewen's party (he is now a judge), on two or three occasions during the year, and liked him as a spirited and even aggressive conversationalist. Dick Ewen remembers in particular that at one party Grahame 'invented a little-known Renaissance writer, Zabaglione I think, who anticipated Melville by writing an epic poem about a whale. Empson joined in, affecting delight that anyone else was familiar with one of his favourite authors, and the two of them spontaneously constructed an extensive history of the man and his oeuvre, one of them (I hope Empson) protesting that we all must have heard Scarlatti's beautiful settings of his love-poems to La Perugina.'[21] Hetta, frowning concentratedly, was among the onlookers who were totally taken in by the joint performance.

There was no doubting the bond of deep love that linked Empson to his wife. At a dinner party given by Win Willis, Empson was suddenly heard to be reciting Coleridge: 'To be beloved is all I need, And whom I love I love indeed.' Hetta gazed at him fondly, if a bit mistily, and proclaimed 'He's a silly old bugger, but I love him.'[22] They had a deep understanding which did not generally need to be articulated or manifested: for instance, at a dinner party given by a colleague named Robert Casto, a specialist in the Romantics and an able poet in his own right, it seemed to them that one of the prime purposes of the occasion was to solicit Empson's response to Casto's poems; but it was Hetta who somehow made it known that her husband 'didn't know this kind of poetry'. As another guest perceived, Empson himself felt no need to utter such comments, for Hetta offered them on his behalf: 'He just sat there and let her transmit his thoughts. Hardly said anything.'[23] At another party, Hetta burst out: 'William: you're stupid in your fucking head.' To which he replied, 'Oh, don't say that, my dear.' There was no offence.

Aviva Layton was far more shocked when Empson announced at one faculty party that he considered his own poetry 'utter rubbish'. She reflects: 'It was almost as if he were deeply ashamed of what he considered his lack of poetic talent. (I heard him make the same remark a few years later when I was living in London and attended a reading of his in Hampstead.)'[24] She was shocked because he seemed to be utterly sincere, though it may be that he did not especially care to discuss his poetry and so cut off that line of talk.

From time to time during the months at Toronto Empson was invited to flit around North America to give speaking appearances at other colleges including New College, Vermont; Vancouver;[25] St John's, Newfoundland; Seattle; and San Francisco. On 5 April 1973, for instance, he was to read his poetry, at the invitation of Marvin Magalaner, at the Graduate Center of the City University of New York. At another occasion, the prestigious Pratt Lecture at the Memorial University in Newfoundland, he again made use of his party piece, 'The Secret Marriage of Andrew Marvell', but his delivery was widely held to have been disastrous: vagarious, self-indulgent, mumbling—he even seemed to be adept at avoiding the microphone provided on the rostrum—and it appeared that his notes had been scribbled on an envelope, so he had to keep turning this small rectangle of paper round and round to catch what he had written. Before he left for Newfoundland, he had borrowed from Dick Ewen a paperback copy of the poems of E. J. Pratt, proposing to open his lecture with a few generous remarks about the very man who was memorialized in the lecture series; but, even as he returned the book to Ewen, he remarked merely: 'I thought it better to say nothing about the matter.' When Ewen enquired if he had enjoyed his encounter with a different, sea-washed Canadian university, Empson simply frowned and said, 'A lot of the people were rather piggy.' It was the most caustic remark that Dick Ewen ever heard Empson make— 'but I thought I understood: it was not he who was unprepared, it was we'. Empson, the august grandee, was never invited to give a public lecture or a poetry reading while at York.

'Happily, it was entirely different when I lured him into giving a lecture on *Paradise Lost* to my big first-year lecture class. That was an occasion of consummate glory.'[26] Initially, when Ewen invited him to give a lecture, Empson amiably responded by proposing a debate between the two of them. Ewen merely questioned, 'Empson and Ewen?' and laughed self-deprecatingly. On the day of the lecture, Ewen chauffered Empson to the lecture theatre; and as they arrived the guest plucked a flask of brandy and water from his coat and drank liberally from it. And then, courteous as ever, he offered the flask to Ewen, who declined. It was 10 o'clock in the morning. The lecture began badly, as Empson's notes fluttered to the floor in disarray. But the audience gradually grew absorbed as he warmed to his theme. Ewen explains further about the effect that Empson's lecture on Milton generated in the first-year survey class: 'It was not so much that my students adored and admired and drank him in: it was that for 50 minutes he made them happy to be alive, and to be students—the room shook with poetry, ideas at full gallop, and the reciprocity of intellectual excitement at its most benign.'[27] At the end, one of them called out: 'I'll never enjoy anything so much again.'[28]

But Empson's most extraordinary encounter of the year was with the seer of popular culture and the media, Marshall McLuhan, whose interpretative works *The Gutenberg Galaxy* (1962), *Understanding Media* (1965), and *The Medium is the Message* (1967) had sold hundreds of thousands of copies; by the late 1960s McLuhan, who taught at St Michael's College, University of Toronto, and was director of the Centre for Culture and Technology, had become famous throughout the global village as cultural commentator and ubiquitous interpeter of the electronic age. Having been made aware that Empson was living and working in Toronto, McLuhan and his wife Corinne were embarrassed by the fact that a critic whose work he enormously admired was being ignored by the premier university, so they invited the Englishman to dinner at their home at 3 Wychwood Park, along with Dr Claude Bissell, then President of the University of Toronto.[29] The evening promised to be all the more remarkable because of the presence of two other noted guests, W. K. Wimsatt and Northrop Frye. McLuhan was an enthusiastic, witty conversationalist who loved to stir things up and challenge his adversaries. 'Conversation has more vitality than books, more fun, more drama,' he had declared in an interview published in 1966. As if to add a further ingredient to the potentially explosive mix, he was a Roman Catholic.

Unhappily, most of the evening has gone unchronicled, passing the way of the food and the wine, though Empson evidently sung well for his supper. There is no question but that Empson was able to set the table on a roar. McLuhan noted too that Empson was 'very noticeably deaf and has a big white mustache and the florid face of a Col. Blimp'. His other guests, on the other hand, disapppointed McLuhan (who would have relished a candid and zestful exchange of views, or even something more like a civil quarrel) by having nothing to say for themselves; they seemed to be shy of Empson—simply starstruck.

McLuhan obviously found Empson much better value than the locals at his dinner table. He noted that 'Empson spoke of his essays as occasional raids on English lit. Mrs Empson is a refreshingly open and boisterous gal socially.' And he was evidently very pleased when the Empsons urged the McLuhans to come and visit them whenever they were next in London.

McLuhan even took the risk of teasing Empson about *Milton's God*, twitting him with the suggestion that it must have been meant as something of a joke. Empson's sole surviving anecdote about the evening, in a letter to his son Jacob, characteristically picks up on McLuhan's temerarious tease, and yet the tone in which he tells of it here shows that he had appreciated the gracious lightness of McLuhan's taunt; above all, he is respectful of his host:

> We were asked to dinner by Marshal [*sic*] McLuhan (The Medium is the Message), who seemed well-intentioned enough, but asked me whether my book on Milton hadn't been all spoof, assuming that to a brother publicist I wouldn't mind confessing that it was; so I thought I had to explain to him that he was worshipping the Devil, being a Roman Catholic. It was at his own dinner-table, but the ladies had gone for their pee, so it wasn't really rude.[30]

What is evident from those few reflections is that Empson was concerned to maintain his mannerliness at McLuhan's table, especially since he had recognized the pleasantness underpinning his host's risky tease. Empson could be brusque and peremptory with wrong-headedness or rudeness, but a sublime kind-heartedness was a predominant characteristic of his nature. He later told Shyamal Bagchee that he had much enjoyed meeting the illustrious 'young man' McLuhan—who was in fact only five years his junior.

Empson was enough of a success at the dinner to earn an invitation to give a public lecture at the University of Toronto early in 1973, when he again spoke (in Sidney Smith Hall) on one of his pet topics of the time, 'The Secret Marriage of Andrew Marvell'. But McLuhan, when he tried to relay what he could gather of Empson's argument to his former colleague Bissell (who had just resigned as President of the University), offered a muddled account that was entirely the consequence of the lecturer's whistlingly inaudible delivery:

One overwhelming fact that emerged was that Andrew Marvell was the master of seventy-seven types of ambiguity. Marvell turns out to have been a quadruple agent for various political groups, all of whom paid him for undermining all the others. He was an extremely worldly man who lived in terror of damnation, and his secret marriage to his landlady was to facilitate certain inheritances, but also motivated by his hatred of women.

Marvell's 'The Coy Mistress' poem ['To His Coy Mistress'] takes on some rather startling meanings in the light of Empson's analysis.[31]

Better still is McLuhan's finely indulgent account of Empson's manner as a lecturer which may also serve to epitomize the experience of those of Empson's students in Canada who found it hard simply to comprehend him:

Would that we had a video tape of his delivery. His rubicund face, bound by a drooping white moustache, had also some histrionics such as I had never seen. He read aloud from a volume which he seldom saw since it was above eye level, with the spine of the book dangling by one string, while he flapped 30 or 40 pages at a time, back and forth. He recited constantly, both from the book and from a great mass of lecture notes that were distributed for several feet around him. These notes he examined with convulsive and darting movements, which were like the action of a card shark shuffling several decks simultaneously. However, I have saved the most amazing part for the last—namely, his voice. Overall it was somewhat like the sound of air escaping from a tire, punctuated by occasional sounds of words. Tiny phrases of three or four words could definitely be heard every minute or so, as he rose suddenly above the general hissing noise that came through the moustache. Several times he alluded to the contemptible P.A. mechanism that lay beside him, unused. The audience was strongly impelled to seize this equipment and wrap it around his neck, if only to strangle him. If one had heard of Marvell before, and even read a bit, the scattered stabbings of tiny phrase bits were very tantalizing indeed. For those who had not heard of Marvell, there were the histrionics! It was a good show at worst, and unforgettable, at best.[32]

In mid-April Empson flew East, first to visit Wellesley College, then for a few days in New York (where he stayed at the Greenwich Village apartment of his American publisher James Laughlin), and from there he travelled on to Cambridge, Massachusetts, to fulfil a couple of speaking engagements at Harvard. He asked the Richardses if he might stay with them for a few days, but Richards had recently been unwell and Dorothea felt she could not cope with Empson. All the same, he went along to a party at their apartment at 1000 Memorial Drive, where the other guests included the academic Reuben Brewer and his wife, the poet William Alfred, and the poet Adrienne Rich. Dorothea recorded in her diary, with relief: 'William behaved well. I. A. R. still has a daunting effect.' Later, however, William Alfred told Dorothea he had found Empson 'truculent and contradictory' towards Richards—his mentor and father-figure— 'who was incredibly patient ... Said Empson seemed to contradict everything I. A. R. said.' Not surprisingly, Dorothea Richards thought Alfred, in a parenthetical word, 'Observant'. On another page of her diary Dorothea reflected: 'William Empson what a problem character so curious, rich & rare & impossible in all sorts of ways. Not house trained, like a naughty child in so many ways, reaching for what he wants & *regardless*.'[33] Empson's uncouth behaviour should probably be put down to nervous agitation, and to his drinking too much in consequence. He had definitely drunk too much by the time he was driven back to his hotel by the critic John Paul Russo (who was dogging Richards like a latterday Boswell). Russo subsequently reported (as Dorothea was prompt to note in her diary, with prejudice against her husband's protégé) that Empson had 'jumped out of the moving car to vomit, & then nearly was in signing the Coleridge book'—though Russo has recalled for me that Empson did not actually leap from his car, though he had certainly tried to get out while it was still moving.[34]

John Paul Russo has confirmed in his biography of Richards, published sixteen years later, that Richards was indeed 'very distressed at Empson's seemingly flippant remarks about the older Coleridge's religious motives ... Richards was "furious" over the last paragraph [of *Coleridge's Verse: A Selection*], where Empson analyzes Coleridge's "Epitaph"; he called Empson an "impudent horsefly" and accused him of "near treason" in the friendship.' Russo goes on to cite in the biography a comment that he penned in his own journal just after the treacherous talk on Coleridge: ' "It was the *strongest* state of anger I have ever seen displayed" by Richards, up to that time or after.'[35] (According to the Cambridge don George Watson, Empson during a visit to his alma mater in his last decade took to uttering severe criticisms of Richards—perhaps in retaliation to the fierce manner in which Richards was speaking to and of himself—even saying that he thought his mentor a fraud who should be brought down a peg or two. 'He's had far too easy a time.')[36]

Empson put on a far better show when he gave a poetry reading for the Woodberry Poetry Room at Harvard University, on Friday, 13 April, as part of the Morris Gray Lecture Series (with a fee of $800). Though slightly nervous and at moments hesitant, he was in amiably discursive mood and took pains for his American audience both to comment on the political and literary background to his verses and to offer beguiling glosses to each of the several poems he read. Realizing that he ought to start off by locating his own poetry in the context of the 'Auden Generation', he was keen to put on record his sense of unwavering admiration for Auden himself, and for his politically-engaged poems of the 1930s. Auden and his friends created 'very powerful propaganda, very effective propaganda', he insisted. It seemed categorically necessary at the time to have 'more socialism' and 'to avoid the effects of the slump', along with a 'Popular Front' to deal with the international threat. He regretted only that he had 'not been in on this movement', which as always he put down to his having been a student not at Oxford but at Cambridge. On some of his other contemporaries, he was equally forthright. 'Dylan Thomas was very deliberately left-wing,' he declared from first-hand acquaintance, 'but never put it in his poetry.' On the importance of T. S. Eliot: 'I hope you won't deduce my opinions from the kind of poetry I wrote. The influence of T. S. Eliot was very strong . . . compared to the final decay of Victorian poetry.' As for the influence of French Symbolism, he went on: 'There have been some tremendous poems written in the Symbolist method, it would be absurd to deny. But I think for young people writing poetry it has been an incubus . . . I was imitating only the English Metaphysicals.'

As for elucidating the specific poems he chose to read out, he called 'Legal Fiction' 'a slight poem in a way.' He then remembered that for some time in the *New Statesman* there was a lady who wrote under the nom-de-plume 'Sagittarius' and who 'wrote exactly this kind of thing: witty comparisons in tidy rhyming verse that drove home the socialist policies of the magazine.' Pausing for a moment, he amusingly recommended his own poem: 'This breathes a larger air.' 'Legal Fiction' had been very popular, he went on, both with his Chinese Communist students in the late 1940s and with American capitalists. 'I was approached by a group of American international lawyers who were doing a brochure about space travel, and they paid me five dollars to reproduce this poem . . . They thought it was funny, do you see.' Reflecting further upon the evidence that his little poem about property, death, and the universe had proved to go down so well with extreme ends of the political spectrum, he remarked: 'The number of poems which satisfy both American international lawyers and Chinese communist students is not very large.' His voice gave out a characteristically sardonic chuckle as he contemplated that huge irony. 'Camping Out' he said he considered 'a rather bad poem, really', primarily because the first stanza is too clumsy, although the second 'can be said'.

Then, thinking about the carved figure of the ancient god who embraced all creeds and peoples and who was the inspiration for his poem 'Homage to the British Museum', he observed: 'It was a remarkable effort of mind for a primitive people.' As for the poem itself, he joked superbly: 'As Matthew Arnold wrote to his mother, the merit of my poetry is to be literal and sincere, do you see?'

'Doctrinal Point' he summed up as being—'really'—about 'Deism...If you arrive at the point of grace, you no longer require a personal god.' 'Missing Dates', he noted, has been 'more widely accepted than anything else I've written, and I think it is probably the best poem.' The poem 'Villanelle', on the other hand, had been 'very hard to write'; after all, the villanelle is a demanding form, and 'making it come to life is I think hard...My villanelles sound very stiff, like tombstones.' Furthermore, he went on, 'what it says is *untrue*'—he meant that the apparently facile moral of his poem, that being tidy and orderly will somehow stop you from growing old, had no foundation. Recalling that I. A. Richards had once remarked to him that 'Villanelle' struck him as very funny, Empson reflected aloud: 'Max Brod records that Kafka's friends thought *The Trial* very funny. If *The Trial* is funny, I'm very willing to believe that my little poem is funny too.' And before reading out the whole of his epic 'Bacchus', Empson reassured his audience—not without a large helping of irony— 'Dylan Thomas used to describe it as my good poem.'

Finally, of 'Let It Go'—his clear-eyed, decisive, melancholy lyric about his giving up the writing of poetry—he noted with modest conviction: 'This little poem is slightly self-important, perhaps'; it was 'rather too portentous.'

Hetta and her son returned home to England at the end of the teaching year; but Empson stayed on for a while, principally so that he might be available on the day of the finals examination board—just in case there were questions to be answered. Shortly before Hetta left, a valedictory party was thrown—not by the Department, but by the Empsons themselves. Dick Ewen remembers of the occasion: 'In a notable reversal of established custom, both Empsons remained steadfastly sober throughout that evening of leave-taking: it was the Department that got drunk.' One of the more dull members of staff offered some farewell words and added, 'I'll be sure to look you up when I come to London.' Empson witheringly replied, 'I have no doubt you will.'

Since the Empsons had surrendered the tenure of their apartment on Potsdam Road, Ewen forthwith arranged for Empson to be accommodated in the ground-floor guest suite of one of the graduate student residences (there were four identical, sixteen-storeyed monstrosities)— 'Extremely considerate of you, my dear Ewen,' said Empson[37]—and Hetta bade the Bagchees, who had an apartment on the fourteenth floor of the same tower block, to 'look after William': it was a flattering task which they undertook with solicitude. Often they would invite him to come up and dine with them, but he always refused, explaining that he could only manage the 'gruel' (soup) he made for himself—as Sumana observed, he loved to put on 'his frail old man act'. All the same, almost every evening, he would appear at their door with an open bottle of Scotch. Bagchee and his wife, along with Dick Ewen who lived in the same block and would often join them for drinks, grew fond of their 'brilliant, witty, gentle and generous-minded' guest, whose conversation knew no bars, who would reveal private facets of himself, and who never hesitated to offer candid opinions. Through all his chats with the Bagchees, he voiced only one regret: 'I cannot understand, Mrs Bagchee'—he never addressed her informally—'how with all your good taste you will not try to appreciate the taste of a good Scotch.'

Just before Empson's departure, Dick Ewen asked him to autograph each of his books—'which he did with his unfailing courtesy.' There was only one snag: 'He spelled my name differently on every single fly-leaf, a remarkable feat, considering the relative fewness of the alphabeti-cals.'[38]

He remembers too that when, a year or so later, he called on the Empsons in London, Empson kindly offered to help him shop for a memento that a friend in Canada had asked him to bring home, uttering the unforgettable sentence: 'Let us see what Hampstead souk can provide us with, m'dear.'[39]

At some point during the outing, Empson remarked:

'I live in unlikely places. Is there anywhere more ridiculous than Hamp-stead?'

'Torremolinos?' offered Ewen.

'I meant, in this world.'

Ewen reflects further: 'I always had the feeling that Empson was a deeply lonely man who did not in the least mind being alone, not that he often was. His dearest companions were ideas. Another thing is that he had the gift of unquenchable happiness. Critical happiness. Confident criticality.' As Empson went out shoppping with Ewen, he strode along 'light-heartedly and with elastic step...with an almost child-like zest'. Ewen thought to himself:

'I am not just in the company of a Grade A genius, I am happy to be with a very happy, very contented, very witty, very helpful and quite extraordinarily generous and magnanimous man.' But his contempt, when it was elicited, was unambiguous and not in the least pastoral.[40]

Empson flew back from Canada to England on Thursday, 10th May. It was a timely return, for his brother Arthur, with whom he had always been concerned to keep on terms, and to handle very gingerly, died on the Friday. Empson went to immense trouble to kit himself out with a mourning suit and top hat. It was an inalienable family tradition, he told his friend Biddy Crozier, that he should tip his topper by the graveside in precisely the right manner.

In the late summer of 1974, at the age of 67, Empson took off for another session as a visiting professor in a curious corner of the USA. This time, he fetched up at Pennsylvania State University, where the fee for his labours was to be $20,000—and most of that remuneration would indeed go straight into his bank, untaxed at source except for a deduction of $500 by way of State Tax. His visit was financed in part by a research unit, the Institute for the Arts and Humanistic Studies, directed by Professor Stanley Weintraub. Penn State University is situated at the exact geographical centre of the state, in a region of rolling wooded hills and agricultural lands. In one sense, the university is in the middle of nowhere; in another sense, it is within reasonable reach of almost everywhere in the eastern USA. Penn State started life as an agricultural college; by the late nineteenth century, there were courses in engineering; and the liberal arts had grown up by the turn of the century (the college was the first in the nation to run a course in American literature, thanks to Fred Pattee—for whom the university library is named).

Empson rented a furnished apartment (number 514) on the fifth floor of a block called 1000A Plaza Drive; it had two bedrooms, and cost $1,000 for the nine months ending in May 1975, and it was convenient enough. There was a supermarket in the plaza, and the walk to work took him about twenty minutes. However, he was neurotic about noise, and this was a real bugbear:

My digs are terribly noisy [he wrote home to Hetta], looking out on a kind of well between two great blocks of flats, where students keep their cars and motorbicycles. It is absurd to remember that the noises made by Simon [now 17] and his young friends (using the motorbicycle as a musical instrument) made me feel I could not work in Studio House; this is the same thing on a vastly greater scale...My study at the university is too uncomfortable to work in much.[41]

He asked to be moved to another apartment on the outside of the building, away from the fiercely revving cauldron of the court, just as soon as anything became vacant; but in the event he stayed where he was put for the duration.

He was put down for the first of the three ten-week terms to teach two courses; the first was on Shakespeare, and the other was an interdisciplinary course he was requested to confect for the Interdisciplinary Program: thus he nervously proposed the hair-raisingly learned title 'The Revival of Belief in the Spirits of Nature, from the late Fifteenth Century: Ficino's translation of Trismegistus; Paracelsus; Cornelius Agrippa; Bruno; with some examples of their influence on English writers till the late seventeenth century.' It looked on the face of it to be suitable only for a small number of students of rarefied taste—though the example of a belief in Spirits of Nature that was foremost in his mind throughout the 1970s was that of Marlowe's *Dr Faustus*. Each course was to take up three periods a week of one-and-a-quarter hours each, and with each period being run on a different day of the week. It seemed a tall order after his much lighter load at York University, Toronto, where he had taught one course over three consecutive hours: there, for the first hour, he had lectured, and for the remainder he had split the class to read out their papers and hold discussions. 'I doubt if that would be enough of the nose to the grindstone for Penn State, but thank God the students are sure to want to speak up and stop listening. I expect something can be worked out.'[42]

He began the first term feeling, he said, 'very exhausted, and just lying up, which has happened fairly often in the last few years, and passes off with vitamin tablets'—so he was relieved to fancy that Penn was an academic lay-by where he could teach without hassle and otherwise get on with his own work. 'Well, it seems all right, a good place to write a book,' he wrote home. 'The students are friendly and sensible; the dons very cagey.'[43] All too soon, however, his initial sense of the pleasant solitariness of his condition at Penn State turned into one of unhappy isolation. While some of his colleagues were friendly and invited him out once or twice, he felt on the whole left out of whatever social swim there was to be found; it was as if the geographical remoteness of the town had entered the souls of its residents. Often he would consume a liquid lunch by himself, and in the evening, after a day's teaching and a raid on the library, he would invariably scuttle back to his bland apartment, eat frugally, and drink and read himself to bed: 'there is no lunch and beer place for teachers...,' he regretted. 'However there is a pleasant basement across the street which gives me a bowl of soup and an icy American beer. I suppose I am getting tetchy...'[44] The sad, ultra-passive turn of phrase 'which gives me a bowl of soup' seems to betray a hint that he was unconsciously seeing himself as a Dickensian waif. He was to tell Hetta too, a few days before Christmas: 'I am never out in the evening.'[45] Not allowing himself to feel self-pity, he would simply work all the harder. Still, he could not but feel himself to be biding his time in a spiritual void, kicking his heels in a little hell at Plaza Drive, unstimulated by any society or friends. Solitary drinking and smoking to excess would take the edge off the evenings.

Even at an early stage in the term, he would frankly admit to Hetta, 'I don't really feel comfortable here; I feel all the time that they don't want what I have to offer.... However, I don't mean they are unfriendly, not at all; they hope there won't be any bother.'[46] He resolved that this post should be the last such visiting appointment overseas he would take up; the prospect of gathering his Old Age Pension at 70 looked so inviting. He was grateful to Hetta for sending him crossword puzzles from the *Times* to fill out the staring hours. 'Thank you so much for the Times Crossword puzzles; I have sometimes finished a New York Times one, so I don't dislike them merely because they expect me to know famous names of baseball and Broadway. The Times (London) has a better style.'[47]

The highlight of the first term was a visit at the end of October by C. P. Snow and his wife, who were surprised and delighted to discover Empson in residence at Penn State. Empson was invited to join the Snows at the head table for a formal dinner, whereupon Snow made great play, in his speech, of knowing Empson. Charles W. Mann remembers that Snow went out of his way to introduce Empson to the assembly, and 'complimented him upon being dismissed from university for having been found with a contraceptive'.[48] Empson was charmed by the company of the Snows, as he related to Hetta:

> It was rather fun having the Snows here. He was firm about our being old friends, and it rather raised my stock; I hadn't realised he was so highly thought of. He made a speech in the main auditorium, very large and almost full, about how you ought to trust in science and not superstition, ... I thought it was an impressive speech.[49]

Otherwise, his own performance as a teacher in his late sixties seemed hit-or-miss, with the students being of varying ages and varying quality, and variously engaged with the subject. The Shakespeare class was basically an undergraduate group: 'the students at the Shakespeare course are now quite well disposed,' he told Hetta in a spirit of valiant hopefulness, 'and auditors (who are older) tend to speak up, so the basic facts are not too bad.'[50] Oddly enough, the first term ended after ten weeks in mid-November, when there was a two-week break for Thanksgiving. Empson was tempted to offer to go and visit the Richardses at Harvard, but hung fire on sending them a letter.

Instead, he headed north for a speaking engagement at Connecticut College, and then flew back to the local airport in one of those 'little bucketing planes that carry you about New England'. To get to his apartment he shared a limousine with some other university employees, and was impressed by the lordly ease with which they directed the driver to take them right up to their front doors, and even to pick up their children on the way. He sat in anxiety, hoping against hope to make it back before the liquor stores shut for the weekend at six o'clock on a Saturday; still, encouraged by the example of his local colleagues, he told the driver just what he wanted and was delighted to be whisked up to the liquor store with a quarter of an hour to spare.[51] Unlike during the year at Toronto, where he and Hetta gadded about all over the place, the Connecticut trip was his sole outing of the year at Penn State; as he wrote to Hetta, praising her initiative, her vim for travelling, 'You see what a difference it is when you aren't present; no more coast-to-coast stuff.'[52]

On the other hand, to mark the welcome end to his first ten weeks of teaching, he revealed to Hetta that he had endured a dispiriting term, finding his class bovine and unresponsive. (They would have found him just as egregiously, exasperatingly, difficult in other ways—to them he would seem geriatric, an alien oddball: weird, abstracted, shabby.)

But only when Christmas came around, after four long months of enervating exile, did he disclose to Hetta the extra difficulty under which he had laboured. He had been to the dentist, even before leaving England, to have a number of rotten teeth pulled from his lower jaw; but the temporary plate that had been fitted had got broken in the aircraft during his flight to the USA. Still worse, he had developed at Penn State an abscess under two of the back teeth and been put on a long course of penicillin by a local dentist. In due course, one of the two infected teeth was extracted, though for some reason the other remained to bother him in its searing place:

> so I have been living entirely on slops since I got to America [he finally admitted to Hetta]. I did not tell you because I thought it would cause

alarm; I have been feeling very well, with no stomach trouble, though I had been afraid that I might not last out the year—I am getting back onto solid food now, because they say it is dangerous in other ways to have no turds...I really couldn't eat out at all, except in the student lunchtime beerhall which provided soup, so there was no problem. But anyway I hate outside food here. Funny [*sic*] enough, taking a little thought in the supermarket, I can get perfectly delicious food to eat at home.[53]

He was anxious not to appear piteous—he knew that she might browbeat him into finding an immediate solution to the problem ('I thought it would cause false alarm')—but there was something feeble or functionally derelict about a grown man in his late sixties who would put up with eating nothing but liquids for four months on end for want of getting his teeth fixed without undue delay. He made out that he was worried about the expense of having such treatment done on his teeth while in the USA, which was no doubt the case—he always hated to eat into his salary by spending money on himself.

The British-born writer Paul West, who was a member of staff at Penn State, was officially on sabbatical leave throughout the period of Empson's visit; nevertheless, he was able to take some measure of the famous visitor during a few worrying encounters: Empson was drinking a lot of cognac, and would talk in a lively way about Isaac Newton, China, and Yorkshire, until he would fell asleep in his revolving office chair; whereupon students would creep up and gently spin him around—'as if he were an astronaut being tested for vertigo,' as West saw it. He was never woken up by the motion. 'He went back at night to a place full of rotting oranges, used tissues, and odd socks.' Empson's abstracted eccentricity was much in evidence: 'He once, for some minutes, watched my neighbor's door lamp through my telescope, thinking it Mars.'[54] While he abhorred self-pity, there was evidently much pathos in his bearing.

Increasingly, as the years passed, he was becoming dependent on Hetta to deal with the practicalities of life; but to outsiders it could seem as if she was quasi-maternal in her brusque or strong-arm efforts to sort him out. Still, if he looked to her to be practical, there is no doubt that she acceded to his expectations in that respect. In the case of his dental problems, there may have been a perverse kind of stoicism in his sad, fossicking or unworldly way of dealing with such a challenge ('taking a little thought in the supermarket'), but if he thought himself to be masterfully discreet in handling his personal difficulties, it is almost certain that others would have been put out by any evasive carry-on. It is not impossible that his worrying obsession with taking only liquid foods, which evidently went on for the whole of his first term, caused him to turn down some invitations to dinner parties and so on, since he was keen to duck any occasion where he might be expected to partake of solid food of any sort. In addition, the lack of teeth might well have inhibited his speech, which was already impaired by a slight muscle paralysis to one side of his mouth in consequence of the radiotherapy treatment he had been given just a few years before. As a younger man, he had enjoyed a fine firm voice; now he had started to speak like an old man, with occasionally obscure or bodiless or fluting intonations fighting against his residual mellifluousness. American students would certainly find it a real strain to follow his talking.

On top of all such difficulty, he was (as West remarked) drinking quite heavily at Penn State: partly, as he would have believed, to anneal some of the pain of the abscessed teeth; primarily to help him through the loneliness. Colleagues and students would be sure to notice the smell, and any possible lack of attention on his part. In any event, it does seem to have been the case that a number of his colleagues thought twice about the onus of hospitality that rested upon them, even if they did not actually mean to neglect or shun him. He was to spend even Christmas Day alone at his lodgings, though he purported in a letter to Hetta written on 26 December that he felt buoyant and busy: 'I was very glad you telephoned on Christmas Day (though actually I was having a very interesting time, in my solitude, with a whole lot of library books) . . . '[55]

He explained further in his pre-Christmas letter home, self-justifyingly:

> However, I do feel outside the place; and if the economic situation or perhaps some family need does not drive the old horse over the jump I do not want to take this type of assignment again. In the long run, and if there is a long run, I will earn more by writing my books, and I have only just time to do that before old age.[56]

That assessment was true enough, but the depth of defensiveness in the telling of it is unhappily transparent. He was putting on a brave face. Indeed, as he typed on, he was faltering more and more, so that the last lines of the page became a splurge of mistaken phrases with heavy deletions and emendations. The likelihood is that he was drinking himself little by little into incoherence, for the very last sentence of the whole lengthy letter stumbles over grammar as it flourishes some bravado for Hetta's sake. 'However it really is a lot of goodwill, and if you came here in early March with a motorcar you would be given a knock-down welcome.' He failed to sign the letter before posting it.

He was rather more candid when writing to Ricks less than a month later: 'I . . . find America very numbing this trip, and can write very little.'[57]

His course on the revival of a belief in the Spirits of Nature, focusing on *Dr Faustus* and other sixteenth-century texts, did not get off to a good start. For one matter, even at a late stage he found it difficult to persuade the university library to purchase the texts he wanted for the course; and, just as deflating, without doubt, was the fact that only two students—'one of each sex, both very severe and highly qualified'—signed up for his esoteric new course. However, the weeks of solitary drinking, and desocialization in general, must have started to take their toll, for he found a testiness bubbling up in himself.

> I said, what was obvious, that we could not maintain a merely lecturing relation, and I needed to know what interests they had in the subject which I was myself still learning about. The lady said: 'I took the course, Mr Empson, merely because I was interested in you', and it seemed to me automatic to say: 'Thank you, but that is no help to me, in planning the course' . . . [T]he idea that you are only interested in gossip about Empson, not in whether what he says is true, is obviously one I have to resist. I ought to have been sweet to these children as they obviously expected me to be— well, I was eager to be, until the fatal words were said. I would always presume that she had to pretend some interest in what the enormous money investment of the whole surrounding demanded, but no, she pretended she was only interested in gossip about the visitor.[58]

Both of the students seem to have stayed for at least most of the course, though it is likely they felt somewhat intimidated by Empson's snappish introduction. After a few weeks, by mid-February, he reported to Hetta:

> My two students for Arthur Waley [*170 Chinese Poems*] and Gilgamesh and Ecclesiastes now seem quite friendly and on the verge of confidences, but still very shy. Come to think of it, that goes for my adult acquaintances too; solitary confinement it could still be called. But . . . don't feel I am crying out for help . . .[59]

It was not the first time he had referred so frankly to his isolation. In January he had noted baldly that by the end of February he would have had 'almost six months of solitary confinement'.[60] The second term was to end on 24 February, followed by a three-week break before the summer term. He had hoped from the beginning of his solitary sojourn at Penn State that Hetta would be able to come out for a while, so they might drive about a bit. But in nearly all of his letters to Hetta since the start he had worried away about two things in particular: the geographical isolation of State College, and how he might keep Hetta entertained, given the nullity (so far as he could judge) of social life at the university. 'If you arrive here with a friend, and use the flat as a basis for driving about,' he wrote in October, 'that would be very agreeable and easy; but if you come here alone you will be terribly bored and I will continually feel that I ought to be trying to entertain you instead of earning my salary.'[61] The reason she had not come out with him in the first place was almost certainly because the teenager Simon had been involved in a road crash and was hospitalized for some time in the autumn. To make matters worse, she herself had been banned from driving for three years because of an accident while being drunk in charge of a car; there was talk for a while of her going to Ireland and taking out a new driving licence there; or maybe she could take a fresh driving test in the USA? 'This place is so cut off that without a car it isn't even a jumping-off place,' Empson forewarned her.[62]

Just two weeks before she did finally turn up, he even managed to turn the whole sorry scene into a good wry joke: 'I just feel you deserve an interesting trip; you might sensibly prefer to go to the oilfields of DILMUN.'[63]

It is all too probable that as the weeks passed into 1975 Empson had continued to drink himself into a bad state, so much so that his self-neglect became apparent to everyone who came across him, not least the students. Evidently some of his colleagues—it is not known how many—came to consider him dishevelled and rather reprehensible. Professor Weintraub has recalled for me that it was Henry Sams, Head of the Department of English, who had petitioned the research unit run by Weintraub to meet some of the expenses of Empson's visiting professorship—even though 'it was a chancy thing given Empson's reputation for being difficult'. Weintraub has provided this stern summary of the situation that ensued, as he saw it:

> [Empson] arrived late and rumpled, and seemed always late and rumpled. One could then smoke in faculty offices, and his office when he turned up was fog-shrouded by cigarette smoke. He also drank to excess, and was warned to be careful about putting out cigarettes in his furnished flat. That didn't help, as one night, befuddled by drink, he set fire to his bed and nearly did himself in. We had to send urgently for his wife, who had declined to accompany him here. Her freedom interrupted, she came glumly to superintend the remainder of the visit. He did teach a seminar in criticism, or nominally did so. Students were put off by his crankiness and attendance dwindled. Henry Sams felt obliged to cover for him when Empson didn't show up. We were relieved when the term ended and he

returned home. We had bought, briefly, a literary reputation of little or no practical value. He was not involved with students or faculty in any useful way.[64]

Strangely, the alarming message that reached London from the secretaries at Penn State was that Empson had been 'walking into cars'—presumably because he was drinking so much that he would forget which way the traffic was flowing. He needed rescuing in a hurry. Mogador was therefore enlisted at the last minute to fly out with Hetta to the USA: they would need another family head in the crisis. At the age of 33, Mogador had presence and experience: he was a man to sort out a mess. *Pace* Weintraub's memory of the crisis, it was of course the case that Hetta was about to go and visit her husband in any event, but Empson's petty but potentially dangerous accident in setting light to the bed would have made the timing imperative.[65] Yet there is no gainsaying the gist of Weintraub's account. Even a kindly witness, Charles W. Mann (Chief of Rare Books and Special Collections at the Pattee Library, Pennsylvania State University), has recalled of Empson's visit:

> He needed a lot of care on campus, and his well-known penchant for getting lost was quite evident. There are many anecdotes about his visit, and the faculty enjoyed him. The students, however, were mystified and several of our professors, one in philosophy and another in anthropology, simply had to intercede as the students abandoned his class . . .
>
> Despite his vagueness, he was a distinctly likeable man, free of any pompousness or ceremony, but sometimes absent-minded to the point of near helplessness.[66]

Advancing years, too much drinking, and a gradual but marked degree of self-abandonment had got the better of Empson at Penn State. He had been lonely, he felt harried by his teaching, and so he simply let himself go. *'Don't you know who he is?'* Hetta raged at people round the university.

She stayed with him at State College until his contract terminated. After two further months, they flew up to Michigan to spend some welcome pleasant days with their old friend Walter Brown, and they were safely back in London by the end of May. They were met at the airport by Mogador with a car, and Empson then passed a number of days unwinding at Studio House.

> He is settling down to his interminable soups [Hetta cheerily reported of her husband] and lying down a good deal, but good-tempered withal, and pleased to be home.[67]

Having been long kept awake by the nocturnal motorcyclists outside his apartment in College Park, he resolved henceforth to secure quieter nights for himself at home. Simon, a motorcycling fan, would be asked to shift his bulky, greasy paraphernalia out of Studio House, and Empson insisted too that Simon should therefore remove himself from the spare room adjacent to his own and go back to his real bedroom, so he need no longer be woken up when the teenager kept his odd hours and knocked about in the small hours. Arguably the most peaceful companion at Studio House was the ginger cat, which liked to lie on his chest. 'He lives in a silent world, like the older Coleridge,' said Empson. 'As Tennyson said, with no language but a cry.' And again, of the cat's miaowing: 'The terrible cry, "Do you still love me?" '[68]

In the summer Empson and Hetta made a reinvigorating visit to the fair quiet of the Wordsworth Conference at Ambleside in the Lake District.

In 1976, the new chairman of the English Department at Delaware University, Zack Bowen, was looking forward to receiving the first distinguished visitor of his period of office, the novelist Anthony Burgess. But when Burgess failed to show up to meet the enormous classes that had been long arranged, and failed even to send a message to explain himself, Bowen began to worry that no arrangements for a visiting scholar-writer could ever possibly work out. (Burgess was much later to try to explain to Bowen, at a Joyce conference in London, that at the time he had not dared to leave the Principality of Monaco, where he was resident, for fear of the punitive income tax implications.) The next visitor on the cards was to be Empson, and Bowen felt immensely gratified when Empson, together with his wife, arrived in good time in September 1976 and duly met all his classes. Being propped up by the robust and vigorous Hetta, Empson was to make a more solid showing than he had achieved at Penn State in the session 1974–5.

The Empsons enjoyed Delaware, driving out to local beauty spots as the weather remained sunny and even pretty hot well into the autumn. 'It is very odd that the first English settlers didn't come to the banks of the Delaware, which must have been sheltered and can never have been swamp,' noted Empson, who must have been comparing the location with his own original home on the ever boggy banks of the River Ouse in Yorkshire. 'I thought they had to go to swamp land because the Red Indians wouldn't allow them to come further in, but here they had decent farm land on the banks. Maybe it was something to do with their delusions about finding gold.'[69] One day they drove just thirty miles from home to a place called Bombay Hook, where they delighted in a vision of Snow Geese and a myriad duck; and at Thanksgiving, they travelled further down the Delaware Bay to eat seafood and to watch the sunset. 'It is so like Africa,' sighed Hetta. 'A great orange balloon beyond the scrubby horizon, and then, puff, and it has sunk, and it is night, and the stars are out, all over the great wide sky.'[70]

They lived for the duration at W12 Conover Apartments, at the busy junction of Elkton Road and Amstel Avenue in Newark; it was a comfortable and spacious apartment from which it took him just ten minutes to walk to the campus. Hetta would go swimming almost every day in the university pool, and smoke and drink to excess betweenwhiles. 'I am smoking these silly Marlboroughs (no rolling tobacco to be had),' she wrote, 'and liquor comes in half-gallons, dirt cheap across the State Line in Maryland, two miles away.'[71] One good local attraction, two blocks from their apartment, was called the Deer Park, which was the closest thing to an English 'pub' that Newark offered; Empson would repair there after his ten-o'clock class for a glass of beer and to read the *Times*.

Zack Bowen delighted in Empson's bluntness when argufying, and took pleasure in putting him into contact with individuals who might try his patience. 'Our Provost at Delaware was anxious to meet him,' he has recalled. 'A blunt Texan who wore cowboy boots but was a respected scientist in his own right, the Provost had opinions about nearly everything. When my wife and I joined the Provost and his wife as dinner guests at the Empsons, who unfortunately lived near the railway tracks running through Newark, Delaware, the evening train made its noisy way past, its whistle/horn loudly announcing its presence as it passed the intersection with the state highway it was crossing, [and] the Provost used the occasion to go into a lengthy disquisition on the inefficiencies of the British railway system. The Empsons sat through the diatribe without a word, and then William turned to me and forcefully demanded, "Who *is* this man?" '[72]

One of the most promising encounters of the visit to Delaware should have taken place on Thursday, 14 October (four weeks into the Empsons' visit), when the poet W. D. Snodgrass, who was then teaching at the university, gave a reading which the Empsons attended. Snodgrass, who had long been passionate about Empson's poetry, was very eager to meet Empson at a party that was held after the reading at the home of a colleague, but he was dashed by the distraction of his hero, and by Hetta's seemingly overbearing ways—though this anecdote may well say more about Snodgrass's inability to understand Hetta's sense of humour than about either of the Empsons:

With him at the party was his wife, a much younger woman [Snodgrass was to remember for an interview], who treated him and everyone else with absolute contempt. I told her at one point how much I'd wanted to meet her husband, and do you know what she said? 'You *may* have been in time.'

He *was* rather a sad figure by this time. When I told him how much his poems had meant to me, he didn't seem to understand what I was saying. We happened to leave the party at the same time, and I remember him hurrying across the lawn to catch up with his wife and another man. It was raining, and she was shouting, 'Bill! Bill! Get off that grass! You'll catch your death of cold! Have you no sense!?' It was said that the other man was her lover, and that Empson used to take them their breakfast every morning.[73]

Zack Bowen, by contrast, enjoyed Hetta's characteristically exuberant carry-on. 'If Empson was a character, his wife was an even bigger one. Tall, athletic, and still beautiful, she swam laps every day at the university pool. She was both a gracious, sophisticated person, and, when she had a few drinks (a not infrequent occurrence), a thoroughly uninhibited one. I thought she was wonderful. She almost always said exactly what she wanted, and occasionally it caused a bit of embarrassment.'[74]

Bowen recalls of Empson and his teaching at Delaware:

He was physically frail, but his mind was certainly intact, his observations and reasoning profound, and our conversations were as rewarding for me as any I ever had had with anyone. . . . we decided that if his comparatively faint and heavily accented voice were to be heard and understood by American undergraduates in the lecture hall, he would have to have a microphone attached to him. Empson liked to use the blackboard behind him and he frequently moved about when he was teaching classes. The umbilical cord attached to his already attached microphone spelled a disaster during his first lecture when he became trussed up in the arrangement and was brought down about thirty minutes into his presentation.[75]

Once Bowen had provided him with a cordless microphone, the course turned into 'a monumental success'. Empson himself noted, 'It is fairly dull here but quite friendly; my health seems to be better when I am allowed to lecture too.'[76] Hetta observed with succinct and sardonic affection: 'William is happy with his students, screwing them out of their minds, I imagine.'[77] Empson also gave several lectures for the university faculty and general public, and according to Zack Bowen every word he uttered from the rostrum 'was as clear as his own not inconsiderable and still highly original insights'.

Just after Christmas, at the annual convention of the Modern Language Association—which had elected Empson to an Honorary Fellowship back in April (Honorary Fellowship being limited to forty distinguished men and women of letters)—the Empsons were put up at the Hilton Hotel, and Empson was awarded an honorarium of $150 ('spending money', as he called it), to facilitate his participation at a panel discussion on the subject 'What is avant-garde criticism?' The convention was one of the largest to date, staging more than 600 separate meetings and with an expected attendance of over 10,000 academics and would-be academics, and the colloquium on theory attracted one of the very largest turn-outs. His fellow panellists were Professors Geoffrey Hartman of Yale, Ihab Hassan of Wisconsin, and Richard Poirier of Rutgers, with Jonathan Arac of Princeton as the 'discussant'. The whole show was chaired by Edward Said of Columbia University, who kindly explained to Empson in a letter, that he hoped the discussion might focus on the merits of 'advanced' or 'new new' criticism—the kinds of criticism practised by recent theorists, some of them drawing on French and continental philosophers, linguists, and literary theorists (critics like Roland Barthes, Jacques Derrida, or Harold Bloom)—as against the virtues of traditional historical scholarship: 'Criticism as a *conservative* activity vs. criticism as an avant garde activity.'[78]

A young scholar and teacher named William Vesterman, who was sitting in the front row of the Hilton 'ballroom', observed that Empson looked like 'an American's idea of a retired British Major'; though very red-faced, he seemed fit and spry and vigorous. For some reason, Empson left his place for a short while before the proceedings got under way: he did so by jumping down from the stage, which was about three feet high. When he came back, he surprised everyone by reversing his direct steps and so trying to spring back onto the stage; unfortunately, his leap left him too near the edge and he stood there trying to regain his balance by waving his arms in circles like the backstrokes of a swimmer for some two or three seconds. He succeeded in recovering his balance, but it was a very near thing: had he fallen backwards he might have been seriously hurt, since it would have been impossible to get his feet under him before hitting the audience level. All the same, Vesterman remembers, Empson seemed to be unconcerned and completely unafraid in the course of all his 'cliffhanging'; for a moment, indeed, it looked as though he might have been joking, exaggerating his predicament in mock-heroic fashion—just to make fun of himself for the sake of amusing the audience.[79]

Empson spoke last of all the panel, recalls Vesterman too. Whereas most of the panellists were poised to pontificate upon the very latest critical positions, Empson preferred to revisit the old-hat issues of the New Criticism, including what he believed the relevance of authorial intention to the analysis of a literary work. It was his old pitch: he had published it many times. Of a fellow-panellist [Geoffrey Hartman] he wrote some five years later: 'I liked Hartman when I met him, and wish we could have talked more, but I feel sure we could have done one another no good. He is a good man someone tricked into Yale, and now languishes there, Yaled for life. He really does, fairly often, know what an author felt or intended, but his principles forbid him to mention it.' There is no question but that Empson had come to feel radically out of sympathy, and largely out of touch, with recent critical theory; for years he had been disdainful of New Critical dogmatics, and of late he had set himself against all theory, especially any theory putatively informed by philosophy.

Two days later, on 29 December 1976, the Empsons flew home from JFK.

Awards and honours were steadily being bestowed upon the ageing eagle. In July 1976, at the instigation of Sir Isaiah Berlin, he was elected a Fellow of the British Academy. Fearing that Empson might disdain the offer of a fellowship, Berlin wrote him an indiscreet personal plea: 'If I may say so, you shine so brightly by your own light that you confer distinction on institutions rather than derive it from them . . . So let me . . . entreat you not to spurn us; if only as a pure, private act of kindness to myself.'[80] Two months later, Empson was gracious enough to accept the proffered fellow-ship (though he was not pleased when, a year or two later, the Academy said it could not offer to support his friend David Jones's private labour in translating the German Faust Book). Then in Queen Elizabeth II's Silver Jubilee summer of 1977—getting on for nearly half a century after he had been dismissed from Cambridge—he was awarded an honorary degree by his alma mater ('high time too,' remarked Hetta[81]), having been nomin-ated by his old friend Hugh Sykes Davies and by George Watson (both dons of St John's).[82] On 10 June he was conferred by the 56-year-old Duke of Edinburgh, who was himself freshly installed as Chancellor, with a Doctorate of Letters. At the selfsame ceremony, I. A. Richards was made a Doctor of Laws, and Mother Teresa of the Congregation of the Mis-sionaries of Charity in Calcutta, a Doctor of Divinity.[83] Empson's old friend Muriel Bradbrook was to note; 'Empson appeared as a country gentleman, a reformed Tom Jones in a canary yellow sporting waistcoat. The proctors would have removed it from anyone taking a degree by examination, and fined the presenter, in this case the Public Orator, a bottle of port; but they could no more object to this sartorial impropriety than to the Queen Mother's hatpin, with which she firmly skewered her doctoral bonnet in place.'[84] Empson immensely enjoyed the occasion, being especially happy in the knowledge that it marked his formal re-admission to the Cambridge fold—as Professor Bradbrook was to recall, he seemed always 'so lively, warm and charming' in his later appearances at Cambridge[85]—though all eyes were on the more elderly and frail figure of Richards. Dorothea Richards related to Richards's biographer John Paul Russo: 'IAR went through the brave ordeal of the Degree Ceremony in a wheel chair & standing for the citation (6 mi.) but it was so exhausting [that he] did not even remember the 10 m. talk from kind Prince Philip at the garden party we attended briefly.'[86]

Also in June 1977, Empson was awarded a further accolade. The BBC recorded an hour-long programme about his life and work, produced by David Perry, and with an ably accessible commentary by Christopher Ricks, which was to be broadcast on Radio 3 on 22 October 1977. Empson's own contribution was to reflect upon some of his ideas, to read and comment upon some favourite poems—'Letter II', 'Chinese Ballad', 'Note on Local Flora', 'To an Old Lady', 'Just a Smack at Auden'—and to answer some easygoing questions put to him by Christopher Ricks. Old friends including Janet Adam Smith and John Wain contributed reminiscences and praise, as did a younger American admirer in the person of the biographer Richard Ellmann, who in 1970 had taken up residence in England as Goldsmiths' Professor of English Literature at Oxford University. (Of Ellmann's superb biography of James Joyce, he once rather impishly—and yet so acutely—remarked to a friend that Ellmann had talked to everyone who knew Joyce and carefully took down everything they said—'but then he believed it all, do you see!')[87] The programme concluded with Ricks's invitation to Empson to defend his conviction that it was valuable to seek to comprehend an author's intentions: 'trying to get inside the author's mind,' said Empson without demur, 'trying to understand his intention and his state of feeling, or his unconscious intention... I think is what it's all about.' And when Ricks suggested that Empson seemed in his work to observe a line beyond which the exercise of criticism seemed pointless or tactless, Empson countered:

> There was a fine statement by G. K. Chesterton, a very good critic I've always thought, who said that if criticism means anything... [it] means saying about the author the very things that would have made him jump out of his skin. And the idea that you should avoid making the author jump out of his skin, I really do hope hasn't occurred to me. That would be falling down on the great duty... [T]here's a grand case of it in the nineties when Frank Harris... greatly admired, very rightly, the poems of the Shropshire Lad, the poems of A. E. Housman. And so he took a taxi

to the north of London and insisted on dragging Housman...out to lunch, and Housman recited a poem about God Save the Queen and praising the first, second and third Zulu wars, and various wars of that kind which were going on in the nineties, and said 'Oh God will save her, fear you not, be you the man you've been, get you the sons your father got, and God will save the Queen.' And Harris said, 'and so he will, and so the old bitch will be saved till the men can be fooled no longer', or something. At any rate, 'old bitch' came in and Housman rose up, white and shaking, and said 'You must allow me to go, I had no intention of meaning anything of the kind', and it is very baffling to see how he could have written those poems without knowing that they were being ironical or at any rate saying that the [soldiers] were being wasted for trivial purposes...I mean, here is a case where the author was made to jump out of his skin. And this could only be because in some mysterious way he knew what was inside his skin.

Two years later, in 1979, Empson was to be made an honorary fellow of Magdalene College, an honour which really did lay history to rest. According to Hetta, it was 'high time' for such an award, though one great benefit which she hoped would flow from the honour did not actually come to pass. 'I rather hoped it would mean he has to spend a day or so a week there, chatting up the young scholars (mad to get him out of the house a bit), but no such luck—it only means dining in Hall two or three times a year.'[88]

In 1983 he was to be elected a Fellow of the Royal Society of Literature.

I. A. Richards, in his brief contribution to the broadcast 'The Ambiguity of William Empson', remembered his pupil's precociousness; he recalled among other things that as a student at Cambridge Empson had passed up a very promising career in mathematics: 'A. S. Ramsey, the father of the ex-archbishop, was his supervisor and told me that Empson was one of the best mathematicians he'd ever had, and he was sorry he was leaving mathematics.'

A few months after adding his mite to the programme, the 86-year-old Richards was to venture in the summer of 1979 upon a return visit to China in order to sheer up the flagging cause of Basic English. Empson was in favour of the brave belated enterprise, telling Ricks in April: 'I. A. Richards goes off to Peking, on the first of May, to establish Basic English there after all. It will be a splendid last-minute scoop if he brings it off. Perhaps you might telephone him with congratulations?'[89] But Richards was taken ill in China, and flown home for medical treatment. Empson visited him at the hospital not long before the end, and was to speak of the visit with sweet tact in a memorial piece written for the *London Review of Books* in June 1980:

> he seemed so full of life that I felt sure he would recover: but he was delirious, and not much could be understood. Two recurring sentences were clear: 'It's time for me to go' and 'I ought to come back', meaning he was ready for death except that the work was incomplete. I said, 'Of course you must come back; you are urgently needed', and he looked at me quizzically, entirely himself for a moment. He was doubting my competence to pronounce upon the question. This of course was charming, but also, taken with some other phrases, suggested that he had done as much on this visit to China as he could usefully do. A too sustained pressure becomes irritating, he had long understood; they must now have time to think it over. He was struggling for life, with the tireless support of Mrs Richards, but he did not feel an immediate exasperating regret.[90]

Richards died on 7 September, and Empson and Hetta went up to Cambridge to attend the cremation on the 18th.

When he was invited to participate in a Memorial Meeting to commemorate the life and work of Ivor Richards to be held in the Senate House on Saturday 2 February 1980, Empson felt doubtful about his capacity for the task; he wrote accordingly to Richard Luckett, Richards' learned young friend and literary executor (who was Pepys Librarian at Magdalene):

> I am bad at this kind of thing and thought I had best refuse, but one plan does seem possible. I could read the Hopkins sonnet *Earnest Earthless Equal* Etc., which would come as a refreshing contrast. When the book came out, with a rather dubious sponsoring by Bridges, Richards praised it heartily at once, with special attention to this sonnet. In those days he was a very pioneering literary critic, picking out the good things even when he might seem out of sympathy with them. It was one of the earliest bits of his criticism I read. Something to the effect should be said, and then the recital, and nothing after it.
>
> Do you think this would do?[91]

Luckett was pleased to know that the prize pupil would attend the occasion, and so Empson duly rose on the day to present his piece, along with other luminaries including Theodore Redpath, Elsie Duncan-Jones, L. C. Knights, A. Alvarez, Sir Ernst Gombrich, Janet Adam Smith, and Richards's friend and putative biographer John Paul Russo. But in the event, Luckett felt at once amazed and amused by Empson's mien and mumbling:

Empson was a predictable and fully anticipated disaster, so he probably shouldn't count [Luckett recorded in a notebook entry two days later]. In its way his act supplied what would otherwise have been an unbearable absence of comedy: though his suit was pressed, his shoes clean, his shirt spotless, he contrived, as he shuffled forward and, swaying slightly, spoke inaudibly and inexactly against his own brilliantly simulated atmospherics of squeaks and high-pitched whistles modulated through a slightly damp moustache, to look exactly as though he had just risen from an Embankment bench.[92]

Later, Janet Adam Smith rather unconsolingly reported to Luckett how Empson had explained to her at the memorial meeting 'that, in order to be sure he was audible, he had removed his teeth before reading'.[93] The muttering was one thing; but there was also the suspicion that he may have taken advantage of his toothlessness to utter some disobliging and even outrageously discourteous remarks about the poet Hopkins as 'a gloomy Jesuit', and perhaps even about Richards himself: specifically, that he really could not understand why Richards had so admired Hopkins. L. C. Knights understood Empson to have expressed himself to that effect, though he later told me that Empson was not very audible—and that in any case his own memory was 'clearly faulty'.[94]

In any event, Empson must have been aware that his muttering or *sotto voce* remarks could be taken as rude, and that his comments had indeed been gossiped about afterwards. A month later, he was writing to Mrs Richards with the obvious intention of putting his face straight, of glossing the record for the sake of the much-respected relict:

Nobody could hear anything in the Senate House—the speakers ought to have been warned.

I said that Richards' article on Hopkins had been my first introduction to his writing, and to Hopkins, and that in the twenties, when much good and novel work was coming out, he did valuable work in picking out the best ones. And he did it in a very large-minded way; one would not expect him to admire Hopkins, anyhow at that stage of his life.

Pretty flat I am afraid.[95]

After tea on the afternoon of the memorial service, there followed an address by Frank Kermode, the King Edward VII Professor of English Literature, who happened also to be an old sparring partner of Empson's: Empson thought the poet Donne much more subversive and challenging than Kermode ever allowed. Empson did not care to stay on to hear Kermode's memorial talk, claiming that he found lectures intolerable because he could never hear the speaker. Nonetheless, he did read Kermode's address when it was published in the *London Review of Books*, and he was greatly impressed by it. He told Dorothea Richards he liked it, and he asked Ricks to convey his compliments to Kermode. He did not like Kermode well enough to tell him so directly, though it would not have been at all difficult to write him a personal note.[96]

Two years before, on the death in Boston of the poet Robert Lowell at the untimely age of 60, Empson had figured among the celebrity mourners who contributed to a memorial service held in London. Janet Adam Smith reported on the event to Dorothea Richards: 'Bill looked very handsome. I really prefer him without the beard. And Hetta looked a bit thinner, a bit less overpowering, & handsome too!' She felt annoyed by the weak and largely inaudible readings from Lowell's poetry at the event, though Empson had been one of only two speakers who 'tried to project their voices; the others seemed to mumble at the lectern'.[97] Nevertheless, Lowell's old friend and associate Grey Gowrie had made a better job of being heard than had Empson.

As for Hetta seeming to Janet Adam Smith to be less overpowering, she had in fact lost none of her vigour with the passing years: at the age of 62, and after long training with Josh, she could still pick a brawl with anyone. At a party thrown that spring to launch a book of poems by her good friend Elizabeth Smart, ex-wife of the poet George Barker, Hetta was reported in the gossip column of the London *Evening Standard* to have assaulted the Scottish poet and editor Eddie Linden on account of a racist remark he had made in her hearing. 'Where is the little beast?' she cried while pursuing him across the room. 'Nobody calls my friends a chink!' The reporter bore this delighted witness:

> In vain Lyndon [*sic*] cowered against the wall. Mrs Empson swung a powerful right to his jaw and followed up by hurling her glass of whisky in his face. Three strong men were needed to haul her off the cringing Celt.[98]

Four years later, aged 66, she was still hale and energetic enough to whizz off with her 18-year-old grandson Saul (elder son of Mogador) to trek and camp in the desert of Algeria. 'The nights were miraculous,' she later related, 'except they seemed to go on forever, lying as I was in my sandy sarcophagus with a dirty old blanket over my head, being kept awake by shooting stars and the blazing moon, and feeling a bit edgy thinking the dreaded horned viper might want to creep into Sye's [Simon's] old sleeping bag with me, out of the cold.'[99]

Empson, for his part, was succumbing more and more to the ills that elderly flesh must be heir to. He seemed never quite to have recovered his vigour after the rough treatment to which he had been subjected for suspected cancer in his sixties; thereafter he looked older than his years, and the deformations of his voice added to the impression that he was quickening into old age. In the first week of April 1978, after an evening spent greatly enjoying himself at a feast at Christ's College, Cambridge, where he was the guest of Christopher Ricks, he felt suddenly so disablingly ill that he immediately took the train back to London instead of calling on Richards for lunch the next day. Later he uncharacteristically admitted to Ricks that he had endured 'several days of really very bad stomach trouble, thinking the cancer had come back'.[100] Hetta had been away from England for a while, but she arrived home just in time to take charge of her wracked husband. She recorded in her diary for 21 April, with unusual starkness: 'Wm very ill.' The following day, Mogador drove him over to the Royal Free Hospital, where on 8 May a surgeon operated on him to bypass an old ulcer. 'We have had a rather harrowing time', Hetta told a friend in late June.

> It was a mighty relief that they did not find anything worse. He has healed fast and been home for three weeks. But of course any operation is weakening and he sometimes looks very frail. But he trots out to buy his cans of soup and biscuits and sweeties. Mostly he lies down and reads old murders. He is still on anti-biotics, so he can't even have a tiny noggin—which I suspect is why he feels what he calls 'rather flat'. However.[101]

Convalescence took up a good deal of the summer, so Hetta treated him to a number of days out. In early July, they motored over to Kent to take a look at Penshurst and Sissinghurst Castles. Later that month, they went to see an exhibition of Henry Moore sculptures mounted by the Serpentine. 'William is no longer poorly—,' she related at that time, 'very much his old self-centred self, and typing away.'[102] For a treat on his seventy-second birthday they drove to Chesham, and to the village of Chalfont St Giles to have a look at John Milton's cottage. Further outings included a visit to Jacob Empson's home at Beverley in Yorkshire. The sad news was that the marriage of Jacob and Janet broke up at this time.

But Empson's own troubles were not done. During the summer of 1978 he was diagnosed with a hernia as an outcome of the ulcer operation—and it seems he would try just about anything to alleviate it, as Hetta wrote:

> I took William to an Indian homeopathic quack about his hernia, who prescribed raw food till six at night, so William simply laid low all day and

had three sloppy meals in a row after six. He lasted about five days, and then said it made him feel ill, so now we are sharing the Royal Jelly (cost £30) and he is happily knocking it back...[103]

That was in October 1978. Five months later, in March 1979, Hetta would remark of his condition, merely: 'they say he should not worry about it.'[104] Late in 1980 he suffered for a period from bad back pain but slowly got over it—'and then said he had a boil on his bum. The doctor said it was piles—he recovered.' Hetta was not about to fuss over his every little ill. Two years later, in the summer of 1981, he reportedly tripped over a flagstone near Studio House and suffered a 'nuisance fracture' in his right arm. It could have happened to anyone, but he was liable to the accidents of age or alcohol.

A grand consolation for his distracting and protracted health problems turned up in the post at the end of November 1978, when he received a letter from 10 Downing Street advising him that the Prime Minister proposed, 'on the occasion of the forthcoming New Year Honours, to submit your name to The Queen with a recommendation that Her Majesty may be graciously pleased to approve that the honour of knighthood be conferred upon you.'[105] It was an honour which the younger Empson, during the 1920s and 1930s, might have snubbed; then, he had expressed strong socialist leanings and had little respect for privilege or royal flummery. But ever since he had hailed the present Queen with his masque at Sheffield University in 1954 he had become an ardent monarchist—or at least he enormously admired this Queen.[106]

He and Hetta, accompanied by Mogador and Jacob, arrived at Buckingham Palace on 7 February 1979—'William in his funeral suit,' as Hetta was to relate a few days later. 'They played Gilbert & Sullivan in the Minstrels Gallery. William looked very splendid & in control.'[107] Hetta, for her part, looked slightly less splendid: she had recently broken an arm, so she was got up in a plaster cast—'and is rather piano', joked Empson. 'She had much better stop fighting.'[108] At lunchtime (as a friend bore witness), 'he made a happy progress into Hampstead village where he was greeted with loud cheers.'[109] In the evening, the family hosted a party at Studio House—'a small boasting party after the dubbing,' as Empson called it— for which eighty people turned out. The boys donated a case of champagne and a Parma ham.

'The knighthood came as a surprise,' the 72-year-old Empson told the *Observer*. 'But I was pleased to receive the acknowledgement. It's been years since I wrote any poetry, and I haven't published a book for 10 years, but I have written a lot of magazine articles—so you couldn't say it was digging up an old relic.'[110] Peter Porter went on record to opine that Empson was 'probably the best poet, together with Auden, writing in the generation after Eliot—the pre-eminent poet between the wars.' (Mrs Valerie Eliot, writing to Dorothea Richards, expressed her puzzlement as to how Empson had come by a knighthood—'though perhaps Ivor had a hand in it. Anyway I am glad his work is being recognized'.[111]) In the local newspaper, the *Hampstead & Highgate Express*, Empson was reported to have said: 'I'm very pleased... This sort of thing gives us old people a bit of entertainment!'[112] When asked in the local pubs why he thought the Queen had given him this honour, he would reply, 'I told Her She was God'—and then, after a pause, he would explain how he had once written a masque for the Queen's visit to Sheffield in 1954, invoking her as a goddess. All the same, he knowingly confided: 'They don't like to reward you at the time— it looks too like bribery.'

Christopher Ricks tells a better tale that Empson told him out of court:

> He admired and relished the Queen, but he did not think it *lèse-majesté* to speak of the awed moment when he was about to rise Sir William. 'She touched my shoulder, and then, in a rather strangled voice, as though She were telling me my flies were undone, She said "I'm so glad". It was the nearest She came to pretending we were old friends.'[113]

As a knight of the realm, Empson would be invited on occasion to go with his lady to garden parties at Buckingham Palace; and he would enjoy turning out to greet his Queen. The new Lady Empson also became much more patriotic upon her elevation; in April 1982, for example, while they were spending time in the USA (where Empson was a visiting professor at the University of Miami), she reacted unambiguously when Americans teased or patronized Britain's actions after General Altieri of Argentina sought to seize the British Falkland Islands.

> Everyone is expressing pity, tinged with good-natured contempt, for the failing British Empire [she wrote]. I think the whole nineteenth century operation—the fleet solemnly steaming ahead for 8000 miles, is admirable, and just the thing to scare the shit out of that Dago upstart dictator.[114]

Empson himself was to comment, in one of the few remarks on politics of his later years that have been recorded, while chatting to a friend: 'Poor Mrs Thatcher will throw the baby out with the bathwater rather than give up the Falklands.' It seems very likely that he shared his wife's sense of pride in the grand, post-imperial gesture.[115] For his birthday in 1982 he was given a collection of stories by Jorge Luis Borges entitled *Dr Brodie's Report*, and commented on it: 'It's all about the Argentines being tough, and I'm rather tired of hearing about the toughness of the Argentines; I'd much rather they were bank clerks'—no doubt recalling the humble occupation in London of the young T. S. Eliot.

At Christmas 1980, a short-term lodger at Studio House was surprised when Hetta silenced a quarrel that had blown up during the festive lunch by informing everyone that the Queen's Christmas Message was about to come 'on telly':

> [It was] an event she had formerly considered an empty ritual but one whose significance she now appreciated . . . I have no idea what Mrs Windsor may have said that afternoon, but William somehow conveyed to me, above all, how enormously proud he was of the energy and vivacity of this fascinating creature to whom he had the good fortune to be married.[116]

The knighthood was hugely enhancing to his morale; and it enhanced his sense of goodwill—so much so that Sir William Empson even graciously consented to bestow upon Dame Helen Gardner—his old éminence grise and enemy—the Rose Mary Crawshay Prize, for her book *The Composition of 'Four Quartets'*, at a ceremony held at the British Academy on 10 July 1980.

A further honour followed for him in May 1982, when he was made a Foreign Honorary Member of the American Academy of Arts and Sciences.

On 15 January 1982 they flew to Florida, where the 74-year-old Empson was to be visiting professor for one semester (with a salary of $19,500) at the University of Miami at Coral Gables. They leased a ground-floor apartment in a condominium at C 102 Lakewood Villas, 7821 Miller Road, just a couple of miles to the north of the university campus. Outside there was a communal garden with tropical trees, and a swimming pool which Hetta was to use on a daily basis. While most of the USA was being assailed by severe winter weather, the temperatures when they arrived in Miami had already started to climb into the 70s and 80s, so they delighted in having the air conditioning in their apartment 'belting away ha-ha', as Hetta put it.[117] A huge shopping mall lay at a convenient distance of just 16 blocks up the road.

Hetta rented a four-year-old Dodge Charger so they could get out and about; 'but finding the way across town is terrible,' said Empson. 'It pretends to have the grid system but keeps bucking you off on roads going sideways, and names and numbers are only put up when they feel like it.'[118] Presently they ventured into the Everglades and went for a ride on an airboat (powered by an aircraft propellor) which 'went crashing through the reeds in a huge swamp very like a Yokefleet warping; we might have been flighting for duck. There were graceful herons. Pretty country but not specially tropical.'[119] Hetta thought it thrilling to go roaring over the saw grass; and in the weeks to come she would take off on many excursions—sometimes with her husband, at other times with various visitors including an English friend, John Saxby, and Empson's sometime pupil, Jin Di, from China—to fabled locations including Key Largo, Key West, Palm Beach, and Cape Florida, and to Parrot Jungle and a Seaquarium. Once, William swam in the sea and spotted sharks.

At the University he was treated well, being provided with a highly willing teaching assistant named Morris Fink who had to dedicate nine hours a week to his bidding. He was given a good office only two doors away from another esteemed visitor, Isaac Bashevis Singer, and within days of their arrival they were invited to a reception for Singer. Unusually for her, Hetta felt too shy of Singer other than to say she was happy to meet him. Ross C. Murfin, a recent member of the faculty, took the Empsons for a Sunday morning picnic, and could not fail to notice that when Empson emerged from the public changing room he was wearing what at first appeared to be swimming trunks but on closer inspection proved to be his boxer shorts. Murfin was less amused when Empson told him and his children, with assurance—he looked old and tired, and had to be wise— that they could increase the speed at which tadpoles grow by tossing bits of liver into their pond: the result of his advice was the death of all their tadpoles.[120]

'William is in FINE FETTLE,' Hetta wrote home early in February; and he did indeed enjoy his students. One of his tasks was to teach an advanced group for Modern English Poetry, so he regaled them with poetry by Eliot and Auden and Dylan Thomas, as well as some lesser poets. 'All I could do was tell anecdotes,' he would later say; but equally he liked teasing and challenging them. 'Look!' he declared one morning. 'I've found two good poems by Stephen Spender. Who'd have thought it possible!?' When asked during a later conversational exchange what the American students had made of Spender's poetry, he continued with his own train of thought. Oh, he reflected, Spender *was* a poet to begin with; the pity is that he had to keep going. He and the students crossed views over the nationality of Auden—'but as I was willing to let them have everything after he moved to America', he had not insisted upon Auden's Englishness.[121] It was anyway clear that he believed the best of Auden was undoubtedly the early English Auden.

One of the class declared an interest in David Gascoyne—'that re-habilitated Surrealist who claims to have been mad,' as Empson cava-lierly described him (in a letter written later in the year).[122] Empson made it clear in a later conversation with a friend that he felt sceptical about what he saw as Gascoyne's pride in having experienced 'that exalted condition'.[123] For similar reasons he expressed scepticism about the manic depression of another friend, the poet Robert Lowell, which he virtually refused to recognise as an illness. To the writer Jonathan Raban (whom he came to know after spending a weekend in the summer of 1971 with Lowell and his wife at their mansion in Kent), he had expostulated of Lowell: 'The only reason people think he's mad is because he's an American.'[124] In truth, he felt sincerely indignant when he talked down the reality of Lowell's mental illness. Like Dr Johnson, he saw no merit whatever in madness, for sanity and rationality was the only wear; as he had insisted in the poem 'Let It Go': 'You don't want madhouse and the whole thing there'.

In general, he would say in his later years, he had not liked very much poetry since Dylan Thomas and Philip Larkin, though he did find he admired the work of Seamus Heaney when he came to assist a grandson with his school exams; and he would state at one time that he thought George Barker 'a real poet'. When Mark Thompson—a young admirer and friend who would assist him in his last months in gathering together copies of uncollected and obscurely published essays—mentioned the name of George Fraser, Empson would curiously remark that he thought Fraser had been a good poet until he got married. Many critics have delved into the question of why Empson himself had virtually stopped writing poetry after his marriage in the early 1940s, and so maybe he was projecting onto Fraser his own sense of having surrendered the muse; in a poem from the 1930s, he wrote, 'I have mislaid the torment and the fear. | You should be praised for taking them away.' From what he also said to Thompson about Fraser's generosity with his time and gifts, he seemed likewise to suggest that Fraser had squandered his talent, or diffused it. A strange remark in his work on James Joyce seems relevant here: 'Joyce was a self-important man, as he needed to be . . . ' The writer who is true to himself was always, in Empson's estimate, some sort of avatar of the pastoral hero who has to sustain the 'self-centred emotional life imposed by the detached intelligence'. But the price of the detached intelligence is 'a painful isolation'.

Not everything was to go smoothly in Miami. Within a month of their arrival, Empson developed a backache which was almost certainly connected with his alcohol intake. When not teaching, he would be working hard at a manual typewriter that Morris Fink had brought along for him to use at home—on his study of *Dr Faustus* to accompany his friend David Jones's translation of the German *Faustbook*, and on a revision of his piece on Joyce's *Ulysses* that he was to deliver at the Joyce centenary conference in Dublin in June—and as always when working on an essay he would speed the plough by pouring unnumbered drinks for himself. Hetta noted on more than one page of her diary, 'Wm poorly'; and at the end of February, Morris Fink took him to be x-rayed at the nearby Baptist Hospital. There was no apparent damage to the back, it turned out, so the cause was probably a transferred pain. He was enjoined not to drink alcohol—'No voddy,' as Hetta put it.

The previous year, I had first approached him about the possibility of writing his biography, and Empson had guardedly welcomed the idea; he was even willing to make available to me any papers and letters that lay around his study, though he did not wish to allow me access to any such papers until he had completed work on the books he was projecting—most notably a revised collection of his essays on Shakespeare, a volume about other Elizabethan playwrights, and his putative introduction to David Jones's translation of the German Faust Book. But he wrote to me at this time:

> I have had a long attack of backache, when I could do practically nothing but lie flat on my back reading old whodunits, all day and most of the night. It seemed to me that I actually could not compose sentences. Two Xrays concluded that I had not got either cancer or stone in the kidney, so it was merely what old men have to expect. I still have a bit of pain and cannot walk far without sitting down, but am in working order again. It seemed to me that I actually could not compose sentences. However, it has altered my view of the prospects; I have left the collection of unfinished work far too late, and so far as my part is concerned in your *Life* of me it had better be put off for two or three years. I hope you will still do it, certainly I do not want anyone else to do it; what I can't do is hunt around for 'papers in my possession'. I must refuse all distractions.[125]

At the end of March, more than a month after he started to complain of severe back pain, Hetta would write to their friend David Jones: 'William was right poorly. A little time ago I thought we should bail out. But he is a right hard-ass, determined to see it through, and is recovering & says he can get out of bed alright today without pain. (No Voddy)'[126] The next day,

Hetta noted again in her diary: 'William poorly'. A little later, Empson wrote again to me—there is no doubt that the pain and discomfort affected his judgement—'I cannot recommend Miami. Friendly enough, though.'[127] Yet within the week he seems to have bounced back; he was looking well again, said Hetta, and was 'cheery'—albeit he was still drinking only Diet Coke—and working 'furiously' at his typewriter. 'I've got to get this ready for Jones,' he exclaimed to Hetta, 'and then there is the Bloomsday thing.'[128]

They flew home to London even as the term closed on Friday, 29 April.

On Sunday, 13 June 1982, Empson and his wife flew to Dublin to participate in the week-long jamboree marking the centenary of James Joyce. There were in fact two distinct conferences held that week. One of them was an academic affair called the Eighth International James Joyce Symposium, which brought together more than 500 scholars: a series of big plenary lectures included contributions by major Joyce scholars including Hugh Kenner, A. Walton Litz, and Richard Ellmann (the last of whom read over Empson's paper—at his particular request—and made some helpful suggestions), along with special lectures by the likes of the screenwriter Dennis Potter (who brilliantly extemporized his speech) and the novelist and critic Anthony Burgess. In all, over a period of five hectic days, there were more than sixty panels and workshops, and over 300 people spoke through the course of the festival.

The complementary conference was organized by an umbrella committee set up by the Taoiseach of Eire. The novelist and critic Anthony Cronin (author of a monograph on Joyce), who was acting as Cultural and Artistic Adviser to the office of the Prime Minister, chaired a subcommittee to select a group of distinguished international writers who would be invited as honoured guests. The writers gathered together in this way were, in addition to Empson, Jorge Luis Borges, Hans Magnus Enzensberger, Chinua Achebe, Angela Carter, and Sorley Maclean. The Empsons were put up at the Shelbourne Hotel, which was splendid— though it did not seem quite so splendid to them that they were obliged to share a room with one another: balefully Hetta noted in her diary, 'Wm snored all night.' According to Cronin, Empson seemed also to suffer from 'memory lapses': he would appear at times not to know where he was or what he was supposed to be doing.[129] Empson was billed to address a capacity audience in the Round Room of the Mansion House on the Tuesday afternoon—he gave a version of his passionately-held thesis that the critical key to the advanced morality of *Ulysses* is that Bloom no longer

has sex with his wife Molly but seeks to enable Stephen to sleep with her—
but unhappily, as Hetta recorded in her diary, 'they mostly left as he was
inaudible'. (At one point Empson left the stage without explanation, and
indeed he also disappeared entirely from the auditorium for about five
minutes—he had perhaps decided to relieve himself *in medias res*.) Fritz
Senn, who came to the talk, thought it 'a sad occasion'.[130] Empson
comforted himself with the reflection that perhaps it was as well that his
argument could not be heard by his audience; when broadcast in such a
fashion, without all the persuasive critical detail of the full essay, it might
have seemed snide, he felt. 'Declaiming like a Roman general to an army is
a skill I have never learned,' he wrote in an apologetic letter to Cronin, 'but
perhaps I ought to have made a shot at it. However, I do think that this
stuff would have made a bad impression if declaimed; it would come out as
an attempt at debunking Joyce, which was not at all my intention.'[131]

Notwithstanding, the following day brought an enormous Bloomsday
Banquet at Dublin Castle at which the Empsons were still treated as
presiding figures. Nevertheless, as all of the innumerable guests filed in to
be greeted by the Taoiseach, Empson attempted to duck out of the line-
up—but Hetta visibly restrained him. The principal guest of honour for the
evening was Jorge Luis Borges—'the Irish did well to bring over the
Argentine great man,' said Empson.[132] At the banquet in Dublin, Borges
had proposed a moving toast in honour of Joyce, but Empson may have
been seeking to find a whimsical similarity between his own notorious
inaudibility and Borges's supposed failure to make himself understood
when he later joked to Mark Thompson that Borges's speech seemed to
him to be given in the style of *Finnegans Wake*—'as was proper and fitting, but
no one could understand. Afterwards, of course, we all applauded . . .'[133]

On another evening, the international writers gave a collective reading;
even the blind Borges recited a couple of poems in English he had learned
by heart. Anthony Cronin, who was sitting just behind the row of writers,
noted that when Empson read his poems he did so 'with a peculiar bowing
motion with his knees'. Hans Magnus Enzensberger, who was quite obviously delighted by Empson's performance, declared to Cronin: 'Look, he's
dancing!'

The excursion to Dublin was one of the last of the fully public engagements that Empson would undertake during his final months, though
he would do his best for the Cambridge Poetry Festival on 17 April
1983—albeit the audience had to strain to catch his words. His brother
Charles died on 17 August 1983, and he attended the funeral. For the
sessions 1978–9, 1982–3 and 1983–4 he was an Honorary Research Fellow

in the Department of English Language and Literature at University College, London, and he would turn out to the occasional seminar presentation. He and Hetta would happily receive visitors at Studio House: in January 1983, for example, Jon Stallworthy came over to tap into his memory for his biography of Louis MacNeice. From time to time, I would show up too, collecting material for this biography. But for a good deal of the time he would dash back and forth between home and the British Museum, intent upon finishing off his writings before his time ran out.

19

Faustus: Finale

I N preparation for the BBC programme about his life and work that was
broadcast in 1977, Empson had advised Christopher Ricks: 'I think our
discussion had much better be about the present state of Lit. Crit, here and
in America; not trying to elicit historical memories about the old buffer.
I think the situation is bad, especially by the Wimsatt Law that no reader
may know the intention of an author—hence there must be no Intuition or
spontaneity and no biography or grasp of the author's character and style.
Are you prepared to defend all that, or say it isn't as bad as I think? The
neo-Christian movement (which I used to think so bad) seems to have
melted away, except for the age-old routine lying, and instead we have this
Inhumanism which is far worse.'[1] He was not reneging on his inveterate
campaign, waged for well over a quarter of a century, against 'neo-
Christian' critical readings, albeit his fixation on the evils of the practice
was at times extreme and even obsessional; rather it was the case that for
his last ten years he was to become increasingly determined to recover the
fullest possible interpretative picture of any particular text and its author:
biography, culture, ideology, intention. So it was that he would give the
final book of essays he was to put together the provocative title *Using
Biography*, seeking to plot his portraits of, *inter alia*, Marvell, Yeats and
Joyce in the context of their lives, times and purposes.

In addition to that volume, throughout his last ten years he worked on a
thoroughgoing study of Marlowe's *Doctor Faustus* which began as an essay
and inexorably became a book. Sickened by the muddle of the surviving
texts of *Doctor Faustus*, in particular the 'harmful' status of the B-text, and by
the sanctimoniousness of many of its critics, he sought to reconstruct the
whole play against the background of its known sources—specifically, the

English Faust Book (EFB) (*The Damnable Life and Deserved Death of Doctor John Faustus*, 1592), which was itself an imaginative translation of the German Faust Book of 1597 (many passages from the GFB were omitted or modified by the clever translator, or author, of the EFB, who is known only by the initials 'P. F. Gent'.)—and also in the context of the hermetic tradition, Marlowe's likeliest intentions, and contemporary theatrical expectations. He was aided in his quest for the secret meaning of the play by the fortuitous arrival at Studio House of a new lodger in the person of John Henry Jones, who liked to be known as 'David'. Jones, who was then in his early forties, had read Chemistry at Bristol University (B.Sc., 1954; Ph.D., 1960), and spent part of his early research career at Heidelberg University (1957-8), where he had also learned German. At some point too, it is said, he got married, but apparently he split from his wife after a very short while. For two years, from 1963 to 1965, he was a Lecturer at Cambridgeshire College of Arts & Technology; but he suddenly abandoned that career in order to come to London to paint and write. An amiable, generous-spirited and perennially impecunious man, he supported himself precariously thereafter by translating German text-books on chemistry, and by coding market research returns in an advertising agency, and by a variety of odd jobs including selling ice-creams and gardening; and now and then he would give piano lessons. In the late 1960s he wrote poems and plays (including *The Caveman Cometh*, which was broadcast on BBC Radio 3 in September 1968) as well as an attempted novel. In 1970 he was involved (as science editor and then editor) with Ted Hughes, Daniel Weissbort and David Ross in their environmental quarterly, *Your Environment*). This gifted, hand-to-mouth, kind-hearted and loyal character, who sustained a multiplicity of interests, came to rest in the nest at Studio House in the spring of 1975; and he found there more than a bare lodging, a diverse and rather dynamic community. 'The tenants were carefully chosen,' he would recall not long after Empson's death; 'they needed to be hardy, resourceful, likeable and interesting, as indeed they mostly were, if not notable.' Tenants during the few years of his own occupation included 'Peter Cadogen, left-wing humanist and champion of lost causes; [along with] a typographer, a batique artist and a dress designer ... and in the basement there lived ... Barry Carman, Australian-born author and writer of radio documentaries, a great traveller (Fellow of the Royal Geographical Society), the most entertaining raconteur I have ever met, and a very close friend of the Empsons for many years. But the geniality, the warmth of the Empsons, both Hetta and William, and their sons, made them a focus for friendship and it was scarcely possible to live as their tenant ...

without being drawn into this extended family circle, sharing their wonderful hospitality, their lack of reserve, their fullness of living.'[2]

Jones moved into Studio House with no prior notions about his host:

> [T]o my shame, I did not know who he was. As a former chemist turned
> translator and playwright I had never had much time for literary criticism
> or for 'thirties poets, nor had I suffered the 'ruination' of a university Eng.
> Lit. course, a mark in my favour with Empson. I soon discovered
> his reputation but had no idea of his stature; and his own manner was
> sufficiently disaffecting of any personal distinction that one could be
> excused for failing to regard him as anything more than a most interesting
> person. So I did not come to him as an Eckermann longing to serve at the
> feet of greatness, far less did I record our conversations. Indeed it was
> some time before I could understand much of what he said; quite apart
> from its occasional gnomic quality, he had a tendency to intone his
> words and, when he was passionate, to roll his head as he spoke so that
> what sound there was streamed off in sundry directions, as from Socrates in
> a basket.[3]

As for the relations between Empson and his wife, which Jones saw at close
quarters, he wrote in his memoir (published four years after Empson's
death):

> Hetta and William complemented one another in a most remarkable
> manner; fire and water are they both, unpredictable, relentlessly enthusias-
> tic, still and concentrated, effecting slow, planned labours, lashing into
> flame. Hetta is an accomplished and talented goldsmith and they shared
> an interest in the graphic arts, yet essentially they inhabited different
> planets. William was the centre of Hetta's life, but William's centre was
> his own mind, a place apart to which he had constant resort and where he
> was to some extent imprisoned. He was emotionally reserved. That they
> loved one another deeply is beyond question yet explicit demonstrations of
> affection were rare. But there was as much love in their breakfast bickerings
> (better than a sit-com) as in any amount of turtle-dovery.[4]

Though open-eyed about Empson's slight foibles and downright peculiarities, Jones yet developed a deep respect for the disciplined integrity of his
way of life:

> [H]e couldn't bear gossip or dullness and he seemed particularly sensitive to
> a potential outbreak of one or the other. He delighted in active minds, his
> own being perpetually at work. This is his distinction from the majority of
> people: he thought critically (in the positive sense) *all the time*. I never once
> heard him refer to anything reported without illuminating some deeper or
> unconsidered significance, or demonstrating its stupidity. He was obsessed

with thought, and this demand upon his time excluded him from much genial society. By the time I met him, the friends of his youth were mostly dead, and they are never replaceable. He shared Hetta's friends, but though everyone loved William, ultimately, apart from his family, he had no great friends.

But he had no time for sentimentality and never complained of loneliness. He liked to be solitary and was at great pains to be alone . . . If he was not visiting libraries, he would spend most of the day in his study bashing at his old Remington; it could still be heard rattling away at three in the morning. His work was his life.[5]

Jones saw too how Empson used drink to oil his critical wheels:

He drank freely, sometimes a great deal, even to the point of unsteadiness, but he was no lush and was never loud, boorish or disgusting. He used alcohol as an essential concomitant to his work, especially when beginning a new piece. Having done all the necessary reading and mentally formulated his thesis he would deliberately make himself 'tipsy' before sitting at the typewriter and dashing out the first few pages (always foolscap); he wanted to establish a flow, to get a 'gut reaction'. Then he would sleep until sober and retype from the beginning, expanding the material but striving not to disturb the line he had set up. More drink was required for each continuation, each new draft being corrected and reworked in sobriety. The labour was prodigious . . . [6]

Upon discovering that Jones knew German, Empson asked him for help with rendering passages from the German Faust Book (there had never been a definitive translation). The upshot was that, beginning in March 1976, Jones undertook to translate the entire work, and he would spend fifteen years in studying all aspects of the Faust theme. To begin with, Empson proposed to write an appendix on the differences between the GFB and the EFB, but as the seasons passed, and he became ever more closely involved with the material, he produced so many draft sections that they ultimately added up to a full book. By early 1982, just before leaving for Miami, he had 300 draft pages ready for Jones.

It is Empson's contention that both the English Faust Book and *Doctor Faustus* were subjected to severe censorship. The earliest surviving copy of the EFB is the 1592 edition (printed by Thomas Orwin, to be sold by Edward White), with the words 'Newly imprinted, and in conuenient places imperfect matter amended . . . Seene and allowed' on the title page. Empson argues with considerable thoroughness that the earlier edition was suppressed by the censors. Marlowe's *Doctor Faustus* survives in two basic texts, the A-text of 1604 and the B-text of 1616, the latter being plumped out with scenes by another hand. Empson's contention is that the A-text is material remaining from a censored prompt-copy of the play and, with very slight changes, would be the basis for any reconstruction.

He then turns to consider why the play and the book were censored: that is, what was the nature of the offending material which had to be cut out? His guiding light here is the conviction that Marlowe would not have allowed Faustus to go to Hell. He once remarked to me: 'I think Marlowe meant Faustus to get away with it. He'd been cursed by a Pope, and Marlowe's audience would know he was a good man.' Marlowe, Empson argues, reworked the Faust story with an underpinning double-plot which allows Faustus to escape eternal torment. The suggestion is that Mephostophiles (whom Empson, for reasons he explains, likes to call 'Meph') comes from neither Heaven nor Hell but is a spirit of nature, a Middle Spirit, who wishes to gain Faustus' soul for his own use: he tricks Faustus by pretending to be an emissary of Lucifer when, in fact, the devil has no part in the business. Faustus must no longer be seen as an overreaching dope who deserves eternal punishment: he is reinstated as a true Renaissance hero, a resourceful and roguish magician who 'lives next door to Punch' (as Empson puts it) and makes a business deal with the 'freelance' Meph. By the terms of his pact Faustus becomes not a member of the Devil, as he supposes, but a Middle Spirit having no soul and therefore not liable to immortal suffering. He will die like an animal, and find oblivion. This is something that 'Meph' reveals to him only at the moment of his death. The result is a fascinatingly detailed and vigorous new construction. The wealth of meticulous argument and analysis that Empson sets out helps the argument to become at least tenable, highly controversial though it is. The essay abounds with illuminating sidelights of the sort we expect from Empson, and throughout there is wit, verve and charm. In all, it is a brilliant piece of work. It depends heavily upon the textual comparison of the EFB and the GFB (and Empson's commentary is well worth having in any context), but much is devoted to a consideration of the role of Middle Spirits, the place of magic in the Elizabethan world, and the staging of Doctor Faustus—and this gives us Empson in a thematic environment that was truly his own, with a lifetime's knowledge and thought at his disposal. He clearly aimed to put the cat among the pietists, and the evidence from his scholarship and close criticism goes far to expand the possible meanings of the play. He concedes that 'most of this essay consists of scouting round for evidence, and thinking up supporting detail in plot or production'; but even when he seems to be quite contrary, he is never less than enlivening.

It is a most valuable work—though it has to be said in the final analysis that the thesis is not totally convincing, not irresistibly sustained.

Faustus and the Censor: The English Faust-book and Marlowe's 'Doctor Faustus' was edited after Empson's death by John Henry Jones (1987), who would also go on to publish his own finely-wrought labour of love, *The English Faust Book: A critical edition based on the text of 1592* (1994). Paul H. Fry, one of Empson's nimblest critics, has acutely pointed out that *Faustus and the Censor* 'is a meditation on last things, and I will say boldly that I think Empson found Middle Spirits consoling'.[7] There can be no doubt that Empson would indeed have wished for himself the very fate that he argued for in the case of Doctor Faustus—something positively at odds with the Christian Heaven or Hell—a happy dissolution, a reabsorption into the divine ground of the world he loved.

Empson felt he would be allowed at least four score of years—ten more than the proverbial biblical span. His brothers had lived beyond 80, so he saw no reason why he should not do likewise. After 80, he maintained, one's best work would be done with. He told his publisher in 1973: 'When I am past anything else maybe I will be able to dictate my memoirs.'[8] Ten years later he joked to Mark Thompson that he would not be writing any memoirs before he reached the age of 80—and by that time 'my memory will be so poor that I shan't be able to do much harm.'[9] Thompson heard the remark more than once, and was left with the firm impression that in reality Empson had no intention of ever writing such things: he needed to conserve all his energies for further literary-critical writing. Just before Christmas 1983 (four months before the end, as things turned out), he told Thompson, 'I said I would try to arrange a lunch party and have done nothing, but I am feeling exhausted by this book and am still having to do odd bits of tidying & tracking evidence. I hope we will meet early next year.'[10] The book was *Using Biography*—for which he would end up writing a preface on his death-bed—and after that, he wanted to collect his essays on Shakespeare.

In the event, his body betrayed his will and he was to die in his 78th year. He felt unwell in the first week of February 1984, and quickly became so poorly that he had to be taken by ambulance to the Royal Free Hospital— just a short stretch from the house in Hampstead. He was diagnosed with a liver complaint. A week later, Mark Thompson came to visit him at the hospital early one afternoon and found him 'asleep—dozing—the bed strewn with the Sunday papers. The flesh on his face was sunken, his eyelids were dark grey, and the skin on his hands was grey.' They talked about George Fraser, about Borges, and about the recent coup by the army in Nigeria (where Thompson had been working for some weeks). After a while, Empson said: 'Well, you don't have to stay thinking up jokes for me.' It was a very kindly way of winding up the visit. Just as Thompson was taking his leave, Empson ventured: 'Years ago, the *New Statesman*, which used to be a much more literary paper, had a competition for people to write their own obituaries. Rose Macaulay, who I'm sorry to say died soon afterward—she thought she'd live to be ninety—wrote: "International affairs, disastrous as they invariably have been, never failed to shock and entertain her." ' Empson chuckled and smiled at this.' Thompson reflects on the implications of the anecdote: 'That he should have quoted this piece of wit by Rose Macaulay then, when I was leaving (with a smile more forced than spontaneous) and we had already said goodbye; and that he should have made it clear he enjoyed and admired her *brio* (and even implied that it was somehow more valuable because death had turned the comments into a real obituary), seems to have been his immensely tactful way of communicating something about his profounder expectations—of saying a larger goodbye, even—without the embarrassment or clumsiness of confession (which from him to me is inconceivable) to someone who was only an acquaintance, after all, not a friend.'[11]

By the end of the month Empson had recuperated himself so far as to be allowed home again, though he was still weak and would need to he assisted in and out of the bath; for much of the time he just stayed in bed. Mogador would call at the house every day to give his father a hand in getting out of the bath, or in guiding him back to bed; so did their staunch friend David Jones. A physiotherapist named Dorothy Ross would drop by to give some ease to Empson. One day, Hetta tried in vain to cheer him up with beer and champagne. Mogador recalls, 'I must have given him his last bath on Monday or Tuesday, which he said was delicious. He found it very difficult to lever himself out after the relaxing hot bath, and I had quite a job heaving him upright and out. We then tottered together to his bedroom.'[12]

Mogador had been to China for a few weeks from 9 March (returning home on 6 April), and would constantly call Studio House to ask after his father. For ten days at the end of the business trip he had arranged to go on a recreational trip to south-west China—to the province of Yunnan where his father had lived and taught at the end of the 1930s—but was fully prepared to call off the add-on vacation if he was needed in London. 'I recall ringing Hetta and William several times from Peking and Yunnan as I was worried about his state of health, and both of them reassured me that he was OK and that they wanted me to carry on. William was especially insistent, as he remembered his Yunnan days fondly. When I got back and called on him I was astonished to hear that he had skied down Jade Dragon Snow Mountain, Lijiang, where I had been. I had climbed up to the beginning of the snow line, at about 16,000 feet, with a great deal of puffing and panting. When I recounted this feat he recalled that he had carried his skis much higher and skied down—he said—from the top! The top is over 20,000 feet. I remember asking: really from the top? and him lying there saying: yes, from the top.'

On Thursday, 12 April, Empson was taken back to the hospital. Mogador rode with him and stayed in Accident and Emergency while his father was put on a trolley and examined by a young male doctor. Mogador was then asked to leave, and Empson was admitted to the hospital. The next day, when Mogador asked his father what he wanted him to do—Hetta was shaky, and becoming loud and emotional—Empson said, 'Yes, that's a good idea: take the old girl to the Creek [her cottage by the River Orwell in Suffolk]. She will just have to tough it out.' Those were the last words he ever spoke to his elder born. 'As we left I looked back and he gave me a long look; for some reason he did not have his glasses on, and his dark eyes looked enormous and round. It was very moving, as if he was making a final farewell.'

Jacob had been working at the University in Hull during the early weeks of the decline, and he had little idea that his father was so gravely ill. It was an insidious process, and no one had thought to warn him. However, on Saturday, 14 April, he was asked to come down to London to keep an eye on things while Mogador and Hetta, with a friend of hers named John Saxby, went for their much-needed break in the Essex countryside. After a quick drink with his brother Simon, Jacob went to the hospital at about noon and was shocked to find his father looking so drawn and in considerable pain. 'He had a catheter which was giving him a lot of trouble. I made a lot of fuss with the nursing staff, and eventually he was given a pain-killer, but this all took some time. I returned later in the afternoon, to find that they'd moved him to a different ward. He was more composed, and pretended to take an interest in a *New Scientist* I'd brought with me, which had a piece about hot-blooded dinosaurs, I believe. But it was obviously a great effort, and he wanted to rest.'[13] (David Jones was to recall that Empson 'maintained strong interests in subjects which intigued him, notably dinosaurs and stone circles (Stonehenge in particular), cosmology and scientific matters').[14] By the early evening, however, Jacob found his father barely conscious. A young doctor attempted to be diplomatic with Jacob, murmuring that no one could live for ever, or something of the sort. When Jacob demanded to know whether his mother and brother should be recalled, the word was given that they should come back immediately. His father had developed pneumonia.

Hetta and Mogador were back in London by 10.30 that night. Empson was no longer speaking, and his breathing had grown very hard. 'He didn't speak again,' recalls Jacob, 'so there were no "last words" for us.' Mogador, Jacob, and David Jones took it in turns to stay with Empson round the clock. Mogador and Jacob were on shift, so to speak, into the small hours. By that time, Empson was evidently in great distress, fighting desperately for breath with great shuddering gasps and with his eyes shut. Both sons feared for an officious prolongation of suffering, if that was all that could be done for him. 'I had to shout at the young female registrar to get him some more morphine,' remembers Mogador. At first the doctor demurred at such a desperate measure, knowing full well that Empson was dying of cirrhosis of the liver and naturally anxious that overdosing the patient could land her in trouble. Jacob recalls: 'She rather oddly said, "He'll be gone by morning, I guarantee", which may have been simply an unfortunate turn of phrase.' Still, it is likely that she was generous with the morphine. 'His breathing was very loud and rasping, hour after hour, and it was painful to hear.' Mogador went out in search of a quiet spot—he fell asleep in the corridor, exhausted—and Jacob was on his own with his father when the sound of breathing ceased. Empson died at 2.30 a.m., and the others woke Mogador when it was all over. Jacob reflects too that it was an extremely painful couple of days for Mogador, who had been worrying for his father for a good many weeks—'and Pa was being typically stoical, so it is perhaps not surprising that he didn't come up with anything to tell us before he lost consciousness.'[15]

Nevertheless, David Jones was to recollect not long after the death: 'There had been no famous last words in that day-long fight for breath, but I have little doubt what they might have been, for he had said them on a previous occasion when he thought he was about to die. I was visiting him on the eve of his last operation, which he fancied he would not survive; Hetta was to visit him later that evening but she had been earlier that day and maybe he thought he would not see her again. After a brief pause in our conversation, without any display of emotion but with deeply moving sincerity he said: "If I die, tell Hetta I love her very much." Then he squeezed my hand briefly and we parted.'[16]

A postmortem without inquest was conducted by no less a person than the Coroner for Greater London, D. R. Chambers, who determined that the cause of death was hepatic failure as a consequence of idiopathic cirrhosis of the liver. 'Idiopathic' merely designates a cause unknown: the certifying doctor was very probably being tactful in using the term to conceal the necessity to register alcohol as a cause of death. This showed sensitivity to the family of the deceased (such deference is often exercised by doctors when dealing with a famous person), because in 1984 the implications of an alcohol-related death would almost certainly have invoked a Coroner's Inquest—since deaths due directly or indirectly to alcohol poisoning required such an enquiry—and an inquest could well have attracted inappropriate media and public attention. (The requirement has been somewhat relaxed in more recent years.) Empson had consumed excessive amounts of alcohol for a good part of his adult life, and it had finally taken its toll. Of recent years, following his various operations, he had abstained from drinking for longish periods, but he never gave up completely. In November 1982, Hetta had written to a friend: 'William is drinking only TAB, but looks jolly healthy.'[17] (Her 'but' is ironically humorous.) In that same month, Empson happened to reflect upon the example of Malcolm Lowry, his acquaintance at Cambridge University, and stated, as Mark Thompson has recalled, that he 'did not admire the adult Lowry's "seeming somehow to make a virtue of alcoholism", for it is no boasting matter—he, Empson, had felt the danger of alcoholism before, and saw nothing in it to be proud of'.[18] Then in mid-February 1984, when admitted for the first time to the hospital where he would die just a few weeks later, he spoke again to Thompson about alcohol and its effects. 'Of George Fraser: "They said he had to give up drinking . . . and he lived for ten years afterwards. I don't think *I'll* survive for another ten years, but long enough to finish a couple of books at any rate." He had "a sort of sleeping sickness"; he "stoked himself up with drink" but still fell asleep when he went to his typewriter. The drink wasn't having any effect, so he might as well stop drinking. "I think I'll have a long period of sobriety when I get out of here." '[19] It was almost as if he was innocent of the long-term effects of drinking too much, for his inveterate habit had been to fuel ('stoke up') his writing with alcohol.

In his last Will and Testament, dated 28 April 1970, he left everything to his wife (she was anyway to retain a life interest in the freehold of Studio House, as a tenant in common in equal shares); and he showed a very fine generosity in providing that every one of her sons—Mogador and Jacob, and Simon Duval Smith as well—should be the residuary legatees. In the final clause he expressed the wish that his eyes might be offered to the Moorfields Eye Hospital for therapeutic purposes, and that his body be used for medical research. Probate was granted on 17 September 1984 in the sum of £193,666.

Not long after his death, on Friday, 25 May 1984, Cambridge University, the *alma mater* which had cast out the gifted young student back in 1929, put on a memorial celebration in the Old Library at Emmanuel College. A fine line-up of distinguished dons—they included Muriel Bradbrook, Graham Hough, Elsie Duncan-Jones, L. C. Knights, J. H. Prynne, Christopher Ricks, Richard Luckett, Geoffrey Hill, John Holloway and Frank Kermode—read poems and prose extracts by Empson. For a finale, Hetta Empson recited 'Chinese Ballad' in an intensely clear, electrifying, haunting voice, and gave especially poignant and deeply affecting expression to the final line: 'Come back in a few days.'

William Empson once remarked in passing, in the midst of *Milton's God*: 'As for myself, when I was a little boy I was very afraid I might not have the courage which I knew life to demand of me'.[20] The record tells that he met the multiple challenges of his extraordinarily varied and demanding life—extending as it did from Yorkshire to Cambridge, and from Japan to China and the USA, and not forgetting the rich, difficult, entertaining and productive years at Sheffield—with rare resolution and resourcefulness. His genius made of him one of the foremost literary critics of the twentieth century, and in many senses he really did invent modern literary criticism in English; and his aptitude and application produced some of the masterpieces of the century: *Seven Types of Ambiguity, Some Versions of Pastoral, The Structure of Complex Words*, and *Milton's God*—all of which abound with clarifying ideas and fresh insights, and with conceptual brilliance, as well as the courage of risk. As a poet—stirred by science and facing up to profound fears—he produced a modest body of rich and compelling verses. His poetry takes the measure of conflict and self-conflict with deep, impeccable courage and sheer good sense. As a man, though sometimes difficult and contrary, contentious, provocative and stubborn, he was above all a figure of humane grace, wide generosity and world-embracing wisdom. He was also—what is surprising to many who met him—a really rather shy and humble man, though always brave-hearted and forceful in speaking up for the causes he believed in. On a sheet of paper that survives in his extensive archive, he once scratched out some Benthamite thoughts—possibly even at some point during the very last weeks of his life—about how one might seek to reckon up the good life: the life that brought the fullest satisfaction. Might it be a good idea, he asked himself, to set up an ad hoc committee to adjudicate such a thing? John Maynard Keynes, he reflected, 'speaks of an economist restless and un-happy in old age—himself happily worked to death, never seeing final effect. Collingwood speaks of misery among old philosophers. Seems rare for literary men to end up like this. One needs to consider all kinds of lives—there would be a willing committee to each. Painters seem satisfied, even bad ones . . . The committee should consider whether a course of life is to be recommended to a young person as likely to produce contentment.' Then, breaking off from this musing before it could become morose or perhaps even morbid, he characteristically added a joke: 'Rather few fret as much as they should, I daresay.' As for himself, he wrote too: 'I have been lucky without much endowment.' The modesty was typical of him.

At a late date too, he wrote out these notes from Charles Darwin's *Autobiography*: 'Whenever I have found out that I have blundered, or that my work has been imperfect, and when I have been contemptuously criticized, and even when I have been overpraised, so that I have felt mortified, it has been my greatest comfort to say hundreds of times to myself that "I have worked as hard and as well as I could, and no man can do more than this." ' Immediately below that noble (and not self-satisfied) sentence, he noted that Darwin died at the age of 82. It is evident that Empson—very possibly taking down Darwin's thoughts in the year of his own death at 77—was justifiably reckoning the same of himself.

Hetta Empson stayed on at Studio House for the next several years, until her death on 22 December 1996 (three months into her eighty-first year). She continued to lead a very full and vigorous social life, amply supported by, and always delighting in, her expanding family of children, grandchil-dren, and great-grandchildren, and by close friends including the loyal David Jones; enjoying visits to art exhibitions in London; and relishing opportunities for foreign travel. In 1985, for instance, she told Walter Brown, her dear friend and sometime lover, that she had been to see an exhibition of Chagall at the Royal Academy, adding: 'I am besotted with that ancient Hassidic Jew of a painter.'[21]

At her funeral, her grandson Saul recounted some of the innumerable ways in which she had struck him as an amazing person and astonishing grandmother:

> I realised from an early age that my grandmother was different from other grandmothers. I remember clearly other children at school talking about

their grandmas along the lines of 'She's a nice old lady with her hair in a bun, and she sits in the corner drinking tea and knitting. What's yours like?' This was always fun to answer, and one of my friends, when he retold some of my tales to his parents, got smacked for lying.

Elegantly dressed, and driving an eclectic variety of vehicles from an ambulance to an Alvis, Hetta never failed to impress me hugely.

When I was a small child, Hetta always took a keen interest in my reading. Appalled to find me reading the *Beano* album, she deftly substituted *The Epic of Gilgamesh*, which I have to confess I found a rather confusing read.

When I was sent to a prep school in Belsize Park, Hetta thoughtfully pressed into my hand a copy of Mao's Little Red Book. I found this very interesting—and also a little confusing. In fact, it was so intriguing that I read out passages to my school chums to get their interpretation of certain passages. This resulted in a huge argument within the staff common-room between the right-wing Leavisite teacher and a Trotskyite history teacher who anyway always addressed his pupils as 'Comrade' and 'Brother'.

Trips with Hetta were always special, and different from those with my friends' grandmas. When I was ten, we went to an archaeological dig near Andover and camped in a nearby field. Arriving in the middle of the night, Hetta and I made camp with consummate ease and went to sleep. In the morning, we looked out to see a party of our fellow Archaeologists Aspirant sitting in a forlorn tangle of canvas, tent-poles and guy-ropes—drenched to the skin. Hetta was always resourceful.

When we travelled on camels through the Sahara Desert, looking for Neolithic cave paintings, Hetta taught me to mash hashish into butter to make Afghan Butter, and to mix screwdrivers based on surgical spirit. As I said, always resourceful . . .

Hetta always gave voice to the pithy *mot juste* in a tricky situation. Once when we were rowing back down the Orwell from the Butt & Oyster to the Creek, a large sailing ship bore down on us. Try as we might, the crew did not seem to respond to any of our desperate shouts. Suddenly, Mogador noticed a Dutch flag flying from the mast. 'They're Dutch, Ma! Try saying something in Dutch!' So Hetta tottered to her feet and shouted, 'Piss off!'

Hetta was also a deft hand at dealing with boring, foolish or pretentious party guests. A rather mediocre painter confided to Hetta that she thought that she—the painter—could paint better than Picasso. Hetta fixed her with a baleful look and said: 'Not even children talk like that.'

The black oxen of the years had trod on, but they could never tread her down. Still, when the time came, she seemed ready for her end. David Jones noted, also at the funeral: 'she had begun to feel it was soon time to be packing up—"tickets time," she called it. With her fiercely independent spirit, she hated the frailties of old age and did not relish a long, dependent haul into senility; she was mentally prepared for death.'

Her eldest son, Mogador, extolled her 'lion-hearted' qualities:

> Ma was fiercely loyal to all of us; she was our truest friend and loved us with an unconditional jealous passion. And we loved her madly in return, knowing we had the real thing, the purest gold. She has left a rich harvest of ten glorious grandchildren: Saul, Ben, Henrietta, Rachel, Rebecca, James, Johanna, Amelia, Nancy, and the newest, little Rory, who all carry her memory, her love and her genes . . . She drank, loved, swore her way through the years, and was always terrific fun to be with. She seduced us all with her honesty and nobility of spirit. She was simply magnificent, blazing through life, leaving us dazzled, spellbound and now bereft. You will be pleased to hear that true to herself to the end her last words were 'Get me a strong Scotch'. And when I hesitated and said I'm not sure you're strong enough, she replied 'Oh yes I am'.

It cannot be gainsaid that Hetta and William Empson did not enjoy a conventional marriage (indeed, it is unlikely that either of them could have endured one). Nevertheless, they had been married some forty-three years when William died, and Hetta often ached with grief for her deceased husband. 'I never met a more lovely man,' she told me once; and from time to time she would phone close friends to ask them movingly, 'Tell me about William.'

The Wife is Praised

An unpublished draft poem
by William Empson

THE WIFE IS PRAISED

Much astonished to find you were handy
   I proposed when we first got to bed;
This was viewed as too pushing or randy
   And not what was usually said;
I urged you have lovers beside me
   O lots, and I'd just as soon know.
It took time and an angel to guide me
     To make the thing go.

Did I love you as mine for possessing?
   Absurd as it seems, I forget;
For the vision of love that was pressing
   And time has not falsified yet
Was always a love with three corners
   I loved you in bed with young men,
Your arousers and foils and adorners
     Who would yield to me then.

It was true and is why one should be male
   That this makes a viable plan;
Taking turns at a generous female
   Is the best act of love with a man.
But I may not have thought to begin with
   That this would make you such a power;
That so nameless a sin is akin with
     The heart of the flower.

It is chiefly to know you are willing
   And not what I get on the side
That I find at once quieting and thrilling,
   A peace, an insurance, a pride.

And indeed when they care for you only
   And think me a price they must pay
That is proof I should really be lonely
    With Hetta away.

But one likes to have something to offer
   And how vain to assume it is charm;
It is low to fling open the coffer;
    To give wisdom—the thought is a qualm.
There is really no other proposal
   One can make to the ones that will do
But "a stunner, and at my disposal,
    And be nice to me too".

And besides, it is that situation
   Two thirds of the men would prefer;
I make a reclassification
   By which few are left buggers that were.
And the third are the men who see double
   For whom *two* girls in bed would be It;
So the Lesbians are out of their trouble
    And the numbers fit.

Indeed I propose a policeman
   Ought nightly to raid the retired
And demand why a Moral Release man
   Is not in this bed as required.
"The State will not stand for a couple;
   It makes all its beds to hold three;
And you are not permitted to tup all
    Alone like I see".

The practice of marriage however
   Outlasts this great change in the law;
There are two whom no time will dissever
   And a third who is quick on the draw.
He comes as a learner or teacher
   Or he comes as a breath of the air;
And O may we happen to reach a
    Ground yet more fair.

And how nice when the man brings the tea-things
  And knows that three cups are required,
And my children so eager to see things
  See nothing that need be admired.
They may all patter in in the morning
  And the bed is no cause for surprise;
And if that isn't heaven—the warning
  Is not to fear eyes.

There is need for a quantum of terror
  In handling this secular theme;
It is hubris and brash and an error
  To present it as strawberries and cream.
The queen of the gods and of mortals
  Insatiate and searching and rich
Who must open for all men her portals—
  They call her a bitch;

She is death and the craving for torture;
  She alone is the Muse, but the price
They all paid—they report her a scorcher;
  They are glad to agree she is Vice.
And for thousands of years on her altar
  Her man was castrated and flayed
Ere he died lest fertility falter
  O mother and maid.

We must all take advice and our bearings
  But what are these tortures to me?
I deduce that the practice of sharing's
  A lust on which all men agree.
A unnameable horror, a monster,
  No torture can blast it enough,
But while it is being well sconced, a
  Thought "That's the stuff".

I shall not assume then there follow
  Desertion, castration, and death
From retracing the source of Apollo
  Resaying the older Thus Saith.

But I dare not be sure it's not tragic
   When all the first sources agree
And (God knows) it is patently magic;
   We must see what we see.

I am rather too readily injured
   And you have no lust to endure;
If I feel the match powerfully cinctured
   It is where one might think it needs cure.
Oh the kindness of each loving two ways
   And one man not tied up at all.
A neurosis? Angelica Lues
   That holds love thrall.

[One might claim this ideal is mere fancy
   Since no man can lust after both,
This presumes a man's either a nancy
   Or not, and thus totally loath.
He is not to reject my affection,
   But how little I have to require;
The mechanics are under direction
   And the central fire.]*

The Triangle called the Eternal
   Here asks for a passing surprise;
For the history of love is a journal
   Of fashions in whom to excise.
They would cut out the first or the second
   Or revolt and then cut out the third,
Proving only that Nature had beckoned
   Absurdly unheard.

For the wife was locked up in the kitchen
   When Greeks got ideas in the gym;
And the troubadour's lady was rich in
   A husband both powerful and dim.
The Reformers then claimed a fantastic
   Reversal of all men adored
And screwed up love parts for domestic
   Bed and board.

And then for three centuries of printing
   We get a great gush every year
About what may the husband be hinting
   And is the young woman sincere;
And there must be one loser however
   They shuffle their sins and their suits.
They could jump into bed all together
     The silly coots.

Not by me are reformers resented;
   I too offer practical norms.
For the marvellous thing was invented
   In two over-specialised forms.
Love is sodomy, love is adultery,
   Say the sources; in pain you must roam.
Nearly true, but I give to each cult a re-
     Vision at home.

It is fair to recall contraception
   (Perhaps about seventy years old)
Was required for the easy reception
   Of truths men went mad to behold.
Granting this, I am surely belated;
   It is time the machine was employed
If three generations have grated
     Desire on a void.

And the great homosexual story
   (Well I know) was the message half read;
I have always felt men were the glory
   And found them quite pointless in bed.
Not that love did not make it a splendour
   But how acid the things one must do,
And what milk when permitted to send your
     Own cocks to you.

I revere the Swinburnian Dolores
   With 28 rhymes upon Pain,
But the lust to spread hurt through this whore is
   A puritan taint in the grain;

He had got in his bones, before Fraser,
    The White Goddess of Graves and her power,
And made that great marvel to praise her
      Both true and too sour.

I want it more homely and jolly—
    This is coarse and like Leopold Bloom—
But he craves to bed Stephen with Molly
    On more grounds than the critics assume.
With this Son in his bed he could sire one;
    Ten years (since the death) he's felt barred;
The theme is a bold and entire one;
    Joyce hiding it hard.

And the answer comes after the story:
    Jeering Stephen became Mr Joyce
Knowing all of both Blooms to his glory,
    And how he got healed is your choice.
But I would not agree it's refining
    Not to care whether Bloom had a son.
Perhaps Joyce was ashamed he kept whining;
    The book's name says they won.

What I want to say, dragging reviews in,
    Is these things have happened before.
What a bore to be smart with a new sin;
    I trace out a natural law.
But it's true that few women can handle
    What so many men want to do,
Or (the phrase is) can "hold up a candle"
    To rival you.

* Note: Stanza deleted on typescript

NOTES

NOTES

I. THE BBC WAR

1. WE, 'Orwell at the BBC', *The Listener*, 4 Feb. 1971; *A*, 496.
2. WE, 'Yes and No', *Essays in Criticism*, 5: 1 (Jan. 1955), 88. See also a letter to Christopher Ricks, 6 May 1962: 'The reason why the greater poet Auden clung to America was that to become Britain's wartime bard would have meant unbearable phoniness, and the poet Dylan though so much less political had to insist on his purity.'
3. T. S. Eliot, letter to John Hayward, 16 Feb. 1940 (Hayward Bequest, Modern Archive Centre, King's College, Cambridge).
4. John Davenport, letter to Julian Trevelyan, 16 Feb. 1940 (Wren Library, Trinity College, Cambridge: JOT 4/41).
5. T. S. Eliot, letter to John Hayward, 3 April 1940 (Hayward Bequest).
6. Professor Sir Ernst Gombrich (1909–2001) was born in Vienna and came to the UK in 1936; he did not meet WE during his time at the monitoring service. 'The organisation of the service was pretty hieratic and one did not easily meet members of other departments' (letter to JH, 23 Sept. 1987). See also Helena de Bertodano, 'Casting ever darker shadows', *Sunday Telegraph Review*, 21 May 1995, 3.
7. See George Weidenfeld, *Remembering My Good Friends: An Autobiography* (London: HarperCollins, 1994), 96–100.
8. See Michael Eaude, 'Arturo Barea: Exile Without Resentment', *London Magazine*, NS 34: 1 & 2 (April/May 1994), 58: 'During the six war years she spent with the BBC, Ilsa's linguistic ability and mental speed made her one of the most valuable monitors. She not only listened to speeches by the German leaders and afterwards typed out a full text from her crude notes, but also monitored, often in poor reception conditions, broadcasts from Spain.' See also Arturo Barea, *The Forging of a Rebel*, trans. Ilsa Barea (London: Granta Books, 2002).
9. Martin Esslin never met WE, but he was aware of his presence; he often spotted him, from 1941 onwards, in the canteen at Bush House: 'He usually sat by himself, reading a book or journal. With his black pointed beard and sharply etched saturnine, sardonic mien he was a most impressive figure' (letter to JH, 6 Oct. 1987).
10. WE, letter to James Jesus Angleton, 12 June 1940 (Beinecke Library, Yale: YCAL MSS 75, Box 1, folder 30). Angleton (1917–1987) was born in the USA

and educated at Malvern School in England and then at Yale University, 1937–41. He worked on *Yale Lit*, and in 1939 founded the magazine *Furioso* which—fuelled by Angleton's liking for WE—put out an essay by I. A. Richards, 'William Empson', *Furioso: A Special Note* (12 Jan. 1940), as an unpaginated supplement to *Furioso* 1: 3 (Spring 1940). As a littérateur, he was friendly also with T. S. Eliot and with Ezra Pound (whom he visited at Rapallo in 1938). During World War II Angleton was to join the US Office of Strategic Services (precursor of the CIA), and in 1943 he was sent to London to be trained by MI5 officers including Dick White and Harold A. R. (Kim) Philby. (Angleton came to know Philby well during the latter's tour of duty in Washington, 1949–51; and Philby's defection to the USSR in 1963 may have aggravated Angleton's apprehension of a monolithic Communist conspiracy seeking to penetrate the intelligence services of the West.) Having won renown for his work in counter-intelligence, after 1949 Angleton was to turn into the paranoid chief of the CIA's Office of Special Operations, in charge of the Agency's Counterintelligence Staff, until being dismissed in 1974 by William Colby, Director of Central Intelligence. (He was disgraced for his involvement in illegal espionage activities.)

11. George Weidenfeld quoted in Olive Renier and Vladimir Rubinstein, *Assigned to Listen: The Evesham Experience 1939–43* (London: British Broadcasting Corporation, 1986), 61.
12. Renier and Rubinstein, *Assigned to Listen*, 92.
13. WE, letter to I. A. Richards, 8 Dec. 1940 (Magdalene).
14. WE, letter to J. J. Angleton, 29 July 1940 (Beinecke Library, Yale: YCAL MSS 75, Box 1, folder 30).
15. Richard Usborne, letter to Olive Renier, 7 March (no year).
16. Olive Renier, letter to JH, 1 Oct. 1987.
17. WE, letter to John Hayward, 7 Dec. 1940 (King's).
18. Asa Briggs, *The History of Broadcasting in the United Kingdom*, III: *The War of Words* (London: Oxford University Press, 1970), 486.
19. See Robert Fraser, *The Chameleon Poet: A Life of George Barker* (London: Weidenfeld & Nicolson, 2001), 159–60.
20. WE, 'Dylan Thomas in Maturity' (book review), *New Statesman*, 29 Oct. 1965; *A*, 407.
21. WE, 'The Ancient Mariner', *Critical Quarterly* 6: 4 (Winter 1964), 312–13.
22. WE, 'Dylan Thomas in Maturity', *A*, 407.
23. Augustus John, OM, 'Dylan Thomas and Company', *The Sunday Times Magazine Section*, 28 Sept. 1958, 17.
24. WE, 'Some More Dylan Thomas' (book review), *Listener*, 28 Oct. 1971; *A*, 412.
25. WE, 'The Collected Dylan Thomas', *A*, 392.
26. WE, *GS*, 9.
27. WE, letter to Christopher Ricks, 19 Jan. 1975.

28. Hayward collection, King's College, Cambridge: JDH/FVM/15). WE had at first offered his new poetry book to Ian Parsons at Chatto & Windus, his regular publishers, but acted swiftly to retrieve it as soon as he heard of Eliot's interest: letter to Ian Parsons, 15 March 1940 (Reading).

29. WE, letter to Andrew Motion, 14 Aug. 1983 (Reading: Chatto & Windus files).

30. WE, letter to Hugh Major, 30 July 1978 (courtesy of Hugh Major).

31. WE, *A*, 277.

32. Rochester, *The Complete Works*, ed. Frank H. Ellis (Harmondsworth, 1994), 75.

33. Hugh Kenner, 'The Son of Spiders', *Poetry*, 56 (June 1950), 150–5.

34. G. S. Fraser in *Contemporary Poets* (London, 1974).

35. T. S. Eliot, letter to Ian Parsons, 24 Jan. 1951 (Reading). 'The great difficulty, of course,' TSE added to his letter, 'is getting in touch with Empson [in Peking], and then getting him to answer letters.' TSE sent off another letter with the same pressing burden on 19 Feb. 1951.

36. Briggs, *The War of Words*, 497. Sir John Pratt (1876–1970) was head of the Far Eastern Section of the Ministry of Information, 1939–41.

37. Sir Stephen Tallents (1884–1958) was BBC Controller (Public Relations), 1935–40; Controller (Overseas Services), 1940–1.

38. WE, letter to the BBC, 12 Feb. 1941 (Houghton carbon, incomplete).

39. Ibid. See also Michael Balfour, *Propaganda in War 1939–1945: Organisations, Policies and Publics in Britain and Germany* (London: Routledge & Kegan Paul, 1979).

40. WE, letter to Ronald Bottrall, 24 Feb. 1941 (Texas).

41. Ibid.

42. WE, 'Propaganda to Japanese', 18 Dec. 1941 (TS in Houghton).

43. WE, undated letter to mother (Houghton). On Professor L. F. Rushbrook Williams, see obituary in *The Times*, 5 Oct. 1978, 19.

44. 'He was thoughtful and exceptionally well-informed with a strong streak of the statesman in him, but he had a schoolboy vein too and could on occasion be more lighthearted than any of us. He was quite at home amongst the administrators of Whitehall but he had too much humanity and too many sympathies to be a real Whitehall type' (Maurice Gorham, *Sound and Fury: Twenty-One Years in the BBC* (London: Percival Marshall, 1948), 97). See also *The Complete Works of George Orwell*, ed. Peter Davison, 13 (London: Secker & Warburg, 1998), 14 note 1.

45. Memorandum in BBC WAC

46. Briggs, *The War of Words*, 500.

47. WE, memo to ESD on 'Broadcasts to Japan', 10 Oct. 1941 (BBC WAC).

48. L. F. Rushbrook Williams, memo to AC(OS), 'Japanese Broadcasts', 19 Feb. 1942 (BBC WAC).

49. 'Extracts from notes on Far Eastern Service meeting', 16 March 1942 (BBC WAC). See also Bruce Lockhart, *Comes the Reckoning* (London: Putnam, 1947),

331–2: 'I had been worried for a long time about the propaganda services to the Far East. When Japan had entered the war, the propaganda to that country and to the territories occupied by the Japanese should have become automatically the function of P.W.E. [Political Warfare Executive]. But we had no Far Eastern experts; the Ministry of Information had . . . I therefore submitted a paper to Mr Eden recommending that the control of all propaganda to the Far East should formally be confirmed as the function of the Ministry of Information. [But Mr Sterndale Bennett, the head of the Far Eastern Department of the Foreign Office] came out flatly against my proposal. Propaganda to the Far East was now closely linked to operations, and operational secrets could not be divulged to the Ministry of Information. It must, he said, come under P.W.E.'

50. WE, memo to ESD on 'Broadcast to Japan', 10 Oct. 1941 (BBC WAC).

51. Karl Miller, 'Empson Agonistes', in Gill, 45.

52. WE quoted in Miller, 'Empson Agonistes', 46. According to Edrita Fried, 'The Nazi assortment of vile names for the British ruling classes and single individuals, especially for Winston Churchill, may well go down as a unique collection in the history of name-calling' ('Techniques of Persuasion', in *Propaganda by Short Wave*, ed. Harwood L. Childs and John B. Whitton (1942; repr. New York: Arno Press, 1972), 293).

53. *MG*, 123.

54. 'Man of many letters' (obituary), *Henley Standard*, 18 March 1988, 22.

55. Ralf Bonwit, letter to JH, 20 March 1985.

56. WE, letter to Sir William Haley, 24 Jan. 1946 (Houghton).

57. WE, undated memo to FESD, 'Mr Bonwit' (Houghton).

58. From MacNeice's entry on WE in *The Concise Encyclopedia of English and American Poets and Poetry*, ed. Stephen Spender and Donald Hall (London: Hutchinson, 1963).

59. Text in Houghton. WE's old associate Tom Harrisson loyally reported in his column on 'Radio', *The Observer*, 10 May 1942: 'A series on Japanese methods started on May 4, fortnightly, the main script written by William Empson, in itself a guarantee of interest.'

60. See David Bergamini, *Japan's Imperial Conspiracy* (London: Heinemann, 1971), 44.

61. Quoted Ibid. 467.

62. Ibid. 481–2.

63. Ibid. 468.

64. WE, 'China and the Future', script in BBC WAC; corrected draft in Houghton.

65. First draft in Houghton.

66. WE, 'Propaganda about China for home audiences', undated (Houghton).

67. R. Bonwit, ' "Don'ts" in relation to China', Intelligence memorandum no. 142, 14 May 1942 (BBC WAC).

68. WE, 'China and the Future' (March 1942), 2 (Houghton).

69. Bonwit, '"Don'ts" in relation to China'.

70. WE, 'Orwell at the BBC', *The Listener*, 4 Feb. 1971; *A*, 498.

71. *Orwell: The War Broadcasts*, ed. W. J. West (London: Duckworth/British Broadcasting Corporation, 1985), 21.

72. 'Security censorship was meant to avoid giving the enemy any useful information; policy scrutiny was meant to avoid annoying our friends and allies, or giving them a bad opinion of Britain and its war effort . . . The outstanding example of security censorship was, of course, the weather' (Gorham, *Sound and Fury*, 112–13).

73. Michael Shelden, *Orwell: The Authorised Biography* (London: Heinemann, 1991), 372.

74. Cited in C. Fleay and M. L. Sanders, 'Looking into the Abyss: George Orwell at the BBC', *Journal of Contemporary History*, 24 (1989), 508. See also Douglas Kerr, 'Orwell's BBC Broadcasts: Colonial Discourse and the Rhetoric of Propaganda', *Textual Practice*, 16: 3 (Winter 2002), 473–90.

75. Henry Swanzy, letter to Bernard Crick, 26 Oct. 1972 (Crick).

76. Bryan Smith speaking at Hetta Empson's funeral, Jan. 1997.

77. Hetta Empson, letter to 'Mr Weight', 28 July 1941 (copy in Sheffield).

78. See further the introduction by Elizabeth Shaw, 'Wenn ich an René denke . . .', to the catalogue of *René Graetz 1908–1974: Grafik & Plastik*, an exhibition held at the State Museum of Berlin, August–October 1978.

79. HE, letter to Rhoda, 22 June 1939 (copy in Sheffield).

80. HE, letter to Frieda, 21 June 1939 (copy in Sheffield).

81. HE, letter to Lorna, 20 Nov. 1940 (copy in Sheffield).

82. HE, letter to Mrs Kibel, 7 Oct. 1940 (copy in Sheffield).

83. HE, letter to R Graetz, 24 March 1941 (copy in Sheffield).

84. HE, letter to Lorna, 6 Nov. 1940 (copy in Sheffield).

85. HE, letter to R. Graetz 24 March 1941 (copy in Sheffield).

86. HE, letters to R. Graetz, 31 Jan. 1941, 2 March 1941 (both at Sheffield). It was at the express invitation of Robert Helpmann (1909–86), the celebrated Australian ballet dancer and actor, that Leslie Hurry (1909–78) designed the set and costumes for a brilliantly realized dance-mime production of *Hamlet* (1942), set to Tchaikovsky's fantasy overture and choreographed by Helpmann. Thereafter, over a period of thirty-five years, Hurry designed more than sixty productions for major companies ranging from Sadler's Wells to the Royal Shakespeare Company.

87. Future leader of the insurrection in Kenya, and subsequently President.

88. WE, 'Orwell at the BBC', 495.

89. Ibid.

90. Humphrey Jennings quoted in *The Humphrey Jennings Film Reader*, ed. Kevin Jackson (Manchester: Carcanet, 1993), 36. (René Graetz, who was released from internment and returned to London in 1941, was to become involved with the 'Freier Deutscher Kulturbund' and—along with Hetta—with the Artists' International Organisation, in assisting refugees from Nazi Germany; in 1944 he was to marry the graphic artist Elizabeth Shaw, and in 1946 the couple would move to East Berlin.)

91. Gwenda David, funeral eulogy for Hetta Empson.

92. Laura Empson, letter to WE, 21 Nov. 1942 (Houghton).

93. WE, letter to mother, 28 June 1943 (Houghton).

94. Hetta Empson, holograph notes: 'Letters of a Wayward Wife' (Sheffield).

95. WE, letter to IAR, 12 June 1943 (Houghton).

96. WE, undated letter to mother, 'Thursday' (Houghton).

97. WE, letter to mother, 28 June (Houghton).

98. On figuring Orwell as a subversive Trotskyite, see Christopher Hitchens, *Orwell's Victory* (London: Allen Lane/Penguin, 2002).

99. Interview with HE, 14 Jan. 1990. See also Peter Davison, 'Orwell and the women', *The Guardian*, 27 June 1998, 3.

100. 'We remained friends afterwards, and sometimes had dinner together' ('Orwell at the BBC', 495).

101. George Woodcock, *The Crystal Spirit: A Study of George Orwell* (1967; repr. London: Fourth Estate, 1984), 19.

102. T. R. Fyvel, *George Orwell: a personal memoir* (London: Hutchinson, 1983), 121.

103. John Morris, 'That Curiously Crucified Expression' (originally 'Some Are More Equal Than Others', in *Penguin New Writing*, 1950), in *Orwell Remembered*, ed. Audrey Coppard and Bernard Crick (London: British Broadcasting Corporation, 1984), 173. 'When we were alone together he always tried to behave in an aggressively working-class manner, and the effect was to make me talk like an unrepentant reactionary' (176).

104. WE, 'Orwell at the BBC', *A*, 496.

105. Ibid.

106. Gerard Mansell, *Let Truth Be Told: 50 Years of BBC External Broadcasting* (London: Weidenfeld & Nicolson, 1982), 117.

107. Gorham, *Sound and Fury*, 131.

108. WE, letter to I. A. Richards, 12 Jan. 1943 (Houghton).

109. See WE, *SL*, 146–7.

110. WE, 'Orwell at the BBC', *A*, 500.

111. George Ivan Smith, letter to *The Guardian*, 16 Nov. 1991. See obituaries of George Ivan Smith in *The Guardian* (by Conor Cruise O'Brien), 22 Nov. 1995, 17; *The Times*, 23 Nov. 1995, 23.

112. Ralf Bonwit, 'Newspeak and the New Year' (letter), *Financial Times*, 5 Jan. 1984.

113. Morris, 'That Curiously Crucified Expression', 172.

114. War-time Diary, 14 March 1942, in *The Complete Works of George Orwell*, ed. Peter Davison (London: Secker & Warburg, 1998), vol. 14, 229; Orwell, letter to Alex Comfort, ? 11 July 1943, ibid, vol. 15, 166. See also Abha Sharma Rodrigues, Orwell's War: George Orwell, the BBC and India, 1939–1945 *(London: Cassell Academic, 1998)*.
115. Fyvel, *George Orwell*, 121.
116. See Bernard Crick, *George Orwell: A Life* (Harmondsworth, Middx.: Penguin, 1982), 427–30. Cf. Michael Meyer's account of the evening with Orwell and Wells, in *Not Prince Hamlet: Literary and Theatrical Memoirs* (London: Secker & Warburg, 1989), 66. See also Gordon Bowker, *George Orwell* (London: Little, Brown, 2003), 288–9; D. J. Taylor, *Orwell* (London: Chatto & Windus, 2003), 305. Inez Holden (1906–1974) was author of *Sweet Charlatan* (1929), *Death in High Society and Other Stories* (1933), and *The Owner* (1952), among other works.
117. Celia Goodman, 'Inez Holden: A Memoir', 5–6 (courtesy of the late Mrs Celia Goodman).
118. WE, 'Obscurity and Annotation' (*c.* 1930), *A*, 83.
119. WE, 'Orwell at the BBC', *A*, 498. Cf. D. J. Taylor's account of his discovery, following the completion of his biography, of an 'intriguing item' in the Buswell Memorial Library at Wheaton College, Illinois: 'a letter from Orwell, dated June 21 1945, to the editor of the Glasgow-based *Million* magazine, complaining about an article entitled "George Orwell and Our Time". Its author, J. E. Miller, had repeated a claim first levelled by the British Communist party leader Harry Pollitt in the *Daily Worker* in 1937, that in *The Road to Wigan Pier*, Orwell asserts that the working classes "smell". Time had not softened Orwell's asperity. "I not only did not say that the working classes "smell", I said almost the opposite of this. What I said, as anyone who chooses to consult the books can see, is that 20 or 30 years ago, when I was a child, middle-class children were taught to believe that the working class "smell" and that this was a psychological fact which had to be taken into consideration"' ('The Ever-Longer Road to Wigan Pier', *Guardian Review*, 21 Feb. 2004, 37).
120. WE, 'Orwell at the BBC', 498–9.
121. Ibid. 499.
122. West, *Orwell: The War Broadcasts*, 37. The five surviving scripts of 'Voice' are printed in *The War Broadcasts*, 80–94.
123. Reflections by Mulk Raj Anand are from 'Reminiscences of William Empson', a letter to JH, 2 March 1989. Obituaries of Anand are in *Daily Telegraph*, 29 Sept. 2004, p. 27; *Guardian* (by Jai Kumar and Haresh Pandya), 29 Sept. 2004, 25; *The Independent* (by Alistair Niven), 29 Sept. 2004, 32; *The Times*, 30 Sept. 2004, p. 65.
124. The late W. W. Robson recalled, in a letter to JH: 'I was introduced to Empson by John Crow, in Finch's Bar in the Strand, in 1945. He had a

brown face and no beard. He was doing the *Times* crossword puzzle and occasionally joining in the conversation. Dylan Thomas was among those present. Empson said he was employed at the BBC turning Ernest Bevin's speeches into intelligible English, so that they could be translated into Japanese for transmission by the Overseas Service.' (Bevin was Foreign Secretary.)

125. Anand, letter to JH, 2 March 1989. Cf. Bowker, *George Orwell*, 287: '[Orwell] favoured independence but (with some reservations) despised Gandhi, whose pacifist tactics he thought played into British hands and illustrated the worthlessness of non-violence in the face of ruthless oppression.'

126. WE, 'Orwell at the BBC', 496.

127. See Crick, *George Orwell*, 22; and a letter by Sydney D. Bailey, 'George Orwell', in *TLS*, 7 Jan. 1983, 15.

128. The BBC Director of Talks turned down 'The Traps of Idealism' on 2 Sept. 1936: 'your analysis of the Pacifist ideal would be a breach of our policy of dealing with controversial subjects only in such a way that there is adequate presentation of both points of view by representatives of both sides.'

129. WE, unpublished letter to the *Spectator* on 'Pacifism and Pacificism', 4 Sept. 1940 (Houghton); *SL*, 129–31.

130. WE, 'Orwell at the BBC', 497.

131. WE, 'Sartre Resartus' (a review originally written for *The Nation* by 2 May 1947), *New York Review of Books*, 48: 10 (21 June 2001), 64–5.

132. See *The Complete Works of George Orwell*, 20, App. 9, 240–58. See also Michael Shelden, 'Revealed: George Orwell's Big Brother Dossier', *Daily Telegraph*, 22 June 1998, 12–13; Timothy Garton Ash, 'Love, Death and Treachery', *The Guardian*, 21 June 2003, 4–7; Garton Ash, 'Orwell's List', *New York Review of Books*, 2 Sept. 2003, 6–12.

133. George Orwell, letter to Robert Giroux, 19 May 1949, in *Complete Works*, 20, 117 (item 3627).

134. See Caroline Davies, 'Orwell's Debutante Friend Tells of Role in Writer's "Betrayal" List', *Daily Telegraph*, 13 July 1996, 7; Robert Conquest, 'In Celia's Office', *TLS*, 21 Aug. 1998, 4–5; obituaries of Celia Goodman in *The Guardian* (by D. J. Taylor), 6 Nov. 2002, 20; *The Times*, 29 Oct. 2002, 33.

2. THE WAR WITHIN THE BBC

1. See Sir Hugh Cortazzi, 'Sir Vere Redman, 1901–1975', in *Britain & Japan: Biographical Portraits*, 3 (London: Japan Library, 1997); and obituary in *The Times*, 31 Jan. 1975, 16.

2. WE, letter to I. A. Richards, 12 Jan. 1943 (Houghton).

3. WE, letter to Richards, 12 Jan. 1943. Arthur Waley, who looked like the actor Leslie Howard playing a don, had a 'very acute mind', according to Ralf Bonwit. They thought of him as their 'guilty conscience'.

4. See *Tambimuttu: Bridge between Two Worlds*, ed. Jane Williams (London: Peter Owen, 1989).

5. Ralf Bonwit, letter to JH, 20 March 1983. In 1975 Tambimuttu would recall an episode from 1939: 'Another beautiful girl of our circle was the tall and buxom but most perfectly proportioned Hetta Crouse from South Africa who graced our parties with fellow South African sculptor René Graetz. But we soon lost her to unambiguous William Empson. She invited me to do some gardening with her and dutifully I went down to Bill's garden. When we were in the drawing-room I said, "Come and sit on my lap, Hetta." "That is not your style, Tambi dear," she said. "I hear you have been gardening with Hetta," Bill told me the next day. That's how close we were in those days in Fitzrovia' (quoted in *Tambimuttu: Bridge between Two Worlds*, 229).

6. T. S. Eliot, letter to Dorothea Richards, 16 Feb. 1942 (Magdalene).

7. R. A. Rendall, memo to ESD on 'Chinese News Commentaries', 10 August 1942 (BBC E1/614/1).

8. Rushbrook Williams, undated response on verso of Randall's memo of 10 Aug. 1942 (BBC E1/614/1).

9. 'Advance list of postscripts: Chinese Service', 17 Dec. 1942 (E1/619/1).

10. Desmond Hawkins, letter to JH, 30 Sept. 1987. See also Hawkins, *When I Was: A Memoir of the Years between the Wars* (London: Macmillan London, 1989), 213: 'I accepted Empson's invitation to broadcast to China, where there was most improbably alleged to be an audience for my views on the novels of Ivy Compton-Burnett.' See obituary of Hawkins in *The Times*, 13 May 1999, 29.

11. Hsiao Ch'ien (Xiao Qian) was born in 1910; his publications include *Etchings of a Tormented Age* (1942)..

12. Mary Somerville, Director of School Broadcasting, memo on 'Dr George Yeh' to Controller (News), 14 Sept. 1942 (BBC Yeh Talks 42–45).

13. A. P. Ryan, handwritten note on Somerville's memo of 14 Sept.

14. WE must have prompted Orwell too: see Orwell letter to Dr Yeh, 2 Sept. 1942 (BBC Yeh Talks 42-45): (*Complete Works*, vol. 14, 4.)

15. Eleen Sam (Mrs Thierry-Mieg) later worked as a Programme Specialist in the Natural Science Department (Sector) of UNESCO in Paris, 1946–79.

16. Empire News Editor, memo to ESD on 'Chinese News Service', 10 Dec. 1942 (BBC E1/614/1).

17. WE, memo to ESD on 'Policy of Chinese News Broadcasts', Dec. 1942 (Houghton).

18. WE, undated memo to ESD on 'Propaganda to China' (Aug. 1942) (Houghton).

19. 'Common Cause of China and Britain: Mr. Eden's Pledge', *The Times*, 29 July 1943, 7.

20. Ministry of Information, Overseas Planning Committee: Plan of Propaganda to China, 2 Dec. 1942 (PRO FO 371/31704).

21. WE, letter to I. A. Richards, 12 Jan. 1943 (Houghton carbon).
22. WE, memo to Mr Farquharson, 'Request from Chungking', 12 Feb. 1943 (BBC E1/619/1).
23. Ibid.
24. J. B. Clark, letter to G. Yeh, 15 March 1943 (BBC E1/619/1).
25. WE, memo to ESD, 'Propaganda to China', 15 May 1943 (Houghton).
26. WE, memo to Controller, 'News Talk for Double Seventh', 20 June 1943 (BBC Yeh Talks 42–45).
27. Ibid.
28. WE, letter to mother, 28 June 1943 (Houghton).
29. 'Plan of Propaganda to China', Dec. 1942, p. 3 (FO 371/31704).
30. 'Chinese Victory on Yangtze: Japanese Divisions in Retreat: Heavy Casualties', *The Times*, 4 June 1943, 3.
31. Text dated 10 Oct. 1943 (Houghton).
32. R. Bonwit, memo to ESD, 'News, News Talks and Features about China', 22 June 1943 (BBC E1/614/1).
33. WE, memo to ESD on 'Home News Treatment of Chinese Communiqué', 17 Nov. 1943 (Houghton).
34. WE, letter to I. A. Richards, 12 Jan. 1943 (Houghton).
35. 'The King's Basic English' (leading article), *The Times*, 10 March 1944.
36. Winston S. Churchill quoted in 'A Joint Staff in Peace: Mr Churchill on Allied Unity', *The Times*, 7 Sept. 1943, 3; see further Churchill, *His Complete Speeches, 1897–1963*, 7: *1943–1949*, ed. Robert Rhodes James (New York: Chelsea House Publishers, 1994), 6826.
37. WE, 'The Hammer's Ring' (1973), *A*, 223.
38. See notes in Ogden Papers, Box 16, file 7 (McMaster University Library).
39. See WE, 'Basic English and the Modern World', *Tribune*, 18 Feb. 1944, 18.
40. WE, letter to C. K. Ogden, 27 Sept. 1944 (BBC WAC). The text of WE's letter is published in West, *Orwell: The War Broadcasts*, 63–4.
41. R. Bonwit, Intelligence Extract, 23 Dec. 1942; copying from 'Cable Intercept, New York to News Chronicle' of 18 Dec. (BBC E1/614/1).
42. Briggs, *War of Words*, 503.
43. Memo from Professor E. R. Dodds on 'Cultural Co-operation between British and Chinese Universities', enclosed with letter from Sir H. Seymour to Mr Anthony Eden, Chungking, 21 April 1943 (E1/614/1).
44. Memo from WE to ESD, 15 May 1943 (Houghton).
45. WE, letter to mother, 28 June 1943 (letter in Houghton). John Morris reported in a memo to the ESD, 'Overseas Planning Committee of Ministry of Information', 13 March 1943, that 'Mr Redman frequently stated ... that he wished at all costs to obtain control of all broadcasting to the Far East' (cited in West, *Orwell: The War Broadcasts*, 50).
46. Orwell, letter to Alex Comfort, 11 [?] July 1943, *Complete Works*, vol. 15, 166.
47. W. J. West, *The Larger Evils* (Edinburgh: Canongate Press, 1992), 59.

48. C. S. Wang, memo to WE, copy to ESD, 7 June 1944 (E1/614/2).
49. See WE, memo to ESD on 'Distribution of texts sent to China', 30 March 1944 (Houghton). The ESD equivocated: 'I think you are taking too pessimistic a view. As I read these papers, the position seems to be that we don't know what distribution is taking place. This is very different from knowing that distribution is *not* taking place.'
50. WE, memo to ESD on 'MOI and China', 9 May 1944.
51. WE, memo to ESD, 22 May 1944.
52. Rushbrook Williams, note to Acting Controller (Overseas), written on WE's memo of 22 May 1944.
53. Ralf Bonwit, memo ('China') to ESD, 30 May 1944 (BBC E1/614/2).
54. WE, handwritten draft of letter to Harold Nicolson, 1 July 1944 (ALS in Houghton).
55. See Briggs, *The War of Words*, 403. Raymond Gram Swing (1887–1968) worked for the *Philadelphia Public Ledger* and the *New York Evening Post* before becoming a commentator for the BBC, 1935–45.
56. Harold Nicolson, letter to WE, 3 July 1944 (Houghton).
57. WE, undated letter to mother, 'Saturday 5th' [Sept. 1944] (Houghton).
58. Jacob Empson, letter to Roma Gill, 3 Oct. 1972.
59. WE recalled, in 'Orwell at the BBC', 499: 'At that time the government, or Churchill himself probably, had put into action a scheme for keeping up the birth-rate during the war by making it in various ways convenient to have babies, for mothers going out to work; government nurseries were available after the first month, I think, and there were extra eggs and other goodies on the rations, clearly a reward for Mum, or even Dad, since they could not be digested by baby. We took advantage of this plan to have two children; it seems rather athletic, looking back, as one or other parent had to retrieve them from the nursery as soon as the official worktime stopped, and the arrangements in case of illness were left to be improvised. I was saying to George one evening after dinner what a pleasure it was to cooperate with so enlightened a plan when, to my horror, I saw the familiar look of settled loathing come over his face. Rich swine boasting over our privileges, that was what we had become; "but it's *true*, George," I cried out piteously, already knowing that nothing would alter his mind. True, that is, that these arrangements had been designed for the whole population, and did apply to all factory workers. He did not refer to the subject again, but at the time his disapproval was absolute.'
60. WE, 'Wartime Nurseries': typescript text in Houghton.
61. HE said in 1990 that she believed Mrs Empson had left £3,000 to WE: £2,500 went to purchase the leasehold of Studio House, £500 to do it up.
62. WE, letter to mother, 'Saturday 5th' (Sept. 1944).
63. WE, undated letter (1972) to Geoffrey Posner (carbon in Houghton). Posner, who worked at the Centre for Television Research, University of Leeds, sent

WE in 1972 a paper on the topic of 'Recruitment Policy and Training in Broadcasting, 1939–45'.

64. Morris wrote in 1943 that 'for the last three years' the Japanese armies 'have been using the China battle front largely as a training ground on which to prepare for the present struggle' (*Traveller from Tokyo* (Harmondsworth, Middx.: Penguin, 1946), 218). That observation *per se* infuriated WE. But Morris went on: 'What they failed to realise, however, was the degree to which the China war was to unify, arouse, and inspire the Chinese people' (ibid.). He also took the view, unexceptional at the time (Empson shared it), that the Japanese militarists had probably bounced the Emperor into the World War (154). In general, Morris's book is balanced, and unequivocally condemns Japan's aggression. See also Mansell, *Let Truth Be Told*, 209: 'The proportion of short wave receivers was probably lowest in Japan, where only a small number of privileged officials were allowed to own one and there were probably not more than one hundred listeners to the limited service of news in Japanese which was started in July 1943.'

65. WE, letter to Sir William Haley, 24 Jan. 1946 (Houghton).

66. WE, undated memo (20 Oct. 1944) to ESD on 'Broadcasts to China' (BBC E1/614/2).

67. C. Lawson-Reece, 'BBC Relations with China on broadcasting affairs', 7 Dec. 1944 (BBC E1/619/3). On Donald Stephenson (1909–1993), who became BBC Controller of Overseas Services, 1956–58, see obituary in *The Times*, 9 Jan. 1993, 15.

68. R. A. Rendall, 'Record of Interview with Dr Joseph Needham', 8 Jan. 1945 (BBC WAC).

69. WE, memo to ESD on 'Chinese Programmes', 15 Jan.1945 (BBC WAC; copy in Houghton).

70. Ibid.

71. WE, letter to Sir William Haley, 24 Jan. 1946 (carbon in Houghton).

72. Director, New Delhi Office, memo to Acting Controller (Overseas), 'Broadcasting in and to China', 29 Jan. 1945 (BBC E1/614/2).

73. WE, memo to FESD, 'Chinese Service, Double Seventh', 1 June 1945 (BBC E1/614/2).

74. James Langham, 'Double Seventh Day', 12 June 1945 (Houghton).

75. WE, letter to Sterndale Bennett, 1 Oct. 1945 (Houghton). See obituary of Sir John Sterndale-Bennett (1895–1969) in *The Times*, 31 May 1969, 10

76. WE, undated memo to John Morris, 'Home propaganda on Japan' (Houghton).

77. WE, 'Yenan and Chungking' (review of *The Challenge of Red China*, by Gunther Stein), *Tribune*, 28 Dec. 1945, 15.

78. 'China and the World': text in Houghton.

79. WE, letter to I. A. Richards, 1 July 1945 (Magdalene).

80. WE, letter to John Hayward, 28 Jan. 1944 (King's WE/JDH/11).

81. WE, memo to FESD, 'China in the War', 29 June 1945 (E1/619/3).
82. Briggs, *War of Words*, 504.
83. WE, letter to T. Tunnard Moore, British Council, 3 Sept. 1945 (Houghton carbon).
84. 'I am not sure whether to congratulate you on your knighthood,' wrote Bonwit on 30 Dec. 1978, 'or to congratulate the Establishment on your having accepted it' (Houghton).
85. John Jordan, letter to JH, 5 Nov. 1987.
86. Dorothea Richards, diary entry, 1 July 1946 (Magdalene).
87. Joan Wyndham, *Anything Once* (London: Sinclair-Stevenson, 1992), 8.
88. Elias Canetti, *Party in the Blitz: The English Years*, trans. Michael Hofmann (London: Harvill Press, 2005), 57; originally *Party im Blitz: Die englischen Jahre* (2003). See also Sven Hanuschek, *Elias Canetti: Biographie* (Carl Hanser Verlag, 2005), 404.
89. WE, letter to Kathleen Raine, 26 March 1948 (BL: Raine Papers).
90. Canetti, *Party in the Blitz*, 55.
91. See Joseph Pearce, *Bloomsbury and Beyond: The Friends and Enemies of Roy Campbell* (London, 2001), 219, 263–4, 268–74.
92. WE, 'Talking Bronco' (letter), *Tribune*, 26 July 1946, 13.
93. See a letter by G. S. Fraser and Erik de Mauny, 'Roy Campbell', *Observer*, 13 Oct.: 'Might we say something, against Mr Grigson, on behalf of a brave, warm-hearted and generous man, who cannot now answer for himself? We were two members of a group of younger writers mainly poets, who got to know Roy Campbell fairly well after 1945. He knew quite well that we did not share his political opinions, but that never interfered with his friendliness. One of his closest friends, indeed, in those years, was George Orwell, who had fought on the other side in Spain. And the two English poets whom he got on with best, William Empson and Dylan Thomas, shared none of Campbell's opinions, either... No doubt he was an archaic figure, but he was also a gallant one... Mr Grigson's beetle-faced thug is not the Campbell that those who had the privilege of being at ease with him remember.'
94. John Heath-Stubbs, *Hindsights: An Autobiography* (London: Hodder & Stoughton, 1993), 120.
95. Ibid. 121.
96. G. S. Fraser, *A Stranger and Afraid: the autobiography of an intellectual* (Manchester: Carcanet New Press, 1983), 181–2.
97. Anne Ridler, letter to JH, 6 Oct. 1986. See also Ridler, *Memoirs* (Oxford: The Perpetua Press, 2004), 141.
98. T. S. Eliot, letter to John Hayward, 25 Sept. 1943 (Hayward Bequest).
99. Anne Ridler, letter to JH, 6 Oct. 1986. On 14 May 1951 Ridler wrote to WE: 'I have to report that I answered G. S. Fraser's letter, but before we could meet, he was off to the Far East, so now I suppose we shall have to converse by magazine again.' (Houghton)

100. George Watson in conversation with JH, 5 July 1996.
101. Fraser, *A Stranger and Afraid*, 181.
102. Canetti, *Party in the Blitz*, 49.
103. Paddy Fraser, 'G. S. Fraser: A Memoir', 10, 13.
104. Paddy Fraser, letter to JH, 15 May 2005. Janet Hopewell, who has written a doctoral dissertation on Fraser, adds that 'there is evidence from students and colleagues to suggest that the GSF/WE rapport was, at times, less than cordial! At a party given by the Frasers in Leicester in the late Sixties, WE needled his host to the extent that he stormed out into the street, on an icy evening, fell and smashed his spectacles, and had to be ferried to Coventry to have broken glass removed from his face. This GSF (not surprisingly) found terrifying.

    'If there was a rivalry between GSF and WE, then I think it would have been one-sided, and fuelled by Fraser's own feelings of inadequacy. He certainly felt that as a poet, he had failed to meet Empson's expectations of him, after his early "Letter to Anne Ridler". And I think he knew that as a critic, he was not in Empson's class' (Letter to JH, 8 Feb. 1990.)
105. 'George Fraser really would be a good appointment,' WE wrote to Bonamy Dobrée at Leeds (6 May 1955). 'I hear that the poets to whom he is always being kind are always suspecting that he is playing some deep ploy, merely *because* he is always doing justice and acting as sensibly as he can all the time … I would rather have him out of London because there he can't stop looking after too many lame dogs all the time' (Leeds).
106. Fraser, *A Stranger and Afraid*, 182.
107. Ibid. 180.
108. Tom Scott quoted ibid.
109. Paddy Fraser, 'G. S. Fraser: A Memoir', 4: http://jacketmagazine.com/20/fraser.html
110. Ibid. 11.
111. 'A Nest of Singing Birds', *Picture Post*, 10 Aug. 1946, 23–5.
112. T. S. Eliot quoted in WE, letter to John Hayward, 28 Jan. 1944 (King's WE/JDH/11).
113. Woodrow Wyatt, *Confessions of an Optimist* (London: Collins, 1985), 96.

3. CHINABOUND

1. Peter Quennell, *A Superficial Journey through Tokyo and Peking* (London: Faber & Faber, 1932), 217.
2. *Peita* is the abbreviation of *Kuo-li Pei-ching Ta-hsueh* ('National Peking University'): this full name includes the elements *Pei* (as in the first syllable of Peiping or Beijing), meaning 'north', *ta* 'large', and *hsueh* 'study'. See further L. C. Arlington and William Lewisohn, *In Search of Old Peking* (1935, reprinted Oxford, 1987); George N. Kates, *The Years That Were Fat: The Last of*

Old China (1952; Cambridge, Mass.: MIT Press, 1967); John Blofeld, *City of Lingering Splendour: A Frank Account of Old Peking's Exotic Pleasures* (London: Hutchinson, 1961).

3. HE, letter to Molly Empson, 15 July 1947 (Sheffield).
4. Quennell, *A Superficial Journey*, 187.
5. WE, 'India on China' (book review), *The Listener*, 8 Oct. 1953, 596.
6. WE, letter to John Hayward (WE/JDH/13); King's.
7. HE, letter to Molly Empson, 15 July 1947 (Sheffield).
8. Nicholas R. Lardy, 'Economic recovery and the 1st Five-Year Plan', in *The Cambridge History of China*, 14: *The People's Republic, Part I: The Emergence of Revolutionary China 1949–1965*, ed. Roderick MacFarquhar and John K. Fairbank (Cambridge: Cambridge University Press, 1987), 149–50. Compare Beverley Hooper (*China Stands Up*, 86): 'Hyper-inflation had taken the gold yuan, issued in August 1948 at four to US$1, to 205,000 to US$1, when the Communists entered Nanjing in late April 1949 and over 23 million to US$1 on the eve of their victory in Shanghai a month later.'
9. Translation courtesy of Christopher Heywood. Cf. Suzanne Pepper, *Civil War in China: The Political Struggle, 1945–1949* (Berkeley, Los Augeles, and London: University of California Press, 1976), 63.
10. WE, letter to John Hayward, 13 April 1948 (King's: WE/JDH/12).
11. WE, letter to Ian Parsons, 21 Nov. 1947 (Reading).
12. A. Doak Barnett, *China on the Eve of Communist Takeover* (London: Thames & Hudson, 1963), 40–1.
13. WE, letter to John Hayward, 18 May 1948; King's College (WE/JDH/13).
14. WE, 'Pei-Ta before the Siege', 6.
15. Jin Di, 'The Voice of an English Poet—In Memory of Professor William Empson', *Shijie Wenxue* (*World Literature*, Beijing), no. 5 (1984), 294–302; translation courtesy of Professor Jin Di.
16. WE, letter to John Hayward, 13 April 1948 (King's WE/JDH/12).
17. Interviews with Professor Huang Ming-yeh, 14 March 1984; Professor Qi Sheng-qiao, 27 March 1984.
18. HE, letter to Irene and John Vincent, 27 Dec. 1949 (Sheffield).
19. HE, letter to Walter Brown, 17 April 1950 (Sheffield).
20. James J. Y. Liu, letter to JH, 14 May 1984. Liu was enrolled to study English Literature at National Tsing Hua University, but attended Empson's lectures on Shakespeare and modern poetry at both Tsing Hua and Peita. 'I also struggled through his *Seven Types of Ambiguity*, even though he had warned us to keep off it. After one semester at Tsing Hua I left for England, having been awarded a British Council scholarship' (James J. Y. Liu, *The Interlingual Critic* (Bloomington: Indiana University Press, 1982), p.xiv).
21. WE, letter to Linda Grier (British Council), 18 Nov. 1948 (Houghton carbon).
22. WE, fragment of letter to an unknown recipient (Houghton carbon).

23. WE, 'Preface' to a collection of essays (TS copy in Houghton).
24. Interview with Liu Jo-tuan, Beijing, 26 March 1984.
25. Zhang Jin-yan, 'Reminiscences of William Empson', with letter to JH of 14 Feb. 1986.
26. WE, fragment of a letter to an unknown recipient (Houghton carbon).
27. Interview with Huang Ming-yeh, Beijing, 14 March 1984.
28. WE, letter to Linda Grier (British Council), 18 Nov. 1948 (Houghton carbon).
29. Interview with Liu Jo-tuan, Beijing, 26 March 1984.
30. See obituary of Linda Grier (1880–1967) in *The Times*, 23 Aug. 1967, 8.
31. Linda Grier, letter to WE, 24 Dec. 1948 (Houghton).
32. WE, letter to Linda Grier, British Council, 18 Nov. 1948 (Houghton carbon).
33. Ibid.
34. *SCW*, 362.
35. Pepper, *Civil War in China*, 76.
36. WE, letter to John Hayward, 18 May 1948; King's College, Cambridge: Hayward Collection: WE/JDH/13.
37. WE, 'Pei-Ta before the Siege', *Arrows* (Sheffield University), no. 78, 7.
38. WE, letter to Ian Parsons, 29 Feb. 1948 (Reading).

4. KENYON COLLEGE, SUMMER 1948

1. WE, letter to HE, 24 June 1948 (Sheffield). 'This is very English country,' WE wrote to his publisher on 12 July 1948, 'with rain and big trees and mixed farming, but at present very muggy and hot.' (Reading).
2. John Crowe Ransom, memo, 9 March 1949 (Kenyon College Archives).
3. Lois Chevalier, letter to Dayle Frazier (*Columbus Despatch*), 9 March 1949 (carbon copy in Kenyon Archives).
4. WE, letter to HE, 8 Aug. 1948.
5. WE, letter to HE, 29 June 1948.
6. WE, letter to HE, 21 Aug. 1948.
7. Ed Watkins, memo, 9 March 1949 (Kenyon College Archives).
8. *Newsweek* quoted in Thomas Boardman Greenslade, *Kenyon College - Its Third Half Century* (Kenyon College, 1975), 118.
9. WE, letter to Ian Parsons, 12 July 1948 (Reading). F. O. Matthiessen (1902–1950) was a prestigious left-wing intellectual; author of the influential *American Renaissance* (1941) and of *From the Heart of Europe* (1948). Depressed by world conditions, he was to commit suicide on 1 April 1950. See William E. Cain, *F. O. Matthiessen and the Politics of Criticism* (Madison: University of Wisconsin Press, 1988); Leo Marx, 'The Double Consciousness and the Cultural Politics of F. O. Matthiessen', *Monthly Review* 34 (February 1983); Frederick C. Stern, *F. O. Matthiessen: Christian Socialist as Critic* (Chapel Hill: University of South Carolina Press, 1981).

10. WE, letter to HE, 29 June 1948.
11. Ibid.
12. John Crowe Ransom, memo, 9 March 1949 (Kenyon College Archives).
13. WE, letter to HE, 8 Aug. 1948.
14. WE, letter to HE, 29 June 1948.
15. Ibid.
16. Charles Coffin, memo, 9 March 1949 (Kenyon College Archives).
17. Eric Bentley, letter to JH, 30 July 1988.
18. Ed Watkins, memo, 9 March 1949 (Kenyon College Archives).
19. John Crowe Ransom, *The New Criticism*, (Norfolk, Conn.: New Directions, 1941), 280.
20. Ibid. 184–5; cited in Young, *Gentleman in a Dustcoat*, 353.
21. Ransom quoted in Thomas Daniel Young, *Gentleman in a Dustcoat: A Biography of John Crowe Ransom* (Baton Rouge: Louisiana State University Press), 355.
22. Ransom, *New Criticism*, cited in Young, *Gentleman in a Dustcoat*, 355.
23. WE, 'A Theoretical Point', in *John Crowe Ransom: A Tribute from the Community of Letters*', supplement to the *Kenyon Collegian*, 90 (1964), 36.
24. WE, letter to HE, 13 July 1948.
25. Ibid.
26. Bernard Heringman, letter to WE, 9 Aug. 1989.
27. John Unterecker, letter to JH, 25 Sept. 1987. The exchange has been published as 'Three Critics on One Poem: Hart Crane's "Voyages III" ', in *Essays in Criticism* 46: 1 (January 1996), 16–27; in *SSS*, 233–42.
28. WE, letter to HE, 29 June 1948.
29. WE, letter to HE, 13 July 1948.
30. Lois Chevalier, letter to Dayle Frazier, 9 March 1949 (Kenyon College Archives).
31. WE, letter to HE, 30 July 1948.
32. Ibid.
33. William Troy, *Poetry*. July 1949.
34. Richard Wilbur, *Sewanee Review*, Jan.–March 1950.
35. WE, letter to HE, 8 Aug. 1948.
36. WE, letter to Ian Parsons, 23 Aug. 1948 (Reading).
37. WE, letter to HE, 21 Aug. 1948.
38. John Crowe Ransom, memo, 9 March 1949 (Kenyon College Archives).

5. SIEGE AND LIBERATION

1. WE, letter to Linda Grier, 19 Nov. 1948 (Houghton carbon).
2. Derk Bodde, *Peking Diary: A Year of Revolution* (London: Jonathan Cape, 1951), 18.
3. *The Cambridge History of China*, 13: *Republican China 1912–1949, Part 2*, ed. John King Fairbank and Albert Feuerwerker (Cambridge, 1986), 744.

4. Maria Yen, *The Umbrella Garden: A Picture of Student Life in Red China* (New York: Macmillan, 1954), 63.

5. Yen, *The Umbrella Garden*, 9–10.

6. Van der Sprenkel, 'Report on my tenure of the subsidized post at National Nankai University—1948–1949', 1 (Courtesy of Mrs Sybille van der Sprenkel). Otto van der Sprenkel was Empson's counterpart at the National Nankai University in Tientsin. A scholarly and genial man of Dutch extraction, the same age as Empson, he had graduated from LSE and lectured in political science at Toronto University, then for the Workers' Educational Association in London (under Harold Laski, R. H. Tawney, and G. D. H. Cole), before starting to study Chinese in his late thirties and becoming a part-time lecturer in history at the School of Oriental and African Studies just prior to his appointment in China (he would later become a professor of Oriental Civilization at the Australian National University in Canberra).

7. C. P. Fitzgerald, *The Birth of Communist China* (Harmondsworth, Middx.: Pelican Books, 1965), 105–6.

8. WE, 'Pei-Ta before the Siege', *Arrows* (Sheffield University), no. 78, 7.

9. David Finkelstein, '57 Years Inside China: An American's Odyssey', *ASIA*, 2: 5 (Jan./Feb. 1980), 10. The *Daily Telegraph* noted on Winter's death (27 Jan. 1987, 16): 'Prof. Robert Winter, who has died in Peking, aged 100, was an American academic who taught English and Shakespeare studies to Chinese for more than 60 years... Winter grew up in rural Indiana and studied at Wabash University under the poet Ezra Pound before going to the Sorbonne and Italy. He lectured at Wabash, Northwestern and Chicago universities before taking up his first Chinese post at Nanking in 1923.'

10. Interview with Liu Yuan Zi, Kunming, 4 Nov. 1988.

11. Zhu Yongiang, 'Thank You, Professor Winter', offprint from *Beijing Ribao* (Dec. 1984), in Richards Collection, Magdalene College, Cambridge.

12. Finkelstein, '57 Years Inside China', 11.

13. HE, letter to WE, 5 July 1948 (Sheffield).

14. Finkelstein, '57 Years Inside China', 11.

15. HE, untitled TS (2pp.) beginning 'Amongst democratic elements in China', Peiping, 30 Aug. 1948 (copy in Sheffield).

16. HE, letter to Dorothy Woodman, 30 Aug. 1948 (Sheffield).

17. See also Tom Fisher, 'Wu Han: The "Upright Official" as a Model in the Humanities', in *China's Establishment Intellectuals*, ed. by Carol Lee Hamrin and Timothy Cheek (Armonk, New York: M. E. Sharpe, 1986), 155–84.

18. WE, 'Pei-Ta before the Siege', 7.

19. Interview with Mrs Sybille van der Sprenkel, 27 Dec. 1988.

20. HE, letter to WE, 21 Sept. 1948 (Sheffield). David Kidd was to publish a memoir, *All the Emperor's Horses* (London: John Murray, 1961), which included this account of the silly preliminaries to his marriage to a Chinese woman named Aimee (Amy) Wu:

'Hetta was to sponsor me, and I asked her if she had brought her seal.

'I should explain that everyone in China has a seal. It is the equivalent of a signature, which is not valid there, the Chinese being convinced that a signature can easily be copied but that no two seals are alike ...

' "I brought a whole bloody sackful," Hetta said, dumping a collection of seals of all sizes from her handbag onto a table. "Some of them are mine, and some are William's, and some are the ones the children use, and I don't know where we got the others. But we must use all of them on your certificate. They'll look *very* important" ' (18).

See also Kidd, 'Outrage in China', *Connoisseur*, March 1984.

21. JH, interview with David Kidd (Kyoto), 10 April 1984.
22. WE wrote of Walter Brown, in an undated draft testimonial: 'I gladly recommend Mr Brown as a teacher of English language to Asiatics, at all levels. I have seen him in operation at Peking and realise his great ability at such work, chiefly from his energy sympathy and powers of encouragement. He is also well acquainted with the theory of the subject; he would be very capable of drawing up a scheme for other teachers to follow, and to advise on the results.'
23. WE was to write of Parker, in a later reference: 'I thought he showed great energy and efficiency. He got together a considerable library, well housed and catalogued, arranged lectures, gramophone recitals, plays, and so on; and made the Council centre well thought of by the Chinese, because it was obviously useful, at a time when there was considerable political suspicion to be overcome. He took to giving classes to teach the English language, which is not usual for a British Council centre, perhaps feeling it was less open to suspicion than more cultural activities. These were well attended and were considered to be giving rapid results. I think Mr Parker adaptable, and able to get on with people, as well as enterprising and energetic' (Houghton).
24. Interview with Sybille van der Sprenkel, 27 Dec. 1988.
25. Yen, *The Umbrella Garden*, 11.
26. *The Cambridge History of China*, 13: *Republican China 1912–1949, Part 2*, 777.
27. Bodde, *Peking Diary*, 59.
28. WE, letter to Ian Parsons, 20 Nov. 1948 (Reading).
29. WE, letter to Molly Empson, 11 Dec. 1948 (Houghton carbon).
30. C. P. Fitzgerald, *The Birth of Communist China*, 113–14.
31. See obituary of Martin Buxton in *The Times*, 20 Oct. 1966, 14.
32. Interview with Sybille van der Sprenkel, 27 Dec. 1988.
33. WE, letter to Molly Empson, 11 Dec. 1948 (Houghton carbon).
34. Quoted in A. Doak Barnett, *China on the Eve of Communist Takeover* (London: Thames & Hudson), 318.
35. Fitzgerald, *The Birth of Communist China*, 115.
36. Yen, *The Umbrella Garden*, 12.
37. Barnett, *China on the Eve*, 322.

38. WE, letter to John Crowe Ransom, 8 Jan. 1949.
39. WE, letter to Ian Parsons, 'New Year 1949' (Reading).
40. Bodde, *Peking Diary*, 89.
41. WE, letter to C. P. Fitzgerald, 14 Aug. 1951 (Houghton carbon).
42. Barnett, *China on the Eve of Communist Takeover*, 328.
43. WE, letter to Ian Parsons, 'New Year 1949' (Reading).
44. WE, letter to John Crowe Ransom, 8 Jan. 1949.
45. WE, *MG*, 255.
46. See also Beverley Hooper, *China Stands Up: Ending the Western Presence, 1948–1950* (Sydney: Allen & Unwin, 1986), 44.
47. Fitzgerald, *The Birth of Communist China*, 115.
48. Mao Tse-tung quoted in Barnett, *China on the Eve*, 331. The new Political Consultative Conference was eventually convened in Peiping (Beijing), 21–28 Oct.; attended by a huge number of representatives from the CCP, the Democratic League and other groups, it adopted among other measures the Common Programme of the PRC.
49. Barnett, *China on the Eve*, 334.
50. Hu Shih quoted in Philip West, *Yenching University and Sino-Western Relations, 1916–1952* (Cambridge, Mass., and London: Harvard University Press, 1976), 182.
51. Suzanne Pepper, *Civil War in China: The Political Struggle, 1945–1949* (Berkeley, Los Angeles, London: University of California Press, 1978), 227.
52. K. M. Panikkar, *In Two Chinas: Memoirs of a Diplomat* (London: Allen & Union, 1955), 45.
53. Alan Winnington, *Breakfast with Mao: Memoirs of a Foreign Correspondent* (London: Lawrence & Wishart, 1986), 103.
54. Bodde, *Peking Diary*, 100–1.
55. Barnett, *China on the Eve*, 342.
56. See Andrew Roth, 'Peiping's New Look', *The Nation*, 5 March 1949, 273.
57. WE, 'Teaching English in the Far East and England', *SSS*, 214.
58. WE, letter to Ian Parsons, 19 June 1949 (Reading).
59. Bertrand Russell (with Dora Russell), *The Prospects of Industrial Civilization* (London: George Allen & Unwin, 1923; second edn., 1959), 146.
60. WE, letter to Martin Buxton, no date, 1949 (Houghton carbon).
61. WE, fragment of undated letter, no date (Houghton carbon).
62. WE, notebook (Houghton).
63. Ernest Bevin quoted in Donald R. McCoy, *The Presidency of Harry S Truman* (Lawrence, Kan.: University Press of Kansas, 1984), 195.
64. Russell, *The Prospects of Industrial Civilization*, 79.
65. WE, undated letter to John Crowe Ransom (Kenyon archive).
66. Mao Tse-tung quoted in O. van der Sprenkel, N. Guillain, and M. Lindsay, *New China: Three Views* (London: Turnstile Press, 1950), 186, 198.

67. Michael Lindsay's later publications include *China and The Cold War* (1955) and *The Unknown War: North China 1937–1945* (London: Bergström & Boyle Books, 1975). See obituary by John Gittings in the *Guardian*, 8 March 1994. Of Lindsay, HE wrote at the time, in a letter to an unknown recipient: 'I thought Michael Lindsay was pretty awful, all he did here was to say how stinking Soviet Russia is and I rather think he won't be invited to come again. Also he didn't have anything to say about England and got very cagey whenever British foreign policy was brought up. He seems to be some kind of a mouldy Liberal intellectual and for an intellectual his thinking is about as muddled and outdated as is possible, even for a liberal' (Sheffield).

68. Michael Lindsay, 'China: Report of a Visit', *International Affairs*, Jan. 1950, 27–8.

69. WE, letter to Jin Di, 13 March 1980 (Jin Di).

70. John King Fairbank, *The Great Chinese Revolution: 1800–1985* (New York: Perennial Library, 1987), 278.

71. Winnington, *Breakfast with Mao*, 104–5.

72. Barnett, *China on the Eve of Communist Takeover*, 353.

73. Roth, 'Peiping's New Look', 275.

74. WE, letter to Ian Parsons, 19 June 1949 (Reading).

75. Barnett, *China on the Eve of Communist Takeover*, 355.

76. WE, letter to Ian Parsons, 19 June 1949 (Reading).

77. Hooper, *China Stands Up*, 73.

78. HE, letter to 'Pat', 7 Sept. 1949 (Sheffield).

79. HE, letter to unknown recipient (Sheffield).

80. Winter went on in the same letter (7 May 1972): '[Ch'i] really came because he was fascinated by the personal freedom of William and myself - unimaginable to a Chinese, and he acquired an unfortunate taste for such freedom. During the five years of the cultural revolution he was tortured by the same people who tortured me - but infinitely worse; his health is quite broken - and of course we never spoke to each other, Then one day last April he walked into my house and asked me to start work again. I understood at once that he had again been appointed to watch the foreigners as no one else was qualified, and that he would have to make a verbatim report of everything we said' (Richards Papers, Magdalene, Box 53).

81. Pepper, *Civil War in China*, 414.

82. WE, letter to Ian Parsons, 19 June 1949 (Reading).

83. Michael Lindsay, 'China: Report of a Visit', International Affairs (January 1950), 22–31.

84. Pepper, *Civil War in China*, 194.

85. WE, TS draft letters to IAR, n.d. (? Sept. 1948); Houghton.

86. WE, letter to IAR, 22 January 1949: typescript transcript in Rockefeller Archive Center: Harvard U - I. A. Richards collection, record group 1.1, series 200, box 234, folder 2797.

87. IAR, letter to John Marshall, 3 February 1949, in ibid.

88. WE, unfinished and undated letter ('Dear Sir') (Houghton carbon)

89. WE, letter to Chao Hsiung Chao, 1 July 1949 (Houghton carbon).

90. WE, letter to IAR, 6 Sept. 1949 (Magdalene).

91. WE, letter to IAR, 3 July 1949 (Magdalene).

92. WE, letter to Chao Hsiung Chao, 1 July 1949 (Houghton carbon).

93. WE, letter to IAR, 6 Sept. 1949 (Magdalene).

94. WE, letter to IAR, 3 July 1949 (Magdalene).

95. WE, letter to IAR, 6 Sept. 1949 (Magdalene).

96. WE, letter to IAR, 3 July 1949 (Magdalene).

97. WE, letter to IAR, 6 Sept. 1949 (Magdalene).

98. WE, letter to IAR, 3 July 1949 (Magdalene).

99. Kidd, *All the Emperor's Horses*, 49.

100. HE, letter to 'Dear Comrade' (probably Eva Ricketts in London), 10 Oct. 1949 (Sheffield).

101. Ibid.

102. Peter Townsend, *China Phoenix: The Revolution in China* (London: Cape, 1955), 217.

103. Quoted in Richard L. Walker, *China Under Communism: The First Five Years* (London: George Allen & Unwin, 1956), 181.

104. HE, letter addressed 'Dear Comrade' (probably Eva Ricketts), 10 October 1949 (Sheffield). For the ceremonial in 1950, see Nicolas Guillen, 'My Second Visit to Peking', *China Reconstructs*, 3: 1 (Jan.-Feb. 1954), 18–19. The occasion in 1951 is related in Peter Lum, *Peking 1950–1953* (London: Robert Hale, 1958), 95–6.

6. THE NEW CHINA

1. The spelling 'Beijing' is the product of the Pinyin system of romanization: it corresponds to a fairly exact pronunciation of the city's name in Mandarin.

2. Quoted in Otto van der Sprenkel, Robert Guillain, and Michael Lindsay, *New China: Three Views* (London: Turnstile Press, 1950), 213.

3. Philip West, *Yenching University and Sino-Western Relations, 1916–1952* (Cambridge, Mass., and London: Harvard University Press, 1976), 206–7.

4. Maria Yen, *The Umbrella Garden: A Picture of Student Life in Red China* (New York: Macmillan, 1954), 130.

5. Ibid.

6. Ibid. 172–3.

7. WE, 'Teaching English in the Far East and England', *SSS*, 207.

8. WE, letter to Dean Coffin, 14 October 1949 (Houghton carbon).

9. Yen, *The Umbrella Garden*, 146.

10. Ibid. 134.

11. Kuo Mo-jo, report on the Chinese People's Political Consultative Conference, June 1950, quoted in Theodore H. E. Chen, *Thought Reform of the Chinese Intellectuals* (Hong Kong: Hong Kong University Press, 1960), 16–17.
12. Yen, *The Umbrella Garden*, 169.
13. Robert Winter diary, Rockefeller Archives, 352–3.
14. WE, letter to John Hayward, 25 Aug. 1950 (King's: WE/JDH/14).
15. Peter Townsend, *China Phoeuix: The Revolution in China* (London: Cape, 1955), 315.
16. HE, letter to Dick (Carline), 30 March 1950 (Sheffield); cf. 'Foreword' to *Contemporary Chinese Woodcuts* (London: Fore Publications & Collet's Holdings, Ltd., 1950).
17. Jack Chen, *Inside the Cultural Revolution* (London: Sheldon Press, 1974), 64–5.
18. Robert Winter, 'Tsing Hua University', *China Monthly Review*, Oct. 1960, 57.
19. Robert Winter, Rockefeller Archive collection, Robert Winter Diary, 348–50.
20. Theodore H. E. Chen, *Thought Reform of the Chinese Intellectuals* (Hong Kong, 1960), 25.
21. Mineo Nakajima, 'Foreign Relations: from the Korean War to the Bandung Line', 266.
22. Townsend, *China Phoenix*, 390.
23. WE, letter to John Hayward, 25 Aug. 1950 (King's: WE/JDH/14).
24. HE, letter to Irene and John (Vincent), 27 Dec. 1949 (Sheffield).
25. Ibid.
26. Ibid.
27. HE, letter to unknown recipient (Sheffield).
28. See K.M. Panikkar, *In Two Chinas: Memoirs of a Diplomat* (London: Allen & Unwin, 1955), 77.
29. WE, 'Fei Hsiao-tung' (letter), *Encounter*, 5: 6 (Nov. 1955), 60.
30. O. Edmund Clubb, 'Chinese Communist Strategy in Foreign Relations', *The Annals of The American Academy*, Sept. 1951, 164–6.
31. David Caute, *The Fellow-Travellers: Intellectual Friends of Communism* (New Haven and London: Yale University Press, 1988), 359.

7. CHANGES IN CHINA; AND KENYON AGAIN

1. Peter Townsend, *China Phoenix: The Revolution in China* (London: Cape, 1955), 390.
2. See obituary of Sir John Hutchison (1890–1965) in *The Times*, 15 July 1965, 14.
3. WE, draft TS letter to John Hayward, 2 July 1950 (Houghton). David Hawkes (b. 1923) read Chinese at Oxford, and was a Research Student at the National Peking University, 1948–51; later Professor of Chinese at Oxford University, 1959–71, and a Research Fellow of All Souls, 1973–83.

His publications include *The Songs of the South: An Ancient Chinese Anthology of Poems by Qu Yuan and Other Poets* (1985); a 3-volume translation of *The Story of the Stone* (1973, 1977, 1980); *Classical, Modern and Humane: essays in Chinese Literature*, ed. J. Munford and Siu-kit Wong (1989).

4. WE, letter to John Hayward, 25 Aug. 1950: King's WE/JDH/14.

5. ' "Fundamentally, I'm an inventor": I. A. Richards at Eighty' (interview by Jane Watkins), *Harvard Magazine* (Sept. 1973), 54.

6. IAR Diary, entry under June Cash Account.

7. IAR Diary, entries on 4 Aug. 1950, and under May Cash Account.

8. IAR Diary, entries on 3 Aug. 1950, and under May Cash Account.

9. IAR Diary, entry under Nov. Cash Account.

10. IAR, undated letter to Langdon [Warner], transcribed in diary under 'Cash Accounts: April', 1950; also in Nov. Cash Account.

11. IAR Diary, entry on 3 Aug. 1950 (Magdalene).

12. IAR Diary, entry on 13 May 1950.

13. ' "Fundamentally, I'm an inventor" ', 53.

14. 'William Empson Remembers I. A. Richards', *LRB*, 5 June–18 June 1980, 14.

15. WE, draft TS letter to John Hayward, 2 July 1950 (Houghton).

16. Memo by John Marshall re interview with IAR, 17 Nov. 1950; Rockefeller Archives 1. 1., series 200, box 235, folder 2798.

17. Charles B. Fahs, letter to IAR, 18 Jan. 1950; Rockefeller Archives 1. 1, series 200 R, box 235, folder 2798.

18. Memo by CBF re. interview with IAR, 17 Nov. 1950; Rockefeller Archives, Harvard U - I. A. Richards, Record Group 1. 1, Series 200, Box 235, folder 2798.

19. IAR Diary, entry on 10 April 1950.

20. HE, letter to Walter Brown, 11 April 1950 (Sheffield).

21. IAR Diary, Monday 29 May 1950. HE was to write to Walter Brown in mid-1950: 'I never argue any more, I've learned the precious art of listening with sympathy and agreeing without the appearance of fawning, so all tongues are miraculously loosened and out it pours.' (Sheffield) More commonly, she was prone to indulge herself with too many 'voddies' (as she called them).

22. HE, letter to Walter Brown, April–May 1950 (Sheffield). Andrew Roth remarked in conversation with JH that WE was 'always drunk by 10.30 in the morning, and incomprehensible'.

23. K. M. Panikkar, *In Two Chinas: Memoirs of a Diplomat* (London: Allen & Unwin, 1955), 97.

24. Frank Moraes, *Report on Mao's China* (New York: Macmillan, 1953), 17. With the onset of the Korean crisis, HE wrote to WE on 19 July 1950: 'Panekar the Indian Ambassador to whom I spoke today at the [Peking] Club seems very pessimistic - he says he gives it till September to blow up but I think he's rather given to alarums' (Sheffield).

25. HE, letter to Walter Brown, 'Tuesday 20th' [June-July 1950] (Sheffield).

26. HE, letter to WE, 13 July 1950 (Sheffield).

27. HE, letter to WE, 18 July 1950 (Sheffield).

28. C. P. Fitzgerald's account is reported to JH in a letter from Vieta Dyer (Svetlana Rimsky-Korsakoff), 19 Feb. 1989. See also Michael Hollington, 'Richards and Empson in China: The Recollections of Professor C. P. ('Possum') Fitzgerald', *A.U.M.L.A.: Journal of the Australian University Modern Language Association*, no. 86 (Nov. 1986), 89.

29. HE, letter to 'Dick' (Carline), 30 March 1950 (Sheffield). To John Blofeld she wrote likewise on 14 April 1950: 'The children wax like weeds' (Sheffield).

30. WE, letter to Kathleen Raine, 30 Nov. 1951 (BL).

31. WE, draft TS letter to John Hayward, 2 July 1950 (Houghton).

32. Ibid.

33. See John Kobler, *Henry Luce: His Time, Life and Fortune* (London: Macdonald, 1968).

34. Don Wiener, letter to JH, 16 Oct. 1988.

35. WE, draft TS letter to John Hayward, 2 July 1950 (Houghton).

36. Ibid.

37. WE, letter to HE, 25 June 1950 (Sheffield).

38. *Selected Letters of John Crowe Ransom*, ed. Thomas Daniel Young and George Core (Baton Rouge and London: Louisiana State University Press, 1985), 355.

39. WE, draft TS letter to John Hayward, 2 July 1950 (Houghton).

40. Interview with Lauro Martines, Jan. 1994.

41. George Lanning, 'Memories of the School of English', in *John Crowe Ransom: A Tribute from the Community of Letters*, supplement to the *Kenyon Collegian*, 90 (1964), 33.

42. Priscilla Sutcliffe, letter to J. H. Willis, Jr., 15 Sept. 1966 (Kenyon College Archives).

43. Ibid.

44. Maurice Charney, letter to JH, 23 Aug. 1988.

45. Don Wiener, letter to JH, 16 Oct. 1988.

46. Lanning, 'Memories of the School of English', p. 35.

47. Ibid.

48. Interview with Lauro Martines.

49. Interview with Lauro Martines.

50. George Soule, letter to JH, 3 and 19 June 1985.

51. *The Letters of Robert Lowell*, ed. Saskia Hamilton (New York and London, 2005), 310

52. Don Wiener, letter to JH, 16 Oct. 1988.

53. Soule, letter to JH, 3 June 1985.

54. WE, letter to HE, 25 June 1950 (Sheffield).

55. Don Wiener, letter to JH, 16 Oct. 1988.

56. WE interviewed by Christopher Norris and David Wilson, 20 Dec. 1970.

57. Marian Janssen, *The Kenyon Review, 1939–1970: A Critical History* (Baton Rouge and London: Louisiana State University Press, 1990), 169.

58. WE, draft TS letter to John Hayward, 2 July 1950 (Houghton).

59. Don Wiener, letter to JH, 16 Oct. 1988.

60. WE, undated letter to IAR (1950), from 'Redman's house' (Magdalene). John Crowe Ransom was to write to Empson on 6 Sept. 1952, following the first season at Indiana University (where the summer school had just been relocated): 'in your place we had Burke again. He has not reformed his views and practices in any way but had become possibly a little more gingerly in extending himself in public; I got to liking him more than ever, as his modesty and good will were unfailing' (Houghton).

61. F. O. Matthiessen committed suicide on 1 April 1950. A week later, when IAR reported the sorry news to the Empsons in Beijing, HE wrote to Walter Brown (11 April): 'Matthiesson [*sic*] (Harvard) has committed suicide by jumping out of a window and William says Richards thinks it's because he was being shot at so much for having Left sympathies. William knew him and thought him a very sober and balanced chap who was rather in favour of Wallace's policies' (Sheffield). Within a few weeks, it seems, WE was being informally sounded out as a possible replacement for Matthiessen at Harvard, for HE wrote again to Brown on 19 May: '[William] had a curious letter from Hightower at Harvard today saying in brackets, "I suppose you heard of Matthiessen's suicide, why don't you talk to Richards about coming here?" A difficult offer to answer' (Sheffield).

62. James Atlas, *Delmore Schwartz: The Life of an American Poet* (New York: Farrar, Straus & Giroux, 1977), 289–90.

63. WE, undated letter to IAR (1950), from 'Redmans' house' (Magdalene).

64. WE, draft TS letter to John Hayward, 2 July 1950 (Houghton).

65. WE, letter to HE, 25 June 1950 (Sheffield).

66. WE, 'Teaching English in the Far East and England', *SSS*, 204–5.

67. WE, letter to John Hayward, 25 Aug. 1950: King's: WE/JDH/14/. HE wrote to WE on 24 July 1950, 'I wish I could be with you for your speech but of course you will have made out alright' (Sheffield).

68. WE, letter to HE, 25 June 1950 (Sheffield).

69. Don Wiener, letter to JH, 16 Oct. 1988.

70. WE, letter to HE, 25 June 1950 (Sheffield).

71. WE, letter to John Hayward, 25 Aug. 1950: King's WE/JDH/14.

72. Paddy Fraser, 'G. S. Fraser: A Memoir', *Jacket* magazine 20 (Dec. 2002), p. 17 (hhttp://jacketmagazine.com/20/html)

73. R. Fukuhara in *The Rising Generation*, 1 Nov. 1950.

74. WE, 'Rintaro Fukuhara', *The Rising Generation*, 1 June 1981, p. 16.

8. QUITTING COMMUNIST CHINA

1. WE, letter to Raine, 2 Oct. 1950 (Houghton carbon).
2. Ibid.
3. Peter Townsend, *China Phoenix: The Revolution in China* (London: Cape, 1955), 217.
4. WE, letter to Raine, 2 Oct. 1950 (Houghton carbon).
5. McCoy, *The Presidency of Harry S. Truman*, 245.
6. 'Ko min-chu tang-p'ai lien-ho hsuan-yen' (Joint Declaration of the Democratic Parties, 4 November 1950), *JMJP*, 5 Nov. 1950; in Nakajima, 'Foreign Relations', 275.
7. Townsend, *China Phoenix*, 388.
8. Ibid. 388–9.
9. Theodore H. E. Chen, *Thought Reform of the Chinese Intellectuals* (Hong Kong: Hong Kong University Press, 1960), 27.
10. Chen, *Thought Reform*, 26.
11. Interview with Jin Di, 24 Sept. 1983.
12. JH, interview with Professor Bian Zhi-lin, Beijing, April 1984.
13. 'Resolutions of the First National Congress on Higher Education', trans. Hung Fan Wang, *People's Education* 1: 5 (September 1950); reprinted in *Chinese Communist Education: Records of the First Decade*, ed. Stewart Fraser (Nashville, Tenn.: Vanderbilt University Press, 1965), 95. HE had anticipated the progress of educational reform with unequivocal eagerness, in a letter to Walter Brown on 2 June 1950: 'It's good news about the changes in the university. A big conference is being held to thrash out a policy on education, and I think in particular on English teaching' (Sheffield).
14. WE, recommendations of texts: untitled and undated (Houghton carbon).
15. The phrase is taken from an article by Lu Tingi-yi (chief propagandist for the Communist Party), 'Education and Culture in New China', *People's China*, 1: 8 (16 April 1950); reprinted in *Chinese Communist Education*, ed. Fraser, 90.
16. WE, letter to Mr Emslie, 15 July 1951 (Houghton carbon). WE had written to Kathleen Raine on 14 May 1951 that HE might be returning to England with the boys, leaving WE to follow after a final year of teaching in Peking (BL).
17. Chou En-lai quoted in Chen, *Thought Reform*, 32.
18. Chen, *Thought Reform*, 31.
19. Cited ibid. 33.
20. Ma Yin-ch'u, 'Political Study Movement of the Faculty of Peking University', *Jen Min Jih Pao (People's Daily)*, 23 Oct. 1951; reprinted in *Chinese Communist Education*, ed. Fraser, 117–19. See also Fei Hsiao-t'ung, 'Educating the Educators', *China Weekly Review*, 29 July 1950, 157.
21. Maria Yen, *The Umbrella Garden: A Picture of Student Life In Red China* (New York, 1954), 254.
22. Ma, 'Political Study Movement of the Faculty of Peking University', 118.

23. WE, letter to IAR, 4 March 1951 (Magdalene).

24. WE, letter to Mr Hedley (British Council), 1 Nov. 1951 (Houghton carbon). Geoffrey Hedley responded with remarkable tortuousness on 8 Jan. 1952: 'in view of the higher cost of living in the United Kingdom it has been decided to increase your subsidy *outside* China from £720 per annum to £900 per annum. With the increase of £350 per annum *inside* China of which I have already informed you, your total subsidy *inside* China is brought up to £1,420 per annum but *outside* China your subsidy has been brought up from £720 to £900. In other words your subsidy *outside* China from 1st January 1951 is £900 per annum bringing your total subsidy *inside* China up to £1,420 per annum instead of a subsidy outside China of £720 with a Cost of Living allowance of £700 per annum which also gives a total of £1,420. This, you will see, is to your advantage.'

25. WE, letter to Pien Chih Lin (Bian Zhi-lin), 'Friday' (copy in Houghton). In the 1930s Bian Zhi-lin (1910–2000), distinguished poet and translator, corresponded with Christopher Isherwood, who admired his stories; one story, 'Red Trousers', was published in *Life & Letters* in 1939/40. After Liberation, when Bian returned from a spell at Oxford, he consulted WE about the poems he was writing. (JH, interview with Bian Zhi-lin, Beijing, March 1984).

26. WE, *A*, 143.

27. WE, undated report on teaching (Houghton carbon).

28. WE, draft letter to John Hayward, no date (1951)(Houghton).

29. WE, letter to John Hayward, no date, 1951 (King's WE/JDH/15).

30. WE, letter to John Hayward, 24 July 1951 (T. Hofmann).

31. Quoted in T.T., 'The Intellectual in the New China', *Problems of Communism*, 2: 2 (Washington, D C: International Information Administration, 1953), 2.

32. Mao Tse-tung quoted ibid.

33. Ibid.

34. Ibid. 3

35. Ibid. 7.

36. Ibid. 3–4.

37. WE, letter to Pien Chih Lin, 'Friday' (Houghton carbon).

38. Ibid.

39. WE, draft letter to John Hayward, 1951 (Houghton).

40. WE, letter to unknown addressee, 10 Sept. 1951 (Houghton carbon).

41. Ibid.

42. WE, 'Teaching English in the Far East and England', *SSS*, 214.

43. WE, letter to Martin Buxton, no date, 1949 (Houghton carbon).

44. WE, 'Report on Work in Progress. April 6th /50' (Houghton carbon).

45. WE, 'Teaching English in the Far East and England', *SSS*, 216.

46. Ralph and Nancy Lapwood, *Through the Chinese Revolution* (London: Spalding & Levy, 1954), 165.

47. William Vogt, *Road to Survival* (London: Victor Gollancz, 1949), 222–3, 222–5.
48. WE, 'Teaching English in the Far East and England', *SSS*, 215.
49. See also Peter Townsend, *China Phoenix: The Revolution in China* (London: Cape, 1955), 360.
50. WE, *MG*, 261.
51. WE, 'Teaching English in the Far East and England', *SSS*, 216.
52. W. M. Emslie, letter to Lionel Lamb, 31 May 1951 (PRO ref FO 924 930). Emslie went on, in the same letter, to reveal that Hetta had been making plans to return with the two boys to England in mid-1951: 'Professor Empson has been finding living difficult owing to the devaluation of sterling in China, and has twice written asking for consideration of subsidy adjustment without any reply. Mrs Empson has been taking English conversation classes at the University but with her projected return to England in the summer with their two children this contribution will have to cease.'
53. A. J. S. White, letter to J. P. G. Finch, 13 July 1951 (PRO FO 924 930).
54. Lionel Lamb, letter to Foreign Office, London, 8 Oct. 1951 (PRO FO 924 930).
55. Lionel Lamb, letter to Foreign Office, 10 Dec. (PRO FO 924 930).
56. WE, undated letter to Pien Chi-lin (Bian Zhi-lin) (Houghton carbon).
57. E. E. R. Church, Director of Personnel Department, British Council, letter to WE, 9 Jan. 1952.
58. Angela Udall, The British Council, letter to JH, 25 Aug. 1983. 'Unfortunately, the papers were destroyed in 1972.'
59. WE, letter to Pien Chih Lin, 2 Feb. 1952 (Houghton carbon).
60. WE, letter to Professor Pien Chih Lin, 2 Feb. 1952 (Houghton carbon).
61. PRO FO 924 799.
62. WE, *MG*, 263.
63. Interview with Mogador Empson, 9 Dec. 2005.
64. WE, letter to Martin Buxton, 30 March 1953 (ALS in Houghton; it is not known whether any version of this letter was ever posted).
65. Dorothea Hayward Scott, letter to JH, 15 July 1985.
66. WE, *MG*, 264.

9. FINAL RECKONING: THE AFFAIR OF FEI HSIAO-T'UNG

1. Mao Tse-tung quoted in Robert Jay Lifton, *Thought Reform and the Psychology of Totalism: A Study of 'brainwashing' in China* (London: Gollancz, 1961, 1962), 433.
2. John Gittings, *China Changes Face: The Road from Revolution 1949–1989* (Oxford: Oxford University Press, 1989), x.
3. WE, 'Teaching English in the Far East and England', *SSS*, 217.
4. The term 'brain-washing' was coined in 1951 by an American journalist, Edward Hunter, as a translation of the Chinese colloquialism *hsi nao* (literally 'wash brain').

5. Lifton, *Thought Reform*, 435–6.
6. Ralph and Nancy Lapwood, *Through the Chinese Revolution* (London: Spalding & Levy, 1954), 165, 171, and Svetlana Rimsky-Korsakoff, unpublished essay entitled 'Morning'.
7. Merle Goldman, 'The Party and the Intellectuals', in *The Cambridge History of China*, 14: *The People's Republic, Part I: The Emergence of Revolutionary China 1949–1965*, ed. Roderick MacFarquhar and John K. Fairbank (Cambridge, 1987), 224.
8. Lapwood, *Through the Chinese Revolution*, 169.
9. Lifton, *Thought Reform and the Psychology of Totalism*, 385.
10. See ibid. 260.
11. Quoted in Richard L. Walker, *China Under Communism: The First Five Years* (London: George Allen & Unwin, 1956), 212.
12. Chin Yueh-lin, 'Criticizing My Decadent Bourgeois Ideology', *Kuang Ming Jih Pao*, 17 April 1952; in *Chinese Communist Education*, 147–58.
13. Maria Yen, *The Umbrella Garden: A Picture of Student Life In Red China* (New York, 1954), 264.
14. Lionel Lamb, letter to Anthony Eden, 13 March 1952, FC 1741/2 (PRO ref. FO371/99B66).
15. Lifton, *Thought Reform and the Psychology of Totalism*, 15.
16. Ibid. 244, 383.
17. Ibid. 376.
18. Ibid. 376–7.
19. Ibid. 385, 378–9.
20. C. P. Fitzgerald, *Flood Tide in China* (London: Cresset Press, 1958), 42, 54.
21. Peter Townsend, *China Phoenix: The Revolution in China* (London: Cape, 1955), 342.
22. Townsend, *China Phoenix*, 343.
23. Lifton, *Thought Reform and the Psychology of Totalism*, 426.
24. Tsui Shu-chin, *From Academic Freedom to Brainwashing: The Tragic Ordeal of Professors in the Chinese Mainland*, Pamphlets on Chinese Affairs no. 17 (Taipei: China Culture Publishing Foundation, 1953), 43–4.
25. Fitzgerald, *Flood Tide in China*, 58.
26. Draft of 'Teaching English in the Far East and England' (Houghton).
27. Frank Moraes, *Report on Mao's China* (New York: Macmillan, 1953), 182.
28. WE, 'Report on China' (review of *Mandarin Red*, by James Cameron), *The Listener*, 9 June 1955, 1039.
29. WE, 'India on China' (review of *Report on Mao's China*, by Frank Moraes, and *Window on China*, by Raja Hutheesing), *The Listener*, 8 Oct. 1953, 595.
30. Frank Moraes, *Report on Mao's China*, 33.
31. Ibid. 596.
32. Ibid.

33. WE, 'China' (review of Basil Davidson, *Daybreak in China*), *New Statesman and Nation*, 20 June 1953, 750.

34. C. P. Fitzgerald, letter to Dorothea Richards, 18 Nov. 1952 (Magdalene College, Cambridge).

35. Ibid.

36. Fitzgerald, *Flood Tide in China*, 46–7.

37. Ibid., 53, 48.

38. Ibid. 195, 197.

39. See entry on Fei Xiaotong in Wolfgang Bartke, *Who's Who in the People's Republic of China* (K. G. Saur, 1987).

40. Helen Foster Snow, *My China Years* (London: Harrap, 1984), 98–9.

41. 'Report on China', *The Annals of the American Academy of Political and Social Science*, 277 (Sept. 1951), preface by H. Arthur Steiner, viii.

42. Karl A. Wittfogel, 'The Historical Position of Communist China: Doctrine and Reality', *The Review of Politics*, 16: 4 (Oct. 1954), 463–74.

43. See also the obituary of Wittfogel in *The Times*, 18 June 1988.

44. Karl A. Wittfogel, 'China—Then and Now (II)', *Encounter*, 4: 1 (Jan. 1955), 78–80.

45. Cedric Dover, 'Fei Hsiao-tung' (letter), *Encounter*, 5: 2 (Aug. 1955), 74. Gordon Bowker notes that George Orwell during his period at the wartime BBC 'was particularly generous to the young Eurasian writer Cedric Dover... although later he concluded that he was "dishonest" and too pro-Russian' (*George Orwell* (London: Little, Brown, 2003), 286).

46. WE, 'Fei Hsiao-tung' (letter), *Encounter*, 5: 2 (Aug. 1955), 74.

47. Karl A. Wittfogel, 'Fei Hsiao-tung' (letter), *Encounter*, 5: 2 (Aug. 1955), 74–5.

48. WE, 'Fei Hsiao-tung' (letter), *Encounter*, 5: 6 (Nov. 1955), 60.

49. Editorial comment on WE's letter, *Encounter*, 5: 6 (Nov. 1955), 60–1.

50. Leslie Fiedler (1917–2003), the son of American immigrants—'an urban American Jew... influenced by Marxist ideas, communist and Trotskyist', as he called himself—was born in New Jersey and educated at New York University. For a while he was a member of the Young Communist League and the Socialist Workers Party, but became fiercely anti-communist by the 1940s. Fiedler became known as an *enfant terrible* of American letters when he published in *Partisan Review* in 1948 a ground-breaking essay 'Come Back to the Raft Ag'in, Huck Honey' analysing the infantilistic and homoerotic elements in Mark Twain's fiction; it was an iconoclastic argument he developed into *Love and Death in the American Novel* (1960), a comprehensive psychosexual examination of American literature from the beginnings to Hemingway and Faulkner which emphasizes the theme of male escapism from a female-dominated society. Later works include *Waiting for the End: The American Literary Scene from Hemingway to Baldwin* (1964); *Fiedler on the Roof* (1991); and a collection of stories and two novels. In 1954–73 he was a fellow of the Indiana School of Letters (where he argued politics with WE in the summer

of 1954). See Mark Royden Winchell, *"Too Good to be True": The Life and Work of Leslie Fiedler* (Columbia and London: University of Missouri Press, 2002); obituaries in *The Daily Telegraph*, 3 Feb. 2003, 23; *The Guardian* (by Christopher Bigsby), 1 Feb. 2003; *The Independent* (by Andrew Rosenheim), 3 Feb. 2003, 16; *The Times*, 4 Feb. 2003, 3.

51. For a defence of Fiedler on the Rosenbergs, see Winchell, *"Too Good To Be True"*, 65–70. John Sutherland in his biography of Spender gives this single-sentence summary of Fiedler's case: 'Fiedler's thesis was that the spies had indubitably been guilty of passing atomic secrets to the Soviets' (*Stephen Spender: The Authorized Biography* (London: Viking, 2004), 372.

52. Leslie A. Fiedler, 'The Middle Against Both Ends', *Encounter*, 5: 5 (Aug. 1955), 16–23.

53. WE, letter to Leslie Fiedler, 4 Jan. 1956 (courtesy of the late Leslie Fiedler). In a follow-up letter to Fiedler (13 Feb. 1956), WE explained: 'It occurs to me, after the week-end, that my last letter to you was too solemn for the occasion; also that you may actually not know what the occasion was if you very reasonably don't take the magazine *Encounter*, in which case it is all bound to seem rather surprising.

     'Spender had published an article containing a "smear" on a distinguished Chinese acquaintance of mine (and of plenty of other people in England); so I thought it ought to be driven into his head that this practice was not welcome in England, and having started on this I have been trying to rout him out of a few of his innumerable bolt-holes in the matter. The chief object of writing to you was to send a carbon copy to him; I wouldn't have thought there was any need to tease you about your articles otherwise, though of course I meant what I said.' (Courtesy of the late Leslie Fiedler)

54. Stephen Spender, letter to Leslie Fiedler, 9 Jan. 1956 (copy in Houghton); Spender, letter to Alexander Korda, quoted in Sutherland, *Stephen Spender*, 372.

55. Frances Stonor Saunders, *Who Paid the Piper? The CIA and the Cultural Cold War* (London: Granta Books, 1999), 188.

56. Sutherland, *Stephen Spender*, 372. On Kristol, see Stonor Saunders, *Who Paid the Piper?*, 170.

57. Leslie A. Fiedler, letter to WE, 18 Jan. 1956 (Fiedler carbon; Houghton original).

58. Stonor Saunders, *Who Paid the Piper?*, 186.

59. Ibid.

60. Ibid. 187.

61. WE, letter to Leslie Fiedler, 10 Feb. 1956 (courtesy of the late Leslie Fiedler).

62. JH, interview with Sir Stephen Spender, 1989.

63. WE, letter to Stephen Spender, 14 June 1961 (courtesy of Lady Spender).

64. Stonor Saunders, *Who Paid the Piper?*, 314.

65. Conor Cruise O'Brien, 'Journal de Combat', collected in *Writers and Politics* (1965; reprinted Harmondsworth, Middx.: Penguin, 1976), 217–19.

66. Stephen Spender, interviewed by Paul Ableman, *Literary Review*, Nov. 1985, 48.

67. WE, letter to Richard Luckett, 11 June 1983 (Richard Luckett). In 1971, when it was suggested to WE that Spender might edit a selection of his poetry for a volume in the Penguin Modern Poets series (where he would appear alongside Edwin Muir and Adrian Stokes), WE had cannily responded to his publisher Ian Parsons on 20 November: 'Yes, I am sure you are right. To put my verse in such company would be practically asking to have it misread, one way or another.' (Reading)

68. Fei Hsiao-tung, letter to the editors, *Encounter*, 6: 2 (Feb. 1956), 68–9.

69. Karl Wittfogel, reply to Fei Hsiao-t'ung, *Encounter*, 6: 2 (Feb. 1956), 70.

70. Fei Hsiao-t'ung, 'Old friends and a new understanding', *People's China* (1 June 1956), 12–17; quoted in Theodore H. E. Chen, *Thought Reform of the Chinese Intellectuals* (Hong Kong: Hong Kong University Press, 1960), 192.

71. Yue Daiyun quoted in Gittings, *China Changes Face*, 203. See also Yue Daiyun and Carolyn Wakeman, *To the Storm* (Berkeley, California: University of California Press, 1985).

72. Zhou Enlai quoted in Gittings, *China Changes Face*, 203.

73. Quoted in Robert Guillain, 'Not by Rice Alone . . .', *Encounter*, 10: 1 (Dec. 1957), 24.

74. Ibid.

75. Ibid., 29.

76. Fei Hsiao-t'ung quoted in Chen, *Thought Reform*, 193.

77. 'From the Other Shore', *Encounter* (9: 6), 65.

78. WE, 'Fei Hsiao-tung' (letter), *Encounter*, 10: 2 (Feb. 1958), 65. On 19 Jan. 1958 WE wrote to HE, who had been visiting Peking for a week: 'Did you see or hear much of poor Fei Hsiao-tung? Dirty *Encounter* had an article last December challenging me and others to admit we were wrong to defend him against the American's attack earlier, now that he had been attacked in Peking. (I had also said in my letter there was no reason to suppose he was sacked). Anyway of course poor Fei would take it very hard; it would upset his feelings very much. Lo Hui-Min has also been much shocked, and said xhax C. C. Yeh has been xesxifying slanders againsx Hsiao Chien (a lexxer has broken); very sordid small beer ix seemed, and he seemed raxher less eager xo go xhere while xhey were in xhax mood' (Sheffield).

    HE's reply has been lost, but WE wrote again on 16 Feb.: 'Your report of the visit to Peking didn't say anything about poor Fei Hsiao-tung . . . Has he been sacked from his job? Spender has published my answer with a long jeering reply . . . (Sheffield).

    A letter from HE (12 Feb.) crossed in the post with the preceding letter from WE: 'Fei has not been dismissed from his job, but has been taken off the Assembly with about ten others. I really do not know much about the Rectification campaign and in Peking they were not talking about it because it was still going on and I was told that the findings would be published complete at the end' (Sheffield).

79. J. E. M. Arden, 'More Trouble in Tartary', *The Spectator*, 22 Aug. 1958, 240.

80. WE, 'Purging Intellectuals' (letter), *The Spectator*, 29 Aug. 1958, 282.

81. WE, 'Purging Intellectuals' (letter), *The Spectator*, 3 Oct. 1958, 442.

82. J. E. M. Arden, 'Purging Intellectuals' (letter), *The Spectator*, 12 Sept. 1958, p.

83. WE, 'Purging Intellectuals' (letter), *The Spectator*, 19 Sept. 1958, 377.

84. Fei Hsiao-t'ung quoted in Chen, *Thought Reform*, 193.

85. Frederick C. Teiwes, *Politics & Purges in China* (1979), 292.

86. WE, 'Fei Hsiao-tung' (letter), *Encounter*, 10: 2 (Feb. 1958), 65.

87. Frederick C. Teiwes has pointed out: 'Where the Chairman had previously raised important questions about the nature of Party leadership in a changing society, he now reaffirmed an orthodox definition of Party control. Where he earlier had assumed a basic consensus so firm that various "weeds" could be tolerated simply because they would be unable to attract a significant following, he subsequently argued that the left had been in danger of cracking under the onslaught of the bourgeois intellectuals. In addition, some of Mao's postures during the anti-rightist struggle can only be viewed as examples of either political duplicity or remarkable rationalisation . . . [I]t appears that Mao was not above political expediency in an effort to escape responsibility for the Hundred Flowers miscalculation.'

88. HE, letter to Dinah Stock, 19 Aug. 1950 (Sheffield).

89. WE, letter to Kathleen Raine, 2 Oct. 1950 (Houghton carbon).

90. K. M. Panikkar, the Indian Ambassador, wrote to WE (20 Dec. 1950): 'It is undoubtedly the most painful book that I have ever come across and I have somehow the feeling that somewhere deep in Orwell's make-up there was a streak of extraordinary sadism. For the first 50 pages the book read like an effective satire, but afterwards it developed such intensity of horror as to leave one gasping' (Houghton).

91. Lifton, *Thought Reform and the Psychology of Totalism*, 427–9.

92. Ibid. 431.

93. *SCW*, 39.

94. Ibid. 42.

95. Ibid. 44.

96. Ibid. 351–2.

97. Ibid. 361.

98. Ibid. 361–2.

99. Lifton, *Thought Reform and the Psychology of Totalism*, 428.

100. *MG* 244–45.

101. *SCW*, 83.

102. Lifton, *Thought Reform and the Psychology of Totalism*, 429.

103. WE, letter to Ian Parsons, 24 Nov. 1950 (Reading). The phrase 'sheer madness' originally read more moderately, 'cases of turbulence'. See also Richard W. Bailey, 'George Orwell and the English Language', in *The Future of "Nineteen Eighty-Four"*, ed. Ejner J. Jensen (Ann Arbor: The University of Michigan Press, 1984), 23–43; Mary Jo Morris, 'Bentham and Basic English: The "Pious Founders" of Newspeak', in *George Orwell: A Reassessment*, ed. Peter Buitenhuis and Ira B. Nadel (Basingstoke, Hampshire: Macmillan Press, 1988), 102–13.

104. *MG*, 245.

105. WE, 'Herbert's Quaintness' (review of *George Herbert*, by T. S. Eliot); *A*, 257.

106. WE, letter to J. G. Ritz, 16 Dec. 1955 (Houghton carbon).

107. WE, 'Christianity and *1984*' (letter to *Critical* Quarterly, 1: 2 (Summer 1959); in *A*, 602. Also: 'All the current accusations against the Totalitarian state are simply inherited from anti-Christian polemic; "brain-washing" is not a new scientific invention, and Hitler had no opportunity to use "the technique of the biggest lie" as grandly as the Christians—since they worship as the source of all goodness a God who, as soon as you are told the basic story about him, is evidently the Devil' (255). In a review of Northrop Frye's *Five Essays on Milton's Epics*, WE was to write: 'Professor Northrop Frye has a powerful intelligence, which told him for example that *1984* is a satire on Christianity as well as on totalitarianism— I knew this because I knew George Orwell, but to deduce it from Structural Theory is a real achievement for the man' ('Senator Milton', *The Listener*, 28 July 1966). In *MG* he testified too: 'I heard nothing from George Orwell after leaving England early in 1947, but I well remember how dreadful he could make you feel if he considered your political understanding of a question inadequate. Passionately indignant with Stalin's betrayal of the Left, he considered that one of the most shocking things about it was that Commmunism had nearly got back to being as bad as Christianity.' (235) See also Bernard Crick's article, 'Why are radicals so eager to give up one of their own?', *Independent on Sunday*, 14 July 1996, 10: 'But don't misread *Nineteen Eighty-Four*. It warned not just against communism but against any kind of total power.'

108. *MG*, 235.

109. WE, 'Two Electrified Curtains' (review of *Return to China*, by James Bertram, and *The Blue Ants*, by Robert Guillain), *New Statesman*, 2 Nov. 1957, 574. Empson mocked what he called 'a spanking chapter' by Guillain that sought to show 'that all Chinese have had their minds destroyed by a committee process so that they are positively imbecile... Still, I warmly agreed with M. Guillain when he quietened his prose style and summed up. He thinks that... Communism is a very rough horse-doctoring, which probably became the only hope for China... [and] that though it is very severe for the Chinese intellectuals they will quite likely become able to handle it later on...'

10. 'A MIGHTY RASPBERRY': *THE STRUCTURE OF COMPLEX WORDS*

1. WE, letter to Ian Parsons, n.d.; answered 18 Oct 1935 (Reading).
2. WE, letter to Ian Parsons, 11 Feb. 1939 (Reading).
3. WE, letter to Michael Roberts, 12 Jan. 1939 (the late Janet Adam Smith).
4. WE, letter to Michael Roberts, 22 Feb. 1939 (Janet Adam Smith).
5. WE, letter to Ian Parsons, 21 Nov. 1947 (Reading).
6. Ian Parsons, letter to WE, 4 Dec. 1947 (Houghton).
7. WE, letter to Ian Parsons, 12 July 1948 (Reading).
8. WE, letter to HE, 21 Aug. 1948 (Sheffield).
9. WE, letter to Ian Parsons, 23 Aug. 1948 (Reading).
10. WE, letter to Ian Parsons, 16 Nov. 1951 (Reading). The letter goes on: 'There was a reviewer of Pastoral who said it was obviously improvised and printed without any second thoughts, but maybe this was better than trying to be accurate; which pleased me as I had spent so many years trying to make the style natural.'
11. WE, letter to Richard Eberhart, 27 Aug. 1948 (Dartmouth College Library).
12. HE, letter to Irene and John Vincent, 27 Dec. 1949 (Sheffield).
13. WE, letter to Ian Parsons, 24 Nov. 1950: 'I have been complaining about delay, but it doesn't hurt me to have time to think the thing over so long as the book doesn't feel out of date by the time it is published; that is why I keep wanting to thrust in extra bits. I should imagine that this little bit is more likely to be quoted in reviews than anything else, because it is fairly contemporary; and I am very anxious that the book should feel fairly contemporary. I realise your difficulties, and that these additions are a nuisance, but am sure you don't want it to appear feeling out of date.' (Reading)
14. Ian Parsons, letter to WE, 27 July 1951 (Houghton).
15. WE, letter to Ian Parsons, 29 Feb. 1948 (Reading).
16. WE, 'Answers to Comments', *Essays in Criticism*, 3 (1953), 120.
17. Richard Sleight, 'Mr Empson's Complex Words', *Essays in Criticism* 2 (1952), 329.
18. *SCW* 49.
19. Ibid. 318.
20. WE, 'He Lisped In Numbers' (review of G. K. Zipf, *The Psycho-Biology of Language*), *The Spectator*, 14 Feb. 1936, 270.
21. Cleanth Brooks, 'Hits and Misses', *Kenyon Review* (Fall 1952), 670.
22. *SCW* 56. Compare WE's discussion of a passage from Wordsworth's *The Prelude* (1805 text), IV, ll. 330–4, in his radio talk 'Basic English and Wordsworth' (1940): 'the nerve of the poetry is in this complex group of ideas, which are inside words like *magnificent* and *pomp*, ideas which we take in reading simply as feelings. We do not commonly get the ideas opened up, and see the reasons for the feelings' (*A*, 238).
23. WE, undated typescript in Houghton.

24. *SCW* 332.
25. Ibid. 74.
26. Ibid. 158.
27. Ibid. 175.
28. One critic who gently took WE to task on the meanings of the word 'wit' was C. S. Lewis, who—approaching the question as a semasiologist or philologist—urged in his book *Studies in Words* (1960, 93–6) that the older sense *ingenium*, variously meaning human quality, talent and even 'imagination', and which he denotes by the terms 'the *ingenium* sense' or '*wit-ingenium*', must be distinguished from the more modern and 'dangerous' sense of wit. 'The error has, I believe, been committed by a critic to whose ingenium we all owe a willing debt . . . ' WE was equally gracious when he came to review Lewis's book, albeit anonymously, in the *TLS*, 30 Sept. 1960, 627; *A*, 142–6.
29. *SCW*, 113.
30. Ibid. 168.
31. Patrick Parrinder, *The Failure of Theory: Essays on Criticism and Contemporary Fiction* (Brighton, Sussex: The Harvester Press, 1987), 59.
32. *SCW*, 168.
33. Ibid. 187–8.
34. Ibid. 156–7.
35. See George Orwell, 'Lear, Tolstoy and the Fool' (1947), in *Inside the Whale*, (Harmondsworth, Middx.: Penguin, 1962), 108.
36. Barbara Everett, 'The New King Lear', *Critical Quarterly*, 2: 4 (Winter 1960), 325–39.
37. WE, *Critical Quarterly*, 3:1 (Spring 1961); *SL*, 309.
38. WE, reply to Cleanth Brooks.
39. *SCW*, 191.
40. Ibid. 211, 213.
41. Ibid. 218.
42. Ibid. 218.
43. Ibid. 224.
44. Ibid. 227.
45. Ibid. 235.
46. Ibid. 245.
47. 'Linguistics and Criticism', *TLS*, 27 June 1952, 420.
48. *SCW* 255–6, 260–1, 266.
49. Ibid. 271, 281–2, 284.
50. Ibid. 284, 288.
51. Ibid. 304.
52. Ibid. 305.
53. Ibid. 300.
54. WE, letter to IAR, 8 Aug. 1939 (Magdalene).
55. *SCW*, 308–9.

56. WE, letter to Ian Parsons, 12 Oct. 1951 (Reading).
57. C. W. M. Johnson, 'Complex Work', *Accent*, Autumn 1951, 236. Kathleen Raine was to review the book twice, each time with considerable praise: 'The Implication of Words', *Observer*, 19 Aug. 1951; 'The World of Words', *New Republic*, 9 Dec. 1952, 23–4.
58. WE, letter to Ian Parsons, 24 Jan. 1952 (Reading).
59. Hugh Kenner did well to decode the formula: 'one can work out that one use of the word, 3b+=1a—.1£1, assembles the following parts: Poet or artist (3), acting as judge (b), and on that account admired (+), implies (=) a bright social talker (1) mocking (a) and so giving rise to satirical amusement (—) but still to be valued as one values such talkers (1£1). The Empsonian paraphrase elucidates this use of the word "wit" like a shot: "Even in authoritative writers one must expect a certain puppyishness."' ('Alice in Empsonland', 139). The consensus was expressed by Brower: 'it is the machinery and the bewildering routines it sanctions that give one pause—to put it most charitably... Empson's operations are often obscure and wasteful. The "types" as defined, and especially as used, are exceedingly slippery classifying devices'(74).
60. Austin Duncan-Jones, untitled review in *Mind*, 62 (1953), 415.
61. Brooks, 'Hits and Misses', 670.
62. Sleight, 'Mr Empson's Complex Words', 336–7.
63. Duncan-Jones, review, 416.
64. WE, unpublished letter to the editor of *Mind* (Houghton).
65. WE, letter to editor of *Mandrake*, 2: 2 (Autumn–Winter 1955–6), 448.
66. Robert Gorham Davis, 'The Complexity of Words', *Partisan Review*, May–June 1952, 371.
67. Hugh Kenner, 'Alice in Empsonland', *Hudson Review*, 1 (Spring 1952), 137, 139–41, 144.
68. Brooks, 'Hits and Misses', 669, 676–8.
69. Ibid. 673–4. The *TLS* remarked: 'Mr Empson admits that ideally a whole pattern of related key-words should be examined, and he sometimes briefly considers alternatives to the one chosen, but without fully arguing the reasons for his choice' ('Linguistics and Criticism', 420l). R. A. Brower objected that 'he never describes—beyond noting the number of times a word occurs—how he selects a key term in a particular work. As a result, he seldom considers rival key words (untitled review, *Furioso*, Spring 1952, 76).
70. Cf. WE's remarks to Christopher Norris and David Wilson (1970): 'There was a rather failed chapter on 'all' in *Paradise Lost* which I added. I was at an American summer school and they were talking about this material and saying "these examples are all selected to fit your theory," which they weren't really. They were the kind of examples I was interested in. But they said: "Take some very general word which recurs, but on the face of it doesn't seem to carry a complexity of meaning." And 'all' in *Paradise Lost* did

fulfil that very much. That was the only time I took a case for a theoretical reason—because I was challenged to. But otherwise I think that the kind of example I'd been puzzling about and the theory I was making up in general, not surprisingly, fitted each other almost too neatly, but it wasn't because they were planned to.'

71. WE, letter to Cleanth Brooks, 16 Sept. 1955 (Yale: YCAL MSS 30: Box 3, folder 85).

72. Ronald Shusterman, 'Blindness and Anxiety: I. A. Richards and some current trends of criticism', *Études Anglaises*, 39: 4 (Oct.–Dec. 1986), 419–20.

73. Christopher Norris, 'The Importance of Empson (II): The Criticism', *Essays in Criticism*, 35: 1, Jan. 1985 (25–44), 41. See also Norris's monograph, *William Empson and the Philosophy of Literary Criticism*, with a Postscript by WE (London: The Athlone Press, 1978). Jonathan Culler, in his 'Foreword to the 1989 Edition' of *SCW* (p. xi), points to WE's connections with contemporary critical debates; he notes, for example, that *Complex Words*, 'despite its posture of eccentric rumination, which one can find winning or maddening depending on one's mood, is especially important today since it offers a new position in debates about meaning and context, about the literary in its relation to the social and the historical. Empson's brilliant discussions of words which express complex social attitudes toward one's fellows or toward moral principles open rich chapters of social and literary history, and possibilities of textual investigation that remain to be explored.' He also compares aspects of *SCW* with the work of Derrida. See too Terry Eagleton, 'The Critic as Clown', *Against the Grain: Essays 1975–1985* (London: Verso, 1986), 149–65.

74. WE, 'An Anatomy of Taste', *New Statesman*, 2 Dec. 1966; *A*, 174.

75. Letter to Christopher Norris, 7 Oct. 1971 (Norris).

76. WE, 'The Verbal Analysis', *Kenyon Review*, 12 (Autumn 1950); *A*, 105.

77. Geoffrey Strickland, 'The Criticism of William Empson', *Mandrake*, 2 (Autumn/Winter 1954/55).

78. H. A. Mason, *The Cambridge Review*, 14 (1985), 141.

79. Campbell Crockett, untitled review, *Journal of Aesthetics*, March 1953, 269.

80. *SCW*, 6.

81. WE, letter to Ian Parsons, 29 Feb. 1948 (Reading).

82. *SCW*, 379, 372.

83. IAR's copy of *Complex Words* is in the Old Library, Magdalene College, Cambridge.

84. See W. H. N. Hotopf, *Language, Thought and Comprehension: A Case Study of the Writings of I. A. Richards* (London: Routledge & Kegan Paul, 1965), esp. 169–76. For a decent short account of Richards's critical career, see John Paul Russo, 'I. A. Richards in Retrospect', *Critical Inquiry*, 8 (Summer 1982), 743–60.

85. WE, letter to Philip Hobsbaum, 2 Aug. 1969 (copy in Empson Papers).

86. Norris, 'The Importance of Empson (II): The Criticism', 32. See also his excellent *William Empson and the Philosophy of Literary Criticism*, London: Athlone Press, 1978.

87. WE, letter to Ian Parsons, New Year 1949 (Reading). In a later year WE conceded that the book did not quite function as whole; writing on 4 July 1976 to the US publisher James Laughlin about progress with his lengthening study of Marlowe's *Doctor Faustus*, he noted: 'But there are a lot of other things in the book, which will perhaps become too large; though not larger than *Complex Words*, and with the same kind of partial unity' (Houghton: New Directions archive).

88. WE, letter to Michael Roberts, 12 Nov. 1932 (the late Janet Adam Smith).

89. IAR, Principles of Literary Criticism (1924); reset edn. (London: Routledge & Kegan Paul, 1967), Ibid., 42, 38.

90. Ibid., 229.

91. C. K. Ogden, I. A. Richards, James Wood, *The Foundations of Aesthetics* (London: Allen & Unwin, 1922), 75, 91. E. D. Hirsch Jr. is not alone in his significant misrepresentation: 'Psychologically, the most beneficial literature, in Richards's view, is the kind that harmonizes a large number of different and conflicting psychic impulses. Thus, a formal or purely literary criterion of excellence, according to the kind proposed by Coleridge, is altogether concordant with Richards's psychological criterion. Literature that is formally rich and complex, and brings into unity a great many opposite and discordant elements achieves excellence both as literature and as therapy. Since the two kinds of criteria coincide, the psychological values of literature can be accommodated to literary categories' (*The Aims of Interpretation*, (University of Chicago Press, 1976), 125).

92. WE, 'O Miselle Passer', *Oxford Outlook*, 19 (May 1930); *A*, 196.

93. WE, ' "The Philosophy of Rhetoric" ', *Criterion*, 17 (Oct. 1937); *A*, 207.

94. WE, 'The Verbal Analysis', *Kenyon Review*, 12 (Autumn 1950); *A*, 107.

95. I. A. Richards, *Speculative Instruments* (London: Routledge & Kegan Paul, 1955), 9.

96. I. A. Richards, *Poetries and Sciences*, 60 footnote.

97. Ibid. 60–1.

98. *SCW*, 432.

99. Robert Gorham Davis, 'The Complexity of Words', *Partisan Review*, May–June 1952, 370.

100. *SCW*, 421, 426–8.

101. WE, letter to IAR, 2 April 1933 (Houghton).

102. I. A. Richards, *Principles of Literary Criticism*, 36, 40.

103. WE, 'The Hammer's Ring' (1973), in *A*, 217.

104. WE, 'A Doctrine of Aesthetics', *Hudson Review*, 2 (Spring 1949); *A*, 214.

105. WE, 'Teaching the Meaning in Poetry', *Criterion*, 15 (April 1936); *A*, 100.

106. WE, 'Rhythm and Imagery in English Poetry', *British Journal of Aesthetics*, 2 (Jan. 1962); *A*, 147.

107. Letter to Mark Roberts, 8 Feb. 1959 (copy in Empson Papers).

108. Michael Roberts, untitled rev. of *Some Versions of Pastoral*, in *Criterion*, Jan. 1936, 345.

109. *SCW*, 168.

110. Ibid. 159.

111. Ibid. 169.

112. Ibid. 176.

113. Ibid. 192.

114. Ibid. 218.

115. Ibid. 104.

116. WE, letter to Roger Sale, ?1973 (Houghton).

11. HOMING TO YORKSHIRE

1. Interview with Biddy Crozier, January 2002. Hetta met John Wright in South Africa in the 1930s. See obituaries of Wright in *The Guardian* (by Sarah McAlister), 7 March 1991); *The Times*, 9 March 1991, both of which mention that he set up his puppet studio in the Empsons' house, 1 Hampstead Hill Gardens.

2. HE to Walter Brown, 13 Feb. 1953.

3. Bob Harris, *The Whispering Years* (London: BBC Worldwide, 2001), 14..

4. WE, undated draft ALS. He added: 'Also I have read the thesis for which he has now received a Ph.D., and formed a high opinion of it; besides, I knew of his frequent visits to libraries in Europe to complete the research which it required.'

5. WE wrote to HE in the spring of 1954 ('Sunday'): 'By the way [Desmond] Lee who was headmaster of Clifton has just been made headmaster of Winchester; I wrote and congratulated him and he answered that he hoped both my children would be coming to him later. I can't help feeling it gives a tiny bit of pull to have the dear old friend in the job now' (Sheffield).

6. Interview with Mogador Empson, 9 Dec. 2005.

7. W. W. Robson, letter to JH, undated.

8. HE, letter to Walter Brown, 4 April 1953 (Sheffield).

9. HE, letter to Walter Brown, 19 May 1954 (Sheffield).

10. David Jones, 'Empson Soup', *The CEA Forum*, 18: 2–4 (1988), 7.

11. WE, letter to the *Sunday Times*, 27 May 1962 (in response to extracts from Maurice Collis's biography *Stanley Spencer*).

12. WE, letter to the Bursar, Sheffield University, 7 Aug. 1957 (Registrar's Dept.). HE reported to Walter Brown (13 Feb. 1953): 'William's drinking rather. He got a scare from a pain in his middle & now he just takes sherry.'

13. HE, letter to Walter Brown, 6 Dec. 1953 (Sheffield).

14. Kenneth Lo, *The Feast of My Life* (London: Doubleday, 1993), 163–4. See also obituaries of Lo in *The Times*, 14 Aug. 1995; *Daily Telegraph*, 12 Aug. 1995.

15. Dorothea Richards journal, 30 June 1953 (Sheffield).

16. Interview with Sybille van der Sprenkel, 1989.

17. HE, letter to Walter Brown, 13 Feb. 1953 (Sheffield).

18. WE, letter to Mr MacColl, *SL*, 187–8. Yann Lovelock, who was a research student at Sheffield from 1964, remembers that WE liked to tell stories in the pub. 'One he commonly told was of the BBC recording made soon after his return to England. As a former broadcaster he was used enough to a microphone but responded best to an audience. The reading was clipped and dry and so the producer decided to take him drinking as a way of loosening him up. After quite a while he was taken back to the studio and did the same reading again. Thereafter they spliced the two tapes so that the sober Empson introduced the poem but the lubricated Empson performed it ... According to Empson, the one question on everyone's lips after the broadcast was "Was William drunk or wasn't he?" Unless you'd actually worked for radio, you wouldn't have known about splicing in those days. It wasn't just your gross pints of beer that had raised William to the point of exultation either. The producer had introduced him to his own favourite tipple, a concoction of (a good) naval rum and Guinness' ('Empson's Sheffield', 23 Jan. 2003).

    Trevor Baxter was once told by Duval Smith the story of 'how he had been sent for by the Head of the Third Programme who said to him, "Mr. Duval Smith, when Mr. Empson broadcast his poems on Friday evening it sounded to me as if he was drunk." Peter, who had directed the programme, replied, "Well, he'd had nine pints of Guinness before he went on air so he probably was" ' (e-mail to JH, 1 Aug. 2005).

19. G. S. Fraser, *The Modern Writer and His World*, rev. edn. (Harmondsworth, Middx.: Penguin, 1964), 316.

20. Naomi Lewis, 'Radio Notes', *New Statesman*, 10 Jan. 1953. On another occasion, 'C.W.', in a review of *The Poet Speaks*, no 7, edited by Peter Orr (Argo RG 517)—a miscellany of poets recorded in association with the British Council and the Poetry Room in the Lamont Library of Harvard University—would dismiss as 'professorial dustiness' WE's reading of 'Legal Fiction' and 'To an Old Lady' (*Records and Recording*, April 1967).

21. Maurice Wiggin, 'Dr. Schweitzer, I Presume', *Sunday Times*, 1 March 1953. The Chief Assistant for Talks (Home Sound) likewise lauded WE's performance, in an internal memo: 'I much enjoyed him in Third on February 27th about Macbeth. I think his voice and manner admirable, human and communicative and would have no hesitation over using him in Home Service.' (BBC Written Archives)

22. HE, letter to Walter Brown, 13 Feb. 1953.

23. WE, letter to C. M. Coffin, 14 October 1949 (Houghton carbon).

24. WE, letter to Mr Phelps, 27 Jan. 1953 (BBC Written Archives).

25. D. R. Cousin, letter to JH, 6 Feb. 1984. WE was to tell his publisher Ian Parsons on 23 June 1957: 'the Shakespeare stuff... I have nearly ready and would hope to make a book of some time, but would hope to make better by letting it lie around while the surge of opinion continues' (Reading).

26. Byron Rogers reported in 1967: ' "The beard? It used to be the old Yorkshire farmer's beard. It's what is known as the Newgate beard. Useful when you're hanged: it stops the rope hurting. In my case my method was just to cut that which cuts easily"—he drew a hand down the side of his face—"and to avoid that which bleeds." He patted the underside of his chin' ('Man of words', *The Star* [Sheffield], 31 March 1967, 4).

27. WE, letter to Antony Brett-James, 13 Feb. 1953 (Reading); *SL*, 216.

28. Bonamy Dobrée (1891–1974) was Professor of English at Leeds. He and WE greatly liked one another; and WE gave talks and readings for Dobrée at Leeds.

29. L. C. Knights (1906–97) was long associated with F. R. Leavis, being co-editor of *Scrutiny* for twenty years until 1953 when the periodical folded. A leading scholar of Shakespeare and Elizabethan drama, he made his name with *How many children had Lady Macbeth?* (1933).

30. WE, letter to the Registrar, 10 July 1952 (Registrar's Dept, Univ. of Sheffield).

31. Ronald Bottrall, who sent references to Hull, Manchester, and Sheffield, wrote to WE on 29 Aug. 1952: 'They are pretty handsome and I did all the canvassing I could.' (Houghton).

32. Eric Laughton (1911–88), who began as an Assistant Lecturer in Latin in 1936, was later Firth Professor of Latin 1952–76; Pro-Vice-Chancellor, 1968–72), Dean of the Faculty of Arts, 1961–4, and Public Orator, 1955–68; his publications included *Latin for Latecomers* and *The Participle in Cicero*. Richard M. Wilson (1909–95) was Senior Lecturer and then Prof. of English Language from 1946 until his retirement in 1973. A separate Department of English Language had been formed in 1926.

33. Interview with Professor Eric Laughton, 28 June 1984; Prof. D. R. Cousin, letter to JH, 6 Feb. 1984.

34. Professor J. S. Deas, letter to JH, 19 Jan. 1984.

35. WE, letter to A. W. Chapman (registrar), 24 Feb. 1953.

36. Ian Sainsbury, 'An "old fogey" retires', *Morning Telegraph*, 20 July 1971.

37. *The University of Sheffield Gazette*, no. 54 (Nov. 1974), 29–30.

38. John Horder, 'William Empson, straight', *The Guardian*, 12 Aug. 1969.

39. Sainsbury, 'An "old fogey" retires", *Morning Telegraph*, 20 July 1971.

40. HE, letter to Walter Brown, 19 May 1954 (Sheffield).

41. WE, undated letter ('Saturday') to HE. On 3 March 1954 he explained to HE how he would try to deal with the regular chores: 'I am particularly glad to have some shirts just now; I let the washing pile up because this nice careless house has let a batch of washing go to the laundry and be lost somewhere on

the way; this morning (and weekly in future) I took my bits to the Chinese one by bicycle, and took it into my head I would at last wash the Nylon myself for a week, daily, which now needs to be done.'

42. 'Goodnight sweet,' HE was to write to her lover, Walter Brown, on 28 April 1953; 'every night I climb into my red flannel pyjamas and crawl into my little bed if that's what you want to know alone—it's the nights that matter and not the days and it's sad and lonely all through the dark.' Brown wrote to her in Aug. 1953, en route to Japan: 'No one has ever or will ever love you as well as I do. Remember' (Sheffield).

43. Paddy Fraser, 'G. S. Fraser: A Memoir', *Jacket* magazine, 20 (Dec. 2002), 11 (hhtp://jacketmagazine.com/20/html)

44. Despite her jauntiness during the holiday, HE was still feeling profoundly alienated from life in England; she wrote late in 1953: 'Mog & Jake are heaven. I won't have them go through the horrible system.' For herself, she added: 'I won't stay here. I'm so sick & not yet even done my work cleaning up this house so I can leave it with a clean conscience . . . I don't want to live here forever like this' (letter to Walter Brown, 6 Dec. 1953). She was in a state of near-depression for nearly two years after returning to England.

45. In a letter to HE of 23 Jan. 1956, WE related: 'The police invaded, the day before yesterday, apparently wanting to catch someone believed to be hiding in the house. We (that is, I and the two police) could hear someone moving about on the floor above, and they wanted to move up from the back door unexpected. But I (without any plan except to be friendly) said in the passage in the dark that they really mustn't come upstairs until I had gone up feeling my way and turned on the light for them, and they came back still pretty suspicious saying that the place seemed to be empty upstairs.'

46. WE, letter to Francis Berry, 24 March 1959 (Francis Berry).

47. HE, letter to Walter Brown, 13 Oct. 1953 (Sheffield).

48. HE, letter to Robert Winter, 11 May 1964 (courtesy of Herbert Stern).

49. Francis Berry, 'William Empson', in Gill, 210. Berry's five-part poem is reprinted in his *Collected Poems* (Bristol: Redcliffe Press, 1994), 343–6. WE's first Christmas at Sheffield was passed like an East Riding squire. The whole family spent a few days with his brother Arthur at Yokefleet Hall, where HE looked upon the hieratic manners of the place with a mocking eye. She wrote to Walter Brown: 'Pa and I have only just stopped talking at each other in the high-pitched screaming rolling of eyes way that is habitual when addressing his relations. He and the children each got a watch—I needless to say was given a scarf—rayon this time. But never mind, I'm going to far places and they can look at their time-pieces' (letter, 3 Jan. 1954: Sheffield).

WE's prowess as a walker was to be remembered by many, including Prof. Brian Cox—who remembered his speed and range: 'From 5–7 April 1963 I organised a *Critical Quarterly* conference for teachers at Hull. WE lectured on Saturday afternoon on "The Romantic Principle of Coleridge's Historical

Poems". After the lecture he insisted on a walk. The other tutors, Malcolm Bradbury and David Palmer, went with me in a car to Brantingham. Empson set a strong pace down the valley, and it was like a relay as we took it in turns to keep up with him and to talk with him. At the end of the valley, I suggested we return. He asked if there was a different route back, and I foolishly admitted there was. He walked us up the side of the valley and across fields with a bitter cold wind from the sea making the walk for the three of us increasingly unpleasant. We arrived back at the car with me jogging at his side, and David and Malcolm several hundred yards in the rear.

'To my surprise he insisted on attending my lecture on Sunday morning and took part in the discussion. At coffee time he invited us to his room and produced a bottle of whisky' (C. B. Cox, letter to JH, 12 June 1985). See also Cox, *The Great Betrayal* (London: Chapmans, 1992), 118.

50. WE, letter to John Hayward, 15 Jan. 1955. (Theodore Hofmann)

51. Annemarie Heywood, e-mail letter to JH, 7 Nov. 2001.

52. Christopher Heywood, e-mail letter to JH, 31 Oct. 2001.

53. Asked in 1967 if he considered himself eccentric, WE responded simply: 'No, I don't worry about it. I've known some really eccentric people' (Byron Rogers, 'Man of words', *The Star* (Sheffield), 31 March 1967, 4).

54. Ann Dovey, 'Person to Person (1): Francis Berry', *Arrows*, no 75 (Spring 1960), 24.

55. Ibid. 23.

56. Andrew Braybrook, memoir, Jan. 2003.

57. WE, letter to A. R. Humphreys, 22 Nov. 1957 (Houghton). WE's other comments on Berry included: 'He is a poet and critic of distinction . . . I see the appointment is for an expert on 16th and 17th century literature, and thus so certainly his main field. He is a Roman Catholic, with a great sense of the tension of paradox in Christian doctrine; and I take it admires the metaphysical poets chiefly because their methods bring that out. He is also much interested in late medieval work, as his publications show. I arrange a voluntary course every year for Honours Students in English Literature on the other major literatures, and he does an hour on Dante very well.'

58. Kenneth Muir, letter to JH, 30 Dec. 1993.

59. Interview with the late Professor Harry Armytage, 15 April 1983.

60. Janet Martin, letter to JH, 24 Sept. 1987. 'I am sorry to write in such a way, but the years when WE was at Sheffield were a time of considerable unhappiness for [my parents] . . . I think I only met [WE] once myself, at a dinner party at my parents' house, & have rarely spent a more uncomfortable evening.' She remembers too another WE occasion, 'which was a public lecture at Leicester University and as awful as the dinner party. Richard Hoggart . . . had the unenviable task of pulling the evening together after Empson's drunken and shambling performance.'

Hamer's major work to date was an edition of *The Works of Sir David Lindsay of the Mount (1490–1555)*, published by the Scottish Text Society in 4 volumes (1931–6); he had also researched the biography and bibliography of Edmund Spenser, with various periodical appearances; and during the war he had worked on a long-projected collection of English nursery rhymes (compiling over nearly nine years about 20,000 variant forms of over two thousand children's rhymes, each of which he proposed to study historically)—though he relinquished his task in 1951 when Iona and Peter Opie began publishing the fruits of their similar undertaking. Enid Hamer is best known for her study *The Metres of English Poetry* (1930).

61. Harry M. Geduld, who was a student during WE's first year at Sheffield, recalls (letter to JH, 11 March 2001) that Hamer 'wasted much time during tutorials getting us to pore over Hogarth when we should have been studying Dryden, Pope and Johnson. He also had an obsessive antipathy to sentences that began with "And" or "But".' (Geduld notes too: 'I recall Empson as something of a cold fish towards students—unlike L. C. Knights who was most charming, affable and encouraging.')

62. WE, letter to HE, 20 June 1957 (Sheffield). On 29 March 1958 he wrote to HE: 'Hamer is getting more and more irritable and inclined to flaunt his coming retirement' (Sheffield). On 7 March 1963, WE would admit to Robert Winter: 'my No. 2 here, who had been doing it for many years and knew all the ropes, was made to resign [*sic*] at the age of 65 last year, and I have been having to run the department myself for the first time. It is rather a badger...' (Herbert Stern).

63. WE, letter to 'Mr Walker', no date (1958) (carbon in Houghton). 'We are having a palace revolution in Sheffield because Hamer refuses to act as a secretary any more,' WE wrote to HE on 25 April 1958, 'and unless I can squeeze a real secretary out of the Bursar I am in a fix' (Sheffield).

64. WE, letter to HE, 16 Nov. 1956.

65. I am grateful to Derek Roper, here and elsewhere, for undated reminiscences.

66. Eric Mackerness (1920–99), who specialized in nineteenth-century literature, was to retire as Reader in English Literature in 1982.

67. E. D. Mackerness, 'Emeritus Professor Sir William Empson', *University of Sheffield Newsletter*, 6.

68. Harry M. Geduld, e-mail letter to JH, 9 March 2001.

69. WE, letter to Mary Fraser (Edith Sitwell's secretary), 12 Dec. 1953 (Texas); letter to HE, 'Tuesday 15th' (May 1954). WE liked Edith Sitwell, with whom he was quickly on first-name terms. In early July 1955, in return for his hospitality at Sheffield, she invited him over for lunch at Renishaw. 'Dear Edith... I am very glad to have seen Renishaw,' he wrote in his bread-and-butter note on 11 July, 'particularly on a day which brought it out so strongly' (Texas).

70. 'Professor Empson's Reply on behalf of the Honorary Graduates', *The University of Sheffield Gazette*, no. 54 (Nov. 1974), 30.

71. WE, postscript to F. Berry and E. D. Mackerness, 'The Idea of an English School: English at Sheffield', *The Critical Survey* 1: 4 (Summer 1964), 245.

72. The phrase is taken from James Joyce, 'I smell the public sweat of monks', which WE was to quote in 'The Theme of *Ulysses*', *Kenyon Review*, 18: 1 (Winter 1956), 45.

73. WE, letter to HE, n. d. ('Friday'); (Sheffield).

74. Elizabeth M. Brennan, e-mail to JH, 19 Nov. 2001.

75. Ibid.

76. JH, interview with Roma Gill, 25 April 1991.

77. WE in *University of Sheffield Gazette*, no. 54 (Nov. 1974), 23.

78. Roger Ebbatson, according to a letter from David Parker to JH, 4 July 1989.

79. Mackerness, 'Professor William Empson', *University of Sheffield Gazette*, 59. Nor was he inclined to pull his punches when marking student papers: on one script submitted by an English General student in May 1956 (courtesy of the late Eric Mackerness) his concluding remarks read: 'I hope this flatulent pretentiousness is only due to pretending you have read the plays when you haven't. If that is all, and you read them in the coming year, you may be able to use this gift of the gab to some purpose. Otherwise you will certainly fail. 10%.'

80. Mackerness, 'Professor William Empson', 59–60.

81. Harry Armytage had a distinguished career as Lecturer, Senior Lecturer and, later, as Professor of Education at Sheffield, 1946–80. He was Pro-Vice-Chancellor (1964–8), and was instrumental in the establishment of the Faculty of Educational Studies and its first Dean in 1970. He was a member of the planning committee for the New University of Ulster in Coleraine, where he was awarded an hon. degree in 1977. After retirement he taught for two years as Kent State University, Ohio, as the Gerald H. Read Professor of Comparative and International Education. See *A Celebration of the Life and Work of Professor Harry Armytage (1915–1998)* (Department of Educational Studies, University of Sheffield, 1998).

82. Interview with Pat Smith, 23 Sept. 1993.

83. WE, 'Old Men Remember with advantages', *Arrows*, no. 102 (1971), 8.

84. Mackerness, 'Professor William Empson' (1971), 59.

85. WE, letter to Bonamy Dobrée, no date ('Sunday') (Brotherton). WE wrote to HE, on 22 Nov. 1953: 'I am smacking out my silly Inaugural on the typewriter, which depresses me very much because it seems nothing at all but show-off, but I think that's what they want and it will soon be over . . . I told them to send Arthur [his eldest brother] an invitation to the Inaugural, because I thought his address gave a bit more swank. I shouldn't think he'd be fool enough to come, but he might feel he would like to have a look at the set-up in general, and there is no reason to shut him out, after all.' (Sheffield)

86. WE, 'Teaching English in the Far East and England', *SSS*, 201. The lecture was reported in the *Sheffield Telegraph* (3 Dec. 1953), under the title 'Basic English Defended by Professor'.

87. Interview with Professor Armytage, 1983.

88. L. C. Knights was to recall in a letter to me (9 Oct. 1983) an occasion in the mid-1950s when WE gave the opening talk to a conference of teachers and lecturers in education, at the London Institute of Education. 'He was supposed to talk about School Examinations—the public ones—and I don't think he knew much about the subject, though he had tried to brief himself. He came up to me immediately afterwards as we all made for drinks and asked anxiously, "Was it all right?", to which I made the disingenuous reply, "My dear Empson, you can't say anything without being interesting", which seemed to reassure him. "Jolly decent of you to come," he said, "I'll come to your lecture tomorrow, as soon as I have met my wife who is returning from . . . "—where was it? I said he couldn't do that, but he did turn up. Had he met his wife? Yes—"Wonderful the conveniences of modern life. Did you know that on railway stations you can get peppermints from slot-machines? Wonderful." He then sat himself immediately below my rostrum, unfolded the *Times* and did the crossword. I assumed he wasn't listening, but at one point he looked up, "That was a splendid remark. Would you mind repeating it?" My momentary glow at this sign of approval was immediately dissipated when I realized that my last remark had been a quotation from Eliot (which I think he wrote down in the margin of the *Times*).'

89. J. S. Deas, letter to JH, 19 Jan. 1984.

90. WE wrote to HE in the spring of 1954 ('Sunday'): 'The only thing I could induce myself to do recently was to issue a little challenge to the Mathematical Department (the Mathematics Prof. being a nice fellow)—an enormously long and cumbrous bit of mathematics was sent in with a request to them to tell me the right answer; I have just been doing still more of it, after a dismal day . . . and then a huge pointless Senate meeting' (Sheffield).

91. Edward Miller, letter to JH, 10 Sept. 1995.

92. Francis Berry, letter to JH, 9 May 1983.

93. WE, 'Old men remember with advantages', 10.

94. WE, letter to HE, 8 February 1968 (Sheffield).

95. Francis Berry, letter to JH, 7 May 1983.

96. Interview with Frank Pierce, 16 Feb. 1984.

97. Maurice Bruce wrote on the development of the social services; his works include *The Coming of the Welfare State* and *The Rise of the Welfare State: English Social Policy 1601–1971*. See *University of Sheffield Gazette*, no. 55 (Dec. 1975), 11; obits. in *Times*, 25 May 1988; *University of Sheffield Newsletter*, 12: 14 (8 June 1988).

98. Harry Kay, letter to JH, 18 Feb. 1992.

99. Neville Moray, letter to JH, 10 Aug. 1992.
100. Wilf Saunders, letter to JH, 9 Aug.1993. Saunders was Deputy University Librarian (1956–63); Director of the Postgraduate School of Librarianship and Information Science (1963–82).
101. Interview with Frank Pierce, 16 Feb. 1984.
102. WE, letter to HE, 26 Jan. 1954.
103. 'I have been feeling nearly crazy at having to write a whole lot of examination papers all at once,' he wrote to HE on 23 Jan. 1956, 'but now I have done the first batch I feel more confident. As soon as I have done a few more of the essentials I shall go out and buy a new electric fire.' Again, on 2 Feb. 1965: 'I can't tell you how lunatic inventing examination papers makes me feel; I am emerging from the pit.'
104. WE, letter to HE, 3 March 1954. See also a letter to HE of 16 March 1956: 'I am so near the edge towards the end of term . . . [J]ust now I have to do a lot of things decently enough in the last week [of term], while all hands are feeling rather exhausted, not only papa. My dearest love, William.'
105. WE, letter to HE, 22 April 1954.
106. HE, letter to Walter Brown, 19 May 1954.
107. WE, letter to Boris Ford, 28 April 1959 (copy in Houghton).

12. FROM POETRY TO THE QUEEN

1. Thom Gunn, *London Magazine*, Feb. 1956.
2. F. W. Bateson, 'Auden's (and Empson's) Heirs', *Essays in Criticism*, Jan. 1957.
3. G. S. Fraser, 'Not wrongly moved . . .', *TLS*, 7 Oct. 1955.
4. Kathleen Raine, 'And Learn a Style from a Despair', *New Statesman and Nation*, 5 Nov. 1955.
5. Charles Madge, 'Empson Agonistes', *Listen*, Summer 1956.
6. Hilary Corke, 'Riding a Hare', *The Observer*, 30 Oct. 1955.
7. Naomi Lewis, 'Sir Oracle', *The Observer*, 30 Oct. 1955.
8. Anne Ridler, 'Passion into Thought', *Manchester Guardian*, 4 Nov. 1955.
9. Austin Clarke, 'The Cryptic Key', *The Irish Times*, 5 Nov. 1955.
10. John Betjeman, *Daily Telegraph*, 18 Nov. 1955.
11. Ian Parsons, letter to WE, 4 January 1956 (Reading).
12. Charles Monteith, letter to Chatto & Windus, 14 July 1972; Chatto responded on 20 July. (Reading).
13. WE, letter to Ian Parsons, undated; Parsons responded on 5 March 1954.
14. See Humphrey Carpenter, *The Angry Young Men: A Literary Comedy of the 1950s* (London: Allen Lane, 2002), and a review of Carpenter by Frank Kermode, 'The outsiders', *London Review of Books*, 25 November 2002.
15. John Wain, *Hurry On Down* (1953; reprinted Harmondsworth, Middx.: Penguin), 1979), 29–30.

16. A. Alvarez, *Where Did It All Go Right?* (London: Richard Cohen Books, 1999), 117.

17. Ibid., 136.

18. John Wain, 'Ambigious Gifts: Notes on the Poetry of William Empson', *Penguin New Writing* 40 (1950), 120.

19. John Wain, *Sprightly Running: Part of an Autobiography* (London: Macmillan, 1962), 173. Years later, in 1982, Empson told another young admirer, Mark Thompson: 'I hope you won't stay freelance for long. It may be cowardly of me, but I think a regular salary is best' ('Notes on meetings with William Empson', June 1986).

20. Alvarez, *Where Did It All Go Right?*, 117.

21. Ibid.

22. John Wain, 'A Gulp of Rough Red Wine', *Observer Weekend Review*, 19 Feb. 1961, 26 (a review of the disc *William Empson Reading Selected Poems*).

23. Alan Brownjohn, 'A Preference for Poetry: Oxford Undergraduate Writing of the Early 1950s', *The Yearbook of English Studies*, 17 (1987), 72–3.

24. John Heath-Stubbs (citing a recollection by Sidney Keyes), *Hindsights: An Autobiography* (London: Hodder & Stoughton, 1993), 76.

25. George Watson, *Never Ones for Theory? England and the War of Ideas* (Cambridge: The Lutterworth Press, 2000), 63.

26. Ibid. 65.

27. It is not possible to know the exact dates of WE's visits to Oxford. HE was to write to Walter Brown (6 Dec. 1953): 'William has gone to Oxford for the weekend to be admired & dined & wined by admiring undergraduates ... I thought it better not to go—not mark you that I am not found to be surprisingly attractive & well-dressed but puzzling. And my God how un-attractive & ill-dressed & furtive are all the ones who think so.' She must have been referring to a later visit than the one so gloomily preserved in the memories of Alvarez and Robson which evidently took place before WE started at Sheffield—or her remarks are very ironic.

28. Alvarez, *Where Did It All Go Right?*, 118.

29. W. W. Robson, letter to JH.

30. Alvarez, *Where Did It All Go Right?*, 119.

31. Ibid., p. 119. Late in 1955 John Wain felt he had cause to ask WE if a veiled but very critical reference in a piece of WE's writing, or possibly in a talk by him, was actually a reference to Leavis; WE responded on 1 December: 'Well, as a matter of fact I *did* mean Leavis, and I am rather shocked to hear you think anybody is drilled into writing like me. But maybe it is all the better if I don't seem to be picking an irrelevant quarrel, so I hope you won't tell anybody "Empson tells me he did mean Leavis"—that seems a typical piece of literary fuss (but it would also be rather fussy not to answer your letter).' (Courtesy of Seamus Perry, who discovered WE's letter in Wain's copy of *SVP*, sold at Waterfields', Oxford, in 2000.)

32. WE, letter to A. Alvarez, 29 August 1956 (Alvarez).

33. See Anthony Hartley, 'Poets of the Fifties', *Spectator*, 193 (1954), 260–1.

34. Empson, 'Literary Opinion' (broadcast 20 Oct. 1954); copy in Houghton. Parodies of WE include Dylan Thomas's incomplete villanelle, written in 1940, 'Request to Leda: Homage to William Empson', first published in *Horizon*, 6: 31 (July 1942), 6. Asked by Christopher Norris and David Wilson (interview, 20 Dec. 2005) about the parodies of his work, WE responded: 'They all seem to be as dull as mutton, the truth is. But I thought that Dylan's one, though a bit rough, was fairly funny. I thought that was all right, but the other ones I've seen I didn't think were very funny—they weren't sufficiently pointed. But I haven't made any study of it, I'm afraid. I agree in general that parody is a very important mode of criticism, and when Leavis denies it that is only because Leavis cannot afford to be parodied, of course.'

35. David Laird, letter to JH, 24 Oct. 1991. Paul Allen, who also attended, recalls that WE 'was very friendly towards the small audience as well as eccentric with his mandarin's beard and tightly fitting hat' (letter to JH, 19 Feb. 1991).

36. WE, letter to the Dean, 19 Jan. 1960.

37. WE, letter to Richard B. Hudson, 1 Feb. 1953 (Stallknecht Papers, Lilly Library, Indiana University, Bloomington, Indiana).

38. Empson's brother Charles was Minister (Commercial) at the British Embassy in Washington, 1950–5; he was later to be Ambassador to Chile, 1955–8.

39. WE, letter to Hudson, 13 May 1953 (Stallknecht Papers).

40. WE, letter to HE, 23 July 1954. The Empson boys, Mogador and Jacob, went off for the summer to stay with the MacNeice family in Ireland. Mogador adored Hedli MacNeice and came to think of her almost as a second mother. HE took a holiday in Morocco (where she proposed to meet up with her lover).

41. WE, letter to HE, 18 July 1954. John Crowe Ransom had written to WE on 6 Sept. 1952: 'I found Indiana hotter than Kenyon, and very different in the general background. The university is a big State one, huge and repellent as to the machinery it takes to run the thing... But the educators there are... wholeheartedly behind the School of Letters. Our little colony is fairly isolated, and some of the bigness shows in library facilities and more eating-places, real advantages as compared to Kenyon. It was pleasant there. The School was never better, I think, in respect to good courses and able students.' (Houghton)

42. WE, letter to HE, 22 June 1954.

43. WE, letter to Newton P. Stallknecht, 22 March 1954. WE would write to Ransom on 12 Aug. 1955: 'It is high time I wrote down some of the opinions about Shakespeare which I could talk out so easily at Bloomington; it would be a great convenience to have a stenographer at lectures who would type

the flow, but we can't afford that in our line of work, and I daresay it is a mercy if we only knew.'

44. WE, letter to HE, 10 July 1954.
45. WE, letter to Newton P. Stallknecht, 12 March 1954.
46. Mark Royden Winchell, *"Too Good To Be True": The Life and Work of Leslie Fiedler* (Columbia and London: University of Missouri Press, 2002), 74.
47. Newton P. Stallknecht, letter to WE, 12 March 1954.
48. WE, letter to Stallknecht, 12 March 1954.
49. Stallknecht, letter to WE, 16 March 1954.
50. WE, letter to Stallknecht, 22 March 1954 (misdated by WE). In a letter to Leslie A. Fiedler (10 Feb. 1956), he explained himself: 'I was made to sign an affidavit, as a condition for my visa to lecture at Bloomington, that I would "support American policy", that is, act as a traitor to my own country for American pay. At a time when the two countries were seriously disagreeing about foreign policy the demand could hardly be regarded otherwise; and what I think extraordinary is that the Americans can make such demands without realising that foreigners feel they ought to be resisted' (ALS in Houghton; TLS Fiedler).
51. *The Ambiguity of William Empson*, produced by David Perry (BBC Radio 3, broadcast 22 Oct. 1977).
52. It is equally possible, on the other hand, that he extemporized a speech along the lines of his inaugural lecture at Sheffield. Even three years later, when he was asked whether he would care to repeat his inaugural for a student literary society, Empson responded that it would give him no difficulty to recover it: 'That was simply chattering about my teaching experience in China and Japan . . . (there is no question of requiring a text to read out)' (letter to Michael Freeman, 22 June 1957).
53. His personal anecdotes included this recollection: 'Around 1949, in Peking, I happened to be moving behind some visitor looking at the work of the universities, and a Chinese biologist (while we were gaping at the rabbits) came up and shook me warmly by the hand, because, he said, he remembered how I had arrived drunk on some great occasion when The Rockefeller Man had visited the refugee Chinese universities in Kunming in 1939. He knew nothing else about me, but this was quite enough; everybody had felt it showed real good feeling from the resident foreigner. I was rather startled by this tribute, because the way the afternoon had worked out [in Kunming] had only seemed to me unfortunate; but they had felt it as extremely unpleasant to be reviewed by the silent Rockefeller Man, obviously thinking "You might be worth sixpence. As for you, I'm not sure I wouldn't give you ninepence." I know it's very unfair, but that's the way it worked.'
54. WE, 'China', unpublished essay, 23 July 1953 (Houghton).
55. Winchell, *"Too Good To Be True"*, p. 75.

56. WE, letter to HE, 10 July 1954.
57. Leslie A. Fiedler, letter to WE, 18 Jan. 1956 (copy courtesy of Leslie A. Fiedler; quoted in Winchell, *"Too Good To Be True"*, 142–43).
58. Quoted in Winchell, *"Too Good To Be True"*, 143.
59. WE, letter to Leslie Fiedler, 10 Feb. 1956 (ALS in Houghton; TLS Fiedler).
60. Memo from SAC, Indianapolis, to the Director of the FBI, 17 Sept. 1954.
61. Office Memo to Director, FBI, 27 July 1954 (the interview took place on 14 July).
62. Office Memo to Director, FBI, 17 Sept. 1954.
63. WE, letter to HE, 2 Aug. 1954.
64. WE, letter to HE, 9 Aug. 1954. WE grew fond of his niece Robin, daughter of his brother Charles. In 1966, when she became engaged to a young publisher, Alan Maclean, brother of the spy Donald Maclean who had defected to Moscow, HE wrote to WE: 'Poor old Robin had William Hickey being snide about her engagement to the man Maclean (didn't Charles or Monica tell you he is the brother of the man who defected to Moscow?). It seems it has taken six years for them to agree to the marriage, possibly hoping the man in Moscow would die' (Sheffield). (See also Alan Maclean's memoirs, *No, I Tell a Lie, It Was the Tuesday* (London: Kyle Cathie, 1997)). WE did not respond to the gossipy possibilities of Robin's match; he was concerned only that she be given a nice wedding present (which was not something he would normally be bothered to think about), writing to HE on 4 March 1966: 'Robin said she wanted a wooden salad bowl for a wedding present—or some other household gadget, but not a pressure cooker, which frightens her. Do you think you could look for something? A rather grand salad-bowl, with nice wood or something, seems a good idea' (Sheffield).
65. WE, 2-page typescript; possibly a draft for 'The Queen and I'.
66. Roma Gill, letter to the editor, *TLS*, 31 July 1987.
67. Unpublished interview with Christopher Norris and David Wilson.
68. WE, 'The Queen and I', *SSS*, 222.
69. WE, letter to HE, 'Tuesday evening' (19 Oct. 1954).
70. 'The Queen and I', 224.
71. Ibid. 224–5.
72. Lord Halifax had been Viceroy of India and Ambassador to the USA, and Home Secretary in the critical period immediately before and during the early days of the Second World War; he was Chancellor of Sheffield University from 1947 to 1959.
73. Quoted in *Darts* (The Newspaper of Sheffield University Union), no. III (Royal Visit and Rag Edition), 4 Nov. 1954, 1.
74. Although Dr Gilbert Kennedy worked in the University's Cancer Research Unit, he was actually an expert not on cancer but on natural pigments.
75. WE, 'The Queen and I', 225–6.

76. Ibid. 227–8.
77. Ibid. 228.
78. WE, letter to Ian Parsons, 6 Nov. 1954 (Reading).
79. The only comparable undertaking in the modern era had been a satirical *Masque of Hope* devised by Oxford University Dramatic Society for Princess Elizabeth's visit to the University in May 1948: produced by Glynne Wickham, it had notably starred Robert Hardy, John Schlesinger, and Kenneth Tynan (Graham Binns, 'Hope's Half Century', *Oxford Today*, 10: 3 (Trinity issue, 1998), 30–2).
80. See WE, 'The Queen and I', *SSS*, 220–31.
81. He was so pleased by Peter Cheeseman's production of the masque that he wrote him a superb reference (now lost) when he came to apply to be Director of the Derby Playhouse in Dec. 1959—'one of the longest and most helpful references that anyone has ever given to a prospective employer,' he was told. Cheeseman got the job.

13. MÉNAGE À TROIS

1. Inga-Stina Ewbank, letter to JH, 15 March 2001. After taking her MA at Sheffield, Ewbank (1932–2004), who was to become a distinguished Shakespeare scholar and linguist, and an inspirational teacher, would teach at the Shakespeare Institute, Birmingham University; then at Bedford College, London, where she became Hildred Carlile Professor, 1974–84; and finally as Professor of English Literature at Leeds University, 1985–97. Her publications include *Their Proper Sphere: A Study of the Bronte Sisters as Early Victorian Female Novelists* (1966), studies of Shakespeare, George Peele, John Webster, and Thomas Middleton; an edition of Ben Jonson's *Catiline*; and, with Peter Hall, collaborative translations of Ibsen. See obituaries in the *Guardian* (by David Fairer), 17 June 2004, 25; *Times*, 1 July 2004, 72.
2. WE, letter to Bonamy Dobrée, 24 October 1954 (Brotherton Library).
3. He did not hold with celibacy or any need for self-denial; he wrote for example in a typescript draft of a passage of *Milton's God*: 'sexual desire when unsatisfied is particularly good at producing a sense of uncleanness.'
4. Trevor Baxter, e-mail to JH, 1 Aug. 2005. 'His was a most engaging personality... [T]here was a legend that he had been dared to walk the length of some posh brasserie in Bond Street that B.B.C. people frequented at that time with his penis out. He picked up a large silver tray of salmon mayonnaise, which always stood at the centre of the room, and placed his virile member amongst the salad. He then strutted down the room and back again. It was a time when childish games seemed a natural corollary of intellectual brilliance.'
5. Jacob Empson, letter to Walter Brown, undated (Sheffield).

6. Kathleen Raine, letter to Dorothea Richards, postmarked 19 July 1955 (Magdalene). It was not the first time Raine had reported a breakdown in the Empson marriage. Six years earlier, she had picked up from Michael Roberts some gossip to the effect that Hetta might be leaving Empson in Peking (there is no corroborative evidence), and so wrote to Julian Trevelyan on 7 April 1949: 'I am distressed to hear of Bill's misfortune—I do not know whether Michael's story is true, but as you say it sounds probable. It is sad that he should be left with the two little boys, but he will be a better mother than Hetta and her day-nurseries. He may have loved her, but he has scarcely written a poem since he set eyes on her, which does not suggest that she was good for him, and he has seemed most unhappy all these years. I cannot think that her departure can hurt Bill as much as her continued presence. Beauty's impact is strongest from a distance and stupid insensitiveness at close proximity is disastrous—and Hetta, God knows, was every kind of fool. But as you know, I am the last person to be fair to her, admiring Bill as I do. And it may only drive him more hopelessly within himself than ever, to lose her.' (Wren Library, Trinity College, Cambridge)

7. See obituary of Peter Duval Smith in *The Times*, 10 Feb. 1967, 14.

8. Paul Johnson, 'London Diary', *New Statesman*, 17 Feb. 1967, 218.

9. Richard West, *Victory in Vietnam* (London: Private Eye Publications/André Deutsch, 1974), 3–4, 6–7. West gives a notable account of Duval Smith's later career and his death in Vietnam in February 1967.

10. John Press, letter to JH, 4 March 2001.

11. See also John Stallworthy, *Louis MacNeice* (London: Faber and Faber, 1995), 384–5.

12. See ibid. 429.

13. From a funeral oration by Gwenda David.

14. John Willett, 'Unambiguously magnificent' (obit.), *The Guardian*, 10 Jan. 1997.

15. Interview with Professor Lewis Wolpert, 25 Nov. 1994.

16. WE, letter to Edmund Blunden, 11 April 1956 (Houghton copy).

17. In the late 1950s Duval Smith wrote a number of reviews for the *New Statesman*; his review of William Golding's *Free Fall* gives an example of his forthright judgement: 'he is preaching a sermon against callousness. It is an excellent thing to do, but his examples are too lurid, and he pitches his voice too stridently' ('Hear the Preacher', *New Statesman*, 24 Oct. 1959, 551).

18. Interview with Alice Stewart, 23 March 1991.

19. Max Bickerton, letter to Walter Brown, 18 Jan. 1956 (Sheffield).

20. WE, 'The Marriage of Marvell', *UB*, 81.

21. To Mark Thompson WE would repeatedly say in the early 1980s that the research on his essay about Marvell's marriage was all done, 'but that the result was *dull*: he was at great pains to make it enjoyable to read; he revised and revised' ('Notes on meetings with William Empson', June 1986).

22. WE, 'Natural Magic and Populism in Marvell's Poetry', *UB*, 14–15.

23. WE, 'The Marriage of Marvell', *UB*, 80.
24. Ibid. 87.
25. Interview with Alice Stewart, 23 March 1991.
26. Cf. WE's remark in 'The Theme of *Ulysses*', *Kenyon Review*, 18: 1 (Winter 1956), 47: 'In general, where the only holy or classy pleasure is inflicting and gloating over torture, a merely sexual scoptophilia is the very lowest pleasure of all.'
27. WE, 'The Just Man Made Innocent', *New Statesman* (19 April 1963).
28. *SVP*, 226.
29. WE, letter to HE, 21 Sept. 1948 (Sheffield).
30. WE, 'The Theme of *Ulysses*' (1956), 30–1, 37, 43, 48. 'I can claim, at any rate,' he wrote further, 'that an impulse to adventurous treatment of the Eternal Triangle was pressing on his mind when he started *Ulysses*' (44). Rachel Harris (Mrs Richard Harris), who became friendly with the Empsons in Peking in the late 1940s, recalled for me in an undated memo: 'My first acquaintance with William and Hetta was a weekend we stayed with them in their courtyard house in Peking. On the Saturday evening we had a Chinese meal in the centre of the city and had a great deal to drink—Hetta was anxious to prolong the evening but William wanted to go home and I agreed to go back with him in a pedicab leaving Hetta with Richard. The conversation I had with William on the way was somewhat unexpected. We already knew about Hetta's "young men" and it seemed as if he wanted in some way to explain the situation. He confided in me that he very much wanted to father another child and that he was saving himself for this occasion and was glad that Hetta was able to enjoy herself in her own way.' (She recalls too, 'When William stayed with us in Shanghai I was able to see for myself the almost dual personality, the charm of the sober man and the terrible bouts of drunken aggressiveness.' And of a later period, in England: 'We were often with them in later years in Hampstead when my hearing was already becoming affected and I shall always remember the way in which he would talk to me as if I were an intellectual equal, never becoming impatient.')
31. Conversation with Professor David Hawkes, Jan. 1997.
32. WE, letter to Ian Parsons, 20 Aug. 1949 (Reading).
33. Peter Duval Smith, memorandum to H. F., 17 May 1954 (BBC Written Archives). WE's published version of the talk, 'The Theme of *Ulysses*' (1956), includes this sentence among other ambiguities: 'Now there seems nothing in the book to stop you from assuming . . . that Stephen *did* go to bed with Molly, very soon after the one day of the book; and, what is more, that Joyce when he looks back thinks it probably saved his life and anyhow made it possible for him to become the great author who tells the story' (28). Compare too: '[Joyce] seems very unhomosexual and rather short even of ordinary intimacy with other men . . . [T]o find himself in a triangular

relation with the Ur-Bloom would be striking for him. After trying to look at the arguments all round, I cannot get away from feeling that at least an approach to the situation really happened.' (51)

34. WE, 'The Theme of *Ulysses*', *20th Century Studies*, no. 2 (Nov. 1969), 40.

35. Ibid. 253.

36. Ibid. 224, 254. See also WE's discussion of cuckoldry and jealousy in a play by Fernand Crommelynck, *Le Cocu Magnifique* (which James Joyce believed had preempted *Exiles*): 'Magnificent Cuckolds', in *SSS*, 156–60.

37. *SVP*, 161.

38. Raymond Southall was at the time an Assistant Lecturer in the Department of English Literature.

39. *MG*, 264.

40. *MG*, 106.

41. WE, letter to G. Wilson Knight, 3 Feb. 1957 (Brotherton). 'I was astonished,' WE continued in the same letter, 'to have a bit of linguistics talked at me by a distinguished Chinese pansy my wife and I met at a Peking dance-hall; he said that in Chinese there were many words for a male invert like himself but no word meaning men who enjoyed them, because it was presumed that any man did, as he claimed to have proved; but the English word implied that only special men did, and he could go right on with anecdotes about how it wasn't only special men, among any of the distinguished conquerors of China during his time.'

   With regard to what he termed the 'bisexual integration', Wilson Knight had written: 'Roughly we may note certain conditions and characteristics of such abnormal persons . . . There is, often, a close relationship to the mother, with the father playing a less emphatic part, a well-known condition often associated with the name "Oedipus". A strong feminine element is preserved, which is less "effeminacy" than spiritual insight, and the result is "bisexual". Such men are . . . ill-attuned for marriage; they may be ascetic, licentious, homosexual, or incestuous in tendency' (*Lord Byron's Marriage* (London: Routledge and Kegan Paul, 1957), 281).

42. WE, draft letter to Darcy O'Brien, 9 March 1970.

43. WE, draft letter to Darcy O'Brien, 13 Feb. 1970 (Houghton).

44. Interview with Jill Neville, 7 Dec. 1994.

45. WE, 'The Theme of *Ulysses*' (1956), 27.

46. HE, letter to Walter Brown, 9 Dec. 1955.

47. Interview with Alice Stewart, 23 March 1991.

48. Biddy Crozier, a close friend of the Empson family, was left with the decided impression that Hetta had indeed pushed Empson towards Alice, as if to balance out Hetta's own 'bad' behaviour (interview, Jan. 2002).

49. HE, letter to Walter Brown, 25 Nov. 1955.

50. Hetta's feeling of alienation from her Empson in-laws continued through the following Easter, when Empson had to take the children by himself to

Yokefleet Hall while Hetta stayed in London. Once again, the good old goat served for an excuse. 'Thank you . . . for asking us all for Easter,' WE wrote to Arthur on 19 March 1956. 'Hetta writes to me that *she* can't come, for one thing because of the goat, but the children would like to' (C. C. Empson).

51. WE, letter to Alice Stewart, 30 Nov. 1955 (Sheffield).

52. Interview with Alice Stewart, 23 March 1991.

53. See Michael Wharton, *The Missing Will* (London: Chatto & Windus, 1984), 182.

54. WE, letter to Edmund Blunden, 11 April 1956 (carbon copy in Hull).

55. G. S. Fraser, 'For William Empson's Fiftieth Birthday', *New Statesman*, 3 November 1956.

56. WE, letter to HE, 18 May 1956 (Sheffield).

57. WE, letter to HE, 12 Oct. 1956 (Sheffield).

58. WE, letter to HE, 'Wednesday' (? 14 Nov. 1956).

59. Ibid.

60. C. S. Lewis, letter to WE, 29 Sept. 1957 (Houghton).

61. John Horder, 'William Empson, straight', *The Guardian*, 12 Aug. 1969. However, in his notes on Lewis's later study, *The Discarded Image* (1964), WE was to adjudge: 'Leaves little room for *any* novelty in the Renaissance.'

62. WE, letter to HE, 'Wednesday' (? 14 Nov. 1956). The 'new man' to whom he referred was Christopher Heywood—a 27-year-old from Cape Town who had been a Rhodes Scholar at Oxford (B.Litt) and then for a time a research fellow at Birmingham—with his wife Annemarie.

63. WE, letter to HE, 'Wednesday' (late Nov. 1956).

64. WE, letter to HE, 'Tuesday, 27th' (Nov. 1956).

65. HE, letter to Duval Smith, 'Thurs. 6th 8 pm.' (Sheffield).

66. Peter Duval Smith, letter to HE, 10 Dec. 1956 (Sheffield).

67. WE, letter to HE, Saturday 8th (Dec. 1956). (Sheffield)

68. WE, letter to Arthur Empson, 11 Dec. 1956 (C. C. Empson).

69. Gwenda David, funeral oration for HE.

70. Blofeld had gone from Beijing to the Chair of English at Chulalongkorn University in Bangkok; a prolific author, his learned and graceful books— they include *The Wheel of Life* (1959), *City of Lingering Splendour* (1961), and *The Way of Power* (1970)—are acknowledged as modern classics.

71. WE, letter to Peter Duval Smith, 21 Jan. 1957 (Sheffield).

72. WE, letter to HE, 23 Jan. 1957 (Sheffield).

73. WE, letter to HE, 25 Jan. 1957 (Sheffield).

74. Ibid.

75. C. D. Wickenden (solicitor), letter to WE, 4 Jan. 1957 (Sheffield).

76. WE, letter to Peter Duval Smith, 7 Feb. 1958 (Sheffield).

77. WE, letter to HE, 17 Feb. 1957 (Sheffield).

78. HE, letter to WE, 19 Feb. 1957 (Sheffield). Max Bickerton was to do duty as rent-collector at Studio House. On 9 April she reconfirmed in a letter to Walter Brown and David Kidd in Japan: 'I left Jake, Mog & Pa in the care of

Mei Fang Blofeld in London, saying I'd be away a year. We're all friends and you'd like my Peter' (Sheffield).

79. WE, letter to Peter Duval Smith, 7 Feb. 1957 (Sheffield).
80. Peter Duval Smith, letter to WE, 24 Feb. 1957 (Sheffield).
81. HE, letter to Walter Brown, 15 April 1957 (Sheffield).
82. WE, letter to Edmund Blunden, 23 March 1957 (Texas).
83. HE, letter to Walter Brown, 9 April 1957 (Sheffield).
84. WE, letter to Ian Parsons, 24 March 1957 (Reading).
85. Annemarie Heywood, e-mail letter to JH, 7 Nov. 2001.
86. WE, letter to HE, 8 April 1957 (Sheffield). On 24 Nov. 1957 he would write to Hetta about Blunden: 'You may feel I might have done more, but if he thinks I wronged him over appointing Peter (that is, recommended Peter for personal reasons) there isn't really anything I can say about it; the only question is whether the appointment turns out to have been a good one, as I really thought it would and expect it is doing, and that he must decide for himself' (Sheffield).
87. HE, letter to WE, 15 April 1957 (Sheffield). In his own letter, WE respectfully referred to Blunden as 'Professor Edmund Blunden'.
88. HE, letter to WE, 2 May 1957 (Sheffield).
89. HE, letter to WE, 15 April 1957 (Sheffield).
90. HE, letter to WE, 14 July 1957 (Sheffield).
91. We, letter to HE, 7 Aug. 1957 (Sheffield).
92. Interview with Jill Neville, 7 Dec. 1994.
93. WE, letter to HE, 4 Nov. 1957 (Sheffield).
94. WE, letter to HE, 24 Nov. 1957 (Sheffield).
95. WE, letter to HE, 20 June 1957 (Sheffield).
96. Ibid.
97. WE, letter to John Crowe Ransom, 5 May 1957. He told HE too (24 April 1957): 'I had the more difficult experience in a way of trying to coax the old Anglican gentleman into meeting the devil alone. They thought it great fun and quite unhurting, and I was so interested in how they reacted that I came home typing about that instead of the many other things the poor old horse ought to be typing about. Oh well, it's been my most badgered holiday so far, but tum can hold.'
98. WE, letter to HE, 7 Aug. 1957 (Sheffield).
99. WE, letter to HE, 24 April 1957 (Sheffield).
100. WE, letter to HE, 20 June 1957 (Sheffield).
101. WE, letter to HE, 7 Sept. 1957 (Sheffield).
102. WE, letter to Arthur Empson, 5 Sept. 1957 (Sheffield).
103. WE, letter to HE, 21 Sept. 1957 (Sheffield).
104. WE, letter to HE, 19 Jan. 1958 (Sheffield).
105. WE, letter to Alice Stewart, 'Sunday' (March 1958). (Sheffield)
106. WE, letter to HE, 25 April 1958 (Sheffield).

107. See WE, letter to Arthur Empson, 15 Nov. 1958: 'I went to London two weeks ago and saw the kids at their half-term leave. Jacobus Arthur likes school but finds his lessons too easy; it is all revising and the last fortnight he had come out top. This bears out a grave warning given me earlier by Mog, that they were putting him in too low a form, which might in the end mean keeping him there for another year. Mog wanted me to write to the Headmaster about it, which I am sure would annoy him as I obviously don't know enough. I expect they will find him his place soon enough; anyhow I thought it showed Mog was taking the right attitude to having a younger brother there' (C. C. Empson).

108. Interview with Biddy Crozier, Jan. 2002.

109. A. M. Stewart, 'The lethal habit' (letter to the editor), *The Times*, 16 Jan. 1971, 13.

110. Interview with Alice Stewart, 23 March 1991.

111. Jacob Empson noted, in an e-mail to JH (3 July 2002), that Alice Stewart 'was very kind to us boys during the time that Hetta was away with Peter Duval Smith, and devoted a lot of her time to us, although one never felt that she was trying to be mumsy. Rather being a good sport, really.'

112. WE, letter to Alice Stewart (March 1958) (Stewart).

113. WE, letter to HE, 29 March 1958 (Sheffield).

114. WE, letter to Alice Stewart, 1 May 1958 (Stewart).

115. WE, letter to HE, 25 April 1958 (Sheffield).

116. In the event, the only book ever published over his name was the posthumous collection of broadcast essays, *Ends of the Earth: Some Collected Travels*, with an introd. by James Cameron (London: Hamish Hamilton, 1969); he was a very fine journalist and travel writer. To the very end he remained avid for excitement. 'To say that war is fun is wrong,' he was to write in one uncollected article, 'but that's what you feel sometimes' ('In the Jungle', *New Statesman*, 18 Dec. 1964, 960).

117. WE, letter to HE, 17 June 1958 (Sheffield).

118. WE, letter to Dorothea Richards, 23 June 1958 (Magdalene).

119. Peter Duval Smith, letter to HE, 4 July 1958 (Sheffield).

120. WE, letter to Arthur Empson, 1 Dec. 1958 (C. C. Empson).

121. Interview with Jill Neville, 7 Dec. 1994.

122. Lewis Wolpert, '"I trusted her and she trusted me... We really did love each other"' (a tribute), *The Times*, 5 Aug. 1997, 13.

123. HE, letter to WE, 26 Jan. 1960 (Sheffield).

124. Jill Neville, *Fall-Girl* (London, 1966), 59.

125. For an idiosyncratic study of Michael Avery, see Nigel Richardson, *Dog Days in Soho: One Man's Adventures in 1950s Bohemia* (London: Victor Gollancz, 2000).

126. WE, letter to *Paunch*, no. 25 (Feb. 1966); *A*, p. 493.

127. WE, letter to Alice Stewart, 6 Dec. 1959 (Stewart). HE, who was determined to be as complaisant towards his affair as he was to hers, wrote to him on one occasion, after an outburst of bad temper on her part, in an undated letter:

'Dearest William,

'I'm so very sorry you should feel you have to go to gloomy Sheffield—or to *make* evasive arrangements in order to have your pleasure.

'Please explain to Alice that I have a temper which makes me say & do what I have to, but once said and done it is the end of the matter.

'I certainly did not want to make an uneasy situation of this kind and I do want you, and us all, to be happy and comfortable. So that naturally I want Alice to come and go as always. I'm sorry I behaved badly' (Sheffield).

128. HE, letter to WE, Wednesday, 20 Jan. 1960 (Sheffield).

129. WE, letter to HE, 25 Jan. 1960 (Sheffield).

130. HE, letter to WE, 26 Jan. 1960 (Sheffield).

131. WE, letter to Jill Neville, 14 Feb. 1960. (The late Jill Neville). I have quoted all that survives of the letter; at least one further page has been lost.

132. A. Alvarez, *Where Did It All Go Right?* (London: Richard Cohen Books, 1999), 312–13. See also obituaries of Neville in the *Daily Telegraph*, 13 June 1997; *The Independent*, 12 June 1997; *The Times*, 14 June 1997.

133. Interview with Lewis Wolpert, 25 Nov. 1994.

134. Richardson reports the recollections of 'Frank', one of Josh's drinking partners in Hampstead: 'Hetta Empson, with whom Josh was then sleeping, off and on, was always attacking him—with a broken bottle or a heavy ashtray—and he was forever turning up at their favourite pub, the Rosslyn Arms, covered in blood. One story struck a chord, though. Josh had got into a fight in a restaurant and been arrested and bound over to keep the peace. When the story appeared in the *Hampstead & Highgate Express*, Josh was described as a poet. "He loved it," said Frank. "The thought of being a poet. He was always telling people at Hetta's he was a poet. But then he'd come unstuck sometimes 'cos he'd meet a real poet. Then Hetta would say something like, 'Oh, don't worry, he's an absolute poet in bed and that's all that matters,' and of course no one dared take Josh on 'cos he could handle himself..." (*Dog Days in Soho*, 152–3).

Richardson notes too (225–6): 'In time [Josh] would move in with Hetta and William Empson, and over twelve years this arrangement would evolve into the classic French triangle. By way of rent he slept with Hetta and, on William's returns from Sheffield, he slept, or at least would share a bed, with William and allow the author of *Seven Types of Ambiguity* and *Milton's God* to rub himself off against the small of his back.'

135. *MG*, 265.

136. Interview with Margaret 'Biddy' Crozier, Jan. 2002.

137. Telephone interview with Geoff Hill.

138. Kenneth Tynan, 'Shouts and Murmurs', *Observer Review*, 16 June 1968, 26.
139. WE, letter to HE, n.d. (17 June 1968) (Sheffield).
140. Interview with George Watson, 5 July 1996.
141. Fay Weldon, oration at HE's funeral, Jan. 1997. See also Weldon, *Mantrapped* (London: Fourth Estate, 2004), 111–12.

14. THE ANTI-CHRISTIAN: *MILTON'S GOD*

1. WE, letter to Bonamy Dobrée, Oct. 1954 (Brotherton).
2. WE, letter to Ian Parsons, 29 Oct. 1956 (Reading).
3. WE, letter to Ian Parsons, 27 April 1957 (Reading).
4. *STA*, viii.
5. Rosemund Tuve, letter to WE, 14 Feb. 1953 (Houghton).
6. 'Herbert's Quaintness', *A*, 258.
7. *STA*, 225–6.
8. Anon, 'Pied Beauty in Spanish', *TLS*, 13 Aug. 1954, 509–10.
9. Derwent May, *Critical Times: The History of the Times Literary Supplement* (London: HarperCollins, 2001), 340.
10. WE, '"The Windhover"' (letter), *TLS*, 20 May 1955, 269; *SL*, 231–3.
11. T. S. Eliot, 'Donne in Our Time', in *A Garland for John Donne*, ed. Theodore Spencer (Oxford, 1931), 11–12.
12. *MG*, 263. See also an editorial, 'Puzzling about Godot', *TLS*, 13 April 1956.
13. WE, '"Waiting for Godot"' (letter), *TLS*, 30 March 1956, 195. See also a notable letter from WE to Francis Doherty, 7 Dec. 1971, in *SL*, 523–5.
14. WE, 'The Loss of Paradise', *The Northern Miscellany*, no. 1 (Autumn 1953), 17–18. Cf. David Reid, *The Humanism of 'Paradise Lost'* (Edinburgh: Edinburgh University Press, 1993). In one of his notebooks WE returned, presumably after the publication of *Milton's God*, to a second reading of Waldock's book; his notes then included these observations: 'Very good, rings like a gong on every page. I ought to have acknowledged how much I was using it. But radically wrong because he cannot conceive of Milton as *really* wanting to justify God, *really* distressed by his incapacity to do it; and he seems to refuse to invent more in the story to explain apparent contradictions in a quite arbitrary way—sometimes it is allowed, sometimes not. The idea that Milton *could* not have seen any need to justify his God, because *everybody* then saw no need, seems to cripple his mind; a result of ignorance of what Milton's contemporaries were saying. Powerful strokes of imagination have to be called impudent laziness (God exercising his troops).'
15. WE, letter to Rosemond Tuve, 25 Feb. 1953; *SSS*, 127.'
16. WE, letter to Ian Parsons, 19 March 1959 (Reading).
17. WE, letter to Ian Parsons, 14 May 1959 (Reading).
18. WE, letter to Ian Parsons, 29 Nov. 1959 (Reading).
19. WE, letter to Ian Parsons, 6 Sept. 1960 (Reading).

20. WE, letter to Ian Parsons, 22 Jan. 1961 (Reading).
21. F. W. Bateson, 'Empson's Godot', *Sunday Telegraph*, 10 Sept. 1961.
22. WE, letter to Ian Parsons, 25 March 1960 (Reading); letter to Robert Winter, 7 March 1963 (Herbert Stern).
23. WE was not fully informed: see Nicolas Walter, *Blasphemy Ancient and Modern* (London: Rationalist Press Association, 1990).
24. WE, 'A Full-Blown Lily', *New Statesman*, 6 Jan. 1961; *A*, 605–7.
25. 'Arthur Koestler', *New Statesman*, 20 Jan. 1961, 90.
26. WE, letter to Ian Parsons, 22 Jan. 1961 (Reading).
27. WE, letter to Norah Smallwood, 27 April 1961 (Reading). His professional title was put back on the title page for the second edition.
28. In response to the first of WE's radio talks, 'Satan Argues His Case', in *The Listener*, 64 (7 July 1960), C. S. Lewis protested in a letter (21 July 1960, p. 109): 'Professor Empson is mistaken when he says I have argued that Milton's Satan "must be meant to be funny". I took *Paradise Lost* as a tragic, and *The Egoist* as a comic, treatment of "the satanic predicament". I said that Milton has subordinated the absurdity of Satan to his misery; but that, just as Meredith cannot exclude all pathos from Sir Willoughby, so Milton cannot exclude all that is ridiculous from Satan. Surely the distinction between saying this and saying that Satan is "meant to be funny" is not imperceptibly fine?' WE responded with respectful tact (*The Listener*, 28 July 1960, p. 157): 'I was saying that God laughs at Satan, in his first words in the poem, and that this supports Professor Lewis's view, though it is rather coarse of God. I know that Professor Lewis would show better feeling. But his account of Satan as morally absurd in *A Preface to Paradise Lost* is very impressive, and clearly true up to a point. Milton would think it in order to be sardonic about the enemy of mankind, and seems to have disliked the character he imagined. My point is that, at the same time, he was scrupulously careful to give the character the strongest arguments he could invent. So it did not occur to me that fairness demanded my recalling the qualifications of tone in Professor Lewis's position; though I readily agree that he put them in.'
29. Christopher Ricks wrote with justice, in a review of the second edition ('The Ways of God', *New Statesman*, 27 Aug. 1965, 292): 'In one respect . . . Empson's position has hardened, and to me unconvincingly. Granted, Milton's poem is, among many things, a fierce argument about God's justice. And it could well be agreed . . . that the notorious narrative inconsistencies, all of which damage God's standing unless they are explained away as technical blunderings, press coincidence too far, and manifest an unconscious hostility towards, and criticism of, Milton's God . . . But this is very different from arguing that Milton *consciously* doubted that God was just.'
30. WE, letter to Ian Parsons, 5 Jan. 1963 (Reading).
31. Letter to *New Statesman*, 31 March 1967, 437.

32. In 'Handling Milton' (*The Guardian*, 16 Sept. 1960), his review of *The Living Milton* (ed. Kermode), WE had anticipated the objection: 'In the final chapter, Mr Bergonzi discusses the old controversy with breadth and decides that the attacks of the anti-Miltonists have not been answered "because they are, quite simply, unanswerable ... within the terms of reference in which they are made"; but as he still finds the poetry good he concludes that the terms must be wrong. Above all, it is "grossly imperceptive" to read the poem as if it were a novel. Several other contributors warn us against doing this, and I think they are all engaged in escapism. Various people in the controversy had shown, most of them while attacking Milton's God, that the motivation of the characters is remarkably well imagined; the only reason for denying this is to avoid calling his God unfair.' See also Helen Gardner, *A Reading of 'Paradise Lost'* (Oxford: Clarendon Press, 1965), and WE's review, 'Not Like a Novel', *New Statesman*, 70 (24 December 1965), 1004.

33. John N. Morris, 'Empson's Milton', *Sewanee Review*, Autumn 1962, 676. John Wain remarked that Empson's reading of *Paradise Lost* has the effect of turning the poem into 'an unselfish attempt to argue a hopeless cause' ('Milton for the defence', *Observer*, 10 September 1961).

34. John Bayley, ' ... The Ways of Man to Man', *Spectator*, 30 July 1965.

35. Letter to Karunakar Jha, 20 June 1971 (copy in Houghton). Cf. Harold Beaver: '[WE] is at heart a generous critic, on the look-out for "decent feelings", temperamentally averse to ironic or aesthetic closures, persuaded that an author's intention (be he Milton or Joyce) "is inherently likely to be the best possible, the richest or most humanly responsive, construction we can place upon his work". So interpretation in *Milton's God*, as Stanley Fish remarked, "developed in the space *between* the explorations of verbal texture rather than as a result of them" ' ('Tilting at Windbags', *New Statesman* 11 Aug. 1978, 185–6).

36. WE, 'Handling Milton' (review of *The Living Milton*, ed. Frank Kermode), *The Guardian*, 16 Sept. 1960. See also Kermode's review of *MG*: 'Empson's Milton', *The Guardian*, 13 Sept. 1961. The beginnings of a helpful re-evaluation of WE's treatment of *Paradise Lost* can be found in an essay by Tobias Gregory, 'In Defense of Empson: A Reassesssment of *Milton's God*', in *Fault Lines and Controversies in the Study of Seventeenth-Century English Literature*, ed. Claude J. Summers and Ted-Larry Pebworth (Columbia: University of Missouri Press, 2002), 73–87.

37. F. N. Lees, 'Empson Contra Gentiles', *The Tablet*, 29 Sept. 1961.

38. Anon, 'God and Mr. Empson', *TLS*, 29 Sept. 1961, 646.

39. WE, ' "Milton's God" ' (letter), *TLS*, 6 Oct. 1961, 663.

40. WE, letter to Robert Winter, 8 February 1964 (Herbert Stern).

41. Helen Gardner, 'Empson's Milton', *The Listener*, 5 Oct. 1961, 522.

42. Graham Hough, 'Mr Empson on Milton's God', BBC Third Programme broadcast, 21 Oct. 1961.

43. WE wrote in an undated letter to John Wain: 'When I said that one can't discuss whether a man believes in the Trinity, I gave the reason: that it is a set of verbal contradictions (in Athanasius at least), so that he can only inure his mind to accepting them' (copy in Houghton).

44. S. G. F. Brandon, *The Judgment of the Dead* (London: Weidenfeld & Nicolson, 1967), 104, 108, 98, 134–5, 196.

45. Kenneth Burke, 'Invective Against the Father', *The Nation*, 16 June 1962, 541.

46. WE interviewed by Christopher Norris and David Wilson, 20 Dec. 1970.

47. Graham Hough, 'Mr. Empson on Milton's God'.

48. E. M. W. Tillyard, letter to WE, 27 Oct. 1961 (Houghton).

49. WE, letter to Arthur Empson, n.d. (C. C. Empson). Of Tillyard's book *Studies in Milton* (1951), WE wrote in his notes: 'Strangest part the cool admission that most Christians don't believe in this wicked old father—seems I am making a fuss about nothing; but this is very bad behaviour from intellectuals—they have comfort and approval, and the ignorant or direct-minded people, encouraged by the intellectuals to think the religion is believed, are driven into suffering and evil. It ought not to be supported unless it publicly stops worshipping its monster.'

50. Letter to Frank Kermode, 27 March 1961 (copy in Houghton).

51. Letter to 'Mr Montague', n.d. (copy in Houghton).

52. Reported in 'Four Women in Union Society Debate', *Cambridge Daily News*, 28 Nov. 1962.

53. Undated and unpublished draft letter to the editor of the *Hudson Review* (in response to Roger Sale's article 'The Achievement of William Empson', *Hudson Review*, 19, Autumn 1966, 369–90). See also WE's published letter, *Hudson Review*, 20, 1967, 434–8; *SL* 462–7.

54. WE, 'Milton's God' (letter), *PMLA*, Jan. 1978, 118; *SL* 639–40.

55. In a letter about his article 'The Variants for the Byzantium Poems' (see *UB*, 163–86), WE wrote to Prof. Kim Jong-Gil on 23 April 1965: 'It is not offensive in Asia, being concerned to say that Christian critics fail to understand what the Byzantium poems were about because Yeats genuinely did think like a Buddhist or Hindu' (Kim Jong-Gil).

56. In 1972 WE contributed to a BBC broadcast, 'Tennyson: Eighty Years On', produced by Hallam Tennyson: see 'Empson on Tennyson', *The Tennyson Research Bulletin*, 4: 3 (Nov. 1984), 107–9. 'I wrote a piece about Mouldy Wedding Cake for Hallam Tennyson,' he reported in a letter to Christopher Ricks on 27 Aug. 1972, 'and he wouldn't believe that Tithonus was kept back for twenty years before printing, till he had searched through your edition. He thought it a rude insinuation to suppose that the poet thought the wish for Nirvana a bit rakish and unChristian. But I don't know why else he would hold it back, do you?—except simply as saying the opposite of *In Memoriam*, which might I suppose be commented on.'

57. Edward L. Hirsh, untitled review, *America*, 28 April 1962. See also W. W. Robson, 'Mr Empson on *Paradise Lost*', *Critical Essays* (London: Routledge & Kegan Paul, 1966), 94–5.

58. *Daily Telegraph*, 20 Oct. 1961.

59. WE stuck to his guns: see his letter to the *New York Review of Books* (1 June 1978), in *SL*, 643–5.

'The chief new defence invented for God is that he intends to resign, and will do so as soon as he conscientiously can, as soon as a workable alternative to his rule has been prepared . . . Christopher Hill gives me welcome support for the idea that God is going to abdicate, saying that it is found in a number of Ranters and suchlike bold men. But they seem to have expected a kind of palace revolution, whereas Milton presents it as a plan which the Creator has been evolving since the start of time.

'Such being what my book says . . . , it is not really an answer to say I "claim" that Milton hated God. But I welcome Christopher Hill saying things rather near it, such as

Empson is right to suggest that Milton was in some sense aware of the terrible collapse which is always possible . . .

if the widespread hatred of God could no longer be contained.'

60. Anon. 'Pastoral and Proletarian', *TLS*, 30 Nov. 1935.

61. Cf. Sigmund Freud's observation, in *The Future of an Illusion* (Anchor Books, 1984), 56: 'If men are taught that there is no almighty and all-just God, no divine world order and no future life, they will feel exempt from all obligation to obey the precepts of civilization. Everyone will, without inhibition or fear, follow asocial, egoistic instincts and seek to exercise his power.'

62. Guy Hunter, 'Science and Magic', *London Mercury*, Feb. 1936.

63. WE, 'Preface' to John R. Harrison, *The Reactionaries* (London: Gollancz, 1966), 11–12.

64. WE, letter to Ian Parsons, 31 Jan. 1967 (Reading).

15. FROM SHEFFIELD TO LEGON

1. WE, letter to Ian Parsons, 6 Dec. 1960 (Reading).

2. WE, letter to the Dean (D. R. Cousin), 19 July 1960 (Houghton).

3. WE, letter to Ian Parsons, 6 Dec. 1960 (Reading). W. W. Robson was to reflect, in a letter to JH: 'I organized Graves's campaign and got the statute changed so that he could run (which he otherwise could not have, as he had not graduated MA in the ordinary course). This was an inexplicable mistake: I knew what Graves was capable of, having read his Clark Lectures. But I went ahead. Graves was not a success as Professor of Poetry (in contrast to Auden). Empson might have been better, but as he was so unpredictable this cannot be said with confidence. In any case, he would not have been elected. Convocation usually chooses someone from Oxford.' On 6 Oct. 1968

F. W. Bateson was to ask WE if he might be 'available' for election when Edmund Blunden stood down from the Chair of Poetry.

4. WE, letter to the Bursar, 24 July 1960 (Sheffield).

5. D. R. Cousin, letter to WE, 13 Sept. 1960 (Houghton). Cousin (1904–84) was Professor of Philosophy from 1949 until 1969; he was the second holder of the Chair of Philosophy at Sheffield; Dean of Arts, 1958–61. Deeply well versed in the rules, regulations, ordinances, and statutes of the university, he was also reputed for his kindness, tolerance, and courtesy.

6. WE, letter to Arthur Empson, 6 Oct. 1960 (C. C. Empson).

7. WE, letter to Arthur Empson, 22 Jan. 1961 (C. C. Empson). Eric Laughton, Professor of Latin, told me that throughout his own tenure as Dean, 1961–64, WE was continually anxious to avoid the succession.

8. WE, letter to Christopher Ricks, 18 Oct. 1965 (Ricks).

9. Hetta wrote to WE on 28 Jan. 1966: 'I spoke to Elizabeth Barker (Smart) about the Oxford professorship and said she should drum up support for Lowell which she was keen to do. She has just telephoned to suggest that you write a piece for her magazine, called Queen, so I said I'd ask. I don't know how much good it could do, but Elizabeth thinks a lot of people peer at Queen and it might help. What do you think? A jolly, witty, short piece saying Lowell is the man. The thing is the next issue comes out on 16th Feb. and I don't know when the Oxford decision is to be made' (Sheffield).

10. WE, letter to Robert Winter, 8 Feb. 1964 (Herbert Stern).

11. See George Hartley, 'The domestic school of publishing', *The Guardian*, 20 Oct. 1961; and *Selected Letters of Philip Larkin, 1940–1985*, ed. Anthony Thwaite (London: Faber & Faber, 1992), pp. xxvii–xxviii.

12. WE to Parsons, 14 May 1959.

13. 'The first pressing was of 100 copies only and was out of pressing by 4th June,' George Hartley wrote to Chatto & Windus on 26 Nov. 1961. 'We issued a new pressing at the beginning of this month' (Reading University Library).

14. John Wain, 'A gulp of rough red wine', *The Observer Weekend Review*, 19 February 1961, 26.

15. WE, letter to Ian Parsons, 25 March 1960 (Reading).

16. WE, letter to Ian Parsons, 20 Nov. 1961 (Reading).

17. See 'Court and Social' in *The Times*, 1 June 1961, 16.

18. John Heath-Stubbs, *Hindsights: An Autobiography* (London: Hodder & Stoughton, 1993), 258–9.

19. John Coleman, 'Centres and Ceremonies', *New Statesman*, 28 July 1961, 130.

20. National Sound Archive: 360R (Poetry at the Mermaid, 23 July 1961).

21. Interview with Prof. and Mrs Eric Laughton, 28 June 1984. Auden was still drinking when he returned for the night to the Laughtons' house. The following morning, he reappeared with his eyes fast closed; he refused breakfast, but then observed that he could probably manage a grapefruit.

22. WE, letter to David Holbrook, 23 March 1962 (Houghton; possibly a draft: *SL*, 328). A year later, in response to Holbrook's *Llareggub Revisited: Dylan Thomas and the State of Modern Poetry*, WE reiterated in a published piece his belief that Auden and Thomas 'had the real fire' ('Dylan Thomas', *E in C*, 13: 3 (April 1963); *A*, 398).

23. See WE, letters to Robert Lowell, 9 March and 12 Oct. 1959 (Houghton: MS Am 1905). Lowell wrote to WE on 20 March 1959: 'I've got a new book of poems coming out here and in England sometime in April, a big thing maybe, heavily autobiographical, in prose and verse and which has taken me about ten years to figure and hammer out' (Houghton).

24. Robert Lowell, letter to WE, 12 Nov. 1959 (Houghton).

25. Robert Lowell, letter to WE, 29 Jan. 1958 (Houghton).

26. Ian Hamilton, 'A Conversation with Robert Lowell', *The Review* 26 (Summer 1971), reprinted in *Robert Lowell: Interviews and Memoirs*, ed. Jeffrey Meyers (Ann Arbor, Michigan: The University of Michigan Press, 1988), 154. Philip Booth, 'Summers in Castine: Contact Prints, 1955–1965', *Salmagundi* 37 (Spring 1977), reprinted in *Robert Lowell*, ed. Meyers, 196. Robert Lowell, 'Digressions from Larkin's 20th-Century Verse', *Encounter*, 40: 5 (May 1973), 68. When Christopher Ricks approached Lowell to see if he would contribute to the *festschrift* edited by Roma Gill (*William Empson*, 1974), Lowell replied on a postcard (16 Jan. 1973): 'Doing something on William has long defeated me, I'm afraid. No poem comes; a considered critical essay is beyond my uncritical talents; I can't somehow catch hold of him briefly in a paragraph or two. My kind of judgment edged out of reminiscence would be impertinent in a festschrift. I've been through this with my old friend Allen Tate, and finally did nothing. William is one of the few (only?) people I read every scrap of and am never disappointed. I don't want to disappoint by promising a piece I won't write' (Christopher Ricks).

27. Robert Fitzgerald speaks of the influence of WE on Lowell's *Lord Weary's Castle*, in 'The Things of the Eye', *Poetry* 132 (May 1978), reprinted in *Robert Lowell: Interviews and Memoirs*, 225.

28. Robert Lowell, letter to WE, 16 May 1960 (Houghton).

29. Robert Lowell, letter to Elizabeth Bishop, 12 Aug. 1963.

30. Mark Thompson, 'Notes on meetings with William Empson', June 1986. WE's recollection of the exchange with Lowell followed on from a brief discussion of the present writer's biography of John Berryman, which (WE noted) had been made plump and comprehensive by the number of letters and personal manuscripts I was able to cite or quote—'and then [WE went on] he quotes the poetry, but it turns out not to be poetry at all, do you see; parts of his diary chopped up.' After a pause, WE proceeded: 'It's an extraordinary thing, the development of free verse in my lifetime.' Of the Berryman archive: 'But no one in my family keeps such things, any more

than I do.' WE wondered how I was going to cope with writing his biography without a collection of such letters and manuscripts.

31. Father Peter A. Fiore, OFM, e-mail to JH, 22 Aug. 2002. Fiore was Dean of the School of Liberal Arts at Siena College, a liberal arts undergraduate institution in New York State; and knowing he was being put up for promotion he asked Empson if he would support his application with a testimonial. 'He obliged with a short letter that he sent directly to the CEO of the college (but he shared the content with me) and which I found humorous and interesting. Humorous in that he wrote that I had very good taste since I had asked him to contribute to the Donne volume, and interesting in that I had definite opinions and was never shy about expressing them.'

32. Robert Lowell, letter to WE, 5 Dec. 1966 (Houghton).

33. 'University Library opened', *The Times*, 13 May 1959, 12. See also University of Sheffield 54th annual report, 1958–59, 23–6.

34. Recorded in Robert Lowell, letter to Gertrude Buckman (10 June 1947).

35. WE, 'Eliot and Politics', *T. S. Eliot Review*, 2: 2 (Fall 1975); *A*, 365.

36. WE, 'Marina' (*c.*1931), *A*, 360.

37. Interview with Kim Jong-gil, 27 April 1985.

38. Michael Freeman, letter to JH, 13 July 1984. 'You naturally feel bothered by the duty of organising, depressed by the lack of response, and so forth,' WE wrote to Freeman about the literary society on 22 June 1957. 'I don't think it shows poor spirit if the students don't want extra lectures; I hate going to lectures myself, and expect it is more important for students to read books, also of course discuss them while they are interested, and feel that advice is easily available' (courtesy of Michael Freeman).

39. Philip Hobsbaum, letter to JH, 27 June 1985.

40. Deidre (Heeton) Sanders, letter to JH, 14 Dec. 1994.

41. WE must have committed the poem to memory back in 1948, when Bernard Heringman, a student at the Kenyon Summer School, chose to write a close criticism of the poem to which WE added a written response (and Heringman's friend John Unterecker added further analytical comments): see *SSS*, 'Appendix. Three Critics on One Poem: An Informal Correspondence in Hart Crane's "Voyages III"', 233–42.

42. David Fuller, letter to JH, 30 July 1989.

43. Interview with Kim Jong-gil, 27 April 1985.

44. John S. Whitley, letter to JH, 24 Aug. 1992.

45. John S. Whitley remembers further that WE came 'down to Sussex in 1965 or 1966 to speak to the Literary Society. I had dinner with him and remember that he was rather deferential to his wife and drank only water. He assured me that the Sheffield undergraduates talked as much nonsense as they did "in your day". His talk, loosely about Yeats' "Byzantium" poems, was astonishingly well attended, with some students left outside in the

corridor. He was clearly famous to the students of the new Universities' (letter to JH, 24 Aug. 1992).

46. Roger Ebbatson, letter to JH, 21 Dec. 1988.

47. Freeman, letter to JH, 13 July 1984. One person who never got the chance to study under WE was the critic Lorna Sage, who recorded in a memoir that in 1960 she and her husband Victor 'both wanted very much to go and sit at his feet' as students (*Bad Blood* (London: Fourth Estate, 2000), 273).

48. Philip Hobsbaum, 27 June 1985.

49. Hobsbaum quoted in a profile by Neal Ascherson, 'Great Brain Spotter', *The Independent on Sunday*, 28 February 1993, 30.

50. 'Philip Hobsbaum in conversation with Nicholas Tredell', *PN Review* 119 (Jan.-Feb. 1998), 24.

51. WE, letter to George Fraser, 29 July 1963 (National Library of Scotland).

52. Ken Livingstone quoted in Ascherson, 'Great Brain Spotter', 30.

53. 'Philip Hobsbaum in conversation with Nicholas Tredell', 24.

54. Philip Hobsbaum, 'Empson as Teacher: The Sheffield Years', in *William Empson: The Critical Achievement*, ed. Christopher Norris and Nigel Mapp (Cambridge, 1993), 294.

55. WE quoted in Hobsbaum, 'Empson as Teacher', 295.

56. WE quoted ibid. 296.

57. Ibid. 298.

58. Ibid. 299.

59. WE, letter to Philip Hobsbaum, 3 Feb. 1962 (Victoria).

60. WE quoted in Hobsbaum, 'Empson as Teacher', 300–1.

61. Ibid. 301–3.

62. WE on *King Lear* (letter), *CQ*, 3: 1 (Spring 1961); *SL*, 308–9.

63. Hobsbaum, 'Empson as Teacher', 305–6.

64. WE was to write to HE on 28 Sept. 1968: 'George Fraser and his wife have been here, giving Hobsbaum a Ph. D. Very jolly, but he [Fraser] is getting rather alarmingly sodden.' (Hull)

65. WE, letter to Hobsbaum, 2 Aug. 1969 (Victoria).

66. Hobsbaum, 'Empson as Teacher', 306.

67. Hobsbaum, 'Some reasons for the great variety of response to literature among modern literary critics' (Ph.D. thesis, Sheffield, May 1968), 272.

68. See WE's 'Fool in Lear', *SCW*, 125–57; and his letter in reply to Everett, *Critical Quarterly*, 3: 1 (Spring 1961).

69. Quoted in Hobsbaum, 'Empson as teacher', 306. WE's immediate response had been to write these comments: 'An "inescapable" work of art would be simply a man-trap, I suppose ... When you have decided what the author meant, why can't you decide that the meaning was bad (dull, etc)? ... To decide between two variants in a text, or two ways of producing a play, you need to consider which the author is likely to have wanted—to forbid that is merely silly ... ' (ibid. 306–7).

70. Hobsbaum, untitled review, *The Listener*, 74 (9 Sept. 1965), 389.
71. WE, 'Milton's God' (letter), The Listener, 16 Sept. 1965, 422.
72. WE, letter to Hobsbaum, 31 Jan. 1966 (Victoria); quoted in part by Hobsbaum, 'Empson as teacher', 307.
73. Hobsbaum, 'Empson as Teacher', 307.
74. WE, letter to Hobsbaum, 2 Aug.1969 (Victoria).
75. Hobsbaum, 'Empson as teacher', 307.
76. Unpublished interview by Christopher Norris and David B. Wilson. Philip Hobsbaum wrote to Wilson on 28 Oct. 2002, after seeing a transcript of the interview: 'it cannot be true that he refused to teach me, since he remained my very active research supervisor until my PhD was conferred. That was in 1968, at an examiners' meeting over which he presided... [H]e caricatures my view regarding the demise of King Lear. That may be found in a chapter entitled "Survival Values" in my book *A Theory of Communication* (London: Macmillan, 1970). The chapter in question is identical with that of the same title found in my PhD thesis. In that chapter I dissented from any simply Christian interpretation of the play's denouement, such as Empson mischievously ascribes to me.

    'It is a pity to see so distinguished a mind distorting a pupil's contribution to argument in this way. The root of this dissension is little to do with my views on *King Lear* and a great deal to do with the fact that I disagreed—in a review of *Milton's God* which appeared in *The Listener*—with the intentionalism that bedevils that book. Where intentionalism led Empson may be seen in *Using Biography*, especially in the misleading essays on Marvell.' (courtesy of David B. Wilson)
77. Hobsbaum quoted in the *TLS* (14 April 1961), 234. A few months earlier, Hobsbaum had published in *E in C* (10: 4 [Oct. 1960], 436) a rather good joke poem entitled 'Lines for an Assistant Lecturer', and subtitled 'Imitated from William Empson'—it was a parody-villanelle taking off from Empson's 'Reflection from Anita Loos'—which opens:

    No don is sure he will not need a rise.
    You can't be sure until you've made a name.
    A don must edit Milton till he dies.
78. WE, 'Academic Caste' (letter), *TLS*, 28 April 1961, 263.
79. WE, letter to HE, 11 Feb. 1962 (Sheffield).
80. A few years later, WE was to exchange letters with Raymond Southall on the subject of *The Merchant of Venice*, following WE's determination that the play was centrally concerned with gambling and his perverse assumption that it would therefore be of special interest to 'our Marxist' (as he liked to call Southall). Southall recalls: 'If he believed that the Marxist objection to mercantilism was a moral one directed against certain kinds of risk-taking, then he was simply obtuse. If, on the other hand, he was only pretending to this belief, then he was simply being mischievous... Empson was often

provocative when we spoke, but not always and . . . I'm not sure that all of his provocations were intended. He didn't mind being chaffed, although he would at times appear genuinely put out, as when I mentioned once that some view he was declaring sounded like Spender circa 1936' (e-mail letter to JH, 19 Nov. 2001). Southall remembers further: 'During my first week of teaching, Empson dropped into my room one morning and asked me to accompany him to a lecture he was to give. When we arrived at the lecture room he indicated that I should take a seat on the rostrum and after speaking on sixteenth century poetry for about ten minutes, introduced me to the students as a "sixteenth century poetry man" and declared that it would be better if I gave the lecture. I have always entertained a suspicion that he was putting me through my paces and wishing to see how I'd perform' (e-mail letter to JH, 13 Nov. 2001).

81. Seamus Heaney, who participated in Hobsbaum's writing group in Belfast in the sixties, said 'he was impatient, dogmatic, relentlessly literary: yet he was patient with those he trusted, unpredictably susceptible to a wide variety of poems and personalities . . . If he drove some people mad with his absolutes and hurt others with his overbearingness, he confirmed as many with his enthusiasms' (Ascherson, 'Great Brain Spotter', 31). Other poets included Derek Mahon and Michael Longley. Writers fostered in Glasgow included James Kelman, Liz Lochhead and Jeff Torrington.

82. Hobsbaum, letter to JH, 27 June 1985.

83. Christopher Ricks, 'Empson as a Man of Letters in the 1960s', *News from the Republic of Letters*, no. 7 (Sept. 1997), 7.

84. WE, letter to Christopher Ricks, 29 March 1963 (Ricks).

85. Interview with Christopher Ricks, 14 Aug. 1995.

86. WE, letter to Norah Smallwood, 7 Nov. 1970 (Reading).

87. WE, letter to Christopher Ricks, 2 Dec. 1962 (Ricks).

88. 'It occurs to me,' WE had written to Ricks (16 Jan. 1963) about a first version of the third sentence from the end, 'that the end of my quarrel piece about Dylan Thomas is tiresome in talking about "two generations" meaning Auden and Thomas—"the last generation" or the "previous" one is all that's needed. But perhaps I will get a proof later on' (Ricks).

89. Ian Hamilton (1938–2001) edited *The Review* (1962–72)—in 1969 he was to edit *The Modern Poet*, an anthology gathered from the magazine—and *The New Review* (fifty issues, 1974–9). His later publications included a biography of Robert Lowell (1983), *In Search of J. D. Salinger* (1988) and *A Gift Imprisoned: The Poetic Life of Matthew Arnold* (1998). His collections of poetry include *The Visit* (1970) and *Fifty Poems* (1988). See obituaries in *Daily Telegraph* and *The Times*, both 31 Dec. 2001; *The Guardian* (by Karl Miller), 2 Jan. 2002.

90. WE, letter to Christopher Ricks, 5 March 1963 (Ricks).

91. WE, letter to Arthur Empson, 26 Aug. 1961 (C. C. Empson). Li'l (not Little) Abner, and his girlfriend Daisy Mae, of Dogpatch, were created by Al Capp

in the 1930s. There have been two movies based on the cartoon: one with Buster Keaton in 1940, and a better widescreen musical in 1959 with Stubby Kaye (and music by Johnny Mercer). (But it seems not impossible that WE was in fact interviewed by Reg Smythe (1917–98), creator of the cartoon character Andy Capp, which first appeared in the *Daily Mirror* in 1957.)

92. WE, 'Early Auden', from *the Review*, no. 5 (Feb. 1961); *A*, 375–7.

93. HE, letter to WE, 3 Nov. 1962 (Sheffield).

94. *Modern Poetry: American and British*, ed. Kimon Friar and John Malcolm Brinnin (New York: Appleton-Century-Crofts, 1951), 498–9.

95. WE, letter to Arthur Empson, 21 March 1964 (C. C. Empson).

96. Anthony Burgess, 'The arts', *The Listener*, 18 Feb. 1965.

97. WE, letter to Arthur Empson, 19 Jan. 1965 (C. C. Empson).

98. WE, letter to Arthur Empson, 2 Feb. 1965 (C. C. Empson).

99. Molly Kitching, letter to WE, 27 Jan. 1965 (Sheffield).

100. See *The CND Story*, ed. John Minnion and Philip Bolsover (London: Allison & Busby, 1983).

101. Irving Kristol, 'The Question of the Bomb' (*The Spectator*, 18 April 1958), 479–81.

102. WE, 'The Question of the Bomb', *The Spectator*, 25 April 1958, 16.

103. WE, letter to Alice Stewart, 1 May 1958 (Alice Stewart).

104. WE, letter to Robert Lowell, 20 June 1962. (Houghton *73M—90, bMS Am 1905 (442–451)

105. Mark Thompson, 'Notes on meetings with William Empson', June 1986.

106. Alan Brownjohn, 'William Empson at Aldermaston', in *Collected Poems 1952–1988* (London: Hutchinson, 1988), 22.

107. The Earl Russell, letter to WE, 27 May 1964 (copy in Bertrand Russell Archives, McMaster University).

108. WE, letter ('Warren Report') to the *New Statesman*, 16 Oct. 1964.

109. Bertrand Russell, letter to WE, 3 Nov. 1964 (Bertrand Russell Archives, McMaster University). WE would later support Russell's campaign against the lunatic foreign policies of Senator Barry Goldwater.

110. 'Everybody's doin' it', *Peace News*, 22 July 1966.

111. 'William Empson in conversation with Christopher Ricks', 34.

112. WE, letter to Arthur Empson, 6 Oct. 1960 (C. C. Empson).

113. WE, letter to Arthur Empson, 22 Jan. 1961 (C. C. Empson).

114. HE, letter to WE, 5 March 1965 (Sheffield). Linden defended her father's reputation (against aspersions cast by Auberon Waugh) in a letter to the *Independent*, 17 July 1989: 'Having lived through two world wars, and fearful of the consequences of a third, he believed in and fought for a policy of détente between the Western and Eastern powers. To hold those views during the era of McCarthyism and the cold war, was to be branded a Communist, a traitor, dangerous heretic.'

115. WE, letter to Arthur Empson, 17 March 1963 (C. C. Empson). See further Robert P. Newman, *Owen Lattimore and the "Loss" of China* (Berkeley and Los Angeles: University of California Press, 1992), esp. ch. 29, 'Ascendancy at Leeds'; Jonathan Mirsky, 'The Hounding of a Pioneer', *TLS* (8 May 1992), 7–8.

116. WE, letter to IAR, 9 June 1964 (Magdalene).

117. WE, letter to Arthur Empson, 8 Sept. 1963 (C. C. Empson).

118. HE, letter to Robert Winter, 11 May 1964 (Herbert Stern).

119. WE, letter to Mr Wright, 31 July 1961 (carbon in Houghton).

120. WE, letter to Arthur Empson, 17 March 1963 (C. C. Empson).

121. Derek Roper, WE's colleague at Sheffield, recalls that while Hetta could observe proprieties in public, at home 'she was less inhibited, and the scene I chiefly remember [*c*.1960–3] if that of her wrestling with Jake for a bottle of beer that he had taken from her, crying "For fuck's sake, Jake, give me mah bottle!" She was a bit tight, but not much, and the two of them were laughing a lot, and seemed very fond of each other. She made him a fringed garment to go on the CND demo with, that must have taken quite a bit of work; he liked it but was in doubt whether it wasn't "camp", a word just then (I think) getting into circulation over here.' Roper remembers too that he and his wife had felt apprehensive on an earlier occasion when Hetta was due to stay a night at their house in Victoria Road, Sheffield. 'In the event she was a perfectly charming, perfectly conventional guest, and sent us a nice bread-and-butter note afterwards. Conceivably she had been warned that we were a stuffy couple and was minding her ps and qs. We had just acquired the first of our mongrels, and she suggested the name Fred for it, which would have been exactly right if it had been of the other sex.'

122. WE, letter to Robert Winter, 8 February 1964 (Herbert Stern).

123. WE, letter to Arthur Empson, 23 April 1965 (C. C. Empson).

124. WE, letter to Alice Stewart, 4 Oct. 1965 (Stewart).

125. WE, 'The Hammer's Ring', in *I. A. Richards: Essays in His Honor*, ed. Reuben Brower, Helen Vendler, John Hollander (New York, 1973), 77; *A*, 219.

126. Interview with Conor Cruise O'Brien, 12 Jan. 2002. WE wrote to his old friend Robert Winter on 8 Feb. 1964: 'I. A. Richards is in Ghana this winter, invited by Conor Cruise O'Brien (who was a U.N. official in the Congo and is now Vice-Chancellor of Ghana University) to advise them on English textbooks. There are a lot of tribal languages but nothing widely spoken enough to rival English, so they urgently need a mass elementary language-teaching program. O'Brien wrote to me about it and I could not induce Richards to play ball, but finally O'B flew to Boston and won him over. I hope to God he gets results' (Herbert Stern).

127. Conor Cruise O'Brien, letter to WE, 25 June 1965 (Houghton).

128. Conor Cruise O'Brien, *Memoir: My Life and Themes* (London: Profile Books, 1998, 1999), 131.

129. WE's remarks were quoted back at him in a letter from O'Brien, 14 Aug. 1964. O'Brien defended himself: ' "Sordid" the article may be. I think that most of the existing writing on Yeats is influenced by a prevailing tendency in England to make an excessive number of charitable assumptions; these make the writer, as well as his subject, feel and look good. In the case of Yeats this has led biographers to play down, e.g., his pronounced and enduring fascist tendencies into being a "passing flirtation" ' (Houghton).

130. WE, letter to Ian Parsons, 2 Nov. 1964 (Reading).

131. Donald Harman Akenson, *Conor: A Biography of Conor Cruise O'Brien* (Montreal and Kingston: McGill-Queen's University Press, 1994), 222.

132. Douglas Duncan, letter to JH, 21 Feb. 1992.

133. WE, letter to Ian Parsons, 2 Nov. 1964 (Reading).

134. Conor Cruise O'Brien, 'The Fall of Africa', *Passion and Cunning and Other Essays* (London: Weidenfeld & Nicolson, 1988), 274.

135. WE, letter to Arthur Empson, 29 Nov. 1964 (C. C. Empson).

136. Ibid.

137. WE, letter to Arthur Empson, 17 Oct. 1964 (C. C. Empson).

138. WE, letter to Ian Parsons, 2 Nov. 1964 (Reading).

139. Quoted from memory by Douglas Duncan, letter to JH, 21 Feb. 1992. WE's letter has been lost.

140. Duncan, letter to JH, 21 Feb. 1992.

141. WE, letter to Arthur Empson, 17 Oct. 1964 (C. C. Empson).

142. WE, letter to Arthur Empson, 29 Nov. 1964 (C. C. Empson).

143. Douglas Duncan, letter to JH, 21 Feb. 1992.

144. JH, Interview with John Willett.

145. Conor Cruise O'Brien wrote on 22 Jan. 1965: 'At the time when you were invited the strain on the balance of payments had not manifested itself and it therefore could not have occurred to me to warn you that there might be delays in transferring a balance ... Your suggestion that people are being invited under false pretences is both unnecessary and regrettable.' (Houghton).

146. Conor Cruise O'Brien, letter to WE, 25 June 1965 (Houghton).

16. THE ROAD TO RETIREMENT

1. WE, letter to Francis Berry, 27 Aug. 1964 (Francis Berry).

2. JH, interview with John Willett.

3. WE, letter to Ian Parsons, 16 April 1966 (Reading).

4. WE, letter to HE, 2 Feb. 1965 (Sheffield).

5. HE, letter to WE, 15 Feb. 1965 (Sheffield).

6. WE, letter to Arthur Empson, 23 April 1965 (C. C. Empson).

7. HE, letter to WE, 27 May 1965 (Sheffield).

8. HE, letter to Alice Stewart, 5 July 1965 (Alice Stewart).

9. George Melly, *Hooked! Fishing Memories* (London: Robson Books, 2000), 113–14.

10. Melly, *Hooked!*, 115.

11. HE, letter to Alice Stewart, 4 Oct. 1965 (Alice Stewart).

12. Jacob Empson, e-mail to JH, 27 May 2005.

13. In general, WE was not averse to awarding Firsts; in a letter to HE of 12 June 1959, he enthused: 'We have been interviewing the Final Honours people all day, giving three Firsts which is rather a triumph ...' (Sheffield).

14. Roger Sale, e-mail to JH, 8 May 2001.

15. WE, 'To whom it may concern', 14 Dec. 1972 (Houghton).

16. WE, letter to David Parker, 28 Feb. 1966 (Parker).

17. WE, letter 'To whom it may concern', 14 Dec. 1972 (Houghton).

18. David Parker, letter to JH, 4 July 1989.

19. WE, letter to 'Doctor Slay', 25 Feb. 1977 (Houghton).

20. WE, letter 'To whom it may concern', 14 Dec. 1972 (Houghton).

21. David Parker, letter to JH, 4 July 1989.

22. Andrew Braybrook, memo, 12 Jan 2003.

23. John Brown, letter to JH, 29 Nov. 1996.

24. WE wrote to George Fraser (who had been taken ill) on 29 Jan. 1974: 'When you are convalescent I will send you some of the best American whodunit writer, REX STOUT, out of fashion now. Or have you read them all long ago? They are on the side of the angels but have none of the false heroics of Raymond Chandler.' (National Library of Scotland) Francis Berry noted in his verses 'William Empson':

     Detective novel for his evening ease;
     At puzzling out this game of intellects
     No-one shrewder. (*Collected Poems* (Bristol: Redcliffe Press, 1994), 346)

    Mark Thompson noted in the 1970s that WE's bedside table was crammed with paperback detective stories in various stages of disintegration. 'Not strong enough for our love,' said WE as he rooted through the packed shelves for a Nero Wolfe story to lend to Thompson (letter to JH, 25 Sept. 1986).

    On depression, WE remarked in 1967, 'I'm very liable to go into depression. I wouldn't have written the poetry if I'd been satisfied.' (Byron Rogers, 'Man of words', *The Star* (Sheffield), 31 March 1967, 4.)

25. John Brown, letter to JH, 29 Nov. 1996.

26. Richard Sylvester, letter to JH, 1 July 2005.

27. WE, letter to Arthur Empson, 14 May 1966 (C. C. Empson).

28. WE, letter to Christopher Ricks, 1 June 1966 (Ricks).

29. John Brown, letter to JH. 29 Nov. 1996.

30. Telephone interview with Geoff Hill, May 1996.

31. WE said of Josh, rather too bluffly, that he was 'very fond of the dear boy': he was a 'good chap' (telephone interview with Geoff Hill, May 1996).

32. Geoff Hill, letter to JH, 11 May 1996.

33. WE was to write to Christopher Ricks, in an undated letter (1970s): 'Obviously vapouring about structure takes practically no prep. at all' (Ricks).

34. Telephone interview with Geoff Hill, May 1996.

35. WE, 'To Whom It May Concern', 4 April 1969 (Geoff Hill).

36. Personal information from Derek Roper (who had taken a small part in the production of *Othello* that WE fairly obviously lamented).

37. WE, letter to Francis Dillon, no date (Houghton).

38. Passages from *The Heroes of Samsara* appeared in *Arrows*, no. 96 (1968), 22.

39. *MG*, 142

40. Francis Berry, untitled review in *New Poetry* magazine, 42–3.

41. WE, letter to Nick Malone, 19 Aug. 1971 (Malone).

42. WE, letter to Nick Malone, 11 Dec. 1973 (Malone).

43. WE, 'Introduction' to Nick Malone, *The Burial of Crispin Pike* (London: Workshop Press, 1974), 5–6.

44. WE, letter to Nick Malone, 9 Jan. 1974 (Malone).

45. WE, letter to Nick Malone, 5 Nov. 1974 (Malone).

46. WE, letter to Nick Malone, 9 Oct. 1979 (Malone).

47. WE, letter to HE, 14 March 1967 (Sheffield).

48. WE, letter to Ian Parsons, 31 Jan. 1967 (Reading).

49. WE, letter to HE, 28 Sept. 1968 (Sheffield).

50. WE, letter to Francis Berry, 8 June 1967 (Francis Berry).

51. Robert Lowell, letter to WE, 26 Feb. 1967 (Houghton).

52. WE, letter to HE, 18 Feb. 1967 (Sheffield).

53. Interview with Pat Smith, 23 Sept. 1993. Alan Usher (1930–98) joined the University of Sheffield as a lecturer in 1961 and became Head of Department in 1964, when he was appointed Consultant Pathologist to the Home Office and Senior Police Surgeon to the South Yorkshire Police Service. In 1978 he was appointed to a new Chair in Forensic Pathology. His high-profile investigations included one of the Yorkshire Ripper cases, the Helen Smith case in Jedda, the Cannock Chase murders, and the Perera dismemberment case. Sometime President of the British Association in Forensic Medicine, he received an OBE in 1980. In addition, he enjoyed a national reputation as a brilliant after-dinner speaker.

54. WE, letter to Alice Stewart, 22 March 1967 (Alice Stewart).

55. WE, letter to Arthur Empson, 30 April 1967 (C. C. Empson).

56. WE, letter to C. B. Cox, 16 April 1967 (John Rylands Library).

57. WE, letter to Arthur Empson, 12 April 1967 (C. C. Empson).

58. HE, letter to Mogador Empson, 6 April 1967 (Sheffield: DEN(3)/104).

59. WE, letter to Arthur Empson, 12 April 1967 (C. C. Empson). Professor G. K. Hunter has recalled of this period: 'I was in Cambridge, to examine a PhD

candidate with Muriel Bradbrook. Empson called in to Muriel's rooms to announce that he had been diagnosed as having throat cancer. He had shaved off his "Chinese" beard and was determined to stay drunk (he told us) till ...—I can't remember what the terminal event was supposed to be' (letter to JH, 17 Dec. 1994).

60. WE, letter to Arthur Empson, 2 April 1967 (C. C. Empson).
61. WE, letter to Francis Berry, 21 April 1967 (Berry).
62. WE, letter to Arthur Empson, 30 April 1967 (C. C. Empson). Nonetheless, he wrote a precautionary letter to Buffalo, advising the administration that he was having treatment for the cancer but that he felt confident of being able to do his teaching as long as he could start a week later than scheduled (letter to William Sylvester, 21 April 1967; Buffalo).
63. WE, letter to Francis Berry, 3 June 1967 (Berry).
64. WE, letter to Ian Parsons, 17 June 1967 (Reading).
65. Several months later, on 5 May 1968, Hetta would for some reason write to WE: 'I see Alvarez is blaming you for John Berryman's twitchiness—I think Al himself is rather twitchy, don't you?'(Sheffield). In an uncollected lyric in the style of the *Dream Songs* published after his death, Berryman himself would gnomically remark: 'I have never forgiven Empson for one remark | about ebullient Henry's ebullience' (*Henry's Fate & Other Poems*, ed. John Haffenden (New York: Farrar, Straus & Giroux, 1977; London: Faber & Faber, 1978, 17)—from which it may be possible to deduce that Empson had made an uncomplimentary remark about Berryman's reading of his poetry.
66. Charles Osborne, *Giving it Away: The Memoirs of an Uncivil Servant* (London: Secker & Warburg, 1986), 197.
67. WE, letter to Robert Lowell, 13 May 1968 (Houghton).
68. WE, letter to Alice Stewart, 5 July 1965 (Alice Stewart).
69. WE, letter to Christopher Ricks, 10 Aug. 1967 (Ricks).
70. WE, letter to Christopher Ricks, 3 Aug. 1967 (Ricks).
71. WE, letter to Ian Parsons, 25 Aug. 1967 (Reading).
72. HE, letter to Francis Berry, 11 Sept. 1967 (Berry).
73. Mogador Empson, letter to Francis Berry, 22 Aug. 1967 (Berry).
74. WE, draft letter to Douglas Duncan, 12 Sept. 1967 (Houghton).
75. WE, letter to Molly Empson, 3 Oct. 1967 (C. C. Empson). It must have felt like more bother that R. M. Wilson, his counterpart in the Department of English Language, was on leave of absence (as a visiting professor at the University of Pittsburgh) until the end of April 1968, since Wilson often took care to look after the interests of his sister Department; Mr Hands stood in.
76. Christopher Heywood, e-mail letter to JH, 1 Nov. 2001.
77. Harry Kay, letter to JH, 18 Feb. 1992.
78. John Myers, Secretary of the selection committee of The Ingram Merrill Foundation, letter to WE, 19 Feb. 1968 (Houghton).

79. Harry Ford, Ingram Merrill Foundation, letter to WH, 15 Jan. 1968 (Houghton).

80. WE, letter to HE, 13 Oct. 1966 (Sheffield).

81. WE, letter to HE, 20 Oct. 1966 (Sheffield).

82. Ibid.

83. WE, letter to I. A. Richards, 11 April 1968 (Magdalene).

84. WE, letter to William Sylvester, 20 Oct. 1966 (Buffalo).

85. WE, letter to Phyllis Faruga, 5 April 1967 (Buffalo).

86. WE, letter to Thomas E. Connolly, 7 April 1968 (Buffalo).

87. See *The Times*, 26 Feb. 1968; *Eastern Daily Press* (Norwich), 10 June 1968.

88. WE, letter to Ian Parsons, postmarked 16 Jan. 1973 (Reading).

89. HE, letter to Walter Brown, 12 Oct. 1968 (Sheffield).

90. WE, letter to Robert Lowell, 3 Aug. 1968 (Houghton).

91. WE, letter to Thomas E. Connolly, 7 April 1968 (Buffalo). On Kenner (1923–2003), see obits in *The Daily Telegraph*, 28 Nov. 2003, 31; *The Times*, 27 Nov. 2003, 43.

92. WE, 'Humanism and Mr Bloom', *New Statesman and Nation*, 11 Aug. 1956; *A*, 477–8.

93. Thomas E. Connolly, letter to JH, 16 Oct. 1986.

94. Fritz Senn, e-mail to JH, 17 April 2002. Another participant at the summer school, Professor Leonard Nathan, remembers the atmosphere of disputatiousness in general: 'What still stands out for me is that the arguments did not stop at the lectern, but were pursued hotly out under the stars or even the summer sun. The issues raised were deadly serious to the participants and went far beyond literary topics . . . The finale was a debate among the critics; the poets and story writers read from their own work. To me the debate was at least as remarkable as the readings perhaps because the former had by no means become reconciled to their opponents. It was, as I remember, a long hot summer' (letter to JH, 17 June 2002). Recalling the specific contretemps, Nathan adds (e-mail to JH, 3 July 2002): 'the host introduced the participants, Empson turned to Kenner and the fun began, mostly one-sided, but not lacking in spirit for that. Empson was relentless, but Kenner took it pretty well, even to making a little joke about it after.'

95. Hugh Kenner, 'The Politics of the Plain Style', *New York Times Book Review*, 15 Sept. 1985, 40. Cf. Bernard Crick, 'Why are radicals so eager to give up one of their own?', *Independent on Sunday*, 14 July 1996, 10: 'But don't misread *Nineteen Eighty-Four*. It warned not just against communism but against any kind of total power.'

96. Hugh Kenner, *A Sinking Island: The Modern English Writers* (London: Barrie & Jenkins, 1988), 212–13 and footnote.

97. Interview with Frank Pierce, 16 Feb. 1984.

98. WE, letter to Alice Stewart, 11 Sept. 1968 (Stewart).

99. WE, letter to HE, 15 Feb. 1969 (Sheffield).

100. WE letter to HE, 10 Oct. 1968 (Sheffield). HE wrote on 12 Oct. 1968 in exuberant vein to Walter Brown: 'Jake's got a grant to do post-graduate, and commutes between two looney bins on a scooter, writing down idle chatter (I suppose) in a little black note-book, and inventing tests to confuse the poor sods' (Sheffield).

101. WE, letter to Jacob Empson, 15 July 1969 (Jacob Empson).

102. HE was to write to Walter Brown on 12 Oct. 1968: 'Mog and Linden and Saul and Ben (the new one) still live below stairs, making sporadic sallies, investigating costly houses in Hampstead, and then returning spent to subside in the womb tomb cosiness of Studio House once more' (Sheffield).

103. HE, letter to WE, 18 May 1969 (Sheffield).

104. 'Mog wants to become China correspondent of the Daily Telegraph—I do hope he gets that' (WE, letter to Alice Stewart, 3 Feb. 1970).

105. In June 1979 Jacob Empson, even while still pursuing his career as an academic at Hull University, was to open and run a restaurant called *Restaurant Duval*; and his elder brother was kindly able to provide the restaurant with a dozen windfall cases of Mouton Cadet at £1 a bottle.

106. WE wrote to his accountant Wickenden on 24 Aug. 1968: 'we have just scored a success, at great cost to my shaky nerves but I had to prove to my elder son Mogador that I was backing him seriously; we had a show-down with my eldest brother Arthur, at which Arthur appeared impenetrable, but today a letter arrives saying that Arthur will lend Mogador money to buy a house. We are not clear whether he realises that Mogador intends to buy a large house, with tenants, but in any case the whole behaviour of Arthur has long been baffling to a romantic degree. When Mogador asked him point-blank how he meant to leave the property, he simpered in an elderly way and said that was his secret' (Sheffield).

107. WE, letter to Jacob Empson, 15 July 1969 (Jacob Empson).

108. WE, letter to G. S. Fraser, 6 Oct. 1970 (National Library of Scotland). Hetta was to write to WE on 30 Oct. 1970, 'All hell is breaking loose on every floor here. The first floor bathroom has been ripped out (no floor) and they found a great fruiting BODY' (Sheffield).

109. WE, letter to HE, 19 June 1970 (Sheffield).

110. George Kane, letter to WE, 7 July 1971 (Houghton).

111. WE, letter to HE, 28 Sept. 1968 (Sheffield).

112. WE, letter to Alice Stewart, 24 Sept. 1968 (Alice Stewart).

113. HE, letter to Walter Brown, 12 Oct. 1968 (Sheffield).

114. HE, interview with Norris and Wilson, 20 Dec. 1970.

115. WE, letter to HE, 11 May 1969 (Sheffield).

116. Kenneth Muir, letter to JH, 30 Dec. 1993.

117. John Horder, 'William Empson, straight', *The Guardian*, 12 Aug. 1969.

118. WE, letter to HE, 17 Jan. 1971 (Sheffield).

119. John Brown, letter to JH, 29 Nov. 1996.

120. WE, letter to HE, 22 Nov. 1969 (Sheffield).
121. WE, letter to John Webb, 15 June 1969. To Hetta he had written similarly on 22 May 1969: 'The Vice-Chancellor's daughter has become engaged to the President of the Students' Union, the Chief of the Revolt. Almost too cosy perhaps' (Sheffield). The V-C (since 1966) was Prof. Hugh Robson, who was to be knighted in 1974.
122. WE, letter to John Webb, 15 June 1969. He wrote to Hetta on the same day: 'Only twice more; it encourages me to remember that' (Sheffield).
123. WE, 'Old Men remember with advantages', *Arrows*, no. 102 (1971), 10.
124. 'An Introduction to the Drama Studio . . .', *The University of Sheffield Newsletter*, 24 Nov. 1995, 7.
125. WE, letter to Francis Berry, n.d. (March 1970) (Houghton).
126. WE, letter to G. S. Fraser, 6 Oct. 1970 (National Library of Scotland).
127. E. D. Mackerness, 'Professor William Empson', *University of Sheffield Gazette*, no. 51 (Nov. 1971), 60.
128. Francis Berry, 'William Empson', *Collected Poems* (Bristol: Redcliffe Press, 1994), 345–6. The only person to rain on the parade was F. R. Leavis, who wrote to R. T. Jones, a colleague at the University of York (where Leavis was then teaching, having retired from Cambridge, and where he had got to know Brian Morris, a senior lecturer in English who was to become Empson's successor at Sheffield) on 12 Nov. 1970: 'Empson will almost have justified his existence in vacating the Chair. As his first backer (I. A. R[ichards] having politicly refrained), I judge him odious and a bad influence; but he leaves, I imagine, a less hope-defeating situation for B. M. [Morris] than (say) a B. Willey, a Kermode or a L. C. Knights would have done.'
129. Ian Sainsbury, 'Man with an option on existence', *Morning Telegraph* (Sheffield), 6 June 1974.
130. Ian Sainsbury, 'An "old fogey" retires: What will Professor Empson do next?', *Morning Telegraph*, 20 July 1971.
131. Byron Rogers, 'Man of words', *The Star* (Sheffield), 31 March 1967, 4.
132. Details recalled by John Webb in a letter to WE, 12 January 1980.
133. Kathleen Raine, letter to Dorothea Richards, no date (Magdalene). An article by WE's old friend N. W. Pirie was indeed turned down by Gill.
134. 'Annual Degree Congregations', *The University of Sheffield Gazette*, no. 53 (Nov. 1974), 22.
135. 'Professor Empson's reply on behalf of the honorary graduates', ibid. 29–31.

17. RESCUING DONNE AND COLERIDGE

1. WE, letter to Kim Jong-Gil, 23 April 1965 (Kim Jong-Gil).
2. WE, letter to David Kidd, 1 June 1969 (David Kidd).

3. Peter Levi, 'Hot gin and peppermint' [on *RB*], *Independent*, 4 Dec. 1986.

4. Leo Salingar, letter to JH, 21 Sept. 1987.

5. George Watson in conversation with JH, 5 July 1996.

6. F. R. Leavis, who also attended Forster's lectures in 1927, said he was 'astonished at the intellectual nullity' of the series (quoted in Ian MacKillop, *F. R. Leavis: A Life in Criticism* (London: Allen Lane/Penguin Press, 1995), 97).

7. Wordsworth and Coleridge, *Lyrical Ballads*, ed. R. L. Brett and A. R. Jones (London: Methuen, 1962), 276–7.

8. *CV*, 48.

9. Seamus Perry, 'Empson's Coleridge's (a paper given at the conference, 'Versions of Empson', at Sheffield University, July 2003); courtesy of Seamus Perry.

10. Coleridge, *Lectures 1795 on Politics and Religion*, ed. Lewis Patton and Peter Mann (Princeton University Press, 1971), 204.

11. David Pirie, letter to WE, 15 April 1970 (Houghton). Zachary Leader argues to the contrary: 'One difficulty with this view ... is that Coleridge's supposed religious, political, and socio-cultural apostasies are not accompanied by poetical apostasy or "decline" ' ('Coleridge's Revisionary Complexity' in *Revision and Romantic Authorship* (Oxford, 1996), 127. Yet WE and Pirie happily accept that in various particular places Coleridge did enhance his poem in the later editions.

12. David Pirie, letter to WE, 15 April 1970 (Houghton).

13. Charles Monteith, letter to David Pirie, 7 Aug. 1970 (copy in Houghton). It was Monteith who approached WE with a view to his producing a volume on Coleridge in the Faber 'Poet to Poet' series. See too WE's letter, 'The Rights of Editors'—'we put all the rejected verses back (though not all the rejected lines) except the ones that would not fit in, as by making a contradiction'—in *NYRB*, 20: 14 (20 Sept. 1973), 44).

14. *CV*, 52–3.

15. 'In the present edition we sometimes need to restore verses from the first one [edition], which the author would have altered if they had been retained' (*CV*, 61).

16. Jack Stillinger, *Coleridge and Textual Instability: The Multiple Versions of the Major Poems* (New York and Oxford: OUP, 1994), 61.

17. Ibid. 120.

18. Ibid. 123, 121.

19. Ibid. 229–30.

20. J. C. C. Mays, 'Editing Coleridge in the Historicized Present', *Text*, 8 (1995), 226.

21. Charles Rosen, 'Isn't It Romantic', *NYRB*, 20: 10 (14 June 1973), 12–18.

22. Martin Amis (anon), 'Guilty rimer', *TLS*, 15 Dec. 1972, 1524; *Critical Essays on William Empson*, ed. John Constable (Aldershot, Hants.: Scolar Press, 1993), 461–2.

23. WE, 'The Ancient Mariner', *Critical Quarterly*, 6:4 (Winter 1964), 298, 304–5.

24. *CV*, 29–30.

25. See J. R. Ebbatson, 'Coleridge's Mariner and the Rights of Man', *Studies in Romanticism* 11 (1972); Peter J. Kitson, 'Coleridge, the French Revolution and "The Ancient Mariner": Collective Guilt and Individual Salvation', *Yearbook of English Studies*, 19 (1989), 197–207; Kitson, 'Coleridge, the French Revolution and "The Ancient Mariner": A Reassessment', *Coleridge Bulletin*, 7 (1996), 30–48; Patrick J. Keane, *Coleridge's Submerged Politics: the ancient mariner and Robinson Crusoe* (Columbia: University of Missouri Press, 1994).

26. Debbie Lee, *Coleridge and the Romantic Imagination* (Philadelphia: University of Pennsylvania Press, 2002), ch. 3.

27. WE, 'The Ancient Mariner', 308.

28. Coleridge's 1817 gloss to ll. 135–8;

29. H. W. Piper, *The Active Universe: Pantheism and the concept of Imagination in the English Romantic poets* (London: The Athlone Press, 1962), 4.

30. Ibid. 46.

31. Ibid. 99.

32. Ibid. 102.

33. H. W. Piper, ' "The Ancient Mariner": Biblical Allegory, Poetic Symbolism and Religious Crisis', *Southern Review* (Australia), 10: 3 (Nov. 1977), 238, 241.

34. WE, letter to H. W. Piper, 5 March 1978 (draft in Houghton). WE was to write of Piper in the draft of an undated testimonial: 'I reviewed his *Active Universe* for Critical Quarterly of Autumn '63, and hoped then he was my ally about the *Ancient Mariner*. (The later versions ruined the story by making *angels* of the spirits operating the corpses, with changes needed to make that just plausible . . .) Piper understood very well the importance of the nature-spirits for the Renaissance view of the world, and the baffled urge of the Romantics to recover it; and he was talking about it very plainly . . . But he now refuses to say that the young Coleridge had believed in nature-spirits *directly*, he had done it in a philosophical manner. He insisted that we had almost no difference of opinion' (Houghton).

35. H. W. Piper, letter to WE, postmarked 14 March 1978 (Houghton).

36. H. W. Piper, letter to JH, 16 Oct. 1982. Thanks among other considerations to Empson's timely challenge, Piper chose to revise his essay quite extensively before reprinting it as a chapter of his book *Singing of Mount Abora: Coleridge's use of biblical imagery and natural symbolism* (Fairleigh Dickinson University Press, 1987).

37. James Twitchell, 'The World above the Ancient Mariner', *Texas Studies in Literature and Language*, 17: 1 (Spring 1975), 104.

38. Ibid. 111.

39. See e.g. David Perkins, who in an article entitled 'The "Ancient Mariner" and Its Interpreters: Some Versions of Coleridge' dismisses Empson's view of Coleridge as differing '*toto caelo* from Coleridge's, not only from that of the

older Coleridge, a pious hypocrite in Empson's opinion, but also from that of the younger one. Naturally and inevitably, Empson found his own view expressed in the poem . . . He thought of his interpretation as a "rescuing" of the poem for modern readers, a redeeming of it from the "false sentiment and cranky self-righteousness" infiltrated by the parsonical reviser (31). By his hermeneutical principles, Empson could not put forth his interpretation as simply his own. It was not the valid interpretation unless it was also Coleridge's. Hence by selective quotation Empson constructed an un- or even an anti-Christian author and cited this invention as evidence for his interpretation. We should not think badly of him, because, as I have said, it is a common practice' (*Modern Language Quarterly*, 57: 3 (1996), 425–8 [442]).

40. Andrew Bennett, untitled review, in *Romanticism on the Net* 5 (Feb. 1997).

41. WE, letter to HE, 16 July 1971. (Sheffield).

42. WE, letter to Christopher Ricks, 1 March 1966 (Ricks).

43. John Carey, 'Creating canon fodder', *Sunday Times*, 26 Nov. 1989, p. G3. Frank Kermode's essay appeared first as a review of *RB*, 'On a Chinese Mountain', in *LRB*, 20 November 1986; repr., in *An Appetite for Poetry* (London: William Collins, 1989), as 'William Empson: The Critic as Genius': '[A]t a time when there are so many models and techniques that can be got up and assiduously applied, there are individual and eccentric gifts which remain the prerequisite of the best criticism; and Empson possessed them in the degree of genius. Second, there are at the moment attempts to enlist him posthumously in the ranks of a theoretical avant-garde; one sees why, but he does not belong there, and would have said so with his customary asperity and emphasis' (3–4). On WE's interpretation of Donne, he believes: 'Though it may take a bourgeois professor to say so, Empson was wrong about Donne and the New Philosophy. Donne knew about Copernicus and made jokes about Kepler and Tycho Brahe and Galileo, but he habitually thought about the world in pre-Copernican terms . . . ' (127–8).

44. John Carey, *John Donne: Life, Mind and Art* (London: Faber & Faber, 1981), 252.

45. 'Preface to 1974 edition', *SVP*, London: Chatto & Windus, 1974, n.p.

46. Ibid. 73, 75.

47. Ibid. 78, 82–4; Empson is slightly (tellingly?) misquoting Jonson's reported remark to Donne, 'if it had been written of ye Virgin Marie it had been something' (Jonson, *Works*, ed. C. H. Herford & P. Simpson, vol. i (Oxford: Clarendon Press, 1925), 133).

48. Jonson, *Works*, i. 133.

49. Unpublished TS in Houghton.

50. Cf. Deborah Aldrich Larson, who argues that while Tuve's work may serve its purpose as 'a rebuff to the New Critics' it overemphasizes the poet's traditionalism: 'it leaves unanswered the question of why Donne *seems* so different from his contemporaries' (*John Donne and Twentieth-Century Criticism* (London & Toronto: Associated University Presses, 1989), 109).

51. Frank Kermode, *John Donne* (1957), rev. edn. (Harlow, Essex: Longman, 1978), 11, 18.

52. Frank Kermode, letter to WE, 26 Jan. 1958 (Houghton).

53. Kermode, *John Donne*, 24.

54. Charles Monroe Coffin, *John Donne and the New Philosophy* (1937) (New York: The Humanities Press, 1958), 150.

55. Herbert J. C. Grierson, *The Poems of John Donne* (Oxford: Clarendon Press, 1912), ii. 90.

56. It is now understood that Elegy XIX 'circulated in manuscripts with other elegies that we know from their association and circulation with early verse letters were composed before the marriage' (M. Thomas Hester, 'Donne's (Re)Annunciation of the Virgin(ia Colony) in *Elegy XIX*', *South Central Review*, 4: 2 (Summer 1987), 51).

57. Frank Kermode, letter to WE, 1 May 1958 (Houghton).

58. WE, letter to Frank Kermode, 24 Nov. 1957 (copy in Houghton). John T. Shawcross, in his fine edition, prints 'There is no pennance due to innocence'; and yet his gloss overlooks the strategic argument of the poem: 'You will not receive penance for remaining innocent of sin or me, or for remaining in your virginal white; you should not wear penitential vestment (as white clothing was considered), for innocence does not require penance.' (*The Complete Poetry of John Donne* (New York: Anchor Books, 1967), 58.) A. J. Smith admits, 'The textual evidence for the *1669* reading is weaker, and I print the other one for that reason alone' (*The Complete English Poems* (Harmondsworth, Middx.: Penguin, 1971), 451).

59. J. B. Leishman, *The Monarch of Wit* (1951), 6th edn. (London: Hutchinson, 1962), 122.

60. See e.g. Barbara Everett's salutary judgement that 'Donne re-works Ovid as radically and as originally as he reworked Horace, Persius, and Juvenal in his figurative narrative. He seems to be learning something both from the early comic Shakespeare and from the brilliant Marlowe of the poems, as he creates here and there an almost purely comical relation between the sober and judicious voice of the narrator and the foolish presence of his own zany desires, or of his mistress's body.' The 'cool and amused element' in the Elegies offsets 'that more prevalent image of Donne as the lewd seducer that takes support from the more apparently simply sensual of the Elegies . . . [F]ew first readers of "Going to Bed" have not, I imagine, been surprised to realize when the poem ends that the proposed event has yet to begin, and that the speaker has so far managed to undress no one but himself' ('Donne: A London Life', *Poets in Their Time: Essays on English poetry from Donne to Larkin* (London & Boston: Faber & Faber, 1986), 8–9).

61. Carey, *John Donne*, 99.

62. John Donne, *The Elegies and The Songs and Sonnets* ed. Helen Gardner (Oxford: Clarendon Press, 1965), p. li. Cited hereinafter as *ESS*.

63. Carey, *John Donne*, 116, 124. *Cf.* Larson: 'Carey has been severely censured for this distorted reading of a poem most find delightfully erotic, but the point here is that he has merely carried to extremes the kind of treatment possible when only one side of Donne's mind is emphasized and, incidentally, when little or no distinction is made between *persona* and poet' (*John Donne and Twentieth-Century Criticism*, 138).

64. Thomas Docherty, *John Donne, Undone* (London & New York: Methuen, 1986), 81–2. R. V. Young argues that the woman in the poem most certainly has a value, but not what you might think: a 'lust for gold and power, rather than sexual desire', is the principal theme of the *Elegies*, it seems; so that 'the signifier/signified relationship of the imperialist tropes is inverted, and the aporia between missionary piety and lust for gain and conquest is discovered and laid bare as surely as the gold mines of America or the body of a submissive mistress' (' "O my America, my new-found-land": Pornography and Imperial Politics in Donne's *Elegies*', *South Central Review*, 3: 2 (Summer 1987), 36, 45). M. Thomas Hester argues that 'this complex literary event' is at once 'a hyperbolic send-up of Renaissance epithalamia and ... an equivocal rewriting of the English myth of America ... The act of "going to bed" ... is being compared throughout the poem to the discovery of America and to "knowing" the Virgin Mary. Thus, the unvoiced word that lay behind the poem from the beginning was the English name of the English colony in America—*Virgin*(ia).' Furthermore, in what amounts to a hermeneutic stew, Hester seeks to show that Elegy XIX 'is even more blasphemous or outrageous than critics have therefore supposed.' Donne's 'amphibolous wit', he claims, extends to 'a critique of the Establishment poet [Spenser] and patron [Ralegh] who were rivals of his coterie'; and yet Hester disarmingly concedes after all: 'I must admit that I do not know where the mockery of Ralegh's adoration of the Virgin Queen (and its personal motives) begins and Donne's delightful play with the dynamics of the bedroom leaves off.' In any event, Hester is happy to reveal the secret of line 46, 'There is no pennance due to innocence', by way of a jocose pun: 'we should not overlook the full thrust of Donne's blasphemy here—the comparison of the speaker's sexual partner to the Virgin Mary'—who 'surely requires "no pennance".' ('Donne's (Re)Annunciation of the Virgin(ia Colony) in *Elegy XIX*', 52, 59, 61, 53, 55, 56.)

65. Empson, ' "There Is No Penance Due to Innocence" ' (on *John Donne: Life, Mind and Art*, by John Carey), *The New York Review of Books*, 28: 19 (Dec. 3, 1981), 42.

66. Ibid. 42–3. 'I agree that the poem ... is pornographic,' Empson acknowledged; 'it describes the greatest bit of luck in this kind that a male reader can imagine, and eggs him on to be pleased. But it is not sadistic' (42). He wrote to Christopher Ricks on 22 Nov. 1981: 'Perhaps I had been coarsely rude

[about Carey], I rather feared, so I was relieved to hear that you didn't' (Ricks).

67. *The Songs and Sonets of John Donne*, ed. Theodore Redpath, 2nd edn. (London: Methuen, 1983), 262. Cited hereinafter as *SS*.

68. Gardner, *ESS*, xxix.

69. Gardner, *ESS*, 222.

70. Redpath, *SS*, 286.

71. Helen Gardner, letter to WE, 19 Oct. 1956 (Houghton).

72. WE, letter to Gardner, 26 Oct. 1956 (copy in Houghton).

73. Helen Gardner, letter to WE, 28 Oct. 1956 (Houghton).

74. WE, letter to Helen Gardner, Guy Fawkes' Day 1956 (copy in Houghton). John T. Shawcross gives 'A something else' the gloss 'perhaps a Christ' (*The Complete Poetry of John Donne*, 142); A. J. Smith notes that the phrase signifies 'possibly "a Jesus Christ"', if the "mis-devotion" denies his resurrection; but more probably one of Mary Magdalen's lovers in her riotous youth. Christopher Ricks points out that "a Jesus Christ" and "a something else" are metrically equivalent" (*The Complete English Poems*, 398). James S. Baumlin has recently remarked upon the outrageousness of "the poet's own implicit apotheosis, his claim to become "a something else"—that is, a resurrected Christ to the lady's Mary Magdalen." *Pace* Helen Gardner, he poses the question: 'Does "mis-devotion" reign *because* of an age's superstitious belief in relics and miracles? Or might this relic and the "miracles" (22) of love be curative to an age's mis-devotion?' (*John Donne and the Rhetorics of Renaissance Discourse* (Columbia & London: University of Missouri Press, 1991), 173.)

75. Cf. WE's pre-emptive observation in *SVP*, 75: 'if Christ went to all the planets his appearances on each take on a different character; it is a more symbolical matter, and you can apply the ideas about Christ to any one who seems worthy of it.'

76. C. S. Lewis, letter to WE, 29 Sept. 1957 (Houghton).

77. Coffin, *John Donne and the New Philosophy*, 263. WE commented, in his notes: 'Coffin is mainly concerned [with] (and very good on) the complications around 1610; whereas the most interesting part of Donne's thought about the matter had happened earlier.' (Houghton)

78. Michael Francis Moloney, *John Donne: His Flight from Medievalism* (New York: Russell & Russell, 1965), 210.

79. Frank Kermode, letter to WE, 26 Jan. 1958 (Houghton).

80. Frank Kermode, letter to WE, 1 May 1958 (Houghton).

81. Transcript of a recorded conversation between WE and Frank Kermode (copy in Houghton). This was a trial run for the script of *John Donne—An Illumination*, a show devised by WE, Kermode, and Andrew Hilton, and performed (as part of *A City Tribute to John Donne: Poet and Dean of St Paul's*, a celebration of the 400th anniversary of his birth) at the Mermaid Theatre, London, 2–8 Oct. 1972. Neither WE nor Kermode appeared in person, the

'agreed' text of their discussion being delivered by actors. WE explained in a letter to the French cultural attaché on 13 Jan. 1973, 'it was part of the backstairs work for arranging a performance. I wrote many pages recommending what should be done and said in the performance, and what should be shown, and then I did this recording, just to do all I could before I had to fly to Canada. I am thankful for my safety when the terrible struggle of devising the performance went on for a sheer fortnight as I am told. But you should realize that in this recording both Kermode and I were pulling our punches, we were *imitating* a discussion, trying to sketch what had better occur in the play. As it went on, it almost broke through into being real, but never on my side and nor I expect on Kermode's' (copy in Houghton). Richard Holmes reviewed it: 'The *Illumination* is semi-dramatic, with ... George Benson and Antony Brown as a pair of faintly buffoon-like modern critics in spectacles and leather armchairs' (*The Times*, 3 Oct. 1972). Kermode's regretful account of the affair is included in *An Appetite for Poetry*: 'The piece was hardly a success, and I am glad to think the Empson scholars are unlikely to trace *that* manuscript' (129). The typescript is in Houghton.

82. There is a small textual crux in line 14, where the great majority of manuscripts, including all manuscripts of Groups II and III, reject 'Let us possesse one world' in favour of 'our world', though it makes no material difference to WE's interpretation. Redpath persuasively suggests that 'our' has even more intimacy than the sonorous 'one' that WE favoured.

83. Draft of the text for *John Donne—An Illumination*, Oct. 1972.

84. Redpath, *SS*, 230; letter to WE, 24 Feb. 1957 (Houghton).

85. John Donne, *The Divine Poems*, ed. Helen Gardner (Oxford: Clarendon Press, 1952), 76. Cited hereinafter as *DP*.

86. Carey, *John Donne*, 50.

87. Gardner, *DP*, 75–6. WE sometime wrote in his notes: 'I had not realised that *I am a little world* was written, on her theory, just before or after Galileo published. Absurd to say he [Donne] didn't know.' (Houghton)

88. WE, draft of a discussion document (copy in Houghton).

89. WE, *SVP*, 75.

90. *SVP*, 76.

91. WE, letter to Frank Kermode, n.d. (copy in Houghton).

92. WE, draft of a discussion document (copy in Houghton).

93. Robert Hues, one of 'the three Magi' retained by the Earl of Northumberland (the others being Walter Warner and Thomas Harriot), published a work on the use of the terrestrial and celestial globes, *Tractatus de globis et eorum usu*, in 1594.

94. Leishman, *The Monarch of Wit*, 200.

95. Redpath, *SS*, 231.

96. Gardner, *ESS*, 199.

97. Gardner, *ESS*, p. liv. R. E. Pritchard ably argues that the poem speaks for a 'new, ideal and transforming relationship', a 'unique love [that] will be a catalytic miracle, cancelling the effect of the Fall': ' "The Good Morrow" presents a new love, different from ordinary sexuality, that is associated with the discovery of reality, the establishment of the true faith, a replacement of the familiar world, an image of perfection and eternity, that recalls an original happy state, and involves an activity unlike that consequent upon the Fall' ('Dying in Donne's "The Good Morrow" ', *Essays in Criticism*, 35: 3 (July 1985), 220).

98. Cf. an anonymous review of *The Elegies and The Songs and Sonnets*, ed. Helen Gardner: 'on the question of dating [WE] has an irrefragable case... [A]bove all, he is right in contending that if the poems of the second group are attributed to the period of Donne's marriage, it becomes impossible to suggest for many of them a psychologically plausible explanation' (*TLS*, 6 April 1967, 279–80).

99. *Letters*, 147; *Selected Prose*, 127.

100. Leishman, *The Monarch of Wit*, 41.

101. Gosse, *The Life and Letters of John Donne* (London: William Heinemann, 1899), ii. 48. R. C. Bald quotes this letter to illustrate Donne's marital happiness (*John Donne: A Life* (London: Oxford University Press, 1970), 326). See Larson, *John Donne and Twentieth-Century Criticism*, for a survey of the divergent views of the letters; 'to support his assessment of Donne's character, Carey must emphasize the egotistical, ambitious elements in the letters' (88).

102. Gardner, *ESS*, p. li.

103. Carey, *John Donne*, 91.

104. Kermode, *John Donne*, 14.

105. Carey, *John Donne*, 253.

106. Ibid. 250.

107. Tycho Brahe, who discovered the fleeting new star in 1572, was one of the most assiduous astronomers of the late sixteenth century. Though an admirer of Copernicus' hypothesis, he did not think it physically demonstrable and in 1588 published his own diagram of the universe, a spherical version of the Copernican system which retained the centrality of a stationary earth with the moon, sun and fixed stars revolving round it. His hybrid or 'half-way theory', as Empson calls it, has been described by J. L. E. Dreyer as 'a stepping-stone from the Ptolemaic to the Copernican system.' See J. L. E. Dreyer, *History of the Planetary Systems from Thales to Kepler* (Cambridge, 1906), 363–4. See also Kristian P. Moesgaard, 'Copernican Influence on Tycho Brahe', in *The Reception of Copernicus' Heliocentric Theory*, ed. Jerzy Dobrzycki (Dordrecht, Holland: D. Reidel, 1972), 31–55; Victor Thoren, *The Lord of Uraniborg: A Biography of Tycho Brahe* (Cambridge: Cambridge University Press, 1991); and John W. Shirley's summary of the

controversy aroused by the conception of 'celestial phenomena which could discredit the ideas of perfection and circular motion' (*Thomas Harriot: A Biography*, 393–4). *Cf.* Anthony Low's remark that 'Donne may not have accepted the literal details of Copernican theory, since "The Progresse of the Soule" (1612) pictures Elizabeth Drury reaching heaven through Tycho Brahe's system' ('Love and Science: cultural change in Donne's *Songs and Sonnets*', *Studies in the Literary Imagination*, 22: 1 (Spring 1989), 14). Low credits John T. Shawcross (*The Complete Poetry of John Donne*, 296 n.) with solving the problem of 'Donne's curious ordering of the spheres in that poem'. But Empson deserves the credit for being the first to suggest that Donne may have settled for Tycho's system.

108. John Donne, *Complete Poetry and Selected Prose*, ed. John Hayward (London: The Nonesuch Press, 1929), 674.

109. Carey, *John Donne*, 18. On Donne's anxieties about censorship, see Annabel Patterson, 'Misinterpretable Donne: The Testimony of the Letters', *John Donne Journal*, 1 (1982), 39–53; M. Thomas Hester, *Kinde Pitty and Brave Scorn: John Donne's Satyres* (Durham, NC: Duke University Press, 1982).

110. Grant McColley, 'The Seventeenth-century Doctrine of a Plurality of Worlds', *Annals of Science*, 1: 3 (1936) 412–13. *Cf.* Robert S. Westman, 'The Melanchthon Circle, Rheticus, and the Wittenberg Interpretation of the Copernican Theory', *Isis*, 66 (1975), 165–93.

111. Helen Gardner, letter to WE, 19 Oct. 1956 (Houghton).

112. WE, draft letter to *Critical Quarterly*, 1967 (copy in Houghton).

113. John Hayward (ed.), *Complete Poetry and Selected Prose*, 514; cited in McColley, 'The Seventeenth-century Doctrine of a Plurality of Worlds', 422; Nicolson, 'The 'New Astronomy' and English Literary Imagination', 459.

114. John Sparrow, letter to WE, 13 Aug. 1972 (Houghton). WE and Sparrow chatted at a reception following a lecture by WE in January 1972, and Sparrow became greatly taken in general with WE's theories regarding the texts of Donne.

115. Gardner, *ESS*, p. lii.

116. Cf. Baumlin, *John Donne and the Rhetorics of Renaissance Discourse*, 284–9.

117. Redpath, *SS*, 178.

118. Gardner, *ESS*, p. lxiv.

119. Ibid., p. xci.

120. Ibid. 209.

121. Redpath, *SS*, 179. I put to Dr Redpath the notion that 'so' could mean 'thus' or 'accordingly'—which would require the unproblematical introduction of a full period in the previous line, or else the grammar goes awry—and he commented: 'I am tempted by the possibility that "so" could mean "in such a way". However, the possibility of catching "truth" from line 8 seems almost a probability' (letter to JH, 17 March 1990).

122. Gardner, *ESS*, 210.

123. Redpath, *SS*, 179.
124. Gardner, *ESS*, 210.
125. See Mark Roberts, "The New Edition of Donne's Love Poems", *Essays in Criticism*, 17 (1967), 277.
126. Redpath, *SS*, App. IV, 315–17.
127. Mark Roberts, 'If It Were Done When 'Tis Done', *Essays in Criticism*, 16: 3 (July 1966), 318; Roberts discusses Gardner's inconsistency vis-à-vis 'The Dreame' on 317.
128. Roberts, 'If It Were Done When 'Tis Done', 326. Roberts later judged that Group III 'seems much further from Donne's papers than either of the other two . . . In general, I take it that the Group I tradition represents the earliest substantive version of the *Songs and Sonets* that comes down to us; that Group II represents what may be called a revision . . . and that Group III, though commonly closer to the "revised" version, presents a number of readings from an early version or versions of which we have no substantive record' ('Problems in Editing Donne's Songs and Sonets', in *Editing Poetry from Spenser to Dryden*, ed. A. H. de Quehen (New York and London: Garland Publishing, 1981), 27).
129. Redpath, *SS*, 101.
130. Ibid. 317.
131. Gardner, *ESS*, 210. Empson spotted the problem: 'Why not?' he observed in his notes. Gardner '[w]on't let us know which these MS are' (Houghton).
132. Redpath, *SS*, 315. It should be noted, however, that Shawcross's textual apparatus includes the entry: 'Profanenes *C57*, *TCD*, *Dob*, *O'F* (> Profane)' (*The Complete Poetry of John Donne*, 452).
133. Gardner, *ESS*, 133.
134. WE, letter to W. D. Maxwell McMahon, 21 Aug. 1973 (copy in Houghton). WE wrote to Ricks on 1 March 1972, 'Of course I admit that plenty of arguing-away can still go on, after starting from her text, but it still feels foul even when a decent meaning has been argued out of it' (Ricks).
135. WE, letter to Christopher Ricks, 'Good Friday' (Ricks). Graham Hough wrote to Empson on 25 March 1972 (Houghton). Despite her all-embracing brief—*John Donne and Twentieth-Century Criticism* (1989)—Deborah Aldrich Larson takes no account of Empson's writings on Donne.
136. John Crowe Ransom, letter to WE, 18 Jan. 1957 (Houghton).
137. Helen Gardner, letter to WE, 15 Sept. 1956 (Empson Papers). 'A lot in Grierson is just slightly unreliable,' Gardner added, 'and people will go on arguing on the basis of statements which are not true.'
138. A. L. French, 'Dr. Gardner's Dating of the *Songs and Sonets*', *Essays in Criticism*, 17 (1967), 119.
139. Ted-Larry Pebworth, 'Manuscript Poems and Print Assumptions: Donne and His Modern Editors', *John Donne Journal*, 3: 1 (1984), 12–17.

140. WE, 'Correspondence', *Critical Quarterly*, 9 (1967), 89; Helen Gardner, 'Correspondence', *Critical Quarterly*, 8 (1966), 376.
141. WE, letter to the Editors of *Critical Quarterly*, n.d. (copy in Houghton).
142. Hugh Sykes Davies in conversation with JH, 9 Aug. 1983.
143. Courtesy of John Fuller.
144. Peter A. Fiore, e-mail to JH, 22 Aug. 2002.
145. Reported by George Watson in conversation with JH, 5 July 1996.

18. ROAMINGS IN RETIREMENT: FROM TORONTO TO MIAMI

1. WE, letter to Ricks, 18 Oct. 1965.
2. Ken McLean, e-mail to JH, 26 June 2002.
3. Dick Ewen, letter to JH, 13 July 2002.
4. WE, letter to Ian Parsons, 4 Nov. 1972 (Reading).
5. WE, letter to Frank Kermode, 14 Oct. 1972 (Kermode).
6. Nicholas Howe, e-mail to JH, 28 July 2002.
7. 'Dear Sir . . . Bagchee . . . was in my seminar at York University Toronto last year. He is a naturally powerful literary critic,' wrote WE in a reference on 5 Sept. 1973 (addressee unknown; carbon in Houghton).
8. Aviva Layton, e-mail to JH, 30 May 2002.
9. John Morgenstern, e-mail to JH, 21 May 2002.
10. Bagchee, 'William Empson in Toronto, 1972–73' (Letter to JH, 27 Nov. 2002).
11. Ken McLean, e-mail to JH, 2 July 2002.
12. John Morgenstern, e-mail to JH, 21 May 2002.
13. Nicholas Howe, e-mail to JH, 28 July 2002.
14. John Morgenstern, e-mail to JH, 21 May 2002.
15. WE quoted by Ken McLean, e-mail to JH, 26 June 2002.
16. John Morgenstern, e-mail to JH, 21 May 2002.
17. Sumana Sen-Bagchee, e-mail to JH, 14 Nov. 2002. Dick Ewen recalls, with additional detail, 'the occasion when I poured him a glass of brown sherry and water in mistake for the brandy he requested. "To err is divine. Please don't do it again." Equipped with a large brandy, he was then free to say, when his sozzled wife rambled on about a famous American novelist, "Who is William Fuggoner, I wonder?" ' (e-mail letter to JH, 6 June 2005).
18. Ken McLean, e-mail to JH, 2 July 2002.
19. Aviva Layton, e-mail to JH, 20 May 2002.
20. Ewen, letter to JH, 19 July 2002.
21. Ibid.
22. Dick Ewen, letter to JH, 13 July 2002. Ewen reports further: 'He was by far the most favourite guest I ever had,' Mrs Willis said of Empson; '—so witty, so charming, so erudite, so handsome, so loveable.'
23. Information from Ewen, letter to JH, 13 July 2002.

24. Aviva Layton, e-mail to JH, 20 May 2002.

25. John R. Doheny recalls of WE's lectures at Simon Fraser University and the University of British Columbia: 'I remember clearly what an excellent speaker he was then. He kept the attention of a large and general audience for an hour each time while he developed his thesis carefully and clearly. We had two days of pleasant talk ranging over Marlowe, Marvell, and Keats' (letter to JH, 2 Jan. 1986).

26. Dick Ewen, letter to JH, 12 Aug. 2002.

27. Dick Ewen, e-mail to JH, 15 Jan. 2003.

28. Ewen, e-mails to JH, 24 Jan. 2004.

29. On McLuhan's admiration for *STA*, which he read at Cambridge in 1935, see *Letters of Marshall McLuhan*, ed. Matie Molinaro, Corinne McLuhan, William Toye (Toronto: Oxford University Press, 1987), 462 n. 3.

30. WE, letter to Jacob Empson, 16 Dec. 1972 (Jacob Empson).

31. Marshall McLuhan, letter to Claude Bissell, 9 Feb. 1973; *Letters of Marshall McLuhan*, 468–9.

32. Ibid. 469. Roger Kuin, of York University, remembers another public lecture at which WE was again barely audible: 'I remember the little I could hear as being amusing and sardonic' (Kuin, e-mail to JH, 16 June 2002).

33. IAR diary, entries for 12, 15 and 16 April, and back matter.

34. IAR diary: Dorothea's entry for 15 April 1973. 'I was asked to drive WE the ten or so blocks back to the center of Harvard after the cocktail party. There were just the two of us. After about halfway, near the corner of Lowell House, WE opened the door while the car was in motion (though it was only going slow, owing to traffic). He wanted to get out immediately. Why? I was stunned and asked him to be very careful and shut the door—we were not yet arrived. Then, I realized he was vomiting out the window and door and trying to get out in the street. Very graciously he said to me that he did not want to mess up my car. I recall telling him not to worry about my car—the important thing was not to get hurt. Eventually I got him to close the door and everything settled down. When he got out a few blocks later, he was fine' (Russo, e-mail to JH, 16 Sept. 2002).

35. John Paul Russo, *I. A. Richards: His Life and Work*, 795 n. 41.

36. George Watson in conversation with JH, 5 July 1996. According to Watson, IAR wanted to be loved by everybody; he needed company, an audience; but he was a 'spellbinder'—'he had us eating out of his hand.' Of WE, IAR said to Watson: 'I wish him articulacy'—which may have been a smack at WE's incoherence when drinking.

37. Dick Ewen, letter to JH, 5 Sept. 2002.

38. Ewen, e-mail to JH, 25 July 2002.

39. Ewen, e-mail to JH, 19 July 2002.

40. Ewen, e-mail to JH, 6 June 2005.

41. WE, letter to HE, 8 October 1974 (Sheffield).

42. WE, letter to HE, 14 Nov. 1974 (Sheffield).

43. WE, undated (? Sept. 1974) letter to HE (Sheffield). Classes began on 9 Sept.

44. WE, letter to HE, 8 Oct. 1974 (Sheffield).

45. WE, letter to HE, 22 Dec. 1974 (Sheffield).

46. WE, letter to HE, 1 Oct. 1974 (Sheffield).

47. WE, letter to HE, 14 Nov. 1974 (Sheffield).

48. Charles W. Mann, letter to JH, 10 Aug. 1995.

49. WE, letter to HE, 5 Nov. 1974 (Sheffield).

50. WE, letter to HE, 8 Oct. 1974 (Sheffield).

51. WE, letter to HE, 22 Dec. 1974 (Sheffield).

52. WE, letter to HE, 14 Nov. 1974 (Sheffield).

53. WE, letter to HE, 22 Dec. 1974 (Sheffield).

54. Paul West, 'Portable People', *The Paris Review*, 115 (vol. 32), Summer 1990, 103–4.

55. WE, letter to HE, 26 Dec. 1974 (Sheffield).

56. WE, letter to HE, 22 Dec. 1974 (Sheffield). 'The kind of life here is just what suits me, really, if only I can get it a bit more convenient,' he had written to Hetta on 16 Nov. 1974 (Sheffield).

57. WE, letter to Christopher Ricks, 19 Jan. 1975 (Ricks).

58. WE, letter to HE, 22 Dec. 1974 (Sheffield).

59. WE, letter to HE, 13 Feb. 1975 (Sheffield).

60. WE, letter to HE, 24 Jan. 1975 (Sheffield).

61. WE, letter to HE, 28 Oct. 1974 (Sheffield).

62. WE, letter to HE, 26 Dec. 1974 (Sheffield).

63. WE, letter to HE, 13 Feb. 1975 (Sheffield).

64. Stanley Weintraub, e-mail to JH, 21 May 2002. WE had first been sounded about the possibility of visiting Penn State by Ralph Condee in May 1972.

65. WE gave no hint of a crisis in a letter to Ricks (6 March 1975), asking if anyone at Harvard could put up Hetta and himself for a weekend: 'Hetta and Mogador have just arrived here (Mog for ten days or so only), and I am rather concerned to provide enough entertainment for Hetta.' (Ricks)

66. Charles W. Mann, letter to JH, 10 Aug. 1995.

67. HE, letter to Walter Brown, 6 June 1975 (Sheffield).

68. Mark Thompson, 'Notes on meetings with William Empson', June 1986.

69. WE, letter to David Jones, 10 Oct. 1976 (Sheffield).

70. HE, letter to David Jones, 26 Nov. 1976 (Sheffield).

71. HE, letter to David Jones, Nov. 1976 (Sheffield).

72. Zack Bowen, 'Memories of William Empson': letter to JH, 27 July 2002. Hetta otherwise enjoyed the Provost's company, as she told David Jones (letter, 13 Oct.): 'William and I went to a grand dinner last night with the President (of the Univ) which was quite fun—I chatted to a Physicist, who was very matey and oddly enough rather pro-Soviet' (Sheffield).

73. *W. D. Snodgrass in conversation with Philip Hoy* (London: Between the Lines, 1998), 24. Snodgrass mentions in the same interview (18) that at the outset of his career, 'I was writing under the influence of William Empson. I'd fallen for that intense, and very intellectual, style. I wrote several villanelles during that period.' In an essay on his own work, 'Finding a Poem' in *In Radical Pursuit* (1975), he notes too: 'I was raised, poetically, in a highly intellectual atmosphere; William Empson was my first love.' Though abashed by the Empsons' brusque and sardonic wit, he was not humourless; he enjoyed relating the story of how WE would smoke a pipe and a cigarette at the same time: 'Apparently, one of WE's students got up the courage one day, and said, "Professor Empson, do you mind if I ask you why you do that?" Empson was momentarily thrown, but quickly recovered himself, and said, "Oh, that's easy: I started smoking cigarettes while I was an undergraduate, but then I went to China, where they didn't have cigarettes, and that's when I took up the pipe' (*W. D. Snodgrass in conversation with Philip Hoy*, 24).

74. Zack Bowen, 'Memories of William Empson': letter to JH 27 July 2002.

75. Ibid.

76. WE, letter to David Jones, 10 Oct. 1976 (Sheffield).

77. HE, letter to David Jones, 13 Oct. 1976 (Sheffield).

78. Edward Said, letter to WE, 13 Oct. 1976 (Houghton).

79. William Vesterman, e-mail message to JH, 28 Feb. 2004.

80. David Walker, 'Research aid for British Academy', *The Times*, 2 July 1976, p. 19. Isaiah Berlin had written to WE on 20 May 1976, expressing the hope that he would accept election even though it was shameful of the British Academy not to have elected him much earlier in his career (Houghton). On 28 Oct. 1976 Berlin wrote again with the news that the Council of the Academy had put WE's name forward to receive one of the international Antonio Feltrinelli prizes to be awarded by the Accademia dei Lincei. The prize in prospect was L. 25.000.000 (£15,000), but nothing seems to have come of the nomination.

81. WE, letter to Walter Brown, 21 April 1977 (Sheffield).

82. WE was formally proposed for an honorary doctorate at Cambridge by Hugh Sykes Davies and George Watson on 17 Nov. 1976.

83. 'Cambridge greets its birthday Chancellor', *The Times*, 11 June 1977, p. 2.

84. M. C. Bradbrook, 'Sir William Empson (1906–84)', *Shakespeare in his Context: the Constellated Globe*, The Collected Papers of Muriel Bradbrook, vol. iv (Hemel Hempstead, Herts.: Harvester Wheatsheaf, 1989), 200.

85. Interview with Muriel Bradbrook, 16 Sept. 1992.

86. Dorothea Richards, letter to John Paul Russo, 21 June 1977 (Magdalene).

87. Thompson, 'Notes on meetings with William Empson'.

88. HE, letter to Walter Brown, 13 March 1979.

89. WE, letter to Christopher Ricks, 25 April 1979 (Ricks).

90. 'William Empson remembers I. A. Richards', *London Review of Books*, 5 June–18 June 1980, 14.

91. WE, letter to Richard Luckett, 4 Jan. 1980 (Luckett).

92. Quoted in letter from Richard Luckett to JH, 22 Sept. 1993.

93. Janet Adam Smith, letter to Luckett (7 Feb. 1980), quoted in Luckett letter to JH, 22 Sept. 1993.

94. L. C. Knights, letter to JH, 9 Oct. 1983.

95. WE, letter to Dorothea Richards, 5 March 1980 (Magdalene).

96. 'He came to the I. A. Richards Memorial thing, lunched at Magdalene but didn't feel up to the big affair that followed in the Senate House, where I gave an address. He read the address in *LRB* and wrote a word of congratulation, but not to me. Instead he wrote to Ricks, asking him to pass the message on and claiming not to know my college' (Frank Kermode, letter to JH, 21 Feb. 1990).

97. Janet Adam Smith, letter to Dorothea Richards, 10 Oct. 1977 (IAR Papers, Box 40, Magdalene College).

98. 'Londoner's Diary', *Evening Standard*, 28 Feb. 1977, 12.

99. HE, letter to Walter Brown, 22 Nov. 1981 (Sheffield).

100. WE, letter to Christopher Ricks, 7 April 1978 (Ricks).

101. HE, letter to Walter Brown, 24 June 1978 (Sheffield).

102. HE, letter to Walter Brown, 28 July 1978 (Sheffield).

103. HE, letter to Walter Brown, 13 Oct. 1978 (Sheffield).

104. HE, letter to Walter Brown, 13 March 1979 (Sheffield).

105. Principal Private Secretary, Prime Minister's Office, letter to WE, 27 Nov. 1978 (Houghton).

106. See also John Henry Jones, 'Empson Soup', *The CEA Forum*, 18: 2–4 (1988), 9: 'He was incensed that the Pope was to meet [the Queen], maintaining that he was not a fit person to do so, since he had failed to encourage or allow artificial birth-control in South America.'

107. HE, letter to Walter Brown, 3–7 Feb. 1979 (Sheffield).

108. WE, letter to Christopher Ricks, 29 Jan. 1979 (Ricks).

109. Jones, 'Empson Soup', p. 9.

110. WE quoted in Geoffrey Wansell, 'Honour at last for silent poet', *Observer*, 31 Dec. 1978.

111. Valerie Eliot, letter to Dorothea Richards, 11 Jan. 1979 (Magdalene).

112. *Hampstead & Highgate Express*, 5 Jan. 1979.

113. Christopher Ricks, 'Empson as a Man of Letters in the 1960s', *News from the Republic of Letters*, no. 2 (Sept. 1997), 7.

114. HE, letter to David Jones, 11 April 1982 (Sheffield).

115. Thompson, 'Notes on meetings with William Empson'.

116. Leroy Desmantries, 'The Old Man and the Critic', *CEA-Forum* 18: 2–4 (1988), 11.

117. HE, letter to David Jones, 4 Feb. 1982 (Sheffield).

118. WE, letter to Jacob Empson, 14 Feb. 1982 (Jacob Empson).
119. Ibid. The phrase 'flighting for duck' refers to WE's poem with that title.
120. Ross C. Murfin, letter to JH, 4 January 1995. Cf. Jones, 'Empson Soup', 9.
121. Thompson, 'Notes on meetings with William Empson'.
122. WE, letter to Christopher Ricks, 6 Dec. 1982 (Ricks).
123. Thompson, 'Notes on meetings with William Empson'.
124. Telephone interview with Jonathan Raban, 9 Feb. 1990.
125. WE, letter to Haffenden, 21 March 1982 (JH).
126. HE, letter to David Jones, 28 March 1982 (Sheffield).
127. WE, letter to Haffenden, 4 April 1982.
128. HE, letter to David Jones, 11 April 1982 (Sheffield).
129. Telephone interview with Anthony Cronin, 23 June 2005.
130. Fritz Senn, e-mail to JH, 17 April 2002.
131. WE, letter to Anthony Cronin, 5 Sept. 1981 (Houghton draft).
132. Thompson, 'Notes on meetings with William Empson'.
133. Ibid.

19. *FAUSTUS*: FINALE

1. WE, letter to Christopher Ricks, 14 Feb. 1977 (Ricks).
2. John Henry Jones, 'Empson Soup: A personal memory of William Empson', *The CEA Forum*, 18: 2–4 (1988), 7; reprinted, as 'Diary', in LRB, 11: 15 (17 Aug. 1989), 20–1. Barry Carman's productions included an edition, with John McPherson, of the legendary Joseph McPherson's writings about Egypt: *Bimbashi McPherson* (1983).
3. Ibid.
4. Ibid.
5. Ibid. 8.
6. Ibid. 9.
7. Paul H. Fry, *William Empson: Prophet Against Sacrifice* (London and New York: Routledge, 1991), 143.
8. WE, letter to Ian Parsons, 16 Jan. 1973 (Reading).
9. Mark Thompson, 'Notes on Meetings with William Empson, June 1986'.
10. WE, letter to Mark Thompson, 17 Dec. 1983.
11. Mark Thompson, 'Notes on Meetings with William Empson'.
12. Mogador Empson, e-mail to JH, 9 Feb. 2003.
13. Jacob Empson, e-mail to JH, 29 Sept. 2005.
14. Jones, 'Empson Soup', 9.
15. Empson's quondam student, Jin Fa-xin, who had inspired aspects of his work on Milton, received a letter from Hetta, dated 2 May 1984, saying of Empson: 'He had been ill for some ten weeks, but we all hoped he might recover. Then suddenly, the last two days, he simply faded away. There was no pain, just a gradual weakening; and he was writing away to the end.'

16. Jones, 'Empson Soup', p. 10.
17. HE, letter to Walter Brown, 3 Nov. 1982 (Sheffield).
18. Thompson, 'Notes on Meetings with William Empson'.
19. Ibid.
20. WE, *MG*, 89
21. HE, letter to Walter Brown, 1 Feb. 1985 (Sheffield).

INDEX

HE   HETTA EMPSON
WE   WILLIAM EMPSON